ArtScroll Mesorah Series®

Rabbi Nosson Scherman / Rabbi Meir Zlotowitz
General Editors

THE SEIF EDITION

שבת / שלש רגלים

AN ORTHODOX UNION CENTENNIAL PUBLICATION

ORTHODOX UNION
1 8 9 8 - 1 9 9 8
דור לדור ישבח מעשיך

Published by

Mesorah Publications, ltd.

ArtScroll
Transliterated Linear
SIDDUR

SABBATH AND FESTIVAL

based on
The Complete ArtScroll Siddur
with translation and commentary by
Rabbi Nosson Scherman

Introductory Essays and Comments by
Rabbi Benjamin Yudin

Designed by
Rabbi Sheah Brander

A PROJECT OF THE

Mesorah Heritage Foundation

AN ORTHODOX UNION CENTENNIAL PUBLICATION

FIRST EDITION
First Impression . . . March 1998
Second Impression . . . August 2000
Third Impression . . . January 2002
Fourth Impression . . . March 2004

THE ARTSCROLL SERIES ®
"SIDDUR ZICHRON AVRAHAM"
THE SEIF EDITION OF THE ARTSCROLL TRANSLITERATED LINEAR SIDDUR
SABBATH AND FESTIVAL — NUSACH ASHKENAZ
© *Copyright 1998 by* MESORAH PUBLICATIONS, Ltd.
4401 Second Avenue / Brooklyn, N.Y. 11232 / (718) 921-9000 / www.artscroll.com

ISBN: 1-57819-150-5 (hard cover)

Typography by CompuScribe at ArtScroll Studios, Ltd.
Printed in the United States of America by Noble Book Press
Bound by Sefercraft, Inc. / 4401 Second Avenue / Brooklyn, N.Y. 11232

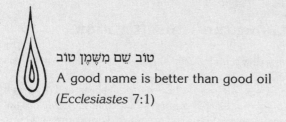

טוֹב שֵׁם מִשֶּׁמֶן טוֹב

A good name is better than good oil

(*Ecclesiastes* 7:1)

This Siddur
is dedicated to the memory of

Abraham Seif ע״ה

אברהם בן יהודה אריה ע״ה

נפטר ה׳ שבט, תשנ״ז / January 13, 1997

He built his good name with uncompromising
devotion to *mitzvot,* unwavering morality,
and tenacious integrity,
all blended with a profound love of
family and *Am Yisrael.*

This Siddur is dedicated
on the occasion of his first *yahrzeit.*
It is our sincere hope that this Siddur
will inspire countless Jews
to engage in quiet conversation
with God, through prayer.

Harriet and Herbert Seif

৵ Guide to Reading the Transliteration

Consonants are read as they sound in English, except for "ch" (ח, כ, ך) which is pronounced as in *challah*.

The "silent" Hebrew letters — א and ע, whenever they appear, and ה, when it appears at the end of a word — are not represented. Although the letter ה is not usually pronounced when it appears at the end of a word, there are exceptions to the rule. These exceptions are indicated in Hebrew by a dot inside the letter — הּ. In transliteration the ה appears as a final h and is preceded by a vowel.

A consonant is usually pronounced together with the vowel following it. Thus, הַמֶּלֶךְ, "hamelech," is pronounced "ha-me-lech," and not "ham-el-ech." Hyphens are used to indicate exceptions to this rule.

When two consonants appear in tandem (except for those that are pronounced as a single sound, such as, ch, sh, tz), the first ends a syllable and the second begins a new syllable. Thus, וּבְנֵה "uvnay," is pronounced "uv-nay"; אֶקְרָא, "ekro," is pronounced "ek-ro" not "e-kro."

Vowels are pronounced as follows:

a	אַ	as in	**hurr**ah
o	אָ	as in	**o**ften
ō	או or אֹ	as in	**po**st
ay	אֵ or אֵי	as in	**pay**
e	אֶ	as in	**le**g
i	אִ or אִי	as in	ma**chi**ne
u	אֻ or אוּ	as in	**lu**nar
oy	אֹי	as in	**boy**
ai	אַי	as in	**ai**sle

The sounded *sh'va* (בְ) is represented by an apostrophe (b') and is pronounced similarly to the indistinct **a** in **a**go.

Hyphens are used to separate syllables that might otherwise be slurred into each other (e.g., מֵעַתָּה is transliterated "may-ato" not "ma-yato").

Capital letters are not used in Hebrew. However, for the convenience of the reader, the transliteration uses a capital letter to indicate the beginning of a verse or a sentence. Additionally, capitals are used to indicate Divine Names which may not be pronounced except as part of a Scriptural verse or within a prayer.

Note: Phrases in the translation or instructions that are followed by an asterisk (*) are discussed in the commentary below, usually on the same page, but sometimes on the facing or following pages.

THE NAMES OF GOD

The Four-Letter Name of HASHEM [י־ה־ו־ה Adōnoy] indicates that God is timeless and infinite, since the letters of this Name are those of the words הָיָה הֹוֶה וְיִהְיֶה, *He was, He is, and He will be*. This Name appears in some editions with vowel points [יְ־הֹ־וָ־ה] and in others, such as the present edition, without vowels. In either case, this Name is *never* pronounced as it is spelled.

During prayer, or when a blessing is recited, or when Torah verses are read, the Four-Letter Name should be pronounced as if it were spelled אֲדֹנָי, *Adōnoy*, the Name that identifies God as the Master of All. At other times, it should be pronounced הַשֵׁם, *HASHEM*, literally, "the Name."

According to the *Shulchan Aruch*, one should have both meanings — the Master of All and the Timeless, Infinite One — in mind when reciting the Four-Letter Name during prayer (*Orach Chaim* ch. 5). According to *Vilna Gaon*, however, one need have in mind only the meaning of the Name as it is pronounced — the Master of All (ibid.).

When the Name is spelled אֲדֹנָי in the prayer or verse, all agree that one should have in mind that God is the Master of All.

The Name of אֱלֹהִים, *Elōhim*, God, refers to Him as the One Who is all-powerful and Who is in direct overlordship of the universe (ibid.). This is also used as a generic name for the angels, a court, rulers, and even idols. However, when the term אֱלֹהִים is used for the God of Israel, it means the One Omniscient God, who is uniquely identified with His Chosen People.

In this work, the Four-Letter Name of God is translated "HASHEM," the pronunciation traditionally used for the Name to avoid pronouncing it unnecessarily. This pronunciation should be used when studying the meanings of the prayers. However, if one prays from the English translation, he should say "God" or "Lord," or he should pronounce the Name in the proper Hebrew way — Adōnoy — in accord with the ruling of most halachic authorities.

PRONOUNCING THE NAMES OF GOD

The following table gives the pronunciations of the Name when it appears with a prefix. In all these cases, the accent is on the last syllable (noy).

בַּי־ה־ו־ה	— *Ba-dōnoy*
הַי־ה־ו־ה	— *Ha- adōnoy*
וַי־ה־ו־ה	— *Va-dōnoy*
כַּי־ה־ו־ה	— *Ka-dōnoy*
לַי־ה־ו־ה	— *La-dōnoy*
מֵי־ה־ו־ה	— *May-adōnoy*
שֵׁי־ה־ו־ה	— *She-adōnoy*

Sometimes the Name appears with the vowelization יְ־הֹ־וִ־ה. This version of the Name is pronounced as if it were spelled אֱלֹהִים, *Elōhim*, the Name that refers to God as the One Who is all-powerful. When it appears with a prefix לֵי־הֹ־וִ־ה, it is pronounced *Lay-lōhim*. We have translated this name as *HASHEM/ ELOHIM* to indicate that it refers to the aspects inherent in each of those Names.

❖ TABLE OF CONTENTS ❖

חֲנוּכָּה / CHANUKAH

פּוּרִים / PURIM

THE ORDER OF PRAYER FOR *CHOL HAMOED*

For the convenience of those using this *Siddur* on the weekdays of *Chol HaMoed* (the Intermediate Days of Pesach and Succos), following is a detailed sequence of the prayers: Those who don *tefillin* on *Chol HaMoed*, see page 837.

Shacharis: Upon Arising (p. 220) through the beginning of *Pesukei D'Zimrah* (p. 286); Continuation of *Pesukei D'Zimrah, Shema* and its Blessings, following instructions for weekdays (pp. 282-295, 318-340, 347-351, 357-372); Weekday *Shemoneh Esrei* (p. 34 — but say *Sim Shalom* instead of *Shalom Rav* [p. 54]); [on Succos, the Four Species (p. 645)]; *Hallel* (p. 647); Full *Kaddish* (p. 58); Removal of the Torah and Torah Reading Service (p. 511); Returning the Torah (p. 516); *Ashrei/U'va L'Tzion* / Half-*Kaddish* (pp. 502-510); *Mussaf* (p. 708); [on Succos, *Hoshanos* (p. 772)]; Full *Kaddish* (p. 454); *Aleinu,* Mourner's *Kaddish* (pp. 463-468); Song of the Day (pp. 473-487); Mourner's *Kaddish* (pp. 466-468) [on Succos, Psalm 27 (pp. 488-490)].

Minchah: The weekday *Minchah* (pp. 30-63).

Maariv: The weekday *Maariv* (pp. 564-596, 604, 620-629).

↵§ *Preface*

In his quest to express our yearning for the joy of God's ultimate redemption, King David writes: זֶה הַיּוֹם עָשָׂה ה׳ נָגִילָה וְנִשְׂמְחָה בוֹ, *This is the day HASHEM has made; let us rejoice and be glad on it.*

This verse includes two distinct expressions of joy: *simchah* and *gilah*. The *Vilna Gaon* explains the difference between the two. *Simchah* is reflected in the thrill of a quick accomplishment; the *simchah* of resolving a difficult problem; the exhilaration of a successful business transaction; the joy of assuming an exalted position of responsibility; or the excitement of finding an item of great worth. *Gilah*, on the other hand, is the joy that comes with the completion of a long process. Where *simchah* is instantaneous, *gilah* is beyond the moment, but well worth the wait and toil. Ultimately, it is a far more fulfilling joy.

While King David yearns for the *simchah* and *gilah* of God's eternal embrace, our quest for purpose in service of God can at times also be reflected in these two expressions. It is with a boundless sense of *simchah* that we introduce to a searching Jewish world this transliterated linear Seif Edition of the Artscroll Siddur. The joy of creating a project and working towards its fulfillment is truly a moment of *simchah*. *Gilah*, however, is the status we confidently aspire to enjoy in the months and years ahead. It will be the joy of seeing the benefits that this transliterated linear Siddur will bring to countless people, in the form of enhanced prayer and understanding. It will be the joy of contributing to man's quest for dialogue with our Creator, through the eloquent verses of prayer.

King Solomon also expressed the joys of *simchah* and *gilah*. He wrote: נָגִילָה וְנִשְׂמְחָה בָּךְ, *We will be glad and rejoice in You (Song of Songs* 1:4). The Midrash asks: What does בָּךְ, *in You*, signify? *Yalkut Shimoni* teaches us that the word represents Your [God's] Torah, Your redemption, and, finally, the numerical value of the word, twenty-two, which represents the twenty-two letters of the Hebrew alphabet. Solomon, therefore, prays for the opportunity for Jews to use the twenty-two letters of the holy Hebrew language as a vehicle toward unbridled joy. With the introduction of the Seif Siddur, the full creative potential of the Hebrew

alphabet is now available to all who yearn for a mystical opportunity to engage God in His holy language.

To praise and beseech God in *L'shon HaKodesh*, the holy language of Hebrew, is an opportunity that is now within the grasp of every Jew. To explore the brilliance of the structure of *tefillah* (prayer) and allow it to penetrate the soul, is now open to every searching Jew. To give the gift of prayer and spiritual meaning to fellow Jews, is, in fact, to grant them a gift of eternity — a dialogue with our Creator — at home and in a synagogue.

As the Orthodox Union celebrates its Centennial Year, this gift of prayer may be its grandest expression of service to the English-speaking Jewish world. It is fitting, therefore, that one of the highlights of the Centennial Celebration is this overture to all Jews to join in the sublime and uplifting experience of prayer — by making it available to all. As the burgeoning spiritually inspired Jewish community seeks greater opportunities to understand the essence of a Jew, the two-volume Seif Edition of the Artscroll Transliterated Linear Siddur will act as a vehicle of inspiration, motivation and guidance.

We hope and expect that, with God's help, this Siddur will turn *tefillah* (prayer) into an all-embracing experience, from which no Jew will feel excluded by shortcomings of language or background. The line-by-line transliterated and translated Hebrew page is designed to encourage the development of skills to help users eventually read the Siddur in the original Hebrew. At the same time, the treatment allows the reader to progress at his own pace, with translation in place, as he prays.

We are deeply appreciative of the spirit of partnership and purpose that we have shared over the decades with Mesorah Publications and its guiding forces, Rabbi Meir Zlotowitz and Rabbi Nosson Scherman. Their contribution to the revitalization of Torah life is perhaps their greatest legacy. We are grateful to Rabbi Benjamin Yudin, noted *Rav,* educator and thinker, for his scholarly and inspirational essays and notes on prayer that will distinguish this Siddur as a book of study as well as a book of prayer. We thank Reb Shea Brander who created the format of the Siddur and whose graphics genius and dedication have made the Seif Edition such a work of beauty. Phyliss Meiner of the Orthodox Union and Avrohom Biderman of Mesorah have coordinated this project from its inception, and this undertaking is a testimony to their diligence and concern. Rabbi Avie Gold did the final editing with his customary skill. Akiva Atwood provided the transliteration. We thank them and all who have toiled in making this Siddur a reality.

The two-volume Seif Edition of the Artscroll Siddur has been dedicated by Mr. and Mrs. Herbert Seif in memory of Abraham Seif, of

blessed memory. May the millions of *tefillos* that will be offered through the creation of the Siddur act as a living legacy to a man of sterling qualities, integrity, and a good name.

Finally, may we, as a united Jewish community, use this newly expanded collective gift of prayer *lehagdil Torah ulehadirah*, to raise the banner of Torah and to extol its values to a searching world.

Rabbi Raphael B. Butler
Executive Vice-President
Orthodox Union

Mandell I. Ganchrow, M.D.
President
Orthodox Union

⋙ Introduction

by Rabbi Benjamin Yudin

⋙ Language of Creation

Why transliterate the Siddur — do we not find in the Talmud (*Sotah* 32a) that prayer may be recited in any language? Moreover, are we not taught (*Sanhedrin* 106b) that Hashem is concerned primarily with the sincerity of man, literally that "He desires the heart" of man? The answers to these questions are significant, as the emergence of this Siddur will, it is hoped, enable people who are not yet comfortable and capable of reading Hebrew to pray in Hebrew with the congregation.

Rabbi Avraham Yitzchok Kook comments on the daily prayer *Baruch She'amar,* which speaks of God as having uttered the words that brought the universe into being, that words most often are descriptive; they *describe* events or things, but words do not create. God's words were of a different order; the very words themselves were the medium of Creation. God "spoke and the world came into being." What is true regarding Hashem is equally true regarding man's prayer. When he prays he is not only praising God, presenting his needs, and expressing thanksgiving, but he is creating the means, text and opportunity to have a dialogue with Hashem.

⋙ The Holy Tongue

Hebrew is called לְשׁוֹן הַקֹּדֶשׁ, *the holy tongue*. Rambam suggests that the reason for this designation is that there are no words in the Hebrew language for the sexual organs or relations. In other words, the language is sacred because it instills within its people a sense of modesty and purity. Ramban proposes that it is called the holy language because it is the language with which Hashem created the world, the language that Adam and Eve spoke. The Midrash (*Bereishis Rabbah* 18:6) cites the response of Adam upon seeing Eve — "This shall be called woman for from man was she taken" (*Genesis* 2:23) — as proof that the Torah was given in Hebrew, for the verse teaches that the name *ishah*, woman, comes from the Hebrew word *ish*, man. Moreover, the above cited Midrash teaches that "As the Torah was written by Hashem in Hebrew, so too the world was created with the holy language." As Hashem creates the world anew every day and man is privileged to create dialogue with Hashem, it is most fitting to approach His Divine Presence in His holy language, thereby approaching Him with greater respect, honor and dignity.

The primary reason for praying in Hebrew is its richness in spiritual connotations. The holy tongue contains many hidden meanings, nuances, and

references that cannot be communicated in a translation. Even if a translation is correct and accurate, by definition it falls short of the mark, because it can capture only one of the meanings of a phrase. The prophet Jeremiah (23:29) describes the Torah's many meanings in terms of "a hammer that shatters a rock," which splinters into countless fragments; similarly the words of God are so rich in meaning that each word has many varied and legitimate explanations. Thus, praying in Hebrew arms the worshiper with the many forms of praise, petition, and thanksgiving that are inherent in the language.

The Arizal taught that no prayer is for naught. Even if a particular prayer is not effective for a person at the specific time he utters it, it is deposited in the Heavenly "bank of prayer," where it is safeguarded and subsequently validated at a time when Hashem sees fit. The richness of Hebrew, therefore, permits us to deposit much more.

⋙ Caliber of the Composers

The Talmud (*Megillah* 17b) teaches that the Men of the Great Assembly, which included many prophets, composed the *Shemoneh Esrei* prayer. Rabbi Joseph B. Soloveitchik, in his *Lonely Man of Faith*, teaches that it was necessary that people of such stature compose the prayers, so that they would be meaningful and expressive of the needs of the Jewish people — not only then, but for the next 2,000 years. A case in point: The Talmud (*Berachos* 28b) teaches that when the Sages deemed it necessary to formulate a nineteenth blessing in the *Amidah* against the heretics who were slandering Jews to the Roman government, all agreed that only Shmuel HaKatan was qualified to compose the blessing, because only he could invest it with the perfect balance of love for fellow Jews, and devotion and dedication to the word of Hashem.

We are taught (*Sofrim* 1:7) that when the Torah was translated into Greek, a fast day was declared and darkness descended on the world, and that this tragedy is comparable to the making of the Golden Calf, because "the Torah could not possibly be translated properly." What is true regarding the Torah is equally true regarding prayer; many different meanings are contained in the many psalms and Scriptural verses that abound in our prayer service. By reciting prayers in their original text we invoke the many meanings to help on our behalf, whether we understand them or not. An example is the way the Sfas Emes understood the verse recited prior to the blowing of the *shofar:* זַמְּרוּ אֱלֹהִים זַמֵּרוּ, usually translated as: *Make music for Hashem, make music*, or *Sing praises to Hashem, sing praises (Psalms 47:7)*. The brilliant chassidic master taught that the Hebrew root זמר also means *to prune*, as in *Leviticus* 25:4. Thus, he interprets the above verse homiletically to mean we cut through a strict, harsh measure of judgment, which is alluded to by the Name *Elokim*, which connotes God's strict judgment. Clearly there is much more than meets the eye when we pray in Hebrew.

⋙ Why Hebrew?

True, the Talmud teaches that prayer and the *Shema* may be recited in any

language, but the commentators offer the following explanation as to why Hebrew is preferable. The Chasam Sofer (*T'shuvos Choshen Mishpat* 193) writes that it is interesting to note that the debate as to whether it is preferable to pray in a language one understands, or to pray in Hebrew, is not a new one. In the days of the Men of the Great Assembly, Hebrew was not the vernacular; the Jewish community, as we are taught in the Book of *Ezra*, spoke Ashdudis, yet the prayers were composed in Hebrew. Moreover, writes Rabbi Ephraim Zalman Margolios in his essay *Safah Berurah*, the Mishnah's teaching that prayer may be recited in all languages was only in effect until the composition of the prayers by the Men of the Great Assembly; subsequently we are to pray preferably in Hebrew. Similarly, the great *gaon* Rabbi Akiva Eiger, as well, writes that it is forbidden to deviate from the enactment of the Men of the Great Assembly.

Another significant reason for praying in Hebrew is suggested by Rabbi Zvi Hirsh Chayes, who notes the powerful unifying effect that praying in Hebrew has had on the Jewish people. Whenever and wherever a Jew was dispersed he was able to join in prayer with other Jews. Moreover, had we accepted the perhaps more logical approach of praying in the vernacular, thus making the service more accessible to all, then the Torah, being written in Hebrew, might, God forbid, have been forgotten and neglected. *Avodah*/prayer — which, with Torah and kind deeds, is part of the tripod upon which the world stands (*Avos* 1:2) — helped preserve and safeguard our holy Torah.

This Siddur enables every worshiper to join the congregation in the fullest sense of the word, as a participant, not as a spectator, stranger, or outsider. In addition, the translation below each line is there to help the worshiper understand his prayers and become more proficient in his knowledge of Hebrew. It is my fervent hope that many newcomers using this Siddur will not only pray from left to right with the transliteration, but use the transliteration to help them learn the Hebrew language, as well.

৶৳ Acknowledgments

I begin with boundless praise to Hashem for assisting and enabling me to participate in this holy endeavor. I am truly humbled at the completion of the first volume of the Seif Edition of the Siddur. Over the past nine months I have been privileged to delve into and explore the world of prayer as never before. I have found boundless treasure, much of which I have shared within this volume.

When approached by **Rabbi Raphael B. Butler** of the Orthodox Union and **Rabbis Nosson Scherman** and **Meir Zlotowitz** of Artscroll/Mesorah to write essays that would make the Siddur more open, understandable, and friendly to those not-yet comfortable with the traditional Hebrew Siddur, as well as to the rest of us who want to know more about the prayers we have been reciting all our lives, I soon realized how much there is to learn regarding the background, meaning and philosophy of our prayers. I am grateful for the trust that these colleagues placed in me and appreciative of the friendship, direction and support that Rabbi Butler has provided me in this project. His excitement and creativity was a personal source of inspiration. Rabbi Nosson Scherman's meticulous editing has breathed additional life and greater clarity into my essays; for this and for his constant encouragement, I am very grateful. May he together with **Rabbi Avie Gold** and **Rabbi Avrohom Biderman**, whose efforts improved the work considerably, be afforded the opportunity to continue to challenge and uplift the Jewish community through their magnificent *harbotzas haTorah*. Rabbis Butler, Scherman, and Zlotowitz have given me the opportunity to enrich my spirit with the precious hours carved out of my life that I spent trying to open the doors of prayer to a wider universe of our fellow Jews.

My task was made easier by the privilege I have had for the past many years of studying on Monday nights with dear friends from the former Soviet Union. Bright men and women, denied the opportunity of any Jewish education in their youth, they have taught me that "beginners" can comprehend sophisticated material if it is presented clearly and logically. In the preparation of these essays I often envisioned myself amid my loyal students, who became the barometer as to what materials would be included in this Siddur. To them I affectionately proclaim the Talmudic statement (*Taanis* 7a): "I learned much from my teachers, more from my colleagues, but from my students most of all." Their remarkable religious growth and devotion has inspired me in this entire effort. Their successful strides in Torah and *mitzvos* give me great joy.

The completed work has emerged with an identity unexpected at its outset. At first, the concept of a transliterated Siddur was novel unto itself and I wondered how the page could be structured to make it visually attractive and easy to use — but **Reb Sheah Brander** did it! I applaud him and his staff — particularly **Mrs. Judi Dick, Mrs. Mindy Stern, Mrs. Faigy Weinbaum,** and **Toby Heilbrun** — for their painstaking difficult labor of love in producing this work. My thanks as well to **Rabbi Moshe Schapiro** and **Akiva Atwood** who developed the excellent transliteration. The work of all these individuals has not only opened

this Siddur to countless Jews, but, I trust, the doors of many more synagogues will be open to them as well. They will now have the opportunity of becoming an integral part of the congregation and its prayers.

The essays are based on my research, in which I utilized many classic works of *tefillah*, among them *Avudraham, Otzar HaTefillos, Siddur HaGra*, and *Iyun Tefillah*. In addition, the following works: *World of Prayer* by Rabbi Elie Munk, *Meditations on the Siddur* by Rabbi Jacobson and *Encyclopedia of Jewish Prayer* by Dr. Macy Nulman, were most helpful in providing background information and scholarship. I thank the especially capable librarians of the Gottesman Library at Yeshiva University, where I did most of my writing, for their eagerness to assist and for introducing me to Rabbi Luban's essay on the *Kaddish,* published by Yeshiva University.

A meeting with **Rabbi Benjamin Blech**, former Rabbi of Young Israel of Oceanside and dear colleague at Yeshiva University, yielded the suggestion for headings or captions to summarize the content of each individual prayer, and thereby help the worshiper to understand the nature and essence of the prayer. These headings were very challenging. A prayer often contains many different themes, and choosing a particular synopsis was most difficult. My son, **Rabbi Nisanel Yudin**, joined in these deliberations. It was truly a fulfillment of אֶת וָהֵב בְּסוּפָה (*Numbers* 21:14), which the Talmud (*Kiddushin* 30b) understands to refer to the only ideal strife between father and son, namely in the quest for the truth of Torah, which generates even greater love between them. My son **Aryeh**, who became a *chasan* during the course of the work, also played an important role in formulating the headings. The family's involvement continued, with my son **Alexander** reading and editing most of the essays; his constructive suggestions have been incorporated into the essays. I am grateful also to my son-in-law **Rabbi Larry Rothwax**, for his assistance in the *Hallel* prayer. I would like to thank my other children, **Joel** and **Susan**, **Nisanel** and **Ruthie**, **Steven** and **Devorah**, **Larry** and **Chaviva**, **Arye**, **Atara** and **Penina** for their encouragement, support and patience throughout this project, which entailed my spending many hours away from them.

I am grateful to my mother, **Mrs. Adele Yudin**, to my in-laws, **Irving** and **Sarah Werner,** who have always been foundations of strength, love and inspiration. May they be blessed with good health to lead our family for many more years. The memory of my father, **Alexander Ziskind זצ״ל**, a man who worked all his life for the betterment and enhancement of Jewish communities and synagogues, inspires me constantly.

I am most grateful to **Rabbi Baruch Simon**, Rosh Yeshiva and colleague at Yeshiva University, for his time, patience and vast encyclopedic array of knowledge that he made available to me. His insights and guidance significantly enhanced this project. May Hashem reward him with the fulfillment of his prayers, enabling him to continue teaching Torah at our Yeshiva for many years.

Rabbi Aharon Kreiser, whom I am proud to call my rebbe, provided important guidance since the beginning of this project. As we go to print, he is in need of a *refuah sheleimah*, and we pray for Aharon Gedalia ben Chana Baila.

I am grateful to **Rabbi Eliyahu Swerdloff**, Rosh Yeshiva of Yeshiva Gedola of Paterson, and a dear friend and neighbor, who enhanced the work and guided me; and to **Rabbi Hershel Schachter**, Rosh Yeshiva at Yeshiva University, for his friendship, availability and his offering insights of Rabbi Soleveitchik זצ״ל on prayer. I feel myself most fortunate that I was able to complete this volume in *Eretz Yisrael*, and appreciate the time I learned with **Rabbi Yaacov Wiener** of the Torah and Science Institute.

I would like to thank my congregational family, Shomrei Torah of Fair Lawn, and its distinguished president, **Mr. Rodney Grundman,** for their encouragement and support of my Friday morning radio programs on the *parashah*, enabling me to reach out to a listening audience, and now for their enthusiasm and support for my work on behalf of a reading audience.

I thank **Debby Friedman** of Fair Lawn for being an enthusiastic and efficient intermediary between myself and the Orthodox Union; and I am grateful to **Phyllis Meiner** for her meticulous transcribing and cheerful encouragement throughout.

On a personal note, now fortuitous that I was privileged to be raised in Crown Heights and knew the late **Abraham Seif** as a warm, friendly mainstay of the community. His son **Heshe Seif,** a loyal helping friend over the years, and his grandson, **Dr. Jordan Alter**, an officer in my congregation, have refined his legacy through their ongoing devoted service to Klal Yisrael.

Finally, in a category all unto herself, there really are no words to describe the debt of gratitude I owe my dear wife **Shevi**. I can only borrow the words of Rabbi Akiva, who proudly declared told all that his Torah and that which he was privileged to teach and disseminate to others was only thanks to his wife's righteousness and total self-sacrifice. Shevi has not only encouraged me but has been a rebbe of *chesed* to me. All of the lessons of sensitivity, compassion, and kindness that I was able to cull from the depths of our *tefillah* stem from her character. May she be blessed with good health and continue to mold our children and grandchildren in her beautiful *middos* of Torah and *maasim tovim*.

Benjamin Yudin

אדר תשנ״ח / March 1998

The Background of the Prayers

✒ The Sources of Our Prayers

✒ The Patriarchs

The Talmud (*Berachos* 26b) cites two sources as the origin of our daily prayers. The first is our Patriarchs, each of whom instituted a prayer which reflected his life experience. *Shacharis*, the morning prayer, which is recited when the sun is rising, reflects the life of Abraham. Faced with many challenges and difficulties as he embarked on the new mission to proclaim the word of God to an idolatrous world, he emerged triumphant and was treated respectfully by his peers and neighbors.

Minchah, which is recited in the afternoon, when the sun is descending, reflects the circumstance of Isaac, who composed it. In comparison with his father, Abraham, his life was one of subtle decline; he never enjoyed the fame or acceptance that his father did. Nevertheless, Isaac maintained Abraham's teachings and continued his legacy.

Maariv, the evening prayer, was composed by Jacob, whose life was filled with one problem after another, reflected by the dark of night when his prayer is recited. His faith and inspiration during even the darkest times has helped sustain his descendants throughout the "nights" of our history, including the past two millennia of dispersion and frequent oppression.

Maharsha suggests that each of the Patriarchs surely prayed all three times, in keeping with the verse *Evening, morning, and noon, I supplicate and moan, and He has heard my voice* (*Psalms* 55:18), but the life experiences of each was closely identified with a particular prayer.

In all circumstances, each Patriarch turned to God for thanksgiving, guidance, comfort, and inspiration. We, their descendants, proudly maintain this Divine encounter.

✒ Korbanos / Offerings

The second source for our prayers is the *Korbanos*, the daily offerings that were brought in the Holy Temple in Jerusalem. The Torah ordains that one lamb was to be offered in the morning and a second lamb in the afternoon (*Numbers* 28:4). This was done every day without exception. On the Sabbath and *Yom Tov,* in addition to the morning offering, the Jewish community brought the *mussaf*, or additional offering.

These daily offerings brought atonement to the Jewish nation and renewed the close ties between Hashem and His people. Indeed, the word *korban*, generally — but erroneously — translated as sacrifice, comes from the root *karov* [קרב], which means coming close. Far from a "sacrifice," a word that implies loss, a *korban* is a positive thing — a means of drawing close to God. The Jew begins his day by reiterating his love for Hashem and his willingness to place all of his possessions and resources in His hands, as a means of drawing closer to Him.

◄§ Symbolism of the Offerings

Rabbi Samson Raphael Hirsch explains the symbolism of the offerings as follows. Hashem is our Shepherd, we are taught in Psalm 23. By offering two lambs daily, we proclaim that He leads us morning and evening, through all the different periods of our lives. The flour and wine offerings brought in the Temple signify that all our possessions, from the bare essentials to the luxuries, come from Him and are at His disposal. The institution of *korbanos* represents a reciprocal process: God gives life to man, and man dedicates his life back to Hashem.

The animal that was slaughtered may be seen as man's animalistic elements being placed in the service of God. We control our natural inclinations and attempt to channel them toward Divine service rather than mundane, even unholy, pursuits. Likewise, the fats offered on the Altar symbolize man's excessive indulgence and unused energy, his untapped resources, which could be used more constructively when applied to a higher cause. And the blood sprinkled by the Altar symbolizes man's passions, all of which should be consecrated to Hashem.

The Talmud (*Taanis* 27b) teaches that Abraham asked how the Jewish nation would attain forgiveness without the Temple. God replied that when the people of Israel recite the Scriptural order of the offerings, God will consider it as if they had actually brought the offerings and they will be forgiven. This principle is cited by the prophet who said, "Let our lips substitute for bulls" (*Hosea* 14:3).

◄§ Time Frames

Offerings, as the origin of prayer, impact upon our prayers both legally and philosophically. Prayer must come at fixed times, following the same schedule that governed the sacrificial order, as opposed to randomly chosen moments of individual inspiration. Thus, one should complete the *Shemoneh Esrei* within the first third of the day, just as the morning offering was brought during the first third of the day. (If, however, one was delayed, the *Shacharis Shemoneh Esrei* may be recited until midday, just as the morning *korban* could have been brought until that time, if it had not been brought in its preferred time.)

Similarly, just as our morning prayer corresponds to the daily morning offering, *Minchah*, the afternoon prayer, corresponds to the daily afternoon offering. *Maariv*, the evening prayer, by contrast, is not tied to a specific offering, as no offerings were brought at night. *Maariv* does, however, correspond to the nighttime burning on the Altar of all the fats and organs left over from the preceding day's offerings. It is because *Shacharis* and *Minchah* correspond to specific, required offerings that they are of primary importance, and, therefore, they include the *chazzan*'s repetition of *Shemoneh Esrei*. *Maariv*, however, has no such repetition because it does not come in place of a required offering.

The daily recitation of the offering of *Ketores*, the eleven spices that comprised the incense offering, substitutes today for the actual daily offering of *Ketores* every morning and evening on the Golden Altar in the Temple. The Talmud

(*Yoma* 44a) teaches that the *Ketores* atoned for evil speech and served as a daily reminder to the people that there is life and death in the power of the tongue, just as intentional changes in the formula of *Ketores* could incur the Heavenly imposed death penalty.

◆§ Not Recitation Alone

Rabbeinu Bachya notes in his commentary on the Torah that it is not the mere recitation of the sacrificial order that is dear to Hashem and that attains its desired end, but rather it is possessing an understanding of the proceedings and their symbolic lessons that achieves this. Thus, our *Shacharis* prayer corresponds to the morning offering that dedicates to God the incoming day's potential; *Minchah* corresponds to the offering that acknowledges Him as Master of all that we have accomplished; and *Maariv* proclaims that even when man is inactive during the night, we declare His absolute and uncontested sovereignty.

The *Levush*, however, contends that our recitation of *Korbanos* is for a different reason. There is a *mitzvah* to study Torah daily and through the recitation of the *Korbanos*, with its combination of Scripture, Mishnah and Talmud, we accomplish this minimum fulfillment of our daily obligation. That these subject matters were chosen may be more fully understood with the philosophical ideas enumerated above, namely, that the *Korbanos* represent our yearning to become close to God.

◆§ Shemoneh Esrei

Shemoneh Esrei, literally "Eighteen" (the number of blessings it originally comprised), is the most important of our prayers. In a sense, every word that precedes it has been but preparation.

The Talmud (*Megillah* 17b) teaches that Ezra and the Men of the Great Assembly composed these eighteen blessings from Scriptural sources in the early years of the Second Temple Era. Why do we continue to use a prescribed prayer that was written over two thousand years ago? Why do we not compose our own spontaneous, personal prayers?

Rabbi Joseph B. Soloveitchik provides an answer by pointing to the Talmud's statement: "Rabbi Yochanon taught, One who connects the blessing of redemption [which concludes the Blessings of the *Shema*] to the evening prayer [the *Shemoneh Esrei*] is worthy of the World to Come" (*Berachos* 4b).

What is the connection between prayer and redemption? Rabbi Soloveitchik explains. After recording that Moses killed an Egyptian for beating a Jew, the Torah writes, "And it happened during those many days that the king of Egypt died, and the Children of Israel groaned because of the work, and they cried out"

(*Exodus* 2:23). The slaves had been subjected to a miserable existence, yet not even a sigh was heard from them until now. Why had they suffered silently?

Because they were born into slavery and knew no other way of life, they believed that this was their natural lot and they were not impelled to cry out. Not only were their bodies enslaved, notes the *Zohar*, but their power of expression was enslaved as well. The Kabbalists comment that the name of our festival of freedom, Pesach, alludes to the Hebrew words פֶּה שָׂח, *the mouth speaks*, to signify the Jews' newfound freedom to express themselves cogently, an ability that had been robbed from them during their long years of servitude.

Moses' actions changed all that. He demonstrated that a superior lifestyle existed and the people came to recognize their pain and call out to God for redemption. The realization that they were victims of injustice triggered a response from them.

Even so, their response was nothing more than וַיִּזְעָקוּ , a groan, a cry (*Exodus* 2:23). Though they were no longer silent, they did not actually pray, as they did not yet have the capacity to articulate their needs. Speech only follows understanding, and at that point in time, after centuries of enslavement, they did not know how their needs could be addressed and their situation rectified. The redemptive process of the Jewish people thus began with their first recognition of a need — with their emergence from being an enslaved and silent people to being a vocal people.

This historical episode, says Rabbi Soloveitchik, reflects the story of the individual man and sheds light upon why we pray as we do. Man often leads a silent existence, unaware of his genuine needs. He may know what he *wants*, but does not know what he needs. Often, his desires are not in his best spiritual or moral interests, and he loses sight of what his fundamental needs are.

Man's challenge, therefore, is to fashion his personality, to arrange his hierarchy of values so that he can discover and identify those needs and cry out for them, converting his silence into articulate speech. In this manner, he is free to move from a mute, peripheral existence to a speaking part at center stage.

The Torah informs us that Hashem declared, "Let us make man in Our image, after Our likeness" (*Genesis* 1:26). Rabbi Soloveitchik suggests that Hashem says, "Let **us** make." He is addressing man directly, inviting him to join in the process of creation and development. In this world, man is constantly challenged to develop himself. Unlike the animals who are born with almost their full natural capacity, man has the power to advance his potential by controlling his impulses and fashioning his character.

The primary purpose of prayer is not to change Hashem, but to change us. Prayer thus begins in the heart. It is, in fact, called עֲבוֹדָה שֶׁבְּלֵב, service of the heart. Prayer differs in this regard from most of the Torah's proactive commandments. *Mitzvos* such as eating in a *succah* and affixing a *mezuzah* can be fulfilled simply with a physical act, even without the proper focus upon its Biblical requirement. The *mitzvah* is achieved even without putting one's heart into it.

Prayer is different. Prayer without awareness, without knowing what one is saying or to Whom one is saying it, is drained of its meaning. Prayer has the

power to transform each of us into a different person with different values, and it frees us to speak up on our own behalf.

Man alone cannot solve his problems or satisfy his needs. Nor can he ignore them. Judaism rejects the notion of man suffering silently; rather the Torah wants man to cry out to God to rescue him from affliction. But though man's Biblical obligation to pray is satisfied simply by crying out, the Rabbinic structure of prayer calls for identifying, clarifying, and prioritizing one's needs. Enter the *Shemoneh Esrei*, introduced by the Men of the Great Assembly as a litany of specific requests, designed to classify every need.

The development of a fixed prayer, moreover, allows the worshiper not only to be aware of his sundry needs — spiritual, dietary, financial, emotional, and so on — but to understand how to respond to them. They must be channeled properly, toward service of God, as expressed by King Solomon, "In all your activities, know Him" (*Proverbs* 3:6).

This is the great contribution of the Men of the Great Assembly. *Shemoneh Esrei* teaches man thrice daily what his needs really are. Instead of focusing on material acquisitions, we are given the opportunity to clearly find and define our true needs. *Shemoneh Esrei* educates and gives dignity to the worshiper, enabling him to achieve his own private redemption.

◆§ Structure of Shemoneh Esrei

"Rabbi Chanina taught, The first three blessings are compared to a servant who thoughtfully praises his master. The middle blessings [of the weekday *Shemoneh Esrei*] are likened to a servant requesting reward from his master; and the three concluding blessings reflect the servant who received his bounty, who thanks the master and takes leave" (*Megillah* 18a).

◆§ The First Blessing: Patriarchs

The first blessing of the *Shemoneh Esrei* is called *Avos*, or Patriarchs. It invokes Abraham, Isaac, and Jacob, whose personal precedents of prayer serve as one of the sources for our obligation to pray. The Talmud (*Berachos* 28b) teaches that this recital of eighteen blessings corresponds to the eighteen times Hashem's Name is mentioned by King David in Psalm 29.

The first three blessings of the *Shemoneh Esrei* correspond not only in number, but in theme to the first three phrases of Psalm 29 (*Megillah* 17b). "Render unto Hashem, you sons of the powerful" is understood by the Talmud to refer to the Patriarchs. The second blessing, praising Hashem's might, corresponds to the second phrase "Render unto Hashem honor and might," and the third phrase "Render unto Hashem honor worthy of His Name" inspired the third blessing, which speaks of the holiness of God's Name.

This first blessing differs from most blessings, as the phrase, *Melech ha'olam*, King of the universe, is distinctly missing. The Tur suggests that praising Hashem as the "God of Abraham" constitutes an expression of His Kingship, as Abraham promulgated Hashem's rule over the entire world by spreading His

word.

We praise Hashem separately as "God of Abraham, God of Isaac, and God of Jacob," because each individual mention denotes a personal discovery of and relationship with Hashem. Each of our Patriarchs labored on his own to perceive God and find the way to serve Him; he did not simply cling to a blind faith as it was passed down to son and grandson (*Panim Me'iros*).

The great Chassidic master Rabbi Menachem Mendel of Kotzk explains that this individualized association with Hashem reflects the specialty of each. Thus, "God of Abraham" reflects Abraham's service of Hashem through kindness and good deeds to man; "God of Isaac" focuses on Isaac's service of Hashem through prayer and introspection; and "God of Jacob" refers to Jacob's service of Hashem through Torah study and the pursuit of truth.

The sensitivity of Jews throughout the millennia to respond to the needs of the downtrodden may be attributed to the spiritual genes we inherited from our father Abraham. The phenomenal faith our people have displayed, even with the sword at our necks, to believe and trust in His salvation comes to us from our father Isaac. The designation of Israel as the "People of the Book" and our dedication to the study of Torah emanates from our father Jacob. Consequently, each Jew is charged not to be content with the performance of the Torah's commandments, but also to discover and relate to Hashem in accordance with his unique talents, character, and potential, to forge a personal bond between himself and Hashem.

In addition, this blessing praises Hashem for responding to us in the merit of the Patriarchs, even when we are unworthy. As Hashem protected Abraham, the founder of the Jewish people, when he was cast into the fire by Nimrod (*Genesis* 11:28), so has He safeguarded Abraham's descendants through the ages, despite innumerable attempts to destroy us.

The blessing is also a charge to emulate the kindness and compassion of Abraham and incorporate it into one's everyday activities. For how, asks Rabbi Yonason Eibeschutz, can one invoke the merit of Abraham if he does not personally aspire to that end?

The importance of this first blessing cannot be underscored enough. Ideally, one should understand what one is saying during the entire *Shemoneh Esrei*, but doing so during the first blessing is crucial. In fact, many authorities hold that one who prays without this minimum concentration during the first blessing must repeat the entire *Shemoneh Esrei*.

⋙ The Second Blessing: God's Might

The second blessing describes the incomparable power of Hashem, by listing miracles only He can perform. The *sine qua non* of these powers is His ability to revive the dead; man can destroy life, but only Hashem can create life. This phenomenon is completely beyond the realm of anything we personally experience, yet it is one of the cardinal tenets of our faith.

Further, understanding and appreciation of this concept is gleaned from the seemingly natural occurrence of rainfall. The Talmud (*Taanis* 7a) teaches, in the

name of Rabbi Abahu, "A day of rain is greater than the day of the resurrection of the dead, for the latter is only for the righteous" (*Isaiah* 66:24), whereas rain benefits both the righteous and the wicked. For this reason, continues the Talmud, the mention of rain was introduced by our Sages in the blessing of the resurrection of the dead. Most natural phenomena occur with regularity, and thus the role of Hashem is not openly evident in them, the Vilna Gaon explains. Rain, though, is unpredictable, and is thus a clearer indication of His control over the world. In this way, rain, which sustains human life by causing produce to grow and providing water for human use, is comparable to the resurrection of the dead.

Shibbolei HaLekket points out that the second blessing corresponds to the *Akeidah*, the binding of Isaac on the altar (*Genesis* 22). *Pirkei d'Rabbi Eliezer* (ch. 31) notes that when Abraham lifted up the knife to slaughter Isaac, Isaac's soul temporarily left him, allowing him to experience firsthand the miracle of resurrection.

Finally, the constant reaffirmation that our physical body will once again come to life challenges us to view our bodies with greater sanctity. The Torah teaches: "Hashem formed [וַיִּיצֶר] Man from the dust of the earth" (*Genesis* 2:7). The word וַיִּיצֶר, *formed*, is spelled with an additional letter *yud*, to imply that there were two aspects in the creation of Adam, and indeed of all people − one for his present existence, and the other for the time of his resurrection.

◄§ The Third Blessing: God's Holiness

In his classic philosophic work, *The Kuzari*, the medieval philosopher, Rabbi Yehudah HaLevi, classifies creation into five groups: inanimate objects, vegetation, animals, man, and the Jewish people. The Jew resides at the top of the chain, because at Sinai God designated us as "a kingdom of ministers and a holy nation" (*Exodus* 19:6).

How do we embrace that holiness?

Rashi defines "holy" as separate, apart. The holiness of Hashem lies in the fact that He is completely beyond human comprehension. Man, who is finite and corporeal, cannot comprehend the infinite and the incorporeal, nor can he fully comprehend all the manifestations of Hashem − such as His compassion and graciousness, His judgment and might. The Jewish nation was chosen to lead the world toward an understanding and acceptance of Hashem's mission.

With each recital of the *Shemoneh Esrei* we renew that commitment toward holiness. This blessing, therefore, exhorts us to emulate Hashem by imparting sanctity to all that we do. The blessing prepares the worshiper for his presentation of requests by putting values in the right perspective. *Mabit* notes that in the *Shemoneh Esrei* we ask Hashem only for what we truly need. By focusing on His holiness and being reminded of our own potential holiness, we elevate the dignity of our requests, because we undertake to use what we receive toward Divine service, subsequently bringing further glory to Hashem's holy Name.

Declaring to Hashem, "You are holy," communicates the readiness of the Jew to sacrifice all, even his life if need be, to sanctify God's Name. In addition, we

ought to be mindful of the interpretation of *Nachmanides*, who understands the command to be holy as a call for moderation in all physical pleasures and materialistic pursuits.

⧉ The Thirteen Middle Blessings

On the Sabbath the thirteen middle blessings of the weekday *Shemoneh Esrei*, which contain specific requests, are omitted. These blessings will be discussed in the Weekday Siddur. In their place, a new blessing is inserted. See *"Kabbalas Shabbos,"* below.

⧉ Expressions of Thanks

The last three blessings of the *Shemoneh Esrei* are the same for every *Amidah*. As a group, they are called *Hoda'ah*, literally Thanksgiving, which is also the theme of the second blessing of the group. While at first glance both the first blessing, *Retzei,* and the final blessing, *Shalom*, Peace, are requests — that God restore the Temple service and endow us with peace — a more careful analysis will show why all three blessings collectively are expressions of thanks.

In essence, in the last section of *Shemoneh Esrei* we are thanking God for granting us the privilege of an audience with Him. In *Retzei*, realizing how fortunate we have been to communicate with Hashem through prayer, we beg that this relationship be expanded, developed, and heightened by the restoration of the Temple Service. In *Modim*, which means not only to thank, but also to acknowledge or confess, we bow in recognition that we are in the actual presence of the Divine, as it were. Finally, in the last blessing, we say that though in a physical sense we are taking leave of God's Presence, may His spirit accompany us in all our endeavors.

The common denominator is that these three blessings were recited by the *Kohanim* (the Priests), in the Temple, at the conclusion of the morning service. All three elements — the people, the place, and the time — relate to our having entered the Divine Presence, and for this privilege we are grateful.

⧉ Curse of Independence

In cursing the serpent for tempting Eve to sin, God said, "Upon your belly shall you go and dust shall you eat all the days of your life" (*Genesis* 13:14). Rabbi Menachem Mendel of Kotzk asked wherein lies the curse to the serpent; after all, there is never a shortage of earth and dust to supply the serpent with his needs. Incisively, the Rabbi explained that it was precisely because God provided the serpent with all that he needed, that he was cursed. In essence God said to the serpent, "There will be no need for any communication nor relationship between us; whatever you will need you will have, and you will have no reason to turn to Me, to beseech Me, or to have a relationship with Me." This teaches what a privilege it is for man to have a relationship with God, and this is why we thank God in these blessings, for having granted us the privilege of an audience with Him.

◆§ Restoration of the Temple Service

I believe there are three new concepts in this blessing. The first is one of relationship. We ask God to respond favorably to our prayers not because He *has* to, but because He *wants* to. There is a difference between fulfilling a commitment because one is bound by contract to do so, and a situation where the donor extends himself because he wants to do so, not motivated by the legal obligation. A husband is obligated by Halachah to support his wife, but if the relationship is good and loving, he will view his support as a privilege, not a burden. Similarly, we pray that God accept our prayers with favor, because He wishes to, and not because of His covenant with our forefathers, or because He must insure our survival since His Name is inextricably associated with ours.

Thus, in the first theme of this blessing, we plead, "May we find favor in Your eyes; may You be pleased with Your people Israel." Enable us to be even closer to You than the direct relationship we are privileged to have by petitioning You through prayer — and that is to restore the Temple service, for the offerings are a means for people to become close to You [קָרְבָּן, *offering*, is from the root קרב, *close*]. As close a rapport as petition and praise of Hashem can bring, the bringing of offerings is an even closer and more intimate relationship.

Secondly, Rabbi Joseph B. Soloveitchik suggested that in this blessing we are asking God not merely to accept our prayers, but rather that we ourselves be elevated in His eyes as if we were offerings. This concept has a basis in Halachah. *Mishkanos Yaakov* maintains that our recitation of *Retzei*, with its reference to offerings, converts our prayer into an offering. On a personal level, the individual's prayer is ideally looked upon as if it were a personal offering, and when the *chazzan* (reader) repeats this blessing, it converts the public prayer into a public sacrifice. This explains why, when the *Kohanim* ascend to bless the congregation on festivals, we recite the prayer וְתֶעֱרַב, asking God to be pleased with our prayer as if it were a burnt offering and sacrifice. This prayer is inserted in the middle of *Retzei*, because it is the theme of this blessing. It is thus understandable that if the *Kohen* does not ascend the platform in preparation for the Priestly Blessings while the *chazzan* is reciting *Retzei*, then he may no longer ascend. It is this blessing that enables the *Kohanim* to bless the congregants, as it transforms prayer into sacrifice.

◆§ National Merit

The third new concept in this blessing is expressed by the commentary of the *Maggid Tzedek*, a student of the Vilna Gaon. He notes that this prayer asks Hashem to find our prayers acceptable in the merit of "Your people Israel." Even if anyone or particular group of people are not worthy of their prayers being answered, the collective merit of *Am Yisrael,* the metaphysical entity of our people, should warrant this special request. Finally, *Midrash Shocher Tov* (*Psalms* 17:5) observes that many thousands died in the days of King David because the Jewish people had not petitioned Hashem for His Temple to be built and for His presence to reside in their midst. Now if they, who had never had a

Temple, were held responsible for not praying for one, we, who have had two Temples, should appreciate the loss and spiritual vacuum created by its destruction. How much more so must we pray for its rebuilding.

The historical background to this blessing is provided in the *Shibbolei HaLekket* that when the Jewish people sinned with the Golden Calf, Hashem showed his displeasure and announced He was moving out of the camp. It was not until months later, on Yom Kippur, that He forgave the Jewish people and ordered that a sanctuary be built (*Exodus* 25:8) that He may dwell again in their midst. They began on the morrow after Yom Kippur and the sanctuary was dedicated on *Rosh Chodesh* Nissan. When the heavenly fire descended symbolizing that God's Presence was in their midst (*Leviticus* 9:24), the angels responded with the blessing of "Who returns His Divine Presence to Zion."

◆§ Ya'aleh V'Yavo

Ya'aleh V'Yavo is the prayer that is added to the *Amidah* and Grace After Meals on *Rosh Chodesh* and Festivals. The Talmud (*Shabbos* 24a) teaches that on days where there is an obligation to bring a *mussaf* (additional offering beyond the required daily morning offering) in the *Amidah*, one recites a prayer "that reflects the occasion" in the blessing for the return of the Temple service. It is fitting that this prayer which mentions the occasion of *Rosh Chodesh* or *Chol HaMoed* be incorporated in the blessing of the Temple service, for *Ya'aleh V'Yavo* petitions God to have compassion on Israel and Jerusalem and to reinstate the Temple service, so that we can fulfill the obligation to bring the offerings mandated by the Torah for the particular occasion. If one did not include this prayer, continues the Talmud, we require him to rectify the omission. [See "Laws."]

The eight expressions beginning "*Rise, come, reach, be noted,* etc." are attributed by the Vilna Goan in his commentary *Avnei Eliyahu* to the fact that the *Shechinah,* Divine Presence, has withdrawn itself to above the seven heavens and therefore the eight expressions denote the many stages that our prayers must penetrate.

◆§ The Blessing of Thanksgiving

The Talmud (*Megillah* 18a) emphasizes the close connection between the preceding blessing of restoring the Temple service and thanksgiving; that in reality they form one unit, for the rendering of thanks and gratitude is part of the service of Hashem. Rabbi Elie Munk writes strongly that "Any expression of gratitude not preceded by the acceptance to observe the Divine law is blasphemy." The word *hoda'ah*, thanksgiving, has three connotations: Firstly, to bow down, therefore we bow at the beginning and end of this *berachah*. Secondly, it is an expression of admission and faith, as in the words of gratitude and recognition recited upon arising in the morning that Hashem has restored our soul. Finally, it refers to thanksgiving (*World of Prayer*, pp. 151-2).

Ideally one should have proper *kavanah*, concentration and understanding of

what is being recited throughout the *Amidah*, but the Sages have taught that the first blessing of the faith of the Patriarchs and this blessing of Thanksgiving warrant special attention and concentration.

The *Mabit* (*Bais Elokim*) notes that we bow at the beginning and end of this blessing because it encompasses all of the praises and the Oneness of Hashem. Thus, to demonstrate that we are humbled by the recitation, we bow in humility. According to *Rokeach*, we bow to signify our personal acceptance of His Kingship, like a servant prostrating himself before his master. It is thus understandable that a perfunctory mechanical bowing without realizing who, what or why is almost meaningless.

In *Modim* we thank Hashem that He has seen fit to bind our identity with His, in the past, present, and future. We offer gratitude that He has maintained His oath to Israel never to exchange us for another as His chosen people. We thank Him for our lives and for our souls that He returns to us daily. Notes the *Zohar*, the norm among people is that if one has entrusted a precious object to someone else and he owes that person a great debt, the lender will keep the object as collateral. Similarly, we owe Hashem everything, and each night we entrust our soul to Him. Only due to His abundant kindness does He return our souls daily. *Eitz Yosef* notes that the numerical value of the word מוֹדִים, *Modim* is one hundred, reminding us of the Rabbinic obligation to recite one hundred blessings daily, thus acknowledging throughout the day that He is our Provider, and making our thanksgiving a constant refrain of life.

◆§ Open and Hidden Miracles

Included in this blessing is our thanks to Hashem for "Your miracles that are with us daily, and for Your wonders every evening, morning, and afternoon. *Miracles*, explains the *Eitz Yosef*, are extraordinary events that everyone recognizes to be the result of Hashem's intervention. *Wonders* are the familiar things that we do not regard as miracles, because we have become accustomed to them, such as breathing, raining, and growing. In *Modim,* we are reminded that we are all daily beneficiaries of Hashem's miracles and wonders — but we have become so blasé that we don't even realize their source, and therefore do not adequately thank Hashem. In this blessing, therefore, we offer thanks for the miracles and wonders of which we are aware, and also for the ones that we do not recognize as such.

The basic philosophical principle contained in this blessing is the attribute of *hakaras hatov,* acknowledging the good done for us. All too often man resists this practice as an unwelcome reminder that we are dependent on others. It humbles us to be forced to say thank you or, in other words, I couldn't do it without you. The Talmud (*Bava Kama* 92a) teaches that one must even thank a waiter. One might argue that, firstly, he is being paid, and secondly, it is not even his food that he is serving. Yet we must accustom ourselves to express appreciation, for unless we recognize the good extended to us by man, we will fail to acknowledge the constant good provided us by God.

The Sages note disapprovingly that Pharaoh was an ingrate. In describing his

plan to enslave and persecute the Jews, the Torah says of Pharaoh that he "did not know of Joseph" (*Exodus* 1:8), implying that the new king was unaware of the enormous debt of gratitude he and his people owed their Jewish savior. Our Rabbis tell us that indeed he *did* know of Joseph, but conducted himself as if he did not. The same Pharaoh later on responded to Moses' request that he set free the Jewish nation: "I do not know Hashem, nor will I send out Israel" (5:2). Because Pharaoh did not recognize the good extended to him by man, he was led to deny the good extended to him by God.

⊷ Modim D'Rabbanan

The Talmud (*Sotah* 40b) teaches that when the *chazzan* repeats the blessing of thanksgiving aloud, the congregation is to join with its own declaration of thanks. *Avudraham* suggests that the congregation cannot rely on the *chazzan's Modim*, because only the beneficiaries can express sincere thanks to one who has helped them. Whereas petitions and requests may be submitted on behalf of another, declarations of faith can be uttered only by each individual himself. Similarly, one Jew cannot recite the *Shema*, thereby accepting the tenets of the existence, Oneness, and love of Hashem on behalf of another, just as one cannot don *tefillin* or shake a *lulav* on behalf of another. Such commandments, like the recitation of *Modim*, must be performed personally, and not through an intermediary.

The Talmud cites the personal declarations used by a number of rabbis (Rav, Shmuel, Rav Simlai, and Rabbi Acha bar Yaakov). Rav Papa held that it is best to include them all, which we do in our text of *Modim D'Rabbanan*, which is appropriately named *Modim* of the Rabbis.

⊷ Conclusion

The blessing ends with praise to God as the One Who deserves thanks. The historical background for this ending, according to *Shibbolei HaLekket*, is found in the Talmud (*Shabbos* 30a). When King Solomon brought the Ark into his newly built Temple, the gates of the Holy of Holies clung to each other miraculously and could not be opened. Solomon recited twenty-four expressions of prayer, but the gates remained closed. Finally, he pleaded, "Hashem, O God, turn not away the face of Your anointed one. Remember the pieties of David Your servant." As soon as he mentioned the name of David, he was answered and the gates opened. At that moment the angels exclaimed, "Blessed are You, Hashem, Whose Name is good, and to You it is fitting to give thanks."

⊷ Peace: The Final Blessing

The last blessing is that of Peace. As we have pointed out before, our prayers take the place of the sacrificial order that was brought in the Temple. In the Temple, the *Kohanim* would bless the people at the conclusion of the service (*Leviticus* 9:22). Their blessings concluded with a plea for peace, and we, too, conclude our prayers with the blessing of peace and the Priestly Blessing, when

appropriate. The Midrash (*Vayikra Rabbah* 9:9) notes that all blessings from God end with peace. Interestingly, the first substantiation of this concept is offered by Rabbi Shimon Ben Yochai from the last verse of Psalm 29, the psalm which, as noted, is the source for the structure of both the weekday and Shabbos *Shemoneh Esrei*. The psalm deals with the revelation at Sinai and ends with "Hashem will bless His people with Peace." The commentaries understand this to mean not only that He will bless His people with peace, but that He will bestow all His blessings in an environment of peace, so that the blessings will endure.

The Talmudic sage Chizkiah derived the great importance of peace from Scripture. He noted that many of the 248 positive commandments of the Torah are conditional. For example, if one chances upon his friend's lost object he must return it (*Exodus* 23:4-5), but one is not required to initiate a search for such objects. Similarly, only if one encounters a mother bird roosting on its chicks or eggs must one carry out the prescribed ritual (*Deuteronomy* 22:6-7). However, regarding peace we are taught: "Seek peace and pursue it" (*Psalms* 34:15) — peace is so vital that one is charged to go out of his way to foster it.

The blessing of peace should be understood as an injunction to every one to pursue peace at all costs. The final blessing after the *Shema* on Friday evenings concludes with "Who spreads the shelter of **peace** upon us, upon all of His people and upon Jerusalem." The last blessing of the *Amidah* and the Priestly Blessings ends with the blessing of peace. And the *Kaddish* concludes with "He Who makes peace in His heights, may He in His compassion make peace upon us and upon all Israel."

Indeed the last Mishnah of the Talmud informs us that the necessary environment to receive blessing is that of peace (*Uktzin* 3:12). Thus, explains Rabbi Yonason Eibeschutz, we pray for peace and unity and harmony among our people thereby making us worthy to receive all the diverse blessings of the *Amidah*. One should pray for genuine peace and that strife and argumentation should not characterize the Jewish community. On a personal note, one is to pray that one be rid of anger, for that, too, is an impediment to peace.

Rabbi Zvi Mecklenburg, in his commentary *Eyun Tefillah*, understands the petition of "Bless us with the light of Your countenance" to mean the gift of greater understanding of Your Torah, on all its levels, including those that are beneath the surface and can be understood only with great toil in study of the Oral Law. In this blessing we ask not only for peace of mind but Divine assistance in mastering the inner hidden secrets of Torah.

◆§ Rabbi Meir Makes Peace

This duty of everyone to seek peace is illustrated by a story found in the Jerusalem Talmud (*Sotah* 1:4). The great sage Rabbi Meir used to lecture on Friday evenings at the synagogue in Chamas, and a certain woman attended his lecture religiously. Once the lecture ran longer than usual and, when she returned home late, her husband, who disliked rabbis, vowed that she could not enter his home until she spat in Rabbi Meir's eye. After three weeks of

banishment from her home, her friends persuaded her to go to Rabbi Meir, who had been informed by Elijah the Prophet that he was the indirect cause of the marital disharmony. When she arrived, Rabbi Meir feigned distress in his eye. He asked the woman visitor, "Can you assist me by spitting in my eye?" He instructed her to spit seven times, assuring her it would help cure him. She did!

Thereupon he instructed her to tell her husband: "You insisted that I spit once, and I spat seven times." When his students asked why the great Torah scholar demeaned himself so, he responded, "I, Meir, take my lead from none other than Hashem Himself." As we are taught, for the sake of restoring peace between husband and wife, the Holy Name of God is erased in the waters of the *sotah* (*Numbers* 5:23).

◄§ Positive Unity Through Peace

Ashkenazic practice is to recite the *Sim Shalom* text of the blessing for peace only at the times that the Priests offered their blessing in the Temple. This includes every *Shacharis*, and *Mussaf*, and *Minchah* on a fast day. In *Avnei Eliyahu*, the Vilna Gaon shows how the six forms of goodness we request in *Sim Shalom* correspond to the six blessings contained in the verses of the Priestly Blessings. Thus, the "peace, goodness, blessing, graciousness, kindness, and compassion" mentioned in *Sim Shalom* parallel the six attributes in *Bircas Kohanim*: Bless you, safeguard you, illuminate, be gracious, turn . . . to you, be gracious. The Talmud (*Sotah* 39b) highlights the connection between the Priestly Blessing and the final blessing of the *Amidah* by mandating that the *Kohanim* are not to leave the platform, where they stood as they blessed the congregation, until the *chazzan* has completed the blessing of *Sim Shalom*.

The *Shibbolei HaLekket* ascribes the text of this blessing to the angels who recited it after Joshua's fourteen years of conquest and division of the Land, whereupon the Jewish nation attained peace, "each man under his vine and under his fig tree" (I *Kings* 5:5).

Rabbi Baruch HaLevi Epstein in his commentary, *Baruch She'amar*, notes that there is a difference between the verb שִׂים, literally *place*, and תֵּן, *grant*. The former has the connotation of something being carefully placed, in contrast to the latter, which does not denote careful placing (see *Temurah* 34a). Thus when Abraham sent away Hagar and Ishmael, he carefully placed and arranged [שָׂם] the provisions on her shoulder (*Genesis* 21:18). Similarly in our blessing of peace, we pray for "*sim shalom*," meaning that we pray for peace that unifies in a positive way, through common values, purpose and goals, as opposed to the unity that comes from without, through crises and troubles.

◄§ Times of Day — and Life

There is a fascinating parallel and symmetry between *Modim*, the blessing of thanksgiving, and *Sim Shalom*, the blessing for peace. In the former we thank God for His wonders and favors in every season, "evening, morning, and afternoon." In the latter we ask for "graciousness, kindness, and compassion."

One of my congregants excitedly shared the following thought with me. The times enumerated in *Modim* may refer not only to the literal times of the day, but to the different times in our lives. Unlike the rest of society, in which elderly people try to resist growing old with dignity, by dressing and acting like the young, our tradition associates the "evening" of life with *chein*, charm. Judaism does not spurn its elderly, or regard them as nonproductive members of society; rather the Torah says, "Ask your father and he will relate it to you and your elders and they will tell you" (*Deuteronomy* 32:7).

The *boker*, morning, is representative of the early, younger years of life, when one sees not only the rising sun, but new opportunities. At this time we recognize God's constant *chessed*, kindness, in guiding our morning, our young selves, toward maturity. Finally, the afternoon represents middle age, which requires a special dose of "His compassion," so that we should be pleased with ourselves, with our accomplishments, and with our contributions to society. The Talmud (*Berachos* 57b) insightfully notes that God implants a positive feeling and desire in each individual artisan and craftsman, so that however one serves society, one should enjoy one's work and perform it with a positive sense of privilege of enhancing society.

Rabbi Moshe Lichtenstein suggests that the main part of the *Amidah* prayer is concluded with the blessing of *Modim* and the recitation of the Priestly Blessings, as was the case in the Temple, when the blessing of the *Kohanim* followed the morning sacrifice. That we bow at the beginning and end of *Modim* is a further demonstration that the formal prayer is over and that we are respectfully taking leave of God's Presence. What then is the *Sim Shalom* blessing? It is our request to God that He extend His blessing even after we have left His Divine presence.

⋙ Kaddish

The *Kaddish* is one of the most important and misunderstood prayers in our liturgy. Although most people think of *Kaddish* as a prayer for the dead, it contains no mention of death whatsoever. Rather, the word *Kaddish* means "sanctification" of Hashem's Name, and that is the function it serves: to declare the holiness of God.

⋙ Its Significance

Why is *Kaddish* so significant? Its opening words and the context of where and when they were recited shed light on this question. The prophet Ezekiel warned Israel of the impending destruction of the First Temple and at the same time assured them that eventually the Jewish people will be restored to their former position of spiritual preeminence and enjoy an ideal relationship with Hashem, centered around the Third Temple. Of that time God says וְהִתְגַּדִּלְתִּי וְהִתְקַדִּשְׁתִּי, *I will be exalted and I will be sanctified* (*Ezekiel* 38:23), the phrase after which the beginning of *Kaddish* is patterned. The prophet says that not only will the people of Israel be redeemed, but, as difficult as it is for us to comprehend, God Himself will be redeemed at that time. When Israel suffers so does He, and when there is evil in this world, not only does man suffer, but God suffers as well. His destiny is inextricably bound to that of the Jewish nation, as we are taught by the symbolism of the burning bush, when He revealed Himself to Moses from the lowly, prickly bush.

The single most important part of *Kaddish* is יְהֵא שְׁמֵהּ רַבָּא מְבָרַךְ לְעָלַם וּלְעָלְמֵי עָלְמַיָּא, May *His great Name be blessed forever and ever*. According to *Machzor Vitri* (cited by *Tosafos*, *Berachos* 3a), it refers to the Amalekite nation's sneak attack upon Israel shortly after the Exodus from Egypt (*Exodus* 17:8). Amalek thus became the symbol and personification of evil in this world, for it attacked Israel not because it wanted land or possessions; rather, Amalek wanted to destroy Israel. At that time God vowed to blot out the remembrance of Amalek from under the heavens, saying, כִּי יָד עַל כֵּס יָהּ, *For the hand* [of God] *is on the throne of God: HASHEM maintains a war against Amalek from generation to generation* (*Exodus* 17:16). Interestingly, both the word for the throne, כֵּס, instead of כִּסֵּא, and the Name of God are shortened (God's Name in the verse has only two letters instead of all four letters [י-ה-ו-ה]). This suggests that neither His Name, meaning our perception of His essence, nor His throne will be complete until the evil represented by Amalek is eradicated from this world. Thus, when we declare in *Kaddish* that His Name be blessed forever, we express the wish that His Name and throne be complete.

⋙ Faith Amid Crisis

The significance of the *Kaddish* is that it manifests man's ability to express his faith, while acknowledging crisis and difficulties, be they national calamities or

personal tragedies. This interpretation can be seen from a fascinating understanding of a Talmudic teaching (*Chullin* 91b). Contrasting the heavenly angels with the nation of Israel, the Talmud concludes that the children of Israel are more beloved and have greater merit before God than even the angels. This is shown by the fact that when the angels praise Hashem, they are permitted to utter His Name only after reciting the three words, "*Kadosh, Kadosh Kadosh*," *Holy. holy, holy* — קָדוֹש, קָדוֹש, קָדוֹש, ה׳ צְבָאוֹת — while Israel recites His Name after the two words, "*Shema Yisrael*" — שְׁמַע יִשְׂרָאֵל ה׳ .

In commenting on this passage, the *Maharsha* suggests that each *Kadosh* of the angels is inspired by a careful scrutiny and analysis of the Divine Presence in a different sphere, as is seen in the explication of these three levels of holiness that is found in the *Uva L'Tzion* prayer:

> Holy in the most exalted heaven, the abode of His Presence; Holy on earth, product of His strength; Holy forever and ever is HASHEM, Master of Legions.

The Maharsha explains that the angels have a complete understanding of the workings of Hashem. They see how His plan emanates from on high and is executed here on earth and will finally be clear to all in the World to Come. Only when they see the totality of His plan, program and actions, do they respond with an enthusiastic sanctification of His Name.

The Jewish people, on the other hand, by virtue of their mortality, are privileged to see and comprehend only the first two stages of holiness. They have faith in His dominion on high and His control of events on earth. Yet mortal man starting from Moses our Teacher cannot understand the totality of His plan, such as the eternal question "Why do the righteous suffer and the wicked prosper (*Berachos* 7a). In his limited vision and understanding, man cannot see how "everything that Hashem does is for the good," as Rabbi Nachum, the illustrious teacher of Rabbi Akiva, was wont to say (*Taanis* 21a).

This lack of comprehension, however, does not deter the Jew from reciting both the *Shema*, which testifies to our faith in Hashem, and the *Kaddish,* which is based on the trust that He knows how and why even death — which is so tragic to the mortal eye — has a far-reaching purpose and meaning beyond our comprehension. We therefore proclaim "*May His Name*" — meaning His essence — "*become great.*" May our understanding be expanded from the Two-letter Name of Amalek's time to the full Four-letter Name, and may His throne become unblemished from a perspective of man's noncomprehension to one of recognition and understanding of the Divine way, thereby enhancing God's position and stature in our world today.

◆§ The Bond Between God and Israel

We are accustomed to regard prayer as man either praising God or requesting something from Him. Rabbi Chaim of Volozhin, in his *Nefesh HaChaim* (Ch. 2), presents another intriguing aspect of prayer. Given the special relationship between Hashem and His people, when Israel is in pain, Hashem suffers, too. The *Kaddish* then assumes a most unique role in that man prays not only for the

alleviation for his own suffering, but for that of Hashem as well. The Mishnah (*Sanhedrin* 46a) expresses this idea in the following dramatic way. Rabbi Meir taught that when a sinner is executed, Hashem Himself complains that His head and arm hurt, as it were. The Mishnah continues that if He suffers even when the wicked are punished, then how much more so does He feel the suffering of the righteous. What, however, is the meaning of His "head and arm hurt"? Reb Chaim of Volozhin explains that just as a Jew dons *tefillin* to express the appreciation that Hashem has a relationship with Israel, similarly, the Talmud (*Berachos* 6a) teaches, Hashem, as well, "dons" *tefillin*, as it were, to symbolize that He and Israel are bound together. When this connection is broken by sin, God's "head and arm," the organs where *tefillin* are worn, are where He feels pain. *Kaddish* is thus man's expression of concern for God's suffering, and a prayer that His Name be sanctified.

◆§ Five Circumstances

Kaddish is recited in five different situations and circumstances:

(1) The *chazzan* (reader) recites it between the different sections of prayer, such as between the *Pesukei D'Zimrah* and the Blessings of the *Shema* to signify that a section has been completed. This *Kaddish* is referred to as *Chatzi Kaddish*, the Half-*Kaddish*, because it does not include the last two or three verses that are recited at other times. Perhaps the role of this *Kaddish* may be understood in light of the following Talmudic passage (*Berachos* 33b). A *chazzan* leading the prayer service before Rabbi Chanina said in his *Amidah* prayer, "The great, the mighty, the awesome, the glorious, the potent, the feared, the strong, the powerful, the certain and the esteemed God." After the service, Rabbi Chanina said to him, "Did you complete all the praises of your Master?" — meaning that his effusive list of adjectives implied that he was capable of listing *all* of God's praises, something that is clearly impossible. Indeed, the praises that we recite at the beginning of the *Amidah* — *the great, mighty and awesome* — are permitted only because they are found in the Torah (*Deuteronomy* 10:17). Similarly in the case of the Half-*Kaddish*, having concluded a section of His praises, we make it clear that we have not exhausted His praises by reciting *Kaddish*, which states that God's ultimate praise is yet to come, and moreover that *"He is beyond any blessing and song, praise and consolation that are uttered in the world."*

(2) The second *Kaddish* is the *Kaddish Shaleim*, the Full *Kaddish*, which is recited by the reader after the conclusion of the *Shemoneh Esrei*, and which includes *Tiskabeil*, a plea that God accept the just-completed prayer.

(3) The third form is *Kaddish Yasom*, the Mourner's *Kaddish*, which is recited by a son for eleven months after the death of a parent.

(4) The fourth *Kaddish*, *Kaddish D'Rabbanan*, or the Rabbis' *Kaddish*, which is recited after the study of Rabbinic Torah teachings, and especially teachings of an Aggadic nature. It includes a prayer for the welfare of the teachers and students of Torah, for they are essential to Israel's welfare. Indeed, the Talmud teaches that the world survives thanks to this *Kaddish* (*Sotah* 48a).

(5) The fifth *Kaddish* is recited at the cemetery by the son after the completion the interment. Interestingly, an almost identical *Kaddish* is recited by someone who celebrates a *Siyum*, the completion of a tractate of Talmud or an order of the Mishnah. A possible reason for the applicability of the same *Kaddish* to both situations may be that this *Kaddish* introduces the concept of תְּחִיַּת הַמֵּתִים, the *Resurrection of the Dead*, and it speaks of perfect service of God. This *Kaddish* symbolizes continuity: Just as the dead will live again, so must we strive in our learning to attain a complete state of service to God.

◆§ The Key Phrase

The Talmud (*Sotah* 49a) refers to the entire *Kaddish* as *Y'hei Sh'mei Rabba M'varach*, "May His great Name be blessed," the response recited by the congregation upon hearing the recitation of *Kaddish*. This response is so important that Rabbi Yehoshua ben Levi teaches (*Shabbos* 119b): "Whoever responds to the *Kaddish* by saying, '*Amen, may His great Name be blessed for ever and ever*,' with all his might" — meaning with great concentration (*Rashi*) — "any evil decree rendered against that individual is nullified."

Kaddish is so important that the response in it of *Amen, Y'hei Sh'mei Rabba* takes precedence over even that of *Kedushah*, which is recited in the *chazzan's* repetition of the *Amidah*. (In a practical sense, therefore, someone who encounters one *minyan* reciting *Kedushah*, and another reciting *Kaddish*, should respond to the *Kaddish* rather than to *Kedushah* (*Orach Chaim* Ch. 56).

Elijah the Prophet taught Rabbi Yose a lesson that sheds understanding on the *Kaddish* (*Berachos* 3a). Three times every night, God laments the fate of the Jewish nation and exclaims, "Woe to the sons because of whose sins I destroyed My House, burned My Temple, and exiled them among the nations of the world." But when Jews enter their synagogues and houses of study and respond in the *Kaddish*, "*May His great Name be blessed*," God shakes His head, as it were, and says, "Fortunate is the King Who is praised this way in His house. What is there for the Father Who has exiled His sons, and woe to the sons who have been exiled from their Father's table."

Tosafos (*Berachos* 3a) explains why *Kaddish* is in Aramaic. In Babylonia, the Torah was taught in that language, which was the vernacular of the people. Since the *Kaddish* that follows Torah study is so important, the Rabbis wanted it to be understood by all, so they formulated it in Aramaic. The reason we do not recite *Kaddish* in the vernacular of our respective countries is explained by the *Zohar* (*Terumah*). Since *Y'hei Sh'mei Rabba* is so important, as noted above, and since the portion that is added to the *Kaddish* following Torah study of great significance, the Rabbis wanted them to be understood by everyone. Aramaic was the common vernacular, so the Sages formulated those parts of Kaddish in the language understood by everyone.

The *Zohar* (*Terumah*) teaches that *Yehei Sh'mei Rabba*, recited with proper concentration and vigor, can destroy evil forces that result from man's misdeeds and prevent God's splendor from being revealed to His children. For this reason it was composed in Aramaic, a language that is utilized by the forces of evil. By

exalting God in Aramaic, we bring holiness to the dark corners of earth, where it could not otherwise penetrate. (This would explain why these portions of *Kaddish* were not recited in other languages.)

⋙ Connection to Death

While the subject of death is not mentioned in the *Kaddish*, the connection between this prayer and death can be seen both from early sources in our tradition and from the philosophical religious response to this personal tragedy.

In *Kallah Rabbasi* (Ch. 2), one of the minor tractates of the Talmud, we are taught that Rabbi Akiva chanced to meet what appeared to be a man carrying wood in a cemetery. According to one text, the wood was for his own burning in *Gehinnom* (Purgatory). The load was so heavy he could hardly walk. He was moaning and groaning.

"Is there no one," asked Rabbi Akiva, "who can rescue you from this terrible suffering?"

"No one, unless my son could recite *Kaddish* for my sake." Rabbi Akiva taught the son Torah and the boy recited the *Kaddish*, whereupon the father was released from his punishment.

The idea that a child can earn merit on behalf of a wicked father is found in *Sanhedrin* (104a): "A righteous son can earn merit for a wicked father, but a righteous father cannot earn merit for a wicked son." The Talmud continues, Abraham could not save his wicked son Ishmael from Divine punishment nor could Isaac save his wicked son Esau from Divine punishment. But Abraham could rescue his father Terach. Rashba explains this phenomenon. Since parents are the cause of the child's existence in this world, they live on through their progeny. Thus if the child performs righteous deeds, the parents are regarded as partners in the deed, and therefore part of the reward for that deed goes to the parents. The reverse, however, is not true. The existence of the parent is not due to the child. Thus, the righteous deeds of a parent may not be viewed as being performed by the child.

In addition, the benefit of recitation of *Kaddish* by a child may be understood in the following way. In sports there is the concept of an "assist," which means that if one player sets up the play enabling his teammate to score, the one who facilitated the play is also given recognition. Similarly, in the realm of the holy and spiritual, if someone positively motivates and inspires the next one to perform good deeds, then part of the credit is attributed to the one who had the positive influence.

The recitation of *Kaddish* on behalf of a parent is a way of saying, "Though I don't understand why my loved one was snatched from me, his/her faith and courage have motivated me to accept the Divine judgment." This is known as *Tzidduk HaDin*, or justification of the Divine judgment.

Finally, the *Kaddish*, in which we pray for the ultimate sanctification of His Name, is simultaneously a pledge on our part to accept the obligation to help create this sanctification. To live a life of *Kiddush Hashem* is to bring honor and glory to Hashem through our actions. With each recitation of the *Kaddish*, we

acknowledge: "All is destined from on high including one's health and wealth, and all accept the fear of Heaven." By not only loving Hashem ourselves, but as taught in *Yoma* (86a), by living in a way that influences others to love Him, we sanctify His Name. The recitation of *Kaddish* is certainly important, but of even greater value is the commitment to live a life of Torah and *mitzvos* that truly sanctifies His Name.

⋗ Worth of an Individual

Moreover, the potential and worth of each individual is highlighted with the recitation of *Kaddish* specifically for a particular person. The late Rabbi Meir Shapiro, who introduced the concept of *Daf Yomi*, the daily study of a folio of Talmud, noted the significance of each person in the following Talmudic teaching. The Mishnah (*Berachos* 49b) teaches that if three or more men ate a meal together that required the recitation of the Grace After Meals, they preface their blessings with the introductory *"Zimun."* The formula for this introduction changes according to the number of participants. If there are ten men present, the Name of God is added. According to one view in the Talmud, if there are a hundred, a thousand, or ten thousand, respectively, the formula of praise for Hashem is increased. Thus if there are 99 or 999, only one person is missing, but this manifests itself in a noticeable diminution in the praise of His Name and essence. This illustrates the importance of even one Jew. The recitation of *Kaddish* for a departed one proclaims that though the army of Hashem has been diminished by one — thus creating a void, a vacuum of holiness, and a diminution of good deeds in the Jewish community — the life that remains behind must continue to be sanctified.

Erev
Shabbos

⋖§ Minchah

⋖§ Elijah's Proof

One should be especially careful regarding the prayer of *Minchah*. Rabbi Chelbo said in the name of Rav Huna, "A person should be diligent with regard to the *Minchah* prayer for Elijah the Prophet was answered only through the *Minchah* prayer" (see *I Kings* 18:19-39). Elijah challenged almost a thousand false prophets, "Let them give us two bulls; let them choose one bull for themselves, cut it, and put it on the wood, but not apply fire, and I will prepare one bull and place it on the wood, and I will not apply fire. You shall call out in the name of your god and I shall call out in the Name of HASHEM, and whichever God responds with fire, He is the [true] God" (vs. 23-24). The false prophets shouted their incantations and mortified their bodies, but to no avail. No "god" heeded them. When they were done, Elijah drenched his offering with water, uttered a simple prayer — and a Heavenly fire consumed the offering. Masses of Jews had gathered to see who would prevail. thunderstruck, they called out, "HASHEM is the God! HASHEM is the God!"

Rashba comments that the false prophets believed that the sun had independent power and that God does not control the world. Therefore Elijah waited until the end of the day when the sun was setting, demonstrating that precisely when their god was waning, the fire would descend and Hashem would manifest His absolute dominion and control. Our daily recitation of *Minchah* echoes Elijah's demonstration that Hashem controls nature always.

⋖§ Minchah's Uniqueness

The *Tur* (*Orach Chaim* Ch. 232) explains the special significance of *Minchah* by contrasting it with the other prayers of the day. Whereas *Shacharis* is recited before a person becomes preoccupied with all the pressures and details of earning a livelihood, and *Maariv* is recited in the evening, after one has distanced himself from the concerns of the workday, *Minchah* is often recited while one is still at work. To extricate oneself not only physically but mentally, and to focus on the Jew's special relationship with God and the responsibilities that accompany that relationship, is often a great challenge and sacrifice. In the words of Ben Hei Hei (*Pirkei Avos* 5:26): "The reward is in proportion to the exertion."

Avudrahum comments that the afternoon prayer is called *Minchah* to allude to the translation of Onkelos on the verse "They [i.e., Adam and Eve] heard the sound of HASHEM God manifesting Itself in the garden toward evening" (*Genesis* 3:8). Onkelos translates the latter phrase *limnach yuma*, "as the day was setting." Adam and Eve transgressed the word of God late in the afternoon, the

time of *Minchah*, and God responded by granting them an audience with Himself, as it were, an opportunity to reflect upon their actions and repent. Similarly, we are given the same opportunity as the day wanes; it is an *opportune time* (*Psalms* 69:14) to reflect upon the day's activities. Perhaps the Aramaic *limnach yuma* can also mean "when the day is coming to a rest"; just as on Shabbos, a day of rest, *yom menuchah*, we should reflect on the activities of the week, and on Yom Kippur we review the activities of the year, each day at *Minchah* we review and scrutinize the proceedings of the day.

Avudraham further suggests that as the setting sun "bows" respectfully to God, we, too, should emulate nature and utilize the moment to draw closer to Him.

At *Minchah*, with the day drawing to a close, we should be filled with pride at having had the privilege to serve Hashem that day. We draw this lesson from the Vilna Gaon's comment on a passage from the liturgical poem *Keil Adon*, which is added to the first blessing of the *Shema* on Shabbos morning: [The sun and the heavenly bodies are] "Glad as they go forth and exultant as they return." They embark on their daily mission with happy anticipation that they will serve God, and upon completion of their mission at sunset, they are filled with exultation stemming from the satisfaction of fulfilling His mission.

⊰{ KINDLING LIGHTS }⊱

──────────── OVER THE SABBATH LIGHTS: ────────────

[ONE WHO IS BOTH LIGHTING SABBATH CANDLES AND RECITING *MINCHAH* MUST RECITE *MINCHAH* BEFORE LIGHTING THE CANDLES.] LIGHT THE CANDLES, THEN COVER THE EYES AND RECITE THE BLESSING. UNCOVER THE EYES AND GAZE BRIEFLY AT THE CANDLES. [WHEN A FESTIVAL COINCIDES WITH THE SABBATH, RECITE THE FESTIVAL BLESSINGS (BELOW).]

BORUCH ato Adōnoy · · · · · · · · · · · · · · בָּרוּךְ אַתָּה יהוה

*Blessed are You, H*ASHEM*,*

Elōhaynu melech ho-ōlom, · · · · · · · · · · אֱלֹהֵינוּ מֶלֶךְ הָעוֹלָם,

our God, King of the universe,

asher kid'shonu b'mitzvōsov, · · · · · · · אֲשֶׁר קִדְּשָׁנוּ בְּמִצְוֹתָיו,

Who has sanctified us with His commandments,

v'tzivonu l'hadlik nayr shel shabos. · · וְצִוָּנוּ לְהַדְלִיק נֵר שֶׁל שַׁבָּת.

and has commanded us to kindle the light of the Sabbath.

──────────── OVER THE FESTIVAL LIGHTS: ────────────

BORUCH ato Adōnoy · · · · · · · · · · · · · · בָּרוּךְ אַתָּה יהוה

*Blessed are You, H*ASHEM*,*

Elōhaynu melech ho-ōlom, · · · · · · · · · · אֱלֹהֵינוּ מֶלֶךְ הָעוֹלָם,

our God, King of the universe,

asher kid'shonu b'mitzvōsov, · · · · · · · אֲשֶׁר קִדְּשָׁנוּ בְּמִצְוֹתָיו,

Who has sanctified us with His commandments,

v'tzivonu l'hadlik nayr · · · · · · · · · · · · · · וְצִוָּנוּ לְהַדְלִיק נֵר

and has commanded us to kindle the light

ON THE SABBATH ADD:

shel shabos v' . . . · · · · · · · · · · · · · · · · · · . . . שֶׁל שַׁבָּת וְ

of the Sabbath and

──────────── ON YOM KIPPUR THIS BLESSING CONCLUDES: ────────────

shel yōm hakipurim. · · · · · · · · · · · · · · שֶׁל יוֹם הַכִּפּוּרִים.

of Yom Kippur.

──────────── ON OTHER FESTIVALS THIS BLESSING CONCLUDES: ────────────

shel yōm tōv. · שֶׁל יוֹם טוֹב.

of the Festival.

────────────────────────

⊰§ **Kindling lights**

The Sabbath lights are kindled approximately eighteen minutes before sunset.

Since women are found in the home more often than their husbands, and since women are generally in charge of household matters, the *mitzvah* of kindling the lights has devolved upon the mistress of the house. Nevertheless, a man living alone, or residing with other men, is required to kindle the lights and recite the proper blessing. Similarly, if a woman is too ill to light, her husband should light the candles and recite the blessing.

There should be some light in every room where it will be needed — and indeed this is a halachic requirement — nevertheless, the blessing is recited upon the candles that are kindled in the room where the Sabbath meal will be eaten. A brightly lit festive table represents one form of fulfillment of the prophet's

ON ALL FESTIVALS EXCEPT THE LAST TWO DAYS OF PESACH
THE FOLLOWING BLESSING IS ALSO RECITED:

BORUCH ato Adōnoy   בָּרוּךְ אַתָּה יהוה

Blessed are You, HASHEM,

Elōhaynu melech ho-ōlom,   אֱלֹהֵינוּ מֶלֶךְ הָעוֹלָם,

our God, King of the universe,

shehecheyonu v'kiy'manu v'higionu   שֶׁהֶחֱיָנוּ וְקִיְּמָנוּ וְהִגִּיעָנוּ

Who has kept us alive, sustained us, and brought us

laz'man ha-ze.   לַזְּמַן הַזֶּה.

to this season.

IT IS CUSTOMARY TO RECITE THE FOLLOWING PRAYER AFTER THE KINDLING.
[THE WORDS IN BRACKETS ARE INCLUDED AS THEY APPLY.]

Y'hi ratzōn l'fonecho,   יְהִי רָצוֹן לְפָנֶיךָ,

May it be Your will,

Adōnoy Elōhai Vaylōhay avōsai,   יהוה אֱלֹהַי וֵאלֹהֵי אֲבוֹתַי,

HASHEM, my God and God of my forefathers,

shet'chōnayn ōsi   שֶׁתְּחוֹנֵן אוֹתִי

that You show favor to me

[v'es ishi, v'es bonai,   [וְאֶת אִישִׁי, וְאֶת בָּנַי,

[my husband, my sons,

v'es b'nōsai, v'es ovi,   וְאֶת בְּנוֹתַי, וְאֶת אָבִי,

my daughters, my father,

v'es imi] v'es kol k'rōvai,   וְאֶת אִמִּי] וְאֶת כָּל קְרוֹבַי,

my mother] and all my relatives;

v'siten lonu ulchol yisro-ayl   וְתִתֵּן לָנוּ וּלְכָל יִשְׂרָאֵל

and that You grant us and all Israel

cha-yim tōvim va-aruchim,   חַיִּים טוֹבִים וַאֲרוּכִים,

a good and long life;

v'sizk'raynu b'zichron   וְתִזְכְּרֵנוּ בְּזִכְרוֹן

tōvo uvrocho,   טוֹבָה וּבְרָכָה,

that You remember us with a beneficent memory and blessing;

v'sifk'daynu bifkudas   וְתִפְקְדֵנוּ בִּפְקֻדַּת

y'shu-o v'rachamim,   יְשׁוּעָה וְרַחֲמִים,

that You consider us with a consideration of salvation and compassion;

---

instructions: "If you proclaim the Sabbath 'a delight', the holy one of HASHEM 'honored' ... then you shall be granted delight with HASHEM ..." (*Isaiah* 58:13-14). The candles honor the Sabbath by imparting dignity and importance to the festive meal.

usvor'chaynu b'rochōs g'dōlōs, וּתְבָרְכֵנוּ בְּרָכוֹת גְּדוֹלוֹת,
that You bless us with great blessings;

v'sashlim botaynu, וְתַשְׁלִים בָּתֵּינוּ,
that You make our households complete;

v'sashkayn sh'chinos'cho baynaynu, וְתַשְׁכֵּן שְׁכִינָתְךָ בֵּינֵינוּ,
that You cause Your Presence to dwell among us.

V'zakayni l'gadayl bonim וְזַכֵּנִי לְגַדֵּל בָּנִים
uvnay vonim וּבְנֵי בָנִים
Privilege me to raise children and grandchildren

chachomim unvōnim, חֲכָמִים וּנְבוֹנִים,
who are wise and understanding,

ōhavay Adōnoy, yir-ay Elōhim, אוֹהֲבֵי יהוה, יִרְאֵי אֱלֹהִים,
who love HASHEM *and fear God,*

anshay emes, אַנְשֵׁי אֱמֶת,
people of truth,

zera kōdesh, Badōnoy d'vaykim, זֶרַע קֹדֶשׁ, בַּיהוה דְּבֵקִים,
holy offspring, attached to HASHEM,

um-irim es ho-ōlom וּמְאִירִים אֶת הָעוֹלָם
who illuminate the world

batōro uvma-asim tovim, בַּתּוֹרָה וּבְמַעֲשִׂים טוֹבִים,
with Torah and good deeds

uvchol m'leches avōdas habōray. וּבְכָל מְלֶאכֶת עֲבוֹדַת הַבּוֹרֵא.
and with every labor in the service of the Creator.

Ono sh'ma es t'chinosi אָנָּא שְׁמַע אֶת תְּחִנָּתִי
Please, hear my supplication

bo-ays hazōs, בָּעֵת הַזֹּאת,
at this time,

bizchus בִּזְכוּת
in the merit of

soro, v'rivko, v'rochayl v'layo שָׂרָה וְרִבְקָה וְרָחֵל וְלֵאָה
i-mōsaynu, אִמּוֹתֵינוּ,
Sarah, Rebecca, Rachel, and Leah, our mothers,

v'ho-ayr nayraynu וְהָאֵר נֵרֵנוּ
and cause our light to illuminate

shelō yichbe l'ōlam vo-ed, שֶׁלֹּא יִכְבֶּה לְעוֹלָם וָעֶד,
that it not be extinguished forever and ever,

v'ho-ayr ponecho v'nivoshay-o. Omayn. וְהָאֵר פָּנֶיךָ וְנִוָּשֵׁעָה. אָמֵן.
and let Your countenance shine so that we are saved. Amen.

⊰ WEEKDAY MINCHAH ⊱

■ We begin *Minchah* with the *Ashrei** prayer — "Praiseworthy are those who dwell in Your house" — extolling those who sit, pause, and reflect on God's greatness. The focus on Scriptural verses of praise and consolation enables us to rise and stand before God in a more cheerful disposition.

The alphabetic acrostic of *Ashray* motivates the supplicant to praise God, His Kingship, and His providing the needs of every living creature. The Sages highlight the importance of *Ashray* by declaring that whoever recites this psalm three times daily is directing himself towards meriting a place in the World to Come (*Berachos* 4b).

ASHRAY yōsh'vay vay-secho,

אַשְׁרֵי יוֹשְׁבֵי בֵיתֶךָ,

Praiseworthy are those who dwell in Your house;

ōd y'hal'lucho selo.

עוֹד יְהַלְלוּךָ סֶּלָה.

may they always praise You, Selah!

Ashray ho-om shekocho lō,

אַשְׁרֵי הָעָם שֶׁכָּכָה לּוֹ,

Praiseworthy is the people for whom this is so,

ashray ho-om she-Adōnoy Elōhov.

אַשְׁרֵי הָעָם שֶׁיהוה אֱלֹהָיו.

praiseworthy is the people whose God is HASHEM.

T'hilo l'dovid,

תְּהִלָּה לְדָוִד,

A psalm of praise by David:

arōmimcho Elōhai hamelech,

אֲרוֹמִמְךָ אֱלוֹהַי הַמֶּלֶךְ,

I will exalt You, my God the King,

va-avor'cho shimcho l'ōlom vo-ed.

וַאֲבָרְכָה שִׁמְךָ לְעוֹלָם וָעֶד.

and I will bless Your Name forever and ever.

B'chol yōm avor'cheko,

בְּכָל יוֹם אֲבָרְכֶךָ,

Every day I will bless You,*

va-ahal'lo shimcho l'ōlom vo-ed.

וַאֲהַלְלָה שִׁמְךָ לְעוֹלָם וָעֶד.

and I will laud Your Name forever and ever.

Godōl Adōnoy umhulol m'ōd,

גָּדוֹל יהוה וּמְהֻלָּל מְאֹד,

HASHEM is great and exceedingly lauded,

v'ligdulosō ayn chayker.

וְלִגְדֻלָּתוֹ אֵין חֵקֶר.

and His greatness is beyond investigation.

⊰⊱ **Ashrei**

Ashrei comprises Psalm 145, with the addition of two introductory verses and a closing verse from elsewhere in *Psalms*. This psalm was chosen because no other psalm possesses both of two virtues: (a) The initials of the psalm's respective verses follow the order of the *alef-beis;* and (b) its sixteenth verse contains the inspiring and the reassuring testimony to God's mercy, "You open Your hand and satisfy the desire of every living thing."

The Midrash records that the Psalmist and Sages used the *alef-beis* formula in chapters that they wanted people to follow more easily or to memorize. Moreover, the *alef-beis* structure symbolizes that we praise God with every sound available to our organs of speech.

בְּכָל יוֹם אֲבָרְכֶךָ — *Every day I will bless You.* True, no mortal can pretend to know God's essence, but each of us *is* equipped to appreciate life, health, sustenance, sunshine, rainfall, and so on. For these and their daily renewal,

Dōr l'dōr y'shabach ma-asecho,

דּוֹר לְדוֹר יְשַׁבַּח מַעֲשֶׂיךָ,

*Each generation will praise Your deeds to the next,**

ugvurōsecho yagidu.

וּגְבוּרֹתֶיךָ יַגִּידוּ.

and of Your mighty deeds they will tell.

Hadar k'vōd hōdecho,

הֲדַר כְּבוֹד הוֹדֶךָ,

The splendrous glory of Your power

v'divray nifl'ōsecho osicho.

וְדִבְרֵי נִפְלְאֹתֶיךָ אָשִׂיחָה.

and Your wondrous deeds I shall discuss.

Ve-ezuz nōr'ōsecho yōmayru,

וֶעֱזוּז נוֹרְאוֹתֶיךָ יֹאמֵרוּ,

And of Your awesome power they will speak,

ugdulos'cho asap'reno.

וּגְדוּלָתְךָ אֲסַפְּרֶנָּה.

and Your greatness I shall relate.

Zecher rav tuv'cho yabi-u,

זֵכֶר רַב טוּבְךָ יַבִּיעוּ,

A recollection of Your abundant goodness they will utter

v'tzidkos'cho y'ranaynu.

וְצִדְקָתְךָ יְרַנֵּנוּ.

and of Your righteousness they will sing exultantly.

Chanun v'rachum Adōnoy,

חַנּוּן וְרַחוּם יהוה,

Gracious and merciful is HASHEM,

erech apa-yim ugdol chosed.

אֶרֶךְ אַפַּיִם וּגְדָל חָסֶד.

slow to anger, and great in [bestowing] kindness.

Tōv Adōnoy lakōl,

טוֹב יהוה לַכֹּל,

HASHEM *is good to all,*

v'rachamov al kol ma-asov.

וְרַחֲמָיו עַל כָּל מַעֲשָׂיו.

and His mercies are on all His works.

Yōducho Adōnoy kol ma-asecho,

יוֹדוּךָ יהוה כָּל מַעֲשֶׂיךָ,

All Your works shall thank You, HASHEM,

vachasidecho y'vor'chucho.

וַחֲסִידֶיךָ יְבָרְכוּכָה.

and Your devout ones will bless You.

K'vōd malchus'cho yōmayru,

כְּבוֹד מַלְכוּתְךָ יֹאמֵרוּ,

Of the glory of Your kingdom they will speak,

ugvuros'cho y'dabayru.

וּגְבוּרָתְךָ יְדַבֵּרוּ.

and of Your power they will tell,

L'hōdi-a livnay ho-odom g'vurōsov,

לְהוֹדִיעַ לִבְנֵי הָאָדָם גְּבוּרֹתָיו,

to inform human beings of His mighty deeds,

we give daily blessings.

דּוֹר לְדוֹר יְשַׁבַּח מַעֲשֶׂיךָ — *Each generation will praise Your deeds to the next.* We cannot under- stand God's essence or His ways, for He is infinite. We must rely on the traditions from earlier generations.

uchvōd hadar malchusō.

וּכְבוֹד הֲדַר מַלְכוּתוֹ.

and the glorious splendor of His kingdom.

Malchus'cho malchus kol ōlomim,

מַלְכוּתְךָ מַלְכוּת כָּל עֹלָמִים,

Your kingdom is a kingdom spanning all eternities,

u-memshalt'cho b'chol dōr vodōr.

וּמֶמְשַׁלְתְּךָ בְּכָל דּוֹר וָדֹר.

and Your dominion is throughout every generation.

Sōmaych Adōnoy l'chol hanōf'lim,

סוֹמֵךְ יהוה לְכָל הַנֹּפְלִים,

HASHEM supports all the fallen ones*

v'zōkayf l'chol hak'fufim.

וְזוֹקֵף לְכָל הַכְּפוּפִים.

and straightens all the bent.

Aynay chōl aylecho y'sabayru,

עֵינֵי כֹל אֵלֶיךָ יְשַׂבֵּרוּ,

The eyes of all look to You with hope

v'ato nōsayn lohem
es ochlom b'ito.

וְאַתָּה נוֹתֵן לָהֶם
אֶת אָכְלָם בְּעִתּוֹ.

and You give them their food in its proper time.

CONCENTRATE INTENTLY WHILE RECITING THE NEXT VERSE.

Pōsay-ach es yodecho,

פּוֹתֵחַ אֶת יָדֶךָ,

You open Your hand*

u-masbi-a l'chol chai rotzōn.

וּמַשְׂבִּיעַ לְכָל חַי רָצוֹן.

and satisfy the desire of every living thing.

Tzadik Adōnoy b'chol d'rochov,

צַדִּיק יהוה בְּכָל דְּרָכָיו,

Righteous is HASHEM in all His ways

v'chosid b'chol ma-asov.

וְחָסִיד בְּכָל מַעֲשָׂיו.

and magnanimous* in all His deeds.

Korōv Adōnoy l'chol kōr'ov,

קָרוֹב יהוה לְכָל קֹרְאָיו,

HASHEM is close to all who call upon Him —

l'chōl asher yikro-uhu ve-emes.

לְכֹל אֲשֶׁר יִקְרָאֻהוּ בֶאֱמֶת.

to all who call upon Him sincerely.

סוֹמֵךְ ה' לְכָל הַנֹּפְלִים — *HASHEM supports all the fallen ones.* Although *Ashrei* follows an alphabetical format, the fourteenth letter of the *alef-beis*, the נ, is omitted. That letter begins the Hebrew word נְפִילָה, ''downfall,'' and in context with the verse of the next letter ס — ''HASHEM supports all the fallen ones'' — could be taken as an allusion to Israel's future downfall, Heaven forbid; but the Psalmist refused to use a letter that could suggest such tragedy. That omission implies that even when Israel does suffer reverses, those reverses will never be final. Rather, as the next verse declares, God supports the fallen.

פּוֹתֵחַ אֶת יָדֶךָ — *You open Your hand.* This verse

should be recited with great joy at the knowledge that God cares for every creature.

יָדֶךָ — *Your hand.* It is axiomatic to Jewish belief that God has no physicality, not even that of the invisible, intangible angels. Because we are physical beings, we cannot grasp God's essence. We cannot conceive of a Being totally unaffected by material conditions or the laws of nature and physics. When Scripture speaks of ''the hand of God'' or ''the eyes of God'' and so forth, it does not imply that God has corporeality. Rather, it speaks this way to enable us to understand the concepts being conveyed.

צַדִּיק ... וְחָסִיד — *Righteous ... and magnanimous.* God judges people righteously, accord-

R'tzōn y'ray-ov ya-ase,   רְצוֹן יְרֵאָיו יַעֲשֶׂה,

The will of those who fear Him He will do,

v'es shav-osom yishma v'yōshi-aym.   וְאֶת שַׁוְעָתָם יִשְׁמַע וְיוֹשִׁיעֵם.

and their cry He will hear, and save them.

Shōmayr Adōnoy es kol ōhavov,   שׁוֹמֵר יהוה אֶת כָּל אֹהֲבָיו,

HASHEM protects all who love Him,

v'ays kol hor'sho-im yashmid.   וְאֵת כָּל הָרְשָׁעִים יַשְׁמִיד.

but all the wicked He will destroy.

T'hilas Adōnoy y'daber pi,   ❖ תְּהִלַּת יהוה יְדַבֶּר פִּי,

May my mouth declare the praise of HASHEM

vivoraych kol bosor shaym kodshō,   וִיבָרֵךְ כָּל בָּשָׂר שֵׁם קָדְשׁוֹ
l'ōlom vo-ed.   לְעוֹלָם וָעֶד.

and may all flesh bless His Holy Name forever and ever.

Va-anachnu n'voraych Yoh,   וַאֲנַחְנוּ נְבָרֵךְ יָהּ,

We will bless God

may-ato v'ad ōlom, hal'lu-yoh.   מֵעַתָּה וְעַד עוֹלָם, הַלְלוּיָהּ.

from this time and forever: Praise God!

THE *CHAZZAN* RECITES *HALF-KADDISH.*
(Congregational responses are indicated by parentheses.)

יִתְגַּדַּל וְיִתְקַדַּשׁ שְׁמֵהּ רַבָּא. (אָמֵן – Omayn). בְּעָלְמָא דִי בְרָא
כִרְעוּתֵהּ. וְיַמְלִיךְ מַלְכוּתֵהּ, בְּחַיֵּיכוֹן וּבְיוֹמֵיכוֹן וּבְחַיֵּי דְכָל
בֵּית יִשְׂרָאֵל, בַּעֲגָלָא וּבִזְמַן קָרִיב. וְאִמְרוּ: אָמֵן.
(אָמֵן. יְהֵא שְׁמֵהּ רַבָּא מְבָרַךְ לְעָלַם וּלְעָלְמֵי עָלְמַיָּא.)

(Omayn. Y'hay sh'mayh rabo m'vorach l'olam ul-ol'may ol'ma-yo.)

יְהֵא שְׁמֵהּ רַבָּא מְבָרַךְ לְעָלַם וּלְעָלְמֵי עָלְמַיָּא. יִתְבָּרַךְ וְיִשְׁתַּבַּח
וְיִתְפָּאַר וְיִתְרוֹמַם וְיִתְנַשֵּׂא וְיִתְהַדָּר וְיִתְעַלֶּה וְיִתְהַלָּל שְׁמֵהּ
דְקֻדְשָׁא בְּרִיךְ הוּא (בְּרִיךְ הוּא – B'rich hu). °לְעֵלָּא מִן כָּל
[°לְעֵלָּא לְעֵלָּא מִכָּל – from Rosh Hashanah to Yom Kippur substitute]
בִּרְכָתָא וְשִׁירָתָא תֻּשְׁבְּחָתָא וְנֶחֱמָתָא, דַּאֲמִירָן בְּעָלְמָא. וְאִמְרוּ: אָמֵן.
(אָמֵן – Omayn).

ON PUBLIC FAST DAYS: The only public fast that can occur on a Friday is the Tenth of Teves. If at least seven members of the *minyan* are fasting, the Torah and *Haftarah* are read. The services of removing the Torah from the Ark and returning it to the Ark appear on pages 511-519. After the Torah has been returned to the Ark, the *chazzan* repeats Half-*Kaddish* and *Shemoneh Esrei* is recited.

---

ing to their deeds. Nevertheless, even when justice calls for grievous punishment, He is   magnanimous in softening the blow, for He is merciful.

◈[SHEMONEH ESREI — AMIDAH]◈

■ *Shemoneh Esrei* (or the *Amidah*) is known as "Service of the Heart." By definition, it must be understood and comprehended. Failure to do so is compared by the Sages to a "body without a soul." Two independent kinds of awareness are necessary for the *Amidah*:

1. To understand the meaning of that which we are saying. The format of this *siddur* is most helpful in this regard. Please take your time to recite the prayer with the conviction that accompanies comprehension.

2. To visualize that we are privileged literally to be standing before God. You are talking to Him directly. In each blessing, when we recite the word *ato*, "You," we should understand to Whom the "You" is referring.

IN THE SYNAGOGUE THE *SHEMONEH ESREI* * IS RECITED WHILE FACING THE ARK; ELSEWHERE IT IS RECITED WHILE FACING THE DIRECTION OF THE LAND OF ISRAEL. TAKE THREE STEPS BACKWARD, LEFT, RIGHT, LEFT, THEN THREE STEPS FORWARD, RIGHT, LEFT, RIGHT. REMAIN STANDING WITH FEET TOGETHER DURING *SHEMONEH ESREI*. RECITE IT WITH QUIET DEVOTION AND WITHOUT ANY INTERRUPTION. ALTHOUGH IT SHOULD NOT BE AUDIBLE TO OTHERS, ONE MUST PRAY LOUDLY ENOUGH TO HEAR ONESELF.

Ki shaym Adōnoy ekro,   כִּי שֵׁם יהוה אֶקְרָא,

When I call out the Name of HASHEM,

hovu gōdel Laylōhaynu.   הָבוּ גֹדֶל לֵאלֹהֵינוּ.

ascribe greatness to our God.

Adōnoy s'fosai tiftoch,   אֲדֹנָי שְׂפָתַי תִּפְתָּח,

My Lord, open my lips,

u-fi yagid t'hilosecho.   וּפִי יַגִּיד תְּהִלָּתֶךָ.

that my mouth may declare Your praise. *

■ **First Blessing:** In the merit of our Patriarchs whose actions reflected Godliness, Hashem pledged to always be with Israel and protect them.

BEND THE KNEES AT Boruch; BOW AT ato; STRAIGHTEN UP AT Adōnoy.

BORUCH ato Adōnoy   בָּרוּךְ אַתָּה יהוה

Blessed are You, HASHEM, *

⋘ Shemoneh Esrei

Moses advanced through three levels of holiness as he approached God when he ascended Mount Sinai. Therefore, as we approach God with our requests, we take three steps backward to symbolize our separation from the mundane, then three steps forward to symbolize our advance toward God.

Shemoneh Esrei has three sections: (a) In the first three blessings, we pay homage to God, like a slave praising his master before daring to make a request; (b) in the middle section of thirteen (originally twelve) blessings, we make our requests; (c) in the last three blessings, we take leave, expressing our gratitude and confidence in our Master's graciousness.

But even the middle section is not merely a catalogue of selfish requests. Rather, in each blessing, we first acknowledge God's mastery, and only then make our request. Thus, each blessing is an affirmation of God's power.

וּפִי יַגִּיד תְּהִלָּתֶךָ — *That my mouth may declare Your praise.* This introductory verse acknowledges that one needs God's help to articulate and comprehend the prayers properly. But why do we ask God for assistance "to declare Your praise"? We should ask, "Assist me to formulate my requests." The answer is that our thrice-daily approach with our requests is in itself a constant praise of God, for it demonstrates that He alone can fulfill our needs.

בָּרוּךְ אַתָּה ה — *Blessed are You, HASHEM.* This formula, used to begin and/or end every bless-

Elōhaynu Vaylōhay avōsaynu,
אֱלֹהֵינוּ וֵאלֹהֵי אֲבוֹתֵינוּ,

our God and the God of our forefathers,

Elōhay avrohom, Elōhay yitzchok,
אֱלֹהֵי אַבְרָהָם, אֱלֹהֵי יִצְחָק,

Vaylōhay ya-akōv,
וֵאלֹהֵי יַעֲקֹב,

God of Abraham, God of Isaac, and God of Jacob;

ho-Ayl hagodōl hagibōr v'hanōro,
הָאֵל הַגָּדוֹל הַגִּבּוֹר וְהַנּוֹרָא,

Ayl elyōn,
אֵל עֶלְיוֹן,

the great, mighty, and awesome God, the supreme God,

gōmayl chasodim tōvim
גּוֹמֵל חֲסָדִים טוֹבִים

v'kōnay hakōl,
וְקוֹנֵה הַכֹּל,

Who bestows beneficial kindnesses and creates everything,

v'zōchayr chasday ovōs,
וְזוֹכֵר חַסְדֵי אָבוֹת,

Who recalls the kindnesses of the Patriarchs

u-mayvi gō-ayl livnay v'nayhem,
וּמֵבִיא גוֹאֵל לִבְנֵי בְנֵיהֶם,

and brings a Redeemer to their children's children,

l'ma-an sh'mō b'ahavo.
לְמַעַן שְׁמוֹ בְּאַהֲבָה.

for His Name's sake, with love.

FROM ROSH HASHANAH TO YOM KIPPUR ADD:

Zochraynu l'cha-yim,
זָכְרֵנוּ לְחַיִּים,

melech chofaytz bacha-yim,
מֶלֶךְ חָפֵץ בַּחַיִּים,

Remember us for life, O King Who desires life,

v'chosvaynu b'sayfer hacha-yim,
וְכָתְבֵנוּ בְּסֵפֶר הַחַיִּים,

l'ma-ancho Elōhim cha-yim.
לְמַעַנְךָ אֱלֹהִים חַיִּים.

and inscribe us in the Book of Life — for Your sake, O Living God.

Melech ōzayr u-mōshi-a u-mogayn.
מֶלֶךְ עוֹזֵר וּמוֹשִׁיעַ וּמָגֵן.

O King, Helper, Savior, and Shield.

BEND THE KNEES AT Boruch; BOW AT ato; STRAIGHTEN UP AT Adōnoy.

Boruch ato Adōnoy,
בָּרוּךְ אַתָּה יהוה,

mogayn avrohom.
מָגֵן אַבְרָהָם.

Blessed are You, HASHEM, Shield of Abraham.

■ Second Blessing: God's might as it is manifest in nature and man

ATO gibōr l'ōlom Adōnoy,
אַתָּה גִבּוֹר לְעוֹלָם אֲדֹנָי,

You are eternally mighty, my Lord,

ing, is a declaration of fact: God *is* blessed in the sense that He is perfect and complete. Addi- tionally, the phrase means, "You, HASHEM, are the source of blessing."

m'cha-yay maysim ato,   מְחַיֶּה מֵתִים אַתָּה,
the Resuscitator of the dead are You;*

rav l'hōshi-a.   רַב לְהוֹשִׁיעַ.
abundantly able to save,

BETWEEN SHEMINI ATZERES AND PESACH, ADD:

Mashiv horu-ach u-mōrid hageshem.   מַשִּׁיב הָרוּחַ וּמוֹרִיד הַגֶּשֶׁם.
Who makes the wind blow and makes the rain descend;

M'chalkayl cha-yim b'chesed,   מְכַלְכֵּל חַיִּים בְּחֶסֶד,
Who sustains the living with kindness;

m'cha-yay maysim b'rachamim rabim,   מְחַיֶּה מֵתִים בְּרַחֲמִים רַבִּים,
resuscitates the dead with abundant mercy;

sōmaych nōf'lim, v'rōfay chōlim,   סוֹמֵךְ נוֹפְלִים, וְרוֹפֵא חוֹלִים,
supports the fallen, heals the sick,

u-matir asurim,   וּמַתִּיר אֲסוּרִים,
releases the confined,

umka-yaym emunosō li-shaynay ofor.   וּמְקַיֵּם אֱמוּנָתוֹ לִישֵׁנֵי עָפָר.
and maintains His faith to those asleep in the dust.

Mi cho-mōcho ba-al g'vurōs,   מִי כָמוֹךָ בַּעַל גְּבוּרוֹת,
Who is like You, O Master of mighty deeds,

u-mi dōme loch,   וּמִי דּוֹמֶה לָּךְ,
and who is comparable to You,

melech maymis umcha-ye   מֶלֶךְ מֵמִית וּמְחַיֶּה
u-matzmi-ach y'shu-o.   וּמַצְמִיחַ יְשׁוּעָה.
O King Who causes death and restores life and makes salvation sprout!

FROM ROSH HASHANAH TO YOM KIPPUR ADD:

Mi cho-mōcho av horachamim,   מִי כָמוֹךָ אַב הָרַחֲמִים,
Who is like You, O Merciful Father,

zōchayr y'tzurov l'cha-yim   זוֹכֵר יְצוּרָיו לְחַיִּים
b'rachamim.   בְּרַחֲמִים.
Who recalls His creatures mercifully for life!

V'ne-emon ato l'hacha-yōs maysim.   וְנֶאֱמָן אַתָּה לְהַחֲיוֹת מֵתִים.
And You are faithful to resuscitate the dead.

Boruch ato Adōnoy,   בָּרוּךְ אַתָּה יהוה,
     m'cha-yay hamaysim.   מְחַיֶּה הַמֵּתִים.
Blessed are You, HASHEM, Who resuscitates the dead.

מְחַיֶּה מֵתִים — *The Resuscitator of the dead are You.* The concept that God restores life is found

three times in this section, alluding to the three kinds of resuscitation: He causes man to

■ Third Blessing: Regarding the holiness of God's Name

DURING THE *CHAZZAN'S* REPETITION, *KEDUSHAH** IS RECITED; INDIVIDUALS CONTINUE ON P. 38.

STAND WITH FEET TOGETHER AND AVOID ANY INTERRUPTIONS. RISE ON TOES
WHEN SAYING Kodōsh, kodōsh, kodōsh; Boruch; AND Yimlōch.

CONGREGATION, THEN *CHAZZAN:*

N'KADAYSH es shimcho bo-ōlom,　　נְקַדֵּשׁ אֶת שִׁמְךָ בָּעוֹלָם,

We shall sanctify Your Name in this world,

k'shaym shemakdishim ōsō　　כְּשֵׁם שֶׁמַּקְדִּישִׁים אוֹתוֹ

bishmay morōm,　　בִּשְׁמֵי מָרוֹם,

just as they sanctify it in heaven above,

Kakosuv al yad n'vi-echo,　　כַּכָּתוּב עַל יַד נְבִיאֶךָ,

as it is written by the hand of Your prophet,

v'koro ze el ze v'omar:　　וְקָרָא זֶה אֶל זֶה וְאָמַר:

"And one [angel] will call another and say:

ALL IN UNISON:

Kodōsh, kodōsh, kodōsh　　קָדוֹשׁ קָדוֹשׁ קָדוֹשׁ

Adōnoy Tz'vo-ōs,　　יהוה צְבָאוֹת,

'*Holy, holy, holy** *is* HASHEM, *Master of Legions,*

m'lō chol ho-oretz k'vōdō.　　מְלֹא כָל הָאָרֶץ כְּבוֹדוֹ.

the whole world is filled with His glory.'"

CHAZZAN:

L'u-mosom boruch yōmayru:　　לְעֻמָּתָם בָּרוּךְ יֹאמֵרוּ:

Those facing them say, "Blessed":

ALL IN UNISON:

Boruch k'vōd Adōnoy, mim'kōmō.　　בָּרוּךְ כְּבוֹד יהוה, מִמְּקוֹמוֹ.

"Blessed is the glory of HASHEM *from His place."*

CHAZZAN:

Uvdivray kodsh'cho kosuv laymōr:　　וּבְדִבְרֵי קָדְשְׁךָ כָּתוּב לֵאמֹר:

And in Your holy Writings the following is written:

ALL IN UNISON:

Yimlōch Adōnoy l'ōlom,　　יִמְלֹךְ יהוה לְעוֹלָם,

"HASHEM *shall reign forever —*

Elōha-yich tziyōn l'dōr vodōr,　　אֱלֹהַיִךְ צִיּוֹן לְדֹר וָדֹר,

hal'luyoh.　　הַלְלוּיָהּ.

your God, O Zion — from generation to generation: Praise God!"

---

awaken every morning after deathlike slumber; He sends the rain that has the life-sustaining quality of making vegetation grow; and He will bring about the literal resuscitation of the dead in the Messianic era.

◄§ **Kedushah,** "Sanctification," expresses the concept that God is exalted above and separated from the limitations of material exis-

tence. A *minyan* (quorum of ten men over the age of *bar mitzvah*) becomes the representative of the nation and echoes the angels who sing God's praises in Heaven by proclaiming His holiness and glory.

קָדוֹשׁ קָדוֹשׁ קָדוֹשׁ — *Holy, holy, holy.* God is holy with relation to the physical world, holy with relation to the spiritual world and holy with

מנחה לחול / 38

CHAZZAN CONCLUDES:

לְדוֹר וָדוֹר נַגִּיד גׇּדְלֶךָ וּלְנֵצַח נְצָחִים קְדֻשָּׁתְךָ נַקְדִּישׁ, וְשִׁבְחֲךָ אֱלֹהֵינוּ מִפִּינוּ לֹא יָמוּשׁ לְעוֹלָם וָעֶד, כִּי אֵל מֶלֶךְ גָּדוֹל וְקָדוֹשׁ אָתָּה. בָּרוּךְ אַתָּה יהוה, °הָאֵל הַקָּדוֹשׁ.

°הַמֶּלֶךְ הַקָּדוֹשׁ. — from Rosh Hashanah to Yom Kippur substitute

THE CHAZZAN CONTINUES ato chōnayn BELOW.

ATO kodōsh v'shimcho kodōsh,
You are holy and Your Name is holy,

אַתָּה קָדוֹשׁ וְשִׁמְךָ קָדוֹשׁ,

ukdōshim b'chol yōm
y'hal'lucho, selo.
and holy ones praise You, every day, forever.

וּקְדוֹשִׁים בְּכָל יוֹם יְהַלְלוּךָ סֶּלָה.

Boruch ato Adōnoy,
°ho-Ayl hakodōsh.
Blessed are You, HASHEM, the holy God.

בָּרוּךְ אַתָּה יהוה,
°הָאֵל הַקָּדוֹשׁ.

FROM ROSH HASHANAH TO YOM KIPPUR SUBSTITUTE:

°hamelech hakodōsh.
the holy King.

°הַמֶּלֶךְ הַקָּדוֹשׁ.

■ Fourth Blessing: Supplication for the gift of intellect

ATO chōnayn l'odom da-as,
You graciously endow man with wisdom*

אַתָּה חוֹנֵן לְאָדָם דַּעַת,

umlamayd le-enōsh bino.
and teach insight to a frail mortal.

וּמְלַמֵּד לֶאֱנוֹשׁ בִּינָה.

Chonaynu may-it'cho
day-o bino v'haskayl.
Endow us graciously from Yourself with wisdom, insight, and discernment.

חָנֵּנוּ מֵאִתְּךָ
דֵּעָה בִּינָה וְהַשְׂכֵּל.

Boruch ato Adōnoy,
chōnayn hado-as.
Blessed are You, HASHEM, gracious Giver of wisdom.

בָּרוּךְ אַתָּה יהוה,
חוֹנֵן הַדָּעַת.

■ Fifth Blessing: Supplication for Divine assistance in repentance

HASHIVAYNU ovinu l'sōrosecho,
Bring us back,* our Father, to Your Torah,

הֲשִׁיבֵנוּ אָבִינוּ לְתוֹרָתֶךָ,

relation to the World to Come.

אַתָּה חוֹנֵן לְאָדָם דַּעַת — *You graciously endow man with wisdom.* This blessing begins the middle section of the *Shemoneh Esrei*, in which man makes his requests of God. The first plea

is for wisdom and understanding, because man's intelligence is the characteristic that sets him apart from animals.

הֲשִׁיבֵנוּ — *Bring us back.* God never compels anyone to repent, but if we make a sincere

v'kor'vaynu malkaynu
la-avōdosecho,

וְקָרְבֵנוּ מַלְכֵּנוּ
לַעֲבוֹדָתֶךָ,

and bring us near, our King, to Your service,

v'hachaziraynu bis-shuvo sh'laymo
l'fonecho.

וְהַחֲזִירֵנוּ בִּתְשׁוּבָה שְׁלֵמָה
לְפָנֶיךָ.

and return us in perfect repentance before You.

Boruch ato Adōnoy,
horōtze bis-shuvo.

בָּרוּךְ אַתָּה יהוה,
הָרוֹצֶה בִּתְשׁוּבָה.

Blessed are You, HASHEM, Who desires repentance.

■ Sixth Blessing: Supplication for forgiveness

STRIKE THE LEFT SIDE OF THE CHEST WITH THE RIGHT FIST
WHILE RECITING THE WORDS ki chotonu AND ki fo-shonu.

S'LACH lonu ovinu ki chotonu,

סְלַח לָנוּ אָבִינוּ כִּי חָטָאנוּ,

Forgive us, our Father, for we have erred;

m'chal lonu malkaynu ki fo-shonu,

מְחַל לָנוּ מַלְכֵּנוּ כִּי פָשָׁעְנוּ,

pardon us, our King, for we have willfully sinned;

ki mōchayl v'sōlay-ach oto.

כִּי מוֹחֵל וְסוֹלֵחַ אָתָּה.

for You pardon and forgive.

Boruch ato Adōnoy,
chanun hamarbe lislō-ach.

בָּרוּךְ אַתָּה יהוה,
חַנּוּן הַמַּרְבֶּה לִסְלוֹחַ.

Blessed are You, HASHEM,
the gracious One Who pardons abundantly.

■ Seventh Blessing: Supplication for personal redemption
from the perils and problems of daily life

R'AY v'on-yaynu, v'rivo rivaynu,

רְאֵה בְעָנְיֵנוּ, וְרִיבָה רִיבֵנוּ,

Behold our affliction, take up our grievance,

ug-olaynu m'hayro
l'ma-an sh'mecho,

וּגְאָלֵנוּ מְהֵרָה
לְמַעַן שְׁמֶךָ,

and redeem us speedily for Your Name's sake,

ki gō-ayl chozok oto.

כִּי גוֹאֵל חָזָק אָתָּה.

for You are a powerful Redeemer.

Boruch ato Adōnoy,
gō-ayl yisro-ayl.

בָּרוּךְ אַתָּה יהוה,
גּוֹאֵל יִשְׂרָאֵל.

Blessed are You, HASHEM, Redeemer of Israel.

beginning, God will make our way easier.

ON A FAST DAY, THE *CHAZZAN* RECITES THE FOLLOWING BLESSING AT THIS POINT:

עֲנֵנוּ יהוה עֲנֵנוּ, בְּיוֹם צוֹם תַּעֲנִיתֵנוּ, כִּי בְצָרָה גְדוֹלָה אֲנָחְנוּ. אַל תֵּפֶן אֶל רִשְׁעֵנוּ, וְאַל תַּסְתֵּר פָּנֶיךָ מִמֶּנּוּ, וְאַל תִּתְעַלַּם מִתְּחִנָּתֵנוּ. הֱיֵה נָא קָרוֹב לְשַׁוְעָתֵנוּ, יְהִי נָא חַסְדְּךָ לְנַחֲמֵנוּ, טֶרֶם נִקְרָא אֵלֶיךָ עֲנֵנוּ, כַּדָּבָר שֶׁנֶּאֱמַר: וְהָיָה טֶרֶם יִקְרָאוּ וַאֲנִי אֶעֱנֶה, עוֹד הֵם מְדַבְּרִים וַאֲנִי אֶשְׁמָע. כִּי אַתָּה יהוה הָעוֹנֶה בְּעֵת צָרָה, פּוֹדֶה וּמַצִּיל בְּכָל עֵת צָרָה וְצוּקָה. בָּרוּךְ אַתָּה יהוה, הָעוֹנֶה בְּעֵת צָרָה.

■ Eighth Blessing: Supplication for health and healing of body and soul

R'FO-AYNU Adōnoy, v'nayrofay,

רְפָאֵנוּ יהוה וְנֵרָפֵא,

Heal us, HASHEM — then we will be healed;*

hōshi-aynu v'nivoshay-ō,
ki s'hilosaynu oto,

הוֹשִׁיעֵנוּ וְנִוָּשֵׁעָה,
כִּי תְהִלָּתֵנוּ אָתָּה,

save us — then we will be saved, for You are our praise;

v'ha-alay r'fu-o sh'laymo
l'chol makōsaynu,

וְהַעֲלֵה רְפוּאָה שְׁלֵמָה
לְכָל מַכּוֹתֵינוּ,

and bring complete recovery for all our ailments,

ki Ayl melech
rōfay ne-emon v'rachamon oto.

כִּי אֵל מֶלֶךְ
רוֹפֵא נֶאֱמָן וְרַחֲמָן אָתָּה.

for You are God, King, the faithful and compassionate Healer.

Boruch ato Adōnoy,
rōfay chōlay amō yisro-ayl.

בָּרוּךְ אַתָּה יהוה,
רוֹפֵא חוֹלֵי עַמּוֹ יִשְׂרָאֵל.

Blessed are You, HASHEM, Who heals the sick of His people Israel.

■ Ninth Blessing: Supplication for a year of prosperity

FOR THE FOLLOWING BLESSING, SUMMER IS DEFINED AS THE PERIOD FROM PESACH
THROUGH *MINCHAH* OF DECEMBER 4TH (OR 5TH, IN THE YEAR BEFORE A CIVIL LEAP YEAR);
WINTER IS DEFINED AS THE REST OF THE YEAR.

BORAYCH olaynu, Adōnoy Elōhaynu,
es hashono hazōs

בָּרֵךְ עָלֵינוּ יהוה אֱלֹהֵינוּ
אֶת הַשָּׁנָה הַזֹּאת

Bless on our behalf, O HASHEM, our God, this year

v'es kol minay s'vu-oso l'tōvo,

וְאֶת כָּל מִינֵי תְבוּאָתָהּ לְטוֹבָה,

and all its kinds of crops for the best,

IN SUMMER SAY

v'sayn b'rocho

וְתֵן בְּרָכָה

and give a blessing

רְפָאֵנוּ ה' וְנֵרָפֵא — *Heal us, HASHEM — then we
will be healed.* The *Zohar* teaches that at
times human beings or angels are sent as

God's agents to heal illness. In such cases,
however, the cure may be only partial or
temporary. Or the pain or other symptoms

IN WINTER SAY

v'sayn tal u-motor livrocho
וְתֵן טַל וּמָטָר לִבְרָכָה

and give dew and rain for a blessing

al p'nay ho-adomo,
עַל פְּנֵי הָאֲדָמָה,

on the face of the earth,

v'sab'aynu mituvecho,
וְשַׂבְּעֵנוּ מִטּוּבֶךָ,

and satisfy us from Your bounty,

u-voraych sh'nosaynu
וּבָרֵךְ שְׁנָתֵנוּ

kashonim hatōvōs.
כַּשָּׁנִים הַטּוֹבוֹת.

and bless our year like the best years.

Boruch ato Adōnoy,
בָּרוּךְ אַתָּה יהוה,

m'voraych hashonim.
מְבָרֵךְ הַשָּׁנִים.

Blessed are You, HASHEM, Who blesses the years.

■ Tenth Blessing: Supplication for the ingathering of the exiles

T'KA b'shōfor godōl l'chayrusaynu,
תְּקַע בְּשׁוֹפָר גָּדוֹל לְחֵרוּתֵנוּ,

Sound the great shofar for our freedom,

v'so nays l'kabaytz golu-yōsaynu,
וְשָׂא נֵס לְקַבֵּץ גָּלֻיּוֹתֵינוּ,

raise a banner to gather our exiles

v'kab'tzaynu yachad
וְקַבְּצֵנוּ יַחַד

may-arba kanfōs ho-oretz.
מֵאַרְבַּע כַּנְפוֹת הָאָרֶץ.

and gather us together from the four corners of the earth.

Boruch ato Adōnoy,
בָּרוּךְ אַתָּה יהוה,

m'kabaytz nidchay amō yisro-ayl.
מְקַבֵּץ נִדְחֵי עַמּוֹ יִשְׂרָאֵל.

Blessed are You, HASHEM, Who gathers in the dispersed of His people Israel.

■ Eleventh Blessing: Supplication for the restoration of justice to the Jewish judiciary

HOSHIVO shōf'taynu k'vorishōno,
הָשִׁיבָה שׁוֹפְטֵינוּ כְּבָרִאשׁוֹנָה,

v'yō-atzaynu k'vat'chilo,
וְיוֹעֲצֵינוּ כְּבַתְּחִלָּה,

Restore our judges as in earliest times and our counselors as at first;

v'hosayr mimenu yogōn va-anocho,
וְהָסֵר מִמֶּנּוּ יָגוֹן וַאֲנָחָה,

remove from us sorrow and groan;

may be relieved, while the illness itself remains uncured. But if God Himself undertakes to cure the patient, the result will not be a temporary or a partial measure, "then we will be healed."

מְטּוּבֶךָ — *From Your bounty.* Food acquired through tainted means lacks the holiness to nourish the soul. Therefore, we ask that God satisfy us from His bounty, not from earnings to which we are not entitled.

umlōch olaynu
   ato, Adōnoy, l'vad'cho

וּמְלוֹךְ עָלֵינוּ
אַתָּה יהוה לְבַדֶּךָ

and reign over us, You, HASHEM, alone,

b'chesed uvrachamim,

בְּחֶסֶד וּבְרַחֲמִים,

with kindness and with compassion,

v'tzad'kaynu bamishpot.

וְצַדְּקֵנוּ בַּמִּשְׁפָּט.

and justify us through judgment.

Boruch ato Adōnoy,
°melech ōhayv tz'doko u-mishpot.

בָּרוּךְ אַתָּה יהוה,
°מֶלֶךְ אוֹהֵב צְדָקָה וּמִשְׁפָּט.

Blessed are You, HASHEM, the King Who loves righteousness and judgment.

FROM ROSH HASHANAH TO YOM KIPPUR SUBSTITUTE:

°hamelech hamishpot.   °הַמֶּלֶךְ הַמִּשְׁפָּט.

the King of Judgment.

■ Twelfth Blessing: Supplication for the eradication
of heretic influences that threaten Jewish life

V'LAMALSHINIM al t'hi sikvo,   וְלַמַּלְשִׁינִים אַל תְּהִי תִקְוָה,

And for the slanderers* let there be no hope;

v'chol horish-o k'rega tōvayd,   וְכָל הָרִשְׁעָה כְּרֶגַע תֹּאבֵד,

and may all wickedness perish in an instant;

v'chol ō-y'vecho m'hayro yikoraysu.   וְכָל אֹיְבֶיךָ מְהֵרָה יִכָּרֵתוּ.

and may all Your enemies be cut down speedily.

V'hazaydim m'hayro s'akayr   וְהַזֵּדִים מְהֵרָה תְעַקֵּר

The wanton sinners — may You speedily uproot

us-shabayr usmagayr v'sachni-a   וּתְשַׁבֵּר וּתְמַגֵּר וְתַכְנִיעַ

smash, cast down, and humble —

bimhayro v'yomaynu.   בִּמְהֵרָה בְיָמֵינוּ.

speedily in our days.

Boruch ato Adōnoy,   בָּרוּךְ אַתָּה יהוה,
shōvayr ō-y'vim u-machni-a zaydim.   שׁוֹבֵר אֹיְבִים וּמַכְנִיעַ זֵדִים.

Blessed are You, HASHEM, Who breaks enemies and humbles wanton sinners.

וְלַמַּלְשִׁינִים — *And for the slanderers.* This blessing is not one of the original eighteen blessings of the *Shemoneh Esrei.* It was composed, and approved, by the Sanhedrin, a short time after the destruction of the Second Temple, in response to the threats of such heretical Jewish sects as the Sadducees, Boethusians, Essenes, and early Christians. These sects tried to lead Jews astray through example and persuasion, and they used their political power to oppress observant Jews and to slander them to the anti-Semitic Roman government.

It was incorporated into the *Shemoneh Esrei* so that the populace would be aware of the danger posed by these sects.

Despite the disappearance from within Israel of the particular sects against whom it was directed, it is always relevant, because there are still those who seek to destroy the spiritual continuity of Israel.

■ Thirteenth Blessing: Supplication on behalf of the righteous
and recognition of their significance

AL hatzadikim v'al hachasidim   עַל הַצַּדִּיקִים וְעַל הַחֲסִידִים,

On the righteous, on the devout,

v'al ziknay am'cho bays yisro-ayl,   וְעַל זִקְנֵי עַמְּךָ בֵּית יִשְׂרָאֵל,

on the elders of Your people the Family of Israel,

v'al p'laytas sōf'rayhem,   וְעַל פְּלֵיטַת סוֹפְרֵיהֶם,

on the remnant of their scholars,

v'al gayray hatzedek v'olaynu,   וְעַל גֵּרֵי הַצֶּדֶק וְעָלֵינוּ,

on the righteous converts and on ourselves —

yehemu rachamecho,   יֶהֱמוּ רַחֲמֶיךָ

    Adōnoy Elōhaynu,   יהוה אֱלֹהֵינוּ,

may Your compassion be aroused, HASHEM, our God;

v'sayn sochor tōv   וְתֵן שָׂכָר טוֹב

and give goodly reward

l'chol habōt'chim b'shimcho be-emes,   לְכָל הַבּוֹטְחִים בְּשִׁמְךָ בֶּאֱמֶת,

to all who sincerely believe in Your Name;

v'sim chelkaynu imohem l'ōlom,   וְשִׂים חֶלְקֵנוּ עִמָּהֶם לְעוֹלָם,

and place our lot with them forever,

v'lō nayvōsh ki v'cho botoch-nu.   וְלֹא נֵבוֹשׁ כִּי בְךָ בָטָחְנוּ.

and we will not feel ashamed, for we trust in You.

Boruch ato Adōnoy,   בָּרוּךְ אַתָּה יהוה,

mish-on u-mivtoch latzadikim.   מִשְׁעָן וּמִבְטָח לַצַּדִּיקִים.

Blessed are You, HASHEM, Mainstay and Assurance of the righteous.

■ Fourteenth Blessing: Supplication for the physical
and spiritual rebuilding of Jerusalem

V'LIRUSHOLA-YIM ir'cho   וְלִירוּשָׁלַיִם עִירְךָ

b'rachamim toshuv,   בְּרַחֲמִים תָּשׁוּב,

And to Jerusalem,* Your city, may You return in compassion,

v'sishkōn b'sōchoh ka-asher dibarto,   וְתִשְׁכּוֹן בְּתוֹכָהּ כַּאֲשֶׁר דִּבַּרְתָּ,

and may You rest within it, as You have spoken;

uvnay ōsoh b'korōv b'yomaynu   וּבְנֵה אוֹתָהּ בְּקָרוֹב בְּיָמֵינוּ

binyan ōlom,   בִּנְיַן עוֹלָם,

may You rebuild it soon in our days as an eternal structure,

וְלִירוּשָׁלַיִם — *And to Jerusalem.* After having sought God's blessing on Israel's leaders and righteous people, we seek His blessing for the Holy City. No blessing is complete until the seat of holiness, Jerusalem, is rebuilt in all its grandeur.

v'chisay dovid   וְכִסֵּא דָוִד
    m'hayro l'sōchoh tochin   מְהֵרָה לְתוֹכָהּ תָּכִין.
and the throne of David may You speedily establish within it.

Boruch ato Adōnoy,   בָּרוּךְ אַתָּה יהוה,
    bōnay y'rusholo-yim.   בּוֹנֵה יְרוּשָׁלָיִם.
Blessed are You, HASHEM, the Builder of Jerusalem.

■ Fifteenth Blessing: Supplication that the Messiah restore the Davidic reign

ES TZEMACH dovid avd'cho   אֶת צֶמַח דָּוִד עַבְדְּךָ
The offspring of Your servant David

m'hayro satzmi-ach,   מְהֵרָה תַצְמִיחַ,
may You speedily cause to flourish,

v'karnō torum bi-shu-osecho,   וְקַרְנוֹ תָּרוּם בִּישׁוּעָתֶךָ,
and enhance his pride through Your salvation,

ki lishu-os'cho kivinu kol hayom.   כִּי לִישׁוּעָתְךָ קִוִּינוּ כָּל הַיּוֹם.
for we hope for Your salvation all day long.

Boruch ato Adōnoy,   בָּרוּךְ אַתָּה יהוה,
    matzmi-ach keren y'shu-o.   מַצְמִיחַ קֶרֶן יְשׁוּעָה.
Blessed are You, HASHEM, Who causes the pride of salvation to flourish.

■ Sixteenth Blessing: Supplication for God's acceptance of our prayer

SH'MA KŌLAYNU Adōnoy Elōhaynu,   שְׁמַע קוֹלֵנוּ יהוה אֱלֹהֵינוּ,
Hear our voice, * HASHEM our God,*

chus v'rachaym olaynu,   חוּס וְרַחֵם עָלֵינוּ,
pity and be compassionate to us,

v'kabayl b'rachamim uvrotzōn   וְקַבֵּל בְּרַחֲמִים וּבְרָצוֹן
    es t'filosaynu,   אֶת תְּפִלָּתֵנוּ,
and accept — with compassion and favor — our prayer,

ki Ayl shōmay-a   כִּי אֵל שׁוֹמֵעַ
    t'filōs v'sachanunim oto,   תְּפִלּוֹת וְתַחֲנוּנִים אָתָּה.
for God Who hears prayers and supplications are You;

umil'fonecho, malkaynu,   וּמִלְּפָנֶיךָ מַלְכֵּנוּ
from before Yourself, our King,

raykom al t'shivaynu,   רֵיקָם אַל תְּשִׁיבֵנוּ,
turn us not away empty-handed,

שְׁמַע קוֹלֵנוּ — *Hear our voice.* In the middle section of *Shemoneh Esrei* we have asked God to grant our specific needs. We now close the section with a general plea that He take note of our call and grant our requests.

ON A FAST DAY, ONE WHO IS FASTING RECITES THE FOLLOWING.

ANAYNU, Adōnoy, anaynu,
עֲנֵנוּ יהוה עֲנֵנוּ,
Answer us, HASHEM, answer us,

b'yōm tzōm ta-anisaynu,
בְּיוֹם צוֹם תַּעֲנִיתֵנוּ,
on this day of our fast,

ki v'tzoro g'dōlo anoch'nu,
כִּי בְצָרָה גְדוֹלָה אֲנָחְנוּ,
for we are in great distress;

al tayfen el rish-aynu,
אַל תֵּפֶן אֶל רִשְׁעֵנוּ,
do not pay attention to our wickedness,

v'al tastayr ponecho mimenu,
וְאַל תַּסְתֵּר פָּנֶיךָ מִמֶּנוּ,
do not hide Your Face from us,

v'al tisalam mit'chinosaynu,
וְאַל תִּתְעַלַּם מִתְּחִנָּתֵנוּ,
and do not ignore our supplication;

heyay no korōv l'shav-osaynu,
הֱיֵה נָא קָרוֹב לְשַׁוְעָתֵנוּ,
please be near to our outcry;

y'hi no chasd'cho l'nachamaynu,
יְהִי נָא חַסְדְּךָ לְנַחֲמֵנוּ,
please let Your kindness comfort us —

terem nikro aylecho anaynu,
טֶרֶם נִקְרָא אֵלֶיךָ עֲנֵנוּ,
before we call to You answer us,

kadovor shene-emar:
כַּדָּבָר שֶׁנֶּאֱמַר:
as it is said:

V'hoyo terem yikro-u va-ani e-ene,
וְהָיָה טֶרֶם יִקְרָאוּ וַאֲנִי אֶעֱנֶה,
"And it will be that before they call, I will answer;

ōd haym m'dab'rim va-ani eshmo.
עוֹד הֵם מְדַבְּרִים וַאֲנִי אֶשְׁמָע.
while they yet speak, I will hear."

Ki ato, Adōnoy,
כִּי אַתָּה יהוה
ho-ōne b'ays tzoro,
הָעוֹנֶה בְּעֵת צָרָה,
For You, HASHEM, are the One Who responds in time of distress,

pōde u-matzil
פּוֹדֶה וּמַצִּיל
b'chol ays tzoro v'tzuko.
בְּכָל עֵת צָרָה וְצוּקָה.
Who redeems and rescues in every time of distress and woe.

Ki ato shōmay-a t'filas
כִּי אַתָּה שׁוֹמֵעַ תְּפִלַּת
am'cho yisro-ayl b'rachamim.
עַמְּךָ יִשְׂרָאֵל בְּרַחֲמִים.
for You hear the prayer of Your people Israel with compassion.

Boruch ato Adōnoy,
בָּרוּךְ אַתָּה יהוה,
shōmay-a t'filo.
שׁוֹמֵעַ תְּפִלָּה.
Blessed are You, HASHEM, Who hears prayer.

■ Seventeenth Blessing: Prayer for restoration of the Temple service

R'TZAY, Adōnoy Elōhaynu   רְצֵה יהוה אֱלֹהֵינוּ

Be favorable,* HASHEM, our God,

b'am'cho yisro-ayl u-visfilosom,   בְּעַמְּךָ יִשְׂרָאֵל וּבִתְפִלָּתָם,

toward Your people Israel and their prayer

v'hoshayv es ho-avōdo   וְהָשֵׁב אֶת הָעֲבוֹדָה

    lidvir bay-secho.   לִדְבִיר בֵּיתֶךָ.

and restore the service to the Holy of Holies of Your Temple.

V'i-shay yisro-ayl, usfilosom   וְאִשֵּׁי יִשְׂרָאֵל וּתְפִלָּתָם

    b'ahavo s'kabayl b'rotzōn,   בְּאַהֲבָה תְקַבֵּל בְּרָצוֹן,

The fire-offerings of Israel and their prayer accept with love and favor,

us-hi l'rotzōn tomid   וּתְהִי לְרָצוֹן תָּמִיד

    avōdas yisro-ayl amecho.   עֲבוֹדַת יִשְׂרָאֵל עַמֶּךָ.

and may the service of Your people Israel always be favorable to You.

■ Yaaleh Veyavo: We petition God to have compassion on Israel and Jerusalem,
and to reinstate the Temple service, to enable us to bring
the appropriate offerings for the particular occasion.

ON *ROSH CHODESH* AND *CHOL HAMOED* RECITE THE FOLLOWING:

ELŌHAYNU Vaylōhay avōsaynu,   אֱלֹהֵינוּ וֵאלֹהֵי אֲבוֹתֵינוּ,

Our God and the God of our forefathers,

ya-a-le v'yovō v'yagi-a v'yayro-e   יַעֲלֶה, וְיָבֹא, וְיַגִּיעַ, וְיֵרָאֶה,

may there rise, come, reach, be noted,

v'yayro-tze v'yi-shoma v'yipokayd   וְיֵרָצֶה, וְיִשָּׁמַע, וְיִפָּקֵד,

be favored, be heard, be considered,

v'yizochayr zichrōnaynu u-fikdōnaynu,   וְיִזָּכֵר זִכְרוֹנֵנוּ וּפִקְדוֹנֵנוּ,

and be remembered — the remembrance and consideration of ourselves;

v'zichrōn avōsaynu,   וְזִכְרוֹן אֲבוֹתֵינוּ,

the remembrance of our forefathers;

v'zichrōn moshi-ach   וְזִכְרוֹן מָשִׁיחַ

    ben dovid avdecho,   בֶּן דָּוִד עַבְדֶּךָ,

the remembrance of Messiah, son of David, Your servant;

v'zichrōn y'rushola-yim   וְזִכְרוֹן יְרוּשָׁלַיִם

    ir kod-shecho,   עִיר קָדְשֶׁךָ,

the remembrance of Jerusalem, Your Holy City;

רְצֵה — *Be favorable.* This begins the final section of *Shemoneh Esrei*. Like a servant who is
grateful for having had the opportunity to express himself before his master, we thank God
for hearing us out.

v'zichrōn kol am'cho bays yisro-ayl וְזִכְרוֹן כָּל עַמְּךָ בֵּית יִשְׂרָאֵל
and the remembrance of Your entire people the Family of Israel —

l'fonecho, לְפָנֶיךָ,
before You

lif-layto l'tōvo לִפְלֵיטָה לְטוֹבָה
for deliverance, for goodness,

l'chayn ul-chesed ul-rachamim, לְחֵן וּלְחֶסֶד וּלְרַחֲמִים,
for grace, for kindness, and for compassion,

l'cha-yim ul-sholōm לְחַיִּים וּלְשָׁלוֹם
for life, and for peace

———————— ON *ROSH CHODESH* ————————

b'yōm rōsh hachōdesh ha-ze. בְּיוֹם רֹאשׁ הַחֹדֶשׁ הַזֶּה.
on this day of Rosh Chodesh

———————— ON *PESACH* ————————

b'yōm chag hamatzōs ha-ze. בְּיוֹם חַג הַמַּצּוֹת הַזֶּה.
on this day of the Festival of Matzos.

———————— ON *SUCCOS* ————————

b'yōm chag hasukōs ha-ze. בְּיוֹם חַג הַסֻּכּוֹת הַזֶּה.
on this day of the Succos Festival.

Zoch-raynu Adōnoy Elōhaynu זָכְרֵנוּ יהוה אֱלֹהֵינוּ
bō l'tōvo, בּוֹ לְטוֹבָה,
Remember us on it, HASHEM, our God, for goodness,

u-fokdaynu vō livrocho, וּפָקְדֵנוּ בּוֹ לִבְרָכָה,
consider us on it for blessing

v'hōshi-aynu vō l'cha-yim. וְהוֹשִׁיעֵנוּ בּוֹ לְחַיִּים.
and help us on it for life.

U-vidvar y'shu-o v'rachamim, וּבִדְבַר יְשׁוּעָה וְרַחֲמִים,
In the matter of salvation and compassion,

chus v'chonaynu חוּס וְחָנֵּנוּ
v'rachaym olaynu v'hōshi-aynu, וְרַחֵם עָלֵינוּ וְהוֹשִׁיעֵנוּ,
pity, be gracious and compassionate with us and help us,

ki aylecho aynaynu, כִּי אֵלֶיךָ עֵינֵינוּ,
for our eyes are turned to You,

ki Ayl melech כִּי אֵל מֶלֶךְ
chanun v'rachum oto. חַנּוּן וְרַחוּם אָתָּה.
because You are God, the gracious and compassionate King.

V'SECHEZENO aynaynu

וְתֶחֱזֶינָה עֵינֵינוּ

May our eyes behold

b'shuv'cho l'tziyōn b'rachamim.

בְּשׁוּבְךָ לְצִיּוֹן בְּרַחֲמִים.

Your return to Zion in compassion.

Boruch ato Adōnoy,

בָּרוּךְ אַתָּה יהוה,

hamachazir sh'chinosō l'tziyōn.

הַמַּחֲזִיר שְׁכִינָתוֹ לְצִיּוֹן.

Blessed are You, HASHEM, Who restores His Presence unto Zion.

■ Eighteenth Blessing: Acknowledgment of our debt of gratitude

BOW AT Mōdim anachnu loch; STRAIGHTEN UP AT Adōnoy.
IN HIS REPETITION THE *CHAZZAN* SHOULD RECITE THE ENTIRE *MODIM* ALOUD,
WHILE THE CONGREGATION RECITES *MODIM OF THE RABBIS* (P. 23) SOFTLY.

MŌDIM anachnu loch,

מוֹדִים אֲנַחְנוּ לָךְ,

We gratefully thank You,

sho-ato hu Adōnoy Elōhaynu

שָׁאַתָּה הוּא יהוה אֱלֹהֵינוּ

for it is You Who are HASHEM, our God,

Vaylōhay avōsaynu

וֵאלֹהֵי אֲבוֹתֵינוּ

and the God of our forefathers

l'ōlom vo-ed,

לְעוֹלָם וָעֶד,

forever and ever;

tzur cha-yaynu, mogayn yish-aynu

צוּר חַיֵּינוּ, מָגֵן יִשְׁעֵנוּ

Rock of our lives,* Shield of our salvation

ato hu l'dōr vodōr.

אַתָּה הוּא לְדוֹר וָדוֹר.

are You from generation to generation.

Nō-de l'cho unsapayr t'hilosecho

נוֹדֶה לְּךָ וּנְסַפֵּר תְּהִלָּתֶךָ

We shall thank You and relate Your praise —

al cha-yaynu ham'surim b'yodecho,

עַל חַיֵּינוּ הַמְּסוּרִים בְּיָדֶךָ,

for our lives, which are committed to Your power

v'al nishmōsaynu hap'kudōs loch,

וְעַל נִשְׁמוֹתֵינוּ הַפְּקוּדוֹת לָךְ,

and for our souls that are entrusted to You

v'al nisecho sheb'chol yōm imonu,

וְעַל נִסֶּיךָ שֶׁבְּכָל יוֹם עִמָּנוּ,

and for Your miracles that are with us every day

v'al nifl'ōsecho v'tōvōsecho
sheb'chol ays,

וְעַל נִפְלְאוֹתֶיךָ וְטוֹבוֹתֶיךָ
שֶׁבְּכָל עֵת,

and for Your wonders and favors in every season —

erev vovōker v'tzohoro-yim.

עֶרֶב וָבֹקֶר וְצָהֳרָיִם.

evening, morning, and afternoon.

צוּר חַיֵּינוּ — *Rock of our lives.* Our parents are the "rocks" from which our bodies are hewn, but it is from You that we receive life itself.

Hatōv ki lō cholu rachamecho,   הַטוֹב כִּי לֹא כָלוּ רַחֲמֶיךָ,

The Beneficent One, for Your compassions were never exhausted,

v'ham'rachaym ki lō samu chasodecho,   וְהַמְרַחֵם כִּי לֹא תַמּוּ חֲסָדֶיךָ,

and the Compassionate One, for Your kindnesses never ended —

may-ōlom kivinu loch.   מֵעוֹלָם קִוִּינוּ לָךְ.

always have we put our hope in You.

MODIM OF THE RABBIS*

RECITED SOFTLY BY CONGREGATION WHILE *CHAZZAN* RECITES THE REGULAR MODIM ALOUD

MŌDIM anachnu loch,   **מוֹדִים** אֲנַחְנוּ לָךְ,

We gratefully thank You,

sho-ato hu Adōnoy Elōhaynu   שָׁאַתָּה הוּא יהוה אֱלֹהֵינוּ

    Vaylōhay avōsaynu,   וֵאלֹהֵי אֲבוֹתֵינוּ,

for it is You Who are HASHEM, our God and the God of our forefathers,

Elōhay chol bosor,   אֱלֹהֵי כָל בָּשָׂר,

the God of all flesh,

yōtz'raynu, yōtzayr b'rayshis.   יוֹצְרֵנוּ, יוֹצֵר בְּרֵאשִׁית.

our Molder, the Molder of the universe.

B'rochōs v'hōdo-ōs l'shimcho   בְּרָכוֹת וְהוֹדָאוֹת לְשִׁמְךָ

    hagodōl v'hakodōsh,   הַגָּדוֹל וְהַקָּדוֹשׁ,

Blessings and thanks are due Your great and holy Name

al sheheche-yisonu v'ki-yamtonu.   עַל שֶׁהֶחֱיִיתָנוּ וְקִיַּמְתָּנוּ.

for You have given us life and sustained us.

Kayn t'cha-yaynu uska-y'maynu,   כֵּן תְּחַיֵּנוּ וּתְקַיְּמֵנוּ,

So may You continue to give us life and sustain us

v'se-esōf golu-yōsaynu   וְתֶאֱסוֹף גָּלֻיּוֹתֵינוּ

    l'chatzrōs kod-shecho,   לְחַצְרוֹת קָדְשֶׁךָ,

and gather our exiles to the Courtyards of Your Sanctuary,

lishmōr chukecho v'la-asōs r'tzōnecho,   לִשְׁמוֹר חֻקֶּיךָ וְלַעֲשׂוֹת רְצוֹנֶךָ,

to observe Your decrees, to do Your will

ul-ovd'cho b'layvov sholaym,   וּלְעָבְדְּךָ בְּלֵבָב שָׁלֵם,

and to serve You wholeheartedly.

al she-anachnu mōdim loch.   עַל שֶׁאֲנַחְנוּ מוֹדִים לָךְ.

[We thank You] for inspiring us to thank You.

Boruch Ayl hahōdo-ōs.   בָּרוּךְ אֵל הַהוֹדָאוֹת.

Blessed is the God of thanksgivings.

◄§ **Modim of the Rabbis**

When the *chazzan* bows and recites *Modim* in the manner of a slave accepting the total authority of his master, the congregation must join him in accepting God's sovereignty. Therefore, each member of the congregation must make his own declaration of submission.

ON CHANUKAH AND PURIM CONTINUE BELOW. ON ALL OTHER DAYS TURN TO P. 53.

ON CHANUKAH AND PURIM ADD THE FOLLOWING:

AL hanisim, v'al hapurkon,   עַל הַנִּסִּים, וְעַל הַפֻּרְקָן,

For the miracles, and for the salvation,

v'al hag'vurōs, v'al hat'shu-ōs,   וְעַל הַגְּבוּרוֹת, וְעַל הַתְּשׁוּעוֹת,

and for the mighty deeds, and for the victories,

v'al hamilchomōs,   וְעַל הַמִּלְחָמוֹת,

and for the battles

she-osiso la-avōsaynu   שֶׁעָשִׂיתָ לַאֲבוֹתֵינוּ

which You performed for our forefathers

ba-yomim hohaym baz'man ha-ze.   בַּיָּמִים הָהֵם בַּזְּמַן הַזֶּה.

in those days, at this time.

ON CHANUKAH CONTINUE HERE; ON PURIM TURN TO P. 52.

BIMAY matisyohu ben yōchonon   בִּימֵי מַתִּתְיָהוּ בֶּן יוֹחָנָן

In the days of Mattisyahu, the son of Yochanan,

kōhayn godōl chashmōno-i u-vonov,   כֹּהֵן גָּדוֹל חַשְׁמוֹנַאִי וּבָנָיו,

the High Priest, the Hasmonean, and his sons —

k'she-om'do malchus yovon   כְּשֶׁעָמְדָה מַלְכוּת יָוָן

hor'sho-o al am'cho yisro-ayl,   הָרְשָׁעָה עַל עַמְּךָ יִשְׂרָאֵל,

when the wicked Greek kingdom rose up against Your people Israel

l'hashkichom tōrosecho,   לְהַשְׁכִּיחָם תּוֹרָתֶךָ,

to make them forget Your Torah

ulha-avirom maychukay r'tzōnecho,   וּלְהַעֲבִירָם מֵחֻקֵּי רְצוֹנֶךָ.

and compel them to stray from the statutes of Your Will —

v'ato b'rachamecho horabim,   וְאַתָּה בְּרַחֲמֶיךָ הָרַבִּים,

But You, in Your abundant mercy,

omadto lohem b'ays tzorosom,   עָמַדְתָּ לָהֶם בְּעֵת צָרָתָם,

stood up for them in the time of their distress;

ravto es rivom, danto es dinom,   רַבְתָּ אֶת רִיבָם, דַּנְתָּ אֶת דִּינָם,

You took up their grievance, You judged their claim,

nokamto es nikmosom.   נָקַמְתָּ אֶת נִקְמָתָם.

and You avenged their wrong.

Mosarto gibōrim b'yad chaloshim,   מָסַרְתָּ גִבּוֹרִים בְּיַד חַלָּשִׁים,

You delivered the strong into the hand of the weak,

᲌ Chanukah

לְהַשְׁכִּיחָם תּוֹרָתֶךָ וּלְהַעֲבִירָם מֵחֻקֵּי רְצוֹנֶךָ — *To make them forget Your Torah and compel them to stray from the statutes of Your Will.*

The Syrian-Greeks knew that the key to the Jewish religion is the study of Torah; if Torah study were neglected, then the decline of ritual observance would be inevitable and

ON CHANUKAH CONTINUE HERE:

v'rabim b'yad m'atim,

וְרַבִּים בְּיַד מְעַטִּים,

the many into the hand of the few,

utmay-im b'yad t'hōrim,

וּטְמֵאִים בְּיַד טְהוֹרִים,

the impure into the hand of the pure,

ursho-im b'yad tzadikim

וּרְשָׁעִים בְּיַד צַדִּיקִים,

the wicked into the hand of the righteous,

v'zaydim b'yad ōs'kay sōrosecho.

וְזֵדִים בְּיַד עוֹסְקֵי תוֹרָתֶךָ.

and the wanton into the hand of the diligent students of Your Torah.

Ulcho osiso

וּלְךָ עָשִׂיתָ

For Yourself You made

shaym godōl v'kodōsh b'ōlomecho,

שֵׁם גָּדוֹל וְקָדוֹשׁ בְּעוֹלָמֶךָ,

a great and holy Name in Your world,

ul-am'cho yisro-ayl

וּלְעַמְּךָ יִשְׂרָאֵל

and for Your people Israel

osiso t'shu-o g'dōlo u-furkon

עָשִׂיתָ תְּשׁוּעָה גְדוֹלָה וּפֻרְקָן

You performed a great victory and salvation

k'ha-yōm ha-ze.

כְּהַיּוֹם הַזֶּה.

as this very day.

V'achar kayn bo-u vonecho

וְאַחַר כֵּן בָּאוּ בָנֶיךָ

lidvir bay-secho,

לִדְבִיר בֵּיתֶךָ,

Thereafter, Your children came to the Holy of Holies of Your House,

u-finu es haycholecho,

וּפִנּוּ אֶת הֵיכָלֶךָ,

they cleansed Your Temple,

v'tiharu es mikdoshecho,

וְטִהֲרוּ אֶת מִקְדָּשֶׁךָ,

they purified the site of Your Holiness

v'hidliku nayrōs

וְהִדְלִיקוּ נֵרוֹת

b'chatzrōs kod-shecho,

בְּחַצְרוֹת קָדְשֶׁךָ,

and they kindled lights in the Courtyards of Your Sanctuary;

v'kov'u

וְקָבְעוּ

sh'mōnas y'may chanuko aylu,

שְׁמוֹנַת יְמֵי חֲנֻכָּה אֵלּוּ,

and they established these eight days of Chanukah

l'hōdōs ulhalayl

לְהוֹדוֹת וּלְהַלֵּל

l'shimcho hagodōl.

לְשִׁמְךָ הַגָּדוֹל.

to express thanks and praise to Your great Name.

CONTINUE ON P. 53.

swift. Therefore, they concentrated first on causing Torah to be forgotten, knowing that the deterioration of observance would soon follow.

ON PURIM CONTINUE HERE:

BIMAY mord'chai v'estayr   בִּימֵי מָרְדְּכַי וְאֶסְתֵּר
In the days of Mordechai and Esther,

b'shushan habiro,   בְּשׁוּשַׁן הַבִּירָה,
in Shushan, the capital,

k'she-omad alayhem   כְּשֶׁעָמַד עֲלֵיהֶם
homon horosho,   הָמָן הָרָשָׁע,
when Haman, the wicked, rose up against them*

bikaysh l'hashmid   בִּקֵּשׁ לְהַשְׁמִיד
laharōg ul-abayd   לַהֲרֹג וּלְאַבֵּד
and sought to destroy, to slay, and to exterminate

es kol ha-y'hudim,   אֶת כָּל הַיְּהוּדִים,
mina-ar v'ad zokayn, taf v'noshim   מִנַּעַר וְעַד זָקֵן, טַף וְנָשִׁים
all the Jews, young and old, infants and women,

b'yōm echod,   בְּיוֹם אֶחָד,
on the same day,

bishlōsho osor l'chōdesh   בִּשְׁלוֹשָׁה עָשָׂר לְחֹדֶשׁ
sh'naym osor, hu chōdesh ador,   שְׁנֵים עָשָׂר, הוּא חֹדֶשׁ אֲדָר,
on the thirteenth of the twelfth month which is the month of Adar,

ushlolom lovōz.   וּשְׁלָלָם לָבוֹז.
and to plunder their possessions.

V'ato b'rachamecho horabim   וְאַתָּה בְּרַחֲמֶיךָ הָרַבִּים
But You, in Your abundant mercy,

hayfarto es atzosō,   הֵפַרְתָּ אֶת עֲצָתוֹ,
nullified his counsel

v'kilkalto es machashavtō,   וְקִלְקַלְתָּ אֶת מַחֲשַׁבְתּוֹ,
and frustrated his intention

vahashayvōso lō g'mulō b'rōshō,   וַהֲשֵׁבוֹתָ לּוֹ גְמוּלוֹ בְּרֹאשׁוֹ,
and caused his design to return upon his own head.

V'solu ōsō v'es bonov al ho-aytz.   וְתָלוּ אוֹתוֹ וְאֶת בָּנָיו עַל הָעֵץ.
And they hanged him and his sons on the gallows.

⊷§ Purim

כְּשֶׁעָמַד עֲלֵיהֶם — *When ... rose up against them.* The paragraph describing the miracle of Purim is far briefer than that describing Chanukah. The danger of Purim was straightforward — the extermination of the nation — and requires no elaboration. The peril of Chanukah was more subtle. It involved assimilation and impurity. The unaware do not perceive danger unless it is starkly physical in nature. Therefore, it requires a more elaborate explanation.

V'AL kulom yisborach v'yisrōmam
shimcho, malkaynu

וְעַל כֻּלָּם יִתְבָּרַךְ וְיִתְרוֹמַם
שִׁמְךָ מַלְכֵּנוּ

For all these, may Your Name be blessed and exalted, our King,

tomid l'ōlom vo-ed.

תָּמִיד לְעוֹלָם וָעֶד.

continually forever and ever.

FROM ROSH HASHANAH TO YOM KIPPUR ADD:

Uchsōv l'cha-yim tōvim
kol b'nay v'risecho.

וּכְתוֹב לְחַיִּים טוֹבִים
כָּל בְּנֵי בְרִיתֶךָ.

And inscribe all the children of Your covenant for a good life.

V'chōl hacha-yim yōducho selo,

וְכֹל הַחַיִּים יוֹדוּךָ סֶּלָה,

Everything alive* will gratefully acknowledge You, Selah!

vihal'lu es shimcho be-emes,

וִיהַלְלוּ אֶת שִׁמְךָ בֶּאֱמֶת,

and praise Your Name sincerely,

ho-Ayl y'shu-osaynu
v'ezrosaynu selo.

הָאֵל יְשׁוּעָתֵנוּ
וְעֶזְרָתֵנוּ סֶלָה.

O God of our salvation and help, Selah!

BEND THE KNEES AT Boruch; BOW AT ato; STRAIGHTEN UP AT Adōnoy.

Boruch ato Adōnoy,
hatōv shimcho
ulcho no-e l'hōdōs.

בָּרוּךְ אַתָּה יהוה,
הַטּוֹב שִׁמְךָ
וּלְךָ נָאֶה לְהוֹדוֹת.

*Blessed are You, HASHEM, Your Name is "The Beneficent One"
and to You it is fitting to give thanks.*

■ Nineteenth Blessing: Prayer for peace and harmony
amongst the Jewish people

ON PUBLIC FAST DAYS THE *CHAZZAN* RECITES THE PRIESTLY BLESSING
DURING HIS REPETITION, EXCEPT IN A HOUSE OF MOURNING.

אֱלֹהֵינוּ, וֵאלֹהֵי אֲבוֹתֵינוּ, בָּרְכֵנוּ בַּבְּרָכָה הַמְשֻׁלֶּשֶׁת בַּתּוֹרָה
הַכְּתוּבָה עַל יְדֵי מֹשֶׁה עַבְדֶּךָ, הָאֲמוּרָה מִפִּי אַהֲרֹן וּבָנָיו,
כֹּהֲנִים עַם קְדוֹשֶׁךָ, כָּאָמוּר:

(kayn y'hi rotzōn – Cong.)	יְבָרֶכְךָ יהוה, וְיִשְׁמְרֶךָ. כֵּן יְהִי רָצוֹן – Cong.
(kayn y'hi rotzōn – Cong.)	יָאֵר יהוה פָּנָיו אֵלֶיךָ וִיחֻנֶּךָּ. כֵּן יְהִי רָצוֹן – Cong.
(kayn y'hi rotzōn – Cong.)	יִשָּׂא יהוה פָּנָיו אֵלֶיךָ וְיָשֵׂם לְךָ שָׁלוֹם. כֵּן יְהִי רָצוֹן – Cong.

וְכֹל הַחַיִּים – *Everything alive.* As long as there is life, people can express their thanks to God.

This passage refers specifically to the universal praise that will come in the time of the Messiah.

ON PUBLIC FAST DAYS Sim sholōm (BELOW) IS RECITED INSTEAD OF Sholōm rov.

SHOLŌM ROV al yisro-ayl
    am'cho tosim l'ōlom,

שָׁלוֹם רָב עַל יִשְׂרָאֵל
עַמְּךָ תָּשִׂים לְעוֹלָם,

Establish abundant peace upon Your people Israel forever,

ki ato hu melech,
    odōn l'chol ha-sholōm.

כִּי אַתָּה הוּא מֶלֶךְ
אָדוֹן לְכָל הַשָּׁלוֹם.

for You are King, Master of all peace.

V'tōv b'aynecho l'voraych
    es am'cho yisro-ayl,

וְטוֹב בְּעֵינֶיךָ לְבָרֵךְ
אֶת עַמְּךָ יִשְׂרָאֵל,

And may it be good in Your eyes to bless Your people Israel

b'chol ays uvchol sho-o bish-lōmecho.

בְּכָל עֵת וּבְכָל שָׁעָה בִּשְׁלוֹמֶךָ.

at every time and every hour with Your peace.

ON PUBLIC FAST DAYS SUBSTITUTE:

SIM SHOLŌM tōvo uvrocho,

שִׂים שָׁלוֹם, טוֹבָה, וּבְרָכָה,

Establish peace, goodness, blessing,

chayn vochesed v'rachamim

חֵן וָחֶסֶד וְרַחֲמִים

graciousness, kindness, and compassion

olaynu v'al kol yisro-ayl amecho.

עָלֵינוּ וְעַל כָּל יִשְׂרָאֵל עַמֶּךָ.

upon us and upon all of Your people Israel.

Bor'chaynu, ovinu, kulonu k'e-chod

בָּרְכֵנוּ, אָבִינוּ, כֻּלָּנוּ כְּאֶחָד

Bless us, our Father, all of us as one,

b'ōr ponecho,

בְּאוֹר פָּנֶיךָ,

with the light of Your countenance,

ki v'ōr ponecho nosato lonu,
    Adōnoy Elōhaynu,

כִּי בְאוֹר פָּנֶיךָ נָתַתָּ לָנוּ,
יהוה אֱלֹהֵינוּ,

for with the light of Your countenance, You, HASHEM, our God, gave us

tōras cha-yim v'ahavas chesed,

תּוֹרַת חַיִּים וְאַהֲבַת חֶסֶד,

the Torah of life and a love of kindness,

utz-doko uvrocho v'rachamim
v'cha-yim v'sholōm.

וּצְדָקָה וּבְרָכָה וְרַחֲמִים
וְחַיִּים וְשָׁלוֹם.

righteousness, blessing, compassion, life, and peace.

V'tōv b'aynecho l'voraych
    es am'cho yisro-ayl,

וְטוֹב בְּעֵינֶיךָ לְבָרֵךְ
אֶת עַמְּךָ יִשְׂרָאֵל,

And may it be good in Your eyes to bless Your people Israel

b'chol ays uvchol sho-o
    bishlōmecho.

בְּכָל עֵת וּבְכָל שָׁעָה
בִּשְׁלוֹמֶךָ.

at every time and at every hour, with Your peace.

°Boruch ato Adōnoy,
ham'voraych es amō yisro-ayl
ba-sholōm.

°בָּרוּךְ אַתָּה יהוה,
הַמְבָרֵךְ אֶת עַמּוֹ יִשְׂרָאֵל
בַּשָׁלוֹם.

°Blessed are You, HASHEM, Who blesses His people Israel with peace.

° FROM ROSH HASHANAH TO YOM KIPPUR SUBSTITUTE THE FOLLOWING:

B'sayfer cha-yim
b'rocho v'sholōm,
ufarnoso tōvo,

בְּסֵפֶר חַיִּים
בְּרָכָה וְשָׁלוֹם,
וּפַרְנָסָה טוֹבָה,

In the book of life, blessing, and peace, and good livelihood,

nizochayr v'nikosayv l'fonecho,

נִזָּכֵר וְנִכָּתֵב לְפָנֶיךָ,

may we be remembered and inscribed before You —

anachnu v'chol am'cho
bays yisro-ayl,

אֲנַחְנוּ וְכָל עַמְּךָ
בֵּית יִשְׂרָאֵל,

we and Your entire people the Family of Israel —

l'cha-yim tōvim ulsholōm.

לְחַיִּים טוֹבִים וּלְשָׁלוֹם.

for a good life and for peace.

Boruch ato Adōnoy,
ō-se ha-sholōm.

בָּרוּךְ אַתָּה יהוה,
עוֹשֶׂה הַשָּׁלוֹם.

Blessed are You, HASHEM, Who makes the peace.

THE *CHAZZAN'S* REPETITION ENDS HERE (TURN TO PAGE 58). INDIVIDUALS CONTINUE:

Yih-yu l'rotzōn imray fi
v'hegyōn libi l'fonecho,

יִהְיוּ לְרָצוֹן אִמְרֵי פִי
וְהֶגְיוֹן לִבִּי לְפָנֶיךָ,

*May the expressions of my mouth and the thoughts of my heart
find favor* before You,*

Adōnoy tzuri v'gō-ali.

יהוה צוּרִי וְגֹאֲלִי.

HASHEM, my Rock and my Redeemer.

■ I pray that, having completed my *Amidah*, I have been changed in a positive way,
especially in regard to my interpersonal relationships.

ELŌHAI, n'tzōr l'shōni mayro,

אֱלֹהַי, נְצוֹר לְשׁוֹנִי מֵרָע,

My God, guard my tongue from evil*

usfosai midabayr mirmo,

וּשְׂפָתַי מִדַּבֵּר מִרְמָה,

and my lips from speaking deceitfully.

יְהִיוּ לְרָצוֹן — *May . . . find favor.* We conclude
Shemoneh Esrei with this brief prayer that our
prayers find favor before God. Kabbalistic literature attaches great sanctity to this verse
and stresses that it be recited slowly and fervently.

אֱלֹהַי נְצוֹר לְשׁוֹנִי מֵרָע — *My God, guard my
tongue from evil.* We pray that God protect us
from situations that would tempt us to speak
ill of others.

The Midrash relates that Rabban Shimon
ben Gamliel once sent his servant, Tavi, to buy

V'limkal'lai nafshi sidōm,
וְלִמְקַלְלַי נַפְשִׁי תִדּוֹם,

To those who curse me, let my soul be silent;

v'nafshi ke-ofor lakōl tih-ye.
וְנַפְשִׁי כֶּעָפָר לַכֹּל תִּהְיֶה.

and let my soul be like dust* to everyone.

P'sach libi b'sōrosecho,
פְּתַח לִבִּי בְּתוֹרָתֶךָ,

Open my heart to Your Torah,*

uvmitzvōsecho tirdōf nafshi.
וּבְמִצְוֹתֶיךָ תִּרְדּוֹף נַפְשִׁי.

then my soul will pursue Your commandments.

V'chol hachōsh'vim olai ro-o,
וְכֹל הַחוֹשְׁבִים עָלַי רָעָה,

As for all those who design evil against me,

m'hayro hofayr atzosom
מְהֵרָה הָפֵר עֲצָתָם

speedily nullify their counsel

v'kalkayl machashavtom.
וְקַלְקֵל מַחֲשַׁבְתָּם.

and disrupt their design.

Asay l'ma-an sh'mecho,
עֲשֵׂה לְמַעַן שְׁמֶךָ,

Act for Your Name's sake;

asay l'ma-an y'minecho,
עֲשֵׂה לְמַעַן יְמִינֶךָ,

act for Your right hand's sake;

asay l'ma-an k'dushosecho,
עֲשֵׂה לְמַעַן קְדֻשָּׁתֶךָ,

act for Your sanctity's sake;

asay l'ma-an tōrosecho.
עֲשֵׂה לְמַעַן תּוֹרָתֶךָ.

act for Your Torah's sake.

L'ma-an yaychol'tzun y'didecho,
לְמַעַן יֵחָלְצוּן יְדִידֶיךָ,

That Your beloved ones may be given rest;

hōshi-o y'min'cho va-anayni.
הוֹשִׁיעָה יְמִינְךָ וַעֲנֵנִי.

let Your right hand save, and respond to me.

Yih-yu l'rotzōn imray fi
יִהְיוּ לְרָצוֹן אִמְרֵי פִי

v'hegyōn libi l'fonecho,
וְהֶגְיוֹן לִבִּי לְפָנֶיךָ,

May the expressions of my mouth and the thoughts of my heart find favor before You,

Adōnoy tzuri v'gō-ali.
יהוה צוּרִי וְגֹאֲלִי.

HASHEM, my Rock and my Redeemer.

"good food." Tavi, who was famous for his wisdom, brought back a tongue. Thereupon Rabban Shimon sent him to buy some "bad food." Again, he returned with a tongue. Rabban Shimon asked him to explain how the same food could be both good and bad. Tavi said, "From a tongue can come good or bad.

When a tongue speaks *good*, there is nothing better, but when a tongue speaks *ill*, there is nothing worse."

נַפְשִׁי ... תִדּוֹם ... כֶּעָפָר — *Let my soul be silent ... like dust.* We should ignore barbs and insults, because the less we care about our prestige, the less we will allow selfishness to

BOW. TAKE THREE STEPS BACK. BOW LEFT AND SAY:

Ō-se sholōm bimrōmov,

עֹשֶׂה שָׁלוֹם בִּמְרוֹמָיו,

He Who makes peace in His heights,

BOW RIGHT AND SAY:

hu ya-a-se sholōm olaynu,

הוּא יַעֲשֶׂה שָׁלוֹם עָלֵינוּ,

may He make peace upon us,

BOW FORWARD AND SAY:

v'al kol yisro-ayl. V'imru: Omayn.

וְעַל כָּל יִשְׂרָאֵל. וְאִמְרוּ: אָמֵן.

and upon all Israel. Now respond: Amen.

Y'HI ROTZŌN mil'fonecho,

יְהִי רָצוֹן מִלְּפָנֶיךָ

May it be Your will,

Adōnoy Elōhaynu

יהוה אֱלֹהֵינוּ

Vaylōhay avōsaynu,

וֵאלֹהֵי אֲבוֹתֵינוּ,

HASHEM, our God and the God of our forefathers,

she-yibo-ne bays hamikdosh

שֶׁיִּבָּנֶה בֵּית הַמִּקְדָּשׁ

bimhayro v'yomaynu,

בִּמְהֵרָה בְיָמֵינוּ,

that the Holy Temple be rebuilt, speedily in our days;

v'sayn chelkaynu b'sōrosecho,

וְתֵן חֶלְקֵנוּ בְּתוֹרָתֶךָ,

and grant us our share in Your Torah;

v'shom na-avod-cho b'yiro,

וְשָׁם נַעֲבָדְךָ בְּיִרְאָה,

and may we serve You there with reverence,

kimay ōlom

כִּימֵי עוֹלָם

uchshonim kadmōniyōs.

וּכְשָׁנִים קַדְמוֹנִיּוֹת.

as in days of old and in former years.

V'or'vo Ladōnoy

וְעָרְבָה לַיהוה

minchas y'hudo virusholo-yim

מִנְחַת יְהוּדָה וִירוּשָׁלָיִם,

Then the offering of Judah and Jerusalem will be pleasing to HASHEM,

kimay ōlom

כִּימֵי עוֹלָם

uchshonim kadmōniyōs.

וּכְשָׁנִים קַדְמוֹנִיּוֹת.

as in days of old and in former years.

THE INDIVIDUAL'S RECITATION OF *SHEMONEH ESREI* ENDS HERE.

REMAIN STANDING IN PLACE UNTIL THE *CHAZZAN* REACHES *KEDUSHAH* —
OR AT LEAST FOR A FEW MOMENTS — THEN TAKE THREE STEPS FORWARD.

interfere with our service of God, our relations with others and our efforts at self-improvement.

פְּתַח לִבִּי בְּתוֹרָתֶךְ — *Open my heart to Your*

Torah. Our goal is to serve God in a positive manner by studying Torah and fulfilling its commandments: both those between man and God and those between man and man.

THE *CHAZZAN* RECITES FULL *KADDISH*

(congregational responses are indicated by parentheses):

יִתְגַּדַּל וְיִתְקַדַּשׁ שְׁמֵהּ רַבָּא. (אָמֵן – Omayn). בְּעָלְמָא דִּי בְרָא כִרְעוּתֵהּ, וְיַמְלִיךְ מַלְכוּתֵהּ, בְּחַיֵּיכוֹן וּבְיוֹמֵיכוֹן וּבְחַיֵּי דְכָל בֵּית יִשְׂרָאֵל, בַּעֲגָלָא וּבִזְמַן קָרִיב. וְאִמְרוּ: אָמֵן.

(אָמֵן. יְהֵא שְׁמֵהּ רַבָּא מְבָרַךְ לְעָלַם וּלְעָלְמֵי עָלְמַיָּא.)

(Omayn. Y'hay sh'mayh rabo m'vorach l'olam ul-ol'may ol'ma-yo.)

יְהֵא שְׁמֵהּ רַבָּא מְבָרַךְ לְעָלַם וּלְעָלְמֵי עָלְמַיָּא. יִתְבָּרַךְ וְיִשְׁתַּבַּח וְיִתְפָּאַר וְיִתְרוֹמַם וְיִתְנַשֵּׂא וְיִתְהַדָּר וְיִתְעַלֶּה וְיִתְהַלָּל שְׁמֵהּ דְקֻדְשָׁא בְּרִיךְ הוּא (בְּרִיךְ הוּא – B'rich hu). °לְעֵלָּא מִן כָּל

[substitute from Rosh Hashanah to Yom Kippur – °לְעֵלָּא לְעֵלָּא מִכָּל]

בִּרְכָתָא וְשִׁירָתָא תֻּשְׁבְּחָתָא וְנֶחֱמָתָא, דַּאֲמִירָן בְּעָלְמָא. וְאִמְרוּ: אָמֵן. (אָמֵן – Omayn).

תִּתְקַבֵּל צְלוֹתְהוֹן וּבָעוּתְהוֹן דְּכָל (בֵּית) יִשְׂרָאֵל קֳדָם אֲבוּהוֹן דִּי בִשְׁמַיָּא. וְאִמְרוּ: אָמֵן. (אָמֵן – Omayn).

יְהֵא שְׁלָמָא רַבָּא מִן שְׁמַיָּא, וְחַיִּים עָלֵינוּ וְעַל כָּל יִשְׂרָאֵל. וְאִמְרוּ: אָמֵן. (אָמֵן – Omayn).

Bow. Take three steps back. Bow left and say, ... עֹשֶׂה; bow right and say, ... הוּא יַעֲשֶׂה; bow forward and say, ... וְעַל כָּל. Remain in place for a few moments, then take three steps forward.

עֹשֶׂה שָׁלוֹם בִּמְרוֹמָיו, הוּא יַעֲשֶׂה שָׁלוֹם עָלֵינוּ, וְעַל כָּל יִשְׂרָאֵל. וְאִמְרוּ: אָמֵן. (אָמֵן – Omayn).

■ As we take leave of the synagogue and God's presence, we fortify ourselves with the resolve and commitment that the lofty ideals of prayer can be implemented and actualized in our mundane pursuits.

STAND WHILE RECITING *ALEINU*.

OLAYNU l'shabay-ach la-adōn hakōl,   **עָלֵינוּ** לְשַׁבֵּחַ לַאֲדוֹן הַכֹּל,

It is our duty to praise* the Master of all,

losays g'dulo l'yōtzayr b'rayshis,   לָתֵת גְּדֻלָּה לְיוֹצֵר בְּרֵאשִׁית,

to ascribe greatness to the Molder of primeval Creation,

shelō osonu k'gōyay ho-arotzōs,   שֶׁלֹּא עָשָׂנוּ כְּגוֹיֵי הָאֲרָצוֹת,

for He has not made us like the nations of the lands

v'lō somonu   וְלֹא שָׂמָנוּ

k'mishp'chōs ho-adomo,   כְּמִשְׁפְּחוֹת הָאֲדָמָה.

and has not emplaced us like the families of the earth;

עָלֵינוּ לְשַׁבֵּחַ — *It is our duty to praise.* According to many early sources, this declaration of faith and dedication was composed by Joshua after he led Israel across the Jordan. It was added to the daily prayers to implant faith in the One-ness of God's kingship, and the conviction that

shelō som chelkaynu kohem,
שֶׁלֹּא שָׂם חֶלְקֵנוּ כָּהֶם,

for He has not assigned our portion like theirs

v'gōrolaynu k'chol hamōnom
וְגוֹרָלֵנוּ כְּכָל הֲמוֹנָם.

nor our lot like all their multitudes.

SOME CONGREGATIONS OMIT THE PARENTHESIZED VERSE:

(Shehaym mishta-chavim
(שֶׁהֵם מִשְׁתַּחֲוִים

l'hevel vorik
לְהֶבֶל וָרִיק,

(For they bow to vanity and emptiness

u-mispal'lim el ayl lō yōshi-a.)
וּמִתְפַּלְּלִים אֶל אֵל לֹא יוֹשִׁיעַ.)

and pray to a god which helps not.)

BOW WHILE RECITING THE NEXT PHRASE.

Va-anachnu kōr'im u-mishta-chavim
וַאֲנַחְנוּ כּוֹרְעִים וּמִשְׁתַּחֲוִים

u-mōdim,
וּמוֹדִים,

But we bend our knees, bow, and acknowledge our thanks

lifnay melech malchay ham'lochim,
לִפְנֵי מֶלֶךְ מַלְכֵי הַמְּלָכִים,

before the King Who reigns over kings,

Hakodōsh boruch hu.
הַקָּדוֹשׁ בָּרוּךְ הוּא.

the Holy One, Blessed is He.

Shehu nō-te shoma-yim
שֶׁהוּא נוֹטֶה שָׁמַיִם

v'yōsayd oretz,
וְיֹסֵד אָרֶץ,

He stretches out heaven and establishes earth's foundation,

u-mōshav y'korō
וּמוֹשַׁב יְקָרוֹ

ba-shoma-yim mima-al,
בַּשָּׁמַיִם מִמַּעַל,

the seat of His homage is in the heavens above

ushchinas u-zō
וּשְׁכִינַת עֻזּוֹ

b'gov-hay m'rōmim.
בְּגָבְהֵי מְרוֹמִים.

and His powerful Presence is in the loftiest heights.

Hu Elōhaynu ayn ōd.
הוּא אֱלֹהֵינוּ, אֵין עוֹד.

He is our God and there is none other.

Emes malkaynu, efes zulosō,
אֱמֶת מַלְכֵּנוּ, אֶפֶס זוּלָתוֹ,

True is our King, there is nothing beside Him,

kakosuv b'sōrosō:
כַּכָּתוּב בְּתוֹרָתוֹ:

as it is written in His Torah:

V'yodato ha-yōm vaha-shayvōso
וְיָדַעְתָּ הַיּוֹם וַהֲשֵׁבֹתָ

el l'vovecho,
אֶל לְבָבֶךָ,

"You are to know this day and take to your heart

He will one day "remove detestable idolatry from the earth . . .," thus preventing Jews from being tempted to follow the beliefs and life styles of the nations among whom they dwell.

ki Adōnoy hu ho-Elōhim

כִּי יהוה הוּא הָאֱלֹהִים

that HASHEM is the only God —

ba-shoma-yim mima-al

בַּשָּׁמַיִם מִמַּעַל

in heaven above

v'al ho-oretz mitochas, ayn ōd.

וְעַל הָאָרֶץ מִתָּחַת, אֵין עוֹד.

and on the earth below — there is none other."

AL KAYN n'kave l'cho

עַל כֵּן נְקַוֶּה לְּךָ

Adōnoy Elōhaynu

יהוה אֱלֹהֵינוּ

Therefore we put our hope in You, HASHEM, our God,

lir-ōs m'hayro b'sif-eres u-zecho,

לִרְאוֹת מְהֵרָה בְּתִפְאֶרֶת עֻזֶּךָ,

that we may soon see Your mighty splendor,

l'ha-avir gilulim min ho-oretz,

לְהַעֲבִיר גִּלּוּלִים מִן הָאָרֶץ,

to remove detestable idolatry from the earth,

v'ho-elilim korōs yikoraysun,

וְהָאֱלִילִים כָּרוֹת יִכָּרֵתוּן,

and false gods will be utterly cut off,

l'sakayn ōlom b'malchus Shadai.

לְתַקֵּן עוֹלָם בְּמַלְכוּת שַׁדַּי.

to perfect the universe through the Almighty's sovereignty.

V'chol b'nay vosor yikr'u vishmecho,

וְכָל בְּנֵי בָשָׂר יִקְרְאוּ בִשְׁמֶךָ,

Then all humanity will call upon Your Name,

l'hafnōs aylecho

לְהַפְנוֹת אֵלֶיךָ

kol rish-ay oretz.

כָּל רִשְׁעֵי אָרֶץ.

to turn all the earth's wicked toward You.

Yakiru v'yayd'u kol yōsh'vay sayvayl,

יַכִּירוּ וְיֵדְעוּ כָּל יוֹשְׁבֵי תֵבֵל,

All the world's inhabitants will recognize and know

ki l'cho tichra kol berech,

כִּי לְךָ תִּכְרַע כָּל בֶּרֶךְ,

that to You every knee should bend,

tishova kol loshōn.

תִּשָּׁבַע כָּל לָשׁוֹן.

every tongue should swear.

L'fonecho Adōnoy Elōhaynu

לְפָנֶיךָ יהוה אֱלֹהֵינוּ

yichr'u v'yipōlu,

יִכְרְעוּ וְיִפֹּלוּ,

Before You, HASHEM, our God, they will bend every knee and cast themselves down,

v'lichvōd shimcho y'kor yitaynu,

וְלִכְבוֹד שִׁמְךָ יְקָר יִתֵּנוּ,

and to the glory of Your Name they will render homage,

vikab'lu chulom

וִיקַבְּלוּ כֻלָּם

es ōl malchusecho,

אֶת עוֹל מַלְכוּתֶךָ,

and they will all accept upon themselves the yoke of Your kingship

v'simlōch alayhem m'hayro
l'ōlom vo-ed.

וְתִמְלֹךְ עֲלֵיהֶם מְהֵרָה
לְעוֹלָם וָעֶד.

that You may reign over them soon and for all eternity.

Ki hamalchus shel'cho hi

כִּי הַמַּלְכוּת שֶׁלְּךָ הִיא

For the kingdom is Yours

ul-ōl'may ad timlōch b'chovōd,

וּלְעוֹלְמֵי עַד תִּמְלוֹךְ בְּכָבוֹד,

and You will reign for all eternity in glory,

kakosuv b'sōrosecho:

כַּכָּתוּב בְּתוֹרָתֶךְ:

as it is written in Your Torah:

Adōnoy yimlōch l'ōlom vo-ed.

יהוה יִמְלֹךְ לְעֹלָם וָעֶד.

"HASHEM shall reign for all eternity."

V'ne-emar:

❖ וְנֶאֱמַר:

And it is said:

V'ho-yo Adōnoy l'melech
al kol ho-oretz,

וְהָיָה יהוה לְמֶלֶךְ
עַל כָּל הָאָרֶץ,

"HASHEM will be King over all the world —

ba-yōm hahu yih-ye
Adōnoy e-chod, ushmō e-chod.

בַּיּוֹם הַהוּא יִהְיֶה
יהוה אֶחָד וּשְׁמוֹ אֶחָד.

on that day HASHEM will be One and His Name will be One."

SOME CONGREGATIONS RECITE THE FOLLOWING AT THIS POINT.

AL TIRO mipachad pis-ōm,

אַל תִּירָא מִפַּחַד פִּתְאֹם,

Do not fear sudden terror,

u-mishō-as r'sho-im ki sovō.

וּמִשֹּׁאַת רְשָׁעִים כִּי תָבֹא.

or the holocaust of the wicked when it comes.

Utzu aytzo v'sufor,

עֻצוּ עֵצָה וְתֻפָר,

Plan a conspiracy and it will be annulled;

dab'ru dovor v'lō yokum,

דַּבְּרוּ דָבָר וְלֹא יָקוּם,

speak your piece and it shall not stand,

ki i-monu Ayl.

כִּי עִמָּנוּ אֵל.

for God is with us.

V'ad zikno ani hu,

וְעַד זִקְנָה אֲנִי הוּא,

Even till your seniority, I remain unchanged;

v'ad sayvo ani esbōl,

וְעַד שֵׂיבָה אֲנִי אֶסְבֹּל,

and even till your ripe old age, I shall endure;

ani osisi va-ani eso,

אֲנִי עָשִׂיתִי וַאֲנִי אֶשָּׂא,

I created [you] and I shall bear [you];

va-ani esbōl va-amalayt.

וַאֲנִי אֶסְבֹּל וַאֲמַלֵּט.

I shall endure and rescue.

⅏ MOURNER'S KADDISH ⅏

■ Man was created to serve God and sanctify His Name. This service and sanctification is actualized by living one's life in accordance with the laws and customs of Judaism. This includes both commandments directed toward God and those that govern our relationship to man.

When an individual passes on, there is a void in this world which is caused by the loss of the sanctification that the deceased had contributed. Therefore, the surviving son (or other relative) addresses this void by announcing through the *Kaddish*, "May the great Name of God continue to be holy." There is no specific reference to death in the *Kaddish*, for it is a message of life. And life that continues is to be sanctified.

The recitation of the *Kaddish* is a great merit for the soul of the deceased. *Kaddish* is recited for eleven months following the death, and is also recited on the *Yahrzeit* (anniversary of the passing).

KADDISH IS RECITED ONLY IN THE PRESENCE OF A MINYAN.

MOURNER:

YISGADAL v'yiskadash   יִתְגַּדַּל וְיִתְקַדַּשׁ

sh'mayh rabo.   שְׁמֵהּ רַבָּא.

May His great Name grow exalted and sanctified

CONGREGATION RESPONDS: Omayn — אָמֵן

B'ol'mo di v'ro chir-usayh.   בְּעָלְמָא דִּי בְרָא כִרְעוּתֵהּ.

In the world that He created as He willed.

V'yamlich malchusayh,   וְיַמְלִיךְ מַלְכוּתֵהּ,

May He give reign to His kingship

b'cha-yaychōn uvyōmaychōn   בְּחַיֵּיכוֹן וּבְיוֹמֵיכוֹן

in your lifetimes and in your days

uvcha-yay d'chol bays yisro-ayl,   וּבְחַיֵּי דְכָל בֵּית יִשְׂרָאֵל,

and in the lifetimes of the entire Family of Israel,

ba-agolo u-vizman koriv.   בַּעֲגָלָא וּבִזְמַן קָרִיב.

swiftly and soon.

V'imru: Omayn.   וְאִמְרוּ: אָמֵן.

Now respond: Amen.

CONGREGATION RESPONDS:

Omayn. Y'hay sh'mayh rabo m'vorach   אָמֵן. יְהֵא שְׁמֵהּ רַבָּא מְבָרַךְ

l'olam ul-ol'may ol'ma-yo.   לְעָלַם וּלְעָלְמֵי עָלְמַיָּא.

Amen. May His great Name be blessed forever and ever;

MOURNER CONTINUES:

Y'hay sh'mayh rabo m'vorach   יְהֵא שְׁמֵהּ רַבָּא מְבָרַךְ

l'olam ul-ol'may ol'ma-yo,   לְעָלַם וּלְעָלְמֵי עָלְמַיָּא,

May His great Name be blessed forever and ever;

yisborach v'yishtabach v'yispo-ar   יִתְבָּרַךְ וְיִשְׁתַּבַּח וְיִתְפָּאַר

blessed, praised, glorified,

v'yisrōmam v'yisnasay   וְיִתְרוֹמַם וְיִתְנַשֵּׂא

exalted, extolled,

v'yis-hador v'yis-ale v'yis-halol   וְיִתְהַדָּר וְיִתְעַלֶּה וְיִתְהַלָּל
mighty, upraised, and lauded

sh'mayh d'kudsho b'rich hu   שְׁמֵהּ דְּקֻדְשָׁא בְּרִיךְ הוּא
be the Name of the Holy One, Blessed is He,

CONGREGATION RESPONDS:

B'rich hu.   *Blessed is He.*   בְּרִיךְ הוּא.

MOURNER CONTINUES:

°l'aylo min kol   °לְעֵלָּא מִן כָּל
beyond any

FROM ROSH HASHANAH TO YOM KIPPUR SUBSTITUTE:

°l'aylo l'aylo mikol   °לְעֵלָּא לְעֵלָּא מִכָּל
exceedingly beyond any

birchoso v'shiroso   בִּרְכָתָא וְשִׁירָתָא
blessing and song,

tushb'choso v'nechemoso,   תֻּשְׁבְּחָתָא וְנֶחֱמָתָא,
praise and consolation

da-amiron b'ol'mo.   דַּאֲמִירָן בְּעָלְמָא.
that are uttered in the world.

V'imru: Omayn.   וְאִמְרוּ: אָמֵן.
Now respond: Amen.

CONGREGATION RESPONDS: Omayn — אָמֵן

Y'hay sh'lomo rabo min sh'mayo   יְהֵא שְׁלָמָא רַבָּא מִן שְׁמַיָּא,
May there be abundant peace from Heaven,

v'cha-yim olaynu   וְחַיִּים עָלֵינוּ
   v'al kol yisro-ayl.   וְעַל כָּל יִשְׂרָאֵל.
and life, upon us and upon all Israel.

V'imru: Omayn.   וְאִמְרוּ: אָמֵן.
Now respond: Amen.

CONGREGATION RESPONDS: Omayn — אָמֵן

MOURNER BOWS, THEN TAKES THREE STEPS BACK, BOWS LEFT AND SAYS:

Ō-se sholōm bimrōmov   עֹשֶׂה שָׁלוֹם בִּמְרוֹמָיו,
He Who makes peace in His heights,

MOURNER BOWS RIGHT AND SAYS:

hu ya-a-se sholōm olaynu   הוּא יַעֲשֶׂה שָׁלוֹם עָלֵינוּ,
may He make peace upon us,

MOURNER BOWS FORWARD AND SAYS:

v'al kol yisro-ayl. V'imru: Omayn.   וְעַל כָּל יִשְׂרָאֵל. וְאִמְרוּ: אָמֵן.
and upon all Israel. Now respond: Amen.

CONGREGATION RESPONDS: Omayn — אָמֵן

MOURNER REMAINS IN PLACE FOR A FEW MOMENTS, THEN TAKES THREE STEPS FORWARD.

The Friday Night Service

✍ Kabbalas Shabbos / Welcoming the Sabbath

✍ Vital Spiritual Organ

It is impossible to capture the essence of the Shabbos in only a few paragraphs. Only by studying the many aspects of Shabbos and by experiencing and living the beauty of Shabbos is one privileged to taste and understand its essence. In his introduction to the laws of Shabbos, the Chafetz Chaim refers to the well-known dictum that the 248 positive commandments correspond to the 248 limbs and organs of the human body, and finds an allusion to it in the verse: "You shall observe My decrees and My laws, which man shall carry out and by which he shall live" (*Leviticus* 18:5). Not only are the laws of our Torah the blueprint for meaningful and productive life, but each positive commandment gives spiritual nourishment to its corresponding organ, sustaining the body not only in our present existence, but in the World to Come, as we recite in the second blessing over the Torah, "Who . . . implanted eternal life within us." The observance of the Torah assures us of a share in the World to Come and of participation in the Resurrection of the Dead. (See Maimonides' *Thirteen Principles of Faith* §13.)

The Chafetz Chaim continues that just as we want our bodies to be completely intact, so we should be scrupulous to observe all the commandments. Nevertheless, a body can live without certain limbs, such as a finger or a toe, although it will be blemished or crippled, but it cannot exist without its head or its heart. Shabbos is one of those indispensable spiritual organs, like the head or the heart. It is our testimony that Hashem is the Creator and Master of the world, Who invited us to participate in the development of His world in the six workdays, and ordained that we cease all material, physical productivity on the seventh day. One cannot live as a Jew in this world without the Shabbos. As a wise man once said, "More than the Jewish people have safeguarded the Shabbos the Shabbos has preserved the Jewish people."

✍ Israel's Mate

Rabbi Shimon bar Yochai (one of the greatest leaders of the Jewish community shortly after the destruction of the Second Temple) taught that the Sabbath complained to God that each day had a mate; the creation of the first day is nurtured and developed by the second; that of the third day by the fourth, and that of the fifth by the sixth. But the Sabbath had no mate. God responded, "The Jewish people is your mate" (*Bereishis Rabbah* 11:8). This teaching suggests the personal attachment and involvement that Jews should feel for the Sabbath. This is why the Sages would don their finest clothing and, as the the Sabbath

approached, would rise saying, "Let us go out to greet the the Sabbath Queen" (*Shabbos* 119a).

Indeed, in his commentary on the text of the the Sabbath service, Avudraham likens it to a marriage service that unites Israel and the the Sabbath as "mates."

◄§ The Friday Night Service

◄§ Origin of the Service

The text of our *Kabbalas Shabbos / Welcoming the the Sabbath* service stems from the Kabbalist masters of 16th-century Safed, in *Eretz Yisrael*, who would literally walk out to the fields to greet the incoming Queen. The custom of reciting six psalms, the liturgical poem *L'chah Dodi*, and then two more psalms was instituted by Rabbi Moshe Cordovero (1522-1570) and his brother-in-law, Rabbi Shlomo HaLevi Alkabetz, the composer of *L'chah Dodi*. From Safed the new liturgy spread, until it was adopted by virtually the entire Jewish nation. According to many commentators, it is because the *Kabbalas Shabbos* service was of later origin that, in many communities, the *chazzan* leads the service from the *bimah*, the table from which the Torah is read, rather than from the regular lectern. This is to set off this part of the service from the rest of *Maariv*, and indicate that it is a later "appendage" to the standard evening service.

◄§ Symbolism of the Psalms

The six psalms correspond to the just-completed six workdays. The positive message of these psalms point to the time when the entire world will recognize Hashem as the Creator, and to man's ability to imbue every day with spirituality. Ideally, the sanctity of the Sabbath should overflow and influence the rest of the week, infusing every day with the realization that God is the Creator and King of the universe. These six psalms portray the ideal spiritual preparation for the Sabbath by demonstrating that not only on the Sabbath do we view Hashem as the Creator, but on each of the weekdays, as well, making the transition to the Sabbath an easier one. Thus, Shammai (colleague of Hillel the Elder) used to designate tasty foods for the Sabbath from the beginning of the week, demonstrating that the day is part of our consciousness throughout the week.

◄§ Symbolism of the Bimah

Rabbi Yitzchok Prag in his *Tzitz HaSadeh* suggests a fascinating reason for the practice in many communities that the cantor leads the *Kabbalas Shabbos* service from the Torah reading table, the *bimah*, instead of the usual location at the front of the congregation. All agree that the Torah was given to the Jewish nation on the Sabbath (*Shabbos* 86b), so it is appropriate that we recite these psalms at the Torah reading table, highlighting the connection between the Sabbath and the Torah. Moreover, the last of these introductory psalms is Psalm 29, which according to the Sages highlights the giving of the Torah, and the impact that it had on the entire world. Since the Jewish people stood at the foot

of Mount Sinai when they received the Torah, it is customary to stand while reciting Psalm 29.

Another aspect of the Sabbath service alludes to the relationship of the Sabbath to the giving of the Torah. The Talmud (*Bava Basra* 14b) credits Moses as the composer of eleven psalms beginning with Psalm 90. All except one of them are included in the Sabbath prayers: *Kabbalas Shabbos* begins with Psalms 95-99; Psalms 92-93 follow *L'chah Dodi*, and Psalms 90-91 are incorporated into the *Pesukei D'Zimrah* of the Sabbath morning. [As for Psalm 94, which is not part of the Shabbos service, some suggest that it is deleted because the Kohanim recited it when the Temple was destroyed, and therefore we do not mar the joy of the Sabbath by including Psalm 94.]

It is advisable that when reciting the six psalms, the worshiper should think of the six respective working days: *L'chu Neranenah* corresponding to the first day, and so on. When a festival or one of the intermediate days of a festival occurs on the Sabbath, *Nusach Ashkenaz* omits all six psalms, so as not to demean the festival. *Nusach Sfard*, however, retains Psalm 29, because it recalls the giving of the Torah.

↞§ L'chah Dodi

This beautiful and inspiring song to the Sabbath was composed by the 16th-century Kabbalistic master, Rabbi Shlomo HaLevi Alkabetz, whose name, Shlomo HaLevi, is formed by the acrostic of the first eight stanzas. Stanzas 1, 2, and 9 deal with various praises of the Sabbath while the remaining stanzas deal with the redemption of Israel and our return to Jerusalem. While custom varies as to whether one stands or sits during the singing or recitation of the poem, it is prevalent everywhere to stand and face the rear door of the synagogue when reciting the last stanza and to bow while saying בֹּאִי כַלָּה, *Enter, O bride*, symbolically greeting and ushering in the Sabbath.

Siddur HaGra suggests another reason for turning to the rear of the synagogue. In King Solomon's Temple, there were separate entrances for bridegrooms and mourners, so that those in the Temple would know how and to whom to respond for various personal circumstances. This practice has been perpetuated, so that mourners during the week of *shivah* enter the synagogue, and the entire congregation extends the Jewish formula of consolation ("May the Omnipresent console you and the other mourners of Zion and Jerusalem"). This is done immediately after *L'chah Dodi* because the recitation of the psalm following *L'chah Dodi* — *Mizmor Shir L'Yom HaShabbos* — constitutes to many a formal acceptance of the Sabbath, and it is forbidden to console mourners on the Sabbath. Thus, this is the last opportunity to extend consolation with most worshipers present.

↞§ The Additional Soul

With the acceptance of the Shabbos a person experiences a heightened spiritual awareness, which the Sages call a נְשָׁמָה יְתֵרָה, *additional soul (Beitzah*

16a). Our sages, who treasure every word and indeed every letter of our liturgy, note that the numerical value of the first letters of these six psalms is 430, which is equal to that of the word נֶפֶשׁ, *soul*. Rabbi Elie Munk explains that this symbolizes that these psalms should imbue us with the spiritual exaltation and serenity that are indicative of the "*neshama yeseirah*," the additional soul that is granted to Jews on the Sabbath (*World of Prayer*, vol. II, p. 5).

This additional soul enhances the Shabbos on essential levels. The first point is psychological. Not only must one abstain from prohibited activities, one must consider all his work as if it is completed and done. In other words, all the worry and concern, pressures and deadlines that one often brings home from work during the week must disappear on Shabbos. On Shabbos people should feel as if they had retired on Friday afternoon, and that the heavy load of responsibility had been completely lifted from their shoulders. I was privileged to see this in my home, growing up, from my late father.

This is certainly no easy task. Not only should our speech on Shabbos be different than during the week — and therefore it is inappropriate to discuss business on Shabbos — but even to think of one's business is wrong. The Jew's capacity to withdraw from the mundane and focus on the spiritual stems from the blessing of the additional soul. Moreover, this gift helps the Jew to adjust physically to the change in diet that often comes with Shabbos. Throughout the millennia the Jew often was needy and impoverished, and the quality of his meals was poor, but on Shabbos it was prevalent to eat "*chamim*," hot food, and the additional soul helped the gastronomical system function. Even today, Shabbos menu often includes rich foods that one may avoid during the week, and the *neshamah yeseirah* still plays its ancient role.

In addition, on the Sabbath, ideally we take on *panim chadashos*, a new appearance and radiance. Great and saintly Jews were suffused with a visage of holiness and serenity on Shabbos, so much so that they actually looked different. Regarding Rabbi Yerucham Levovitz, the late *mashgiach* (spiritual head) of the pre-War Mirrer Yeshiva, it is told that some new students, who had interacted with him during the week, did not recognize him on Shabbos. Apparently he was enveloped by the *panim chadashos* of Shabbos to the point where there was a tangible change in his appearance.

⋞ Maariv

Jacob instituted *Maariv* (*Berachos* 26b). A cursory look at his life indicates why he became the composer of the prayer of the night. The Torah tells us "And a man wrestled with him [Jacob] until the break of dawn" (*Genesis* 32:25). The Sages explain that the "man" was the guardian angel of Esau, who tried to overcome Jacob. Ramban comments that the "night" of this prophetic text refers to the long exile that Jacob's offspring would experience at the hands of Esau's

descendants — Israel's current, seemingly endless exile. Away from the land of Israel, facing foes that attempt either to exterminate or absorb us, Jacob's struggle with the guardian angel of Esau portended the future travail of the Jewish people. Furthermore, as Jacob was about to leave *Eretz Yisrael* for Egypt, God appeared to him in "night visions" (*Genesis* 46:2). *Meshech Chochmah* notes that the term "night visions" is used only with regard to Jacob. As he was about to leave *Eretz Yisrael* and venture into the darkness of exile, God taught him that even in the dark of night, the Divine Presence would still be found in Israel. As our Rabbis have comforted us, when the Jewish people go into exile, the Divine Presence joins them in exile (*Megillah* 29a).

Jacob's trials and difficulties seem endless. He was forced to flee from family, home, and country because his brother wished to kill him. He worked honestly and diligently for his father-in-law for twenty years, was deceived countless times, and because of the great resentment that others had for his success, he had to flee again. Only Divine intervention saved his life. He had problems with his children. His daughter was kidnapped and defiled, his firstborn failed to show him proper respect, and his favored treatment of Joseph led his other sons to sell Joseph, lie to their father, and plunge him into sadness for twenty-two years.

◆§ Prayer of Faith

For close to two thousand years, the Jewish nation has been exiled from its land and has suffered communal and personal persecution, humiliation, and difficulty. Nevertheless, they derived strength from the great faith of Jacob, as expressed in his *Maariv*, the prayer of the distressed. "To relate Your kindness in the dawn and Your faith in the nights," exclaims the psalmist (*Psalms* 92:3). The Sages (*Berachos* 12a) understood this verse as a reflection of the *Shacharis* and *Maariv* prayers. *Dawn* symbolizes the hope-filled time when we can see the redemption, success, and prosperity of our nation; *nights* symbolize times when we are beset by failure, problems, and foreboding. The prayer of the night, which is characterized by *faith*, calls upon Israel to believe that God will redeem His chosen ones in the future, as He had saved them from exile and persecution from Egyptian times onward. On a personal note, faith and trust are understood by the Chazon Ish not to mean that the outcome of every problem will be as we desire or that we will understand why it should be so, but rather the comforting knowledge that God is in control, that the outcome is not haphazard, and "whatever the Omnipotent does is for the best," though we may not understand how (*Emunah U'Vitachon*).

I recently heard of two Jewish mothers sitting in the intensive care waiting room, while their children were undergoing serious surgery. One mother, a Torah-observant, believing Jewess, was reciting *Tehillim / Psalms*. The other was not-yet observant and had no way to cope with the situation, other than bite her nails and curse the day. The *Maariv* prayer, in effect, declares: To the faithful, committed Jew there are no questions; to the Jew bereft of faith there are no answers.

⋖§ Structure of Maariv

The structure of *Maariv* consists of the Biblical recitation of the *Shema* — the declaration of our faith — as the Torah legislates, "Speak of them [the words of the *Shema*] . . . when you retire and when you arise" (*Deuteronomy* 6:7) and the recitation of the *Shemoneh Esrei*. As in the *Shacharis* prayer, the *Shema* is surrounded by blessings. While in the morning there are three blessings, in the evening there are two blessings before and two after the recitation of the *Shema*. The total number of seven blessings that encompass the two recitations of the *Shema* reflect the sentiment "Seven times a day I have praised You for Your righteous ordinances" (*Psalms* 119:164; *Berachos* 11a, *Rashi*).

⋖§ The Blessings

The themes of the evening and morning blessings are identical. The first blessing extols God as the Creator Who still controls the cosmos. The second blessing is an expression of our deeply felt gratitude to God for the gift of His Torah and His unconditional love for the Jewish people. It is most appropriate that we focus on the Torah at night, for we recognize that it is only due to our loyalty to Torah study and observance that we have endured the many, long, difficult exiles. Moreover, the Sages teach that while there is a commandment to study Torah both day and night, one acquires the majority of one's Torah insight and understanding in the quietude of the night (*Eruvim* 65a). Rambam extols the virtues of Torah study at night (*Hil. Talmud Torah* 3:13).

The third blessing, immediately after the *Shema*, recounts the wondrous events that gave way to the Exodus from Egypt. It begins "True and faithful is all this" and *Chiddushei HaRim* explains that *truth* refers to something we know to be true because our senses tell us so, or we have conclusive evidence. *Faith*, on the other hand, refers to that which we believe, though we have never seen it nor do we have proof that it happened. We know the Exodus to be true, because it was witnessed by millions of people. The future redemption is not yet an accomplished fact, but we have perfect faith that God will bring it about, as He promised through the Prophets

The fourth blessing, *Hashkiveinu*, is understood by the Sages (*Berachos* 4a) as an extension of the previous blessing of redemption. We affirm that He is our Protector from the challenges and afflictions associated with the terrors of night, literally and figuratively..

⋖§ Additional Blessings

Ashkenazic Jews outside of Israel add *Baruch Hashem L'Olam*, a collection of Scriptural verses. *Tur Orach Chaim* 236 explains its origin. In the Geonic Era (750-1000 C.E.) the synagogues were located in the fields and people were afraid to remain there until after the conclusion of the complete *Shemoneh Esrei*, so the rabbis of the time composed a shorter prayer, containing the Name Hashem eighteen times, corresponding to the eighteen blessings of *Shemoneh Esrei*.

Tosafos (*Berachos* 4b) suggests that *Baruch Hashem L'Olam* was added to enable latecomers to catch up to the congregation, thus enabling all to leave in safety together. Though the full *Maariv* has been recited in synagogues for many centuries, the former custom was not abandoned, and *Baruch Hashem* is still recited before *Shemoneh Esrei* by nearly all Ashkenazi congregations.

✌§ The Shema and Its Blessings

The *Shema* is the only text that the Torah obligates a Jew to recite daily. It is our pledge of allegiance to God, acknowledging His sovereignty and Oneness. It is not sufficient merely to recite the *Shema*; one must understand and internalize the content of the declaration, "Hear, O Israel: HASHEM is our God, HASHEM, the One and Only." One who fails to do so, though one has pronounced the words, has not fulfilled the Biblical command.

The Sages ordained blessings in order to enhance our performance of commandments. By reciting a blessing, we focus on the *mitzvah* we are about to perform and on the privilege and responsibility we have in serving Hashem through its performance.

An analogy might help us appreciate the blessings that come before and after the *Shema*. Customarily, a groom gives his fiancée a ring, denoting their serious intention and commitment to a lifetime of devotion to each other. The stone in the center of the ring is its central and most costly aspect. Yet, without the actual ring and setting to house the stone and keep it in place, the precious gem could not be exhibited or fully appreciated. Like this precious gem, the *Shema* has blessings before it and after it, to highlight it and help us appreciate it.

The Sages teach that the morning *Shema* is preceded by two blessings and followed by one blessing. The evening *Shema* is both preceded and followed by two blessings (*Berachos* 11a).

✌§ Themes of the Blessings

The morning and evening blessings begin with inspirational commitments. The opening blessing of the morning describes God's renewal of nature, for we welcome the daylight with excitement, anticipating new opportunities to develop ourselves and our environment. Every night we acknowledge that He brings on evenings, affording us the opportunity to rest our bodies and refresh our souls.

The second blessing of the *Shema*, both morning and evening, which acknowledges the preciousness of Torah, our responsibility to study it, and the gratitude we must feel that God entrusted it to us, is directly related to the *Shema*, the recitation of which is the minimum fulfillment of the commandment to study the Torah, day and night. Thus, the blessing *Ahavah Rabbah*, which precedes the *Shema*, doubles as a form of *Birkas HaTorah*, a blessing for Torah study. (In fact, one who forgot to recite the Torah blessings at the beginning of the *Shacharis* service may discharge that obligation with his recitation of *Ahavah Rabbah*.

In the morning blessing, we pray movingly, "Our Father, the merciful Father, Who acts mercifully, have mercy upon us, instill in our hearts to understand and elucidate, to listen, learn, teach, safeguard, perform, and fulfill all the words of Your Torah's teaching with love." But after such an impassioned request, what if anything do we do about it?

The Chafetz Chaim, of blessed memory, in a famous parable, compares our request to that of a poor man who approached a wealthy member of his community and asked for a substantial loan, with which he would establish himself in business. The wealthy man agreed, and asked the borrower to come to his home that evening for the money.

That night the lender stayed home looking forward to the opportunity to help his friend — but the poor man never came. The next day they met in the street and once again the poor man asked his neighbor for the sizable loan, explaining excitedly the potential of his business plan and his genuine need for the money. The rich man responded, "I told you yesterday that the money was yours. All you had to do was come and get it. I will be prepared for you again tonight." That night, as well, the rich man did not leave his home. Again the poor man did not come.

The following day they met again and again the poor man began to ask for the loan. This time the frustrated businessman cut him off. "I was ready every night," he said angrily, "but you never followed through."

Similarly, God surely wishes to enable us to understand, elucidate, listen, learn, teach, safeguard, perform, and fulfill all of His Torah. All He asks is that we come to the house of study. All too often we don't.

◆§ Commandment to Love

The second blessing of the *Shema* concludes with God's love for Israel. Why is this blessing said exclusively prior to the recitation of the *Shema*, and not in conjunction with the performance of any other *mitzvah*?

The paragraph of *Shema* commands a Jew to love God "with all your heart, with all your soul, and with all your resources." It is understandable that the Torah can demand or prohibit various activities: Return a lost object, do not charge interest when lending money, eat matzah on Pesach. Such *mitzvos* require our physical ability to perform them or strength of character not to violate them — but how can the Torah demand our love, an emotion that swells from within? Love is not something we can control; what tugs at the emotions of one individual might leave the next one unmoved.

The *Sifre* teaches that one comes to love God by studying His Torah and seeing the infinite depths of His wisdom. To know Him is to love Him. No code of morals and ethics composed by mortals, who are bound by their environment and culture, has stood the test of time. Only Hashem, Who created man's nature, is able to legislate eternal ethics and teachings.

It is thus understandable that what follows our declaration of His Oneness is the commandment to love Him and to study His Torah. Commensurate with one's study of Torah is one's love for Hashem.

Rabbi Boruch Epstein (*Baruch She'amar*) offers a different explanation. Love is reciprocal. When someone extends unconditional love to someone else, that person usually responds in turn. Therefore, before we recite the *Shema*, we declare God's unconditional, absolute love for Israel, prompting us to respond with love toward Him.

✥ With Every Organ

There are 248 proactive or positive commandments in the Torah, corresponding to the 248 organs in the human body. This phenomenon is given great significance by the Sages, as it signals that man's physical body was created in harmony with the commandments of the Torah; that the commandments do not go against man's nature. This correspondence of *mitzvos* to organs symbolizes that the purpose of our physical existence is to obey the precepts of the Torah.

The total number of words in the three paragraphs of the *Shema* is 245. To help convey the parallelism of 248 organs to the words of the *Shema*, the Sages added three words to the recitation: In the synagogue, the congregation listens to the *chazzan* repeat aloud the final three words, ה׳ אֱלֹהֵיכֶם אֱמֶת, *"Hashem, your God, is true,"* which is considered as if the listeners had uttered the words. One who prays alone prefaces the *Shema* with three words, אֵל מֶלֶךְ נֶאֱמָן, *"God, trustworthy King."* These words were chosen because their initials spell *amen*, which means faithful or true, thus testifying to our faith in the truths we are about to recite.

✥ No Contradictions

There is one more critical theme that binds the blessings of the *Shema* with the declaration of the *Shema*: God's absolute Oneness. The text of the opening blessing praises God "Who forms light and creates darkness, makes peace and creates all." The Talmud (*Berachos* 11b) teaches that this blessing is based on the verse in *Isaiah* 45:7 in which God declares that He "forms light and creates darkness, makes peace and creates evil". Our Sages changed the text from "and creates evil" to "and creates all," because, explains the Talmud, it is unseemly to praise God by saying that He creates evil. We speak, rather, in general terms, of God creating everything — including that which appears to be evil.

In the evening service, too, the first blessing describes God as the One "Who removes light from before darkness and darkness from before light." The terms day and night are used extensively both by the prophets and in our liturgy to refer to prosperous or troubled times. Light symbolizes life, wisdom, and happiness. Darkness is associated with suffering, failure, and death. Thus we speak of God as the Master of all aspects of life. This refutes the contention of heretical philosophers who reasoned that the "good god" who creates light cannot be the same "bad god" who creates darkness. Therefore, they argued, there must be at least two gods.

Judaism believes that there is One God, that He is good, and that light and darkness, joy and sadness, are all ultimately good, though it is often — or even usually — beyond human capacity to understand how. As the Midrash states: God tells us, "Do not treat Me as the Canaanites and Egyptians treat their

deities. When they experience good, they honor their gods, and when misfortune befalls them, they curse their gods. However, when you are showered with blessings, praise Me, and when you experience suffering and travail, praise Me as well."

This charge is beautifully substantiated by the sixth paragraph of the *Hallel* prayer, Psalm 116. Says David the Psalmist, "How can I repay Hashem for all His kindness to me? I will raise the cup of salvations and the Name of Hashem I will invoke." Earlier in the same paragraph, he declares, "The pains of death encircled me; the confines of the grave have found me; trouble and sorrow I would find. Then I would invoke the Name of Hashem." No matter what the circumstances, David invokes God's Name.

◆§ Omnipresent and Indivisible

God's omnipresence allows us to more fully appreciate our declaration: "Hear, O Israel, *Hashem* (the Name of God signifying His Attribute of Love) *Eloheinu* (the Name of God pointing to His Attribute of Justice), Hashem, the One and Only." Both attributes come from the One and only God, writes Rabbi Elie Munk in *World of Prayer*, "for only if mercy and justice, joy and pain, life and death flow from one source, only if our health and wealth are granted and withheld by the order of the One God, only then are we His, with every fiber of our being, with all our heart, all our soul and all our wealth. Therefore the immediate consequence of His Oneness is וְאָהַבְתָּ, *and you shall love HASHEM*, not a theoretical concept echoing in a vacuum, but the direct challenge to lead a moral existence, that we should love and serve God in all the diverse phases of our life and being. Complete, unreserved submission to the One indivisible God makes man into a harmonious and integrated personality."

Rabbi Gedalia Schorr likened this understanding of God to light seen through a prism. Though the viewer sees a myriad of different colors, they all come from a single ray of light. So, too, God's many manifestations are truly one.

◆§ The Unique One

Finally the word אֶחָד, *One,* in the context of the *Shema* has the connotation of "unique." While one often speaks of "one of a kind," by definition there are many others of that kind in different variations. The "one and only ring," for example, that a spouse may receive is invaluable and especially sentimental to her, but it is not truly unique, for there are many other rings like it in the world, or imitations of it can be made. Only, God, however, is unique in the sense that He is incomparable; he is in a category and class unto Himself.

Moreover, we declare that Hashem, Who at present is acknowledged and recognized only by His people Israel — He is now אֱלֹקֵינוּ, **our** *God* — will one day be recognized as the only One, and will be worshiped by all.

◆§ Mode of Recitation

Traditional practice is to recite the first sentence of the *Shema* in a loud voice, with the right hand covering the eyes, thereby blocking all distractions and

helping us concentrate on accepting God's absolute sovereignty. This is our testimony to God's Oneness. In the Torah scroll, the letter *ayin* of *Shema* and the letter *daled* of Echad are enlarged — אחד . . . שמע. Together these two letters form the word עד, *witness*. By pronouncing the *Shema*, every Jew bears witness to God's unity and declares it to all the world.

Immediately after proclaiming God's Kingship with *Shema Yisrael*, we declare, in an undertone, "Blessed is the Name of His glorious Kingdom for all eternity."

The Talmud (*Pesachim* 56a) explains why this verse is said quietly. Prior to his passing, our Patriarch Jacob wanted to reveal to his family future events of Jewish history, including when the Messiah would come. But God, in His infinite wisdom, shut down Jacob's spiritual antenna and withheld this information from him. Jacob feared that perhaps his children were not worthy of hearing this prophecy.

His sons reassured him emphatically, "*Shema Yisrael*, Hear [our father], O Israel, there is no generational or cultural gap; your God is ours, the One and the same."

Hearing this, Jacob immediately responded, "Blessed is the Name of His glorious Kingdom for all eternity."

Nonetheless, the verse *Shema Yisrael* appears in the Torah, but not the verse that Jacob spoke in reply. We wish to include Jacob's words, states the Talmud, but because they are not found in the Torah, we recite them in a whisper.

Aruch HaShulchan suggests that the story of Jacob and his sons may also provide insight into the recitation of the *Shema* itself. Twice daily we address our grandfather Jacob, who was also given the name Israel — "Hear, O Israel" — and reassure him that there is still no generational or cultural gap between us and previous generations of dedicated Jews. We are perpetuating our national belief in the Oneness of Hashem.

◄§ Order of the Passages

The Talmud (*Berachos* 13a) explains the order of the three Biblical paragraphs that make up the *Shema*. In the first paragraph, the Jew accepts upon himself the yoke of the Kingdom of Heaven, for without acknowledgment that the commandments are God given, their performance would have no sanctity. In the second paragraph, he submits to the Divine law, to perform all the *mitzvos* properly, and acknowledges the concept of reward and punishment. And the third paragraph refers to sanctification of the individual, by stressing the responsibility to avoid temptation and to remember God's commandments. The third paragraph also fulfills the commandment to remember the Exodus from Egypt. Simply put, *Krias Shema* comprises the origin of the law, its demands, and its purpose.

Rabbi Joseph B. Soloveitchik notes that both the second and third paragraphs include our acceptance of the commandments. Why twice? He answered that the second paragraph deals with accepting those *mitzvos* that we are capable of doing, while the third paragraph refers to our acceptance of even those *mitzvos*

from which we are technically exempt. For example, nowadays, as our garments are not four-cornered cloaks, a man in his regular garb would never be required to wear *tzitzis*. Yet, in our love for God and His *mitzvos,* we commit ourselves to wear special four-cornered garments in order to put *tzitzis* on them. To us, all *mitzvos* are a privilege, and we are eager to find ways to fulfill them.

This attitude, the *Chinuch* maintains, is the purpose of the morning *Shema* — to assist the Jew in sanctifying the challenges of the upcoming day. Realizing that one is an ambassador of the King of kings imposes certain responsibilities and restrictions. Indeed, the word וְאָהַבְתָּ means more than *you shall love* [*Hashem*]; it also implies that you shall want others to love Him, and that you should act in such a way that your speech, actions, demeanor, honesty, and integrity will influence *others* to love God — that your conduct will set an example that will cause others to love the God you serve (*Yoma* 86a). Society ought to see that you are galvanized by the principles of the *Shema* and be motivated to emulate your ways.

◆§ How to Love

God commands the Jew to love Him בְּכָל לְבָבְךָ, *with all your heart*. Our Sages point out that the Hebrew word for *your heart* is spelled with two *lameds,* when it should be לְבָּךָ, with one *lamed*. From the structure of this word, the Talmud famously infers that you must serve God with your "two" hearts, i.e., with both of your inclinations, good and evil.

One loves God, Rabbeinu Yonah explains, by following one's good inclination to perform *mitzvos* and one loves God just the same by rejecting the evil inclination that presses him to sin.

The Rambam takes a different approach to loving God with your "evil" inclination. This, he says, refers to one's baser instincts, his earthly cravings, such as his desire for food and other physical gratifications. By channeling even the most temporal features of one's humanity toward the service of God — by eating kosher food in proper moderation, by having sexual relations only with one's spouse at the permitted time — one elevates the activity and thereby succeeds in serving God with that inclination as well.

God further commands the Jew to love Him בְּכָל נַפְשְׁךָ, *with all your soul*, even if, explains the Mishnah (*Berachos* 61b), your devotion to God costs you your life. This self-sacrifice is demanded of us only in very rare situations: where we are asked to choose between death and one of three cardinal sins — idolatry, adultery or incest, and murder. It is also demanded when the alternative is public desecration of God's Name. In these cases, Jewish law requires that one die rather than sin, and to offer his life in happiness, in martyrdom. The great Rabbi Akiva was joyous while being tortured to death. To his amazed disciples he explained, "All my life I prayed that if faced with this situation, I would be able to maintain my love of God. Now that I succeeded in so doing, should I not be happy?" (ibid.).

The final step is to love God בְּכָל מְאֹדֶךָ, *with all your resources*. A Jew must be prepared to forfeit financial gain rather than violate Torah law. Moreover, those

foolish people in every generation who value their money above their lives and will risk their lives to save their money are reminded that they, too, must put their love of God first.

In addition, the Mishnah notes, the phrase means "in whatever measure [מדה] He measures out to you, you should give thanks to Him." This includes any talent with which you are blessed. Channel your pleasant voice, artistic skill, mathematical acumen, to serve Him and the Jewish community, and maintain your faith even if God serves you an apparently bitter portion in life.

◄§ Further Commandments

There are three specific commandments in both the first and second paragraphs of the *Shema* — to study and teach Torah, to don the head and arm *tefillin*, and to affix a *mezuzah* to one's doorpost. The obligation to teach Torah to one's children is written in each of the two paragraphs, once referring to one's actual children and once referring to one's students.

The first paragraph of *Shema* closes with the *mitzvos* of *tefillin* and *mezuzah*. These *mitzvos* writes the Malbim, are the actualization of the start of the paragraph: The *tefillin* are worn on the arm across from the heart, directing the Jew to serve Hashem "with all your heart." The head *tefillin* signifies the subjugation of one's intellect to God; this corresponds to "with all your soul." Lastly, the *mezuzah* on the doorpost of one's home shows love of God "with all your resources," as one's home represents his wealth.

The second paragraph of the *Shema* differs from the first in that it is written in the plural form. The first paragraph addresses the individual Jew; the second addresses the Jews as a nation and introduces the concept of reward and punishment. This communicates to us that the good and bad that befall our nation is contingent upon the behavior of all. Reward and punishment, financial gain and drought, security and exile, are not part of some natural process, as Rambam explains. Do not be fooled into thinking that some years you are more productive, other years less. Rather, your yield is commensurate with your service and dedication to Hashem.

God's miraculous intervention in human affairs occurs on a national level, based on the merit of the populace as a whole; for the individual, it is not as apparent. It is for this reason that the concept of reward and punishment is not found in the first paragraph, which talks to the individual Jew.

The punishment listed for turning away from God is in the material realm. God promises that "He will restrain the heaven so there will be no rain and the ground will not yield its produce." In the ninth chapter of the Laws of Repentance, Rambam notes that lack of financial security causes the individual to devote all of his time and effort toward eking out a living. The dreadful effect is that he will be left with no qualitative time to study Torah or perform acts of kindness, which earn him his share in the World to Come. Thus the ultimate blessing and curse of the second paragraph of the *Shema* is that man's actions determine his ability to attain that lofty reward.

The third paragraph of the *Shema* concludes with the declaration, "I am

Hashem your God who has removed you from the land of Egypt." By saying these words we fulfill the daily obligation "that you will remember the day you left Egypt all the days of your life" (*Deuteronomy* 16:3).

◆§ The Shemoneh Esrei of the Sabbath

◆§ Continuation and Purpose

One word in the Friday evening service stands out and helps provide a proper perspective of the nature of the Sabbath. In the opening paragraph of the central blessing we recite, "You sanctified the seventh day for Your Name's sake, the [תַּכְלִית, *tachlis*] conclusion of the creation of heaven and earth." The word *tachlis* means not only *conclusion*, meaning that God's six days of labor ended on the Sabbath; the word *tachlis* has the additional meaning of "purpose." Accordingly, a second look at this opening prayer teaches that the very purpose of heaven and earth, of Creation, was the Sabbath. In complete opposition to the secular perspective all around us, that the weekend is for rest and relaxation, so that man can return to his productive work refreshed and rejuvenated, we declare that the world was created for the Sabbath.

The purpose of Creation was this day when man can reflect on his Maker and declare that the world has a Creator and that His creatures are here to do His bidding and perfect the universe according to the Torah, His blueprint of Creation.

This theme is advanced by Abarbanel in his commentary on *Genesis* 2:1-3, which is incorporated into the Friday night *Shemoneh Esrei*, immediately after the *Amidah*, and into *Kiddush*. וַיְכֻלּוּ הַשָּׁמַיִם וְהָאָרֶץ is usually translated *Thus the heaven and earth were finished* [וַיְכֻלּוּ] — but Abarbanel breathes new life into the verse and explains that the root of *vayechulu* is the same as that of *tachlis*, meaning *purpose*. With the coming of the Sabbath, heaven and earth attained their purpose, their primary purpose for being.

◆§ The Amidah (Shemoneh Esrei) for Friday Evening

Originally the regular weekday *Amidah / Shemoneh Esrei* was recited on the Sabbath, with the inclusion of an appropriate paragraph indicating the holiness of Shabbos, as is done on *Rosh Chodesh* and the intermediate days of the festivals (*Berachos* 21a). However, the Sages removed the section of supplications and requests, as one is not permitted to petition for one's personal needs on the Sabbath. This is based on *Isaiah* (58:13): "Refrain from accomplishing your own needs on My holy day" (*Jerusalem Talmud, Shabbos* 15:3). *Midrash Tanchuma* explains that the thirteen middle blessings of the *Shemoneh Esrei*, which deal with human concerns and needs, are not appropriate for the Sabbath, the sacred day when we turn from our daily preoccupations and occupy ourselves with spiritual values and priorities. Technically, therefore, the name *Shemoneh Esrei*, literally *Eighteen [19 blessings]*, is a misnomer for the seven-blessing Sabbath prayer; the name *Amidah*, standing prayer, would be

more correct. However since both titles are used interchangeably, we will follow the popular practice and usage, *Shemoneh Esrei*.

⋯ Introductory and Closing Blessings

Every *Shemoneh Esrei* begins with the same three blessings of praise. The first blessing highlights the Patriarchs and God's assurance to preserve their descendants. The second blessing acknowledges God's might, focusing primarily on His revival of the dead: be it man's awakening every morning after deathlike slumber, the life-giving gift of rain, sustenance, and the literal resuscitation of the dead, that will take place in the Messianic Age. The third blessing is that of *Kedushah* / Sanctification and Holiness, declaring that God is exalted above and separated from the limitations of material existence.

Similarly every *Shemoneh Esrei* ends with three blessings of *Hoda'ah* / Thanksgiving. The first one is a call for God to restore the Temple service and view our prayers as if they were actual sacrifices. The second blessing acknowledges that He constantly renews the precious gift of life and provides miracles on our behalf, often unbeknown to us. Finally the last blessing of every *Shemoneh Esrei* is that of peace, acknowledging that peace of mind and peace among our people is a prerequisite for all other blessings to take effect.

⋯ The Essential Middle Blessing

Since the first three and the last three blessings are constant, the essence of the Sabbath and Yom Tov *Shemoneh Esrei* is the fourth blessing, which is unique to the day and gives the prayer its special character. It is noteworthy that there is a significant difference between the *Shemoneh Esrei* of the Sabbath and that of the festivals. The latter *Shemoneh Esrei* is identical for the evening, morning, and afternoon prayers (with the exception of *Mussaf*, the Additional Service). Not so on the Sabbath. when the middle blessing of each *Shemoneh Esrei* has its own text.

On Friday night the middle blessing begins "You have sanctified the seventh day"; in the morning we pray "Moses rejoiced in the gift of his portion"; and in the afternoon "You are One and Your Name is One." True, all the middle blessings end the same way: "Blessed are You, Hashem, Who sanctifies the Sabbath," but the theme of each *Amidah* varies. Why?

Avudraham suggests an emotionally uplifting response, based on the above-cited *midrash* that the Sabbath is the mate of the Jewish people. Every Sabbath we "renew our vows," as it were, refreshing the relationship between ourselves and God through the Sabbath. The Jewish wedding ceremony consists of three distinct parts. The first is *Kiddushin*, the ring ceremony that sanctifies the relationship and that is performed before two witnesses. The second stage of the ceremony is *Nesuin*, the seven blessings recited under the *chuppah,* the wedding canopy. The third phase is *Yichud*, the private union of the bride and groom, alone and separate from all.

The three *Shemoneh Esreis* of the Sabbath symbolize these three stages. On Friday night, "You have sanctified," refers to the *Kiddushin*, the ritual of

betrothal. This ceremony is valid only if it is performed before witnesses, and on Friday night our recitation of *Vayechulu* constitutes our "testimony" that God created the earth in six days and rested on the seventh. On the Sabbath morning with *Yismach Moshe*, we have the celebration of receiving the Torah and many understand that our *chuppah* was Mount Sinai, which, according to the Sages, hovered over Israel when they received the Torah.

Even the *Mussaf* prayer symbolically joins the celebration. The word *Mussaf* means "to add," and in the context of prayers it refers to the additional sacrifices that were offered on the Sabbath and hence our additional prayer. In also symbolizes our additional commitment to our mates, to the Sabbath and to God, beyond the normal commitment that is contained in the *kesubah*, the marriage contract. This translates itself in greater participation in Torah and *mitzvos*. Finally, the Sabbath *Minchah* prayer reflects the oneness, closeness, and consummation of the relationship, our private communion with God, as it were.

⮂ The Variations

The above explanation can be related to the custom cited by the *Magen Avraham* (O.C. 268:3) that the central blessing of the Sabbath *Shemoneh Esrei* alternates between the feminine, masculine, and plural forms. On Friday night, the blessing concludes: "May Israel, the sanctifiers of Your Name, rest בָּהּ [feminine singular] on it." In the morning, the same paragraph uses the word בּוֹ, in the masculine singular form. In the afternoon, at *Minchah*, the same paragraph ends with בָּם, *them*, in the plural. In terms of the marriage ceremony being reenacted: Friday night focuses on the bride, therefore the feminine form; Sabbath morning, on the groom, therefore the masculine form. Sabbath afternoon focuses on them both, bride and groom, therefore the plural.

Rabbi Elie Munk offers another explanation for the above variations. In the evening, which represents the Sabbath of Creation, the feminine form is used because the newly created Shabbos — without a nation to observe it and realize its potential — was like a lonely woman without a husband. In the morning, which recalls the Sabbath when the Torah was given, the masculine form alludes to Israel's acceptance of the Torah, when the Sabbath was "betrothed" to Israel, the nation that activated the ideals of the day. Finally, the afternoon prayer represents the Sabbath of the Ultimate Redemption, when every day — *all* the days (plural) — will have the serenity and holiness of the Sabbath.

⳥{ YEDID NEFESH }⳥

SOME CONGREGATIONS RECITE *YEDID NEFESH*, AT THIS POINT.

■ Some congregations recite *yedid nefesh*, which declares the intense love that a Jew must feel for Hashem, as a prelude to the prayers that usher in the Shabbos, which Hashem presented to Israel to show His intense love for them.

Y'DID NEFESH ov horachamon,
יְדִיד נֶפֶשׁ אָב הָרַחֲמָן,

Beloved of the soul, Compassionate Father,

m'shōch avd'cho el r'tzōnecho,
מְשֹׁךְ עַבְדְּךָ אֶל רְצוֹנֶךָ,

draw Your servant* to Your will;

yorutz avd'cho k'mō a-yol,
יָרוּץ עַבְדְּךָ כְּמוֹ אַיָּל,

then Your servant will hurry like a hart

yishtachave el mul hadorecho,
יִשְׁתַּחֲוֶה אֶל מוּל הֲדָרֶךָ,

to bow before Your majesty;

ye-erav lō y'didōsecho,
יֶעֱרַב לוֹ יְדִידוֹתֶיךָ,

to him Your friendship will be sweeter

minōfes tzuf v'chol to-am.
מִנֹּפֶת צוּף וְכָל טָעַם.

than the dripping of the honeycomb* and any taste.

Hodur na-e ziv ha-ōlam,
הָדוּר נָאֶה זִיו הָעוֹלָם,

Majestic, Beautiful, Radiance of the universe —

nafshi chōlas ahavosecho,
נַפְשִׁי חוֹלַת אַהֲבָתֶךָ,

my soul pines for Your love.*

ono Ayl no r'fo no loh,
אָנָּא אֵל נָא רְפָא נָא לָהּ,

Please, O God, heal her now

b'har-ōs loh nō-am zivecho,
בְּהַרְאוֹת לָהּ נֹעַם זִיוֶךָ,

by showing her the pleasantness of Your radiance;

oz tis-chazayk v'sisrapay,
אָז תִּתְחַזֵּק וְתִתְרַפֵּא,

then she will be strengthened and healed,*

v'ho-y'so loh simchas ōlom.
וְהָיְתָה לָהּ שִׂמְחַת עוֹלָם.

and eternal gladness will be hers.

מְשֹׁךְ עַבְדְּךָ — *Draw Your servant.* We plead with God to take the first step toward bringing us closer to His Will. We assure Him that if He takes such an initiative, then we will continue with the alacrity of a swift hart.

יֶעֱרַב לוֹ יְדִידוֹתֶיךָ מִנֹּפֶת צוּף — *To him Your friendship will be sweeter than the dripping of the honeycomb.* To the human taste, honey is the sweetest of delicacies. Nevertheless, its taste lingers for only a brief while, and too much of

it can cause discomfort. God's friendship, however, endures forever and it becomes more beneficial the more one draws closer to Him.

נַפְשִׁי חוֹלַת אַהֲבָתֶךָ — *My soul pines for Your love.* The soul which yearns for God's closeness grows lovesick, much like a person who is denied the closeness of his beloved.

אָז תִּתְחַזֵּק וְתִתְרַפֵּא — *Then she will be strengthened and healed.* Generally, a patient is healed first, and later regains strength. In this case,

Vasik yehemu no rachamecho,

וָתִיק יֶהֱמוּ נָא רַחֲמֶיךָ,

All-worthy One, may Your mercy, be aroused

v'chuso no al bayn ahuvecho,

וְחוּסָה נָא עַל בֵּן אֲהוּבֶךָ,

and please take pity on the son of Your beloved,*

ki ze kamo nichsōf nichsafti,

כִּי זֶה כַּמָּה נִכְסֹף נִכְסַפְתִּי,

because it is so very long that I have yearned intensely

lir-ōs m'hayro

לִרְאוֹת מְהֵרָה

b'siferes u-zecho,

בְּתִפְאֶרֶת עֻזֶּךָ,

to see speedily the splendor of Your strength;

ayle chom'do libi,

אֵלֶּה חָמְדָה לִבִּי,

only these my heart desired,

v'chuso no v'al tis-alom.

וְחוּסָה נָא וְאַל תִּתְעַלָּם.

so please take pity* and do not conceal Yourself.

Higolay no

הִגָּלֶה נָא

ufrōs chavivi olai,

וּפְרֹשׂ חֲבִיבִי עָלַי,

Please be revealed and spread upon me, my Beloved,

es sukas sh'lōmecho,

אֶת סֻכַּת שְׁלוֹמֶךָ,

the shelter of Your peace;

ta-ir eretz mich-vodecho,

תָּאִיר אֶרֶץ מִכְּבוֹדֶךָ,

illuminate the world with Your glory,

nogilo v'nism'cho boch.

נָגִילָה וְנִשְׂמְחָה בָּךְ.

that we may rejoice and be glad with You;

Mahayr ehōv ki vo mō-ayd,

מַהֵר אֱהֹב כִּי בָא מוֹעֵד,

hasten, show love,* for the time has come,

v'chonaynu kimay ōlom.

וְחָנֵּנוּ כִּימֵי עוֹלָם.

and show us grace as in days of old.

---

however, the illness came about only because the spiritual level of the soul was weakened. Once that holiness is strengthened once again, the healing will come naturally.

וְחוּסָה נָא עַל בֵּן אֲהוּבֶךָ — *And please take pity on the son of Your beloved.* We beseech God to take pity on Israel which is the offspring of Abraham, whom God loved.

וְחוּסָה — *Take pity. Malbim* (Ezekiel 7:4,9) explains the difference between the two Hebrew words for pity: חוּס and חָמַל. The first one, חוּס, represents the concern which one feels for selfish reasons; a farmer may be reluctant to destroy a mule because he needs it to do his own work. The second, חָמַל, refers to concern for the sake of another; one feels compassion for a sick child because of his true love for the child. Therefore, we may interpret our stich as a plea that God take pity on Israel for His Own sake, since His people, whatever their deficiencies, are the only ones who study His Torah, obey His commandments, and teach His word.

מַהֵר אֱהֹב — *Hasten, show love.* That God retains His love for Israel is unquestioned, but in the length and severity of the exile, this love is barely perceptible. Therefore, we ask God to makes His love manifest.

⚜ KABBALAS SHABBOS ⚜

THE REGULAR *KABBALAS SHABBOS** BEGINS HERE.
WHEN A FESTIVAL OR *CHOL HAMOED* FALLS ON FRIDAY OR ON THE SABBATH,
MOST CONGREGATIONS RECITE AN ABRIDGED VERSION, BEGINNING WITH PSALM 92 (P. 99).

■ Psalm 95: I sing confidently, knowing that Hashem controls both nature and history, and that if the Jewish people keep the Torah, they will be redeemed from exile.

L'CHU N'RAN'NO Ladōnoy,
לְכוּ נְרַנְּנָה לַיהוה,
Come! Let us sing* to HASHEM,

nori-o l'tzur yish-aynu.
נָרִיעָה לְצוּר יִשְׁעֵנוּ.
let us call out to the Rock of our salvation.

N'kad'mo fonov b'sōdo,
נְקַדְּמָה פָנָיו בְּתוֹדָה,
Let us greet Him with thanksgiving,

bizmirōs nori-a lō.
בִּזְמִרוֹת נָרִיעַ לוֹ.
with praiseful songs let us call out to Him.

Ki Ayl godōl Adōnoy,
כִּי אֵל גָּדוֹל יהוה,
For a great God is HASHEM,

u-melech godōl al kol elōhim.
וּמֶלֶךְ גָּדוֹל עַל כָּל אֱלֹהִים.
and a great King above all heavenly powers.

Asher b'yodō mechk'ray oretz,
אֲשֶׁר בְּיָדוֹ מֶחְקְרֵי אָרֶץ,
For in His power are the hidden mysteries of earth,

v'sō-afōs horim lō.
וְתוֹעֲפוֹת הָרִים לוֹ.
and the mountain summits are His.

Asher lō ha-yom v'hu osohu,
אֲשֶׁר לוֹ הַיָּם וְהוּא עָשָׂהוּ,
v'yabeshes yodov yotzru.
וְיַבֶּשֶׁת יָדָיו יָצָרוּ.
For His is the sea and He perfected it, and the dry land — His hands fashioned it.

⛵ Kabbalas Shabbos

The Talmud (*Shabbos* 119a) teaches that as the Sabbath drew near, the Sages would don their finest clothing and say to one another, "Let us go out to greet the Sabbath queen." A thousand years later, the Kabbalists of Safed embellished the Talmudic custom by actually walking out to the fields to welcome the incoming Sabbath. It was there in Safed that the *Kabbalas Shabbos* (Welcoming the Sabbath) service was first formulated and subsequently spread to the entire Jewish world. Jews regard the Sabbath as a queen that brings majesty to their midst, and consider it their privilege to usher her in.

Since this service was an innovation, and many congregations wished to signify that it was not part of the established service, their *chazzan* would stand in the center of the synagogue, at the *bimah*, until after *Lechah Dodi*, whereupon he would move to his accustomed place at the front of the synagogue.

The *Kabbalas Shabbos* service begins with six psalms [95-99 and 29] that allude to the six weekdays, which we elevate by dedicating them to the service of God and by preparing on them for the Sabbath day of spiritual elevation. These six psalms are followed by the *Lechah Dodi* song that greets the incoming queen, and Psalms 92-93, the songs of not only every Sabbath, but of the eternal Sabbath of Messianic days.

לְכוּ נְרַנְּנָה — *Come! Let us sing.* This psalm is composed of two parts. The first seven verses are the Psalmist's call to his people: Come with alacrity to sing to God, to praise Him, to thank Him, to acknowledge Him as the sole Creator and Guiding Force of the universe in general and of Israel in particular.

The second section is in the form of a direct

Bō-u nishtachave v'nichro-o,   בֹּאוּ נִשְׁתַּחֲוֶה וְנִכְרָעָה,
Come! Let us prostrate ourselves and bow,

nivr'cho lifnay Adōnoy ōsaynu.   נִבְרְכָה לִפְנֵי יהוה עֹשֵׂנוּ.
let us kneel before HASHEM, our Maker.

Ki hu Elōhaynu   כִּי הוּא אֱלֹהֵינוּ
For He is our God

va-anachnu am mar-isō   וַאֲנַחְנוּ עַם מַרְעִיתוֹ
   v'tzōn yodō   וְצֹאן יָדוֹ,
and we can be the flock He pastures, and the sheep in His charge

ha-yōm im b'kōlō sishmo-u.   הַיּוֹם אִם בְּקֹלוֹ תִשְׁמָעוּ.
— even today, if we but heed His call!

Al takshu l'vavchem kimrivo,   אַל תַּקְשׁוּ לְבַבְכֶם כִּמְרִיבָה,
Do not harden your heart as at Meribah,

k'yōm maso bamidbor.   כְּיוֹם מַסָּה בַּמִּדְבָּר.
as on the day of Massah in the Wilderness;

Asher nisuni avōsaychem,   אֲשֶׁר נִסּוּנִי אֲבוֹתֵיכֶם,
when Your ancestors tried Me,

b'chonuni gam ro-u fo-oli.   בְּחָנוּנִי גַּם רָאוּ פָעֳלִי.
they tested Me, though they had seen My deed.

Arbo-im shono okut b'dōr,   ✧ אַרְבָּעִים שָׁנָה אָקוּט בְּדוֹר,
For forty years I was angry with the generation;

vo-ōmar am tō-ay layvov haym,   וָאֹמַר עַם תֹּעֵי לֵבָב הֵם,
then I said, "An errant-hearted people are they,

v'haym lō yod'u d'rochoy.   וְהֵם לֹא יָדְעוּ דְרָכָי.
and they know not My ways.

Asher nishbati v'api,   אֲשֶׁר נִשְׁבַּעְתִּי בְאַפִּי,
Therefore, I have sworn in My wrath

im y'vō-un el m'nuchosi.   אִם יְבֹאוּן אֶל מְנוּחָתִי.
that they shall not enter My [land of] contentment."

■ Psalm 96: I join the Jewish nation in inviting the rest of mankind
to unite in praise of Hashem.

SHIRU LADŌNOY shir chodosh,   **שִׁירוּ לַיהוה** שִׁיר חָדָשׁ,
Sing to HASHEM a new song,

shiru Ladōnoy kol ho-oretz.   שִׁירוּ לַיהוה כָּל הָאָרֶץ.
sing to HASHEM — everyone on earth.

exhortation from God to Israel, in which He recalls the disastrous outcome of our ancestors' sins in the wilderness and urges us not to emulate that course.

שִׁירוּ לַה' שִׁיר חָדָשׁ — *Sing to Hashem a new song.* What is new about this song? It is a song for the

Shiru Ladōnoy bor'chu sh'mō,   שִׁירוּ לַיהוה בָּרְכוּ שְׁמוֹ,
Sing to HASHEM, bless His Name;

bas'ru miyōm l'yōm y'shu-osō.   בַּשְּׂרוּ מִיּוֹם לְיוֹם יְשׁוּעָתוֹ.
announce His salvation daily. *

Sap'ru vagōyim k'vōdō,   סַפְּרוּ בַגּוֹיִם כְּבוֹדוֹ,
Relate His glory among the nations,

b'chol ho-amim nifl'ōsov.   בְּכָל הָעַמִּים נִפְלְאוֹתָיו.
among all peoples, His wonders:

Ki godōl Adōnoy umhulol m'ōd,   כִּי גָדוֹל יהוה וּמְהֻלָּל מְאֹד,
that HASHEM is great and exceedingly lauded,

nōro hu al kol elōhim.   נוֹרָא הוּא עַל כָּל אֱלֹהִים.
awesome is He above all heavenly powers.

Ki kol elōhay ho-amim elilim,   כִּי כָּל אֱלֹהֵי הָעַמִּים אֱלִילִים,
For all the gods of the peoples are nothings —

(PAUSE BRIEFLY)

Vadōnoy shoma-yim oso.   וַיהוה שָׁמַיִם עָשָׂה.
but HASHEM made heaven!

Hōd v'hodor l'fonov,   הוֹד וְהָדָר לְפָנָיו,
Glory and majesty are before Him,

ōz v'sif-eres b'mikdoshō.   עֹז וְתִפְאֶרֶת בְּמִקְדָּשׁוֹ.
might and splendor are in His Sanctuary.

Hovu Ladōnoy mishp'chōs amim,   הָבוּ לַיהוה מִשְׁפְּחוֹת עַמִּים,
Render unto HASHEM, O families of the peoples,

hovu Ladōnoy kovōd vo-ōz.   הָבוּ לַיהוה כָּבוֹד וָעֹז.
render unto HASHEM honor and might.

Hovu Ladōnoy k'vōd sh'mō,   הָבוּ לַיהוה כְּבוֹד שְׁמוֹ,
Render unto HASHEM honor worthy of His Name,

s'u mincho uvō-u l'chatzrōsov.   שְׂאוּ מִנְחָה וּבְאוּ לְחַצְרוֹתָיו.
take an offering and come to His Courtyards.

Hishtachavu Ladōnoy   הִשְׁתַּחֲווּ לַיהוה
b'hadras kōdesh,   בְּהַדְרַת קֹדֶשׁ,
Bow to HASHEM in His intensely holy place,

chilu miponov kol ho-oretz.   חִילוּ מִפָּנָיו כָּל הָאָרֶץ.
tremble before Him, everyone on earth.

---

future, for the time when God "will have arrived to judge the earth" and all its inhabitants. It will come at the unique stage of history when all the nations on earth will join in acknowledging Hashem as the true God.

בַּשְּׂרוּ מִיּוֹם לְיוֹם יְשׁוּעָתוֹ — *Announce His salvation daily.* Do not acknowledge God only for openly miraculous interventions. Recognize that even seemingly innocuous daily events are Heavenly gifts.

Imru vagōyim Adōnoy moloch,

אִמְרוּ בַגּוֹיִם יהוה מָלָךְ,

Declare among the nations, "HASHEM reigns,

af tikōn tayvayl bal timōt,

אַף תִּכּוֹן תֵּבֵל בַּל תִּמּוֹט,

indeed, the world is fixed so that it cannot falter,

yodin amim b'mayshorim.

יָדִין עַמִּים בְּמֵישָׁרִים.

He will judge the peoples with fairness."

Yism'chu hashoma-yim

❖ יִשְׂמְחוּ הַשָּׁמַיִם

v'sogayl ho-oretz,

וְתָגֵל הָאָרֶץ,

The heavens will be glad and the earth will rejoice, ✳

yir-am ha-yom umlō-ō.

יִרְעַם הַיָּם וּמְלֹאוֹ.

the sea and its fullness will roar;

Ya-alōz sodai v'chol asher bō,

יַעֲלֹז שָׂדַי וְכָל אֲשֶׁר בּוֹ,

the field and everything in it will exult,

oz y'ran'nu kol atzay yo-ar.

אָז יְרַנְּנוּ כָּל עֲצֵי יָעַר.

then all the trees of the forest will sing with joy —

Lifnay Adōnoy ki vo,

לִפְנֵי יהוה כִּי בָא,

before HASHEM, for He will have arrived,

ki vo lishpōt ho-oretz,

כִּי בָא לִשְׁפֹּט הָאָרֶץ,

He will have arrived to judge the earth.

yishpōt tayvayl b'tzedek,

יִשְׁפֹּט תֵּבֵל בְּצֶדֶק,

He will judge the world with righteousness,

v'amim be-emunosō.

וְעַמִּים בֶּאֱמוּנָתוֹ.

and peoples with His truth.

■ Psalm 97: The enemies of God need to be eradicated
as a prerequisite for the ultimate redemption.

ADŌNOY moloch togayl ho-oretz,

יהוה מָלָךְ תָּגֵל הָאָרֶץ,

When HASHEM will reign, the world will rejoice;

yism'chu iyim rabim.

יִשְׂמְחוּ אִיִּים רַבִּים.

numerous islands will be glad.

Onon va-arofel s'vivov,

עָנָן וַעֲרָפֶל סְבִיבָיו,

Cloud and dense darkness will surround Him; ✳

tzedek u-mishpot m'chōn kis-ō.

צֶדֶק וּמִשְׁפָּט מְכוֹן כִּסְאוֹ.

righteousness and justice are His throne's foundation.

. . . יִשְׂמְחוּ הַשָּׁמַיִם — *The heavens will be glad and
the earth will rejoice.* The components of nature signify their joy by carrying out the functions assigned to them by God. The heavens
give abundant rain and dew, the earth gives
bountiful crops, and so on.

עָנָן וַעֲרָפֶל סְבִיבָיו — *Cloud and dense darkness
will surround Him.* To us it often seems as if
God's guidance of events is masked by cloud
and darkness. In reality, however, "righteousness and justice [are] His throne's foundation"; everything He does is for a reason.

Aysh l'fonov taylaych,
אֵשׁ לְפָנָיו תֵּלֵךְ,
Fire will advance before Him

uslahayt soviv tzorov.
וּתְלַהֵט סָבִיב צָרָיו.
and consume His enemies all around.

Hay-iru v'rokov tayvayl,
הֵאִירוּ בְרָקָיו תֵּבֵל,
His lightning bolts will light up the world,

ro-aso vatochayl ho-oretz.
רָאֲתָה וַתָּחֵל הָאָרֶץ.
the inhabitants of the earth will see and tremble.

Horim kadōnag nomasu
milifnay Adōnoy,
הָרִים כַּדּוֹנַג נָמַסּוּ
מִלִּפְנֵי יהוה,
Mountains will melt like wax* from before HASHEM,

milifnay adōn kol ho-oretz.
מִלִּפְנֵי אֲדוֹן כָּל הָאָרֶץ.
before the Lord of all the earth.

Higidu hashoma-yim tzidkō,
הִגִּידוּ הַשָּׁמַיִם צִדְקוֹ,
The heavens will declare His righteousness,

v'ro-u chol ho-amim k'vōdō.
וְרָאוּ כָל הָעַמִּים כְּבוֹדוֹ.
and all the peoples will see His glory.

Yayvōshu kol ōv'day fesel
יֵבֹשׁוּ כָּל עֹבְדֵי פֶסֶל
Humiliated will be all who worship idols,

hamis-hal'lim bo-elilim,
הַמִּתְהַלְלִים בָּאֱלִילִים,
who pride themselves in worthless gods;

hishtachavu lō kol elōhim.
הִשְׁתַּחֲווּ לוֹ כָּל אֱלֹהִים.
to Him all the powers will bow.

Shom'o vatismach tziyōn
שָׁמְעָה וַתִּשְׂמַח צִיּוֹן
Zion will hear and be glad,

vatogaylno b'nōs y'hudo,
וַתָּגֵלְנָה בְּנוֹת יְהוּדָה,
and the daughters of Judah will exult,

l'ma-an mishpotecho Adōnoy.
לְמַעַן מִשְׁפָּטֶיךָ יהוה.
because of Your judgments, HASHEM.

Ki ato Adōnoy
elyōn al kol ho-oretz,
כִּי אַתָּה יהוה
עֶלְיוֹן עַל כָּל הָאָרֶץ,
For You, HASHEM, are supreme above all the earth,

m'ōd na-alayso al kol elōhim.
מְאֹד נַעֲלֵיתָ עַל כָּל אֱלֹהִים.
exceedingly exalted above all powers.

Ōhavay Adōnoy sin-u ro,
❖ אֹהֲבֵי יהוה שִׂנְאוּ רָע,
O lovers of HASHEM — despise evil!

---

leaders whose pretensions of grandeur will
melt like wax before God's wrath.

shōmayr nafshōs chasidov,   שֹׁמֵר נַפְשׁוֹת חֲסִידָיו,

He guards the lives of His devout ones,

miyad r'sho-im yatzilaym.   מִיַּד רְשָׁעִים יַצִּילֵם.

from the hand of the wicked He rescues them.

Ōr zoru-a latzadik,   אוֹר זָרֻעַ לַצַּדִּיק,

Light is sown for the righteous,*

ulyishray layv simcho.   וּלְיִשְׁרֵי לֵב שִׂמְחָה.

and for the upright of heart, gladness.

Simchu tzadikim Badōnoy,   שִׂמְחוּ צַדִּיקִים בַּיהוה,

Be glad, O righteous, in HASHEM,

v'hōdu l'zaycher kodshō.   וְהוֹדוּ לְזֵכֶר קָדְשׁוֹ.

and give grateful praise at the mention of His Holy Name.

■ Psalm 98: When Hashem redeems the Jewish people,
the rest of mankind and all of nature will burst forth in song.

MIZMŌR,   מִזְמוֹר,

shiru Ladōnoy shir chodosh,   שִׁירוּ לַיהוה שִׁיר חָדָשׁ,

A Psalm! Sing to HASHEM a new song

ki niflo-ōs oso,   כִּי נִפְלָאוֹת עָשָׂה,

for He has done wonders;

hōshi-o lō y'minō uzrō-a kodshō.   הוֹשִׁיעָה לּוֹ יְמִינוֹ וּזְרוֹעַ קָדְשׁוֹ.

His own right hand and holy arm have helped Him.

Hōdi-a Adōnoy y'shu-osō,   הוֹדִיעַ יהוה יְשׁוּעָתוֹ,

HASHEM has made known His salvation;

l'aynay hagō-yim gilo tzidkosō.   לְעֵינֵי הַגּוֹיִם גִּלָּה צִדְקָתוֹ.

in the sight of the nations He revealed His righteousness.

Zochar chasdō ve-emunosō   זָכַר חַסְדּוֹ וֶאֱמוּנָתוֹ
    l'vays yisro-ayl,   לְבֵית יִשְׂרָאֵל,

He recalled His kindness and faithfulness to the House of Israel;

ro-u chol afsay oretz   רָאוּ כָל אַפְסֵי אָרֶץ
    ays y'shu-as Elōhaynu.   אֵת יְשׁוּעַת אֱלֹהֵינוּ.

all ends of the earth have seen the salvation of our God.

Hori-u Ladōnoy kol ho-oretz,   הָרִיעוּ לַיהוה כָּל הָאָרֶץ,

Call out to HASHEM, all inhabitants of the earth,*

אוֹר זָרֻעַ לַצַּדִּיק — *Light is sown for the righteous.*
The spiritual light — the reward for good
deeds and the personal perfection that are their
natural outgrowth — is like seeds sown in
fertile soil.

הָרִיעוּ לַה׳ כָּל הָאָרֶץ — *Call out to HASHEM, all*

inhabitants of the earth.

    A czarist official in Russia once asked the
Netziv, rabbi of Volozhin, why many psalms
call upon the nations to praise God for His
salvation of Israel. It should be *Israel,* not its
oppressors, who praise Him!

pitzchu v'ran'nu v'zamayru.
open your mouths, sing joyous songs and play music.

פִּצְחוּ וְרַנְּנוּ וְזַמֵּרוּ.

Zam'ru Ladōnoy b'chinōr,
Play music to HASHEM on a harp,

זַמְּרוּ לַיהוה בְּכִנּוֹר,

b'chinōr v'kōl zimro.
with harp and sound of chanted praise.

בְּכִנּוֹר וְקוֹל זִמְרָה.

Bachatzōtz'rōs v'kōl shōfor,
With trumpets and shofar sound,

בַּחֲצֹצְרוֹת וְקוֹל שׁוֹפָר,

hori-u lifnay hamelech Adōnoy.
call out before the King, HASHEM.

הָרִיעוּ לִפְנֵי הַמֶּלֶךְ יהוה.

Yir-am ha-yom umlō-ō,
The sea and its fullness will roar,

יִרְעַם הַיָּם וּמְלֹאוֹ,

tayvayl v'yōsh'vay voh.
the world and those who dwell therein.

תֵּבֵל וְיֹשְׁבֵי בָהּ.

N'horōs yimcha-u chof,
Rivers will clap hands,

נְהָרוֹת יִמְחֲאוּ כָף,

yachad horim y'ranaynu.
mountains will exult together —

יַחַד הָרִים יְרַנֵּנוּ.

Lifnay Adōnoy
before HASHEM,

לִפְנֵי יהוה

ki vo lishpōt ho-oretz,
for He will have arrived to judge the earth.

כִּי בָא לִשְׁפֹּט הָאָרֶץ,

Yishpōt tayvayl b'tzedek,
He will judge the world with righteousness

יִשְׁפֹּט תֵּבֵל בְּצֶדֶק,

v'amim b'mayshorim.
and peoples with fairness.

וְעַמִּים בְּמֵישָׁרִים.

■ **Psalm 99:** The Torah values of justice and righteousness, which have been safeguarded by Israel throughout history, will emerge as the foundation of society.

ADŌNOY MOLOCH yirg'zu amim,
When HASHEM will reign, peoples will tremble;

יהוה מָלָךְ יִרְגְּזוּ עַמִּים,

yōshayv k'ruvim tonut ho-oretz.
[before] Him Who is enthroned on Cherubim, the earth will quake.

יֹשֵׁב כְּרוּבִים תָּנוּט הָאָרֶץ.

Adōnoy b'tziyōn godōl,
Before HASHEM Who is great in Zion

יהוה בְּצִיּוֹן גָּדוֹל,

v'rom hu al kol ho-amim.
and Who is exalted above all peoples.

וְרָם הוּא עַל כָּל הָעַמִּים.

The *Netziv* replied, "We have no way of knowing the extent of your conspiracies against us. Only you know how many times you have plotted against us, but have been

Yōdu shimcho godōl v'nōro
kodōsh hu.

יוֹדוּ שִׁמְךָ גָּדוֹל וְנוֹרָא
קָדוֹשׁ הוּא.

They will gratefully praise Your great and awesome Name; it is holy!

V'ōz melech mishpot o-hayv,

וְעֹז מֶלֶךְ מִשְׁפָּט אָהֵב,

Mighty is the King Who loves justice.

ato kōnanto may-shorim.

אַתָּה כּוֹנַנְתָּ מֵישָׁרִים,

You founded fairness.

Mishpot utzdoko b'ya-akōv
ato osiso.

מִשְׁפָּט וּצְדָקָה בְּיַעֲקֹב
אַתָּה עָשִׂיתָ.

The justice and righteousness of Jacob, You have made.

Rōm'mu Adōnoy Elōhaynu,

רוֹמְמוּ יהוה אֱלֹהֵינוּ,

Exalt HASHEM, our God,

v'hishtachavu lahadōm raglov,

וְהִשְׁתַּחֲווּ לַהֲדֹם רַגְלָיו,

and bow at His footstool;

kodōsh hu.

קָדוֹשׁ הוּא.

He is holy!

Mōshe v'aharōn b'chōhanov,

מֹשֶׁה וְאַהֲרֹן בְּכֹהֲנָיו,

*Moses and Aaron were among His priests,**

ushmu-ayl b'kōr'ay sh'mō,

וּשְׁמוּאֵל בְּקֹרְאֵי שְׁמוֹ,

*and Samuel among those who invoke His Name** —*

kōrim el Adōnoy v'hu ya-anaym.

קֹרִאים אֶל יהוה וְהוּא יַעֲנֵם.

they called upon HASHEM and He answered them.

❖ B'amud onon y'dabayr alayhem,

❖ בְּעַמּוּד עָנָן יְדַבֵּר אֲלֵיהֶם,

In a pillar of cloud He spoke to them;

shom'ru aydōsov v'chōk nosan lomō.

שָׁמְרוּ עֵדֹתָיו וְחֹק נָתַן לָמוֹ.

they obeyed His testimonies and whatever decree He gave them.

Adōnoy Elōhaynu ato anisom,

יהוה אֱלֹהֵינוּ אַתָּה עֲנִיתָם,

HASHEM, our God, You answered them.

Ayl nōsay ho-yiso lohem,

אֵל נֹשֵׂא הָיִיתָ לָהֶם,

A forgiving God were You for them —

v'nōkaym al alilōsom.

וְנֹקֵם עַל עֲלִילוֹתָם.

and an Avenger for their iniquities.

---

thwarted by God. You are far more conscious than we are, therefore, of the magnitude of God's miraculous salvations. Only *you* can appreciate the full extent of His greatness."

מֹשֶׁה וְאַהֲרֹן בְּכֹהֲנָיו — *Moses and Aaron were among His priests.* How did Israel merit the gifts of God's Torah and His Sanctuary on earth? Because it had — and was obedient to — leaders such as Moses, Aaron, and Samuel.

וּשְׁמוּאֵל בְּקֹרְאֵי שְׁמוֹ — *And Samuel among those who invoke His Name.* Samuel is singled out from among the multitude of prophets "who invoke His Name," because he was the greatest prophet [after Moses].

Rōm'mu Adōnoy Elōhaynu
רוֹמְמוּ יהוה אֱלֹהֵינוּ
Exalt HASHEM, our God,

v'hishtachavu l'har kodshō,
וְהִשְׁתַּחֲווּ לְהַר קָדְשׁוֹ,
and bow at His holy mountain;

ki kodōsh Adōnoy Elōhaynu.
כִּי קָדוֹשׁ יהוה אֱלֹהֵינוּ.
for holy is HASHEM, our God.

■ Psalm 29: We stand in awe and recognition of Hashem's control of the destiny of man, culminating with the Jewish people's attainment of peace and harmony.

IT IS CUSTOMARY TO STAND DURING THE RECITATION OF THE FOLLOWING PSALM
AND TO RECITE IT SLOWLY, FERVENTLY, AND ALOUD.

MIZMŌR L'DOVID,
מִזְמוֹר לְדָוִד,
A psalm of David.

hovu Ladōnoy b'nay aylim,
הָבוּ לַיהוה בְּנֵי אֵלִים,
Render unto HASHEM you sons of the powerful, *

hovu Ladōnoy kovōd vo-ōz.
הָבוּ לַיהוה כָּבוֹד וָעֹז.
render unto HASHEM * honor and might.*

Hovu Ladōnoy k'vōd sh'mō,
הָבוּ לַיהוה כְּבוֹד שְׁמוֹ,
Render unto HASHEM honor worthy of His Name;

hishta-chavu Ladōnoy
הִשְׁתַּחֲווּ לַיהוה
b'hadras kōdesh.
בְּהַדְרַת קֹדֶשׁ.
prostrate Yourselves before HASHEM in His intensely holy place.

Kōl Adōnoy al hamo-yim,
קוֹל יהוה עַל הַמָּיִם,
The voice of HASHEM * is upon the waters,*

Ayl hakovōd hir-im,
אֵל הַכָּבוֹד הִרְעִים,
the God of Glory thunders,

Adōnoy al ma-yim rabim.
יהוה עַל מַיִם רַבִּים.
HASHEM is upon vast waters.

Kōl Adōnoy bakō-ach,
קוֹל יהוה בַּכֹּחַ,
The voice of HASHEM is in power!

Kōl Adōnoy behodor.
קוֹל יהוה בֶּהָדָר.
The voice of HASHEM is in majesty!

Kōl Adōnoy shōvayr arozim,
קוֹל יהוה שֹׁבֵר אֲרָזִים,
The voice of HASHEM breaks the cedars, *

בְּנֵי אֵלִים — *Sons of the powerful.* The Psalmist addresses himself to the descendants of Abraham, Isaac and Jacob, the Patriarchs who were powerful in righteousness.

קוֹל ה׳ — *The voice of HASHEM.* Throughout Scripture, the "voice" of God refers only to His communication with man, never to a loud natural sound, such as thunder.

שֹׁבֵר אֲרָזִים — *Breaks the cedars.* An allusion to haughty alien kings.

vaishaber Adōnoy   וַיְשַׁבֵּר יהוה
    es arzay hal'vonōn.   אֶת אַרְזֵי הַלְּבָנוֹן.

HASHEM shatters the cedars of Lebanon!

Va-yarkidaym k'mō aygel,   וַיַּרְקִידֵם כְּמוֹ עֵגֶל,

He makes them prance about like a calf;

l'vonōn v'siryōn k'mō ven r'aymim.   לְבָנוֹן וְשִׂרְיוֹן כְּמוֹ בֶן רְאֵמִים.

Lebanon and Siryon like young re'eimim.

Kōl Adōnoy chōtzayv lahavōs aysh.   קוֹל יהוה חֹצֵב לַהֲבוֹת אֵשׁ.

The voice of HASHEM carves with shafts of fire.

Kōl Adōnoy yochil midbor,   קוֹל יהוה יָחִיל מִדְבָּר,

The voice of HASHEM convulses the wilderness;

yochil Adōnoy midbar kodaysh.   יָחִיל יהוה מִדְבַּר קָדֵשׁ.

HASHEM convulses the wilderness of Kadesh.

Kōl Adōnoy y'chōlayl a-yolōs,   ❖ קוֹל יהוה יְחוֹלֵל אַיָּלוֹת,

The voice of HASHEM frightens the hinds,

va-yechesōf y'orōs,   וַיֶּחֱשֹׂף יְעָרוֹת,

and strips the forests bare;

uvhaycholō, kulō ōmayr kovōd.   וּבְהֵיכָלוֹ, כֻּלּוֹ אֹמֵר כָּבוֹד.

while in His Temple all proclaim, "Glory!"

Adōnoy lamabul yoshov,   יהוה לַמַּבּוּל יָשָׁב,

HASHEM sat enthroned at the Deluge;

va-yayshev Adōnoy melech l'ōlom.   וַיֵּשֶׁב יהוה מֶלֶךְ לְעוֹלָם.

HASHEM sits enthroned as King forever.*

Adōnoy ōz l'amō yitayn,   יהוה עֹז לְעַמּוֹ יִתֵּן,

HASHEM will give might to His people,

Adōnoy y'voraych es amō   יהוה יְבָרֵךְ אֶת עַמּוֹ
    vasholōm.   בַּשָּׁלוֹם.

HASHEM will bless His people with peace.

■ Utilizing the close relationship that my additional soul,
bestowed upon me by the Shabbos, creates between Hashem and me,
I pray on behalf of my people Israel.

ONO b'chō-ach g'dulas y'min'cho   **אָנָּא** בְּכֹחַ גְּדֻלַּת יְמִינְךָ

We beg You! With the strength of Your right hand's greatness,

---

ה׳ לַמַּבּוּל יָשָׁב . . . מֶלֶךְ לְעוֹלָם — *HASHEM sat en-*
throned at the Deluge . . . King forever. Seldom
has God's omnipotence been as pronounced as

during the Deluge in the time of Noah. Then,
the universe came to a standstill and life was
virtually wiped out. When the entire earth was

tatir tz'ruro.

תַּתִּיר צְרוּרָה.

untie the bundled sins.

Kabayl rinas am'cho

קַבֵּל רִנַּת עַמְּךָ

Accept the prayer of Your people;

sag'vaynu taharaynu nōro.

שַׂגְּבֵנוּ טַהֲרֵנוּ נוֹרָא.

strengthen us, purify us, O Awesome One.

No, gibōr,

נָא גִבּוֹר

Please, O Strong One,

dōr'shay yichud'cho
   k'vovas shomraym.

דּוֹרְשֵׁי יִחוּדְךָ
כְּבָבַת שָׁמְרֵם.

guard like the pupil of an eye
those who foster Your Oneness.

Bor'chaym taharaym rachamaym

בָּרְכֵם טַהֲרֵם רַחֲמֵם

Bless them, purify them, show them pity,

tzidkos'cho tomid gom-laym.

צִדְקָתְךָ תָּמִיד גָּמְלֵם.

may Your righteousness always recompense them.

Chasin kodōsh

חֲסִין קָדוֹשׁ

Powerful Holy One,

b'rōv tuv'cho nahayl adosecho.

בְּרוֹב טוּבְךָ נַהֵל עֲדָתֶךָ.

with Your abundant goodness guide Your congregation.

Yochid gay-e

יָחִיד גֵּאֶה

One and only Exalted One,

l'am'cho p'nay
   zōch'ray k'dushosecho.

לְעַמְּךָ פְּנֵה
זוֹכְרֵי קְדֻשָּׁתֶךָ.

turn to Your pepole, which proclaims Your holiness.

Shavosaynu kabayl

שַׁוְעָתֵנוּ קַבֵּל

Accept our entreaty

ush-ma tza-akosaynu

וּשְׁמַע צַעֲקָתֵנוּ

and hear our cry,

yōday-a ta-alumōs.

יוֹדֵעַ תַּעֲלֻמוֹת.

O Knower of mysteries.

Boruch shaym k'vōd malchusō
   l'ōlom vo-ed.

בָּרוּךְ שֵׁם כְּבוֹד מַלְכוּתוֹ
לְעוֹלָם וָעֶד.

Blessed is the Name of His glorious Kingdom forever and ever.

---

covered with water, God reigned alone in silence, while man and beast who had disobeyed Him were washed away. That degree of sovereignty will be manifest again in Messianic times when idolatry and wickedness will be uprooted.

■ This treasured poem, which describes the heightened spiritual encounter with the Shabbos bride, motivates me to yearn for the redemption of my people.

THE *LECHAH DODI* SONG IS RECITED RESPONSIVELY. IN MOST CONGREGATIONS, THE *CHAZZAN* REPEATS EACH VERSE AFTER THE CONGREGATION; IN SOME THE PROCEDURE IS REVERSED; AND IN OTHERS, THE ENTIRE SONG IS SUNG IN UNISON.

L'CHO DŌDI likras kalo,　　　　　לְכָה דוֹדִי לִקְרַאת כַּלָּה,
　　Come my Beloved* to greet the bride* —

p'nay shabos n'kab'lo.　　　　　פְּנֵי שַׁבָּת נְקַבְּלָה.
　　the Sabbath presence, let us welcome!

L'cho dōdi likras kalo,　　　　　לְכָה דוֹדִי לִקְרַאת כַּלָּה,
　　p'nay shabos n'kab'lo.　　　　פְּנֵי שַׁבָּת נְקַבְּלָה.
Come my Beloved to greet the bride — the Sabbath presence, let us welcome!

Shomōr v'zochōr b'dibur e-chod,　　　שָׁמוֹר וְזָכוֹר בְּדִבּוּר אֶחָד,
　　"Safeguard" and "Remember" — in a single utterance —

hishmi-onu Ayl ham'yuchod,　　　　הִשְׁמִיעָנוּ אֵל הַמְיֻחָד,
　　the One and Only God made us hear. *

Adōnoy e-chod ush-mō e-chod,　　　יהוה אֶחָד וּשְׁמוֹ אֶחָד,
　　HASHEM is One and His Name is One,

l'shaym ulsif-eres v'lis-hilo,　　　לְשֵׁם וּלְתִפְאֶרֶת וְלִתְהִלָּה.
　　for renown, for splendor, and for praise.

L'cho dōdi likras kalo,　　　　　לְכָה דוֹדִי לִקְרַאת כַּלָּה,
　　p'nay shabos n'kab'lo.　　　　פְּנֵי שַׁבָּת נְקַבְּלָה.
Come my Beloved to greet the bride — the Sabbath presence, let us welcome!

Likras shabos l'chu v'nayl'cho,　　　לִקְרַאת שַׁבָּת לְכוּ וְנֵלְכָה,
　　To welcome the Sabbath, come let us go,

ki hi m'kōr hab'rocho,　　　　　כִּי הִיא מְקוֹר הַבְּרָכָה,
　　for it is the source of blessing; *

לְכָה דוֹדִי — *Come my Beloved.* Our "Beloved" is God Himself. We invite Him to join us in ushering in the Sabbath.

כַּלָּה — *The bride.* The Midrash teaches that God told the newly created Sabbath, "Israel shall be your mate." Accordingly, every week, Israel greets the approaching Sabbath like a groom awaiting his bride as she advances to the wedding canopy.

שָׁמוֹר וְזָכוֹר בְּדִבּוּר אֶחָד הִשְׁמִיעָנוּ — *"Safeguard" and "Remember" — in a single utterance . . . made us hear.* The Talmud (*Shavuos* 20b) teaches that when God gave the Ten Commandments, He miraculously spoke and caused Israel to hear the two complementary aspects of the Sabbath commandment simultaneously: שָׁמוֹר, "Safeguard" (*Deuteronomy* 5:12), the injunction to avoid the desecration of the Sabbath; and זָכוֹר, "Remember" (*Exodus* 20:8), the commandment to keep the Sabbath in our minds and hearts, and give verbal expression to its holiness. Although the Torah writes these commandments separately, God combined them into a single utterance at Sinai so that Israel would know that they are inseparable. To observe the "spirit of the Sabbath" while ignoring its practice, and vice versa, is a travesty.

לִקְרַאת . . . כִּי הִיא מְקוֹר הַבְּרָכָה — *To welcome . . . for it is the source of blessing.* The *Zohar*

mayrosh mikedem n'sucho,

מֵרֹאשׁ מִקֶּדֶם נְסוּכָה,

from the beginning, from antiquity she was honored,

sōf ma-ase.

סוֹף מַעֲשֶׂה

    b'machashovo t'chilo.

בְּמַחֲשָׁבָה תְּחִלָּה.

Last in deed, but first in thought.*

L'cho dōdi likras kalo,

לְכָה דוֹדִי לִקְרַאת כַּלָּה,

    p'nay shabos n'kab'lo.

פְּנֵי שַׁבָּת נְקַבְּלָה.

Come my Beloved to greet the bride — the Sabbath presence, let us welcome!

Mikdash melech ir m'lucho,

מִקְדַּשׁ מֶלֶךְ עִיר מְלוּכָה,

O Sanctuary of the King, royal city,*

kumi tz'i mitōch hahafaycho,

קוּמִי צְאִי מִתּוֹךְ הַהֲפֵכָה,

arise and depart from amid the upheaval,

rav loch sheves b'aymek habocho,

רַב לָךְ שֶׁבֶת בְּעֵמֶק הַבָּכָא,

too long have you dwelled in the valley of weeping,

v'hu yachamōl ola-yich chemlo.

וְהוּא יַחֲמוֹל עָלַיִךְ חֶמְלָה.

He will shower compassion upon you.

L'cho dōdi likras kalo,

לְכָה דוֹדִי לִקְרַאת כַּלָּה,

    p'nay shabos n'kab'lo.

פְּנֵי שַׁבָּת נְקַבְּלָה.

Come my Beloved to greet the bride — the Sabbath presence, let us welcome!

Hisna-ari may-ofor kumi,

הִתְנַעֲרִי מֵעָפָר קוּמִי,

Shake off the dust; arise!*

livshi bigday sif-artaych ami,

לִבְשִׁי בִּגְדֵי תִפְאַרְתֵּךְ עַמִּי,

Don your splendid clothes, My people,

al yad ben yishai bays halachmi,

עַל יַד בֶּן יִשַׁי בֵּית הַלַּחְמִי,

through the son of Jesse,* the Bethlehemite!

kor'vo el nafshi g'oloh.

קָרְבָה אֶל נַפְשִׁי גְאָלָהּ.

Draw near to my soul — redeem it!

---

teaches that all the blessings and success of the week come as a result of the Sabbath.

סוֹף מַעֲשֶׂה בְּמַחֲשָׁבָה תְּחִלָּה — *Last in deed, but first in thought* [i.e., the Sabbath was the final act of Creation, but primary in God's purpose]. Whenever a great project is envisioned, a host of preparations must be made before the goal can be achieved. That there would be a day of holiness in Creation was uppermost in God's thought, but first the entire universe had to be created.

מִקְדַּשׁ מֶלֶךְ — *O Sanctuary of the King, royal city* [i.e., Jerusalem]. From this point until the last stanza, the theme shifts from the Sabbath to Israel's longing for its return to Jerusalem and

the Holy Temple therein. This is a logical extension of our welcome of the Sabbath, because the Talmud (*Shabbos* 118b) teaches that the Messiah will come if Israel observes two Sabbaths properly.

הִתְנַעֲרִי מֵעָפָר קוּמִי — *Shake off the dust; arise!* The reference is to *Isaiah* 52:2 where the prophet addresses Jerusalem as if she were a woman wallowing in the dust. He urges her to rise up, dress in her finery, and resume her noble ways.

בֶּן יִשַׁי — *The son of Jesse.* A reference to the Messiah, who will be a descendant of David, son of Jesse.

הִתְעוֹרְרִי — *Wake up!* The poet addresses

L'cho dōdi likras kalo,
　p'nay shabos n'kab'lo.

לְכָה דוֹדִי לִקְרַאת כַּלָּה,
פְּנֵי שַׁבָּת נְקַבְּלָה.

Come my Beloved to greet the bride — the Sabbath presence, let us welcome!

His-ōr'ri his-ōr'ri,

הִתְעוֹרְרִי הִתְעוֹרְרִי,

Wake up!* Wake up!

ki vo ōraych kumi ōri,

כִּי בָא אוֹרֵךְ קוּמִי אוֹרִי,

For your light has come, rise up and shine;

uri uri shir dabayri,

עוּרִי עוּרִי שִׁיר דַּבֵּרִי,

awaken, awaken, utter a song,

k'vōd Adōnoy ola-yich niglo.

כְּבוֹד יהוה עָלַיִךְ נִגְלָה.

the glory of HASHEM is revealed on you.

L'cho dōdi likras kalo,
　p'nay shabos n'kab'lo.

לְכָה דוֹדִי לִקְרַאת כַּלָּה,
פְּנֵי שַׁבָּת נְקַבְּלָה.

Come my Beloved to greet the bride — the Sabbath presence, let us welcome!

Lō sayvōshi v'lō sikol'mi,

לֹא תֵבוֹשִׁי וְלֹא תִכָּלְמִי,

Feel not ashamed, be not humiliated,

ma tishtōchachi uma tehemi,

מַה תִּשְׁתּוֹחֲחִי וּמַה תֶּהֱמִי,

why are you downcast? Why are you disconsolate?

boch yechesu aniyay ami,

בָּךְ יֶחֱסוּ עֲנִיֵּי עַמִּי,

In you will My people's afflicted find shelter

v'nivn'so ir al tiloh.

וְנִבְנְתָה עִיר עַל תִּלָּהּ.

as the City is built upon its hilltop.

L'cho dōdi likras kalo,
　p'nay shabos n'kab'lo.

לְכָה דוֹדִי לִקְרַאת כַּלָּה,
פְּנֵי שַׁבָּת נְקַבְּלָה.

Come my Beloved to greet the bride — the Sabbath presence, let us welcome!

V'ho-yu limshiso shōso-yich,

וְהָיוּ לִמְשִׁסָּה שֹׁאסָיִךְ,

May your oppressor be downtrodden,

v'rochaku kol m'val'o-yich,

וְרָחֲקוּ כָּל מְבַלְּעָיִךְ,

and may those who devoured you be cast far off.

yosis o-la-yich Elōho-yich,

יָשִׂישׂ עָלַיִךְ אֱלֹהָיִךְ,

Your God will rejoice over you

kimsōs choson al kalo.

כִּמְשׂוֹשׂ חָתָן עַל כַּלָּה.

like a groom's rejoicing over his bride.

L'cho dōdi likras kalo,
　p'nay shabos n'kab'lo.

לְכָה דוֹדִי לִקְרַאת כַּלָּה,
פְּנֵי שַׁבָּת נְקַבְּלָה.

Come my Beloved to greet the bride — the Sabbath presence, let us welcome!

Yomin usmōl tifrōtzi,

יָמִין וּשְׂמֹאל תִּפְרֹצִי,

Rightward and leftward, you shall spread out mightily,

v'es Adōnoy ta-aritzi,

וְאֶת יהוה תַּעֲרִיצִי,

and you shall extol the might of HASHEM,

al yad ish ben partzi,

עַל יַד אִישׁ בֶּן פַּרְצִי,

through the man descended from Peretz,*

v'nism'cho v'nogilo.

וְנִשְׂמְחָה וְנָגִילָה.

then we shall be glad and mirthful.

L'cho dōdi likras kalo,

לְכָה דוֹדִי לִקְרַאת כַּלָּה,

p'nay shabos n'kab'lo.

פְּנֵי שַׁבָּת נְקַבְּלָה.

Come my Beloved to greet the bride — the Sabbath presence, let us welcome!

RISE AND FACE THE REAR OF THE SYNAGOGUE. WHEN SAYING THE WORDS bō-i chalo,
bō-i chalo, BOW AND TURN, AS IF TO ACKNOWLEDGE THE ENTRANCE OF THE SABBATH.

BŌ-I v'sholōm ateres baloh,

בּוֹאִי בְשָׁלוֹם עֲטֶרֶת בַּעְלָהּ,

Enter in peace,* O crown of her husband,

gam b'simcho uvtzoholo,

גַּם בְּשִׂמְחָה וּבְצָהֳלָה,

even in gladness and good cheer,

tōch emunay am s'gulo,

תּוֹךְ אֱמוּנֵי עַם סְגֻלָּה,

among the faithful of the treasured people.

bō-i chalo, bō-i chalo.

בּוֹאִי כַלָּה, בּוֹאִי כַלָּה.

Enter, O bride! Enter, O bride!

L'cho dōdi likras kalo,

לְכָה דוֹדִי לִקְרַאת כַּלָּה,

p'nay shabos n'kab'lo.

פְּנֵי שַׁבָּת נְקַבְּלָה.

Come my Beloved to greet the bride — the Sabbath presence, let us welcome!

IN MANY CONGREGATIONS, MOURNERS, DURING THE WEEK OF *SHIVAH*, ENTER THE
SYNAGOGUE AT THIS POINT AND ARE GREETED BY THE LEADERS OF THE CONGREGATION,
WHEREUPON THE CONGREGATION OFFERS THE FOLLOWING WORDS OF CONSOLATION:

Hamokōm y'nachaym eschem

הַמָּקוֹם יְנַחֵם אֶתְכֶם

May the Omnipresent console you*

b'sōch sh'or avaylay

בְּתוֹךְ שְׁאָר אֲבֵלֵי

tziyōn virusholo-yim.

צִיּוֹן וִירוּשָׁלָיִם.

among the other mourners of Zion and Jerusalem.

Jerusalem again, exhorting her to rise from the
spiritual sluggishness of exile and exhibit the
brilliance that once made her great. The stanza
closes by declaring that God's glory has returned,
as if the redemption has already taken place.

אִישׁ בֶּן פַּרְצִי — *The man descended from Peretz.*
Another reference to the Messiah, a descendant
of David, whose lineage began with Judah's son
Peretz.

בּוֹאִי בְשָׁלוֹם — *Enter in peace.* At this point, the
holiness of the Sabbath enters and with it the
additional soul which enables a Jew to appreciate
and benefit from the enhanced holiness of the
day. For this reason, the congregation turns to
face the rear of the synagogue, as if to welcome
the queen as she makes her entrance.

הַמָּקוֹם יְנַחֵם אֶתְכֶם — *May the Omnipresent console you.* Because the holiness of the Sabbath

WHEN A FESTIVAL OR *CHOL HAMOED* FALLS ON FRIDAY OR ON THE SABBATH,
MOST CONGREGATIONS BEGIN *KABBALAS SHABBOS* HERE.

■ Psalm 92: While the Shabbos day is not mentioned in the body of this psalm, the psalm speaks of the faith in Hashem — in the face of evil — that sustained our people through the various exiles and that enables us to excitedly anticipate the "day of everlasting Sabbath."

MIZMŌR SHIR l'yōm ha-shabos.   מִזְמוֹר שִׁיר לְיוֹם הַשַּׁבָּת.

A psalm, a song for the Sabbath day.*

Tōv l'hōdōs Ladōnoy,   טוֹב לְהֹדוֹת לַיהוה,

It is good to thank HASHEM

ulzamayr l'shimcho elyōn.   וּלְזַמֵּר לְשִׁמְךָ עֶלְיוֹן.

and to sing praise to Your Name, O Exalted One;

L'hagid babōker chasdecho,   לְהַגִּיד בַּבֹּקֶר חַסְדֶּךָ,

to relate Your kindness in the dawn

ve-emunos'cho balaylōs.   וֶאֱמוּנָתְךָ בַּלֵּילוֹת.

and Your faith in the nights.*

Alay osōr va-alay no-vel,   עֲלֵי עָשׂוֹר וַעֲלֵי נָבֶל,

Upon ten-stringed instrument* and lyre,

alay higo-yōn b'chinōr.   עֲלֵי הִגָּיוֹן בְּכִנּוֹר.

with singing accompanied by a harp.

Ki simachtani Adōnoy b'fo-olecho,   כִּי שִׂמַּחְתַּנִי יהוה בְּפָעֳלֶךָ,

For You have gladdened me, HASHEM, *with Your deeds;*

b'ma-asay yodecho aranayn.   בְּמַעֲשֵׂי יָדֶיךָ אֲרַנֵּן.

at the works of Your Hands I sing glad song.

---

enters at this point and public observance of the regulations of mourning are not permitted on this sacred day, mourners during the *shivah* week now enter the synagogue to pray with the congregation. In many congregations it is customary to mark this interruption of mourning with a brief ceremony. The leaders of the congregation invite the mourners to enter the synagogue whereupon they are welcomed with the traditional formula of consolation: *May the Omnipresent console you . . .*

מִזְמוֹר שִׁיר לְיוֹם הַשַּׁבָּת — *A psalm, a song for the Sabbath day.* Although this psalm is identified as belonging particularly to the theme of the Sabbath, the text contains not a single direct reference to the Sabbath. What is the connection? Among the many explanations are:

— The psalm refers not to the weekly Sabbath, but to the World to Come, when man will achieve the spiritual perfection which we only glimpse during the Sabbath. The psalm is thus well suited to the Sabbath which is a semblance of that future spiritual perfection.

— Praise of God is necessary, but difficult in the weekdays when people must struggle for a livelihood. On the Sabbath, when Jews are free from the strictures of the workweek, they can turn their minds and hearts to the perception of God's ways and His praise — which are the topics of this psalm.

בַּבֹּקֶר . . . בַּלֵּילוֹת — *In the dawn . . . in the nights.* Dawn alludes to redemption, while night symbolizes exile. We express our faith that even though there are times when God makes us suffer, those, too, are manifestations of His *kindness,* because He does it for our ultimate benefit.

עָשׂוֹר — *Ten-stringed instrument.* The Talmudic Sages teach that the lyre of Messianic times will be ten stringed, representing a beautiful enhancement of music, which is now limited to the octave of eight notes. Every period in life calls for its own unique expression of praise, just as each day has its own song of praise and each part of Creation serves God in its own way. The enhanced spirituality of Messianic times will demand a heightened form of song.

Ma god'lu ma-asecho Adōnoy,
מַה גָּדְלוּ מַעֲשֶׂיךָ יהוה,
How great are Your deeds, HASHEM;

m'ōd om'ku machsh'vōsecho.
מְאֹד עָמְקוּ מַחְשְׁבֹתֶיךָ.
*exceedingly profound are Your thoughts.**

Ish ba-ar lō yaydo,
אִישׁ בַּעַר לֹא יֵדָע,
A boor cannot know,

uchsil lō yovin es zōs.
וּכְסִיל לֹא יָבִין אֶת זֹאת.
nor can a fool understand this:

Bifrō-ach r'sho-im k'mō aysev,
בִּפְרֹחַ רְשָׁעִים כְּמוֹ עֵשֶׂב,
*When the wicked bloom** like grass*

va-yotzitzu kol pō-alay o-ven,
וַיָּצִיצוּ כָּל פֹּעֲלֵי אָוֶן,
and all the doers of iniquity blossom —

l'hi-shom'dom aday ad.
לְהִשָּׁמְדָם עֲדֵי עַד.
it is to destroy them till eternity.

V'ato morōm l'ōlom Adōnoy.
וְאַתָּה מָרוֹם לְעֹלָם יהוה.
But You remain exalted forever, HASHEM.

Ki hinay ō-y'vecho, Adōnoy,
כִּי הִנֵּה אֹיְבֶיךָ יהוה,
For behold! — Your enemies, HASHEM,

ki hinay ō-y'vecho yōvaydu,
כִּי הִנֵּה אֹיְבֶיךָ יֹאבֵדוּ,
for behold! — Your enemies shall perish,

yispor'du kol pō-alay o-ven.
יִתְפָּרְדוּ כָּל פֹּעֲלֵי אָוֶן.
dispersed shall be all doers of iniquity.

Vatorem kir-aym karni,
וַתָּרֶם כִּרְאֵים קַרְנִי,
As exalted as a re'eim's shall be my pride,

balōsi b'shemen ra-anon.
בַּלֹּתִי בְּשֶׁמֶן רַעֲנָן.
I will be saturated with ever-fresh oil.

Vatabayt ayni b'shuroy,
וַתַּבֵּט עֵינִי בְּשׁוּרָי,
My eyes have seen my vigilant foes;

bakomim olai m'ray-im,
בַּקָּמִים עָלַי מְרֵעִים,
when those who would harm me rise up against me,

tishma-no oznoy.
תִּשְׁמַעְנָה אָזְנָי.
my ears have heard their doom.

❖ Tzadik katomor yifroch,
❖ צַדִּיק כַּתָּמָר יִפְרָח,
A righteous man will flourish like a date palm,

מַעֲשֶׂיךָ ... מַחְשְׁבֹתֶיךָ — *Your deeds ... Your thoughts.* God's "deeds" are the tangible parts of Creation and the events we perceive with our senses. His "thoughts" are His purposes and goals; they are profound beyond human comprehension.

בִּפְרֹחַ רְשָׁעִים — *When the wicked bloom.* Most

people can find no answer to the eternal human dilemma: Why do the wicked prosper? If only these inquisitors could look beyond what their senses tell them, they would realize that God gives temporal success and happiness to the wicked as reward for whatever good deeds they may have done. Having been recompensed,

k'erez bal'vonōn yisge.   כְּאֶרֶז בַּלְּבָנוֹן יִשְׂגֶּה.
like a cedar in the Lebanon he will grow tall.

Sh'sulim b'vays Adōnoy,   שְׁתוּלִים בְּבֵית יהוה,
Planted in the House of HASHEM,

b'chatzrōs Elōhaynu yaf-richu.   בְּחַצְרוֹת אֱלֹהֵינוּ יַפְרִיחוּ.
in the Courtyards of our God they will flourish.

Ōd y'nuvun b'sayvo,   עוֹד יְנוּבוּן בְּשֵׂיבָה,
They will still be fruitful in old age,

d'shaynim v'ra-ananim yih-yu.   דְּשֵׁנִים וְרַעֲנַנִּים יִהְיוּ.
vigorous and fresh they will be —

L'hagid ki yoshor Adōnoy,   לְהַגִּיד כִּי יָשָׁר יהוה,
to declare that HASHEM is just,

tzuri v'lō avloso bō.   צוּרִי וְלֹא עַוְלָתָה בּוֹ.
my Rock in Whom there is no wrong.

■ **Psalm 93:** This is a continuation of the previous theme that God's greatness will be recognized by all in the Messianic era. It spans all of time by describing Hashem in His full grandeur at the completion of Creation, and His "dressing" Himself like a person adorned in special Shabbos clothing.

ADŌNOY MOLOCH gay-us lovaysh,   יהוה מָלָךְ גֵּאוּת לָבֵשׁ,
HASHEM will have reigned, He will have donned grandeur,*

lovaysh Adōnoy ōz his-azor,   לָבֵשׁ יהוה עֹז הִתְאַזָּר,
HASHEM will have donned might and girded Himself;

af tikōn tayvayl bal timōt.   אַף תִּכּוֹן תֵּבֵל בַּל תִּמּוֹט.
even firmed the world that it should not falter.

Nochōn kis-acho may-oz,   נָכוֹן כִּסְאֲךָ מֵאָז,
Your throne was established from of old;

may-ōlom oto.   מֵעוֹלָם אָתָּה.
eternal are You.

Nos'u n'horōs, Adōnoy,   נָשְׂאוּ נְהָרוֹת, יהוה,
Like rivers they raised, O HASHEM,

nos'u n'horōs kōlom,   נָשְׂאוּ נְהָרוֹת קוֹלָם,
like rivers they raised their voice;

yis-u n'horōs dochyom.   יִשְׂאוּ נְהָרוֹת דָּכְיָם.
like rivers they shall raise their destructiveness.

---

they will sink to destruction, while the righteous gain eternal reward.

גֵּאוּת לָבֵשׁ — *He will have donned grandeur.* God dons grandeur. This is similar to a person donning a garment; our comprehension of him is guided by the contours and quality of the garment, but the garment is hardly his essence. No matter how much of God's greatness we think we understand, our puny intellect grasps but the minutest fraction of His infinite greatness. He does us the favor of allowing mankind this degree of perception so that we can aspire to the privilege of praising Him.

❖ Mikōlōs ma-yim rabim
❖ מִקֹּלוֹת מַיִם רַבִּים
More than the roars of many waters,

adirim mishb'ray yom,
אַדִּירִים מִשְׁבְּרֵי יָם,
mightier than the waves of the sea,

adir bamorōm Adōnoy.
אַדִּיר בַּמָּרוֹם יהוה.
HASHEM is mighty on high.

Aydōsecho ne-emnu m'ōd
עֵדֹתֶיךָ נֶאֶמְנוּ מְאֹד
Your testimonies are exceedingly trustworthy,

l'vays'cho no-avo kōdesh,
לְבֵיתְךָ נָאֲוָה קֹדֶשׁ,
about Your House, the Sacred Dwelling —

Adōnoy, l'ōrech yomim.
יהוה, לְאֹרֶךְ יָמִים.
O HASHEM, may it be for lengthy days.

MOURNER'S KADDISH

MOURNER:

YISGADAL v'yiskadash
sh'mayh rabo.
יִתְגַּדַּל וְיִתְקַדַּשׁ
שְׁמֵהּ רַבָּא.
May His great Name grow exalted and sanctified

CONGREGATION RESPONDS: Omayn — אָמֵן

B'ol'mo di v'ro chir-usayh.
בְּעָלְמָא דִּי בְרָא כִרְעוּתֵהּ.
in the world that He created as He willed.

V'yamlich malchusayh,
וְיַמְלִיךְ מַלְכוּתֵהּ,
May He give reign to His kingship

b'cha-yaychōn uvyōmaychōn
בְּחַיֵּיכוֹן וּבְיוֹמֵיכוֹן
in your lifetimes and in your days

uvcha-yay d'chol bays yisro-ayl,
וּבְחַיֵּי דְכָל בֵּית יִשְׂרָאֵל,
and in the lifetimes of the entire Family of Israel,

ba-agolo u-vizman koriv.
בַּעֲגָלָא וּבִזְמַן קָרִיב.
swiftly and soon.

V'imru: Omayn.
וְאִמְרוּ: אָמֵן.
Now respond: Amen.

CONGREGATION RESPONDS:

Omayn. Y'hay sh'mayh rabo m'vorach
l'olam ul-ol'may ol'ma-yo.
אָמֵן. יְהֵא שְׁמֵהּ רַבָּא מְבָרַךְ
לְעָלַם וּלְעָלְמֵי עָלְמַיָּא.
Amen. May His great Name be blessed forever and ever;

MOURNER CONTINUES:

Y'hay sh'mayh rabo m'vorach
l'olam ul-ol'may ol'ma-yo,
יְהֵא שְׁמֵהּ רַבָּא מְבָרַךְ
לְעָלַם וּלְעָלְמֵי עָלְמַיָּא,
May His great Name be blessed forever and ever,

yisborach v'yishtabach v'yispo-ar
יִתְבָּרַךְ וְיִשְׁתַּבַּח וְיִתְפָּאַר
blessed, praised, glorified,

v'yisrōmam v'yisnasay   וְיִתְרוֹמַם וְיִתְנַשֵּׂא
exalted, extolled,

v'yis-hador v'yis-ale v'yis-halol   וְיִתְהַדָּר וְיִתְעַלֶּה וְיִתְהַלָּל
mighty, upraised, and lauded

sh'mayh d'kudsho b'rich hu   שְׁמֵהּ דְּקֻדְשָׁא בְּרִיךְ הוּא
be the Name of the Holy One, Blessed is He,

CONGREGATION RESPONDS:

B'rich hu.   *Blessed is He.*   בְּרִיךְ הוּא.

MOURNER CONTINUES:

°l'aylo min kol   °לְעֵלָּא מִן כָּל
beyond any

FROM ROSH HASHANAH TO YOM KIPPUR SUBSTITUTE:

°l'aylo l'aylo mikol   °לְעֵלָּא לְעֵלָּא מִכָּל
exceedingly beyond any

birchoso v'shiroso   בִּרְכָתָא וְשִׁירָתָא
blessing and song,

tushb'choso v'nechemoso,   תֻּשְׁבְּחָתָא וְנֶחֱמָתָא,
praise and consolation

da-amiron b'ol'mo.   דַּאֲמִירָן בְּעָלְמָא.
that are uttered in the world.

V'imru: Omayn.   וְאִמְרוּ: אָמֵן.
Now respond: Amen.

CONGREGATION RESPONDS: Omayn — אָמֵן

Y'hay sh'lomo rabo min sh'mayo   יְהֵא שְׁלָמָא רַבָּא מִן שְׁמַיָּא,
May there be abundant peace from Heaven,

v'cha-yim olaynu v'al kol yisro-ayl.   וְחַיִּים עָלֵינוּ וְעַל כָּל יִשְׂרָאֵל.
and life, upon us and upon all Israel.

V'imru: Omayn.   וְאִמְרוּ: אָמֵן.
Now respond: Amen.

CONGREGATION RESPONDS: Omayn — אָמֵן

MOURNER BOWS THEN TAKES THREE STEPS BACK, BOWS LEFT AND SAYS:

Ō-se sholōm bimrōmov   עֹשֶׂה שָׁלוֹם בִּמְרוֹמָיו,
He Who makes peace in His heights,

MOURNER BOWS RIGHT AND SAYS:

hu ya-a-se sholōm olaynu   הוּא יַעֲשֶׂה שָׁלוֹם עָלֵינוּ,
may He make peace upon us,

MOURNER BOWS FORWARD AND SAYS:

v'al kol yisro-ayl. V'imru: Omayn.   וְעַל כָּל יִשְׂרָאֵל. וְאִמְרוּ: אָמֵן.
and upon all Israel. Now respond: Amen.

CONGREGATION RESPONDS: Omayn — אָמֵן

MOURNER REMAINS IN PLACE FOR A FEW MOMENTS, THEN TAKES THREE STEPS FORWARD.

◄[BAMEH MADLIKIN]►

■ Throughout Jewish history the synagogue was often located at the outskirts of the
city. The recitation of this section of Mishnah was therefore instituted to prolong the
service allowing latecomers to complete their prayers, and join the other congregants
on their way home without fear and danger. It consists of the second chapter of
Mishnah Shabbos: a series of laws focusing on the lighting of Shabbos candles and
other Shabbos preparations.

MOST CONGREGATIONS RECITE THE SECOND CHAPTER OF MISHNAH TRACTATE *SHABBOS**
AT THIS POINT; SOME RECITE IT AFTER *MAARIV.*

WHEN A FESTIVAL OR *CHOL HAMOED* FALLS ON EITHER FRIDAY OR THE SABBATH, THIS CHAPTER
IS USUALLY OMITTED, AND THE SERVICE CONTINUES WITH *"BORCHU . . ."* (P. 114).

MISHNAH ONE

BA-ME MADLIKIN   בַּמֶּה מַדְלִיקִין
With what may we light [the Sabbath lamp]

u-vamo ayn madlikin?   וּבַמֶּה אֵין מַדְלִיקִין?
and with what may we not light?

Ayn madlikin lō v'lechesh,   אֵין מַדְלִיקִין לֹא בְלֶכֶשׁ,
We may not light with cedar bast,*

v'lō v'chōsen, v'lō v'chaloch,   וְלֹא בְחֹסֶן, וְלֹא בְכַלָּךְ,
nor with uncombed flax, nor with floss-silk,

v'lō bifsilas ho-idon,   וְלֹא בִּפְתִילַת הָאִידָן,
nor with willow bast,

v'lō bifsilas hamidbor,   וְלֹא בִּפְתִילַת הַמִּדְבָּר,
nor with desert silk,

v'lō virōko she-al p'nay hamo-yim.   וְלֹא בִירוֹקָה שֶׁעַל פְּנֵי הַמָּיִם.
nor with seaweed.

Lō v'zefes, v'lo v'sha-avo,   לֹא בְזֶפֶת, וְלֹא בְשַׁעֲוָה,
Nor [may we light] with pitch, wax,*

**The second chapter of Mishnah Tractate
Shabbos** discusses the laws of providing light
in the home during the Sabbath and also mentions tangentially the *eruv* requirement, which
makes it permissible to carry from one domain
to another, and the giving of tithes, which provides the Levites with food and permits the
remaining food for consumption by its owner.
These three *mitzvos* — light, *eruv,* and tithes
— enhance the feeling of peace within the
home. Light makes the meal more festive and
prevents accidents and frayed nerves that can
result from stumbling in the dark; *eruv* im-
proves relationships with neighbors; and tithes
provide for others. In consonance with this
theme of peace, the Sages appended teachings

in praise of the Sages, who foster peace among
people.

1. אֵין מַדְלִיקִין — *We may not light . . .* The mishnah first lists wicks that are unacceptable because they do not burn evenly. As a result,
someone may forget it is the Sabbath and tip
the lamp so that more fuel will flow to the wick,
an act forbidden on the Sabbath because it
promotes burning.

לֹא בְזֶפֶת — *Nor [may we light] with pitch.* Now
the mishnah lists the unacceptable fuels. Except for one of them (see below) the reason they
are unfit is because they do not burn well,
leading to the fear that the user may tip the
lamp.

v'lō v'shemen kik,

וְלֹא בְּשֶׁמֶן קִיק,

nor with cottonseed oil,

v'lō v'shemen s'rayfo,

וְלֹא בְּשֶׁמֶן שְׂרֵפָה,

nor with oil that must be destroyed by burning,*

v'lō v'al-yo, v'lō v'chaylev.

וְלֹא בָאַלְיָה, וְלֹא בְחֵלֶב.

nor with fat from sheeps' tails, nor with tallow.*

Nachum hamodi ōmayr:

נַחוּם הַמָּדִי אוֹמֵר:

[The Sage] Nachum the Mede says:

Madlikin b'chaylev m'vushol.

מַדְלִיקִין בְּחֵלֶב מְבֻשָּׁל.

We may light with boiled tallow.

Vachachomim ōm'rim:

וַחֲכָמִים אוֹמְרִים:

But the [other] Sages say:

Echod m'vushol

אֶחָד מְבֻשָּׁל

v'e-chod she-ayno m'vushol

וְאֶחָד שֶׁאֵינוֹ מְבֻשָּׁל

Whether it is boiled or it is not boiled,

ayn madlikin bō.

אֵין מַדְלִיקִין בּוֹ.

we may not light with it.

MISHNAH TWO

Ayn madlikin

אֵין מַדְלִיקִין

b'shemen s'rayfo b'yōm tōv.

בְּשֶׁמֶן שְׂרֵפָה בְּיוֹם טוֹב.

We may not light on a Festival day*
with oil that must be destroyed by burning.

Rabi yishmo-ayl ōmayr:

רַבִּי יִשְׁמָעֵאל אוֹמֵר:

Rabbi Yishmael says:

Ayn madlikin b'itron

אֵין מַדְלִיקִין בְּעִטְרָן

We may not light with tar,*

mip'nay k'vōd hashabos.

מִפְּנֵי כְּבוֹד הַשַּׁבָּת.

out of respect for the honor due the Sabbath.

Vachachomim matirin

וַחֲכָמִים מַתִּירִין

b'chol hash'monim:

בְּכָל הַשְּׁמָנִים:

But the [other] Sages permit [lighting] with all [these] oils:*

שֶׁמֶן שְׂרֵפָה — *Oil that must be destroyed by burning.* Oil of *terumah* [the priest's tithe] must be burned if it becomes *tamei* [ritually contaminated]. Even if such oil is of the sort that burns well, there is a fear that one may tip the lamp in order to more efficiently fulfill the *mitzvah* of burning the oil.

וְלֹא בְחֵלֶב — *Nor with tallow.* Although this may not be used as fuel in lamps, it may be made into candles.

2. בְּיוֹם טוֹב — *On a Festival day.* Although kindling (from an existing flame) is permitted on Festivals, it is forbidden to burn contaminated *terumah* on Festivals.

בְּעִטְרָן — *With tar.* Although it burns well, tar has a foul odor and will cause people to dishonor the Sabbath by refusing to remain at the table.

בְּכָל הַשְּׁמָנִים — *With all [these] oils.* The Sages maintain that all the following oils, in-

b'shemen shumsh'min, בְּשֶׁמֶן שֻׁמְשְׁמִין,

 b'shemen egōzim, בְּשֶׁמֶן אֱגוֹזִים,

with sesame-seed oil, with nut oil,

b'shemen tz'nōnōs, b'shemen dogim, בְּשֶׁמֶן צְנוֹנוֹת, בְּשֶׁמֶן דָּגִים,

with radish oil, with fish oil,

b'shemen paku-ōs, בְּשֶׁמֶן פַּקֻעוֹת,

 b'itron, uvnayft. בְּעִטְרָן, וּבְנֵפְט.

with gourd oil, with tar, or with naphtha.

Rabi tarfōn ōmayr: רַבִּי טַרְפוֹן אוֹמֵר:

Rabbi Tarfon says:

Ayn madlikin אֵין מַדְלִיקִין

 elo b'shemen za-yis bilvod. אֶלָּא בְּשֶׁמֶן זַיִת בִּלְבָד.

We may light only with olive oil.

MISHNAH THREE

Kol hayōtzay min ho-aytz כָּל הַיּוֹצֵא מִן הָעֵץ

*All products of trees**

ayn madlikin bō elo fishton. אֵין מַדְלִיקִין בּוֹ אֶלָּא פִשְׁתָּן.

we may not light with, with the exception of linen.

V'chol ha-yōtzay min ho-aytz וְכָל הַיּוֹצֵא מִן הָעֵץ

And all products of trees

aynō mitamay tum-as ōholim אֵינוֹ מְטַמֵּא טֻמְאַת אֹהָלִים

*cannot contract contamination from sheltering [a contaminated object],**

elo fishton. אֶלָּא פִשְׁתָּן.

with the exception of linen.

P'silas habeged shekip'loh פְּתִילַת הַבֶּגֶד שֶׁקִּפְּלָהּ

 v'lō hivhavoh — וְלֹא הִבְהֲבָהּ —

If a wick was made from a cloth that was twisted but not singed —

rabi eli-ezer ōmayr: רַבִּי אֱלִיעֶזֶר אוֹמֵר:

Rabbi Eliezer says:

T'may-o hi v'ayn madlikin boh. טְמֵאָה הִיא וְאֵין מַדְלִיקִין בָּהּ.

It contracts contamination and we may not light with it.

---

cluding tar, may be used. They are not concerned with the smell, as long as the fuel burns well.

3. כָּל הַיּוֹצֵא מִן הָעֵץ — *All products of trees.* The mishnah returns to discussing the wicks and forbids wicks made from trees because they do not burn well. Linen, made from the flax plant which Scripture sometimes refers to as a tree

(e.g., *Joshua* 2:6), is the exception.

טֻמְאַת אֹהָלִים — *Contamination from sheltering [a contaminated object].* If a corpse is under the shelter of a roof or canopy, everything else under the shelter becomes contaminated. The shelter itself, however, does not become contaminated if it was a tree product, unless it was made of linen.

Rabi akivo ōmayr:

רַבִּי עֲקִיבָא אוֹמֵר:

Rabbi Akiva says:

T'hōro hi u-madlikin boh.

טְהוֹרָה הִיא וּמַדְלִיקִין בָּהּ.

It does not contract contamination and we may light with it.

MISHNAH FOUR

Lō yikōv odom

לֹא יִקּוֹב אָדָם

sh'fōferes shel baytzo

שְׁפוֹפֶרֶת שֶׁל בֵּיצָה

*One may not pierce an eggshell,** *

vimal'eno shemen

וִימַלְאֶנָה שֶׁמֶן

fill it with oil,

v'yit'neno al pi hanayr

וְיִתְּנֶנָּה עַל פִּי הַנֵּר

and put it over the mouth of a lamp

bishvil shet'hay m'natefes,

בִּשְׁבִיל שֶׁתְּהֵא מְנַטֶּפֶת,

so that [the oil] will drip down,

va-afilu hi shel cheres.

וַאֲפִילוּ הִיא שֶׁל חֶרֶס.

even if [the container is] of earthenware.

V'rabi y'hudo matir.

וְרַבִּי יְהוּדָה מַתִּיר.

But Rabbi Yehudah permits this.

Avol im chib'roh hayōtzayr

אֲבָל אִם חִבְּרָהּ הַיּוֹצֵר

mit'chilo — mutor,

מִתְּחִלָּה — מֻתָּר,

*But if the potter attached it** * originally — it is permitted,*

mip'nay shehu k'li e-chod.

מִפְּנֵי שֶׁהוּא כְּלִי אֶחָד.

because it is a single vessel.

Lō y'ma-lay odom k'oro shemen

לֹא יְמַלֵּא אָדָם קְעָרָה שֶׁמֶן

One may not fill a bowl with oil,

v'yit'neno b'tzad hanayr

וְיִתְּנֶנָּה בְּצַד הַנֵּר

put it next to a lamp,

v'yitayn rōsh hap'silo v'sōchoh

וְיִתֵּן רֹאשׁ הַפְּתִילָה בְּתוֹכָהּ

*and put the end of the wick into [the bowl]** *

---

4. לֹא יִקּוֹב — *One may not pierce an eggshell.* The pierced eggshell, in effect, becomes a spare reservoir of fuel for the lamp, increasing its oil capacity and allowing it to burn longer, but it does not become an integral part of the lamp. The Sages feared that the owner might remove some oil from the shell on the Sabbath, thus decreasing the life of the flame (by denying it more oil) and causing it to become extinguished, an act that is forbidden on the Sabbath.

אֲבָל אִם חִבְּרָהּ — *But if . . . attached it.* If the reservoir and lamp were attached, they are regarded as a single lamp, and we do not fear that someone will forget that it is the Sabbath and remove oil from a lamp.

וְיִתֵּן רֹאשׁ הַפְּתִילָה בְּתוֹכָהּ — *And put the end of the wick into [the bowl].* The intent is that the wick will burn longer because it has two sources of oil, the lamp and the bowl. Here, too, the Sages feared that one might not realize that the second bowl is also supplying oil to the wick and

bishvil shet'hay shō-oves.

בִּשְׁבִיל שֶׁתְּהֵא שׁוֹאָבֶת.

so that it will draw [oil].

V'rabi y'hudo matir.

וְרַבִּי יְהוּדָה מַתִּיר.

Rabbi Yehudah permits this.

MISHNAH FIVE

Ham'chabe es hanayr

הַמְכַבֶּה אֶת הַנֵּר

If one extinguishes a lamp

mip'nay shehu misyoray

מִפְּנֵי שֶׁהוּא מִתְיָרֵא

because he fears*

mip'nay gōyim, mip'nay listim,

מִפְּנֵי גוֹיִם, מִפְּנֵי לִסְטִים,

from idolaters, from bandits,

mip'nay ru-ach ro-o,

מִפְּנֵי רוּחַ רָעָה,

[or] from melancholia,

ō bishvil hachōle sheyishon,

אוֹ בִּשְׁבִיל הַחוֹלֶה שֶׁיִּישָׁן,

or so that a sick person can fall asleep,

potur.

פָּטוּר.

he is not liable.*

K'chos al hanayr,

כְּחָס עַל הַנֵּר,

But if he does so to spare the lamp,

k'chos al hashemen,

כְּחָס עַל הַשֶּׁמֶן,

to spare the oil,

k'chos al hap'silo, chayov.

כְּחָס עַל הַפְּתִילָה, חַיָּב.

or to spare the wick, he is liable.

Rabi yōsi pōtayr b'chulon,

רַבִּי יוֹסֵי פוֹטֵר בְּכֻלָּן,

Rabbi Yose exempts in all these cases,

chutz min hap'silo,

חוּץ מִן הַפְּתִילָה,

except that of the wick,

mip'nay shehu ōsoh pechom.

מִפְּנֵי שֶׁהוּא עָשָׂה פֶחָם.

because he makes it into charcoal.

---

may remove oil from that bowl.

5. הַמְכַבֶּה . . . מִפְּנֵי שֶׁהוּא מִתְיָרֵא — *If one extinguishes . . . because he fears.* This mishnah's first four cases involve life-and-death considerations: Certain idolatrous sects made it a capital offense to light any fire on their holidays except in their temples; the light may disclose one's whereabouts to a band of cutthroats; one suffers from a mental illness that causes a morbid fear of light; or a patient's condition is critical and he requires sleep.

פָּטוּר — *He is not liable.* The phrase, "he is not liable," does not necessarily mean that the act is permitted, merely that it does not entail any penalty or punishment from the *beis din* (court). It may, nevertheless, be prohibited.

רַבִּי יוֹסֵי פוֹטֵר — *Rabbi Yose exempts,* because Rabbi Yose holds that to be culpable for desecrating the Sabbath, the prohibited labor must be performed for its primary purpose. For example, if one extinguished the flame so that he would be left with charcoal or a singed wick, he is liable.

MISHNAH SIX

Al sholōsh avayrōs
For three transgressions*

עַל שָׁלֹשׁ עֲבֵרוֹת

noshim may-sōs bishas laydoson:
women die during childbirth:

נָשִׁים מֵתוֹת בִּשְׁעַת לֵדָתָן:

Al she-aynon z'hirōs
for being careless regarding [the laws of]

עַל שֶׁאֵינָן זְהִירוֹת

b'nido, b'chalo uvhadlokas hanayr.
menstruation, the tithe from dough, and kindling the [Sabbath] light.

בְּנִדָּה, בְּחַלָּה, וּבְהַדְלָקַת הַנֵּר.

MISHNAH SEVEN

Sh'lōsho d'vorim
tzorich odom lōmar b'sōch baysō
A person must say three things in his home

שְׁלֹשָׁה דְבָרִים צָרִיךְ אָדָם לוֹמַר בְּתוֹךְ בֵּיתוֹ

erev shabos im chashaycho:
on the eve of the Sabbath just before dark:

עֶרֶב שַׁבָּת עִם חֲשֵׁכָה:

Isartem, ayravtem,
"Have you tithed?* Have you prepared the eruv?*

עִשַּׂרְתֶּם, עֵרַבְתֶּם,

hadliku es hanayr.
Kindle the [Sabbath] lights!"

הַדְלִיקוּ אֶת הַנֵּר.

Sofayk chashaycho
If there is a doubt* whether it is dark

סָפֵק חֲשֵׁכָה

sofayk aynoh chashaycho —
or it is not dark,

סָפֵק אֵינָהּ חֲשֵׁכָה —

ayn m'as'rin es havadoy,
we may not tithe definitely untithed produce,

אֵין מְעַשְּׂרִין אֶת הַוַּדַּאי,

v'ayn matbilin es hakaylim,
we may not immerse vessels,

וְאֵין מַטְבִּילִין אֶת הַכֵּלִים,

v'ayn madlikin es hanayrōs;
and we may not kindle the lights;

וְאֵין מַדְלִיקִין אֶת הַנֵּרוֹת;

---

6. עַל שָׁלֹשׁ עֲבֵרוֹת — *For three transgressions.* These three *mitzvos* are designated for women; therefore they bear great responsibility for transgressing them.

בִּשְׁעַת לֵדָתָן — *During childbirth.* Punishments are most likely to occur in time of danger.

7. עִשַּׂרְתֶּם — *Have you tithed?* It is forbidden to tithe on the Sabbath and untithed food may not be eaten. Thus, it is appropriate to ask the question before the Sabbath begins. Similarly regarding the next two things.

עֵרַבְתֶּם — *Have you prepared the eruv?* This

refers to two types of *eruv: eruvei chatzeiros,* which permits people to carry from one domain to another; and *eruvei techumin,* which permits one to walk (in one direction) more than would normally be permitted on the Sabbath.

סָפֵק — *If there is a doubt.* If one is not sure whether or not the Sabbath has begun, it is forbidden to risk performing labors that are definitely forbidden on the Sabbath, even though the prohibitions are of Rabbinic, not Scriptural, origin. The time when such a doubt exists is during twilight, whose halachic status is in question.

avol m'as'rin es had'moy,
אֲבָל מְעַשְּׂרִין אֶת הַדְּמָאי,
but we may tithe questionable produce, *

um-or'vin, v'tōm'nin es hachamin.
וּמְעָרְבִין, וְטוֹמְנִין אֶת הַחַמִּין.
we may make an eruv, and we may insulate * hot food.*

TANYO, chananyo ōmayr:
תַּנְיָא חֲנַנְיָא אוֹמֵר:
It has been taught; [The Sage] Chanania says:

Chayov odom l'mashmaysh b'godov
חַיָּב אָדָם לְמַשְׁמֵשׁ בִּגְדָיו
A person is required to examine * his clothing*

b'erev shabos im chashaycho,
בְּעֶרֶב שַׁבָּת עִם חֲשֵׁכָה,
on the eve of the Sabbath just before dark

shemo yishkach v'yaytzay.
שֶׁמָּא יִשְׁכַּח וְיֵצֵא.
for he may forget himself and go out.

Omar rav yōsayf:
אָמַר רַב יוֹסֵף:
Rav Yosef said:

Hilch'so rab'so l'shab'so.
הִלְכְתָא רַבְּתָא לְשַׁבְּתָא.
This is a significant law regarding the Sabbath. *

OMAR rabi el-ozor
אָמַר רַבִּי אֶלְעָזָר
omar rabi chanino:
אָמַר רַבִּי חֲנִינָא:
Rabbi Elazar said in the name of Rabbi Chanina:

Talmiday chachomim
תַּלְמִידֵי חֲכָמִים
Torah Scholars

marbim sholōm bo-ōlom,
מַרְבִּים שָׁלוֹם בָּעוֹלָם,
increase peace in the world, *

shene-emar. V'chol bona-yich
שֶׁנֶּאֱמַר. וְכָל בָּנַיִךְ
limuday Adōnoy,
לִמּוּדֵי יהוה,
as it is said: "And all your children will be students of HASHEM,

---

הַדְּמָאי — *Questionable produce.* Although the majority of unlearned farmers *do* tithe their produce, the Sages require one who purchases from them to set aside tithes because a minority of farmers are not observant of this *mitzvah.* Since it is only a precautionary measure, the Sages permitted such tithes to be taken on the Sabbath.

וְטוֹמְנִין — *And we may insulate.* Hot food may be wrapped and bundled to retain its warmth. This wrapping is permitted at twilight but not on the Sabbath day.

לְמַשְׁמֵשׁ — *To examine* [lit., *to tap*]. One should examine one's pockets to be sure not to unwittingly carry items into the public domain when leaving home.

הִלְכְתָא רַבְּתָא לְשַׁבְּתָא — *This is a significant law regarding the Sabbath.* In the law of examining clothing there is a major deterrent against violating the Sabbath. The principle here is important: One should not rely on memory or good intentions; rather one should make plans and institute procedures to develop habits of proper Sabbath observance.

תַּלְמִידֵי חֲכָמִים מַרְבִּים שָׁלוֹם בָּעוֹלָם — *Torah scholars increase peace in the world.* Torah scholars increase peace in two ways: They engage in Torah study, the activity for which the universe was created; and God promises peace as a reward for the diligent study of Torah (see *Leviticus* 26:5).

v'rav sh'lōm bono-yich　　　　　　וְרַב שָׁלוֹם בָּנָיִךְ
and your children will have abundant peace.''

al tikray bono-yich elo bōno-yich.　　אַל תִּקְרֵי בָּנָיִךְ אֶלָּא בּוֹנָיִךְ.
Do not read* bono-yich [your children], but bōno-yich [your builders].

❖ Sholōm rov l'ōhavay sōrosecho,　　שָׁלוֹם רָב לְאֹהֲבֵי תוֹרָתֶךָ,
There is abundant peace for the lovers of Your Torah,

v'ayn lomō michshōl.　　　　　　וְאֵין לָמוֹ מִכְשׁוֹל.
and there is no stumbling block for them.

Y'hi sholōm b'chaylaych,　　　　יְהִי שָׁלוֹם בְּחֵילֵךְ,
May there be peace within your wall,

shalvo b'arm'nōso-yich.　　　　שַׁלְוָה בְּאַרְמְנוֹתָיִךְ.
serenity within your palaces.

L'ma-an achai v'ray-oy,　　　　לְמַעַן אַחַי וְרֵעָי,
For the sake of my brethren and my comrades,

adab'ro no sholōm boch.　　　　אֲדַבְּרָה נָּא שָׁלוֹם בָּךְ.
I shall speak of peace in your midst.

L'ma-an bays Adōnoy Elōhaynu,　　לְמַעַן בֵּית יהוה אֱלֹהֵינוּ,
For the sake of the House of HASHEM, our God,

avaksho tōv loch.　　　　　　אֲבַקְשָׁה טוֹב לָךְ.
I will request good for you.

Adōnoy ōz l'amō yitayn,　　　　יהוה עֹז לְעַמּוֹ יִתֵּן,
HASHEM will give might to His people,

Adōnoy y'voraych es amō vasholōm.　יהוה יְבָרֵךְ אֶת עַמּוֹ בַשָּׁלוֹם.
HASHEM will bless His people with peace.

THE RABBIS' KADDISH

IN THE PRESENCE OF A *MINYAN,* MOURNERS RECITE THE RABBIS' *KADDISH.*

MOURNER:

YISGADAL v'yiskadash　　　　**יִתְגַּדַּל** וְיִתְקַדַּשׁ
sh'mayh rabo.　　　　　　　שְׁמֵהּ רַבָּא.
May His great Name grow exalted and sanctified

CONGREGATION RESPONDS: Omayn — אָמֵן

אַל תִּקְרֵי — *Do not read.* As in all cases where the Talmudic Sages use this expression, they do not intend to change the Masoretic text, but to suggest an additional implication. Since the expression, "your children," already appears in the verse, the repetition of the same word can only mean to introduce a new concept — that children are also builders — in this case that the students of Torah are the builders of abundant peace.

⇜§ **The Rabbis' Kaddish**

Whenever ten or more Israelites join for the study of the Oral Law — for example, Mishnah, Halachah, Midrash or Aggadah — one of them recites the Rabbis' *Kaddish* upon conclusion of the study. It has become customary in most communities for this *Kaddish* to be recited by mourners.

B'ol'mo di v'ro chir-usayh.   בְּעָלְמָא דִי בְרָא כִרְעוּתֵהּ.
in the world that He created as He willed.

V'yamlich malchusayh,   וְיַמְלִיךְ מַלְכוּתֵהּ,
May He give reign to His kingship

b'cha-yaychōn uvyōmaychōn   בְּחַיֵּיכוֹן וּבְיוֹמֵיכוֹן
in your lifetimes and in your days

uvcha-yay d'chol bays yisro-ayl,   וּבְחַיֵּי דְכָל בֵּית יִשְׂרָאֵל,
and in the lifetimes of the entire Family of Israel,

ba-agolo u-vizman koriv.   בַּעֲגָלָא וּבִזְמַן קָרִיב.
swiftly and soon.

V'imru: Omayn.   וְאִמְרוּ: אָמֵן.
Now respond: Amen.

CONGREGATION RESPONDS:

Omayn. Y'hay sh'mayh rabo m'vorach   אָמֵן. יְהֵא שְׁמֵהּ רַבָּא מְבָרַךְ
l'olam ul-ol'may ol'ma-yo.   לְעָלַם וּלְעָלְמֵי עָלְמַיָּא.
Amen. May His great Name be blessed forever and ever;

MOURNER CONTINUES:

Y'hay sh'mayh rabo m'vorach   יְהֵא שְׁמֵהּ רַבָּא מְבָרַךְ
l'olam ul-ol'may ol'ma-yo,   לְעָלַם וּלְעָלְמֵי עָלְמַיָּא,
May His great Name be blessed forever and ever,

yisborach v'yishtabach v'yispo-ar   יִתְבָּרַךְ וְיִשְׁתַּבַּח וְיִתְפָּאַר
blessed, praised, glorified,

v'yisrōmam v'yisnasay   וְיִתְרוֹמַם וְיִתְנַשֵּׂא
exalted, extolled,

v'yis-hador v'yis-ale v'yis-halol   וְיִתְהַדָּר וְיִתְעַלֶּה וְיִתְהַלָּל
mighty, upraised, and lauded

sh'mayh d'kudsho b'rich hu   שְׁמֵהּ דְּקֻדְשָׁא בְּרִיךְ הוּא
be the Name of the Holy One, Blessed is He,

CONGREGATION RESPONDS:

B'rich hu.   *Blessed is He.*   בְּרִיךְ הוּא.

MOURNER CONTINUES:

°l'aylo min kol   °לְעֵלָּא מִן כָּל
beyond any

FROM ROSH HASHANAH TO YOM KIPPUR SUBSTITUTE:

°l'aylo l'aylo mikol   °לְעֵלָּא לְעֵלָּא מִכָּל
exceedingly beyond any

The ultimate sanctification of God's Name will come when Israel is redeemed; in this sense *Kaddish* is a plea for the final Redemption. It is also an expression of Israel's mission to bring recognition of His sovereignty primarily upon the community as a whole, and *Kaddish* is therefore recited only in the presence of a *minyan* [a quorum of ten males over the age of *bar mitzvah*].

עַל יִשְׂרָאֵל וְעַל רַבָּנָן — *Upon Israel, (and) upon*

birchoso v'shiroso   בִּרְכָתָא וְשִׁירָתָא
blessing and song,

tushb'choso v'nechemoso,   תֻּשְׁבְּחָתָא וְנֶחֱמָתָא,
praise and consolation

da-amiron b'ol'mo.   דַּאֲמִירָן בְּעָלְמָא.
that are uttered in the world.

V'imru: Omayn.   וְאִמְרוּ: אָמֵן.
Now respond: Amen.

CONGREGATION RESPONDS: Omayn — אָמֵן

Al yisro-el v'al rabo-non   עַל יִשְׂרָאֵל וְעַל רַבָּנָן,
Upon Israel, and upon the teachers,*

v'al talmiday-hōn,   וְעַל תַּלְמִידֵיהוֹן,

v'al kol talmiday salmiday-hōn,   וְעַל כָּל תַּלְמִידֵי תַלְמִידֵיהוֹן,
their disciples and all of their disciples

v'al kol man d'os'kin b'ōrai-so,   וְעַל כָּל מָאן דְּעָסְקִין בְּאוֹרַיְתָא,
and upon all those who engage in the study of Torah,

dee v'as-ro hodayn,   דִּי בְאַתְרָא הָדֵין,

v'dee b'chol asar va-asar.   וְדִי בְכָל אֲתַר וַאֲתַר.
who are here or anywhere else.

Y'hay l'hōn ulchōn sh'lomo rabo,   יְהֵא לְהוֹן וּלְכוֹן שְׁלָמָא רַבָּא,
May they and you have* abundant peace,

chi-no v'chis-do v'racha-min,   חִנָּא וְחִסְדָּא וְרַחֲמִין,
grace, kindness, and mercy,

v'cha-yin arichin, um-zōnay r'vichay,   וְחַיִּין אֲרִיכִין, וּמְזוֹנֵי רְוִיחֵי,
long life, ample nourishment,

u-furkono min kodom a-vu-hōn   וּפֻרְקָנָא מִן קֳדָם אֲבוּהוֹן
and salvation from before their Father

dee vishma-yo (v'ar-o).   דִּי בִשְׁמַיָּא (וְאַרְעָא).
Who is in Heaven (and on earth).

V'imru: Omayn.   וְאִמְרוּ: אָמֵן.
Now respond: Amen.

CONGREGATION RESPONDS: Omayn — אָמֵן

---

the teachers. It is because of this section that this *Kaddish* is called the Rabbis' *Kaddish.* Though this is a prayer for the benefit of the Torah community, it begins with mention of Israel. Any prayer for Torah scholars is a prayer for the nation, because Israel's welfare depends on its Torah study and on the leadership of its Sages.

יְהֵא לְהוֹן וּלְכוֹן — *May they and you have.* The blessing is extended not only to the Torah teachers and their students, but to all the people present in their congregation.

Y'hay sh'lomo rabo min sh'mayo   יְהֵא שְׁלָמָא רַבָּא מִן שְׁמַיָּא,
May there be abundant peace from Heaven,

v'cha-yim olaynu v'al kol yisro-ayl.   וְחַיִּים עָלֵינוּ וְעַל כָּל יִשְׂרָאֵל.
and life, upon us and upon all Israel.

V'imru: Omayn.   וְאִמְרוּ: אָמֵן.
Now respond: Amen.

CONGREGATION RESPONDS: Omayn — אָמֵן

MOURNER BOWS, THEN TAKES THREE STEPS BACK, BOWS LEFT AND SAYS:

Ō-se sholōm bimrōmov   עֹשֶׂה שָׁלוֹם בִּמְרוֹמָיו,
He Who makes peace in His heights,

MOURNER BOWS RIGHT AND SAYS:

hu b'racha-mov ya-a-se sholōm   הוּא בְּרַחֲמָיו יַעֲשֶׂה שָׁלוֹם
olaynu   עָלֵינוּ,
may He, in His compassion, make peace upon us,

MOURNER BOWS FORWARD AND SAYS:

v'al kol yisro-ayl. V'imru: Omayn.   וְעַל כָּל יִשְׂרָאֵל. וְאִמְרוּ: אָמֵן.
and upon all Israel. Now respond: Amen.

CONGREGATION RESPONDS: Omayn — אָמֵן

MOURNER REMAINS IN PLACE FOR A FEW MOMENTS, THEN TAKES THREE STEPS FORWARD.

⊰ MAARIV FOR SABBATH AND FESTIVALS ⊱

THE *CHAZZAN* SUMMONS THE CONGREGATION TO JOIN IN THE FORTHCOMING PRAYERS,

BOWING AT Bor'chu AND STRAIGHTENING UP AT Adōnoy.

BOR'CHU es Adōnoy ham'vōroch.   **בָּרְכוּ** אֶת יהוה הַמְבֹרָךְ.
Bless HASHEM, the blessed One.

CONGREGATION, FOLLOWED BY *CHAZZAN*, RESPONDS:

Boruch Adōnoy   בָּרוּךְ יהוה
ham'vōroch l'ōlom vo-ed.   הַמְבֹרָךְ לְעוֹלָם וָעֶד.
Blessed is HASHEM, the blessed One, for all eternity.

■ First blessing preceding the *Shema:* We recognize God's ongoing management of the world, as He allows us to benefit from the recurring cycles of night and day.

BORUCH ato Adōnoy,   **בָּרוּךְ** אַתָּה יהוה
Blessed are You, HASHEM,

Elōhaynu melech ho-ōlom,   אֱלֹהֵינוּ מֶלֶךְ הָעוֹלָם,
our God, King of the universe,

asher bidvorō ma-ariv arovim,   אֲשֶׁר בִּדְבָרוֹ מַעֲרִיב עֲרָבִים,
*Who by His word brings on evenings,**

אֲשֶׁר בִּדְבָרוֹ מַעֲרִיב עֲרָבִים — *Who by His word brings on evenings.* Every moment of the day and night has a purpose in God's plan. Recognition of God's everpresent will is especially

b'chochmo pōsay-ach sh'orim,   בְּחָכְמָה פּוֹתֵחַ שְׁעָרִים,
*with wisdom opens gates,**

u-visvuno m'shane itim,   וּבִתְבוּנָה מְשַׁנֶּה עִתִּים,
*with understanding alters periods,**

u-machalif es haz'manim,   וּמַחֲלִיף אֶת הַזְּמַנִּים,
changes the seasons,

umsadayr es hakōchovim,   וּמְסַדֵּר אֶת הַכּוֹכָבִים
and orders the stars

b'mishm'rōsayhem boroki-a   בְּמִשְׁמְרוֹתֵיהֶם בָּרָקִיעַ
in their heavenly constellations

kirtzōnō.   כִּרְצוֹנוֹ.
as He wills.

Bōray yōm voloylo,   בּוֹרֵא יוֹם וָלָיְלָה,
He creates day and night,

gōlayl ōr mip'nay chōshech,   גּוֹלֵל אוֹר מִפְּנֵי חֹשֶׁךְ
v'chōshech mip'nay ōr,   וְחֹשֶׁךְ מִפְּנֵי אוֹר,
removing light before darkness and darkness before light;

u-ma-avir yōm u-mayvi loylo,   וּמַעֲבִיר יוֹם וּמֵבִיא לָיְלָה,
He causes day to pass and brings night,

u-mavdil bayn yōm u-vayn loylo,   וּמַבְדִּיל בֵּין יוֹם וּבֵין לָיְלָה,
and separates between day and night —

Adōnoy Tz'vo-ōs sh'mō.   יהוה צְבָאוֹת שְׁמוֹ.
HASHEM, Master of Legions, is His Name.*

❖ Ayl chai v'ka-yom,   ❖ אֵל חַי וְקַיָּם,
   tomid yimlōch olaynu   תָּמִיד יִמְלוֹךְ עָלֵינוּ,
May the living and enduring God continuously reign over us,

l'ōlom vo-ed.   לְעוֹלָם וָעֶד.
for all eternity.

Boruch ato Adōnoy,   בָּרוּךְ אַתָּה יהוה,
   hama-ariv arovim.   הַמַּעֲרִיב עֲרָבִים.
Blessed are You, HASHEM, Who brings on evenings.

CONGREGATION RESPONDS AMEN: Omayn — אָמֵן

---

important at night, which represents the period of fear, failure, and exile.

שְׁעָרִים — *gates.* A figurative reference to the gates which open to release the light of the morning sun and "close" upon it in the evening — as if the sun were brought out at dawn and put to rest at dusk.

וּבִתְבוּנָה מְשַׁנֶּה עִתִּים — *With understanding al-*

ters periods. With deep understanding of the needs of a particular time segment, God varies weather conditions from day to day and from hour to hour.

צְבָאוֹת — *Master of Legions.* God takes the infinite number of forces and conditions that form the universe and harmonizes them to perform His will.

■ Second blessing preceding the *Shema:* God's love of Israel manifested itself by His giving the Jewish people the Torah and *mitzvos.* We reciprocate with our pledge to study and observe His Torah and *mitzvos.*

AHAVAS ŌLOM   אַהֲבַת עוֹלָם

*[With] an eternal love**

bays yisro-ayl am'cho ohovto,   בֵּית יִשְׂרָאֵל עַמְּךָ אָהָבְתָּ,
have You loved the House of Israel, Your people;

tōro u-mitzvōs,   תּוֹרָה וּמִצְוֹת,
   chukim u-mishpotim,   חֻקִּים וּמִשְׁפָּטִים,
Torah and commandments, decrees and ordinances

ōsonu limadto   אוֹתָנוּ לִמַּדְתָּ.
have You taught us.

Al kayn Adōnoy Elōhaynu,   עַל כֵּן יהוה אֱלֹהֵינוּ,
Therefore HASHEM, our God,

b'shoch-vaynu uvkumaynu   בְּשָׁכְבֵנוּ וּבְקוּמֵנוּ
upon our retiring and our arising,

nosi-ach b'chukecho,   נָשִׂיחַ בְּחֻקֶּיךָ,
we will discuss Your decrees

v'nismach b'divray sōrosecho   וְנִשְׂמַח בְּדִבְרֵי תוֹרָתֶךָ,
*and we will rejoice * with the words of Your Torah*

uvmitzvōsecho l'ōlom vo-ed,   וּבְמִצְוֹתֶיךָ לְעוֹלָם וָעֶד,
and with Your commandments for all eternity,

ki haym cha-yaynu   ❖ כִּי הֵם חַיֵּינוּ,
   v'ōrech yomaynu,   וְאֹרֶךְ יָמֵינוּ,
for they are our life and the length of our days

u-vohem neh-ge yōmom voloylo.   וּבָהֶם נֶהְגֶּה יוֹמָם וָלָיְלָה.
and about them we will meditate day and night.

V'ahavos'cho   וְאַהֲבָתְךָ,
   al tosir mimenu l'ōlomim.   אַל תָּסִיר מִמֶּנּוּ לְעוֹלָמִים.
May You not remove Your love from us forever.

Boruch ato Adōnoy,   בָּרוּךְ אַתָּה יהוה,
   ōhayv amō yisro-ayl.   אוֹהֵב עַמּוֹ יִשְׂרָאֵל.
Blessed are You, HASHEM, Who loves His people Israel.

CONGREGATION RESPONDS: Omayn — אָמֵן

אַהֲבַת עוֹלָם — *[With] an eternal love.* The second blessing begins with an expression of an axiom of Jewish existence: God loves us. The fact that He chose to give us His Torah proves that it is the vehicle for our national fulfill-ment. Therefore we dedicate ourselves to study it — constantly, joyously, and devotedly.

וְנִשְׂמַח — *And we will rejoice.* Torah study must be seen not as a chore, but as a source of joy.

THE SHEMA

■ The *Shema* is our acceptance of and submission to the absolute Sovereignty of God.

IMMEDIATELY BEFORE THE RECITATION OF THE *SHEMA*, CONCENTRATE ON FULFILLING THE POSITIVE COMMANDMENT OF RECITING THE *SHEMA* DAILY, ONCE IN THE EVENING AND ONCE IN THE MORNING. IT IS IMPORTANT TO ENUNCIATE EACH WORD CLEARLY AND NOT TO RUN WORDS TOGETHER.

ONE PRAYING WITHOUT A *MINYAN* BEGINS WITH THE FOLLOWING THREE-WORD FORMULA:

Ayl melech ne-emon.   אֵל מֶלֶךְ נֶאֱמָן.

God, trustworthy King.

RECITE THE FIRST VERSE ALOUD, WITH YOUR RIGHT HAND COVERING YOUR EYES, AND CONCENTRATE INTENSELY UPON ACCEPTING GOD'S ABSOLUTE SOVEREIGNTY.

SH'MA yisro-ayl,   שְׁמַע יִשְׂרָאֵל,

Adōnoy Elōhaynu, Adōnoy e-chod.   יהוה אֱלֹהֵינוּ, יהוה אֶחָד.

Hear, O Israel: HASHEM *is our God,** HASHEM, *the One [and Only].**

In an undertone:

Boruch shaym k'vōd malchusō   בָּרוּךְ שֵׁם כְּבוֹד מַלְכוּתוֹ

l'ōlom vo-ed.   לְעוֹלָם וָעֶד.

Blessed is the Name* of His glorious kingdom for all eternity.

■ We return God's love by studying His Torah and committing ourselves to observe the Torah with all our resources and being.

WHILE RECITING THE FOLLOWING PARAGRAPH, CONCENTRATE ON ACCEPTING THE COMMANDMENT TO LOVE GOD.

V'OHAVTO ays Adōnoy Elōhecho,   וְאָהַבְתָּ אֵת יהוה ׀ אֱלֹהֶיךָ,

You shall love* HASHEM, *your God,*

b'chol l'vov'cho, uvchol nafsh'cho,   בְּכָל לְבָבְךָ, וּבְכָל נַפְשְׁךָ,

uvchol m'ōdecho.   וּבְכָל מְאֹדֶךָ.

with all your heart, with all your soul and with all your resources.

V'ho-yu had'vorim ho-ayle,   וְהָיוּ הַדְּבָרִים הָאֵלֶּה,

asher onōchi m'tzav'cho ha-yōm,   אֲשֶׁר אָנֹכִי מְצַוְּךָ הַיּוֹם,

Let these matters that I command you today*

שְׁמַע יִשְׂרָאֵל — *Hear, O Israel:* HASHEM *is our God.*" At this point in history, He is only "our God," for He is not acknowledged universally. Ultimately, however, all will recognize Him as "the One and Only" God.

אֶחָד — *The One [and Only].* The Hebrew word has two connotations: (a) There is no God other than HASHEM and, (b) though we perceive God in many roles — kind, angry, merciful, wise, judging, and so on — these different attitudes are not contradictory, even though human intelligence does not comprehend their harmony. This can be compared to a ray of light seen through a prism. Though one may

see a myriad of different colors, they are all a single ray of light. So, too, God's many manifestations are truly one.

בָּרוּךְ שֵׁם — *Blessed is the Name.* Having proclaimed God as our King, we show gratitude for the privilege of serving the One Whose kingdom is eternal and unbounded.

וְאָהַבְתָּ — *You shall love.* We should serve God with all our emotions and desires ("with all your heart"), even to the point of giving up our life ("with all your soul"), and our wealth ("with all your resources") for God.

אֲשֶׁר אָנֹכִי מְצַוְּךָ הַיּוֹם — *That I command you today.* But have they all been commanded

al l'vovecho.
עַל לְבָבֶךָ.
be upon your heart.

V'shinantom l'vonecho,
וְשִׁנַּנְתָּם לְבָנֶיךָ,
Teach them thoroughly to your children

v'dibarto bom
וְדִבַּרְתָּ בָּם,
and speak of them

b'shivt'cho b'vaysecho,
בְּשִׁבְתְּךָ בְּבֵיתֶךָ,
   uvlecht'cho vaderech
וּבְלֶכְתְּךָ בַדֶּרֶךְ,
while you sit in your home, while you walk on the way,

uv'shochb'cho, uvkumecho.
וּבְשָׁכְבְּךָ וּבְקוּמֶךָ.
when you retire and when you arise.

Ukshartom l'ōs al yodecho,
וּקְשַׁרְתָּם לְאוֹת עַל יָדֶךָ,
And you shall bind them* as a sign upon your arm

v'ho-yu l'tōtofōs bayn aynecho.
וְהָיוּ לְטֹטָפֹת בֵּין עֵינֶיךָ.
and they shall be tefillin between your eyes.

Uchsavtom al m'zuzōs baysecho
וּכְתַבְתָּם עַל מְזֻזוֹת בֵּיתֶךָ,
   u-vish-orecho.
וּבִשְׁעָרֶיךָ.
And write them on the doorposts of your house and upon your gates.

■ We declare Israel's collective commitment to observe God's *mitzvos,* and the recognition that our national success or failure is dependent on this observance.

V'HO-YO im shomō-a tishm'u
וְהָיָה, אִם־שָׁמֹעַ תִּשְׁמְעוּ
   el mitzvōsai,
אֶל מִצְוֹתַי,
And it will come to pass that if you continually hearken to My comandments

asher onōchi
אֲשֶׁר אָנֹכִי
   m'tza-ve eschem ha-yōm,
מְצַוֶּה אֶתְכֶם הַיּוֹם,
that I command you today,

l'ahavo es Adōnoy Elōhaychem,
לְאַהֲבָה אֶת יהוה אֱלֹהֵיכֶם
to love HASHEM, your God,

ul-ovdō
וּלְעָבְדוֹ,
and to serve Him,

b'chol-l'vavchem uvchol nafsh'chem.
בְּכָל לְבַבְכֶם, וּבְכָל נַפְשְׁכֶם.
with all your heart and with all your soul —

V'nosati m'tar artz'chem b'itō,
וְנָתַתִּי מְטַר אַרְצְכֶם בְּעִתּוֹ,
then I will provide rain for your land in its proper time,

---

today? — This teaches that although the Torah and *mitzvos* were given to us thousands of years ago, we are not to regard the commandments as an ancient rite that we follow out of loyalty and habit. Rather, we are to regard them with as much freshness and enthusiasm as if God had given them to us this very day.

וּקְשַׁרְתָּם — *And you shall bind them.* By binding

yōre u-malkōsh,   יוֹרֶה וּמַלְקוֹשׁ,

the early rains and the late rains,

v'osafto d'gonecho v'sirōsh'cho   וְאָסַפְתָּ דְגָנֶךָ וְתִירֹשְׁךָ

v'yitzhorecho.   וְיִצְהָרֶךָ.

that you may gather in your grain, your wine, and your oil.

V'nosati aysev   וְנָתַתִּי עֵשֶׂב

b'sod'cho livhemtecho,   בְּשָׂדְךָ לִבְהֶמְתֶּךָ,

I will provide grass in your field for your cattle

v'ochalto v'sovo-to.   וְאָכַלְתָּ וְשָׂבָעְתָּ.

and you will eat and you will be satisfied.

Hi-shom'ru lochem,   הִשָּׁמְרוּ לָכֶם,

Beware* for yourselves,

pen yifte l'vavchem,   פֶּן יִפְתֶּה לְבַבְכֶם,

lest your heart be seduced

v'sartem va-avadtem   וְסַרְתֶּם וַעֲבַדְתֶּם

elōhim a-chayrim   אֱלֹהִים אֲחֵרִים,

and you turn astray and serve gods of others

v'hishtachavisem lohem.   וְהִשְׁתַּחֲוִיתֶם לָהֶם.

and bow to them.*

V'choro af Adōnoy bochem,   וְחָרָה אַף יהוה בָּכֶם,

Then the wrath of HASHEM *will blaze against you;*

v'otzar es ha-shoma-yim   וְעָצַר אֶת הַשָּׁמַיִם,

v'lō yih-ye motor,   וְלֹא יִהְיֶה מָטָר,

He will restrain the heaven so there will be no rain

v'ho-adomo lō sitayn es y'vuloh   וְהָאֲדָמָה לֹא תִתֵּן אֶת יְבוּלָהּ,

and the ground will not yield its produce;

va-avadtem m'hayro   וַאֲבַדְתֶּם מְהֵרָה

and you will swiftly be banished

may-al ho-oretz hatōvo   מֵעַל הָאָרֶץ הַטֹּבָה

from the goodly land

asher Adōnoy nōsayn lochem.   אֲשֶׁר יהוה נֹתֵן לָכֶם.

which HASHEM *gives you.*

---

tefillin on our arm, next to our heart, and on our head, we consecrate our physical, emotional, and intellectual capacities to God's service. The *mezuzah* on our doorpost consecrates our home to Him.

וְאָכַלְתָּ וְשָׂבָעְתָּ הִשָּׁמְרוּ — *And you will eat and You will be satisfied. Beware ...* Prosperity is often the greatest challenge to religious devotion. People who are rich in wealth but poor in sophistication often succumb to temptation.

יִפְתֶּה ... וְהִשְׁתַּחֲוִיתֶם לָהֶם — *Be seduced ... and bow to them,* i.e., to strange gods. An imperceptible, seemingly innocent surrender to temptation can be the beginning of a course that will end in the basest of sins.

V'samtem es d'vorai ayle — וְשַׂמְתֶּם אֶת דְּבָרַי אֵלֶּה,
You shall place these words of Mine

al l'vavchem v'al nafsh'chem — עַל לְבַבְכֶם וְעַל נַפְשְׁכֶם,
upon your heart and upon your soul;

ukshartem ōsom l'ōs al yedchem, — וּקְשַׁרְתֶּם אֹתָם לְאוֹת עַל יֶדְכֶם,
and you shall bind them for a sign upon your arm

v'ho-yu l'tōtofōs bayn aynaychem. — וְהָיוּ לְטוֹטָפֹת בֵּין עֵינֵיכֶם.
and they shall be tefillin between your eyes.

V'limadtem ōsom es b'naychem, — וְלִמַּדְתֶּם אֹתָם אֶת בְּנֵיכֶם,
You shall teach to your children,

l'dabayr bom, — לְדַבֵּר בָּם,
to discuss them,

b'shivt'cho b'vay-secho, uvlecht'cho vaderech, — בְּשִׁבְתְּךָ בְּבֵיתֶךָ, וּבְלֶכְתְּךָ בַדֶּרֶךְ,
while you sit in your home, while you walk on the way,

uv'shochb'cho uvkumecho. — וּבְשָׁכְבְּךָ וּבְקוּמֶךָ.
when you retire and when you arise.

Uchsavtom al m'zuzōs baysecho uvish-orecho. — וּכְתַבְתָּם עַל מְזוּזוֹת בֵּיתֶךָ, וּבִשְׁעָרֶיךָ.
And write them on the doorposts of your house and upon your gates.

L'ma-an yirbu y'maychem vimay v'naychem — לְמַעַן יִרְבּוּ יְמֵיכֶם וִימֵי בְנֵיכֶם,
In order to prolong your days and the days of your children

al ho-adomo asher nishba Adōnoy la-avōsaychem — עַל הָאֲדָמָה אֲשֶׁר נִשְׁבַּע יהוה לַאֲבֹתֵיכֶם
upon the ground that HASHEM has sworn to your ancestors

losays lohem, — לָתֵת לָהֶם,
to give them,

kimay ha-shoma-yim al ho-oretz. — כִּימֵי הַשָּׁמַיִם עַל הָאָרֶץ.
like the days of the heavens on the earth.

■ We acknowledge the Divine providence over Israel as demonstrated by the Exodus from Egypt, thus obligating us to observe His *mitzvos*.

VA-YŌMER Adōnoy el mōshe laymōr. — **וַיֹּאמֶר** יהוה אֶל מֹשֶׁה לֵּאמֹר.
And HASHEM said to Moses saying:

Dabayr el b'nay yisro-ayl   דַּבֵּר אֶל בְּנֵי יִשְׂרָאֵל,

v'omarto alayhem,   וְאָמַרְתָּ אֲלֵהֶם,

Speak to the Children of Israel and say to them

v'osu lohem tzitzis   וְעָשׂוּ לָהֶם צִיצִת,

that they are to make themselves tzitzis

al kanfay vigdayhem   עַל כַּנְפֵי בִגְדֵיהֶם

on the corners of their garments,

l'dōrōsom,   לְדֹרֹתָם,

throughout their generations.

v'nos'nu al tzitzis hakonof   וְנָתְנוּ עַל צִיצִת הַכָּנָף,

p'sil t'chayles.   פְּתִיל תְּכֵלֶת.

And they are to place upon the tzitzis of each corner a thread of turquoise wool.

V'hoyo lochem l'tzitzis,   וְהָיָה לָכֶם לְצִיצִת,

And it shall constitute tzitzis for you,

ur-isem ōsō   וּרְאִיתֶם אֹתוֹ,

that you may see it

uz-chartem   וּזְכַרְתֶּם

es kol mitzvōs Adōnoy,   אֶת כָּל מִצְוֹת יהוה,

and remember all the commandments of HASHEM

va-asisem ōsom,   וַעֲשִׂיתֶם אֹתָם,

and perform them;

v'lō sosuru acharay l'vavchem   וְלֹא תָתוּרוּ אַחֲרֵי לְבַבְכֶם

v'acharay aynaychem,   וְאַחֲרֵי עֵינֵיכֶם,

and you shall not explore after your heart and after your eyes

asher atem zōnim acharayhem.   אֲשֶׁר אַתֶּם זֹנִים אַחֲרֵיהֶם.

after which you stray.

L'ma-an tizk'ru   לְמַעַן תִּזְכְּרוּ

va-asisem es kol mitzvōsoy,   וַעֲשִׂיתֶם אֶת כָּל מִצְוֹתָי,

So that you may remember and perform all My commandments;

vih-yisem k'dōshim Laylōhaychem.   וִהְיִיתֶם קְדֹשִׁים לֵאלֹהֵיכֶם.

and be holy to your God.

CONCENTRATE ON FULFILLING THE COMMANDMENT TO REMEMBER THE EXODUS FROM EGYPT.

Ani Adōnoy Elohaychem,   אֲנִי יהוה אֱלֹהֵיכֶם,

I am HASHEM, *your God,*

asher hōtzaysi eschem   אֲשֶׁר הוֹצֵאתִי אֶתְכֶם

may-eretz mitzra-yim,   מֵאֶרֶץ מִצְרָיִם,

Who has removed you from the land of Egypt*

מֵאֶרֶץ מִצְרַיִם — *From the land of Egypt.* By freeing Israel from Egypt, God laid claim to the   nation's eternal allegiance. No Jew is free to absolve himself of that obligation.

lih-yōs lochem Laylōhim,

לִהְיוֹת לָכֶם לֵאלֹהִים,

to be a God to you;

ani Adōnoy Elōhaychem. Emes . . . . . .

אֲנִי יהוה אֱלֹהֵיכֶם. אֱמֶת

I am HASHEM *your God. It is true . . .*

יהוה אֱלֹהֵיכֶם אֱמֶת. — *Chazzan repeats*

■ First blessing following *Shema*: Our national deliverance in the past, exemplified by the Egyptian Exodus, serves as a source of trust in God in difficult times, strengthening our faith and commitment in the future Redemption.

VE-EMUNO kol zōs,

וֶאֱמוּנָה כָּל זֹאת,

v'ka-yom olaynu,

וְקַיָּם עָלֵינוּ,

. . . and faithful is all this, and it is firmly established for us

ki hu Adōnoy Elōhaynu

כִּי הוּא יהוה אֱלֹהֵינוּ

that He is HASHEM *our God,*

v'ayn zulosō,

וְאֵין זוּלָתוֹ,

and there is none but Him,

va-anachnu yisro-ayl amō.

וַאֲנַחְנוּ יִשְׂרָאֵל עַמּוֹ.

and we are Israel, His people.

Hapōdaynu mi-yad m'lochim,

הַפּוֹדֵנוּ מִיַּד מְלָכִים,

He redeems us from the power of kings,

malkaynu hagō-alaynu
mikaf kol he-oritzim,

מַלְכֵּנוּ הַגּוֹאֲלֵנוּ
מִכַּף כָּל הֶעָרִיצִים,

our King Who delivers us from the hand of all the cruel tyrants;

ho-Ayl hanifro lonu mitzoraynu,

הָאֵל הַנִּפְרָע לָנוּ מִצָּרֵינוּ,

the God Who exacts vengeance for us from our foes

v'ham'shalaym g'mul
l'chol ōy'vay nafshaynu,

וְהַמְשַׁלֵּם גְּמוּל
לְכָל אֹיְבֵי נַפְשֵׁנוּ,

and Who brings just retribution upon all enemies of our soul;

ho-ō-se g'dōlōs ad ayn chayker,

הָעֹשֶׂה גְדֹלוֹת עַד אֵין חֵקֶר,

He performs great deeds that are beyond comprehension,*

v'niflo-ōs ad ayn mispor,

וְנִפְלָאוֹת עַד אֵין מִסְפָּר,

and wonders beyond number;

hasom nafshaynu ba-cha-yim,

הַשָּׂם נַפְשֵׁנוּ בַּחַיִּים,

He set our soul in life

v'lō nosan lamōt raglaynu,

וְלֹא נָתַן לַמּוֹט רַגְלֵנוּ,

and did not allow our foot to falter;

גְדֹלוֹת עַד אֵין חֵקֶר — *Great deeds that are beyond comprehension.* If our entire solar system were to disappear, the loss would hardly be noticed in the vastness of the universe that God created.

hamad-richaynu al bomōs ōy'vaynu,   הַמַּדְרִיכֵנוּ עַל בָּמוֹת אוֹיְבֵינוּ,
He led us upon the heights of our enemies

va-yorem karnaynu al kol sōn'aynu,   וַיָּרֶם קַרְנֵנוּ עַל כָּל שׂוֹנְאֵינוּ,
and raised our pride above all who hate us;

ho-ōse lonu   הָעֹשֶׂה לָנוּ
nisim un-komō b'faro,   נִסִּים וּנְקָמָה בְּפַרְעֹה,
He wrought for us miracles and vengeance upon Pharaoh,

ōsōs u-mōf'sim   אוֹתוֹת וּמוֹפְתִים
b'admas b'nay chom,   בְּאַדְמַת בְּנֵי חָם,
signs and wonders on the land of the offspring of Ham;

hama-ke v'evrosō   הַמַּכֶּה בְעֶבְרָתוֹ
kol b'chōray mitzroyim,   כָּל בְּכוֹרֵי מִצְרָיִם,
He struck with His anger all the firstborn of Egypt

va-yōtzay es amō yisro-ayl   וַיּוֹצֵא אֶת עַמּוֹ יִשְׂרָאֵל
mitōchom,   מִתּוֹכָם,
and removed His people Israel from their midst

l'chayrus ōlom,   לְחֵרוּת עוֹלָם,
to everlasting freedom;

hama-avir bonov   הַמַּעֲבִיר בָּנָיו
bayn gizray yam suf,   בֵּין גִּזְרֵי יַם סוּף,
He brought His children through the split parts of the Sea of Reeds

es rōd'fayhem v'es sōn'ayhem,   אֶת רוֹדְפֵיהֶם וְאֶת שׂוֹנְאֵיהֶם
bis-hōmōs tiba.   בִּתְהוֹמוֹת טִבַּע.
while their pursuers and their enemies He caused to sink into the depths.

V'ro-u vonov g'vurosō,   וְרָאוּ בָנָיו גְּבוּרָתוֹ,
When His children perceived His power,

shib'chu v'hōdu lishmō,   שִׁבְּחוּ וְהוֹדוּ לִשְׁמוֹ,
they lauded and gave grateful praise to His Name;

u-malchusō v'rotzōn   ✧ וּמַלְכוּתוֹ בְּרָצוֹן
kib'lu alayhem.   קִבְּלוּ עֲלֵיהֶם.
and His Kingship they willingly accepted upon themselves.

Mōshe uvnay yisro-ayl   מֹשֶׁה וּבְנֵי יִשְׂרָאֵל
l'cho onu shiro,   לְךָ עָנוּ שִׁירָה,
Moses and the Children of Israel exclaimed to You in song,

b'simcho rabo,   בְּשִׂמְחָה רַבָּה,
with abundant gladness —

v'om'ru chulom: וְאָמְרוּ כֻלָּם:
and they said unanimously:

MI chomōcho bo-aylim Adōnoy,
מִי כָמְׄכָה בָּאֵלִם יהוה,
Who is like You among the heavenly powers, HASHEM!

mi komōcho nedor bakōdesh,
מִי כָּמְׄכָה נֶאְדָּר בַּקֹּֽדֶשׁ,
Who is like You, mighty in holiness,

nōro s'hilōs, ōsay fele.
נוֹרָא תְהִלֹת עֹֽשֵׂה פֶֽלֶא.
too awesome for praise,* doing wonders!

❖ Malchus'cho ro-u vonecho
❖ מַלְכוּתְׄךָ רָאוּ בָנֶֽיךָ
Your children beheld Your majesty,

bōkay-a yom lifnay mōshe,
בּוֹקֵֽעַ יָם לִפְנֵי מֹשֶׁה,
as You split the sea before Moses,

zeh Ayli onu v'om'ru:
זֶה אֵלִי עָנוּ וְאָמְֽרוּ:
"This is my God!" they exclaimed, then they said:

ADŌNOY yimlōch l'ōlom vo-ed.
יהוה יִמְלֹךְ לְעוֹלָם וָעֶד.
"HASHEM shall reign for all eternity!"

❖ V'ne-emar:
❖ וְנֶאֱמַר:

Ki fodo Adōnoy es ya-akōv,
כִּי פָדָה יהוה אֶת יַעֲקֹב,
And it is further said: "For HASHEM has redeemed Jacob

ug-olō mi-yad chozok mimenu.
וּגְאָלוֹ מִיַּד חָזָק מִמֶּֽנּוּ.
and delivered him from a power mightier than he."

Boruch ato Adōnoy,
בָּרוּךְ אַתָּה יהוה,
go-al yisro-ayl.
גָּאַל יִשְׂרָאֵל.
Blessed are You, HASHEM, Who redeemed Israel.

CONGREGATION RESPONDS: Omayn — אָמֵן

■ Second blessing following *Shema:* We have complete trust in the protection that God grants us always. We request that He assist us to utilize the tranquility of the night for personal resolutions and to plan for a better tomorrow.

HASHKIVAYNU Adōnoy Elōhaynu
l'sholōm,
הַשְׁכִּיבֵֽנוּ יהוה אֱלֹהֵֽינוּ לְשָׁלוֹם,
Lay us down to sleep,* HASHEM, our God, in peace,

v'ha-amidaynu malkaynu l'cha-yim,
וְהַעֲמִידֵֽנוּ מַלְכֵּֽנוּ לְחַיִּים,
raise us erect, our King, to life;

ufrōs olaynu sukas sh'lōmecho,
וּפְרוֹשׂ עָלֵֽינוּ סֻכַּת שְׁלוֹמֶֽךָ,
spread over us the shelter of Your peace;

נוֹרָא תְהִלֹת — *Too awesome for praise.* It is impossible for people to praise God adequately; the only way to laud Him is by simply recounting His awe-inspiring deeds.

הַשְׁכִּיבֵֽנוּ — *Lay us down to sleep.* The Talmud (*Berachos* 4a) describes this blessing as an extension of the previous blessing of redemption. It describes God as our Savior from the dangers

v'sak'naynu
  b'aytzo tōvo mil'fonecho, וְתַקְּנֵנוּ בְּעֵצָה טוֹבָה מִלְּפָנֶיךָ,

set us aright with good counsel* from before Your Presence;

v'hōshi-aynu l'ma-an sh'mecho. וְהוֹשִׁיעֵנוּ לְמַעַן שְׁמֶךָ.

and save us for Your Name's sake.

V'hogayn ba-adaynu, וְהָגֵן בַּעֲדֵנוּ,

Shield us,

v'hosayr may-olaynu ōyayv, וְהָסֵר מֵעָלֵינוּ אוֹיֵב,

  dever v'cherev v'ro-ov v'yogōn, דֶּבֶר, וְחֶרֶב, וְרָעָב, וְיָגוֹן,

remove from us foe, plague, sword, famine, and woe;

v'hosayr soton mil'fonaynu וְהָסֵר שָׂטָן מִלְּפָנֵינוּ

  u-may-acharaynu, וּמֵאַחֲרֵינוּ,

and remove spiritual impediment from before us and from behind us,

uvtzayl k'nofecho tastiraynu, וּבְצֵל כְּנָפֶיךָ תַּסְתִּירֵנוּ,

and in the shadow of Your wings* shelter us —

ki Ayl shōm'raynu כִּי אֵל שׁוֹמְרֵנוּ

  u-matzilaynu oto, וּמַצִּילֵנוּ אָתָּה,

for God Who protects and rescues us are You;

ki Ayl melech chanun כִּי אֵל מֶלֶךְ חַנּוּן

  v'rachum oto. וְרַחוּם אָתָּה.

for God, the Gracious and Compassionate King, are You.

❖ Ushmōr tzaysaynu u-vō-aynu, וּשְׁמוֹר צֵאתֵנוּ וּבוֹאֵנוּ,

Safeguard our going and coming,

l'cha-yim ulsholōm לְחַיִּים וּלְשָׁלוֹם

for life and for peace,

mayato v'ad ōlom, מֵעַתָּה וְעַד עוֹלָם,

from now to eternity.

ufrōs olaynu sukas sh'lōmecho. וּפְרוֹשׂ עָלֵינוּ סֻכַּת שְׁלוֹמֶךָ.

Spread over us the shelter of Your peace.

Boruch atoh Adōnoy, בָּרוּךְ אַתָּה יהוה,

Blessed are You, Hashem,

hapōrays sukas sholōm olaynu, הַפּוֹרֵשׂ סֻכַּת שָׁלוֹם עָלֵינוּ

Who spreads the shelter of peace upon us,

---

and afflictions associated with the terrors of night, literally and figuratively.

וְתַקְּנֵנוּ בְּעֵצָה טוֹבָה — *Set us aright with good counsel.* Help us plan well at night for the activity of the next day, and let the relaxation

of the night give us a clearer perspective for the deliberations of the day.

וּבְצֵל כְּנָפֶיךָ — *And in the shadow of Your wings.* Psalms (91:4) liken God's protection to the wings of a bird sheltering her young.

v'al kol amō yisro-ayl,
וְעַל כָּל עַמּוֹ יִשְׂרָאֵל

v'al y'rusholo-yim.
וְעַל יְרוּשָׁלָיִם.

and upon all His people Israel, and upon Jerusalem.

CONGREGATION RESPONDS: Omayn — אָמֵן

ON THE SABBATH, THE CONGREGATION, FOLLOWED BY THE *CHAZZAN*, RECITES:

■ The Jewish people exclusively are invited to contribute
to the observance and character of the Shabbos day.

V'SHOM'RU v'nay yisro-ayl
וְשָׁמְרוּ בְנֵי יִשְׂרָאֵל

es ha-shabos,
אֶת הַשַּׁבָּת,

And the Children of Israel shall keep the Sabbath,

la-asōs es ha-shabos l'dōrōsom
לַעֲשׂוֹת אֶת הַשַּׁבָּת לְדֹרֹתָם

b'ris ōlom.
בְּרִית עוֹלָם.

to make the Sabbath* for their generations an eternal covenant.

Bayni uvayn b'nay yisro-ayl
בֵּינִי וּבֵין בְּנֵי יִשְׂרָאֵל

Between Me and the Children of Israel*

ōs hi l'ōlom,
אוֹת הִיא לְעֹלָם,

it is a sign forever

ki shayshes yomim
כִּי שֵׁשֶׁת יָמִים

that in six days

oso Adōnoy
עָשָׂה יהוה

es hashoma-yim v'es ho-oretz,
אֶת הַשָּׁמַיִם וְאֶת הָאָרֶץ,

HASHEM has made the heavens and the earth,

uva-yōm hash'vi-i shovas va-yinofash.
וּבַיּוֹם הַשְּׁבִיעִי שָׁבַת וַיִּנָּפַשׁ.

and on the seventh day He rested and was refreshed.

ON PESACH, SHAVUOS, AND SUCCOS, EXCEPT ON *CHOL HAMOED,*
THE CONGREGATION, FOLLOWED BY THE *CHAZZAN*, RECITES:

VAIDABAYR mōshe
וַיְדַבֵּר מֹשֶׁה

And Moses declared

es mō-aday Adōnoy
אֶת מוֹעֲדֵי יהוה

HASHEM's appointed Festivals

el b'nay yisro-ayl.
אֶל בְּנֵי יִשְׂרָאֵל.

to the Children of Israel.

לַעֲשׂוֹת אֶת הַשַּׁבָּת — *To make the Sabbath.* Each generation must "make" the Sabbath, by teaching its importance and holiness to those who are lax in sanctifying it because they fail to appreciate its importance.

בֵּינִי וּבֵין בְּנֵי יִשְׂרָאֵל — *Between Me and the*

Children of Israel. Only Israel is commanded to observe the Sabbath, thereby bearing witness to God's creation of heaven and earth in six days. Consequently, the Sabbath is a *sign* of God's special relationship with Israel.

ON AN ORDINARY SABBATH AND ON THE SABBATH OF *CHOL HAMOED*
CONTINUE WITH THE SABBATH *SHEMONEH ESREI* BELOW.
ON FESTIVALS, EVEN THOSE THAT FALL ON THE SABBATH,
THE FESTIVAL *SHEMONEH ESREI* (P. 675) IS RECITED.

ᛜ **SHEMONEH ESREI FOR THE SABBATH** ᛜ

IN THE SYNAGOGUE THE *SHEMONEH ESREI* IS RECITED WHILE FACING THE ARK; ELSEWHERE IT IS
RECITED WHILE FACING THE DIRECTION OF THE LAND OF ISRAEL. TAKE THREE STEPS BACKWARD,
LEFT, RIGHT, LEFT, THEN THREE STEPS FORWARD, RIGHT, LEFT, RIGHT. REMAIN STANDING WITH
FEET TOGETHER DURING *SHEMONEH ESREI*. RECITE IT WITH QUIET DEVOTION AND WITHOUT ANY
INTERRUPTION. ALTHOUGH IT SHOULD NOT BE AUDIBLE TO OTHERS, ONE MUST PRAY LOUDLY
ENOUGH TO HEAR ONESELF.

Adōnoy s'fosai tiftoch, אֲדֹנָי שְׂפָתַי תִּפְתָּח,

My Lord, open my lips,

U-fi yagid t'hilosecho. וּפִי יַגִּיד תְּהִלָּתֶךָ.

that my mouth may declare Your praise.

■ First Blessing: In the merit of our Patriarchs whose actions reflected Godliness, Hashem pledged to always be with Israel and protect them.

BEND THE KNEES AT Boruch; BOW AT ato; STRAIGHTEN UP AT Adōnoy.

BORUCH ato Adōnoy בָּרוּךְ אַתָּה יהוה

Blessed are You, HASHEM,

Elōhaynu Vaylōhay avōsaynu, אֱלֹהֵינוּ וֵאלֹהֵי אֲבוֹתֵינוּ,

our God and the God of our forefathers,

Elōhay avrohom, Elōhay yitzchok, אֱלֹהֵי אַבְרָהָם, אֱלֹהֵי יִצְחָק,
Vaylōhay ya-akōv, וֵאלֹהֵי יַעֲקֹב,

God of Abraham, God of Isaac, and God of Jacob;

ho-Ayl hagodōl hagibōr v'hanōro, הָאֵל הַגָּדוֹל הַגִּבּוֹר וְהַנּוֹרָא,
Ayl elyōn, אֵל עֶלְיוֹן,

the great, mighty, and awesome God, the supreme God,

gōmayl chasodim tōvim גּוֹמֵל חֲסָדִים טוֹבִים
v'kōnay hakōl, וְקוֹנֵה הַכֹּל,

Who bestows beneficial kindnesses and creates everything,

v'zōchayr chasday ovōs, וְזוֹכֵר חַסְדֵי אָבוֹת,

Who recalls the kindnesses of the Patriarchs

u-mayvi gō-ayl livnay v'nayhem, וּמֵבִיא גוֹאֵל לִבְנֵי בְנֵיהֶם,

and brings a Redeemer to their children's children,

l'ma-an sh'mō b'ahavo. לְמַעַן שְׁמוֹ בְּאַהֲבָה.

for His Name's sake, with love.

ᥱᥱ **Shemoneh Esrei/Amidah of Shabbos**
  Technically, the name *Shemoneh Esrei* [lit., eighteen] refers to the weekday prayer which originally contained eighteen blessings. It is a misnomer for the seven-blessing Sabbath prayer, which should correctly be called the *Amidah* [Standing Prayer]. Nevertheless, both names are commonly used interchangeably,

Zochraynu l'cha-yim,   זָכְרֵנוּ לְחַיִּים,

melech chofaytz bacha-yim,   מֶלֶךְ חָפֵץ בַּחַיִּים,

Remember us for life, O King Who desires life,

v'chosvaynu b'sayfer hacha-yim,   וְכָתְבֵנוּ בְּסֵפֶר הַחַיִּים,

l'ma-ancho Elōhim cha-yim.   לְמַעַנְךָ אֱלֹהִים חַיִּים.

and inscribe us in the Book of Life — for Your sake, O Living God.

Melech ōzayr u-mōshi-a u-mogayn.   מֶלֶךְ עוֹזֵר וּמוֹשִׁיעַ וּמָגֵן.

O King, Helper, Savior, and Shield.

BEND THE KNEES AT Boruch; BOW AT ato; STRAIGHTEN UP AT Adōnoy.

Boruch ato Adōnoy,   בָּרוּךְ אַתָּה יהוה,

mogayn avrohom.   מָגֵן אַבְרָהָם.

Blessed are You, HASHEM, Shield of Abraham.

■ Second Blessing: God's might as it is manifest in nature and man

ATO gibōr l'ōlom Adōnoy,   **אַתָּה** גִּבּוֹר לְעוֹלָם אֲדֹנָי,

You are eternally mighty, my Lord,

m'cha-yay maysim ato,   מְחַיֵּה מֵתִים אַתָּה,

the Resuscitator of the dead are You;

rav l'hōshi-a.   רַב לְהוֹשִׁיעַ.

abundantly able to save,

BETWEEN SHEMINI ATZERES AND PESACH, ADD:

Mashiv horu-ach umōrid hageshem.   מַשִּׁיב הָרוּחַ וּמוֹרִיד הַגֵּשֶׁם.

Who makes the wind blow and makes the rain descend;

M'chalkayl cha-yim b'chesed,   מְכַלְכֵּל חַיִּים בְּחֶסֶד,

Who sustains the living with kindness,

m'cha-yay maysim b'rachamim rabim,   מְחַיֵּה מֵתִים בְּרַחֲמִים רַבִּים,

resuscitates the dead with abundant mercy,

sōmaych nōf'lim, v'rōfay chōlim,   סוֹמֵךְ נוֹפְלִים, וְרוֹפֵא חוֹלִים,

supports the fallen, heals the sick,

u-matir asurim,   וּמַתִּיר אֲסוּרִים,

releases the confined,

---

and we follow the popular practice in this *Siddur*, as well. The first and last three blessings are the same for all versions of *Shemoneh Esrei*. The first three are discussed on pages 34-37 above; the last three on pages 46-55.

The *Shemoneh Esrei* of the Sabbath and *Yom Tov* should have been identical to the weekday one, with the inclusion of an appropriate paragraph indicating the holiness of the day, as is done on *Rosh Chodesh*, Chanukah, Purim and *Chol HaMoed*. The Sages, however, wished to make the Sabbath Festival prayers simpler and less burdensome than they would be if we had to beseech God for the entire

umka-yaym emunosō li-shaynay ofor.　　　וּמְקַיֵּם אֱמוּנָתוֹ לִישֵׁנֵי עָפָר.

and maintains His faith to those asleep in the dust.

Mi cho-mōcho ba-al g'vurōs,　　　מִי כָמְוֹךָ בַּעַל גְּבוּרוֹת,

Who is like You, O Master of mighty deeds,

u-mi dōme loch,　　　וּמִי דְוֹמֶה לָךְ,

and who is comparable to You,

melech maymis umcha-ye　　　מֶלֶךְ מֵמִית וּמְחַיֶּה

u-matzmi-ach y'shu-o.　　　וּמַצְמִיחַ יְשׁוּעָה.

O King Who causes death and restores life and makes salvation sprout!

FROM ROSH HASHANAH TO YOM KIPPUR ADD:

Mi cho-mōcho av horachamim,　　　מִי כָמְוֹךָ אַב הָרַחֲמִים,

Who is like You, O Merciful Father,

zōchayr y'tzurov l'cha-yim　　　זוֹכֵר יְצוּרָיו לְחַיִּים

b'rachamim.　　　בְּרַחֲמִים.

Who recalls His creatures mercifully for life!

V'ne-emon ato l'hacha-yōs maysim.　　　וְנֶאֱמָן אַתָּה לְהַחֲיוֹת מֵתִים.

And You are faithful to resuscitate the dead.

Boruch ato Adōnoy,　　　בָּרוּךְ אַתָּה יהוה,

m'cha-yay hamaysim.　　　מְחַיֵּה הַמֵּתִים.

Blessed are You, HASHEM, Who resuscitates the dead.

■ Third Blessing: Regarding the holiness of God's Name

ATO kodōsh v'shimcho kodōsh,　　　אַתָּה קָדוֹשׁ וְשִׁמְךָ קָדוֹשׁ,

You are holy and Your Name is holy,

ukdōshim b'chol yōm　　　וּקְדוֹשִׁים בְּכָל יוֹם

y'hal'lucho, selo.　　　יְהַלְלוּךָ סֶלָה.

and holy ones praise You, every day, forever.

Boruch ato Adōnoy,　　　בָּרוּךְ אַתָּה יהוה,

°ho-Ayl hakodōsh.　　　°הָאֵל הַקָּדוֹשׁ.

Blessed are You, HASHEM, the holy God.

FROM ROSH HASHANAH TO YOM KIPPUR SUBSTITUTE:

°hamelech hakodōsh.　　　°הַמֶּלֶךְ הַקָּדוֹשׁ.

the holy King.

---

catalogue of our personal and national needs. Therefore they replaced the middle thirteen blessings, which are all requests, with a single blessing known as "Sanctity of the Day" (*Berachos* 21a). Moreover, as the Midrash explains, the thirteen middle blessings which deal with human concerns and needs are not appropriate for the Sabbath, the sacred day on which we turn from ordinary preoccupations and occupy ourselves with spiritual values and priorities.

■ **Fourth blessing, relating to the holiness of the day:**
Shabbos is the ultimate purpose of Creation.

ATO kidashto
אַתָּה קִדַּשְׁתָּ

es yōm hash'vi-i lishmecho,
אֶת יוֹם הַשְּׁבִיעִי לִשְׁמֶךָ,

You sanctified the seventh day for Your Name's sake, *

tachlis ma-asay shoma-yim vo-oretz,
תַּכְלִית מַעֲשֵׂה שָׁמַיִם וָאָרֶץ,

the conclusion* of the creation of heaven and earth.

uvayrachtō mikol ha-yomim,
וּבֵרַכְתּוֹ מִכָּל הַיָּמִים,

You blessed it of all days,

v'kidashtō mikol haz'manim,
וְקִדַּשְׁתּוֹ מִכָּל הַזְּמַנִּים,

and You sanctified it of all seasons,

v'chayn kosuv bsōrosecho.
וְכֵן כָּתוּב בְּתוֹרָתֶךָ.

and so it is written in Your Torah:

■ **I offer testimony that the purpose of Hashem's creating**
the world in six days was for man to rest on the Shabbos.

VAICHULU ha-shoma-yim v'ho-oretz
וַיְכֻלּוּ הַשָּׁמַיִם וְהָאָרֶץ

Thus the heavens and the earth were finished,

v'chol tz'vo-om.
וְכָל צְבָאָם.

and all their legion.

Vaichal Elōhim ba-yōm hash'vi-i
וַיְכַל אֱלֹהִים בַּיּוֹם הַשְּׁבִיעִי

On the seventh day God completed

m'lachtō asher oso,
מְלַאכְתּוֹ אֲשֶׁר עָשָׂה,

His work which He had done,

va-yishbōs ba-yōm hash'vi-i
וַיִּשְׁבֹּת בַּיּוֹם הַשְּׁבִיעִי

and He abstained* on the seventh day

mikol m'lachtō asher oso.
מִכָּל מְלַאכְתּוֹ אֲשֶׁר עָשָׂה.

from all His work which He had done.

אַתָּה קִדַּשְׁתָּ ... לִשְׁמֶךָ — *You sanctified ... for Your Name's sake.* God sanctified the Sabbath as an eternal reminder that He rested on that day; and He made it clear that we are not to regard it as a humanly legislated day of rest for personal convenience. Rather, we are to dedicate it to His service.

תַּכְלִית — *The conclusion.* God's six days of labor ended on the Sabbath. The word תַּכְלִית has its secondary meaning of *purpose:* The purpose of Creation was so that God could allow people to enjoy the spiritual pleasure of His Presence. That will occur in its fullest sense only when the Messiah arrives; that era will be known as an unending Sabbath, because its holiness will

be unlimited. Meanwhile, however, a taste of the spiritual bliss of the future is given Israel every week with the advent of the holy Sabbath. Accordingly, it is only on the Sabbath that Creation achieves its purpose.

וַיְכַל ... וַיִּשְׁבֹּת — *Completed ... and He abstained.* These two words have different connotations. "He completed" means that the task at hand was finished; "He abstained" implies that more was to be done, but it was set aside for another day. The Torah uses both words to teach people that even though they are still in the middle of their work, when the Sabbath arrives they should consider it completed and not think about it.

Vaiyvorech Elōhim
  es yōm hash'vi-i,
God blessed the seventh day

וַיְבָרֶךְ אֱלֹהִים
אֶת יוֹם הַשְּׁבִיעִי,

vaikadaysh ōsō,
and sanctified it,

וַיְקַדֵּשׁ אֹתוֹ,

ki vō shovas mikol m'lachtō,
because on it He had abstained from all His work

כִּי בוֹ שָׁבַת מִכָּל מְלַאכְתּוֹ,

asher boro Elōhim la-asōs.
which God created to make.

אֲשֶׁר בָּרָא אֱלֹהִים לַעֲשׂוֹת.

■ I affirm that the sanctity of Shabbos emanates from Hashem,
and I petition that the holiness of the day influence my life.

ELŌHAYNU Vaylōhay avōsaynu
Our God and the God of our forefathers,

אֱלֹהֵינוּ וֵאלֹהֵי אֲבוֹתֵינוּ

r'tzay vimnuchosaynu.
may You be pleased with our rest.*

רְצֵה בִמְנוּחָתֵנוּ.

Kad'shaynu b'mitzvōsecho,
Sanctify us with Your commandments

קַדְּשֵׁנוּ בְּמִצְוֹתֶיךָ,

v'sayn chelkaynu b'sōrosecho,
and grant us our share in Your Torah;

וְתֵן חֶלְקֵנוּ בְּתוֹרָתֶךָ,

sab'aynu mituvecho,
satisfy us from Your goodness

שַׂבְּעֵנוּ מִטּוּבֶךָ,

v'sam'chaynu bi-shu-osecho,
and gladden us with Your salvation,

וְשַׂמְּחֵנוּ בִּישׁוּעָתֶךָ,

v'tahayr libaynu l'ovd'cho be-emes.
and purify our heart* to serve You sincerely.

וְטַהֵר לִבֵּנוּ לְעָבְדְּךָ בֶּאֱמֶת.

V'hanchilaynu Adōnoy Elōhaynu
O HASHEM, our God, grant us as a heritage

וְהַנְחִילֵנוּ יהוה אֱלֹהֵינוּ

b'ahavo uvrotzōn
with love and favor,

בְּאַהֲבָה וּבְרָצוֹן

shabas kodshecho,
Your holy Sabbath

שַׁבַּת קָדְשֶׁךָ,

v'yonuchu voh
  yisro-ayl m'kad'shay sh'mecho.
and may Israel, the sanctifiers of Your Name, rest on it.

וְיָנוּחוּ בָהּ
יִשְׂרָאֵל מְקַדְּשֵׁי שְׁמֶךָ.

אֱלֹהֵינוּ . . . רְצֵה בִמְנוּחָתֵנוּ — *O God . . . may You be pleased with our rest.* Even though we may concentrate more on relaxation and good food than spiritual growth, we ask that You not be displeased by our human frailty.

וְטַהֵר לִבֵּנוּ — *And purify our heart.* The Talmud assures us that "If one comes to purify himself, Heaven helps him" (*Yoma* 38b). Therefore, we are justified in asking God to help us purify ourselves to serve Him better.

Boruch ato Adōnoy,
m'kadaysh hashabos.

בָּרוּךְ אַתָּה יהוה,
מְקַדֵּשׁ הַשַּׁבָּת.

Blessed You, HASHEM, Who sanctifies the Sabbath.

■ Fifth Blessing: Prayer fo restoration of the Temple service

R'TZAYH, Adōnoy Elōhaynu

רְצֵה יהוה אֱלֹהֵינוּ

Be favorable, HASHEM, our God,

b'am'cho yisro-ayl uvisfilosom,

בְּעַמְּךָ יִשְׂרָאֵל וּבִתְפִלָּתָם,

toward Your people Israel and their prayer

v'hoshayv es ho-avōdo
lidvir bay-secho.

וְהָשֵׁב אֶת הָעֲבוֹדָה
לִדְבִיר בֵּיתֶךָ.

and restore the service to the Holy of Holies of Your Temple.

V'ishay yisro-ayl, usfilosom
b'ahavo s'kabayl b'rotzōn,

וְאִשֵּׁי יִשְׂרָאֵל וּתְפִלָּתָם
בְּאַהֲבָה תְקַבֵּל בְּרָצוֹן,

The fire-offerings of Israel and their prayer accept with love and favor,

us'hi l'rotzōn tomid
avōdas yisro-ayl amecho.

וּתְהִי לְרָצוֹן תָּמִיד
עֲבוֹדַת יִשְׂרָאֵל עַמֶּךָ.

and may the service of Your people Israel always be favorable to You.

■ Yaaleh Veyavo: We petition God to have compassion on Israel and Jerusalem,
and to reinstate the Temple service, to enable us to bring
the appropriate offerings for the particular occasion.

ON ROSH CHODESH AND CHOL HAMOED* RECITE THE FOLLOWING:

ELŌHAYNU Vaylōhay avōsaynu,

אֱלֹהֵינוּ וֵאלֹהֵי אֲבוֹתֵינוּ,

Our God and God of our forefathers,

ya-a-le v'yovō v'yagi-a v'yayro-e

יַעֲלֶה, וְיָבֹא, וְיַגִּיעַ, וְיֵרָאֶה,

may there rise, come, reach, be noted,

v'yayrotze v'yishoma v'yipokayd

וְיֵרָצֶה, וְיִשָּׁמַע, וְיִפָּקֵד,

be favored, be heard, be considered,

v'yizochayr zichrōnaynu ufikdōnaynu,

וְיִזָּכֵר זִכְרוֹנֵנוּ וּפִקְדוֹנֵנוּ,

and be remembered — the remembrance and consideration of ourselves;

v'zichrōn avōsaynu,

וְזִכְרוֹן אֲבוֹתֵינוּ,

the remembrance of our forefathers;

v'zichrōn moshi-ach
ben dovid avdecho,

וְזִכְרוֹן מָשִׁיחַ
בֶּן דָּוִד עַבְדֶּךָ,

the remembrance of Messiah, son of David, Your servant;

v'zichrōn y'rushola-yim
ir kod'shecho,

וְזִכְרוֹן יְרוּשָׁלַיִם
עִיר קָדְשֶׁךָ,

the remembrance of Jerusalem, the City; Your Holy

v'zichrōn kol am'cho bays yisro-ayl וְזִכְרוֹן כָּל עַמְּךָ בֵּית יִשְׂרָאֵל
and the remembrance of Your entire people the Family of Israel —

l'fonecho, לְפָנֶיךָ,
before You

liflayto l'tōvo לִפְלֵיטָה לְטוֹבָה
for deliverance, for goodness,

l'chayn ulchesed ulrachamim, לְחֵן וּלְחֶסֶד וּלְרַחֲמִים,
for grace, for kindness, and for compassion,

l'cha-yim ulsholōm לְחַיִּים וּלְשָׁלוֹם
for life, and for peace

─────── ON ROSH CHODESH ───────

b'yōm rōsh hachōdesh ha-ze. בְּיוֹם רֹאשׁ הַחֹדֶשׁ הַזֶּה.
on this day of Rosh Chodesh.

─────── ON PESACH ───────

b'yōm chag hamatzōs ha-ze. בְּיוֹם חַג הַמַּצּוֹת הַזֶּה.
on this day of the Festival of Matzos.

─────── ON SUCCOS ───────

b'yōm chag hasukōs ha-ze. בְּיוֹם חַג הַסֻּכּוֹת הַזֶּה.
on this day of the Succos Festival.

zoch'raynu Adōnoy Elōhaynu זָכְרֵנוּ יהוה אֱלֹהֵינוּ
  bō l'tōvo, בּוֹ לְטוֹבָה,
Remember us on it, HASHEM, our God, for goodness,

u-fok'daynu vō livrocho, וּפָקְדֵנוּ בּוֹ לִבְרָכָה,
consider us on it for blessing

v'hōshi-aynu vō l'cha-yim. וְהוֹשִׁיעֵנוּ בּוֹ לְחַיִּים.
and help us on it for life.

U-vidvar y'shu-o v'rachamim, וּבִדְבַר יְשׁוּעָה וְרַחֲמִים,
In the matter of salvation and compassion,

chus v'chonaynu חוּס וְחָנֵּנוּ
  v'rachaym olaynu v'hōshi-aynu, וְרַחֵם עָלֵינוּ וְהוֹשִׁיעֵנוּ,
pity, be gracious and compassionate with us and help us,

ki aylecho aynaynu, כִּי אֵלֶיךָ עֵינֵינוּ,
for our eyes are turned to You,

ki Ayl melech כִּי אֵל מֶלֶךְ
  chanun v'rachum oto. חַנּוּן וְרַחוּם אָתָּה.
because You are God, the gracious and compassionate King.

V'SECHEZENO aynaynu   וְתֶחֱזֶינָה עֵינֵינוּ
May our eyes behold

b'shuv'cho l'tziyōn b'rachamim.   בְּשׁוּבְךָ לְצִיּוֹן בְּרַחֲמִים.
Your return to Zion in compassion.

Boruch ato Adōnoy,   בָּרוּךְ אַתָּה יהוה,
    hamachazir sh'chinosō l'tziyōn.   הַמַּחֲזִיר שְׁכִינָתוֹ לְצִיּוֹן.
Blessed are You, HASHEM, Who restores His Presence unto Zion.

■ Sixth Blessing: Acknowledgment of our debt of gratitude

BOW AT Mōdim anachnu loch; STRAIGHTEN UP AT Adōnoy.

MŌDIM anachnu loch,   מוֹדִים אֲנַחְנוּ לָךְ,
We gratefully thank You,

sho-ato hu Adōnoy Elōhaynu   שָׁאַתָּה הוּא יהוה אֱלֹהֵינוּ
for it is You Who are HASHEM, our God,

Vaylōhay avōsaynu   וֵאלֹהֵי אֲבוֹתֵינוּ
and the God of our forefathers

l'ōlom vo-ed,   לְעוֹלָם וָעֶד,
forever and ever;

tzur cha-yaynu, mogayn yish-aynu   צוּר חַיֵּינוּ, מָגֵן יִשְׁעֵנוּ
Rock of our lives, Shield of our salvation

ato hu l'dōr vodōr.   אַתָּה הוּא לְדוֹר וָדוֹר.
are You from generation to generation.

Nō-de l'cho unsapayr t'hilosecho   נוֹדֶה לְּךָ וּנְסַפֵּר תְּהִלָּתֶךָ
We shall thank You and relate Your praise —

al cha-yaynu ham'surim b'yodecho,   עַל חַיֵּינוּ הַמְּסוּרִים בְּיָדֶךָ,
for our lives, which are committed to Your power,

v'al nishmōsaynu hap'kudōs loch,   וְעַל נִשְׁמוֹתֵינוּ הַפְּקוּדוֹת לָךְ,
and for our souls that are entrusted to You,

v'al nisecho sheb'chol yōm i-monu,   וְעַל נִסֶּיךָ שֶׁבְּכָל יוֹם עִמָּנוּ,
and for Your miracles that are with us every day,

v'al nifl'ōsecho v'tōvōsecho   וְעַל נִפְלְאוֹתֶיךָ וְטוֹבוֹתֶיךָ
    sheb'chol ays,   שֶׁבְּכָל עֵת,
and for Your wonders and favors in every season —

erev vovōker v'tzohoro-yim.   עֶרֶב וָבְקֶר וְצָהֳרָיִם.
evening, morning, and afternoon.

Hatōv ki lō cholu rachamecho,   הַטּוֹב כִּי לֹא כָלוּ רַחֲמֶיךָ,
The Beneficent One, for Your compassions were never exhausted,

v'ham'rachaym ki lō samu chasodecho, וְהַמְרַחֵם כִּי לֹא תַמּוּ חֲסָדֶיךָ,
and the Compassionate One, for Your kindnesses never ended —

may-ōlom kivinu loch. מֵעוֹלָם קִוִּינוּ לָךְ.
always have we put our hope in You.

ON CHANUKAH CONTINUE BELOW. ON ALL OTHER DAYS TURN TO P. 137.

AL hanisim, v'al hapurkon, **עַל** הַנִּסִּים, וְעַל הַפֻּרְקָן,
For the miracles, and for the salvation,

v'al hag'vurōs, v'al hat'shu-ōs, וְעַל הַגְּבוּרוֹת, וְעַל הַתְּשׁוּעוֹת,
and for the mighty deeds, and for the victories,

v'al hamilchomōs, וְעַל הַמִּלְחָמוֹת,
and for the battles

she-osiso la-avōsaynu שֶׁעָשִׂיתָ לַאֲבוֹתֵינוּ
which You performed for our forefathers

ba-yomim hohaym baz'man ha-ze. בַּיָּמִים הָהֵם בַּזְּמַן הַזֶּה.
in those days, at this time.

BIMAY matisyohu ben yōchonon **בִּימֵי** מַתִּתְיָהוּ בֶּן יוֹחָנָן
In the days of Mattisyahu, the son of Yochanan,

kōhayn godōl chashmōno-i u-vonov, כֹּהֵן גָּדוֹל חַשְׁמוֹנַאי וּבָנָיו,
the High Priest, the Hasmonean, and his sons —

k'she-om'do malchus yovon כְּשֶׁעָמְדָה מַלְכוּת יָוָן
hor'sho-o al am'cho yisro-ayl, הָרְשָׁעָה עַל עַמְּךָ יִשְׂרָאֵל,
when the wicked Greek kingdom rose up against Your people Israel

l'hashkichom tōrosecho, לְהַשְׁכִּיחָם תּוֹרָתֶךָ,
to make them forget Your Torah,

ulha-avirom maychukay r'tzōnecho, וּלְהַעֲבִירָם מֵחֻקֵּי רְצוֹנֶךָ.
and compel them to stray from the statutes of Your Will —

v'ato b'rachamecho horabim, וְאַתָּה בְּרַחֲמֶיךָ הָרַבִּים,
But You, in Your abundant mercy,

omadto lohem b'ays tzorosom, עָמַדְתָּ לָהֶם בְּעֵת צָרָתָם,
stood up for them in the time of their distress.

Ravto es rivom, danto es dinom, רַבְתָּ אֶת רִיבָם, דַּנְתָּ אֶת דִּינָם,
You took up their grievance, You judged their claim,

nokamto es nikmosom. נָקַמְתָּ אֶת נִקְמָתָם.
and You avenged their wrong.

mosarto gibōrim b'yad chaloshim, מָסַרְתָּ גִבּוֹרִים בְּיַד חַלָּשִׁים,
You delivered the strong into the hand of the weak,

v'rabim b'yad m'atim,   וְרַבִּים בְּיַד מְעַטִּים,
the many into the hand of the few,

utmay-im b'yad t'horim,   וּטְמֵאִים בְּיַד טְהוֹרִים,
the impure into the hand of the pure,

ursho-im b'yad tzadikim   וּרְשָׁעִים בְּיַד צַדִּיקִים,
the wicked into the hand of the righteous,

v'zaydim b'yad ōs'kay sōrosecho.   וְזֵדִים בְּיַד עוֹסְקֵי תוֹרָתֶךָ.
and the wanton into the hand of the diligent students of Your Torah.

Ulcho osiso   וּלְךָ עָשִׂיתָ
For Yourself You made

shaym godōl v'kodōsh b'ōlomecho,   שֵׁם גָּדוֹל וְקָדוֹשׁ בְּעוֹלָמֶךָ,
a great and holy Name in Your world,

ul-am'cho yisro-ayl   וּלְעַמְּךָ יִשְׂרָאֵל
and for Your people Israel

osiso t'shu-o g'dōlo u-furkon   עָשִׂיתָ תְּשׁוּעָה גְדוֹלָה וּפֻרְקָן
You performed a great victory and salvation

k'ha-yōm ha-ze.   כְּהַיּוֹם הַזֶּה.
as this very day.

V'achar kayn bo-u vonecho   וְאַחַר כֵּן בָּאוּ בָנֶיךָ
    lidvir bay-secho,   לִדְבִיר בֵּיתֶךָ,
Thereafter, Your children came to the Holy of Holies of Your House,

u-finu es haycholecho,   וּפִנּוּ אֶת הֵיכָלֶךָ,
they cleansed Your Temple,

v'tiharu es mikdoshecho,   וְטִהֲרוּ אֶת מִקְדָּשֶׁךָ,
they purified the site of Your Holiness;

v'hidliku nayrōs   וְהִדְלִיקוּ נֵרוֹת
and they kindled lights

b'chatzrōs kod-shecho,   בְּחַצְרוֹת קָדְשֶׁךָ,
in the Courtyards of Your Sanctuary;

v'kov'u   וְקָבְעוּ
    sh'mōnas y'may chanuko aylu,   שְׁמוֹנַת יְמֵי חֲנֻכָּה אֵלּוּ,
and they established these eight days of Chanukah

l'hōdōs ulhalayl   לְהוֹדוֹת וּלְהַלֵּל
    l'shimcho hagodōl.   לְשִׁמְךָ הַגָּדוֹל.
to express thanks and praise to Your great Name.

V'AL kulom yisborach v'yisrōmam
shimcho, malkaynu

וְעַל כֻּלָּם יִתְבָּרַךְ וְיִתְרוֹמַם
שִׁמְךָ מַלְכֵּנוּ

For all these, may Your Name be blessed and exalted, our King,

tomid l'ōlom vo-ed.

תָּמִיד לְעוֹלָם וָעֶד.

continually forever and ever.

FROM ROSH HASHANAH TO YOM KIPPUR ADD:

Uchsōv l'cha-yim tōvim
kol b'nay v'risecho.

וּכְתוֹב לְחַיִּים טוֹבִים
כָּל בְּנֵי בְרִיתֶךָ.

And inscribe all the children of Your covenant for a good life.

V'chōl hacha-yim yōducho selo,

וְכֹל הַחַיִּים יוֹדוּךָ סֶּלָה,

Everything alive will gratefully acknowledge You, Selah!

vihal'lu es shimcho be-emes,

וִיהַלְלוּ אֶת שִׁמְךָ בֶּאֱמֶת,

and praise Your Name sincerely,

ho-Ayl y'shu-osaynu
v'ezrosaynu selo.

הָאֵל יְשׁוּעָתֵנוּ
וְעֶזְרָתֵנוּ סֶּלָה.

O God of our salvation and help, Selah!

BEND THE KNEES AT Boruch; BOW AT ato; STRAIGHTEN UP AT Adōnoy.

Boruch ato Adōnoy,
hatōv shimcho
ulcho no-e l'hōdōs.

בָּרוּךְ אַתָּה יהוה,
הַטּוֹב שִׁמְךָ
וּלְךָ נָאֶה לְהוֹדוֹת.

*Blessed are You, HASHEM, Your Name is "The Beneficent One"
and to You it is fitting to give thanks.*

■ Seventh Blessing: Prayer for peace and harmony
amongst the Jewish people

SHOLŌM ROV al yisro-ayl
am'cho tosim l'ōlom,

שָׁלוֹם רָב עַל יִשְׂרָאֵל
עַמְּךָ תָּשִׂים לְעוֹלָם,

Establish abundant peace upon Your people Israel forever,

ki ato hu melech,
odōn l'chol ha-sholōm.

כִּי אַתָּה הוּא מֶלֶךְ
אָדוֹן לְכָל הַשָּׁלוֹם.

for You are King, Master of all peace.

V'tōv b'aynecho l'voraych
es am'cho yisro-ayl,

וְטוֹב בְּעֵינֶיךָ לְבָרֵךְ
אֶת עַמְּךָ יִשְׂרָאֵל,

And may it be good in Your eyes to bless Your people Israel

b'chol ays uvchol sho-o bish-lōmecho.

בְּכָל עֵת וּבְכָל שָׁעָה בִּשְׁלוֹמֶךָ.

at every time and at every hour, with Your peace.

°Boruch ato Adōnoy,
　　ham'voraych es amō yisro-ayl
　　ba-sholōm.

°בָּרוּךְ אַתָּה יהוה,
הַמְבָרֵךְ אֶת עַמּוֹ יִשְׂרָאֵל
בַּשָּׁלוֹם.

°*Blessed are You, HASHEM, Who blesses His people Israel with peace.*

° FROM ROSH HASHANAH TO YOM KIPPUR SUBSTITUTE THE FOLLOWING:

B'sayfer cha-yim
　　b'rocho v'sholōm,
　　u-farnoso tōvo,

בְּסֵפֶר חַיִּים
בְּרָכָה וְשָׁלוֹם,
וּפַרְנָסָה טוֹבָה,

In the book of life, blessing, and peace, and good livelihood,

nizochayr v'nikosayv l'fonecho,

נִזָּכֵר וְנִכָּתֵב לְפָנֶיךָ,

may we be remembered and inscribed before You —

anachnu v'chol am'cho
　　bays yisro-ayl,

אֲנַחְנוּ וְכָל עַמְּךָ
בֵּית יִשְׂרָאֵל,

we and Your entire people the Family of Israel —

l'cha-yim tōvim ulsholōm.

לְחַיִּים טוֹבִים וּלְשָׁלוֹם.

for a good life and for peace.

Boruch ato Adōnoy,
　　ō-se ha-sholōm.

בָּרוּךְ אַתָּה יהוה,
עוֹשֶׂה הַשָּׁלוֹם.

Blessed are You, HASHEM, Who makes the peace.

Yih-yu l'rotzōn imray fi
　　v'hegyōn libi l'fonecho,

יִהְיוּ לְרָצוֹן אִמְרֵי פִי
וְהֶגְיוֹן לִבִּי לְפָנֶיךָ,

May the expressions of my mouth and the thoughts of my heart
find favor before You,

Adōnoy tzuri v'gō-ali.

יהוה צוּרִי וְגֹאֲלִי.

HASHEM, my Rock and my Redeemer.

■ I pray that, having completed my *Amidah,* I have been changed in a positive way,
especially with regard to my interpersonal relationships.

ELŌHAI, n'tzōr l'shōni mayro,

אֱלֹהַי, נְצוֹר לְשׁוֹנִי מֵרָע,

My God, guard my tongue from evil

usfosai midabayr mirmo,

וּשְׂפָתַי מִדַּבֵּר מִרְמָה,

and my lips from speaking deceitfully.

V'limkal'lai nafshi sidōm,

וְלִמְקַלְלַי נַפְשִׁי תִדּוֹם,

To those who curse me, let my soul be silent;

v'nafshi ke-ofor lakōl tih-ye.

וְנַפְשִׁי כֶּעָפָר לַכֹּל תִּהְיֶה.

and let my soul be like dust to everyone.

P'sach libi b'sōrosecho,

פְּתַח לִבִּי בְּתוֹרָתֶךָ,

Open my heart to Your Torah,

uvmitzvōsecho tirdōf nafshi.

וּבְמִצְוֹתֶיךָ תִּרְדּוֹף נַפְשִׁי.

then my soul will pursue Your commandments.

V'chol hachōsh'vim olai ro-o,

וְכֹל הַחוֹשְׁבִים עָלַי רָעָה,

As for all those who design evil against me,

m'hayro hofayr atzosom

מְהֵרָה הָפֵר עֲצָתָם

speedily nullify their counsel

v'kalkayl machashavtom.

וְקַלְקֵל מַחֲשַׁבְתָּם.

and disrupt their design.

Asay l'ma-an sh'mecho,

עֲשֵׂה לְמַעַן שְׁמֶךָ,

Act for Your Name's sake;

asay l'ma-an y'minecho,

עֲשֵׂה לְמַעַן יְמִינֶךָ,

act for Your right hand's sake;

asay l'ma-an k'dushosecho,

עֲשֵׂה לְמַעַן קְדֻשָּׁתֶךָ,

act for Your sanctity's sake;

asay l'ma-an tōrosecho.

עֲשֵׂה לְמַעַן תּוֹרָתֶךָ.

act for Your Torah's sake.

L'ma-an yaychol'tzun y'didecho,

לְמַעַן יֵחָלְצוּן יְדִידֶיךָ,

That Your beloved ones may be given rest;

hōshi-o y'min'cho va-anayni.

הוֹשִׁיעָה יְמִינְךָ וַעֲנֵנִי.

let Your right hand save, and respond to me.

Yih-yu l'rotzōn imray fi

יִהְיוּ לְרָצוֹן אִמְרֵי פִי

v'hegyōn libi l'fonecho,

וְהֶגְיוֹן לִבִּי לְפָנֶיךָ,

*May the expressions of my mouth and the thoughts of my heart
find favor before You,*

Adōnoy tzuri v'gō-ali.

יהוה צוּרִי וְגֹאֲלִי.

HASHEM, my Rock and my Redeemer.

BOW. TAKE THREE STEPS BACK. BOW LEFT AND SAY:

Ō-se sholōm bimrōmov,

עֹשֶׂה שָׁלוֹם בִּמְרוֹמָיו,

He Who makes peace in His heights,

BOW RIGHT AND SAY:

hu ya-a-se sholōm olaynu,

הוּא יַעֲשֶׂה שָׁלוֹם עָלֵינוּ,

may He make peace upon us,

BOW FORWARD AND SAY:

v'al kol yisro-ayl. V'imru: Osmayn.

וְעַל כָּל יִשְׂרָאֵל. וְאִמְרוּ: אָמֵן.

and upon all Israel. Now respond: Amen.

Y'HI ROTZŌN mil'fonecho,   יְהִי רָצוֹן מִלְּפָנֶיךָ
May it be Your will,

Adōnoy Elōhaynu   יהוה אֱלֹהֵינוּ
Vaylōhay avōsaynu,   וֵאלֹהֵי אֲבוֹתֵינוּ,
HASHEM, our God and the God of our forefathers,

she-yibo-ne bays hamikdosh   שֶׁיִּבָּנֶה בֵּית הַמִּקְדָּשׁ
bimhayroh v'yomaynu,   בִּמְהֵרָה בְיָמֵינוּ,
that the Holy Temple be rebuilt, speedily in our days;

v'sayn chelkaynu b'sōrosecho,   וְתֵן חֶלְקֵנוּ בְּתוֹרָתֶךָ,
and grant us our share in Your Torah;

v'shom na-avod'cho b'yiro,   וְשָׁם נַעֲבָדְךָ בְּיִרְאָה,
and may we serve You there with reverence,

kimay ōlom   כִּימֵי עוֹלָם
uchshonim kadmōniyōs.   וּכְשָׁנִים קַדְמוֹנִיּוֹת.
as in days of old and in former years.

V'or'vo Ladōnoy   וְעָרְבָה לַיהוה
minchas y'hudo virusholo-yim   מִנְחַת יְהוּדָה וִירוּשָׁלָיִם,
Then the offering of Judah and Jerusalem will be pleasing to HASHEM,

kimay ōlom   כִּימֵי עוֹלָם
uchshonim kadmōniyōs.   וּכְשָׁנִים קַדְמוֹנִיּוֹת.
as in days of old and in former years.

SHEMONEH ESREI ENDS HERE. REMAIN STANDING IN PLACE FOR A FEW MOMENTS
THEN TAKE THREE STEPS FORWARD.

ON THE SABBATH, ALL PRESENT STAND AND RECITE THE FOLLOWING PARAGRAPH
ALOUD IN UNISON:

VAICHULU hashoma-yim v'ho-oretz   וַיְכֻלּוּ הַשָּׁמַיִם וְהָאָרֶץ
Thus the heavens and the earth were finished,

v'chol tz'vo-om.   וְכָל צְבָאָם.
and all their legion.

Vaichal Elōhim ba-yōm hash'vi-i   וַיְכַל אֱלֹהִים בַּיּוֹם הַשְּׁבִיעִי
On the seventh day God completed

m'lachtō asher oso,   מְלַאכְתּוֹ אֲשֶׁר עָשָׂה,
His work which He had done,

va-yishbōs ba-yōm hash'vi-i   וַיִּשְׁבֹּת בַּיּוֹם הַשְּׁבִיעִי
and He abstained on the seventh day

mikol m'lachtō asher oso.   מִכָּל מְלַאכְתּוֹ אֲשֶׁר עָשָׂה.
from all His work which He had done.

Vaiyvorech Elōhim
  es yōm hash'vi-i,

וַיְבָרֶךְ אֱלֹהִים
אֶת יוֹם הַשְּׁבִיעִי,

God blessed the seventh day

vaikadaysh ōsō,

וַיְקַדֵּשׁ אֹתוֹ,

and sanctified it,

ki vō shovas mikol m'lachtō,

כִּי בוֹ שָׁבַת מִכָּל מְלַאכְתּוֹ,

because on it He had abstained from all His work

asher boro Elōhim la-asōs.

אֲשֶׁר בָּרָא אֱלֹהִים לַעֲשׂוֹת.

which God created to make.

THE FOLLOWING THREE PARAGRAPHS (THE SEVEN-FACETED BLESSING*) ARE OMITTED BY AN INDIVIDUAL PRAYING ALONE OR BY AN OCCASIONAL *MINYAN* (SUCH AS IN THE HOME OF A MOURNER). THESE ARE ALSO OMITTED ON THE FIRST NIGHT OF PESACH.

CHAZZAN RECITES:

BORUCH ato Adōnoy
  Elōhaynu Vaylōhay avōsaynu,

בָּרוּךְ אַתָּה יהוה
אֱלֹהֵינוּ וֵאלֹהֵי אֲבוֹתֵינוּ,

Blessed are You, HASHEM, our God and the God of our forefathers,

Elōhay avrohom, Elōhay yitzchok,
  vaylōhay ya-akōv,

אֱלֹהֵי אַבְרָהָם, אֱלֹהֵי יִצְחָק,
וֵאלֹהֵי יַעֲקֹב,

God of Abraham, God of Isaac, and God of Jacob;

ho-Ayl hagodōl hagibōr v'hanōro
  Ayl elyōn,

הָאֵל הַגָּדוֹל הַגִּבּוֹר וְהַנּוֹרָא,
אֵל עֶלְיוֹן,

the great, mighty, and awesome God, the supreme God,

kōnay shoma-yim vo-oretz.

קוֹנֵה שָׁמַיִם וָאָרֶץ.

Creator of heaven and earth.

THE NEXT PARAGRAPH IS RECITED BY THE CONGREGATION, THEN BY THE *CHAZZAN:*

MOGAYN OVŌS bidvorō,

מָגֵן אָבוֹת בִּדְבָרוֹ,

He Who was the shield of our forefathers with His word,

m'cha-yay maysim b'ma-amorō,

מְחַיֶּה מֵתִים בְּמַאֲמָרוֹ,

Who resuscitates the dead with His utterance,

°ho-Ayl hakodōsh

°הָאֵל הַקָּדוֹשׁ

°the Holy God

°FROM ROSH HASHANAH TO YOM KIPPUR SUBSTITUTE:

hamelech hakodōsh

הַמֶּלֶךְ הַקָּדוֹשׁ

the Holy King

◆§ **The Seven-Faceted Blessing**
In Talmudic times, the synagogues were generally located outside town limits, in open fields. Since it was dangerous to walk home alone in the dark after *Maariv*, the Sages instituted an extra prayer for the congregation so that everyone would stay a little longer, in the event someone was slow in finishing his own *Maariv* (*Shabbos* 24b). On the eve of the Sabbath, this extra prayer was formulated as a synopsis of the seven blessings of the *Shemoneh Esrei*.

she-ayn komōhu,
שֶׁאֵין כָּמֽוֹהוּ,

Who is unequaled,

hamayni-ach l'amō
b'yōm shabas kodshō,
הַמֵּנִיחַ לְעַמּוֹ
בְּיוֹם שַׁבַּת קָדְשׁוֹ,

Who grants rest to His people on His holy Sabbath day,

ki vom rotzo l'honi-ach lohem.
כִּי בָם רָצָה לְהָנִיחַ לָהֶם.

for He was pleased with them to grant them rest.

L'fonov na-avōd b'yir-o vofachad,
לְפָנָיו נַעֲבֹד בְּיִרְאָה וָפַחַד,

Before Him we will serve with awe and dread

v'nōde lishmō b'chol yōm tomid
וְנוֹדֶה לִשְׁמוֹ בְּכָל יוֹם תָּמִיד

and give thanks to His Name every day continually

may-ayn hab'rochōs.
מֵעֵין הַבְּרָכוֹת.

with appropriate blessings.

Ayl hahōdo-ōs, adōn hasholōm,
אֵל הַהוֹדָאוֹת, אֲדוֹן הַשָּׁלוֹם,

God of grateful praise, Master of peace,

m'kadaysh ha-shabos,
umvoraych sh'vi-i,
מְקַדֵּשׁ הַשַּׁבָּת,
וּמְבָרֵךְ שְׁבִיעִי,

Who sanctifies the Sabbath and blesses the seventh day,

u-mayni-ach bikdusho
וּמֵנִיחַ בִּקְדֻשָּׁה

and gives rest with holiness

l'am m'dush'nay ōneg,
לְעַם מְדֻשְּׁנֵי עֹנֶג,

to a people saturated with delight —

zaycher l'ma-asay v'rayshis.
זֵכֶר לְמַעֲשֵׂה בְרֵאשִׁית.

in memory of the work of Creation.

CHAZZAN CONTINUES:

ELŌHAYNU Vaylōhay avōsaynu,
אֱלֹהֵינוּ וֵאלֹהֵי אֲבוֹתֵינוּ

Our God and the God of our forefathers,

r'tzay vimnuchosaynu.
רְצֵה בִמְנוּחָתֵנוּ.

may You be pleased with our rest.

Kad'shaynu b'mitzvōsecho,
קַדְּשֵׁנוּ בְּמִצְוֹתֶיךָ,

Sanctify us with Your commandments

v'sayn chelkaynu b'sōrosecho,
וְתֵן חֶלְקֵנוּ בְּתוֹרָתֶךָ,

and grant us our share in Your Torah;

sab'aynu mituvecho,
שַׂבְּעֵנוּ מִטּוּבֶךָ,

satisfy us from Your goodness

v'sam'chaynu bi-shu-osecho,
וְשַׂמְּחֵנוּ בִּישׁוּעָתֶךָ,

and gladden us with Your salvation,

v'tahayr libaynu l'ovd'cho be-emes. וְטַהֵר לִבֵּנוּ לְעָבְדְּךָ בֶּאֱמֶת.

and purify our heart to serve You sincerely.

V'hanchilaynu Adōnoy Elōhaynu וְהַנְחִילֵנוּ יהוה אֱלֹהֵינוּ

O HASHEM, our God, grant us as a heritage,

b'ahavo uvrotzōn בְּאַהֲבָה וּבְרָצוֹן

with love and favor,

shabas kod'shecho, שַׁבַּת קָדְשֶׁךָ,

Your holy Sabbath

v'yonuchu voh וְיָנוּחוּ בָה

yisro-ayl m'kad'shay sh'mecho. יִשְׂרָאֵל מְקַדְּשֵׁי שְׁמֶךָ.

and may Israel, the sanctifiers of Your Name, rest on it.

Boruch ato Adōnoy, בָּרוּךְ אַתָּה יהוה,

m'kadaysh ha-shabos. מְקַדֵּשׁ הַשַּׁבָּת.

Blessed are You, HASHEM, Who sanctifies the Sabbath.

CONGREGATION RESPONDS: Omayn — אָמֵן

THE *CHAZZAN* RECITES FULL *KADDISH*

(congregational responses are indicated by parentheses):

יִתְגַּדַּל וְיִתְקַדַּשׁ שְׁמֵהּ רַבָּא. (אָמֵן–Omayn). בְּעָלְמָא דִּי בְרָא

כִרְעוּתֵהּ. וְיַמְלִיךְ מַלְכוּתֵהּ, בְּחַיֵּיכוֹן וּבְיוֹמֵיכוֹן וּבְחַיֵּי דְכָל

בֵּית יִשְׂרָאֵל, בַּעֲגָלָא וּבִזְמַן קָרִיב. וְאִמְרוּ: אָמֵן.

(אָמֵן. יְהֵא שְׁמֵהּ רַבָּא מְבָרַךְ לְעָלַם וּלְעָלְמֵי עָלְמַיָּא.)

(Omayn. Y'hay sh'mayh rabo m'vorach l'olam ul-ol'may ol'ma-yo.)

יְהֵא שְׁמֵהּ רַבָּא מְבָרַךְ לְעָלַם וּלְעָלְמֵי עָלְמַיָּא. יִתְבָּרַךְ וְיִשְׁתַּבַּח

וְיִתְפָּאַר וְיִתְרוֹמַם וְיִתְנַשֵּׂא וְיִתְהַדָּר וְיִתְעַלֶּה וְיִתְהַלָּל שְׁמֵהּ

דְּקֻדְשָׁא בְּרִיךְ הוּא (בְּרִיךְ הוּא – B'rich hu). °לְעֵלָּא מִן כָּל

[לְעֵלָּא לְעֵלָּא מִכָּל° – from Rosh Hashanah to Yom Kippur substitute]

בִּרְכָתָא וְשִׁירָתָא תֻּשְׁבְּחָתָא וְנֶחֱמָתָא, דַּאֲמִירָן בְּעָלְמָא. וְאִמְרוּ: אָמֵן.

(אָמֵן–Omayn).

תִּתְקַבֵּל צְלוֹתְהוֹן וּבָעוּתְהוֹן דְּכָל (בֵּית) יִשְׂרָאֵל קֳדָם אֲבוּהוֹן דִּי

בִשְׁמַיָּא. וְאִמְרוּ: אָמֵן. (אָמֵן–Omayn).

יְהֵא שְׁלָמָא רַבָּא מִן שְׁמַיָּא, וְחַיִּים עָלֵינוּ וְעַל כָּל יִשְׂרָאֵל. וְאִמְרוּ:

אָמֵן. (אָמֵן–Omayn).

Bow. Take three steps back. Bow left and say, . . . עֹשֶׂה; bow right and say, . . . הוּא יַעֲשֶׂה; bow

forward and say, . . . וְעַל כָּל. Remain in place for a few moments, then take three steps forward.

עֹשֶׂה שָׁלוֹם בִּמְרוֹמָיו, הוּא יַעֲשֶׂה שָׁלוֹם עָלֵינוּ, וְעַל כָּל יִשְׂרָאֵל.

וְאִמְרוּ: אָמֵן. (אָמֵן–Omayn).

KIDDUSH IN THE SYNAGOGUE

IN MANY CONGREGATIONS, THE *CHAZZAN* RECITES *KIDDUSH*.
THE SABBATH *KIDDUSH* APPEARS BELOW; THE *KIDDUSH* FOR FESTIVALS APPEARS ON P. 671.

סַבְרִי מָרָנָן וְרַבָּנָן וְרַבּוֹתַי:

בָּרוּךְ אַתָּה יהוה אֱלֹהֵינוּ מֶלֶךְ הָעוֹלָם, בּוֹרֵא פְּרִי הַגָּפֶן.

(Cong. – Omayn)

בָּרוּךְ אַתָּה יהוה אֱלֹהֵינוּ מֶלֶךְ הָעוֹלָם, אֲשֶׁר קִדְּשָׁנוּ בְּמִצְוֹתָיו וְרָצָה
בָנוּ, וְשַׁבַּת קָדְשׁוֹ בְּאַהֲבָה וּבְרָצוֹן הִנְחִילָנוּ, זִכָּרוֹן לְמַעֲשֵׂה
בְרֵאשִׁית. כִּי הוּא יוֹם תְּחִלָּה לְמִקְרָאֵי קֹדֶשׁ, זֵכֶר לִיצִיאַת מִצְרָיִם. כִּי
בָנוּ בָחַרְתָּ, וְאוֹתָנוּ קִדַּשְׁתָּ, מִכָּל הָעַמִּים. וְשַׁבַּת קָדְשְׁךָ בְּאַהֲבָה וּבְרָצוֹן
הִנְחַלְתָּנוּ. בָּרוּךְ אַתָּה יהוה, מְקַדֵּשׁ הַשַּׁבָּת.

(Cong. – Omayn)

THE *CHAZZAN* SHOULD NOT DRINK THE *KIDDUSH* WINE, BUT SHOULD GIVE SOME
TO A CHILD WHO HAS LISTENED TO THE *KIDDUSH* AND RESPONDED *AMEN*.

BETWEEN PESACH AND SHAVUOS, THE *OMER* IS COUNTED (P. 153).

■ As we take leave of the synagogue and God's presence, we fortify ourselves with the resolve and commitment that the lofty ideals of prayer can be implemented and actualized in our mundane pursuits.

STAND WHILE RECITING *ALEINU*.

OLAYNU l'shabay-ach la-adōn hakōl,   **עָלֵינוּ** לְשַׁבֵּחַ לַאֲדוֹן הַכֹּל,
It is our duty to praise the Master of all,

losays g'dulo l'yōtzayr b'rayshis,   לָתֵת גְּדֻלָּה לְיוֹצֵר בְּרֵאשִׁית,
to ascribe greatness to the Molder of primeval Creation,

shelō osonu k'gōyay ho-arotzōs,   שֶׁלֹּא עָשָׂנוּ כְּגוֹיֵי הָאֲרָצוֹת,
for He has not made us like the nations of the lands

v'lō somonu   וְלֹא שָׂמָנוּ
   k'mishp'chōs ho-adomo,   כְּמִשְׁפְּחוֹת הָאֲדָמָה.
and has not emplaced us like the families of the earth;

shelō som chelkaynu kohem,   שֶׁלֹּא שָׂם חֶלְקֵנוּ כָּהֶם,
for He has not assigned our portion like theirs

v'gōrolaynu k'chol hamōnom   וְגוֹרָלֵנוּ כְּכָל הֲמוֹנָם.
nor our lot like all their multitudes.

SOME CONGREGATIONS OMIT THE PARENTHESIZED VERSE:

(Shehaym mishta-chavim   (שֶׁהֵם מִשְׁתַּחֲוִים
   l'hevel vorik   לְהֶבֶל וָרִיק,
(For they bow to vanity and emptiness

u-mispal'lim el ayl lō yōshi-a.)   וּמִתְפַּלְלִים אֶל אֵל לֹא יוֹשִׁיעַ.)
and pray to a god which helps not.)

BOW WHILE RECITING THE NEXT PHRASE.

Va-anachnu kŏr'im u-mishta-chavim   וַאֲנַחְנוּ כּוֹרְעִים וּמִשְׁתַּחֲוִים

u-mŏdim,   וּמוֹדִים,

But we bend our knees, bow, and acknowledge our thanks

lifnay melech malchay ham'lochim,   לִפְנֵי מֶלֶךְ מַלְכֵי הַמְּלָכִים

before the King Who reigns over kings,

Hakodŏsh boruch hu.   הַקָּדוֹשׁ בָּרוּךְ הוּא.

the Holy One, Blessed is He.

Shehu nŏte shoma-yim   שֶׁהוּא נוֹטֶה שָׁמַיִם

v'yŏsayd oretz,   וְיֹסֵד אָרֶץ,

He stretches out heaven and establishes earth's foundation,

u-mŏshav y'korŏ   וּמוֹשַׁב יְקָרוֹ

ba-shoma-yim mima-al,   בַּשָּׁמַיִם מִמַּעַל,

the seat of His homage is in the heavens above

ush-chinas u-zŏ   וּשְׁכִינַת עֻזּוֹ

b'gov-hay m'rŏmim.   בְּגָבְהֵי מְרוֹמִים.

and His powerful Presence is in the loftiest heights.

Hu Elŏhaynu ayn ŏd.   הוּא אֱלֹהֵינוּ, אֵין עוֹד.

He is our God and there is none other.

Emes malkaynu, efes zulosŏ,   אֱמֶת מַלְכֵּנוּ, אֶפֶס זוּלָתוֹ,

True is our King, there is nothing beside Him,

kakosuv b'sŏrosŏ: כַּכָּתוּב בְּתוֹרָתוֹ:

as it is written in His Torah:

V'yodato ha-yŏm vaha-shayvŏso   וְיָדַעְתָּ הַיּוֹם וַהֲשֵׁבֹתָ

el l'vovecho,   אֶל לְבָבֶךָ,

"You are to know this day and take to your heart

ki Adŏnoy hu ho-Elŏhim   כִּי יהוה הוּא הָאֱלֹהִים

that HASHEM is the only God —

ba-shoma-yim mima-al   בַּשָּׁמַיִם מִמַּעַל

in heaven above

v'al ho-oretz mitochas, ayn ŏd.   וְעַל הָאָרֶץ מִתָּחַת, אֵין עוֹד.

and on the earth below — there is none other."

AL KAYN n'kave l'cho   **עַל כֵּן** נְקַוֶּה לְּךָ

Adŏnoy Elŏhaynu   יהוה אֱלֹהֵינוּ

Therefore we put our hope in You, HASHEM, our God,

lirŏs m'hayro b'sif-eres u-zecho,   לִרְאוֹת מְהֵרָה בְּתִפְאֶרֶת עֻזֶּךָ,

that we may soon see Your mighty splendor,

l'ha-avir gilulim min ho-oretz,

לְהַעֲבִיר גִּלּוּלִים מִן הָאָרֶץ,

to remove detestable idolatry from the earth,

v'ho-elilim korōs yikoraysun,

וְהָאֱלִילִים כָּרוֹת יִכָּרֵתוּן,

and false gods will be utterly cut off,

l'sakayn ōlom b'malchus Shadai.

לְתַקֵּן עוֹלָם בְּמַלְכוּת שַׁדַּי.

to perfect the universe through the Almighty's sovereignty.

V'chol b'nay vosor yikr'u vishmecho,

וְכָל בְּנֵי בָשָׂר יִקְרְאוּ בִשְׁמֶךָ,

Then all humanity will call upon Your Name,

l'hafnōs aylecho

לְהַפְנוֹת אֵלֶיךָ

kol rish-ay oretz.

כָּל רִשְׁעֵי אָרֶץ.

to turn all the earth's wicked toward You.

Yakiru v'yayd'u kol yōsh'vay sayvayl,

יַכִּירוּ וְיֵדְעוּ כָּל יוֹשְׁבֵי תֵבֵל,

All the world's inhabitants will recognize and know

ki l'cho tichra kol berech,

כִּי לְךָ תִּכְרַע כָּל בֶּרֶךְ,

that to You every knee should bend,

tishova kol loshōn.

תִּשָּׁבַע כָּל לָשׁוֹן.

every tongue should swear.

L'fonecho Adōnoy Elōhaynu

לְפָנֶיךָ יהוה אֱלֹהֵינוּ

yichr'u v'yipōlu,

יִכְרְעוּ וְיִפֹּלוּ,

Before You, HASHEM, our God, they will bend every knee and cast themselves down,

v'lichvōd shimcho y'kor yitaynu,

וְלִכְבוֹד שִׁמְךָ יְקָר יִתֵּנוּ,

and to the glory of Your Name they will render homage,

vikab'lu chulom

וִיקַבְּלוּ כֻלָּם

es ōl malchusecho,

אֶת עוֹל מַלְכוּתֶךָ,

and they will all accept upon themselves the yoke of Your kingship

v'simlōch alayhem m'hayro

וְתִמְלֹךְ עֲלֵיהֶם מְהֵרָה

l'ōlom vo-ed.

לְעוֹלָם וָעֶד.

that You may reign over them soon and for all eternity.

Ki hamalchus shelcho hi

כִּי הַמַּלְכוּת שֶׁלְּךָ הִיא

For the kingdom is Yours

ul-ōl'may ad timlōch b'chovōd,

וּלְעוֹלְמֵי עַד תִּמְלוֹךְ בְּכָבוֹד,

and You will reign for all eternity in glory,

kakosuv b'sōrosecho:

כַּכָּתוּב בְּתוֹרָתֶךָ:

as it is written in Your Torah:

Adōnoy yimlōch l'ōlom vo-ed.

יהוה יִמְלֹךְ לְעֹלָם וָעֶד.

"HASHEM shall reign for all eternity."

❖ V'ne-emar: ❖ וְנֶאֱמַר:

And it is said:

V'ho-yo Adōnoy l'melech   וְהָיָה יהוה לְמֶלֶךְ

al kol ho-oretz,   עַל כָּל הָאָרֶץ,

"HASHEM *will be King over all the world —*

ba-yōm hahu yih-ye   בַּיּוֹם הַהוּא יִהְיֶה

Adōnoy e-chod, ushmō e-chod.   יהוה אֶחָד וּשְׁמוֹ אֶחָד.

on that day HASHEM *will be One and His Name will be One."*

SOME CONGREGATIONS RECITE THE FOLLOWING AT THIS POINT.

AL TIRO mipachad pis-ōm,   אַל תִּירָא מִפַּחַד פִּתְאֹם,

Do not fear sudden terror,

u-mishō-as r'sho-im ki sovō.   וּמִשֹּׁאַת רְשָׁעִים כִּי תָבֹא.

or the holocaust of the wicked when it comes.

Utzu aytzo v'sufor,   עֻצוּ עֵצָה וְתֻפָר,

Plan a conspiracy and it will be annulled;

dab'ru dovor v'lō yokum,   דַּבְּרוּ דָבָר וְלֹא יָקוּם,

speak your piece and it shall not stand,

ki i-monu Ayl.   כִּי עִמָּנוּ אֵל.

for God is with us.

V'ad zikno ani hu,   וְעַד זִקְנָה אֲנִי הוּא,

Even till your seniority, I remain unchanged;

v'ad sayvo ani esbōl,   וְעַד שֵׂיבָה אֲנִי אֶסְבֹּל,

and even till your ripe old age, I shall endure;

ani osisi va-ani eso,   אֲנִי עָשִׂיתִי וַאֲנִי אֶשָּׂא,

I created [you] and I shall bear [you];

va-ani esbōl va-amalayt.   וַאֲנִי אֶסְבֹּל וַאֲמַלֵּט.

I shall endure and rescue.

MOURNER'S KADDISH

MOURNER:

YISGADAL v'yiskadash   יִתְגַּדַּל וְיִתְקַדַּשׁ

sh'mayh rabo.   שְׁמֵהּ רַבָּא.

May His great Name grow exalted and sanctified

CONGREGATION RESPONDS: Omayn — אָמֵן

B'ol'mo di v'ro chir-usayh.   בְּעָלְמָא דִּי בְרָא כִרְעוּתֵהּ.

in the world that He created as He willed.

V'yamlich malchusayh,   וְיַמְלִיךְ מַלְכוּתֵהּ,

May He give reign to His kingship

b'cha-yaychōn uvyōmaychōn
בְּחַיֵּיכוֹן וּבְיוֹמֵיכוֹן
in your lifetimes and in your days

uvcha-yay d'chol bays yisro-ayl,
וּבְחַיֵּי דְכָל בֵּית יִשְׂרָאֵל,
and in the lifetimes of the entire Family of Israel,

ba-agolo u-vizman koriv.
בַּעֲגָלָא וּבִזְמַן קָרִיב.
swiftly and soon.

V'imru: Omayn.
וְאִמְרוּ: אָמֵן.
Now respond: Amen.

CONGREGATION RESPONDS:

Omayn. Y'hay sh'mayh rabo m'vorach
אָמֵן. יְהֵא שְׁמֵהּ רַבָּא מְבָרַךְ
l'olam ul-ol'may ol'ma-yo.
לְעָלַם וּלְעָלְמֵי עָלְמַיָּא.
Amen. May His great Name be blessed forever and ever.

MOURNER CONTINUES:

Y'hay sh'mayh rabo m'vorach
יְהֵא שְׁמֵהּ רַבָּא מְבָרַךְ
l'olam ul-ol'may ol'ma-yo,
לְעָלַם וּלְעָלְמֵי עָלְמַיָּא,
May His great Name be blessed forever and ever;

yisborach v'yishtabach v'yispo-ar
יִתְבָּרַךְ וְיִשְׁתַּבַּח וְיִתְפָּאַר
blessed, praised, glorified,

v'yisrōmam v'yisnasay
וְיִתְרוֹמַם וְיִתְנַשֵּׂא
exalted, extolled,

v'yis-hador v'yis-ale v'yis-halol
וְיִתְהַדָּר וְיִתְעַלֶּה וְיִתְהַלָּל
mighty, upraised, and lauded

sh'mayh d'kudsho b'rich hu
שְׁמֵהּ דְּקֻדְשָׁא בְּרִיךְ הוּא
be the Name of the Holy One, Blessed is He,

CONGREGATION RESPONDS:

B'rich hu.   *Blessed is He.*
בְּרִיךְ הוּא.

MOURNER CONTINUES:

°l'aylo min kol
°לְעֵלָּא מִן כָּל
beyond any

FROM ROSH HASHANAH TO YOM KIPPUR SUBSTITUTE:

°l'aylo l'aylo mikol
°לְעֵלָּא לְעֵלָּא מִכָּל
exceedingly beyond any

birchoso v'shiroso
בִּרְכָתָא וְשִׁירָתָא
blessing and song,

tushb'choso v'nechemoso,
תֻּשְׁבְּחָתָא וְנֶחֱמָתָא,
praise and consolation

da-amiron b'ol'mo.
דַּאֲמִירָן בְּעָלְמָא.
that are uttered in the world.

V'imru: Omayn.
וְאִמְרוּ: אָמֵן.
Now respond: Amen.

CONGREGATION RESPONDS: Omayn — אָמֵן

Y'hay sh'lomo rabo min sh'mayo   יְהֵא שְׁלָמָא רַבָּא מִן שְׁמַיָּא,

May there be abundant peace from Heaven,

v'cha-yim olaynu   וְחַיִּים עָלֵינוּ

v'al kol yisro-ayl.   וְעַל כָּל יִשְׂרָאֵל.

and life, upon us and upon all Israel.

V'imru: Omayn: וְאִמְרוּ: אָמֵן.

Now respond: Amen.

CONGREGATION RESPONDS: Omayn — אָמֵן

MOURNER BOWS, THEN TAKES THREE STEPS BACK, BOWS LEFT AND SAYS:

Ō-se sholōm bimrōmov   עֹשֶׂה שָׁלוֹם בִּמְרוֹמָיו,

He Who makes peace in His heights,

MOURNER BOWS RIGHT AND SAYS:

hu ya-a-se sholōm olaynu   הוּא יַעֲשֶׂה שָׁלוֹם עָלֵינוּ,

may He make peace upon us,

MOURNER BOWS FORWARD AND SAYS:

v'al kol yisro-ayl. V'imru: Omayn: וְעַל כָּל יִשְׂרָאֵל. וְאִמְרוּ: אָמֵן.

and upon all Israel. Now respond: Amen.

CONGREGATION RESPONDS: Omayn — אָמֵן

MOURNER REMAINS IN PLACE FOR A FEW MOMENTS, THEN TAKES THREE STEPS FORWARD.

FROM *ROSH CHODESH* ELUL THROUGH SHEMINI ATZERES,
THE FOLLOWING PSALM IS RECITED.

■ *Rosh Chodesh* Elul, forty days after the incident of the Golden Calf, was the third time Moses ascended Mt. Sinai, and forty days later, on Yom Kippur, he brought with him the message of God's forgiveness. Every year we relive this momentous chapter in our history, highlighting the special opportunity for repentance and forgiveness by reciting Psalm 27, which contains allusions to the holidays of Rosh Hashanah, Yom Kippur, and Succos.

L'DOVID, Adōnoy ōri v'yish-i   לְדָוִד, יהוה אוֹרִי וְיִשְׁעִי,

mimi iro,   מִמִּי אִירָא,

Of David:* HASHEM is my light and my salvation, whom shall I fear?

Adōnoy mo-ōz cha-yai, mimi efchod.   יהוה מָעוֹז חַיַּי, מִמִּי אֶפְחָד.

HASHEM is my life's strength, whom shall I dread?

Bikrōv olai m'ray-im   בִּקְרֹב עָלַי מְרֵעִים

When evildoers approach me

le-echōl es b'sori,   לֶאֱכֹל אֶת בְּשָׂרִי,

to devour my flesh,

tzorai v'ō-y'vai li,
צָרַי וְאֹיְבַי לִי,
my tormentors and my foes against me —

haymo kosh'lu v'nofolu.
הֵמָּה כָּשְׁלוּ וְנָפָלוּ.
it is they who stumble and fall.

Im tachane olai machane,
אִם תַּחֲנֶה עָלַי מַחֲנֶה,
Though an army would besiege me,

lō yiro libi,
לֹא יִירָא לִבִּי,
my heart would not fear;

im tokum olai milchomo,
אִם תָּקוּם עָלַי מִלְחָמָה,
though war would arise against me,

b'zōs ani vōtay-ach.
בְּזֹאת אֲנִי בוֹטֵחַ.
in this I trust.

Achas sho-alti may-ays Adōnoy,
אַחַת שָׁאַלְתִּי מֵאֵת יהוה,
One thing I asked of HASHEM,

ōsoh avakaysh,
אוֹתָהּ אֲבַקֵּשׁ,
that shall I seek:

shivti b'vays Adōnoy kol y'may cha-yai,
שִׁבְתִּי בְּבֵית יהוה כָּל יְמֵי חַיַּי,
that I dwell in the House of HASHEM all the days of my life;

la-chazōs b'nō-am Adōnoy,
לַחֲזוֹת בְּנֹעַם יהוה,
to behold the sweetness of HASHEM

ulvakayr b'haycholō.
וּלְבַקֵּר בְּהֵיכָלוֹ.
and to contemplate in His Sanctuary.

Ki yitzp'nayni b'sukō b'yōm ro-o,
כִּי יִצְפְּנֵנִי בְּסֻכֹּה בְּיוֹם רָעָה,
Indeed, He will hide me in His shelter on the day of evil;

yastirayni b'sayser oholō,
יַסְתִּירֵנִי בְּסֵתֶר אָהֳלוֹ,
He will conceal me in the concealment of His Tent,

b'tzur y'rōm'mayni.
בְּצוּר יְרוֹמְמֵנִי.
He will lift me upon a rock.

V'ato yorum rōshi
וְעַתָּה יָרוּם רֹאשִׁי
al ō-y'vai s'vivōsai,
עַל אֹיְבַי סְבִיבוֹתַי,
Now my head is raised above my enemies around me,

v'ezb'cho v'oholō zivchay s'ru-o,
וְאֶזְבְּחָה בְאָהֳלוֹ זִבְחֵי תְרוּעָה,
and in His Tent I will slaughter offerings accompanied by joyous song;

oshiro va-azam'ro Ladōnoy.
אָשִׁירָה וַאֲזַמְּרָה לַיהוה.
I will sing and make music to HASHEM.

Sh'ma Adōnoy kōli ekro,
שְׁמַע יהוה קוֹלִי אֶקְרָא,
HASHEM, hear my voice when I call,

v'chonayni va-anayni.
וְחָנֵּנִי וַעֲנֵנִי.
and be gracious toward me and answer me.

L'cho omar libi bak'shu fonoy,　　　　לְךָ אָמַר לִבִּי בַּקְּשׁוּ פָנָי,
In Your behalf, my heart has said, "Seek My Presence";

es ponecho Adōnoy avakaysh.　　　　אֶת פָּנֶיךָ יהוה אֲבַקֵּשׁ.
Your Presence, HASHEM, do I seek.

Al tastayr ponecho mimeni,　　　　אַל תַּסְתֵּר פָּנֶיךָ מִמֶּנִּי,
Conceal not Your Presence from me,

al tat b'af avdecho,　　　　אַל תַּט בְּאַף עַבְדֶּךָ,
repel not Your servant in anger.

ezrosi ho-yiso,　　　　עֶזְרָתִי הָיִיתָ,
You have been my Helper,

al tit'shayni v'al ta-azvayni,　　　　אַל תִּטְּשֵׁנִי וְאַל תַּעַזְבֵנִי,
abandon me not, forsake me not,

Elōhay yish-i.　　　　אֱלֹהֵי יִשְׁעִי.
O God of my salvation.

Ki ovi v'imi azovuni,　　　　כִּי אָבִי וְאִמִּי עֲזָבוּנִי,
Though my father and mother have forsaken me,

Vadōnoy ya-asfayni.　　　　וַיהוה יַאַסְפֵנִי.
HASHEM will gather me in.

Hōrayni Adōnoy dar-kecho,　　　　הוֹרֵנִי יהוה דַּרְכֶּךָ,
Teach me Your way, HASHEM,

un-chayni b'ōrach mi-shōr,　　　　וּנְחֵנִי בְּאֹרַח מִישׁוֹר,
and lead me on the path of integrity,

l'ma-an shōr'roy.　　　　לְמַעַן שׁוֹרְרָי.
because of my watchful foes.

Al tit'nayni b'nefesh tzoroy,　　　　אַל תִּתְּנֵנִי בְּנֶפֶשׁ צָרָי,
Deliver me not to the wishes of my tormentors,

ki komu vi　　　　כִּי קָמוּ בִי
ayday sheker vifay-ach chomos.　　　　עֵדֵי שֶׁקֶר, וִיפֵחַ חָמָס.
for there have arisen against me false witnesses who breathe violence.

✧ Lulay he-emanti　　　　✧ לוּלֵא הֶאֱמַנְתִּי
Had I not trusted

lir-ōs b'tuv Adōnoy b'eretz cha-yim.　　　　לִרְאוֹת בְּטוּב יהוה בְּאֶרֶץ חַיִּים.
that I would see the goodness of HASHEM in the land of life!

Kavay el Adōnoy,　　　　קַוֵּה אֶל יהוה,
Hope to HASHEM,

chazak v'ya-amaytz libecho,　　　　חֲזַק וְיַאֲמֵץ לִבֶּךָ,
strengthen yourself and He will give your heart courage;

v'kavay el Adōnoy.　　　　וְקַוֵּה אֶל יהוה.
and hope to HASHEM.

MOURNERS RECITE THE MOURNER'S *KADDISH* (P. 147).

MANY CONGREGATIONS RECITE THE FOLLOWING AT THIS POINT.

ADŌN ŌLOM asher molach,

אֲדוֹן עוֹלָם אֲשֶׁר מָלַךְ,

Master of the universe, Who reigned*

b'terem kol y'tzir nivro.

בְּטֶרֶם כָּל־יְצִיר נִבְרָא.

before any form was created.

L'ays na-aso v'cheftzō kōl,

לְעֵת נַעֲשָׂה בְחֶפְצוֹ כֹּל,

At the time when His will brought all into being —

azai melech sh'mō nikro.

אֲזַי מֶלֶךְ שְׁמוֹ נִקְרָא.

then as "King" was His Name proclaimed.

V'a-charay kichlōs hakōl,

וְאַחֲרֵי כִּכְלוֹת הַכֹּל,

After all has ceased to be,

l'vadō yimlōch nōro.

לְבַדּוֹ יִמְלוֹךְ נוֹרָא.

He, the Awesome One, will reign alone.

V'hu ho-yo, v'hu hōve,

וְהוּא הָיָה וְהוּא הֹוֶה,

It is He Who was, He Who is,

v'hu yih-ye, b'siforo.

וְהוּא יִהְיֶה בְּתִפְאָרָה.

and He Who shall remain, in splendor.

V'hu e-chod v'ayn shayni,

וְהוּא אֶחָד וְאֵין שֵׁנִי,

He is One — there is no second

l'hamshil lō l'hachbiro.

לְהַמְשִׁיל לוֹ לְהַחְבִּירָה.

to compare to Him, to declare as His equal.

B'li rayshis b'li sachlis,

בְּלִי רֵאשִׁית בְּלִי תַכְלִית,

Without beginning, without conclusion —

v'lō ho-ōz v'hamisro.

וְלוֹ הָעֹז וְהַמִּשְׂרָה.

His is the power and dominion.

V'hu Ayli v'chai gō-ali,

וְהוּא אֵלִי וְחַי גֹּאֲלִי,

He is my God, my living Redeemer,

v'tzur chevli b'ays tzoro.

וְצוּר חֶבְלִי בְּעֵת צָרָה.

Rock of my pain in time of distress.

V'hu nisi u-monōs li

וְהוּא נִסִּי וּמָנוֹס לִי

He is my banner, a refuge for me,

m'nos kōsi b'yōm ekro.

מְנָת כּוֹסִי בְּיוֹם אֶקְרָא.

the portion in my cup on the day I call.

◆§ **Adon Olam.** The theme of this beautiful poem of praise has motivated many communities to adopt it as the concluding part of *Kabbalas Shabbos.* Adon Olam proclaims God as the One and the Eternal; He existed before Creation and He will survive every form of material existence. Since observance of the Sabbath is Israel's way of bearing witness to God as the Creator, it is fitting that one leave the synagogue bearing the message of God's

B'yodō afkid ruchi,

בְּיָדוֹ אַפְקִיד רוּחִי,

Into His hand I shall entrust my spirit

b'ays ishan v'o-iro.

בְּעֵת אִישָׁן וְאָעִירָה.

when I go to sleep — and I shall awaken!

V'im ruchi g'viyosi,

וְעִם רוּחִי גְּוִיָּתִי,

With my spirit shall my body remain.

Adōnoy li v'lō iro.

יהוה לִי וְלֹא אִירָא.

HASHEM is with me, I shall not fear.

⁘ COUNTING THE OMER ⁘

THE *CHAZZAN*, FOLLOWED BY THE CONGREGATION, RECITES THE BLESSING AND COUNT.
ONE PRAYING WITHOUT A *MINYAN* SHOULD ALSO RECITE THE *OMER* SERVICE.

BORUCH ato Adōnoy

בָּרוּךְ אַתָּה יהוה

Blessed are You, HASHEM,

Elōhaynu melech ho-ōlom,

אֱלֹהֵינוּ מֶלֶךְ הָעוֹלָם,

our God, King of the universe,

asher kid'shonu b'mitzvōsov

אֲשֶׁר קִדְּשָׁנוּ בְּמִצְוֹתָיו

Who has sanctified us with His commandments

v'tzivonu al s'firas ho-ōmer.

וְצִוָּנוּ עַל סְפִירַת הָעוֹמֶר.

and has commanded us regarding the counting of the Omer.

INSERT THE APPROPRIATE DAY'S COUNT. SEE CHART PP. 154-158.

HORACHAMON hu ya-chazir lonu

הָרַחֲמָן הוּא יַחֲזִיר לָנוּ

The Compassionate One! May He return for us

avōdas bays hamikdosh
    limkōmoh,

עֲבוֹדַת בֵּית הַמִּקְדָּשׁ
לִמְקוֹמָהּ,

the service of the Temple to its place,

bimhayro v'yomaynu . Omayn selo.

בִּמְהֵרָה בְיָמֵינוּ. אָמֵן סֶלָה.

speedily in our days. Amen , Selah.

---

eternal sovereignty. The recitation of *Adon Olam* now has a further significance. During the week, we begin the day before *Shacharis* and end it by reciting *Adon Olam* after the Bedtime *Shema*. By reciting it now at the inauguration of the Sabbath, we signify that this is not the start of just one more day, but that the Sabbath is on a far higher spiritual level, and therefore represents a new beginning in our service of God.

⁘**Counting the Omer.** The Torah commands that from the second day of Pesach — the day the *Omer*-offering of new barley is brought in the Temple — forty-nine days are to be counted, and the festival of Shavuos celebrated on the fiftieth day. This period is called

Sefiras HoOmer, the Counting of the *Omer*. The *Sefirah* count also recalls an earlier event. During the seven weeks following the Exodus, our ancestors prepared themselves for receiving the Torah at Mount Sinai. This responsibility to prepare oneself to receive the Torah is present every year, as we relive the Exodus from bondage and materialism, and strive to be worthy of the gift of Torah. In ancient times, the *Sefirah* period was a time of rejoicing, but it is now observed as a time of semi-mourning because of several reasons: the absence of the Temple; the death of Rabbi Akiva's 24,000 students during thirty-three days of the *Sefirah;* and a series of bloody massacres befalling Jewish communities during the Crusades.

1	Ha-yōm yōm echod bo-ōmer. *Today is one day of the Omer.*	הַיּוֹם יוֹם אֶחָד בָּעוֹמֶר.
2	Ha-yōm sh'nay yomim bo-ōmer. *Today is two days of the Omer.*	הַיּוֹם שְׁנֵי יָמִים בָּעוֹמֶר.
3	Ha-yōm sh'lōsho yomim bo-ōmer. *Today is three days of the Omer.*	הַיּוֹם שְׁלֹשָׁה יָמִים בָּעוֹמֶר.
4	Ha-yōm arbo-o yomim bo-ōmer. *Today is four days of the Omer.*	הַיּוֹם אַרְבָּעָה יָמִים בָּעוֹמֶר.
5	Ha-yōm chami-sho yomim bo-ōmer. *Today is five days of the Omer.*	הַיּוֹם חֲמִשָּׁה יָמִים בָּעוֹמֶר.
6	Ha-yōm shisho yomim bo-ōmer. *Today is six days of the Omer.*	הַיּוֹם שִׁשָּׁה יָמִים בָּעוֹמֶר.
7	Ha-yōm shiv-o yomim shehaym shovu-a e-chod bo-ōmer. *Today is seven days, which are one week of the Omer.*	הַיּוֹם שִׁבְעָה יָמִים, שֶׁהֵם שָׁבוּעַ אֶחָד, בָּעוֹמֶר.
8	Ha-yōm sh'mōno yomim shehaym shovu-a e-chod v'yōm e-chod bo-ōmer. *Today is eight days, which are one week and one day of the Omer.*	הַיּוֹם שְׁמוֹנָה יָמִים, שֶׁהֵם שָׁבוּעַ אֶחָד וְיוֹם אֶחָד, בָּעוֹמֶר.
9	Ha-yōm tish-o yomim shehaym shovu-a e-chod ushnay yomim bo-ōmer. *Today is nine days, which are one week and two days of the Omer.*	הַיּוֹם תִּשְׁעָה יָמִים, שֶׁהֵם שָׁבוּעַ אֶחָד וּשְׁנֵי יָמִים, בָּעוֹמֶר.
10	Ha-yōm asoro yomim shehaym shovu-a e-chod ushlōsho yomim bo-ōmer. *Today is ten days, which are one week and three days of the Omer.*	הַיּוֹם עֲשָׂרָה יָמִים, שֶׁהֵם שָׁבוּעַ אֶחָד וּשְׁלֹשָׁה יָמִים, בָּעוֹמֶר.
11	Ha-yōm achad osor yōm shehaym shovu-a e-chod v'arbo-o yomim bo-ōmer. *Today is eleven days, which are one week and four days of the Omer.*	הַיּוֹם אַחַד עָשָׂר יוֹם, שֶׁהֵם שָׁבוּעַ אֶחָד וְאַרְבָּעָה יָמִים, בָּעוֹמֶר.
12	Ha-yōm sh'naym osor yōm shehaym shovu-a e-chod vachami-sho yomim bo-ōmer. *Today is twelve days, which are one week and five days of the Omer.*	הַיּוֹם שְׁנֵים עָשָׂר יוֹם, שֶׁהֵם שָׁבוּעַ אֶחָד וַחֲמִשָּׁה יָמִים, בָּעוֹמֶר.

13	Ha-yōm sh'lōsho osor yōm	הַיּוֹם שְׁלֹשָׁה עָשָׂר יוֹם,
	shehaym shovu-a e-chod	שֶׁהֵם שָׁבוּעַ אֶחָד
	v'shisho yomim bo-ōmer.	וְשִׁשָׁה יָמִים, בָּעוֹמֶר.
	Today is thirteen days, which are one week and six days of the Omer.	
14	Ha-yōm arbo-o osor yōm	הַיּוֹם אַרְבָּעָה עָשָׂר יוֹם,
	shehaym sh'nay shovu-ōs bo-ōmer.	שֶׁהֵם שְׁנֵי שָׁבוּעוֹת, בָּעוֹמֶר.
	Today is fourteen days, which are two weeks of the Omer.	
15	Ha-yōm chami-sho osor yōm	הַיּוֹם חֲמִשָׁה עָשָׂר יוֹם,
	shehaym sh'nay shovu-ōs	שֶׁהֵם שְׁנֵי שָׁבוּעוֹת
	v'yōm e-chod bo-ōmer.	וְיוֹם אֶחָד, בָּעוֹמֶר.
	Today is fifteen days, which are two weeks and one day of the Omer.	
16	Ha-yōm shisho osor yōm	הַיּוֹם שִׁשָׁה עָשָׂר יוֹם,
	shehaym sh'nay shovu-ōs	שֶׁהֵם שְׁנֵי שָׁבוּעוֹת
	ushnay yomim bo-ōmer.	וּשְׁנֵי יָמִים, בָּעוֹמֶר.
	Today is sixteen days, which are two weeks and two days of the Omer.	
17	Ha-yōm shiv-o osor yōm	הַיּוֹם שִׁבְעָה עָשָׂר יוֹם,
	shehaym sh'nay shovu-ōs	שֶׁהֵם שְׁנֵי שָׁבוּעוֹת
	ushlōsho yomim bo-ōmer.	וּשְׁלֹשָׁה יָמִים, בָּעוֹמֶר.
	Today is seventeen days, which are two weeks and three days of the Omer.	
18	Ha-yōm sh'mōno osor yōm	הַיּוֹם שְׁמוֹנָה עָשָׂר יוֹם,
	shehaym sh'nay shovu-ōs	שֶׁהֵם שְׁנֵי שָׁבוּעוֹת
	v'arbo-o yomim bo-ōmer.	וְאַרְבָּעָה יָמִים, בָּעוֹמֶר.
	Today is eighteen days, which are two weeks and four days of the Omer.	
19	Ha-yōm tish-o osor yōm	הַיּוֹם תִּשְׁעָה עָשָׂר יוֹם,
	shehaym sh'nay shovu-ōs	שֶׁהֵם שְׁנֵי שָׁבוּעוֹת
	vachami-sho yomim bo-ōmer.	וַחֲמִשָׁה יָמִים, בָּעוֹמֶר.
	Today is nineteen days, which are two weeks and five days of the Omer.	
20	Ha-yōm esrim yōm	הַיּוֹם עֶשְׂרִים יוֹם,
	shehaym sh'nay shovu-ōs	שֶׁהֵם שְׁנֵי שָׁבוּעוֹת
	v'shisho yomim bo-ōmer.	וְשִׁשָׁה יָמִים, בָּעוֹמֶר.
	Today is twenty days, which are two weeks and six days of the Omer.	
21	Ha-yōm e-chod v'esrim yōm	הַיּוֹם אֶחָד וְעֶשְׂרִים יוֹם,
	shehaym sh'lōsho shovu-ōs bo-ōmer.	שֶׁהֵם שְׁלֹשָׁה שָׁבוּעוֹת, בָּעוֹמֶר.
	Today is twenty-one days, which are three weeks of the Omer.	
22	Ha-yōm sh'na-yim v'esrim yōm	הַיּוֹם שְׁנַיִם וְעֶשְׂרִים יוֹם,
	shehaym sh'lōsho shovu-ōs	שֶׁהֵם שְׁלֹשָׁה שָׁבוּעוֹת
	v'yōm e-chod bo-ōmer.	וְיוֹם אֶחָד, בָּעוֹמֶר.
	Today is twenty-two days, which are three weeks and one day of the Omer.	

23	Ha-yōm sh'lōsho v'esrim yōm shehaym sh'lōsho shovu-ōs ushnay yomim bo-ōmer. *Today is twenty-three days, which are three weeks and two days of the Omer.*	הַיּוֹם שְׁלֹשָׁה וְעֶשְׂרִים יוֹם, שֶׁהֵם שְׁלֹשָׁה שָׁבוּעוֹת וּשְׁנֵי יָמִים, בָּעוֹמֶר.
24	Ha-yōm arbo-o v'esrim yōm shehaym sh'lōsho shovu-ōs ushlōsho yomim bo-ōmer. *Today is twenty-four days, which are three weeks and three days of the Omer.*	הַיּוֹם אַרְבָּעָה וְעֶשְׂרִים יוֹם, שֶׁהֵם שְׁלֹשָׁה שָׁבוּעוֹת וּשְׁלֹשָׁה יָמִים, בָּעוֹמֶר.
25	Ha-yōm chami-sho v'esrim yōm shehaym sh'lōsho shovu-ōs v'arbo-o yomim bo-ōmer. *Today is twenty-five days, which are three weeks and four days of the Omer.*	הַיּוֹם חֲמִשָּׁה וְעֶשְׂרִים יוֹם, שֶׁהֵם שְׁלֹשָׁה שָׁבוּעוֹת וְאַרְבָּעָה יָמִים, בָּעוֹמֶר.
26	Ha-yōm shisho v'esrim yōm shehaym sh'lōsho shovu-ōs vachami-sho yomim bo-ōmer. *Today is twenty-six days, which are three weeks and five days of the Omer.*	הַיּוֹם שִׁשָּׁה וְעֶשְׂרִים יוֹם, שֶׁהֵם שְׁלֹשָׁה שָׁבוּעוֹת וַחֲמִשָּׁה יָמִים, בָּעוֹמֶר.
27	Ha-yōm shiv-o v'esrim yōm shehaym sh'lōsho shovu-ōs v'shisho yomim bo-ōmer. *Today is twenty-seven days, which are three weeks and six days of the Omer.*	הַיּוֹם שִׁבְעָה וְעֶשְׂרִים יוֹם, שֶׁהֵם שְׁלֹשָׁה שָׁבוּעוֹת וְשִׁשָּׁה יָמִים, בָּעוֹמֶר.
28	Ha-yōm sh'mōno v'esrim yōm shehaym arbo-o shovu-ōs bo-ōmer. *Today is twenty-eight days, which are four weeks of the Omer.*	הַיּוֹם שְׁמוֹנָה וְעֶשְׂרִים יוֹם, שֶׁהֵם אַרְבָּעָה שָׁבוּעוֹת בָּעוֹמֶר.
29	Ha-yōm tish-o v'esrim yōm shehaym arbo-o shovu-ōs v'yōm e-chod bo-ōmer. *Today is twenty-nine days, which are four weeks and one day of the Omer.*	הַיּוֹם תִּשְׁעָה וְעֶשְׂרִים יוֹם, שֶׁהֵם אַרְבָּעָה שָׁבוּעוֹת וְיוֹם אֶחָד, בָּעוֹמֶר.
30	Ha-yōm sh'lōshim yōm shehaym arbo-o shovu-ōs ushnay yomim bo-ōmer. *Today is thirty days, which are four weeks and two days of the Omer.*	הַיּוֹם שְׁלֹשִׁים יוֹם, שֶׁהֵם אַרְבָּעָה שָׁבוּעוֹת וּשְׁנֵי יָמִים, בָּעוֹמֶר.
31	Ha-yōm e-chod ushlōshim yōm shehaym arbo-o shovu-ōs ushlōsho yomim bo-ōmer. *Today is thirty-one days, which are four weeks and three days of the Omer.*	הַיּוֹם אֶחָד וּשְׁלֹשִׁים יוֹם, שֶׁהֵם אַרְבָּעָה שָׁבוּעוֹת וּשְׁלֹשָׁה יָמִים, בָּעוֹמֶר.

32	Ha-yōm sh'na-yim ushlōshim yōm shehaym arbo-o shovu-ōs v'arbo-o yomim bo-ōmer. *Today is thirty-two days, which are four weeks and four days of the Omer.*	הַיּוֹם שְׁנַיִם וּשְׁלֹשִׁים יוֹם, שֶׁהֵם אַרְבָּעָה שָׁבוּעוֹת וְאַרְבָּעָה יָמִים, בָּעוֹמֶר.
33	Ha-yōm sh'lōsho ushlōshim yōm shehaym arbo-o shovu-ōs vachami-sho yomim bo-ōmer. *Today is thirty-three days, which are four weeks and five days of the Omer.*	הַיּוֹם שְׁלֹשָׁה וּשְׁלֹשִׁים יוֹם, שֶׁהֵם אַרְבָּעָה שָׁבוּעוֹת וַחֲמִשָּׁה יָמִים, בָּעוֹמֶר.
34	Ha-yōm arbo-o ushlōshim yōm shehaym arbo-o shovu-ōs v'shisho yomim bo-ōmer. *Today is thirty-four days, which are four weeks and six days of the Omer.*	הַיּוֹם אַרְבָּעָה וּשְׁלֹשִׁים יוֹם, שֶׁהֵם אַרְבָּעָה שָׁבוּעוֹת וְשִׁשָּׁה יָמִים, בָּעוֹמֶר.
35	Ha-yōm chami-sho ushlōshim yōm shehaym chami-sho shovu-ōs bo-ōmer. *Today is thirty-five days, which are five weeks of the Omer.*	הַיּוֹם חֲמִשָּׁה וּשְׁלֹשִׁים יוֹם, שֶׁהֵם חֲמִשָּׁה שָׁבוּעוֹת, בָּעוֹמֶר.
36	Ha-yōm shisho ushlōshim yōm shehaym chami-sho shovu-ōs v'yōm e-chod bo-ōmer. *Today is thirty-six days, which are five weeks and one day of the Omer.*	הַיּוֹם שִׁשָּׁה וּשְׁלֹשִׁים יוֹם, שֶׁהֵם חֲמִשָּׁה שָׁבוּעוֹת וְיוֹם אֶחָד, בָּעוֹמֶר.
37	Ha-yōm shiv-o ushlōshim yōm shehaym chami-sho shovu-ōs ushnay yomim bo-ōmer. *Today is thirty-seven days, which are five weeks and two days of the Omer.*	הַיּוֹם שִׁבְעָה וּשְׁלֹשִׁים יוֹם, שֶׁהֵם חֲמִשָּׁה שָׁבוּעוֹת וּשְׁנֵי יָמִים, בָּעוֹמֶר.
38	Ha-yōm sh'mōno ushlōshim yōm shehaym chami-sho shovu-ōs ushlōsho yomim bo-ōmer. *Today is thirty-eight days, which are five weeks and three days of the Omer.*	הַיּוֹם שְׁמוֹנָה וּשְׁלֹשִׁים יוֹם, שֶׁהֵם חֲמִשָּׁה שָׁבוּעוֹת וּשְׁלֹשָׁה יָמִים, בָּעוֹמֶר.
39	Ha-yōm tish-o ushlōshim yōm shehaym chami-sho shovu-ōs v'arbo-o yomim bo-ōmer. *Today is thirty-nine days, which are five weeks and four days of the Omer.*	הַיּוֹם תִּשְׁעָה וּשְׁלֹשִׁים יוֹם, שֶׁהֵם חֲמִשָּׁה שָׁבוּעוֹת וְאַרְבָּעָה יָמִים, בָּעוֹמֶר.
40	Ha-yōm arbo-im yōm shehaym chami-sho shovu-ōs v'chami-sho yomim bo-ōmer. *Today is forty days, which are five weeks and five days of the Omer.*	הַיּוֹם אַרְבָּעִים יוֹם, שֶׁהֵם חֲמִשָּׁה שָׁבוּעוֹת וַחֲמִשָּׁה יָמִים, בָּעוֹמֶר.

41	Ha-yōm e-chod v'arbo-im yōm shehaym chami-sho shovu-ōs v'shisho yomim bo-ōmer.	הַיּוֹם אֶחָד וְאַרְבָּעִים יוֹם, שֶׁהֵם חֲמִשָּׁה שָׁבוּעוֹת וְשִׁשָּׁה יָמִים, בָּעוֹמֶר.
	Today is forty-one days, which are five weeks and six days of the Omer.	
42	Ha-yōm sh'na-yim v'arbo-im yōm shehaym shisho shovu-ōs bo-ōmer.	הַיּוֹם שְׁנַיִם וְאַרְבָּעִים יוֹם, שֶׁהֵם שִׁשָּׁה שָׁבוּעוֹת, בָּעוֹמֶר.
	Today is forty-two days, which are six weeks of the Omer.	
43	Ha-yōm sh'lōsho v'arbo-im yōm shehaym shisho shovu-ōs v'yōm e-chod bo-ōmer.	הַיּוֹם שְׁלֹשָׁה וְאַרְבָּעִים יוֹם, שֶׁהֵם שִׁשָּׁה שָׁבוּעוֹת וְיוֹם אֶחָד, בָּעוֹמֶר.
	Today is forty-three days, which are six weeks and one day of the Omer.	
44	Ha-yōm arbo-o v'ar'bo-im yōm shehaym shisho shovu-ōs ushnay yomim bo-ōmer.	הַיּוֹם אַרְבָּעָה וְאַרְבָּעִים יוֹם, שֶׁהֵם שִׁשָּׁה שָׁבוּעוֹת, וּשְׁנֵי יָמִים, בָּעוֹמֶר.
	Today is forty-four days, which are six weeks and two days of the Omer.	
45	Ha-yōm chamisho v'arbo-im yōm shehaym shisho shovu-ōs ushlōsho yomim bo-ōmer.	הַיּוֹם חֲמִשָּׁה וְאַרְבָּעִים יוֹם, שֶׁהֵם שִׁשָּׁה שָׁבוּעוֹת וּשְׁלֹשָׁה יָמִים, בָּעוֹמֶר.
	Today is forty-five days, which are six weeks and three days of the Omer.	
46	Ha-yōm shisho v'arbo-im yōm shehaym shisho shovu-ōs v'arbo-o yomim bo-ōmer.	הַיּוֹם שִׁשָּׁה וְאַרְבָּעִים יוֹם, שֶׁהֵם שִׁשָּׁה שָׁבוּעוֹת וְאַרְבָּעָה יָמִים, בָּעוֹמֶר.
	Today is forty-six days, which are six weeks and four days of the Omer.	
47	Ha-yōm shiv-o v'arbo-im yōm shehaym shisho shovu-ōs vachami-sho yomim bo-ōmer.	הַיּוֹם שִׁבְעָה וְאַרְבָּעִים יוֹם, שֶׁהֵם שִׁשָּׁה שָׁבוּעוֹת וַחֲמִשָּׁה יָמִים, בָּעוֹמֶר.
	Today is forty-seven days, which are six weeks and five days of the Omer.	
48	Ha-yōm sh'mōno v'arbo-im yōm shehaym shisho shovu-ōs v'shisho yomim bo-ōmer.	הַיּוֹם שְׁמוֹנָה וְאַרְבָּעִים יוֹם, שֶׁהֵם שִׁשָּׁה שָׁבוּעוֹת וְשִׁשָּׁה יָמִים, בָּעוֹמֶר.
	Today is forty-eight days, which are six weeks and six days of the Omer.	
49	Ha-yōm tish-o v'arbo-im yōm shehaym shiv-o shovu-ōs bo-ōmer.	הַיּוֹם תִּשְׁעָה וְאַרְבָּעִים יוֹם, שֶׁהֵם שִׁבְעָה שָׁבוּעוֹת, בָּעוֹמֶר.
	Today is forty-nine days, which are seven weeks of the Omer.	

Kiddush

∾§ Kiddush

The fourth commandment of the Decalogue is that of Shabbos, but it is expressed differently in the Torah's two versions of the Ten Commandments. In the first account (*Exodus* 20:8), we are commanded *Zachor*, to *remember* the Shabbos to sanctify it. In the second account (*Deuteronomy* 5:12), we are taught *Shamor*, *safeguard* the Shabbos day to sanctify it. The Sages understood *Zachor* as a Biblical commandment to articulate verbally the holiness and sanctity of the Shabbos. Just as regarding the *Vidui*, the Confession that must accompany repentance, it is not enough to think about it, contemplate it, or simply be aware of past sins; they must be articulated. Similarly there is a Biblical commandment to recite words of sanctity and praise in honor of the Shabbos (*Rambam*, *Hil. Shabbos* 29:12).

The *Kiddush* on Friday night consists of three parts: 1) the recitation of *Vayechulu* (*Genesis* 2:1-3), which testifies that God completed the labor of creation in six days and rested on the seventh; 2) the blessing over the wine; and 3) the formal declaration of the holiness of the day.

∾§ Two Opinions

Some halachic authorities (*Magen Avraham* 271:1 and *Shulchan Aruch HaRav* 271:2) hold that the middle blessing of the Friday night *Shemoneh Esrei*, which ends "Blessed are You, Hashem, Who sanctifies the Shabbos," constitutes a fulfillment of the Biblical obligation of *Kiddush*. Accordingly, the Talmudic directive (*Pesachim* 106a) "Sanctify the Shabbos over a cup of wine," in conjunction with the Friday night meal, is a Rabbinic *mitzvah*.

However, the Talmud (*Pesachim* 117b) derives exegetically that the commandment of *Zachor* includes mention of the Exodus from Egypt — but the Exodus is not mentioned in the evening *Amidah*. Furthermore, people do not have in mind to satisfy their obligation of *Kiddush* with the recitation of the blessing in the *Shemoneh Esrei*. Consequently, most authorities agree that the recitation of *Kiddush* Friday night constitutes the Biblical *mitzvah* of *Kiddush*.

∾§ Positive Testimony

Abarbanel points out that the two tablets of the Ten Commandments — which contain five commandments on each tablet — actually complement one another. Thus the first commandment, which is "I am your God," and the sixth commandment, which is "You shall not kill," are related to one another. We are forbidden to murder because the first commandment teaches that each person is created in the image of God; thus respect for God dictates that one dare not kill the host of the Godly soul. Incidentally, it would be an exciting enhancement of

the Shabbos table to have family and friends work through the parallel relationships of the other pairs of commandments. For the context of *Kiddush*, we consider the relationship of the fourth and ninth commandments. The fourth is to sanctify the Shabbos and the ninth is the prohibition of false testimony. Our observance of Shabbos, our abstention from creative labor, is not simply an *in*action; rather it is akin to such positive deeds as donning *tefillin*, shaking a *lulav*, or eating in a *succah*. That is to say, by abstaining from weekday activities, we are *doing* something, namely testifying to God's creation of the universe, His control over the world and our acceptance of His commandments.

The converse is also true, unfortunately, of a Jew who is not yet a Sabbath observer. By his disregard of the Shabbos, by failing to sanctify it and by laboring on it, by desecrating the sacredness of the Shabbos, he violates the ninth commandment and gives false testimony. His actions declare that man, not God, is at the center of his universe, and that it is man whom he regards as the ultimate source of values.

When we observe the Shabbos, we bear weekly testimony to His creation of the universe. It is thus understandable why many have the custom to stand for at least the first paragraph of *Kiddush*, *Vayechulu*, as this recitation is viewed as a form of testimony, and the Torah says of witnesses: "And the two men shall stand before Hashem" (*Deuteronomy* 19:17), which means that testimony should be given in a standing, formal position (*Shavuos* 30a). Although this paragraph has already been recited as part of the evening *Amidah*, it is included in *Kiddush* for the benefit of women and children who may not have recited *Maariv*.

◄§ Two reasons

The Ten Commandments are found twice in the Torah, with some variations between the respective texts. One of the differences is in the reason given for the commandment of Shabbos. In the first Decalogue, the Torah states, "For in six days HASHEM made the heaven and the earth" (*Exodus* 20:11). In the second Decalogue, the Torah states, "And you shall remember that you were a slave in the land of Egypt and HASHEM, your God, has taken you out from there ... therefore HASHEM, you God, has commanded you to make the Shabbos day" (*Deuteronomy* 5:15).

Ramban, Nachmanides, suggests brilliantly that there is no contradiction between the two reasons for the observance of Shabbos. Both identify God as the Creator. Like Creation *ex nihilo*, God's total suspension of nature in performing the miracles of the Exodus demonstrate that He is the Creator. The difference is that the teaching "for in six days HASHEM created" would have to be accepted on blind faith, for we were not present at the Creation. In Egypt, however, the Jewish nation came to see for themselves that God is the Creator. The Ten Plagues, which affected only the Egyptians and miraculously spared any inconvenience to the Jews, the splitting of the Sea of Reeds before their eyes, demonstrated clearly that God controls nature, thereby making the belief in Creation most realistic and natural.

◈§ Man's Contribution to Holiness

Rabbi Joseph B. Soloveitchik posits a fascinating additional understanding of the recitation of *Kiddush*. Most often it is man who sanctifies things. A Torah scroll is our holiest physical possession. It is holy because the parchment was prepared by Torah-observant people for the express purpose of having the holy Torah inscribed on it. The scroll imbibes further sanctity because the scribe stated as he wrote that he was writing "for the fulfillment of the holiness of the *Sefer Torah.*" It is for this reason that if a Torah scroll were written by a non-Jew, or a not-yet observant Jew, who had a beautiful calligraphy, that scroll would have no sanctity whatsoever. The man's greatness is that he can invest an object, a place, and even time with sanctity. The Talmud tells us how Jerusalem and the Temple were invested with sanctity by the Sanhedrin (highest court of the Jewish people, consisting of seventy-one judges) and the leadership of the Jewish people (*Shevuos* 15a).

Similarly regarding the holidays, the Torah teaches: "These are the appointed festivals of Hashem, the holy convocations, which **you** shall designate in their appropriate time" (*Leviticus* 23:4). The "you" refers to the members of the Sanhedrin; based upon their knowledge of astronomy and their interrogation of the witnesses who testify that they observed the new moon, the Sanhedrin declares and sanctifies the new moon, thereby proclaiming *Rosh Chodesh*, the new month. Since the new moon, and hence the calendar, is the province of the nation, acting through its Sanhedrin, there is a major difference between the closing blessing of the *Kiddush* of *Yom Tov* and that of Shabbos. The text for the closing blessing for *Kiddush* on *Yom Tov* is "Blessed are You, Hashem, Who sanctifies Israel and the Festivals." This is most appropriate, as it is Israel that sanctifies and determines when each holiday is to be observed. However the text for the *Kiddush* of Shabbos is "Blessed are You, Hashem, Who sanctifies the *Shabbos.*" It is Hashem Who sanctified the Shabbos at the end of the first week of Creation. Every seventh day, every Shabbos, is already blessed and sanctified from that time onward by God, as the Torah states, "God blessed the seventh day and sanctified it" (*Genesis* 2:3).

Based on three other sources, however, Rabbi Soloveitchik suggests that man does indeed play a role in the sanctification of Shabbos. (1) Ramban comments on "Remember [זָכוֹר] the Shabbos to sanctify it" (*Exodus* 20:8) that the sanctification process is similar to that which is executed by the Sanhedrin in declaring the *Yovel,* Jubilee year, where the Torah commands: "You [i.e., the Sanhedrin] shall sanctify the fiftieth year" (*Leviticus* 25:10), and without the formal pronouncement of the High Court, there is no *Yovel*. At first glance this equation between Shabbos and *Yovel* suggests that the Jewish people have some participation in the sanctification of the Shabbos as well. Moreover, (2) in *Leviticus* 23:2-3, the Torah seems to include Shabbos with the Festivals: ". . . these are My appointed Festivals: For six days labor may be done, and the seventh day is a day of complete rest." It appears that in addition to the sanctity of Shabbos that was ordained at the end of Creation, Shabbos is listed first among the Festivals that the Jewish people are to sanctify. (3) Finally, in

Deuteronomy's version of the Ten Commandments, the reason for Shabbos is because "HASHEM took us out of Egypt," which is the common denominator for the observance of the three Festivals. In the *Kiddush* for Pesach, Shavuos, and Succos, we cite זֵכֶר לִיצִיאַת מִצְרָיִם, a *memorial of the Exodus from Egypt,* as a primary factor in observing these holidays.

Based on the above sources, Rabbi Soloveitchik suggests that the *Kiddush* on Shabbos is more than just a recitation of the praise and acknowledgment of the sanctity of Shabbos. Rather the *Kiddush* is actually man's participation with God in the sanctification process. How does man sanctify that which is already holy? The answer is that the holiness of Shabbos has two aspects: the prohibition against work and a sanctity akin to that of the Festivals. The ban against labor is ordained by God alone, regardless of anything said or done by man; this aspect of Shabbos holiness is endowed exclusively by God. However, man is called upon to invest the day with an additional festive character of "*moed*." In this respect Shabbos resembles the other Festivals, which are totally dependent on Israel's sanctification.

This manifests itself in the fact that the Shabbos Temple service, like that of the Festivals, has a *mussaf*, additional offering. It is thus understandable that in the *Shemoneh Esrei* of *Mussaf*, we introduce the concept of the Shabbos offering by saying, "Then from Sinai they [the Jewish people] were instructed about it."

The Sages (*Sanhedrin* 56b) teach that the commandment of Shabbos was given to the Jewish people at Marah (*Exodus* 15:25), several weeks before the revelation at Sinai. There, three days after the miraculous deliverance at the Sea of Reeds, the Jewish people sensed a void of spirituality, and God responded by giving them several laws, including the Shabbos. Why, then, does the *Mussaf* prayer state that Shabbos was given at Sinai?

Rabbi Soloveitchik taught that at Marah we were given the essence and identity of Shabbos, its metaphysical phenomena and the prohibition of labor. At Sinai we were given an additional component, namely that which Shabbos shares with the other Festivals, that it, too, has a *moed* character — and this "festival" component of the day is the basis for the additional *mussaf* offering. True, our blessing for the conclusion of the *Kiddush* is "Blessed are You, Hashem, Who sanctifies the Shabbos," but the text of the Jerusalem Talmud, "Who sanctifies Israel and the Shabbos," gives further credence to the thesis that the recitation of *Kiddush* is man's own participation in the sanctification of the day.

Rabbi Soloveitchik suggests a further substantiation of this thesis, namely the concept of *Tosefes Shabbos*, the law that a Jew has the ability to accept the sanctity of Shabbos before evening, while it is most definitely still Friday (see *Rashi, Genesis* 2:2). One may accept upon oneself the sanctity of Shabbos up to $1^1/_4$ hours prior to sunset. But how one recite the Shabbos *Amidah* and the Shabbos *Kiddush* if the sun is still in the sky and it is clearly the sixth day? The answer is that this is the part of the Shabbos that *man* sanctifies, and he accomplishes through his *Kiddush*.

✺ The Shabbos Atmosphere

Sfas Emes, the great Polish chassidic master, derived an important principle from the rule that women are obligated to hear or recite *Kiddush*, even though it is a positive *mitzvah* governed by time, and women are normally exempt from such commandments (*Kiddushin* 29a). The Talmud expounds that since *Shamor* [שָׁמוֹר], the negative commandment to refrain from forbidden work, and *Zachor* [זָכוֹר], the positive commandment to remember and sanctify the Shabbos, were said by God in the same utterance, whoever is obligated in the *Shamor* of Shabbos, the observance of its restrictions, is likewise obligated in the *Zachor*, the positive *mitzvah* of *Kiddush*. Since men and women are equally obligated regarding the restrictions of Shabbos, they are equally included as well in the mitzvah of *Kiddush* (*Berachos* 20b).

Based on this Talmudic teaching, Sfas Emes expounded that commensurate with one's observance of the restrictions of Shabbos will be the effectiveness of ones *Kiddush* and *zemiros* and positive *mitzvos* of the day. Thus the Torah teaches that sanctity is more often attained by complying with the restrictions of the Torah, as opposed to only performing its positive *mitzvos*. Thus, in *Parashas Kedoshim* (*Leviticus* 19-20), where the Torah commands the Jewish people to live a life of holiness, there is a total of fifty-one commandments, thirty-eight of which are negative commandments, which forbid or curtail behavior, and only thirteen of which are positive. It is only when an environment of sanctity is created by the elimination of improper conduct can the *Kiddush* be effective in establishing the positive tone and environment of Shabbos. If TV and other Shabbos desecrations are included as part of the atmosphere of Shabbos, then the ability of the *Kiddush* to sanctify is severely limited.

⋙ **BLESSING OF THE CHILDREN** ⋘

IT IS CUSTOMARY FOR PARENTS TO BLESS THEIR CHILDREN INDIVIDUALLY — YOUNG AND
OLD — UPON RETURNING FROM THE SYNAGOGUE ON THE EVE OF THE SABBATH.

BLESSING BESTOWED ON A SON:

Y'SIMCHO Elōhim   יְשִׂמְךָ אֱלֹהִים

May God make you

k'efrai-im v'chimnashe.   כְּאֶפְרַיִם וְכִמְנַשֶּׁה.

*like Ephraim and Menashe.**

BLESSING BESTOWED ON A DAUGHTER:

Y'SIMAYCH Elōhim   יְשִׂמֵךְ אֱלֹהִים

May God make you

k'soro rivko rochayl v'layo.   כְּשָׂרָה רִבְקָה רָחֵל וְלֵאָה.

*like Sarah, Rebecca, Rachel and Leah.**

FOR ALL CHILDREN CONTINUE HERE:

Y'VORECH'CHO Adōnoy   יְבָרֶכְךָ יהוה

v'yishm'recho.   וְיִשְׁמְרֶךָ.

*May HASHEM bless you** and safeguard you.*

Yo-ayr Adōnoy panov aylecho   יָאֵר יהוה פָּנָיו אֵלֶיךָ

vichuneko.   וִיחֻנֶּךָּ.

May HASHEM illuminate His countenance for you and be gracious to you.

Yiso Adōnoy panov aylecho   יִשָּׂא יהוה פָּנָיו אֵלֶיךָ,

May HASHEM turn His countenance to you

v'yosaym l'cho sholōm.   וְיָשֵׂם לְךָ שָׁלוֹם.

and establish peace for you.

◆§ **Blessing of the Children**

The flow of Divine beneficence and blessing which comes with the beginning of the Sabbath makes it a particularly auspicious time for such blessings.

When conferring the blessing, parents should have in mind a silent prayer that they should be able to raise their children and grandchildren to lives of Torah, marriage and good deeds. Both hands should be laid upon the head of the child to signify that the blessing is conveyed with complete generosity of spirit.

יְשִׂמְךָ אֱלֹהִים כְּאֶפְרַיִם וְכִמְנַשֶּׁה — *May God make you like Ephraim and Menashe.* This is the blessing that the Patriarch Jacob conferred upon his grandchildren, the two sons of Joseph and the first Jews born and raised in exile. They grew to be sources of pride to the Patriarch, despite having been raised in Pharaoh's court at a time when there was no Jewish religious life in Egypt except for the intimacy of their own family. Jacob himself indicated that this blessing should be given by Jewish parents to their children throughout history.

יְשִׂמֵךְ אֱלֹהִים כְּשָׂרָה רִבְקָה רָחֵל וְלֵאָה — *May God make you like Sarah, Rebecca, Rachel and Leah.* Unlike that of sons, this blessing is not a Scriptural quote. However, it is logical to wish Jewish girls that they emulate the Matriarchs who grew up in alien surroundings and surmounted infertility and other distress to become the mothers of the nation.

יְבָרֶכְךָ ה׳ — *May HASHEM bless you.* These verses form *Bircas Kohanim* [the Priestly Blessings]. The *Kohanim*, descendants of Moses' brother Aaron, were designated as the instruments through which God allows His blessing to rest upon Israel. Similarly, parents in their own families serve as agents to bestow God's blessing upon their children.

⊰⦑ SABBATH EVE MEAL ⦒⊱

EACH OF THE FOLLOWING FOUR STANZAS IS RECITED THREE TIMES.

SHOLŌM ALAYCHEM, שָׁלוֹם עֲלֵיכֶם,
*Peace upon you,**
mal-achay ha-shorays, מַלְאֲכֵי הַשָּׁרֵת
O ministering angels,
mal-achay elyōn, מַלְאֲכֵי עֶלְיוֹן,
angels of the Exalted One —
mimelech malchay ham'lochim, מִמֶּֽלֶךְ מַלְכֵי הַמְּלָכִים
from the King Who reigns over kings,
Hakodōsh boruch hu. הַקָּדוֹשׁ בָּרוּךְ הוּא.
the Holy One, Blessed is He.

BŌ-ACHEM l'sholōm, בּוֹאֲכֶם לְשָׁלוֹם,
*May your coming be for peace,**
mal-achay ha-sholōm, מַלְאֲכֵי הַשָּׁלוֹם,
O angels of peace,
mal-achay elyōn, מַלְאֲכֵי עֶלְיוֹן,
angels of the Exalted One —
mimelech malchay ham'lochim, מִמֶּֽלֶךְ מַלְכֵי הַמְּלָכִים
from the King Who reigns over kings,
hakodōsh boruch hu. הַקָּדוֹשׁ בָּרוּךְ הוּא.
the Holy One, Blessed is He.

BOR'CHUNI l'sholōm, בָּרְכֽוּנִי לְשָׁלוֹם,
*Bless me for peace,**
mal-achay hasholōm, מַלְאֲכֵי הַשָּׁלוֹם,
O angels of peace,
mal-achay elyōn, מַלְאֲכֵי עֶלְיוֹן,
angels of the Exalted One —

⊰ Shalom Aleichem

The Talmud teaches that two ministering angels — one good and one evil — escort a person home from the synagogue on the eve of the Sabbath. If a Jew arrives home and finds a kindled lamp, a set table, and a made bed, the good angel says, "May it be [God's] will that it also be so next Sabbath." The evil angel is compelled to answer, "Amen." But if not — then the evil angel says, "May it be [God's] will that it also be so next Sabbath." The good angel is compelled to answer, "Amen" (*Shabbos* 119b).

The *Shalom Aleichem* song is based on the above passage. If every Jew is accompanied home by two ministering angels, then it is only proper to greet them, bless them, and seek their blessing.

בּוֹאֲכֶם לְשָׁלוֹם — *May your coming be for peace.* If a Jewish home is worthy of the Sabbath's holiness, even the *angels* gain the blessings of peace that emanate from the meritorious deed.

בָּרְכֽוּנִי לְשָׁלוֹם — *Bless me for peace.* This is not a request for an angelic blessing in the usual sense, but should be understood as follows:

If the escorting angels are pleased with the Sabbath preparations awaiting them, they extend the blessing that it may be equally so in succeeding weeks. This is in recognition of

mimelech malchay ham'lochim,   מִמֶּלֶךְ מַלְכֵי הַמְּלָכִים
from the King Who reigns over kings,

hakodōsh boruch hu.   הַקָּדוֹשׁ בָּרוּךְ הוּא.
the Holy One, Blessed is He.

TZAYS'CHEM l'sholōm,   צֵאתְכֶם לְשָׁלוֹם,
May your departure be to peace,

mal-achay ha-sholōm,   מַלְאֲכֵי הַשָּׁלוֹם,
O angels of peace,

mal-achay elyōn,   מַלְאֲכֵי עֶלְיוֹן,
angels of the Exalted One —

mimelech malchay ham'lochim,   מִמֶּלֶךְ מַלְכֵי הַמְּלָכִים
from the King Who reigns over kings,

hakodōsh boruch hu.   הַקָּדוֹשׁ בָּרוּךְ הוּא.
the Holy One, Blessed is He.

SOME ADD THE FOLLOWING TWO VERSES:

Ki malochov y'tzave loch   כִּי מַלְאָכָיו יְצַוֶּה לָּךְ
He will charge His angels for you,

lishmorcho b'chol d'rochecho.   לִשְׁמָרְךָ בְּכָל דְּרָכֶיךָ.
to protect you in all your ways.

Adōnoy yishmor tzays'cho uvō-e-cho   יהוה יִשְׁמָר צֵאתְךָ וּבוֹאֶךָ
May HASHEM protect your going and your returning

may-ato v'ad ōlom.   מֵעַתָּה וְעַד עוֹלָם.
from this time and forever.

■ Alphabetically arranged eulogy that Abraham our Patriarch authored on behalf of Sarah our Matriarch was incorporated by King Solomon as part of the closing chapter of Proverbs. This hymn extols the way virtues of the Jewish wife and mother who sets the tone for Shabbos in the home and in her family.

AYSHES CHA-YIL mi yimtzo,   אֵשֶׁת חַיִל מִי יִמְצָא,
An accomplished woman,* who can find?

v'rochōk mip'ninim michroh.   וְרָחֹק מִפְּנִינִים מִכְרָהּ.
Far beyond pearls is her value.

Botach boh layv baloh,   בָּטַח בָּהּ לֵב בַּעְלָהּ,
Her husband's heart relies on her

---

man's achievement and is an auspicious wish for the future. In seeking this blessing from the angels we do no more than express the hope that our efforts have met with their approval.

אֵשֶׁת חַיִל — *An accomplished woman,* consists of the concluding twenty-two verses of the Book of *Proverbs,* which, on the surface, is a hymn to the perfect wife who is the mainstay of her home. Although the commentators agree

v'sholol lō yechsor.

וְשָׁלָל לֹא יֶחְסָר.

and he shall lack no fortune.

G'molas-hu tōv v'lō ro,

גְּמָלַתְהוּ טוֹב וְלֹא רָע,

She repays his good, but never his harm,

kōl y'may cha-yeho.

כֹּל יְמֵי חַיֶּיהָ.

all the days of her life.

Dor'sho tzemer u-fishtim,

דָּרְשָׁה צֶמֶר וּפִשְׁתִּים,

She seeks out wool and linen,

vata-as b'chayfetz kapeho.

וַתַּעַשׂ בְּחֵפֶץ כַּפֶּיהָ.

and her hands work willingly.

Hoy'so ko-oniyōs sōchayr,

הָיְתָה כָּאֳנִיּוֹת סוֹחֵר,

She is like a merchant's ships,

mimerchok tovi lachmo.

מִמֶּרְחָק תָּבִיא לַחְמָהּ.

from afar she brings her sustenance.

Vatokom b'ōd lailo,

וַתָּקָם בְּעוֹד לַיְלָה,

She arises while it is yet nighttime, *

vatitayn teref l'vaysoh,

וַתִּתֵּן טֶרֶף לְבֵיתָהּ,

and gives food to her household

v'chōk l'na-arōseho.

וְחֹק לְנַעֲרֹתֶיהָ.

and a ration to her maidens.

Zom'mo so-de vatikochayhu,

זָמְמָה שָׂדֶה וַתִּקָּחֵהוּ,

She envisions a field and buys it,

mip'ri chapeho not'o korem.

מִפְּרִי כַפֶּיהָ נָטְעָה כָּרֶם.

from the fruit of her handiwork she plants a vineyard.

Chog'ro b'ōz mosneho,

חָגְרָה בְעוֹז מָתְנֶיהָ,

With strength she girds her loins,

vat'amaytz z'rō-ōseho.

וַתְּאַמֵּץ זְרוֹעֹתֶיהָ.

and invigorates her arms.

To-amo ki tōv sachroh,

טָעֲמָה כִּי טוֹב סַחְרָהּ,

She discerns that her enterprise is good —

lō yichbe valailo nayroh.

לֹא יִכְבֶּה בַלַּיְלָה נֵרָהּ.

so her lamp is not snuffed out by night.

---

that the chapter is allegorical, it is variously interpreted as a reference to either the Divine Presence, the Sabbath, the Torah, wisdom, or the soul — the very fact that the Jewish woman was chosen as the vehicle through which to describe such lofty spiritual manifestations is in itself a profound tribute to her.

וַתָּקָם בְּעוֹד לַיְלָה — *She arises while it is yet nighttime.* With enthusiasm and a sense of responsibility, she arises before dawn to be sure that she can prepare adequately for the needs of her household. She recognizes that only by caring for the physical well-being of her family can she be sure that they will grow spiritually.

Yodeho shil'cho vakishōr,   יָדֶיהָ שִׁלְּחָה בַכִּישׁוֹר,
Her hands she stretches out to the distaff,

v'chapeho tom'chu folech.   וְכַפֶּיהָ תָּמְכוּ פָלֶךְ.
and her palms support the spindle.

Kapoh por'so le-oni,   כַּפָּה פָּרְשָׂה לֶעָנִי,
She spreads out her palm to the poor,

v'yodeho shil'cho lo-evyōn.   וְיָדֶיהָ שִׁלְּחָה לָאֶבְיוֹן.
and extends her hands to the destitute.

Lō siro l'vaysoh mi-sholeg,   לֹא תִירָא לְבֵיתָהּ מִשָּׁלֶג,
She fears not snow for her household,

ki chol baysoh lovush shonim.   כִּי כָל בֵּיתָהּ לָבֻשׁ שָׁנִים.
for her entire household is clothed with scarlet wool.

Marvadim os'so loh,   מַרְבַדִּים עָשְׂתָה לָּהּ,
Luxurious [bed]spreads she made herself,

shaysh v'argomon l'vushoh.   שֵׁשׁ וְאַרְגָּמָן לְבוּשָׁהּ.
linen and purple wool are her clothing.

Nōdo bash'orim baloh,   נוֹדָע בַּשְּׁעָרִים בַּעְלָהּ,
Distinctive in the councils is her husband,

b'shivtō im ziknay oretz.   בְּשִׁבְתּוֹ עִם זִקְנֵי אָרֶץ.
when he sits with the elders of the land.

Sodin os'so vatimkōr,   סָדִין עָשְׂתָה וַתִּמְכֹּר,
She makes a cloak to sell,

vachagōr nos'no lak'na-ani.   וַחֲגוֹר נָתְנָה לַכְּנַעֲנִי.
and delivers a belt to the peddler.

Ōz v'hodor l'vushoh,   עֹז וְהָדָר לְבוּשָׁהּ,
Strength and majesty are her raiment,

vatis-chak l'yōm acharōn.   וַתִּשְׂחַק לְיוֹם אַחֲרוֹן.
*she joyfully awaits the last day.**

Piho pos'cho v'chochmo,   פִּיהָ פָּתְחָה בְחָכְמָה,
She opens her mouth with wisdom,

v'sōras chesed al l'shōnoh.   וְתוֹרַת חֶסֶד עַל לְשׁוֹנָהּ.
*and a lesson of kindness is on her tongue.**

Tzōfiyo halichōs baysoh,   צוֹפִיָּה הֲלִיכוֹת בֵּיתָהּ,
She anticipates the ways of her household,

וַתִּשְׂחַק לְיוֹם אַחֲרוֹן — *She joyfully awaits the last day.* She awaits the inevitable last day of life with confidence that she will have earned respect and honor.

וְתוֹרַת חֶסֶד עַל לְשׁוֹנָהּ — *And a lesson of kindness is on her tongue.* She teaches others to engage in deeds of lovingkindness.

v'lechem atzlus lō sōchayl.   וְלֶחֶם עַצְלוּת לֹא תֹאכֵל.

and partakes not of the bread of laziness.

Komu voneho vai-ash'ruho,   קָמוּ בָנֶיהָ וַיְאַשְּׁרוּהָ,

Her children arise and praise her,*

baloh vai-hal'loh.   בַּעְלָהּ וַיְהַלְלָהּ.

her husband, and he lauds her.

Rabōs bonōs osu cho-yil,   רַבּוֹת בָּנוֹת עָשׂוּ חָיִל,

"Many daughters have amassed achievement,

v'at olis al kulono.   וְאַתְּ עָלִית עַל כֻּלָּנָה.

but you surpassed them all."

Sheker hachayn v'hevel hayōfi,   שֶׁקֶר הַחֵן וְהֶבֶל הַיְּפִי,

False is grace and vain is beauty,*

isho yir-as Adōnoy hi sis-halol.   אִשָּׁה יִרְאַת יהוה הִיא תִתְהַלָּל.

a God-fearing woman — she should be praised.

T'nu loh mip'ri yodeho,   תְּנוּ לָהּ מִפְּרִי יָדֶיהָ,

Give her the fruits of her hand

vihal'luho vash'orim ma-aseho.   וִיהַלְלוּהָ בַשְּׁעָרִים מַעֲשֶׂיהָ.

and let her be praised in the gates by her very own deeds.

THE FOLLOWING *KIDDUSH* IS RECITED ON THE SABBATH AND ON THE SABBATH OF *CHOL HAMOED*.
ON A FESTIVAL (EVEN IF IT FALLS ON THE SABBATH) THE *KIDDUSH* FOR FESTIVALS (P. 671) IS RECITED.

⊰{ SABBATH EVE KIDDUSH* }⊱

■ I offer testimony that the purpose of Hashem's creating
the world in six days was for men to rest on the Shabbos.

(vai-hi erev vai-hi vōker)   (וַיְהִי עֶרֶב וַיְהִי בְקֶר)

(And there was evening and there was morning)

YŌM HA-SHISHI.   יוֹם הַשִּׁשִׁי.

The sixth day.

Vaichulu ha-shoma-yim v'ho-oretz   וַיְכֻלּוּ הַשָּׁמַיִם וְהָאָרֶץ

Thus were finished the heavens and the earth,

v'chol tz'vo-om.   וְכָל צְבָאָם.

and all their array.

קָמוּ בָנֶיהָ וַיְאַשְּׁרוּהָ — *Her children arise and praise her,* in appreciation for, and recognition of, the qualities described above.

שֶׁקֶר הַחֵן וְהֶבֶל הַיְּפִי — *False is grace and vain is beauty.* Grace and beauty are not attributes that are worthy of serious praise for they have no great value. Moreover, they are often only transitory and do not reflect the character and

worth of a person. Only a person's fear of God is deserving of praise.

⊰§ **Kiddush**

The *mitzvah* to recite — or listen to — *Kiddush* over a cup of wine is incumbent upon men and women alike.

The first paragraph of *Kiddush* is in the nature of testimony to the fact that God com-

Vaichal Elōhim ba-yōm hash'vi-i   וַיְכַל אֱלֹהִים בַּיּוֹם הַשְּׁבִיעִי

On the seventh day God completed

m'lachtō asher oso,   מְלַאכְתּוֹ אֲשֶׁר עָשָׂה,

His work which He had done,

va-yishbōs ba-yōm hash'vi-i   וַיִּשְׁבֹּת בַּיּוֹם הַשְּׁבִיעִי

and He abstained on the seventh day

mikol m'lachtō asher oso.   מִכָּל מְלַאכְתּוֹ אֲשֶׁר עָשָׂה.

from all His work which He had done.

Vaivorech Elōhim es yōm hash'vi-i   וַיְבָרֶךְ אֱלֹהִים אֶת יוֹם הַשְּׁבִיעִי

God blessed the seventh day

vaikadaysh ōsō,   וַיְקַדֵּשׁ אֹתוֹ,

and hallowed it,

ki vō shovas miko'l m'lachtō   כִּי בוֹ שָׁבַת מִכָּל מְלַאכְתּוֹ

because on it He had abstained from all His work

asher boro Elōhim la-asōs.   אֲשֶׁר בָּרָא אֱלֹהִים לַעֲשׂוֹת.

which God created to make.

Savri moronon v'rabonon v'rabōsai: סַבְרִי מָרָנָן וְרַבָּנָן וְרַבּוֹתַי:

By your leave, my masters, rabbis and teachers:

BORUCH ato Adōnoy   בָּרוּךְ אַתָּה יהוה

Blessed are You, HASHEM,

Elōhaynu melech ho-ōlom,   אֱלֹהֵינוּ מֶלֶךְ הָעוֹלָם,

our God, King of the universe,

bōray p'ri hagofen.   בּוֹרֵא פְּרִי הַגָּפֶן.

Who creates the fruit of the vine.

ALL PRESENT RESPOND: Omayn — אָמֵן

■ Blessing over the sanctification of the Shabbos day: The love of Hashem for Israel is demonstrated by His crowning us with the observance of Shabbos.

BORUCH ato Adōnoy   בָּרוּךְ אַתָּה יהוה

Blessed are You, HASHEM,

Elōhaynu melech ho-ōlom,   אֱלֹהֵינוּ מֶלֶךְ הָעוֹלָם,

our God, King of the universe,

asher kid'shonu b'mitzvōsov   אֲשֶׁר קִדְּשָׁנוּ בְּמִצְוֹתָיו

Who has sanctified us with His commandments,

v'rotzo vonu,   וְרָצָה בָנוּ,

took pleasure in us,

---

pleted the labor of Creation in six days and rested on the seventh. Thus, by observing the Sabbath we bear weekly testimony to God's Creation of the universe.

v'shabas kodshō
וְשַׁבַּת קָדְשׁוֹ

and His holy Sabbath,

b'ahavo uvrotzōn hinchilonu
בְּאַהֲבָה וּבְרָצוֹן הִנְחִילָנוּ,

with love and with favor He gave us as a heritage,

zikorōn l'ma-asay v'rayshis.
זִכָּרוֹן לְמַעֲשֵׂה בְרֵאשִׁית.

a remembrance of Creation.

Ki hu yōm
כִּי הוּא יוֹם

t'chilo l'mikro-ay kōdesh,
תְּחִלָּה לְמִקְרָאֵי קֹדֶשׁ,

For that day is the prologue to holy convocations,

zaycher litzi-as mitzro-yim.
זֵכֶר לִיצִיאַת מִצְרָיִם.

a memorial of the Exodus from Egypt. *

Ki vonu vocharto, v'ōsonu kidashto
כִּי בָנוּ בָחַרְתָּ, וְאוֹתָנוּ קִדַּשְׁתָּ,

mikol ho-amim
מִכָּל הָעַמִּים.

For us did You choose and us did You sanctify from among all the peoples.

V'shabas kodsh'cho
וְשַׁבַּת קָדְשֶׁךָ

And Your holy Sabbath,

b'ahavo uvrotzōn hinchaltonu.
בְּאַהֲבָה וּבְרָצוֹן הִנְחַלְתָּנוּ.

with love and favor, You gave us as a heritage.

Boruch ato Adōnoy,
בָּרוּךְ אַתָּה יהוה,

m'kadaysh ha-shabos.
מְקַדֵּשׁ הַשַּׁבָּת.

Blessed are You, HASHEM, Who sanctifies the Sabbath.

ALL PRESENT RESPOND: Omayn — אָמֵן

ON THE SABBATH OF *CHOL HAMOED* SUCCOS, IN THE SUCCAH, ADD:

BORUCH ato Adōnoy
בָּרוּךְ אַתָּה יהוה

Blessed are You, HASHEM,

Elōhaynu melech ho-ōlom,
אֱלֹהֵינוּ מֶלֶךְ הָעוֹלָם,

our God, King of the universe,

asher kid'shonu b'mitzvosov
אֲשֶׁר קִדְּשָׁנוּ בְּמִצְוֹתָיו

Who has sanctified us with His commandments

v'tzivonu layshayv basuko.
וְצִוָּנוּ לֵישֵׁב בַּסֻּכָּה.

and has commanded us to dwell in the succah.

ALL PRESENT RESPOND: Omayn — אָמֵן

AFTER THE PERSON WHO RECITED *KIDDUSH* DRINKS, IT IS CUSTOMARY TO GIVE
EACH PERSON PRESENT SOME WINE FROM THE *KIDDUSH* CUP.

זֵכֶר לִיצִיאַת מִצְרָיִם — *A memorial of the Exodus from Egypt.* The Sabbath and the Exodus are intertwined. The Sabbath is symbolic of God's Creation; the Exodus was His demonstration to humanity that He controls nature and manipulates it as His will sees fit. In turn, the events of the Exodus bear witness to God's Creation — and, hence, His mastery — of the universe. The Sabbath, on the other hand, is the backdrop of the Exodus, because the concept it represents explains how the events of the Exodus were possible.

THE FOLLOWING BLESSING IS RECITED UPON WASHING THE HANDS BEFORE EATING BREAD.

BORUCH ato Adōnoy

בָּרוּךְ אַתָּה יהוה

Blessed are You, HASHEM,

Elōhaynu melech ho-ōlom,

אֱלֹהֵינוּ מֶלֶךְ הָעוֹלָם,

our God, King of the universe,

asher kid'shonu b'mitzvōsov,

אֲשֶׁר קִדְּשָׁנוּ בְּמִצְוֹתָיו,

Who has sanctified us with His commandments

v'tzivonu al n'tilas yodo-yim.

וְצִוָּנוּ עַל נְטִילַת יָדָיִם.

and has commanded us regarding washing the hands.

THE FOLLOWING BLESSING IS RECITED BEFORE EATING BREAD.

BORUCH ato Adōnoy

בָּרוּךְ אַתָּה יהוה

Blessed are You, HASHEM,

Elōhaynu melech ho-ōlom,

אֱלֹהֵינוּ מֶלֶךְ הָעוֹלָם,

our God, King of the universe,

ha-mō‑tzi lechem min ho-o-retz.

הַמּוֹצִיא לֶחֶם מִן הָאָרֶץ.

Who brings forth bread from the earth.

◄§ GRACE AFTER MEALS §►

IT IS CUSTOMARY TO RECITE PSALM 126 BEFORE *BIRCAS HAMAZON*
ON THE SABBATH AND FESTIVALS.

SHIR hama-alōs,

שִׁיר הַמַּעֲלוֹת,

A song of ascents.

b'shuv Adōnoy

בְּשׁוּב יהוה

es shivas tziyōn,

אֶת שִׁיבַת צִיּוֹן,

When HASHEM will return the captivity of Zion,*

ho-yinu k'chōl'mim.

הָיִינוּ כְּחֹלְמִים.

we will be like dreamers.*

Oz yimolay s'chōk pinu

אָז יִמָּלֵא שְׂחוֹק פִּינוּ

Then our mouth will be filled with laughter

◄§ **Grace After Meals**

The commandment to thank God after a meal is of Scriptural origin: "And you shall eat and you shall be satisfied and you shall bless HASHEM, your God, for the goodly Land that He gave you" (*Deuteronomy* 8:10). As the verse indicates, the Scriptural requirement applies only when one has eaten his fill — *you shall eat and you shall be satisfied*. From earliest times, however, the Jewish people has undertaken to express its gratitude to God even after a modest meal, provided one had eaten at least as much bread as a *kezayis,* the volume of an olive.

The first to compose a text for Grace After Meals was Moses, whose text is still recited as

the first blessing of the Grace. Although Moses' blessing was composed in gratitude for the manna in the wilderness, it makes no mention of the manna. The message appears rather clear: When we thank God for giving us food, we are recognizing that there is no intrinsic difference between the manna and the livelihood one wrests from the earth through sweat and hard toil; both are gifts from Heaven.

בְּשׁוּב ה׳ אֶת שִׁיבַת צִיּוֹן — *When HASHEM will return the captivity of Zion.* The Psalmist wrote prophetically about the return from the exile.

הָיִינוּ כְּחֹלְמִים — *We will be like dreamers.* When the long-awaited return to Zion finally comes to pass, the recollection of the past oppression of

ulshōnaynu rino,
ולְשׁוֹנֵנוּ רִנָּה,
and our tongue with glad song.

oz yōm'ru vagōyim,
אָז יֹאמְרוּ בַגּוֹיִם,
Then they will declare among the nations,

higdil Adōnoy la-asōs im ayle.
הִגְדִּיל יהוה לַעֲשׂוֹת עִם אֵלֶּה.
"HASHEM has done greatly with these."

Higdil Adōnoy la-asōs imonu
הִגְדִּיל יהוה לַעֲשׂוֹת עִמָּנוּ,
HASHEM has done greatly with us,

ho-yinu s'maychim.
הָיִינוּ שְׂמֵחִים.
we were gladdened.

Shuvo Adōnoy es sh'visaynu
שׁוּבָה יהוה אֶת שְׁבִיתֵנוּ,
O HASHEM — return our captivity

ka-afikim banegev.
כַּאֲפִיקִים בַּנֶּגֶב.
like springs in the desert.

Hazōr'im b'dim-o b'rino yiktzōru.
הַזֹּרְעִים בְּדִמְעָה בְּרִנָּה יִקְצֹרוּ.
Those who tearfully sow* will reap in glad song.

Holōch yaylaych uvochō
הָלוֹךְ יֵלֵךְ וּבָכֹה
nōsay meshech hazora,
נֹשֵׂא מֶשֶׁךְ הַזָּרַע,
He walks along weeping, he who bears the measure of seeds,

bō yovō v'rino, nōsay alumōsov.
בֹּא יָבֹא בְרִנָּה, נֹשֵׂא אֲלֻמֹּתָיו.
but will return in exultation, a bearer of his sheaves.

T'HILAS Adonoy y'daber pi,
תְּהִלַּת יהוה יְדַבֶּר פִּי,
[May my mouth declare the praise of HASHEM

vivoraych kol bosor
וִיבָרֵךְ כָּל בָּשָׂר
shem kodshō l'ōlom vo-ed.
שֵׁם קָדְשׁוֹ לְעוֹלָם וָעֶד.
and may all flesh bless His Holy Name forever.

Va-anachnu n'voraych Yoh,
וַאֲנַחְנוּ נְבָרֵךְ יָהּ,
We will bless HASHEM

may-ato v'ad ōlam, hal'luyoh.
מֵעַתָּה וְעַד עוֹלָם, הַלְלוּיָהּ.
from this time and forever, Praise God!

Hōdu Ladonoy ki tov,
הוֹדוּ לַיהוה כִּי טוֹב,
Give thanks to God for He is good,

---

the exile will swiftly fade away and seem like a bad dream.

הַזֹּרְעִים בְּדִמְעָה — *Those who tearfully sow.* The Psalmist compares those whose primary concern is with the study of Torah and with the performance of the commandments to farmers. The seeds of Israel's spiritual mission may become drenched in tears of unbearable suffer-

ing, but the crop, the eventual harvest of homage to righteousness and truth, will be reaped in joy.

הָלוֹךְ יֵלֵךְ וּבָכֹה נֹשֵׂא מֶשֶׁךְ הַזָּרַע — *He walks along weeping, he who bears the measure of seeds.* The poor man weeps in fear that his precious seeds may go to waste. God sees his plight and has mercy on him, enabling him to reap a

ki l'ōlom chasdo.   כִּי לְעוֹלָם חַסְדּוֹ.

His kindness endures forever.

Mi y'malayl g'vurōs Adonoy,   מִי יְמַלֵּל גְּבוּרוֹת יהוה,

Who can express the mighty acts of HASHEM?

yashmi-a kol t'hilosō.   יַשְׁמִיעַ כָּל תְּהִלָּתוֹ.

Who can declare all His praise?

Hin'ni muchon umzumon   הִנְנִי מוּכָן וּמְזֻמָּן

Behold I am prepared and ready

l'ka-yaym mitzvas asay   לְקַיֵּם מִצְוַת עֲשֵׂה

to perform the positive commandment

shel birkas hamozōn,   שֶׁל בִּרְכַּת הַמָּזוֹן,

of Grace After Meals,

shene-emar: v'ochalto v'sovoto,   שֶׁנֶּאֱמַר: וְאָכַלְתָּ וְשָׂבָעְתָּ,

for it is said: "And you shall eat and you shall be satisfied

u-vayrachto es Adōnoy Elōhecho,   וּבֵרַכְתָּ אֶת יהוה אֱלֹהֶיךָ,

and you shall bless HASHEM, your God,

al ho-oretz hatōvo   עַל הָאָרֶץ הַטֹּבָה

    asher nosan loch.   אֲשֶׁר נָתַן לָךְ.

for the good land which He gave you."

ZIMUN/INVITATION

IF THREE OR MORE MALES, AGED THIRTEEN OR OLDER, PARTICIPATE IN A MEAL, A LEADER IS
APPOINTED TO FORMALLY INVITE THE OTHERS TO JOIN HIM IN RECITING GRACE AFTER MEALS.

LEADER:

Rabōsai n'voraych.   רַבּוֹתַי נְבָרֵךְ.

Gentlemen, let us bless.

OTHERS:

Y'hi shaym Adōnoy m'vōroch   יְהִי שֵׁם יהוה מְבֹרָךְ

Blessed be the Name of HASHEM*

may-ato v'ad ōlom.   מֵעַתָּה וְעַד עוֹלָם.

from this time and forever!

LEADER:

Y'hi shaym Adōnoy m'vōroch   יְהִי שֵׁם יהוה מְבֹרָךְ

Blessed be the Name of HASHEM

may-ato v'ad ōlom.   מֵעַתָּה וְעַד עוֹלָם.

from this time and forever!

---

bountiful crop. So, too, exiled Israel carries the burden of spiritual seeds in a hostile world, fearful lest its efforts be wasted. Yet, God will reward its sacrifice with the bounty of the World to Come.

יְהִי שֵׁם ה׳ מְבֹרָךְ — *Blessed be the Name of HASHEM.* The leader, too, repeats the blessings because it would be sacrilegious for him to ask others to bless God while he, being part of the group, refrains from joining them.

IF TEN MEN JOIN IN THE *ZIMUN*, THE WORD IN PARENTHESES IS ADDED.

Bir-shus moronon v'rabonon v'rabōsai,

בִּרְשׁוּת מָרָנָן וְרַבָּנָן וְרַבּוֹתַי,

With the permission* of my masters, rabbis and teachers,

n'voraych (Elōhaynu) she-ochalnu mi-shelō.

נְבָרֵךְ (אֱלֹהֵינוּ) שֶׁאָכַלְנוּ מִשֶּׁלוֹ.

let us bless [our God,] He of Whose we have eaten.*

THOSE WHO HAVE EATEN RESPOND:

Boruch (Elōhaynu) she-ochalnu mi-shelō

בָּרוּךְ (אֱלֹהֵינוּ) שֶׁאָכַלְנוּ מִשֶּׁלוֹ

Blessed is [our God,] He of Whose we have eaten

uvtuvō cho-yinu.

וּבְטוּבוֹ חָיִינוּ.

and through Whose goodness we live.

THOSE WHO HAVE NOT EATEN RESPOND:

Boruch (Elōhaynu) umvōroch sh'mo

בָּרוּךְ (אֱלֹהֵינוּ) וּמְבֹרָךְ שְׁמוֹ

Blessed is He [our God] and blessed is His Name

tomid l'ōlom vo-ed.

תָּמִיד לְעוֹלָם וָעֶד.

continuously forever and ever.

LEADER:

Boruch (Elōhaynu) she-ochalnu mishelō

בָּרוּךְ (אֱלֹהֵינוּ) שֶׁאָכַלְנוּ מִשֶּׁלוֹ

Blessed is [our God,] He of Whose we have eaten

uvtuvō cho-yinu.

וּבְטוּבוֹ חָיִינוּ.

and through Whose goodness we live.

ALL:

Boruch hu uvoruch sh'mō.

בָּרוּךְ הוּא וּבָרוּךְ שְׁמוֹ.

Blessed is He and Blessed is His Name.

THE *ZIMUN* LEADER SHOULD RECITE GRACE AFTER MEALS (OR, AT LEAST, THE FIRST BLESSING) ALOUD. OTHER THAN TO RESPOND AMEN AT THE CONCLUSION OF EACH BLESSING, IT IS FORBIDDEN TO INTERRUPT GRACE AFTER MEALS FOR ANY RESPONSE OTHER THAN THOSE PERMITTED DURING THE *SHEMA*.

■ **First blessing: for nourishment.** I thank Hashem for miraculously providing and sustaining me and all living beings with nourishment, as He sustained the Jewish people daily for forty years in the wilderness.

BORUCH ato Adōnoy

בָּרוּךְ אַתָּה יהוה

Blessed are You, HASHEM,

בִּרְשׁוּת — *With the permission.* Since one of the group assumes the privilege of leading them all in the recitation, he requests their permission.

שֶׁאָכַלְנוּ מִשֶּׁלוֹ — *Of Whose we have eaten.* This text is ancient. The Talmud relates that Abraham would invite wayfarers to his home and

Elōhaynu melech ho-ōlom,
אֱלֹהֵינוּ מֶלֶךְ הָעוֹלָם,
our God, King of the universe,

hazon es ho-ōlom kulō, b'tuvō,
הַזָּן אֶת הָעוֹלָם כֻּלּוֹ, בְּטוּבוֹ,
Who nourishes the entire world, in His goodness —

b'chayn b'chesed uvrachamim
בְּחֵן בְּחֶסֶד וּבְרַחֲמִים,
with grace, with kindness, and with mercy.

hu nōsayn lechem l'chol bosor,
הוּא נֹתֵן לֶחֶם לְכָל בָּשָׂר,
He gives nourishment to all flesh,

ki l'ōlom chasdō.
כִּי לְעוֹלָם חַסְדּוֹ.
for His kindness is eternal.

Uvtuvō hagodōl,
וּבְטוּבוֹ הַגָּדוֹל,
And through His great goodness,

tomid lō chosar lonu,
תָּמִיד לֹא חָסַר לָנוּ,
we have never lacked,

v'al yechsar lonu
וְאַל יֶחְסַר לָנוּ
mozōn l'ōlom vo-ed.
מָזוֹן לְעוֹלָם וָעֶד.
and may we never lack, nourishment, for all eternity.

ba-avur sh'mō hagodōl,
בַּעֲבוּר שְׁמוֹ הַגָּדוֹל,
For the sake of His Great Name,

ki hu Ayl zon umfarnays lakōl,
כִּי הוּא אֵל זָן וּמְפַרְנֵס לַכֹּל,
because He is God* Who nourishes and sustains all,

u-maytiv lakōl,
וּמֵטִיב לַכֹּל,
and benefits all,

u-maychin mozōn l'chōl b'riyōsov
וּמֵכִין מָזוֹן לְכָל בְּרִיּוֹתָיו
asher boro.
אֲשֶׁר בָּרָא.
and He prepares food for all of His creatures which He has created.

❖ Boruch ato Adōnoy,
בָּרוּךְ אַתָּה יהוה,
hazon es hakōl.
הַזָּן אֶת הַכֹּל.
Blessed are You, HASHEM, Who nourishes all.

ALL PRESENT RESPOND: Omayn — אָמֵן

---

serve them lavishly. When they were sated and refreshed and ready to continue on their way, they would thank him. He would insist that their thanks should go not to him, but to God, the One from Whose bounty they had eaten (*Sotah* 10b).

◾§ **First Blessing: for the Nourishment**

Bircas HaMazon comprises four blessings, of which the first three are Scripturally ordained and the fourth was instituted by the Sages. The

first blessing was, as noted above, composed by Moses in gratitude for the manna with which God sustained Israel daily in the wilderness (*Berachos* 48b).

בַּעֲבוּר שְׁמוֹ הַגָּדוֹל כִּי הוּא אֵל — *For the sake of His Great Name, because He is God.* We declare that the motive of our request for eternally abundant food is not selfish, but for the sake of His Great Name so that we may be better able to serve Him.

■ Second Blessing: for the Land of Israel. I thank Hashem for giving us the Holy Land
and the opportunity it affords me to permeate it with *mitzvos*.

NŌ-DE l'cho, Adōnoy Elōhaynu,　　　נוֹדֶה לְךָ, יהוה אֱלֹהֵינוּ,
We thank You, HASHEM, our God,

al shehinchalto la-avōsaynu　　　עַל שֶׁהִנְחַלְתָּ לַאֲבוֹתֵינוּ
because You have given to our forefathers as a heritage*

eretz chemdo tōvo urchovo,　　　אֶרֶץ חֶמְדָּה טוֹבָה וּרְחָבָה,
a desirable, good and spacious Land;

V'al shehōtzaysonu　　　וְעַל שֶׁהוֹצֵאתָנוּ
because You removed us,

Adōnoy Elōhaynu　　　יהוה אֱלֹהֵינוּ
HASHEM, our God,

may-eretz mitzra-yim,　　　מֵאֶרֶץ מִצְרַיִם,
from the land of Egypt

ufdisonu mibays avodim,　　　וּפְדִיתָנוּ מִבֵּית עֲבָדִים,
and You redeemed us from the house of bondage;

v'al b'ris'cho　　　וְעַל בְּרִיתְךָ
and for Your covenant

shechosamto bivsoraynu,　　　שֶׁחָתַמְתָּ בִּבְשָׂרֵנוּ,
which You sealed in our flesh;*

v'al tōros'cho shelimad-tonu,　　　וְעַל תּוֹרָתְךָ שֶׁלִּמַּדְתָּנוּ,
for Your Torah which You taught us

v'al chu-kecho shehōdatonu,　　　וְעַל חֻקֶּיךָ שֶׁהוֹדַעְתָּנוּ,
and for Your statutes which You made known to us;

v'al cha-yim chayn vo-chesed　　　וְעַל חַיִּים חֵן וָחֶסֶד
shechōnantonu,　　　שֶׁחוֹנַנְתָּנוּ,
for life, grace, and lovingkindness which You granted us;

v'al achilas mozōn　　　וְעַל אֲכִילַת מָזוֹן
and for the provision of food

᛫§ **Second Blessing: for the Land**

The second blessing was formulated by
Joshua (*Berachos* 48a). He saw how much
Moses wanted to enter the Land of Israel and
how anxious the Patriarchs were to be buried
there. Therefore when Joshua was privileged
to enter it, he composed this blessing in its
honor.

עַל שֶׁהִנְחַלְתָּ לַאֲבוֹתֵינוּ — *Because You have given
to our forefathers as a heritage.* The Land of
Israel is referred to as "a heritage," implying
that it remains eternally the inheritance of
Israel. Thus, the long exile means only that

God denied us access to it in punishment for
our sins, not that it ceased to be ours.

וְעַל בְּרִיתְךָ שֶׁחָתַמְתָּ בִּבְשָׂרֵנוּ — *And for Your
covenant which You sealed in our flesh.* The
reference is to circumcision, mention of which
is required in the blessing of the Land because
the Land was promised to Abraham in the
merit of circumcision (see *Genesis* 17:7-8).

Women are not subject to the commandment
of circumcision. Nevertheless, women do say,
"For Your covenant which You sealed in our
flesh." Since women do not require circumcision, they are considered as equivalent to cir-
cumcised men in this regard.

sho-ato zon umfarnays   שָׁאַתָּה זָן וּמְפַרְנֵס
  ōsonu tomid,   אוֹתָנוּ תָּמִיד,

with which You nourish and sustain us constantly,

b'chol yōm uvchol ays   בְּכָל יוֹם וּבְכָל עֵת
  uvchol sho-o.   וּבְכָל שָׁעָה.

in every day, in every season, and in every hour.

ON CHANUKAH CONTINUE BELOW. ON ALL OTHER DAYS TURN TO P. 181.

AL hanisim, v'al hapurkon,   **עַל** הַנִּסִּים, וְעַל הַפֻּרְקָן,

For the miracles, and for the salvation,

v'al hag'vurōs, v'al hat'shu-ōs,   וְעַל הַגְּבוּרוֹת, וְעַל הַתְּשׁוּעוֹת,

and for the mighty deeds, and for the victories,

v'al hamilchomōs,   וְעַל הַמִּלְחָמוֹת,

and for the battles

she-osiso la-avōsaynu   שֶׁעָשִׂיתָ לַאֲבוֹתֵינוּ

which You performed for our forefathers

ba-yomim hohaym baz'man ha-ze.   בַּיָּמִים הָהֵם בַּזְּמַן הַזֶּה.

in those days, at this time.

BIMAY matisyohu ben yōchonon   **בִּימֵי** מַתִּתְיָהוּ בֶּן יוֹחָנָן

In the days of Mattisyahu, the son of Yochanan,

kōhayn godōl chashmōno-i u-vonov,   כֹּהֵן גָּדוֹל חַשְׁמוֹנַאי וּבָנָיו,

the High Priest, the Hasmonean, and his sons —

k'she-om'do malchus yovon   כְּשֶׁעָמְדָה מַלְכוּת יָוָן
  hor'sho-o al am'cho yisro-ayl,   הָרְשָׁעָה עַל עַמְּךָ יִשְׂרָאֵל,

when the wicked Greek kingdom rose up against Your people Israel

l'hashkichom tōrosecho,   לְהַשְׁכִּיחָם תּוֹרָתֶךָ,

to make them forget Your Torah

ulha-avirom maychukay r'tzōnecho.   וּלְהַעֲבִירָם מֵחֻקֵּי רְצוֹנֶךָ.

and compel them to stray from the statutes of Your Will —

V'ato b'rachamecho horabim,   וְאַתָּה בְּרַחֲמֶיךָ הָרַבִּים,

But You, in Your abundant mercy,

omadto lohem b'ays tzorosom,   עָמַדְתָּ לָהֶם בְּעֵת צָרָתָם,

stood up for them in the time of their distress.

Ravto es rivom, danto es dinom,   רַבְתָּ אֶת רִיבָם, דַּנְתָּ אֶת דִּינָם,

You took up their grievance, You judged their claim,

nokamto es nikmosom.   נָקַמְתָּ אֶת נִקְמָתָם.

and You avenged their wrong.

ON CHANUKAH CONTINUE:

mosarto gibōrim b'yad chaloshim,   מָסַרְתָּ גִבּוֹרִים בְּיַד חַלָּשִׁים,
You delivered the strong into the hand of the weak,

v'rabim b'yad m'atim,   וְרַבִּים בְּיַד מְעַטִּים,
the many into the hand of the few,

utmay-im b'yad t'hōrim,   וּטְמֵאִים בְּיַד טְהוֹרִים,
the impure into the hand of the pure,

ursho-im b'yad tzadikim   וּרְשָׁעִים בְּיַד צַדִּיקִים
the wicked into the hand of the righteous,

v'zaydim b'yad ōs'kay sōrosecho.   וְזֵדִים בְּיַד עוֹסְקֵי תוֹרָתֶךָ.
and the wanton into the hand of the diligent students of Your Torah.

Ulcho osiso   וּלְךָ עָשִׂיתָ
For Yourself You made

shaym godōl v'kodōsh b'ōlomecho,   שֵׁם גָּדוֹל וְקָדוֹשׁ בְּעוֹלָמֶךָ,
a great and holy Name in Your world,

ul-am'cho yisro-ayl   וּלְעַמְּךָ יִשְׂרָאֵל
and for Your people Israel

osiso t'shu-o g'dōlo u-furkon   עָשִׂיתָ תְּשׁוּעָה גְדוֹלָה וּפֻרְקָן
You performed a great victory and salvation

k'ha-yōm ha-ze.   כְּהַיּוֹם הַזֶּה.
as this very day.

V'achar kayn bo-u vonecho   וְאַחַר כֵּן בָּאוּ בָנֶיךָ
  lidvir bay-secho,   לִדְבִיר בֵּיתֶךָ,
Thereafter, Your children came to the Holy of Holies of Your House,

u-finu es haycholecho,   וּפִנּוּ אֶת הֵיכָלֶךָ,
they cleansed Your Temple,

v'tiharu es mikdo-shecho,   וְטִהֲרוּ אֶת מִקְדָּשֶׁךָ,
they purified the site of Your Holiness;

v'hidliku nayrōs   וְהִדְלִיקוּ נֵרוֹת
and they kindled lights

b'chatzrōs kod-shecho,   בְּחַצְרוֹת קָדְשֶׁךָ,
in the Courtyards of Your Sanctuary;

v'kov'u   וְקָבְעוּ
  sh'mōnas y'may chanuko aylu,   שְׁמוֹנַת יְמֵי חֲנֻכָּה אֵלּוּ,
and they established these eight days of Chanukah

l'hōdōs ulhalayl   לְהוֹדוֹת וּלְהַלֵּל
  l'shimcho hagodōl.   לְשִׁמְךָ הַגָּדוֹל.
to express thanks and praise to Your great Name.

V'AL HAKŌL, Adōnoy Elōhaynu, וְעַל הַכֹּל יהוה אֱלֹהֵינוּ
For all, HASHEM, our God,

anachnu mōdim loch, אֲנַחְנוּ מוֹדִים לָךְ,

umvor'chim ōsoch, וּמְבָרְכִים אוֹתָךְ,
we thank You and bless You.

yisborach shimcho b'fi kol chai יִתְבָּרַךְ שִׁמְךָ בְּפִי כָּל חַי
May Your Name be blessed by the mouth of all the living,

tomid l'ōlom vo-ed. תָּמִיד לְעוֹלָם וָעֶד.
continuously for all eternity.

Kakosuv: V'ochalto v'sovoto, כַּכָּתוּב: וְאָכַלְתָּ וְשָׂבָעְתָּ,
As it is written: "And you shall eat and you shall be satisfied

u-vayrachto es Adōnoy Elōhecho, וּבֵרַכְתָּ אֶת יהוה אֱלֹהֶיךָ,
and you shall bless HASHEM, your God,

al ho-oretz hatōvo asher nosan loch. עַל הָאָרֶץ הַטֹּבָה אֲשֶׁר נָתַן לָךְ.
for the good land which He gave you."

❖ Boruch ato Adōnoy, בָּרוּךְ אַתָּה יהוה,

al ho-oretz v'al hamozōn. עַל הָאָרֶץ וְעַל הַמָּזוֹן.
Blessed are You, HASHEM, for the land and for the nourishment.

ALL PRESENT RESPOND: Omayn — אָמֵן

■ Third Blessing: for Jerusalem. I ask Hashem to rebuild Jerusalem and the Third Temple which will again enable us to be cognizant of the fact that He provides us with all our needs.

RACHAYM Adōnoy Elōhaynu רַחֵם יהוה אֱלֹהֵינוּ
Have mercy, HASHEM, our God,

al yisro-ayl amecho, עַל יִשְׂרָאֵל עַמֶּךָ,
on Israel Your people;

v'al y'rushola-yim i-recho, וְעַל יְרוּשָׁלַיִם עִירֶךָ,
on Jerusalem, Your city;

v'al tziyōn mishkan k'vōdecho, וְעַל צִיּוֹן מִשְׁכַּן כְּבוֹדֶךָ,
on Zion, the resting place of Your Glory;

v'al malchus bays dovid m'shichecho, וְעַל מַלְכוּת בֵּית דָּוִד מְשִׁיחֶךָ,
on the monarchy of the house of David, Your anointed;*

∽§ Third Blessing: for Jerusalem

The third blessing is the final one required by the Torah. It was composed in stages by David and Solomon. David, who occupied Jerusalem, made reference to "Israel, Your people, and Jerusalem, Your city." Solomon, following his construction of the Temple, added, "the great and holy House" (*Berachos* 48b).

Their blessing was a prayer that God preserve the tranquility of the Land. Following the destruction and exile, the blessing was changed to embody a prayer for the return of the Land, the Temple, and the Davidic dynasty.

וְעַל מַלְכוּת בֵּית דָּוִד מְשִׁיחֶךְ — *(And) on the monar-*

v'al haba-yis hagodōl v'hakodōsh
וְעַל הַבַּיִת הַגָּדוֹל וְהַקָּדוֹשׁ
and on the great and holy House

shenikro shimcho olov.
שֶׁנִּקְרָא שִׁמְךָ עָלָיו.
upon which Your Name is called.

Elōhaynu ovinu,
אֱלֹהֵינוּ אָבִינוּ
Our God, our Father —

r'aynu, zunaynu, parn'saynu
רְעֵנוּ זוּנֵנוּ פַּרְנְסֵנוּ
tend us, nourish us, sustain us,

v'chalk'laynu v'harvichaynu,
וְכַלְכְּלֵנוּ וְהַרְוִיחֵנוּ,
support us, relieve us;

v'harvach lonu Adōnoy Elōhaynu
וְהַרְוַח לָנוּ יהוה אֱלֹהֵינוּ
m'hayro mikol tzorōsaynu.
מְהֵרָה מִכָּל צָרוֹתֵינוּ.
HASHEM, our God, grant us speedy relief from all our troubles.

V'no al tatzrichaynu,
וְנָא אַל תַּצְרִיכֵנוּ,
Please, make us not needful —

Adōnoy Elōhaynu,
יהוה אֱלֹהֵינוּ,
HASHEM, our God —

lō liday mat'nas bosor vodom,
לֹא לִידֵי מַתְּנַת בָּשָׂר וָדָם,
of the gifts of human hands

v'lō liday halvo-osom,
וְלֹא לִידֵי הַלְוָאָתָם,
nor of their loans,

ki im l'yod'cho
כִּי אִם לְיָדְךָ
but only of Your Hand

ham'lay-o hap'su-cho
הַמְּלֵאָה הַפְּתוּחָה
that is full, open,

hak'dōsho v'hor'chovo,
הַקְּדוֹשָׁה וְהָרְחָבָה,
holy, and generous,

shelō nayvōsh v'lō nikolaym
שֶׁלֹּא נֵבוֹשׁ וְלֹא נִכָּלֵם
that we not feel inner shame nor be humiliated

l'ōlom vo-ed.
לְעוֹלָם וָעֶד.
forever and ever.

ON THE SABBATH ADD THE FOLLOWING.

R'TZAY v'hachalitzaynu
רְצֵה וְהַחֲלִיצֵנוּ
Adōnoy Elōhaynu
יהוה אֱלֹהֵינוּ
May it please You, HASHEM, our God — give us rest

---

chy of the house of David, Your anointed. It is required that the monarchy of David's dynasty be mentioned in this blessing; whoever has not mentioned it has not fulfilled his obligation (*Berachos* 49a), because it was David who sanctified Jerusalem, and because the consolation for the exile will not be complete until David's kingdom is restored.

b'mitzvōsecho,
בְּמִצְוֹתֶיךָ,
through Your commandments

uvmitzvas yōm hash'vi-i
וּבְמִצְוַת יוֹם הַשְּׁבִיעִי
and through the commandment of the seventh day,

ha-shabos hagodōl
הַשַּׁבָּת הַגָּדוֹל
v'hakodōsh ha-ze,
וְהַקָּדוֹשׁ הַזֶּה,
this great and holy Sabbath.

ki yōm ze
כִּי יוֹם זֶה
For this day

godōl v'kodōsh hu l'fonecho,
גָּדוֹל וְקָדוֹשׁ הוּא לְפָנֶיךָ,
is great and holy before You

lishbos bō v'lonu-ach bō b'ahavo
לִשְׁבָּת בּוֹ וְלָנוּחַ בּוֹ בְּאַהֲבָה
to rest on it and be content on it in love,

k'mitzvas r'tzōnecho.
כְּמִצְוַת רְצוֹנֶךָ.
as ordained by Your will.

U-virtzōn'cho honi-ach lonu,
וּבִרְצוֹנְךָ הָנִיחַ לָנוּ,
May this be Your will — calm us,

Adōnoy Elōhaynu,
יהוה אֱלֹהֵינוּ,
HASHEM, our God,

shelō s'hay tzoro v'yogōn
שֶׁלֹּא תְהֵא צָרָה וְיָגוֹן
va-anocho
וַאֲנָחָה
so that there be no distress, grief, or lament

b'yōm m'nuchosaynu.
בְּיוֹם מְנוּחָתֵנוּ.
on this day of our contentment.

V'har-aynu Adōnoy Elōhaynu
וְהַרְאֵנוּ יהוה אֱלֹהֵינוּ
And show us, HASHEM, our God,

b'nechomas tziyōn i-recho,
בְּנֶחָמַת צִיּוֹן עִירֶךָ,
the consolation of Zion, Your city,

uv'vinyan y'rushola-yim
וּבְבִנְיַן יְרוּשָׁלַיִם
and the rebuilding of Jerusalem,

ir kodshecho,
עִיר קָדְשֶׁךָ,
City of Your holiness,

ki ato hu ba-al hai-shu-ōs
כִּי אַתָּה הוּא בַּעַל הַיְשׁוּעוֹת
for You are the Master of salvations

uva-al hanechomōs.
וּבַעַל הַנֶּחָמוֹת.
and Master of consolations.

ON *ROSH CHODESH*, FESTIVALS AND *CHOL HAMOED* RECITE THE FOLLOWING:

ELŌHAYNU Vaylōhay avōsaynu,
Our God and the God of our forefathers,

אֱלֹהֵינוּ וֵאלֹהֵי אֲבוֹתֵינוּ,

ya-a-le v'yovō v'yagi-a v'yayro-e
may there rise, come, reach, be noted,

יַעֲלֶה, וְיָבֹא, וְיַגִּיעַ, וְיֵרָאֶה,

v'yayro-tze v'yi-shoma v'yipokayd
be favored, be heard, be considered,

וְיֵרָצֶה, וְיִשָּׁמַע, וְיִפָּקֵד,

v'yizochayr zichrōnaynu u-fikdōnaynu,
and be remembered — the remembrance and consideration of ourselves;

וְיִזָּכֵר זִכְרוֹנֵנוּ וּפִקְדּוֹנֵנוּ,

v'zichrōn avōsaynu,
the remembrance of our forefathers;

וְזִכְרוֹן אֲבוֹתֵינוּ,

v'zichrōn moshi-ach ben dovid avdecho,
the remembrance of Messiah, son of David, Your servant;

וְזִכְרוֹן מָשִׁיחַ בֶּן דָּוִד עַבְדֶּךָ,

v'zichrōn y'rushola-yim ir kod'shecho,
the remembrance of Jerusalem, Your Holy City;

וְזִכְרוֹן יְרוּשָׁלַיִם עִיר קָדְשֶׁךָ,

v'zichrōn kol am'cho bays yisro-ayl
l'fonecho,
and the remembrance of Your entire people the Family of Israel — before You

וְזִכְרוֹן כָּל עַמְּךָ בֵּית יִשְׂרָאֵל לְפָנֶיךָ,

lif-layto l'tōvo
for deliverance, for goodness,

לִפְלֵיטָה לְטוֹבָה

l'chayn ulchesed ulrachamim,
for grace, for kindness, and for compassion,

לְחֵן וּלְחֶסֶד וּלְרַחֲמִים,

l'cha-yim ulsholōm
for life, and for peace

לְחַיִּים וּלְשָׁלוֹם

———————————— ON *ROSH CHODESH* ————————————

b'yōm rōsh hachōdesh ha-ze.
on this day of Rosh Chodesh.

בְּיוֹם רֹאשׁ הַחֹדֶשׁ הַזֶּה.

———————————— ON *PESACH* ————————————

b'yōm chag hamatzōs ha-ze.
on this day of the Festival of Matzos.

בְּיוֹם חַג הַמַּצּוֹת הַזֶּה.

———————————— ON *SHAVUOS* ————————————

b'yōm chag hashovu-ōs ha-ze.
on this day of the Festival of Shavuos.

בְּיוֹם חַג הַשָּׁבֻעוֹת הַזֶּה.

———————————— ON *SUCCOS* ————————————

b'yōm chag hasukōs ha-ze.
on this day of the Succos Festival.

בְּיוֹם חַג הַסֻּכּוֹת הַזֶּה.

——————— ON *SHEMINI ATZERES* AND *SIMCHAS TORAH* ———————

b'yōm hash'mini
chag ho-atzeress ha-ze.
on the eighth day, this Festival of the Assembly.

בְּיוֹם הַשְּׁמִינִי חַג הָעֲצֶרֶת הַזֶּה.

zoch'raynu Adōnoy Elōhaynu bō l'tōvo,   זָכְרֵנוּ יהוה אֱלֹהֵינוּ בּוֹ לְטוֹבָה,

Remember us on it, HASHEM, our God, for goodness,

u-fokdaynu vō livrocho,   וּפָקְדֵנוּ בּוֹ לִבְרָכָה,

consider us on it for blessing

v'hōshi-aynu vō l'cha-yim.   וְהוֹשִׁיעֵנוּ בּוֹ לְחַיִּים.

and help us on it for life.

U-vidvar y'shu-o v'rachamim,   וּבִדְבַר יְשׁוּעָה וְרַחֲמִים,

In the matter of salvation and compassion,

chus v'chonaynu   חוּס וְחָנֵּנוּ

v'rachaym olaynu v'hōshi-aynu,   וְרַחֵם עָלֵינוּ וְהוֹשִׁיעֵנוּ,

pity, be gracious and compassionate with us and help us,

ki aylecho aynaynu,   כִּי אֵלֶיךָ עֵינֵינוּ,

for our eyes are turned to You,

ki Ayl melech chanun v'rachum oto.   כִּי אֵל מֶלֶךְ חַנּוּן וְרַחוּם אָתָּה.

because You are God, the gracious and compassionate King.

❖ **UVNAY** y'rushola-yim ir hakōdesh   וּבְנֵה יְרוּשָׁלַיִם עִיר הַקֹּדֶשׁ

Rebuild Jerusalem,* the Holy City,

bimhayro v'yomaynu.   בִּמְהֵרָה בְיָמֵינוּ.

soon in our days.

Boruch ato Adōnoy,   בָּרוּךְ אַתָּה יהוה,

bōnay (v'rachamov) y'rusholo-yim.   בּוֹנֵה (בְרַחֲמָיו) יְרוּשָׁלָיִם.

Blessed are You, HASHEM, Who rebuilds Jerusalem (in His mercy).

Omayn.   אָמֵן.

Amen.*

ALL PRESENT RESPOND: Omayn — אָמֵן

■ Fourth Blessing: for God's goodness. I thank Hashem for the constant goodness that He provides for me and for the entire Jewish nation, especially in our difficult times.

BORUCH ato Adōnoy   בָּרוּךְ אַתָּה יהוה

Blessed are You, HASHEM,

Elōhaynu melech ho-ōlom,   אֱלֹהֵינוּ מֶלֶךְ הָעוֹלָם,

our God, King of the universe,

וּבְנֵה יְרוּשָׁלַיִם — *Rebuild Jerusalem.* This is the conclusion of the third blessing, and thus returns to the theme with which the blessings began — a plea for God's mercy on Jerusalem (*Pesachim* 104a).

אָמֵן — *Amen.* This blessing is unique in that one responds *Amen* after his own blessing. The purpose of this unusual formula is to serve as a

demarcation between the first three blessings, which are ordained by the Torah, and the next blessing, which is Rabbinic in origin.

◆§ **Fourth Blessing: for God's Goodness**

The essence of this blessing is the phrase "Who is good and Who does good." The blessing was composed by the court of Rabban Gamliel the Elder in Yavneh in gratitude to God for

הָאֵל אָבִינוּ מַלְכֵּנוּ
ho-Ayl ovinu malkaynu
the Almighty, our Father, our King,

אַדִּירֵנוּ בּוֹרְאֵנוּ
adiraynu bōr'aynu
our Sovereign, our Creator,

גּוֹאֲלֵנוּ יוֹצְרֵנוּ,
gō-alaynu yōtz'raynu,
our Redeemer, our Maker,

קְדוֹשֵׁנוּ קְדוֹשׁ יַעֲקֹב,
k'dōshaynu k'dōsh ya-akōv,
our Holy One, Holy One of Jacob,

רוֹעֵנוּ רוֹעֵה יִשְׂרָאֵל.
rō-aynu rō-ay yisro-ayl.
our Shepherd, the Shepherd of Israel,

הַמֶּלֶךְ הַטּוֹב
Hamelech hatōv
the King Who is good

וְהַמֵּטִיב לַכֹּל,
v'hamaytiv lakōl,
and Who does good for all.

שֶׁבְּכָל יוֹם וָיוֹם
sheb'chol yōm vo-yōm
For every single day*

הוּא הֵטִיב, הוּא מֵטִיב,
hu haytiv, hu maytiv,
He did good, He does good,

הוּא יֵיטִיב לָנוּ.
hu yaytiv lonu.
and He will do good to us.

הוּא גְמָלָנוּ, הוּא גוֹמְלֵנוּ,
Hu g'molonu, hu gōm'laynu,
He was bountiful with us, He is bountiful with us,

הוּא יִגְמְלֵנוּ לָעַד,
hu yigm'laynu lo-ad,
and He will forever be bountiful with us —

לְחֵן וּלְחֶסֶד
l'chayn ulchesed
with grace and with kindness,

וּלְרַחֲמִים וּלְרֶוַח,
ulrachamim ulrevach,
with mercy and with relief,

הַצָּלָה וְהַצְלָחָה,
hatzolo v'hatzlocho,
salvation, success,

בְּרָכָה וִישׁוּעָה
b'rocho vi-shu-o,
blessing, help,

נֶחָמָה פַּרְנָסָה וְכַלְכָּלָה
nechomo, parnoso v'chalkolo,
consolation, sustenance, support,

❖ וְרַחֲמִים וְחַיִּים
v'rachamim v'cha-yim
mercy, life,

---

preserving the bodies of the victims of the Roman massacre at Betar, and for eventually allowing them to be brought to burial (*Berachos* 48b).

שֶׁבְּכָל יוֹם וָיוֹם — *For every single day.* It is not nearly sufficient to thank God for His graciousness to past generations of Jews. We must be conscious of the fact that His goodness and

v'sholōm v'chol tōv,

וְשָׁלוֹם וְכָל טוֹב,

peace, and all good;

u-mikol tuv l'ōlom al y'chas'raynu.

וּמִכָּל טוּב לְעוֹלָם אַל יְחַסְּרֵנוּ.

and of all good things may He never deprive us.

ALL PRESENT RESPOND: Omayn — אָמֵן

HORACHAMON,

הָרַחֲמָן,

The compassionate One!

hu yimlōch olaynu l'ōlom vo-ed.

הוּא יִמְלוֹךְ עָלֵינוּ לְעוֹלָם וָעֶד.

May He reign over us forever.

Horachamon, hu yisborach

הָרַחֲמָן, הוּא יִתְבָּרַךְ

The compassionate One! May He be blessed

bashoma-yim uvo-oretz.

בַּשָּׁמַיִם וּבָאָרֶץ.

in heaven and on earth.

Horachamon,

הָרַחֲמָן,

The compassionate One!

hu yishtabach l'dōr dōrim,

הוּא יִשְׁתַּבַּח לְדוֹר דּוֹרִים,

May He be praised throughout all generations,

v'yispo-ar bonu lo-ad

וְיִתְפָּאַר בָּנוּ לָעַד

and may He be glorified through us forever

ulnaytzach n'tzochim,

וּלְנֵצַח נְצָחִים,

to the ultimate ends,

v'yis-hadar bonu lo-ad

וְיִתְהַדַּר בָּנוּ לָעַד

and be honored through us forever

ul-ōl'may ōlomim.

וּלְעוֹלְמֵי עוֹלָמִים.

and for all eternity.

Horachamon,

הָרַחֲמָן

The compassionate One!

hu y'farn'saynu b'chovōd.

הוּא יְפַרְנְסֵנוּ בְּכָבוֹד.

May He sustain us in honor.

Horachamon,

הָרַחֲמָן,

The compassionate One!

hu yishbōr ulaynu

הוּא יִשְׁבּוֹר עֻלֵּנוּ

may-al tzavoraynu,

מֵעַל צַוָּארֵנוּ,

May He break the yoke of oppression from our necks

v'hu yōli-chaynu

וְהוּא יוֹלִיכֵנוּ

kōm'miyus l'artzaynu.

קוֹמְמִיּוּת לְאַרְצֵנוּ.

and guide us erect to our Land.

---

bounty are daily, constant occurrences. הָרַחֲמָן — *The compassionate One!* The four blessings of *Bircas HaMazon* end with לְעוֹלָם

אַל יְחַסְּרֵנוּ, ''may He never deprive us.'' The remainder of *Bircas HaMazon* is a collection of brief prayers for God's compassion.

Horachamon,
The compassionate One!

הָרַחֲמָן,

hu yishlach lonu b'rocho
m'rubo baba-yis ha-ze,

הוּא יִשְׁלַח לָנוּ בְּרָכָה
מְרֻבָּה בַּבַּיִת הַזֶּה,

May He send us abundant blessing to this house

v'al shulchon ze she-ochalnu olov.

וְעַל שֻׁלְחָן זֶה שֶׁאָכַלְנוּ עָלָיו.

and upon this table at which we have eaten.

Horachamon,
The compassionate One!

הָרַחֲמָן,

hu yishlach lonu es
ayliyohu hanovi zochur latōv,

הוּא יִשְׁלַח לָנוּ אֶת
אֵלִיָּהוּ הַנָּבִיא זָכוּר לַטּוֹב,

May He send us Elijah, the Prophet — he is remembered for good —

vivaser lonu b'sōrōs tōvōs

וִיבַשֶּׂר לָנוּ בְּשׂוֹרוֹת טוֹבוֹת

to proclaim to us good tidings,

y'shu-ōs v'nechomōs.

יְשׁוּעוֹת וְנֶחָמוֹת.

salvations, and consolations.

AT ONE'S OWN TABLE (INCLUDE THE APPLICABLE WORDS IN PARENTHESES):

Horachamon,
The compassionate One!

הָרַחֲמָן,

hu y'voraych ōsi
(v'es ishti/v'es bali. v'es zari)

הוּא יְבָרֵךְ אוֹתִי
(וְאֶת אִשְׁתִּי/וְאֶת בַּעְלִי. וְאֶת זַרְעִי)

May He bless me (my wife/husband and my children)

v'es kol asher li.

וְאֶת כָּל אֲשֶׁר לִי.

and all that is mine.

GUESTS RECITE THE FOLLOWING (CHILDREN AT THEIR PARENTS' TABLE
INCLUDE THE APPLICABLE WORDS IN PARENTHESES):

Horachamon,
The compassionate One!

הָרַחֲמָן,

hu y'voraych es (ovi mōri)
ba-al haba-yis ha-ze,

הוּא יְבָרֵךְ אֶת (אָבִי מוֹרִי)
בַּעַל הַבַּיִת הַזֶּה,

May He bless (my father, my teacher) the master of this house,

v'es (imi mōrosi)
ba-alas haba-yis ha-ze,

וְאֶת (אִמִּי מוֹרָתִי)
בַּעֲלַת הַבַּיִת הַזֶּה,

and (my mother, my teacher) lady of this house,

ALL CONTINUE:

ōsom v'es baysom v'es zar-om

אוֹתָם וְאֶת בֵּיתָם וְאֶת זַרְעָם

them, their house, their family,

v'es kol asher lohem, וְאֶת כָּל אֲשֶׁר לָהֶם,
and all that is theirs.

ōsonu v'es kol asher lonu, אוֹתָנוּ וְאֶת כָּל אֲשֶׁר לָנוּ,
Ours and all that is ours —

k'mō shenisbor'chu avōsaynu כְּמוֹ שֶׁנִּתְבָּרְכוּ אֲבוֹתֵינוּ
avrohom yitzchok v'ya-akōv אַבְרָהָם יִצְחָק וְיַעֲקֹב
just as our forefathers Abraham, Isaac, and Jacob were blessed

bakōl mikōl kōl. בַּכֹּל מִכֹּל כֹּל,
in everything, from everything, with everything.

kayn y'voraych ōsonu kulonu yachad כֵּן יְבָרֵךְ אוֹתָנוּ כֻּלָּנוּ יַחַד
So may He bless us all together

bivrocho sh'laymo. בִּבְרָכָה שְׁלֵמָה.
with a perfect blessing.

V'nōmar: Omayn. וְנֹאמַר: אָמֵן.
And let us say: Amen!

BAMORŌM בַּמָּרוֹם
On high,

y'lam'du alayhem v'olaynu z'chus, יְלַמְּדוּ עֲלֵיהֶם וְעָלֵינוּ זְכוּת,
may merit be pleaded upon them and upon us,

shet'hay l'mishmeres sholōm, שֶׁתְּהֵא לְמִשְׁמֶרֶת שָׁלוֹם.
for a safeguard of peace.*

V'niso v'rocho may-ays Adōnoy, וְנִשָּׂא בְרָכָה מֵאֵת יהוה,
May we receive a blessing from HASHEM

utzdoko may-Elōhay yish-aynu, וּצְדָקָה מֵאֱלֹהֵי יִשְׁעֵנוּ,
and just kindness from the God of our salvation,

v'nimtzo chayn v'saychel tōv וְנִמְצָא חֵן וְשֵׂכֶל טוֹב
and find favor and good understanding

b'aynay Elōhim v'odom. בְּעֵינֵי אֱלֹהִים וְאָדָם.
in the eyes of God and man.

ON THE SABBATH ADD:

Horachamon, hu yanchilaynu הָרַחֲמָן, הוּא יַנְחִילֵנוּ
The compassionate One! May He cause us to inherit

yōm shekulō shabos umnucho יוֹם שֶׁכֻּלּוֹ שַׁבָּת וּמְנוּחָה
the day which will be completely a Sabbath* and rest day

l'cha-yay ho-ōlomim. לְחַיֵּי הָעוֹלָמִים.
for eternal life.

לְמִשְׁמֶרֶת שָׁלוֹם — *For a safeguard of peace,* i.e., to assure that the home will be contented and peaceful.

יוֹם שֶׁכֻּלּוֹ שַׁבָּת — *The day which will be completely a Sabbath,* an allusion to the World to Come after the Final Redemption.

ON ROSH CHODESH ADD:

Horachamon,

הָרַחֲמָן

The compassionate One!

hu y'chadaysh olaynu

הוּא יְחַדֵּשׁ עָלֵינוּ

es hachōdesh ha-ze

אֶת הַחֹדֶשׁ הַזֶּה

May He inaugurate this month upon us

l'tōvo v'livrocho.

לְטוֹבָה וְלִבְרָכָה.

for goodness and for blessing.

ON FESTIVALS ADD:

Horachamon, hu yanchilaynu

הָרַחֲמָן הוּא יַנְחִילֵנוּ

The compassionate One! May He cause us to inherit

yōm shekulō tōv.

יוֹם שֶׁכֻּלוֹ טוֹב.

the day which is completely good.

ON SUCCOS ADD:

Horachamon, hu yokim lonu

הָרַחֲמָן הוּא יָקִים לָנוּ

The compassionate One! May He erect for us

es sukas dovid hanōfoles.

אֶת סֻכַּת דָּוִיד הַנֹּפֶלֶת.

David's fallen booth.*

HORACHAMON, hu y'zakaynu

הָרַחֲמָן הוּא יְזַכֵּנוּ

The compassionate One! May He make us worthy

limōs hamoshi-ach

לִימוֹת הַמָּשִׁיחַ

of the days of Messiah

ulcha-yay ho-ōlom habo.

וּלְחַיֵּי הָעוֹלָם הַבָּא.

and the life of the World to Come.

ON THE SABBATH, FESTIVALS, *CHOL HAMOED,* AND *ROSH CHODESH*:

Migdōl y'shu-ōs malkō,

מִגְדּוֹל יְשׁוּעוֹת מַלְכּוֹ

He Who is a tower of salvations to His king

ON WEEKDAYS:

Magdil y'shu-ōs malkō,

מַגְדִּיל יְשׁוּעוֹת מַלְכּוֹ

He Who makes great the salvations of His king

v'ōse chesed limshichō

וְעֹשֶׂה חֶסֶד לִמְשִׁיחוֹ

and does kindness for His anointed,

l'dovid ulzar-ō ad ōlom.

לְדָוִד וּלְזַרְעוֹ עַד עוֹלָם.

to David and to his descendants forever.

סֻכַּת דָּוִיד הַנֹּפֶלֶת — *David's fallen booth.* This phrase was used by God when He promised to restore the kingship of the Davidic dy-nasty which is figuratively called *succah.* The word *succah* means "protection," and refers to the king's protection of his people.

Ō-se sholōm bimrōmov,　　　　　עֹשֶׂה שָׁלוֹם בִּמְרוֹמָיו,

　　He Who makes peace in His heights,*

hu ya-a-se sholōm olaynu　　　　הוּא יַעֲשֶׂה שָׁלוֹם עָלֵינוּ

　　　　may He make peace upon us

v'al kol yisro-ayl. V'imru: Omayn.　וְעַל כָּל יִשְׂרָאֵל. וְאִמְרוּ, אָמֵן.

　　and upon all Israel. Now respond: Amen!

Y'RU es Adōnoy k'dōshov,　　　יְראוּ אֶת יהוה קְדֹשָׁיו,

　　　Fear HASHEM, *you — His holy ones —*

ki ayn machsōr liray-ov.　　　כִּי אֵין מַחְסוֹר לִירֵאָיו.

　　for there is no deprivation for His reverent ones.*

K'firim roshu v'ro-ayvu,　　　כְּפִירִים רָשׁוּ וְרָעֵבוּ,

　　Young lions may be in need and hunger,

v'dōr'shay Adōnoy　　　　וְדֹרְשֵׁי יהוה

　lō yachs'ru chol tōv.　　　לֹא יַחְסְרוּ כָל טוֹב.

　　but those who seek HASHEM *will not lack any good.*

Hōdu Ladōnoy ki tōv,　　　הוֹדוּ לַיהוה כִּי טוֹב,

　　Give thanks to God for He is good;

ki l'ōlom chasdō.　　　כִּי לְעוֹלָם חַסְדּוֹ.

　　His kindness endures forever.

Pōsay-ach es yodecho,　　　פּוֹתֵחַ אֶת יָדֶךָ,

　　You open Your hand

u-masbi-a l'chol chai rotzōn.　　וּמַשְׂבִּיעַ לְכָל חַי רָצוֹן.

　　and satisfy the desire of every living thing.

Boruch hagever　　　　בָּרוּךְ הַגֶּבֶר

　asher yivtach Badōnoy,　　　אֲשֶׁר יִבְטַח בַּיהוה,

　　Blessed is the man who trusts in HASHEM,

v'ho-yo Adōnoy mivtachō.　　וְהָיָה יהוה מִבְטַחוֹ.

　　then HASHEM *will be his security.**

Na-ar ho-yisi gam zokanti,　　נַעַר הָיִיתִי גַּם זָקַנְתִּי,

　　I was a youth and also have aged,

By extension, this also refers to the Temple, which is called David's because he longed to build it and prepared for its construction. As the abode of God's Presence, it, too, protects Israel.

עֹשֶׂה שָׁלוֹם בִּמְרוֹמָיו — *He Who makes peace in His heights.* Even the heavenly beings require God to make peace among them — how much more so fractious man!

יְראוּ . . . כִּי אֵין מַחְסוֹר לִירֵאָיו — *Fear . . . for there*

is no deprivation for His reverent ones. Those who fear God are content, even if they are lacking in material possessions. But the wicked are never satisfied; whatever they have only whets their appetite for more.

אֲשֶׁר יִבְטַח בַּה׳ וְהָיָה ה׳ מִבְטַחוֹ — *Who trusts in* HASHEM, *then* HASHEM *will be his security.* God will be a fortress of trust to a person in direct proportion to the amount of trust one places in God.

v'lō ro-isi tzadik ne-ezov,

וְלֹא רָאִיתִי צַדִּיק נֶעֱזָב,

and I have not seen a righteous man forsaken,

v'zar-ō m'vakaysh lochem.

וְזַרְעוֹ מְבַקֶּשׁ לָחֶם.

with his children begging for bread.*

Adōnoy ōz l'amō yitayn,

יהוה עֹז לְעַמּוֹ יִתֵּן,

HASHEM will give might to His people;

Adōnoy y'voraych es amō

va-sholōm.

יהוה יְבָרֵךְ אֶת עַמּוֹ
בַשָּׁלוֹם.

HASHEM will bless His people with peace.

⚜ BLESSINGS AFTER OTHER FOODS ⚜
THE THREE-FACETED BLESSING*

THE FOLLOWING BLESSING IS RECITED AFTER PARTAKING OF:
(A) GRAIN PRODUCTS (OTHER THAN BREAD OR MATZAH) MADE FROM WHEAT, BARLEY, RYE,
OATS, OR SPELT; (B) GRAPE WINE OR GRAPE JUICE; (C) GRAPES, FIGS, POMEGRANATES, OLIVES,
OR DATES. (IF FOODS FROM TWO OR THREE OF THESE GROUPS WERE EATEN, THEN THE
INSERTIONS FOR EACH GROUP ARE CONNECTED WITH THE CONJUNCTIVE וְ, THUS וְעַל.
THE ORDER IN SUCH A CASE IS GRAIN, WINE, FRUIT.)

Boruch ato Adōnoy,

בָּרוּךְ אַתָּה יהוה

Blessed are You, HASHEM,

Elōhaynu melech ho-ōlom,

אֱלֹהֵינוּ מֶלֶךְ הָעוֹלָם,

our God, King of the universe,

———————————— AFTER GRAIN PRODUCTS: ————————————

al hamichyo v'al hakalkolo,

עַל הַמִּחְיָה וְעַל הַכַּלְכָּלָה,

for the nourishment* and the sustenance*

———————————— AFTER WINE: ————————————

al hagefen v'al p'ri hagefen,

עַל הַגֶּפֶן וְעַל פְּרִי הַגֶּפֶן,

for the vine and the fruit of the vine*

———————————— AFTER FRUITS: ————————————

al ho-aytz v'al p'ri ho-aytz,

עַל הָעֵץ וְעַל פְּרִי הָעֵץ,

for the tree and the fruit of the tree

וְלֹא רָאִיתִי צַדִּיק נֶעֱזָב ... — *And I have not seen a righteous man forsaken, with his children begging for bread.* I have never seen a righteous man consider himself forsaken even if his children must beg for bread. Whatever his lot in life, he trusts that God brings it upon him for a constructive and merciful purpose.

⽔ **The Three-Faceted Blessing**

A special blessing of thanks is recited after partaking of any of the seven species for which the Torah praises the Land of Israel (see *Deuteronomy* 8:8). This blessing is a single blessing that is an abridgment of the three Scripturally

ordained blessings of *Bircas HaMazon*.

הַמִּחְיָה — *Nourishment.* This is a generic term referring to all foods made from five species of grain: wheat, barley, rye, oats, and spelt.

כַּלְכָּלָה — *Sustenance.* This concludes the first part of the Three-Part Blessing. It is parallel to the first blessing of *Bircas HaMazon* which thanks God for the blessing of food.

עַל הַגֶּפֶן וְעַל פְּרִי הַגֶּפֶן — *For the vine and the fruit of the vine.* Wine has its own particular blessings, both before partaking of it and after. The uniqueness of wine is due to its special qualities: In sensible amounts it glad-

v'al t'nuvas haso-de,   וְעַל תְּנוּבַת הַשָּׂדֶה,

and for the produce of the field;

v'al eretz chemdo tova urchovo,   וְעַל אֶרֶץ חֶמְדָּה טוֹבָה וּרְחָבָה,

for the desirable, good, and spacious Land*

sherotziso v'hinchalto la-avōsaynu,   שֶׁרָצִיתָ וְהִנְחַלְתָּ לַאֲבוֹתֵינוּ,

that You were pleased to give our forefathers as a heritage,

le-echōl mipiryoh   לֶאֱכוֹל מִפִּרְיָהּ

to eat of its fruit

v'lisbō-a mituvoh.   וְלִשְׂבּוֹעַ מִטּוּבָהּ.

and to be satisfied with its goodness.

Rachaym no Adōnoy Elōhaynu   רַחֵם נָא יהוה אֱלֹהֵינוּ

Have mercy,* we beg You, HASHEM, our God,

al yisro-ayl amecho,   עַל יִשְׂרָאֵל עַמֶּךָ,

on Israel, Your people;

v'al y'rushola-yim i-recho,   וְעַל יְרוּשָׁלַיִם עִירֶךָ,

on Jerusalem, Your city;

v'al tzi-yōn mishkan k'vodecho,   וְעַל צִיּוֹן מִשְׁכַּן כְּבוֹדֶךָ,

on Zion, the resting place of Your glory;

v'al mizb'checho v'al haycholecho.   וְעַל מִזְבְּחֶךָ וְעַל הֵיכָלֶךָ.

on Your Altar, and on Your Temple.

Uvnay y'rushola-yim ir hakōdesh   וּבְנֵה יְרוּשָׁלַיִם עִיר הַקֹּדֶשׁ

Rebuild Jerusalem, the Holy City,

bimhayro v'yomaynu,   בִּמְהֵרָה בְיָמֵינוּ,

speedily in our days.

v'ha-alaynu l'sōchoh,   וְהַעֲלֵנוּ לְתוֹכָהּ,

Bring us up into it

v'samchaynu b'vinyonoh,   וְשַׂמְּחֵנוּ בְּבִנְיָנָהּ,

and gladden us in its rebuilding

v'nochal mipiryoh,   וְנֹאכַל מִפִּרְיָהּ,

and let us eat from its fruit

v'nisba mituvoh,   וְנִשְׂבַּע מִטּוּבָהּ,

and be satisfied with its goodness

---

dens and satiates and is used in the performance of such commandments as *Kiddush* and *Havdalah* (*Berachos* 35b).

וְעַל אֶרֶץ חֶמְדָּה — *And for the desirable . . . Land.* This begins the second section of the blessing.

It parallels the second blessing of *Bircas HaMazon* in thanking God for *Eretz Yisrael.*

רַחֵם — *Have mercy.* This begins the third section of the blessing, paralleling the third blessing of *Bircas HaMazon.*

unvorech'cho oleho

וּנְבָרֶכְךָ עָלֶיהָ

and bless You upon it

bikdusho uvtohoro.

בִּקְדֻשָּׁה וּבְטָהֲרָה.

in holiness and purity.

──────────── ON THE SABBATH: ────────────

Urtzay v'ha-chalitzaynu
b'yōm ha-shabos ha-ze.

וּרְצֵה וְהַחֲלִיצֵנוּ
בְּיוֹם הַשַּׁבָּת הַזֶּה.

And be pleased to let us rest on this Sabbath day.

──────────── ON *ROSH CHODESH:* ────────────

V'zochraynu l'tōvo
b'yōm rōsh hachōdesh ha-ze.

וְזָכְרֵנוּ לְטוֹבָה
בְּיוֹם רֹאשׁ הַחֹדֶשׁ הַזֶּה.

And remember us (for goodness) on this day of Rosh Chodesh.

──────────── ON PESACH: ────────────

V'sam'chaynu b'yōm
chag hamatzōs ha-ze.

וְשַׂמְּחֵנוּ בְּיוֹם
חַג הַמַּצּוֹת הַזֶּה.

And gladden us on this day of the Festival of Matzos.

──────────── ON SHAVUOS: ────────────

V'sam'chaynu b'yōm
chag ha-shovu-ōs ha-ze.

וְשַׂמְּחֵנוּ בְּיוֹם
חַג הַשָּׁבֻעוֹת הַזֶּה.

And gladden us on this day of the Festival of Shavuos.

──────────── ON SUCCOS: ────────────

V'sam'chaynu b'yōm
chag ha-sukōs ha-ze.

וְשַׂמְּחֵנוּ בְּיוֹם
חַג הַסֻּכּוֹת הַזֶּה.

And gladden us on this day of the Festival of Succos.

──────────── ON SHEMINI ATZERES AND SIMCHAS TORAH: ────────────

V'sam'chaynu b'yōm ha-shmini
chag ho-atzeres ha-ze.

וְשַׂמְּחֵנוּ בְּיוֹם הַשְּׁמִינִי
חַג הָעֲצֶרֶת הַזֶּה.

And gladden us on the eighth day, this Festival of the Assembly.

Ki ato Adōnoy

כִּי אַתָּה יהוה

For You, HASHEM,

tōv u-maytiv lakōl,

טוֹב וּמֵטִיב לַכֹּל,

are good and do good to all*

v'nō-de lecho al ho-oretz

וְנוֹדֶה לְךָ עַל הָאָרֶץ

and we thank You for the Land

──────────────────────────────

אַתָּה . . . טוֹב וּמֵטִיב לַכֹּל — *You . . . are good and do good to all.* This section of the blessing parallels the fourth, Rabbinically instituted, blessing of *Bircas HaMazon.*.

———————— AFTER GRAIN PRODUCTS: ————————

v'al hamichyo,

וְעַל הַמִּחְיָה.

and for the nourishment.

Boruch ato Adōnoy,

בָּרוּךְ אַתָּה יהוה,

al ho-oretz v'al hamichyo.

עַל הָאָרֶץ וְעַל הַמִּחְיָה.

Blessed are You, HASHEM, for the Land and for the nourishment.

———————— AFTER WINE: ————————

IF THE WINE IS FROM *ERETZ YISRAEL*, SUBSTITUTE THE WORD IN BRACKETS.

v'al p'ri hagefen [gafnoh],

וְעַל פְּרִי הַגֶּפֶן [גַפְנָה].

and for the fruit of the [its] vine

Boruch ato Adōnoy, al ho-oretz

בָּרוּךְ אַתָּה יהוה, עַל הָאָרֶץ

v'al p'ri hagefen [gafnoh],

וְעַל פְּרִי הַגֶּפֶן [גַפְנָה].

Blessed are You, HASHEM, for the Land and for the fruit of the [its] vine.

———————— AFTER FRUITS: ————————

IF THE FRUIT IS FROM *ERETZ YISRAEL*, SUBSTITUTE THE WORD IN BRACKETS.

v'al hapayrōs [payrō-seho].

וְעַל הַפֵּרוֹת [פֵּרוֹתֶיהָ].

and for the [its] fruit.

Boruch ato Adōnoy, al ho-oretz

בָּרוּךְ אַתָּה יהוה, עַל הָאָרֶץ

v'al hapayrōs [payrō-seho].

וְעַל הַפֵּרוֹת [פֵּרוֹתֶיהָ].

Blessed are You, HASHEM, for the Land and for the [its] fruit.

BOREI NEFASHOS

AFTER EATING OR DRINKING ANY FOOD TO WHICH NEITHER THE GRACE AFTER MEALS
NOR THE THREE-FACETED BLESSING APPLIES, SUCH AS FRUITS OTHER THAN THE ABOVE,
VEGETABLES, OR BEVERAGES OTHER THAN WINE, RECITE:

Boruch ato Adōnoy,

בָּרוּךְ אַתָּה יהוה

Blessed are You, HASHEM,

Elōhaynu melech ho-ōlom,

אֱלֹהֵינוּ מֶלֶךְ הָעוֹלָם,

our God, King of the universe,

bōray n'foshōs rabōs v'chesrōnon,

בּוֹרֵא נְפָשׁוֹת רַבּוֹת וְחֶסְרוֹנָן,

Who creates numerous living things with their deficiencies;

al kol ma sheboro(so)

עַל כָּל מַה שֶׁבָּרָא(תָ)

for all that You have created

l'hacha-yōs bohem nefesh kol chai.

לְהַחֲיוֹת בָּהֶם נֶפֶשׁ כָּל חָי.

with which to maintain the life of every being.

Boruch chay ho-ōlomim.

בָּרוּךְ חֵי הָעוֹלָמִים.

Blessed is He, the life of the worlds.

⊰ THE BEDTIME SHEMA ⊱

■ Commensurate with our belief and trust in Hashem is the protection He affords each of us. The Talmud (*Berachos* 57b) teaches that sleep constitutes one-sixtieth of death. In response to the need for greater protection, we recite the *Shema* and Scriptural verses portraying Hashem's protection.

RIBŌNO shel ōlom

רִבּוֹנוֹ שֶׁל עוֹלָם

Master of the universe,

harayni mōchayl l'chol mi

הֲרֵינִי מוֹחֵל לְכָל מִי

she-hich-is v'hik-nit ōsi

שֶׁהִכְעִיס וְהִקְנִיט אוֹתִי,

I hereby forgive anyone who angered or antagonized me

ō shechoto k'negdi —

אוֹ שֶׁחָטָא כְּנֶגְדִּי —

or who sinned against me —

bayn b'gufi bayn b'momōni

בֵּין בְּגוּפִי, בֵּין בְּמָמוֹנִי,

whether against my body, my property,

bayn bichvōdi bayn b'chol asher li;

בֵּין בִּכְבוֹדִי, בֵּין בְּכָל אֲשֶׁר לִי;

my honor or against anything of mine;

bayn b'ōnes bayn b'rotzōn

בֵּין בְּאוֹנֶס, בֵּין בְּרָצוֹן,

whether he did so accidentally, willfully,

bayn b'shōgayg bayn b'mayzid;

בֵּין בְּשׁוֹגֵג, בֵּין בְּמֵזִיד;

carelessly, or purposely;

bayn b'dibur bayn b'ma-a-se

בֵּין בְּדִבּוּר, בֵּין בְּמַעֲשֶׂה,

whether through speech, deed,

bayn b'machshovo bayn b'hirhur;

בֵּין בְּמַחֲשָׁבָה, בֵּין בְּהִרְהוּר;

thought, or notion;

bayn b'gilgul ze

בֵּין בְּגִלְגּוּל זֶה,

bayn b'gilgul achayr —

בֵּין בְּגִלְגּוּל אַחֵר —

whether in this transmigration or another transmigration —

l'chol bar yisro-ayl

לְכָל בַּר יִשְׂרָאֵל,

I forgive every Jew.

v'lo yay-onaysh shum odom b'sibosi.

וְלֹא יֵעָנֵשׁ שׁוּם אָדָם בִּסְבָתִי.

May no man be punished because of me.

Y'hi rotzon mil'fonecho

יְהִי רָצוֹן מִלְפָנֶיךָ

Adōnoy Elōhai Vaylōhay avosai

יהוה אֱלֹהַי וֵאלֹהֵי אֲבוֹתַי,

May it be Your will, Hashem, my God and the God of my forefathers,

shelō e-cheto ōd

שֶׁלֹא אֶחֱטָא עוֹד,

that I may sin no more,

u-ma shechotosi l'fonecho

וּמַה שֶּׁחָטָאתִי לְפָנֶיךָ

and whatever sins I have done before You,

m'chok b'rachamecho horabim

מְחוֹק בְּרַחֲמֶיךָ הָרַבִּים,

may You blot out in Your abundant mercies,

avol lō al y'day yisurim

אֲבָל לֹא עַל יְדֵי יִסּוּרִים

vocholo-yim ro-im.

וַחֲלָיִים רָעִים.

but not through suffering or bad illnesses.

Yih-yu l'rotzōn imray fi

יִהְיוּ לְרָצוֹן אִמְרֵי פִי

v'hegyōn libi lifonecho

וְהֶגְיוֹן לִבִּי לְפָנֶיךָ,

May the expressions of my mouth and the thoughts of my heart find favor before You,

Adōnoy tzuri v'gō-ali

יהוה צוּרִי וְגֹאֲלִי.

HASHEM, my Rock and my Redeemer.

BORUCH ato Adōnoy

בָּרוּךְ אַתָּה יהוה

Elōhaynu melech ho-ōlom

אֱלֹהֵינוּ מֶלֶךְ הָעוֹלָם,

Blessed are You, HASHEM, our God, King of the universe,

hamapil chevlay shayno al aynoi

הַמַּפִּיל חֶבְלֵי שֵׁנָה עַל עֵינָי,

Who casts the bonds of sleep upon my eyes

us-numo al af-apoi.

וּתְנוּמָה עַל עַפְעַפָּי.

and slumber upon my eyelids.

Vi-hi rotzōn mil'fonecho

וִיהִי רָצוֹן מִלְּפָנֶיךָ

Adōnoy Elohai Vaylōhay avosai,

יהוה אֱלֹהַי וֵאלֹהֵי אֲבוֹתַי,

May it be Your will, HASHEM, my God, and the God of my forefathers,

shetashkivayni l'sholōm

שֶׁתַּשְׁכִּיבֵנִי לְשָׁלוֹם

v'sa-amidayni l'sholōm.

וְתַעֲמִידֵנִי לְשָׁלוֹם.

that You lay me down to sleep in peace and raise me erect in peace.

V'al y'va-haluni ra-yōnai,

וְאַל יְבַהֲלוּנִי רַעְיוֹנַי,

vachalōmōs ro-im,

וַחֲלוֹמוֹת רָעִים,

v'harhōrim ro-im.

וְהִרְהוּרִים רָעִים.

May my ideas, bad dreams, and bad notions not confound me.

Us-hay mitosi sh'laymo l'fonecho.

וּתְהֵא מִטָּתִי שְׁלֵמָה לְפָנֶיךָ.

May my offspring be perfect before You,

V'ho-ayr aynai pen i-shan hamo-ves,

וְהָאֵר עֵינַי פֶּן אִישַׁן הַמָּוֶת,

and may You illuminate my eyes lest I die in sleep,

ki ato hamayir l'i-shōn bas o-yin.

כִּי אַתָּה הַמֵּאִיר לְאִישׁוֹן בַּת עָיִן.

for it is You Who illuminates the pupil of the eye.

Boruch ato Adōnoy
Blessed are You, HASHEM,
בָּרוּךְ אַתָּה יהוה,

hamay-ir lo-ōlom kulō bichvodō.
Who illuminates the entire world with His glory.
הַמֵּאִיר לָעוֹלָם כֻּלּוֹ בִּכְבוֹדוֹ.

AYL melech ne-emon.
God, trustworthy King.
אֵל מֶלֶךְ נֶאֱמָן.

RECITE THE FIRST VERSE ALOUD, WITH YOUR RIGHT HAND COVERING YOUR EYES, AND
CONCENTRATE INTENSELY UPON ACCEPTING GOD'S ABSOLUTE SOVEREIGNTY.

SH'MA yisro-ayl,
שְׁמַע יִשְׂרָאֵל,

Adōnoy Elōhaynu, Adōnoy e-chod.
יהוה אֱלֹהֵינוּ, יהוה אֶחָד.
Hear, O Israel: HASHEM is our God, HASHEM, the One [and Only].

IN AN UNDERTONE:

Boruch shaym k'vōd malchusō
בָּרוּךְ שֵׁם כְּבוֹד מַלְכוּתוֹ

l'ōlom vo-ed.
לְעוֹלָם וָעֶד.
Blessed is the Name of His glorious kingdom for all eternity.

V'OHAVTO ays
וְאָהַבְתָּ אֵת

Adōnoy Elōhecho,
יהוה ׀ אֱלֹהֶיךָ,
You shall love HASHEM, your God,

b'chol l'vov'cho,
בְּכָל לְבָבְךָ,
with all your heart,

uvchol nafsh'cho, uvchol m'ōdecho.
וּבְכָל נַפְשְׁךָ, וּבְכָל מְאֹדֶךָ.
with all your soul and with all your resources.

V'ho-yu had'vorim ho-ayle,
וְהָיוּ הַדְּבָרִים הָאֵלֶּה,

asher onōchi m'tzav'cho ha-yōm,
אֲשֶׁר אָנֹכִי מְצַוְּךָ הַיּוֹם,
Let these matters that I command you today

al l'vovecho.
עַל לְבָבֶךָ.
be upon your heart.

V'shinantom l'vonecho,
וְשִׁנַּנְתָּם לְבָנֶיךָ,
Teach them thoroughly to your children

v'dibarto bom
וְדִבַּרְתָּ בָּם,
and speak of them

b'shivt'cho b'vay-secho,
בְּשִׁבְתְּךָ בְּבֵיתֶךָ,

uvlecht'cho vaderech
וּבְלֶכְתְּךָ בַדֶּרֶךְ,
while you sit in your home, while you walk on the way,

uv'shochb'cho, uvkumecho.
וּבְשָׁכְבְּךָ וּבְקוּמֶךָ.
when you retire and when you arise.

Ukshartom l'ōs al yodecho,
וּקְשַׁרְתָּם לְאוֹת עַל יָדֶךָ,
And you shall bind them as a sign upon your arm

v'ho-yu l'tōtofōs bayn aynecho.   וְהָיוּ לְטֹטָפֹת בֵּין עֵינֶיךָ.

and they shall be tefillin between your eyes.

Uchsavtom al m'zuzōs bay-secho   וּכְתַבְתָּם עַל מְזֻזוֹת בֵּיתֶךָ,
u-vish-orecho.   וּבִשְׁעָרֶיךָ.

And write them on the doorposts of your house and upon your gates.

VIHI nō-am Adōnoy   **וִיהִי** נֹעַם אֲדֹנָי
Elōhaynu olaynu,   אֱלֹהֵינוּ עָלֵינוּ,

May the pleasantness of my Lord, our God, be upon us —

u-ma-asay yodaynu kōn'no olaynu,   וּמַעֲשֵׂה יָדֵינוּ כּוֹנְנָה עָלֵינוּ,

and our handiwork, may You establish for us;

u-ma-asay yodaynu kōn'nayhu.   וּמַעֲשֵׂה יָדֵינוּ כּוֹנְנֵהוּ.

and our handiwork, may You establish.

YŌSHAYV b'sayser elyōn,   **יֹשֵׁב** בְּסֵתֶר עֶלְיוֹן,

Whoever sits in the refuge of the Most High,

b'tzayl Shadai yislōnon.   בְּצֵל שַׁדַּי יִתְלוֹנָן.

he shall dwell in the shadow of the Almighty.

Ōmar Ladōnoy machsi umtzudosi,   אֹמַר לַיהוה מַחְסִי וּמְצוּדָתִי,

I will say of HASHEM, "He is my refuge and my fortress,

Elōhai evtach bō.   אֱלֹהַי אֶבְטַח בּוֹ.

my God, I will trust in Him."

Ki hu yatzil'cho mipach yokush,   כִּי הוּא יַצִּילְךָ מִפַּח יָקוּשׁ,

For He will deliver you from the ensnaring trap,

mi-dever havōs.   מִדֶּבֶר הַוּוֹת.

from devastating pestilence.

B'evrosō yosech loch,   בְּאֶבְרָתוֹ יָסֶךְ לָךְ,

With His pinion He will cover you,

v'sachas k'nofov techse,   וְתַחַת כְּנָפָיו תֶּחְסֶה,

and beneath His wings you will be protected;

tzino v'sōchayro amitō.   צִנָּה וְסֹחֵרָה אֲמִתּוֹ.

shield and armor is His truth.

Lō siro mipachad loylo,   לֹא תִירָא מִפַּחַד לָיְלָה,

You shall not fear the terror of night;

maychaytz yo-uf yōmom.   מֵחֵץ יָעוּף יוֹמָם.

nor the arrow that flies by day;

Mi-dever bo-ōfel yahalōch,   מִדֶּבֶר בָּאֹפֶל יַהֲלֹךְ,

nor the pestilence that walks in gloom;

miketev yoshud tzohoro-yim.

מִקֶּטֶב יָשׁוּד צָהֳרָיִם.

nor the destroyer who lays waste at noon.

Yipōl mitzid'cho elef,

יִפֹּל מִצִּדְּךָ אֶלֶף,

ur'vovo miminecho,

וּרְבָבָה מִימִינֶךָ,

Let a thousand encamp at your side and a myriad at your right hand,

aylecho lō yigosh.

אֵלֶיךָ לֹא יִגָּשׁ.

but to you they shall not approach.

Rak b'aynecho sabit,

רַק בְּעֵינֶיךָ תַבִּיט,

v'shilumas r'sho-im tir-e.

וְשִׁלֻּמַת רְשָׁעִים תִּרְאֶה.

You will merely peer with your eyes and you will see the retribution of the wicked.

Ki ato Adōnoy machsi,

כִּי אַתָּה יהוה מַחְסִי,

Because [you said,] "You, HASHEM, are my refuge,"

elyōn samto m'ōnecho.

עֶלְיוֹן שַׂמְתָּ מְעוֹנֶךָ.

you have made the Most High your dwelling place.

Lō s'une aylecho ro-o,

לֹא תְאֻנֶּה אֵלֶיךָ רָעָה,

v'nega lō yikrav b'oholecho.

וְנֶגַע לֹא יִקְרַב בְּאָהֳלֶךָ.

No evil will befall you, nor will any plague come near your tent.

Ki mal-ochov y'tza-ve loch,

כִּי מַלְאָכָיו יְצַוֶּה לָּךְ,

lishmorcho b'chol d'rochecho.

לִשְׁמָרְךָ בְּכָל דְּרָכֶיךָ.

He will charge His angels for you, to protect you in all your ways.

Al kapa-yim yiso-uncho,

עַל כַּפַּיִם יִשָּׂאוּנְךָ,

pen tigōf bo-even raglecho.

פֶּן תִּגֹּף בָּאֶבֶן רַגְלֶךָ.

On [their] palms they will carry you, lest you strike your foot against a stone.

Al shachal vofesen tidrōch,

עַל שַׁחַל וָפֶתֶן תִּדְרֹךְ,

Upon the lion and the viper you will tread;

tirmōs k'fir v'sanin.

תִּרְמֹס כְּפִיר וְתַנִּין.

you will trample the young lion and the serpent.

Ki vi choshak va-afal'tayhu,

כִּי בִי חָשַׁק וַאֲפַלְּטֵהוּ,

For he has yearned for Me and I will deliver him;

asag'vayhu ki yoda sh'mi.

אֲשַׂגְּבֵהוּ כִּי יָדַע שְׁמִי.

I will elevate him because he knows My Name.

Yikro-ayni v'e-enayhu,

יִקְרָאֵנִי וְאֶעֱנֵהוּ,

He will call upon Me and I will answer him,

imō onōchi v'tzoro,

עִמּוֹ אָנֹכִי בְצָרָה,

achal'tzayhu va-achab'dayhu.

אֲחַלְּצֵהוּ וַאֲכַבְּדֵהוּ.

I am with him in distress, I will release him and I will honor him.

Ōrech yomim asbi-ayhu,
v'ar-ayhu bishu-osi.

אֹרֶךְ יָמִים אַשְׂבִּיעֵהוּ,
וְאַרְאֵהוּ בִּישׁוּעָתִי.

With long life will I satisfy him, and I will show him My salvation.

Ōrech yomim asbi-ayhu,
v'ar-ayhu bishu-osi.

אֹרֶךְ יָמִים אַשְׂבִּיעֵהוּ,
וְאַרְאֵהוּ בִּישׁוּעָתִי.

With long life will I satisfy him, and I will show him My salvation.

ADONOY mo rabu tzoroy
rabim komim oloy.

יהוה מָה רַבּוּ צָרָי,
רַבִּים קָמִים עָלָי.

HASHEM, how many are my tormentors! The great rise up against me!

Rabim ōm'rim l'nafshi

רַבִּים אֹמְרִים לְנַפְשִׁי,

The great say of my soul,

ayn yishu-oso lō Baylōhim selo.

אֵין יְשׁוּעָתָה לּוֹ בֵאלֹהִים סֶלָה.

"There is no salvation for him from God — Selah!"

V'ato Adōnoy mogayn ba-adi
k'vōdi u-mayrim rōshi.

וְאַתָּה יהוה מָגֵן בַּעֲדִי,
כְּבוֹדִי וּמֵרִים רֹאשִׁי.

But You HASHEM are a shield for me, for my soul, and the One Who raises my head.

kōli el Adōnoy ekro

קוֹלִי אֶל יהוה אֶקְרָא,

With my voice I call out to HASHEM,

va-ya-anayni may-har kodshō selo.

וַיַּעֲנֵנִי מֵהַר קָדְשׁוֹ סֶלָה.

and He answers me from His holy mountain — Selah.

Ani shochavti vo-ishono

אֲנִי שָׁכַבְתִּי וָאִישָׁנָה,

I lay down and slept,

hekitzōsi ki Adōnoy yism'chayni

הֱקִיצוֹתִי, כִּי יהוה יִסְמְכֵנִי.

yet I awoke, for HASHEM supports me.

Lō iro mayriv'vōs om
asher soviv shosu oloy.

לֹא אִירָא מֵרִבְבוֹת עָם,
אֲשֶׁר סָבִיב שָׁתוּ עָלָי.

I fear not the myriad people deployed against me from every side.

Kumo Adōnoy hōshi-ayni Elōhai

קוּמָה יהוה, הוֹשִׁיעֵנִי אֱלֹהַי,

Rise up, HASHEM; save me, my God;

ki hikiso es kōl ō-y'vai lechi

כִּי הִכִּיתָ אֶת כָּל אֹיְבַי לֶחִי,

for You struck all of my enemies on the cheek,

shinay r'sho-im shibarto.

שִׁנֵּי רְשָׁעִים שִׁבַּרְתָּ.

You broke the teeth of the wicked.

Ladōnoy hai-shu-o
al amcho virchosecho selo.

לַיהוה הַיְשׁוּעָה,
עַל עַמְּךָ בִרְכָתֶךָ סֶּלָה.

Salvation is HASHEM's, upon Your people is Your blessing — Selah.

HASHKIVAYNU Adōnoy Elōhaynu
l'sholōm,

הַשְׁכִּיבֵנוּ יהוה אֱלֹהֵינוּ
לְשָׁלוֹם,

Lay us down to sleep, HASHEM, our God, in peace,

v'ha-amidaynu malkaynu l'cha-yim,

וְהַעֲמִידֵנוּ מַלְכֵּנוּ לְחַיִּים,

raise us erect, our King, to life;

ufrōs olaynu sukas sh'lōmecho,

וּפְרוֹשׂ עָלֵינוּ סֻכַּת שְׁלוֹמֶךָ,

spread over us the shelter of Your peace;

v'sak'naynu b'aytzo tōvo
mil'fonecho,

וְתַקְּנֵנוּ בְּעֵצָה טוֹבָה
מִלְּפָנֶיךָ,

set us aright with good counsel from before Your Presence;

v'hōshi-aynu l'ma-an sh'mecho.

וְהוֹשִׁיעֵנוּ לְמַעַן שְׁמֶךָ.

and save us for Your Name's sake.

V'hogayn ba-adaynu,

וְהָגֵן בַּעֲדֵנוּ,

Shield us,

v'hosayr may-olaynu ō-yayv,
dever v'cherev v'ro-ov v'yogōn,

וְהָסֵר מֵעָלֵינוּ אוֹיֵב,
דֶּבֶר, וְחֶרֶב, וְרָעָב, וְיָגוֹן,

remove from us foe, plague, sword, famine, and woe;

v'hosayr soton mil'fonaynu
u-may-acharaynu,

וְהָסֵר שָׂטָן מִלְּפָנֵינוּ
וּמֵאַחֲרֵינוּ,

and remove spiritual impediment from before us and from behind us,

uvtzayl k'nofecho tastiraynu,

וּבְצֵל כְּנָפֶיךָ תַּסְתִּירֵנוּ,

and in the shadow of Your wings shelter us —

ki Ayl shōm'raynu
u-matzilaynu oto,

כִּי אֵל שׁוֹמְרֵנוּ
וּמַצִּילֵנוּ אָתָּה,

for God Who protects and rescues us are You;

ki Ayl melech chanun
v'rachum oto.

כִּי אֵל מֶלֶךְ חַנּוּן
וְרַחוּם אָתָּה.

for God, the Gracious and Compassionate King, are You.

Ushmōr tzaysaynu u-vō-aynu,
l'cha-yim ulsholōm

וּשְׁמוֹר צֵאתֵנוּ וּבוֹאֵנוּ,
לְחַיִּים וּלְשָׁלוֹם

Safeguard our going and coming, for life and for peace,

may-ato v'ad ōlom.

מֵעַתָּה וְעַד עוֹלָם.

from now to eternity.

BORUCH Adōnoy ba-yōm,
boruch Adōnoy baloylo,

בָּרוּךְ יהוה בַּיּוֹם,
בָּרוּךְ יהוה בַּלָּיְלָה,

Blessed is HASHEM by day; blessed is HASHEM by night;

boruch Adōnoy b'shoch'vaynu,　　　　　בָּרוּךְ יהוה בְּשָׁכְבֵנוּ,

boruch Adōnoy b'kumaynu.　　　　　בָּרוּךְ יהוה בְּקוּמֵנוּ.

Blessed is HASHEM *when we retire; blessed is* HASHEM *when we arise.*

Ki v'yod'cho nafshōs　　　　　כִּי בְיָדְךָ נַפְשׁוֹת

hacha-yim v'hamaysim.　　　　　הַחַיִּים וְהַמֵּתִים.

For in Your hand are the souls of the living and the dead.

Asher b'yodō nefesh kol choy,　　　　　אֲשֶׁר בְּיָדוֹ נֶפֶשׁ כָּל חָי,

He in Whose hand is the soul of all the living

v'ru-ach kol b'sar ish.　　　　　וְרוּחַ כָּל בְּשַׂר אִישׁ.

and the spirit of every human being.

B'yod'cho afkid ruchi,　　　　　בְּיָדְךָ אַפְקִיד רוּחִי,

In Your hand I shall entrust my spirit,

podiso ōsi, Adōnoy Ayl emes.　　　　　פָּדִיתָה אוֹתִי, יהוה אֵל אֱמֶת.

You redeemed me, HASHEM, *God of truth.*

Elōhaynu, sheba-shoma-yim,　　　　　אֱלֹהֵינוּ שֶׁבַּשָּׁמַיִם

Our God, Who is in heaven,

yachayd shimcho,　　　　　יַחֵד שִׁמְךָ,

v'ka-yaym malchus'cho tomid,　　　　　וְקַיֵּם מַלְכוּתְךָ תָּמִיד,

bring unity to Your Name; establish Your kingdom forever

umlōch olaynu l'ōlom vo-ed.　　　　　וּמְלוֹךְ עָלֵינוּ לְעוֹלָם וָעֶד.

and reign over us for all eternity.

YIR-U aynaynu v'yismach libaynu　　　　　**יִרְאוּ** עֵינֵינוּ וְיִשְׂמַח לִבֵּנוּ

May our eyes see, our heart rejoice

v'sogayl nafshaynu　　　　　וְתָגֵל נַפְשֵׁנוּ

bishu-os'cho be-emes,　　　　　בִּישׁוּעָתְךָ בֶּאֱמֶת,

and our soul exult in Your salvation in truth,

be-emōr l'tziyōn molach Elōhoyich.　　　　　בֶּאֱמֹר לְצִיּוֹן מָלַךְ אֱלֹהָיִךְ.

when Zion is told, "Your God has reigned!"

Adōnoy melech, Adōnoy moloch,　　　　　יהוה מֶלֶךְ, יהוה מָלָךְ,

Adōnoy yimlōch l'ōlom vo-ed.　　　　　יהוה יִמְלֹךְ לְעֹלָם וָעֶד.

HASHEM *reigns,* HASHEM *has reigned,* HASHEM *will reign for all eternity.*

Ki hamalchus shel'cho hi,　　　　　כִּי הַמַּלְכוּת שֶׁלְּךָ הִיא,

ul-ōl'may ad timlōch b'chovōd,　　　　　וּלְעוֹלְמֵי עַד תִּמְלוֹךְ בְּכָבוֹד,

For the kingdom is Yours and for all eternity You will reign in glory,

ki ayn lonu melech elo oto.　　　　　כִּי אֵין לָנוּ מֶלֶךְ אֶלָּא אָתָּה.

for we have no King but You.

HAMAL-OCH hagō-ayl ōsi mikol ro הַמַּלְאָךְ הַגֹּאֵל אֹתִי מִכָּל רָע
The angel who redeems me from all evil

y'voraych es han'orim יְבָרֵךְ אֶת הַנְּעָרִים,

v'yikoray vohem sh'mi וְיִקָּרֵא בָהֶם שְׁמִי,

may he bless the lads, and may my name be declared upon them —

v'shaym avosai avrohom v'yitzchok וְשֵׁם אֲבֹתַי אַבְרָהָם וְיִצְחָק,

and the names of my forefathers Abraham and Isaac —

v'yidgu lorōv b'kerev ho-oretz. וְיִדְגּוּ לָרֹב בְּקֶרֶב הָאָרֶץ.

and may they proliferate abundantly like fish within the land.

VAYŌMER im shomō-a tishma וַיֹּאמֶר, אִם שָׁמוֹעַ תִּשְׁמַע

l'kōl Adōnoy Elōhecha לְקוֹל יהוה אֱלֹהֶיךָ,

He said: "If you diligently heed the voice of HASHEM, your God,

v'hayoshor b'aynov ta-a-se וְהַיָּשָׁר בְּעֵינָיו תַּעֲשֶׂה,

and do what is proper in His eyes,

v'ha-azanto l'mitzvōsov וְהַאֲזַנְתָּ לְמִצְוֺתָיו,

v'shomarto kol chukov וְשָׁמַרְתָּ כָּל חֻקָּיו,

and you listen closely to His commandments and observe His decrees —

kol hamachalo כָּל הַמַּחֲלָה

asher sam-ti v'mitzra-yim אֲשֶׁר שַׂמְתִּי בְמִצְרַיִם

lō osim olecho לֹא אָשִׂים עָלֶיךָ,

the entire malady that I inflicted upon Egypt I will not inflict upon you,

ki ani Adōnoy ro-f'echo. כִּי אֲנִי יהוה רֹפְאֶךָ.

for I am HASHEM your Healer."

VA-YŌMER Adōnoy el hasoton וַיֹּאמֶר יהוה אֶל הַשָּׂטָן,

HASHEM said to the Satan,

yig-ar Adōnoy b'cho hasoton יִגְעַר יהוה בְּךָ הַשָּׂטָן,

"HASHEM shall denounce you, O Satan,

v'yig-ar Adōnoy b'cho וְיִגְעַר יהוה בְּךָ

habochayr birushalo-yim הַבֹּחֵר בִּירוּשָׁלָיִם,

and HASHEM, Who selects Jerusalem, shall denounce you again.

halō ze ud mutzol may-aysh. הֲלוֹא זֶה אוּד מֻצָּל מֵאֵשׁ.

This is indeed a firebrand rescued from flames."

Hinay mitosō she-lishlōmo הִנֵּה מִטָּתוֹ שֶׁלִּשְׁלֹמֹה,

Behold! The couch of Shlomo!

shishim gibōrim soviv lo שִׁשִּׁים גִּבֹּרִים סָבִיב לָהּ,

Sixty mighty ones round about it,

migibōray yisro-ayl.

מִגִּבֹּרֵי יִשְׂרָאֵל.

of the mighty ones of Israel.

Kulom achuzay cherev
m'lumday milchomo

כֻּלָּם אֲחֻזֵי חֶרֶב,
מְלֻמְּדֵי מִלְחָמָה,

All gripping the sword, learned in warfare,

ish charbō al y'raychō
mipachad balaylōs.

אִישׁ חַרְבּוֹ עַל יְרֵכוֹ
מִפַּחַד בַּלֵּילוֹת.

each with his sword on his thigh, from fear in the nights.

———————— RECITE THREE TIMES: ————————

Y'vorech'cho Adōnoy v'yishm'recho

יְבָרֶכְךָ יהוה וְיִשְׁמְרֶךָ.

May HASHEM bless you and safeguard you.

Yo-air Adōnoy
ponov aylecho vichuneko.

יָאֵר יהוה
פָּנָיו אֵלֶיךָ, וִיחֻנֶּךָּ.

May HASHEM illuminate His countenance for you and be gracious to you.

Yiso Adōnoy ponov ay-lecho
v'yosaym l'cho sholōm.

יִשָּׂא יהוה פָּנָיו אֵלֶיךָ,
וְיָשֵׂם לְךָ שָׁלוֹם.

May HASHEM turn His countenance to you and establish peace for you.

———————— RECITE THREE TIMES: ————————

Hinay lō yonum v'lō yishon
shōmayr yisro-ayl.

הִנֵּה לֹא יָנוּם וְלֹא יִישָׁן,
שׁוֹמֵר יִשְׂרָאֵל.

Behold, the Guardian of Israel neither slumbers nor sleeps.

———————— RECITE THREE TIMES: ————————

Lishu-oscho kivisi Adōnoy.

לִישׁוּעָתְךָ קִוִּיתִי יהוה.

For Your salvation do I long HASHEM.

Kivisi Adōnoy lishu-oscho.

קִוִּיתִי יהוה לִישׁוּעָתְךָ.

I do long, HASHEM, for your salvation.

Adōnoy lishu-oscho kivisi.

יהוה לִישׁוּעָתְךָ קִוִּיתִי.

HASHEM, for Your salvation do I long.

———————— RECITE THREE TIMES: ————————

B'shaym Adonoy Elohay yisro-ayl,

בְּשֵׁם יהוה אֱלֹהֵי יִשְׂרָאֵל,

In the Name of HASHEM, God of Israel:

mi-mini micho-ayl,
umismoli gavri-ayl,

מִימִינִי מִיכָאֵל,
וּמִשְּׂמֹאלִי גַּבְרִיאֵל,

may Michael be at my right, Gabriel at my left,

umilfonai uri-el,
u-may-achorai r'fō-ayl,

וּמִלְּפָנַי אוּרִיאֵל,
וּמֵאֲחוֹרַי רְפָאֵל,

Uriel before me, and Rephael behind me;

v'al rōshi sh'chinas Ayl.

וְעַל רֹאשִׁי שְׁכִינַת אֵל.

and above my head the Presence of God.

SHIR HAMA-ALŌS

שִׁיר הַמַּעֲלוֹת,

A song of ascents:

ashray kol y'ray Adōnoy,

אַשְׁרֵי כָּל יְרֵא יהוה,

hahōlaych bidrochov.

הַהֹלֵךְ בִּדְרָכָיו.

Praiseworthy is each person who fears HASHEM, who walks in His paths.

Y'gi-a kapecho ki sōchayl,

יְגִיעַ כַּפֶּיךָ כִּי תֹאכֵל,

When you eat the labor of your hands,

ashrecho v'tōv loch.

אַשְׁרֶיךָ וְטוֹב לָךְ.

you are praiseworthy, and it is well with you.

Esht'cho k'gefen pōriyo

אֶשְׁתְּךָ כְּגֶפֶן פֹּרִיָּה

b'yark'say vay-secho

בְּיַרְכְּתֵי בֵיתֶךָ,

Your wife shall be like a fruitful vine in the inner chambers of your home;

bonecho kish-silay zaysim,

בָּנֶיךָ כִּשְׁתִלֵי זֵיתִים,

soviv l'shulchonecho.

סָבִיב לְשֻׁלְחָנֶךָ.

your children shall be like olive shoots surrounding your table.

Hinay chi chayn y'vōrach gover

הִנֵּה כִי כֵן יְבֹרַךְ גָּבֶר

y'ray Adōnoy.

יְרֵא יהוה.

Behold! For so is blessed the man who fears HASHEM.

Y'vorech'cho Adōnoy mitziyōn,

יְבָרֶכְךָ יהוה מִצִּיּוֹן,

May HASHEM bless you from Zion,

ur-ay b'tuv y'rusholo-yim,

וּרְאֵה בְּטוּב יְרוּשָׁלָיִם,

and may you gaze upon the goodness of Jerusalem,

kōl y'may cha-yecho.

כֹּל יְמֵי חַיֶּיךָ.

all the days of your life.

Ur-ay vonim l'vonecho,

וּרְאֵה בָנִים לְבָנֶיךָ,

sholōm al yisro-ayl.

שָׁלוֹם עַל יִשְׂרָאֵל.

And may you see children born to your children, peace upon Israel.

--- RECITE THREE TIMES: ---

Rigzu v'al techeto-u

רִגְזוּ וְאַל תֶּחֱטָאוּ,

Tremble and sin not.

imru vilvavchem al mishkavchem

אִמְרוּ בִלְבַבְכֶם עַל מִשְׁכַּבְכֶם,

Reflect in your hearts while on your beds,

v'dōmu selo.

וְדֹמּוּ סֶלָה.

and be utterly silent. Selah.

ADŌN ŌLOM asher molach,   אֲדוֹן עוֹלָם אֲשֶׁר מָלַךְ,
Master of the universe, Who reigned

b'terem kol y'tzir nivro.   בְּטֶרֶם כָּל־יְצִיר נִבְרָא.
before any form was created.

L'ays na-aso v'cheftzō kōl,   לְעֵת נַעֲשָׂה בְחֶפְצוֹ כֹּל,
At the time when His will brought all into being —

a-zai melech sh'mō nikro.   אֲזַי מֶלֶךְ שְׁמוֹ נִקְרָא.
then as "King" was His Name proclaimed.

V'a-charay kichlōs hakōl,   וְאַחֲרֵי כִּכְלוֹת הַכֹּל,
  l'vadō yimlōch nōro.   לְבַדּוֹ יִמְלוֹךְ נוֹרָא.
After all has ceased to be, He, the Awesome One, will reign alone.

V'hu ho-yo, v'hu hō-ve,   וְהוּא הָיָה וְהוּא הֹוֶה,
  v'hu yih-ye, b'siforo.   וְהוּא יִהְיֶה בְּתִפְאָרָה.
It is He Who was, He Who is, and He Who shall remain, in splendor.

V'hu e-chod v'ayn shayni,   וְהוּא אֶחָד וְאֵין שֵׁנִי,
He is One — there is no second

l'hamshil lō l'hachbiro.   לְהַמְשִׁיל לוֹ לְהַחְבִּירָה.
to compare to Him, to declare as His equal.

B'li rayshis b'li sachlis,   בְּלִי רֵאשִׁית בְּלִי תַכְלִית,
Without beginning, without conclusion —

v'lō ho-ōz v'hamisro.   וְלוֹ הָעֹז וְהַמִּשְׂרָה.
His is the power and dominion.

V'hu Ayli v'chai gō-ali,   וְהוּא אֵלִי וְחַי גֹּאֲלִי,
He is my God, my living Redeemer,

v'tzur chevli b'ays tzoro.   וְצוּר חֶבְלִי בְּעֵת צָרָה.
Rock of my pain in time of distress.

V'hu nisi u-monōs li   וְהוּא נִסִּי וּמָנוֹס לִי
  m'nos kōsi b'yōm ekro.   מְנָת כּוֹסִי בְּיוֹם אֶקְרָא.
He is my banner, a refuge for me, the portion in my cup on the day I call.

B'yodō afkid ruchi,   בְּיָדוֹ אַפְקִיד רוּחִי,
  b'ays i-shan v'o-iro.   בְּעֵת אִישַׁן וְאָעִירָה.
Into His hand I shall entrust my spirit when I go to sleep — and I shall awaken!

V'im ruchi g'viyosi,   וְעִם רוּחִי גְּוִיָּתִי,
With my spirit shall my body remain.

Adōnoy li v'lō iro.   יהוה לִי וְלֹא אִירָא.
HASHEM is with me, I shall not fear.

The Shabbos Morning Service

⋖§ Donning the Tallis

Prayer is a great and challenging privilege. To be granted an audience with Hashem, regardless of the outcome, is rewarding. The very encounter is uplifting. Yet, though Hashem grants us this opportunity, too often man fails to capitalize upon the experience. Prayer is called "service of the heart," for Hashem desires our heartfelt commitment when we pray to Him. One way to help accomplish this is by wearing a garment especially for prayer. This is why our rabbis instituted the custom for married men — and, in many communities, single males, as well — to wear a *tallis* in conjunction with the morning prayers, to help us focus on our lofty mission, our personal encounter with Hashem.

⋖§ Tzitzis — the Reminder

The Torah teaches that *tzitzis* (the ritual fringes affixed to a four-cornered garment) help us remember all of God's commandments (see the third paragraph of the *Shema*). Thus we cloak ourselves in a *tallis,* as if to separate ourselves from the mundane pressures and lures of society and envelop ourselves in a special wrap that reminds us of our unique calling and responsibility to observe the 613 *mitzvos*.

When he stands in prayer, man wishes to be remembered, to be noticed, by God. We therefore don a garment whose essence is remembering, and in remembering Hashem, we hope to be remembered by Him. Perhaps this is why we are taught to give charity before praying (on Shabbos, one may pledge to do so): Though we may not be worthy of having all our requests granted, by giving charity we symbolize our plea that Hashem will reciprocate and be charitable to us.

The Torah ordains that only a four-cornered garment must have *tzitzis,* but since modern wardrobes do not include such garments, we would not have occasion to perform the commandment. Our love for God and desire to carry out His will is so strong, however, that we wear a four-cornered garment in order to affix *tzitzis*, such as the *tallis* during services and the smaller *tallis-katan* worn by males under their shirts. This insistence on creating a means to perform the commandment demonstrates our proactive commitment to find ways to observe even *mitzvos* that do not find their way to us.

The *tallis* is worn by males at every morning service, Shabbos, festivals, and weekdays, except on Tishah B'Av. It is also worn at all the Yom Kippur services and at the afternoon service on Tishah B'Av.

The Talmud teaches that covering one's head with the *tallis* is a sign of respect as well as an aid to concentration. Therefore, many follow this practice during the recitation of the *Amidah*, the most important prayer. Others cover their heads earlier in the service, some just before the *Kaddish* prior to *Borchu*, or even before.

৺ Verses of Song and Praise: Pesukei D'Zimrah

Pesukei D'Zimrah is a collection of psalms and verses from all three sections of the Written Torah: Torah, Prophets, and Writings. Most of it — indeed its very essence — is composed of chapters and selected verses from King David's Book of *Psalms*.

৺ Praising and Pruning

Rav Simlai taught that prior to beseeching Hashem to allow him to enter *Eretz Yisrael*, Moses first praised Hashem: "You have begun to show Your servant Your greatness and Your strong hand" (*Deuteronomy* 3:24). According to Rashi, Moses referred to God's boundless mercy and willingness to forgive sinners. So too, prior to our petition of prayer, our *Shemoneh Esrei*, we are to praise Hashem (*Berachos* 32a).

Pesukei D'Zimrah helps to prepare us for the *Shemoneh Esrei* by reminding us before Whom we are about to have a personal audience. In addition, the psalms that constitute *Pesukei D'Zimrah* communicate that no one other than Hashem can grant our requests and desires.

Elaborating on this concept, *Menoras HaMaor* suggests that the term *Pesukei D'Zimrah* might have an additional meaning stemming from the Hebrew verb, זמר, *to prune*. Thus the introduction to the *Shacharis* prayer is designated as "Verses of Pruning." Just as a gardener prunes his vines, removing the unhealthy branches in order to improve the fruit-bearing ability of the superior ones, so too, our recitation of *Pesukei D'Zimrah* removes all spiritual and metaphysical obstructions and hindrances from our prayers, enabling our *tefillos* to enter before the Divine Throne. *Pesukei D'Zimrah* may thus be seen as man's struggle to break through the many layers of impurity in his environment and enable him to connect with the Holy. Our recitation of these verses is our way of sending praises to God and of asking him to decipher our prayers, to cut and paste our yearnings into something worthwhile, as it were. Perhaps this notion is included in the words of the *Yishtabach*, the blessing that concludes *Pesukei D'Zimrah*. There we extol God as הַבּוֹחֵר בְּשִׁירֵי זִמְרָה, *the One Who chooses musical songs of praise*.

Moreover, the Talmud (ibid.) continues, one is not to pray out of sadness, but rather with the happiness that comes from the performance of a *mitzvah*. For this reason, one should recite these verses slowly and with a great deal of feeling and emotion. In fact, the *Shulchan Aruch* writes, one should recite these psalms just as one would count his money; carefully, deliberately, happily. *Quality* of prayer, as opposed to quantity, is the ideal.

Since *Pesukei D'Zimrah* is not a requirement in and of itself, but is a preparation for the *Shema* and *Shemoneh Esrei* — the more essential parts of the service — it is understandable that one who comes to the synagogue late and finds the congregation about to begin the section of *Shema* with its blessings should skip *Pesukei D'Zimrah*, and join the *minyan* for the *Shema* and *Shemoneh Esrei*. As important as *Pesukei D'Zimrah* is in preparing the individual for prayer, not every page of the *siddur* has equal significance. Recitation of the *Amidah* together with the congregation is the primary purpose and fulfillment of congregational prayer.

◄§ Independent Importance

The second Talmudic source for *Pesukei D'Zimrah* is found in Talmud (*Shabbos* 118b). Rav Yosei taught, "Let my portion be with those who complete the *Hallel* every day." (The Talmud explains that the term *Hallel*, as it is used here, means *Pesukei D'Zimrah*, and not what is commonly referred to as *Hallel*, the special collection of psalms recited on Festivals and *Rosh Chodesh*.) The final six chapters of the Book of *Psalms* comprise the essence of *Pesukei D'Zimrah*. They do not contain petitions to God, but uniquely and exclusively praise Him.

◄§ The Blessings

Pesukei D'Zimrah is preceded and concluded by blessings. The introductory blessing is *Baruch She'amar* and the concluding blessing is *Yishtabach*. According to tradition, the Men of the Great Assembly received the text of *Baruch She'amar* on a note that fell from heaven. Its eighty-seven words correspond to the Hebrew word for refined gold, פָּז, which has the numerical value of eighty-seven. This alludes to the verse in *Song of Songs* (5:11), *His opening words* — i.e. the introductory words of *Pesukei D'Zimrah* — *are of* פָּז, *the finest gold*.

The concluding blessing, *Yishtabach*, does not include the words אֱלֹקֵינוּ מֶלֶךְ הָעוֹלָם, *our God, King of the universe*, as do most blessings, do, for *Yishtabach* is, in a sense, the conclusion of *Baruch She'amar*. This shows that all of *Pesukei D'Zimrah* is one unit, and therefore one is not permitted to engage in unnecessary conversation during its *entirety*. Such prayer responses as *amen*, however, are permitted.

◄§ The Central Core

In *Baruch She'amar*, the worshiper says, *through the psalms of David your servant. We shall laud You, Hashem our God, with praises and songs*. *Yehi Chevod* then captures the major themes and motifs of David's psalms. It is a collection of verses taken primarily from *Psalms*, but also from *Chronicles* and *Proverbs*. Incidentally, this helps us understand why this section of the *siddur* is called *Pesukei D'Zimrah*, or *verses* of praise and song. Whereas the *Hallel* recited on Festivals consists of complete psalms, this daily *Hallel* is literally

pesukim or *verses* of praise, culled from different sources.

∾§ Yehi Chevod

Yehi Chevod contains three separate units. The first discusses God's immanence in the world and how, in this way, man discovers Him as the Creator of the universe. The second section refers to Him as the Master of history, leading mankind towards the realization of His plan, with the chosenness of Israel. Finally, it closes with the assurance that God will forgive our sins when we call to Him, and that He will restore us to our glory when He returns to Zion.

In a sense, *Yehi Chevod* encapsulates the entire Book of *Psalms*. The glory of God, His Kingdom, His relation to His people; petitions for forgiveness; and entreaties for salvation — fundamental ideas that permeate *Psalms* (*Tehillim*) — are encapsulated in the twenty-one verses of *Yehi Chevod*.

∾§ Ashrei and Its Companion Psalms

Yehi Chevod is followed by *Ashrei* (*Psalms* 145) and the final five chapters of *Psalms*.

The Talmud (*Berachos* 4b) states that one reason *Ashrei* was chosen as the primary chapter of *Pesukei D'Zimrah* is because the initials of its verses follow the order of the Hebrew alphabet, from *aleph* to *tav*. This symbolizes that our praise and service of God are complete. But, the Talmud asks, why was *Ashrei* chosen when two other psalms also contain complete alphabetic acrostics? The Talmud responds that *Ashrei* includes the verse, *You open Your hand and satisfy the desire of every living thing,* an inspiring and reassuring testimony to God's mercy. The Maharsha understands the significance of *Ashrei* to be that God nourishes us both physically and spiritually.

After *Ashrei,* in Psalm 146, the Psalmist addresses the concept of Divine Providence directed to each and every person. Each member of *Klal Yisrael* has a purpose, a mission for which God created him, and God cares about him as an individual. This psalm encourages the Jew in exile, promising that God will reign forever, despite the current ascendancy of our enemies.

Psalm 147 extends His Divine Providence to the community of Israel. It is no longer the voice of the individual praising God, but the communal voice recognizing *our* God. If their voice, if their emotion is lacking, then the national symphony of His praise is incomplete. As God heals all wounds so will He heal Israel's wounds. We are reminded that as we endure exile, the Heavenly Jerusalem is being developed by our good deeds and is waiting to descend. Throughout our exile, we must continue to develop the treasures of the Jewish people, our moral and spiritual values.

The psalm makes a striking comparison between nature's obedience to God's command, and our own responsibility to obey His Torah just as unquestioningly, because the Torah way of life should be the natural way for the Jew.

Psalm 148 brings our praises to the next level, rejoicing in the moment when even the non-Jewish nations of the world will recognize and praise the Creator.

This will occur only after the Temple in Jerusalem is rebuilt, and the people of Israel will have risen to surpass their former glory.

Psalm 149 reminds us that every generation is confronted with unique challenges and new problems. At the same time, God provides us with the opportunities and wherewithal to solve them. Thus our songs of praise are always infused with new meanings, they never grow stale. The greatest, newest song of all will emanate from Israel's lips when history reaches its climax with the coming of *Mashiach*.

The last psalm contains thirteen variations of the word הַלְלוּ, *give praise*, extolling God for his Thirteen Attributes of Mercy. It concludes with the admission that, while the entire Book of *Psalms* consists of beautifully articulated songs of praise, feelings that words cannot express may best be communicated by the sounds of music or without emitting any sound whatsoever. The human soul can often express God's praises more eloquently than anything else.

∞§ Intercessors and Utterances

Avudraham suggests that the above six psalms serve as "intercessors" for our prayers. They help man attain a purity of soul and an elevation of spirit, enabling him to properly recite the *Shema* and *Shemoneh Esrei*. He suggests further that *Pesukei D'Zimrah* provides a daily reminder of the ten utterances with which Hashem created the world (*Pirkei Avos* 5:1). In his formulation, *Vayevarech David*, which comes after the above six psalms, corresponds to the final statement of Creation, "God blessed them and said to them, Be fruitful and multiply; fill the earth and subdue it" (*Bereishis* 1:28). This final charge for man to conquer the world finds its parallel in *Vayevareich David*, where King David says, "Wealth and honor come from You and You rule everything." This is man's response to the trust and faith that God has invested in him, by recognizing that whatever success he might achieve is due only to the fact that God rules everything and provides man with talent and resources.

David was not allowed to build the First Temple, but nevertheless made the necessary preparations for that purpose. When he entrusted these funds to his son Solomon, he recited this praise, reminding us, writes Rabbi Samson Raphael Hirsch, that it is not God Who needs a dwelling place, but we who need His sanctuary and His Presence in our midst.

Moreover, David reminds the people that whatever they donated was given them by God. For this reason, many either give charity at this point of the prayer or set aside money to be given later in the service.

The daily *Pesukei D'Zimrah* closes with the song that Moses and Israel sang at the occasion of the splitting of the Sea of Reeds. Heretofore, all the praises have been within the context of the natural world, as controlled and supervised by God. This song extols Him for His miraculous involvement in the world. Indeed, suggests Rabbi Elie Munk, the most perfect praise of God is not found in the inspired songs of David, but grows out of the actual events that our ancestors beheld with their own eyes. Only since the day of the miracle at the Sea, when

God revealed His mastery of nature and mankind before the eyes of an astonished world, has "His Throne been established for all times."

In his commentary on the Torah, Ramban teaches that through God's miraculous control over nature, exhibited by the ten plagues in Egypt and culminating with the splitting of the Sea of Reeds, we come to appreciate and accept Him as the Creator. This song is thus a fitting finale to *Pesukei D'Zimrah.*

As noted above, *Yishtabach* is the closing blessing of *Pesukei D'Zimrah.* It contains fifteen expressions of praise, which alludes to *Psalms* 120-134, the fifteen Songs of Ascent composed by David. We now "ascend" to the next stage of our prayers.

◄§ Shemoneh Esrei of Shabbos Morning

◄§ Moses and the Shabbos

While the theme of the Friday night *Shemoneh Esrei* is that of the Shabbos of nature and creation, the theme of the Shabbos morning *Amidah* is the revelation at Sinai, the creation of the Jewish nation. This relationship between God and His people took place on Shabbos morning. The Torah (*Exodus* 19:16) informs us that the revelation occurred on the "third day when it was morning," and that third day was Shabbos (*Shabbos* 86b).

The *Amidah*'s theme begins with "Moses rejoiced at the gift of his portion," thus identifying the Shabbos with Moses. While the Jews were yet slaves in Egypt, Moses appealed to Pharaoh on their behalf. The Midrash (*Shemos Rabbah* 1:28) teaches that when the young Moses went out to his brethren and saw that they had no rest whatsoever from their slavery, he told Pharaoh that all masters give their slaves one day to rest, lest they die of exhaustion. Pharaoh agreed and said, "Pick a day for their rest." Moses responded, "Let the day of rest be the seventh day." Years later when God ordained the commandment of Shabbos, Moses was overjoyed that he had anticipated the Divine command many years earlier.

Moreover, the last prophecy of the last prophet was "Remember the Torah of Moses My servant" (*Malachi* 3:22). At Sinai all Israel was present. Every man, woman, and child personally witnessed and heard God communicating with Moses. It is thus understandable that at Sinai God said to Moses ". . . so that the people will hear as I speak to you, and they will also believe in you forever" (*Exodus* 19:9). We believe in the binding authenticity of Torah, as we, like no other people or religion, do not rely on the testimony of any one individual or group of individuals. Rather, the entire nation, old and young, heard God

proclaim and deliver His Torah to Israel. Each Shabbos morning we reaffirm our belief in God and His Torah.

⋙ Torah and Shabbos

It is thus understandable that every Shabbos, immediately following the *Shacharis Shemoneh Esrei*, we read from the Torah that was given to us on Shabbos. In fact, the Sages teach us that one of the primary purposes of the Shabbos is to study Torah. While there is a commandment to study Torah daily, our busy weekday schedule and the pressures of earning a livelihood preoccupy most of our time. On Shabbos we have the time and, more important, the peace of mind, to study our precious Torah. In codifying the laws of Shabbos, *Tur Orach Chaim* 290 cites the Midrash that the Torah was troubled when the Jewish nation entered and settled the land of Israel. When will they study and grow? God responded that this is one of the primary purposes of the Shabbos.

It is interesting that in acknowledging Moses as the one who brought down the two stone tablets that contain the commandment to observe the Shabbos, the *Shemoneh Esrei* states, "A crown of splendor You placed on his head." The Sages explain that this refers to *Exodus* 34:29, which states that when Moses descended from Sinai with the Second Tablets, his face glowed with a Divine radiance. Rabbi Joseph B. Soloveitchik asked why Moses' face radiated specifically at this point in his career. Why not at the burning bush? Or at the splitting of the Sea of Reeds? Or when he brought down the First Tablets?

Rabbi Soloveitchik suggested that in all Moses' encounters with God prior to the giving of the Second Tablets, he was but an emissary of either God or the Jewish people — a most important go-between, but ultimately just that — with no personal contribution to the dialogue. Now Moses is being elevated to the status of teacher, and is transmitting the Second Tablets, which symbolize the Oral Law that accompanies and explains the Written Law (see *Beis Halevi*). Only now, when Moses — and subsequently all future teachers — becomes an active participant in the development of the Torah, does his face shine, as he personally becomes involved in teaching the understanding of the Torah.

⋙ Shabbos Mussaf

The term *mussaf* means extra or additional, and it refers to the additional prayer that is added on Shabbos, Festivals, and *Rosh Chodesh,* and also to the additional offering in the Temple service on those days. As mentioned earlier, there are two reasons for our prayers (*Berachos* 26b). We pray as did our forefathers, and our prayers correspond to the daily offerings in the Temple. *Mussaf*, however, has one motivation exclusively; it is, as the prophet Hosea

(14:3) taught, "Let our lips substitute for bulls." That is to say, let God view the *Mussaf Amidah* as if we actually brought the offering in the Temple.

Rabbi Yitzchok Hutner noted that we do not mention the daily *tamid*, continual offering, in the *Shacharis* or *Minchah* prayer, but we do recount the exact composition of the various *Mussaf* offerings that were brought in the Temple. He explains that the daily prayers focus on various motifs, not only the offerings; these prayers *correspond* to the offerings, but are not devoted exclusively to them. Regarding the *Mussaf* prayer, however, the offerings are their exclusive focus (*Pachad Yitzchak*, *Pesach* §67).

⋖§ Double Measure of Shabbos

There are fewer animals in the *mussaf* offerings of Shabbos than in those of the Festivals. In fact, the *mussaf* of Shabbos is but double the daily *tamid*, the regular daily communal offering. The Midrash explains this with the following parable. A king asked that a meal be prepared for his son, and the servants prepared two delicacies. Afterwards, the king asked that a meal be prepared for himself. When asked what he wanted, he responded, "Whatever you prepared for my son." Similarly, God gave the Jewish people a double measure of manna on Friday, one for Friday and one for Shabbos (which is why we have two loaves at each of the three Shabbos meals), and He requested that for Him, likewise, a double measure be given on Shabbos. Therefore, in addition to the "one sheep that is offered in the morning and one sheep in the afternoon" every day, the *mussaf* for Shabbos is two sheep. So not only we, but also God enjoys *lechem mishneh*, a double portion, on Shabbos, as it were. This aspect of the *Mussaf* prayer reflects the intimacy between God and His people. As noted above, the word קָרְבָּן, *offering,* comes from the root קרב, *near,* because the offerings are devices to bring people closer to God.

⋖§ God's Favor

The blessing of *Kedushas HaYom*, the "Holiness of the Day," i.e., the middle blessing of the *Mussaf Shemoneh Esrei* begins, "You established the Sabbath; found favor in its offerings . . ." Tur (*Orach Chaim* 283) explains this "favor" in two ways. Firstly, the offering of sacrifices should have been prohibited on Shabbos, since slaughter of an animal constitutes a Biblical violation of Shabbos. It is for this reason that our Rabbis teach (*Shemos Rabbah* 28) that Hashem uttered two statements simultaneously, namely "Remember the Shabbos to sanctify it," and the commandment to offer two sheep as the day's *mussaf* (*Numbers* 28:9). Thus offerings are brought on Shabbos only in accordance with His expressed will, hence the expression that God "found favor" in its offerings (*Tur, Levush, Orach Chaim* 286).

A second explanation is that the *mussaf* offering of Shabbos is unique in that it does not include a sin offering. This is in order not to disturb the tranquillity of the Shabbos by focusing on man's sin. Indeed, this is a reason that the Talmud refers to Shabbos as ¹⁄₆₀th of the World to Come (*Berachos* 57b). Abraham was

concerned that at a time that there will not be a Temple and offerings, what will intercede on behalf of his descendants? God responded that He will regard the recitation of the order of the offerings as if they were actually brought, "and Hashem will then pardon them for their sins" *(Taanis* 27b). This applies to all the holidays, when sin offerings comprised a significant part of the sacrificial order of the day. On Shabbos, however, there was no sin offering. Because this *mussaf* is sin-free, it is especially pleasing to God, and that is the origin of the phrase "He takes pleasure in its offerings" *(Tur* 283).

In the prayer *Tikanta Shabbos*, the worshiper includes a strong plea for Israel's return to our homeland and the restoration of the Temple service. It is sad that this petition has been deleted from the prayerbook of some Jews, who distance themselves from our holy Temple worship.

◆§ Mussaf and the Temple

Ashkenazic tradition includes the prayer *Yismachu V'Malchuscha*, "They shall rejoice in your Kingship," only in *Mussaf*. This indicates that joy has a special relationship to *Mussaf*, that does not apply to other aspects of the day. The Festivals, however, are basically different; the component of *simchah*, happiness and joy, is part of the very essence and character of the Festivals. For this reason, the Talmud teaches that the festivals are incompatible with mourning *(Moed Kattan* 14b). Thus if one began the *shivah*, the seven-day period of mourning, before a Festival, *Yom Tov* cancels the remaining days of this mourning observance; the *simchah* frame of mind for the holiday, which is a communal *mitzvah,* cannot coexist with the somber introspection that is incumbent on but the closest relatives of the departed. Instead, Jewish law dictates that the individual conform to the communal *simchah*, as it is manifested on the *Yom Tov.*

Shabbos is different. Although public manifestations of mourning are forbidden, Shabbos does not end the *shivah* observance, as there is no *mitzvah* of *simchah* on Shabbos. Instead, Shabbos has two commandments: *kavod,* to honor the Shabbos, by preparing oneself and one's home; and *oneg*, to delight in the Shabbos with specially prepared foods *(Isaiah* 58:13).

The only place where *simchah*, happiness, is mentioned in conjunction with Shabbos is in the *Mussaf*. This is because the *mussaf* offering was brought in the Temple. As we find in the case of the Four Species taken on Succos, only when mentioning its seven-day observance in the Temple, the Torah specifically mandates "And you shall rejoice before Hashem" *(Leviticus* 23:40). Similarly, when the Torah speaks of the commandment to sound trumpets in the Temple in conjunction with the offerings of sacred days, Shabbos is referred to as "Your day of happiness" *(Sifrei, Numbers* 10:10), thus suggesting the special connection of *simchah* with the Temple.

Rabbi Soloveitchik suggested that there is a special level of happiness associated with the Temple, where one is in the personal abode of God's Presence, for when one understands with greater clarity that everything emanates from Hashem, one is filled with *simchah*. Wherever Jews are, Shabbos

has *kavod* and *oneg*; in the Temple it has *simchah* as well. For this reason, *Yismechu V'Malchusecha*, which speaks of gladness, is added only in *Mussaf*.

Finally another characteristic is unique to *Mussaf*, namely there is no *tashlumim* or make-up for this prayer. The general rule is that if one failed to recite a prayer before the end of its assigned time, one should recite a second, "make-up" *Shemoneh Esrei* during the next prayer period. Thus if one missed *Maariv* at night, he would recite two *Shemoneh Esreis* at the next *Shacharis*. This rule, however, does not apply to *Mussaf*; for a forgotten *Mussaf* there is no make-up. Here again, the exclusive relationship of the *Mussaf Amidah* to the offering of the day is the explanation. The Talmud teaches that once the time for the offering has passed, it may no longer be brought, and therefore its corresponding *Shemoneh Esrei* can no longer be recited. Regarding every other *Amidah*, however, in addition to the theme of sacrifices that comprise its character, there is the element of pleading for mercy and compassion from Hashem, and this may be done even at a later time. After all, explains the Talmud, "If only man would pray the entire day!" (*Berachos* 21a).

∙◦§ Reverse Order

It is interesting to note that the first twenty-two words of the middle blessing, *Tikanta Shabbos*, begin with the letters of the *Aleph-Bais* in reverse order, from *tav* to *aleph*. This Kabbalistic device symbolizes that after man reaches the full extent of his understanding — the letter *tav* representing completion — he must not be content. Rather, he must go back to the beginning and deepen his spiritual understanding even more. For a discussion of this concept, see Rabbi M.L. Munk, *Wisdom of the Hebrew Alphabet*, page 221; Mesorah Publications.

⊰{ UPON ARISING }⊱

■ The essence of a Jew is gratitude to Hashem:
We awake and thank Hashem for restoring our faculties.

IMMEDIATELY UPON WAKING UP FROM HIS SLEEP, A JEW DECLARES:

MŌ-DE ANI l'fonecho,   מוֹדֶה אֲנִי לְפָנֶיךָ,

I gratefully thank You,*

melech chai v'ka-yom,   מֶלֶךְ חַי וְקַיָּם,

O living and eternal King,

shehechezarto bi nishmosi   שֶׁהֶחֱזַרְתָּ בִּי נִשְׁמָתִי

  b'chemlo —   בְּחֶמְלָה —

for You have returned my soul within me with compassion —

rabo emunosecho.   רַבָּה אֱמוּנָתֶךָ.

abundant is Your faithfulness!

WASH THE HANDS ACCORDING TO THE RITUAL PROCEDURE:
PICK UP THE VESSEL OF WATER WITH THE RIGHT HAND, PASS IT TO THE LEFT, AND POUR OVER
THE RIGHT. THEN WITH THE RIGHT HAND POUR OVER THE LEFT. FOLLOW THIS PROCEDURE
UNTIL WATER HAS BEEN POURED OVER EACH HAND THREE TIMES. THEN, RECITE:

RAYSHIS chochmo   רֵאשִׁית חָכְמָה

The beginning of wisdom

yir-as Adōnoy,   יִרְאַת יהוה,

is the fear of HASHEM —

saychel tōv l'chol ōsayhem,   שֵׂכֶל טוֹב לְכָל עֹשֵׂיהֶם,

good understanding to all their practitioners;

t'hilosō ōmedes lo-ad.   תְּהִלָּתוֹ עֹמֶדֶת לָעַד.

His praise endures forever.

Boruch shaym k'vōd malchusō   בָּרוּךְ שֵׁם כְּבוֹד מַלְכוּתוֹ

Blessed is the Name of His glorious kingdom

l'ōlom vo-ed.   לְעוֹלָם וָעֶד.

for all eternity.

⊰{ DONNING THE TZITZIS }⊱

HOLD THE *TALLIS KATTAN* IN READINESS TO PUT ON, INSPECT THE *TZITZIS,* AND RECITE THE
BLESSING. THEN DON THE *TALLIS KATTAN* AND KISS THE *TZITZIS.* ONE WHO WEARS A *TALLIS* FOR
SHACHARIS DOES NOT RECITE THIS BLESSING.

BORUCH ato Adōnoy   בָּרוּךְ אַתָּה יהוה

Blessed are You, HASHEM,

מוֹדֶה אֲנִי לְפָנֶיךָ — *I gratefully thank You.* A Jew
opens his eyes and thanks God for restoring his
faculties to him in the morning. Then, he acknowledges that God did so in the expectation
that he will serve Him, and that He is abundantly faithful to reward those who do.

⊰≶ **Donning the Tzitzis**
    Since *tzitzis* need not be worn at night, the
commandment of *tzitzis* (*Numbers* 15:38) is
classified as a time-related commandment and,
as such, is not required of women. It may be
fulfilled in two ways: (a) by means of the *tallis*

Elōhaynu melech ho-ōlom,
אֱלֹהֵינוּ מֶלֶךְ הָעוֹלָם,

our God, King of the universe,

asher kid'shonu b'mitzvōsov,
אֲשֶׁר קִדְּשָׁנוּ בְּמִצְוֹתָיו,

Who has sanctified us with His commandments,

v'tzivonu al mitzvas tzitzis.
וְצִוָּנוּ עַל מִצְוַת צִיצִת.

and has commanded us regarding the commandment of tzitzis.

Y'HI rotzōn mil'fonecho,
יְהִי רָצוֹן מִלְּפָנֶיךָ,

May it be Your will,

Adōnoy Elōhai Vaylōhay avōsai,
יהוה אֱלֹהַי וֵאלֹהֵי אֲבוֹתַי,

HASHEM, my God and the God of my forefathers,

shet'hay chashuvo
שֶׁתְּהֵא חֲשׁוּבָה

mitzvas tzitzis l'fonecho,
מִצְוַת צִיצִת לְפָנֶיךָ,

that the commandment of tzitzis be as worthy before You

k'ilu kiyamtiho b'chol p'roteho
כְּאִלּוּ קִיַּמְתִּיהָ בְּכָל פְּרָטֶיהָ

as if I had fulfilled it in all its details,

v'dikdukeho v'chav'nōseho,
וְדִקְדּוּקֶיהָ וְכַוָּנוֹתֶיהָ,

implications, and intentions,

v'saryag mitzvōs hat'luyim boh.
וְתַרְיַ"ג מִצְוֺת הַתְּלוּיִם בָּהּ.

as well as the 613 commandments that are dependent upon it.

Omayn selo.
אָמֵן סֶלָה.

Amen, Selah!

⊰ **DONNING THE TALLIS** ⊱

BEFORE DONNING THE *TALLIS,* INSPECT THE *TZITZIS* WHILE RECITING THESE VERSES:

BOR'CHI nafshi es Adōnoy,
בָּרְכִי נַפְשִׁי אֶת יהוה,

Bless HASHEM, O my soul,*

Adōnoy Elōhai godalto m'ōd,
יהוה אֱלֹהַי גָּדַלְתָּ מְּאֹד,

HASHEM, my God, You are very great;

hōd v'hodor lovoshto.
הוֹד וְהָדָר לָבָשְׁתָּ.

You have donned majesty and splendor;

Ōte ōr kasalmo,
עֹטֶה אוֹר כַּשַּׂלְמָה,

cloaked in light as with a garment,

nōte shoma-yim kai-ri-o.
נוֹטֶה שָׁמַיִם כַּיְרִיעָה.

stretching out the heavens like a curtain.

---

katan (lit., small garment), popularly known simply as "the *tzitzis,*" which is worn all day, usually under the shirt; and (b) by means of the familiar large *tallis,* commonly known simply as "the *tallis,*" which is worn during the morn-

ing prayers, in some congregations by all males, and in others only by one who is or has been married.

בָּרְכִי נַפְשִׁי — *Bless … O my soul.* These two verses describe God figuratively as donning

MANY RECITE THE FOLLOWING DECLARATION OF INTENT BEFORE DONNING THE *TALLIS:*

HARAYNI mis-atayf gufi batzitzis,   הֲרֵינִי מִתְעַטֵּף גּוּפִי בַּצִּיצָת,

I am ready to wrap my body in tzitzis,

kayn tis-atayf nishmosi   כֵּן תִּתְעַטֵּף נִשְׁמָתִי

    urmach ayvorai ushso gidai   וּרְמַ״ח אֵבָרַי וּשְׁסָ״ה גִידַי

so may my soul, my 248 organs and my 365 sinews* be wrapped

b'ōr hatzitzis ho-ōle saryag.   בְּאוֹר הַצִּיצָת הָעוֹלֶה תַרְיַ״ג.

in the illumination of tzitzis which has the numerical value of 613 .

uchshaym she-ani miskase b'talis   וּכְשֵׁם שֶׁאֲנִי מִתְכַּסֶּה בְּטַלִּית

    bo-ōlom ha-ze,   בָּעוֹלָם הַזֶּה,

Just as I cover myself with a tallis in this world,

kach ezke lachaluko derabonon   כַּךְ אֶזְכֶּה לַחֲלוּקָא דְרַבָּנָן

    ultalis no-e   וּלְטַלִּית נָאֶה

so may I merit the rabbinical garb and a beautiful cloak

lo-ōlom habo b'gan ayden.   לָעוֹלָם הַבָּא בְּגַן עֵדֶן.

in the World to Come in the Garden of Eden.

V'al y'day mitzvas tzitzis   וְעַל יְדֵי מִצְוַת צִיצָת

Through the commandment of tzitzis

tinotzayl nafshi v'ruchi   תִּנָּצֵל נַפְשִׁי וְרוּחִי

    v'nishmosi usfilosi   וְנִשְׁמָתִי וּתְפִלָּתִי

may my life-force, spirit, soul, and prayer be rescued

min hachitzōnim.   מִן הַחִיצוֹנִים.

from the external forces.

V'hatalis yifrōs k'nofov alayhem   וְהַטַּלִּית יִפְרוֹשׂ כְּנָפָיו עֲלֵיהֶם

    v'yatzilaym   וְיַצִּילֵם

May the tallis spread its wings over them and rescue them

k'nesher yo-ir kinō,   כְּנֶשֶׁר יָעִיר קִנּוֹ,

    al gōzolov y'rachayf.   עַל גּוֹזָלָיו יְרַחֵף.

like an eagle rousing his nest, fluttering over his eaglets.

Us-hay chashuvo mitzvas tzitzis   וּתְהֵא חֲשׁוּבָה מִצְוַת צִיצָת

May the commandment of tzitzis be worthy

lifnay Hakodōsh boruch hu   לִפְנֵי הַקָּדוֹשׁ בָּרוּךְ הוּא

before the Holy One, Blessed is He,

---

garments of majesty and light. Because the *tallis* symbolizes the splendor of God's commandments, we liken our wearing of it to wrapping ourselves in God's glory and brilliance.

רְמַ״ח אֵבָרַי וּשְׁסָ״ה גִידַי — *My 248 organs and my 365 sinews.* The Sages' computation of the important organs, 248, corresponds to the number of positive commandments in the Torah,

k'ilu kiyamtiho b'chōl p'roteho   כְּאִלּוּ קִיַּמְתִּיהָ בְּכָל פְּרָטֶיהָ
as if I had fulfilled it in all its details,

v'dikdukeho v'chav'nōseho   וְדִקְדּוּקֶיהָ וְכַוָּנוֹתֶיהָ
implications, and intentions,

v'saryag mitzvōs hat'luyim boh.   וְתַרְיַ״ג מִצְוֹת הַתְּלוּיִם בָּהּ.
as well as the 613 commandments that are dependent upon it.

Omayn selo.   אָמֵן סֶלָה.
Amen, Selah!

UNFOLD THE *TALLIS*, HOLD IT IN READINESS TO WRAP AROUND YOURSELF,
AND RECITE THE FOLLOWING BLESSING:

BORUCH ato Adōnoy   **בָּרוּךְ** אַתָּה יהוה
Blessed are You, HASHEM,

Elōhaynu melech ho-ōlom,   אֱלֹהֵינוּ מֶלֶךְ הָעוֹלָם,
our God, King of the universe,

asher kid'shonu b'mitzvōsov,   אֲשֶׁר קִדְּשָׁנוּ בְּמִצְוֹתָיו,
Who has sanctified us with His commandments

v'tzivonu l'hisatayf batzitzis.   וְצִוָּנוּ לְהִתְעַטֵּף בַּצִּיצִת.
and has commanded us to wrap ourselves in tzitzis.

WRAP THE *TALLIS* AROUND YOUR HEAD AND BODY, THEN RECITE:

MAH YOKOR chasd'cho Elōhim,   **מַה יָּקָר** חַסְדְּךָ אֱלֹהִים,
How precious is Your kindness, O God!

uvnay odom   וּבְנֵי אָדָם
   b'tzayl k'nofecho yecheso-yun.   בְּצֵל כְּנָפֶיךָ יֶחֱסָיוּן.
The sons of man take refuge in the shadows of Your wings.

Yirv'yun mideshen bay-secho,   יִרְוְיֻן מִדֶּשֶׁן בֵּיתֶךָ,
May they be sated from the abundance of Your house;

v'nachal adonecho sashkaym.   וְנַחַל עֲדָנֶיךָ תַשְׁקֵם.
and may You give them to drink from the stream of Your delights.

Ki im'cho m'kōr cha-yim,   כִּי עִמְּךָ מְקוֹר חַיִּים,
For with You is the source of life —

b'ōr'cho nir-e ōr.   בְּאוֹרְךָ נִרְאֶה אוֹר.
by Your light we shall see light.

M'shōch chasd'cho l'yōd'e-cho,   מְשֹׁךְ חַסְדְּךָ לְיֹדְעֶיךָ,
Extend Your kindness to those who know You,

v'tzidkos'cho l'yishray layv.   וְצִדְקָתְךָ לְיִשְׁרֵי לֵב.
and Your charity to the upright of heart.

---

while the 365 sinews corresponds to the number of negative commandments. This symbol- izes the principle that man was created to perform God's will.

■ The privilege of entering the synagogue fills me
with both reverence and joy.

THE FOLLOWING VERSES ARE RECITED UPON ENTERING THE SYNAGOGUE:

MA TŌVU ōholecho ya-akōv,   **מַה טֹּבוּ** אֹהָלֶיךָ יַעֲקֹב,

How goodly are your tents, *O Jacob,*

mishk'nōsecho yiŝro-ayl.   מִשְׁכְּנֹתֶיךָ יִשְׂרָאֵל.

your dwelling places, O Israel.

va-ani b'rōv chasd'cho   וַאֲנִי בְּרֹב חַסְדְּךָ

As for me, through Your abundant kindness

ovō vay-secho,   אָבוֹא בֵיתֶךָ,

I will enter Your House;

eshtacha-ve el haychal kodsh'cho   אֶשְׁתַּחֲוֶה אֶל הֵיכַל קָדְשְׁךָ
b'yirosecho.   בְּיִרְאָתֶךָ.

I will prostrate myself toward Your Holy Sanctuary in awe of You.

Adōnoy   יהוה

O HASHEM,

ohavti m'ōn bay-secho,   אָהַבְתִּי מְעוֹן בֵּיתֶךָ,

I love the House where You dwell,

umkōm mishkan k'vōdecho.   וּמְקוֹם מִשְׁכַּן כְּבוֹדֶךָ.

and the place where Your glory resides.

Va-ani eshtacha-ve v'echro-o,   וַאֲנִי אֶשְׁתַּחֲוֶה וְאֶכְרָעָה,

I shall prostrate myself and bow,

evr'cho lifnay Adōnoy ōsi.   אֶבְרְכָה לִפְנֵי יהוה עֹשִׂי.

I shall kneel before HASHEM my Maker.

Va-ani,   וַאֲנִי,

As for me,

s'filosi l'cho Adōnoy,   תְפִלָּתִי לְךָ יהוה,

may my prayer to You, HASHEM,

ays rotzōn,   עֵת רָצוֹן,

be at an opportune time;

Elōhim b'rov chasdecho,   אֱלֹהִים בְּרָב חַסְדֶּךָ,

O God, in Your abundant kindness,

anayni be-emes yish-e-cho.   עֲנֵנִי בֶּאֱמֶת יִשְׁעֶךָ.

answer me with the truth of Your salvation.

מַה טֹּבוּ אֹהָלֶיךָ — *How goodly are your tents.* The
Jewish home achieves its highest level when it
incorporates the values of the synagogue and
study hall. This collection of verses expresses

love and reverence for the synagogue that is
the place where God's glory resides among Israel.

■ I begin the morning prayer, instituted by our Patriarch, Abraham,
by referring to Hashem, as did Abraham,
as the Master of the universe — yet involved in my everyday activities.

ADŌN ŌLOM asher molach, אֲדוֹן עוֹלָם אֲשֶׁר מָלַךְ,
Master of the universe, * Who reigned*

b'terem kol y'tzir nivro. בְּטֶרֶם כָּל־יְצִיר נִבְרָא.
before any form was created.

L'ays na-aso v'cheftzō kōl, לְעֵת נַעֲשָׂה בְחֶפְצוֹ כֹּל,
At the time when His will brought all into being —

a-zai melech sh'mō nikro. אֲזַי מֶלֶךְ שְׁמוֹ נִקְרָא.
then as "King" was His Name proclaimed.

V'a-charay kichlōs hakōl, וְאַחֲרֵי כִּכְלוֹת הַכֹּל,
After all has ceased to be,

l'vadō yimlōch nōro. לְבַדּוֹ יִמְלוֹךְ נוֹרָא.
He, the Awesome One, will reign alone.

V'hu ho-yo, v'hu hō-ve, וְהוּא הָיָה וְהוּא הֹוֶה,
It is He Who was, He Who is,

v'hu yih-ye, b'siforo. וְהוּא יִהְיֶה בְּתִפְאָרָה.
and He Who shall remain, in splendor.

V'hu echod v'ayn shayni, וְהוּא אֶחָד וְאֵין שֵׁנִי,
He is One — there is no second

l'hamshil lō l'hachbiro. לְהַמְשִׁיל לוֹ לְהַחְבִּירָה.
to compare to Him, to declare as His equal.

B'li rayshis b'li sachlis, בְּלִי רֵאשִׁית בְּלִי תַכְלִית,
Without beginning, without conclusion —

v'lō ho-ōz v'hamisro. וְלוֹ הָעֹז וְהַמִּשְׂרָה.
His is the power and dominion.

V'hu Ayli v'chai gō-ali, וְהוּא אֵלִי וְחַי גֹּאֲלִי,
He is my God, my living Redeemer,

v'tzur chevli b'ays tzoro. וְצוּר חֶבְלִי בְּעֵת צָרָה.
Rock of my pain in time of distress.

V'hu nisi u-monōs li, וְהוּא נִסִּי וּמָנוֹס לִי,
He is my banner, a refuge for me,

אֲדוֹן עוֹלָם — *Master of the universe.* This song emphasizes that God is timeless, infinite and omnipotent. Mankind can offer Him only one thing: to proclaim Him as King, by doing His will and praising Him. Despite God's greatness, however, He involves Himself with man's personal needs in time of pain and distress, and so man need not fear.

m'nos kōsi b'yōm ekro.   מְנָת כּוֹסִי בְּיוֹם אֶקְרָא.

the portion in my cup on the day I call.

B'yodō afkid ruchi,   בְּיָדוֹ אַפְקִיד רוּחִי,

Into His hand I shall entrust my spirit

b'ays ishan v'o-iro.   בְּעֵת אִישָׁן וְאָעֵירָה.

when I go to sleep — and I shall awaken!

V'im ruchi g'viyosi,   וְעִם רוּחִי גְּוִיָּתִי,

With my spirit shall my body remain.

Adōnoy li v'lō iro.   יהוה לִי וְלֹא אִירָא.

HASHEM is with me, I shall not fear.

■ I affirm daily my belief in the Thirteen Principles of Faith accepted by my ancestors at Sinai, as expounded by Maimonides in his famous *Ani Maamin.*

YIGDAL Elōhim chai v'yishtabach,   **יִגְדַּל** אֱלֹהִים חַי וְיִשְׁתַּבַּח,

Exalted be the Living God* and praised,

nimtzo v'ayn ays el m'tzi-usō.   נִמְצָא וְאֵין עֵת אֶל מְצִיאוּתוֹ.

He exists — unbounded by time is His existence. *

E-chod v'ayn yo-chid k'yi-chudō,   אֶחָד וְאֵין יָחִיד כְּיִחוּדוֹ,

He is One — and there is no unity like His Oneness,

nelom v'gam ayn sōf l'achdusō.   נֶעְלָם וְגַם אֵין סוֹף לְאַחְדוּתוֹ.

inscrutable and infinite is His Oneness.

Ayn lō d'mus haguf v'aynō guf,   אֵין לוֹ דְּמוּת הַגּוּף וְאֵינוֹ גוּף,

He has no semblance of a body nor is He corporeal; *

lō na-arōch aylov k'dushosō.   לֹא נַעֲרוֹךְ אֵלָיו קְדֻשָּׁתוֹ.

nor has His holiness any comparison.

Kadmōn l'chol dovor asher nivro,   קַדְמוֹן לְכָל דָּבָר אֲשֶׁר נִבְרָא,

He preceded every being that was created —

rishōn v'ayn rayshis l'rayshisō.   רִאשׁוֹן וְאֵין רֵאשִׁית לְרֵאשִׁיתוֹ.

the First, and nothing precedes His precedence.

Hinō adōn ōlom l'chol nōtzor,   הִנּוֹ אֲדוֹן עוֹלָם לְכָל נוֹצָר,

Behold! He is Master of the universe* to every creature,

יִגְדַּל אֱלֹהִים חַי — *Exalted be the living God.* This song of uncertain authorship summarizes the Thirteen Principles of Faith expounded by Maimonides and stated succinctly in the famous *Ani Maamin* prayer. They comprise the basic principles that every Jew should believe.

וְאֵין עֵת אֶל מְצִיאוּתוֹ — *Unbounded by time is His existence.* If God's existence were timebound, it would be no different in kind from that of any living, but not eternal, being. The principle of

God's timelessness, with neither beginning nor end, implies that He cannot be dependent in any way on any other being, for the timebound is inherently inferior to the timeless. Nothing can exist without God, but He depends on no one and on no thing.

וְאֵינוֹ גוּף — *Nor is He corporeal.* God has no physicality, not even that of invisible, intangible angels.

הִנּוֹ אֲדוֹן עוֹלָם — *Behold! He is Master of the universe.* Because He is absolute Master, there

Yōre g'dulosō u-malchusō.

יוֹרֶה גְדֻלָּתוֹ וּמַלְכוּתוֹ.

He demonstrates His greatness and His sovereignty.

Shefa n'vu-osō n'sonō,

שֶׁפַע נְבוּאָתוֹ נְתָנוֹ,

He granted His flow of prophecy *

el anshay s'gulosō v'sif-artō.

אֶל אַנְשֵׁי סְגֻלָּתוֹ וְתִפְאַרְתּוֹ.

to His treasured splendrous people.

Lō kom b'yisro-ayl k'mōshe ōd,

לֹא קָם בְּיִשְׂרָאֵל כְּמֹשֶׁה עוֹד,

In Israel none like Moses arose again —*

novi u-mabit es t'munosō.

נָבִיא וּמַבִּיט אֶת תְּמוּנָתוֹ.

a prophet who perceived His vision clearly.

Tōras emes nosan l'amō Ayl,

תּוֹרַת אֱמֶת נָתַן לְעַמּוֹ אֵל,

God gave His people a Torah of truth,

al yad n'vi-ō ne-eman bay-sō.

עַל יַד נְבִיאוֹ נֶאֱמַן בֵּיתוֹ.

by means of His prophet, the most trusted of His household.

Lō yachalif ho-Ayl v'lō yomir dosō,

לֹא יַחֲלִיף הָאֵל וְלֹא יָמִיר דָּתוֹ,

God will never amend nor exchange His law

l'ōlomim l'zulosō.

לְעוֹלָמִים לְזוּלָתוֹ.

for all eternity, for any other one.

Tzōfe v'yōday-a s'soraynu,

צוֹפֶה וְיוֹדֵעַ סְתָרֵינוּ,

He scrutinizes and knows our hiddenmost secrets;

mabit l'sōf dovor b'kadmosō.

מַבִּיט לְסוֹף דָּבָר בְּקַדְמָתוֹ.

He perceives a matter's outcome at its inception.

Gōmayl l'ish chesed k'mif-olō,

גּוֹמֵל לְאִישׁ חֶסֶד כְּמִפְעָלוֹ,

He recompenses man with kindness according to his deed;

nōsayn l'rosho ro k'rishosō.

נוֹתֵן לְרָשָׁע רָע כְּרִשְׁעָתוֹ.

He places evil on the wicked according to his wickedness.

Yishlach l'kaytz ha-yomin m'shichaynu,

יִשְׁלַח לְקֵץ הַיָּמִין מְשִׁיחֵנוּ,

By the End of Days He will send our Messiah,

lifdōs m'chakay kaytz y'shu-osō.

לִפְדּוֹת מְחַכֵּי קֵץ יְשׁוּעָתוֹ.

to redeem those longing for His final salvation.

Maysim y'cha-ye Ayl b'rōv chasdō,

מֵתִים יְחַיֶּה אֵל בְּרֹב חַסְדּוֹ,

God will revive the dead in His abundant kindness —

boruch aday ad shaym t'hilosō.

בָּרוּךְ עֲדֵי עַד שֵׁם תְּהִלָּתוֹ.

Blessed forever is His praised Name.

---

is nothing else to which prayers may be directed.

שֶׁפַע נְבוּאָתוֹ — *His flow of prophecy.* God revealed His will to Israel through His prophets.

כְּמֹשֶׁה — *Like Moses.* Moses' prophecy is peerless; otherwise another "prophet" could conceivably challenge or amend it, thus challenging the authenticity of the Torah.

⊰ **MORNING BLESSINGS** ⊱

■ Upon awakening each day, we wash our hands, as did the *Kohanim* of old,
to dedicate our daily activities to the service of Hashem.

THIS BLESSING IS RECITED IN THE MORNING, EITHER IMMEDIATELY AFTER THE RITUAL WASHING
OF THE HANDS UPON ARISING, OR AT THIS POINT. IT IS REPEATED DURING THE DAY AFTER THE
RITUAL WASHING THAT PRECEDES A MEAL AT WHICH BREAD IS EATEN.

BORUCH ato Adōnoy   בָּרוּךְ אַתָּה יהוה

Blessed are You, Hashem,

Elōhaynu melech ho-ōlom,   אֱלֹהֵינוּ מֶלֶךְ הָעוֹלָם,

our God, King of the universe,

asher kid'shonu b'mitzvōsov,   אֲשֶׁר קִדְּשָׁנוּ בְּמִצְוֹתָיו,

Who has sanctified us with His commandments

v'tzivonu al n'tilas yodo-yim.   וְצִוָּנוּ עַל נְטִילַת יָדָיִם.

and has commanded us regarding washing the hands.*

■ We thank Hashem for the daily maintenance of our bodies
and the wonders of Divine wisdom performed within ourselves.

THIS BLESSING IS RECITED IN THE MORNING, EITHER IMMEDIATELY AFTER THE RITUAL WASHING
OF THE HANDS AFTER RELIEVING ONESELF, OR AT THIS POINT. IT IS REPEATED AFTER THE RITUAL
WASHING AFTER RELIEVING ONESELF ANYTIME DURING THE DAY.

BORUCH ato Adōnoy   בָּרוּךְ אַתָּה יהוה

Blessed are You, Hashem,

Elōhaynu melech ho-ōlom,   אֱלֹהֵינוּ מֶלֶךְ הָעוֹלָם,

our God, King of the universe,

asher yotzar es ho-odom   אֲשֶׁר יָצַר אֶת הָאָדָם
    b'chochmo,   בְּחָכְמָה,

Who fashioned man with wisdom*

u-voro vō n'kovim n'kovim,   וּבָרָא בוֹ נְקָבִים נְקָבִים,
    chalulim chalulim.   חֲלוּלִים חֲלוּלִים.

and created within him many openings and many cavities.

Goluy v'yodu-a   גָּלוּי וְיָדוּעַ
    lifnay chisay ch'vōdecho,   לִפְנֵי כִסֵּא כְבוֹדֶךָ,

It is obvious and known before Your Throne of Glory

she-im yiposay-ach e-chod mayhem,   שֶׁאִם יִפָּתֵחַ אֶחָד מֵהֶם,

that if but one of them were to be ruptured

עַל נְטִילַת יָדָיִם — *Regarding washing the hands.* In the case of blessings, the general rule is that they should be recited in conjunction with the acts to which they apply. Nevertheless, some postpone this blessing for washing the hands and the next blessing for relieving

oneself so that they will be recited as part of *Shacharis.*

אֲשֶׁר יָצַר אֶת הָאָדָם בְּחָכְמָה — *Who fashioned man with wisdom.* This phrase has two meanings: (a) When God created man, He gave him the gift of wisdom; and (b) God used wisdom when

ō yisosaym e-chod mayhem,

אוֹ יִסָּתֵם אֶחָד מֵהֶם,

or but one of them were to be blocked

i efshar l'hiska-yaym

אִי אֶפְשַׁר לְהִתְקַיֵּם

it would be impossible to survive

v'la-amōd l'fonecho.

וְלַעֲמוֹד לְפָנֶיךָ.

and to stand before You.

Boruch ato Adōnoy,

בָּרוּךְ אַתָּה יהוה,

Blessed are You, HASHEM,

rōfay chol bosor u-mafli la-asōs.   רוֹפֵא כָל בָּשָׂר וּמַפְלִיא לַעֲשׂוֹת.

Who heals all flesh and acts wondrously. *

BLESSINGS OVER THE STUDY OF THE TORAH*

ALTHOUGH THE FOLLOWING TWO BLESSINGS ARE RECITED OVER TORAH STUDY, THEY ARE RECITED ONLY ONCE EACH DAY, REGARDLESS OF HOW MANY STUDY SESSIONS ONE HAS DURING THE DAY.

■ First blessing for the Torah: We thank Hashem for the privilege of being commanded to thoroughly study Torah, our most precious possession, and pray for His assistance in our mastering and successfully transmitting the Oral Torah (Talmud).

BORUCH ato Adōnoy

בָּרוּךְ אַתָּה יהוה

Blessed are You, HASHEM,

Elōhaynu melech ho-ōlom,

אֱלֹהֵינוּ מֶלֶךְ הָעוֹלָם,

our God, King of the universe,

asher kid'shonu b'mitzvōsov,

אֲשֶׁר קִדְּשָׁנוּ בְּמִצְוֹתָיו,

Who has sanctified us with His commandments

v'tzivonu la-asōk b'divray sōro.

וְצִוָּנוּ לַעֲסוֹק בְּדִבְרֵי תוֹרָה.

and has commanded us to engross ourselves in the words of Torah.

V'ha-arev no Adōnoy Elōhaynu

וְהַעֲרֶב נָא יהוה אֱלֹהֵינוּ

es divray sōros'cho

אֶת דִּבְרֵי תוֹרָתְךָ

Please, HASHEM, *our God, sweeten the words of Your Torah*

b'finu uvfi am'cho bays yisro-ayl.   בְּפִינוּ וּבְפִי עַמְּךָ בֵּית יִשְׂרָאֵל.

in our mouth and in the mouth of Your people, the House of Israel.

V'nih-ye anachnu v'tze-etzo-aynu

וְנִהְיֶה אֲנַחְנוּ וְצֶאֱצָאֵינוּ

May we and our offspring

v'tze-etzo-ay am'cho bays yisro-ayl,   וְצֶאֱצָאֵי עַמְּךָ בֵּית יִשְׂרָאֵל,

and the offspring of Your people, the House of Israel —

He created man, as is demonstrated in the precise balance of his organs and functions.

וּמַפְלִיא לַעֲשׂוֹת — *And acts wondrously.* The delicate balance of the organs is a wonder of wonders. Alternatively: It is wondrous that the spiritual soul fuses with the physical body to

create a human being.

⋖§ **Blessings of the Torah**

The study of Torah is the paramount commandment. Without it, man cannot know God's will; with it, he can penetrate the wisdom of the Creator Himself.

kulonu yōd'ay sh'mecho
כֻּלָּנוּ יוֹדְעֵי שְׁמֶךָ
all of us — know Your Name

v'lōm'day sōrosecho lishmoh.
וְלוֹמְדֵי תוֹרָתֶךָ לִשְׁמָהּ.
and study Your Torah for its own sake.*

Boruch ato Adōnoy,
בָּרוּךְ אַתָּה יהוה,
Blessed are You, HASHEM,

ham'lamayd tōro l'amō yisro-ayl.
הַמְלַמֵּד תּוֹרָה לְעַמּוֹ יִשְׂרָאֵל.
Who teaches Torah to His people Israel.

■ Second blessing for the Torah: We thank Hashem for His choosing Israel and giving us the gift of the Written Torah (Scripture).

BORUCH ato Adōnoy
בָּרוּךְ אַתָּה יהוה
Blessed are You, HASHEM,

Elōhaynu melech ho-ōlom,
אֱלֹהֵינוּ מֶלֶךְ הָעוֹלָם,
our God, King of the universe,

asher bochar bonu mikol ho-amim
אֲשֶׁר בָּחַר בָּנוּ מִכָּל הָעַמִּים
Who selected us from all the peoples

v'nosan lonu es tōrosō.
וְנָתַן לָנוּ אֶת תּוֹרָתוֹ.
and gave us His Torah.

Boruch ato Adōnoy,
בָּרוּךְ אַתָּה יהוה,
nōsayn hatōro.
נוֹתֵן הַתּוֹרָה.
Blessed are You, HASHEM, Giver of the Torah.

SCRIPTURAL SELECTION*

Y'VORECH'CHO Adōnoy v'yishm'recho.
יְבָרֶכְךָ יהוה וְיִשְׁמְרֶךָ.
May HASHEM bless you and safeguard you.

Yo-ayr Adōnoy ponov aylecho
יָאֵר יהוה פָּנָיו אֵלֶיךָ
vichuneko.
וִיחֻנֶּךָּ.
May HASHEM illuminate His countenance for you and be gracious to you.

Yiso Adōnoy ponov aylecho,
יִשָּׂא יהוה פָּנָיו אֵלֶיךָ,
May HASHEM turn His countenance to you

v'yosaym l'cho sholōm.
וְיָשֵׂם לְךָ שָׁלוֹם.
and establish peace for you.

לִשְׁמָהּ — *For its own sake.* May we study Torah for no other reason than to know it and become imbued with its wisdom.

❧ **Scriptural and Talmudic Selections**

Whenever a blessing is recited for a *mitzvah*, the *mitzvah* must be performed immediately. Having recited the blessings for the study of Torah, we immediately recite selections from the

both the Written and Oral Torah. First we recite the Scriptural verses of the Priestly Blessing, then Talmudic selections from the Mishnah (*Pe'ah* 1:1) and Gemara (*Shabbos* 127a). The Talmudic selections discuss the reward for various commandments and conclude with the declaration that Torah study is equivalent to them all, an appropriate addendum to the Blessings of the Torah.

TALMUDIC SELECTIONS*

AYLU D'VORIM

אֵלּוּ דְבָרִים

These are the precepts

she-ayn lohem shi-ur:

שֶׁאֵין לָהֶם שִׁעוּר:

that have no prescribed measure: *

hapay-o, v'habikurim,

הַפֵּאָה, וְהַבִּכּוּרִים,

the corner of a field [which must be left for the poor], the first-fruit offering,

v'hora-yōn,

וְהָרֵאָיוֹן,

the pilgrimage,

ugmilus chasodim,

וּגְמִילוּת חֲסָדִים,

acts of kindness,

v'salmud tōro.

וְתַלְמוּד תּוֹרָה.

and Torah study.

AYLU D'VORIM

אֵלּוּ דְבָרִים

These are the precepts

she-odom ōchayl payrōsayhem

שֶׁאָדָם אוֹכֵל פֵּרוֹתֵיהֶם

whose fruits a person enjoys

bo-ōlom ha-ze

בָּעוֹלָם הַזֶּה

in this world,

v'hakeren ka-yemes lō

וְהַקֶּרֶן קַיֶּמֶת לוֹ

but whose principal remains intact for him *

lo-ōlom habo.

לָעוֹלָם הַבָּא.

in the World to Come.

V'aylu hayn:

וְאֵלּוּ הֵן:

They are:

kibud ov vo-aym,

כִּבּוּד אָב וָאֵם,

the honor due to father and mother,

ugmilus chasodim,

וּגְמִילוּת חֲסָדִים,

acts of kindness,

v'hashkomas bays hamidrosh

וְהַשְׁכָּמַת בֵּית הַמִּדְרָשׁ

early attendance at the house of study

shacharis v'arvis,

שַׁחֲרִית וְעַרְבִית,

morning and evening,

v'hachnosas ōr'chim,

וְהַכְנָסַת אוֹרְחִים,

hospitality to guests,

uvikur chōlim,

וּבִקּוּר חוֹלִים,

visiting the sick,

אֵלּוּ דְבָרִים שֶׁאֵין לָהֶם שִׁעוּר — *These are the pre-cepts that have no prescribed measure.* The Torah does not prescribe how much is involved in the performance of the following commandments.

וְהַקֶּרֶן קַיֶּמֶת לוֹ — *But whose principal remains intact for him.* Though one is rewarded for these *mitzvos* in this world, his reward in the World to Come is not diminished.

v'hachnosas kalo,   וְהַכְנָסַת כַּלָּה,

providing for a bride,

ulvo-yas hamays,   וּלְוָיַת הַמֵּת,

escorting the dead,

v'iyun t'filo,   וְעִיּוּן תְּפִלָּה,

absorption in prayer,

vahavo-as sholōm   וַהֲבָאַת שָׁלוֹם

  bayn odom lachavayrō.   בֵּין אָדָם לַחֲבֵרוֹ.

bringing peace between man and his fellow.

V'salmud tōro k'neged kulom.   וְתַלְמוּד תּוֹרָה כְּנֶגֶד כֻּלָּם.

And the study of Torah is equivalent to them all.

■ I thank Hashem for the daily restoration of my pure soul.

ELŌHAI,   אֱלֹהַי,

My God,

n'shomo shenosato bi t'hōro hi.   נְשָׁמָה שֶׁנָּתַתָּ בִּי טְהוֹרָה הִיא.

the soul You placed within me is pure.

Ato v'rosoh ato y'tzartoh,   אַתָּה בְרָאתָהּ אַתָּה יְצַרְתָּהּ,

You created it, You fashioned it,

ato n'fachtoh bi,   אַתָּה נְפַחְתָּהּ בִּי,

You breathed it into me,

v'ato m'sham'roh b'kirbi,   וְאַתָּה מְשַׁמְּרָהּ בְּקִרְבִּי,

You safeguard it within me,

v'ato osid lit'loh mimeni,   וְאַתָּה עָתִיד לִטְּלָהּ מִמֶּנִּי,

and eventually You will take it from me,

ulhachaziroh bi le-osid lovō.   וּלְהַחֲזִירָהּ בִּי לֶעָתִיד לָבֹא.

and restore it to me in Time to Come.

Kol z'man shehan'shomo v'kirbi,   כָּל זְמַן שֶׁהַנְּשָׁמָה בְקִרְבִּי,

As long as the soul is within me,

mōde ani l'fonecho,   מוֹדֶה אֲנִי לְפָנֶיךָ,

I gratefully thank You,

Adōnoy Elōhai Vaylōhay avōsai,   יהוה אֱלֹהַי וֵאלֹהֵי אֲבוֹתַי,

HASHEM, my God and the God of my forefathers,

ribōn kol hama-asim,   רִבּוֹן כָּל הַמַּעֲשִׂים,

Master of all works,

Adōn kol han'shomōs.   אֲדוֹן כָּל הַנְּשָׁמוֹת.

Lord of all souls.

Boruch ato Adōnoy,   בָּרוּךְ אַתָּה יהוה,

Blessed are You, HASHEM,

hamachazir n'shomōs

lifgorim maysim.

הַמַּחֲזִיר נְשָׁמוֹת
לִפְגָרִים מֵתִים.

Who restores souls to dead bodies.

THE *CHAZZAN* RECITES THE FOLLOWING BLESSINGS ALOUD, AND THE CONGREGATION
RESPONDS *OMAYN* TO EACH BLESSING. NEVERTHELESS, EACH PERSON MUST RECITE THESE
BLESSINGS EITHER BEFORE OR AFTER THE *CHAZZAN* RECITES THEM ALOUD.

■ We greet each new day with the recognition that Hashem gives us the ability
to make distinctions and to deal with new situations.

BORUCH ato Adōnoy

בָּרוּךְ אַתָּה יהוה

Blessed* are You, HASHEM,

Elōhaynu melech ho-ōlom,

אֱלֹהֵינוּ מֶלֶךְ הָעוֹלָם,

our God, King of the universe,

asher nosan lasechvi vino

אֲשֶׁר נָתַן לַשֶּׂכְוִי בִינָה

Who gave the heart understanding

l'havchin bayn yom u-vayn loylo.

לְהַבְחִין בֵּין יוֹם וּבֵין לָיְלָה.

to distinguish between day and night.

■ We acknowledge daily the special mission of the 613 commandments
which sets us apart from the other nations.

Boruch ato Adōnoy

בָּרוּךְ אַתָּה יהוה

Blessed are You, HASHEM,

Elōhaynu melech ho-ōlom,

אֱלֹהֵינוּ מֶלֶךְ הָעוֹלָם,

our God, King of the universe,

Shelō osani gōy.

שֶׁלֹּא עָשַׂנִי גּוֹי.

for not having made me a gentile.

■ We acknowledge daily that Judaism frees us from enslavement
to passions and desires.

Boruch ato Adōnoy

בָּרוּךְ אַתָּה יהוה

Blessed are You, HASHEM,

Elōhaynu melech ho-ōlom,

אֱלֹהֵינוּ מֶלֶךְ הָעוֹלָם,

our God, King of the universe,

בָּרוּךְ — *Blessed.* This series of fifteen blessings is based on *Berachos* 60b, where the Sages teach that as one experiences the phenomena of the new day, he should bless God for providing them. For example, one thanks God for giving man the crucial ability to make distinctions in life, such as that between day and night; when he rubs his eyes and sees; when he gets dressed, and so on. Some of the phenomena are not so obvious from the text of the blessing. Among them are: sitting up and stretching ["releases the bound"]; getting out of bed ["straightens the bent"]; standing on the floor ["spreads out the earth ..."]; donning shoes which symbolizes man's ability to go on his way comfortably ["provided me my every need"]; setting out on one's destination ["firms ... footsteps"]; fastening one's clothing ["girds Israel ..."]; putting on a hat, which symbolizes the Jew's reminder that Someone is above him ["crowns Israel ..."]; feeling the passing of nighttime exhaustion ["gives

shelō osani oved.

שֶׁלֹּא עָשַׂנִי עָבֶד.

*for not having made me a slave.**

■ We express our gratitude for separate but equal roles:
Men acknowledge daily that they need more *mitzvos* than women do
to heighten their awareness of Hashem and to serve Him.

MEN AND BOYS RECITE:

Boruch ato Adōnoy

בָּרוּךְ אַתָּה יהוה

Blessed are You, HASHEM,

Elōhaynu melech ho-ōlom,

אֱלֹהֵינוּ מֶלֶךְ הָעוֹלָם,

our God, King of the universe,

shelō osani i-sho.

שֶׁלֹּא עָשַׂנִי אִשָּׁה.

*for not having made me a woman.**

■ Women acknowledge the manifestation of Divine beneficence in granting them
greater strength in moral self-discipline.

WOMEN AND GIRLS RECITE:

Boruch ato Adōnoy

בָּרוּךְ אַתָּה יהוה

Blessed are You, HASHEM,

Elōhaynu melech ho-ōlom,

אֱלֹהֵינוּ מֶלֶךְ הָעוֹלָם,

our God, King of the universe,

she-osani kirtzōnō.

שֶׁעָשַׂנִי כִּרְצוֹנוֹ.

*for having made me according to His will.**

■ We acknowledge daily the gift of sight and insight.

Boruch ato Adōnoy

בָּרוּךְ אַתָּה יהוה

Blessed are You, HASHEM,

Elōhaynu melech ho-ōlom,

אֱלֹהֵינוּ מֶלֶךְ הָעוֹלָם,

our God, King of the universe,

pōkay-ach ivrim.

פּוֹקֵחַ עִוְרִים.

Who gives sight to the blind.

---

strength . . . and removes sleep . . .''].

שֶׁלֹּא עָשַׂנִי גוֹי . . . עָבֶד . . . אִשָּׁה — *For not having
made me a gentile . . . a slave . . . a woman.* The
Torah assigns missions to respective groups of
people. Within Israel, for example, the Davidic
family, *Kohanim,* and Levites are set apart by
virtue of their particular callings, in addition to
their shared mission as Jews. All such missions
carry extra responsibilities and call for the performance of the *mitzvos* associated with them.
We thank God, therefore, for the challenge of
improving His universe in accordance with His
will. Male, free Jews have responsibilities and
duties not shared by others. For this, they
express gratitude that, unlike women, they

were *not* freed from the obligation to perform
the time-related commandments. This follows
the Talmudic dictum that an obligatory performance of a commandment is superior to a vol-
untary one, because it is human nature to resist obligations.

שֶׁעָשַׂנִי כִּרְצוֹנוֹ — *For having made me according
to His will.* Women, both historically and because of their nature, are the guardians of
tradition, and the molders of character, children, and family. Furthermore, women have
often been the protectors of Judaism when the
impetuosity and aggressiveness of the male
nature led the men astray. The classic precedent was in the wilderness when the men —

■ We acknowledge daily the gift of our clothing: modesty and dignity.

Boruch ato Adōnoy
בָּרוּךְ אַתָּה יהוה
Blessed are You, HASHEM,

Elōhaynu melech ho-ōlom,
אֱלֹהֵינוּ מֶלֶךְ הָעוֹלָם,
our God, King of the universe,

malbish arumim.
מַלְבִּישׁ עֲרֻמִּים.
Who clothes the naked.

■ We acknowledge daily our appreciation to freely move our limbs
which were bound in sleep all night.

Boruch ato Adōnoy
בָּרוּךְ אַתָּה יהוה
Blessed are You, HASHEM,

Elōhaynu melech ho-ōlom,
אֱלֹהֵינוּ מֶלֶךְ הָעוֹלָם,
our God, King of the universe,

matir asurim.
מַתִּיר אֲסוּרִים.
Who releases the bound.

■ We acknowledge daily our appreciation of the human ability to stand erect.

Boruch ato Adōnoy
בָּרוּךְ אַתָּה יהוה
Blessed are You, HASHEM,

Elōhaynu melech ho-ōlom,
אֱלֹהֵינוּ מֶלֶךְ הָעוֹלָם,
our God, King of the universe,

zōkayf k'fufim.
זוֹקֵף כְּפוּפִים.
Who straightens the bent.

■ We acknowledge daily our appreciation of the separation of land and water
(enabling us to enjoy life on the earth).

Boruch ato Adōnoy
בָּרוּךְ אַתָּה יהוה
Blessed are You, HASHEM,

Elōhaynu melech ho-ōlom,
אֱלֹהֵינוּ מֶלֶךְ הָעוֹלָם,
our God, King of the universe,

rōka ho-oretz al hamo-yim.
רוֹקַע הָאָרֶץ עַל הַמָּיִם.
Who spreads out the earth upon the waters.

■ We acknowledge daily that God provides our needs,
thus enabling us to adapt to our environment.

Boruch ato Adōnoy
בָּרוּךְ אַתָּה יהוה
Blessed are You, HASHEM,

---

not the women — worshiped the Golden Calf. Thus, though women were not given the privilege of the challenge assigned to men, they are created closer to God's ideal of satisfaction. They express their gratitude in the blessing "for having made me according to His will."

Elōhaynu melech ho-ōlom,

אֱלֹהֵינוּ מֶלֶךְ הָעוֹלָם,

our God, King of the universe,

she-oso li kol tzorki.

שֶׁעָשָׂה לִי כָּל צָרְכִּי.

Who has provided me my every need.

■ We acknowledge daily that God paves the way for man's success.

Boruch ato Adōnoy

בָּרוּךְ אַתָּה יהוה

Blessed are You, HASHEM,

Elōhaynu melech ho-ōlom,

אֱלֹהֵינוּ מֶלֶךְ הָעוֹלָם,

our God, King of the universe,

hamaychin mitz-aday gover.

הַמֵּכִין מִצְעֲדֵי גָבֶר.

Who firms man's footsteps.

■ We acknowledge daily our recognition that Hashem has endowed us
with the ability to have self-control.

Boruch ato Adōnoy

בָּרוּךְ אַתָּה יהוה

Blessed are You, HASHEM,

Elōhaynu melech ho-ōlom,

אֱלֹהֵינוּ מֶלֶךְ הָעוֹלָם,

our God, King of the universe,

ōzayr yisro-ayl bigvuro.

אוֹזֵר יִשְׂרָאֵל בִּגְבוּרָה.

Who girds Israel with strength.

■ We acknowledge daily that covering the head is an honor
for the Jewish man and woman.

Boruch ato Adōnoy

בָּרוּךְ אַתָּה יהוה

Blessed are You, HASHEM,

Elōhaynu melech ho-ōlom,

אֱלֹהֵינוּ מֶלֶךְ הָעוֹלָם,

our God, King of the universe,

ōtayr yisro-ayl b'sif-oro.

עוֹטֵר יִשְׂרָאֵל בְּתִפְאָרָה.

Who crowns Israel with splendor.

■ We acknowledge daily the Divine gift of both personal and national endurance.

Boruch ato Adōnoy

בָּרוּךְ אַתָּה יהוה

Blessed are You, HASHEM,

Elōhaynu melech ho-ōlom,

אֱלֹהֵינוּ מֶלֶךְ הָעוֹלָם,

our God, King of the universe,

hanōsayn layo-ayf kō-ach.

הַנּוֹתֵן לַיָּעֵף כֹּחַ.

Who gives strength to the weary.

■ Upon awakening and being energized by Hashem, I pray for Divine assistance in my service of Him.

BORUCH ato Adōnoy

בָּרוּךְ אַתָּה יהוה

Blessed are You, HASHEM,

Elōhaynu melech ho-ōlom,

אֱלֹהֵינוּ מֶלֶךְ הָעוֹלָם,

our God, King of the universe,

hama-avir shayno may-aynoy

הַמַּעֲבִיר שֵׁנָה מֵעֵינַי

Who removes sleep from my eyes

usnumo may-af-apoy;

וּתְנוּמָה מֵעַפְעַפָּי;

and slumber from my eyelids;

vihi rotzōn mil'fonecho,

וִיהִי רָצוֹן מִלְּפָנֶיךָ,

and may it be Your will,

Adōnoy Elōhaynu

יהוה אֱלֹהֵינוּ

Vaylōhay avōsaynu,

וֵאלֹהֵי אֲבוֹתֵינוּ,

HASHEM, our God, and the God of our forefathers,

shetargilaynu b'sōrosecho

שֶׁתַּרְגִּילֵנוּ בְּתוֹרָתֶךָ

that You accustom us to [study] Your Torah

v'dab'kaynu b'mitzvōsecho,

וְדַבְּקֵנוּ בְּמִצְוֹתֶיךָ,

and attach us to Your commandments;

v'al t'vi-aynu lō liday chayt,

וְאַל תְּבִיאֵנוּ לֹא לִידֵי חֵטְא,

that You do not bring us into the power of error,

v'lō liday avayro v'ovōn,

וְלֹא לִידֵי עֲבֵרָה וְעָוֹן,

nor into the power of transgression and sin;

v'lō liday niso-yōn,

וְלֹא לִידֵי נִסָּיוֹן,

nor into the power of challenge,

v'lō liday vizo-yōn,

וְלֹא לִידֵי בִזָּיוֹן,

nor into the power of scorn;

v'al tashlet bonu yaytzer horo,

וְאַל תַּשְׁלֶט בָּנוּ יֵצֶר הָרָע,

let not the Evil Inclination dominate us;

v'harchikaynu may-odom ro

וְהַרְחִיקֵנוּ מֵאָדָם רָע

u-maychovayr ro,

וּמֵחָבֵר רָע,

distance us from an evil person and an evil companion;

v'dab'kaynu b'yaytzer hatōv

וְדַבְּקֵנוּ בְּיֵצֶר הַטּוֹב

attach us to the Good Inclination

uvma-asim tōvim,

וּבְמַעֲשִׂים טוֹבִים,

and to good deeds,

v'chôf es yitzraynu l'hishtabed loch,
וְכוֹף אֶת יִצְרֵנוּ לְהִשְׁתַּעְבֶּד לָךְ,
and compel our Evil Inclination to be subservient to You;

usnaynu ha-yōm uvchol yōm
וּתְנֵנוּ הַיּוֹם וּבְכָל יוֹם
grant us today and every day

l'chayn ulchesed ulrachamim
לְחֵן וּלְחֶסֶד וּלְרַחֲמִים
grace, kindness, and mercy

b'aynecho uv-aynay chol rō-aynu,
בְּעֵינֶיךָ וּבְעֵינֵי כָל רוֹאֵינוּ,
in Your eyes and in the eyes of all who see us;

v'sigm'laynu chasodim tōvim.
וְתִגְמְלֵנוּ חֲסָדִים טוֹבִים.
and bestow beneficent kindnesses upon us.

Boruch ato Adōnoy,
בָּרוּךְ אַתָּה יהוה,
Blessed are You, HASHEM,

gōmayl chasodim tōvim
גּוֹמֵל חֲסָדִים טוֹבִים
l'amō yisro-ayl.
לְעַמּוֹ יִשְׂרָאֵל.
Who bestows beneficent kindnesses upon His people Israel.

Y'HI ROTZŌN mil'fonecho,
יְהִי רָצוֹן מִלְּפָנֶיךָ,
May it be Your will,*

Adōnoy Elōhai Vaylōhay avōsai,
יהוה אֱלֹהַי וֵאלֹהֵי אֲבוֹתַי,
HASHEM, my God, and the God of my forefathers,

shetatzilayni ha-yōm uvchol yōm
שֶׁתַּצִּילֵנִי הַיּוֹם וּבְכָל יוֹם
that You rescue me today and every day

may-azay fonim u-may-azus ponim,
מֵעַזֵּי פָנִים וּמֵעַזּוּת פָּנִים,
from brazen men and from brazenness,

may-odom ro, u-maychovayr ro,
מֵאָדָם רָע, וּמֵחָבֵר רָע,
from an evil man, from an evil companion,

umishochayn ro, u-mipega ro,
וּמִשָּׁכֵן רָע, וּמִפֶּגַע רָע,
from an evil neighbor, from an evil mishap,

umisoton hamashchis,
וּמִשָּׂטָן הַמַּשְׁחִית,
from the destructive spiritual impediment,

midin koshe u-miba-al din koshe,
מִדִּין קָשֶׁה וּמִבַּעַל דִּין קָשֶׁה,
from a harsh trial and from a harsh opponent,

bayn shehu ven b'ris,
בֵּין שֶׁהוּא בֶן בְּרִית,
whether he is a member of the covenant*

יְהִי רָצוֹן — *May it be Your will.* This is a prayer for protection in day-to-day dealings with one's fellowmen. During the recitation, one may add his personal requests for God's help during the day.

בֶּן בְּרִית — *A member of the covenant,* i.e., Abraham's covenant of circumcision, the emblem of Israel's bond with God.

u-vayn she-aynō ven b'ris.　　　　　　וּבֵין שֶׁאֵינוֹ בֶן בְּרִית.

or whether he is not a member of the covenant.

THE AKEIDAH

SOME OMIT THE FOLLOWING SUPPLICATING PARAGRAPH ON THE SABBATH AND FESTIVALS.

ELŌHAYNU Vaylōhay avōsaynu,　　אֱלֹהֵינוּ וֵאלֹהֵי אֲבוֹתֵינוּ,

Our God and the God of our forefathers,

zochraynu b'zikorōn tōv l'fonecho,　　זָכְרֵנוּ בְּזִכָּרוֹן טוֹב לְפָנֶיךָ,

remember us with a favorable memory before You,

u-fokdaynu bifkudas　　　　　　　　וּפָקְדֵנוּ בִּפְקֻדַּת

y'shu-o v'rachamim　　　　　　　　יְשׁוּעָה וְרַחֲמִים

and recall us with a recollection of salvation and mercy

mish'may sh'may kedem.　　　　　　מִשְּׁמֵי שְׁמֵי קֶדֶם.

from the primeval loftiest heavens.

Uzchor lonu Adōnoy Elōhaynu　　　וּזְכָר לָנוּ יהוה אֱלֹהֵינוּ

Remember on our behalf — HASHEM, our God —

ahavas hakadmōnim　　　　　　　　אַהֲבַת הַקַּדְמוֹנִים

the love of the Patriarchs,

avrohom yitzchok v'yisro-ayl　　אַבְרָהָם יִצְחָק וְיִשְׂרָאֵל

avodecho,　　　　　　　　　　　　עֲבָדֶיךָ,

Abraham, Isaac, and Israel, Your servants;

es hab'ris v'es hachesed　　　　אֶת הַבְּרִית וְאֶת הַחֶסֶד

the covenant, the kindness

v'es hash'vu-o　　　　　　　　　　וְאֶת הַשְּׁבוּעָה

shenishbato l'avrohom ovinu　　שֶׁנִּשְׁבַּעְתָּ לְאַבְרָהָם אָבִינוּ

and the oath that You swore to our father Abraham

b'har hamōri-yo,　　　　　　　　בְּהַר הַמּוֹרִיָּה,

at Mount Moriah,

v'es ho-akaydo　　　　　　　　　וְאֶת הָעֲקֵדָה

and the Akeidah,

she-okad es yitzchok b'nō　　שֶׁעָקַד אֶת יִצְחָק בְּנוֹ

al gabay hamizbay-ach,　　　　עַל גַּבֵּי הַמִּזְבֵּחַ,

when he bound his son Isaac atop the altar,

kakosuv b'sōrosecho:　　　　　כַּכָּתוּב בְּתוֹרָתֶךָ:

as it is written in Your Torah:

◆§ The Akeidah

　The *Akeidah* is the story of the most difficult challenge to Abraham's faith in God: He was commanded to sacrifice Isaac, his beloved son and sole heir, to God. Father and son jointly demonstrated their total devotion, upon which God ordered Abraham to release Isaac. The kabbalistic masters have stressed the great

VAI-HI achar had'vorim ho-ayle,
וַיְהִי אַחַר הַדְּבָרִים הָאֵלֶּה,
And it happened after these things

v'ho-Elōhim niso es avrohom,
וְהָאֱלֹהִים נִסָּה אֶת אַבְרָהָם,
that God tested Abraham

va-yōmer aylov, avrohom,
וַיֹּאמֶר אֵלָיו, אַבְרָהָם,
and said to him, "Abraham."

va-yōmer, hinayni.
וַיֹּאמֶר, הִנֵּנִי.
And he replied, "Here I am."

Va-yōmer, kach no es bincho,
וַיֹּאמֶר, קַח נָא אֶת בִּנְךָ,
And He said, "Please take your son,

es y'chid'cho, asher ohavto,
אֶת יְחִידְךָ, אֲשֶׁר אָהַבְתָּ,
es yitzchok,
אֶת יִצְחָק,
your only one, whom you love — Isaac —

v'lech l'cho el eretz hamōri-yo,
וְלֶךְ לְךָ אֶל אֶרֶץ הַמֹּרִיָּה,
and get yourself to the Land of Moriah;

v'ha-alayhu shom l'ōlo
וְהַעֲלֵהוּ שָׁם לְעֹלָה
bring him up there as an offering,

al achad hehorim
עַל אַחַד הֶהָרִים
upon one of the mountains

asher ōmar aylecho.
אֲשֶׁר אֹמַר אֵלֶיךָ.
which I shall indicate to you."

Va-yashkaym avrohom babōker,
וַיַּשְׁכֵּם אַבְרָהָם בַּבֹּקֶר,
So Abraham awoke early in the morning

va-yachavōsh es chamōrō,
וַיַּחֲבֹשׁ אֶת חֲמֹרוֹ,
and he saddled his donkey;

va-yikach es sh'nay n'orov itō,
וַיִּקַּח אֶת שְׁנֵי נְעָרָיו אִתּוֹ,
he took his two young men with him,

v'ays yitzchok b'nō,
וְאֵת יִצְחָק בְּנוֹ,
and Isaac, his son.

vaivaka atzay ōlo,
וַיְבַקַּע עֲצֵי עֹלָה,
He split the wood for the offering,

importance of the daily recitation of the *Akeidah*. In response to their writings, the *Akeidah* has been incorporated into the great majority of *siddurim*, although it is not recited in all congregations. In some congregations, it is recited individually rather than as part of the public morning service. According to the kabbalistic teachings, this recitation of Abraham and Isaac's readiness to put love of God ahead of life itself is a source of Heavenly mercy whenever Jewish lives are threatened; the *Akeidah* should inspire us toward greater love of God, by following the example of Abraham and Isaac; and the recitation brings atonement to someone who repents sincerely, for he identifies himself with these two Patriarchs who placed loyalty to God above all other considerations.

va-yokom va-yaylech el hamokōm   וַיָּקָם וַיֵּלֶךְ אֶל הַמָּקוֹם
and rose and went toward the place

asher omar lō ho-Elōhim.   אֲשֶׁר אָמַר לוֹ הָאֱלֹהִים.
which God had indicated to him.

Ba-yōm hash'lishi,   בַּיּוֹם הַשְּׁלִישִׁי,
On the third day,

va-yiso avrohom es aynov,   וַיִּשָּׂא אַבְרָהָם אֶת עֵינָיו,
Abraham looked up,

va-yar es hamokōm mayrochōk.   וַיַּרְא אֶת הַמָּקוֹם מֵרָחֹק.
and perceived the place from afar.

Va-yōmer avrohom el n'orov,   וַיֹּאמֶר אַבְרָהָם אֶל נְעָרָיו,
And Abraham said to his young men,

sh'vu lochem pō im hachamōr,   שְׁבוּ לָכֶם פֹּה עִם הַחֲמוֹר,
"Stay here by yourselves with the donkey,

va-ani v'hana-ar nayl'cho ad kō   וַאֲנִי וְהַנַּעַר נֵלְכָה עַד כֹּה,
while I and the lad will go yonder;

v'nishtacha-ve   וְנִשְׁתַּחֲוֶה
we will prostrate ourselves

v'noshuvo alaychem.   וְנָשׁוּבָה אֲלֵיכֶם.
and we will return* to you."

Va-yikach avrohom es atzay ho-ōlo,   וַיִּקַּח אַבְרָהָם אֶת עֲצֵי הָעֹלָה,
And Abraham took the wood for the offering,

va-yosem al yitzchok b'nō,   וַיָּשֶׂם עַל יִצְחָק בְּנוֹ,
and placed it on Isaac, his son.

va-yikach b'yodō es ho-aysh   וַיִּקַּח בְּיָדוֹ אֶת הָאֵשׁ
v'es hama-acheles,   וְאֶת הַמַּאֲכֶלֶת,
He took in his hand the fire and the knife,

va-yayl'chu sh'nayhem yachdov.   וַיֵּלְכוּ שְׁנֵיהֶם יַחְדָּו.
and the two of them went together.

Va-yōmer yitzchok el avrohom oviv,   וַיֹּאמֶר יִצְחָק אֶל אַבְרָהָם אָבִיו,
Then Isaac spoke to Abraham his father

va-yōmer, ovi,   וַיֹּאמֶר, אָבִי,
and said, "My father —, "

va-yōmer, hineni v'ni.   וַיֹּאמֶר, הִנֶּנִּי בְנִי.
and he said, "Here I am, my son."

וְנִשְׁתַּחֲוֶה וְנָשׁוּבָה — *We will prostrate ourselves and we will return.* An unintended prophecy issued from Abraham's lips. Instead of saying "I will return," — without Isaac — he said "we," for such, indeed was God's intention.

Va-yōmer, hinay ho-aysh v'ho-aytzim,   וַיֹּאמֶר, הִנֵּה הָאֵשׁ וְהָעֵצִים,
And he said, "Here are the fire and the wood,

v'a-yay ha-se l'ōlo.   וְאַיֵּה הַשֶּׂה לְעֹלָה.
but where is the lamb for the offering?"

Va-yōmer avrohom,   וַיֹּאמֶר אַבְרָהָם,
And Abraham said,

Elōhim yir-e lō, ha-se l'ōlo,   אֱלֹהִים יִרְאֶה לּוֹ הַשֶּׂה לְעֹלָה,
  b'ni.   בְּנִי.
"God will seek out for Himself the lamb* for the offering, my son."

Va-yayl'chu sh'nayhem yachdov.   וַיֵּלְכוּ שְׁנֵיהֶם יַחְדָּו.
And the two of them went together.

Va-yovō-u el hamokōm   וַיָּבֹאוּ אֶל הַמָּקוֹם
They arrived at the place

asher omar lō ho-Elōhim,   אֲשֶׁר אָמַר לוֹ הָאֱלֹהִים,
which God indicated to him.

va-yiven shom avrohom   וַיִּבֶן שָׁם אַבְרָהָם
  es hamizbay-ach,   אֶת הַמִּזְבֵּחַ,
Abraham built the altar there,

va-ya-arōch es ho-aytzim,   וַיַּעֲרֹךְ אֶת הָעֵצִים,
and arranged the wood;

va-ya-akōd es yitzchok b'nō,   וַיַּעֲקֹד אֶת יִצְחָק בְּנוֹ,
he bound Isaac, his son,

va-yosem ōsō al hamizbay-ach   וַיָּשֶׂם אֹתוֹ עַל הַמִּזְבֵּחַ
and he placed him on the altar

mima-al lo-aytzim.   מִמַּעַל לָעֵצִים.
atop the wood.

Va-yishlach avrohom es yodō,   וַיִּשְׁלַח אַבְרָהָם אֶת יָדוֹ,
Abraham stretched out his hand,

va-yikach es hama-acheles   וַיִּקַּח אֶת הַמַּאֲכֶלֶת
  lishchōt es b'nō.   לִשְׁחֹט אֶת בְּנוֹ.
and took the knife to slaughter his son.

Va-yikro aylov mal-ach Adōnoy   וַיִּקְרָא אֵלָיו מַלְאַךְ יהוה
  min hashoma-yim,   מִן הַשָּׁמַיִם,
And an angel of HASHEM called to him from heaven,

אֱלֹהִים יִרְאֶה לּוֹ הַשֶּׂה — *God will seek out for Himself the lamb.* Isaac understood from this reply that he would be the sacrificial lamb. Nevertheless, though Isaac was in the prime of life at the age of thirty-seven and Abraham was a century his senior, "the two of them went together," united in their dedication.

Va-yōmer, avrohom, avrohom,   וַיֹּאמֶר, אַבְרָהָם, אַבְרָהָם,
and he said, "Abraham! Abraham!"

va-yōmer, hinayni.   וַיֹּאמֶר, הִנֵּנִי.
And he said, "Here I am."

Va-yōmer,   וַיֹּאמֶר,
And he [the angel quoting HASHEM] said,

al tishlach yod'cho el hana-ar,   אַל תִּשְׁלַח יָדְךָ אֶל הַנַּעַר,
"Do not stretch out your hand against the lad

v'al ta-as lō m'umo,   וְאַל תַּעַשׂ לוֹ מְאוּמָה,
and do not do anything to him,

ki ato yodati   כִּי עַתָּה יָדַעְתִּי
for now I know

ki y'ray Elōhim ato,   כִּי יְרֵא אֱלֹהִים אַתָּה,
that you are a God-fearing man,

v'lō chosachto es bincho   וְלֹא חָשַׂכְתָּ אֶת בִּנְךָ
es y'chid'cho mimeni.   אֶת יְחִידְךָ מִמֶּנִּי.
since you have not withheld your son, your only one, from Me."

Va-yiso avrohom es aynov   וַיִּשָּׂא אַבְרָהָם אֶת עֵינָיו
And Abraham raised his eyes

va-yar, v'hinay a-yil, achar,   וַיַּרְא, וְהִנֵּה אַיִל, אַחַר,
and saw — behold a ram! — afterwards,

ne-echaz bas'vach b'karnov.   נֶאֱחַז בַּסְּבַךְ בְּקַרְנָיו.
caught in the thicket by its horns.

Va-yaylech avrohom   וַיֵּלֶךְ אַבְרָהָם
va-yikach es ho-a-yil,   וַיִּקַּח אֶת הָאַיִל,
So Abraham went and took the ram

va-ya-alayhu l'ōlo tachas b'nō.   וַיַּעֲלֵהוּ לְעֹלָה תַּחַת בְּנוֹ.
and brought it as an offering instead of his son.

Va-yikro avrohom   וַיִּקְרָא אַבְרָהָם
shaym hamokōm hahu   שֵׁם הַמָּקוֹם הַהוּא
And Abraham named that site

Adōnoy yir-e,   יהוה יִרְאֶה,
"HASHEM Yireh,"

asher yayo-mayr ha-yōm,   אֲשֶׁר יֵאָמֵר הַיּוֹם,
as it is said this day:

b'har Adōnoy yayro-e.   בְּהַר יהוה יֵרָאֶה.
On the mountain HASHEM will be seen.

Va-yikro mal-ach Adōnoy
el avrohom,

וַיִּקְרָא מַלְאַךְ יהוה
אֶל אַבְרָהָם,

The angel of HASHEM called to Abraham,

shaynis min hashomo-yim.

שֵׁנִית מִן הַשָּׁמָיִם.

a second time from heaven,

Va-yōmer,

וַיֹּאמֶר,

and he said,

bi nishbati n'um Adōnoy,

בִּי נִשְׁבַּעְתִּי נְאֻם יהוה,

" 'By Myself I swear,' declared HASHEM,

ki ya-an asher osiso
es hadovor ha-ze,

כִּי יַעַן אֲשֶׁר עָשִׂיתָ
אֶת הַדָּבָר הַזֶּה,

'that since you have done this thing,

v'lō chosachto
es bincho es y'chide-cho.

וְלֹא חָשַׂכְתָּ
אֶת בִּנְךָ אֶת יְחִידֶךָ.

and have not withheld your son, your only one,

Ki voraych avorech'cho,

כִּי בָרֵךְ אֲבָרֶכְךָ,

I shall surely bless you

v'harbo arbe es zar-acho

וְהַרְבָּה אַרְבֶּה אֶת זַרְעֲךָ

and greatly increase your offspring

k'chōch'vay ha-shoma-yim,

כְּכוֹכְבֵי הַשָּׁמַיִם,

like the stars of the heavens

v'chachōl asher al s'fas ha-yom,

וְכַחוֹל אֲשֶׁר עַל שְׂפַת הַיָּם,

and like the sand on the seashore;

v'yirash zar-acho ays sha-ar ōy'vov.

וְיִרַשׁ זַרְעֲךָ אֵת שַׁעַר אֹיְבָיו.

and your offspring shall inherit the gate of its enemy;

V'hisbor'chu v'zar-acho
kōl gō-yay ho-oretz,

וְהִתְבָּרְכוּ בְזַרְעֲךָ
כֹּל גּוֹיֵי הָאָרֶץ,

and all the nations of the earth shall bless themselves by your offspring,

aykev asher shomato b'kōli.

עֵקֶב אֲשֶׁר שָׁמַעְתָּ בְּקֹלִי.

because you have listened to My voice.' "

Va-yoshov avrohom el n'orov,

וַיָּשָׁב אַבְרָהָם אֶל נְעָרָיו,

Abraham returned to his young men,

va-yokumu va-yayl'chu yachdov
el b'ayr shova,

וַיָּקֻמוּ וַיֵּלְכוּ יַחְדָּו
אֶל בְּאֵר שָׁבַע,

and they rose and went together to Beer Sheba,

va-yayshev avrohom biv-ayr shova.

וַיֵּשֶׁב אַבְרָהָם בִּבְאֵר שָׁבַע.

and Abraham stayed at Beer Sheba.

SOME OMIT THE FOLLOWING SUPPLICATION ON THE SABBATH AND ON FESTIVALS.
THEY CONTINUE AT THE BOTTOM OF P. 246.

RIBŌNŌ shel ōlom,   רִבּוֹנוֹ שֶׁל עוֹלָם,
Master of the universe!

y'hi rotzōn mil'fonecho,   יְהִי רָצוֹן מִלְּפָנֶיךָ,
May it be Your will,

Adōnoy Elōhaynu   יהוה אֱלֹהֵינוּ

Vaylōhay avōsaynu,   וֵאלֹהֵי אֲבוֹתֵינוּ,
HASHEM, our God, and the God of our forefathers,

shetizkor lonu b'ris avōsaynu.   שֶׁתִּזְכָּר לָנוּ בְּרִית אֲבוֹתֵינוּ.
that You remember for our sake the covenant of our forefathers.

k'mō shekovash avrohom ovinu   כְּמוֹ שֶׁכָּבַשׁ אַבְרָהָם אָבִינוּ
Just as Abraham our forefather suppressed

es rachamov miben y'chidō,   אֶת רַחֲמָיו מִבֶּן יְחִידוֹ,
his mercy for his only son

v'rotzo lishchōt ōsō   וְרָצָה לִשְׁחוֹט אוֹתוֹ
and was willing to slaughter him

k'day la-asōs r'tzōnecho,   כְּדֵי לַעֲשׂוֹת רְצוֹנֶךָ,
in order to do Your will,

kayn yichb'shu rachamecho   כֵּן יִכְבְּשׁוּ רַחֲמֶיךָ
es ka-ascho may-olaynu,   אֶת כַּעַסְךָ מֵעָלֵינוּ,
so may Your mercy suppress Your anger from upon us

v'yogōlu rachamecho al midōsecho,   וְיָגֹלּוּ רַחֲמֶיךָ עַל מִדּוֹתֶיךָ,
and may Your mercy overwhelm Your attributes.

v'sikonays itonu   וְתִכָּנֵס אִתָּנוּ
May You overstep with us

lifnim mishuras dinecho,   לִפְנִים מִשּׁוּרַת דִּינֶךָ,
the line of Your law

v'sisnahayg imonu,   וְתִתְנַהֵג עִמָּנוּ,
Adōnoy Elōhaynu,   יהוה אֱלֹהֵינוּ,
and deal with us — O HASHEM, our God —

b'midas hachesed   בְּמִדַּת הַחֶסֶד
uvmidas horachamim.   וּבְמִדַּת הָרַחֲמִים.
with the attribute of kindness and the attribute of mercy.

Uvtuv'cho hagodōl,   וּבְטוּבְךָ הַגָּדוֹל,
In Your great goodness

yoshuv charōn ap'cho   יָשׁוּב חֲרוֹן אַפְּךָ
may You turn aside Your burning wrath

may-am'cho u-may-ir'cho
מֵעַמְּךָ וּמֵעִירְךָ

from Your people, Your city,

u-may-artz'cho u-minachalose-cho.
וּמֵאַרְצְךָ וּמִנַּחֲלָתֶךָ.

Your land, and Your heritage.

V'ka-yem lonu, Adōnoy Elōhaynu,
וְקַיֶּם לָנוּ, יהוה אֱלֹהֵינוּ,

Fulfill for us, HASHEM, our God,

es hadovor she-hivtachtonu
אֶת הַדָּבָר שֶׁהִבְטַחְתָּנוּ

the word You pledged

al y'day mōshe avdecho,
עַל יְדֵי מֹשֶׁה עַבְדֶּךָ,

through Moses, Your servant,

ko-omur:
כָּאָמוּר:

as it is said:

V'zocharti es b'risi ya-akōv,
וְזָכַרְתִּי אֶת בְּרִיתִי יַעֲקוֹב,

"I shall remember My covenant with Jacob;

v'af es b'risi yitzchok,
וְאַף אֶת בְּרִיתִי יִצְחָק,

also My covenant with Isaac,

v'af es b'risi avrohom ezkōr,
וְאַף אֶת בְּרִיתִי אַבְרָהָם אֶזְכֹּר,

and also My covenant with Abraham shall I remember;

v'ho-oretz ezkōr.
וְהָאָרֶץ אֶזְכֹּר.

and the land shall I remember."

L'ŌLOM y'hay odom
לְעוֹלָם יְהֵא אָדָם

y'ray shoma-yim
יְרֵא שָׁמַיִם

Always* let a person be God-fearing

b'sayser u-vagoluy,
בְּסֵתֶר וּבַגָּלוּי,

privately and publicly,

u-mōde al ho-emes,
וּמוֹדֶה עַל הָאֱמֶת,

acknowledge the truth,*

v'dōvayr emes bilvovō,
וְדוֹבֵר אֱמֶת בִּלְבָבוֹ,

speak the truth within his heart,

v'yashkaym v'yōmar:
וְיַשְׁכֵּם וְיֹאמַר:

and arise early and proclaim:

לְעוֹלָם — *Always*. The section beginning here and extending until *Offerings* is in its totality a profound and succinct summation of basic Jewish faith and loyalty to God. What is more, it is a ringing declaration of joyous pride in our Jewishness, a pride that overcomes all persecutions and that moves us to pray for the time when all will recognize the truth of the Torah's message, and we will proudly proclaim that message which the anti-Semites of the world attempt to silence.

Furthermore, the declarations contained in this section represent the manner in which a Jew should conduct himself always, not merely on ceremonial occasions.

וּמוֹדֶה עַל הָאֱמֶת — *[Let him] acknowledge the truth.* One who seeks the truth is not ashamed to concede his errors. But if he cares more about his reputation than the truth, he will stubbornly persist in falsehood and sin.

Ribōn kol ho-ōlomim,   רִבּוֹן כָּל הָעוֹלָמִים,
Master of all worlds!

lō al tzidkōsaynu   לֹא עַל צִדְקוֹתֵֽינוּ
Not in the merit of our righteousness

anachnu mapilim   אֲנַחְנוּ מַפִּילִים
  tachanunaynu l'fonecho,   תַּחֲנוּנֵֽינוּ לְפָנֶֽיךָ
do we cast our supplications before You,

ki al rachamecho horabim.   כִּי עַל רַחֲמֶֽיךָ הָרַבִּים.
but in the merit of Your abundant mercy.

Mo anachnu, me cha-yaynu,   מָה אֲנַֽחְנוּ, מֶה חַיֵּֽינוּ,
What are we? What is our life?

me chasdaynu, ma tzidkōsaynu   מֶה חַסְדֵּֽנוּ, מַה צִּדְקוֹתֵֽינוּ,
  ma y'shu-osaynu,   מַה יְשׁוּעָתֵֽנוּ,
What is our kindness? What is our righteousness? What is our salvation?

ma kōchaynu, ma g'vurosaynu.   מַה כֹּחֵֽנוּ, מַה גְּבוּרָתֵֽנוּ.
What is our strength? What is our might?

Ma nōmar l'fonecho,   מַה נֹּאמַר לְפָנֶֽיךָ,
What can we say before You,

Adōnoy Elōhaynu Vaylōhay avōsaynu,   יהוה אֱלֹהֵֽינוּ וֵאלֹהֵי אֲבוֹתֵֽינוּ,
HASHEM, our God, and the God of our forefathers —

halō kol hagibōrim k'a-yin l'fonecho,   הֲלֹא כָּל הַגִּבּוֹרִים כְּאַֽיִן לְפָנֶֽיךָ,
are not all the mighty like nothing before You,

v'anshay hashaym k'lō ho-yu,   וְאַנְשֵׁי הַשֵּׁם כְּלֹא הָיוּ,
the renowned as if they had never existed,

vachachomim kivli mado,   וַחֲכָמִים כִּבְלִי מַדָּע,
the wise as if devoid of wisdom

unvōnim kivli haskayl.   וּנְבוֹנִים כִּבְלִי הַשְׂכֵּל.
and the perceptive as if devoid of intelligence?

Ki rōv ma-asayhem tōhu,   כִּי רוֹב מַעֲשֵׂיהֶם תֹּֽהוּ,
For most of their deeds are desolate

vimay cha-yayhem hevel l'fonecho,   וִימֵי חַיֵּיהֶם הֶֽבֶל לְפָנֶֽיךָ,
and the days of their lives are empty before You.

U-mōsar ho-odom   וּמוֹתַר הָאָדָם
  min hab'haymo o-yin,   מִן הַבְּהֵמָה אָֽיִן,
The pre-eminence of man over beast is non-existent

ki hakōl hovel.   כִּי הַכֹּל הָֽבֶל.
for all is vain.

Avol anachnu am'cho,
b'nay v'risecho,

אֲבָל אֲנַחְנוּ עַמֶּךָ,
בְּנֵי בְרִיתֶךָ,

But we are Your people, members of Your covenant,

b'nay avrohom ōhavcho

בְּנֵי אַבְרָהָם אֹהַבְךָ

children of Abraham, Your beloved,

shenishbato lō b'har hamōri-yo,

שֶׁנִּשְׁבַּעְתָּ לּוֹ בְּהַר הַמּוֹרִיָּה,

to whom You took an oath at Mount Moriah;

zera yitzchok y'chidō

זֶרַע יִצְחָק יְחִידוֹ

the offspring of Isaac, his only son,

shene-ekad al gabay hamizbay-ach,

שֶׁנֶּעֱקַד עַל גַּבֵּי הַמִּזְבֵּחַ,

who was bound atop the altar;

adas ya-akōv bincho b'chōrecho,

עֲדַת יַעֲקֹב בִּנְךָ בְּכוֹרֶךָ,

the community of Jacob, Your firstborn son,

shemay-ahavos'cho she-ohavto ōsō

שֶׁמֵאַהֲבָתְךָ שֶׁאָהַבְתָּ אוֹתוֹ

whom — because of the love with which You adored him

u-misimchos'cho shesomachto bō,

וּמִשִּׂמְחָתְךָ שֶׁשָּׂמַחְתָּ בּוֹ,

and the joy with which You delighted in him —

koroso es shmō yisro-ayl
vishurun.

קָרָאתָ אֶת שְׁמוֹ יִשְׂרָאֵל
וִישֻׁרוּן.

You named Israel and Jeshurun.

L'FI-CHOCH anachnu cha-yovim

לְפִיכָךְ אֲנַחְנוּ חַיָּבִים

Therefore, we are obliged

l'hōdōs l'cho, ulshabaychacho,
ulfo-ercho,

לְהוֹדוֹת לְךָ, וּלְשַׁבֵּחֲךָ,
וּלְפָאֶרְךָ,

to thank You, praise You, glorify You,

ulvoraych ulkadaysh

וּלְבָרֵךְ וּלְקַדֵּשׁ

bless, sanctify,

v'losays shevach v'hōdo-yo lishmecho.

וְלָתֵת שֶׁבַח וְהוֹדָיָה לִשְׁמֶךָ.

and offer praise and thanks to Your Name.

Ashraynu, ma tōv chelkaynu,

אַשְׁרֵינוּ, מַה טּוֹב חֶלְקֵנוּ,

We are fortunate — how good is our portion,

u-ma no-im gōrolaynu,

וּמַה נָּעִים גּוֹרָלֵנוּ,

how pleasant our lot,

u-ma yofo y'rushosaynu.

וּמַה יָּפָה יְרֻשָׁתֵנוּ.

and how beautiful our heritage!

Ashraynu,

❖ אַשְׁרֵינוּ,

We are fortunate

she-anachnu mashkimim   שֶׁאֲנַֽחְנוּ מַשְׁכִּימִים
   uma-arivim,   וּמַעֲרִיבִים,

for we come early and stay late,

erev vovōker,   עֶֽרֶב וָבֹֽקֶר,

evening and morning,

v'ōm'rim pa-ama-yim b'chol yōm.   וְאוֹמְרִים פַּעֲמַֽיִם בְּכָל יוֹם.

and proclaim twice each day.

SH'MA yisro-ayl,   שְׁמַע יִשְׂרָאֵל,

Hear, O Israel.

Adōnoy Elohaynu, Adōnoy e-chod.   יהוה אֱלֹהֵֽינוּ, יהוה אֶחָד.

HASHEM is our God, HASHEM, the One and Only.

IN AN UNDERTONE:

Boruch shaym k'vōd malchuso   בָּרוּךְ שֵׁם כְּבוֹד מַלְכוּתוֹ
   l'ōlom vo-ed.   לְעוֹלָם וָעֶד.

Blessed is the Name of His glorious kingdom for all eternity.

ATO HU   אַתָּה הוּא
   ad she-lo nivro ho-ōlom,   עַד שֶׁלֹּא נִבְרָא הָעוֹלָם,

It was You before the world was created,*

ato hu mi-shenivro ho-ōlom,   אַתָּה הוּא מִשֶּׁנִּבְרָא הָעוֹלָם,

it is You since the world was created,

ato hu bo-ōlom ha-ze,   אַתָּה הוּא בָּעוֹלָם הַזֶּה,

it is You in This World,

v'ato hu lo-ōlom habo.   וְאַתָּה הוּא לָעוֹלָם הַבָּא.

and it is You in the World to Come.

Kadaysh es shimcho   ❖ קַדֵּשׁ אֶת שִׁמְךָ

Sanctify Your Name

al makdi-shay sh'mecho,   עַל מַקְדִּישֵׁי שְׁמֶךָ,

through those who sanctify Your Name,

v'kadaysh es shimcho b'ōlomecho.   וְקַדֵּשׁ אֶת שִׁמְךָ בְּעוֹלָמֶךָ.

and sanctify Your Name in Your universe.

u-vi-shu-os'cho   וּבִישׁוּעָתְךָ

Through Your salvation

שְׁמַע יִשְׂרָאֵל — *Hear, O Israel.* During the fifth century, the Persian king forbade the Jews in his empire to recite the *Shema.* He stationed guards in every synagogue during the time that the *Shema* would ordinarily be recited. To counteract his design, the people recited *Shema* at home, before going to the synagogue. When the ban was lifted, the first verse of the *Shema* was made a part of the introductory prayers of the morning synagogue service.

אַתָּה הוּא — *It was You. . .* God is eternal and unchanging, unaffected by time or place.

torim v'sagbi-ah karnaynu.
תָּרִים וְתַגְבִּיהַּ קַרְנֵנוּ.
may You exalt and raise our pride.

Boruch ato Adōnoy,
בָּרוּךְ אַתָּה יהוה,
Blessed are You, HASHEM,

m'kadaysh es shimcho borabim.
מְקַדֵּשׁ אֶת שִׁמְךָ בָּרַבִּים.
Who sanctifies Your Name among the multitudes.

CONGREGATION RESPONDS: Omayn — אָמֵן

ATO hu Adōnoy Elōhaynu,
אַתָּה הוּא יהוה אֱלֹהֵינוּ,
It is You Who are HASHEM, our God,

ba-shoma-yim u-vo-oretz
בַּשָּׁמַיִם וּבָאָרֶץ
in heaven and on earth

u-vishmay ha-shoma-yim ho-elyōnim.
וּבִשְׁמֵי הַשָּׁמַיִם הָעֶלְיוֹנִים.
and in the loftiest heavens.

Emes, ato hu rishōn,
אֱמֶת, אַתָּה הוּא רִאשׁוֹן,
True — You are the First

v'ato hu acharōn,
וְאַתָּה הוּא אַחֲרוֹן,
and You are the Last, *

umibal-odecho ayn Elōhim.
וּמִבַּלְעָדֶיךָ אֵין אֱלֹהִים.
and other than You there is no God.

Kabaytz kōvecho
קַבֵּץ קֹוֶיךָ
Gather in those who [place] their hope in You,

may-arba kanfōs ho-oretz.
מֵאַרְבַּע כַּנְפוֹת הָאָרֶץ.
from the four corners of the earth.

Yakiru v'yayd'u kol bo-ay ōlom
יַכִּירוּ וְיֵדְעוּ כָּל בָּאֵי עוֹלָם
Let all who walk the earth recognize and know

ki ato hu ho-Elōhim l'vad'cho
כִּי אַתָּה הוּא הָאֱלֹהִים לְבַדֶּךָ
that You alone are the God

l'chōl maml'chōs ho-oretz.
לְכֹל מַמְלְכוֹת הָאָרֶץ.
over all the kingdoms of the earth.

Ato osiso
אַתָּה עָשִׂיתָ
es hashoma-yim v'es ho-oretz,
אֶת הַשָּׁמַיִם וְאֶת הָאָרֶץ,
You have made the heavens, the earth,

es ha-yom, v'es kol asher bom.
אֶת הַיָּם, וְאֶת כָּל אֲשֶׁר בָּם.
the sea, and all that is in them.

ראשׁוֹן ... אַחֲרוֹן — *The First ... the Last.* This means that God pre-existed everything and will survive everything, not that He had a be- ginning or will have an end, for God is infinite and timeless.

U-mi b'chol ma-asay yodecho / וּמִי בְּכָל מַעֲשֵׂה יָדֶיךָ

Who among all Your handiwork,

bo-elyōnim ō vatachtōnim / בָּעֶלְיוֹנִים אוֹ בַתַּחְתּוֹנִים

those above and those below,

she-yōmar l'cho, ma ta-ase. / שֶׁיֹּאמַר לְךָ, מַה תַּעֲשֶׂה.

can say to You, "What are You doing?"

Ovinu shebashoma-yim, / אָבִינוּ שֶׁבַּשָּׁמַיִם,

Our Father in Heaven,

asay imonu chesed / עֲשֵׂה עִמָּנוּ חֶסֶד

do kindness with us

ba-avur shimcho hagodōl / בַּעֲבוּר שִׁמְךָ הַגָּדוֹל

shenikro olaynu, / שֶׁנִּקְרָא עָלֵינוּ,

for the sake of Your great Name that has been proclaimed upon us.

v'ka-yem lonu Adōnoy Elōhaynu / וְקַיֵּם לָנוּ יהוה אֱלֹהֵינוּ

Fulfill for us, HASHEM, our God,

ma shekosuv: / מַה שֶׁכָּתוּב:

what is written:

Bo-ays ha-hi ovi eschem, / בָּעֵת הַהִיא אָבִיא אֶתְכֶם,

" 'At that time I will bring you

u-vo-ays kab'tzi eschem, / וּבָעֵת קַבְּצִי אֶתְכֶם,

and at that time I will gather you in,

ki etayn eschem l'shaym v'lis-hilo / כִּי אֶתֵּן אֶתְכֶם לְשֵׁם וְלִתְהִלָּה

for I will set you up for renown and praise

b'chōl amay ho-oretz, / בְּכֹל עַמֵּי הָאָרֶץ,

among all the peoples of the earth,

b'shuvi es sh'vusaychem / בְּשׁוּבִי אֶת שְׁבוּתֵיכֶם

l'aynaychem, omar Adōnoy. / לְעֵינֵיכֶם, אָמַר יהוה.

when I bring back your captivity, before your own eyes,' said HASHEM. "

⊰{ OFFERINGS }⊱

VAIDABAYR Adōnoy / וַיְדַבֵּר יהוה

el mōshe laymōr. / אֶל מֹשֶׁה לֵּאמֹר.

HASHEM spoke to Moses, saying:

⊷§ Offerings

From the beginning of its existence as a nation, Israel *saw* — whether or not it understood why or how — that the sacrificial service effected a closeness to God and the manifestation of His Presence. The offerings represented the Jew's submission to God of his self and his resources.

In the inspiring words of Rabbi S. R. Hirsch (*Horeb* §624): "The Temple has fallen, the Altar has disappeared, the harps of the singers are heard no more, but their spirit has become the heritage of Israel; it still infuses the word which alone survives as an expression of the

V'osiso kiyōr n'chōshes,
Make a laver of copper, *

וְעָשִׂיתָ כִּיּוֹר נְחֹשֶׁת,

v'chanō n'chōshes, l'rochtzo,
and its base of copper, for washing;

וְכַנּוֹ נְחֹשֶׁת, לְרָחְצָה,

v'nosato ōsō
and place it

וְנָתַתָּ אֹתוֹ

bayn ōhel mō-ayd
u-vayn hamizbay-ach,
between the Tent of Appointment and the Altar

בֵּין אֹהֶל מוֹעֵד
וּבֵין הַמִּזְבֵּחַ,

v'nosato shomo mo-yim.
and put water there.

וְנָתַתָּ שָׁמָּה מָיִם.

V'rochatzu aharōn u-vonov mimenu,
Aaron and his sons are to wash from it

וְרָחֲצוּ אַהֲרֹן וּבָנָיו מִמֶּנּוּ,

es y'dayhem v'es raglayhem.
their hands and feet.

אֶת יְדֵיהֶם וְאֶת רַגְלֵיהֶם.

B'vō-om el ōhel mō-ayd
When they arrive at the Tent of Appointment

בְּבֹאָם אֶל אֹהֶל מוֹעֵד

yirchatzu ma-yim
they are to wash with water

יִרְחֲצוּ מַיִם

v'lō yomusu,
so that they not die, *

וְלֹא יָמֻתוּ,

ō v'gishtom el hamizbay-ach
l'shorays
or when they approach the Altar to serve,

אוֹ בְגִשְׁתָּם אֶל הַמִּזְבֵּחַ
לְשָׁרֵת

l'haktir i-she Ladōnoy.
to burn a fire-offering to HASHEM.

לְהַקְטִיר אִשֶּׁה לַיהוה.

V'rochatzu y'dayhem v'raglayhem
They are to wash their hands and feet

וְרָחֲצוּ יְדֵיהֶם וְרַגְלֵיהֶם

v'lō yomusu,
so that they not die;

וְלֹא יָמֻתוּ,

v'hoy'so lohem chok ōlom,
and this shall be an eternal decree for them —

וְהָיְתָה לָהֶם חָק עוֹלָם,

lō ulzar-ō l'dōrōsom.
for him and for his offspring — throughout their generations.

לוֹ וּלְזַרְעוֹ לְדֹרֹתָם.

---

inward Divine service."

The offerings whose laws are about to be recited are all communal ones; the Sages chose them because they illustrate our wish that Israel become united as a single nation in God's service.

וְעָשִׂיתָ כִּיּוֹר נְחֹשֶׁת — *Make a laver of copper.* Before the *Kohanim* could begin the Temple service, they had to take sanctified water and pour it over their hands and feet. This water was drawn from a large copper laver in the Temple Courtyard. In preparation for our ver-

VAIDABAYR Adōnoy

el mōshe laymōr.

וַיְדַבֵּר יהוה
אֶל מֹשֶׁה לֵּאמֹר.

HASHEM spoke to Moses, saying:

Tzav es aharōn v'es bonov laymōr,

צַו אֶת אַהֲרֹן וְאֶת בָּנָיו לֵאמֹר,

Instruct Aaron and his sons, saying:

zōs tōras ho-ōlo,

זֹאת תּוֹרַת הָעֹלָה,

This is the teaching of the elevation-offering;

hi ho-ōlo al mōk'do

al hamizbay-ach

הִוא הָעֹלָה עַל מוֹקְדָה
עַל הַמִּזְבֵּחַ

it is the elevation-offering that stays on the pyre on the Altar

kol ha-lailo ad habōker,

כָּל הַלַּיְלָה עַד הַבֹּקֶר,

all night until morning,

v'aysh hamizbay-ach tukad bō.

וְאֵשׁ הַמִּזְבֵּחַ תּוּקַד בּוֹ.

and the fire of the Altar should be kept burning on it.

V'lovash hakōhayn midō vad,

וְלָבַשׁ הַכֹּהֵן מִדּוֹ בַד,

The Kohen should don his linen garment,

u-michn'say vad yilbash al b'sorō,

וּמִכְנְסֵי בַד יִלְבַּשׁ עַל בְּשָׂרוֹ,

and he is to don linen breeches upon his flesh;

v'hayrim es hadeshen

וְהֵרִים אֶת הַדֶּשֶׁן

he is to pick up the ashes

asher tōchal ho-aysh

אֲשֶׁר תֹּאכַל הָאֵשׁ

of what the fire consumed

es ho-ōlo al hamizbay-ach,

אֶת הָעֹלָה עַל הַמִּזְבֵּחַ,

of the elevation-offering upon the Altar

v'somō aytzel hamizbay-ach.

וְשָׂמוֹ אֵצֶל הַמִּזְבֵּחַ.

and place it next to the Altar.

U-foshat es b'godov,

וּפָשַׁט אֶת בְּגָדָיו,

Then he should remove his garments *

v'lovash b'godim achayrim,

וְלָבַשׁ בְּגָדִים אֲחֵרִים,

and don other garments;

---

bal sacrificial service therefore, we wash ourselves with water from the laver, as it were.

וְלֹא יָמֻתוּ — *So that they not die.* The offense of performing the service without washing did *not* incur a court-imposed death penalty, but the violator made himself liable to a Heavenly punishment for his display of contempt.

⊰§ The Taking of Ashes

These verses are recited here because they concern the first service of the day: to remove a small portion of the ashes from the previous

day's offerings.

וּפָשַׁט אֶת בְּגָדָיו — *Then he should remove his garments.* Unlike the previous verse that discusses a daily *mitzvah,* this verse discusses the cleaning of the Altar, which was done whenever the accumulation of ashes atop the Altar interfered with the service, but did not need to be done daily. The ashes were removed and taken to a designated place outside of Jerusalem. The verse advises that the *Kohen* should wear less expensive or well-worn

v'hōtzi es hadeshen   וְהוֹצִיא אֶת הַדֶּשֶׁן
then he should remove the ashes

el michutz lamachane,   אֶל מִחוּץ לַמַּחֲנֶה,
to the outside of the camp

el mokōm tohōr.   אֶל מָקוֹם טָהוֹר.
to a pure place.

V'ho-aysh al hamizbay-ach   וְהָאֵשׁ עַל הַמִּזְבֵּחַ
The fire on the Altar

tukad bō, lō sichbe,   תּוּקַד בּוֹ, לֹא תִכְבֶּה,
shall be kept burning on it, it may not be extinguished,

u-vi-ayr oleho hakōhayn aytzim   וּבִעֵר עָלֶיהָ הַכֹּהֵן עֵצִים
and the Kohen shall burn wood upon it

babōker babōker,   בַּבֹּקֶר בַּבֹּקֶר,
every morning.

v'orach oleho ho-ōlo,   וְעָרַךְ עָלֶיהָ הָעֹלָה,
He is to prepare the elevation-offering upon it

v'hiktir oleho   וְהִקְטִיר עָלֶיהָ
and burn upon it

chelvay hash'lomim.   חֶלְבֵי הַשְּׁלָמִים.
the fats of the peace-offering.

Aysh tomid tukad al hamizbay-ach,   אֵשׁ תָּמִיד תּוּקַד עַל הַמִּזְבֵּחַ,
A permanent fire should remain burning on the Altar;

lō sichbe.   לֹא תִכְבֶּה.
it may not be extinguished.

SOME OMIT THE FOLLOWING SUPPLICATION ON THE SABBATH AND ON FESTIVALS.

Y'HI ROTZŌN mil'fonecho,   **יְהִי רָצוֹן** מִלְּפָנֶיךָ,
May it be Your will,

Adōnoy Elōhaynu   יהוה אֱלֹהֵינוּ
    Vaylōhay avōsaynu,   וֵאלֹהֵי אֲבוֹתֵינוּ,
HASHEM, our God, and the God of our forefathers,

shet'rachaym olaynu   שֶׁתְּרַחֵם עָלֵינוּ
that You have mercy on us

v'simchol lonu al kol chatōsaynu,   וְתִמְחָל לָנוּ עַל כָּל חַטֹּאתֵינוּ,
and pardon us for all our errors,

uschaper lonu es kol avonōsaynu,   וּתְכַפֵּר לָנוּ אֶת כָּל עֲוֺנוֹתֵינוּ,
atone for us all our iniquities,

---

priestly garments when performing this service because the ashes would tend to soil his clothing. In the words of the Talmud, "The outfit one wears while cooking his master's meal, one should not wear while filling his master's goblet" (*Yoma* 23a).

v'sislach l'chol p'sho-aynu,

וְתִסְלַח לְכָל פְּשָׁעֵינוּ,

and forgive all our willful sins;

v'sivne bays hamikdosh
   bimhayro v'yomaynu,

וְתִבְנֶה בֵּית הַמִּקְדָּשׁ
בִּמְהֵרָה בְיָמֵינוּ,

and that You rebuild the Holy Temple speedily, in our days,

v'nakriv l'fonecho korban hatomid

וְנַקְרִיב לְפָנֶיךָ קָרְבַּן הַתָּמִיד

so that we may offer to You the continual-offering

she-y'chapayr ba-adaynu,

שֶׁיְּכַפֵּר בַּעֲדֵנוּ,

that it may atone for us,

k'mō shekosavto olaynu
   b'sōrosecho

כְּמוֹ שֶׁכָּתַבְתָּ עָלֵינוּ
בְּתוֹרָתֶךָ

as You have prescribed for us in Your Torah

al y'day mōshe avdecho,

עַל יְדֵי מֹשֶׁה עַבְדֶּךָ,

through Moses, Your servant,

mipi ch'vōdecho, ko-omur:

מִפִּי כְבוֹדֶךָ, כָּאָמוּר:

from Your glorious mouth, as it is said:

SOME STAND WHILE RECITING THE FOLLOWING PARAGRAPH

VAIDABAYR Adōnoy
   el mōshe laymōr.

וַיְדַבֵּר יהוה
אֶל מֹשֶׁה לֵּאמֹר.

HASHEM spoke to Moses, saying:

Tzav es b'nay yisro-ayl
   v'omarto alayhem,

צַו אֶת בְּנֵי יִשְׂרָאֵל
וְאָמַרְתָּ אֲלֵהֶם,

Command the Children of Israel and tell them:

es korboni lachmi l'i-shai,

אֶת קָרְבָּנִי לַחְמִי לְאִשַּׁי,

My offering, My food* for My fires,

ray-ach nichōchi,

רֵיחַ נִיחֹחִי,

My satisfying aroma,

tishm'ru l'hakriv li b'mō-adō.

תִּשְׁמְרוּ לְהַקְרִיב לִי בְּמוֹעֲדוֹ.

you are to be scrupulous to offer Me in its appointed time.

V'omarto lohem,

וְאָמַרְתָּ לָהֶם,

And you are to tell them:

ze ho-i-she asher takrivu Ladōnoy,

זֶה הָאִשֶּׁה אֲשֶׁר תַּקְרִיבוּ לַיהוה,

This is the fire-offering that you are to bring to HASHEM:

וַיְדַבֵּר ה' ... קָרְבָּנִי לַחְמִי — *HASHEM spoke . . . My offering, My food.* The offering referred to here is the *tomid* or continual-offering which is brought continually, day in and day out; it is a communal offering purchased with the annual

half-*shekel* contributions, collected especially for this purpose. The offering is called ''food'' in the figurative sense, referring to the parts that are burned on the Altar. The ''satisfying aroma'' does not refer to the aroma *per se,* for

k'vosim b'nay shono s'mimim,　　כְּבָשִׂים בְּנֵי שָׁנָה תְמִימִם,

[male] first-year lambs, unblemished ,

sh'na-yim la-yōm, ōlo somid.　　שְׁנַיִם לַיּוֹם, עֹלָה תָמִיד.

two a day, as a continual elevation-offering.

Es hakeves e-chod ta-ase vabōker,　　אֶת הַכֶּבֶשׂ אֶחָד תַּעֲשֶׂה בַבֹּקֶר,

One lamb-service you are to perform in the morning

v'ays hakeves hashayni　　וְאֵת הַכֶּבֶשׂ הַשֵּׁנִי

ta-ase bayn ho-arbo-yim.　　תַּעֲשֶׂה בֵּין הָעַרְבָּיִם.

and the second lamb-service you are to perform in the afternoon;

Va-asiris ho-ayfo sōles l'mincho,　　וַעֲשִׂירִית הָאֵיפָה סֹלֶת לְמִנְחָה,

with a tenth-ephah of fine flour for a meal-offering,

b'lulo b'shemen kosis　　בְּלוּלָה בְּשֶׁמֶן כָּתִית

r'vi-is hahin.　　רְבִיעִת הַהִין.

mixed with a quarter-hin of crushed olive oil.

Ōlas tomid, ho-asuyo b'har sinai,　　עֹלַת תָּמִיד, הָעֲשֻׂיָה בְּהַר סִינַי,

It is the continual elevation-offering that was done at Mount Sinai,

l'ray-ach nichō-ach, i-she Ladōnoy.　　לְרֵיחַ נִיחֹחַ, אִשֶּׁה לַיהוה.

for a satisfying aroma, a fire-offering to HASHEM.

v'niskō r'vi-is hahin　　וְנִסְכּוֹ רְבִיעִת הַהִין

lakeves ho-e-chod,　　לַכֶּבֶשׂ הָאֶחָד,

And its libation is a quarter-hin for each lamb,

bakōdesh hasaych　　בַּקֹּדֶשׁ הַסֵּךְ

nesech shaychor Ladōnoy.　　נֶסֶךְ שֵׁכָר לַיהוה.

to be poured on the Holy [Altar], a fermented libation to HASHEM.

V'ays hakeves hashayni　　וְאֵת הַכֶּבֶשׂ הַשֵּׁנִי

And the second lamb-service

ta-ase bayn ho-arbo-yim,　　תַּעֲשֶׂה בֵּין הָעַרְבָּיִם,

you are to perform in the afternoon,

k'minchas habōker　　כְּמִנְחַת הַבֹּקֶר

uchniskō ta-ase,　　וּכְנִסְכּוֹ תַּעֲשֶׂה,

like the meal-offering of the morning and its libation are you to make,

i-shay ray-ach nichō-ach Ladōnoy.　　אִשֵּׁה רֵיחַ נִיחֹחַ לַיהוה.

a fire-offering for a satisfying aroma to HASHEM.

---

just as God does not require our "food," He does not benefit from the aroma of burning flesh. Rather, the aroma of the burning offering is pleasing to God because it represents the culmination of our performance of His will. God is pleased, for He has spoken, and His will has been done.

V'shochat ōsō וְשָׁחַט אֹתוֹ

al yerech hamizbay-ach tzofōno עַל יֶרֶךְ הַמִּזְבֵּחַ צָפֹנָה

He is to slaughter it on the north side of the Altar

lifnay Adōnoy, לִפְנֵי יהוה,

before HASHEM,

v'zor'ku b'nay aharōn hakōhanim וְזָרְקוּ בְּנֵי אַהֲרֹן הַכֹּהֲנִים

es domō אֶת דָּמוֹ

and Aaron's sons the Kohanim are to dash its blood

al hamizbay-ach soviv. עַל הַמִּזְבֵּחַ סָבִיב.

upon the Altar, all around.

SOME OMIT THE FOLLOWING SUPPLICATION ON THE SABBATH AND ON FESTIVALS.

Y'HI ROTZŌN milfonecho, יְהִי רָצוֹן מִלְפָנֶיךָ,

May it be Your will,

Adōnoy Elōhaynu יהוה אֱלֹהֵינוּ

Vaylōhay avōsaynu, וֵאלֹהֵי אֲבוֹתֵינוּ,

HASHEM, *our God and the God of our forefathers,*

shet'hay amiro zu שֶׁתְּהֵא אֲמִירָה זוֹ

that this recital be

chashuvo umkubeles חֲשׁוּבָה וּמְקֻבֶּלֶת

umrutzo l'fonecho וּמְרֻצָּה לְפָנֶיךָ

worthy and acceptable, and favorable before You

k'ilu hikravnu korban hatomid כְּאִלּוּ הִקְרַבְנוּ קָרְבַּן הַתָּמִיד

as if we had offered the continual-offering

b'mō-adō u-vimkōmō uch-hilchosō. בְּמוֹעֲדוֹ וּבִמְקוֹמוֹ וּכְהִלְכָתוֹ.

in its set time, in its place, and according to its requirement.

ATO hu Adōnoy Elōhaynu אַתָּה הוּא יהוה אֱלֹהֵינוּ

It is You, HASHEM, *our God,*

she-hiktiru avōsaynu l'fonecho שֶׁהִקְטִירוּ אֲבוֹתֵינוּ לְפָנֶיךָ

es k'tōres hasamim אֶת קְטֹרֶת הַסַּמִּים

before Whom our forefathers burned the incense-spices

bizman shebays hamikdosh ka-yom, בִּזְמַן שֶׁבֵּית הַמִּקְדָּשׁ קַיָּם,

in the time when the Holy Temple stood,

ka-asher tziviso ōsom כַּאֲשֶׁר צִוִּיתָ אוֹתָם

al y'day mōshe n'vi-e-cho, עַל יְדֵי מֹשֶׁה נְבִיאֶךָ,

as You commanded them through Moses Your prophet,

kakosuv b'sōrosecho: כַּכָּתוּב בְּתוֹרָתֶךָ:

as is written in Your Torah:

VA-YŌMER Adōnoy el mōshe,
וַיֹּאמֶר יהוה אֶל מֹשֶׁה,
HASHEM said to Moses:

kach l'cho samim,
קַח לְךָ סַמִּים,
Take yourself spices *

notof ushchayles v'chelb'no,
נָטָף וּשְׁחֵלֶת וְחֶלְבְּנָה,
— stacte, onycha, and galbanum —

samim ulvōno zako,
סַמִּים וּלְבֹנָה זַכָּה,
spices and pure frankincense;

bad b'vad yih-ye.
בַּד בְּבַד יִהְיֶה.
they shall all be of equal weight. *

V'osiso ōsoh k'tōres,
וְעָשִׂיתָ אֹתָהּ קְטֹרֶת,
You shall make it into incense,

rōkach, ma-asay rōkayach,
רֹקַח, מַעֲשֵׂה רוֹקֵחַ,
a spice-compound, the handiwork of an expert spice-compounder,

m'muloch, tohōr, kōdesh.
מְמֻלָּח, טָהוֹר, קֹדֶשׁ.
thoroughly mixed, pure and holy.

V'shochakto mimeno hodayk,
וְשָׁחַקְתָּ מִמֶּנָּה הָדֵק,
You shall grind some of it finely

v'nosato mimeno lifnay ho-aydus
וְנָתַתָּה מִמֶּנָּה לִפְנֵי הָעֵדֻת
and place some of it before the Testimony

b'ōhel mō-ayd
בְּאֹהֶל מוֹעֵד
in the Tent of Appointment,

asher ivo-ayd l'cho shomo,
אֲשֶׁר אִוָּעֵד לְךָ שָׁמָּה,
where I shall designate a time to meet you;

kōdesh kodoshim tih-ye lochem.
קֹדֶשׁ קָדָשִׁים תִּהְיֶה לָכֶם.
it shall be a Holy of Holies for you.

V'ne-emar:
וְנֶאֱמַר:
It is also written:

v'hiktir olov aharōn
וְהִקְטִיר עָלָיו אַהֲרֹן
    k'tōres samim,
קְטֹרֶת סַמִּים,
Aaron shall burn upon it the incense-spices

◆§ **Incense**

Incense, blended according to a strictly prescribed formula, was burned morning and evening on the Golden Altar, located inside the Temple building.

וַיֹּאמֶר ה׳ ... קַח לְךָ סַמִּים — *HASHEM said to Moses: Take yourself spices.* As enumerated below in the Talmudic passage beginning "The Rabbis taught," eleven different spices were used in the incense mixture, but only four of

them — stacte, onycha, galbanum, and frankincense — are named in the Scriptural verse. It should be noted that the exact translations of the spices are not known with absolute certainty.

בַּד בְּבַד יִהְיֶה — *They shall all be of equal weight.* The four spices given by name are of equal weight. The other seven, however, were different from these four, as will be seen from the Talmudic passage that follows.

babōker babōker,	בַּבֹּקֶר בַּבֹּקֶר,
every morning;	
b'haytivō es hanayrōs yaktireno.	בְּהֵיטִיבוֹ אֶת הַנֵּרֹת יַקְטִירֶנָּה.
when he cleans the lamps he is to burn it.	
Uvha-alōs aharōn es hanayrōs	וּבְהַעֲלֹת אַהֲרֹן אֶת הַנֵּרֹת
bayn ho-arba-yim,	בֵּין הָעַרְבַּיִם,
And when Aaron ignites the lamps in the afternoon,	
yaktireno,	יַקְטִירֶנָּה,
he is to burn it,	
k'tōres tomid lifnay Adōnoy	קְטֹרֶת תָּמִיד לִפְנֵי יהוה
as continual incense before HASHEM	
l'dōrōsaychem.	לְדֹרֹתֵיכֶם.
throughout your generations.	

TONU RABONON,   תָּנוּ רַבָּנָן,

The Rabbis taught:

Pitum hak'tōres kaytzad.	פִּטּוּם הַקְּטֹרֶת כֵּיצַד.
How is the incense mixture formulated? *	
Sh'lōsh may-ōs v'shishim	שְׁלֹשׁ מֵאוֹת וְשִׁשִּׁים
ush'mōno monim ho-yu voh.	וּשְׁמוֹנָה מָנִים הָיוּ בָהּ.
Three hundred sixty-eight maneh were in it:	
Sh'lōsh mayōs	שְׁלֹשׁ מֵאוֹת
v'shishim vachami-sho	וְשִׁשִּׁים וַחֲמִשָּׁה
three hundred sixty-five	
k'minyan y'mōs hachamo —	כְּמִנְיַן יְמוֹת הַחַמָּה —
corresponding to the days of the solar year —	
mone l'chol yōm,	מָנֶה לְכָל יוֹם,
a maneh for each day,	
p'ras b'shacharis	פְּרָס בְּשַׁחֲרִית
half in the morning	
ufras bayn ho-arbo-yim;	וּפְרָס בֵּין הָעַרְבָּיִם;
and half in the afternoon;	
ushlōsho monim y'sayrim,	וּשְׁלֹשָׁה מָנִים יְתֵרִים,
and three extra maneh,	
shemayhem machnis kōhayn godōl	שֶׁמֵּהֶם מַכְנִיס כֹּהֵן גָּדוֹל
from which the Kohen Gadol would bring [into the Holy of Holies]	

תָּנוּ רַבָּנָן פִּטּוּם הַקְּטֹרֶת כֵּיצַד — *The Rabbis taught: How is the incense mixture formulated?* This passage explains how the incense mix-ture was prepared and it gives the names and amounts that are not specified in Scrip-ture.

מְלֹא חָפְנָיו

m'lō chof'nov

both his handfuls

בְּיוֹם הַכִּפֻּרִים.

b'yōm hakipurim.

on Yom Kippur.

וּמַחֲזִירָם לְמַכְתֶּשֶׁת

Umachazirom l'machteshes

He would return them to the mortar

בְּעֶרֶב יוֹם הַכִּפֻּרִים,

b'erev yōm hakipurim,

on the day before Yom Kippur,

וְשׁוֹחֲקָן יָפֶה יָפֶה

v'shōchakon yofe yofe

and grind them very thoroughly

כְּדֵי שֶׁתְּהֵא דַקָּה מִן הַדַּקָּה.

k'day shet'hay dako min hadako.

so that it would be exceptionally fine.

וְאַחַד עָשָׂר סַמָּנִים הָיוּ בָהּ,

v'achad osor samonim ho-yu voh,

Eleven kinds of spices were in it,

וְאֵלּוּ הֵן:

v'aylu hayn:

as follows:

הַצֳּרִי, וְהַצִּפְּרֶן,

hatzori, v'hatzipōren,

(1) stacte, (2) onycha,

הַחֶלְבְּנָה, וְהַלְּבוֹנָה,

hachelb'no, v'hal'vōno,

(3) galbanum, (4) frankincense —

מִשְׁקַל שִׁבְעִים שִׁבְעִים מָנֶה;

mishkal shiv-im shiv-im mone;

each weighing seventy maneh;

מוֹר, וּקְצִיעָה,

mōr, uktzi-o,

(5) myrrh, (6) cassia,

שִׁבֹּלֶת נֵרְדְּ, וְכַרְכֹּם,

shibōles nayrd, v'charkōm,

(7) spikenard, (8) saffron —

מִשְׁקַל שִׁשָּׁה עָשָׂר
שִׁשָּׁה עָשָׂר מָנֶה;

mishkal shisho osor
shisho osor mone;

each weighing sixteen maneh;

הַקֹּשְׁטְ שְׁנֵים עָשָׂר,

hakōsht sh'naym osor,

(9) costus — twelve [maneh];

וְקִלּוּפָה שְׁלֹשָׁה, וְקִנָּמוֹן תִּשְׁעָה.

v'kilufo sh'lōsho, v'kinomōn tish-o.

(10) aromatic bark — three; and (11) cinnamon — nine.

בֹּרִית כַּרְשִׁינָה תִּשְׁעָה קַבִּין,

Bōris karshino tish-o kabin,

[Additionally] Carshinah lye, nine kav;

יֵין קַפְרִיסִין

yayn kafrisin

סְאִין תְּלָתָא וְקַבִּין תְּלָתָא,

s'in t'loso v'kabin t'loso,

Cyprus wine, three se'ah and three kav —

v'im ayn lō yayn kafrisin,
וְאִם אֵין לוֹ יֵין קַפְרִיסִין,

if he has no Cyprus wine,

mayvi chamar chivaryon atik,
מֵבִיא חֲמַר חִוַּרְיָן עַתִּיק,

he brings old white wine;

melach s'dōmis rōva hakov;
מֶלַח סְדוֹמִית רְבַע הַקַּב;

Sodom salt, a quarter-kav;

ma-a-le oshon kol she-hu.
מַעֲלֶה עָשָׁן כָּל שֶׁהוּא.

and a minute amount of maaleh ashan.*

Rabi noson habavli ōmayr:
רַבִּי נָתָן הַבַּבְלִי אוֹמֵר:

Rabbi Nassan the Babylonian says:

af kipas ha-yardayn kol shehu.
אַף כִּפַּת הַיַּרְדֵּן כָּל שֶׁהוּא.

Also a minute amount of Jordan amber.

V'im nosan boh d'vash, p'soloh.
וְאִם נָתַן בָּה דְּבַשׁ, פְּסָלָה.

If he placed fruit-honey into it, he invalidated it.

V'im chisar achas mikol samoneho,
וְאִם חִסַּר אַחַת מִכָּל סַמָּנֶיהָ,

But if he left out any of its spices,

cha-yov miso.
חַיָּב מִיתָה.

he is liable to the death penalty.

RABON shim-ōn ben gamli-ayl ōmayr:
רַבָּן שִׁמְעוֹן בֶּן גַּמְלִיאֵל אוֹמֵר:

Rabban Shimon ben Gamliel says:

Hatzori aynō elo s'rof
הַצֳרִי אֵינוֹ אֶלָּא שְׂרָף

The stacte is simply the sap

hanōtayf may-atzay hak'tof.
הַנּוֹטֵף מֵעֲצֵי הַקְּטָף.

that drips from balsam trees.

Bōris karshino lomo hi vo-o,
בֹּרִית כַּרְשִׁינָה לָמָה הִיא בָאָה,

Why is Carshinah lye used?

k'day l'yapōs boh es hatzipōren,
כְּדֵי לְיַפּוֹת בָּה אֶת הַצִּפְּרֶן,

To bleach the onycha,

k'day shet'hay no-o.
כְּדֵי שֶׁתְּהֵא נָאָה.

to make it pleasing.

Yayn kafrisin lomo hu vo,
יֵין קַפְרִיסִין לָמָה הוּא בָא,

Why is Cyprus wine used?

k'day lishrōs bō es hatzipōren,
כְּדֵי לִשְׁרוֹת בּוֹ אֶת הַצִּפְּרֶן,

So that the onycha could be soaked in it,

מַעֲלֶה עָשָׁן — *Maaleh ashan* [lit. *a smoke-raising herb*]. As implied by its name, the addi-tion of this herb caused the smoke of the in-cense to ascend straight as a pillar.

k'day shet'hay azo.   כְּדֵי שֶׁתְּהֵא עַזָּה.
to make it pungent.

Vahalō may ragla-yim yofin loh,   וַהֲלֹא מֵי רַגְלַיִם יָפִין לָהּ,
Even though mei raglayim more suitable for that,

elo she-ayn machnisin   אֶלָּא שֶׁאֵין מַכְנִיסִין
    may ragla-yim bamikdosh   מֵי רַגְלַיִם בַּמִּקְדָּשׁ
nevertheless they do not bring mei raglayim into the Temple

mip'nay hakovōd.   מִפְּנֵי הַכָּבוֹד.
out of respect.

TANYO, rabi noson ōmayr: תַּנְיָא, רַבִּי נָתָן אוֹמֵר:
It is taught: Rabbi Nassan says:

K'shehu shōchayk,   כְּשֶׁהוּא שׁוֹחֵק,
As one would grind [the incense]

ōmayr: hodayk haytayv,   אוֹמֵר: הָדֵק הֵיטֵב,
another would say, "Grind thoroughly,

haytayv hodayk,   הֵיטֵב הָדֵק,
thoroughly grind,"

mip'nay shehakōl yofe lab'somim.   מִפְּנֵי שֶׁהַקּוֹל יָפֶה לַבְּשָׂמִים.
because the sound is beneficial for the spices.

Pit'moh lachatzo-in, k'shayro;   פִּטְּמָהּ לַחֲצָאִין, כְּשֵׁרָה;
If one mixed it in half-quantities, it was fit for use,

lishlish v'lirvi-a, lō shomonu.   לִשְׁלִישׁ וְלִרְבִיעַ, לֹא שָׁמָעְנוּ.
but as to a third or a quarter — we have not heard the law.

Omar rabi y'hudo: Ze hak'lol —   אָמַר רַבִּי יְהוּדָה: זֶה הַכְּלָל —
Rabbi Yehudah said: This is the general rule —

im k'midosoh, k'shayro lachatzo-in;   אִם כְּמִדָּתָהּ, כְּשֵׁרָה לַחֲצָאִין;
In its proper proportion, it is fit for use in half the full amount;

v'im chisar achas mikol samoneho,   וְאִם חִסַּר אַחַת מִכָּל סַמָּנֶיהָ,
but if he left out any one of its spices,

cha-yov miso.   חַיָּב מִיתָה.
he is liable to the death penalty.

TANYO, bar kaporo ōmayr: תַּנְיָא, בַּר קַפָּרָא אוֹמֵר:
It is taught: [The Sage] Bar Kappara says:

Achas l'shishim ō l'shiv-im shono   אַחַת לְשִׁשִּׁים אוֹ לְשִׁבְעִים שָׁנָה
Once every sixty or seventy years,

hoy'so vo-o   הָיְתָה בָאָה
    shel shira-yim lachatzo-in.   שֶׁל שִׁירַיִם לַחֲצָאִין.
the accumulated leftovers reached half the yearly quantity.

V'ōd tonay bar kaporo:　　　　　　　וְעוֹד תָּנֵי בַּר קַפָּרָא:
Bar Kappara taught further:

Ilu ho-yo nōsayn boh　　　　　　　אִלּוּ הָיָה נוֹתֵן בָּה
　　kōr'tōv shel d'vash,　　　　　קוֹרְטוֹב שֶׁל דְּבַשׁ,
Had one put a kortov of fruit-honey* into it,

ayn odom yochōl la-amōd　　　　אֵין אָדָם יָכוֹל לַעֲמוֹד
　　mip'nay raychoh.　　　　　　מִפְּנֵי רֵיחָה.
no person could have resisted its scent.

V'lomo ayn m'or'vin boh d'vash,　וְלָמָה אֵין מְעָרְבִין בָּה דְּבַשׁ,
Why did they not mix fruit-honey into it?

mip'nay shehatōro om'ro:　　　　מִפְּנֵי שֶׁהַתּוֹרָה אָמְרָה:
Because the Torah says:

Ki chol s'ōr v'chol d'vash　　　　כִּי כָל שְׂאֹר וְכָל דְּבַשׁ
"For any leaven or any fruit-honey,

lō saktiru mimenu　　　　　　　לֹא תַקְטִירוּ מִמֶּנּוּ
　　i-she Ladōnoy.　　　　　　　אִשֶּׁה לַיהוה.
you are not to burn from them a fire-offering to HASHEM."

THE NEXT THREE VERSES ARE EACH RECITED THREE TIMES.

ADŌNOY tz'vo-ōs imonu,　　　**יהוה** צְבָאוֹת עִמָּנוּ,
HASHEM, Master of Legions, is with us,

misgov lonu Elōhay ya-akōv, selo.　מִשְׂגָּב לָנוּ אֱלֹהֵי יַעֲקֹב, סֶלָה.
a stronghold for us is the God of Jacob, Selah!

ADŌNOY tz'vo-ōs,　　　　　　**יהוה** צְבָאוֹת,
HASHEM, Master of Legions,

ashray odom bōtay-ach boch.　　אַשְׁרֵי אָדָם בֹּטֵחַ בָּךְ.
praiseworthy is the person who trusts in You.

ADŌNOY hōshi-o,　　　　　　**יהוה** הוֹשִׁיעָה,
HASHEM, save!

hamelech ya-anaynu v'yōm kor-aynu.　הַמֶּלֶךְ יַעֲנֵנוּ בְיוֹם קָרְאֵנוּ.
May the King answer us on the day we call!

ATO sayser li,　　　　　　　　**אַתָּה** סֵתֶר לִי,
You are a shelter for me;

mitzar titz'rayni,　　　　　　　מִצַּר תִּצְּרֵנִי,
from distress You preserve me;

קוֹרְטוֹב שֶׁל דְּבַשׁ — *A kortov of fruit-honey.* Honey or any other fruit juice or produce would have made the scent irresistible, but the Torah forbids the use of fruit products in the incense.

ronay falayt, t'sōv'vayni, selo.   רָנֵּי פַלֵּט, תְּסוֹבְבֵנִי, סֶלָה.

with glad song of rescue, You envelop me, Selah!

V'or'vo Ladōnoy   וְעָרְבָה לַיהוה

minchas y'hudo virusholo-yim,   מִנְחַת יְהוּדָה וִירוּשָׁלָיִם,

May the offering of Judah and Jerusalem be pleasing to HASHEM,

kimay ōlom uchshonim kadmōni-yōs.   כִּימֵי עוֹלָם וּכְשָׁנִים קַדְמֹנִיּוֹת.

as in days of old and in former years.

ABA-YAY havo m'sadayr   **אַבַּיֵי** הֲוָה מְסַדֵּר

sayder hama-arocho   סֵדֶר הַמַּעֲרָכָה

Abaye listed* the order of the Altar service

mish'mo digmoro   מִשְּׁמָא דִגְמָרָא

v'alibo d'abo sho-ul: וְאַלִּבָּא דְאַבָּא שָׁאוּל:

based on the tradition and according to Abba Shaul:

Ma-arocho g'dōlo   מַעֲרָכָה גְדוֹלָה

The arrangement of the large pyre

kōdemes l'ma-arocho sh'niyo   קוֹדֶמֶת לְמַעֲרָכָה שְׁנִיָּה

shel k'tōres;   שֶׁל קְטְרֶת;

precedes that of the secondary pyre for the incense-offering;

uma-arocho sh'niyo shel k'tōres   וּמַעֲרָכָה שְׁנִיָּה שֶׁל קְטְרֶת

the secondary pyre for the incense-offering

kōdemes l'sidur   קוֹדֶמֶת לְסִדּוּר

sh'nay gizray aytzim;   שְׁנֵי גִזְרֵי עֵצִים;

precedes the placement of two logs;

v'sidur sh'nay gizray aytzim   וְסִדּוּר שְׁנֵי גִזְרֵי עֵצִים

the placement of two logs

kōdaym l'dishun mizbay-ach hap'nimi;   קוֹדֵם לְדִשּׁוּן מִזְבֵּחַ הַפְּנִימִי;

precedes the removal of ashes from the Inner Altar;

v'dishun mizbay-ach hap'nimi   וְדִשּׁוּן מִזְבֵּחַ הַפְּנִימִי

the removal of ashes from the Inner Altar

kōdaym lahatovas chomaysh nayrōs;   קוֹדֵם לַהֲטָבַת חָמֵשׁ נֵרוֹת;

precedes the cleaning of five lamps [of the Menorah];

vahatovas chomaysh nayrōs   וַהֲטָבַת חָמֵשׁ נֵרוֹת

the cleaning of the five lamps

אַבַּיֵי הֲוָה מְסַדֵּר — *Abaye listed.* To conclude the description of the daily Temple service, we recite its full order as transmitted by the Talmudic sage Abaye. Although he lived several generations after the Destruction, he taught the order, as it had been transmitted orally, in the name of Abba Shaul, a sage who lived in the time of the Second Temple.

kōdemes l'dam hatomid; קוֹדֶמֶת לְדַם הַתָּמִיד;
precedes the [dashing of the] blood of the continual-offering;

v'dam hatomid kōdaym וְדַם הַתָּמִיד קוֹדֵם
the blood of the continual offering precedes

lahatovas sh'tay nayrōs; לַהֲטָבַת שְׁתֵּי נֵרוֹת;
the cleaning of the [other] two lamps;

vahatovas sh'tay nayrōs וַהֲטָבַת שְׁתֵּי נֵרוֹת
the cleaning of the two lamps

kōdemes liktōres; קוֹדֶמֶת לִקְטְרֶת;
precedes the incense;

uktōres kōdemes l'ayvorim; וּקְטְרֶת קוֹדֶמֶת לָאֵבָרִים;
the incense precedes the [burning of the] limbs;

v'ayvorim l'mincho; וְאֵבָרִים לְמִנְחָה;
the [burning of the] limbs [precedes] the meal-offering;

u-mincho lachavitin; וּמִנְחָה לַחֲבִתִּין;
the meal-offering [precedes] the pancakes;

vachavitin linsochin; וַחֲבִתִּין לִנְסָכִין;
the pancakes [precede] the wine-libations;

unsochin l'musofin; וּנְסָכִין לְמוּסָפִין;
the wine-libations [precede] the mussaf-offering;

u-musofin l'vozichin; וּמוּסָפִין לְבָזִיכִין;
the mussaf-offering [precedes] the bowls [of frankincense];

u-vozichin kōd'min וּבָזִיכִין קוֹדְמִין
the bowls precede

l'somid shel bayn ho-arbo-yim, לְתָמִיד שֶׁל בֵּין הָעַרְבָּיִם,
the afternoon continual-offering,

shene-emar: שֶׁנֶּאֱמַר:
v'orach oleho ho-ōlo, וְעָרַךְ עָלֶיהָ הָעֹלָה,
for it is said: "And he is to arrange the elevation-offering upon it

v'hiktir oleho וְהִקְטִיר עָלֶיהָ
chelvay hash'lomim. חֶלְבֵי הַשְּׁלָמִים.
and burn the fats of the peace-offering upon it";

oleho hashlaym עָלֶיהָ הַשְׁלֵם
— "upon it" [the elevation-offering] you are to complete

kol hakorbonōs kulom. כָּל הַקָּרְבָּנוֹת כֻּלָם.
all the [day's] offerings.

ONO B'CHŌACH g'dulas y'min'cho   אָנָּא בְּכֹחַ גְּדֻלַּת יְמִינְךָ
We beg You! With the strength* of Your right hand's greatness,

tatir tz'ruro.   תַּתִּיר צְרוּרָה.
untie the bundled sins.

Kabayl rinas am'cho   קַבֵּל רִנַּת עַמְּךָ
Accept the prayer of Your people;

sag'vaynu taharaynu nōro.   שַׂגְּבֵנוּ טַהֲרֵנוּ נוֹרָא.
strengthen us, purify us, O Awesome One.

No, gibōr,   נָא גִבּוֹר
Please, O Strong One —

dōr'shay yichud'cho   דּוֹרְשֵׁי יִחוּדְךָ
those who foster Your Oneness,

k'vovas shom'raym.   כְּבָבַת שָׁמְרֵם.
guard them like the pupil of an eye.

Bor'chaym taharaym rachamaym   בָּרְכֵם טַהֲרֵם רַחֲמֵם
Bless them, purify them, show them pity,

tzidkos'cho tomid gomlaym.   צִדְקָתְךָ תָּמִיד גָּמְלֵם.
may Your righteousness always recompense them.

Chasin kodōsh   חֲסִין קָדוֹשׁ
Powerful Holy One,

b'rov tuv'cho nahayl adosecho.   בְּרוֹב טוּבְךָ נַהֵל עֲדָתֶךָ.
with Your abundant goodness guide Your congregation.

Yochid gay-e l'am'cho p'nay   יָחִיד גֵּאֶה לְעַמְּךָ פְּנֵה
One and only Exalted One, turn to Your people,

zōch'ray k'dushosecho.   זוֹכְרֵי קְדֻשָּׁתֶךָ.
which proclaims Your holiness.

Shav-osaynu kabayl   שַׁוְעָתֵנוּ קַבֵּל
Accept our entreaty

ushma tza-akosaynu   וּשְׁמַע צַעֲקָתֵנוּ
and hear our cry,

yōday-a ta-alumōs.   יוֹדֵעַ תַּעֲלֻמוֹת.
O Knower of mysteries.

Boruch shaym k'vōd malchusō   בָּרוּךְ שֵׁם כְּבוֹד מַלְכוּתוֹ
l'ōlom vo-ed.   לְעוֹלָם וָעֶד.
Blessed is the Name of His glorious Kingdom for all eternity.

אָנָּא בְּכֹחַ — *We beg You! With the strength . . .*
This prayer — ascribed to the *tanna* Rabbi
Nechunia ben Hakanah — has profound mystical significance. It is inserted at this point because it is an eloquent prayer that God save
Israel from Exile. After having recited the order of the Temple service, it is a most fitting
time for us to pray for the Redemption.

SOME OMIT THE FOLLOWING SUPPLICATION ON THE SABBATH AND ON FESTIVALS.

RIBŌN HO-ŌLOMIM,   רִבּוֹן הָעוֹלָמִים,
Master of the worlds,

ato tzivisonu l'hakriv   אַתָּה צִוִּיתָנוּ לְהַקְרִיב
     korban hatomid b'mō-adō,   קָרְבַּן הַתָּמִיד בְּמוֹעֲדוֹ,
You commanded us to bring the continual-offering at its set time,

v'lih-yōs kōhanim ba-avōdosom,   וְלִהְיוֹת כֹּהֲנִים בַּעֲבוֹדָתָם,
and that the Kohanim be at their assigned service,

ulviyim b'duchonom,   וּלְוִיִּם בְּדוּכָנָם,
the Levites on their platform,

v'yisro-ayl b'ma-amodom.   וְיִשְׂרָאֵל בְּמַעֲמָדָם.
and the Israelites at their station.

V'ato ba-avōnōsaynu   וְעַתָּה בַּעֲוֹנוֹתֵינוּ
But now, through our sins,

chorav bays hamikdosh   חָרַב בֵּית הַמִּקְדָּשׁ
     uvotayl hatomid,   וּבָטֵל הַתָּמִיד,
the Holy Temple is destroyed, the continual-offering is discontinued,

v'ayn lonu lō chōhayn ba-avōdosō,   וְאֵין לָנוּ לֹא כֹהֵן בַּעֲבוֹדָתוֹ,
and we have neither Kohen at his service,

v'lō layvi b'duchonō,   וְלֹא לֵוִי בְּדוּכָנוֹ,
nor Levite on his platform,

v'lō yisro-ayl b'ma-amodō.   וְלֹא יִשְׂרָאֵל בְּמַעֲמָדוֹ.
nor Israelite at his station. *

V'ato omarto: וְאַתָּה אָמַרְתָּ:
     Unshal'mo forim s'fosaynu.   וּנְשַׁלְּמָה פָרִים שְׂפָתֵינוּ.
But You said: "Let our lips compensate for the bulls" —

Lochayn y'hi rotzōn mil'fonecho,   לָכֵן יְהִי רָצוֹן מִלְּפָנֶיךָ,
therefore may it be Your will,

Adōnoy Elōhaynu   יהוה אֱלֹהֵינוּ
     Vaylōhay avōsaynu,   וֵאלֹהֵי אֲבוֹתֵינוּ,
HASHEM, our God, and the God of our forefathers,

she-y'hay si-ach sifsōsaynu   שֶׁיְּהֵא שִׂיחַ שִׂפְתוֹתֵינוּ
that the prayer of our lips

לֹא כֹהֵן בַּעֲבוֹדָתוֹ, וְלֹא לֵוִי בְּדוּכָנוּ, וְלֹא יִשְׂרָאֵל בְּמַעֲמָדוֹ — *Neither Kohen at his service, nor Levite on his platform, nor Israelite at his station.* All three categories of Jews were represented in the daily communal service. The *Kohanim* per-

formed the service, the Levites stood on a platform to sing the psalm of the day, and the rest of the nation were represented by delegates who recited special prayers and Scriptural passages.

choshuv umkubol
חָשׁוּב וּמְקֻבָּל

umrutze l'fonecho,
וּמְרֻצֶּה לְפָנֶיךָ,

be worthy, acceptable, and favorable before You,

k'ilu hikravnu
כְּאִלּוּ הִקְרַבְנוּ

korban hatomid b'mō-adō,
קָרְבַּן הַתָּמִיד בְּמוֹעֲדוֹ,

as if we had brought the continual-offering at its set time

v'omadnu al ma-amodō.
וְעָמַדְנוּ עַל מַעֲמָדוֹ.

and we had stood at its station.

THE FOLLOWING PARAGRAPH IS RECITED ONLY ON THE SABBATH:

UVYŌM ha-shabos
וּבְיוֹם הַשַּׁבָּת

On the Sabbath day [the mussaf-offering consists of]

sh'nay ch'vosim
שְׁנֵי כְבָשִׂים

b'nay shono t'mimim,
בְּנֵי שָׁנָה תְּמִימִם,

two [male] first-year lambs, unblemished;

ush-nay esrōnim sō-les mincho
וּשְׁנֵי עֶשְׂרֹנִים סֹלֶת מִנְחָה

and two tenth-ephah of fine flour for a meal-offering

b'lulo va-shemen, v'niskō.
בְּלוּלָה בַשֶּׁמֶן וְנִסְכּוֹ.

mixed with olive oil, and its wine-libation.

Ōlas shabas b'shabatō,
עֹלַת שַׁבַּת בְּשַׁבַּתּוֹ,

The elevation-offering of the Sabbath must be on its particular Sabbath,

al ōlas hatomid v'niskoh.
עַל עֹלַת הַתָּמִיד וְנִסְכָּהּ.

in addition to the continual elevation-offering and its wine-libation.

THE FOLLOWING PARAGRAPH IS RECITED ONLY ON *ROSH CHODESH*:

UVROSHAY chodshaychem
וּבְרָאשֵׁי חָדְשֵׁיכֶם

On the first days of your months

takrivu ōlo Ladōnoy,
תַּקְרִיבוּ עֹלָה לַיהוה,

you are to bring an elevation-offering to HASHEM,

porim b'nay vokor sh'na-yim,
פָרִים בְּנֵי בָקָר שְׁנַיִם,

v'a-yil e-chod,
וְאַיִל אֶחָד,

two young bulls, one ram,

k'vosim b'nay shono shiv-o,
כְּבָשִׂים בְּנֵי שָׁנָה שִׁבְעָה,

t'mimim.
תְּמִימִם.

seven [male] first-year lambs, unblemished.

Ushlōsho esrōnim sō-les mincho
וּשְׁלֹשָׁה עֶשְׂרֹנִים סֹלֶת מִנְחָה

And three tenth-ephah of fine flour for a meal-offering

b'lulo va-shemen
בְּלוּלָה בַשֶּׁמֶן

mixed with olive oil

lapor ho-e-chod,

לַפָּר הָאֶחָד,

for each bull,

ushnay esrōnim sō-les mincho

וּשְׁנֵי עֶשְׂרֹנִים סֹלֶת מִנְחָה

and two tenth-ephah of fine flour for a meal-offering

b'lulo va-shemen

בְּלוּלָה בַשֶּׁמֶן

mixed with olive oil

lo-a-yil ho-e-chod.

לָאַיִל הָאֶחָד.

for each ram.

v'isorōn isorōn, sō-les mincho

וְעִשָּׂרֹן עִשָּׂרוֹן, סֹלֶת מִנְחָה

And a tenth-ephah of fine flour for a meal-offering

b'lulo vashemen,

בְּלוּלָה בַשֶּׁמֶן,

mixed with olive oil

lakeves ho-e-chod,

לַכֶּבֶשׂ הָאֶחָד,

for each lamb —

ōlo ray-ach nichō-ach,

עֹלָה רֵיחַ נִיחֹחַ,

an elevation-offering, a satisifying aroma,

i-she Ladōnoy.

אִשֶּׁה לַיהוה.

a fire-offering to HASHEM.

V'nis-kayhem,

וְנִסְכֵּיהֶם

And their libations —

chatzi hahin yih-ye lapor

חֲצִי הַהִין יִהְיֶה לַפָּר,

there is to be a half-hin for a bull,

ushlishis hahin lo-a-yil,

וּשְׁלִישִׁת הַהִין לָאַיִל,

a third-hin for a ram,

urvi-is hahin lakeves — yo-yin;

וּרְבִיעִת הַהִין לַכֶּבֶשׂ — יָיִן;

a quarter-hin for a lamb — of wine.

zōs ōlas chōdesh b'chodshō

זֹאת עֹלַת חֹדֶשׁ בְּחָדְשׁוֹ

This is the elevation-offering of the month upon its renewal,

l'chodshay hashono.

לְחָדְשֵׁי הַשָּׁנָה.

for the months of the year.

Us-ir izim e-chod

וּשְׂעִיר עִזִּים אֶחָד

l'chatos Ladōnoy,

לְחַטָּאת לַיהוה,

And one he-goat for a sin-offering to HASHEM.

al ōlas hatomid yay-ose,

עַל עֹלַת הַתָּמִיד יֵעָשֶׂה,

In addition to the continual elevation-offering, should it be made —

v'niskō.

וְנִסְכּוֹ.

and its libation.

MISHNAH SELECTION

MISHNAH ONE

AY-ZEHU m'kōmon shel z'vochim.

אֵיזֶהוּ מְקוֹמָן שֶׁל זְבָחִים.

What is the location* of the offerings?

Kodshay kodoshim
sh'chitoson batzofōn,

קָדְשֵׁי קָדָשִׁים
שְׁחִיטָתָן בַּצָּפוֹן.

The most holy offerings, their slaughter is in the north.*

Por v'so-ir shel yōm hakipurim

פָּר וְשָׂעִיר שֶׁל יוֹם הַכִּפּוּרִים

The bull and the he-goat of Yom Kippur

sh'chitoson batzofōn,

שְׁחִיטָתָן בַּצָּפוֹן,

their slaughter is in the north,

v'kibul domon bichli shorays
batzofōn.

וְקִבּוּל דָּמָן בִּכְלִי שָׁרֵת
בַּצָּפוֹן.

and the reception of their blood in a service-vessel is in the north.

V'domon to-un hazo-yo

וְדָמָן טָעוּן הַזָּיָה

Their blood requires sprinkling

al bayn habadim,

עַל בֵּין הַבַּדִּים,

between the poles [of the Holy Ark],*

v'al haporōches,

וְעַל הַפָּרֹכֶת,

and toward the Curtain* [of the Holy of Holies]

v'al mizbach hazohov.

וְעַל מִזְבַּח הַזָּהָב.

and upon the Golden Altar;

matono achas mayhen m'akoves.

מַתָּנָה אַחַת מֵהֶן מְעַכָּבֶת.

[the absence of] any one of these applications [of blood] prevents [atonement].

Sh'yoray hadom ho-yo shōfaych

שְׁיָרֵי הַדָּם הָיָה שׁוֹפֵךְ

The leftover blood he would pour

◆§ What Is the Location

The Talmud (*Kiddushin* 30a) teaches that one should study Scripture, Mishnah [i.e., the compilation of laws that are the basis of the Talmud discussions], and Gemara [i.e., the discussions of the laws] every day. In fulfillment of that injunction, the Sages instituted that appropriate passages from each of these three categories be included in this section of *Shacharis*. Since Scriptural passages regarding the Temple offerings are part of the service in any case, the Sages chose a chapter of the Mishnah on the same subject. Chapter 5 of *Zevachim*, which begins אֵיזֶהוּ מְקוֹמָן, *What is the location,* was chosen for three reasons: (a) It discusses all the sacrifices; (b) it is the only chapter in the Mishnah in which there is no halachic dispute; and (c) its text is of very

ancient origin, possibly even from the days of Moses.

אֵיזֶהוּ מְקוֹמָן — *What is the location* in the Courtyard where they were slaughtered and the part of the Altar upon which their blood was placed?

בַּצָּפוֹן — *In the north,* i.e., in the Courtyard to the north of the Altar.

עַל בֵּין הַבַּדִּים — *Between the poles* [of the Holy Ark]. On Yom Kippur, the *Kohen Gadol* brought the blood of this offering into the Holy of Holies and sprinkled part of it toward the Holy Ark, between the two poles of the Ark that extended from either side of it toward the Sanctuary.

וְעַל הַפָּרֹכֶת — *And toward the Curtain* that separated the Holy of Holies from the Sanctuary. Toward this Curtain, too, the *Kohen Gadol*

al y'sōd ma-arovi
   shel mizbay-ach hachitzōn;

עַל יְסוֹד מַעֲרָבִי
שֶׁל מִזְבֵּחַ הַחִיצוֹן;

onto the western base of the Outer Altar;

im lō nosan, lō ikayv.

אִם לֹא נָתַן, לֹא עִכֵּב.

but if he did not apply it [the leftover blood on the base],
he has not prevented [atonement].

MISHNAH TWO

PORIM hanisrofim

פָּרִים הַנִּשְׂרָפִים

The bulls that are completely burned*

us-irim hanisrofim

וּשְׂעִירִים הַנִּשְׂרָפִים

and he-goats that are completely burned,*

sh'chitoson batzofōn,

שְׁחִיטָתָן בַּצָּפוֹן,

their slaughter is in the north,

v'kibul domon bichli shorays
   batzofōn.

וְקִבּוּל דָּמָן בִּכְלִי שָׁרֵת
בַּצָּפוֹן.

and the reception of their blood in a service-vessel is in the north.

V'domon to-un hazo-yo

וְדָמָן טָעוּן הַזָּיָה

Their blood requires sprinkling

al haporōches

עַל הַפָּרֶכֶת

toward the Curtain

v'al mizbach hazohov.

וְעַל מִזְבַּח הַזָּהָב.

and upon the Golden Altar;

matono achas mayhen m'akoves.

מַתָּנָה אַחַת מֵהֶן מְעַכָּבֶת.

[the absence of] any one of these applications prevents [atonement].

Sh'yoray hadom ho-yo shōfaych

שְׁיָרֵי הַדָּם הָיָה שׁוֹפֵךְ

The leftover blood he would pour

al y'sōd ma-arovi
   shel mizbay-ach hachitzōn;

עַל יְסוֹד מַעֲרָבִי
שֶׁל מִזְבֵּחַ הַחִיצוֹן;

onto the western base of the Outer Altar;

im lō nosan, lō ikayv.

אִם לֹא נָתַן, לֹא עִכֵּב.

but if he did not apply it, he has not prevented [atonement].

---

sprinkled blood.

פָּרִים הַנִּשְׂרָפִים — *The bulls that are completely burned.* With the exception of the Yom Kippur offerings mentioned above, only two kinds of bull offerings are completely burned, no part of them being eaten by the *Kohanim.* They are (a) the bull brought if the Sanhedrin erred in a halachic ruling, and, as a result of following that ruling, a majority of the people violated a commandment; (b) the bull brought

by the *Kohen Gadol* if he made an erroneous halachic decision and himself acted on this ruling.

שְׂעִירִים הַנִּשְׂרָפִים — *He-goats that are completely burned.* If the Sanhedrin (highest court) erroneously permitted an act that was a violation of the laws against idol worship, and a majority of the community followed their ruling, their atonement consists of a he-goat that is completely burned.

Aylu vo-aylu

אֵלּוּ וָאֵלּוּ

Both these and those [the Yom Kippur offerings]

nisrofin b'vays hadoshen.

נִשְׂרָפִין בְּבֵית הַדָּשֶׁן.

are burned in the place where the [Altar] ashes are deposited.

MISHNAH THREE

CHATOS hatzibur v'ha-yochid,

חַטַּאת הַצִּבּוּר וְהַיָּחִיד,

Sin-offerings of the community and of the individual —

aylu hayn chatos hatzibur:

אֵלּוּ הֵן חַטַּאת הַצִּבּוּר:

the communal sin-offerings are the following:

s'iray roshay chodoshim
    v'shel mo-ados,

שְׂעִירֵי רָאשֵׁי חֳדָשִׁים
וְשֶׁל מוֹעֲדוֹת

The he- goats of Rosh Chodesh and Festivals:

sh'chitoson batzofon,

שְׁחִיטָתָן בַּצָּפוֹן,

Their slaughter is in the north,

v'kibul domon bichli shorays
    batzofon.

וְקִבּוּל דָּמָן בִּכְלִי שָׁרֵת
בַּצָּפוֹן.

and the reception of their blood in a service-vessel is in the north.

V'domon to-un arba matonos

וְדָמָן טָעוּן אַרְבַּע מַתָּנוֹת

Their blood requires four applications,

al arba k'ronos.

עַל אַרְבַּע קְרָנוֹת.

[one] on [each of] the four corners [of the Altar].

Kaytzad,

כֵּיצַד,

How is it done?

olo vakevesh, ufono lasovayv

עָלָה בַכֶּבֶשׁ, וּפָנָה לַסּוֹבֵב

He [the Kohen] ascended the [Altar] ramp, and turned to the surrounding ledge

uvo lo l'keren d'romis mizrochis,

וּבָא לוֹ לְקֶרֶן דְּרוֹמִית מִזְרָחִית,

and came (first) to the southeast [corner],

mizrochis tz'fonis,

מִזְרָחִית צְפוֹנִית,

[then to] the northeast [corner],

tz'fonis ma-arovis,

צְפוֹנִית מַעֲרָבִית,

[then to] the northwest,

ma-arovis d'romis.

מַעֲרָבִית דְּרוֹמִית.

and [finally] the southwest.

Sh'yoray hadom ho-yo shofaych

שְׁיָרֵי הַדָּם הָיָה שׁוֹפֵךְ

The leftover blood he would pour out

al y'sod d'romi.

עַל יְסוֹד דְּרוֹמִי.

on the southern base.

V'ne-echolin lifnim min hak'lo-im,　　　וְנֶאֱכָלִין לִפְנִים מִן הַקְּלָעִים,

*They are eaten within the [Courtyard] curtains,**

l'zichray ch'huno, b'chol ma-achol,　　　לְזִכְרֵי כְהֻנָּה, בְּכָל מַאֲכָל,

by males of the priesthood, prepared in any manner,

l'yōm volailo, ad chatzōs.　　　לְיוֹם וָלַיְלָה, עַד חֲצוֹת.

on the day [of offering] and on the following night until midnight.

MISHNAH FOUR

HO-ŌLO kōdesh kodoshim.　　　הָעוֹלָה קֹדֶשׁ קָדָשִׁים.

The elevation-offering is among the most-holy offerings:

sh'chitosoh batzofōn,　　　שְׁחִיטָתָהּ בַּצָּפוֹן,

Its slaughter is in the north,

v'kibul domoh bichli shorays
batzofōn.　　　וְקִבּוּל דָּמָהּ בִּכְלִי שָׁרֵת
בַּצָּפוֹן.

and the reception of its blood in a service-vessel is in the north.

V'domoh to-un sh'tay matonōs
shehayn arba;　　　וְדָמָהּ טָעוּן שְׁתֵּי מַתָּנוֹת
שֶׁהֵן אַרְבַּע;

*Its blood requires two applications that are [equivalent] to four.**

ut-uno hafshayt v'nitu-ach,　　　וּטְעוּנָה הַפְשֵׁט וְנִתּוּחַ,

*It requires flaying and dismemberment,**

v'cholil lo-ishim.　　　וְכָלִיל לָאִשִּׁים.

and it is entirely consumed by the fire.

MISHNAH FIVE

ZIVCHAY shalmay tzibur
va-ashomōs,　　　זִבְחֵי שַׁלְמֵי צִבּוּר
וַאֲשָׁמוֹת,

*Communal peace-offerings and [personal] guilt-offerings —**

aylu hayn ashomōs:　　　אֵלוּ הֵן אֲשָׁמוֹת:

the guilt-offerings are the following:

asham g'zaylōs,　　　אָשָׁם גְּזֵלוֹת,

*the guilt-offering for thefts,**

וְנֶאֱכָלִין לִפְנִים מִן הַקְּלָעִים — *They are eaten within the [Courtyard] curtains.* After the specified fats are removed to be burned on the Altar, the flesh of the sin-offerings is distributed to be eaten by male *Kohanim*. It could be prepared and eaten only within the Temple Courtyard. The term "curtains" is borrowed from the period in the wilderness, when the Tabernacle Courtyard was enclosed not by walls, but by curtains.

שְׁתֵּי מַתָּנוֹת שֶׁהֵן אַרְבַּע — *Two applications that are equivalent to four.* Their blood was thrown from the service-vessel at two corners of the

Altar walls: the northeast and the southwest. The blood would spread out to the two adjacent walls. Thus, the two applications of blood would put blood on all four walls of the Altar.

וְנִתּוּחַ — *And dismemberment.* The elevation-offering was cut up in a prescribed way; only then was it completely burned.

אֲשָׁמוֹת — *Guilt-offerings.* There are six kinds of guilt-offerings, all of which are listed in this mishnah. They are:

(a) אָשָׁם גְּזֵלוֹת — *. . . for thefts.* If someone owed money — whether a loan, a theft, an

asham m'ilōs,
the guilt-offering for misuse of sacred objects,*

אֲשַׁם מְעִילוֹת,

asham shifcho charufo,
the guilt-offering [for violating] a betrothed maidservant,*

אֲשַׁם שִׁפְחָה חֲרוּפָה,

asham nozir, asham m'tzōro,
the guilt-offering of a Nazirite,* the guilt-offering of a metzora,*

אֲשַׁם נָזִיר, אֲשַׁם מְצֹרָע,

oshom toluy.
and a guilt-offering in case of doubt.*

אָשָׁם תָּלוּי.

sh'chitoson batzofōn,
Their slaughter is in the north,

שְׁחִיטָתָן בַּצָּפוֹן,

v'kibul domon bichli shorays
batzofōn,
and the reception of their blood in a service-vessel is in the north.

וְקִבּוּל דָמָן בִּכְלִי שָׁרֵת
בַּצָּפוֹן,

V'domon to-un sh'tay matonōs
shehayn arba.
Their blood requires two applications that are [equivalent to] four.

וְדָמָן טָעוּן שְׁתֵּי מַתָּנוֹת
שֶׁהֵן אַרְבַּע.

V'ne-echolin lifnim min hak'lo-im,
They are eaten within the [Courtyard] curtains,*

וְנֶאֱכָלִין לִפְנִים מִן הַקְּלָעִים,

l'zichray ch'huno, b'chol ma-achol,
by males of the priesthood, prepared in any manner,

לְזִכְרֵי כְהֻנָּה, בְּכָל מַאֲכָל,

l'yōm volailo, ad chatzōs.
on the day [of offering] and on the following night until midnight.

לְיוֹם וָלַיְלָה, עַד חֲצוֹת.

---

article held in safekeeping, or whatever — and intentionally swore falsely that he did not owe it, after returning the money or article he is required to bring a guilt-offering as an atonement. See *Leviticus* 5:20-26.

(b) אֲשַׁם מְעִילוֹת — *... for misuse of sacred objects.* If someone unintentionally used objects belonging to the Sanctuary for his personal benefit he must atone by bringing a guilt-offering. See *Leviticus* 5:14-16.

(c) אֲשַׁם שִׁפְחָה חֲרוּפָה — *... [for violating] a betrothed maidservant.* The woman involved was a non-Jewish slave who had been owned by two Jewish partners. One of the partners freed her, thus making her half free and half slave. But since a freed non-Jewish slave has the same status as a proselyte, this half-free maidservant is half Jewish and half non-Jewish and is forbidden to marry either a non-Jew or a Jew. She is, however, permitted to a Jewish indentured servant, who is permitted to both a Jewish woman and a non-Jewish maidservant. If she became betrothed to a Jewish inden-

tured servant and subsequently had relations with another man, the adulterer must bring a guilt-offering in atonement.

(d) אֲשַׁם נָזִיר — *... of a Nazirite,* who became טָמֵא, *ritually contaminated,* through contact with a corpse. See *Numbers* 6:9-12.

(e) אֲשַׁם מְצֹרָע — *... of a metzora.* One afflicted by the leprous-like disease of *tzaraas* described in *Leviticus* (ch. 13) regains his complete ritual purity upon bringing a series of offerings after he is cured. See *Leviticus* 14:10-12.

(f) אֲשָׁם תָּלוּי — *... in case of doubt.* This is the only guilt-offering not prescribed for a specific offense or phenomenon. It is required whenever there is a question of whether one has become liable to bring a sin-offering. As long as such a doubt exists, the possible transgressor can protect himself from punishment through a guilt-offering. However, if and when it becomes established that the offense was indeed committed, the person must bring his sin-offering. See *Leviticus* 5:17-19.

MISHNAH SIX

HATÔDO v'ayl nozir הַתּוֹדָה וְאֵיל נָזִיר

The thanksgiving-offering* and the ram of a Nazirite*

kodoshim kalim. קָדָשִׁים קַלִּים.

are offerings of lesser holiness:*

Sh'chitoson b'chol mokōm bo-azoro, שְׁחִיטָתָן בְּכָל מָקוֹם בָּעֲזָרָה,

Their slaughter is anywhere in the Courtyard,

v'domon to-un sh'tay matonōs וְדָמָן טָעוּן שְׁתֵּי מַתָּנוֹת

shehayn arba. שֶׁהֵן אַרְבַּע.

and their blood requires two applications that are [equivalent to] four.

V'ne-echolin b'chol ho-ir, וְנֶאֱכָלִין בְּכָל הָעִיר,

They are eaten throughout the City [of Jerusalem],

l'chol odom, b'chol ma-achol, לְכָל אָדָם, בְּכָל מַאֲכָל,

by anyone, prepared in any manner,

l'yōm volailo, ad chatzōs. לְיוֹם וָלַיְלָה, עַד חֲצוֹת.

on the day [of offering] and on the following night until midnight.

Hamurom may-hem ka-yōtzay vohem, הַמּוּרָם מֵהֶם כַּיּוֹצֵא בָהֶם,

The [priestly] portion separated from them is treated like them,

elo she-hamurom ne-echol אֶלָּא שֶׁהַמּוּרָם נֶאֱכָל

except that that separated portion may be eaten

lakōhanim, linshayhem v'livnayhem לַכֹּהֲנִים, לִנְשֵׁיהֶם וְלִבְנֵיהֶם

ul-avdayhem. וְלְעַבְדֵיהֶם.

only by the Kohanim, by their wives, by their children, and by their slaves.

MISHNAH SEVEN

SH'LOMIM kodoshim kalim. שְׁלָמִים קָדָשִׁים קַלִּים.

The peace-offerings* are offerings of lesser holiness:*

sh'chitoson b'chol mokōm bo-azoro, שְׁחִיטָתָן בְּכָל מָקוֹם בָּעֲזָרָה,

Their slaughter is anywhere in the Courtyard,

v'domon to-un sh'tay matonōs וְדָמָן טָעוּן שְׁתֵּי מַתָּנוֹת

shehayn arba. שֶׁהֵן אַרְבַּע.

and their blood requires two applications that are [equivalent to] four.

הַתּוֹדָה — *The thanksgiving-offering.* This offering is brought by someone who survives serious danger or illness. See *Leviticus* 7:12.

אֵיל נָזִיר — *Ram of a Nazirite,* which is brought when a Nazirite completes the period of abstinence he has accepted upon himself. See *Number* 6:13-21.

שְׁלָמִים — *Peace-offerings.* The peace-offerings

may be eaten for two days and the night between them, while thanksgiving-offerings (mishnah 6) are eaten for only one day and a night.

קָדָשִׁים קַלִּים — *Offerings of lesser holiness.* Their greater leniency is obvious from a comparison of the laws in this mishnah with those above.

V'ne-e-cholin b'chol ho-ir,
וְנֶאֱכָלִין בְּכָל הָעִיר,
They are eaten throughout the City [of Jerusalem]

l'chol odom, b'chol ma-achol,
לְכָל אָדָם, בְּכָל מַאֲכָל,
by anyone, prepared in any manner,

lishnay yomim v'lailo e-chod.
לִשְׁנֵי יָמִים וְלַיְלָה אֶחָד.
*for two days and one night [the day of offering,
the following night, and the next day].*

Hamurom mayhem kayōtzay vohem,
הַמּוּרָם מֵהֶם כַּיּוֹצֵא בָהֶם,
The [priestly] portion separated from them is treated like them,

elo shehamurom ne-e-chol
אֶלָּא שֶׁהַמּוּרָם נֶאֱכָל
except that that separated portion may be eaten

lakōhanim, linshayhem v'livnayhem
ulavdayhem.
לַכֹּהֲנִים, לִנְשֵׁיהֶם וְלִבְנֵיהֶם
וּלְעַבְדֵיהֶם.
only by the Kohanim, by their wives, by their children and by their slaves.

MISHNAH EIGHT

HAB'CHŌR v'hama-asayr v'hapesach
הַבְּכוֹר וְהַמַּעֲשֵׂר וְהַפֶּסַח
The firstborn, the animal tithe and the pesach-offering

kodoshim kalim,
קָדָשִׁים קַלִּים,
are offerings of lesser holiness:

sh'chitoson b'chol mokōm bo-azoro,
שְׁחִיטָתָן בְּכָל מָקוֹם בָּעֲזָרָה,
Their slaughter is anywhere in the Courtyard,

v'domon to-un matono e-chos,
וְדָמָן טָעוּן מַתָּנָה אֶחָת,
and their blood requires a single application,

u-vilvod she-yitayn k'neged ha-y'sōd.
וּבִלְבָד שֶׁיִּתֵּן כְּנֶגֶד הַיְסוֹד.
provided he applies it above the base.

Shino va-achiloson:
שִׁנָּה בַּאֲכִילָתָן:
They differ in their consumption:

hab'chōr ne-echol lakōhanim,
הַבְּכוֹר נֶאֱכָל לַכֹּהֲנִים,
The firstborn is eaten by Kohanim,

v'hama-asayr l'chol odom.
וְהַמַּעֲשֵׂר לְכָל אָדָם.
and the tithe by anyone;

v'ne-e-cholin b'chol ho-ir,
וְנֶאֱכָלִין בְּכָל הָעִיר,
they are eaten throughout the City [of Jerusalem],

b'chol ma-achol,
בְּכָל מַאֲכָל,
prepared in any manner,

lishnay yomim v'lailo e-chod.
לִשְׁנֵי יָמִים וְלַיְלָה אֶחָד.
for two days and one night.

Hapesach aynō ne-e-chol elo valailo,   הַפֶּסַח אֵינוֹ נֶאֱכָל אֶלָּא בַלַּיְלָה,

The pesach-offering is not eaten except at night;

v'aynō ne-e-chol elo ad chatzōs,   וְאֵינוֹ נֶאֱכָל אֶלָּא עַד חֲצוֹת,

and it is not eaten except until midnight;

v'aynō ne-e-chol elo limnuyov,   וְאֵינוֹ נֶאֱכָל אֶלָּא לִמְנוּיָו,

and it is not eaten except by those registered for it; *

v'aynō ne-e-chol elo tzoli.   וְאֵינוֹ נֶאֱכָל אֶלָּא צָלִי.

and it is not eaten [in any manner] except roasted.

TALMUD SELECTION

RABI YISHMO-AYL ōmayr: רַבִּי יִשְׁמָעֵאל אוֹמֵר:

Rabbi Yishmael * says:*

Bishlōsh esray midōs   בִּשְׁלֹשׁ עֶשְׂרֵה מִדּוֹת

Through thirteen rules

hatōro nidreshes bo-hayn.   הַתּוֹרָה נִדְרֶשֶׁת בָּהֶן.

is the Torah elucidated:

Mikal vochōmer;   מִקַּל וָחֹמֶר;

*(1) Through a conclusion inferred from a lenient law to a strict one,
and vice versa;*

u-mig'zayro shovo;   וּמִגְּזֵרָה שָׁוָה;

*(2) through tradition that similar words in different contexts
are meant to clarify one another;*

mibinyan ov mikosuv e-chod,   מִבִּנְיַן אָב מִכָּתוּב אֶחָד,

(3) through a general principle derived from one verse,

u-mibinyan ov mish'nay ch'suvim;   וּמִבִּנְיַן אָב מִשְּׁנֵי כְתוּבִים;

and a general principle derived from two verses;

mik'lol ufrot;   מִכְּלָל וּפְרָט;

(4) through a general statement limited by a specification;

לִמְנוּיָו ... הַפֶּסַח — *The pesach-offering ... by those registered for it.* Those who eat from a particular *pesach*-offering must reserve their share in it before the slaughter (see *Exodus* 12:4).

◆§ **Rabbi Yishmael**

As noted above, the Sages prefaced *Shacharis* with selections from Scripture, Mishnah, and Gemara. As used in the Talmud, Mishnah means a listing of laws and Gemara means the logic behind and the application of the laws. As a selection from Gemara, the Sages chose one that gives the thirteen methods used in Scriptural interpretation. It shows us how the very brief statements of the Torah can be mined to reveal a host of principles and

teachings. This is why such use of these thirteen rules is called *derash,* which implies investigation; we seek to elicit principles and laws from the sometimes cryptic words of the Torah.

The Torah was composed by God according to the rules of logic and textual analysis contained in this passage. (These rules are also known as hermeneutic principles.) The oral tradition governs the way in which these rules are applied and we have no authority to use them in a manner that contradicts or is not sanctioned by the Oral Law. Thus, when we speak of Rabbinic exegesis, or the way in which the Torah is expounded, we do not speak of the invention of new laws, but of the means by

u-mip'rot uchlol;

וּמִפְּרָט וּכְלָל;

(5) through a specification broadened by a general statement;

k'lol ufrot uchlol,

כְּלָל וּפְרָט וּכְלָל,

(6) through a general statement followed by a specification
followed, in turn, by another general statement —

i ato don elo k'ayn hap'rot;

אִי אַתָּה דָן אֶלָּא כְּעֵין הַפְּרָט;

you may only infer whatever is similar to the specification;

mik'lol shehu tzorich lifrot,

מִכְּלָל שֶׁהוּא צָרִיךְ לִפְרָט,

(7) when a general statement requires a specification

u-mip'rot shehu tzorich lichlol;

וּמִפְּרָט שֶׁהוּא צָרִיךְ לִכְלָל;

or a specification requires a general statement to clarify its meaning;

kol dovor sheho-yo bichlol

כָּל דָּבָר שֶׁהָיָה בִכְלָל

(8) anything that was included in a general statement,

v'yotzo min hak'lol l'lamayd,

וְיָצָא מִן הַכְּלָל לְלַמֵּד,

but was then singled out from the general statement in order to teach something,

lō l'lamayd al atzmō yotzo,

לֹא לְלַמֵּד עַל עַצְמוֹ יָצָא,

was not singled out to teach only about itself,

elo l'lamayd al hak'lol kulō yotzo;

אֶלָּא לְלַמֵּד עַל הַכְּלָל כֻּלּוֹ יָצָא;

but to apply its teaching to the entire generality;

kol dovor sheho-yo bichlol

כָּל דָּבָר שֶׁהָיָה בִכְלָל

(9) anything that was included in a general statement,

v'yotzo lit-ōn tō-an e-chod
shehu ch'inyonō,

וְיָצָא לִטְעוֹן טוֹעַן אֶחָד
שֶׁהוּא כְעִנְיָנוֹ,

but was then singled out to discuss a provision similar to the general category,

yotzo l'hokayl v'lō l'hachamir;

יָצָא לְהָקֵל וְלֹא לְהַחֲמִיר;

has been singled out to be more lenient rather than more severe;

kol dovor sheho-yo bichlol

כָּל דָּבָר שֶׁהָיָה בִכְלָל

(10) anything that was included in a general statement,

v'yotzo lit-ōn tō-an achayr

וְיָצָא לִטְעוֹן טַעַן אַחֵר

but was then singled out to discuss a provision

shelō ch'inyonō,

שֶׁלֹּא כְעִנְיָנוֹ,

not similar to the general category,

---

which the Oral Law was implied in the Torah itself. It should also be noted that the great majority of the laws had been handed down through the centuries from teacher to student, and they were well known without a need to search for their Scriptural sources. Consequently, in the Talmud era, when the Sages attempted to set forth the Scriptural derivation of such well-known laws, there were disputes concerning the exact Scriptural interpretations.

Unfortunately, even a brief explanation of the Thirteen Rules is not within the purview of this *siddur*.

yotzo l'hokayl ulhachamir;   יָצָא לְהָקֵל וּלְהַחֲמִיר;

has been singled out both to be more lenient and more severe;

kol dovor sheho-yo bichlol   כָּל דָּבָר שֶׁהָיָה בִּכְלָל

(11) anything that was included in a general statement,

v'yotzo lidōn badovor hechodosh,   וְיָצָא לִדּוֹן בַּדָּבָר הֶחָדָשׁ,

but was then singled out to be treated as a new case,

i ato yochōl l'hachazirō lichlolō,   אִי אַתָּה יָכוֹל לְהַחֲזִירוֹ לִכְלָלוֹ,

cannot be returned to its general statement

ad she-yachazirenu hakosuv   עַד שֶׁיַּחֲזִירֶנּוּ הַכָּתוּב
    lichlolō b'fayrush;   לִכְלָלוֹ בְּפֵרוּשׁ;

unless Scripture returns it explicitly to its general statement;

dōvōr halomayd may-inyonō,   דָּבָר הַלָּמֵד מֵעִנְיָנוֹ,

(12) a matter elucidated from its context,

v'dovor halomayd misōfō;   וְדָבָר הַלָּמֵד מִסּוֹפוֹ;

or from the following passage;

v'chayn sh'nay ch'suvim   וְכֵן שְׁנֵי כְתוּבִים
    hamach-chishim ze es ze,   הַמַּכְחִישִׁים זֶה אֶת זֶה,

(13) similarly, two passages that contradict one another —

ad she-yovō hakosuv hash'lishi   עַד שֶׁיָּבוֹא הַכָּתוּב הַשְּׁלִישִׁי

until a third passage comes

v'yachri-a baynayhem.   וְיַכְרִיעַ בֵּינֵיהֶם.

and reconciles them.

Y'HI ROTZŌN mil'fonecho,   **יְהִי רָצוֹן** מִלְּפָנֶיךָ,

May it be Your will,

Adōnoy Elōhaynu   יהוה אֱלֹהֵינוּ
Vaylōhay avōsaynu   וֵאלֹהֵי אֲבוֹתֵינוּ,

HASHEM, our God and the God of our forefathers,

sheyibone bays hamikdosh   שֶׁיִּבָּנֶה בֵּית הַמִּקְדָּשׁ
    bimhayro v'yomaynu,   בִּמְהֵרָה בְיָמֵינוּ,

that the Holy Temple be rebuilt, speedily in our days,

v'sayn chelkaynu b'sōrosecho.   וְתֵן חֶלְקֵנוּ בְּתוֹרָתֶךָ.

and grant us our share in Your Torah,

V'shom na-avodcho b'yir-o   וְשָׁם נַעֲבָדְךָ בְּיִרְאָה

and may we serve You there with reverence

kimay ōlom uchshonim kadmōniyōs.   כִּימֵי עוֹלָם וּכְשָׁנִים קַדְמוֹנִיּוֹת.

as in days of old and in former years.

THE RABBIS' KADDISH

IN THE PRESENCE OF A *MINYAN*, MOURNERS RECITE THE RABBIS' *KADDISH*.

MOURNER:

YISGADAL v'yiskadash
sh'mayh rabo.

יִתְגַּדַּל וְיִתְקַדַּשׁ
שְׁמֵהּ רַבָּא.

May His great Name grow exalted and sanctified

CONGREGATION RESPONDS: Omayn — אָמֵן

B'ol'mo di v'ro chir-usayh.

בְּעָלְמָא דִּי בְרָא כִרְעוּתֵהּ.

in the world that He created as He willed.

V'yamlich malchusayh,

וְיַמְלִיךְ מַלְכוּתֵהּ,

May He give reign to His kingship

b'cha-yaychōn uvyōmaychōn

בְּחַיֵּיכוֹן וּבְיוֹמֵיכוֹן

in your lifetimes and in your days

uvcha-yay d'chol bays yisro-ayl,

וּבְחַיֵּי דְכָל בֵּית יִשְׂרָאֵל,

and in the lifetimes of the entire Family of Israel,

ba-agolo u'vizman koriv.

בַּעֲגָלָא וּבִזְמַן קָרִיב.

swiftly and soon.

V'imru: Omayn.

וְאִמְרוּ: אָמֵן.

Now respond: Amen.

CONGREGATION RESPONDS:

Omayn. Y'hay sh'mayh rabo m'vorach
l'olam ul-ol'may ol'ma-yo.

אָמֵן. יְהֵא שְׁמֵהּ רַבָּא מְבָרַךְ
לְעָלַם וּלְעָלְמֵי עָלְמַיָּא.

Amen. May His great Name be blessed forever and ever;

MOURNER CONTINUES:

Y'hay sh'mayh rabo m'vorach
l'olam ul-ol'may ol'ma-yo,

יְהֵא שְׁמֵהּ רַבָּא מְבָרַךְ
לְעָלַם וּלְעָלְמֵי עָלְמַיָּא,

May His great Name be blessed forever and ever;

yisborach v'yishtabach v'yispo-ar

יִתְבָּרַךְ וְיִשְׁתַּבַּח וְיִתְפָּאַר

blessed, praised, glorified,

v'yisrōmam v'yisnasay

וְיִתְרוֹמַם וְיִתְנַשֵּׂא

exalted, extolled,

v'yis-hador v'yis-ale v'yis-halol

וְיִתְהַדָּר וְיִתְעַלֶּה וְיִתְהַלָּל

mighty, upraised, and lauded

sh'mayh d'kudsho b'rich hu

שְׁמֵהּ דְּקֻדְשָׁא בְּרִיךְ הוּא

be the Name of the Holy One, Blessed is He,

CONGREGATION RESPONDS:

B'rich hu.   *Blessed is He.*

בְּרִיךְ הוּא.

MOURNER CONTINUES:

°l'aylo min kol

°לְעֵלָּא מִן כָּל

beyond any

FROM ROSH HASHANAH TO YOM KIPPUR SUBSTITUTE:

°l'aylo l'aylo mikol   °לְעֵלָּא לְעֵלָא מִכָּל

exceedingly beyond any

birchoso v'shiroso   בִּרְכָתָא וְשִׁירָתָא

blessing and song,

tushb'choso v'nechemoso,   תֻּשְׁבְּחָתָא וְנֶחֱמָתָא,

praise and consolation

da-amiron b'ol'mo.   דַּאֲמִירָן בְּעָלְמָא.

that are uttered in the world.

V'imru: Omayn.   וְאִמְרוּ: אָמֵן.

Now respond: Amen.

CONGREGATION RESPONDS: Omayn — אָמֵן

Al yisro-el v'al rabo-non   עַל יִשְׂרָאֵל וְעַל רַבָּנָן,

Upon Israel, and upon the teachers,

v'al talmiday-hōn,   וְעַל תַּלְמִידֵיהוֹן

v'al kol talmiday salmiday-hōn,   וְעַל כָּל תַּלְמִידֵי תַלְמִידֵיהוֹן,

their disciples and all of their disciples

v'al kol man d'os'kin b'ōrai-so,   וְעַל כָּל מָאן דְּעָסְקִין בְּאוֹרַיְתָא,

and upon all those who engage in the study of Torah,

dee v'as-ro hodayn,   דִּי בְאַתְרָא הָדֵין

v'dee b'chol asar va-asar.   וְדִי בְכָל אֲתַר וַאֲתַר.

who are here or anywhere else.

Y'hay l'hōn ulchōn sh'lomo rabo,   יְהֵא לְהוֹן וּלְכוֹן שְׁלָמָא רַבָּא,

May they and you have abundant peace,

chi-no v'chis-do v'racha-min,   חִנָּא וְחִסְדָּא וְרַחֲמִין,

grace, kindness, and mercy,

v'cha-yin arichin, um-zōnay r'vichay,   וְחַיִּין אֲרִיכִין, וּמְזוֹנֵי רְוִיחֵי,

long life, ample nourishment,

u-furkono min kodom a-vu-hōn   וּפֻרְקָנָא מִן קֳדָם אֲבוּהוֹן

and salvation from before their Father

dee vishma-yo (v'ar-o).   דִּי בִשְׁמַיָּא (וְאַרְעָא).

Who is in Heaven (and on earth).

V'imru: Omayn.   וְאִמְרוּ: אָמֵן.

Now respond: Amen.

CONGREGATION RESPONDS: Omayn — אָמֵן

Y'hay sh'lomo rabo min sh'mayo   יְהֵא שְׁלָמָא רַבָּא מִן שְׁמַיָּא,

May there be abundant peace from Heaven,

v'cha-yim olaynu v'al kol yisro-ayl.   וְחַיִּים עָלֵינוּ וְעַל כָּל יִשְׂרָאֵל.

and life, upon us and upon all Israel.

V'imru: Omayn: וְאִמְרוּ: אָמֵן.

Now respond: Amen.

CONGREGATION RESPONDS: Omayn — אָמֵן

MOURNER BOWS, THEN TAKES THREE STEPS BACK, BOWS LEFT AND SAYS:

Ō-se sholōm bimrōmov עֹשֶׂה שָׁלוֹם בִּמְרוֹמָיו,

He Who makes peace in His heights,

MOURNER BOWS RIGHT AND SAYS:

hu b'racha-mov ya-a-se sholōm olaynu הוּא בְּרַחֲמָיו יַעֲשֶׂה שָׁלוֹם עָלֵינוּ,

may He, in His compassion, make peace upon us,

MOURNER BOWS FORWARD AND SAYS:

v'al kol yisro-ayl. V'imru: Omayn: וְעַל כָּל יִשְׂרָאֵל. וְאִמְרוּ: אָמֵן.

and upon all Israel. Now respond: Amen.

CONGREGATION RESPONDS: Omayn — אָמֵן

MOURNER REMAINS IN PLACE FOR A FEW MOMENTS, THEN TAKES THREE STEPS FORWARD.

■ Psalms 30: This psalm of inauguration provides a perspective on the frequent afflictions and frustrations that commonly precede success. Just as the darkest part of night precedes sunrise, so human agony should be accepted as the preparation for success and jubilation.

MIZMŌR shir **מִזְמוֹר** שִׁיר

chanukas haba-yis l'dovid. חֲנֻכַּת הַבַּיִת לְדָוִד.

A psalm — a song* for the inauguration of the Temple* — by David.

Arōmimcho Adōnoy ki dilisoni, אֲרוֹמִמְךָ יהוה כִּי דִלִּיתָנִי,

I will exalt You, HASHEM, for You have drawn me up

v'lō simachto ōy'vai li. וְלֹא שִׂמַּחְתָּ אֹיְבַי לִי.

and not let my foes rejoice over me.

Adōnoy Elōhoy, יהוה אֱלֹהָי,

HASHEM, my God,

shivati aylecho vatirpo-ayni. שִׁוַּעְתִּי אֵלֶיךָ וַתִּרְפָּאֵנִי.

I cried out to You and You healed me.

Adōnoy he-eliso min sh'ōl nafshi, יהוה הֶעֱלִיתָ מִן שְׁאוֹל נַפְשִׁי,

HASHEM, You have raised my soul from the lower world,

מִזְמוֹר שִׁיר — *A psalm, a song.* Psalm 30 was sung to inaugurate the morning Temple service, and thus is an appropriate prelude to the prayers that take the place of that service. It is also a fitting conclusion to the Scriptural and Talmudical passages regarding the offerings.

חֲנֻכַּת הַבַּיִת — *The inauguration of the Temple.* How is this psalm, which deals only with David's illness, related to the dedication of the Temple? The Temple's purpose is best achieved when each individual Jew recognizes God's presence and help in his personal life. Accordingly, by never losing his faith in God, and by finally being vindicated through God's deliverance, David is the perfect embodiment of the Temple's role in the life of the nation.

chi-yisani mi-yordi vōr.　　　חִיִּיתַנִי מִיָּרְדִי בוֹר.

You have preserved me from my descent to the Pit.

Zam'ru Ladōnoy chasidov,　　זַמְּרוּ לַיהוה חֲסִידָיו,

Make music to HASHEM, His devout ones,

v'hōdu l'zaycher kodshō.　　וְהוֹדוּ לְזֵכֶר קָדְשׁוֹ.

and give thanks to His Holy Name.

Ki rega b'apō,　　　　　כִּי רֶגַע בְּאַפּוֹ,

For His anger endures but a moment;

cha-yim birtzōnō,　　　　חַיִּים בִּרְצוֹנוֹ,

life results from His favor.

bo-erev yolin bechi, v'labōker rino.　בָּעֶרֶב יָלִין בֶּכִי וְלַבְּקֶר רִנָּה.

In the evening one lies down weeping, but with dawn — a cry of joy!

Va-ani omarti v'shalvi,　　וַאֲנִי אָמַרְתִּי בְשַׁלְוִי,

I had said in my serenity,

bal emōt l'ōlom.　　　　בַּל אֶמּוֹט לְעוֹלָם.

"I will never falter."

Adōnoy birtzōn'cho　　　יהוה בִּרְצוֹנְךָ

he-emadto l'har'ri ōz,　　הֶעֱמַדְתָּה לְהַרְרִי עֹז,

But, HASHEM, through Your favor* You supported my greatness with might;

histarto fonecho ho-yisi nivhol.　הִסְתַּרְתָּ פָנֶיךָ הָיִיתִי נִבְהָל.

should You but conceal Your face, I would be confounded.

Aylecho Adōnoy ekro,　　אֵלֶיךָ יהוה אֶקְרָא,

To You, HASHEM, I would call

v'el Adōnoy eschanon.　　וְאֶל אֲדֹנָי אֶתְחַנָּן.

and to my Lord I would appeal.

Mah betza b'domi,　　　מַה בֶּצַע בְּדָמִי,

What gain is there in my death,

b'ridti el shochas,　　　בְּרִדְתִּי אֶל שָׁחַת,

when I descend to the Pit?

ha-yōd'cho ofor, ha-yagid amitecho.　הֲיוֹדְךָ עָפָר, הֲיַגִּיד אֲמִתֶּךָ.

Will the dust acknowledge You? Will it declare Your truth?

Sh'ma Adōnoy v'chonayni,　　שְׁמַע יהוה וְחָנֵּנִי,

Hear, HASHEM, and favor me;

Adōnoy he-yay ōzayr li.　　יהוה הֱיֵה עֹזֵר לִי.

HASHEM, be my Helper!

❖ Hofachto misp'di l'mochōl li,　❖ הָפַכְתָּ מִסְפְּדִי לְמָחוֹל לִי,

You have changed for me my lament into dancing;

pitachto saki, vat'az'rayni simcho.   פִּתַּחְתָּ שַׂקִּי, וַתְּאַזְּרֵנִי שִׂמְחָה.

You undid my sackcloth and girded me with gladness.

L'ma-an y'zamercho chovōd   לְמַעַן יְזַמֶּרְךָ כָבוֹד

v'lō yidōm,   וְלֹא יִדֹּם,

So that my soul might make music to You and not be stilled,

Adōnoy Elōhai l'ōlom ōdeko.   יהוה אֱלֹהַי לְעוֹלָם אוֹדֶךָ.

HASHEM, my God, forever will I thank You.

MOURNER'S KADDISH

IN THE PRESENCE OF A *MINYAN*, MOURNERS RECITE THE MOURNER'S *KADDISH*.

MOURNER:

YISGADAL v'yiskadash   **יִתְגַּדַּל** וְיִתְקַדַּשׁ

sh'mayh rabo.   שְׁמֵהּ רַבָּא.

May His great Name grow exalted and sanctified

CONGREGATION RESPONDS: Omayn — אָמֵן

B'ol'mo di v'ro chir-usayh.   בְּעָלְמָא דִּי בְרָא כִרְעוּתֵהּ.

in the world that He created as He willed.

V'yamlich malchusayh,   וְיַמְלִיךְ מַלְכוּתֵהּ,

May He give reign to His kingship

b'cha-yaychōn uvyōmaychōn   בְּחַיֵּיכוֹן וּבְיוֹמֵיכוֹן

in your lifetimes and in your days

uvcha-yay d'chol bays yisro-ayl,   וּבְחַיֵּי דְכָל בֵּית יִשְׂרָאֵל,

and in the lifetimes of the entire Family of Israel,

ba-agolo u-vizman koriv.   בַּעֲגָלָא וּבִזְמַן קָרִיב.

swiftly and soon.

V'imru: Omayn.   וְאִמְרוּ: אָמֵן.

Now respond: Amen.

CONGREGATION RESPONDS:

Omayn. Y'hay sh'mayh rabo m'vorach   אָמֵן. יְהֵא שְׁמֵהּ רַבָּא מְבָרַךְ

l'olam ul-ol'may ol'ma-yo.   לְעָלַם וּלְעָלְמֵי עָלְמַיָּא.

Amen. May His great Name be blessed forever and ever.

MOURNER CONTINUES:

Y'hay sh'mayh rabo m'vorach   יְהֵא שְׁמֵהּ רַבָּא מְבָרַךְ

l'olam ul-ol'may ol'ma-yo,   לְעָלַם וּלְעָלְמֵי עָלְמַיָּא,

May His great Name be blessed forever and ever;

yisborach v'yishtabach v'yispo-ar   יִתְבָּרַךְ וְיִשְׁתַּבַּח וְיִתְפָּאַר

blessed, praised, glorified,

v'yisrōmam v'yisnasay   וְיִתְרוֹמַם וְיִתְנַשֵּׂא

exalted, extolled,

v'yis-hador v'yis-ale v'yis-halol   וְיִתְהַדָּר וְיִתְעַלֶּה וְיִתְהַלָּל
mighty, upraised, and lauded

sh'mayh d'kudsho b'rich hu   שְׁמֵהּ דְּקֻדְשָׁא בְּרִיךְ הוּא
be the Name of the Holy One, Blessed is He,

CONGREGATION RESPONDS:

B'rich hu.   *Blessed is He.*   בְּרִיךְ הוּא.

MOURNER CONTINUES:

°l'aylo min kol   °לְעֵלָּא מִן כָּל
beyond any

FROM ROSH HASHANAH TO YOM KIPPUR SUBSTITUTE:

°l'aylo l'aylo mikol   °לְעֵלָּא לְעֵלָּא מִכָּל
exceedingly beyond any

birchoso v'shiroso   בִּרְכָתָא וְשִׁירָתָא
blessing and song,

tushb'choso v'nechemoso,   תֻּשְׁבְּחָתָא וְנֶחֱמָתָא,
praise and consolation

da-amiron b'ol'mo.   דַּאֲמִירָן בְּעָלְמָא.
that are uttered in the world.

V'imru: Omayn.   וְאִמְרוּ: אָמֵן.
Now respond: Amen.

CONGREGATION RESPONDS: Omayn — אָמֵן

Y'hay sh'lomo rabo min sh'mayo   יְהֵא שְׁלָמָא רַבָּא מִן שְׁמַיָּא,
May there be abundant peace from Heaven,

v'cha-yim olaynu v'al kol yisro-ayl.   וְחַיִּים עָלֵינוּ וְעַל כָּל יִשְׂרָאֵל.
and life, upon us and upon all Israel.

V'imru: Omayn: וְאִמְרוּ: אָמֵן.
Now respond: Amen.

CONGREGATION RESPONDS: Omayn — אָמֵן

MOURNER BOWS, THEN TAKES THREE STEPS BACK, BOWS LEFT AND SAYS:

Ō-se sholōm bimrōmov   עֹשֶׂה שָׁלוֹם בִּמְרוֹמָיו,
He Who makes peace in His heights,

MOURNER BOWS RIGHT AND SAYS:

hu ya-a-se sholōm olaynu   הוּא יַעֲשֶׂה שָׁלוֹם עָלֵינוּ,
may He make peace upon us,

MOURNER BOWS FORWARD AND SAYS:

v'al kol yisro-ayl. V'imru: Omayn: וְעַל כָּל יִשְׂרָאֵל. וְאִמְרוּ: אָמֵן.
and upon all Israel. Now respond: Amen.

CONGREGATION RESPONDS: Omayn — אָמֵן

MOURNER REMAINS IN PLACE FOR A FEW MOMENTS, THEN TAKES THREE STEPS FORWARD.

⁘ PESUKEI D'ZIMRAH ⁘

SOME RECITE THIS STATEMENT OF INTENT BEFORE *PESUKEI D'ZIMRAH:*

Harayni m'zamayn es pi   הֲרֵינִי מְזַמֵּן אֶת פִּי

I now prepare my mouth

l'hōdōs ulhalayl ulshabay-ach   לְהוֹדוֹת וּלְהַלֵּל וּלְשַׁבֵּחַ

es bo-r'i.   אֶת בּוֹרְאִי

to thank, to laud and to praise my Creator.

SOME INCLUDE THIS KABBALISTIC STATMENT:

L'shaym yichud kudsho brich hu   לְשֵׁם יִחוּד קֻדְשָׁא בְּרִיךְ הוּא

ush-chintayh   וּשְׁכִינְתֵּיה

For the sake of the Unification of the Holy One, Blessed is He, and His Presence,

al y'day hahu tomir v'ne-elam,   עַל יְדֵי הַהוּא טָמִיר וְנֶעְלָם,

through Him Who is hidden and inscrutable —

b'shaym kol yisro-ayl.   בְּשֵׁם כָּל יִשְׂרָאֵל.

[I pray] in the name of all Israel.

CONVERSATION IS FORBIDDEN FROM THIS POINT UNTIL AFTER *SHEMONEH ESREI*
(EXCEPT FOR CERTAIN PRAYER RESPONSES).

■ This blessing consists of two separate sections. The first is an introductory series of thanksgiving sentences focusing on Hashem as the Creator Who manifests Himself through His beneficence to His creations. The second section begins with *Boruch ato,* and is the blessing whereby we extol Hashem for accepting human praise in general, and specifically the praises that follow this blessing.

BORUCH SHE-OMAR   בָּרוּךְ שֶׁאָמַר

v'ho-yo ho-ōlom,   וְהָיָה הָעוֹלָם,

Blessed is He Who spoke,* and the world came into being;*

boruch hu,   בָּרוּךְ הוּא.

blessed is He.

Boruch ōse v'rayshis,   בָּרוּךְ עֹשֶׂה בְרֵאשִׁית,

Blessed is He Who maintains Creation;

boruch ōmayr v'ōse,   בָּרוּךְ אוֹמֵר וְעֹשֶׂה,

blessed is He Who speaks and does;*

◆§ **Pesukei D'Zimrah / Verses of Praise**

The Sages taught that one should set forth the praises of God before making requests of Him (*Berachos* 32a). In this section of *Shacharis,* we concentrate on God's revelation in nature and history — on how His glory can be seen in Creation and in the unfolding of events.

Because it is a separate section of *Shacharis* with a purpose all its own, *Pesukei D'Zimrah* is introduced with a blessing — *Baruch She-amar* — and concluded with a blessing —

Yishtabach (p. 347).

בָּרוּךְ שֶׁאָמַר — *Blessed is He Who spoke.* There is an ancient tradition that this prayer was transcribed approximately 2400 years ago from a script that fell from heaven.

שֶׁאָמַר וְהָיָה הָעוֹלָם — *Who spoke, and the world came into being.* God is the Creator Who brought all of Creation into being and maintains it with no more than His word.

אוֹמֵר וְעֹשֶׂה — *Who speaks and does.* God brings His promise into being even when people no

boruch gōzayr umka-yaym,

בָּרוּךְ גּוֹזֵר וּמְקַיֵּם,

blessed is He Who decrees and fulfills;

boruch m'rachaym al ho-oretz,

בָּרוּךְ מְרַחֵם עַל הָאָרֶץ,

blessed is He Who has mercy on the earth;*

boruch m'rachaym al hab'riyōs,

בָּרוּךְ מְרַחֵם עַל הַבְּרִיּוֹת,

blessed is He Who has mercy on the creatures;

boruch m'shalaym sochor tōv
    liray-ov,

בָּרוּךְ מְשַׁלֵּם שָׂכָר טוֹב
לִירֵאָיו,

blessed is He Who gives goodly reward to those who fear Him;*

boruch chai lo-ad v'ka-yom lonetzach,

בָּרוּךְ חַי לָעַד וְקַיָּם לָנֶצַח,

blessed is He Who lives forever and endures to eternity;*

boruch pōde u-matzil,

בָּרוּךְ פּוֹדֶה וּמַצִּיל,

blessed is He Who redeems and rescues;*

boruch sh'mō.

בָּרוּךְ שְׁמוֹ.

blessed is His Name!*

Boruch ato Adōnoy
    Elōhaynu melech ho-ōlom,

בָּרוּךְ אַתָּה יהוה
אֱלֹהֵינוּ מֶלֶךְ הָעוֹלָם,

Blessed are You, HASHEM, our God, King of the universe,

ho-Ayl ho-ov horachamon

הָאֵל הָאָב הָרַחֲמָן

the God, the merciful Father,*

ham'hulol b'fe amō,

הַמְהֻלָּל בְּפֶה עַמּוֹ,

Who is lauded by the mouth of His people,

m'shuboch umfō-or
    bilshōn chasidov va-avodov,

מְשֻׁבָּח וּמְפֹאָר
בִּלְשׁוֹן חֲסִידָיו וַעֲבָדָיו,

praised and glorified by the tongue of His devout ones and His servants

uvshiray dovid avdecho.

וּבְשִׁירֵי דָוִד עַבְדֶּךָ.

and through the psalms of David Your servant.

---

longer seem to deserve His generosity. Conversely, "He decrees and fulfills"; when He warns of punishment, the sinner cannot escape unless he repents sincerely.

מְרַחֵם עַל הָאָרֶץ — *Who has mercy on the earth.* God has compassion on the earth and all its creatures, human or otherwise.

מְשַׁלֵּם שָׂכָר טוֹב לִירֵאָיו — *Who gives goodly reward to those who fear Him.* His reward may not be dispensed in This World, but it will surely be dispensed in the World to Come. Whatever the case, no good deed goes unrewarded.

חַי לָעַד וְקַיָּם לָנֶצַח — *Who lives forever and endures to eternity.* Not only is God's existence

infinite and eternal, but He continues to involve Himself in the affairs of the universe.

פּוֹדֶה וּמַצִּיל — *Who redeems* people from moral decline *and rescues* them from physical danger.

בָּרוּךְ שְׁמוֹ — *Blessed is His Name!* The Name by which we call God can in no way express His true essence. Nevertheless, in His kindness to man, He allows us to glimpse some of His properties and express them in a Name.

הָאֵל הָאָב הָרַחֲמָן — *The God, the merciful Father.* We acknowledge that He is the all-powerful God, yet is filled with mercy, like a father whose behavior is a constant expression of mercy, even when he must be harsh.

N'halelcho Adōnoy Elōhaynu
נְהַלֶּלְךָ יהוה אֱלֹהֵינוּ,
We shall laud You, HASHEM, our God,

bishvochōs u-vizmirōs.
בִּשְׁבָחוֹת וּבִזְמִרוֹת.
with praises and songs;

n'gadelcho un-shabaychacho
נְגַדֶּלְךָ וּנְשַׁבֵּחֲךָ
we shall exalt You, we shall praise You,

unfo-ercho v'nazkir shimcho
וּנְפָאֶרְךָ וְנַזְכִּיר שִׁמְךָ
we shall glorify You, we shall mention Your Name

v'namlich'cho, malkaynu Elōhaynu.
וְנַמְלִיכְךָ, מַלְכֵּנוּ אֱלֹהֵינוּ.
and we shall proclaim Your reign, our King, our God.

Yochid, chay ho-ōlomim,
❖ יָחִיד, חֵי הָעוֹלָמִים,
O Unique One, Life-giver of the worlds,

melech m'shuboch umfō-or
מֶלֶךְ מְשֻׁבָּח וּמְפֹאָר
a-day ad sh'mō hagodōl.
עֲדֵי עַד שְׁמוֹ הַגָּדוֹל.
King Whose great Name is eternally praised and glorified.

Boruch ato Adōnoy,
בָּרוּךְ אַתָּה יהוה,
Blessed are You, HASHEM,

melech m'hulol batishbochōs.
מֶלֶךְ מְהֻלָּל בַּתִּשְׁבָּחוֹת.
the King Who is lauded with praises.

CONGREGATION RESPONDS: Omayn — אָמֵן

■ The following prayer comprises three parts: In the first, we praise Hashem for His guiding the course of history, whereby we realize that seemingly unrelated events all lead to His ultimate plan for mankind: man living by His Torah. In the second part, beginning *Shiru Ladōnoy,* we excitedly anticipate the time when all nations will acknowledge Hashem. And in the third part, beginning *V'hu rachum,* we plead for Hashem's mercy to actualize our aspirations.

HŌDU Ladōnoy kir-u vishmō,
הוֹדוּ לַיהוה קִרְאוּ בִשְׁמוֹ,
Give thanks to HASHEM,* declare His Name,

hōdi-u vo-amim alilōsov.
הוֹדִיעוּ בָעַמִּים עֲלִילוֹתָיו.
make His acts known among the peoples.

Shiru lō, zam'ru lō,
שִׁירוּ לוֹ, זַמְּרוּ לוֹ,
Sing to Him, make music to Him,

sichu b'chol nifl'ōsov.
שִׂיחוּ בְּכָל נִפְלְאוֹתָיו.
speak of all His wonders.

הוֹדוּ לַה׳ — *Give thanks to HASHEM.* The first twenty-nine verses of this lengthy prayer form a jubilant song that David intended to be sung when the Holy Ark was brought to Jerusalem.

In its entirety this song calls upon Israel to maintain its faith in God and its confidence that He will bring it salvation from exile and persecution.

His-hal'lu b'shaym kodshō,
הִתְהַלְלוּ בְּשֵׁם קָדְשׁוֹ,

Glory in His holy Name,

yismach layv m'vakshay Adōnoy.
יִשְׂמַח לֵב מְבַקְשֵׁי יהוה.

be glad of heart, you who seek HASHEM.

Dirshu Adōnoy v'uzō,
דִּרְשׁוּ יהוה וְעֻזּוֹ,

Search out HASHEM and His might,

bak'shu fonov tomid.
בַּקְשׁוּ פָנָיו תָּמִיד.

seek His Presence always.

Zichru nifl'ōsov asher oso,
זִכְרוּ נִפְלְאֹתָיו אֲשֶׁר עָשָׂה,

Remember His wonders that He wrought,

mōfsov u-mishp'tay fihu.
מֹפְתָיו וּמִשְׁפְּטֵי פִיהוּ.

His marvels and the judgments of His mouth.

Zera yisro-ayl avdō,
זֶרַע יִשְׂרָאֵל עַבְדּוֹ,

O seed of Israel, His servant,

b'nay ya-akōv b'chirov.
בְּנֵי יַעֲקֹב בְּחִירָיו.

O children of Jacob, His chosen ones —

Hu Adōnoy Elōhaynu,
הוּא יהוה אֱלֹהֵינוּ,

He is HASHEM, our God,

b'chol ho-oretz mishpotov.
בְּכָל הָאָרֶץ מִשְׁפָּטָיו.

over all the earth are His judgments.

Zichru l'ōlom b'risō,
זִכְרוּ לְעוֹלָם בְּרִיתוֹ,

Remember His covenant forever —

dovor tzivo l'elef dōr.
דָּבָר צִוָּה לְאֶלֶף דּוֹר.

the word He commanded for a thousand generations —

Asher koras es avrohom,
אֲשֶׁר כָּרַת אֶת אַבְרָהָם,

that He made with Abraham

ushvu-osō l'yitzchok.
וּשְׁבוּעָתוֹ לְיִצְחָק.

and His vow to Isaac.

Va-ya-amideho l'ya-akōv l'chōk,
וַיַּעֲמִידֶהָ לְיַעֲקֹב לְחֹק,

Then He established it for Jacob as a statute,

l'yisro-ayl b'ris ōlom.
לְיִשְׂרָאֵל בְּרִית עוֹלָם.

for Israel as an everlasting covenant,

Laymōr, l'cho etayn eretz k'no-an,
לֵאמֹר, לְךָ אֶתֵּן אֶרֶץ כְּנָעַן,

saying, "To you I shall give the Land of Canaan,

chevel nachalaschem.
חֶבֶל נַחֲלַתְכֶם.

the lot of your heritage."

Bih-yōs'chem m'say mispor,
בִּהְיוֹתְכֶם מְתֵי מִסְפָּר,

When you were but few in number,

kim-at v'gorim boh.
כִּמְעַט וְגָרִים בָּהּ.
hardly dwelling there,

Va-yis-hal'chu migōy el gōy,
וַיִּתְהַלְּכוּ מִגּוֹי אֶל גּוֹי,
and they wandered from nation to nation,

u-mimamlocho el am achayr.
וּמִמַּמְלָכָה אֶל עַם אַחֵר.
from one kingdom to another people.

Lō hini-ach l'ish l'oshkom,
לֹא הִנִּיחַ לְאִישׁ לְעָשְׁקָם,
He let no man rob them,

va-yōchach alayhem m'lochim.
וַיּוֹכַח עֲלֵיהֶם מְלָכִים.
and He rebuked kings for their sake.

Al tig'u bimshichoy,
אַל תִּגְּעוּ בִמְשִׁיחָי,
"Dare not touch My anointed ones,

u-vinvi-ai al toray-u.
וּבִנְבִיאַי אַל תָּרֵעוּ.
and to My prophets do no harm."

Shiru Ladōnoy kol ho-oretz,
שִׁירוּ לַיהוה כָּל הָאָרֶץ,
Sing to HASHEM, everyone on earth,

bas'ru mi-yōm el yōm y'shu-osō.
בַּשְּׂרוּ מִיּוֹם אֶל יוֹם יְשׁוּעָתוֹ.
announce His salvation daily.

Sap'ru vagōyim es k'vōdō,
סַפְּרוּ בַגּוֹיִם אֶת כְּבוֹדוֹ,
Relate His glory among the nations,

b'chol ho-amim nifl'ōsov.
בְּכָל הָעַמִּים נִפְלְאוֹתָיו.
among all the peoples His wonders.

Ki godōl Adōnoy umhulol m'ōd,
כִּי גָדוֹל יהוה וּמְהֻלָּל מְאֹד,
That HASHEM is great and exceedingly lauded,

v'nōro hu al kol elōhim.
וְנוֹרָא הוּא עַל כָּל אֱלֹהִים.
and awesome is He above all heavenly powers.

Ki kol elōhay ho-amim elilim.
❖ כִּי כָּל אֱלֹהֵי הָעַמִּים אֱלִילִים,
For all the gods of the peoples are nothings —
(PAUSE BRIEFLY)

Vadōnoy shoma-yim oso.
וַיהוה שָׁמַיִם עָשָׂה.
but HASHEM made heaven!

Hōd v'hodor l'fonov,
הוֹד וְהָדָר לְפָנָיו,
Glory and majesty are before Him,

ōz v'chedvo bimkōmō.
עֹז וְחֶדְוָה בִּמְקֹמוֹ.
might and delight are in His place.

Hovu Ladōnoy mishp'chōs amim,
הָבוּ לַיהוה מִשְׁפְּחוֹת עַמִּים,
Render to HASHEM, O families of the peoples,

hovu Ladōnoy kovōd vo-ōz.

הָבוּ לַיהוה כָּבוֹד וָעֹז.

render to HASHEM honor and might.

Hovu Ladōnoy k'vōd sh'mō,

הָבוּ לַיהוה כְּבוֹד שְׁמוֹ,

Render to HASHEM honor worthy of His Name,

s'u mincho u-vō-u l'fonov,

שְׂאוּ מִנְחָה וּבֹאוּ לְפָנָיו,

take an offering and come before Him,

hishtachavu Ladōnoy
   b'hadras kōdesh.

הִשְׁתַּחֲווּ לַיהוה
בְּהַדְרַת קֹדֶשׁ.

prostrate yourselves before HASHEM in His intensely holy place.

Chilu mil'fonov kol ho-oretz,

חִילוּ מִלְּפָנָיו כָּל הָאָרֶץ,

Tremble before Him, everyone on earth,

af tikōn tayvayl bal timōt.

אַף תִּכּוֹן תֵּבֵל בַּל תִּמּוֹט.

indeed, the world is fixed so that it cannot falter.

Yism'chu hashoma-yim
   v'sogayl ho-oretz,

יִשְׂמְחוּ הַשָּׁמַיִם
וְתָגֵל הָאָרֶץ,

The heavens will be glad and the earth will rejoice

v'yōm'ru vagōyim Adōnoy moloch.

וְיֹאמְרוּ בַגּוֹיִם, יהוה מָלָךְ.

and say among the nations, "HASHEM has reigned!"

Yir-am ha-yom umlō-ō,

יִרְעַם הַיָּם וּמְלֹאוֹ,

The sea and its fullness will roar,

ya-alōtz hasode v'chol asher bō.

יַעֲלֹץ הַשָּׂדֶה וְכָל אֲשֶׁר בּוֹ.

the field and everything in it will exult.

Oz y'ran'nu atzay ha-yo-ar,

אָז יְרַנְּנוּ עֲצֵי הַיָּעַר,

Then the trees of the forest will sing with joy

milifnay Adōnoy,

מִלִּפְנֵי יהוה,

before HASHEM,

ki vo lishpōt es ho-oretz.

כִּי בָא לִשְׁפּוֹט אֶת הָאָרֶץ.

for He will have arrived to judge the earth.

Hōdu Ladōnoy ki tōv,

הוֹדוּ לַיהוה כִּי טוֹב,

Give thanks to HASHEM, for He is good,

ki l'ōlom chasdō.

כִּי לְעוֹלָם חַסְדּוֹ.

for His kindness endures forever.

V'imru hōshi-aynu Elōhay yish-aynu,

וְאִמְרוּ הוֹשִׁיעֵנוּ אֱלֹהֵי יִשְׁעֵנוּ,

And say, "Save us, O God of our salvation,

v'kab'tzaynu v'hatzilaynu
   min hagōyim,

וְקַבְּצֵנוּ וְהַצִּילֵנוּ
מִן הַגּוֹיִם,

gather us and rescue us from the nations,

l'hōdōs l'shaym kodshecho,
לְהֹדוֹת לְשֵׁם קָדְשֶׁךָ,
to thank Your Holy Name

l'hishtabay-ach bis-hilosecho.
לְהִשְׁתַּבֵּחַ בִּתְהִלָּתֶךָ.
and to glory in Your praise!"

Boruch Adōnoy Elōhay yisro-ayl
בָּרוּךְ יהוה אֱלֹהֵי יִשְׂרָאֵל
Blessed is HASHEM, the God of Israel,

min ho-ōlom v'ad ho-ōlom,
מִן הָעוֹלָם וְעַד הָעֹלָם,
from this world to the World to Come —

va-yōm'ru chol ho-om,
וַיֹּאמְרוּ כָל הָעָם,
and let the entire people say,

omayn, v'halayl Ladōnoy.
אָמֵן, וְהַלֵּל לַיהוה.
"Amen and praise to God!"

❖ Rōm'mu Adōnoy Elōhaynu
❖ רוֹמְמוּ יהוה אֱלֹהֵינוּ
Exalt HASHEM, our God,

v'hishta-chavu lahadōm raglov,
וְהִשְׁתַּחֲווּ לַהֲדֹם רַגְלָיו,
and bow at His footstool;

kodōsh hu.
קָדוֹשׁ הוּא.
He is holy!

Rōm'mu Adōnoy Elōhaynu
רוֹמְמוּ יהוה אֱלֹהֵינוּ
Exalt HASHEM, our God,

v'hishta-chavu l'har kodshō,
וְהִשְׁתַּחֲווּ לְהַר קָדְשׁוֹ,
and bow at His holy mountain;

ki kodōsh Adōnoy Elōhaynu.
כִּי קָדוֹשׁ יהוה אֱלֹהֵינוּ.
for holy is HASHEM, our God.

V'hu rachum y'chapayr ovōn
וְהוּא רַחוּם יְכַפֵּר עָוֹן
He, the Merciful One, is forgiving of iniquity

v'lō yashchis,
וְלֹא יַשְׁחִית,
and does not destroy;

v'hirbo l'hoshiv apō,
וְהִרְבָּה לְהָשִׁיב אַפּוֹ,
frequently, He withdraws His anger,

v'lō yo-ir kol chamosō.
וְלֹא יָעִיר כָּל חֲמָתוֹ.
not arousing His entire rage.

Ato Adōnoy,
אַתָּה יהוה,

lō sichlo rachamecho mimeni,
לֹא תִכְלָא רַחֲמֶיךָ מִמֶּנִּי,
You, HASHEM — withhold not Your mercy from me;

chasd'cho va-amit'cho tomid yitz'runi.
חַסְדְּךָ וַאֲמִתְּךָ תָּמִיד יִצְּרוּנִי.
may Your kindness and Your truth always protect me.

Z'chōr rachamecho Adōnoy   זְכֹר רַחֲמֶיךָ יהוה
    vachasodecho,   וַחֲסָדֶיךָ,

Remember Your mercies, HASHEM, and Your kindnesses,

ki may-ōlom haymo.   כִּי מֵעוֹלָם הֵמָּה.

for they are from the beginning of the world.

T'nu ōz Laylōhim,   תְּנוּ עֹז לֵאלֹהִים,

Render might to God,

al yisro-ayl ga-avosō,   עַל יִשְׂרָאֵל גַּאֲוָתוֹ,

Whose majesty hovers over Israel

v'uzō bash'chokim.   וְעֻזּוֹ בַּשְּׁחָקִים.

and Whose might is in the clouds.

Nōro Elōhim mimikdoshecho,   נוֹרָא אֱלֹהִים מִמִּקְדָּשֶׁיךָ,

You are awesome, O God, from Your Sanctuaries,

Ayl yisro-ayl   אֵל יִשְׂרָאֵל

O God of Israel —

hu nōsayn ōz v'sa-atzumōs lo-om,   הוּא נֹתֵן עֹז וְתַעֲצֻמוֹת לָעָם,

it is He Who grants might and power to the people,

boruch Elōhim.   בָּרוּךְ אֱלֹהִים.

blessed is God.

Ayl n'komōs Adōnoy,   אֵל נְקָמוֹת יהוה,

O God of vengeance, HASHEM,

Ayl n'komōs hōfi-a.   אֵל נְקָמוֹת הוֹפִיעַ.

O God of vengeance, appear!

Hinosay shōfayt ho-oretz,   הִנָּשֵׂא שֹׁפֵט הָאָרֶץ,

Arise, O Judge of the earth,

hoshayv g'mul al gay-im.   הָשֵׁב גְּמוּל עַל גֵּאִים.

render recompense to the haughty.

Ladōnoy hai-shu-o,   לַיהוה הַיְשׁוּעָה,

Salvation is HASHEM's,

al am'cho virchosecho selo.   עַל עַמְּךָ בִרְכָתֶךָ סֶּלָה.

upon Your people is Your blessing, Selah.

Adōnoy tz'vo-ōs imonu,   ❖ יהוה צְבָאוֹת עִמָּנוּ,

HASHEM, Master of Legions, is with us,

misgov lonu, Elōhay ya-akōv selo.   מִשְׂגָּב לָנוּ אֱלֹהֵי יַעֲקֹב סֶלָה.

a stronghold for us is the God of Jacob, Selah.

Adōnoy tz'vo-ōs,   יהוה צְבָאוֹת,

HASHEM, Master of Legions,

ashray odom bōtay-ach boch.   אַשְׁרֵי אָדָם בֹּטֵחַ בָּךְ.
praiseworthy is the person who trusts in You.

Adōnoy hōshi-o,   יהוה הוֹשִׁיעָה,
HASHEM, *save!*

hamelech ya-anaynu v'yōm kor-aynu.   הַמֶּלֶךְ יַעֲנֵנוּ בְיוֹם קָרְאֵנוּ.
May the King answer us on the day we call.

Hōshi-o es amecho,   הוֹשִׁיעָה אֶת עַמֶּךָ,
    u-voraych es nachalosecho,   וּבָרֵךְ אֶת נַחֲלָתֶךָ,
Save Your people and bless Your heritage,

ur-aym v'nas'aym ad ho-ōlom.   וּרְעֵם וְנַשְּׂאֵם עַד הָעוֹלָם.
tend them and elevate them forever.

Nafshaynu chik'so Ladōnoy,   נַפְשֵׁנוּ חִכְּתָה לַיהוה,
Our soul longed for HASHEM —

ezraynu u-moginaynu hu.   עֶזְרֵנוּ וּמָגִנֵּנוּ הוּא.
our help and our shield is He.

Ki vō yismach libaynu,   כִּי בוֹ יִשְׂמַח לִבֵּנוּ,
For in Him will our hearts be glad,

ki v'shaym kodshō votochnu.   כִּי בְשֵׁם קָדְשׁוֹ בָטָחְנוּ.
for in His Holy Name we trusted.

Y'hi chasd'cho Adōnoy olaynu,   יְהִי חַסְדְּךָ יהוה עָלֵינוּ,
May Your kindness, HASHEM, be upon us,

ka-asher yi-chalnu loch.   כַּאֲשֶׁר יִחַלְנוּ לָךְ.
just as we awaited You.

Har-aynu Adōnoy chasdecho,   הַרְאֵנוּ יהוה חַסְדֶּךָ,
Show us Your kindness, HASHEM,

v'yeshacho titayn lonu.   וְיֶשְׁעֲךָ תִּתֶּן לָנוּ.
and grant us Your salvation.

Kumo ezroso lonu,   קוּמָה עֶזְרָתָה לָּנוּ,
Arise — assist us,

ufdaynu l'ma-an chasdecho.   וּפְדֵנוּ לְמַעַן חַסְדֶּךָ.
and redeem us by virtue of Your kindness.

Onōchi Adōnoy Elōhecho,   אָנֹכִי יהוה אֱלֹהֶיךָ
I am HASHEM, your God,

hama-alcho may-eretz mitzroyim,   הַמַּעַלְךָ מֵאֶרֶץ מִצְרָיִם,
Who raised you from the land of Egypt;

harchev picho va-amal-ayhu.   הַרְחֶב פִּיךָ וַאֲמַלְאֵהוּ.
open wide your mouth and I will fill it.

Ashray ho-om shekocho lō,　　אַשְׁרֵי הָעָם שֶׁכָּכָה לּוֹ,

Praiseworthy is the people for whom this is so,

ashray ho-om She-adōnoy Elōhov.　　אַשְׁרֵי הָעָם שֶׁיהוה אֱלֹהָיו.

praiseworthy is the people whose God is HASHEM.

Va-ani b'chasd'cho votachti,　　וַאֲנִי בְּחַסְדְּךָ בָטַחְתִּי,

As for me, I trust in Your kindness;

yogayl libi bishu-osecho,　　יָגֵל לִבִּי בִּישׁוּעָתֶךָ,

my heart will rejoice in Your salvation.

oshiro Ladōnoy, ki gomal oloy.　　אָשִׁירָה לַיהוה, כִּי גָמַל עָלָי.

I will sing to HASHEM, for He dealt kindly with me.

ON *CHOL HAMOED* SUCCOS AND HOSHANA RABBAH, RECITE WHILE STANDING.

■ Psalm 100: In recognition of His daily extricating us from dangers, even from those unbeknownst to us, we view it as a privilege to serve God with joy.

MIZMŌR l'sōdo,　　מִזְמוֹר לְתוֹדָה,

A psalm of thanksgiving,

hori-u Ladōnoy kol ho-oretz.　　הָרִיעוּ לַיהוה כָּל הָאָרֶץ.

call out to HASHEM everyone on earth.

Ivdu es Adōnoy b'simcho,　　עִבְדוּ אֶת יהוה בְּשִׂמְחָה,

Serve HASHEM with gladness,

bō-u l'fonov birnono.　　בֹּאוּ לְפָנָיו בִּרְנָנָה.

come before Him with joyous song.

D'u ki Adōnoy hu Elōhim　　דְּעוּ כִּי יהוה הוּא אֱלֹהִים,

Know that HASHEM, He is God,

hu osonu, v'lō anachnu,　　הוּא עָשָׂנוּ, וְלוֹ אֲנַחְנוּ,

it is He Who made us and we are His,

amō v'tzōn mar-isō.　　עַמּוֹ וְצֹאן מַרְעִיתוֹ.

His people and the sheep of His pasture.

Bō-u sh'orov b'sōdo,　　בֹּאוּ שְׁעָרָיו בְּתוֹדָה,

　chatzayrōsov bis-hilo,　　חֲצֵרֹתָיו בִּתְהִלָּה,

Enter His gates with thanksgiving, His Courtyards with praise,

hōdu lō bor'chu sh'mō.　　הוֹדוּ לוֹ, בָּרְכוּ שְׁמוֹ.

give thanks to Him, bless His Name.

Ki tōv Adōnoy, l'ōlom chasdō,　　כִּי טוֹב יהוה, לְעוֹלָם חַסְדּוֹ,

For HASHEM is good, His kindness endures forever,

v'ad dōr vodōr emunoso　　וְעַד דֹּר וָדֹר אֱמוּנָתוֹ.

and from generation to generation is His faithfulness.

ON WEEKDAY *CHOL HAMOED* CONTINUE ON PAGE 318.

■ Psalm19: Shabbos marks the day when we more fully appreciate Hashem, both as the Creator and as the Giver of the Torah which we are privileged to study and more deeply appreciate on Shabbos. Before the Creator, I stand in awe; with the Giver of the Torah, I have a personal relationship. I am therefore moved to add these additional praises on Shabbos and holy days.*

LAM'NATZAY-ACH mizmōr l'dovid.   לַמְנַצֵּחַ מִזְמוֹר לְדָוִד.

For the Conductor, a song of David.*

Ha-shoma-yim m'sap'rim k'vōd Ayl,   הַשָּׁמַיִם מְסַפְּרִים כְּבוֹד אֵל,

The heavens declare the glory of God,

u-ma-asay yodov magid horoki-a,   וּמַעֲשֵׂה יָדָיו מַגִּיד הָרָקִיעַ.

and the expanse of the sky tells of His handiwork.

Yōm l'yōm yabi-a ōmer,   יוֹם לְיוֹם יַבִּיעַ אֹמֶר,

Day following day brings expressions of praise,

v'lailo l'lailo y'cha-ve do-as.   וְלַיְלָה לְּלַיְלָה יְחַוֶּה דָּעַת.

and night following night bespeaks wisdom.

Ayn ōmer v'ayn d'vorim,   אֵין אֹמֶר וְאֵין דְּבָרִים,

There is no speech and there are no words;

b'li nishmo kōlom.   בְּלִי נִשְׁמָע קוֹלָם.

their sound is unheard.

B'chol ho-oretz yotzo kavom,   בְּכָל הָאָרֶץ יָצָא קַוָּם,

Their line goes forth throughout the earth,*

u-viktzay sayvayl milayhem,   וּבִקְצֵה תֵבֵל מִלֵּיהֶם,

and their words reach the farthest ends of the land.

la-shemesh som ōhel bohem.   לַשֶּׁמֶשׁ שָׂם אֹהֶל בָּהֶם.

He has set up a tent for the sun in their midst.

◅§ **Additional Pesukei D'Zimrah for the Sabbath and Festivals**

The *Zohar* teaches that the prayers of the Sabbath morning symbolize the special spiritual bliss that adorns Israel on the Sabbath. The angels join in their own hymns of praise to God, and they laud Israel, saying that our human spiritual elevation enables the angels themselves to rise to greater heights. This heightened holiness is expressed by the addition of psalms to the morning service. The choice of psalms is based on three fundamental concepts found in the Sabbath: the remembrance that God finished Creation in six days and rested on the Sabbath; the remembrance of the Exodus from Egypt; and the idea that our Sabbath is a semblance of the World to Come.

לַמְנַצֵּחַ — *For the Conductor.* This psalm describes how the wonders of Creation are a testimony to the glory of God Who made them. Nature sings to God in the sense that each part of the universe acts as God wanted it to and in harmony with all other parts. Seen this way, the universe is likened to a symphony orchestra playing a continuous song of praise. But after lyrically recounting the wonders of Creation, the Psalmist says that all of this is merely an example of the greatness of the Torah, the blueprint that enables man to understand God's will and fulfill it.

אֵין אֹמֶר וְאֵין דְּבָרִים — *There is no speech and there are no words.* The heavens do not speak, yet the inner soul of man can discern their message clearly.

קַוָּם — *Their line.* The precision of the universe is likened metaphorically to a surveyor's tape stretched out to the ends of the earth, for the precision of the cosmos is evident to any observer all over the earth.

V'hu k'choson yōtzay maychuposō, וְהוּא כְּחָתָן יֹצֵא מֵחֻפָּתוֹ,

And it is like a groom coming forth from his bridal chamber,

yosis k'gibōr lorutz ōrach. יָשִׂישׂ כְּגִבּוֹר לָרוּץ אֹרַח.

rejoicing like a warrior to run the course.

Miktzay ha-shoma-yim mōtzo-ō, מִקְצֵה הַשָּׁמַיִם מוֹצָאוֹ,

The end of the heavens is its source,

uskufosō al k'tzōsom, וּתְקוּפָתוֹ עַל קְצוֹתָם,

and its circuit is to their other end;

v'ayn nistor maychamosō: וְאֵין נִסְתָּר מֵחַמָּתוֹ.

nothing is hidden from its heat.

Tōras Adōnoy t'mimo, תּוֹרַת יהוה תְּמִימָה,

*The Torah of H*ASHEM* is perfect,*

m'shivas nofesh, מְשִׁיבַת נָפֶשׁ,

restoring the soul;

aydus Adōnoy ne-emono, עֵדוּת יהוה נֶאֱמָנָה,

*the testimony of H*ASHEM* is trustworthy,*

machkimas pesi. מַחְכִּימַת פֶּתִי.

making the simple one wise.

Pikuday Adōnoy y'shorim, פִּקּוּדֵי יהוה יְשָׁרִים,

*The orders of H*ASHEM* are upright,*

m'sam'chay layv, מְשַׂמְּחֵי לֵב,

gladdening the heart;*

mitzvas Adōnoy boro מִצְוַת יהוה בָּרָה,

*the command of H*ASHEM* is clear*

m'i-ras ayno-yim. מְאִירַת עֵינָיִם.

enlightening the eyes.

Yir-as Adōnoy t'hōro, יִרְאַת יהוה טְהוֹרָה,

*The fear of H*ASHEM* is pure,*

ōmedes lo-ad, עוֹמֶדֶת לָעַד,

enduring forever;

mishp'tay Adōnoy emes, מִשְׁפְּטֵי יהוה אֱמֶת,

*the judgments of H*ASHEM* are true,*

tzod'ku yachdov. צָדְקוּ יַחְדָּו.

all together righteous.*

Hanechemodim mizohov u-mipaz rov, הַנֶּחֱמָדִים מִזָּהָב וּמִפַּז רָב,

They are more desirable than gold, than even much fine gold,

מְשַׂמְּחֵי לֵב – *Gladdening the heart.* The wise man will rejoice when his intellect will dominate the passions of his body.

צָדְקוּ יַחְדָּו – *All together righteous.* There is no contradiction between one law of the Torah and another, whereas in secular law one will

umsukim mid'vash v'nōfes tzufim.   וּמְתוּקִים מִדְּבַשׁ וְנֹפֶת צוּפִים.

and sweeter than honey and drippings from the combs.

Gam avd'cho nizhor bohem,   גַּם עַבְדְּךָ נִזְהָר בָּהֶם,

Even Your servant is careful of them,

b'shomrom aykev rov.   בְּשָׁמְרָם עֵקֶב רָב.

for in observing them there is great reward.

Sh'gi-ōs mi yovin,   שְׁגִיאוֹת מִי יָבִין,

Yet, who can discern mistakes?*

minis-torōs nakayni.   מִנִּסְתָּרוֹת נַקֵּנִי.

From unperceived faults cleanse me.

Gam mizaydim chasōch avdecho,   גַּם מִזֵּדִים חֲשֹׂךְ עַבְדֶּךָ,

Also from intentional sins, restrain Your servant;

al yimsh'lu vi,   אַל יִמְשְׁלוּ בִי,

let them not rule me;

oz aysom, v'nikaysi mipesha rov.   אָז אֵיתָם, וְנִקֵּיתִי מִפֶּשַׁע רָב.

then I shall be perfect and cleansed of great transgression.

Yih-yu l'rotzōn imray fi,   ❖ יִהְיוּ לְרָצוֹן אִמְרֵי פִי,

v'hegyōn libi l'fonecho,   וְהֶגְיוֹן לִבִּי לְפָנֶיךָ,

May the expressions of my mouth and the thoughts of my heart* find favor before You,

Adōnoy tzuri v'gō-ali.   יהוה צוּרִי וְגֹאֲלִי.

Hashem, my Rock and my Redeemer.

■ Psalm 34: Continuing with the theme of Shabbos marking Creation, I extol Hashem through this alphabetically arranged psalm for the understanding that all He created has merits and expresses Divine wisdom.

L'DOVID, b'shanōsō es tamō   לְדָוִד, בְּשַׁנּוֹתוֹ אֶת טַעְמוֹ

lifnay avimelech,   לִפְנֵי אֲבִימֶלֶךְ,

Of David, when he disguised his sanity* before Abimelech

vaigor'shayhu va-yaylach.   וַיְגָרְשֵׁהוּ וַיֵּלַךְ.

who drove him out and he left.

---

often find inconsistencies and conflicts between different statutes.

שְׁגִיאוֹת מִי יָבִין — *Yet, who can discern mistakes?* Though I try to keep Your commands, who can be so careful as to never make an error due to imperfect understanding and reasoning, from which no man is immune? Only Divine assistance can protect a person from these inborn human flaws.

וְהֶגְיוֹן לִבִּי — *And the thoughts of my heart.* Please do not limit Your attention to the re-

quests which I express orally. Be aware of the many inner thoughts that I am incapable of expressing.

לְדָוִד בְּשַׁנּוֹתוֹ — *Of David, when he disguised his sanity.* Everything in Creation has its place. The previous psalm spoke of the loftiest physical and spiritual forces in Creation and how they sing to God. Here we see how His greatness can be perceived even in the most painful depths. David once said to God, "All that You created is beautiful, and wisdom is the most

Avor'cho es Adōnoy b'chol ays,

אֲבָרְכָה אֶת יהוה בְּכָל עֵת,

I shall bless* HASHEM at all times,

tomid t'hilosō b'fi.

תָּמִיד תְּהִלָּתוֹ בְּפִי.

always shall His praise be in my mouth.

Badōnoy tis-halayl nafshi,

בַּיהוה תִּתְהַלֵּל נַפְשִׁי,

In HASHEM does my soul glory,

yishm'u anovim v'yismochu.

יִשְׁמְעוּ עֲנָוִים וְיִשְׂמָחוּ.

may humble ones hear and be glad.

Gad'lu Ladōnoy iti,

גַּדְּלוּ לַיהוה אִתִּי,

Declare the greatness of HASHEM with me,*

unrōm'mo sh'mō yachdov.

וּנְרוֹמְמָה שְׁמוֹ יַחְדָּו.

and let us exalt His Name together.

Dorashti es Adōnoy v'ononi,

דָּרַשְׁתִּי אֶת יהוה וְעָנָנִי,

I sought out HASHEM and He answered me,

u-mikol m'gurōsai hitziloni.

וּמִכָּל מְגוּרוֹתַי הִצִּילָנִי.

and from all my terror He delivered me.

Hibitu aylov v'nohoru,

הִבִּיטוּ אֵלָיו וְנָהָרוּ,

They look to Him and become radiant,

ufnayhem al yechporu.

וּפְנֵיהֶם אַל יֶחְפָּרוּ.

and their faces were not shamed.

Ze oni koro Vadōnoy shomay-a,

זֶה עָנִי קָרָא וַיהוה שָׁמֵעַ,

This poor man calls and HASHEM hears —

u-mikol tzorōsov hōshi-ō.

וּמִכָּל צָרוֹתָיו הוֹשִׁיעוֹ.

and from all his troubles He saved him.

Chō-ne mal-ach Adōnoy

חֹנֶה מַלְאַךְ יהוה

soviv liray-ov, vaichal-tzaym.

סָבִיב לִירֵאָיו, וַיְחַלְּצֵם.

The angel of HASHEM encamps around His reverent
ones and releases them.

---

beautiful of all. However, I fail to understand or to appreciate the value of madness. What satisfaction can You derive from having created a lunatic?''

God replied, ''David, you will someday pray that I give this madness to you.''

A short time later, David was forced to flee for his life from King Saul. Only among the Philistines, Israel's sworn enemies, did he find safety. But even there he was recognized as Israel's greatest warrior and threatened with death. He pretended to be a madman and King Abimelech, disgusted by David's insane behavior, drove him out (see *I Samuel* 21:11-16). In-

stead of feeling despair, David composed this beautiful and profound hymn. The initial letters of its verses follow the *alef-beis*, to show that we are to praise God with our every faculty, and to acknowledge that whatever He created — from *alef* to *tav* — is for the good.

אֲבָרְכָה — *I shall bless.* David's frightening experience and miraculous escape inspired him to understand that God's ways are merciful, so he responds with a blessing.

גַּדְּלוּ לַה׳ אִתִּי — *Declare the greatness of HASHEM with me.* Not content merely to have been saved, he wants his salvation to be a lesson to others. Let everyone declare God's greatness.

Ta-amu ur'u ki tōv Adōnoy,

טַעֲמוּ וּרְאוּ כִּי טוֹב יהוה,

Contemplate and see that HASHEM is good —

ashray hagever ye-chese bō.

אַשְׁרֵי הַגֶּבֶר יֶחֱסֶה בּוֹ.

praiseworthy is the man who takes refuge in Him.

Y'ru es Adōnoy k'dōshov,

יְראוּ אֶת יהוה קְדֹשָׁיו,

Fear HASHEM, you — His holy ones —

ki ayn machsōr liray-ov:

כִּי אֵין מַחְסוֹר לִירֵאָיו.

for there is no deprivation for His reverent ones.

K'firim roshu v'ro-ayvu,

כְּפִירִים רָשׁוּ וְרָעֵבוּ,

Young lions may be in need and hunger,

v'dōr'shay Adōnoy
lō yachs'ru chol tōv.

וְדֹרְשֵׁי יהוה
לֹא יַחְסְרוּ כָל טוֹב.

but those who seek HASHEM will not lack any good.*

L'chu vonim shim-u li,

לְכוּ בָנִים שִׁמְעוּ לִי,

Go, O sons, heed me,

yiras Adōnoy alamedchem.

יִרְאַת יהוה אֲלַמֶּדְכֶם.

the fear of HASHEM will I teach you.

Mi ho-ish hechofaytz cha-yim,

מִי הָאִישׁ הֶחָפֵץ חַיִּים,

Which man desires life,*

ōhayv yomim lir-ōs tōv.

אֹהֵב יָמִים לִרְאוֹת טוֹב.

who loves days of seeing good?

N'tzōr l'shōn'cho mayro,

נְצֹר לְשׁוֹנְךָ מֵרָע,

Guard your tongue from evil,

usfosecho midabayr mirmo.

וּשְׂפָתֶיךָ מִדַּבֵּר מִרְמָה.

and your lips from speaking deceit.

Sur mayro va-asay tōv,

סוּר מֵרָע וַעֲשֵׂה טוֹב,

Turn from evil and do good,

bakaysh sholōm v'rodfayhu.

בַּקֵּשׁ שָׁלוֹם וְרָדְפֵהוּ.

seek peace and pursue it.

aynay Adōnoy el tzadikim,

עֵינֵי יהוה אֶל צַדִּיקִים,

The eyes of HASHEM are toward the righteous,

v'oznov el shav-osom.

וְאָזְנָיו אֶל שַׁוְעָתָם.

and His ears to their cry.

P'nay Adōnoy b'ōsay ro,

פְּנֵי יהוה בְּעֹשֵׂי רָע,

The face of HASHEM is against evildoers,

לֹא יַחְסְרוּ כָל טוֹב — *Will not lack any good.* They may not have all the luxuries enjoyed by their neighbors, but they feel no lack of anything because they are content with their lot.

מִי הָאִישׁ הֶחָפֵץ חַיִּים — *Which man desires life.* The Psalmist urges people to better their lives in this world by avoiding gossip and slander. David was the victim of constant slander and

l'hachris may-eretz zichrom.

לְהַכְרִית מֵאֶרֶץ זִכְרָם.

to cut off their memory from earth.

Tzo-aku Vadōnoy shomay-a,

צָעֲקוּ וַיהוה שָׁמֵעַ,

They cried out and HASHEM heeds,

u-mikol tzorōsom hitzilom.

וּמִכָּל צָרוֹתָם הִצִּילָם.

and from all their troubles He rescues them.

Korōv Adōnoy l'nishb'ray layv,

קָרוֹב יהוה לְנִשְׁבְּרֵי לֵב,

HASHEM is close to the brokenhearted;

v'es dak'ay ru-ach yōshi-a.

וְאֶת דַּכְּאֵי רְוּחַ יוֹשִׁיעַ.

and those crushed in spirit, He saves.

Rabōs ro-ōs tzadik,

רַבּוֹת רָעוֹת צַדִּיק,

Many are the mishaps of the righteous,*

u-mikulom yatzilenu Adōnoy.

וּמִכֻּלָּם יַצִּילֶנּוּ יהוה.

but from them all HASHEM rescues him.

Shōmayr kol atzmōsov,

שֹׁמֵר כָּל עַצְמוֹתָיו,

He guards all his bones,

achas mayhayno lō nishboro.

אַחַת מֵהֵנָּה לֹא נִשְׁבָּרָה.

even one of them was not broken.

T'mōsays rosho ro-o,

תְּמוֹתֵת רָשָׁע רָעָה,

The death blow of the wicked is evil,*

v'sōn'ay tzadik ye-shomu.

וְשֹׂנְאֵי צַדִּיק יֶאְשָׁמוּ.

and the haters of the righteous will be condemned.

Pōde Adōnoy nefesh avodov,

✧ פּוֹדֶה יהוה נֶפֶשׁ עֲבָדָיו,

HASHEM redeems the soul of His servants,

v'lō yesh'mu kol hachōsim bō.

וְלֹא יֶאְשְׁמוּ כָּל הַחֹסִים בּוֹ.

and all those who take refuge in Him will not be condemned.

■ Psalm 90: Shabbos affords me the opportunity to reflect on my purpose and mission in life. I therefore beseech Hashem to help me utilize my limited time in this world properly and productively.

T'FILO l'mōshe ish ho-Elōhim,   **תְּפִלָּה** לְמֹשֶׁה אִישׁ הָאֱלֹהִים,

A prayer by Moses, the man of God:*

his generation suffered defeats in battle because they were not careful in their speech.

The Baal Shem Tov taught that every person is allotted a given number of words during his life. When he has used up his quota, he dies. Thus, by guarding his tongue, one assures himself of longevity.

רַבּוֹת רָעוֹת צַדִּיק — *Many are the mishaps of the righteous.* Greatness is a product of challenges, brave attempts, and many mistakes. No one

becomes truly righteous without his share of mishaps.

תְּמוֹתֵת רָשָׁע רָעָה — *The death blow of the wicked is evil.* Wicked people will be destroyed by the very evil they set in motion.

מֹשֶׁה אִישׁ הָאֱלֹהִים — *Moses, the man of God.* The Talmud (*Bava Basra* 14b) states that, in composing *Psalms,* David drew upon the works of ten Psalmists, including Moses, in addition to his own. Though Moses was a flesh-and-blood

Adōnoy mo-ōn ato ho-yiso lonu
b'dōr vodōr.

אֲדֹנָי מָעוֹן אַתָּה הָיִיתָ לָּנוּ
בְּדֹר וָדֹר.

My Lord, You have been an abode for us in all generations;

B'terem horim yulodu

בְּטֶרֶם הָרִים יֻלָּדוּ

before the mountains were born

vat'chōlayl eretz v'sayvayl,

וַתְּחוֹלֵל אֶרֶץ וְתֵבֵל,

and You had not yet fashioned the earth and the inhabited land,

u-may-ōlom ad ōlom ato Ayl.

וּמֵעוֹלָם עַד עוֹלָם אַתָּה אֵל.

and from this world to the World to Come You are God.

Toshayv enōsh ad dako,

תָּשֵׁב אֱנוֹשׁ עַד דַּכָּא,

You reduce man to pulp

vatōmer shuvu v'nay odom.

וַתֹּאמֶר שׁוּבוּ בְנֵי אָדָם.

and You say, "Repent, O sons of man."

Ki elef shonim b'aynecho

כִּי אֶלֶף שָׁנִים בְּעֵינֶיךָ

For a thousand years in Your eyes

k'yōm esmōl ki ya-avōr

כְּיוֹם אֶתְמוֹל כִּי יַעֲבֹר,

are but a bygone yesterday,

v'ashmuro valoylo.

וְאַשְׁמוּרָה בַלָּיְלָה.

and like a watch in the night.

Z'ramtom, shayno yih-yu,

זְרַמְתָּם, שֵׁנָה יִהְיוּ,

You flood them away, they become sleeplike,*

babōker kechotzir yachalōf.

בַּבֹּקֶר כֶּחָצִיר יַחֲלֹף.

by morning they are like grass that withers.

Babōker yotzitz v'cholof,

בַּבֹּקֶר יָצִיץ וְחָלָף,

In the morning it blossoms and is rejuvenated,

lo-erev y'mōlayl v'yovaysh.

לָעֶרֶב יְמוֹלֵל וְיָבֵשׁ.

by evening it is cut down and brittle.

Ki cholinu v'apecho,

כִּי כָלִינוּ בְאַפֶּךָ,

For we are consumed by Your fury;

u-vachamos'cho nivholnu.

וּבַחֲמָתְךָ נִבְהָלְנוּ.

and we are confounded by Your wrath.

Shato avōnōsaynu l'negdecho,

שַׁתָּ עֲוֹנֹתֵינוּ לְנֶגְדֶּךָ,

You have set our iniquities before Yourself,

alumaynu lim-ōr ponecho.

עֲלֻמֵנוּ לִמְאוֹר פָּנֶיךָ.

our immaturity before the light of Your countenance.

---

man, he elevated himself to the level of a Godly being.

זְרַמְתָּם שֵׁנָה יִהְיוּ — *You flood them away, they*

become sleeplike. The Psalmist continues to describe man's transitory nature. His life is like a dream that vanishes without a trace.

Ki chol yomaynu ponu v'evrosecho,   כִּי כָל יָמֵינוּ פָּנוּ בְעֶבְרָתֶךָ,
For all our days passed by* because of Your anger,

kilinu shonaynu ch'mō he-ge.   כִּלִּינוּ שָׁנֵינוּ כְמוֹ הֶגֶה.
we consumed our years like a fleeting thought.

Y'may sh'nōsaynu vohem   יְמֵי שְׁנוֹתֵינוּ בָהֶם
    shiv-im shono,   שִׁבְעִים שָׁנָה,
The days of our years among them are seventy years,

v'im bigvurōs sh'mōnim shono,   וְאִם בִּגְבוּרֹת שְׁמוֹנִים שָׁנָה,
and if with strength, eighty years;

v'robom omol vo-oven,   וְרָהְבָּם עָמָל וָאָוֶן,
their proudest success is but toil and pain,

ki goz chish vano-ufo.   כִּי גָז חִישׁ וַנָּעֻפָה.
for it is cut off swiftly and we fly away.*

Mi yōday-a ōz apecho,   מִי יוֹדֵעַ עֹז אַפֶּךָ,
Who knows the power of Your fury?*

uch-yir-os'cho evrosecho.   וּכְיִרְאָתְךָ עֶבְרָתֶךָ.
As You are feared, so is Your anger.

Limnōs yomaynu kayn hōda,   לִמְנוֹת יָמֵינוּ כֵּן הוֹדַע,
According to the count of our days,* so may You teach us;

v'novi l'vav chochmo.   וְנָבִא לְבַב חָכְמָה.
then we shall acquire a heart of wisdom.

Shuvo Adōnoy ad mosoy,   שׁוּבָה יהוה עַד מָתָי,
Return, HASHEM, how long?*

v'hinochaym al avodecho.   וְהִנָּחֵם עַל עֲבָדֶיךָ.
Relent concerning Your servants.

Sab'aynu vabōker chasdecho,   שַׂבְּעֵנוּ בַבֹּקֶר חַסְדֶּךָ,
Satisfy us in the morning with Your kindness,

unran'no v'nism'cho b'chol yomaynu.   וּנְרַנְּנָה וְנִשְׂמְחָה בְּכָל יָמֵינוּ.
then we shall sing out and rejoice throughout our days.

Sam'chaynu kimōs inisonu,   שַׂמְּחֵנוּ כִּימוֹת עִנִּיתָנוּ,
Gladden us according to the days You afflicted us,*

יָמֵינוּ פָּנוּ — *Our days passed by.* Because we incurred God's wrath, our days passed by unproductively.

כִּי גָז חִישׁ וַנָּעֻפָה — *For it is cut off swiftly and we fly away.* Man's success is fleeting. When our souls fly away, life and accomplishment go with it.

מִי יוֹדֵעַ עֹז אַפֶּךָ — *Who knows the power of Your fury?* Once God's wrath is unleashed, who can

guard against it?

לִמְנוֹת יָמֵינוּ — *According to the count of our days.* Since our lives are so short, make the truth known to us so that we may comprehend it.

שׁוּבָה ה' עַד מָתָי — *Return, HASHEM, how long?* Come back to us — how long will You abandon us?

שַׂמְּחֵנוּ כִּימוֹת עִנִּיתָנוּ — *Gladden us according to the days You afflicted us.* May our joy in the

sh'nōs ro-inu ro-o.
שְׁנוֹת רָאִינוּ רָעָה.

the years when we saw evil.

Yayro-e el avodecho fo-olecho,
יֵרָאֶה אֶל עֲבָדֶיךָ פָעֳלֶךָ,

May Your works be visible to Your servants,

vahador'cho al b'nayhem.
וַהֲדָרְךָ עַל בְּנֵיהֶם.

and Your majesty upon their children.

Vihi nō-am Adōnoy
❖ וִיהִי נֹעַם אֲדֹנָי

Elōhaynu olaynu,
אֱלֹהֵינוּ עָלֵינוּ,

May the pleasantness* of my Lord, our God, be upon us —

u-ma-asay yodaynu kōn'no olaynu,
וּמַעֲשֵׂה יָדֵינוּ כּוֹנְנָה עָלֵינוּ,

and our handiwork, may He establish for us;*

u-ma-asay yodaynu kōn'nayhu.
וּמַעֲשֵׂה יָדֵינוּ כּוֹנְנֵהוּ.

and our handiwork, may He establish .

■ Psalm 91: The Torah intertwines the themes of Shabbos and the Sanctuary. As the Sanctuary — "the shadow of the Almighty" — represents a *place* of refuge, Shabbos serves as a *time* of refuge.

YŌSHAYV b'sayser elyōn,
יֹשֵׁב בְּסֵתֶר עֶלְיוֹן,

Whoever sits* in the refuge of the Most High,*

b'tzayl Shadai yislōnon.
בְּצֵל שַׁדַּי יִתְלוֹנָן.

he shall dwell in the shadow of the Almighty.

Ōmar Ladōnoy machsi umtzudosi,
אֹמַר לַיהוה מַחְסִי וּמְצוּדָתִי,

I will say of HASHEM, "He is my refuge and my fortress,

Elōhai evtach bō.
אֱלֹהַי אֶבְטַח בּוֹ.

my God, I will trust in Him."

Ki hu yatzil'cho mipach yokush,
כִּי הוּא יַצִּילְךָ מִפַּח יָקוּשׁ,

For He will deliver you from the ensnaring trap,

---

future be equal in intensity to our suffering of the past.

וִיהִי נֹעַם — *May the pleasantness.* When the Tabernacle was built, Moses uttered this prayer that it might endure and be blessed by God. The term "pleasantness" refers to the bliss one feels after having done something that achieved its purpose. When man has this feeling of accomplishment, God, too, feels satisfaction that His will has been done.

וּמַעֲשֵׂה יָדֵינוּ כּוֹנְנָה עָלֵינוּ — *And our handiwork, may He establish for us.* Moses repeated the prayer for the success of *our handiwork*, once referring to the newly built Tabernacle and once referring to man's general activities. This can also be understood as a plea that we be independent of human pressures that interfere with our true purpose on earth.

יֹשֵׁב — *Whoever sits.* Moses continues his theme that man achieves fulfillment only through closeness to God. Moreover, God will rescue him from danger and foe. The Talmud (*Shavuos* 15b) calls this hymn "The Song of Plagues," because one who recites it with faith in God will be helped by Him in time of danger. In it, Moses speaks of the faithful believer who finds refuge in the shadow of the Almighty. This is the true hero to whom God promises long life and salvation.

יֹשֵׁב בְּסֵתֶר עֶלְיוֹן — *Whoever sits in the refuge of the Most High.* The person who scorns conventional forms of protection and seeks only the refuge provided by the Most High will find his faith rewarded. He will be enveloped by God's providence so that he can continue to seek holiness and wisdom without fear of those who

mi-dever havōs.   מִדֶּבֶר הַוּוֹת.

from devastating pestilence.

B'evrosō yosech loch,   בְּאֶבְרָתוֹ יָסֶךְ לָךְ,

With His pinion He will cover you,

v'sachas k'nofov techse,   וְתַחַת כְּנָפָיו תֶּחְסֶה,

and beneath His wings you will be protected;

tzino v'sōchayro amitō.   צִנָּה וְסֹחֵרָה אֲמִתּוֹ.

shield and armor is His truth.

Lō siro mipachad loylo,   לֹא תִירָא מִפַּחַד לָיְלָה,

You shall not fear the terror of night;*

maychaytz yo-uf yōmom.   מֵחֵץ יָעוּף יוֹמָם.

nor the arrow that flies by day;

Mi-dever bo-ōfel yahalōch,   מִדֶּבֶר בָּאֹפֶל יַהֲלֹךְ,

nor the pestilence that walks in gloom;

miketev yoshud tzohoro-yim.   מִקֶּטֶב יָשׁוּד צָהֳרָיִם.

nor the destroyer who lays waste at noon.

Yipōl mitzid'cho elef,   יִפֹּל מִצִּדְּךָ אֶלֶף,

Let a thousand encamp at your side

ur'vovo miminecho,   וּרְבָבָה מִימִינֶךָ,

and a myriad at your right hand,

aylecho lō yigosh.   אֵלֶיךָ לֹא יִגָּשׁ.

but to you they shall not approach.

Rak b'aynecho sabit,   רַק בְּעֵינֶיךָ תַבִּיט,

You will merely peer with your eyes

v'shilumas r'sho-im tir-e.   וְשִׁלֻּמַת רְשָׁעִים תִּרְאֶה.

and you will see the retribution of the wicked.

Ki ato Adōnoy machsi,   כִּי אַתָּה יהוה מַחְסִי,

Because [you said,] "You, Hashem, are my refuge,"

elyōn samto m'ōnecho.   עֶלְיוֹן שַׂמְתָּ מְעוֹנֶךָ.

you have made the Most High your dwelling place.

Lō s'une aylecho ro-o,   לֹא תְאֻנֶּה אֵלֶיךָ רָעָה,

No evil will befall you,

v'nega lō yikrav b'oholecho.   וְנֶגַע לֹא יִקְרַב בְּאָהֳלֶךָ.

nor will any plague come near your tent.*

---

would seek to do him harm.

לֹא תִירָא מִפַּחַד לָיְלָה — *You shall not fear the terror of night.* If you put your faith in God, fear will be banished from your heart.

וְנֶגַע לֹא יִקְרַב בְּאָהֳלֶךָ — *Nor will any plague come near your tent.* The Talmud (Sanhedrin 103a) perceives this as a blessing for domestic tranquility and for having worthy

Ki mal-ochov y'tza-ve loch,
He will charge His angels for you,
כִּי מַלְאָכָיו יְצַוֶּה לָּךְ,

lishmorcho b'chol d'rochecho.
to protect you in all your ways.
לִשְׁמָרְךָ בְּכָל דְּרָכֶיךָ.

Al kapa-yim yiso-uncho,
On [their] palms they will carry you,*
עַל כַּפַּיִם יִשָּׂאוּנְךָ,

pen tigōf bo-even raglecho.
lest you strike your foot against a stone.
פֶּן תִּגֹּף בָּאֶבֶן רַגְלֶךָ.

Al shachal vofesen tidrōch,
Upon the lion and the viper you will tread;
עַל שַׁחַל וָפֶתֶן תִּדְרֹךְ,

tirmōs k'fir v'sanin.
you will trample the young lion and the serpent.
תִּרְמֹס כְּפִיר וְתַנִּין.

Ki vi choshak va-afal'tayhu,
For he has yearned for Me* and I will deliver him;
כִּי בִי חָשַׁק וַאֲפַלְּטֵהוּ,

asag'vayhu ki yoda sh'mi.
I will elevate him because he knows My Name.
אֲשַׂגְּבֵהוּ כִּי יָדַע שְׁמִי.

Yikro-ayni v'e-enayhu,
He will call upon Me and I will answer him,
יִקְרָאֵנִי וְאֶעֱנֵהוּ,

imō onōchi v'tzoro,
I am with him in distress,
עִמּוֹ אָנֹכִי בְצָרָה,

achal'tzayhu va-achab'dayhu.
I will release him and I will honor him.
אֲחַלְּצֵהוּ וַאֲכַבְּדֵהוּ.

❖ Ōrech yomim asbi-ayhu,
With long life will I satisfy him,
❖ אֹרֶךְ יָמִים אַשְׂבִּיעֵהוּ,

v'ar-ayhu bishu-osi.
and I will show him My salvation.
וְאַרְאֵהוּ בִּישׁוּעָתִי.

Ōrech yomim asbi-ayhu,
With long life will I satisfy him,
אֹרֶךְ יָמִים אַשְׂבִּיעֵהוּ,

v'arayhu bishu-osi.
and I will show him My salvation.
וְאַרְאֵהוּ בִּישׁוּעָתִי.

---

children and students, who will not shame him.

עַל כַּפַּיִם יִשָּׂאוּנְךָ — *On [your] palms they will carry you.* The angels created by the commandments you perform with your palms [i.e., giving charity and doing acts of kindness] will raise you above all dangers that lurk in your path.

כִּי בִי חָשַׁק — *For he has yearned for Me.* From here to the end of the psalm, God speaks in praise of and with assurances to the person who has faith in Him.

■ Psalm 135: Shabbos is highlighted in the second account as the Ten Commandments as the day and opportunity to remember the Exodus from Egypt. This psalm
recounts the miracles of the Exodus which demonstrates that Hashem not only
created the universe but continues to supervise and guide history.

HAL'LUYOH   הַלְלוּיָהּ

Praise God!

hal'lu es shaym Adōnoy,   הַלְלוּ אֶת שֵׁם יהוה,

Praise the Name of HASHEM!

hal'lu avday Adōnoy.   הַלְלוּ עַבְדֵי יהוה.

Praise, you servants of HASHEM;

She-ōm'dim b'vays Adōnoy,   שֶׁעֹמְדִים בְּבֵית יהוה,

you who stand in the House of HASHEM,

b'chatzrōs bays Elōhaynu.   בְּחַצְרוֹת בֵּית אֱלֹהֵינוּ.

in the Courtyards of the House of our God —

Hal'luyoh ki tōv Adōnoy,   הַלְלוּיָהּ כִּי טוֹב יהוה,

praise God, for HASHEM is good;

zam'ru lishmō ki no-im.   זַמְּרוּ לִשְׁמוֹ כִּי נָעִים.

sing to His Name, for It is pleasant.

Ki ya-akōv bochar lō Yoh,   כִּי יַעֲקֹב בָּחַר לוֹ יָהּ,

For God selected Jacob for His own,

yisro-ayl lisgulosō.   יִשְׂרָאֵל לִסְגֻלָּתוֹ.

Israel as His treasure.*

Ki ani yodati ki godōl Adōnoy,   כִּי אֲנִי יָדַעְתִּי כִּי גָדוֹל יהוה,

For I know that HASHEM is great,

Va-adōnaynu mikol elōhim.   וַאֲדֹנֵינוּ מִכָּל אֱלֹהִים.

amd our Lord [is greater] than all heavenly powers.

Kōl asher chofaytz Adōnoy oso,   כֹּל אֲשֶׁר חָפֵץ יהוה עָשָׂה,

Whatever HASHEM wished, He did,

ba-shoma-yim u-vo-oretz,   בַּשָּׁמַיִם וּבָאָרֶץ,

ba-yamim v'chol t'hōmōs.   בַּיַּמִּים וְכָל תְּהֹמוֹת.

in heaven and on earth; in the seas and all the depths.

הַלְלוּיָהּ — *Praise God!* The Exodus from Egypt
complements the Sabbath. While the Sabbath
testifies that God created the universe, the
miracles of the Exodus testify that he continues to supervise and guide history. This psalm
recounts the miracles of the Exodus and
Israel's trek through the wilderness to the
Land of Israel. It ends with the conclusion that
it is worthless to worship anything except
Hashem.

שֶׁעוֹמְדִים בְּבֵית ה' — *You who stand in the House
of HASHEM.* The prime responsibility to lead
Israel in God's praise falls upon the scholars
and teachers in the synagogues and study
halls.

כִּי יַעֲקֹב ... יִשְׂרָאֵל — *For ... Jacob ... Israel.*
Jacob represents the multitude of Jews while
Israel represents the great people among
them. God chooses even ordinary Jews (Jacob)
for his own, but Israel is His treasure.

Ma-ale n'si-im miktzay ho-oretz,   מַעֲלֶה נְשִׂאִים מִקְצֵה הָאָרֶץ,
He raises clouds from the end of the earth;

b'rokim lamotor oso,   בְּרָקִים לַמָּטָר עָשָׂה,
He made lightning bolts for the rain;

mōtzay ru-ach may-ōtz'rōsov.   מוֹצֵא רְוּחַ מֵאוֹצְרוֹתָיו.
He brings forth wind from His treasuries.

Shehiko b'chōray mitzro-yim,   שֶׁהִכָּה בְּכוֹרֵי מִצְרֶיִם,
It was He Who smote the firstborn of Egypt,

may-odom ad b'haymo.   מֵאָדָם עַד בְּהֵמָה.
from man to beast.

Sholach ōsōs u-mōf'sim   שָׁלַח אוֹתֹת וּמֹפְתִים
   b'sōchaychi mitzro-yim,   בְּתוֹכֵכִי מִצְרֶיִם,
He sent signs and wonders into your midst, O Egypt,

b'far-ō uvchol avodov.   בְּפַרְעֹה וּבְכָל עֲבָדָיו.
upon Pharaoh and upon all of his servants.

Shehiko gō-yim rabim,   שֶׁהִכָּה גּוֹיִם רַבִּים,
It was He Who smote many nations,

v'horag m'lochim atzumim.   וְהָרַג מְלָכִים עֲצוּמִים.
and slew mighty kings —

L'sichōn melech ho-emōri,   לְסִיחוֹן מֶלֶךְ הָאֱמֹרִי,
Sichon, king of the Emorites,

ul-ōg melech haboshon,   וּלְעוֹג מֶלֶךְ הַבָּשָׁן,
Og, king of Bashan,

ulchōl maml'chōs k'no-an.   וּלְכֹל מַמְלְכוֹת כְּנֶעַן.
and all the kingdoms of Canaan —

V'nosan artzom nachalo,   וְנָתַן אַרְצָם נַחֲלָה,
and presented their land as a heritage,

nachalo l'yisro-ayl amō.   נַחֲלָה לְיִשְׂרָאֵל עַמּוֹ.
a heritage for Israel, His people.

Adōnoy shimcho l'ōlom,   יהוה שִׁמְךָ לְעוֹלָם,
Hashem is Your Name forever,

Adōnoy zichr'cho l'dōr vodōr.   יהוה זִכְרְךָ לְדֹר וָדֹר.
Hashem is Your memorial throughout the generations.

Ki yodin Adōnoy amō,   כִּי יָדִין יהוה עַמּוֹ,
When Hashem will judge* [the nations] for the sake of His people,

---

כִּי יָדִין ה׳ — *When Hashem will judge.* Eventually, God will consider the plight of oppressed   Israel, and then He will show mercy to His people.

v'al avodov yisnechom.   וְעַל עֲבָדָיו יִתְנֶחָם.

and He will relent concerning His servants.

Atzabay hagōyim kesef v'zohov,   עֲצַבֵּי הַגּוֹיִם כֶּסֶף וְזָהָב,

The idols of the nations are silver and gold,

ma-asay y'day odom.   מַעֲשֵׂה יְדֵי אָדָם.

human handiwork.

Pe lohem v'lō y'dabayru,   פֶּה לָהֶם וְלֹא יְדַבֵּרוּ,

They have mouths, but they speak not;*

ayna-yim lohem v'lō yir-u.   עֵינַיִם לָהֶם וְלֹא יִרְאוּ.

they have eyes, but they see not;

Ozna-yim lohem v'lō ya-azinu,   אָזְנַיִם לָהֶם וְלֹא יַאֲזִינוּ,

they have ears, but they heed not;

af ayn yesh ru-ach b'fihem.   אַף אֵין יֶשׁ רוּחַ בְּפִיהֶם.

neither is there any breath in their mouths.

K'mōhem yih-yu ōsayhem,   כְּמוֹהֶם יִהְיוּ עֹשֵׂיהֶם,

Like them shall their makers become,*

kōl asher bōtay-ach bohem.   כֹּל אֲשֶׁר בֹּטֵחַ בָּהֶם.

everyone who trusts in them.

Bays yisro-ayl   ❖ בֵּית יִשְׂרָאֵל

  bor'chu es Adōnoy,   בָּרְכוּ אֶת יהוה,

O House of Israel, bless HASHEM;

bays aharōn bor'chu es Adōnoy.   בֵּית אַהֲרֹן בָּרְכוּ אֶת יהוה.

O House of Aaron, bless HASHEM.

Bays halayvi bor'chu es Adōnoy,   בֵּית הַלֵּוִי בָּרְכוּ אֶת יהוה,

O House of Levi, bless HASHEM;

yir-ay Adōnoy bor'chu es Adōnoy.   יִרְאֵי יהוה בָּרְכוּ אֶת יהוה.

O those who fear HASHEM, *bless* HASHEM.

Boruch Adōnoy mitzi-yōn   בָּרוּךְ יהוה מִצִּיּוֹן

Blessed is HASHEM *from Zion,*

shōchayn y'rusholo-yim,   שֹׁכֵן יְרוּשָׁלָיִם,

He Who dwells in Jerusalem.

hal'luyoh.   הַלְלוּיָהּ.

Praise God!

פֶּה לָהֶם וְלֹא יְדַבֵּרוּ — *They have mouths, but they speak not.* Intelligent speech is man's greatest distinction, yet idolaters are foolish enough to worship mute idols!

כְּמוֹהֶם יִהְיוּ עֹשֵׂיהֶם — *Like them shall their makers become.* This can be taken as a prayer, or as a statement of fact that eventually idol worshipers will perish and be as lifeless as the clods

■ Psalm 136: As I acknowledge Hashem as the Creator and as the Controller of Jewish history, I additionally focus and extend praise to Him for His supervision over countless details, even that He provides every creature with its daily needs.

IN MOST CONGREGATIONS THE FOLLOWING PSALM IS RECITED WHILE STANDING.

HŌDU Ladōnoy ki tōv,   הוֹדוּ לַיהוה כִּי טוֹב,
Give thanks to HASHEM* for He is good,

ki l'ōlom chasdō.   כִּי לְעוֹלָם חַסְדּוֹ.
for His kindness endures forever.

Hōdu Laylōhay ho-elōhim,   הוֹדוּ לֵאלֹהֵי הָאֱלֹהִים,
Give thanks to the God of the heavenly powers,

ki l'ōlom chasdō.   כִּי לְעוֹלָם חַסְדּוֹ.
for His kindness endures forever.

Hōdu La-adōnay ho-adōnim,   הוֹדוּ לַאֲדֹנֵי הָאֲדֹנִים,
Give thanks to the Lord of the lords,

ki l'ōlom chasdō.   כִּי לְעוֹלָם חַסְדּוֹ.
for His kindness endures forever.

L'ōsay niflo-ōs g'dōlōs l'vadō,   לְעֹשֵׂה נִפְלָאוֹת גְּדֹלוֹת לְבַדּוֹ,
To Him Who alone performs great wonders,

ki l'ōlom chasdō.   כִּי לְעוֹלָם חַסְדּוֹ.
for His kindness endures forever.

L'ōsay ha-shoma-yim bisvuno,   לְעֹשֵׂה הַשָּׁמַיִם בִּתְבוּנָה,
To Him Who makes the heavens with understanding,*

ki l'ōlom chasdō.   כִּי לְעוֹלָם חַסְדּוֹ.
for His kindness endures forever.

L'rōka ho-oretz al hamo-yim,   לְרוֹקַע הָאָרֶץ עַל הַמָּיִם,
To Him Who spreads out the earth upon the waters,

ki l'ōlom chasdō.   כִּי לְעוֹלָם חַסְדּוֹ.
for His kindness endures forever.

L'ōsay ōrim g'dōlim,   לְעֹשֵׂה אוֹרִים גְּדֹלִים,
To Him Who makes great lights,

they worship.

הוֹדוּ לַה׳ — *Give thanks to HASHEM.* The Talmud (*Pesachim* 118a) calls this psalm (136) *Hallel HaGadol,* "the Great Song of Praise," because it lauds God for giving sustenance to every living being. Thus, although it speaks of a multitude of mighty miracles, including the Creation of the universe and the Exodus from Egypt, the psalm concludes by saying, "He give nourishment [lit., bread] to all flesh," because God's mercy upon every creature is equal to all the great miracles. The twenty-six verses of the psalm are another allusion to God's mercy, because for twenty-six generations before the Torah was given, God provided for all living things out of His mercy. Once the Torah was given, man could earn his keep by performing the commandments. The praises are in present tense because God renews Creation constantly.

בִּתְבוּנָה — *With understanding.* The solar system and the countless galaxies function with a complexity that is beyond human comprehension.

ki l'ōlom chasdō.   כִּי לְעוֹלָם חַסְדּוֹ.

for His kindness endures forever.

Es hashemesh l'memsheles ba-yōm,   אֶת הַשֶּׁמֶשׁ לְמֶמְשֶׁלֶת בַּיּוֹם,

The sun for the reign of the day,

ki l'ōlom chasdō.   כִּי לְעוֹלָם חַסְדּוֹ.

for His kindness endures forever.

Es ha-yoray-ach v'chōchovim   אֶת הַיָּרֵחַ וְכוֹכָבִים

   l'memsh'lōs baloylo,   לְמֶמְשְׁלוֹת בַּלָּיְלָה,

The moon and the stars for the reign of the night,

ki l'ōlom chasdō.   כִּי לְעוֹלָם חַסְדּוֹ.

for His kindness endures forever.

L'makay mitzra-yim bivchōrayhem,   לְמַכֵּה מִצְרַיִם בִּבְכוֹרֵיהֶם,

To Him Who smote Egypt through their firstborn,

ki l'ōlom chasdō.   כִּי לְעוֹלָם חַסְדּוֹ.

for His kindness endures forever.

Va-yōtzay yisro-ayl mitōchom,   וַיּוֹצֵא יִשְׂרָאֵל מִתּוֹכָם,

And brought Israel forth from their midst,

ki l'ōlom chasdō.   כִּי לְעוֹלָם חַסְדּוֹ.

for His kindness endures forever.

B'yod chazoko u-vizrō-a n'tu-yo,   בְּיָד חֲזָקָה וּבִזְרוֹעַ נְטוּיָה,

With strong hand and outstretched arm,

ki l'ōlom chasdō.   כִּי לְעוֹלָם חַסְדּוֹ.

for His kindness endures forever.

L'gōzayr yam suf ligzorim,   לְגֹזֵר יַם סוּף לִגְזָרִים,

To Him Who divided the Sea of Reeds into parts,*

ki l'ōlom chasdō.   כִּי לְעוֹלָם חַסְדּוֹ.

for His kindness endures forever.

V'he-evir yisro-ayl b'sōchō,   וְהֶעֱבִיר יִשְׂרָאֵל בְּתוֹכוֹ,

And caused Israel to pass through it,

ki l'ōlom chasdō.   כִּי לְעוֹלָם חַסְדּוֹ.

for His kindness endures forever.

V'ni-ayr par-ō v'chaylō v'yam suf,   וְנִעֵר פַּרְעֹה וְחֵילוֹ בְיַם סוּף,

And threw Pharaoh and his army into the Sea of Reeds,

ki l'ōlom chasdō.   כִּי לְעוֹלָם חַסְדּוֹ.

for His kindness endures forever.

L'mōlich amō bamidbor,   לְמוֹלִיךְ עַמּוֹ בַּמִּדְבָּר,

To Him Who led His people through the wilderness,

יַם סוּף לִגְזָרִים — *The Sea of Reeds into parts.* The Midrash teaches that the sea was divided into twelve parts, one for each tribe. This shows that each tribe had its own mission and

ki l'olom chasdo.   כִּי לְעוֹלָם חַסְדּוֹ.
for His kindness endures forever.

L'makay m'lochim g'dolim,   לְמַכֵּה מְלָכִים גְּדֹלִים,
To Him Who smote great kings,

ki l'olom chasdo.   כִּי לְעוֹלָם חַסְדּוֹ.
for His kindness endures forever.

Va-yaharog m'lochim adirim,   וַיַּהֲרֹג מְלָכִים אַדִּירִים,
And slew mighty kings,

ki l'olom chasdo.   כִּי לְעוֹלָם חַסְדּוֹ.
for His kindness endures forever.

L'sichon melech ho-emori,   לְסִיחוֹן מֶלֶךְ הָאֱמֹרִי,
Sichon, king of the Emorites,

ki l'olom chasdo.   כִּי לְעוֹלָם חַסְדּוֹ.
for His kindness endures forever.

Ul-og melech ha-boshon,   וּלְעוֹג מֶלֶךְ הַבָּשָׁן,
And Og, king of Bashan,

ki l'olom chasdo.   כִּי לְעוֹלָם חַסְדּוֹ.
for His kindness endures forever.

V'nosan artzom l'nachalo,   וְנָתַן אַרְצָם לְנַחֲלָה,
And presented their land as a heritage,

ki l'olom chasdo.   כִּי לְעוֹלָם חַסְדּוֹ.
for His kindness endures forever.

Nachalo l'yisro-ayl avdo,   נַחֲלָה לְיִשְׂרָאֵל עַבְדּוֹ,
A heritage for Israel, His servant,

ki l'olom chasdo.   כִּי לְעוֹלָם חַסְדּוֹ.
for His kindness endures forever.

Sheb'shiflaynu zochar lonu,   שֶׁבְּשִׁפְלֵנוּ זָכַר לָנוּ,
In our lowliness He remembered us,

ki l'olom chasdo.   כִּי לְעוֹלָם חַסְדּוֹ.
for His kindness endures forever.

Va-yifr'kaynu mitzoraynu,   וַיִּפְרְקֵנוּ מִצָּרֵינוּ,
And He released us from our tormentors,

ki l'olom chasdo.   כִּי לְעוֹלָם חַסְדּוֹ.
for His kindness endures forever.

Nosayn lechem l'chol bosor,   ❖ נֹתֵן לֶחֶם לְכָל בָּשָׂר,
He gives nourishment to all flesh,

ki l'olom chasdo.   כִּי לְעוֹלָם חַסְדּוֹ.
for His kindness endures forever.

---

deserved the miracle for its own sake.

Hōdu l'Ayl ha-shomo-yim,

הוֹדוּ לְאֵל הַשָּׁמָיִם,

Give thanks to God of the heavens,

ki l'ōlom chasdō.

כִּי לְעוֹלָם חַסְדּוֹ.

for His kindness endures forever.

■ Psalm 33: Shabbos constitutes a "taste of the World to Come." As the Jewish nation utilizes the Shabbos to renew its relationship with Hashem, I anticipate with excitement the time when all of mankind will accept His moral law.

RAN'NU tzadikim Badōnoy,

רַנְּנוּ צַדִּיקִים בַּיהוה,

Sing joyfully, O righteous, * before* HASHEM;

laishorim novo s'hilo.

לַיְשָׁרִים נָאוָה תְהִלָּה.

for the upright, praise is fitting.

Hōdu Ladōnoy b'chinōr,

הוֹדוּ לַיהוה בְּכִנּוֹר,

Give thanks to HASHEM *with the harp,*

b'nayvel osōr zam'ru lō.

בְּנֵבֶל עָשׂוֹר זַמְּרוּ לוֹ.

with the ten-stringed lyre make music to Him.

Shiru lō shir chodosh,

שִׁירוּ לוֹ שִׁיר חָדָשׁ,

Sing to Him a new song,

haytivu nagayn bisru-o.

הֵיטִיבוּ נַגֵּן בִּתְרוּעָה.

play well with sounds of deepest feeling.

Ki yoshor d'var Adōnoy,

כִּי יָשָׁר דְּבַר יהוה,

For upright is the word of HASHEM,

v'chol ma-asayhu be-emuno.

וְכָל מַעֲשֵׂהוּ בֶּאֱמוּנָה.

and all His deeds are done with faithfulness. *

Ōhayv tz'doko u-mishpot,

אֹהֵב צְדָקָה וּמִשְׁפָּט,

He loves charity and justice,

chesed Adōnoy mol'o ho-oretz.

חֶסֶד יהוה מָלְאָה הָאָרֶץ.

the kindness of HASHEM *fills the earth.*

Bidvar Adōnoy shoma-yim na-asu,

בִּדְבַר יהוה שָׁמַיִם נַעֲשׂוּ,

By the word of HASHEM *the heavens were made,*

uvru-ach piv kol tz'vo-om.

וּבְרוּחַ פִּיו כָּל צְבָאָם.

and by the breath of His mouth all their host.

Kōnays kanayd may ha-yom,

כֹּנֵס כַּנֵּד מֵי הַיָּם,

He assembles like a wall the waters of the sea,

רַנְּנוּ צַדִּיקִים — *Sing joyfully, O righteous.* Psalm 133 turns to the celebration of the World to Come when all will recognize that God controls events. The Sabbath represents awareness of this truth, and it calls upon us to "sing Him a

new song."

וְכָל מַעֲשֵׂהוּ בֶּאֱמוּנָה — *And all His deeds are done with faithfulness.* The natural forces are reliable and consistent. Otherwise we would be in constant fear of upheaval.

nōsayn b'ōtzorōs t'hōmōs.
He places the deep waters in vaults.

נֹתֵן בְּאוֹצָרוֹת תְּהוֹמוֹת.

Yir'u may-Adōnoy kol ho-oretz,
All the earth shall fear HASHEM,

יִירְאוּ מֵיהוה כָּל הָאָרֶץ,

mimenu yoguru kol yōsh'vay sayvayl.
all inhabitants of the world shall be in dread of Him.

מִמֶּנּוּ יָגוּרוּ כָּל יֹשְׁבֵי תֵבֵל.

Ki hu omar va-yehi,
For He spoke and it came to be,

כִּי הוּא אָמַר וַיֶּהִי,

hu tzivo va-ya-amōd.
He commanded and it stood firm.

הוּא צִוָּה וַיַּעֲמֹד.

Adōnoy hayfir atzas gō-yim,
HASHEM annuls the counsel of nations,

יהוה הֵפִיר עֲצַת גּוֹיִם,

hayni machsh'vōs amim.
He thwarts the designs of peoples.

הֵנִיא מַחְשְׁבוֹת עַמִּים.

Atzas Adōnoy l'ōlom ta-amōd,
The counsel of HASHEM will endure forever,

עֲצַת יהוה לְעוֹלָם תַּעֲמֹד,

machsh'vōs libō l'dōr vodōr.
the designs of His heart throughout the generations.

מַחְשְׁבוֹת לִבּוֹ לְדֹר וָדֹר.

Ashray hagōy asher Adōnoy Elōhov,
Praiseworthy is the nation whose God is HASHEM,

אַשְׁרֵי הַגּוֹי אֲשֶׁר יהוה אֱלֹהָיו,

ho-om bochar l'nachalo lō.
the people He chose for His own heritage.

הָעָם בָּחַר לְנַחֲלָה לוֹ.

Mi-shoma-yim hibit Adōnoy,
From heaven HASHEM looks down,

מִשָּׁמַיִם הִבִּיט יהוה,

ro-o es kol b'nay ho-odom.
He sees all mankind.

רָאָה אֶת כָּל בְּנֵי הָאָדָם.

Mim'chōn shivtō hishgi-ach,
el kol yōsh'vay ho-oretz.
From His dwelling place He oversees all inhabitants of earth.

מִמְּכוֹן שִׁבְתּוֹ הִשְׁגִּיחַ,
אֶל כָּל יֹשְׁבֵי הָאָרֶץ.

Ha-yōtzayr yachad libom,
He fashions their hearts all together,

הַיֹּצֵר יַחַד לִבָּם,

hamayvin el kol ma-asayhem.
He comprehends all their deeds.

הַמֵּבִין אֶל כָּל מַעֲשֵׂיהֶם.

Ayn hamelech nōsho b'rov cho-yil,
A king is not saved by a great army,

אֵין הַמֶּלֶךְ נוֹשָׁע בְּרָב חָיִל,

gibōr lō yinotzayl b'rov kō-ach.
nor is a hero rescued by great strength;

גִּבּוֹר לֹא יִנָּצֵל בְּרָב כֹּחַ.

Sheker hasus lis-shu-o,   שֶׁקֶר הַסּוּס לִתְשׁוּעָה,

sham is the horse for salvation;

uvrōv chaylō lō y'malayt.   וּבְרֹב חֵילוֹ לֹא יְמַלֵּט.

despite its great strength it provides no escape.

Hinay ayn Adōnoy el y'ray-ov,   הִנֵּה עֵין יהוה אֶל יְרֵאָיו,

Behold, the eye of HASHEM is on those who fear Him,

lam'yachalim l'chasdō.   לַמְיַחֲלִים לְחַסְדּוֹ.

upon those who await His kindness.

L'hatzil mimoves nafshom,   לְהַצִּיל מִמָּוֶת נַפְשָׁם,

To rescue their soul from death,

ulcha-yōsom boro-ov.   וּלְחַיּוֹתָם בָּרָעָב.

and to sustain them in famine.

❖ Nafshaynu chik'so Ladōnoy,   נַפְשֵׁנוּ חִכְּתָה לַיהוה,

Our soul longed for HASHEM —

ezraynu u-moginaynu hu.   עֶזְרֵנוּ וּמָגִנֵּנוּ הוּא.

our help and our shield is He.

Ki vō yismach libaynu,   כִּי בוֹ יִשְׂמַח לִבֵּנוּ,

For in Him will our hearts be glad,

ki v'shaym kodshō votochnu.   כִּי בְשֵׁם קָדְשׁוֹ בָטָחְנוּ.

for in His Holy Name we trusted.

Y'hi chasd'cho Adōnoy olaynu,   יְהִי חַסְדְּךָ יהוה עָלֵינוּ,

May Your kindness, HASHEM, be upon us,

ka-asher yichalnu loch.   כַּאֲשֶׁר יִחַלְנוּ לָךְ.

just as we awaited You.

■ Psalm 92: While the Shabbos day is not mentioned in the body of this psalm, the psalm speaks of the faith in Hashem — in the face of evil — that sustained our people through the various exiles and that enables us to excitedly anticipate the ''day of everlasting Shabbos.''

MIZMŌR shir l'yōm ha-shabos.   מִזְמוֹר שִׁיר לְיוֹם הַשַּׁבָּת.

A psalm, a song for the Sabbath day.*

Tōv l'hōdōs Ladōnoy,   טוֹב לְהֹדוֹת לַיהוה,

It is good to thank HASHEM

ulzamayr l'shimcho elyōn.   וּלְזַמֵּר לְשִׁמְךָ עֶלְיוֹן.

and to sing praise to Your Name, O Exalted One;

L'hagid babōker chasdecho,   לְהַגִּיד בַּבֹּקֶר חַסְדֶּךָ,

to relate Your kindness in the dawn

שִׁיר מִזְמוֹר — *A psalm, a song for the Sabbath day,* Psalm 92, is discussed on pages 99-101 above.

ve-emunos'cho balaylōs.
וֶאֱמוּנָתְךָ בַּלֵּילוֹת.

and Your faith in the nights.

Alay osōr va-alay novel,
עֲלֵי עָשׂוֹר וַעֲלֵי נָבֶל,

Upon ten-stringed instrument and lyre,

alay higo-yōn b'chinōr.
עֲלֵי הִגָּיוֹן בְּכִנּוֹר.

with singing accompanied by a harp.

Ki simachtani Adōnoy b'fo-olecho,
כִּי שִׂמַּחְתַּנִי יהוה בְּפָעֳלֶךָ,

For You have gladdened me, HASHEM, with Your deeds;

b'ma-asay yodecho aranayn.
בְּמַעֲשֵׂי יָדֶיךָ אֲרַנֵּן.

at the works of Your Hands I sing glad song.

Ma god'lu ma-asecho Adōnoy,
מַה גָּדְלוּ מַעֲשֶׂיךָ יהוה,

How great are Your deeds, HASHEM;

m'ōd om'ku machsh'vōsecho.
מְאֹד עָמְקוּ מַחְשְׁבֹתֶיךָ.

exceedingly profound are Your thoughts.

Ish ba-ar lō yaydo,
אִישׁ בַּעַר לֹא יֵדָע,

A boor cannot know,

uchsil lō yovin es zōs.
וּכְסִיל לֹא יָבִין אֶת זֹאת.

nor can a fool understand this:

Bifrō-ach r'sho-im k'mō aysev,
בִּפְרֹחַ רְשָׁעִים כְּמוֹ עֵשֶׂב,

When the wicked bloom like grass

va-yotzitzu kol pō-alay o-ven,
וַיָּצִיצוּ כָּל פֹּעֲלֵי אָוֶן,

and all the doers of iniquity blossom —

l'hi-shom'dom aday ad.
לְהִשָּׁמְדָם עֲדֵי עַד.

it is to destroy them till eternity.

V'ato morōm l'ōlom Adōnoy.
וְאַתָּה מָרוֹם לְעֹלָם יהוה.

But You remain exalted forever, HASHEM.

Ki hinay ō-y'vecho, Adōnoy,
כִּי הִנֵּה אֹיְבֶיךָ יהוה,

For behold! — Your enemies, HASHEM,

ki hinay ō-y'vecho, yōvaydu,
כִּי הִנֵּה אֹיְבֶיךָ יֹאבֵדוּ,

for behold! — Your enemies shall perish,

yispor'du kol pō-alay o-ven.
יִתְפָּרְדוּ כָּל פֹּעֲלֵי אָוֶן.

dispersed shall be all doers of iniquity.

Vatorem kir-aym karni,
וַתָּרֶם כִּרְאֵים קַרְנִי,

As exalted as a re'eim's shall be my pride,

balōsi b'shemen ra-anon.
בַּלֹּתִי בְּשֶׁמֶן רַעֲנָן.

I will be saturated with ever-fresh oil.

Vatabayt ayni b'shuroy,   וַתַּבֵּט עֵינִי בְּשׁוּרָי,
My eyes will see my vigilant foes;

bakomim olai m'ray-im,   בַּקָּמִים עָלַי מְרֵעִים,
when those who would harm me rise up against me,

tishma-no oznoy.   תִּשְׁמַעְנָה אָזְנָי.
my ears will hear their doom.

❖ Tzadik katomor yifroch,   ❖ צַדִּיק כַּתָּמָר יִפְרָח,
A righteous man will flourish like a date palm,

k'erez bal'vonōn yisge.   כְּאֶרֶז בַּלְּבָנוֹן יִשְׂגֶּה.
like a cedar in the Lebanon he will grow tall.

Sh'sulim b'vays Adōnoy,   שְׁתוּלִים בְּבֵית יהוה,
Planted in the House of HASHEM,

b'chatzrōs Elōhaynu yaf-richu.   בְּחַצְרוֹת אֱלֹהֵינוּ יַפְרִיחוּ.
in the Courtyards of our God they will flourish.

Ōd y'nuvun b'sayvo,   עוֹד יְנוּבוּן בְּשֵׂיבָה,
They will still be fruitful in old age,

d'shaynim v'ra-ananim yih-yu.   דְּשֵׁנִים וְרַעֲנַנִּים יִהְיוּ.
vigorous and fresh they will be —

L'hagid ki yoshor Adōnoy,   לְהַגִּיד כִּי יָשָׁר יהוה,
to declare that HASHEM is just,

tzuri v'lō avloso bō.   צוּרִי וְלֹא עַוְלָתָה בּוֹ.
my Rock in Whom there is no wrong.

■ Psalm 93: This is a continuation of the previous theme that God's greatness will be recognized by all in the Messianic Era. It spans all of time by describing Hashem in His full grandeur at the completion of Creation, and His "dressing" Himself like a person adorned in special Shabbos clothing.

ADŌNOY MOLOCH gay-us lovaysh,   יהוה מָלָךְ גֵּאוּת לָבֵשׁ,
Hashem will have reigned, He will have donned grandeur;

lovaysh Adōnoy ōz his-azor,   לָבֵשׁ יהוה עֹז הִתְאַזָּר,
HASHEM will have donned might and girded Himself;

af tikōn tayvayl bal timōt.   אַף תִּכּוֹן תֵּבֵל בַּל תִּמּוֹט.
even firmed the world that it should not falter.

Nochōn kis-acho may-oz,   נָכוֹן כִּסְאֲךָ מֵאָז,
may-ōlom oto.   מֵעוֹלָם אָתָּה.
Your throne was established from of old; eternal are You.

Nos'u n'horōs Adōnoy,   נָשְׂאוּ נְהָרוֹת יהוה,
Like rivers they raised, O HASHEM,

nos'u n'horōs kōlom,
נָשְׂאוּ נְהָרוֹת קוֹלָם,

like rivers they raised their voice;

yis-u n'horōs dochyom.
יִשְׂאוּ נְהָרוֹת דָּכְיָם.

like rivers they shall raise their destructiveness.

❖ Mikōlōs ma-yim rabim
❖ מִקֹּלוֹת מַיִם רַבִּים

More than the roars of many waters,

adirim mishb'ray yom,
אַדִּירִים מִשְׁבְּרֵי יָם,

mightier than the waves of the sea,

adir bamorōm Adōnoy.
אַדִּיר בַּמָּרוֹם יהוה.

HASHEM is mighty on high.

Aydōsecho ne-emnu m'ōd
עֵדֹתֶיךָ נֶאֶמְנוּ מְאֹד

Your testimonies are exceedingly trustworthy

l'vays'cho no-avo kōdesh,
לְבֵיתְךָ נָאֲוָה קֹדֶשׁ,

about Your House, the Sacred Dwelling —

Adōnoy, l'ōrech yomim.
יהוה לְאֹרֶךְ יָמִים.

O HASHEM, may it be for lengthy days.

ON ALL DAYS CONTINUE HERE.

■ I sing in anticipation of the time when the kingship, honor and glory of Hashem will be manifested by man's noble ways.

Y'HI CH'VŌD Adōnoy l'ōlom,
יְהִי כְבוֹד יהוה לְעוֹלָם,

May the glory of HASHEM* endure forever,

yismach Adōnoy b'ma-asov.
יִשְׂמַח יהוה בְּמַעֲשָׂיו.

let HASHEM rejoice in His works.

Y'hi shaym Adōnoy m'vōroch,
יְהִי שֵׁם יהוה מְבֹרָךְ,

Blessed be the Name of HASHEM,

may-ato v'ad ōlom.
מֵעַתָּה וְעַד עוֹלָם.

from this time and forever.

Mimizrach shemesh ad m'vō-ō,
מִמִּזְרַח שֶׁמֶשׁ עַד מְבוֹאוֹ,

From the rising of the sun to its setting,

m'hulol shaym Adōnoy.
מְהֻלָּל שֵׁם יהוה.

HASHEM's Name is praised.

יְהִי כְבוֹד ה׳ — *May the glory of HASHEM.* This is a collection of verses, primarily from *Psalms*, that revolves around two themes: the sovereignty of God and the role of Israel. Central to prayer and to the purpose of Creation is the Kingship of Heaven, which means that every being exists as part of God's plan and is dedicated to His service. This idea is found in nature itself, for, as the Psalmist says lyrically, man attains awareness of God when he contemplates the beauty and perfection of the universe. The last five verses speak of God's selec-

Rom al kol gō-yim Adōnoy,　　　רָם עַל כָּל גּוֹיִם יהוה,

High above all nations is HASHEM,

al ha-shoma-yim k'vōdō.　　　עַל הַשָּׁמַיִם כְּבוֹדוֹ.

above the heavens is His glory.

Adōnoy shimcho l'ōlom,　　　יהוה שִׁמְךָ לְעוֹלָם,

"HASHEM" is Your Name forever,

Adōnoy zichr'cho l'dōr vodōr.　　　יהוה זִכְרְךָ לְדֹר וָדֹר.

"HASHEM" is Your memorial throughout the generations.

Adōnoy ba-shoma-yim haychin kis-ō,　　　יהוה בַּשָּׁמַיִם הֵכִין כִּסְאוֹ,

HASHEM has established His throne in the heavens,

u-malchusō bakōl mosholo.　　　וּמַלְכוּתוֹ בַּכֹּל מָשָׁלָה.

and His kingdom reigns over all.

Yism'chu hashoma-yim　　　יִשְׂמְחוּ הַשָּׁמַיִם

v'sogayl ho-oretz,　　　וְתָגֵל הָאָרֶץ,

The heavens will be glad and the earth will rejoice,

v'yōm'ru vagō-yim Adōnoy moloch.　　　וְיֹאמְרוּ בַגּוֹיִם יהוה מָלָךְ.

they will proclaim among the nations, "HASHEM has reigned!"

Adōnoy melech, Adōnoy moloch,　　　יהוה מֶלֶךְ, יהוה מָלָךְ,

HASHEM reigns, HASHEM has reigned,

Adōnoy yimlōch l'ōlom vo-ed.　　　יהוה יִמְלֹךְ לְעֹלָם וָעֶד.

HASHEM shall reign for all eternity.*

Adōnoy melech ōlom vo-ed,　　　יהוה מֶלֶךְ עוֹלָם וָעֶד,

HASHEM reigns forever and ever,

ov'du gō-yim may-artzō.　　　אָבְדוּ גוֹיִם מֵאַרְצוֹ.

when the nations will have perished from His earth.*

Adōnoy hayfir atzas gō-yim,　　　יהוה הֵפִיר עֲצַת גּוֹיִם,

HASHEM annuls the counsel of nations,

hayni machsh'vōs amim.　　　הֵנִיא מַחְשְׁבוֹת עַמִּים.

He balks the designs of peoples.

Rabōs machashovōs b'lev ish,　　　רַבּוֹת מַחֲשָׁבוֹת בְּלֶב אִישׁ,

Many designs are in man's heart,

---

tion of the Jewish people and pleads for His mercy and attentiveness to their prayers.

ה׳ מֶלֶךְ ... — *HASHEM reigns, HASHEM has reigned, HASHEM shall reign for all eternity.* This is one of the most familiar verses in the entire liturgy, but, surprisingly enough, it is not found in Scripture. Rather, each phrase

comes from a different part of Scripture. In combination, the three phrases express the eternity of God's reign.

אָבְדוּ גוֹיִם מֵאַרְצוֹ — *When the nations will have perished from His earth.* The verse refers only to the *evil* people among the nations, for their deeds prevent others from acknowledging God.

va-atzas Adōnoy hi sokum.   וַעֲצַת יהוה הִיא תָקוּם.
but the counsel of HASHEM — only it will prevail.

Atzas Adōnoy l'ōlom ta-amōd,   עֲצַת יהוה לְעוֹלָם תַּעֲמֹד,
The counsel of HASHEM will endure forever,

machsh'vōs libō l'dōr vodōr.   מַחְשְׁבוֹת לִבּוֹ לְדֹר וָדֹר.
the designs of His heart throughout the generations.

Ki hu omar va-yehi,   כִּי הוּא אָמַר וַיֶּהִי,
hu tzivo va-ya-amōd.   הוּא צִוָּה וַיַּעֲמֹד.
For He spoke and it came to be; He commanded and it stood firm.

Ki vochar Adōnoy b'tziyōn,   כִּי בָחַר יהוה בְּצִיּוֹן,
ivoh l'mōshov lō.   אִוָּהּ לְמוֹשָׁב לוֹ.
For God selected Zion, He desired it for His dwelling place.

Ki ya-akōv bochar lō Yoh,   כִּי יַעֲקֹב בָּחַר לוֹ יָהּ,
yisro-ayl lisgulosō.   יִשְׂרָאֵל לִסְגֻלָּתוֹ.
For God selected Jacob as His own, Israel as His treasure.

Ki lō yitōsh Adōnoy amō,   כִּי לֹא יִטֹּשׁ יהוה עַמּוֹ,
For HASHEM will not cast off His people,

v'nachalosō lō ya-azōv.   וְנַחֲלָתוֹ לֹא יַעֲזֹב.
nor will He forsake His heritage.

V'hu rachum y'chapayr ovōn   ❖ וְהוּא רַחוּם יְכַפֵּר עָוֹן
v'lō yashchis,   וְלֹא יַשְׁחִית,
He, the Merciful One, is forgiving of iniquity and does not destroy;

v'hirbo l'hoshiv apō,   וְהִרְבָּה לְהָשִׁיב אַפּוֹ,
frequently He withdraws His anger,

v'lō yo-ir kol chamosō.   וְלֹא יָעִיר כָּל חֲמָתוֹ.
not arousing His entire rage.

Adōnoy hōshi-o,   יהוה הוֹשִׁיעָה,
HASHEM, save!

hamelech ya-anaynu v'yōm koraynu.   הַמֶּלֶךְ יַעֲנֵנוּ בְיוֹם קָרְאֵנוּ.
May the King answer us on the day we call.

■ The alphabetic acrostic of *Ashrei* motivates the supplicant to praise God, His Kingship, and His providing the needs of every living creature. The Sages highlight the importance of *Ashrei* by declaring that whoever recites this psalm three times daily is directing himself towards meriting a place in the World to Come (*Berachos* 4b).

ASHRAY YŌSH'VAY vay-secho,   אַשְׁרֵי יוֹשְׁבֵי בֵיתֶךָ,
Praiseworthy* are those who dwell in Your house;

ōd y'hal'lucho selo.

עוֹד יְהַלְלוּךְ סֶּלָה.

may they always praise You, Selah!

Ashray ho-om shekocho lō,

אַשְׁרֵי הָעָם שֶׁכָּכָה לּוֹ,

Praiseworthy is the people for whom this is so,

ashray ho-om she-Adōnoy Elōhov.

אַשְׁרֵי הָעָם שֶׁיהוה אֱלֹהָיו.

praiseworthy is the people whose God is HASHEM.

T'hilo l'dovid,

תְּהִלָּה לְדָוִד,

A psalm of praise by David.

arōmimcho Elōhai hamelech,

אֲרוֹמִמְךָ אֱלוֹהַי הַמֶּלֶךְ,

I will exalt You, my God the King,

va-avor'cho shimcho l'ōlom vo-ed.

וַאֲבָרְכָה שִׁמְךָ לְעוֹלָם וָעֶד.

and I will bless Your Name forever and ever.

B'chol yōm avor'cheko,

בְּכָל יוֹם אֲבָרְכֶךָ,

Every day I will bless You,

va-ahal'lo shimcho l'ōlom vo-ed.

וַאֲהַלְלָה שִׁמְךָ לְעוֹלָם וָעֶד.

and I will laud Your Name forever and ever.

Godōl Adōnoy umhulol m'ōd,

גָּדוֹל יהוה וּמְהֻלָּל מְאֹד,

HASHEM is great and exceedingly lauded,

v'ligdulosō ayn chayker.

וְלִגְדֻלָּתוֹ אֵין חֵקֶר.

and His greatness is beyond investigation.

Dōr l'dōr y'shabach ma-asecho,

דּוֹר לְדוֹר יְשַׁבַּח מַעֲשֶׂיךָ,

Each generation will praise Your deeds to the next,

ugvurōsecho yagidu.

וּגְבוּרֹתֶיךָ יַגִּידוּ.

and of Your mighty deeds they will tell.

Hadar k'vōd hōdecho,

הֲדַר כְּבוֹד הוֹדֶךָ,

The splendrous glory of Your power

v'divray nifl'ōsecho osicho.

וְדִבְרֵי נִפְלְאֹתֶיךָ אָשִׂיחָה.

and Your wondrous deeds I shall discuss.

Ve-ezuz nōr'ōsecho yōmayru,

וֶעֱזוּז נוֹרְאֹתֶיךָ יֹאמֵרוּ,

And of Your awesome power they will speak,

ugdulos'cho asap'reno.

וּגְדוּלָּתְךָ אֲסַפְּרֶנָּה.

and Your greatness I shall relate.

Zecher rav tuv'cho yabi-u,

זֵכֶר רַב טוּבְךָ יַבִּיעוּ,

A recollection of Your abundant goodness they will utter,

v'tzidkos'cho y'ranaynu.

וְצִדְקָתְךָ יְרַנֵּנוּ.

and of Your righteousness they will sing exultantly.

Chanun v'rachum Adōnoy,

חַנּוּן וְרַחוּם יהוה,

Gracious and merciful is HASHEM,

erech apa-yim ugdol chosed.

אֶרֶךְ אַפַּיִם וּגְדָל חָסֶד.

slow to anger, and great in [bestowing] kindness.

Tōv Adōnoy lakōl,

טוֹב יהוה לַכֹּל,

HASHEM is good to all,

v'rachamov al kol ma-asov.

וְרַחֲמָיו עַל כָּל מַעֲשָׂיו.

and His mercies are on all His works.

Yōducho Adōnoy kol ma-asecho,

יוֹדוּךָ יהוה כָּל מַעֲשֶׂיךָ,

All Your works shall thank You, HASHEM,

vachasidecho y'vor'chucho.

וַחֲסִידֶיךָ יְבָרְכוּכָה.

and Your devout ones will bless You.

K'vōd malchus'cho yōmayru,

כְּבוֹד מַלְכוּתְךָ יֹאמֵרוּ,

Of the glory of Your kingdom they will speak,

ugvuros'cho y'dabayru.

וּגְבוּרָתְךָ יְדַבֵּרוּ.

and of Your power they will tell,

L'hōdi-a livnay ho-odom
g'vurōsov,

לְהוֹדִיעַ לִבְנֵי הָאָדָם
גְּבוּרֹתָיו,

to inform human beings of His mighty deeds,

uchvōd hadar malchusō.

וּכְבוֹד הֲדַר מַלְכוּתוֹ.

and the glorious splendor of His kingdom.

Malchus'cho
   malchus kol ōlomim,

מַלְכוּתְךָ
מַלְכוּת כָּל עֹלָמִים,

Your kingdom is a kingdom spanning all eternities,

u-memshalt'cho b'chol dōr vodōr.

וּמֶמְשַׁלְתְּךָ בְּכָל דּוֹר וָדֹר.

and Your dominion is throughout every generation.

Sōmaych Adōnoy l'chol hanōf'lim,

סוֹמֵךְ יהוה לְכָל הַנֹּפְלִים,

HASHEM supports all the fallen ones

v'zōkayf l'chol hak'fufim.

וְזוֹקֵף לְכָל הַכְּפוּפִים.

and straightens all the bent.

Aynay chōl aylecho y'sabayru,

עֵינֵי כֹל אֵלֶיךָ יְשַׂבֵּרוּ,

The eyes of all look to You with hope

v'ato nōsayn lohem
   es ochlom b'itō.

וְאַתָּה נוֹתֵן לָהֶם
אֶת אָכְלָם בְּעִתּוֹ.

and You give them their food in its proper time.

CONCENTRATE INTENTLY WHILE RECITING THE NEXT VERSE.

Pōsay-ach es yodecho, פּוֹתֵחַ אֶת יָדֶךָ,

u-masbi-a l'chol chai rotzōn. וּמַשְׂבִּיעַ לְכָל חַי רָצוֹן.

You open Your hand, and satisfy the desire of every living thing.

Tzadik Adōnoy b'chol d'rochov, צַדִּיק יהוה בְּכָל דְּרָכָיו,

Righteous is HASHEM *in all His ways*

v'chosid b'chol ma-asov. וְחָסִיד בְּכָל מַעֲשָׂיו.

and magnanimous in all His deeds.

Korōv Adōnoy l'chol kōr'ov, קָרוֹב יהוה לְכָל קֹרְאָיו,

HASHEM *is close to all who call upon Him —*

l'chōl asher yikro-uhu ve-emes. לְכֹל אֲשֶׁר יִקְרָאֻהוּ בֶאֱמֶת.

to all who call upon Him sincerely.

R'tzōn y'ray-ov ya-ase, רְצוֹן יְרֵאָיו יַעֲשֶׂה,

The will of those who fear Him He will do,

v'es shav-osom yishma v'yōshi-aym. וְאֶת שַׁוְעָתָם יִשְׁמַע וְיוֹשִׁיעֵם.

and their cry He will hear, and save them.

Shōmayr Adōnoy es kol ōhavov, שׁוֹמֵר יהוה אֶת כָּל אֹהֲבָיו,

HASHEM *protects all who love Him,*

v'ays kol hor'sho-im yashmid. וְאֵת כָּל הָרְשָׁעִים יַשְׁמִיד.

but all the wicked He will destroy.

❖ T'hilas Adōnoy y'daber pi, ❖ תְּהִלַּת יהוה יְדַבֶּר פִּי,

May my mouth declare the praise of HASHEM

vi-voraych kol bosor shaym kodshō וִיבָרֵךְ כָּל בָּשָׂר שֵׁם קָדְשׁוֹ

l'ōlom vo-ed. לְעוֹלָם וָעֶד.

and may all flesh bless His Holy Name forever and ever.

Va-anachnu n'voraych Yoh, וַאֲנַחְנוּ נְבָרֵךְ יָהּ,

We will bless God

may-ato v'ad ōlom, hal'luyoh מֵעַתָּה וְעַד עוֹלָם, הַלְלוּיָהּ.

from this time and forever. Praise God!

■ Psalm 146: I recognize that You alone can address my material and emotional needs.

HAL'LUYOH, הַלְלוּיָהּ,

Praise God!

hal'li nafshi es Adōnoy. הַלְלִי נַפְשִׁי אֶת יהוה.

Praise HASHEM, *O my soul!**

הַלְלוּיָהּ הַלְלִי נַפְשִׁי אֶת ה׳ — *Praise God! Praise* HASHEM, *O my soul!* Psalm 146 is a a hymn of encouragement for Jews in exile. It begins with the Psalmist insisting that he will praise God as long as he lives and warning his fellow Jews not to rely on human beings. After describing

Ahal'lo Adōnoy b'cha-yoy,
אֲהַלְלָה יהוה בְּחַיָּי,

I will praise HASHEM while I live,

azam'ro Laylōhai b'ōdi.
אֲזַמְּרָה לֵאלֹהַי בְּעוֹדִי.

I will make music to my God while I exist.

Al tivt'chu vindivim,
אַל תִּבְטְחוּ בִנְדִיבִים,

Do not rely on nobles,

B'ven odom she-ayn lō s'shu-o.
בְּבֶן אָדָם שֶׁאֵין לוֹ תְשׁוּעָה.

nor on a human being for he holds no salvation.

Taytzay ruchō, yoshuv l'admosō,
תֵּצֵא רוּחוֹ, יָשֻׁב לְאַדְמָתוֹ,

When his spirit departs he returns to his earth,

ba-yōm hahu ov'du eshtōnōsov.
בַּיּוֹם הַהוּא אָבְדוּ עֶשְׁתֹּנֹתָיו.

on that day his plans all perish.

Ashray she-Ayl ya-akōv b'ezrō,
אַשְׁרֵי שֶׁאֵל יַעֲקֹב בְּעֶזְרוֹ,

Praiseworthy is one whose help is Jacob's God,

sivrō al Adōnoy Elōhov.
שִׂבְרוֹ עַל יהוה אֱלֹהָיו.

whose hope is in HASHEM, his God.

Ō-se shoma-yim vo-oretz,
עֹשֶׂה שָׁמַיִם וָאָרֶץ,

He is the Maker of heaven and earth,

es ha-yom v'es kol asher bom,
אֶת הַיָּם וְאֶת כָּל אֲשֶׁר בָּם,

the sea and all that is in them,

hashōmayr emes l'ōlom.
הַשֹּׁמֵר אֱמֶת לְעוֹלָם.

Who safeguards truth forever.

Ō-se mishpot la-ashukim,
עֹשֶׂה מִשְׁפָּט לַעֲשׁוּקִים,

He does justice for the exploited;

nōsayn lechem lor'ayvim,
נֹתֵן לֶחֶם לָרְעֵבִים,

He gives bread to the hungry;

Adōnoy matir asurim.
יהוה מַתִּיר אֲסוּרִים.

HASHEM releases the bound.

Adōnoy pōkay-ach ivrim,
יהוה פֹּקֵחַ עִוְרִים,

HASHEM gives sight to the blind;

Adōnoy zōkayf k'fufim,
יהוה זֹקֵף כְּפוּפִים,

HASHEM straightens the bent;

Adōnoy ōhayv tzadikim.
יהוה אֹהֵב צַדִּיקִים.

HASHEM loves the righteous.

Adōnoy shōmayr es gayrim,
יהוה שֹׁמֵר אֶת גֵּרִים,

HASHEM protects strangers;

God as the One Who cares for the underprivileged and oppressed, the Psalmist concludes that God will reign forever — despite the current ascendancy of our enemies.

yosōm v'almono y'ōdayd,

יָתוֹם וְאַלְמָנָה יְעוֹדֵד,

orphan and widow He encourages;

v'derech r'sho-im y'avays.

וְדֶרֶךְ רְשָׁעִים יְעַוֵּת.

but the way of the wicked He contorts.

Yimlōch Adōnoy l'ōlom,

⸭ יִמְלֹךְ יהוה לְעוֹלָם,

HASHEM shall reign forever,

Elōha-yich tziyōn, l'dōr vodōr,

אֱלֹהַיִךְ צִיּוֹן, לְדֹר וָדֹר,

your God, O Zion, from generation to generation.

hal'luyoh

הַלְלוּיָהּ.

Praise God!

■ Psalm 147: I, as part of the Jewish people, praise Hashem for His ongoing redemption of Israel and for the Torah that emanates from Jerusalem.

HAL'LUYOH,   הַלְלוּיָהּ,

Praise God!

ki tōv zam'ro Elōhaynu,

כִּי טוֹב זַמְּרָה אֱלֹהֵינוּ,

For it is good* to make music to our God,

ki no-im novo s'hilo.

כִּי נָעִים נָאוָה תְהִלָּה.

for praise is pleasant and befitting.

Bōnay y'rushola-yim Adōnoy,

בּוֹנֵה יְרוּשָׁלַיִם יהוה,

The Builder of Jerusalem is HASHEM,

nidchay yisro-ayl y'chanays.

נִדְחֵי יִשְׂרָאֵל יְכַנֵּס.

the outcast of Israel He will gather in.

Horōfay lishvuray layv,

הָרוֹפֵא לִשְׁבוּרֵי לֵב,

He is the Healer of the brokenhearted,

umchabaysh l'atz'vōsom.

וּמְחַבֵּשׁ לְעַצְּבוֹתָם.

and the One Who binds up their sorrows.

Mōne mispor lakōchovim,

מוֹנֶה מִסְפָּר לַכּוֹכָבִים,

He counts the number of the stars,*

l'chulom shaymōs yikro.

לְכֻלָּם שֵׁמוֹת יִקְרָא.

to all of them He assigns names.

הַלְלוּיָהּ כִּי טוֹב — *Praise God. For it is good!* Psalm 147 continues the theme of redemption, placing its primary focus on Jerusalem, the center from which holiness, redemption, and Torah will emanate. In this sense, Jerusalem cannot be considered rebuilt until the Redemption, because the city's spiritual grandeur cannot be recaptured by mere architecture and growing numbers of people.

מוֹנֶה מִסְפָּר לַכּוֹכָבִים — *He counts the number of*

the stars. Having given the assurance that God will rebuild Jerusalem and gather in Israel with joy, the Psalmist then proceeds to illustrate God's ability to do so. The next series of verses catalogue His might, compassion, and attention to individual needs.

The stars number in the billions, but God is aware of each one and gives it a "name" that denotes its purpose in the universe. Thus, nothing goes unnoticed or unprovided for.

Godōl adōnaynu v'rav kō-ach,   גָּדוֹל אֲדוֹנֵינוּ וְרַב כֹּחַ,
Great is our Lord and abundant in strength,

lisvunosō ayn mispor.   לִתְבוּנָתוֹ אֵין מִסְפָּר.
His understanding is beyond calculation.

M'ōdayd anovim Adōnoy,   מְעוֹדֵד עֲנָוִים יהוה,
HASHEM encourages the humble,

mashpil r'sho-im aday oretz.   מַשְׁפִּיל רְשָׁעִים עֲדֵי אָרֶץ.
He lowers the wicked down to the ground.

enu Ladōnoy b'sōdo,   עֱנוּ לַיהוה בְּתוֹדָה,
Call out to HASHEM with thanks,

zam'ru Laylōhaynu b'chinōr.   זַמְּרוּ לֵאלֹהֵינוּ בְכִנּוֹר.
with the harp sing to our God —

Ham'chase shoma-yim b'ovim,   הַמְכַסֶּה שָׁמַיִם בְּעָבִים,
Who covers the heavens with clouds,

hamaychin lo-oretz motor,   הַמֵּכִין לָאָרֶץ מָטָר,
Who prepares rain for the earth,

hamatzmi-ach horim chotzir.   הַמַּצְמִיחַ הָרִים חָצִיר.
Who makes mountains sprout with grass.

Nōsayn livhaymo lachmoh,   נוֹתֵן לִבְהֵמָה לַחְמָהּ,
He gives to an animal its food,

livnay ōrayv asher yikro-u.   לִבְנֵי עֹרֵב אֲשֶׁר יִקְרָאוּ.
to young ravens that cry out.

Lō vigvuras hasus yechpotz,   לֹא בִגְבוּרַת הַסּוּס יֶחְפָּץ,
Not in the strength of the horse does He desire,

lō v'shōkay ha-ish yirtze.   לֹא בְשׁוֹקֵי הָאִישׁ יִרְצֶה.
and not in the legs of man does He favor.

Rōtze Adōnoy es y'ray-ov,   רוֹצֶה יהוה אֶת יְרֵאָיו,
HASHEM favors those who fear Him,

es ham'yachalim l'chasdō.   אֶת הַמְיַחֲלִים לְחַסְדּוֹ.
those who hope for His kindness.

Shab'chi y'rushola-yim es Adōnoy,   שַׁבְּחִי יְרוּשָׁלַיִם אֶת יהוה,
Praise HASHEM, O Jerusalem,

hal'li Elōha-yich tziyōn.   הַלְלִי אֱלֹהַיִךְ צִיּוֹן.
laud your God, O Zion.

Ki chizak b'richay sh'oro-yich,   כִּי חִזַּק בְּרִיחֵי שְׁעָרָיִךְ,
For He has strengthened the bars of your gates,

bayrach bona-yich b'kirbaych.   בֵּרַךְ בָּנַיִךְ בְּקִרְבֵּךְ.

and blessed your children in your midst.

Hasom g'vulaych sholōm,   הַשָּׂם גְּבוּלֵךְ שָׁלוֹם,

He Who makes your borders peaceful,

chaylev chitim yasbi-aych.   חֵלֶב חִטִּים יַשְׂבִּיעֵךְ.

and with the cream of the wheat He sates you;

Hashōlay-ach imrosō oretz,   הַשֹּׁלֵחַ אִמְרָתוֹ אָרֶץ,

He Who dispatches His utterance earthward;

ad m'hayro yorutz d'vorō.   עַד מְהֵרָה יָרוּץ דְּבָרוֹ.

how swiftly His commandment runs!

Hanōsayn sheleg katzomer,   הַנֹּתֵן שֶׁלֶג כַּצָּמֶר,

He Who gives snow like fleece,

k'fōr ko-ayfer y'fazayr.   כְּפוֹר כָּאֵפֶר יְפַזֵּר.

He scatters frost like ashes.

Mashlich karchō ch'fitim,   מַשְׁלִיךְ קַרְחוֹ כְפִתִּים,

He hurls His ice like crumbs —

lifnay korosō mi ya-amōd.   לִפְנֵי קָרָתוֹ מִי יַעֲמֹד.

before His cold, who can stand?

Yishlach d'vorō v'yamsaym,   יִשְׁלַח דְּבָרוֹ וְיַמְסֵם,

He issues His command and it melts them,*

yashayv ruchō yiz'lu mo-yim.   יַשֵּׁב רוּחוֹ יִזְּלוּ מָיִם.

He blows His wind — the waters flow.

❖ Magid d'vorov l'ya-akōv,   ❖ מַגִּיד דְּבָרָיו לְיַעֲקֹב,

He relates His Word to Jacob,*

chukov u-mishpotov l'yisro-ayl.   חֻקָּיו וּמִשְׁפָּטָיו לְיִשְׂרָאֵל.

His statutes and judgments to Israel.

Lō oso chayn l'chol gōy,   לֹא עָשָׂה כֵן לְכָל גּוֹי,

He did not do so for any other nation,

u-mishpotim bal y'do-um,   וּמִשְׁפָּטִים בַּל יְדָעוּם,

such judgments — they know them not.

hal'luyoh.   הַלְלוּיָהּ.

Praise God!

יִשְׁלַח דְּבָרוֹ וְיַמְסֵם — *He issues His command and it melts them.* The Psalmist had spoken of the many solid forms of moisture: snow, frost, ice — but at God's command, everything melts and flows like water. The Jew should emulate nature by conforming to the will of God.

מַגִּיד דְּבָרָיו לְיַעֲקֹב — *He relates His Word to*

Jacob. Lest you wonder at the many centuries that have gone by without the redemption of Jerusalem and Israel, do not forget that the Torah itself — the very purpose of Creation — was not given to man until 2448 years after Creation. That God sees fit to delay is no cause for despair.

■ Psalm 148: I sing in anticipation and excitement of the time when all the world will be imbued with the knowledge of Hashem.

HAL'LUYOH,
Praise God!

הַלְלוּיָהּ,

הַלְלוּ אֶת יהוה מִן הַשָּׁמַיִם,
hal'lu es Adōnoy min ha-shoma-yim,
Praise HASHEM from the heaven;*

הַלְלוּהוּ בַּמְּרוֹמִים.
hal'luhu bam'rōmim.
praise Him in the heights;

הַלְלוּהוּ כָל מַלְאָכָיו,
Hal'luhu chol mal-ochov,
praise Him, all His angels;

הַלְלוּהוּ כָּל צְבָאָיו.
hal'luhu kol tz'vo-ov.
praise Him, all His legions;*

הַלְלוּהוּ שֶׁמֶשׁ וְיָרֵחַ,
Hal'luhu shemesh v'yoray-ach,
praise Him, sun and moon;

הַלְלוּהוּ כָּל כּוֹכְבֵי אוֹר.
hal'luhu kol kōch'vay ōr.
praise Him, all bright stars;

הַלְלוּהוּ שְׁמֵי הַשָּׁמָיִם,
Hal'luhu sh'may ha-shomo-yim,
praise Him, the most exalted of the heavens

וְהַמַּיִם אֲשֶׁר מֵעַל הַשָּׁמָיִם.
v'hama-yim asher may-al ha-shomo-yim.
and the waters that are above the heavens.

יְהַלְלוּ אֶת שֵׁם יהוה,
Y'hal'lu es shaym Adōnoy,
Let them praise the Name of HASHEM,

כִּי הוּא צִוָּה וְנִבְרָאוּ.
ki hu tzivo v'nivro-u.
for He commanded and they were created.

וַיַּעֲמִידֵם לָעַד לְעוֹלָם,
Va-ya-amidaym lo-ad l'ōlom,
And He established them forever and ever,

חָק נָתַן וְלֹא יַעֲבוֹר.
chok nosan v'lō ya-avōr.
He issued a decree* that will not change.

הַלְלוּ אֶת יהוה מִן הָאָרֶץ,
Hal'lu es Adōnoy min ho-oretz,
Praise HASHEM from the earth,

תַּנִּינִים וְכָל תְּהֹמוֹת.
taninim v'chol t'hōmōs.
sea giants and all watery depths;

הַלְלוּיָהּ הַלְלוּ אֶת ה' מִן הַשָּׁמַיִם, — *Praise God! Praise HASHEM from the heavens.* The Psalmist begins by calling upon the heavenly beings to praise God, and then he directs his call to earthly beings. God's praises echo from the heavens and descend to earth, where the devout echo the heavenly songs with their own praises.

מַלְאָכָיו ... צְבָאָיו — *His angels ... His legions.* The *angels* are spiritual beings without physical form while the *legions* are the heavenly bodies, which are so numerous that they are likened to legions.

Aysh u-vorod, sheleg v'kitōr,　　אֵשׁ וּבָרָד, שֶׁלֶג וְקִיטוֹר,
fire and hail; snow and vapor;

ru-ach s'oro ōso d'vorō.　　רוּחַ סְעָרָה עֹשָׂה דְבָרוֹ.
stormy wind fulfilling His word;

Hehorim v'chol g'vo-ōs,　　הֶהָרִים וְכָל גְּבָעוֹת,
mountains and all hills;

aytz p'ri v'chol arozim.　　עֵץ פְּרִי וְכָל אֲרָזִים.
fruitful trees and all cedars;

Hacha-yo v'chol b'haymo,　　הַחַיָּה וְכָל בְּהֵמָה,
beasts and all cattle;

remes v'tzipōr konof.　　רֶמֶשׂ וְצִפּוֹר כָּנָף.
crawling things and winged fowl;

Malchay eretz v'chol l'umim,　　מַלְכֵי אֶרֶץ וְכָל לְאֻמִּים,
kings of the earth and all governments;

sorim v'chol shōf'tay oretz.　　שָׂרִים וְכָל שֹׁפְטֵי אָרֶץ.
princes and all judges on earth;

Bachurim v'gam b'sulōs,　　בַּחוּרִים וְגַם בְּתוּלוֹת,
young men and also maidens;*

z'kaynim im n'orim.　　זְקֵנִים עִם נְעָרִים.
old men together with youths.

❖ Y'hal'lu es shaym Adōnoy,　　❖ יְהַלְלוּ אֶת שֵׁם יהוה,
Let them praise the Name of HASHEM,

ki nisgov sh'mō l'vadō,　　כִּי נִשְׂגָּב שְׁמוֹ לְבַדּוֹ,
for His Name alone will have been exalted;

hōdō al eretz v'shomo-yim.　　הוֹדוֹ עַל אֶרֶץ וְשָׁמָיִם.
His glory is above earth and heaven.

Va-yorem keren l'amō,　　וַיָּרֶם קֶרֶן לְעַמּוֹ,
And He will have exalted the pride of His people,

t'hilo l'chol chasidov,　　תְּהִלָּה לְכָל חֲסִידָיו,
causing praise for all His devout ones,

livnay yisro-ayl am k'rōvō,　　לִבְנֵי יִשְׂרָאֵל עַם קְרֹבוֹ,
for the Children of Israel, His intimate people.

hal'luyoh.　　הַלְלוּיָהּ.
Praise God!

חָק נָתַן — *He issued a decree* that the sun shine by day and the moon by night, and this *decree* can never be violated.

בַּחוּרִים וְגַם בְּתוּלוֹת — *Young men and also maidens.* The use here of the word וְגַם, "and also," is noteworthy. The Psalmist does not say that

■ Psalm 149: I sing in anticipation of the ultimate redemption and Israel's triumph over the enemies of Hashem.

HAL'LUYOH,   הַלְלוּיָהּ,
Praise God!

shiru Ladōnoy shir chodosh,   שִׁירוּ לַיהוה שִׁיר חָדָשׁ,
Sing to HASHEM a new song, *

t'hilosō bikhal chasidim.   תְּהִלָּתוֹ בִּקְהַל חֲסִידִים.
let His praise be in the congregation of the devout.

Yismach yisro-ayl b'ōsov,   יִשְׂמַח יִשְׂרָאֵל בְּעֹשָׂיו,
Let Israel exult in its Maker,

b'nay tziyōn yogilu v'malkom.   בְּנֵי צִיּוֹן יָגִילוּ בְמַלְכָּם.
let the Children of Zion rejoice in their King.

Y'hal'lu sh'mō v'mochōl,   יְהַלְלוּ שְׁמוֹ בְמָחוֹל,
Let them praise His Name with dancing,

b'sōf v'chinōr y'zam'ru lō.   בְּתֹף וְכִנּוֹר יְזַמְּרוּ לוֹ.
with drums and harp let them make music to Him.

Ki rōtze Adōnoy b'amō,   כִּי רוֹצֶה יהוה בְּעַמּוֹ,
For HASHEM favors His people,

y'fo-ayr anovim bishu-o.   יְפָאֵר עֲנָוִים בִּישׁוּעָה.
He adorns the humble with salvation.

Ya-l'zu chasidim b'chovōd,   יַעְלְזוּ חֲסִידִים בְּכָבוֹד,
Let the devout exult in glory,

y'ran'nu al mishk'vōsom.   יְרַנְּנוּ עַל מִשְׁכְּבוֹתָם.
let them sing joyously upon their beds.

Rōm'mōs Ayl bigrōnom,   רוֹמְמוֹת אֵל בִּגְרוֹנָם,
The lofty praises of God are in their throats,

v'cherev pifiyōs b'yodom.   וְחֶרֶב פִּיפִיּוֹת בְּיָדָם.
and a double-edged sword is in their hand —

La-asōs n'komo bagōyim,   לַעֲשׂוֹת נְקָמָה בַּגּוֹיִם,
to execute vengeance among the nations,

tōchaychōs bal-umim.   תּוֹכֵחוֹת בַּלְאֻמִּים.
rebukes among the governments.

---

young men *and* women will be together, because such mingling would be immodest. Only later, when he speaks of old men and youths does the Psalmist say עִם, "with" — that they will be together.

הַלְלוּיָהּ שִׁירוּ לַה׳ — *Praise God! Sing to HASHEM a new song.* In every generation, God confronts us with new challenges and problems, yet He provides us with the opportunity to solve them. For this, our songs of praise never grow stale, because they are always infused with new meaning. But the greatest, newest song of all will spring from Israel's lips when history reaches its climax with the coming of Messiah.

❖ Lesōr malchayhem b'zikim,

לֶאְסֹר מַלְכֵיהֶם בְּזִקִּים,

To bind their kings with chains,

v'nichb'dayhem b'chavlay varzel.

וְנִכְבְּדֵיהֶם בְּכַבְלֵי בַרְזֶל.

and their nobles with fetters of iron;

La-asōs bohem mishpot kosuv,

לַעֲשׂוֹת בָּהֶם מִשְׁפָּט כָּתוּב,

to execute upon them written judgment — *

hodor hu l'chol chasidov,

הָדָר הוּא לְכָל חֲסִידָיו,

that will be the splendor of all His devout ones.

hal'luyoh.

הַלְלוּיָהּ.

Praise God!

■ Psalm 150: I conclude that the ultimate praise of Hashem can neither be articulated nor played on any instrument, but comes from the soul.

HAL'LUYOH,

הַלְלוּיָהּ,

Praise God!

hal'lu Ayl b'kodshō,

הַלְלוּ אֵל בְּקָדְשׁוֹ,

Praise God in His Sanctuary; *

hal'luhu birki-a uzō.

הַלְלוּהוּ בִּרְקִיעַ עֻזּוֹ.

praise Him in the firmament of His power.

Hal'luhu bigvurōsov,

הַלְלוּהוּ בִּגְבוּרֹתָיו,

Praise Him for His mighty acts;

hal'luhu k'rōv gudlō.

הַלְלוּהוּ כְּרֹב גֻּדְלוֹ.

praise Him as befits His abundant greatness.

Hal'luhu b'sayka shōfor,

הַלְלוּהוּ בְּתֵקַע שׁוֹפָר,

Praise Him with the blast of the shofar;

hal'luhu b'nayvel v'chinōr.

הַלְלוּהוּ בְּנֵבֶל וְכִנּוֹר.

praise Him with lyre and harp.

Hal'luhu b'sōf u-mochōl,

הַלְלוּהוּ בְּתֹף וּמָחוֹל,

Praise Him with drum and dance;

hal'luhu b'minim v'ugov.

הַלְלוּהוּ בְּמִנִּים וְעֻגָב.

praise Him with organ and flute.

Hal'luhu b'tziltz'lay shoma,

הַלְלוּהוּ בְּצִלְצְלֵי שָׁמַע,

Praise Him with clanging cymbals;

לַעֲשׂוֹת בָּהֶם מִשְׁפָּט כָּתוּב — *To execute upon them written judgment.* The future judgment upon the nations has been written in the Prophets. The execution of that judgment will bring the reign of justice to earth, and that will be the splendor — the pride and vindication — of the righteous who have always lived that way.

הַלְלוּיָהּ הַלְלוּ אֵל בְּקָדְשׁוֹ — *Praise God! Praise God*

in His Sanctuary. In this, the final psalm in the Book of *Psalms,* the Psalmist sums up his task by saying that man must enrich his spiritual self by recognizing God's greatness and kindness and by praising Him. The Psalmist's long list of musical instruments reflects the full spectrum of human emotions and spiritual potential, all of which can be aroused by music.

hal'luhu b'tziltz'lay s'ru-o.

הַלְלוּהוּ בְּצִלְצְלֵי תְרוּעָה.

praise Him with resonant trumpets.

Kōl han'shomo t'halayl Yoh

כֹּל הַנְּשָׁמָה תְּהַלֵּל יָהּ, ❖

Let all souls praise* God,

hal'luyoh.

הַלְלוּיָהּ.

Praise God!

Kōl han'shomo t'halayl Yoh

כֹּל הַנְּשָׁמָה תְּהַלֵּל יָהּ,

Let all souls praise God,

hal'luyoh.

הַלְלוּיָהּ.

Praise God!

BORUCH Adōnoy l'ōlom,

בָּרוּךְ יהוה לְעוֹלָם,

Blessed is HASHEM forever,

omayn v'omayn.

אָמֵן וְאָמֵן.

Amen and Amen.

Boruch Adōnoy mitziyōn,
   shōchayn y'rusholoyim,

בָּרוּךְ יהוה מִצִּיּוֹן,
שֹׁכֵן יְרוּשָׁלָיִם,

Blessed is HASHEM from Zion, Who dwells in Jerusalem.

hal'luyoh.

הַלְלוּיָהּ.

Praise God!

Boruch Adōnoy
   Elōhim Elōhay yisro-ayl,

בָּרוּךְ יהוה
אֱלֹהִים אֱלֹהֵי יִשְׂרָאֵל,

Blessed is HASHEM, God, the God of Israel,

ōsay niflo-ōs l'vadō.

עֹשֵׂה נִפְלָאוֹת לְבַדּוֹ.

Who alone does wonders.

U-voruch shaym k'vōdō l'ōlom,

וּבָרוּךְ שֵׁם כְּבוֹדוֹ לְעוֹלָם, ❖

Blessed is His glorious Name forever,

v'yimolay ch'vōdō es kol ho-oretz,

וְיִמָּלֵא כְבוֹדוֹ אֶת כָּל הָאָרֶץ,

and may all the earth be filled with His glory,

omayn v'omayn.

אָמֵן וְאָמֵן.

Amen and Amen.

■ I affirm, as did King David, that beyond the psalms of praise that I have offered, the personal circumstances of my life inspire me to further thank Hashem.

THE FOLLOWING IS RECITED WHILE STANDING:

VAIVORECH dovid es Adōnoy

וַיְבָרֶךְ דָּוִיד אֶת יהוה

And David blessed HASHEM*

כֹּל הַנְּשָׁמָה תְּהַלֵּל — *Let all souls praise.* Far greater than the most sublime instrumental songs of praise is the song of the human soul. God's greatest praise is the soul that utilizes its full potential in His service.

וַיְבָרֶךְ דָּוִיד — *And David blessed HASHEM.* The

first four verses of this prayer (*I Chronicles* 29:10-13) were uttered by David at one of the supreme moments of his life: Although he had been denied Divine permission to build the Holy Temple, he had assembled the necessary contributions and materials so that his heir,

l'aynay kol hakohol,   לְעֵינֵי כָּל הַקָּהָל,

in the presence of the entire congregation —

va-yōmer dovid: וַיֹּאמֶר דָּוִיד:

David said,

Boruch ato Adōnoy,   בָּרוּךְ אַתָּה יהוה,

"Blessed are You, HASHEM,

Elōhay yisro-ayl ovinu,   אֱלֹהֵי יִשְׂרָאֵל אָבִינוּ,

the God of Israel our forefather,

may-ōlom v'ad ōlom.   מֵעוֹלָם וְעַד עוֹלָם.

from this world to the World to Come.

L'cho Adōnoy hag'dulo   לְךָ יהוה הַגְּדֻלָּה

Yours, HASHEM, is the greatness,*

v'hag'vuro v'hatif-eres   וְהַגְּבוּרָה וְהַתִּפְאֶרֶת

the strength, the splendor,

v'hanaytzach v'hahōd,   וְהַנֵּצַח וְהַהוֹד,

the triumph, and the glory,

ki chōl ba-shoma-yim u-vo-oretz;   כִּי כֹל בַּשָּׁמַיִם וּבָאָרֶץ;

even everything in heaven and earth;

l'cho Adōnoy hamamlocho   לְךָ יהוה הַמַּמְלָכָה

Yours, HASHEM, is the kingdom,

v'hamisnasay l'chōl l'rōsh.   וְהַמִּתְנַשֵּׂא לְכֹל לְרֹאשׁ.

and the sovereignty over every leader.

V'ho-ōsher v'hakovōd mil'fonecho,   וְהָעֹשֶׁר וְהַכָּבוֹד מִלְּפָנֶיךָ,

Wealth and honor come from You

v'ato mōshayl bakōl,   וְאַתָּה מוֹשֵׁל בַּכֹּל,

and You rule everything —

uvyod'cho kō-ach ugvuro,   וּבְיָדְךָ כֹּחַ וּגְבוּרָה,

in Your hand is power and strength,

uvyod'cho l'gadayl ulchazayk lakōl.   וּבְיָדְךָ לְגַדֵּל וּלְחַזֵּק לַכֹּל.

and it is in Your hand to make anyone great or strong.

V'ato Elōhaynu   וְעַתָּה אֱלֹהֵינוּ

So now, our God,

mōdim anachnu loch,   מוֹדִים אֲנַחְנוּ לָךְ,

we thank You

Solomon, could be ready to build it upon assuming the throne. In the presence of the assembled congregation, he thanked and blessed God for having allowed him to set aside resources for the Divine service.

לְךָ ה׳ הַגְּדֻלָּה — *Yours, HASHEM, is the greatness.*

In his moment of public glory, David scrupulously made clear that his every achievement was made possible by God and that it was meant to be utilized in His service. Lest anyone think that his attainments are to his own credit, David proclaims that God is Master of

umhal'lim l'shaym tif-artecho.	וּמְהַלְלִים לְשֵׁם תִּפְאַרְתֶּךָ.
and praise Your splendrous Name.''	
Ato hu Adōnoy l'vadecho,	אַתָּה הוּא יהוה לְבַדֶּךָ,
*It is You alone, HASHEM,**	
ato osiso es ha-shoma-yim,	אַתָּה עָשִׂיתָ אֶת הַשָּׁמַיִם,
You have made the heaven,	
sh'may ha-shoma-yim v'chol tz'vo-om,	שְׁמֵי הַשָּׁמַיִם וְכָל צְבָאָם,
the most exalted heaven and all their legions,	
ho-oretz v'chol asher oleho,	הָאָרֶץ וְכָל אֲשֶׁר עָלֶיהָ,
the earth and everything upon it,	
ha-yamim v'chol asher bohem,	הַיַּמִּים וְכָל אֲשֶׁר בָּהֶם,
the seas and everything in them,	
v'ato m'cha-ye es kulom,	וְאַתָּה מְחַיֶּה אֶת כֻּלָּם,
*and You give them all life;**	
utzvo ha-shoma-yim	וּצְבָא הַשָּׁמַיִם
l'cho mishta-chavim.	לְךָ מִשְׁתַּחֲוִים.
and the heavenly legions bow to You.	
Ato hu Adōnoy ho-Elōhim	❖ אַתָּה הוּא יהוה הָאֱלֹהִים
It is You, HASHEM, the God	
asher bocharto b'avrom,	אֲשֶׁר בָּחַרְתָּ בְּאַבְרָם,
*Who selected Abram,**	
v'hōtzaysō may-ur kasdim,	וְהוֹצֵאתוֹ מֵאוּר כַּשְׂדִּים,
and You brought him out of Ur Kasdim	
v'samto sh'mō avrohom.	וְשַׂמְתָּ שְּׁמוֹ אַבְרָהָם.
*and You made his name Abraham.**	
U-motzoso es l'vovō	וּמָצָאתָ אֶת לְבָבוֹ
ne-emon l'fonecho —	נֶאֱמָן לְפָנֶיךָ —
You found his heart faithful before You —	

---

everything in heaven and earth and, because He has "sovereignty over every leader," He decrees who shall gain high positions and who shall be toppled.

אַתָּה הוּא ה' לְבַדֶּךָ — *It is You alone, HASHEM.* The next six verses (*Nechemiah* 9:6-1) were recited by the people, led by the Levites, the day after the newly returned Jews had completed their first Succos festival in Jerusalem after returning from their Babylonian exile. They gathered in devotion and repentance and echoed the resolve voiced by David nearly five hundred years earlier.

וְאַתָּה מְחַיֶּה אֶת כֻּלָּם — *And You give them all life.*

Even inanimate objects have "life" in the sense that they have whatever conditions are necessary for their continued existence.

אֲשֶׁר בָּחַרְתָּ בְּאַבְרָם — *Who selected Abram.* After cataloguing the endless array of Creation and its components, we acknowledge that from them all, God chose Abraham and his offspring as His chosen ones — an astonishing testimony to the first Patriarch and the nation he founded.

וְשַׂמְתָּ שְּׁמוֹ אַבְרָהָם — *And You made his name Abraham.* The change of name signified that Abram's mission had been changed and elevated. His original name — Abram — means "father of Aram," because he had been a spiri-

— V'CHORŌS imō hab'ris   **וְכָרוֹת** עִמּוֹ הַבְּרִית

and You established the covenant with him

losays es eretz hak'na-ani   לָתֵת אֶת אֶרֶץ הַכְּנַעֲנִי

to give the land of the Canaanite,

ha-chiti ho-emōri v'hap'rizi,   הַחִתִּי הָאֱמֹרִי וְהַפְּרִזִּי

v'haivusi v'hagirgoshi,   וְהַיְבוּסִי וְהַגִּרְגָּשִׁי,

Hittite, Emorite, Perizzite, Jebusite, and Girgashite,

losays l'zar-ō,   לָתֵת לְזַרְעוֹ,

to give it to his offspring;

vatokem es d'vorecho,   וַתָּקֶם אֶת דְּבָרֶיךָ,

ki tzadik oto.   כִּי צַדִּיק אָתָּה.

and You affirmed Your word, for You are righteous.

Vatayre es oni avōsaynu   וַתֵּרֶא אֶת עֳנִי אֲבֹתֵינוּ

b'mitzroyim,   בְּמִצְרָיִם,

You observed the suffering of our forefathers in Egypt,

v'es za-akosom shomato   וְאֶת זַעֲקָתָם שָׁמַעְתָּ

al yam suf.   עַל יַם סוּף.

and their outcry You heard at the Sea of Reeds.

Vatitayn ōsōs umōf'sim b'far-ō   וַתִּתֵּן אֹתֹת וּמֹפְתִים בְּפַרְעֹה

You imposed signs and wonders upon Pharaoh

uvchol avodov uvchol am artzō,   וּבְכָל עֲבָדָיו וּבְכָל עַם אַרְצוֹ,

and upon all his servants, and upon all the people of his land.

ki yodato ki hayzidu alayhem,   כִּי יָדַעְתָּ כִּי הֵזִידוּ עֲלֵיהֶם,

For You knew that they sinned willfully* against them,

vata-as l'cho shaym k'ha-yōm ha-ze.   וַתַּעַשׂ לְךָ שֵׁם כְּהַיּוֹם הַזֶּה.

and You brought Yourself renown as [clear as] this very day.

❖ V'ha-yom bokato lifnayhem,   ❖ וְהַיָּם בָּקַעְתָּ לִפְנֵיהֶם,

You split the Sea before them

va-ya-avru v'sōch ha-yom ba-yabosho,   וַיַּעַבְרוּ בְתוֹךְ הַיָּם בַּיַּבָּשָׁה,

and they crossed in the midst of the Sea on dry land;

v'es rōd'fayhem   וְאֶת רֹדְפֵיהֶם

hishlachto vimtzōlōs,   הִשְׁלַכְתָּ בִמְצוֹלֹת,

but their pursuers You hurled into the depths,

k'mō even b'ma-yim azim.   כְּמוֹ אֶבֶן בְּמַיִם עַזִּים.

like a stone into turbulent waters.

---

tual father of his native Aram. The new name — Abraham — means "father of a multitude [of nations]," marking him as the spiritual

mentor of all mankind.

כִּי הֵזִידוּ — *That they sinned willfully.* The Egyptians sinned against the Jews by mistreating

■ Each day I repeat the Song recited by Moses and Israel at the Splitting of the Sea of Reeds. In addition to my appreciation of Hashem in the natural world order, my recognition of His performing miraculous events constitutes the full praise of Hashem.

VA-YŌSHA Adōnoy ba-yōm hahu   וַיּוֹשַׁע יהוה בַּיּוֹם הַהוּא
Hashem saved * — *on that day* —

es yisro-ayl mi-yad mitzro-yim,   אֶת יִשְׂרָאֵל מִיַּד מִצְרָיִם,
Israel from the hand of Egypt,

va-yar yisro-ayl es mitzra-yim   וַיַּרְא יִשְׂרָאֵל אֶת מִצְרַיִם
and Israel saw the Egyptians

mays al s'fas ha-yom.   מֵת עַל שְׂפַת הַיָּם.
dead on the seashore.

Va-yar yisro-ayl   ❖ וַיַּרְא יִשְׂרָאֵל
Israel saw

es ha-yod hag'dōlo   אֶת הַיָּד הַגְּדֹלָה
the great hand

asher oso Adōnoy b'mitzra-yim,   אֲשֶׁר עָשָׂה יהוה בְּמִצְרַיִם,
that Hashem inflicted upon Egypt

va-yir'u ho-om es Adōnoy,   וַיִּירְאוּ הָעָם אֶת יהוה,
and the people feared Hashem,

va-ya-aminu Badōnoy   וַיַּאֲמִינוּ בַּיהוה
and they had faith in Hashem

uvmōshe avdō.   וּבְמֹשֶׁה עַבְדּוֹ.
and in Moses, His servant.

OZ YOSHIR mōshe uvnay yisro-ayl   אָז יָשִׁיר מֹשֶׁה וּבְנֵי יִשְׂרָאֵל
Then Moses and the Children of Israel chose to sing

es ha-shiro ha-zōs Ladōnoy,   אֶת הַשִּׁירָה הַזֹּאת לַיהוה,
this song to Hashem,

va-yōm'ru laymōr,   וַיֹּאמְרוּ לֵאמֹר,
and they said the following:

oshiro Ladōnoy ki go-ō go-o,   אָשִׁירָה לַיהוה כִּי גָאֹה גָּאָה,
I shall sing to Hashem for He is exalted above the arrogant,

sus v'rōch'vō romo va-yom.   סוּס וְרֹכְבוֹ רָמָה בַיָּם.
having hurled horse with its rider into the sea.

---

and enslaving them. Had the servitude not been so harsh and hatefully cruel, the Egyptians would not have suffered such devastation.

וַיּוֹשַׁע ה׳ — *Hashem saved.* In these two verses the Torah sums up the miracle at the Sea as a prelude to Moses' song. The miracles of the Exodus, beginning with the Ten Plagues, illus-

trate that God controls every facet of nature at will. Thus, they remain the testimony to God as the all-powerful Creator: No human being saw the Creation of the universe, but millions of Jews witnessed the Exodus. The climax of those miraculous events was the Splitting of the Sea, an event celebrated by Moses and the

Ozi v'zimros Yoh vai-hi li lishu-o, עָזִּי וְזִמְרָת יָהּ וַיְהִי לִי לִישׁוּעָה,

God is my might and my praise, and He was a salvation for me.

ze Ayli v'anvayhu, זֶה אֵלִי וְאַנְוֵהוּ,

This is my God,* and I will build Him a Sanctuary;

Elōhay ovi va-arōm'menhu. אֱלֹהֵי אָבִי וַאֲרֹמְמֶנְהוּ.

the God of my father, and I will exalt Him.

Adōnoy ish milchomo Adōnoy sh'mō. יהוה אִישׁ מִלְחָמָה, יהוה שְׁמוֹ.

HASHEM is Master of war, through His Name HASHEM.*

Mark'vōs par-ō v'chaylō yoro va-yom, מַרְכְּבֹת פַּרְעֹה וְחֵילוֹ יָרָה בַיָּם,

Pharaoh's chariots and army He threw into the sea;

u-mivchar sholishov tub'u v'yam-suf. וּמִבְחַר שָׁלִשָׁיו טֻבְּעוּ בְיַם־סוּף.

and the pick of his officers were mired in the Sea of Reeds.

T'hōmōs y'chasyumu, תְּהֹמֹת יְכַסְיֻמוּ,

Deep waters covered them;

yor'du vimtzōlōs k'mō oven. יָרְדוּ בִמְצוֹלֹת כְּמוֹ אָבֶן.

they descended in the depths like stone.

Y'min'cho Adōnoy nedori bakō-ach, יְמִינְךָ יהוה נֶאְדָּרִי בַּכֹּחַ,

Your right hand,* HASHEM, is adorned with strength;

Y'min'cho Adōnoy tir-atz ōyayv. יְמִינְךָ יהוה תִּרְעַץ אוֹיֵב.

Your right hand, HASHEM, smashes the enemy.

Uvrōv g'ōn'cho taharōs komecho, וּבְרֹב גְּאוֹנְךָ תַּהֲרֹס קָמֶיךָ,

In Your abundant grandeur You shatter Your opponents;

t'shalach charōn'cho תְּשַׁלַּח חֲרֹנְךָ

yōch'laymō kakash. יֹאכְלֵמוֹ כַּקַּשׁ.

You dispatch Your wrath, it consumes them like straw.

Uvru-ach apecho ne-ermu ma-yim, וּבְרוּחַ אַפֶּיךָ נֶעֶרְמוּ מַיִם,

At a blast from Your nostrils the waters were heaped up;

nitz'vu ch'mō nayd nōz'lim, נִצְּבוּ כְמוֹ נֵד נֹזְלִים,

straight as a wall stood the running water,

kof'u s'hōmōs b'lev yom. קָפְאוּ תְהֹמֹת בְּלֶב יָם.

the deep waters congealed in the heart of the sea.

Omar ōyayv, אָמַר אוֹיֵב,

The enemy declared:

---

entire nation in the glorious Song of the Sea (*Exodus* 14:30-15:19).

זֶה אֵלִי — *This is my God.* So obvious was God's presence that the Jews could point to it, as it were, and say, "This is my God."

ה' שְׁמוֹ — *Through His Name HASHEM.* Mortal kings require legions and armaments, but God overcomes His enemies with nothing more than His Name.

יְמִינְךָ — *Your right hand.* Of course God has no "hand" or any other physical characteristic. All the many Scriptural references to physical-

erdōf asig achalayk sholol,   אֶרְדֹּף אַשִּׂיג אֲחַלֵּק שָׁלָל,

"I will pursue, I will overtake, I will divide plunder;

timlo-aymō nafshi,   תִּמְלָאֵמוֹ נַפְשִׁי,

I will satisfy my lust with them;

orik charbi, tōrishaymō yodi.   אָרִיק חַרְבִּי, תּוֹרִישֵׁמוֹ יָדִי.

I will unsheathe my sword, my hand will impoverish them."

Noshafto v'ruchacho kisomō yom,   נָשַׁפְתָּ בְרוּחֲךָ כִּסָּמוֹ יָם,

You blew with Your wind — the sea enshrouded them;

tzol'lu ka-ōferes b'ma-yim, adirim.   צָלְלוּ כַּעוֹפֶרֶת בְּמַיִם, אַדִּירִים.

the mighty ones sank like lead in the waters.

Mi chomōcho bo-aylim Adōnoy,   מִי כָמֹכָה בָּאֵלִם יהוה,

Who is like You among the heavenly powers, HASHEM!

mi komōcho nedor bakōdesh,   מִי כָּמֹכָה נֶאְדָּר בַּקֹּדֶשׁ,

Who is like You, mighty in holiness,

nōro s'hilōs ōsay fele.   נוֹרָא תְהִלֹּת עֹשֵׂה פֶלֶא.

too awesome for praise, doing wonders!

Notiso y'min'cho, tivlo-aymō oretz.   נָטִיתָ יְמִינְךָ, תִּבְלָעֵמוֹ אָרֶץ.

You stretched out Your right hand — the earth swallowed them.

Nochiso v'chasd'cho am zu go-olto,   נָחִיתָ בְחַסְדְּךָ עַם זוּ גָּאָלְתָּ,

You guided with Your kindness this people that You redeemed;

nayhalto v'oz'cho el n'vay kodshecho.   נֵהַלְתָּ בְעָזְּךָ אֶל נְוֵה קָדְשֶׁךָ.

You led with Your might to Your holy abode.*

Shom'u amim yirgozun,   שָׁמְעוּ עַמִּים יִרְגָּזוּן,

Peoples heard — they were agitated;

chil ochaz yōsh'vay p'loshes.   חִיל אָחַז יֹשְׁבֵי פְּלָשֶׁת.

convulsive terror gripped the dwellers of Philistia.

Oz nivhalu alufay edōm,   אָז נִבְהֲלוּ אַלּוּפֵי אֱדוֹם,

Then the chieftains of Edom were confounded,

aylay mō-ov yōchazaymō ro-ad,   אֵילֵי מוֹאָב יֹאחֲזֵמוֹ רָעַד,

trembling gripped the powers of Moab,

nomōgu kōl yōsh'vay ch'no-an.   נָמֹגוּ כֹּל יֹשְׁבֵי כְנָעַן.

all the dwellers of Canaan dissolved.

Tipōl alayhem aymoso vofachad,   תִּפֹּל עֲלֵיהֶם אֵימָתָה וָפַחַד,

May fear and terror befall them,

---

ity are allegorical. The right hand symbolizes power. Similarly, below God's wrath is described as a blast from His nostrils, because angry people tend to snort.

אֶל נְוֵה קָדְשֶׁךָ — *To Your holy abode,* i.e., the Holy Temple. Although the Temple would not be built for over four hundred years, it is typical for prophetic song to combine the past with

bigdōl z'rō-acho yid'mu ko-oven, בִּגְדֹל זְרוֹעֲךָ יִדְּמוּ כָּאָבֶן,

at the greatness of Your arm may they be still as stone;

ad ya-avōr am'cho Adōnoy, עַד יַעֲבֹר עַמְּךָ יהוה,

until Your people passes through, HASHEM,

ad ya-avōr am zu koniso. עַד יַעֲבֹר עַם זוּ קָנִיתָ.

until this people You have acquired passes through.

T'vi-aymō v'sito-aymō תְּבִאֵמוֹ וְתִטָּעֵמוֹ

You shall bring them and implant them

b'har nachalos'cho, בְּהַר נַחֲלָתְךָ,

on the mount of Your heritage,

mochōn l'shivt'cho po-alto Adōnoy, מָכוֹן לְשִׁבְתְּךָ פָּעַלְתָּ יהוה,

the foundation of Your dwelling-place, which You, HASHEM, have made:

mik'dosh Adōnoy kōn'nu yodecho. מִקְּדָשׁ אֲדֹנָי כּוֹנְנוּ יָדֶיךָ.

the Sanctuary, my Lord, that Your hands established.

Adōnoy yimlōch l'ōlom vo-ed. יהוה יִמְלֹךְ לְעֹלָם וָעֶד.

HASHEM shall reign for all eternity.*

Adōnoy yimlōch l'ōlom vo-ed. יהוה יִמְלֹךְ לְעֹלָם וָעֶד.

HASHEM shall reign for all eternity.

(Adōnoy malchusayh ko-aym, (יהוה מַלְכוּתֵהּ קָאֵם,

l'olam ul-ol'may ol'ma-yo.) לְעָלַם וּלְעָלְמֵי עָלְמַיָּא.)

(HASHEM — His kingdom is established forever and ever.)

Ki vo sus par-ō כִּי בָא סוּס פַּרְעֹה

When Pharaoh's cavalry came —

b'richbō uvforoshov ba-yom, בְּרִכְבּוֹ וּבְפָרָשָׁיו בַּיָּם,

with his chariots and horsemen — into the sea

va-yoshev Adōnoy alayhem וַיָּשֶׁב יהוה עֲלֵהֶם

es may ha-yom, אֶת מֵי הַיָּם,

and HASHEM turned back the waters of the sea upon them,

uvnay yisro-ayl וּבְנֵי יִשְׂרָאֵל

hol'chu va-yabosho b'sōch ha-yom. הָלְכוּ בַיַּבָּשָׁה בְּתוֹךְ הַיָּם.

the Children of Israel walked on the dry bed amid the sea.

❖ Ki Ladōnoy ham'lucho, ❖ כִּי לַיהוה הַמְּלוּכָה,

For the sovereignty is HASHEM's*

---

the future, because in the Divine perception they are interrelated.

הׄ יִמְלֹךְ לְעֹלָם וָעֶד — *HASHEM shall reign for all eternity.* This verse is repeated to signify that it is the climax of the Song — that God's sover-

eignty shall be recognized forever. Because of the importance of this idea the Aramaic Targum of this verse is also recited.

כִּי לַהּ הַמְּלוּכָה — *For the sovereignty is HASHEM's.* The collected verses attached to the

u-mōshayl bagōyim.

וּמֹשֵׁל בַּגּוֹיִם.

and He rules over nations.

V'olu mōshi-im b'har tziyōn,

וְעָלוּ מוֹשִׁעִים בְּהַר צִיּוֹן,

lishpōt es har ay-sov,

לִשְׁפֹּט אֶת הַר עֵשָׂו,

The saviors will ascend Mount Zion to judge Esau's mountain,

v'hoy'so Ladōnoy ham'lucho.

וְהָיְתָה לַיהוה הַמְּלוּכָה.

and the kingdom will be HASHEM's.

V'ho-yo Adōnoy l'melech

וְהָיָה יהוה לְמֶלֶךְ

al kol ho-oretz,

עַל כָּל הָאָרֶץ,

Then HASHEM will be King over all the world,

ba-yōm hahu yih-ye Adōnoy e-chod

בַּיּוֹם הַהוּא יִהְיֶה יהוה אֶחָד

ushmō e-chod.

וּשְׁמוֹ אֶחָד.

on that day HASHEM will be One and His Name will be One.

SOME CONGREGATIONS CONCLUDE:

(Uvsōros'cho kosuv lamōr:

(וּבְתוֹרָתְךָ כָּתוּב לֵאמֹר:

(And in Your Torah it is written:

Sh'ma yisro-ayl Adōnoy Elōhaynu

שְׁמַע יִשְׂרָאֵל יהוה אֱלֹהֵינוּ

Adōnoy E-chod.)

יהוה אֶחָד.)

Hear O Israel: Hashem is our God, Hashem, the One and Only.)

THE FOLLOWING INSPIRATIONAL PRAYER IS RECITED ON THE SABBATH AND FESTIVAL DAYS. IT IS AN INTEGRAL PART OF THE BLESSING OF *YISHTABACH*, THE CLOSING BLESSING OF *PESUKEI D'ZIMRAH,* AND AS SUCH MUST *PRECEDE* THE RECITATION OF *YISHTABACH.*
ON WEEKDAY *CHOL HAMOED* AND ON HOSHANA RABBAH TURN TO PAGE 347.

■ Utilizing the "additional soul" that I am blessed with on Shabbos, I acknowledge my total dependency on Hashem's mercy; my inadequacy to praise Him properly, and my enthusiastic resolve to dedicate myself to His service.

NISHMAS kol chai

נִשְׁמַת כָּל חַי

*The soul of every living being**

t'voraych es shimcho

תְּבָרֵךְ אֶת שִׁמְךָ

shall bless Your Name,

Adōnoy Elōhaynu,

יהוה אֱלֹהֵינוּ,

HASHEM, our God;

v'ru-ach kol bosor

וְרוּחַ כָּל בָּשָׂר

the spirit of all flesh

Song are appropriate to the climactic verse that God will reign forever.

נִשְׁמַת כָּל חַי — *The soul of every living being.* This beautiful and moving prayer is an out-pouring of praise and gratitude to God. Lyrically, it depicts our utter dependence on God's mercy, our total inadequacy to laud Him prop-

erly, and our enthusiastic resolve to dedicate ourselves to His service. It is especially appropriate for recitation on the Sabbath and Festivals — although it contains no mention of the day — because the additional holiness of the Sabbath and the time it affords for extra contemplation make man better able to under-

t'fo-ayr usrōmaym   תְּפָאֵר וּתְרוֹמֵם
    zichr'cho malkaynu tomid.   זִכְרְךָ מַלְכֵּנוּ תָּמִיד.
shall always glorify and exalt Your remembrance, our King.

Min ho-ōlom v'ad ho-ōlom ato Ayl.   מִן הָעוֹלָם וְעַד הָעוֹלָם אַתָּה אֵל,
From this world to the World to Come, You are God,

umi-bal-odecho ayn lonu melech   וּמִבַּלְעָדֶיךָ אֵין לָנוּ מֶלֶךְ
    gō-ayl u-mōshi-a.   גּוֹאֵל וּמוֹשִׁיעַ.
and other than You we have no king, redeemer or savior.

Pōde u-matzil umfarnays umrachaym   פּוֹדֶה וּמַצִּיל וּמְפַרְנֵס וּמְרַחֵם
Liberator, Rescuer, Sustainer and Merciful One

b'chol ays tzoro v'tzuko,   בְּכָל עֵת צָרָה וְצוּקָה,
in every time of distress and anguish,*

ayn lonu melech elo oto.   אֵין לָנוּ מֶלֶךְ אֶלָּא אָתָּה.
we have no king but You!

Elōhay horishōnim v'ho-acharōnim,   אֱלֹהֵי הָרִאשׁוֹנִים וְהָאַחֲרוֹנִים,
God of the first and of the last,*

Elō-ah kol b'riyōs,   אֱלוֹהַּ כָּל בְּרִיּוֹת,
God of all creatures,

adōn kol tōlodōs,   אֲדוֹן כָּל תּוֹלָדוֹת,
Master of all generations,

ham'hulol b'rōv hatishbochōs,   הַמְהֻלָּל בְּרֹב הַתִּשְׁבָּחוֹת,
Who is extolled through a multitude of praises,

ham'nahayg ōlomō b'chesed   הַמְנַהֵג עוֹלָמוֹ בְּחֶסֶד
Who guides His world with kindness

uvri-yōsov b'rachamim.   וּבְרִיּוֹתָיו בְּרַחֲמִים.
and His creatures with mercy.

Vadōnoy lō yonum v'lō yishon.   וַיהוה לֹא יָנוּם וְלֹא יִישָׁן.
HASHEM neither slumbers nor sleeps.

Ham'ōrayr y'shaynim,   הַמְעוֹרֵר יְשֵׁנִים,
    v'hamaykitz nirdomim,   וְהַמֵּקִיץ נִרְדָּמִים,
He Who rouses the sleepers, Who awakens the slumberers,

v'hamaysi-ach il'mim,   וְהַמֵּשִׂיחַ אִלְּמִים,
Who makes the mute speak,

---

stand and express the message of the *Nishmas* prayer.

בְּכָל עֵת צָרָה וְצוּקָה — *In every time of distress and anguish.* Commonly, people express gratitude in happy times and pray for salvation in hard times. We go further, however: Even

when we suffer distress and anguish, we express our gratitude to God for allowing us to survive.

אֱלֹהֵי הָרִאשׁוֹנִים וְהָאַחֲרוֹנִים — *God of the first and of the last.* When God initiates a course of action, He takes into account the results it will

v'hamatir asurim,

וְהַמַּתִּיר אֲסוּרִים,

Who releases the bound,

v'hasōmaych nōf'lim,

וְהַסּוֹמֵךְ נוֹפְלִים,

Who supports the fallen,

v'hazōkayf k'fufim,

וְהַזּוֹקֵף כְּפוּפִים,

and Who straightens the bent —

L'cho l'vad'cho anachnu mōdim.

לְךָ לְבַדְּךָ אֲנַחְנוּ מוֹדִים.

to You alone we give thanks.

Ilu finu molay shiro ka-yom,

אִלּוּ פִינוּ מָלֵא שִׁירָה כַּיָּם,

Were our mouth as full of song as the sea,

ulshōnaynu rino kahamōn galov,

וּלְשׁוֹנֵנוּ רִנָּה כַּהֲמוֹן גַּלָּיו,

and our tongue as full of joyous song as its multitude of waves,

v'sifsōsaynu shevach

וְשִׂפְתוֹתֵינוּ שֶׁבַח

   k'merchavay roki-a,

כְּמֶרְחֲבֵי רָקִיעַ,

and our lips as full of praise as the breadth of the heavens,

v'aynaynu m'irōs

וְעֵינֵינוּ מְאִירוֹת

   ka-shemesh v'cha-yoray-ach,

כַּשֶּׁמֶשׁ וְכַיָּרֵחַ,

and our eyes as brilliant as the sun and the moon,

v'yodaynu f'rusōs

וְיָדֵינוּ פְרוּשׂוֹת

   k'nishray shomo-yim,

כְּנִשְׁרֵי שָׁמָיִם,

and our hands as outspread as eagles of the sky

v'raglaynu kalōs ko-a-yolōs,

וְרַגְלֵינוּ קַלּוֹת כָּאַיָּלוֹת,

and our feet as swift as hinds —

ayn anachnu maspikim

אֵין אֲנַחְנוּ מַסְפִּיקִים

   l'hōdōs l'cho

לְהוֹדוֹת לָךְ,

we still could not thank You sufficiently

Adōnoy Elōhaynu

יהוה אֱלֹהֵינוּ

   Vaylōhay avōsaynu,

וֵאלֹהֵי אֲבוֹתֵינוּ,

HASHEM, our God and God of our forefathers,

ulvoraych es sh'mecho

וּלְבָרֵךְ אֶת שְׁמֶךָ

and to bless Your Name

al achas may-olef

עַל אַחַת מֵאָלֶף

   elef alfay alofim

אֶלֶף אַלְפֵי אֲלָפִים

for even one of the thousand thousand, thousands of thousands

v'ribay r'vovōs p'omim hatōvōs

וְרִבֵּי רְבָבוֹת פְּעָמִים הַטּוֹבוֹת

and myriad myriads of favors

---

engender centuries into the future. Thus, He   as of the last.
is the Master of the first set of events as well

she-osiso im avōsaynu v'imonu.   שֶׁעָשִׂיתָ עִם אֲבוֹתֵינוּ וְעִמָּנוּ.

that You performed for our ancestors and for us.*

Mimitzra-yim g'altonu   מִמִּצְרַיִם גְּאַלְתָּנוּ

You redeemed us from Egypt,

Adōnoy Elōhaynu,   יהוה אֱלֹהֵינוּ,

HASHEM, our God,

u-mibays avodim p'disonu.   וּמִבֵּית עֲבָדִים פְּדִיתָנוּ.

and liberated us from the house of bondage.

B'ro-ov zantonu,   בְּרָעָב זַנְתָּנוּ,

In famine You nourished us

uvsovo kilkaltonu,   וּבְשָׂבָע כִּלְכַּלְתָּנוּ,

and in plenty You sustained us.

maycherev hitzaltonu,   מֵחֶרֶב הִצַּלְתָּנוּ,

From sword You saved us;

u-midever milat-tonu,   וּמִדֶּבֶר מִלַּטְתָּנוּ,

from plague You let us escape;

u-maycholo-yim ro-im v'ne-emonim   וּמֵחֳלָיִם רָעִים וְנֶאֱמָנִים
dilisonu.   דִּלִּיתָנוּ.

and from severe and enduring diseases You spared us.

Ad hayno azorunu rachamecho,   עַד הֵנָּה עֲזָרוּנוּ רַחֲמֶיךָ,

Until now Your mercy has helped us,

v'lō azovunu chasodecho   וְלֹא עֲזָבוּנוּ חֲסָדֶיךָ.

and Your kindness has not forsaken us.

V'al tit'shaynu Adōnoy Elōhaynu   וְאַל תִּטְּשֵׁנוּ יהוה אֱלֹהֵינוּ
lonetzach.   לָנֶצַח.

Do not abandon us, HASHEM, our God, forever.

Al kayn   עַל כֵּן

Therefore,

ayvorim shepilagto bonu,   אֵבָרִים שֶׁפִּלַּגְתָּ בָּנוּ,

the organs that You set within us,

v'ru-ach unshomo   וְרוּחַ וּנְשָׁמָה
shenofachto b'apaynu,   שֶׁנָּפַחְתָּ בְּאַפֵּינוּ,

and the spirit and soul that You breathed into our nostrils,

v'loshōn asher samto b'finu,   וְלָשׁוֹן אֲשֶׁר שַׂמְתָּ בְּפִינוּ,

and the tongue that You placed in our mouth —

עִם אֲבוֹתֵינוּ וְעִמָּנוּ — *For our ancestors and for us.*
Man does not live in a vacuum. The favors

done for previous generations have lasting effects that benefit us as well.

hayn haym yōdu vivor'chu — הֵן הֵם יוֹדוּ וִיבָרְכוּ
all of them shall thank and bless

vishab'chu vifo-aru virōm'mu — וִישַׁבְּחוּ וִיפָאֲרוּ וִירוֹמְמוּ
and praise and glorify and exalt

v'ya-aritzu v'yakdishu — וְיַעֲרִיצוּ וְיַקְדִּישׁוּ
and revere and sanctify

v'yamlichu es shimcho malkaynu. — וְיַמְלִיכוּ אֶת שִׁמְךָ מַלְכֵּנוּ.
and declare the sovereignty of Your Name, our King.

Ki chol pe l'cho yōde, — כִּי כָל פֶּה לְךָ יוֹדֶה,
For every mouth shall offer thanks to You;

v'chol loshōn l'cho si-shova, — וְכָל לָשׁוֹן לְךָ תִשָּׁבַע,
every tongue shall vow allegiance to You;

v'chol berech l'cho sichra, — וְכָל בֶּרֶךְ לְךָ תִכְרַע,
every knee shall bend to You;

v'chol kōmo l'fonecho sishta-chave, — וְכָל קוֹמָה לְפָנֶיךָ תִשְׁתַּחֲוֶה,
every erect spine shall prostrate itself before You;*

v'chol l'vovōs yiro-ucho, — וְכָל לְבָבוֹת יִירָאוּךָ,
all hearts shall fear You,

v'chol kerev uchlo-yōs y'zam'ru lishmecho, — וְכָל קֶרֶב וּכְלָיוֹת יְזַמְּרוּ לִשְׁמֶךָ,
and all innermost feelings and thoughts shall sing praises to Your name,

kadovor shekosuv: — כַּדָּבָר שֶׁכָּתוּב:
as it is written:

Kol atzmōsai tōmarno, — כָּל עַצְמֹתַי תֹּאמַרְנָה,
"All my bones shall say:

Adōnoy mi chomōcho, — יהוה מִי כָמוֹךָ,
'HASHEM, who is like You?'

matzil oni maychozok mimenu, — מַצִּיל עָנִי מֵחָזָק מִמֶּנּוּ,
You save the poor man from one stronger than he,

v'oni v'evyōn migōz'lō. — וְעָנִי וְאֶבְיוֹן מִגֹּזְלוֹ.
the poor and destitute from one who would rob him."

Mi yidme loch, u-mi yishve loch, — ❖ מִי יִדְמֶה לָּךְ, וּמִי יִשְׁוֶה לָּךְ,
Who is like unto You? Who is equal to You?

u-mi ya-aroch loch. — וּמִי יַעֲרָךְ לָךְ.
Who can be compared to You?

וְכָל קוֹמָה לְפָנֶיךָ תִשְׁתַּחֲוֶה — *Every erect spine shall prostrate itself before You.* One must bow to God even while standing erect. "Bowing" is not only a physical action; the heart and mind

Ho-Ayl hagodōl hagibōr v'hanōro,   הָאֵל הַגָּדוֹל הַגִּבּוֹר וְהַנּוֹרָא,

O great, mighty, and awesome God,

Ayl elyōn,   אֵל עֶלְיוֹן,

the supreme God,

kōnay shoma-yim vo-oretz.   קֹנֵה שָׁמַיִם וָאָרֶץ.

Creator of heaven and earth.

N'halelcho unshabaychacho   נְהַלֶּלְךָ וּנְשַׁבֵּחֲךָ

unfo-ercho   וּנְפָאֶרְךָ

We shall laud, praise, and glorify You

unvoraych es shaym kodshecho,   וּנְבָרֵךְ אֶת שֵׁם קָדְשֶׁךָ,

and bless Your holy Name,

ko-omur: L'dovid,   כָּאָמוּר: לְדָוִד,

as it is said: "Of David:

bor'chi nafshi es Adōnoy,   בָּרְכִי נַפְשִׁי אֶת יהוה,

Bless HASHEM, *O my soul,*

v'chol k'rovai es shaym kodshō.   וְכָל קְרָבַי אֶת שֵׁם קָדְשׁוֹ.

and let all my innermost being bless His holy Name!"

ON FESTIVALS, THE *CHAZZAN* OF *SHACHARIS* BEGINS HERE:

HO-AYL b'sa-atzumōs u-zecho,   **הָאֵל** בְּתַעֲצֻמוֹת עֻזֶּךָ,

O God, in the omnipotence of Your strength,

hagodōl bichvōd sh'mecho,   הַגָּדוֹל בִּכְבוֹד שְׁמֶךָ,

great in the glory of Your Name,

hagibōr lonetzach   הַגִּבּוֹר לָנֶצַח

v'hanōro b'nōr'ōsecho.   וְהַנּוֹרָא בְּנוֹרְאוֹתֶיךָ.

mighty forever and awesome through Your awesome deeds.

Hamelech ha-yōshayv   הַמֶּלֶךְ הַיּוֹשֵׁב

al kisay rom v'niso.   עַל כִּסֵּא רָם וְנִשָּׂא.

O King enthroned upon a high and lofty throne!

ON THE SABBATH, THE *CHAZZAN* OF *SHACHARIS* BEGINS HERE:

SHŌCHAYN AD   **שׁוֹכֵן עַד**

He Who abides forever,

morōm v'kodōsh sh'mō.   מָרוֹם וְקָדוֹשׁ שְׁמוֹ.

exalted and holy is His Name.

V'chosuv: Ran'nu tzadikim Badōnoy   וְכָתוּב: רַנְּנוּ צַדִּיקִים בַּיהוה

And it is written: "Sing joyfully, O righteous, before HASHEM;

---

must also participate.

שׁוֹכֵן עַד — *He Who abides forever.* Although God is *exalted and holy,* He nevertheless makes His abode on earth, for it is only here —

through the deeds of the righteous — that His commandments can be carried out. Therefore, this paragraph goes on to say that the primary praise of God comes from such people. The key,

lai-shorim novo s'hilo.
לַיְשָׁרִים נָאוָה תְהִלָּה.

for the upright, praise is fitting.''

❖ B'fi y'shorim tis-halol,
❖ בְּפִי יְשָׁרִים תִּתְהַלָּל,

By the mouth of the upright shall You be lauded;

Uvdivray tzadikim tisborach,
וּבְדִבְרֵי צַדִּיקִים תִּתְבָּרַךְ,

by the words of the righteous shall You be blessed;

U-vilshōn chasidim tisrōmom,
וּבִלְשׁוֹן חֲסִידִים תִּתְרוֹמָם,

by the tongue of the devout shall You be exalted;

Uvkerev k'dōshim tiskadosh.
וּבְקֶרֶב קְדוֹשִׁים תִּתְקַדָּשׁ.

and amid the holy shall You be sanctified.

UVMAK-HALŌS riv'vōs
וּבְמַקְהֲלוֹת רִבְבוֹת

am'cho bays yisro-ayl,
עַמְּךָ בֵּית יִשְׂרָאֵל,

And in the assemblies of the myriads of Your people, the House of Israel,

b'rino yispo-ar shimcho malkaynu
בְּרִנָּה יִתְפָּאַר שִׁמְךָ מַלְכֵּנוּ

with joyous song shall Your Name be glorified, our King,

b'chol dōr vodōr.
בְּכָל דּוֹר וָדוֹר.

throughout every generation.

❖ Shekayn chōvas kol ha-y'tzurim,
❖ שֶׁכֵּן חוֹבַת כָּל הַיְצוּרִים,

*For such is the duty of all creatures — ***

l'fonecho Adōnoy Elōhaynu
לְפָנֶיךָ יהוה אֱלֹהֵינוּ

Vaylōhay avōsaynu,
וֵאלֹהֵי אֲבוֹתֵינוּ,

before You, HASHEM, our God and God of our forefathers,

l'hōdōs l'halayl l'shabay-ach
לְהוֹדוֹת לְהַלֵּל לְשַׁבֵּחַ

to thank, laud, praise,

l'fo-ayr l'rōmaym l'hadayr
לְפָאֵר לְרוֹמֵם לְהַדֵּר

glorify, exalt, adore,

l'voraych l'alay ul-kalays,
לְבָרֵךְ לְעַלֵּה וּלְקַלֵּס,

bless, raise high, and sing praises —

al kol divray shirōs v'sishb'chōs
עַל כָּל דִּבְרֵי שִׁירוֹת וְתִשְׁבָּחוֹת

even beyond all expressions of the songs and praises

dovid ben yishai
דָּוִד בֶּן יִשַׁי

avd'cho m'shichecho.
עַבְדְּךָ מְשִׁיחֶךָ.

of David the son of Jesse, Your servant, Your anointed.

---

however, is not in their rhetoric but in the "song" of their good deeds.

שֶׁכֵּן חוֹבַת כָּל הַיְצוּרִים — *For such is the duty of all creatures.* It is their duty because of the simple

fact that they are God's creatures; since He fashioned them, they must feel obligated to pay Him homage.

ON ALL DAYS CONTINUE HERE:

■ The praises of Hashem are never ending. In the closing blessing of Pesukei D'Zimrah I pray that the Name of Hashem will be praised forever.

STAND WHILE RECITING THE FOLLOWING BLESSING:

YISHTABACH shimcho lo-ad malkaynu,

יִשְׁתַּבַּח שִׁמְךָ לָעַד מַלְכֵּנוּ,

May Your Name be praised forever — our King,

ho-Ayl hamelech hagodōl v'hakodōsh, ba-shoma-yim uvo-oretz.

הָאֵל הַמֶּלֶךְ הַגָּדוֹל וְהַקָּדוֹשׁ, בַּשָּׁמַיִם וּבָאָרֶץ.

the God, the great and holy King — in heaven and on earth.

Ki l'cho no-e Adōnoy Elōhaynu Vaylōhay avōsaynu,

כִּי לְךָ נָאֶה יהוה אֱלֹהֵינוּ וֵאלֹהֵי אֲבוֹתֵינוּ,

Because for You is fitting — O HASHEM, our God and the God of our forefathers —

shir ushvocho, halayl v'zimro,

שִׁיר וּשְׁבָחָה, הַלֵּל וְזִמְרָה,

song and praise, lauding and hymns,

ōz u-memsholo,

עֹז וּמֶמְשָׁלָה,

netzach, g'dulo ugvuro,

נֶצַח גְּדֻלָּה וּגְבוּרָה,

power and dominion, triumph, greatness and strength,

t'hilo v'sif-eres,

תְּהִלָּה וְתִפְאֶרֶת,

k'dusho u-malchus,

קְדֻשָּׁה וּמַלְכוּת,

praise and splendor, holiness and sovereignty,

b'rochōs v'hōdo-ōs may-ato v'ad ōlom.

בְּרָכוֹת וְהוֹדָאוֹת מֵעַתָּה וְעַד עוֹלָם.

blessings and thanksgivings from this time and forever.

❖ Boruch ato Adōnoy,

❖ בָּרוּךְ אַתָּה יהוה,

Blessed are You, HASHEM,

Ayl melech godōl batishbochōs,

אֵל מֶלֶךְ גָּדוֹל בַּתִּשְׁבָּחוֹת,

God, King exalted through praises,*

Ayl hahōdo-ōs, adōn haniflo-ōs,

אֵל הַהוֹדָאוֹת, אֲדוֹן הַנִּפְלָאוֹת,

God of thanksgivings, Master of wonders,

habōchayr b'shiray zimro,

הַבּוֹחֵר בְּשִׁירֵי זִמְרָה,

Who chooses musical songs of praise —

melech Ayl chay ho-ōlomim.

מֶלֶךְ אֵל חֵי הָעוֹלָמִים.

King, God, Life-giver of the world.*

CONGREGATION RESPONDS: **Omayn** — אָמֵן

גָּדוֹל בַּתִּשְׁבָּחוֹת — *Exalted through praises.* The implication is not that God requires our praises in order to become exalted, for His infinite greatness is beyond our capacity to compre- hend, much less express. Rather, it is His will that we have the privilege of exalting Him, despite our inability to do so adequately.

חֵי הָעוֹלָמִים — *Life-giver of the world.* This

FROM ROSH HASHANAH UNTIL YOM KIPPUR AND ON HOSHANA RABBAH, SOME CONGREGATIONS RECITE THE FOLLOWING (PSALM 130). THE ARK IS OPENED. EACH VERSE IS RECITED ALOUD BY THE CHAZZAN, THEN REPEATED BY THE CONGREGATION.

SHIR HAMA-ALŌS,

שִׁיר הַמַּעֲלוֹת,

A song of ascents:

mima-amakim k'rosicho Adōnoy.

מִמַּעֲמַקִּים קְרָאתִיךָ יהוה.

From the depths I called You, HASHEM.

Adōnoy shim-o v'kōli,

אֲדֹנָי שִׁמְעָה בְקוֹלִי,

My Lord, hear my voice,

tih-yeno oznecho kashuvōs l'kōl tachanunoy.

תִּהְיֶינָה אָזְנֶיךָ קַשֻּׁבוֹת לְקוֹל תַּחֲנוּנָי.

may Your ears be attentive to the sound of my pleas.

Im avonōs tishmor Yoh,

אִם עֲוֹנוֹת תִּשְׁמָר יָהּ,

If You preserve iniquities, O God,

Adōnoy mi ya-amōd.

אֲדֹנָי מִי יַעֲמֹד.

my Lord, who could survive?

Ki im'cho has'licho,

כִּי עִמְּךָ הַסְּלִיחָה,

For with You is forgiveness,

l'ma-an tivoray.

לְמַעַן תִּוָּרֵא.

that You may be feared.

Kivisi Adōnoy kiv'so nafshi,

קִוִּיתִי יהוה קִוְּתָה נַפְשִׁי,

I put my confidence in HASHEM, my soul put confidence,

v'lidvorō hōcholti.

וְלִדְבָרוֹ הוֹחָלְתִּי.

and I hoped for His word.

Nafshi LaAdōnoy, mishōm'rim labōker,

נַפְשִׁי לַאדֹנָי, מִשֹּׁמְרִים לַבֹּקֶר,

I yearn for my Lord, among those longing for the dawn,

shōm'rim labōker.

שֹׁמְרִים לַבֹּקֶר.

those longing for the dawn.

Yachayl yisro-ayl el Adōnoy,

יַחֵל יִשְׂרָאֵל אֶל יהוה,

Let Israel hope for HASHEM,

ki im Adōnoy ha-chesed,

כִּי עִם יהוה הַחֶסֶד,

for with HASHEM is kindness,

v'harbay imō f'dus.

וְהַרְבֵּה עִמּוֹ פְדוּת.

and with Him is abundant redemption.

V'hu yifde es yisro-ayl, mikōl avonōsov.

וְהוּא יִפְדֶּה אֶת יִשְׂרָאֵל, מִכֹּל עֲוֹנוֹתָיו.

And He shall redeem Israel from all its iniquities.

THE *CHAZZAN* RECITES *HALF-KADDISH.*
(Congregational responses are indicated by parentheses.)

יִתְגַּדַּל וְיִתְקַדַּשׁ שְׁמֵהּ רַבָּא. (Omayn – אָמֵן). בְּעָלְמָא דִּי בְרָא
כִרְעוּתֵהּ. וְיַמְלִיךְ מַלְכוּתֵהּ, בְּחַיֵּיכוֹן וּבְיוֹמֵיכוֹן וּבְחַיֵּי דְכָל
בֵּית יִשְׂרָאֵל, בַּעֲגָלָא וּבִזְמַן קָרִיב. וְאִמְרוּ: אָמֵן.
(אָמֵן. יְהֵא שְׁמֵהּ רַבָּא מְבָרַךְ לְעָלַם וּלְעָלְמֵי עָלְמַיָּא.)

(Omayn. Y'hay sh'mayh rabo m'vorach l'olam ul-ol'may ol'ma-yo.)

יְהֵא שְׁמֵהּ רַבָּא מְבָרַךְ לְעָלַם וּלְעָלְמֵי עָלְמַיָּא. יִתְבָּרַךְ וְיִשְׁתַּבַּח
וְיִתְפָּאַר וְיִתְרוֹמַם וְיִתְנַשֵּׂא וְיִתְהַדָּר וְיִתְעַלֶּה וְיִתְהַלָּל שְׁמֵהּ
דְקֻדְשָׁא בְּרִיךְ הוּא (בְּרִיךְ הוּא – B'rich hu). °לְעֵלָּא מִן כָּל
[°לְעֵלָּא לְעֵלָּא מִכָּל – from Rosh Hashanah to Yom Kippur substitute]
בִּרְכָתָא וְשִׁירָתָא תֻּשְׁבְּחָתָא וְנֶחֱמָתָא, דַּאֲמִירָן בְּעָלְמָא. וְאִמְרוּ: אָמֵן.
(אָמֵן – Omayn).

THE *CHAZZAN* SUMMONS THE CONGREGATION TO JOIN IN THE FORTHCOMING PRAYERS,
BOWING AT Bor'chu AND STRAIGHTENING UP AT Adōnoy.

BOR'CHU es Adōnoy ham'vōroch. בָּרְכוּ אֶת יהוה הַמְבֹרָךְ.

Bless HASHEM, the blessed One.

CONGREGATION, FOLLOWED BY *CHAZZAN,* RESPONDS,
BOWING AT Boruch AND STRAIGHTENING UP AT Adōnoy:

Boruch Adōnoy בָּרוּךְ יהוה
ham'vōroch l'ōlom vo-ed. הַמְבֹרָךְ לְעוֹלָם וָעֶד.

Blessed is HASHEM, the blessed One, for all eternity.

BLESSINGS OF THE SHEMA*

■ First blessing preceding the *Shema:* I praise Hashem for His governing the universe
and acknowledge that everything emanates from Hashem — both that which is visibly
and understandably good and that which is not.

BORUCH ato Adōnoy בָּרוּךְ אַתָּה יהוה
Elōhaynu melech ho-ōlom, אֱלֹהֵינוּ מֶלֶךְ הָעוֹלָם,
Blessed are You, HASHEM, our God, King of the universe,

essential principle of Jewish belief reiterates
that Creation is an ongoing process — God
created and continues to create. Because He
gives life constantly our thanks and praise are
likewise constant.

◆§ **Blessings of the Shema**
The blessing of the *Shema* comprise the
third section of *Shacharis,* whose central feature is the *Shema.* The recitation of *Shema* is
required by the Torah and is the basic acknowledgment of God's sovereignty and Oneness.
The morning *Shema* is accompanied by three

blessings (two before it and one after it), which
(a) express God's mastery over nature, (b) pray
for intellectual and moral attainment through
the study of Torah, and (c) describe God's role
in the flow of history.

Essentially, this part of the Sabbath
Shacharis is no different from that of weekdays. Each contains two blessings before the
Shema and one after it. Since the first blessing
discusses the miracles of Creation, and it is the
Sabbath that commemorates the completion of
the universe, this blessing is augmented on the

yōtzayr ōr u-vōray chōshech,

יוֹצֵר אוֹר וּבוֹרֵא חֹשֶׁךְ,

Who forms light and creates darkness,*

ō-se sholōm u-vōray es hakōl.

עֹשֶׂה שָׁלוֹם וּבוֹרֵא אֶת הַכֹּל.

makes peace and creates all.

ON A FESTIVAL WHICH FALLS ON A WEEKDAY CONTINUE HERE:

HAMAY-IR lo-oretz

הַמֵּאִיר לָאָרֶץ

v'ladorim oleho b'rachamim,

וְלַדָּרִים עָלֶיהָ בְּרַחֲמִים,

He Who illuminates the earth and those who dwell upon it,* with compassion;

uvtuvō m'chadaysh b'chol yōm

וּבְטוּבוֹ מְחַדֵּשׁ בְּכָל יוֹם

tomid ma-asay v'rayshis.

תָּמִיד מַעֲשֵׂה בְרֵאשִׁית.

and in His goodness renews daily, perpetually, the work of Creation.

Mo rabu ma-asecho Adōnoy,

מָה רַבּוּ מַעֲשֶׂיךָ יהוה,

How great are Your works, HASHEM,

kulom b'chochmo osiso,

כֻּלָּם בְּחָכְמָה עָשִׂיתָ,

You make them all with wisdom,

mol'o ho-oretz kinyonecho.

מָלְאָה הָאָרֶץ קִנְיָנֶךָ.

the world is full of Your possessions.

Hamelech ham'rōmom

הַמֶּלֶךְ הַמְרוֹמָם

l'vadō may-oz,

לְבַדּוֹ מֵאָז,

The King Who was exalted in solitude before Creation,

ham'shuboch v'ham'fō-or

הַמְשֻׁבָּח וְהַמְפֹאָר

v'hamisnasay mimōs ōlom.

וְהַמִּתְנַשֵּׂא מִימוֹת עוֹלָם.

Who is praised, glorified, and upraised since days of old.

Elōhay ōlom,

אֱלֹהֵי עוֹלָם,

Eternal God,

b'rachamecho horabim

בְּרַחֲמֶיךָ הָרַבִּים

rachaym olaynu,

רַחֵם עָלֵינוּ,

with Your abundant compassion be compassionate to us —

Sabbath with additional prayers and songs of praise.

יוֹצֵר אוֹר וּבוֹרֵא חֹשֶׁךְ — *Who forms light and creates darkness.* Since the beginning of time, the term light has symbolized new life, wisdom, happiness — all the things associated with goodness. Darkness, however, is associated with suffering, failure and death. The philosophers of idolatry claimed that the good god who creates light cannot also be the bad one who creates darkness. Therefore, they reasoned, there must be at least two gods. In modern times, the same argument is presented in different terms: How can there be a God if

He allows bad things to happen? This blessing refutes the argument that anything people find unpleasant either is not an act of God or proves that He lacks power. To the contrary, we believe unequivocally that God is One; what appears to our limited human intelligence to be contradictory or evil is really part of the plan of the One Merciful God, despite our failure to understand it.

הַמֵּאִיר לָאָרֶץ וְלַדָּרִים עָלֶיהָ — *He Who illuminates the earth and those who dwell upon it.* The earth's dwellers enjoy the light, but so does the earth itself, because sunlight makes vegetation possible.

adōn u-zaynu, tzur misgabaynu,   אֲדוֹן עֻזֵּנוּ, צוּר מִשְׂגַּבֵּנוּ,
O Master of our power, our rocklike stronghold,

mogayn yish-aynu, misgov ba-adaynu.   מָגֵן יִשְׁעֵנוּ, מִשְׂגָּב בַּעֲדֵנוּ.
O Shield of our salvation, be a stronghold for us.

Ayl boruch g'dōl day-o,   אֵל בָּרוּךְ גְּדוֹל דֵּעָה,
The blessed God, Who is great in knowledge,*

haychin u-fo-al zohoray chamo,   הֵכִין וּפָעַל זָהֲרֵי חַמָּה,
prepared and worked on the rays of the sun;

tōv yotzar kovōd lishmō,   טוֹב יָצַר כָּבוֹד לִשְׁמוֹ,
the Beneficent One fashioned honor for His Name,

m'ōrōs nosan s'vivōs u-zō,   מְאוֹרוֹת נָתַן סְבִיבוֹת עֻזּוֹ,
emplaced luminaries all around His power;

pinōs tz'vo-ov k'dōshim   פִּנּוֹת צְבָאָיו קְדוֹשִׁים
   rōm'may Shadai,   רוֹמְמֵי שַׁדַּי,
the leaders of His legions, holy ones, Who exalt the Almighty,

tomid m'sap'rim   תָּמִיד מְסַפְּרִים
   k'vōd Ayl ukdushosō.   כְּבוֹד אֵל וּקְדֻשָּׁתוֹ.
constantly relate the honor of God and His sanctity.

Tisborach Adōnoy Elōhaynu   תִּתְבָּרַךְ יהוה אֱלֹהֵינוּ
May You be blessed, Hashem, our God,

al shevach ma-asay yodecho,   עַל שֶׁבַח מַעֲשֵׂה יָדֶיךָ,
beyond the praises of Your handiwork

v'al m'ōray ōr she-osiso,   וְעַל מְאוֹרֵי אוֹר שֶׁעָשִׂיתָ,
and beyond the bright luminaries that You have made —

y'fo-aru-cho, selo.   יְפָאֲרוּךָ, סֶלָה.
may they glorify You — Selah!

CONTINUE ON P. 357

ON THE SABBATH CONTINUE HERE:

HAKŌL YŌDUCHO,   הַכֹּל יוֹדוּךָ,
   v'hakōl y'shab'chucho,   וְהַכֹּל יְשַׁבְּחוּךָ,
All will thank You and all will praise You —*

v'hakōl yōm'ru   וְהַכֹּל יֹאמְרוּ
   ayn kodōsh Kadōnoy.   אֵין קָדוֹשׁ כַּיהוה.
and all will declare: "Nothing is as holy as Hashem!"

אֵל בָּרוּךְ — *The blessed God.* From here, the next twenty-two words follow the order of the *alefbeis.*

הַכֹּל יוֹדוּךְ — *All will thank You.* Every facet of the universe will join in thanking and lauding God. Only man and the angels do this verbally;

Hakōl y'rōm'mucho selo,
yōtzayr hakōl.

הַכֹּל יְרוֹמְמוּךָ סֶּלָה,
יוֹצֵר הַכֹּל.

All will exalt You, Selah! — You Who forms everything.

Ho-Ayl hapōsay-ach b'chol yōm

הָאֵל הַפּוֹתֵחַ בְּכָל יוֹם

The God Who opens daily

dalsōs sha-aray mizroch,

דַּלְתוֹת שַׁעֲרֵי מִזְרָח,

the doors of the gateways of the East,

u-vōkay-a chalōnay roki-a,

וּבוֹקֵעַ חַלּוֹנֵי רָקִיעַ,

and splits the windows of the firmament,

mōtzi chamo mim'kōmoh

מוֹצִיא חַמָּה מִמְּקוֹמָה

Who removes the sun from its place

ulvono mim'chōn shivtoh,

וּלְבָנָה מִמְּכוֹן שִׁבְתָּהּ,

and the moon from the site of its dwelling,

u-may-ir lo-ōlom kulō ul-yōsh'vov,

וּמֵאִיר לָעוֹלָם כֻּלּוֹ וּלְיוֹשְׁבָיו,

and Who illuminates all the world and its inhabitants,

sheboro b'midas rachamim.

שֶׁבָּרָא בְּמִדַּת רַחֲמִים.

which He created with the attribute of mercy.

Hamay-ir lo-oretz
v'ladorim oleho, b'rachamim,

הַמֵּאִיר לָאָרֶץ
וְלַדָּרִים עָלֶיהָ, בְּרַחֲמִים,

He Who illuminates the earth and those who dwell upon it, with compassion;

uvtuvō m'chadaysh b'chol yōm
tomid ma-asay v'rayshis.

וּבְטוּבוֹ מְחַדֵּשׁ בְּכָל יוֹם
תָּמִיד מַעֲשֵׂה בְרֵאשִׁית.

and in His goodness renews daily, perpetually, the work of Creation.

Hamelech ham'rōmom l'vadō may-oz,

הַמֶּלֶךְ הַמְרוֹמָם לְבַדּוֹ מֵאָז,

The King Who was exalted in solitude from before Creation,

ham'shuboch v'ham'fō-or
v'hamisnasay mimōs ōlom.

הַמְשֻׁבָּח וְהַמְפֹאָר
וְהַמִּתְנַשֵּׂא מִימוֹת עוֹלָם.

Who is praised, glorified, and extolled since days of old.

Elōhay ōlom,

אֱלֹהֵי עוֹלָם,

Eternal God,

b'rachamecho horabim
rachaym olaynu,

בְּרַחֲמֶיךָ הָרַבִּים,
רַחֵם עָלֵינוּ,

with Your abundant compassion be compassionate to us —

adōn u-zaynu, tzur misgabaynu,

אֲדוֹן עֻזֵּנוּ, צוּר מִשְׂגַּבֵּנוּ,

O Master of our power, our rocklike stronghold;

---

the rest of Creation does so by carrying out its assigned tasks and inspiring man to recognize

the Guiding Hand that created and orders everything.

mogayn yish-aynu,　　　　　　　　　　מָגֵן יִשְׁעֵנוּ,

misgov ba-adaynu.　　　　　　　　　מִשְׂגָּב בַּעֲדֵנוּ.

O Shield of our salvation, be a stronghold for us.

Ayn k'erkecho, v'ayn zulosecho,　　אֵין כְּעֶרְכֶּךָ, וְאֵין זוּלָתֶךָ,

There is no comparison to You, there is nothing except for You,

efes biltecho, umi dōme loch.　　אֶפֶס בִּלְתֶּךָ, וּמִי דוֹמֶה לָּךְ.

there is nothing without You, for who is like You?

❖ Ayn k'erk'cho Adōnoy Elōhaynu　　❖ אֵין כְּעֶרְכְּךָ יהוה אֱלֹהֵינוּ

bo-ōlom ha-ze,　　　　　　　　　בָּעוֹלָם הַזֶּה,

There is no comparison to You, HASHEM, our God, in this world;

v'ayn zulos'cho malkaynu　　　　וְאֵין זוּלָתְךָ מַלְכֵּנוּ

and there will be nothing except for You, our King,

l'cha-yay ho-ōlom habo.　　　　לְחַיֵּי הָעוֹלָם הַבָּא.

in the life of the World to Come;

Efes bilt'cho gō-alaynu　　　　אֶפֶס בִּלְתְּךָ גּוֹאֲלֵנוּ

limōs hamoshi-ach,　　　　　　לִימוֹת הַמָּשִׁיחַ,

there will be nothing without You, our Redeemer, in Messianic days;

v'ayn dōme l'cho mōshi-aynu　　וְאֵין דוֹמֶה לְךָ מוֹשִׁיעֵנוּ

and there will be none like You, our Savior,

lischiyas hamaysim.　　　　לִתְחִיַּת הַמֵּתִים.

at the Resuscitation of the Dead.

THE FOLLOWING LITURGICAL SONG IS RECITED RESPONSIVELY IN MOST CONGREGATIONS. IN
SOME CONGREGATIONS, THE *CHAZZAN* AND CONGREGATION SING THE STANZAS TOGETHER.

■ With this alphabetically arranged poem we praise Hashem for creating the
heavenly hosts — the sun, the moon and the stars. The alphabetical arrangement
teaches that Hashem created the world for the sake of the Torah which is written
using the twenty-two letters of the *alef-beis.*

AYL ODŌN al kol hama-asim,　　אֵל אָדוֹן עַל כָּל הַמַּעֲשִׂים,

God — the Master over all works;

boruch umvōroch b'fi kol n'shomo,　　בָּרוּךְ וּמְבֹרָךְ בְּפִי כָּל נְשָׁמָה,

the Blessed One — and He is blessed* by the mouth of every soul;

godlō v'tuvō molay ōlom,　　גָּדְלוֹ וְטוּבוֹ מָלֵא עוֹלָם,

His greatness and goodness fill the world,

da-as usvuno sōv'vim ōsō.　　דַּעַת וּתְבוּנָה סוֹבְבִים אֹתוֹ.

wisdom and insight surround Him.

בָּרוּךְ וּמְבֹרָךְ — *The Blessed One — and He is*
blessed, i.e., God is the source of all blessing. In

addition, His creatures bless Him in their prayers and through their obedience to His will.

Hamisgo-e al cha-yōs hakōdesh,   הַמִּתְגָּאֶה עַל חַיּוֹת הַקֹּדֶשׁ,
He Who exalts Himself* over the holy Chayos

v'nedor b'chovōd al hamerkovo,   וְנֶהְדָּר בְּכָבוֹד עַל הַמֶּרְכָּבָה,
and is splendrous in glory above the Chariot.

z'chus u-mishōr lifnay chis-ō,   זְכוּת וּמִישׁוֹר לִפְנֵי כִסְאוֹ,
Merit and fairness are before His throne,

chesed v'rachamim lifnay ch'vōdō.   חֶסֶד וְרַחֲמִים לִפְנֵי כְבוֹדוֹ.
kindness and mercy are before His glory.

Tōvim m'ōrōs sheboro Elōhaynu,   טוֹבִים מְאוֹרוֹת שֶׁבָּרָא אֱלֹהֵינוּ,
Good are the luminaries that our God has created,

y'tzorom b'da-as   יְצָרָם בְּדַעַת
   b'vino uvhaskayl,   בְּבִינָה וּבְהַשְׂכֵּל,
He has fashioned them with wisdom, with insight and discernment;

kō-ach ugvuro nosan bohem,   כֹּחַ וּגְבוּרָה נָתַן בָּהֶם,
strength and power has He granted them,

lih-yōs mōsh'lim b'kerev tayvayl.   לִהְיוֹת מוֹשְׁלִים בְּקֶרֶב תֵּבֵל.
to be dominant within the world.

M'lay-im ziv umfikim nōgah,   מְלֵאִים זִיו וּמְפִיקִים נֹגַהּ,
Filled with luster and radiating brightness,

no-e zivom b'chol ho-ōlom,   נָאֶה זִיוָם בְּכָל הָעוֹלָם,
their luster is beautiful throughout the world.

S'maychim b'tzaysom   שְׂמֵחִים בְּצֵאתָם
   v'sosim b'vō-om,   וְשָׂשִׂים בְּבוֹאָם,
Glad as they go forth* and exultant as they return,

ōsim b'aymo r'tzōn kōnom.   עוֹשִׂים בְּאֵימָה רְצוֹן קוֹנָם.
they do with awe their Creator's will.

P'ayr v'chovōd nōs'nim lishmō,   פְּאֵר וְכָבוֹד נוֹתְנִים לִשְׁמוֹ,
Splendor and glory they bestow upon His Name,

tzoholo v'rino l'zaycher malchusō,   צָהֳלָה וְרִנָּה לְזֵכֶר מַלְכוּתוֹ,
jubilation and glad song upon the mention of His reign —

koro la-shemesh va-yizrach ōr,   קָרָא לַשֶּׁמֶשׁ וַיִּזְרַח אוֹר,
He called out to the sun and it glowed with light,

הַמִּתְגָּאֶה — *He Who exalts Himself.* The *Chayos* are the highest category of angels and the Chariot refers to the order of angelic praises of God. Both were seen by Ezekiel in his vision of the Heavenly Chariot (Ch. 1). Thus they represent the highest degree of holiness accessible to human understanding. Nevertheless, God is exalted far above even this.

שְׂמֵחִים בְּצֵאתָם — *Glad as they go forth.* The heavenly bodies are likened to a loyal servant entrusted with an important mission. He is proud and happy when he sets out, but is

ro-o v'hiskin tzuras hal'vono.   רָאָה וְהִתְקִין צוּרַת הַלְּבָנָה.

He saw and fashioned the form of the moon.*

Shevach nōs'nim lō   שֶׁבַח נוֹתְנִים לוֹ
   kol tz'vo morōm.   כָּל צְבָא מָרוֹם.

All the host above bestows praise on Him,

Tiferes ugdulo,   תִּפְאֶרֶת וּגְדֻלָּה,

splendor and greatness —

s'rofim v'ōfanim   שְׂרָפִים וְאוֹפַנִּים
   v'cha-yōs hakōdesh   וְחַיּוֹת הַקֹּדֶשׁ —

the Seraphim, Ophanim, and holy Chayos —

LO-AYL asher shovas   לָאֵל אֲשֶׁר שָׁבַת
   mikol hama-asim,   מִכָּל הַמַּעֲשִׂים,

To the God Who rested* from all works,

ba-yōm hash'vi-i his-alo   בַּיּוֹם הַשְּׁבִיעִי הִתְעַלָּה

Who ascended on the seventh day

v'yoshav al kisay ch'vōdō.   וְיָשַׁב עַל כִּסֵּא כְבוֹדוֹ.

and sat on the Throne of His Glory.

Tif-eres oto l'yōm ham'nucho,   תִּפְאֶרֶת עָטָה לְיוֹם הַמְּנוּחָה,

With splendor He enwrapped the Day of Contentment —

ōneg koro l'yōm ha-shabos.   עֹנֶג קָרָא לְיוֹם הַשַּׁבָּת.

He declared the Sabbath day a delight!

Ze shevach shel yōm hash'vi-i,   זֶה שֶׁבַח שֶׁל יוֹם הַשְּׁבִיעִי,

This is the praise of the Sabbath day:*

shebō shovas Ayl   שֶׁבּוֹ שָׁבַת אֵל
   mikol m'lachtō.   מִכָּל מְלַאכְתּוֹ.

that on it God rested from all His work.

V'yōm hash'vi-i   וְיוֹם הַשְּׁבִיעִי
   m'shabay-ach v'ōmayr: מְשַׁבֵּחַ וְאוֹמֵר.

And the seventh day gives praise saying:

Mizmōr shir l'yōm ha-shabos,   מִזְמוֹר שִׁיר לְיוֹם הַשַּׁבָּת,

"A psalm, a song for the Sabbath Day.

---

even more joyous when he returns to his master.

צוּרַת הַלְּבָנָה — *The form of the moon.* With insight, God shaped the phases of the moon so that it would enable Israel to order the calendar as commanded by the Torah.

לָאֵל אֲשֶׁר שָׁבַת — *To the God Who rested.* To

Whom are directed the praises mentioned above? — to the God Who rested on the Sabbath from His six days of Creation.

זֶה שֶׁבַח שֶׁל יוֹם הַשְּׁבִיעִי — *This is the praise of the Sabbath Day.* The glory of the Sabbath is not in the leisure it offers, but in its witness to the Creator and its stimulus to man to join it in

tōv l'hōdōs Ladōnoy.　　　　טוֹב לְהוֹדוֹת לַיהוה.

It is good to thank HASHEM . . ."

L'fichoch y'fo-aru vivor'chu lo-Ayl
kol y'tzurov.　　　　לְפִיכָךְ יְפָאֲרוּ וִיבָרְכוּ לָאֵל כָּל יְצוּרָיו.

Therefore let all that He has fashioned glorify* and bless God

Shevach y'kor ugdulo　　　　שֶׁבַח יְקָר וּגְדֻלָה

Praise, honor, and greatness

yit'nu l'Ayl melech yōtzayr kōl,　　　　יִתְּנוּ לָאֵל מֶלֶךְ יוֹצֵר כֹּל,

let them render to God, the King Who fashioned everything,

hamanchil m'nucho
l'amō yisro-ayl　　　　הַמַּנְחִיל מְנוּחָה לְעַמּוֹ יִשְׂרָאֵל

Who gives a heritage of contentment to His People, Israel,

bikdushoso　　　　בִּקְדֻשָּׁתוֹ

in His holiness

b'yōm shabas kōdesh　　　　בְּיוֹם שַׁבַּת קֹדֶשׁ.

on the holy Sabbath Day.

Shimcho Adōnoy Elōhaynu
yiskadash,　　　　שִׁמְךָ יהוה אֱלֹהֵינוּ יִתְקַדַּשׁ,

May Your Name, HASHEM, our God, be sanctified

v'zichr'cho malkaynu yispo-ar,　　　　וְזִכְרְךָ מַלְכֵּנוּ יִתְפָּאַר,

and may Your remembrance, Our King, be glorified

ba-shoma-yim mima-al　　　　בַּשָּׁמַיִם מִמַּעַל

in the heaven above

v'al ho-oretz mitochas.　　　　וְעַל הָאָרֶץ מִתָּחַת.

and upon the earth below.

Tisborach mōshi-aynu　　　　תִּתְבָּרַךְ מוֹשִׁיעֵנוּ

May You be blessed, our Savior,

al shevach ma-asay yodecho,　　　　עַל שֶׁבַח מַעֲשֵׂה יָדֶיךָ,

beyond the praises of Your handiwork

v'al m'ōray ōr she-osiso,　　　　וְעַל מְאוֹרֵי אוֹר שֶׁעָשִׂיתָ,

and beyond the brilliant luminaries that You have made —

y'fo-arucho selo.　　　　יְפָאֲרוּךָ, סֶלָה.

may they glorify You — Selah.

---

praising God. In this sense, the very existence of the Sabbath is a praise to God.

לְפִיכָךְ יְפָאֲרוּ ... כָּל יְצוּרָיו — *Therefore let all that He has fashioned. . . glorify.* As the prayer goes on to say, the reason that Creation glorifies

God is because He has given the Sabbath to Israel. By observing the Sabbath and absorbing its holiness, Israel brings a higher degree of fulfillment and holiness to the entire universe.

ON ALL DAYS CONTINUE HERE:

■ We recount the daily praise of Hashem respectfully offered by the angels and celestial beings.

TISBORACH tzuraynu malkaynu v'gō-alaynu,

תִּתְבָּרַךְ צוּרֵנוּ מַלְכֵּנוּ וְגוֹאֲלֵנוּ,

May You be blessed, our Rock,* our King and our Redeemer,

bōray k'dōshim.

בּוֹרֵא קְדוֹשִׁים.

Creator of holy ones;

Yishtabach shimcho lo-ad malkaynu,

יִשְׁתַּבַּח שִׁמְךָ לָעַד מַלְכֵּנוּ,

may Your Name be praised forever, our King,

yōtzayr m'shor'sim,

יוֹצֵר מְשָׁרְתִים,

O Fashioner of ministering angels;

va-asher m'shor'sov
kulom ōm'dim b'rum ōlom,

וַאֲשֶׁר מְשָׁרְתָיו
כֻּלָּם עוֹמְדִים בְּרוּם עוֹלָם,

all of Whose ministering angels stand at the summit of the universe

u-mashmi-im b'yiro yachad b'kōl

וּמַשְׁמִיעִים בְּיִרְאָה יַחַד בְּקוֹל

and proclaim — with awe, together, loudly —

divray Elōhim cha-yim
u-melech ōlom.

דִּבְרֵי אֱלֹהִים חַיִּים
וּמֶלֶךְ עוֹלָם.

the words of the living God and King of the universe.

Kulom ahuvim, kulom b'rurim,
kulom gibōrim,

כֻּלָּם אֲהוּבִים, כֻּלָּם בְּרוּרִים,
כֻּלָּם גִּבּוֹרִים,

They are all beloved; they are all flawless; they are all mighty;

v'chulom ōsim b'aymo uvyir-o
r'tzōn kōnom.

וְכֻלָּם עֹשִׂים בְּאֵימָה וּבְיִרְאָה
רְצוֹן קוֹנָם.

they all do the will of their Maker with dread and reverence.

❖ V'chulom pōs'chim es pihem

❖ וְכֻלָּם פּוֹתְחִים אֶת פִּיהֶם

And they all open their mouth

bikdusho uvtohoro,
b'shiro uvzimro,

בִּקְדֻשָּׁה וּבְטָהֳרָה,
בְּשִׁירָה וּבְזִמְרָה,

in holiness and purity, in song and hymn —

umvor'chim umshab'chim

וּמְבָרְכִים וּמְשַׁבְּחִים

and bless, praise,

תִּתְבָּרַךְ צוּרֵנוּ — *May You be blessed, our Rock.* The previous paragraph expressed man's praise of God. Now we turn to the angels' praise of Him. Since there have been people who worshiped the heavenly bodies as independent gods, we now cite the prayers of the heavenly legions, for they know that the sun and the moon are but God's creations and servants.

umfo-arim uma-aritzim	וּמְפָאֲרִים וּמַעֲרִיצִים
umakdishim umamlichim —	וּמַקְדִּישִׁים וּמַמְלִיכִים —

glorify, revere, sanctify and declare the kingship of —

ES SHAYM ho-Ayl,   אֶת שֵׁם הָאֵל

the Name of God,

hamelech hagodōl hagibōr v'hanōro,	הַמֶּלֶךְ הַגָּדוֹל הַגִּבּוֹר וְהַנּוֹרָא
kodōsh hu.	קָדוֹשׁ הוּא.

the great, mighty, and awesome King; holy is He.

V'chulom m'kab'lim alayhem	❖ וְכֻלָּם מְקַבְּלִים עֲלֵיהֶם

Then they all accept upon themselves

ōl malchus shoma-yim ze mi-ze,	עֹל מַלְכוּת שָׁמַיִם זֶה מִזֶּה,

the yoke of heavenly sovereignty from one another,*

v'nōs'nim r'shus ze lo-ze,	וְנוֹתְנִים רְשׁוּת זֶה לָזֶה,

and grant permission to one another

l'hakdish l'yōtz'rom,	לְהַקְדִּישׁ לְיוֹצְרָם,

to sanctify the One Who formed them,

b'nachas ru-ach	בְּנַחַת רוּחַ

with tranquility,

b'sofo v'ruro u-vin-imo.	בְּשָׂפָה בְרוּרָה וּבִנְעִימָה.

with clear articulation, and with sweetness.

K'dusho kulom k'e-chod	קְדֻשָּׁה כֻלָּם כְּאֶחָד
ōnim v'ōm'rim b'yir-o:	עוֹנִים וְאוֹמְרִים בְּיִרְאָה:

All of them as one proclaim His holiness and say with awe:

CONGREGATION RECITES ALOUD:

kodōsh kodōsh kodōsh	קָדוֹשׁ קָדוֹשׁ קָדוֹשׁ
Adōnoy tz'vo-ōs,	יהוה צְבָאוֹת,

"Holy, holy, holy* is HASHEM, *Master of Legions,*

m'lō chol ho-oretz k'vōdō.	מְלֹא כָל הָאָרֶץ כְּבוֹדוֹ.

the whole world is filled with His glory."

V'ho-ōfanim v'cha-yōs hakōdesh	❖ וְהָאוֹפַנִּים וְחַיּוֹת הַקֹּדֶשׁ

Then the Ofanim* and the holy Chayos,

וְכֻלָּם מְקַבְּלִים . . . זֶה מִזֶּה — *Then they all accept . . . from one another.* Unlike people whose competitive jealousies cause them to thwart and outdo one another, the angels urge one another to take the initiative in serving and praising God. Conflict is the foe of perfection, harmony is its ally.

קָדוֹשׁ קָדוֹשׁ קָדוֹשׁ — *Holy, holy, holy.* God is holy with relation to the physical world, *holy* with relation to the spiritual world and *holy* with relation to the World to Come.

וְהָאוֹפַנִּים — *Then the Ofanim.* The categories of angels are not translated since we lack the vocabulary to define them. Maimonides notes that there are ten levels of angels: *Chayos, Ōfanim, Eraylim, Chashmalim, Serafim,*

b'ra-ash godōl   בְּרַעַשׁ גָּדוֹל

with great noise,

misnas'im l'umas s'rofim.   מִתְנַשְּׂאִים לְעֻמַּת שְׂרָפִים.

raise themselves towards the Seraphim.

L'u-mosom m'shab'chim v'ōm'rim: לְעֻמָּתָם מְשַׁבְּחִים וְאוֹמְרִים:

Facing them they give praise saying:

CONGREGATION RECITES ALOUD:

Boruch k'vōd adōnoy mim'kōmō.   בָּרוּךְ כְּבוֹד יהוה מִמְּקוֹמוֹ.

"Blessed is the glory of HASHEM from His place."

■ We complete the first blessing citing Hashem's continuing renewal of Creation and His addressing the specific needs of mankind.

L'AYL boruch n'imōs yitaynu.   לְאֵל בָּרוּךְ נְעִימוֹת יִתֵּנוּ.

To the blessed God they shall offer sweet melodies;

L'melech Ayl chai v'ka-yom,   לְמֶלֶךְ אֵל חַי וְקַיָּם,

to the King, the living and enduring God,

z'mirōs yōmayru,   זְמִרוֹת יֹאמֵרוּ,

v'sishbochōs yashmi-u.   וְתִשְׁבָּחוֹת יַשְׁמִיעוּ.

they shall sing hymns and proclaim praises.

Ki hu l'vadō pō-ayl g'vurōs,   כִּי הוּא לְבַדּוֹ פּוֹעֵל גְּבוּרוֹת,

For He alone effects mighty deeds,

ōse chadoshōs, ba-al milchomōs,   עֹשֶׂה חֲדָשׁוֹת, בַּעַל מִלְחָמוֹת,

makes new things, is Master of wars,

zōray-a tz'dokōs,   זוֹרֵעַ צְדָקוֹת,

matzmi-ach y'shu-ōs,   מַצְמִיחַ יְשׁוּעוֹת,

sows kindnesses,* makes salvations flourish,

bōray r'fu-ōs, nōro s'hilōs,   בּוֹרֵא רְפוּאוֹת, נוֹרָא תְהִלּוֹת,

creates cures, is too awesome for praise,

adōn haniflo-ōs.   אֲדוֹן הַנִּפְלָאוֹת.

is Lord of wonders.

Ham'chadaysh b'tuvō   הַמְחַדֵּשׁ בְּטוּבוֹ

b'chol yōm tomid   בְּכָל יוֹם תָּמִיד

In His goodness He renews daily, perpetually,

ma-asay v'rayshis.   מַעֲשֵׂה בְרֵאשִׁית.

the work of Creation.

Melachim, Elohim, B'nei Elohim, Cheruvim and Ishim.

זוֹרֵעַ צְדָקוֹת — *Sows kindnesses.* God does not merely reward man for his good deeds; He rewards him even for the chain reaction that results from human kindness. Thus, an act of kindness is like a seed that can produce luxuriant vegetation.

Ko-omur: L'ōsay ōrim g'dōlim,   כָּאָמוּר: לְעֹשֵׂה אוֹרִים גְּדֹלִים,

As it is said: "[Give thanks] to Him Who makes the great luminaries,

ki l'ōlom chasdō.   כִּי לְעוֹלָם חַסְדּוֹ.

for His kindness endures forever."

Ōr chodosh al tziyōn to-ir,   ❖ אוֹר חָדָשׁ עַל צִיּוֹן תָּאִיר,

May You shine a new light* on Zion,

v'nizke chulonu m'hayro l'ōrō.   וְנִזְכֶּה כֻלָּנוּ מְהֵרָה לְאוֹרוֹ.

and may we all speedily merit its light.

Boruch ato Adōnoy,   בָּרוּךְ אַתָּה יהוה,

Blessed are You, Hashem,

yōtzayr ham'ōrōs.   יוֹצֵר הַמְּאוֹרוֹת.

CONGREGATION RESPONDS: Omayn — אָמֵן

■ Second blessing preceding the *Shema:* We appreciate the love of Israel that God demonstrated by choosing Israel and giving them the gift of Torah; and we request Divine assistance in living according to His Torah.

AHAVO rabo ahavtonu   **אַהֲבָה** רַבָּה אֲהַבְתָּנוּ

Adōnoy Elōhaynu,   יהוה אֱלֹהֵינוּ,

With an abundant love* have You loved us, Hashem, our God;

chemlo g'dōlo visayro   חֶמְלָה גְדוֹלָה וִיתֵרָה

chomalto olaynu.   חָמַלְתָּ עָלֵינוּ.

with exceedingly great pity have You pitied us.

Ovinu malkaynu,   אָבִינוּ מַלְכֵּנוּ,

Our Father, our King,

ba-avur avōsaynu shebot'chu v'cho,   בַּעֲבוּר אֲבוֹתֵינוּ שֶׁבָּטְחוּ בְךָ,

for the sake of our forefathers who trusted in You

vat'lam'daym chukay cha-yim,   וַתְּלַמְּדֵם חֻקֵּי חַיִּים,

and whom You taught the decrees of life,

kayn t'chonaynu uslam'daynu.   כֵּן תְּחָנֵּנוּ וּתְלַמְּדֵנוּ.

may You be equally gracious to us and teach us.

Ovinu ho-ov horachamon,   אָבִינוּ הָאָב הָרַחֲמָן,

Our Father, the merciful Father,

ham'rachaym, rachaym olaynu,   הַמְרַחֵם, רַחֵם עָלֵינוּ,

Who acts mercifully, have mercy upon us,

אוֹר חָדָשׁ — *A new light.* The *new* light is actually a return of the original brilliance of Creation. That light was concealed for the enjoyment of the righteous in the Messianic era. May it soon shine upon Zion.

אַהֲבָה רַבָּה — *With an abundant love.* Up to now, we have blessed God for having created the luminaries, but there is a light even greater than that of the brightest stars and the sun — the light of the Torah. Now, in this second

v'sayn b'libaynu l'hovin ulhaskil,   וְתֵן בְּלִבֵּנוּ לְהָבִין וּלְהַשְׂכִּיל,

instill in our hearts to understand and elucidate,

lishmō-a lilmōd ul'lamayd,   לִשְׁמֹעַ לִלְמֹד וּלְלַמֵּד,

to listen, learn, teach,

lishmōr v'la-asōs ul-ka-yaym   לִשְׁמֹר וְלַעֲשׂוֹת וּלְקַיֵּם

safeguard, perform, and fulfill

es kol divray   אֶת כָּל דִּבְרֵי

salmud tōrosecho b'ahavo.   תַּלְמוּד תּוֹרָתֶךָ בְּאַהֲבָה.

all the words of Your Torah's teaching with love.

V'ho-ayr aynaynu b'sōrosecho,   וְהָאֵר עֵינֵינוּ בְּתוֹרָתֶךָ,

Enlighten our eyes* in Your Torah,

v'dabayk libaynu b'mitzvōsecho,   וְדַבֵּק לִבֵּנוּ בְּמִצְוֺתֶיךָ,

attach our hearts to Your commandments,

v'yachayd l'vovaynu   וְיַחֵד לְבָבֵנוּ

l'a-havo ul-yiro es sh'mecho,   לְאַהֲבָה וּלְיִרְאָה אֶת שְׁמֶךָ,

and unify our hearts to love and fear Your Name,

v'lō nayvōsh l'ōlom vo-ed: וְלֹא נֵבוֹשׁ לְעוֹלָם וָעֶד.

and may we not feel inner shame for all eternity.*

Ki v'shaym kod-sh'cho   כִּי בְשֵׁם קָדְשְׁךָ

hagodōl v'hanōro botoch'nu,   הַגָּדוֹל וְהַנּוֹרָא בָּטָחְנוּ,

Because we have trusted in Your great and awesome holy Name,

nogilo v'nism'cho bi-shu-osecho.   נָגִילָה וְנִשְׂמְחָה בִּישׁוּעָתֶךָ.

may we exult and rejoice in Your salvation.

ONE WHO IS WEARING *TZITZIS* SHOULD GATHER THE FOUR *TZITZIS* (FRINGES) INTO HIS
LEFT HAND AND HOLD THEM UNTIL AFTER THE *SHEMA,* AS INDICATED BELOW (P. 367).

Vahavi-aynu l'sholōm   וַהֲבִיאֵנוּ לְשָׁלוֹם

Bring us in peacefulness

may-arba kanfōs ho-oretz,   מֵאַרְבַּע כַּנְפוֹת הָאָרֶץ,

from the four corners of the earth

v'sōlichaynu kōm'miyus l'artzaynu,   וְתוֹלִיכֵנוּ קוֹמְמִיּוּת לְאַרְצֵנוּ.

and lead us with upright pride to our land.

---

blessing before *Shema,* we thank God for the
Torah and pray that He grant us the wisdom to
understand it properly.

וְהָאֵר עֵינֵינוּ — *Enlighten our eyes.* This begins a
series of brief supplications with one general
purpose: A Jew's involvement with Torah study
and observance must saturate all his activities,
even his business, leisure, and social life.

וְלֹא נֵבוֹשׁ לְעוֹלָם וָעֶד — *And may we not feel inner*

shame for all eternity. "Inner shame" refers to
the humiliation one feels deep within himself
when he knows he has done wrong — even
though the people around him may sing his
praises. The cost of such shame is borne primarily in the World to Come, where it can
diminish one's eternal bliss or even destroy it
entirely. Therefore we pray that our eternity
not be marred by inner shame.

Ki Ayl pō-ayl y'shu-ōs oto,   כִּי אֵל פּוֹעֵל יְשׁוּעוֹת אָתָּה,

For You effect salvations, O God;

u-vonu vocharto mikol am v'loshōn.   וּבָנוּ בָחַרְתָּ מִכָּל עַם וְלָשׁוֹן.

and You have chosen us from among every people and tongue.

V'kayravtonu l'shimcho hagodōl   ❖ וְקֵרַבְתָּנוּ לְשִׁמְךָ הַגָּדוֹל

selo be-emes   סֶלָה בֶּאֱמֶת,

And You have brought us close to Your great Name forever, in truth,

l'hōdōs l'cho ul-yachedcho b'ahava.   לְהוֹדוֹת לְךָ וּלְיַחֶדְךָ בְּאַהֲבָה.

to offer praiseful thanks to You, and proclaim Your Oneness with love.

Boruch ato Adōnoy,   בָּרוּךְ אַתָּה יהוה,

habōchayr b'amō yisro-ayl   הַבּוֹחֵר בְּעַמּוֹ יִשְׂרָאֵל

b'ahavoh.   בְּאַהֲבָה.

Blessed are You, HASHEM Who chooses His people Israel with love.

CONGREGATION RESPONDS: Omayn — אָמֵן

THE SHEMA

■ The *Shema* is our acceptance of and submission to the absolute Sovereignty of God.

IMMEDIATELY BEFORE THE RECITATION OF THE *SHEMA*, CONCENTRATE ON FULFILLING THE POSITIVE COMMANDMENT OF RECITING THE *SHEMA* DAILY, ONCE IN THE EVENING AND ONCE IN THE MORNING. IT IS IMPORTANT TO ENUNCIATE EACH WORD CLEARLY AND NOT TO RUN WORDS TOGETHER.

ONE PRAYING WITHOUT A *MINYAN* BEGINS WITH THE FOLLOWING THREE-WORD FORMULA:

Ayl melech ne-emon.   אֵל מֶלֶךְ נֶאֱמָן.

God, trustworthy King.

RECITE THE fiRST VERSE ALOUD, WITH YOUR RIGHT HAND COVERING YOUR EYES, AND CONCENTRATE INTENSELY UPON ACCEPTING GOD'S ABSOLUTE SOVEREIGNTY.

SH'MA yisro-ayl,   **שְׁמַע** יִשְׂרָאֵל,

Adōnoy Elōhaynu, Adōnoy e-chod.   יהוה אֱלֹהֵינוּ, יהוה אֶחָד.

Hear, O Israel: HASHEM is our God, HASHEM, the One [and Only].

In an undertone:

Boruch shaym k'vōd malchusō   בָּרוּךְ שֵׁם כְּבוֹד מַלְכוּתוֹ

l'ōlom vo-ed.   לְעוֹלָם וָעֶד.

Blessed is the Name of His glorious kingdom for all eternity.

■ We return God's love by studying His Torah and committing ourselves to observe the Torah with all our resources and being.

WHILE RECITING THE FOLLOWING PARAGRAPH, CONCENTRATE ON ACCEPTING THE COMMANDMENT TO LOVE GOD.

V'OHAVTO ays   **וְאָהַבְתָּ** אֵת

Adōnoy Elōhecho,   יהוה ׀ אֱלֹהֶיךָ,

You shall love HASHEM, your God,

b'chol l'vov'cho,   בְּכָל לְבָבְךָ,

with all your heart,

uvchol nafsh'cho, uvchol m'ōdecho.   וּבְכָל נַפְשְׁךָ, וּבְכָל מְאֹדֶךָ.

with all your soul and with all your resources.

V'ho-yu had'vorim ho-ayle,   וְהָיוּ הַדְּבָרִים הָאֵלֶּה,

asher onōchi m'tzav'cho ha-yōm,   אֲשֶׁר אָנֹכִי מְצַוְּךָ הַיּוֹם,

Let these matters that I command you today be

al l'vovecho.   עַל לְבָבֶךָ.

upon your heart.

V'shinantom l'vonecho,   וְשִׁנַּנְתָּם לְבָנֶיךָ,

Teach them thoroughly to your children

v'dibarto bom   וְדִבַּרְתָּ בָּם,

and speak of them

b'shivt'cho b'vaysecho,   בְּשִׁבְתְּךָ בְּבֵיתֶךָ,

uvlecht'cho vaderech   וּבְלֶכְתְּךָ בַדֶּרֶךְ,

while you sit in your home, while you walk on the way,

uv'shochb'cho, uvkumecho.   וּבְשָׁכְבְּךָ וּבְקוּמֶךָ.

when you retire and when you arise.

Ukshartom l'ōs al yodecho,   וּקְשַׁרְתָּם לְאוֹת עַל יָדֶךָ,

And you shall bind them* as a sign upon your arm

v'ho-yu l'tōtofōs bayn aynecho.   וְהָיוּ לְטֹטָפֹת בֵּין עֵינֶיךָ.

and they shall be tefillin between your eyes.

Uchsavtom al m'zuzōs bay-secho   וּכְתַבְתָּם עַל מְזֻזוֹת בֵּיתֶךָ,

u-vish-orecho.   וּבִשְׁעָרֶיךָ.

And write them on the doorposts of your house and upon your gates.

■ We declare Israel's collective commitment to observe God's *mitzvos,* and the recognition that our national success or failure is dependent on this observance.

V'HO-YO im shomō-a tishm'u   **וְהָיָה,** אִם־שָׁמֹעַ תִּשְׁמְעוּ

el mitzvōsai,   אֶל מִצְוֹתַי,

And it will come to pass that if you continually hearken to My commandments

asher onōchi   אֲשֶׁר אָנֹכִי

m'tza-ve eschem ha-yōm,   מְצַוֶּה אֶתְכֶם הַיּוֹם,

that I command you today,

l'ahavo es Adōnoy Elōhaychem,   לְאַהֲבָה אֶת יהוה אֱלֹהֵיכֶם,

to love HASHEM, *your God,*

ul-ovdō   וּלְעָבְדוֹ,

and to serve Him,

b'chol l'vavchem uvchol nafsh'chem.   בְּכָל לְבַבְכֶם, וּבְכָל נַפְשְׁכֶם.
with all your heart and with all your soul —

V'nosati m'tar artz'chem b'itō,   וְנָתַתִּי מְטַר אַרְצְכֶם בְּעִתּוֹ,
then I will provide rain for your land in its proper time,

yōre u-malkōsh,   יוֹרֶה וּמַלְקוֹשׁ,
the early rains and the late rains,

v'osafto d'gonecho v'sirōsh'cho   וְאָסַפְתָּ דְגָנֶךָ וְתִירֹשְׁךָ
v'yitzhorecho.   וְיִצְהָרֶךָ.
that you may gather in your grain, your wine, and your oil.

V'nosati aysev   וְנָתַתִּי עֵשֶׂב
b'sod'cho livhemtecho,   בְּשָׂדְךָ לִבְהֶמְתֶּךָ,
I will provide grass in your field for your cattle

v'ochalto v'sovo-to.   וְאָכַלְתָּ וְשָׂבָעְתָּ.
and you will eat and you will be satisfied.

Hi-shom'ru lochem,   הִשָּׁמְרוּ לָכֶם,
Beware for yourselves,

pen yifte l'vavchem,   פֶּן יִפְתֶּה לְבַבְכֶם,
lest your heart be seduced

v'sartem va-avadtem   וְסַרְתֶּם וַעֲבַדְתֶּם
elōhim a-chayrim   אֱלֹהִים אֲחֵרִים,
and you turn astray and serve gods of others

v'hishtachavisem lohem.   וְהִשְׁתַּחֲוִיתֶם לָהֶם.
and bow to them.

V'choro af Adōnoy bochem,   וְחָרָה אַף יהוה בָּכֶם,
Then the wrath of HASHEM will blaze against you;

v'otzar es ha-shoma-yim   וְעָצַר אֶת הַשָּׁמַיִם,
v'lō yih-ye motor,   וְלֹא יִהְיֶה מָטָר,
He will restrain the heaven so there will be no rain

v'ho-adomo lō sitayn es y'vuloh,   וְהָאֲדָמָה לֹא תִתֵּן אֶת יְבוּלָהּ,
and the ground will not yield its produce;

va-avadtem m'hayro   וַאֲבַדְתֶּם מְהֵרָה
and you will swiftly be banished

may-al ho-oretz hatōvo   מֵעַל הָאָרֶץ הַטֹּבָה
from the goodly land

asher Adōnoy nōsayn lochem.   אֲשֶׁר יהוה נֹתֵן לָכֶם.
which HASHEM gives you.

V'samtem es d'vorai ayle   וְשַׂמְתֶּם אֶת דְּבָרַי אֵלֶּה,
You shall place these words of Mine

al l'vavchem v'al nafsh'chem

עַל לְבַבְכֶם וְעַל נַפְשְׁכֶם,

upon your heart and upon your soul;

ukshartem ōsom l'ōs
  al yedchem,

וּקְשַׁרְתֶּם אֹתָם לְאוֹת
עַל יֶדְכֶם,

and you shall bind them for a sign upon your arm

v'ho-yu l'tōtofōs bayn aynaychem.

וְהָיוּ לְטוֹטָפֹת בֵּין עֵינֵיכֶם.

and they shall be tefillin between your eyes.

V'limadtem ōsom es b'naychem,

וְלִמַּדְתֶּם אֹתָם אֶת בְּנֵיכֶם,

You shall teach them to your children,

l'dabayr bom,

לְדַבֵּר בָּם,

to discuss them,

b'shivt'cho b'vay-secho,
  uvlecht'cho vaderech,

בְּשִׁבְתְּךָ בְּבֵיתֶךָ,
וּבְלֶכְתְּךָ בַדֶּרֶךְ,

while you sit in your home, while you walk on the way,

uv'shochb'cho uvkumecho.

וּבְשָׁכְבְּךָ וּבְקוּמֶךָ.

when you retire and when you arise.

Uchsavtom al m'zuzōs bay-secho
  u-vish-orecho.

וּכְתַבְתָּם עַל מְזֻזוֹת בֵּיתֶךָ,
וּבִשְׁעָרֶיךָ.

And write them on the doorposts of your house and upon your gates.

L'ma-an yirbu y'maychem
  vimay v'naychem

לְמַעַן יִרְבּוּ יְמֵיכֶם
וִימֵי בְנֵיכֶם,

In order to prolong your days and the days of your children

al ho-adomo asher nishba
  Adōnoy la-avōsaychem

עַל הָאֲדָמָה אֲשֶׁר נִשְׁבַּע
יהוה לַאֲבֹתֵיכֶם

upon the ground that HASHEM has sworn to your ancestors

losays lohem,

לָתֵת לָהֶם,

to give them,

kimay ha-shoma-yim al ho-oretz.

כִּימֵי הַשָּׁמַיִם עַל הָאָרֶץ.

like the days of the heavens on the earth.

■ We acknowledge the Divine providence over Israel as demonstrated by the Exodus from Egypt, thus obligating us to observe His *mitzvos*.

BEFORE RECITING THIS PARAGRAPH, THE *TZITZIS*, WHICH HAVE BEEN HELD IN THE LEFT HAND, ARE TAKEN IN THE RIGHT HAND ALSO. THE *TZITZIS* ARE KISSED AT EACH MENTION OF *TZITZIS*, AND AT THE END OF THE PARAGRAPH, AND ARE PASSED BEFORE THE EYES AT ur'isem ōsō.

VA-YŌMER Adōnoy
  el mōshe laymōr.

וַיֹּאמֶר יהוה
אֶל מֹשֶׁה לֵּאמֹר.

And HASHEM said to Moses saying:

Dabayr el b'nay yisro-ayl   דַּבֵּר אֶל בְּנֵי יִשְׂרָאֵל,

v'omarto alayhem,   וְאָמַרְתָּ אֲלֵהֶם,

Speak to the Children of Israel and say to them

v'osu lohem tzitzis   וְעָשׂוּ לָהֶם צִיצִת,

that they are to make themselves tzitzis

al kanfay vigdayhem   עַל כַּנְפֵי בִגְדֵיהֶם

on the corners of their garments,

l'dōrōsom,   לְדֹרֹתָם,

throughout their generations.

v'nos'nu al tzitzis hakonof   וְנָתְנוּ עַל צִיצִת הַכָּנָף,

p'sil t'chayles.   פְּתִיל תְּכֵלֶת.

And they are to place upon the tzitzis of each corner a thread of turquoise wool.

V'ho-yo lochem l'tzitzis,   וְהָיָה לָכֶם לְצִיצִת,

And it shall constitute tzitzis for you,

ur-isem ōsō   וּרְאִיתֶם אֹתוֹ,

that you may see it

uz-chartem es kol mitzvōs Adōnoy,   וּזְכַרְתֶּם אֶת כָּל מִצְוֹת יהוה,

and remember all the commandments of HASHEM

va-asisem ōsom,   וַעֲשִׂיתֶם אֹתָם,

and perform them;

v'lō sosuru acharay l'vavchem   וְלֹא תָתוּרוּ אַחֲרֵי לְבַבְכֶם

v'acharay aynaychem,   וְאַחֲרֵי עֵינֵיכֶם,

and you shall not explore after your heart and after your eyes

asher atem zōnim acharayhem.   אֲשֶׁר אַתֶּם זֹנִים אַחֲרֵיהֶם.

after which you stray.

L'ma-an tizk'ru   לְמַעַן תִּזְכְּרוּ

va-asisem es kol mitzvōsoy,   וַעֲשִׂיתֶם אֶת כָּל מִצְוֹתָי,

So that you may remember and perform all My commandments;

vih-yisem k'dōshim Laylōhaychem.   וִהְיִיתֶם קְדֹשִׁים לֵאלֹהֵיכֶם.

and be holy to your God.

CONCENTRATE ON FULFILLING THE COMMANDMENT TO REMEMBER THE EXODUS FROM EGYPT.

Ani Adōnoy Elohaychem,   אֲנִי יהוה אֱלֹהֵיכֶם,

I am HASHEM, *your God,*

asher hōtzaysi eschem   אֲשֶׁר הוֹצֵאתִי אֶתְכֶם

may-eretz mitzra-yim,   מֵאֶרֶץ מִצְרַיִם,

Who has removed you from the land of Egypt

lih-yōs lochem Laylōhim,   לִהְיוֹת לָכֶם לֵאלֹהִים,

to be a God to you;

ani Adōnoy Elōhaychem.

אֲנִי יהוה אֱלֹהֵיכֶם.

Emes . . .

אֱמֶת . . .

I am HASHEM your God. It is true . . .

יהוה אֱלֹהֵיכֶם אֱמֶת. — Chazzan repeats

■ The blessing following the *Shema:* This blessing marks our transition from the *Shema* to the *Shemoneh Esrei* with profuse expressions of praise for His manifold acts of redemption.

V'YATZIV v'nochōn v'ka-yom

וְיַצִּיב וְנָכוֹן וְקַיָּם

And certain,* established and enduring,

v'yoshor v'ne-emon v'ohuv v'choviv

וְיָשָׁר וְנֶאֱמָן וְאָהוּב וְחָבִיב

fair and faithful, beloved and cherished,

v'nechmod v'no-im v'nōro v'adir

וְנֶחְמָד וְנָעִים וְנוֹרָא וְאַדִּיר

delightful and pleasant, awesome and powerful,

umsukon umkubol v'tōv v'yofe

וּמְתֻקָּן וּמְקֻבָּל וְטוֹב וְיָפֶה

correct and accepted, good and beautiful

hadovor ha-ze olaynu l'ōlom vo-ed.

הַדָּבָר הַזֶּה עָלֵינוּ לְעוֹלָם וָעֶד.

is this affirmation to us forever and ever.

Emes Elōhay ōlom malkaynu,

אֱמֶת אֱלֹהֵי עוֹלָם מַלְכֵּנוּ,

True — the God of the universe is our King;

tzur ya-akōv mogayn yish-aynu,

צוּר יַעֲקֹב מָגֵן יִשְׁעֵנוּ,

the Rock of Jacob is the Shield of our salvation.

l'dōr vodōr hu ka-yom,

לְדֹר וָדֹר הוּא קַיָּם,

From generation to generation He endures

ushmō ka-yom, v'chis-ō nochōn,

וּשְׁמוֹ קַיָּם, וְכִסְאוֹ נָכוֹן,

and His Name endures and His throne is well established;

umalchusō ve-emunosō

וּמַלְכוּתוֹ וֶאֱמוּנָתוֹ

lo-ad ka-yomes.

לָעַד קַיָּמֶת.

His sovereignty and faithfulness endure forever.

Udvorov cho-yim v'ka-yomim,

וּדְבָרָיו חָיִים וְקַיָּמִים,

His words are living and enduring,

ne-emonim v'nechemodim lo-ad

נֶאֱמָנִים וְנֶחֱמָדִים לָעַד

faithful and delightful forever

(ONE WHO IS WEARING A TALLIS KISSES THE TZITZIS AND RELEASES THEM)

אֱמֶת . . . וְיַצִּיב — *True . . . and certain.* This paragraph begins the third and final blessing of the *Shema*, which ends with "Who redeemed Israel." Like its counterpart in the Evening Service, this blessing continues our fulfillment of the requirement to recall the Exodus, morning and evening.

ul-ōl'may ōlomim.   וּלְעוֹלְמֵי עוֹלָמִים.

and to all eternity;

Al avōsaynu v'olaynu,   עַל אֲבוֹתֵינוּ וְעָלֵינוּ,

for our forefathers and for us,

al bonaynu v'al dōrōsaynu,   עַל בָּנֵינוּ וְעַל דּוֹרוֹתֵינוּ,

for our children and for our generations,

v'al kol dōrōs   וְעַל כָּל דּוֹרוֹת

zera yisro-ayl avodecho.   זֶרַע יִשְׂרָאֵל עֲבָדֶיךָ.

and for all the generations of Your servant Israel's offspring.

■ Our expressions of confidence that Hashem, in His goodness,
will continue to redeem Israel

AL HORISHŌNIM   עַל הָרִאשׁוֹנִים

v'al ho-acharōnim,   וְעַל הָאַחֲרוֹנִים,

Upon the earlier and upon the later generations,

dovor tōv v'ka-yom l'ōlom vo-ed,   דָּבָר טוֹב וְקַיָּם לְעוֹלָם וָעֶד,

this affirmation is good and enduring forever.

emes ve-emuno   אֱמֶת וֶאֱמוּנָה

True and faithful,

chōk v'lō ya-avōr.   חֹק וְלֹא יַעֲבֹר.

it is an unbreachable decree.

Emes sho-ato hu Adōnoy   אֱמֶת שָׁאַתָּה הוּא יהוה

It is true that You are HASHEM,

Elōhaynu Vaylōhay avōsaynu,   אֱלֹהֵינוּ וֵאלֹהֵי אֲבוֹתֵינוּ,

our God and the God of our forefathers,

malkaynu melech avōsaynu,   ❖ מַלְכֵּנוּ מֶלֶךְ אֲבוֹתֵינוּ,

our King and the King of our forefathers,

gō-alaynu gō-ayl avōsaynu,   גֹּאֲלֵנוּ גֹּאֵל אֲבוֹתֵינוּ,

our Redeemer, the Redeemer of our forefathers;

yōtz'raynu tzur y'shu-osaynu,   יוֹצְרֵנוּ צוּר יְשׁוּעָתֵנוּ,

our Molder, the Rock of our salvation;

pōdaynu u-matzilaynu   פּוֹדֵנוּ וּמַצִּילֵנוּ

our Liberator and our Rescuer —

may-ōlom sh'mecho,   מֵעוֹלָם שְׁמֶךָ,

this has ever been Your Name.

ayn Elōhim zulosecho.   אֵין אֱלֹהִים זוּלָתֶךָ.

There is no God but You.

■ A detailed description of our past redemption and the joy we expressed then provides the basis for our confidence and surety of future redemption.

EZRAS avōsaynu   עֶזְרַת אֲבוֹתֵינוּ
*The Helper of our forefathers**

ato hu may-ōlom,   אַתָּה הוּא מֵעוֹלָם,
have You ever been,

mogayn u-mōshi-a   מָגֵן וּמוֹשִׁיעַ
Shield and Savior

livnayhem acharayhem   לִבְנֵיהֶם אַחֲרֵיהֶם
b'chol dōr vodōr.   בְּכָל דּוֹר וָדוֹר.
for their children after them in every generation.

B'rum ōlom mōshovecho,   בְּרוּם עוֹלָם מוֹשָׁבֶךָ,
At the zenith of the universe is Your dwelling,

u-mishpotecho v'tzidkos'cho   וּמִשְׁפָּטֶיךָ וְצִדְקָתְךָ
ad afsay oretz.   עַד אַפְסֵי אָרֶץ.
and Your justice and Your righteousness extend to the ends of the earth.

Ashray ish she-yishma l'mitzvōsecho,   אַשְׁרֵי אִישׁ שֶׁיִּשְׁמַע לְמִצְוֹתֶיךָ,
Praiseworthy is the person who obeys Your commandments

v'sōros'cho udvor'cho yosim al libō.   וְתוֹרָתְךָ וּדְבָרְךָ יָשִׂים עַל לִבּוֹ.
and takes to his heart Your teaching and Your word.

Emes ato hu odōn l'amecho   אֱמֶת אַתָּה הוּא אָדוֹן לְעַמֶּךָ
True — You are the Master for Your people

u-melech gibōr loriv rivom.   וּמֶלֶךְ גִּבּוֹר לָרִיב רִיבָם.
and a mighty King to take up their grievance.

Emes ato hu rishōn   אֱמֶת אַתָּה הוּא רִאשׁוֹן
True — You are the First

v'ato hu acharōn,   וְאַתָּה הוּא אַחֲרוֹן,
and You are the Last,

u-mibal-odecho ayn lonu melech   וּמִבַּלְעָדֶיךָ אֵין לָנוּ מֶלֶךְ
and other than You we have no king,

gō-ayl u-mōshi-a.   גּוֹאֵל וּמוֹשִׁיעַ.
redeemer, or savior.

Mimitzra-yim g'altonu   מִמִּצְרַיִם גְּאַלְתָּנוּ
From Egypt You redeemed us,

Adōnoy Elōhaynu,   יהוה אֱלֹהֵינוּ,
Hashem, our God,

עֶזְרַת אֲבוֹתֵינוּ — *The Helper of our forefathers.* This passage elaborates upon the Exodus within the context of God's eternal supervision of Israel and mastery over its destiny.

u-mibays avodim p'disonu.   וּמִבֵּית עֲבָדִים פְּדִיתָנוּ.
and from the house of slavery You liberated us.

Kol b'chōrayhem horogto,   כָּל בְּכוֹרֵיהֶם הָרָגְתָּ,
All their firstborn You slew,

uvchōr'cho go-olto,   וּבְכוֹרְךָ גָּאָלְתָּ,
but Your firstborn You redeemed;

v'yam suf bokato,   וְיַם סוּף בָּקַעְתָּ,
the Sea of Reeds You split;

v'zaydim tibato,   וְזֵדִים טִבַּעְתָּ,
the wanton sinners You drowned;

vididim he-evarto,   וִידִידִים הֶעֱבַרְתָּ,
the dear ones You brought across;

vaichasu ma-yim tzorayhem,   וַיְכַסּוּ מַיִם צָרֵיהֶם,
and the water covered their foes

e-chod mayhem lō nōsor.   אֶחָד מֵהֶם לֹא נוֹתָר.
— not one of them was left.

Al zōs shib'chu ahuvim   עַל זֹאת שִׁבְּחוּ אֲהוּבִים
   v'rōm'mu Ayl,   וְרוֹמְמוּ אֵל,
For this, the beloved praised and exalted God;

v'nos'nu y'didim   וְנָתְנוּ יְדִידִים
the dear ones offered

z'mirōs shirōs v'sishbochōs,   זְמִרוֹת שִׁירוֹת וְתִשְׁבָּחוֹת,
hymns, songs, praises,

b'rochōs v'hōdo-ōs,   בְּרָכוֹת וְהוֹדָאוֹת,
blessings, and thanksgivings

l'melech Ayl chai v'ka-yom,   לְמֶלֶךְ אֵל חַי וְקַיָּם,
to the King, the living and enduring God —

rom v'niso, godōl v'nōro,   רָם וְנִשָּׂא, גָּדוֹל וְנוֹרָא,
exalted and uplifted, great and awesome,

mashpil gay-im,   מַשְׁפִּיל גֵּאִים,
   u-magbi-ah sh'folim,   וּמַגְבִּיהַּ שְׁפָלִים,
Who humbles the haughty and lifts the lowly;

mōtzi asirim, u-fōde anovim,   מוֹצִיא אֲסִירִים, וּפוֹדֶה עֲנָוִים,
   v'ōzayr dalim,   וְעוֹזֵר דַּלִּים,
withdraws the captive, liberates the humble, and helps the poor;

v'ōne l'amō   וְעוֹנֶה לְעַמּוֹ
   b'ays shav-om aylov.   בְּעֵת שַׁוְּעָם אֵלָיו.
Who responds to His people upon their outcry to Him.

RISE FOR *SHEMONEH ESREI*. SOME TAKE THREE STEPS BACKWARD
AT THIS POINT; OTHERS DO SO BEFORE *TZUR YISRO-AYL*, "ROCK OF ISRAEL."

❖ T'hilōs l'Ayl elyōn,　　　　　　　　　❖ תְּהִלּוֹת לְאֵל עֶלְיוֹן,

Praises to the Supreme God,

boruch hu umvōroch.　　　　　　　　　　בָּרוּךְ הוּא וּמְבֹרָךְ.

the blessed One Who is blessed.

Mōshe uvnay yisro-ayl　　　　　　　　מֹשֶׁה וּבְנֵי יִשְׂרָאֵל

　l'cho onu shiro　　　　　　　　　　　　לְךָ עָנוּ שִׁירָה

Moses and the Children of Israel exclaimed a song to You

b'simcho rabo v'om'ru chulom:　　　　בְּשִׂמְחָה רַבָּה וְאָמְרוּ כֻלָּם:

with great joy and they all said:

mi chomōcho bo-aylim Adōnoy,　　　　מִי כָמֹכָה בָּאֵלִם יהוה,

"Who is like You among the heavenly powers, HASHEM!

mi komōcho nedor bakōdesh,　　　　　מִי כָּמֹכָה נֶאְדָּר בַּקֹּדֶשׁ,

Who is like You, mighty in holiness,

nōro s'hilōs ōsay fele.　　　　　　　　נוֹרָא תְהִלֹת עֹשֵׂה פֶלֶא.

too awesome for praise, doing wonders."

❖ Shiro chadosho　　　　　　　　　　　❖ שִׁירָה חֲדָשָׁה

With a new song

shib'chu g'ulim l'shimcho　　　　　　　שִׁבְּחוּ גְאוּלִים לְשִׁמְךָ

the redeemed ones praised Your Name

al s'fas ha-yom,　　　　　　　　　　　עַל שְׂפַת הַיָּם,

at the seashore,

yachad kulom　　　　　　　　　　　　יַחַד כֻּלָּם

　hōdu v'himlichu v'om'ru:　　　　　　הוֹדוּ וְהִמְלִיכוּ וְאָמְרוּ:

all of them in unison gave thanks, acknowledged [Your] sovereignty, and said:

Adōnoy yimlōch l'ōlom vo-ed.　　　　יהוה יִמְלֹךְ לְעֹלָם וָעֶד.

"HASHEM shall reign for all eternity."

❖ **TZUR** yisro-ayl,　　　　　　　　　❖ **צוּר** יִשְׂרָאֵל,

Rock of Israel,*

kumo b'ezras yisro-ayl,　　　　　　　קוּמָה בְּעֶזְרַת יִשְׂרָאֵל,

arise to the aid of Israel

ufday chin-umecho　　　　　　　　　וּפְדֵה כִנְאֻמֶךָ

　y'hudo v'yisro-ayl.　　　　　　　　יְהוּדָה וְיִשְׂרָאֵל.

and liberate, as You pledged, Judah and Israel.

צוּר יִשְׂרָאֵל — *Rock of Israel.* Since the end of *Shema,* we have concentrated on an elaboration of the miracles of the Exodus. We do not lose sight, however, of our faith that there is another, greater redemption yet to come. Thus we conclude with a plea that God rise up again to redeem Israel from this exile as He did in ancient Egypt.

Gō-alaynu Adōnoy tz'vo-ōs sh'mō,   גֹּאֲלֵנוּ יהוה צְבָאוֹת שְׁמוֹ,

Our Redeemer — HASHEM, Master of Legions, is His Name —

k'dōsh yisro-ayl.   קְדוֹשׁ יִשְׂרָאֵל.

the Holy One of Israel.

Boruch ato Adōnoy go-al yisro-ayl.   בָּרוּךְ אַתָּה יהוה, גָּאַל יִשְׂרָאֵל.

Blessed are You, HASHEM, Who redeemed Israel.

ON AN ORDINARY SABBATH AND ON THE SABBATH OF *CHOL HAMOED*
CONTINUE WITH THE SABBATH *SHEMONEH ESREI* BELOW.
ON FESTIVALS, EVEN THOSE THAT FALL ON THE SABBATH,
THE FESTIVAL *SHEMONEH ESREI* (P. 675) IS RECITED.

⊰ SHEMONEH ESREI FOR SABBATH MORNING ⊱

IN THE SYNAGOGUE THE *SHEMONEH ESREI* IS RECITED WHILE FACING THE ARK; ELSEWHERE IT IS
RECITED WHILE FACING THE DIRECTION OF THE LAND OF ISRAEL. TAKE THREE STEPS BACKWARD,
LEFT, RIGHT, LEFT, THEN THREE STEPS FORWARD, RIGHT, LEFT, RIGHT. REMAIN STANDING WITH
FEET TOGETHER DURING *SHEMONEH ESREI*. RECITE IT WITH QUIET DEVOTION AND WITHOUT ANY
INTERRUPTION. ALTHOUGH IT SHOULD NOT BE AUDIBLE TO OTHERS, ONE MUST PRAY LOUDLY
ENOUGH TO HEAR ONESELF.

Adōnoy s'fosai tiftoch,   אֲדֹנָי שְׂפָתַי תִּפְתָּח,

My Lord, open my lips,

u-fi yagid t'hilosecho.   וּפִי יַגִּיד תְּהִלָּתֶךָ.

that my mouth may declare Your praise.

■ First Blessing: In the merit of our Patriarchs whose actions reflected Godliness,
Hashem pledged to always be with Israel and protect them.

BEND THE KNEES AT Boruch; BOW AT ato; STRAIGHTEN UP AT Adōnoy.

BORUCH ato Adōnoy   בָּרוּךְ אַתָּה יהוה

Blessed are You, HASHEM,＊

Elōhaynu Vaylōhay avōsaynu,   אֱלֹהֵינוּ וֵאלֹהֵי אֲבוֹתֵינוּ,

our God and the God of our forefathers,

Elōhay avrohom, Elōhay yitzchok,   אֱלֹהֵי אַבְרָהָם, אֱלֹהֵי יִצְחָק,

Vaylōhay ya-akōv,   וֵאלֹהֵי יַעֲקֹב,

God of Abraham, God of Isaac, and God of Jacob;

ho-Ayl hagodōl hagibōr v'hanōro,   הָאֵל הַגָּדוֹל הַגִּבּוֹר וְהַנּוֹרָא,

Ayl elyōn,   אֵל עֶלְיוֹן,

the great, mighty, and awesome God, the supreme God,

gōmayl chasodim tōvim   גּוֹמֵל חֲסָדִים טוֹבִים

v'kōnay hakōl,   וְקוֹנֵה הַכֹּל,

Who bestows beneficial kindnesses and creates everything,

The first three and last three blessings are the   The first three are discussed on pages 34-37
same for all versions of the *Shemoneh Esrei*.   above; the last three on pages 46-55.

v'zōchayr chasday ovōs, וְזוֹכֵר חַסְדֵי אָבוֹת,
Who recalls the kindnesses of the Patriarchs

u-mayvi gō-ayl livnay v'nayhem, וּמֵבִיא גוֹאֵל לִבְנֵי בְנֵיהֶם,
and brings a Redeemer to their children's children,

l'ma-an sh'mō b'ahavo. לְמַעַן שְׁמוֹ בְּאַהֲבָה.
for His Name's sake, with love.

FROM ROSH HASHANAH TO YOM KIPPUR ADD:

Zochraynu l'cha-yim, זָכְרֵנוּ לְחַיִּים,

melech chofaytz bacha-yim, מֶלֶךְ חָפֵץ בַּחַיִּים,
Remember us for life, O King Who desires life,

v'chosvaynu b'sayfer hacha-yim, וְכָתְבֵנוּ בְּסֵפֶר הַחַיִּים,

l'ma-ancho Elōhim cha-yim. לְמַעַנְךָ אֱלֹהִים חַיִּים.
and inscribe us in the Book of Life — for Your sake, O Living God.

Melech ōzayr u-mōshi-a u-mogayn. מֶלֶךְ עוֹזֵר וּמוֹשִׁיעַ וּמָגֵן.
O King, Helper, Savior, and Shield.

BEND THE KNEES AT Boruch; BOW AT ato; STRAIGHTEN UP AT Adōnoy.

Boruch ato Adōnoy, בָּרוּךְ אַתָּה יהוה,

mogayn avrohom. מָגֵן אַבְרָהָם.
Blessed are You, HASHEM, Shield of Abraham.

■ Second Blessing: God's might as it is manifest in nature and man

---

ATO gibōr l'ōlom Adōnoy, אַתָּה גִּבּוֹר לְעוֹלָם אֲדֹנָי,
You are eternally mighty, my Lord,

m'cha-yay maysim ato, מְחַיֵּה מֵתִים אַתָּה,
the Resuscitator of the dead are You;

rav l'hōshi-a. רַב לְהוֹשִׁיעַ.
abundantly able to save,

BETWEEN SHEMINI ATZERES AND PESACH, ADD:

Mashiv horu-ach u-mōrid hageshem. מַשִּׁיב הָרוּחַ וּמוֹרִיד הַגֶּשֶׁם.
Who makes the wind blow and makes the rain descend;

M'chalkayl cha-yim b'chesed, מְכַלְכֵּל חַיִּים בְּחֶסֶד,
Who sustains the living with kindness;

m'cha-yay maysim b'rachamim rabim, מְחַיֵּה מֵתִים בְּרַחֲמִים רַבִּים,
resuscitates the dead with abundant mercy;

sōmaych nōf'lim, v'rōfay chōlim, סוֹמֵךְ נוֹפְלִים, וְרוֹפֵא חוֹלִים,
supports the fallen, heals the sick,

u-matir asurim,

וּמַתִּיר אֲסוּרִים,

releases the confined,

umka-yaym emunosō li-shaynay ofor.

וּמְקַיֵּם אֱמוּנָתוֹ לִישֵׁנֵי עָפָר.

and maintains His faith to those asleep in the dust.

Mi chomōcho ba-al g'vurōs,

מִי כָמְוֹךָ בַּעַל גְּבוּרוֹת,

Who is like You, O Master of mighty deeds,

u-mi dōme loch,

וּמִי דְוֹמֶה לָּךְ,

and who is comparable to You,

melech maymis umcha-ye

מֶלֶךְ מֵמִית וּמְחַיֶּה

u-matzmi-ach y'shu-o.

וּמַצְמִיחַ יְשׁוּעָה.

O King Who causes death and restores life and makes salvation sprout!

FROM ROSH HASHANAH TO YOM KIPPUR ADD:

Mi chomōcho av horachamim,

מִי כָמְוֹךָ אַב הָרַחֲמִים,

Who is like You, O Merciful Father,

zōchayr y'tzurov l'cha-yim
b'rachamim.

זוֹכֵר יְצוּרָיו לְחַיִּים
בְּרַחֲמִים.

Who recalls His creatures mercifully for life!

V'ne-emon ato l'hacha-yōs maysim.

וְנֶאֱמָן אַתָּה לְהַחֲיוֹת מֵתִים.

And You are faithful to resuscitate the dead.

Boruch ato Adōnoy,
m'cha-yay hamaysim.

בָּרוּךְ אַתָּה יהוה,
מְחַיֵּה הַמֵּתִים.

Blessed are You, HASHEM, Who resuscitates the dead.

■ Third Blessing: Regarding the holiness of God's Name

DURING THE *CHAZZAN'S* REPETITION, *KEDUSHAH* IS RECITED; INDIVIDUALS CONTINUE ON P. 376.

STAND WITH FEET TOGETHER AND AVOID ANY INTERRUPTIONS. RISE ON TOES
WHEN SAYING Kodōsh, kodōsh, kodōsh; Boruch; AND Yimlōch.

CONGREGATION, THEN *CHAZZAN:*

N'KADAYSH es shimcho bo-ōlom,

נְקַדֵּשׁ אֶת שִׁמְךָ בָּעוֹלָם,

We shall sanctify Your Name in this world,

k'shaym shemakdishim ōsō
bishmay morōm,

כְּשֵׁם שֶׁמַּקְדִּישִׁים אוֹתוֹ
בִּשְׁמֵי מָרוֹם,

just as they sanctify it in heaven above,

Kakosuv al yad n'vi-echo,

כַּכָּתוּב עַל יַד נְבִיאֶךָ,

as it is written by the hand of Your prophet,

◄§ **Kedushah**

Kedushah, Sanctification, expresses the concept that God is exalted above and separated from the limitations of material existence. When a *minyan* (quorum of ten) is present, it

becomes the representative of the nation and echoes the angels who sing God's praise by proclaiming His holiness and glory. We do this by reciting *Kedushah,* a prayer based on that of the angels themselves, and with feet together,

v'koro ze el ze v'omar:

וְקָרָא זֶה אֶל זֶה וְאָמַר:

"And one [angel] will call another and say:

ALL IN UNISON:

Kodōsh, kodōsh, kodōsh

קָדוֹשׁ קָדוֹשׁ קָדוֹשׁ

Adōnoy tz'vo-ōs,

יהוה צְבָאוֹת,

'Holy, holy, holy is HASHEM, *Master of Legions,*

m'lō chol ho-oretz k'vōdō.

מְלֹא כָל הָאָרֶץ כְּבוֹדוֹ.

the whole world is filled with His glory.' "

CONGREGATION, THEN *CHAZZAN*:

Oz b'kōl ra-ash godōl

אָז בְּקוֹל רַעַשׁ גָּדוֹל

adir v'chozok

אַדִּיר וְחָזָק

Then, with a sound of great noise, mighty and powerful,

mashmi-im kōl,

מַשְׁמִיעִים קוֹל,

they make heard a voice,

misnas'im l'u-mas s'rofim,

מִתְנַשְּׂאִים לְעֻמַּת שְׂרָפִים,

raising themselves toward the Seraphim;

l'u-mosom boruch yōmayru:

לְעֻמָּתָם בָּרוּךְ יֹאמֵרוּ:

those facing them say, "Blessed . . .":

ALL IN UNISON:

Boruch k'vōd Adōnoy, mim'kōmō.

בָּרוּךְ כְּבוֹד יהוה, מִמְּקוֹמוֹ.

"Blessed is the glory of HASHEM *from His place."*[*]

CONGREGATION, THEN *CHAZZAN*:

Mim'kōm'cho malkaynu sōfi-a,

מִמְּקוֹמְךָ מַלְכֵּנוּ תוֹפִיעַ,

From Your place, our King, You will appear

v'simlōch olaynu,

וְתִמְלֹךְ עָלֵינוּ,

and reign over us,

ki m'chakim anachnu loch.

כִּי מְחַכִּים אֲנַחְנוּ לָךְ.

for we await You.

Mosai timlōch b'tziyōn,

מָתַי תִּמְלֹךְ בְּצִיּוֹן,

When will You reign in Zion?

in the manner of the angels (*Ezekiel* 1:7). When reciting the key words — *Kodōsh, kodōsh, kodōsh; Boruch* and *Yimlōch* — we rise up on our toes to symbolize that we seek to break loose from the bonds of earth and unite our service with that of the angels.

The *Kedushah* of the Sabbath is expanded to indicate the special significance of the Sabbath in attaining the goal of sanctification. The home of God's Presence was — and will be again — the Temple in Jerusalem. If we properly appreciate the great holiness of the Sabbath, we can better comprehend the song of the angels and elevate ourselves to the level where we are worthy of the coming of Messiah and the return of the Temple. Therefore, these two themes are stressed in the Sabbath additions to *Kedushah*.

מִמְּקוֹמוֹ — *From His place.* Maimonides interprets "place" figuratively as meaning level or degree, in the sense that we say that someone takes his father's place. However, even the angels do not know what God's place really is; He is beyond all understanding. Therefore, when we say that God's glory comes "from His place," we are purposely being vague because

b'korov b'yomaynu,
Soon, in our days —
בְּקָרוֹב בְּיָמֵינוּ,

l'olom vo-ed tishkon.
forever and ever — may You dwell there.
לְעוֹלָם וָעֶד תִּשְׁכּוֹן.

Tisgadal v'siskadash
May You be exalted and sanctified
תִּתְגַּדַּל וְתִתְקַדַּשׁ

b'soch y'rushola-yim ir'cho,
within Jerusalem, Your city,
בְּתוֹךְ יְרוּשָׁלַיִם עִירְךָ,

l'dor vodor ulnaytzach n'tzochim.
from generation to generation and for all eternity.
לְדוֹר וָדוֹר וּלְנֵצַח נְצָחִים.

V'aynaynu sir-eno malchusecho,
May our eyes see Your kingdom,
וְעֵינֵינוּ תִרְאֶינָה מַלְכוּתֶךָ,

kadovor ho-omur b'shiray u-zecho,
as it is expressed in the songs of Your might,
כַּדָּבָר הָאָמוּר בְּשִׁירֵי עֻזֶּךָ,

al y'day dovid m'shi-ach tzidkecho:
written by David, Your righteous anointed:
עַל יְדֵי דָוִד מְשִׁיחַ צִדְקֶךָ:

ALL IN UNISON:

Yimloch Adonoy l'olom,
"HASHEM shall reign* forever;
יִמְלֹךְ יהוה לְעוֹלָם,

Eloha-yich tziyon l'dor vodor,
your God, O Zion, from generation to generation.
אֱלֹהַיִךְ צִיּוֹן לְדֹר וָדֹר,

hal'luyoh.
Praise God!"
הַלְלוּיָהּ.

CHAZZAN CONCLUDES:

לְדוֹר וָדוֹר נַגִּיד גָּדְלֶךָ וּלְנֵצַח נְצָחִים קְדֻשָּׁתְךָ נַקְדִּישׁ, וְשִׁבְחֲךָ אֱלֹהֵינוּ מִפִּינוּ לֹא יָמוּשׁ לְעוֹלָם וָעֶד, כִּי אֵל מֶלֶךְ גָּדוֹל וְקָדוֹשׁ אָתָּה. בָּרוּךְ אַתָּה יהוה, °הָאֵל הַקָּדוֹשׁ.

°הַמֶּלֶךְ הַקָּדוֹשׁ. — from Rosh Hashanah to Yom Kippur substitute

THE *CHAZZAN* CONTINUES *Yismach moshe* (P. 377).

INDIVIDUALS CONTINUE HERE:

ATO kodosh v'shimcho kodosh,
You are holy and Your Name is holy,
אַתָּה קָדוֹשׁ וְשִׁמְךָ קָדוֹשׁ,

ukdoshim b'chol yom
y'hal'lucho, selo.
and holy ones praise You, every day, forever.
וּקְדוֹשִׁים בְּכָל יוֹם יְהַלְלוּךָ סֶּלָה.

---

we cannot know the extent of His true glory. We are saying that whatever the true level of God's perfection may be, let it be implicit in the limited words with which we praise Him.

יִמְלֹךְ ה' — *HASHEM shall reign.* The Sages inserted this verse into *Kedushah* because all prayers should include an implied or direct plea for the rebuilding of Jerusalem [Zion].

Boruch ato Adōnoy,
°ho-Ayl hakodōsh.

בָּרוּךְ אַתָּה יהוה,
°הָאֵל הַקָּדוֹשׁ.

Blessed are You, HASHEM, the holy God.

FROM ROSH HASHANAH TO YOM KIPPUR SUBSTITUTE:

°hamelech hakodōsh.

°הַמֶּלֶךְ הַקָּדוֹשׁ.

the holy King.

■ Fourth Blessing: relating to the holiness of the day. The Torah, which was given to Moses and Israel on a Shabbos day, is to be especially revered and studied each Shabbos.

YISMACH MŌSHE
יִשְׂמַח מֹשֶׁה

b'mat'nas chelkō,
בְּמַתְּנַת חֶלְקוֹ,

Moses rejoiced* in the gift of his portion:

ki eved ne-emon koroso lō.
כִּי עֶבֶד נֶאֱמָן קָרֵאתָ לּוֹ.

that You called him a faithful servant.

K'lil tif-eres b'rōshō
nosato (lō),

כְּלִיל תִּפְאֶרֶת בְּרֹאשׁוֹ
נָתַתָּ (לּוֹ),

A crown of splendor* You placed on his head

B'omdō l'fonecho al har sinoy.
בְּעָמְדוֹ לְפָנֶיךָ עַל הַר סִינָי.

when he stood before You on Mount Sinai.

Ushnay luchōs avonim
hōrid b'yodō,

וּשְׁנֵי לוּחוֹת אֲבָנִים
הוֹרִיד בְּיָדוֹ,

He brought down two stone Tablets in his hand,

v'chosuv bohem sh'miras shabos,
וְכָתוּב בָּהֶם שְׁמִירַת שַׁבָּת,

on which is inscribed the observance of the Sabbath;

v'chayn kosuv b'sōrosecho:
וְכֵן כָּתוּב בְּתוֹרָתֶךָ:

and so it is written in Your Torah:

■ The Jewish people exclusively are invited to contribute to the observance and character of the Shabbos day.

V'SHOM'RU v'nay yisro-ayl
es ha-shabos,

וְשָׁמְרוּ בְנֵי יִשְׂרָאֵל
אֶת הַשַּׁבָּת,

"And the Children of Israel shall keep the Sabbath,

la-asōs es ha-shabos l'dōrōsom
לַעֲשׂוֹת אֶת הַשַּׁבָּת לְדֹרֹתָם

to make the Sabbath for their generations

יִשְׂמַח מֹשֶׁה — *Moses rejoiced* that God considered him a faithful servant (*Numbers* 12:7) and that, in reward for his dedication, God chose him to receive the Tablets of the Ten

Commandments, which included the *mitzvah* of the Sabbath.

כְּלִיל תִּפְאֶרֶת — *A crown of splendor.* When Moses descended from Sinai, his face glowed

b'ris ōlom.   בְּרִית עוֹלָם.

an eternal covenant.

Bayni u-vayn b'nay yisro-ayl   בֵּינִי וּבֵין בְּנֵי יִשְׂרָאֵל

Between Me and the Children of Israel

ōs hi l'ōlom,   אוֹת הִיא לְעֹלָם,

it is a sign forever

ki shayshes yomim oso Adōnoy   כִּי שֵׁשֶׁת יָמִים עָשָׂה יהוה

that in six days HASHEM *made*

es ha-shoma-yim v'es ho-oretz,   אֶת הַשָּׁמַיִם וְאֶת הָאָרֶץ,

heaven and earth,

u-va-yōm hash'vi-i shovas va-yinofash.   וּבַיּוֹם הַשְּׁבִיעִי שָׁבַת וַיִּנָּפַשׁ.

and on the seventh day He rested and was refreshed.''

V'LŌ N'SATŌ Adōnoy Elōhaynu   **וְלֹא נְתַתּוֹ** יהוה אֱלֹהֵינוּ

l'gōyay ho-arotzōs,   לְגוֹיֵי הָאֲרָצוֹת,

And You did not give it,* HASHEM, *our God, to the nations of the lands,*

v'lō hinchaltō malkaynu   וְלֹא הִנְחַלְתּוֹ מַלְכֵּנוּ

l'ōv'day f'silim,   לְעוֹבְדֵי פְסִילִים,

nor did You make it the inheritance, our King, of the worshipers of graven idols.

v'gam bimnuchosō   וְגַם בִּמְנוּחָתוֹ

lō yishk'nu araylim.   לֹא יִשְׁכְּנוּ עֲרֵלִים.

And in its contentment the uncircumcised shall not abide —

Ki l'yisro-ayl am'cho   כִּי לְיִשְׂרָאֵל עַמְּךָ

n'satō b'ahavo,   נְתַתּוֹ בְּאַהֲבָה,

for to Israel, Your people, have You given it in love,

l'zera ya-akōv asher bom bochorto.   לְזֶרַע יַעֲקֹב אֲשֶׁר בָּם בָּחָרְתָּ.

to the seed of Jacob, whom You have chosen.

Am m'kad'shay sh'vi-i,   עַם מְקַדְּשֵׁי שְׁבִיעִי,

The people that sanctifies the Seventh —

kulom yisb'u v'yis-an'gu mituvecho,   כֻּלָּם יִשְׂבְּעוּ וְיִתְעַנְּגוּ מִטּוּבֶךָ,

they will all be satisfied and delighted from Your goodness.

---

with a Divine radiance, signifying that he was worthy to be a bearer of God's splendor (see *Exodus* 34:29).

וְלֹא נְתַתּוֹ — *And You did not give it.* If the Sabbath were nothing more than a day of rest, it could be the equal property of all nations. But the Sabbath is a day of holiness and, as such, it could be given only to the nation that accepts the mission of sanctity. God did not give the Sabbath to "the nations of the lands," i.e., who worship the land and the power its possession implies; nor to "the worshipers of graven idols," who ascribe mastery of the world to such natural forces as the heavenly bodies, fertility, nature, etc. that they symbolize by means of idols; nor to "the uncircumcised," who are unwilling to curb their lusts for the sake of a higher goal.

uvash'vi-i rotziso bō v'kidashtō,   וּבַשְּׁבִיעִי רָצִיתָ בּוֹ וְקִדַּשְׁתּוֹ,
And the Seventh — You found favor in it and sanctified it!

chemdas yomim ōsō koroso,   חֶמְדַּת יָמִים אוֹתוֹ קָרֵאתָ,
"Most coveted of days," You called it,

zaycher l'ma-asay v'rayshis.   זֵכֶר לְמַעֲשֵׂה בְרֵאשִׁית.
a remembrance of the act of Creation.

■ I affirm that the sanctity of Shabbos emanates from Hashem,
and I petition that the holiness of the day influence my life.

ELŌHAYNU Vaylōhay avōsaynu   אֱלֹהֵינוּ וֵאלֹהֵי אֲבוֹתֵינוּ
Our God and the God of our forefathers,

r'tzay vimnuchosaynu.   רְצֵה בִמְנוּחָתֵנוּ.
may You be pleased with our rest.

Kad'shaynu b'mitzvōsecho,   קַדְּשֵׁנוּ בְּמִצְוֹתֶיךָ,
Sanctify us with Your commandments

v'sayn chelkaynu b'sōrosecho,   וְתֵן חֶלְקֵנוּ בְּתוֹרָתֶךָ,
and grant us our share in Your Torah;

sab'aynu mituvecho,   שַׂבְּעֵנוּ מִטּוּבֶךָ,
satisfy us from Your goodness

v'sam'chaynu bi-shu-osecho,   וְשַׂמְּחֵנוּ בִּישׁוּעָתֶךָ,
and gladden us with Your salvation,

v'tahayr libaynu l'ovd'cho be-emes.   וְטַהֵר לִבֵּנוּ לְעָבְדְּךָ בֶּאֱמֶת.
and purify our heart to serve You sincerely.

V'hanchilaynu Adōnoy Elōhaynu   וְהַנְחִילֵנוּ יהוה אֱלֹהֵינוּ
O HASHEM, our God, grant us as a heritage

b'ahavo uvrotzōn   בְּאַהֲבָה וּבְרָצוֹן
with love and favor,

shabas kodshecho,   שַׁבַּת קָדְשֶׁךָ,
Your holy Sabbath

v'yonuchu vō   וְיָנוּחוּ בוֹ
yisro-ayl m'kad'shay sh'mecho.   יִשְׂרָאֵל מְקַדְּשֵׁי שְׁמֶךָ.
and may Israel, the sanctifiers of Your Name, rest on it.

Boruch ato Adōnoy,   בָּרוּךְ אַתָּה יהוה,
m'kadaysh ha-shabos.   מְקַדֵּשׁ הַשַּׁבָּת.
Blessed are You, HASHEM, Who sanctifies the Sabbath.

■ Fifth Blessing: Prayer for restoration of the Temple service

R'TZAY, Adōnoy Elōhaynu   רְצֵה יהוה אֱלֹהֵינוּ
Be favorable, HASHEM, our God,

b'am'cho yisro-ayl u-visfilosom,   בְּעַמְּךָ יִשְׂרָאֵל וּבִתְפִלָּתָם,
toward Your people Israel and their prayer

v'hoshayv es ho-avōdo   וְהָשֵׁב אֶת הָעֲבוֹדָה
lidvir bay-secho.   לִדְבִיר בֵּיתֶךָ.
and restore the service to the Holy of Holies of Your Temple.

V'i-shay yisro-ayl, usfilosom   וְאִשֵּׁי יִשְׂרָאֵל וּתְפִלָּתָם
b'ahavo s'kabayl b'rotzōn,   בְּאַהֲבָה תְקַבֵּל בְּרָצוֹן,
The fire-offerings of Israel and their prayer accept with love and favor,

us-hi l'rotzōn tomid   וּתְהִי לְרָצוֹן תָּמִיד
avōdas yisro-ayl amecho.   עֲבוֹדַת יִשְׂרָאֵל עַמֶּךָ.
and may the service of Your people Israel always be favorable to You.

■ *Yaaleh Veyavo:* We petition God to have compassion on Israel and Jerusalem,
and to reinstate the Temple service, to enable us to bring
the appropriate offerings for the particular occasion.

ON *ROSH CHODESH* AND *CHOL HAMOED* RECITE THE FOLLOWING:

ELŌHAYNU Vaylōhay avōsaynu,   אֱלֹהֵינוּ וֵאלֹהֵי אֲבוֹתֵינוּ,
Our God and the God of our forefathers,

ya-a-le v'yovō v'yagi-a v'yayro-e   יַעֲלֶה, וְיָבֹא, וְיַגִּיעַ, וְיֵרָאֶה,
may there rise, come, reach, be noted,

v'yayrotze v'yishoma v'yipokayd   וְיֵרָצֶה, וְיִשָּׁמַע, וְיִפָּקֵד,
be favored, be heard, be considered,

v'yizochayr zichrōnaynu ufikdōnaynu,   וְיִזָּכֵר זִכְרוֹנֵנוּ וּפִקְדוֹנֵנוּ,
and be remembered — the remembrance and consideration of ourselves;

v'zichrōn avōsaynu,   וְזִכְרוֹן אֲבוֹתֵינוּ,
the remembrance of our forefathers;

v'zichrōn moshi-ach   וְזִכְרוֹן מָשִׁיחַ
ben dovid avdecho,   בֶּן דָּוִד עַבְדֶּךָ,
the remembrance of Messiah, son of David, Your servant;

v'zichrōn y'rushola-yim   וְזִכְרוֹן יְרוּשָׁלַיִם
ir kod-shecho,   עִיר קָדְשֶׁךָ,
the remembrance of Jerusalem, Your Holy City;

v'zichrōn kol am'cho bays yisro-ayl   וְזִכְרוֹן כָּל עַמְּךָ בֵּית יִשְׂרָאֵל
l'fonecho,   לְפָנֶיךָ,
and the remembrance of Your entire people the Family of Israel — before You

liflayto l'tōvo   לִפְלֵיטָה לְטוֹבָה
for deliverance, for goodness,

l'chayn ulchesed ulrachamim,   לְחֵן וּלְחֶסֶד וּלְרַחֲמִים,
for grace, for kindness, and for compassion,

l'cha-yim ulsholōm   לְחַיִּים וּלְשָׁלוֹם
for life, and for peace

——————————— ON ROSH CHODESH ———————————
b'yōm rōsh hachōdesh ha-ze.   בְּיוֹם רֹאשׁ הַחֹדֶשׁ הַזֶּה.
on this day of Rosh Chodesh.

——————————— ON PESACH ———————————
b'yōm chag hamatzōs ha-ze.   בְּיוֹם חַג הַמַּצּוֹת הַזֶּה.
on this day of the Festival of Matzos.

——————————— ON SUCCOS ———————————
b'yōm chag hasukōs ha-ze.   בְּיוֹם חַג הַסֻּכּוֹת הַזֶּה.
on this day of the Succos Festival.

Zoch'raynu Adōnoy Elōhaynu   זָכְרֵנוּ יהוה אֱלֹהֵינוּ
    bō l'tōvo,   בּוֹ לְטוֹבָה,
Remember us on it, HASHEM, our God, for goodness,
u-fokdaynu vō livrocho,   וּפָקְדֵנוּ בּוֹ לִבְרָכָה,
consider us on it for blessing
v'hōshi-aynu vō l'cha-yim.   וְהוֹשִׁיעֵנוּ בּוֹ לְחַיִּים.
and help us on it for life.
U-vidvar y'shu-o v'rachamim,   וּבִדְבַר יְשׁוּעָה וְרַחֲמִים,
In the matter of salvation and compassion,
chus v'chonaynu   חוּס וְחָנֵּנוּ
    v'rachaym olaynu v'hōshi-aynu,   וְרַחֵם עָלֵינוּ וְהוֹשִׁיעֵנוּ,
pity, be gracious and compassionate with us and help us,
ki aylecho aynaynu,   כִּי אֵלֶיךָ עֵינֵינוּ,
for our eyes are turned to You,
ki Ayl melech   כִּי אֵל מֶלֶךְ
    chanun v'rachum oto.   חַנּוּן וְרַחוּם אָתָּה.
because You are God, the gracious and compassionate King.

V'SECHEZENO aynaynu   **וְתֶחֱזֶינָה** עֵינֵינוּ
May our eyes behold
b'shuv'cho l'tziyōn b'rachamim.   בְּשׁוּבְךָ לְצִיּוֹן בְּרַחֲמִים.
Your return to Zion in compassion.
Boruch ato Adōnoy,   בָּרוּךְ אַתָּה יהוה,
    hamachazir sh'chinosō l'tziyōn.   הַמַּחֲזִיר שְׁכִינָתוֹ לְצִיּוֹן.
Blessed are You, HASHEM, Who restores His Presence unto Zion.

■ Sixth Blessing: Acknowledgment of our debt of gratitude

BOW AT Mōdim anachnu loch; STRAIGHTEN UP AT Adōnoy.
IN HIS REPETITION THE *CHAZZAN* SHOULD RECITE THE ENTIRE *MODIM* ALOUD,
WHILE THE CONGREGATION RECITES *MODIM OF THE RABBIS* (P. 383) SOFTLY.

MŌDIM anachnu loch,   **מוֹדִים** אֲנַחְנוּ לָךְ,

We gratefully thank You,

sho-ato hu Adōnoy Elōhaynu   שָׁאַתָּה הוּא יהוה אֱלֹהֵינוּ

for it is You Who are HASHEM, our God,

Vaylōhay avōsaynu   וֵאלֹהֵי אֲבוֹתֵינוּ

and the God of our forefathers

l'ōlom vo-ed,   לְעוֹלָם וָעֶד,

forever and ever;

tzur cha-yaynu, mogayn yish-aynu   צוּר חַיֵּינוּ, מָגֵן יִשְׁעֵנוּ

Rock of our lives, Shield of our salvation

ato hu l'dōr vodōr.   אַתָּה הוּא לְדוֹר וָדוֹר.

are You from generation to generation.

Nō-de l'cho unsapayr t'hilosecho   נוֹדֶה לְּךָ וּנְסַפֵּר תְּהִלָּתֶךָ

We shall thank You and relate Your praise —

al cha-yaynu ham'surim b'yodecho,   עַל חַיֵּינוּ הַמְּסוּרִים בְּיָדֶךָ,

for our lives, which are committed to Your power,

v'al nishmōsaynu hap'kudōs loch,   וְעַל נִשְׁמוֹתֵינוּ הַפְּקוּדוֹת לָךְ,

and for our souls that are entrusted to You,

v'al nisecho sheb'chol yōm imonu,   וְעַל נִסֶּיךָ שֶׁבְּכָל יוֹם עִמָּנוּ,

and for Your miracles that are with us every day,

v'al nifl'ōsecho v'tōvōsecho   וְעַל נִפְלְאוֹתֶיךָ וְטוֹבוֹתֶיךָ
sheb'chol ays,   שֶׁבְּכָל עֵת,

and for Your wonders and favors in every season —

erev vovōker v'tzohoro-yim.   עֶרֶב וָבֹקֶר וְצָהֳרָיִם.

evening, morning, and afternoon.

Hatōv ki lō cholu rachamecho,   הַטּוֹב כִּי לֹא כָלוּ רַחֲמֶיךָ,

The Beneficent One, for Your compassions were never exhausted,

v'ham'rachaym   וְהַמְרַחֵם

and the Compassionate One,

ki lō samu chasodecho,   כִּי לֹא תַמּוּ חֲסָדֶיךָ,

for Your kindnesses never ended —

may-ōlom kivinu loch.   מֵעוֹלָם קִוִּינוּ לָךְ.

always have we put our hope in You.

MODIM OF THE RABBIS

RECITED SOFTLY BY CONGREGATION WHILE *CHAZZAN* RECITES THE REGULAR MODIM ALOUD

MŌDIM anachnu loch,

מוֹדִים אֲנַחְנוּ לָךְ,

We gratefully thank You,

sho-ato hu Adōnoy Elōhaynu

שָׁאַתָּה הוּא יהוה אֱלֹהֵינוּ

Vaylōhay avōsaynu,

וֵאלֹהֵי אֲבוֹתֵינוּ,

for it is You Who are HASHEM, our God and the God of our forefathers,

Elōhay chol bosor,

אֱלֹהֵי כָל בָּשָׂר,

the God of all flesh,

yōtz'raynu, yōtzayr b'rayshis.

יוֹצְרֵנוּ, יוֹצֵר בְּרֵאשִׁית.

our Molder, the Molder of the universe.

B'rochōs v'hōdo-ōs l'shimcho

בְּרָכוֹת וְהוֹדָאוֹת לְשִׁמְךָ

hagodōl v'hakodōsh,

הַגָּדוֹל וְהַקָּדוֹשׁ,

Blessings and thanks are due Your great and holy Name

al sheheche-yisonu v'ki-yamtonu.

עַל שֶׁהֶחֱיִיתָנוּ וְקִיַּמְתָּנוּ.

for You have given us life and sustained us.

Kayn t'cha-yaynu uska-y'maynu,

כֵּן תְּחַיֵּנוּ וּתְקַיְּמֵנוּ,

So may You continue to give us life and sustain us,

v'se-esōf golu-yōsaynu

וְתֶאֱסוֹף גָּלֻיּוֹתֵינוּ

l'chatzrōs kod-shecho,

לְחַצְרוֹת קָדְשֶׁךָ,

and gather our exiles to the Courtyards of Your Sanctuary,

lishmōr chukecho v'la-asōs r'tzōnecho,

לִשְׁמוֹר חֻקֶּיךָ וְלַעֲשׂוֹת רְצוֹנֶךָ,

to observe Your decrees, to do Your will

ul-ovd'cho b'layvov sholaym,

וּלְעָבְדְּךָ בְּלֵבָב שָׁלֵם,

and to serve You wholeheartedly.

al she-anachnu mōdim loch.

עַל שֶׁאֲנַחְנוּ מוֹדִים לָךְ.

[We thank You] for inspiring us to thank You.

Boruch Ayl hahōdo-ōs.

בָּרוּךְ אֵל הַהוֹדָאוֹת.

Blessed is the God of thanksgivings.

ON CHANUKAH CONTINUE BELOW. ON ALL OTHER DAYS TURN TO P. 385.

AL hanisim, v'al hapurkon,

עַל הַנִּסִּים, וְעַל הַפֻּרְקָן,

For the miracles, and for the salvation,

v'al hag'vurōs, v'al hat'shu-ōs,

וְעַל הַגְּבוּרוֹת, וְעַל הַתְּשׁוּעוֹת,

and for the mighty deeds, and for the victories,

v'al hamilchomōs,

וְעַל הַמִּלְחָמוֹת,

and for the battles

she-osiso la-avôsaynu
שֶׁעָשִׂיתָ לַאֲבוֹתֵינוּ

which You performed for our forefathers

ba-yomim hohaym baz'man ha-ze.
בַּיָּמִים הָהֵם בַּזְּמַן הַזֶּה.

in those days, at this time.

BIMAY matisyohu ben yôchonon
בִּימֵי מַתִּתְיָהוּ בֶּן יוֹחָנָן

In the days of Mattisyahu, the son of Yochanan,

kôhayn godôl chashmôno-i u-vonov,
כֹּהֵן גָּדוֹל חַשְׁמוֹנַאִי וּבָנָיו,

the High Priest, the Hasmonean, and his sons —

k'she-om'do malchus yovon
כְּשֶׁעָמְדָה מַלְכוּת יָוָן

hor'sho-o al am'cho yisro-ayl,
הָרְשָׁעָה עַל עַמְּךָ יִשְׂרָאֵל,

when the wicked Greek kingdom rose up against Your people Israel

l'hashkichom tôrosecho,
לְהַשְׁכִּיחָם תּוֹרָתֶךָ,

to make them forget Your Torah

ulha-avirom maychukay r'tzônecho,
וּלְהַעֲבִירָם מֵחֻקֵּי רְצוֹנֶךָ.

and compel them to stray from the statutes of Your Will —

v'ato b'rachamecho horabim,
וְאַתָּה בְּרַחֲמֶיךָ הָרַבִּים,

But You, in Your abundant mercy,

omadto lohem b'ays tzorosom,
עָמַדְתָּ לָהֶם בְּעֵת צָרָתָם,

stood up for them in the time of their distress.

Ravto es rivom, danto es dinom,
רַבְתָּ אֶת רִיבָם, דַּנְתָּ אֶת דִּינָם,

You took up their grievance, You judged their claim,

nokamto es nikmosom.
נָקַמְתָּ אֶת נִקְמָתָם.

and You avenged their wrong.

Mosarto gibôrim b'yad chaloshim,
מָסַרְתָּ גִבּוֹרִים בְּיַד חַלָּשִׁים,

You delivered the strong into the hand of the weak,

v'rabim b'yad m'atim,
וְרַבִּים בְּיַד מְעַטִּים,

the many into the hand of the few,

utmay-im b'yad t'hôrim,
וּטְמֵאִים בְּיַד טְהוֹרִים,

the impure into the hand of the pure,

ursho-im b'yad tzadikim
וּרְשָׁעִים בְּיַד צַדִּיקִים,

the wicked into the hand of the righteous,

v'zaydim b'yad ôs'kay sôrosecho.
וְזֵדִים בְּיַד עוֹסְקֵי תוֹרָתֶךָ.

and the wanton into the hand of the diligent students of Your Torah.

Ulcho osiso
וּלְךָ עָשִׂיתָ

shaym godôl v'kodôsh b'ôlomecho,
שֵׁם גָּדוֹל וְקָדוֹשׁ בְּעוֹלָמֶךָ,

For Yourself You made a great and holy Name in Your world,

ul-am'cho yisro-ayl
וּלְעַמְּךָ יִשְׂרָאֵל
and for Your people Israel

osiso t'shu-o g'dōlo u-furkon
עָשִׂיתָ תְּשׁוּעָה גְדוֹלָה וּפֻרְקָן
You performed a great victory and salvation

k'ha-yōm ha-ze.
כְּהַיּוֹם הַזֶּה.
as this very day.

V'achar kayn bo-u vonecho
וְאַחַר כֵּן בָּאוּ בָנֶיךָ
lidvir bay-secho,
לִדְבִיר בֵּיתֶךָ,
Thereafter, Your children came to the Holy of Holies of Your House,

u-finu es haycholecho,
וּפִנּוּ אֶת הֵיכָלֶךָ,
they cleansed Your Temple,

v'tiharu es mikdoshecho,
וְטִהֲרוּ אֶת מִקְדָּשֶׁךָ,
they purified the site of Your Holiness;

v'hidliku nayrōs
וְהִדְלִיקוּ נֵרוֹת
b'chatzrōs kod-shecho,
בְּחַצְרוֹת קָדְשֶׁךָ,
and they kindled lights in the Courtyards of Your Sanctuary;

v'kov'u
וְקָבְעוּ
sh'mōnas y'may chanuko aylu,
שְׁמוֹנַת יְמֵי חֲנֻכָּה אֵלּוּ,
and they established these eight days of Chanukah

l'hōdōs ulhalayl l'shimcho hagodōl.
לְהוֹדוֹת וּלְהַלֵּל לְשִׁמְךָ הַגָּדוֹל.
to express thanks and praise to Your great Name.

V'AL kulom yisborach v'yisrōmam
וְעַל כֻּלָּם יִתְבָּרַךְ וְיִתְרוֹמַם
shimcho, malkaynu
שִׁמְךָ מַלְכֵּנוּ
For all these, may Your Name be blessed and exalted, our King,

tomid l'ōlom vo-ed.
תָּמִיד לְעוֹלָם וָעֶד.
continually forever and ever.

FROM ROSH HASHANAH TO YOM KIPPUR ADD:

Uchsōv l'cha-yim tōvim
וּכְתוֹב לְחַיִּים טוֹבִים
kol b'nay v'risecho.
כָּל בְּנֵי בְרִיתֶךָ.
And inscribe all the children of Your covenant for a good life.

V'chōl hacha-yim yōducho selo,
וְכֹל הַחַיִּים יוֹדוּךָ סֶּלָה,
Everything alive will gratefully acknowledge You, Selah!

vihal'lu es shimcho be-emes,
וִיהַלְלוּ אֶת שִׁמְךָ בֶּאֱמֶת,
and praise Your Name sincerely,

ho-Ayl y'shu-osaynu
הָאֵל יְשׁוּעָתֵנוּ
v'ezrosaynu selo.
וְעֶזְרָתֵנוּ סֶלָה.
O God of our salvation and help, Selah!

BEND THE KNEES AT Boruch; BOW AT ato; STRAIGHTEN UP AT Adōnoy.

Boruch ato Adōnoy,
                  בָּרוּךְ אַתָּה יהוה,

Blessed are You, HASHEM,

hatōv shimcho ulcho no-e l'hōdōs.
      הַטּוֹב שִׁמְךָ וּלְךָ נָאֶה לְהוֹדוֹת.

Your Name is "The Beneficent One" and to You it is fitting to give thanks.

■ Seventh Blessing: Prayer for peace and harmony
amongst the Jewish people

THE *CHAZZAN* RECITES THE PRIESTLY BLESSING DURING HIS REPETITION.

אֱלֹהֵֽינוּ, וֵאלֹהֵי אֲבוֹתֵֽינוּ, בָּרְכֵֽנוּ* בַּבְּרָכָה הַמְשֻׁלֶּֽשֶׁת בַּתּוֹרָה
הַכְּתוּבָה עַל יְדֵי מֹשֶׁה עַבְדֶּֽךָ, הָאֲמוּרָה מִפִּי אַהֲרֹן וּבָנָיו,
כֹּהֲנִים עַם קְדוֹשֶֽׁךָ, כָּאָמוּר:

יְבָרֶכְךָ יהוה,* וְיִשְׁמְרֶֽךָ.*   (Cong. – כֵּן יְהִי רָצוֹן – kayn y'hi rotzōn)

יָאֵר יהוה פָּנָיו אֵלֶֽיךָ* וִיחֻנֶּֽךָ.*   (Cong. – כֵּן יְהִי רָצוֹן – kayn y'hi rotzōn)

יִשָּׂא יהוה פָּנָיו אֵלֶֽיךָ* וְיָשֵׂם לְךָ שָׁלוֹם.*   (Cong. – כֵּן יְהִי רָצוֹן – kayn y'hi rotzōn)

SIM SHOLŌM tōvo uvrocho,
              שִׂים שָׁלוֹם, טוֹבָה, וּבְרָכָה,

Establish peace, goodness, blessing,

chayn vochesed v'rachamim
                חֵן וָחֶֽסֶד וְרַחֲמִים

graciousness, kindness, and compassion

olaynu v'al kol yisro-ayl amecho.
       עָלֵֽינוּ וְעַל כָּל יִשְׂרָאֵל עַמֶּֽךָ.

upon us and upon all of Your people Israel.

◄§ The Priestly Blessing

God commanded Aaron and his descendants to bless the Jewish people by pronouncing the blessings written in the Torah (*Numbers* 6:22-27). Although in earlier times the *Kohanim* pronounced these blessings every day, a centuries-old custom has developed in the Diaspora that they do so only on Festivals when the Jewish people still feel the joy that should accompany these blessings. On other days the following prayer is recited by the *chazzan* at *Shacharis* and *Mussaf*. It contains the text of the Priestly Blessing and the prayer that God fulfill it upon us.

אֱלֹהֵֽינוּ ... בָּרְכֵֽנוּ — *Our God ... bless us.* Although the blessing is pronounced by the *Kohanim*, it is God who actually gives the blessing. This is made clear in the Scriptural commandment, which ends with God's pledge "and I will bless them" (*Numbers* 2:27).

יְבָרֶכְךָ ה׳ — *May* HASHEM *bless you,* with increasing wealth and long lives.

וְיִשְׁמְרֶֽךָ — *And safeguard you.* May the above

blessings be preserved against loss or attack. Only God can guarantee that no one or nothing can tamper with the gifts He confers upon His loved ones.

יָאֵר ה׳ פָּנָיו אֵלֶֽיךָ — *May Hashem illuminate His countenance for you.* This is the blessing of spiritual growth, the light of Torah, which is symbolized by God's countenance.

וִיחֻנֶּֽךָ — *And be gracious to you.* May you find favor in God's eyes; and may you find favor in the eyes of others, for all a person's talents and qualities will avail him little if others dislike him.

יִשָּׂא ה׳ פָּנָיו אֵלֶֽיךָ — *May* HASHEM *turn His countenance to you.* One's face is indicative of his attitude toward someone else. If he is angry, he will turn away from the one he dislikes. God turns His face *toward* Israel to show that He loves them.

וְיָשֵׂם לְךָ שָׁלוֹם — *And establish peace for you.* Peace is the seal of all blessings, because without peace — prosperity, health, food and drink are worthless.

Bor'chaynu, ovinu, kulonu k'e-chod b'ōr ponecho,

בָּרְכֵנוּ, אָבִינוּ, כֻּלָּנוּ כְּאֶחָד בְּאוֹר פָּנֶיךָ,

Bless us, our Father, all of us as one, with the light of Your countenance,

ki v'ōr ponecho nosato lonu, Adōnoy Elōhaynu,

כִּי בְאוֹר פָּנֶיךָ נָתַתָּ לָּנוּ, יהוה אֱלֹהֵינוּ,

for with the light of Your countenance You, HASHEM, our God, gave us

tōras cha-yim v'ahavas chesed,

תּוֹרַת חַיִּים וְאַהֲבַת חֶסֶד,

*the Torah of life and a love of kindness,**

utz-doko uvrocho v'rachamim v'cha-yim v'sholōm.

וּצְדָקָה וּבְרָכָה וְרַחֲמִים וְחַיִּים וְשָׁלוֹם.

righteousness, blessing, compassion, life, and peace.

V'tōv b'aynecho l'voraych es am'cho yisro-ayl,

וְטוֹב בְּעֵינֶיךָ לְבָרֵךְ אֶת עַמְּךָ יִשְׂרָאֵל,

And may it be good in Your eyes to bless Your people Israel

b'chol ays uvchol sho-o bishlōmecho.

בְּכָל עֵת וּבְכָל שָׁעָה בִּשְׁלוֹמֶךָ.

at every time and at every hour, with Your peace.

°Boruch ato Adōnoy, ham'voraych es amō yisro-ayl ba-sholōm.

°בָּרוּךְ אַתָּה יהוה, הַמְבָרֵךְ אֶת עַמּוֹ יִשְׂרָאֵל בַּשָּׁלוֹם.

°Blessed are You, HASHEM, Who blesses His people Israel with peace.

° FROM ROSH HASHANAH TO YOM KIPPUR SUBSTITUTE THE FOLLOWING:

B'sayfer cha-yim b'rocho v'sholōm, u-farnoso tōvo,

בְּסֵפֶר חַיִּים בְּרָכָה וְשָׁלוֹם, וּפַרְנָסָה טוֹבָה,

In the book of life, blessing, and peace, and good livelihood,

nizochayr v'nikosayv l'fonecho,

נִזָּכֵר וְנִכָּתֵב לְפָנֶיךָ,

may we be remembered and inscribed before You —

anachnu v'chol am'cho bays yisro-ayl,

אֲנַחְנוּ וְכָל עַמְּךָ בֵּית יִשְׂרָאֵל,

we and Your entire people the Family of Israel —

l'cha-yim tōvim ulsholōm.

לְחַיִּים טוֹבִים וּלְשָׁלוֹם.

for a good life and for peace.

Boruch ato Adōnoy, ō-se ha-sholōm.

בָּרוּךְ אַתָּה יהוה, עוֹשֶׂה הַשָּׁלוֹם.

Blessed are You, HASHEM, Who makes the peace.

וְאַהֲבַת חֶסֶד — *And a love of kindness.* God is not content if we merely act kindly toward others. He wants us to love kindness. What someone loves to do is never a chore.

THE *CHAZZAN'S* REPETITION ENDS HERE (TURN TO PAGE 390). INDIVIDUALS CONTINUE:

Yiyu l'rotzōn imray fi
v'hegyōn libi l'fonecho,

יִהְיוּ לְרָצוֹן אִמְרֵי פִי
וְהֶגְיוֹן לִבִּי לְפָנֶיךָ,

May the expressions of my mouth and the thoughts of my heart
find favor before You,

Adōnoy tzuri v'gō-ali.

יהוה צוּרִי וְגֹאֲלִי.

HASHEM, my Rock and my Redeemer.

■ I pray that, having completed my *Amidah,* I have been changed in a positive way,
especially with regard to my interpersonal relationships.

ELŌHAI, n'tzōr l'shōni mayro,

אֱלֹהַי, נְצוֹר לְשׁוֹנִי מֵרָע,

My God, guard my tongue from evil

usfosai midabayr mirmo,

וּשְׂפָתַי מִדַּבֵּר מִרְמָה,

and my lips from speaking deceitfully.

V'limkal'lai nafshi sidōm,

וְלִמְקַלְלַי נַפְשִׁי תִדּוֹם,

To those who curse me, let my soul be silent;

v'nafshi ke-ofor lakōl tih-ye.

וְנַפְשִׁי כֶּעָפָר לַכֹּל תִּהְיֶה.

and let my soul be like dust to everyone.

P'sach libi b'sōrosecho,

פְּתַח לִבִּי בְּתוֹרָתֶךָ,

Open my heart to Your Torah,

uvmitzvōsecho tirdōf nafshi.

וּבְמִצְוֹתֶיךָ תִּרְדּוֹף נַפְשִׁי.

then my soul will pursue Your commandments.

V'chol hachōsh'vim olai ro-o,

וְכָל הַחוֹשְׁבִים עָלַי רָעָה,

As for all those who design evil against me,

m'hayro hofayr atzosom

מְהֵרָה הָפֵר עֲצָתָם

speedily nullify their counsel

v'kalkayl machashavtom.

וְקַלְקֵל מַחֲשַׁבְתָּם.

and disrupt their design.

asay l'ma-an sh'mecho,

עֲשֵׂה לְמַעַן שְׁמֶךָ,

Act for Your Name's sake;

asay l'ma-an y'minecho,

עֲשֵׂה לְמַעַן יְמִינֶךָ,

act for Your right hand's sake;

asay l'ma-an k'dushosecho,

עֲשֵׂה לְמַעַן קְדֻשָּׁתֶךָ,

act for Your sanctity's sake;

asay l'ma-an tōrosecho.

עֲשֵׂה לְמַעַן תּוֹרָתֶךָ.

act for Your Torah's sake.

L'ma-an yaychol'tzun y'didecho,

לְמַעַן יֵחָלְצוּן יְדִידֶיךָ,

That Your beloved ones may be given rest;

hōshi-o y'min'cho va-anayni. הוֹשִׁיעָה יְמִינְךָ וַעֲנֵנִי.

let Your right hand save, and respond to me.

Yih-yu l'rotzōn imray fi יִהְיוּ לְרָצוֹן אִמְרֵי פִי

v'hegyōn libi l'fonecho, וְהֶגְיוֹן לִבִּי לְפָנֶיךָ,

May the expressions of my mouth and the thoughts of my heart
find favor before You,

Adōnoy tzuri v'gō-ali. יהוה צוּרִי וְגֹאֲלִי.

HASHEM, my Rock and my Redeemer.

BOW. TAKE THREE STEPS BACK. BOW LEFT AND SAY:

Ō-se sholōm bimrōmov, עֹשֶׂה שָׁלוֹם בִּמְרוֹמָיו,

He Who makes peace in His heights,

BOW RIGHT AND SAY:

hu ya-a-se sholōm olaynu, הוּא יַעֲשֶׂה שָׁלוֹם עָלֵינוּ,

may He make peace upon us,

BOW FORWARD AND SAY:

v'al kol yisro-ayl. V'imru: Omayn. וְעַל כָּל יִשְׂרָאֵל. וְאִמְרוּ: אָמֵן.

and upon all Israel. Now respond: Amen.

Y'HI ROTZŌN mil'fonecho, **יְהִי רָצוֹן** מִלְּפָנֶיךָ

May it be Your will,

Adōnoy Elōhaynu יהוה אֱלֹהֵינוּ

Vaylōhay avōsaynu, וֵאלֹהֵי אֲבוֹתֵינוּ,

HASHEM, our God and the God of our forefathers,

she-yibo-ne bays hamikdosh שֶׁיִּבָּנֶה בֵּית הַמִּקְדָּשׁ

bimhayro v'yomaynu, בִּמְהֵרָה בְיָמֵינוּ,

that the Holy Temple be rebuilt, speedily in our days;

v'sayn chelkaynu b'sōrosecho, וְתֵן חֶלְקֵנוּ בְּתוֹרָתֶךָ,

and grant us our share in Your Torah;

v'shom na-avod-cho b'yiro, וְשָׁם נַעֲבָדְךָ בְּיִרְאָה,

and may we serve You there with reverence,

kimay ōlom כִּימֵי עוֹלָם

uchshonim kadmōniyōs. וּכְשָׁנִים קַדְמֹנִיּוֹת.

as in days of old and in former years.

V'or'vo Ladōnoy וְעָרְבָה לַיהוה

minchas y'hudo virusholo-yim מִנְחַת יְהוּדָה וִירוּשָׁלָיִם,

Then the offering of Judah and Jerusalem will be pleasing to HASHEM,

kimay ōlom כִּימֵי עוֹלָם

uchshonim kadmōniyōs. וּכְשָׁנִים קַדְמֹנִיּוֹת.

as in days of old and in former years.

THE INDIVIDUAL'S RECITATION OF *SHEMONEH ESREI* ENDS HERE.

REMAIN STANDING IN PLACE UNTIL THE *CHAZZAN* REACHES *KEDUSHAH* —
OR AT LEAST FOR A FEW MOMENTS — THEN TAKE THREE STEPS FORWARD.

THE *CHAZZAN* RECITES FULL *KADDISH*

(congregational responses are indicated by parentheses):

יִתְגַּדַּל וְיִתְקַדַּשׁ שְׁמֵהּ רַבָּא. (אָמֵן – Omayn). בְּעָלְמָא דִּי בְרָא
כִרְעוּתֵהּ. וְיַמְלִיךְ מַלְכוּתֵהּ, בְּחַיֵּיכוֹן וּבְיוֹמֵיכוֹן וּבְחַיֵּי דְכָל
בֵּית יִשְׂרָאֵל, בַּעֲגָלָא וּבִזְמַן קָרִיב. וְאִמְרוּ: אָמֵן.

(אָמֵן. יְהֵא שְׁמֵהּ רַבָּא מְבָרַךְ לְעָלַם וּלְעָלְמֵי עָלְמַיָּא.)

(Omayn. Y'hay sh'mayh rabo m'vorach l'olam ul-ol'may ol'ma-yo.)

יְהֵא שְׁמֵהּ רַבָּא מְבָרַךְ לְעָלַם וּלְעָלְמֵי עָלְמַיָּא. יִתְבָּרַךְ וְיִשְׁתַּבַּח
וְיִתְפָּאַר וְיִתְרוֹמַם וְיִתְנַשֵּׂא וְיִתְהַדָּר וְיִתְעַלֶּה וְיִתְהַלָּל שְׁמֵהּ
דְּקֻדְשָׁא בְּרִיךְ הוּא (בְּרִיךְ הוּא – B'rich hu). °לְעֵלָּא מִן כָּל
[substitute Kippur Yom to Hashanah Rosh from – °לְעֵלָּא לְעֵלָּא מִכָּל]
בִּרְכָתָא וְשִׁירָתָא תֻּשְׁבְּחָתָא וְנֶחֱמָתָא, דַּאֲמִירָן בְּעָלְמָא. וְאִמְרוּ: אָמֵן.
(אָמֵן – Omayn).

תִּתְקַבֵּל צְלוֹתְהוֹן וּבָעוּתְהוֹן דְּכָל (בֵּית) יִשְׂרָאֵל קֳדָם אֲבוּהוֹן דִּי
בִשְׁמַיָּא. וְאִמְרוּ: אָמֵן. (אָמֵן – Omayn).

יְהֵא שְׁלָמָא רַבָּא מִן שְׁמַיָּא, וְחַיִּים עָלֵינוּ וְעַל כָּל יִשְׂרָאֵל. וְאִמְרוּ:
אָמֵן. (אָמֵן – Omayn).

Bow. Take three steps back. Bow left and say, . . . עֹשֶׂה; bow right and say, . . . הוּא יַעֲשֶׂה; bow forward and say, . . . וְעַל כָּל. Remain in place for a few moments, then take three steps forward.

עֹשֶׂה שָׁלוֹם בִּמְרוֹמָיו, הוּא יַעֲשֶׂה שָׁלוֹם עָלֵינוּ, וְעַל כָּל יִשְׂרָאֵל.
וְאִמְרוּ: אָמֵן. (אָמֵן – Omayn).

⊰ REMOVAL OF THE TORAH FROM THE ARK ⊱

■ After completing the prayer service in which man communicates with Hashem, by extolling His greatness, I prepare myself for the Torah reading where Hashem communicates with us.

ALL RISE AND REMAIN STANDING UNTIL THE TORAH IS PLACED ON THE *BIMAH*. ALL RECITE:

AYN KOMŌCHO vo-elōhim, Adōnoy, אֵין כָּמוֹךָ בָאֱלֹהִים, אֲדֹנָי,

There is none like You* among the powers, my Lord,

v'ayn k'ma-asecho. וְאֵין כְּמַעֲשֶׂיךָ.

and there is nothing like Your works.

אֵין כָּמוֹךָ – *There is none like You.* On the Sabbath and Festivals the service of removing the Torah from the Ark begins with an in- | troductory series of verses that emphasize God's greatness and plead for the rebuilding of Zion and Jerusalem. Since we are about to read

Malchus'cho malchus kol ōlomim,　　מַלְכוּתְךָ מַלְכוּת כָּל עֹלָמִים,
Your kingdom is a kingdom spanning all eternities,

u-memshalt'cho b'chol dōr vodōr.　　וּמֶמְשַׁלְתְּךָ בְּכָל דּוֹר וָדֹר.
and Your dominion is throughout every generation.

Adōnoy melech, Adōnoy moloch,　　יהוה מֶלֶךְ, יהוה מָלָךְ,
HASHEM reigns, HASHEM has reigned,

Adōnoy yimlōch l'ōlom vo-ed.　　יהוה יִמְלֹךְ לְעֹלָם וָעֶד.
HASHEM shall reign for all eternity.

Adōnoy ōz l'amō yitayn,　　יהוה עֹז לְעַמּוֹ יִתֵּן,
HASHEM will give might to His people;

Adōnoy y'voraych es amō va-sholōm.　　יהוה יְבָרֵךְ אֶת עַמּוֹ בַשָּׁלוֹם.
HASHEM will bless His people with peace.

AV HORACHAMIM,　　אַב הָרַחֲמִים,
Father of compassion,

haytivo virtzōn'cho es tziyōn,　　הֵיטִיבָה בִרְצוֹנְךָ אֶת צִיּוֹן,
do good with Zion* according to Your will;

tivne chōmōs y'rusholo-yim.　　תִּבְנֶה חוֹמוֹת יְרוּשָׁלָיִם.
rebuild the walls of Jerusalem.

Ki v'cho l'vad botochnu,　　כִּי בְךָ לְבַד בָּטָחְנוּ,
For we trust in You alone,

melech Ayl rom v'niso,　　מֶלֶךְ אֵל רָם וְנִשָּׂא,
adōn ōlomim.　　אֲדוֹן עוֹלָמִים.
O King, God, exalted and uplifted, Master of worlds.

THE ARK IS OPENED. BEFORE THE TORAH IS REMOVED THE CONGREGATION RECITES:

VAIHI BINSŌ-A ho-orōn　　וַיְהִי בִּנְסֹעַ הָאָרֹן
va-yōmer mōshe,　　וַיֹּאמֶר מֹשֶׁה,
When the Ark would travel,* Moses would say,

kumo Adōnoy v'yofutzu ōy'vecho　　קוּמָה יהוה וְיָפֻצוּ אֹיְבֶיךָ
"Arise, HASHEM, and let Your foes be scattered,

v'yonusu m'san-echo miponecho.　　וְיָנֻסוּ מְשַׂנְאֶיךָ מִפָּנֶיךָ.
let those who hate You flee from You."

---

from God's word to Israel, it is fitting that we first call to mind that the One Who speaks to us is our All-powerful King.

הֵיטִיבָה... אֶת צִיּוֹן — *Do good with Zion.* Only in God's chosen Sanctuary can His kingdom come to full flower among mankind. Only there can the Torah reading attain its greatest meaning.

וַיְהִי בִּנְסֹעַ הָאָרֹן — *When the Ark would travel.*

When the Ark is opened we declare, as Moses did when the Ark traveled for forty years in the wilderness, that God's word is invincible. Having acknowledged this, we can read from the Torah with the proper awareness. We continue that it is God's will that the Torah's message go forth to the entire world, and by blessing Him for having given us the Torah, we accept

Ki mitziyōn taytzay sōro,
כִּי מִצִּיּוֹן תֵּצֵא תוֹרָה,

For from Zion the Torah will come forth

udvar Adōnoy mirusholo-yim.
וּדְבַר יהוה מִירוּשָׁלָיִם.

and the word of HASHEM from Jerusalem.

Boruch shenosan tōro
בָּרוּךְ שֶׁנָּתַן תּוֹרָה

l'amō yisro-ayl bikdushosō.
לְעַמּוֹ יִשְׂרָאֵל בִּקְדֻשָּׁתוֹ.

Blessed is He Who gave the Torah to His people Israel in His holiness.

ON THE SABBATH CONTINUE WITH *B'RICH SH'MAYH*, ON PAGE 397.
ON A FESTIVAL THAT FALLS ON A WEEKDAY AND ON HOSHANA RABBAH CONTINUE BELOW.

ON FESTIVALS (EXCEPT ON THE SABBATH) THE THIRTEEN ATTRIBUTES OF MERCY*
[BOLD TYPE ARE RECITED THREE TIMES.]

Adōnoy, Adōnoy,
יהוה, יהוה,

HASHEM, HASHEM,

Ayl, rachum, v'chanun,
אֵל, רַחוּם, וְחַנּוּן,

God, Compassionate and Gracious,

erech apa-yim,
אֶרֶךְ אַפַּיִם,

Slow to anger,

v'rav chesed, ve-emes,
וְרַב חֶסֶד, וֶאֱמֶת,

and Abundant in Kindness and Truth.

nōtzayr chesed lo-alofim,
נֹצֵר חֶסֶד לָאֲלָפִים,

Preserver of kindness for thousands of generations,

nōsay ovōn, vofesha, v'chato-o,
נֹשֵׂא עָוֺן, וָפֶשַׁע, וְחַטָּאָה,

Forgiver of iniquity, willful sin, and error,

v'nakay.
וְנַקֵּה.

and Who cleanses.

ON FESTIVAL DAYS CONTINUE HERE; ON HOSHANA RABBAH TURN TO PAGE 395.

RIBŌNŌ shel ōlom,
רִבּוֹנוֹ שֶׁל עוֹלָם,

Master of the universe,

malay mish-alōs libi l'tōvo,
מַלֵּא מִשְׁאֲלוֹת לִבִּי לְטוֹבָה,

fulfill my heartfelt requests for good,

---

our responsibility to carry out its commands and spread its message.

**•⊰ Special Festival Prayers /
Thirteen Attributes of Mercy**

On Pesach, Shavuos, and Succos, a special prayer requesting God's help in attaining His goals for us is recited at this point. Similarly, on Rosh Hashanah, Yom Kippur, and Hoshana Rabbah, a prayer is recited that reflects the theme of repentance and forgiveness. Each of these prayers is preceded by the "Thirteen Attributes of Mercy," the prayer that God Himself taught Moses after Israel worshiped

the Golden Calf. Although Moses, quite understandably, thought that prayers could not help the nation that had bowed to and danced around an idol less than six weeks after hearing the Ten Commandments, God showed him that it was never too late for prayer and repentance. Instead, Moses was given a Divine covenant that "the Thirteen Attributes are never turned back unanswered" (*Rosh Hashanah* 17b).

מַלֵּא מִשְׁאֲלוֹת לִבִּי לְטוֹבָה — *Fulfill my heartfelt requests for good.* Often man's personal goals are not to his real benefit. May my requests be filled in a way that will be truly good.

v'hofayk r'tzōni, v'sayn sh'aylosi,　　　וְהָפֵק רְצוֹנִי, וְתֵן שְׁאֵלָתִי,
satisfy my desire, and grant my request,

―――――――――――――――― MEN SAY: ――――――――――――――――

li avd'cho　　　　　(SUPPLICANT'S HEBREW NAME)　　　לִי עַבְדְּךָ
　ben　　　　　　　　　　　　　　　　　　　　　　בֶּן
　amosecha,　　　(SUPPLICANT'S MOTHER'S HEBREW NAME)　　אֲמָתֶךָ,
　　me — Your servant (. . .) son of (. . .) Your maidservant

v'zakayni (v'es ishti),　　　　　　　וְזַכֵּנִי (וְאֶת אִשְׁתִּי),
　　and privilege me (and my wife),

―――――――――――――――― WOMEN SAY: ――――――――――――――――

li avd'cho　　　　　(SUPPLICANT'S HEBREW NAME)　　　לִי עַבְדְּךָ
　bas　　　　　　　　　　　　　　　　　　　　　　בַּת
　amosecha,　　　(SUPPLICANT'S MOTHER'S HEBREW NAME)　　אֲמָתֶךָ,
　　me — Your servant (. . .) daughter of (. . .) Your maidservant

v'zakayni (v'es ba-li),　　　　　　　וְזַכֵּנִי (וְאֶת בַּעְלִי),
　　and privilege me (and my husband),

―――――――――――ALL CONTINUE, INSERTING THE APPROPRIATE PHRASES:――――――――――

(uvni/u-vonai),　　　*(and my son/and my sons),*　　(וּבְנִי/וּבָנַי),
(u-viti/uvnōsai),　*(and my daughter/and my daughters),*　(וּבִתִּי/וּבְנוֹתַי)
v'chol b'nay vaysi　　　　　　　　וְכָל בְּנֵי בֵיתִי
　　and everyone in my household

la-asōs r'tzōn'cho b'layvov sholaym.　לַעֲשׂוֹת רְצוֹנְךָ בְּלֵבָב שָׁלֵם.
　　to do Your will wholeheartedly.

U-mal'taynu mi-yaytzer horo,　　　וּמַלְּטֵנוּ מִיֵּצֶר הָרָע,
　　Rescue us from the Evil Inclination

v'sayn chelkaynu b'sōrosecho.　　וְתֵן חֶלְקֵנוּ בְּתוֹרָתֶךָ.
　　and grant our share in Your Torah.

V'zakaynu　　　　　　　　　　　וְזַכֵּנוּ
　shetishre sh'chinos'cho olaynu,　שֶׁתִּשְׁרֶה שְׁכִינָתְךָ עָלֵינוּ,
　　Privilege us that Your Presence may rest upon us

v'hōfa olaynu　　　　　　　　　וְהוֹפַע עָלֵינוּ
　ru-ach chochmo u-vino.　　　　רוּחַ חָכְמָה וּבִינָה.
　　and radiate upon us a spirit of wisdom and insight.

V'yiska-yaym bonu mikro shekosuv:　וְיִתְקַיֵּם בָּנוּ מִקְרָא שֶׁכָּתוּב:
　　Let there be fulfilled in us the verse that is written:

V'nocho olov ru-ach Adōnoy,　　וְנָחָה עָלָיו רוּחַ יהוה,
　　"The spirit of HASHEM shall rest upon him,

ru-ach chochmo u-vino,	רוּחַ חָכְמָה וּבִינָה,
the spirit of wisdom and insight,	
ru-ach aytzo ugvuro,	רוּחַ עֵצָה וּגְבוּרָה,
the spirit of counsel and strength,	
ru-ach da-as v'yir-as Adōnoy.	רוּחַ דַּעַת וְיִרְאַת יהוה.
the spirit of knowledge and fear of HASHEM."	
V'chayn y'hi rotzōn mil'fonecho,	וְכֵן יְהִי רָצוֹן מִלְּפָנֶיךָ,
Similarly may it be Your will,	
Adōnoy Elōhaynu	יהוה אֱלֹהֵינוּ
Vaylōhay avōsaynu,	וֵאלֹהֵי אֲבוֹתֵינוּ,
HASHEM, our God and the God of our forefathers,	
shet'zakaynu la-asōs	שֶׁתְּזַכֵּנוּ לַעֲשׂוֹת
ma-asim tōvim b'aynecho,	מַעֲשִׂים טוֹבִים בְּעֵינֶיךָ,
that You privilege us to do deeds that are good in Your eyes	
v'loleches b'darchay y'shorim	וְלָלֶכֶת בְּדַרְכֵי יְשָׁרִים
l'fonecho	לְפָנֶיךָ.
and to walk before You in upright paths.	
V'kad'shaynu b'mitzvōsecho	וְקַדְּשֵׁנוּ בְּמִצְוֹתֶיךָ
Sanctify us with Your commandments	
k'day shenizke	כְּדֵי שֶׁנִּזְכֶּה
so that we may be worthy	
l'cha-yim tōvim va-aruchim,	לְחַיִּים טוֹבִים וַאֲרֻכִּים,
of a good and long life,	
limōs hamoshi-ach,	לִימוֹת הַמָּשִׁיחַ,
to the days of the Messiah,	
ulcha-yay ho-ōlom habo.	וּלְחַיֵּי הָעוֹלָם הַבָּא.
and to the life of the World to Come.	
V'sishm'raynu mima-asim ro-im,	וְתִשְׁמְרֵנוּ מִמַּעֲשִׂים רָעִים,
May You protect us against evil deeds	
u-misho-ōs ro-ōs	וּמִשָּׁעוֹת רָעוֹת
and from bad times	
hamisrag'shōs lovō lo-ōlom.	הַמִּתְרַגְּשׁוֹת לָבֹא לָעוֹלָם.
that surge upon the world.	
V'habōtay-ach Badōnoy	וְהַבּוֹטֵחַ בַּיהוה
He who trusts in HASHEM —	
chesed y'sōv'venhu, omayn.	חֶסֶד יְסוֹבְבֶנְהוּ, אָמֵן.
may kindness surround him. Amen.	

CONTINUE ON PAGE 396.

ON HOSHANA RABBAH CONTINUE HERE:

RIBŌNŌ shel ōlam   רִבּוֹנוֹ שֶׁל עוֹלָם,
Master of the universe,

malay mish-alōsai l'tōva,   מַלֵּא מִשְׁאֲלוֹתַי לְטוֹבָה,
fulfill my requests for good,

v'hofayk r'tzōni, v'sayn sh'aylosi,   וְהָפֵק רְצוֹנִי, וְתֵן שְׁאֵלָתִי,
satisfy my desire, and grant my request.

umchol li al kol avōnōsai   וּמְחוֹל לִי עַל כָּל עֲוֹנוֹתַי,
Pardon all my iniquities

v'al kol avōnōs anshay vaysi,   וְעַל כָּל עֲוֹנוֹת אַנְשֵׁי בֵיתִי,
and all the iniquities of my household —

m'chilo b'chesed,   מְחִילָה בְּחֶסֶד,
a pardon with kindness,

m'chilo b'rachamim,   מְחִילָה בְּרַחֲמִים,
a pardon with compassion,

v'taharayni maychato-ai   וְטַהֲרֵנִי מֵחֲטָאַי
u-may-avōnōsai u-mip'sho-ai.   וּמֵעֲוֹנוֹתַי וּמִפְּשָׁעַי.
and purify me of my errors, my iniquities, and my willful sins.

V'zochrayni b'zikarōn tōv l'fonecho,   וְזָכְרֵנִי בְּזִכָּרוֹן טוֹב לְפָנֶיךָ,
Remember me with a favorable memory before You,

u-fokdayni bifkudas y'shu-o   וּפָקְדֵנִי בִּפְקֻדַּת יְשׁוּעָה
v'rachamim,   וְרַחֲמִים,
and consider me for salvation and compassion.

v'zochrayni l'cha-yim aruchim,   וְזָכְרֵנִי לְחַיִּים אֲרֻכִּים,
Remember me for long life,

l'cha-yim tōvim ulsholōm,   לְחַיִּים טוֹבִים וּלְשָׁלוֹם,
for good life and for peace,

u-farnoso tōvo v'chalkolo,   וּפַרְנָסָה טוֹבָה וְכַלְכָּלָה,
good livelihood and sustenance,

v'lechem le-echol,   וְלֶחֶם לֶאֱכוֹל,
bread to eat,

u-veged lilbōsh,   וּבֶגֶד לִלְבּוֹשׁ,
clothes to wear,

v'ōsher v'chovōd va-arichus yomim   וְעֹשֶׁר וְכָבוֹד וַאֲרִיכוּת יָמִים
wealth, honor, a long life

lahagōs b'sōresecho uvmitzvōsecho,   לַהֲגוֹת בְּתוֹרָתֶךָ וּבְמִצְוֹתֶיךָ,
to engage in Your Torah and Your commandments;

v'saychel u-vino   וְשֵׂכֶל וּבִינָה
and intelligence and insight

l'hovin ulhaskil
imkay sōdōsecho.

לְהָבִין וּלְהַשְׂכִּיל
עָמְקֵי סוֹדוֹתֶיךָ.

to understand and discern the depths of Your mysteries.

V'hofayk r'fu-o sh'laymo
l'chol mach-ōvaynu,

וְהָפֵק רְפוּאָה שְׁלֵמָה
לְכָל מַכְאוֹבֵינוּ,

Grant a complete recovery to all our sufferings

usvorach es kol ma-asay yodaynu.

וּתְבָרֵךְ אֶת כָּל מַעֲשֵׂה יָדֵינוּ.

and bless all our handiwork.

V'sigzōr olaynu g'zayrōs tōvōs
y'shu-ōs v'nechomōs.

וְתִגְזוֹר עָלֵינוּ גְּזֵרוֹת טוֹבוֹת
יְשׁוּעוֹת וְנֶחָמוֹת.

Decree upon us good decrees, salvations, and consolations.

Usvatayl may-olaynu
kol g'zayrōs ko-shōs v'ro-ōs,

וּתְבַטֵּל מֵעָלֵינוּ
כָּל גְּזֵרוֹת קָשׁוֹת וְרָעוֹת,

Nullify all harsh and evil decrees against us

v'sayn b'layv malchus v'yō-atzov
v'sorov

וְתֵן בְּלֵב מַלְכוּת וְיוֹעֲצָיו
וְשָׂרָיו

and dispose the feelings of the government, its counselors and ministers,

olaynu l'tovo.

עָלֵינוּ לְטוֹבָה.

upon us for good.

Omayn v'chayn y'hi rotzōn.

אָמֵן וְכֵן יְהִי רָצוֹן.

Amen, and so be Your will.

ON A FESTIVAL THAT FALLS ON A WEEKDAY AND ON HOSHANA RABBAH CONTINUE HERE:

Yih-yu l'rotzon imray fi
v'hegyōn libi l'fonecho,

יִהְיוּ לְרָצוֹן אִמְרֵי פִי
וְהֶגְיוֹן לִבִּי לְפָנֶיךָ,

*May the expressions of my mouth and the thoughts of my heart
find favor before You,*

Adonoy tzuri v'gō-ali.

יהוה צוּרִי וְגֹאֲלִי.

HASHEM, my Rock and my Redeemer.

RECITE THE FOLLOWING VERSE THREE TIMES:

VA-ANI s'filosi l'cho Adōnoy
ays rotzōn,

וַאֲנִי תְפִלָּתִי לְךָ יהוה
עֵת רָצוֹן,

As for me, may my prayer to You, HASHEM, be at an opportune time;

Elōhim b'rov chasdecho,

אֱלֹהִים בְּרָב חַסְדֶּךָ,

O God, in Your abundant kindness,

anayni be-emes yish-echo.

עֲנֵנִי בֶּאֱמֶת יִשְׁעֶךָ.

answer me with Your true salvation.

ON ALL DAYS CONTINUE HERE:

■ I pray that Hashem crown His Third Temple with mercy and love, and I declare my absolute faith in Him and His Torah.

B'RICH SH'MAYH d'moray ol'mo,   בְּרִיךְ שְׁמֵהּ דְּמָרֵא עָלְמָא,

Blessed is the Name* of the Master of the universe,

b'rich kisroch v'asroch.   בְּרִיךְ כִּתְרָךְ וְאַתְרָךְ.

blessed is Your crown and Your place.

Y'hay r'usoch im amoch yisro-ayl   יְהֵא רְעוּתָךְ עִם עַמָּךְ יִשְׂרָאֵל
l'olam,   לְעָלַם,

May Your favor remain with Your people Israel forever;

u-furkan y'minoch achazay l'amoch   וּפֻרְקַן יְמִינָךְ אַחֲזֵי לְעַמָּךְ

may You display the salvation of Your right hand* to Your people

b'vays makd'shoch   בְּבֵית מַקְדְּשָׁךְ,

in Your Holy Temple,

ul-amtuyay lono mituv n'hōroch,   וּלְאַמְטְוּיֵי לָנָא מִטּוּב נְהוֹרָךְ,

and to benefit us with the goodness of Your luminescence

ulkabayl tz'lōsono b'rachamin.   וּלְקַבֵּל צְלוֹתָנָא בְּרַחֲמִין.

and to accept our prayers with mercy.

Y'hay ra-avo kodomoch   יְהֵא רַעֲוָא קֳדָמָךְ,

May it be Your will

d'sōrich lon cha-yin b'tivuso,   דְּתוֹרִיךְ לָן חַיִּין בְּטִיבוּתָא,

that You extend our lives with goodness

v'lehevay ano f'kido   וְלֶהֱוֵי אֲנָא פְּקִידָא
b'gō tzadika-yo,   בְּגוֹ צַדִּיקַיָּא,

and that I be numbered among the righteous;

l'mircham olai   לְמִרְחַם עָלַי

that You have mercy on me

ulmintar yosi v'yas kol di li,   וּלְמִנְטַר יָתִי וְיַת כָּל דִּי לִי,

and protect me, all that is mine

v'di l'amoch yisro-ayl.   וְדִי לְעַמָּךְ יִשְׂרָאֵל.

and that is Your people Israel's.

בְּרִיךְ שְׁמֵהּ — *Blessed is the Name.* The *Zohar* declares that when the congregation prepares to read from the Torah, the heavenly gates of mercy are opened and God's love for Israel is aroused. Therefore, it is an auspicious occasion for the recital of this prayer which asks for God's compassion; pleads that He display His salvation in the finally rebuilt Holy Temple;

declares our faith in Him and His Torah; and asks that He make us receptive to its wisdom.

יְמִינָךְ — *Your right hand.* It is axiomatic to Jewish belief that God had no physicality, not even that of the invisible, intangible angels. Because we are physical beings, we cannot grasp God's essence. We cannot conceive of a Being totally unaffected by material conditions

Ant hu zon l'chōlo,
    umfarnays l'chōlo,
אַנְתְּ הוּא זָן לְכֹלָּא,
וּמְפַרְנֵס לְכֹלָּא,

It is You Who nourishes all and sustains all;

ant hu shalit al kōlo,
אַנְתְּ הוּא שַׁלִּיט עַל כֹּלָּא,

it is You Who controls everything;

ant hu d'shalit al malcha-yo,
    u-malchuso diloch hi.
אַנְתְּ הוּא דְּשַׁלִּיט עַל מַלְכַיָּא,
וּמַלְכוּתָא דִילָךְ הִיא.

it is You Who controls kings, and kingship is Yours.

Ano avdo d'kudsho b'rich hu,
אֲנָא עַבְדָּא דְקֻדְשָׁא בְּרִיךְ הוּא,

I am a servant of the Holy One, Blessed is He,

d'sogidno kamayh
    u-mikamo dikar ōraisayh
דְּסָגִידְנָא קַמֵּהּ
וּמִקַּמָּא דִיקַר אוֹרַיְתֵהּ

and I prostrate myself before Him and before the glory of His Torah

b'chol idon v'idon.
בְּכָל עִדָּן וְעִדָּן.

at all times.

Lo al enosh rochitzno,
לָא עַל אֱנָשׁ רָחִיצְנָא,

Not in any man do I put trust,

v'lo al bar elohin somichno,
וְלָא עַל בַּר אֱלָהִין סָמִיכְנָא,

nor on any angel do I rely —

elo be-Eloho dishma-yo,
אֶלָּא בֶּאֱלָהָא דִשְׁמַיָּא,

only on the God of heaven

d'hu Eloho k'shōt,
דְּהוּא אֱלָהָא קְשׁוֹט,

Who is the God of truth,

v'ōraisayh k'shōt,
וְאוֹרַיְתֵהּ קְשׁוֹט,

Whose Torah is truth

unvi-ōhi k'shōt,
וּנְבִיאוֹהִי קְשׁוֹט,

and Whose prophets are true

u-masgay l'mebad tav-von ukshōt.
וּמַסְגֵּא לְמֶעְבַּד טַבְוָן וּקְשׁוֹט.

and Who acts liberally with kindness and truth.

Bayh ano rochitz,
בֵּהּ אֲנָא רָחִיץ,

In Him do I trust,

v'lishmayh kadisho yakiro
    ano aymar tushb'chon.
וְלִשְׁמֵהּ קַדִּישָׁא יַקִּירָא
אֲנָא אֲמַר תֻּשְׁבְּחָן.

and to His glorious and holy Name do I declare praises.

Y'hay ra-avo kodomoch,
יְהֵא רַעֲוָא קֳדָמָךְ,

May it be Your will

---

or the laws of nature and physics. When Scripture speaks of "the hand of God" or "the eyes of God" and so forth, it does not imply that God has corporeality. Rather, it speaks this way to enable us to understand the concepts being conveyed.

d'siftach libo-i b'ōraiso,

דְּתִפְתַּח לִבָּאִי בְּאוֹרַיְתָא,

that You open my heart to the Torah,

v'sashlim mish-alin d'libo-i,

וְתַשְׁלִים מִשְׁאֲלִין דְּלִבָּאִי,

and that You fulfill the wishes of my heart

v'libo d'chol amoch yisro-ayl,

וְלִבָּא דְכָל עַמָּךְ יִשְׂרָאֵל,

and the heart of Your entire people Israel,

l'tav ulcha-yin v'lishlom. Omayn.

לְטַב וּלְחַיִּין וְלִשְׁלָם. אָמֵן.

for good, for life, and for peace. Amen.

THE TORAH SCROLL IS REMOVED FROM THE ARK AND PRESENTED TO THE *CHAZZAN,* WHO ACCEPTS IT IN HIS RIGHT ARM. (WHEN TWO OR MORE TORAH SCROLLS ARE REMOVED, THE *CHAZZAN* IS PRESENTED WITH THE FIRST ONE.) FACING THE CONGREGATION, THE *CHAZZAN* RAISES THE TORAH AND, FOLLOWED BY THE CONGREGATION, RECITES ALOUD:

Sh'ma yisro-ayl, Adōnoy Elōhaynu

שְׁמַע יִשְׂרָאֵל יהוה אֱלֹהֵינוּ

Adōnoy e-chod.

יהוה אֶחָד.

Hear, O Israel:* HASHEM is our God, HASHEM, the One and Only.

THE *CHAZZAN* RAISES THE TORAH AND, FOLLOWED BY CONGREGATION, RECITES:

E-chod Elōhaynu, godōl Adōnaynu,

אֶחָד אֱלֹהֵינוּ גָּדוֹל אֲדוֹנֵינוּ,

One is our God, great is our Master,

kodōsh [v'nōro] sh'mō.

קָדוֹשׁ [וְנוֹרָא] שְׁמוֹ.

Holy [ON HOSHANA RABBAH: *and awesome*] *is His Name.*

THE *CHAZZAN* TURNS TO THE ARK, BOWS WHILE RAISING THE TORAH, AND RECITES:

Gad'lu Ladōnoy iti

גַּדְּלוּ לַיהוה אִתִּי

Declare the greatness of HASHEM with me,

unrōm'mo sh'mō yachdov.

וּנְרוֹמְמָה שְׁמוֹ יַחְדָּו.

and let us exalt His Name together.

THE *CHAZZAN* TURNS TO HIS RIGHT AND CARRIES THE TORAH TO THE *BIMAH.* THE TORAH IS KISSED AS IT IS CARRIED TO THE *BIMAH.* THE CONGREGATION RESPONDS:

L'CHO Adōnoy hag'dulo

לְךָ יהוה הַגְּדֻלָּה

Yours, HASHEM, is the greatness,

v'hag'vuro v'hatif-eres

וְהַגְּבוּרָה וְהַתִּפְאֶרֶת

the strength, the splendor,

v'hanaytzach v'hahōd,

וְהַנֵּצַח וְהַהוֹד,

the triumph, and the glory;

ki chōl ba-shoma-yim u-vo-oretz,

כִּי כֹל בַּשָּׁמַיִם וּבָאָרֶץ,

even everything in heaven and earth;

שְׁמַע יִשְׂרָאֵל — *Hear, O Israel.* Holding the Torah Scroll and facing the congregation, the *chazzan* leads them in reciting three verses that help set the majestic tone of reading pub- licly from the word of God. The verses form a logical progression: God is One; He is great and holy; therefore we join in declaring His great- ness.

l'cho Adōnoy hamamlocho
v'hamisnasay l'chōl l'rōsh.

לְךָ יהוה הַמַּמְלָכָה
וְהַמִּתְנַשֵּׂא לְכֹל לְרֹאשׁ.

Yours, HASHEM, is the kingdom, and the sovereignty over every leader.

Rōm'mu Adōnoy Elōhaynu,
v'hishta-chavu lahadōm raglov,
kodōsh hu.

רוֹמְמוּ יהוה אֱלֹהֵינוּ,
וְהִשְׁתַּחֲווּ לַהֲדֹם רַגְלָיו,
קָדוֹשׁ הוּא.

Exalt HASHEM, our God, and bow at His footstool; He is Holy!

Rōm'mu Adōnoy Elōhaynu,
v'hishta-chavu l'har kodshō,
ki kodōsh Adōnoy Elōhaynu.

רוֹמְמוּ יהוה אֱלֹהֵינוּ,
וְהִשְׁתַּחֲווּ לְהַר קָדְשׁוֹ,
כִּי קָדוֹשׁ יהוה אֱלֹהֵינוּ.

Exalt HASHEM, our God, and bow to His holy mountain; for holy is HASHEM, our God.

AS THE *CHAZZAN* CARRIES THE TORAH TO THE *BIMAH*, THE CONGREGATION RECITES:

AL HAKŌL, yisgadal v'yiskadash

עַל הַכֹּל, יִתְגַּדַּל וְיִתְקַדַּשׁ

For all this,* may it grow exalted, sanctified,

v'yishtabach v'yispo-ar
v'yisrōmam v'yisnasay

וְיִשְׁתַּבַּח וְיִתְפָּאַר
וְיִתְרוֹמַם וְיִתְנַשֵּׂא

praised, glorified, exalted, and extolled —

sh'mō shel melech malchay ham'lochim
hako'dōsh boruch hu,

שְׁמוֹ שֶׁל מֶלֶךְ מַלְכֵי הַמְּלָכִים
הַקָּדוֹשׁ בָּרוּךְ הוּא,

the Name of the King of kings, the Holy One, Blessed is He,

bo-ōlomōs sheboro,
ho-olom ha-ze v'ho-ōlom habo,

בָּעוֹלָמוֹת שֶׁבָּרָא,
הָעוֹלָם הַזֶּה וְהָעוֹלָם הַבָּא,

in the worlds that He has created — this world and the World to Come —

kirtzōnō, v'chirtzōn y'ray-ov,

כִּרְצוֹנוֹ, וְכִרְצוֹן יְרֵאָיו,

according to His will, and the will of those who fear Him,

v'chirtzōn kol bays yisro-ayl.

וְכִרְצוֹן כָּל בֵּית יִשְׂרָאֵל.

and the will of the entire House of Israel.

Tzur ho-ōlomim,
adōn kol hab'riyōs,
Elō-ah kol han'foshōs,

צוּר הָעוֹלָמִים,
אֲדוֹן כָּל הַבְּרִיּוֹת,
אֱלוֹהַּ כָּל הַנְּפָשׁוֹת,

Rock of the eternities, Master of all creatures, God of all souls,

ha-yōshayv b'merchavay morōm,
ha-shōchayn bishmay sh'may kedem.

הַיּוֹשֵׁב בְּמֶרְחֲבֵי מָרוֹם,
הַשּׁוֹכֵן בִּשְׁמֵי שְׁמֵי קֶדֶם.

He Who sits in the expanses on high, Who rests in the loftiest primeval heavens.

עַל הַכֹּל — *For all this.* Although He is sanctified in the heavens by spiritual beings, we long
to become worthy vehicles through which His
greatness can be manifested on earth, as well.

K'dushosō al hachāyōs,
קְדֻשָּׁתוֹ עַל הַחַיּוֹת,

ukdushosō al kisay hakovōd.
וּקְדֻשָּׁתוֹ עַל כִּסֵּא הַכָּבוֹד.

His holiness is upon the Chayos; His holiness is upon the Throne of Glory.

Uvchayn yiskadash shimcho bonu,
וּבְכֵן יִתְקַדַּשׁ שִׁמְךָ בָּנוּ,

Adōnoy Elōhaynu,
יהוה אֱלֹהֵינוּ,

And so, may Your Name be sanctified within us, Hashem, our God,*

l'aynay kol choy.
לְעֵינֵי כָּל חָי.

in the sight of all the living.

V'nōmar l'fonov shir chodosh,
וְנֹאמַר לְפָנָיו שִׁיר חָדָשׁ,

kakosuv:
כַּכָּתוּב:

May we chant before Him a new song as it is written:

Shiru Laylōhim zam'ru sh'mō,
שִׁירוּ לֵאלֹהִים זַמְּרוּ שְׁמוֹ,

"Sing to God, make music for His Name,

sōlu lorōchayv bo-arovōs b'Yoh sh'mō,
סֹלּוּ לָרֹכֵב בָּעֲרָבוֹת בְּיָהּ שְׁמוֹ,

v'ilzu l'fonov.
וְעִלְזוּ לְפָנָיו.

extol the One Who rides in the highest heavens, with His Name — God — and exult before Him."

V'nir-ayhu a-yin b'a-yin
וְנִרְאֵהוּ עַיִן בְּעַיִן

b'shuvō el novayhu,
בְּשׁוּבוֹ אֶל נָוֵהוּ,

May we see Him with a perceptive view upon His return to His Abode,

kakosuv: Ki a-yin b'a-yin yir-u
כַּכָּתוּב: כִּי עַיִן בְּעַיִן יִרְאוּ

b'shuv Adōnoy tziyōn.
בְּשׁוּב יהוה צִיּוֹן.

as is written: "For they shall see with a perceptive view as Hashem returns to Zion."

V'ne-emar: V'niglo k'vōd Adōnoy,
וְנֶאֱמַר: וְנִגְלָה כְּבוֹד יהוה,

And it is said: "The glory of Hashem shall be revealed

v'ro-u chol bosor yachdov,
וְרָאוּ כָל בָּשָׂר יַחְדָּו

ki pi Adōnoy dibayr.
כִּי פִּי יהוה דִּבֵּר.

and all flesh together shall see that the mouth of Hashem has spoken."

AV horachamim,
אַב הָרַחֲמִים,

hu y'rachaym am amusim,
הוּא יְרַחֵם עַם עֲמוּסִים,

May the Father of compassion have mercy on the people that is borne by Him,

v'yizkōr b'ris aysonim,
וְיִזְכּוֹר בְּרִית אֵיתָנִים,

and may He remember the covenant of the spiritually mighty.

v'yatzil nafshōsaynu
וְיַצִּיל נַפְשׁוֹתֵינוּ

May He rescue our souls

יִתְקַדַּשׁ שִׁמְךָ בָּנוּ — *May Your Name be sanctified within us.* The goal of people should be to demonstrate that God's greatness should not be reserved for the higher, spiritual spheres. Rather, the most noble purpose of life is for mortal man to become a bearer of Godliness.

min ha-sho-ōs horo-ōs,
מִן הַשָּׁעוֹת הָרָעוֹת,
from the bad times,

v'yig-ar b'yaytzer hora min han'su-im,
וְיִגְעַר בְּיֵצֶר הָרָע מִן הַנְּשׂוּאִים,
and upbraid the Evil Inclination to leave those borne by Him;

v'yochōn ōsonu liflaytas ōlomim,
וְיָחָן אוֹתָנוּ לִפְלֵיטַת עוֹלָמִים,
graciously make us an eternal remnant,

vimalay mish-alōsaynu
וִימַלֵּא מִשְׁאֲלוֹתֵינוּ
b'mido tōvo y'shu-o v'rachamim.
בְּמִדָּה טוֹבָה יְשׁוּעָה וְרַחֲמִים.
and fulfill our requests in good measure, for salvation and mercy.

THE TORAH IS PLACED ON THE *BIMAH* AND PREPARED FOR READING.
THE *GABBAI* USES THE FOLLOWING FORMULA TO CALL A *KOHEN* TO THE TORAH:

וְיַעֲזוֹר וְיָגֵן וְיוֹשִׁיעַ לְכָל הַחוֹסִים בּוֹ, וְנֹאמַר, אָמֵן. הַכֹּל הָבוּ גֹדֶל לֵאלֹהֵינוּ וּתְנוּ כָבוֹד לַתּוֹרָה, כֹּהֵן° קְרָב, יַעֲמֹד (NAME) בֶּן הַכֹּהֵן. (FATHER'S NAME)

°IF NO *KOHEN* IS PRESENT, THE *GABBAI* SAYS:

אֵין כַּאן כֹּהֵן,יַעֲמֹד (NAME) בֶּן (FATHER'S NAME) יִשְׂרָאֵל (לֵוִי) בִּמְקוֹם כֹּהֵן. בָּרוּךְ שֶׁנָּתַן תּוֹרָה לְעַמּוֹ יִשְׂרָאֵל בִּקְדֻשָּׁתוֹ.

CONGREGATION, THEN *GABBAI*:

V'atem had'vaykim
וְאַתֶּם הַדְּבֵקִים
Badōnoy Elōhaychem,
בַּיהוה אֱלֹהֵיכֶם,
You who cling to HASHEM, your God,

cha-yim kul'chem ha-yōm.
חַיִּים כֻּלְּכֶם הַיּוֹם
you are all alive today.

⊰⊱ **READING OF THE TORAH** ⊰⊱

THE READER SHOWS THE *OLEH* (PERSON CALLED TO THE TORAH) THE PLACE IN THE TORAH. THE *OLEH* TOUCHES THE TORAH WITH A CORNER OF HIS *TALLIS*, OR THE BELT OR MANTLE OF THE TORAH, AND KISSES IT. HE THEN BEGINS THE BLESSING, BOWING AT Bor'chu AND STRAIGHTENING UP AT Adōnoy.

BOR'CHU es Adōnoy ham'vōroch.
בָּרְכוּ אֶת יהוה הַמְּבֹרָךְ.
Bless HASHEM, the blessed One.

CONGREGATION, FOLLOWED BY *OLEH*, RESPONDS,
BOWING AT Boruch AND STRAIGHTENING UP AT Adōnoy.

Boruch Adōnoy ham'vōroch
בָּרוּךְ יהוה הַמְּבֹרָךְ
l'ōlom vo-ed.
לְעוֹלָם וָעֶד.
Blessed is HASHEM, the blessed One, for all eternity.

OLEH CONTINUES:

BORUCH ato Adōnoy
בָּרוּךְ אַתָּה יהוה
Elōhaynu melech ho-ōlom,
אֱלֹהֵינוּ מֶלֶךְ הָעוֹלָם,
Blessed are You, HASHEM, our God, King of the universe,

asher bochar bonu mikol ho-amim
אֲשֶׁר בָּחַר בָּנוּ מִכָּל הָעַמִּים,

v'nosan lonu es tōrosō.
וְנָתַן לָנוּ אֶת תּוֹרָתוֹ.

Who selected us from all the peoples and gave us His Torah.

Boruch ato Adōnoy, nōsayn hatōro.
בָּרוּךְ אַתָּה יהוה, נוֹתֵן הַתּוֹרָה.

Blessed are You, HASHEM, Giver of the Torah.

CONGREGATION RESPONDS: Omayn — אָמֵן

AFTER HIS TORAH PORTION HAS BEEN READ, THE *OLEH* RECITES:

BORUCH ato Adōnoy
בָּרוּךְ אַתָּה יהוה

Elōhaynu melech ho-ōlom,
אֱלֹהֵינוּ מֶלֶךְ הָעוֹלָם,

Blessed are You, HASHEM, our God, King of the universe,

asher nosan lonu tōras emes,
אֲשֶׁר נָתַן לָנוּ תּוֹרַת אֱמֶת,

v'cha-yay ōlom nota b'sōchaynu.
וְחַיֵּי עוֹלָם נָטַע בְּתוֹכֵנוּ.

Who gave us the Torah of truth and implanted eternal life within us.

Boruch ato Adōnoy, nōsayn hatōro.
בָּרוּךְ אַתָּה יהוה, נוֹתֵן הַתּוֹרָה.

Blessed are You, HASHEM, Giver of the Torah.

CONGREGATION RESPONDS: Omayn — אָמֵן

THANKSGIVING BLESSING

THE FOLLOWING IS RECITED BY ONE WHO SURVIVED A DANGEROUS SITUATION:

BORUCH ato Adōnoy
בָּרוּךְ אַתָּה יהוה

Elōhaynu melech ho-ōlom,
אֱלֹהֵינוּ מֶלֶךְ הָעוֹלָם,

Blessed are You, HASHEM, our God, King of the universe,

hagōmayl l'chayovim tōvōs,
הַגּוֹמֵל לְחַיָּבִים טוֹבוֹת,

Who bestows good things upon the guilty,

sheg'molani kol tōv.
שֶׁגְּמָלַנִי כָּל טוֹב.

Who has bestowed every goodness upon me.

CONGREGATION RESPONDS:

Omayn. Mi sheg'mol'cho kol tōv,
אָמֵן. מִי שֶׁגְּמָלְךָ כָּל טוֹב,

Amen. May He Who has bestowed goodness upon you

hu yigmol'cho kol tōv selo.
הוּא יִגְמָלְךָ כָּל טוֹב, סֶלָה.

continue to bestow every goodness upon you, Selah.

⊷§ Reading of the Torah

Moses and his court ordained that the Torah be read publicly on the mornings of the Sabbath, Monday and Thursday so that no three-day period would ever go by without a minimum of Torah study.

There is a basic difference between the reading of the Torah and the prayers. When we pray, we call upon God; that is why the *chazzan* stands in front of the congregation as its representative. But the Torah reading is reminiscent of God's revelation to Israel, when the nations gathered around Mount Sinai to hear Him communicate His word to Israel. That is why the Torah is read from a *bimah*, platform, usually elevated and in the center of the congregation, like Israel gathered around the mountain.

⊷§ Thanksgiving Blessing

When the Temple stood, a person who had been spared from a life-threatening situation would bring a thanksgiving -offering. Now, the obligation to thank God is discharged by reciting the thanksgiving blessing during the Torah

BAR MITZVAH BLESSING*

AFTER A *BAR MITZVAH* BOY COMPLETES HIS FIRST *ALIYAH*, HIS FATHER RECITES:

Boruch shep'torani   בָּרוּךְ שֶׁפְּטָרַנִי

Blessed is the One Who has freed me

may-ônshô shelo-ze.   מֵעָנְשׁוֹ שֶׁלָזֶה.

from the punishment* due this boy.*

PRAYER FOR THE OLEH

מִי שֶׁבֵּרַךְ אֲבוֹתֵינוּ אַבְרָהָם יִצְחָק וְיַעֲקֹב, הוּא יְבָרֵךְ אֶת (OLEH'S NAME)
בֶּן (OLEH'S FATHER'S NAME) בַּעֲבוּר שֶׁעָלָה לִכְבוֹד הַמָּקוֹם,
לִכְבוֹד הַתּוֹרָה, [ON FESTIVALS – לִכְבוֹד הַשַּׁבָּת – ON THE SABBATH / לִכְבוֹד
הָרֶגֶל]. בִּשְׂכַר זֶה, הַקָּדוֹשׁ בָּרוּךְ הוּא יִשְׁמְרֵהוּ וְיַצִּילֵהוּ מִכָּל צָרָה
וְצוּקָה, וּמִכָּל נֶגַע וּמַחֲלָה, וְיִשְׁלַח בְּרָכָה וְהַצְלָחָה בְּכָל מַעֲשֵׂה יָדָיו,
[ON FESTIVALS – וְיִזְכֶּה לַעֲלוֹת לָרֶגֶל,] עִם כָּל יִשְׂרָאֵל אֶחָיו. וְנֹאמַר. אָמֵן.
CONGREGATION RESPONDS: Omayn – אָמֵן

PRAYER FOR OTHERS

מִי שֶׁבֵּרַךְ אֲבוֹתֵינוּ אַבְרָהָם יִצְחָק וְיַעֲקֹב, הוּא יְבָרֵךְ אֶת (NAMES OF THE
RECIPIENTS) בַּעֲבוּר שֶׁ(NAME OF OLEH) יִתֵּן לִצְדָקָה בַּעֲבוּרָם.
בִּשְׂכַר זֶה, הַקָּדוֹשׁ בָּרוּךְ הוּא יִשְׁמְרֵם וְיַצִּילֵם מִכָּל צָרָה וְצוּקָה, וּמִכָּל נֶגַע
וּמַחֲלָה, וְיִשְׁלַח בְּרָכָה וְהַצְלָחָה בְּכָל מַעֲשֵׂה יְדֵיהֶם, [ON FESTIVALS – וְיִזְכּוּ
לַעֲלוֹת לָרֶגֶל,] עִם כָּל יִשְׂרָאֵל אֲחֵיהֶם. וְנֹאמַר. אָמֵן.
CONGREGATION RESPONDS: Omayn – אָמֵן

PRAYER FOR MOTHER AND HER NEWBORN SON

מִי שֶׁבֵּרַךְ אֲבוֹתֵינוּ אַבְרָהָם יִצְחָק וְיַעֲקֹב, הוּא יְבָרֵךְ אֶת הָאִשָּׁה
הַיּוֹלֶדֶת (NEW MOTHER'S NAME) בַּת (HER FATHER'S NAME) וְאֶת בְּנָהּ
הַנּוֹלָד לָהּ בְּמַזָּל טוֹב, בַּעֲבוּר שֶׁבַּעְלָהּ וְאָבִיו יִתֵּן לִצְדָקָה. בִּשְׂכַר זֶה יִגְדְּלוֹ
לְתוֹרָה וּלְחֻפָּה וּלְמַעֲשִׂים טוֹבִים. (וְיַכְנִיסוֹ בִּבְרִיתוֹ שֶׁל אַבְרָהָם אָבִינוּ
בְּעִתּוֹ וּבִזְמַנּוֹ) וְנֹאמַר. אָמֵן.
CONGREGATION RESPONDS: Omayn – אָמֵן

---

reading, within three days of the event, if possible. The types of events that require one to recite the blessing are derived from Psalm 107. They are: (a) completion of a sea journey; (b) completion of a hazardous land journey; (c) recovery from a major illness; (d) release from captivity. By extension, however, the blessing should be recited whenever someone has been spared from a life-threatening situation.

◆§ Bar Mitzvah Blessing

This blessing is recited by a father when his son becomes a *bar mitzvah*. Since the calling to

the Torah is symbolic of religious adulthood, the father recites the blessing after his son has completed his *aliyah*.

שֶׁפְּטָרַנִי מֵעָנְשׁוֹ — *Who has freed me from the punishment.* There are two interpretations of the word "punishment": (a) Until the *bar mitzvah,* the father was responsible for his child's behavior and could be punished if it was deficient; or, (b) until the *bar mitzvah,* the child could have suffered for the failures of his parents. According to the second interpretation, the father is grateful that his own sins will no longer harm his child.

PRAYER FOR MOTHER AND HER NEWBORN DAUGHTER (AND NAMING GIRL)

מִי שֶׁבֵּרַךְ אֲבוֹתֵינוּ אַבְרָהָם יִצְחָק וְיַעֲקֹב, הוּא יְבָרֵךְ אֶת הָאִשָּׁה הַיּוֹלֶדֶת

(NEW MOTHER'S NAME) בַּת (HER FATHER'S NAME) וְאֶת בִּתָּהּ הַנּוֹלְדָה

לָהּ בְּמַזָּל טוֹב, [וְיִקָּרֵא שְׁמָהּ בְּיִשְׂרָאֵל (BABY'S NAME) בַּת (BABY'S FATHER'S NAME)]

בַּעֲבוּר שֶׁבַּעְלָהּ וְאָבִיהָ יִתֵּן לִצְדָקָה. בִּשְׂכַר זֶה יִגְדְּלָהּ (לְתוֹרָה) וּלְחֻפָּה

ולמעשים טובים. וְנֹאמַר. אָמֵן.   CONGREGATION RESPONDS: Omayn – אָמֵן

PRAYER FOR A SICK PERSON

מִי שֶׁבֵּרַךְ אֲבוֹתֵינוּ אַבְרָהָם יִצְחָק וְיַעֲקֹב, מֹשֶׁה אַהֲרֹן דָּוִד וּשְׁלֹמֹה,

—— FOR A MAN ——

הוּא יְבָרֵךְ וִירַפֵּא אֶת הַחוֹלֶה (PATIENT'S NAME) בֶּן (PATIENT'S MOTHER'S NAME)

בַּעֲבוּר שֶׁ(SUPPLICANT'S NAME) יִתֵּן לִצְדָקָה בַּעֲבוּרוֹ.° בִּשְׂכַר זֶה, הַקָּדוֹשׁ בָּרוּךְ

הוּא יִמָּלֵא רַחֲמִים עָלָיו, לְהַחֲלִימוֹ וּלְרַפֹּאתוֹ וּלְהַחֲזִיקוֹ וּלְהַחֲיוֹתוֹ, וְיִשְׁלַח

לוֹ מְהֵרָה רְפוּאָה שְׁלֵמָה מִן הַשָּׁמַיִם, לִרְמַ"ח אֵבָרָיו, וּשְׁסָ"ה גִּידָיו,

—— FOR A WOMAN ——

הוּא יְבָרֵךְ וִירַפֵּא אֶת הַחוֹלֶה (PATIENT'S NAME) בַּת (PATIENT'S MOTHER'S NAME)

בַּעֲבוּר שֶׁ(SUPPLICANT'S NAME) יִתֵּן לִצְדָקָה בַּעֲבוּרָהּ.° בִּשְׂכַר זֶה, הַקָּדוֹשׁ בָּרוּךְ

הוּא יִמָּלֵא רַחֲמִים עָלֶיהָ, לְהַחֲלִימָהּ וּלְרַפֹּאתָהּ וּלְהַחֲזִיקָהּ וּלְהַחֲיוֹתָהּ,

וְיִשְׁלַח לָהּ מְהֵרָה רְפוּאָה שְׁלֵמָה מִן הַשָּׁמַיִם, לְכָל אֵבָרֶיהָ, וּלְכָל גִּידֶיהָ,

—— FOR ALL CONTINUE HERE ——

בְּתוֹךְ שְׁאָר חוֹלֵי יִשְׂרָאֵל, רְפוּאַת הַנֶּפֶשׁ, וּרְפוּאַת הַגּוּף,

[ON THE SABBATH—שַׁבָּת הִיא מִלְּזְעֹק, וּרְפוּאָה קְרוֹבָה לָבֹא,]

[ON A FESTIVAL—יוֹם טוֹב הוּא מִלְּזְעֹק, וּרְפוּאָה קְרוֹבָה לָבֹא,]

הַשְׁתָּא, בַּעֲגָלָא וּבִזְמַן קָרִיב, וְנֹאמַר. אָמֵן.

CONGREGATION RESPONDS: Omayn – אָמֵן

°בַּעֲבוּר שֶׁכָּל הַקָּהָל מִתְפַּלְּלִים בַּעֲבוּרוֹ (בַּעֲבוּרָהּ) – SOME SUBSTITUTE

PRAYER FOR MEMBERS OF THE ISRAEL DEFENSE FORCE

מִי שֶׁבֵּרַךְ אֲבוֹתֵינוּ אַבְרָהָם יִצְחָק וְיַעֲקֹב, הוּא יְבָרֵךְ אֶת חַיָּלֵי צְבָא הֲגַנָּה

לְיִשְׂרָאֵל, הָעוֹמְדִים עַל מִשְׁמַר אַרְצֵנוּ וְעָרֵי אֱלֹהֵינוּ, מִגְּבוּל

הַלְּבָנוֹן וְעַד מִדְבַּר מִצְרַיִם, וּמִן הַיָּם הַגָּדוֹל עַד לְבוֹא הָעֲרָבָה, בַּיַּבָּשָׁה בָּאֲוִיר

וּבַיָּם. יִתֵּן יהוה אֶת אוֹיְבֵינוּ הַקָּמִים עָלֵינוּ נִגָּפִים לִפְנֵיהֶם. הַקָּדוֹשׁ בָּרוּךְ הוּא

יִשְׁמֹר וְיַצִּיל אֶת חַיָּלֵינוּ מִכָּל צָרָה וְצוּקָה, וּמִכָּל נֶגַע וּמַחֲלָה, וְיִשְׁלַח בְּרָכָה

וְהַצְלָחָה בְּכָל מַעֲשֵׂה יְדֵיהֶם. יַדְבֵּר שׂוֹנְאֵינוּ תַּחְתֵּיהֶם, וִיעַטְּרֵם בְּכֶתֶר יְשׁוּעָה

וּבַעֲטֶרֶת נִצָּחוֹן. וִיקֻיַּם בָּהֶם הַכָּתוּב: כִּי יהוה אֱלֹהֵיכֶם הַהֹלֵךְ עִמָּכֶם, לְהִלָּחֵם

לָכֶם עִם אֹיְבֵיכֶם לְהוֹשִׁיעַ אֶתְכֶם. וְנֹאמַר: אָמֵן.

CONGREGATION RESPONDS: Omayn – אָמֵן

WHEN THE TORAH READING HAS BEEN COMPLETED (BUT BEFORE THE *ALIYAH* FOR *MAFTIR*),
THE READER RECITES HALF-*KADDISH*.
(Congregational responses are indicated by parentheses.)

יִתְגַּדַּל וְיִתְקַדַּשׁ שְׁמֵהּ רַבָּא. (אָמֵן–Omayn). בְּעָלְמָא דִּי בְרָא
כִרְעוּתֵהּ. וְיַמְלִיךְ מַלְכוּתֵהּ, בְּחַיֵּיכוֹן וּבְיוֹמֵיכוֹן וּבְחַיֵּי דְכָל
בֵּית יִשְׂרָאֵל, בַּעֲגָלָא וּבִזְמַן קָרִיב. וְאִמְרוּ: אָמֵן.

(אָמֵן. יְהֵא שְׁמֵהּ רַבָּא מְבָרַךְ לְעָלַם וּלְעָלְמֵי עָלְמַיָּא.)
(Omayn. Y'hay sh'mayh rabo m'vorach l'olam ul-ol'may ol'ma-yo.)

יְהֵא שְׁמֵהּ רַבָּא מְבָרַךְ לְעָלַם וּלְעָלְמֵי עָלְמַיָּא. יִתְבָּרַךְ וְיִשְׁתַּבַּח
וְיִתְפָּאַר וְיִתְרוֹמַם וְיִתְנַשֵּׂא וְיִתְהַדָּר וְיִתְעַלֶּה וְיִתְהַלָּל שְׁמֵהּ
דְּקֻדְשָׁא בְּרִיךְ הוּא (בְּרִיךְ הוּא – B'rich hu). °לְעֵלָּא מִן כָּל
[°לְעֵלָּא לְעֵלָּא מִכָּל – from Rosh Hashanah to Yom Kippur substitute]
בִּרְכָתָא וְשִׁירָתָא תֻּשְׁבְּחָתָא וְנֶחֱמָתָא, דַּאֲמִירָן בְּעָלְמָא. וְאִמְרוּ: אָמֵן.
(אָמֵן–Omayn).

HAGBAHAH AND GELILAH/RAISING THE TORAH

THE TORAH IS RAISED FOR ALL TO SEE. EACH PERSON LOOKS AT THE TORAH AND RECITES ALOUD:

V'ZŌS hatōro asher som mōshe   **וְזֹאת** הַתּוֹרָה אֲשֶׁר שָׂם מֹשֶׁה
lifnay b'nay yisro-ayl   לִפְנֵי בְּנֵי יִשְׂרָאֵל,

This is the Torah* that Moses placed before the Children of Israel,

al pi Adōnoy b'yad mōshe.   עַל פִּי יהוה בְּיַד מֹשֶׁה.

upon the command of HASHEM, through Moses' hand.

BLESSING BEFORE THE HAFTARAH

AFTER THE TORAH SCROLL HAS BEEN WOUND, TIED AND COVERED,
THE *OLEH* FOR *MAFTIR* RECITES THE *HAFTARAH* BLESSINGS.

BORUCH ato Adōnoy   **בָּרוּךְ** אַתָּה יהוה

Blessed are You, HASHEM,

Elōhaynu melech ho-ōlom,   אֱלֹהֵינוּ מֶלֶךְ הָעוֹלָם,

our God, King of the universe,

וְזֹאת הַתּוֹרָה — *This is the Torah.* As the congregation looks at the words and columns of the unrolled, upheld Torah Scroll, it declares the cardinal tenet of faith that the Torah we now have is the same one that God transmitted to Moses.

⸗§ **The reading of the Haftarah** was instituted during the Second Temple era, when, in his attempts to rid the Jewish people of their religion, the infamous Antiochus (who ruled and persecuted Israel prior to the time of the Chanukah miracle) forbade any public reading from the Torah. Unable to refresh their spiri-

tual thirst from the Torah itself, the people resorted to readings from the Prophets, calling seven people to read at least three verses each. Later, when the ban was lifted, the people retained their custom of having someone read from the Prophets. However, in order not to let it seem as though the reading from the Prophets had equal standing with the reading from the Torah, the Sages decreed that the person reading the *Haftarah* must first read a portion from the Torah. The *Haftarah* selection is always one that is related to the subject of the weekly Torah reading or the Festival or

asher bochar binvi-im tōvim,   אֲשֶׁר בָּחַר בִּנְבִיאִים טוֹבִים,

Who has chosen good prophets*

v'rotzo v'divrayhem   וְרָצָה בְדִבְרֵיהֶם

hane-emorim be-emes.   הַנֶּאֱמָרִים בֶּאֱמֶת.

and took pleasure with their words that were uttered with truth.

Boruch ato Adōnoy,   בָּרוּךְ אַתָּה יהוה,

Blessed are You, HASHEM,

habōchayr batōro uvmōshe avdō,   הַבּוֹחֵר בַּתּוֹרָה וּבְמֹשֶׁה עַבְדּוֹ,

Who chooses the Torah; Moses, His servant;

uvyisro-ayl amō,   וּבְיִשְׂרָאֵל עַמּוֹ,

Israel, His people;

u-vinvi-ay ho-emes votzedek.   וּבִנְבִיאֵי הָאֱמֶת וָצֶדֶק.

and the prophets of truth and righteousness.

CONGREGATION RESPONDS: Omayn – אָמֵן

BLESSINGS AFTER THE HAFTARAH

AFTER THE *HAFTARAH* IS READ, THE *OLEH* RECITES THE FOLLOWING BLESSINGS:

BORUCH ato Adōnoy   **בָּרוּךְ** אַתָּה יהוה

Blessed are You, HASHEM,

Elōhaynu melech ho-ōlom,   אֱלֹהֵינוּ מֶלֶךְ הָעוֹלָם,

our God, King of the universe,

tzur kol ho-ōlomim,   צוּר כָּל הָעוֹלָמִים,

tzadik b'chol hadōrōs,   צַדִּיק בְּכָל הַדּוֹרוֹת,

Rock of all eternities, Righteous in all generations,*

ho-Ayl hane-emon, ho-ōmayr v'ōse,   הָאֵל הַנֶּאֱמָן הָאוֹמֵר וְעֹשֶׂה,

ham'dabayr umka-yaym,   הַמְדַבֵּר וּמְקַיֵּם,

the trustworthy God, Who says and does, Who speaks and fulfills,

shekol d'vorov emes votzedek.   שֶׁכָּל דְּבָרָיו אֱמֶת וָצֶדֶק.

all of Whose words are true and righteous.

Ne-emon ato hu Adōnoy Elōhaynu,   נֶאֱמָן אַתָּה הוּא יהוה אֱלֹהֵינוּ,

v'ne-emonim d'vorecho,   וְנֶאֱמָנִים דְּבָרֶיךָ,

Trustworthy are You HASHEM, our God, and trustworthy are Your words;

---

event being celebrated.

בִּנְבִיאִים טוֹבִים — *Good prophets.* The theme of the *Haftarah* blessings is the integrity of the prophets and their teachings. Even when it is their mission to criticize and threaten, they are good to the Jewish people, Also, they are chosen because they are good people: learned,

righteous, impressive, etc. Our tradition does not accept prophets who are lacking in any of the attributes of Jewish greatness.

צַדִּיק בְּכָל הַדּוֹרוֹת — *Righteous in all generations.* Whether a generation enjoys good fortune or suffers tragic oppression, God is righteous and His judgments are justified.

v'dovor e-chod mid'vorecho   וְדָבָר אֶחָד מִדְּבָרֶיךָ

   ochōr lō yoshuv raykom,   אָחוֹר לֹא יָשׁוּב רֵיקָם,

not one of Your words is turned back to its origin unfulfilled,

ki Ayl melech ne-emon oto.   כִּי אֵל מֶלֶךְ נֶאֱמָן אָתָּה.

for You are God, trustworthy King.

Boruch ato Adōnoy,   בָּרוּךְ אַתָּה יהוה,

   ho-Ayl hane-emon b'chol d'vorov.   הָאֵל הַנֶּאֱמָן בְּכָל דְּבָרָיו.

Blessed are You, HASHEM, the God Who is trustworthy in all His words.

CONGREGATION RESPONDS: Omayn – אָמֵן

RACHAYM al tziyōn   רַחֵם עַל צִיּוֹן

   ki hi bays cha-yaynu,   כִּי הִיא בֵּית חַיֵּינוּ,

Have mercy on Zion* for it is the source of our life;

v'la-aluvas nefesh tōshi-a   וְלַעֲלוּבַת נֶפֶשׁ תּוֹשִׁיעַ

to the one who is deeply humiliated bring salvation

tōshi-a bimhayro v'yomaynu.   בִּמְהֵרָה בְיָמֵינוּ.

speedily, in our days.

Boruch ato Adōnoy,   בָּרוּךְ אַתָּה יהוה,

   m'samay-ach tziyōn b'voneho.   מְשַׂמֵּחַ צִיּוֹן בְּבָנֶיהָ.

Blessed are You, HASHEM, Who gladdens Zion through her children.

CONGREGATION RESPONDS: Omayn – אָמֵן

SAM'CHAYNU Adōnoy Elōhaynu   שַׂמְּחֵנוּ יהוה אֱלֹהֵינוּ

Gladden us, HASHEM, our God,

b'ayliyohu hanovi avdecho,   בְּאֵלִיָּהוּ הַנָּבִיא עַבְדֶּךָ,

with Elijah the prophet Your servant,

uvmalchus bays dovid m'shichecho,   וּבְמַלְכוּת בֵּית דָּוִד מְשִׁיחֶךָ,

and with the kingdom of the House of David,* Your anointed,

bimhayro yovō v'yogayl libaynu,   בִּמְהֵרָה יָבֹא וְיָגֵל לִבֵּנוּ,

may he come speedily and cause our heart to exult.

al kis-ō lō yayshayv zor   עַל כִּסְאוֹ לֹא יֵשֶׁב זָר

On his throne let no stranger sit

v'lō yinchalu ōd achayrim   וְלֹא יִנְחֲלוּ עוֹד אֲחֵרִים

   es k'vōdō,   אֶת כְּבוֹדוֹ,

nor let others continue to inherit his honor,

רַחֵם עַל צִיּוֹן — *Have mercy on Zion.* The holiness of the Temple on Mount Zion is the source of our spiritual life. Exiled and without it, we are humiliated. Without her children, Zion,

too, is despondent.

בְּאֵלִיָּהוּ . . . בֵּית דָּוִד — *With Elijah . . . the House of David.* Elijah will be the herald of the Messiah, a descendant of the Davidic dynasty.

ki v'shaym kodsh'cho nishbato lō,   כִּי בְשֵׁם קָדְשְׁךָ נִשְׁבַּעְתָּ לּוֹ,

for by Your holy Name You swore to him

shelō yichbe nayrō l'ōlom vo-ed.   שֶׁלֹּא יִכְבֶּה נֵרוֹ לְעוֹלָם וָעֶד.

that his lamp will not be extinguished forever and ever.

Boruch ato Adōnoy, mogayn dovid.   בָּרוּךְ אַתָּה יהוה, מָגֵן דָּוִד.

Blessed are You, HASHEM, Shield of David. *

CONGREGATION RESPONDS: Omayn — אָמֵן

ON A REGULAR SABBATH AND ON THE SABBATH OF *CHOL HAMOED* PESACH CONTINUE HERE.
ON A FESTIVAL AND ON THE SABBATH OF *CHOL HAMOED* SUCCOS CONTIUE ON P. 410.

AL HATŌRO, v'al ho-avōdo,   **עַל הַתּוֹרָה**, וְעַל הָעֲבוֹדָה,

For the Torah reading, * for the prayer service,*

v'al han'vi-im,   וְעַל הַנְּבִיאִים,

for the reading from the Prophets

v'al yōm ha-shabos ha-ze,   וְעַל יוֹם הַשַּׁבָּת הַזֶּה,

and for this Sabbath day

shenosato lonu Adōnoy Elōhaynu,   שֶׁנָּתַתָּ לָּנוּ יהוה אֱלֹהֵינוּ,

that You, HASHEM, our God, have given us

likdusho v'limnucho,   לִקְדֻשָּׁה וְלִמְנוּחָה,

l'chovōd ulsif-ores.   לְכָבוֹד וּלְתִפְאָרֶת.

for holiness and contentment, for glory and splendor:

Al hakōl, Adōnoy Elōhaynu,   עַל הַכֹּל, יהוה אֱלֹהֵינוּ,

For all this, HASHEM, our God,

anachnu mōdim loch,   אֲנַחְנוּ מוֹדִים לָךְ,

umvor'chim ōsoch,   וּמְבָרְכִים אוֹתָךְ,

we gratefully thank You and bless You.

yisborach shimcho b'fi kol chai   יִתְבָּרַךְ שִׁמְךָ בְּפִי כָּל חַי

May Your Name be blessed by the mouth of all the living,

tomid l'ōlom vo-ed.   תָּמִיד לְעוֹלָם וָעֶד.

always, for all eternity.

Boruch ato Adōnoy,   בָּרוּךְ אַתָּה יהוה,

Blessed are You, HASHEM,

m'kadaysh ha-shabos.   מְקַדֵּשׁ הַשַּׁבָּת.

Who sanctifies the Sabbath.

CONGREGATION RESPONDS: Omayn — אָמֵן

מָגֵן דָּוִד — *Shield of David.* In *II Samuel* (22:36) and *Psalms* (18:36), David praised God for shielding him against defeat.

עַל הַתּוֹרָה — *For the Torah reading.* This final blessing sums up the entire Torah-reading service: not only the reading from the Prophets, but also the Torah reading, the prayers and the holiness of the Sabbath or Festival day.

ON A FESTIVAL AND ON THE SABBATH OF *CHOL HAMOED* SUCCOS:
[ON THE SABBATH ADD THE WORDS IN BRACKETS.]

AL HATÔRO, v'al ho-avôdo,   עַל הַתּוֹרָה, וְעַל הָעֲבוֹדָה,
For the Torah reading, for the prayer service,

v'al han'vi-im   וְעַל הַנְּבִיאִים,
for the reading from the Prophets

v'al [yôm ha-shabos ha-ze v'al]   וְעַל [יוֹם הַשַּׁבָּת הַזֶּה וְעַל]
[and for this Sabbath day] and for this day of the

——————————— ON PESACH: ———————————

yôm chag hamatzôs ha-ze,   יוֹם חַג הַמַּצּוֹת הַזֶּה,
this day of the Festival of Matzos

——————————— ON SHAVUOS: ———————————

yôm chag hashovu-ôs ha-ze,   יוֹם חַג הַשָּׁבֻעוֹת הַזֶּה,
this day of the Shavuos Festival

——————————— ON SUCCOS: ———————————

yôm chag hasukôs ha-ze,   יוֹם חַג הַסֻּכּוֹת הַזֶּה,
this day of the Succos Festival

————————— ON SHEMINI ATZERES/SIMCHAS TORAH: —————————

yôm hash'mini chag ho-atzeres ha-ze,   יוֹם הַשְּׁמִינִי חַג הָעֲצֶרֶת הַזֶּה,
the eighth day, this Festival of the Assembly

——————————— ON ALL DAYS CONTINUE HERE: ———————————

shenosato lonu Adônoy Elôhaynu,   שֶׁנָּתַתָּ לָּנוּ יהוה אֱלֹהֵינוּ,
that You, HASHEM, our God, have given us

[likdusho v'limnucho]   [לִקְדֻשָּׁה וְלִמְנוּחָה,]
[for holiness and contentment,]

l'sosôn ulsimcho,   לְשָׂשׂוֹן וּלְשִׂמְחָה,
for gladness and joy,

l'chovôd ulsif-ores.   לְכָבוֹד וּלְתִפְאָרֶת.
for glory and splendor.

Al hakôl, Adônoy Elôhaynu,   עַל הַכֹּל יהוה אֱלֹהֵינוּ,
For all this, HASHEM, our God,

anachnu môdim loch,   אֲנַחְנוּ מוֹדִים לָךְ,
we gratefully thank You

umvor'chim ôsoch,   וּמְבָרְכִים אוֹתָךְ,
and bless You.

yisborach shimcho b'fi kol chai   יִתְבָּרַךְ שִׁמְךָ בְּפִי כָּל חַי
May Your Name be blessed by the mouth of all the living,

tomid l'ôlom vo-ed.   תָּמִיד לְעוֹלָם וָעֶד.
always, for all eternity.

——————— EVERY DAY EXCEPT THE SABBATH, THE BLESSING CONCLUDES: ———————

Boruch ato Adōnoy,   בָּרוּךְ אַתָּה יהוה,

Blessed are You, HASHEM,

m'kadaysh yisro-ayl v'haz'manim.   מְקַדֵּשׁ יִשְׂרָאֵל וְהַזְּמַנִּים.

Who sanctifies Israel and the festival seasons.

CONGREGATION RESPONDS: Omayn — אָמֵן

——————— ON THE SABBATH THE BLESSING CONCLUDES: ———————

Boruch ato Adōnoy,   בָּרוּךְ אַתָּה יהוה,

Blessed are You, HASHEM,

m'kadaysh hashabos v'yisro-ayl   מְקַדֵּשׁ הַשַּׁבָּת וְיִשְׂרָאֵל
v'haz'manim.   וְהַזְּמַנִּים.

Who sanctifies the Sabbath, Israel and the festival seasons.

CONGREGATION RESPONDS: Omayn — אָמֵן

ON EVERY SABBATH OF THE YEAR (INCLUDING FESTIVALS), CONTINUE WITH *YEKUM PURKAN* (BELOW). ON FESTIVALS THAT DO NOT FALL ON THE SABBATH, THE SERVICE CONTINUES WITH *KAH KEILI* (P. 693), EXCEPT ON THE LAST DAY OF PESACH, THE LAST DAY OF SHAVUOS, AND SHEMINI ATZERES, WHEN *YIZKOR* (P. 695) IS RECITED.

Y'KUM purkon min sh'ma-yo,   יְקוּם פֻּרְקָן מִן שְׁמַיָּא,

May salvation arise* from heaven —

chino v'chisdo v'rachamay,   חִנָּא וְחִסְדָּא וְרַחֲמֵי,

grace, kindness, compassion,

v'cha-yay arichay, umzōnay r'vichay,   וְחַיֵּי אֲרִיכֵי, וּמְזוֹנֵי רְוִיחֵי,

long life, abundant sustenance,

v'siyato dishma-yo,   וְסִיַּעְתָּא דִשְׁמַיָּא,
    u-varyus gufo,   וּבַרְיוּת גּוּפָא,

heavenly assistance, physical health,

unhōro ma-alyo,   וּנְהוֹרָא מַעַלְיָא,

lofty vision,

zar-o cha-yo v'ka-yomo,   זַרְעָא חַיָּא וְקַיָּמָא,

living and surviving offspring,

zar-o di lo yifsōk v'di lo yivtōl   זַרְעָא דִי לָא יִפְסוֹק וְדִי לָא יִבְטוֹל
mipisgomay ōraiso.   מִפִּתְגָּמֵי אוֹרַיְתָא.

offspring who will neither interrupt nor cease from words of the Torah —

יְקוּם פֻּרְקָן — *May salvation arise.* Very fittingly, the reading from the Torah is followed by a series of prayers for those who uphold the Torah — by teaching, study, and support, and especially by undertaking the difficult responsibilities of leadership. The first is a general prayer for all such people wherever they may be; consequently, it is written in the third person. The second is a prayer for the congregation with which one is praying, and it is written in the second person. These two prayers were composed by the Babylonian *geonim* after the close of the Talmudic period; therefore they were written in Aramaic, the spoken language

L'moronon v'rabonon   לְמָרָנָן וְרַבָּנָן

chavuroso kadishoso   חֲבוּרָתָא קַדִּישָׁתָא

for our masters and sages, the holy fellowships

di v'ar-o d'yisro-ayl v'di b'vovel,   דִּי בְאַרְעָא דְיִשְׂרָאֵל וְדִי בְּבָבֶל,

that are in the Land of Israel and that are in the Diaspora:*

l'rayshay chalay, ulrayshay galvoso,   לְרֵישֵׁי כַלֵּי, וּלְרֵישֵׁי גַלְוָתָא,

for the leaders of the Torah assemblages, the leaders of the exile communities,

ulrayshay m'sivoso,   וּלְרֵישֵׁי מְתִיבָתָא,

ulda-yonay di vovo,   וּלְדַיָּנֵי דִי בָבָא,

the leaders of the academies, the judges at the gateways,

l'chol talmidayhōn,   לְכָל תַּלְמִידֵיהוֹן,

ulchol talmiday salmidayhōn,   וּלְכָל תַּלְמִידֵי תַלְמִידֵיהוֹן,

and all their students and to all the students of their students,

ulchol mon d'os'kin b'ōraiso.   וּלְכָל מָן דְּעָסְקִין בְּאוֹרַיְתָא.

and to everyone who engages in Torah study.

Malko d'ol'mo y'voraych yas-hōn,   מַלְכָּא דְעָלְמָא יְבָרֵךְ יַתְהוֹן,

May the King of the universe bless them,

yapish cha-yayhōn, v'yasgay yōmayhōn,   יַפִּישׁ חַיֵּיהוֹן, וְיַסְגֵּא יוֹמֵיהוֹן,

make their lives fruitful, increase their days

v'yitayn archo lishnayhōn,   וְיִתֵּן אַרְכָה לִשְׁנֵיהוֹן,

and grant length to their years.

v'yispor'kun v'yishtayz'vun   וְיִתְפָּרְקוּן וְיִשְׁתֵּזְבוּן

May He save them and rescue them

min kol oko   מִן כָּל עָקָא

u-min kol mar-in bi-shin.   וּמִן כָּל מַרְעִין בִּישִׁין.

from every distress and from all serious ailments.

Moron di vishma-yo   מָרָן דִּי בִשְׁמַיָּא

May the Master in heaven

y'hay v'sa-d'hōn, kol z'man v'idon   יְהֵא בְסַעְדְּהוֹן, כָּל זְמַן וְעִדָּן.

come to their assistance at every season and time.

V'nōmar: Omayn.   וְנֹאמַר: אָמֵן.

Now let us respond: Amen.

CONGREGATION RESPONDS: Omayn — אָמֵן

---

of that country.

דִּי בְאַרְעָא דְיִשְׂרָאֵל וְדִי בְּבָבֶל — *That are in the Land of Israel and that are in the Diaspora* [literally, *Babylonia*]. Although the Jewish community in the Land of Israel at the time

this prayer was composed was comparatively insignificant, the authors of the prayer gave honor and precedence to the Holy Land. The original text of the prayer has been maintained throughout the centuries of exile — even when

ONE WHO IS PRAYING ALONE OMITS THE NEXT TWO PARAGRAPHS.

Y'KUM purkon min sh'ma-yo,   יְקוּם פֻּרְקָן מִן שְׁמַיָּא,
May salvation arise from heaven —

chino v'chisdo v'rachamay,   חִנָּא וְחִסְדָּא וְרַחֲמֵי,
grace, kindness, compassion,

v'cha-yay arichay, umzōnay r'vichay,   וְחַיֵּי אֲרִיכֵי, וּמְזוֹנֵי רְוִיחֵי,
long life, abundant sustenance,

v'siyato dishma-yo, u-varyus gufo,   וְסִיַּעְתָּא דִשְׁמַיָּא, וּבַרְיוּת גּוּפָא,
heavenly assistance, physical health,

unhōro ma-alyo,   וּנְהוֹרָא מַעַלְיָא,
lofty vision,

zar-o cha-yo v'ka-yomo,   זַרְעָא חַיָּא וְקַיָּמָא,
living and surviving offspring,

zar-o di lo yifsōk v'di lo yivtōl   זַרְעָא דִּי לָא יִפְסוֹק וְדִי לָא יִבְטוֹל
mipisgomay ōraiso.   מִפִּתְגָּמֵי אוֹרַיְתָא.
offspring who will neither interrupt nor cease from words of the Torah —

l'chol k'holo kadisho hodayn,   לְכָל קְהָלָא קַדִּישָׁא הָדֵין,
to this entire holy congregation,

ravr'va-yo im z'ayra-yo,   רַבְרְבַיָּא עִם זְעֵרַיָּא,
taflo unsha-yo,   טַפְלָא וּנְשַׁיָּא,
adults along with children, infants and women.

malko d'ol'mo y'voraych yaschōn,   מַלְכָּא דְעָלְמָא יְבָרֵךְ יַתְכוֹן,
May the King of the universe bless you,

yapish cha-yaychōn,   יַפִּישׁ חַיֵּיכוֹן,
v'yasgay yōmaychōn,   וְיַסְגֵּא יוֹמֵיכוֹן,
make your lives fruitful, increase your days,

v'yitayn archo lishnaychōn,   וְיִתֵּן אַרְכָה לִשְׁנֵיכוֹן,
and grant length to your years.

v'sispor'kun v'sishtayz'vun   וְתִתְפָּרְקוּן וְתִשְׁתֵּזְבוּן
May He save you and rescue you

min kol oko   מִן כָּל עָקָא
u-min kol mar-in bishin.   וּמִן כָּל מַרְעִין בִּישִׁין.
from every distress and from all serious ailments.

---

the great masses of Jewry no longer lived in Babylonia. By extension, however, this timeless prayer refers to all Jewish communities; the word Babylonia is a general term for all Jewish communities outside the Land of Israel.

יְקוּם פֻּרְקָן — *May salvation arise.* This prayer refers specifically to the congregation with which one is praying. Therefore it omits mention of national teachers and leaders, and is written in the second person. It also mentions all segments of the congregation, young and

Moron di vishma-yo   מָרָן דִּי בִשְׁמַיָּא
May the Master in heaven

y'hay v'sad'chōn, kol z'man v'idon   יְהֵא בְסַעְדְּכוֹן, כָּל זְמַן וְעִדָּן.
come to your assistance at every season and time.

V'nōmar: Omayn.   וְנֹאמַר: אָמֵן.
Now let us respond: Amen.

CONGREGATION RESPONDS: Omayn — אָמֵן

MI SHEBAYRACH avōsaynu   **מִי שֶׁבֵּרַךְ** אֲבוֹתֵינוּ
He Who blessed* our forefathers,

avrohom yitzchok v'ya-akōv,   אַבְרָהָם יִצְחָק וְיַעֲקֹב,
Abraham, Isaac, and Jacob —

hu y'voraych   הוּא יְבָרֵךְ
es kol hakohol hakodōsh ha-ze,   אֶת כָּל הַקָּהָל הַקָּדוֹשׁ הַזֶּה,
may He bless this entire holy congregation

im kol k'hilōs hakōdesh,   עִם כָּל קְהִלּוֹת הַקֹּדֶשׁ,
along with all the holy congregations;

haym, unshayhem,   הֵם, וּנְשֵׁיהֶם,
uvnayhem, uvnōsayhem,   וּבְנֵיהֶם, וּבְנוֹתֵיהֶם,
them, their wives, sons, and daughters

v'chol asher lohem.   וְכָל אֲשֶׁר לָהֶם.
and all that is theirs;

U-mi shem'yachadim   וּמִי שֶׁמְּיַחֲדִים
botay ch'naysiyōs lisfilo,   בָּתֵּי כְנֵסִיּוֹת לִתְפִלָּה,
and those who dedicate synagogues for prayer

u-mi shebo-im b'sōchom   וּמִי שֶׁבָּאִים בְּתוֹכָם
l'hispalayl,   לְהִתְפַּלֵּל,
and those who enter them to pray,

u-mi shenōs'nim nayr lamo-ōr,   וּמִי שֶׁנּוֹתְנִים נֵר לַמָּאוֹר,
and those who give lamps for illumination

v'ya-yin l'kidush ulhavdolo,   וְיַיִן לְקִדּוּשׁ וּלְהַבְדָּלָה,
and wine for Kiddush and Havdalah,

u-fas lo-ōr'chim,   וּפַת לָאוֹרְחִים,
bread for guests

---

old, man and woman, because it prays for the welfare of each member of the community.

מִי שֶׁבֵּרַךְ — *He Who blessed.* This prayer asks that God bless this and all other congregations. It also singles out the people who unselfishly provide the means and services for the general good. These charitable causes are stressed so that the entire community will hear how great is the reward of those who provide for others. Knowing this, others will emulate their deeds.

utzdoko lo-aniyim, וּצְדָקָה לָעֲנִיִּים,

and charity for the poor;

v'chol mi she-ōs'kim וְכָל מִי שֶׁעוֹסְקִים

b'tzorchay tzibur be-emuno, בְּצָרְכֵי צִבּוּר בֶּאֱמוּנָה,

and all who are involved faithfully
in the needs of the community —

hakodōsh boruch hu הַקָּדוֹשׁ בָּרוּךְ הוּא

y'shalaym s'chorom, יְשַׁלֵּם שְׂכָרָם,

may the Holy One, Blessed is He, pay their reward

v'yosir mayhem kol machalo, וְיָסִיר מֵהֶם כָּל מַחֲלָה,

v'yirpo l'chol gufom, וְיִרְפָּא לְכָל גּוּפָם,

and remove from them every affliction, heal their entire body

v'yislach l'chol avōnom, וְיִסְלַח לְכָל עֲוֹנָם,

and forgive their every iniquity,

v'yishlach b'rocho v'hatzlocho וְיִשְׁלַח בְּרָכָה וְהַצְלָחָה

b'chol ma-asay y'dayhem, בְּכָל מַעֲשֵׂה יְדֵיהֶם,

and send blessing and success to all their handiwork,

im kol yisro-ayl achayhem. עִם כָּל יִשְׂרָאֵל אֲחֵיהֶם.

along with all Israel, their brethren.

V'nōmar: Omayn. וְנֹאמַר: אָמֵן.

And let us say: Amen.

CONGREGATION RESPONDS: Omayn — אָמֵן

PRAYER FOR THE WELFARE OF THE STATE

HANŌSAYN t'shu-o lam'lochim **הַנּוֹתֵן** תְּשׁוּעָה לַמְּלָכִים

u-memsholo lan'sichim וּמֶמְשָׁלָה לַנְּסִיכִים,

He Who grants salvation to kings and dominion to rulers,

malchusō malchus kol ōlomim מַלְכוּתוֹ מַלְכוּת כָּל עוֹלָמִים,

Whose kingdom is a kingdom spanning all eternities;

hapō-tze es dovid avdō הַפּוֹצֶה אֶת דָּוִד עַבְדּוֹ

maycherev ro-o, מֵחֶרֶב רָעָה,

Who releases David, His servant, from the evil sword;

hanōsayn ba-yom derech הַנּוֹתֵן בַּיָּם דֶּרֶךְ

uv-mayim azim n'sivo, וּבְמַיִם עַזִּים נְתִיבָה,

Who places a road in the sea and a path in the mighty waters —

hu y'voraych es hanosi הוּא יְבָרֵךְ אֶת הַנָּשִׂיא

v'es mish-nayhu וְאֶת מִשְׁנֵהוּ

may He bless the President, the Vice President,

v'es kol so-ray ham'dinōs ho-aylu. וְאֵת כָּל שָׂרֵי הַמְּדִינוֹת הָאֵלוּ.

and all the constituted officers of government of this land.

Melech malchay ham'lochim מֶלֶךְ מַלְכֵי הַמְּלָכִים,

The King Who reigns over kings,

b'rachamov y'cha-yaym v'yish-m'raym, בְּרַחֲמָיו יְחַיֵּם וְיִשְׁמְרֵם

in His mercy may He sustain them and protect them;

u-mikol tzoro v'yogōn vonezek וּמִכָּל צָרָה וְיָגוֹן וָנֶזֶק
yatzilaym, יַצִּילֵם.

from every trouble, woe and injury, may He rescue them;

v'yitayn b'libom וְיִתֵּן בְּלִבָּם

and put into their heart

uv-layv kol yō-atzay-hem v'sorayhem וּבְלֵב כָּל יוֹעֲצֵיהֶם וְשָׂרֵיהֶם

and into the heart of all their counselors [compassion]

la-asōs tōvōs imonu לַעֲשׂוֹת טוֹבוֹת עִמָּנוּ
v'im kol yisrō-ayl achaynu. וְעִם כָּל יִשְׂרָאֵל אַחֵינוּ.

to do good with us and with all Israel, our brethren.

Bi-mayhem uv-yomaynu בִּימֵיהֶם וּבְיָמֵינוּ
tivōsha y'hudo, תִּוָּשַׁע יְהוּדָה,

In their days and in ours, may Judah be saved

v'yisrō-ayl tishkōn lovetach. וְיִשְׂרָאֵל יִשְׁכּוֹן לָבֶטַח.

and may Israel dwell securely,

U-vo l'tzi-yōn gō-ayl. וּבָא לְצִיּוֹן גּוֹאֵל.

and may the Redeemer come to Zion.

V'chayn y'hi rotzton. וְכֵן יְהִי רָצוֹן.

So may it be His will.

V'nomar: Omayn. וְנֹאמַר: אָמֵן.

Now let us respond: Amen.

CONGREGATION RESPONDS: Omayn – אָמֵן

PRAYER FOR THE WELFARE OF THE STATE OF ISRAEL

OVINU SHEBA-SHOMA-YIM **אָבִינוּ שֶׁבַּשָּׁמַיִם,**
tzur yisrō-ayl v'gō-alo, צוּר יִשְׂרָאֵל וְגוֹאֲלוֹ,

Our Father Who is in heaven, Rock of Israel and its Redeemer,

boraych es m'dinas yisrō-ayl, בָּרֵךְ אֶת מְדִינַת יִשְׂרָאֵל,

bless the State of Israel,

rayshis tz'michas g'ulosaynu. רֵאשִׁית צְמִיחַת גְּאֻלָתֵנוּ.

the first sprouting of our redemption.

Hogayn o-le-ho b'evras chasdecho,   הָגֵן עָלֶיהָ בְּאֶבְרַת חַסְדֶּךָ,
Shield her with the pinion of Your kindness,

uvfrōs ole-ho sukas sh'lōmecho,   וּפְרֹשׂ עָלֶיהָ סֻכַּת שְׁלוֹמֶךָ,
and spread over her the shelter of Your peace;

ushlach ōr'cho v'amit'cho   וּשְׁלַח אוֹרְךָ וַאֲמִתְּךָ
send Your light and truth

l'ro-she-ho sore-ho v'yō-atze-ho   לְרָאשֶׁיהָ שָׂרֶיהָ וְיוֹעֲצֶיהָ,
to her leaders, ministers, and counselors,

v'sak-naym b'aytzo tōvo mil'fonecho.   וְתַקְּנֵם בְּעֵצָה טוֹבָה מִלְּפָנֶיךָ.
and set them aright with good counsel, from before Your Presence.

Chazayk es y'day   חַזֵּק אֶת יְדֵי
m'ginay eretz kod-shaynu,   מְגִנֵּי אֶרֶץ קָדְשֵׁנוּ,
Strengthen our Holy Land's defenders;

v'hanchilaym Elōhaynu y'shu-o,   וְהַנְחִילֵם אֱלֹהֵינוּ יְשׁוּעָה,
give them, our God, a heritage of salvation

va-ateres nitzochōn t'atraym   וַעֲטֶרֶת נִצָּחוֹן תְּעַטְּרֵם,
and adorn them with a diadem of triumph;

v'nosato sholōm bo-oretz   וְנָתַתָּ שָׁלוֹם בָּאָרֶץ
emplace peace in the Land

v'simchas ōlom l'yosh've-ho.   וְשִׂמְחַת עוֹלָם לְיוֹשְׁבֶיהָ.
and eternal gladness for its inhabitants.

V'es achaynu kol bays yisrō-ayl   וְאֶת אַחֵינוּ כָּל בֵּית יִשְׂרָאֵל,
And our brethren, the entire Family of Israel,

p'kod no   פְּקָד נָא
b'chol artzōs p'zuray-hem   בְּכָל אַרְצוֹת פְּזוּרֵיהֶם,
recall them in all the lands of their dispersion

v'sōlichaym m'hayro kom'miyus   וְתוֹלִיכֵם מְהֵרָה קוֹמְמִיּוּת
and lead them quickly, with upright pride,

l'tzi-yōn i-recho,   לְצִיּוֹן עִירֶךָ,
to Zion, Your City,

v'lirushola-yim mishkan sh'mecho,   וְלִירוּשָׁלַיִם מִשְׁכַּן שְׁמֶךָ,
and to Jerusalem, the resting place of Your Name,

kakosuv b'sōras moshe avdecho: כַּכָּתוּב בְּתוֹרַת מֹשֶׁה עַבְדֶּךָ:
as it is written in the Torah of Your servant Moses:

Im yih-ye nida-chacho   אִם יִהְיֶה נִדַּחֲךָ
biktzay ha-shoma-yim,   בִּקְצֵה הַשָּׁמָיִם,
Though you be banished to the end of heaven,

mishom y'kabetzcho Adōnoy Elōhecho   מִשָּׁם יְקַבֶּצְךָ יהוה אֱלֹהֶיךָ,
from there HASHEM, your God, will gather you

u-mishom yikochecho.   וּמִשָּׁם יִקָּחֶךָ.
and from there He will take you.

Ve-hevi-acho Adōnoy Elōhecho   וֶהֱבִיאֲךָ יהוה אֱלֹהֶיךָ
    el ho-oretz   אֶל הָאָרֶץ
HASHEM, your God, will bring you to the Land

asher yor'shu avōsecho virishtoh   אֲשֶׁר יָרְשׁוּ אֲבֹתֶיךָ וִירִשְׁתָּהּ,
that your forefathers inherited and you will inherit it,

v'haytivcho v'hirb'cho may-avōsecho.   וְהֵיטִבְךָ וְהִרְבְּךָ מֵאֲבֹתֶיךָ.
and He will benefit you and make you more numerous than your forefathers.

V'yachayd l'vovaynu l'ahavo   וְיַחֵד לְבָבֵנוּ לְאַהֲבָה
Unify our heart to love

ulyir-o es sh'mecho,   וּלְיִרְאָה אֶת שְׁמֶךָ,
and fear Your Name

v'lishmōr es kol divray sorosecho,   וְלִשְׁמֹר אֶת כָּל דִּבְרֵי תוֹרָתֶךָ,
and to observe all the words of Your Torah;

ush-lach lonu m'hayro   וּשְׁלַח לָנוּ מְהֵרָה
and send us quickly

ben dovid m'shi-ach tzidkecho,   בֶּן דָּוִד מְשִׁיחַ צִדְקֶךָ,
the offspring of David, Your righteous Messiah,

lifdōs m'chakay kaytz y'shu-osecho.   לִפְדּוֹת מְחַכֵּי קֵץ יְשׁוּעָתֶךָ.
to redeem those who long for Your salvation.

V'hōfa bahadar g'ōn u-zecho   וְהוֹפַע בַּהֲדַר גְּאוֹן עֻזֶּךָ,
Shine forth in the glorious majesty of Your might

al kol yōsh'vay sayvel artzecho   עַל כָּל יוֹשְׁבֵי תֵבֵל אַרְצֶךָ,
upon all inhabitants of Your populated world,

v'yōmar kōl asher n'shomo v'apō: וְיֹאמַר כֹּל אֲשֶׁר נְשָׁמָה בְאַפּוֹ:
and let every creature with breath in its nostrils proclaim:

Adōnoy Elōhay yisrō-ayl melech   יהוה אֱלֹהֵי יִשְׂרָאֵל מֶלֶךְ,
HASHEM, the God of Israel, is King,

u-malchusō bakol mosholo.   וּמַלְכוּתוֹ בַּכֹּל מָשָׁלָה.
and His kingdom has dominion over all.

Omayn, selo.   אָמֵן, סֶלָה.
Amen, Selah!

⊰⊱ BLESSING OF THE NEW MONTH ⊰⊱

■ I join the Jewish people in prayer that the forthcoming month be one of blessing, fulfilling our physical and spiritual needs.

ON THE SABBATH PRECEDING *ROSH CHODESH*, A SPECIAL BLESSING FOR THE NEW MONTH IS RECITED. THE *CHAZZAN* STANDS AT THE *BIMAH* AND HE OR A CONGREGANT HOLDS THE TORAH SCROLL. CONGREGATION, STANDING, FOLLOWED BY THE *CHAZZAN*:

Y'HI ROTZŌN mil'fonecho,   יְהִי רָצוֹן מִלְּפָנֶיךָ,

May it be Your will,

Adōnoy Elōhaynu   יהוה אֱלֹהֵינוּ

HASHEM, *our God*

Vaylōhay avōsaynu,   וֵאלֹהֵי אֲבוֹתֵינוּ,

and the God of our forefathers,

shet'chadaysh olaynu   שֶׁתְּחַדֵּשׁ עָלֵינוּ

es hachōdesh ha-ze   אֶת הַחֹדֶשׁ הַזֶּה

that You inaugurate this month upon us

l'tōvo v'livrocho.   לְטוֹבָה וְלִבְרָכָה.

for goodness and for blessing.

V'siten lonu cha-yim arukim,   וְתִתֶּן לָנוּ חַיִּים אֲרֻכִּים,

May You give us long life —

cha-yim shel sholōm,   חַיִּים שֶׁל שָׁלוֹם,

a life of peace,

cha-yim shel tōvo,   חַיִּים שֶׁל טוֹבָה,

a life of goodness,

cha-yim shel b'rocho,   חַיִּים שֶׁל בְּרָכָה,

a life of blessing,

cha-yim shel parnoso,   חַיִּים שֶׁל פַּרְנָסָה,

a life of sustenance,

cha-yim shel chilutz atzomōs,   חַיִּים שֶׁל חִלּוּץ עֲצָמוֹת,

a life of physical health,

cha-yim she-yaysh bohem   חַיִּים שֶׁיֵּשׁ בָּהֶם

yir-as shoma-yim v'yir-as chayt,   יִרְאַת שָׁמַיִם וְיִרְאַת חֵטְא,

a life in which there is fear of heaven and fear of sin,

cha-yim she-ayn bohem   חַיִּים שֶׁאֵין בָּהֶם

busho uchlimo,   בּוּשָׁה וּכְלִמָּה,

a life in which there is no shame nor humiliation,

⊰⊱ **Blessing of the New Month**

On the Sabbath before each new month begins, we pray that it will be a good and blessed month for all Israel. The purpose of this blessing is to inform the congregation of the date of *Rosh Chodesh*, so that the people will keep an

cha-yim shel ōsher v'chovōd,
חַיִּים שֶׁל עֹשֶׁר וְכָבוֹד,
a life of wealth and honor,

cha-yim shet'hay vonu
חַיִּים שֶׁתְּהֵא בָנוּ
a life in which we will have

ahavas tōro v'yir-as shoma-yim,
אַהֲבַת תּוֹרָה וְיִרְאַת שָׁמַיִם,
love of Torah and fear of heaven,*

cha-yim she-yimol'u
חַיִּים שֶׁיִּמָּלְאוּ
mish-alōs libaynu l'tōvo.
מִשְׁאֲלוֹת לִבֵּנוּ לְטוֹבָה.
a life in which the requests of our heart will be fulfilled for the good.

Omayn, selo.
אָמֵן, סֶלָה.
Amen, Selah.

THE MOLAD* IS ANNOUNCED AT THIS POINT.

CONGREGATION, STILL STANDING, FOLLOWED BY THE THE *CHAZZAN:*

MI SHE-OSO nisim
מִי שֶׁעָשָׂה נִסִּים
la-avōsaynu,
לַאֲבוֹתֵינוּ,
He Who performed miracles* for our forefathers

v'go-al ōsom may-avdus l'chayrus,
וְגָאַל אוֹתָם מֵעַבְדוּת לְחֵרוּת,
and redeemed them from slavery to freedom —

hu yig-al ōsonu b'korōv,
הוּא יִגְאַל אוֹתָנוּ בְּקָרוֹב,
may He redeem us soon

vikabaytz nidochaynu
וִיקַבֵּץ נִדָּחֵינוּ
and gather in our dispersed

may-arba kanfōs ho-oretz,
מֵאַרְבַּע כַּנְפוֹת הָאָרֶץ,
from the four corners of the earth;

chavayrim kol yisro-ayl.
חֲבֵרִים כָּל יִשְׂרָאֵל.
all Israel becoming comrades.

V'nōmar: Omayn.
וְנֹאמַר: אָמֵן.
Now let us respond: Amen.

CONGREGATION RESPONDS: Omayn — אָמֵן

---

accurate calendar. It is said on the Sabbath because that is when the greatest number of people are congregated.

אַהֲבַת תּוֹרָה וְיִרְאַת שָׁמַיִם — *Love of Torah and fear of heaven.* Knowledge and appreciation of Torah enhances a person's feeling of reverence and awe of God.

◢§ The *Molad* — the precise time at which the new moon begins to appear in Jerusalem — is customarily announced. The cycle of the moon is symbolic of renewal and it teaches that Is-

rael's glory may fade and disappear, but the nation will always re-emerge and grow to fullness, as does the moon. Thus, the monthly blessing of the new month is a source of inspiration and significance.

מִי שֶׁעָשָׂה נִסִּים — *He Who performed miracles.* Since the *mitzvah* of Rosh Chodesh and its symbolism of national renewal are related to the Exodus and every Jewish redemption, the blessing of the new month is, in effect, a prayer for the sequence of salvation.

CHAZZAN THEN CONGREGATION [SEE CHART BELOW]:

Rōsh chōdesh　　　　(NAME OF MONTH)　　　　רֹאשׁ חֹדֶשׁ

The new month of (. . .)

yih-ye bayōm　　　　(DAY OF THE WEEK)　　　　יִהְיֶה בַּיּוֹם

will be on the (. . .) day* of the week

habo olaynu v'al kol yisro-ayl　　　　הַבָּא עָלֵינוּ וְעַל כָּל יִשְׂרָאֵל

l'tōvo.　　　　לְטוֹבָה.

which is coming to us and all Israel for goodness.

NAMES OF THE MONTHS				DAYS OF THE WEEK		
Nison	נִיסָן	(Mar)cheshvon	(מַר)חֶשְׁוָן	ho-rishōn	*first*	הָרִאשׁוֹן
I-yor	אִיָּר	Kislayv	כִּסְלֵו	ha-shayni	*second*	הַשֵּׁנִי
Sivon	סִיוָן	Tayvays	טֵבֵת	ha-sh'lishi	*third*	הַשְּׁלִישִׁי
Tamuz	תַּמּוּז	Sh'vot	שְׁבָט	hor'vi-i	*fourth*	הָרְבִיעִי
(M'nachaym) Ov	(מְנַחֵם) אָב	Ador [Rishōn]	אֲדָר [רִאשׁוֹן]	ha-chamishi	*fifth*	הַחֲמִישִׁי
Elul	אֱלוּל	[Ador Shayni]	[אֲדָר שֵׁנִי]	ha-shishi	*sixth*	הַשִּׁשִּׁי
Note: When there are two days *Rosh Chodesh*, the second day's number is preceded by the word וּבַיּוֹם, uvayōm.				shabas kōdesh　　שַׁבַּת קֹדֶשׁ *the holy Sabbath*		

CONGREGATION THEN CHAZZAN:

Y'CHAD'SHAYHU　　　　יְחַדְּשֵׁהוּ

hakodōsh boruch hu　　　　הַקָּדוֹשׁ בָּרוּךְ הוּא

May the Holy One, Blessed is He, renew it

olaynu v'al kol amō bays yisro-ayl,　　　　עָלֵינוּ וְעַל כָּל עַמּוֹ בֵּית יִשְׂרָאֵל,

upon us and upon all His people, the Family of Israel,

l'cha-yim ulsholōm,　　　　לְחַיִּים וּלְשָׁלוֹם,

for life and for peace,

l'sosōn ulsimcho,　　　　לְשָׂשׂוֹן וּלְשִׂמְחָה,

for joy and for gladness,

li-shu-o ulnechomo.　　　　לִישׁוּעָה וּלְנֶחָמָה.

for salvation and for consolation.

V'nōmar: Omayn.　　　　וְנֹאמַר: אָמֵן.

Now let us respond: Amen.

CONGREGATION RESPONDS: Omayn — אָמֵן

יִהְיֶה בְּיוֹם — *Will be on the . . . day.* The day of the week is not given as "Sunday," "Monday," etc., but as "the first day," "the second day," etc., in fulfillment of the Torah's command to always remember the Sabbath. By counting the days of the week with references to the Sabbath we tie our existence to the Sabbath. This is in sharp contrast to the non-Jewish custom of assigning names to the days in commemoration of events or gods, such as Sunday for the sun, Monday for the moon and so on.

ON THE LAST DAY OF PESACH AND SHAVUOS, AND ON SHEMINI ATZERES,
YIZKOR (P. 695) IS RECITED.

IN MANY CONGREGATIONS THE *GABBAI* RECITES THE FOLLOWING PRAYER FOR THOSE WHO
PASSED AWAY DURING THE YEAR AND, IN MANY CONGREGATIONS, FOR THOSE WHOSE
YAHRTZEIT FALLS DURING THE COMING WEEK.

אֵל מָלֵא רַחֲמִים, שׁוֹכֵן בַּמְּרוֹמִים, הַמְצֵא מְנוּחָה נְכוֹנָה עַל
כַּנְפֵי הַשְּׁכִינָה, בְּמַעֲלוֹת קְדוֹשִׁים וּטְהוֹרִים כְּזֹהַר הָרָקִיעַ
מַזְהִירִים, אֶת נִשְׁמַת (NAME OF THE DECEASED) [בֶּן/בַּת] (FATHER'S NAME)
[שֶׁהָלַךְ לְעוֹלָמוֹ/שֶׁהָלְכָה לְעוֹלָמָהּ], בַּעֲבוּר שֶׁבְּלִי נֶדֶר אֶתֵּן
צְדָקָה בְּעַד הַזְכָּרַת [נִשְׁמָתוֹ/נִשְׁמָתָהּ], בְּגַן עֵדֶן תְּהֵא [מְנוּחָתוֹ/
מְנוּחָתָהּ], לָכֵן בַּעַל הָרַחֲמִים [יַסְתִּירֵהוּ/יַסְתִּירֶהָ] בְּסֵתֶר כְּנָפָיו
לְעוֹלָמִים, וְיִצְרוֹר בִּצְרוֹר הַחַיִּים אֶת [נִשְׁמָתוֹ/נִשְׁמָתָהּ], יהוה
הוּא [נַחֲלָתוֹ/נַחֲלָתָהּ], [וְיָנוּחַ/ וְתָנוּחַ] בְּשָׁלוֹם עַל [מִשְׁכָּבוֹ/
מִשְׁכָּבָהּ.] וְנֹאמַר: אָמֵן. (אָמֵן – CONG: Omayn)

EXCEPT ON CERTAIN FESTIVE SABBATHS, THE FOLLOWING PRAYER,
IN MEMORY OF THE DEPARTED, IS RECITED.

AV HORACHAMIM,

אַב הָרַחֲמִים,

shōchayn m'rōmim,

שׁוֹכֵן מְרוֹמִים,

Father of compassion,* Who dwells on high,

b'rachamov ho-atzumim

בְּרַחֲמָיו הָעֲצוּמִים

in His powerful compassion

hu yifkōd b'rachamim,

הוּא יִפְקוֹד בְּרַחֲמִים,

may He recall with compassion

hachasidim v'hai-shorim
v'hat'mimim,

הַחֲסִידִים וְהַיְשָׁרִים
וְהַתְּמִימִים,

the devout, the upright, and the perfect ones,

k'hilōs hakōdesh

קְהִלּוֹת הַקֹּדֶשׁ

the holy congregations

shemos'ru nafshom
al k'dushas ha-shaym,

שֶׁמָּסְרוּ נַפְשָׁם
עַל קְדֻשַּׁת הַשֵּׁם,

who gave their lives for the sanctification of the Name —

hane-ehovim v'han'imim
b'cha-yayhem,

הַנֶּאֱהָבִים וְהַנְּעִימִים
בְּחַיֵּיהֶם,

who were beloved and pleasant in their lifetimes

אַב הָרַחֲמִים — *Father of compassion.* This is a
memorial prayer, as the text makes clear, written
at the time of the atrocities of the Crusades for
the martyrs who died to sanctify God's Name.

uvmōsom lō nifrodu.

וּבְמוֹתָם לֹא נִפְרָדוּ.

and in their death were not parted [from God].

Min'shorim kalu,

מִנְּשָׁרִים קַלּוּ,

They were swifter than eagles

u-may-aro-yōs govayru,

וּמֵאֲרָיוֹת גָּבֵרוּ,

and stronger than lions

la-asōs r'tzōn kōnom

לַעֲשׂוֹת רְצוֹן קוֹנָם

to do their Creator's will

v'chayfetz tzurom.

וְחֵפֶץ צוּרָם.

and their Rock's desire.

Yiz-k'raym Elōhaynu l'tōvo,

יִזְכְּרֵם אֱלֹהֵינוּ לְטוֹבָה,

May our God remember them for good

im sh'or tzadikay ōlom,

עִם שְׁאָר צַדִּיקֵי עוֹלָם,

with the other righteous of the world.

v'yinkōm l'aynaynu

וְיִנְקוֹם לְעֵינֵינוּ

May He, before our eyes, exact retribution*

nikmas dam avodov hashofuch,

נִקְמַת דַּם עֲבָדָיו הַשָּׁפוּךְ,

for the spilled blood of His servants,

kakosuv b'sōras mōshe

כַּכָּתוּב בְּתוֹרַת מֹשֶׁה

as it is written in the Torah of Moses,

ish ho-Elōhim:

אִישׁ הָאֱלֹהִים:

the man of God:

Harninu gōyim amō

הַרְנִינוּ גוֹיִם עַמּוֹ

O nations, sing the praise of His people

ki dam avodov yikōm,

כִּי דַם עֲבָדָיו יִקּוֹם,

for He will avenge the blood of His servants

v'nokom yoshiv l'tzorov,

וְנָקָם יָשִׁיב לְצָרָיו,

and He will bring retribution upon His foes;

v'chiper admosō amō.

וְכִפֶּר אַדְמָתוֹ עַמּוֹ.

and He will appease His land and His people.

V'al y'day avodecho han'vi-im

וְעַל יְדֵי עֲבָדֶיךָ הַנְּבִיאִים

And by Your servants, the prophets,

וְיִנְקוֹם — *May He ... exact retribution.* We do not pray that we be strong enough to avenge our martyrs; Jews are not motivated by a lust to repay violence and murder with violence and murder. Rather we pray that God choose how and when to atone for the blood of His fallen martyrs. For the living, decency and integrity remain the primary goals of social behavior.

kosuv laymōr:

כָּתוּב לֵאמֹר:

it is written, saying:

V'nikaysi domom lō nikaysi,

וְנִקֵּיתִי דָּמָם לֹא נִקֵּיתִי,

Though I cleanse [the enemy] — their bloodshed
I will not cleanse

VaAdōnoy shōchayn b'tziyōn.

וַיהוה שֹׁכֵן בְּצִיּוֹן.

when HASHEM dwells in Zion.

Uvchisvay hakōdesh ne-emar:

וּבְכִתְבֵי הַקֹּדֶשׁ נֶאֱמַר:

And in the Holy Writings it is said:

Lomo yōm'ru hagōyim,

לָמָּה יֹאמְרוּ הַגּוֹיִם,

Why should the nations say,

a-yay Elōhayhem,

אַיֵּה אֱלֹהֵיהֶם,

"Where is their God?"

yivoda bagōyim l'aynaynu,

יִוָּדַע בַּגּוֹיִם לְעֵינֵינוּ,

Let there be known among the nations,
before our eyes,

nikmas dam avodecho hashofuch.

נִקְמַת דַּם עֲבָדֶיךָ הַשָּׁפוּךְ.

revenge for Your servants' spilled blood.

V'ōmayr:

וְאוֹמֵר:

And it says:

Ki dōraysh domim

כִּי דֹרֵשׁ דָּמִים

ōsom zochor,

אוֹתָם זָכָר,

For the Avenger of blood has remembered them;

lō shochach tza-akas anovim.

לֹא שָׁכַח צַעֲקַת עֲנָוִים.

He has not forgotten the cry of the humble.

V'ōmayr:

וְאוֹמֵר:

And it says:

Yodin bagōyim molay g'viyōs,

יָדִין בַּגּוֹיִם מָלֵא גְוִיּוֹת,

He will judge the corpse-filled nations,

mochatz rōsh

מָחַץ רֹאשׁ

al eretz rabo.

עַל אֶרֶץ רַבָּה.

He will crush the leader of the mighty land.

Minachal ba-derech yishte

מִנַּחַל בַּדֶּרֶךְ יִשְׁתֶּה,

From a river along the way he shall drink —

al kayn yorim rōsh.

עַל כֵּן יָרִים רֹאשׁ.

therefore he may proudly lift his head.

ON ALL DAYS THE SERVICE CONTINUES HERE:

ASHRAY yōsh'vay vay-secho,

אַשְׁרֵי יוֹשְׁבֵי בֵיתֶךָ,

Praiseworthy are those who dwell in Your house;

ōd y'hal'lucho selo.

עוֹד יְהַלְלוּךָ סֶּלָה.

may they always praise You, Selah!

Ashray ho-om shekocho lō,

אַשְׁרֵי הָעָם שֶׁכָּכָה לּוֹ,

Praiseworthy is the people for whom this is so,

ashray ho-om she-Adōnoy Elōhov.

אַשְׁרֵי הָעָם שֶׁיהוה אֱלֹהָיו.

praiseworthy is the people whose God is HASHEM.

T'hilo l'dovid,

תְּהִלָּה לְדָוִד,

A psalm of praise by David:

arōmimcho Elōhai hamelech,

אֲרוֹמִמְךָ אֱלוֹהַי הַמֶּלֶךְ,

I will exalt You, my God the King,

va-avor'cho shimcho l'ōlom vo-ed.

וַאֲבָרְכָה שִׁמְךָ לְעוֹלָם וָעֶד.

and I will bless Your Name forever and ever.

B'chol yōm avor'cheko,

בְּכָל יוֹם אֲבָרְכֶךָּ,

Every day I will bless You,

va-ahal'lo shimcho l'ōlom vo-ed.

וַאֲהַלְלָה שִׁמְךָ לְעוֹלָם וָעֶד.

and I will laud Your Name forever and ever.

Godōl Adōnoy umhulol m'ōd,

גָּדוֹל יהוה וּמְהֻלָּל מְאֹד,

HASHEM is great and exceedingly lauded,

v'ligdulosō ayn chayker.

וְלִגְדֻלָּתוֹ אֵין חֵקֶר.

and His greatness is beyond investigation.

Dōr l'dōr y'shabach ma-asecho,

דּוֹר לְדוֹר יְשַׁבַּח מַעֲשֶׂיךָ,

Each generation will praise Your deeds to the next,

ugvurōsecho yagidu.

וּגְבוּרֹתֶיךָ יַגִּידוּ.

and of Your mighty deeds they will tell.

Hadar k'vōd hōdecho,

הֲדַר כְּבוֹד הוֹדֶךָ,

The splendrous glory of Your power

v'divray nifl'ōsecho osicho.

וְדִבְרֵי נִפְלְאֹתֶיךָ אָשִׂיחָה.

and Your wondrous deeds I shall discuss.

Ve-ezuz nōr'ōsecho yōmayru,

וֶעֱזוּז נוֹרְאוֹתֶיךָ יֹאמֵרוּ,

And of Your awesome power they will speak,

ugdulos'cho asap'reno.

וּגְדוּלָּתְךָ אֲסַפְּרֶנָּה.

and Your greatness I shall relate.

Zecher rav tuv'cho yabi-u,

זֵכֶר רַב טוּבְךָ יַבִּיעוּ,

A recollection of Your abundant goodness they will utter

v'tzidkos'cho y'ranaynu.

וְצִדְקָתְךָ יְרַנֵּנוּ.

and of Your righteousness they will sing exultantly.

Chanun v'rachum Adōnoy,

חַנּוּן וְרַחוּם יהוה,

Gracious and merciful is HASHEM,

erech apa-yim ugdol chosed.

אֶרֶךְ אַפַּיִם וּגְדָל חָסֶד.

slow to anger, and great in [bestowing] kindness.

Tōv Adōnoy lakōl,

טוֹב יהוה לַכֹּל,

HASHEM is good to all,

v'rachamov al kol ma-asov.

וְרַחֲמָיו עַל כָּל מַעֲשָׂיו.

and His mercies are on all His works.

Yōducho Adōnoy kol ma-asecho,

יוֹדוּךָ יהוה כָּל מַעֲשֶׂיךָ,

All Your works shall thank You, HASHEM,

vachasidecho y'vor'chucho.

וַחֲסִידֶיךָ יְבָרְכוּכָה.

and Your devout ones will bless You.

K'vōd malchus'cho yōmayru,

כְּבוֹד מַלְכוּתְךָ יֹאמֵרוּ,

Of the glory of Your kingdom they will speak,

ugvuros'cho y'dabayru.

וּגְבוּרָתְךָ יְדַבֵּרוּ.

and of Your power they will tell,

L'hōdi-a livnay ho-odom g'vurōsov,

לְהוֹדִיעַ לִבְנֵי הָאָדָם גְּבוּרֹתָיו,

to inform human beings of His mighty deeds,

uchvōd hadar malchusō.

וּכְבוֹד הֲדַר מַלְכוּתוֹ.

and the glorious splendor of His kingdom.

Malchus'cho malchus kol ōlomim,

מַלְכוּתְךָ מַלְכוּת כָּל עֹלָמִים,

Your kingdom is a kingdom spanning all eternities,

umemshalt'cho b'chol dōr vodōr.

וּמֶמְשַׁלְתְּךָ בְּכָל דּוֹר וָדֹר.

and Your dominion is throughout every generation.

Sōmaych Adōnoy l'chol hanōf'lim,

סוֹמֵךְ יהוה לְכָל הַנֹּפְלִים,

HASHEM supports all the fallen ones

v'zōkayf l'chol hak'fufim.

וְזוֹקֵף לְכָל הַכְּפוּפִים.

and straightens all the

Aynay chōl aylecho y'sabayru,

עֵינֵי כֹל אֵלֶיךָ יְשַׂבֵּרוּ,

The eyes of all look to You with hope

v'ato nōsayn lohem
es ochlom b'ito.

וְאַתָּה נוֹתֵן לָהֶם
אֶת אָכְלָם בְּעִתּוֹ.

and You give them their food in its proper time.

CONCENTRATE INTENTLY WHILE RECITING THE NEXT VERSE.

Pōsay-ach es yodecho,

פּוֹתֵחַ אֶת יָדֶךָ,

You open Your hand

u-masbi-a l'chol chai rotzōn.

וּמַשְׂבִּיעַ לְכָל חַי רָצוֹן.

and satisfy the desire of every living thing.

Tzadik Adōnoy b'chol d'rochov,

צַדִּיק יהוה בְּכָל דְּרָכָיו,

Righteous is HASHEM in all His ways

v'chosid b'chol ma-asov.

וְחָסִיד בְּכָל מַעֲשָׂיו.

and magnanimous in all His deeds.

Korōv Adōnoy l'chol kōr'ov,

קָרוֹב יהוה לְכָל קֹרְאָיו,

HASHEM is close to all who call upon Him —

l'chōl asher yikro-uhu ve-emes.

לְכֹל אֲשֶׁר יִקְרָאֻהוּ בֶאֱמֶת.

to all who call upon Him sincerely.

R'tzōn y'ray-ov ya-ase,

רְצוֹן יְרֵאָיו יַעֲשֶׂה,

The will of those who fear Him He will do,

v'es shav-osom yishma v'yōshi-aym.

וְאֶת שַׁוְעָתָם יִשְׁמַע וְיוֹשִׁיעֵם.

and their cry He will hear, and save them.

Shōmayr Adōnoy es kol ōhavov,

שׁוֹמֵר יהוה אֶת כָּל אֹהֲבָיו,

HASHEM protects all who love Him,

v'ays kol hor'sho-im yashmid.

וְאֵת כָּל הָרְשָׁעִים יַשְׁמִיד.

but all the wicked He will destroy.

T'hilas Adōnoy y'daber pi,

✧ תְּהִלַּת יהוה יְדַבֶּר פִּי,

May my mouth declare the praise of HASHEM

vi-voraych kol bosor shaym kod'shō,
l'ōlom vo-ed.

וִיבָרֵךְ כָּל בָּשָׂר שֵׁם קָדְשׁוֹ
לְעוֹלָם וָעֶד.

and may all flesh bless His Holy Name forever and ever.

Va-anachnu n'voraych Yoh,

וַאֲנַחְנוּ נְבָרֵךְ יָהּ,

We will bless God

may-ato v'ad ōlom, hal'lu-yoh.

מֵעַתָּה וְעַד עוֹלָם, הַלְלוּיָהּ.

from this time and forever: Praise God!

RETURNING THE TORAH

THE CHAZZAN TAKES THE TORAH IN HIS RIGHT ARM AND RECITES:

Y'hal'lu es shaym Adōnoy,   יְהַלְלוּ אֶת שֵׁם יהוה,

Let them praise the Name of Hashem,

ki nisgov sh'mō l'vadō —   כִּי נִשְׂגָּב שְׁמוֹ לְבַדּוֹ —

for His Name alone will have been exalted —

CONGREGATION RESPONDS:

— hōdō al eretz v'shomōyim   הוֹדוֹ עַל אֶרֶץ וְשָׁמָיִם.

— His glory is above earth and heaven.

Va-yorem keren l'amō,   וַיָּרֶם קֶרֶן לְעַמּוֹ,

And He will have exalted the pride of His people,

t'hilo l'chol chasidov,   תְּהִלָּה לְכָל חֲסִידָיו,

causing praise for all His devout ones,

livnay yisro-ayl am k'rōvō,   לִבְנֵי יִשְׂרָאֵל עַם קְרֹבוֹ,

for the Children of Israel, His intimate people.

hal'luyoh.   הַלְלוּיָהּ.

Praise God!

AS THE TORAH IS CARRIED TO THE ARK THE APPROPRIATE PSALM IS RECITED.
ON THE SABBATH CONTINUE HERE; ON FESTIVALS THAT FALL ON WEEKDAYS TURN TO P. 430:

MIZMOR L'DOVID,   מִזְמוֹר לְדָוִד,

A psalm of David. *

hovu Ladōnoy b'nay aylim,   הָבוּ לַיהוה בְּנֵי אֵלִים,

Render unto Hashem, you sons of the powerful;

hovu Ladōnoy kovōd vo-ōz.   הָבוּ לַיהוה כָּבוֹד וָעֹז.

render unto Hashem honor and might.

Hovu Ladōnoy k'vōd sh'mō,   הָבוּ לַיהוה כְּבוֹד שְׁמוֹ,

Render unto Hashem the honor worthy of His Name;

hishta-chavu Ladōnoy   הִשְׁתַּחֲווּ לַיהוה

prostrate yourselves before Hashem

b'hadras kōdesh.   בְּהַדְרַת קֹדֶשׁ.

in His intensely holy place.

Kōl Adōnoy al hamo-yim,   קוֹל יהוה עַל הַמָּיִם,

The voice of Hashem is upon the waters,

Ayl hakovōd hir-im,   אֵל הַכָּבוֹד הִרְעִים,

the God of Glory thunders,

Adōnoy al ma-yim rabim.   יהוה עַל מַיִם רַבִּים.

Hashem is upon vast waters.

מִזְמוֹר לְדָוִד — *A psalm of David.* Psalm 29, discussed on page 92-93 above.

Kōl Adōnoy bakō-ach,
קוֹל יהוה בַּכֹּחַ,

The voice of HASHEM is in power!

kōl Adōnoy behodor.
קוֹל יהוה בֶּהָדָר.

The voice of HASHEM is in majesty!

Kōl Adōnoy shōvayr arozim,
קוֹל יהוה שֹׁבֵר אֲרָזִים,

The voice of HASHEM breaks the cedars,

vaishaber Adōnoy
וַיְשַׁבֵּר יהוה

es arzay hal'vonōn.
אֶת אַרְזֵי הַלְּבָנוֹן.

HASHEM shatters the cedars of Lebanon!

Va-yarkidaym k'mō aygel,
וַיַּרְקִידֵם כְּמוֹ עֵגֶל,

He makes them prance about like a calf;

l'vonōn v'siryōn k'mō ven r'aymim.   לְבָנוֹן וְשִׂרְיוֹן כְּמוֹ בֶן רְאֵמִים.

Lebanon and Siryon like young re'eimim.

Kōl Adōnoy
קוֹל יהוה

chōtzayv lahavōs aysh.
חֹצֵב לַהֲבוֹת אֵשׁ.

The voice of HASHEM carves with shafts of fire.

Kōl Adōnoy yochil midbor,
קוֹל יהוה יָחִיל מִדְבָּר,

The voice of HASHEM convulses the wilderness.

yochil Adōnoy midbar kodaysh.
יָחִיל יהוה מִדְבַּר קָדֵשׁ.

HASHEM convulses the wilderness of Kadesh.

Kōl Adōnoy y'chōlayl a-yolōs,
קוֹל יהוה יְחוֹלֵל אַיָּלוֹת,

The voice of HASHEM frightens the hinds,

va-yechesōf y'orōs,
וַיֶּחֱשׂף יְעָרוֹת,

and strips the forests bare,

uvhaycholō, kulō ōmayr kovōd.
וּבְהֵיכָלוֹ, כֻּלּוֹ אֹמֵר כָּבוֹד.

while in His Temple all proclaim, "Glory!"

Adōnoy lamabul yoshov,
יהוה לַמַּבּוּל יָשָׁב,

HASHEM sat enthroned at the Deluge;

va-yayshev Adōnoy melech l'ōlom.
וַיֵּשֶׁב יהוה מֶלֶךְ לְעוֹלָם.

HASHEM sits enthroned as King forever.

Adōnoy ōz l'amō yitayn,
יהוה עֹז לְעַמּוֹ יִתֵּן,

HASHEM will give might to His people,

Adōnoy y'voraych es amō
יהוה יְבָרֵךְ אֶת עַמּוֹ

vasholōm.
בַשָּׁלוֹם.

HASHEM will bless His people with peace.

CONTINUE Uvnuchō ON P. 431.

ON FESTIVALS THAT FALL ON WEEKDAYS CONTINUE HERE:

L'DOVID MIZMÔR,   לְדָוִד מִזְמוֹר,
        Of David a psalm:*

Ladônoy ho-oretz umlô-oh,   לַיהוה הָאָרֶץ וּמְלוֹאָהּ,
    Hashem's is the earth and its fullness,

tayvayl v'yôsh'vay voh.   תֵּבֵל וְיֹשְׁבֵי בָהּ.
    the inhabited land and those who dwell in it.

Ki hu al yamim y'sodoh,   כִּי הוּא עַל יַמִּים יְסָדָהּ,
    For He founded it upon seas,

v'al n'horôs y'chôn'neho.   וְעַל נְהָרוֹת יְכוֹנְנֶהָ.
    and established it upon rivers.

Mi ya-ale v'har Adônoy,   מִי יַעֲלֶה בְהַר יהוה,
    Who may ascend the mountain of Hashem,

u-mi yokum bimkôm kodshô.   וּמִי יָקוּם בִּמְקוֹם קָדְשׁוֹ.
    and who may stand in the place of His sanctity?

N'ki chapa-yim u-var layvov,   נְקִי כַפַּיִם וּבַר לֵבָב,
    One with clean hands and pure heart,

asher lô noso la-shov nafshi   אֲשֶׁר לֹא נָשָׂא לַשָּׁוְא נַפְשִׁי
    who has not sworn in vain by My soul

v'lô nishba l'mirmo.   וְלֹא נִשְׁבַּע לְמִרְמָה.
    and has not sworn deceitfully.

Yiso v'rocho may-ays Adônoy,   יִשָּׂא בְרָכָה מֵאֵת יהוה,
    He will receive a blessing from Hashem

utzdoko may-Elôhay yish-ô.   וּצְדָקָה מֵאֱלֹהֵי יִשְׁעוֹ.
    and just kindness from the God of his salvation.

Ze dôr dôrshov,   זֶה דּוֹר דֹּרְשָׁיו,
    This is the generation of those who seek Him,

m'vakshay fonecho, ya-akôv, selo.   מְבַקְשֵׁי פָנֶיךָ, יַעֲקֹב, סֶלָה.
    those who strive for Your Presence — Jacob, Selah.

S'u sh'orim ro-shaychem,   שְׂאוּ שְׁעָרִים רָאשֵׁיכֶם,
    Raise up your heads, O gates,

v'hinos'u pischay ôlom,   וְהִנָּשְׂאוּ פִּתְחֵי עוֹלָם,
    and be uplifted, you everlasting entrances,

v'yovô melech hakovôd.   וְיָבוֹא מֶלֶךְ הַכָּבוֹד.
    so that the King of Glory may enter.

לְדָוִד מִזְמוֹר — *Of David a psalm.* Psalm 24, discussed on page 473-474 below.

Mi ze melech hakovōd,   מִי זֶה מֶלֶךְ הַכָּבוֹד,
Who is this King of Glory? —

Adōnoy izuz v'gibōr,   יהוה עִזּוּז וְגִבּוֹר,
HASHEM, the mighty and strong,

Adōnoy gibōr milchomo.   יהוה גִּבּוֹר מִלְחָמָה.
HASHEM, the strong in battle.

S'u sh'orim ro-shaychem,   שְׂאוּ שְׁעָרִים רָאשֵׁיכֶם,
Raise up your heads, O gates,

us-u pischay ōlom,   וּשְׂאוּ פִּתְחֵי עוֹלָם,
and raise up, you everlasting entrances,

v'yovō melech hakovōd.   וְיָבֹא מֶלֶךְ הַכָּבוֹד.
so that the King of Glory may enter.

Mi hu ze melech hakovōd,   מִי הוּא זֶה מֶלֶךְ הַכָּבוֹד,
Who then is the King of Glory?

Adōnoy tz'vo-ōs   יהוה צְבָאוֹת
HASHEM, Master of Legions,

hu melech hakovōd, selo.   הוּא מֶלֶךְ הַכָּבוֹד, סֶלָה.
He is the King of Glory. Selah!

ON ALL DAYS CONTINUE HERE.
AS THE TORAH IS PLACED INTO THE ARK, THE FOLLOWING VERSES ARE RECITED:

UVNUCHŌ yōmar,   **וּבְנֻחֹה** יֹאמַר,
And when it rested he would say,*

shuvo Adōnoy   שׁוּבָה יהוה
    riv'vōs alfay yisro-ayl.   רִבְבוֹת אַלְפֵי יִשְׂרָאֵל.
"Reside tranquilly, O HASHEM, among the myriad thousands of Israel."

Kumo Adōnoy limnuchosecho,   קוּמָה יהוה לִמְנוּחָתֶךָ,
Arise, HASHEM, to Your resting place,

ato va-arōn u-zecho.   אַתָּה וַאֲרוֹן עֻזֶּךָ.
You and the Ark of Your strength.

Kōhanecho yilb'shu tzedek,   כֹּהֲנֶיךָ יִלְבְּשׁוּ צֶדֶק,
Let Your priests be clothed in righteousness,

vachasidecho y'ranaynu.   וַחֲסִידֶיךָ יְרַנֵּנוּ.
and Your devout ones will sing joyously.

וּבְנֻחֹה יֹאמַר — *And when it rested he would say.*
This is the companion verse to that which
Moses said (above p. 391) when the Ark began
to journey. When it came to rest, he expressed
the hope that God's Presence would find comfortable repose among the multitudes of the
Jewish people; in other words, that Israel

should be worthy of being host to God's holiness.

The rest of this paragraph is a selection of
verses from Scripture on the themes of a resting place for God's Law, the greatness of the
Torah, and the hope that God will see fit to
draw us closer to His service.

Ba-avur dovid avdecho,　　　בַּעֲבוּר דָּוִד עַבְדֶּךָ,

For the sake of David, Your servant,

al toshayv p'nay m'shichecho.　　אַל תָּשֵׁב פְּנֵי מְשִׁיחֶךָ.

turn not away the face of Your anointed.

Ki lekach tōv nosati lochem,　　כִּי לֶקַח טוֹב נָתַתִּי לָכֶם,

For I have given you a good teaching,

tōrosi al ta-azōvu.　　　　תּוֹרָתִי אַל תַּעֲזֹבוּ.

do not forsake My Torah.

Aytz cha-yim hi　　　　❖ עֵץ חַיִּים הִיא
　lamachazikim boh,　　　　לַמַּחֲזִיקִים בָּהּ,

It is a tree of life for those who grasp it,

v'sōm'cheho m'u-shor.　　　וְתֹמְכֶיהָ מְאֻשָּׁר.

and its supporters are praiseworthy.

D'rocheho darchay nō-am,　　דְּרָכֶיהָ דַרְכֵי נֹעַם,

Its ways are ways of pleasantness

v'chol n'sivōseho sholōm.　　וְכָל נְתִיבֹתֶיהָ שָׁלוֹם.

and all its paths are peace.

Hashivaynu Adōnoy aylecho　　הֲשִׁיבֵנוּ יהוה אֵלֶיךָ
　v'noshuvo,　　　　　　וְנָשׁוּבָה,

Bring us back to You, HASHEM, and we shall return,

chadaysh yomaynu k'kedem.　　חַדֵּשׁ יָמֵינוּ כְּקֶדֶם.

renew our days as of old.

THE *CHAZZAN* RECITES *HALF-KADDISH.*
(Congregational responses are indicated by parentheses.)

יִתְגַּדַּל וְיִתְקַדַּשׁ שְׁמֵהּ רַבָּא. (אָמֵן–Omayn). בְּעָלְמָא דִּי בְרָא כִרְעוּתֵהּ. וְיַמְלִיךְ מַלְכוּתֵהּ, בְּחַיֵּיכוֹן וּבְיוֹמֵיכוֹן וּבְחַיֵּי דְכָל בֵּית יִשְׂרָאֵל, בַּעֲגָלָא וּבִזְמַן קָרִיב. וְאִמְרוּ: אָמֵן.

(אָמֵן. יְהֵא שְׁמֵהּ רַבָּא מְבָרַךְ לְעָלַם וּלְעָלְמֵי עָלְמַיָּא.)

(Omayn. Y'hay sh'mayh rabo m'vorach l'olam ul-ol'may ol'ma-yo.)

יְהֵא שְׁמֵהּ רַבָּא מְבָרַךְ לְעָלַם וּלְעָלְמֵי עָלְמַיָּא. יִתְבָּרַךְ וְיִשְׁתַּבַּח וְיִתְפָּאַר וְיִתְרוֹמַם וְיִתְנַשֵּׂא וְיִתְהַדָּר וְיִתְעַלֶּה וְיִתְהַלָּל שְׁמֵהּ דְּקֻדְשָׁא בְּרִיךְ הוּא (בְּרִיךְ הוּא – B'rich hu). °לְעֵלָּא מִן כָּל

[substitute Rosh Hashanah to Yom Kippur from – °לְעֵלָּא לְעֵלָּא מִכָּל]

בִּרְכָתָא וְשִׁירָתָא תֻּשְׁבְּחָתָא וְנֶחֱמָתָא, דַּאֲמִירָן בְּעָלְמָא. וְאִמְרוּ: אָמֵן.
(אָמֵן–Omayn).

MUSSAF FOR A FESTIVAL AND *CHOL HAMOED* (EVEN ON THE SABBATH) BEGINS ON P. 708

◀{ MUSSAF FOR SABBATH/SABBATH ROSH CHODESH }▶

IN THE SYNAGOGUE THE *SHEMONEH ESREI* IS RECITED WHILE FACING THE ARK; ELSEWHERE IT IS RECITED WHILE FACING THE DIRECTION OF THE LAND OF ISRAEL. TAKE THREE STEPS BACKWARD, LEFT, RIGHT, LEFT, THEN THREE STEPS FORWARD, RIGHT, LEFT, RIGHT. REMAIN STANDING WITH FEET TOGETHER DURING *SHEMONEH ESREI.* RECITE IT WITH QUIET DEVOTION AND WITHOUT ANY INTERRUPTION. ALTHOUGH IT SHOULD NOT BE AUDIBLE TO OTHERS, ONE MUST PRAY LOUDLY ENOUGH TO HEAR ONESELF.

Ki shaym Adōnoy ekro,   כִּי שֵׁם יהוה אֶקְרָא,

When I call out the Name of HASHEM,

hovu gōdel Laylōhaynu.   הָבוּ גֹדֶל לֵאלֹהֵינוּ.

ascribe greatness to our God.

Adōnoy s'fosai tiftoch,   אֲדֹנָי שְׂפָתַי תִּפְתָּח,

My Lord, open my lips,

ufi yagid t'hilosecho.   וּפִי יַגִּיד תְּהִלָּתֶךָ.

that my mouth may declare Your praise.

■ First Blessing: In the merit of our Patriarchs whose actions reflected Godliness, Hashem pledged to always be with Israel and protect them.

BEND THE KNEES AT Boruch; BOW AT ato; STRAIGHTEN UP AT Adōnoy.

BORUCH ato Adōnoy   בָּרוּךְ אַתָּה יהוה

Blessed are You, HASHEM,

Elōhaynu Vaylōhay avōsaynu,   אֱלֹהֵינוּ וֵאלֹהֵי אֲבוֹתֵינוּ,

our God and the God of our forefathers,

Elōhay avrohom, Elōhay yitzchok,   אֱלֹהֵי אַבְרָהָם, אֱלֹהֵי יִצְחָק,

Vaylōhay ya-akōv,   וֵאלֹהֵי יַעֲקֹב,

God of Abraham, God of Isaac, and God of Jacob;

ho-Ayl hagodōl hagibōr v'hanōro,   הָאֵל הַגָּדוֹל הַגִּבּוֹר וְהַנּוֹרָא,

Ayl elyōn,   אֵל עֶלְיוֹן,

the great, mighty, and awesome God, the supreme God,

gōmayl chasodim tōvim   גּוֹמֵל חֲסָדִים טוֹבִים

v'kōnay hakōl,   וְקוֹנֵה הַכֹּל,

Who bestows beneficial kindnesses and creates everything,

v'zōchayr chasday ovōs,   וְזוֹכֵר חַסְדֵי אָבוֹת,

Who recalls the kindnesses of the Patriarchs

u-mayvi gō-ayl livnay v'nayhem,   וּמֵבִיא גוֹאֵל לִבְנֵי בְנֵיהֶם,

and brings a Redeemer to their children's children,

◀§ **Mussaf**

The *Mussaf* [additional] prayer commemorates the special communal offerings that were brought in the Temple to symbolize the added holiness and joy of the Sabbath or Festival. This is reflected in the emphasis on joy that is found in the *Mussaf Shemoneh Esrei* and in the expanded version of the *Mussaf Kedushah.*

l'ma-an sh'mō b'ahavo.   לְמַעַן שְׁמוֹ בְּאַהֲבָה.

for His Name's sake, with love.

FROM ROSH HASHANAH TO YOM KIPPUR ADD:

Zochraynu l'cha-yim,   זָכְרֵנוּ לְחַיִּים,

melech chofaytz bacha-yim,   מֶלֶךְ חָפֵץ בַּחַיִּים,

Remember us for life, O King Who desires life,

v'chosvaynu b'sayfer hacha-yim,   וְכָתְבֵנוּ בְּסֵפֶר הַחַיִּים,

l'ma-ancho Elōhim cha-yim.   לְמַעַנְךָ אֱלֹהִים חַיִּים.

and inscribe us in the Book of Life — for Your sake, O Living God.

Melech ōzayr u-mōshi-a u-mogayn.   מֶלֶךְ עוֹזֵר וּמוֹשִׁיעַ וּמָגֵן.

O King, Helper, Savior, and Shield.

BEND THE KNEES AT Boruch; BOW AT ato; STRAIGHTEN UP AT Adōnoy.

Boruch ato Adōnoy,   בָּרוּךְ אַתָּה יהוה,

mogayn avrohom.   מָגֵן אַבְרָהָם.

Blessed are You, HASHEM, Shield of Abraham.

■ Second Blessing: God's might as it is manifest in nature and man

ATO gibōr l'ōlom Adōnoy,   אַתָּה גִּבּוֹר לְעוֹלָם אֲדֹנָי,

You are eternally mighty, my Lord,

m'cha-yay maysim ato,   מְחַיֵּה מֵתִים אַתָּה,

the Resuscitator of the dead are You;

rav l'hōshi-a.   רַב לְהוֹשִׁיעַ.

abundantly able to save,

BETWEEN SHEMINI ATZERES AND PESACH, ADD:

Mashiv horu-ach u-mōrid hageshem.   מַשִּׁיב הָרוּחַ וּמוֹרִיד הַגֶּשֶׁם.

Who makes the wind blow and makes the rain descend;.

M'chalkayl cha-yim b'chesed,   מְכַלְכֵּל חַיִּים בְּחֶסֶד,

Who sustains the living with kindness;

m'cha-yay maysim b'rachamim rabim,   מְחַיֵּה מֵתִים בְּרַחֲמִים רַבִּים,

resuscitates the dead with abundant mercy;

sōmaych nōf'lim, v'rōfay chōlim,   סוֹמֵךְ נוֹפְלִים, וְרוֹפֵא חוֹלִים,

supports the fallen, heals the sick,

u-matir asurim,   וּמַתִּיר אֲסוּרִים,

releases the confined,

umka-yaym emunosō li-shaynay ofor.   וּמְקַיֵּם אֱמוּנָתוֹ לִישֵׁנֵי עָפָר.

and maintains His faith to those asleep in the dust.

Mi cho-mōcho ba-al g'vurōs,   מִי כָמְוֹךָ בַּעַל גְּבוּרוֹת,

Who is like You, O Master of mighty deeds,

u-mi dōme loch,   וּמִי דְּוֹמֶה לָּךְ,

and who is comparable to You,

melech maymis umcha-ye   מֶלֶךְ מֵמִית וּמְחַיֶּה

u-matzmi-ach y'shu-o.   וּמַצְמִיחַ יְשׁוּעָה.

O King Who causes death and restores life and makes salvation sprout!

FROM ROSH HASHANAH TO YOM KIPPUR ADD:

Mi chomōcho av horachamim,   מִי כָמְוֹךָ אַב הָרַחֲמִים,

Who is like You, O Merciful Father,

zōchayr y'tzurov l'cha-yim   זוֹכֵר יְצוּרָיו לְחַיִּים

b'rachamim.   בְּרַחֲמִים.

Who recalls His creatures mercifully for life!

V'ne-emon ato l'hacha-yōs maysim.   וְנֶאֱמָן אַתָּה לְהַחֲיוֹת מֵתִים.

And You are faithful to resuscitate the dead.

Boruch ato Adōnoy,   בָּרוּךְ אַתָּה יהוה,

m'cha-yay hamaysim.   מְחַיֵּה הַמֵּתִים.

Blessed are You, Hᴀsʜᴇᴍ, Who resuscitates the dead.

■ Third Blessing: Regarding the holiness of God's Name

DURING THE *CHAZZAN'S* REPETITION, *KEDUSHAH* IS RECITED; INDIVIDUALS CONTINUE ON P. 437. STAND WITH FEET TOGETHER AND AVOID ANY INTERRUPTIONS. RISE ON TOES WHEN SAYING Kodōsh, kodōsh, kodōsh; Boruch; AND Yimlōch.

CONGREGATION, THEN *CHAZZAN*:

NA-ARITZ'CHO v'nakdish'cho   **נַעֲרִיצְךָ** וְנַקְדִּישְׁךָ

We shall revere You and sanctify You

k'sōd si-ach sarfay kōdesh,   כְּסוֹד שִׂיחַ שַׂרְפֵי קֹדֶשׁ,

according to the counsel of the holy Seraphim,

hamakdishim shimcho bakōdesh,   הַמַּקְדִּישִׁים שִׁמְךָ בַּקֹּדֶשׁ,

who sanctify Your Name in the Sanctuary,

kakosuv al yad n'vi-echo,   כַּכָּתוּב עַל יַד נְבִיאֶךָ,

as it is written by Your prophet,

v'koro ze el ze v'omar: וְקָרָא זֶה אֶל זֶה וְאָמַר:

"And one [angel] will call another and say:

ALL IN UNISON:

Kodōsh kodōsh kodōsh   קָדוֹשׁ קָדוֹשׁ קָדוֹשׁ

Adōnoy Tz'vo-ōs,   יהוה צְבָאוֹת,

'Holy, holy, holy* is Hᴀsʜᴇᴍ, Master of Legions,

קָדוֹשׁ קָדוֹשׁ קָדוֹשׁ — *Holy, holy, holy.* God is holy with relation to the physical world, holy with relation to the spiritual world and holy with relation to the World to Come.

m'lō chol ho-oretz k'vōdō.   מְלֹא כָל הָאָרֶץ כְּבוֹדוֹ.

the whole world is filled with His glory.' "

CONGREGATION, THEN *CHAZZAN:*

K'vōdō molay ōlom,   כְּבוֹדוֹ מָלֵא עוֹלָם,

His glory fills the world.

m'shor'sov shō-alim ze lo-ze,   מְשָׁרְתָיו שׁוֹאֲלִים זֶה לָזֶה,

His ministering angels ask one another,

a-yay m'kōm k'vōdō,   אַיֵּה מְקוֹם כְּבוֹדוֹ,

"Where is the place of His glory?" *

l'umosom boruch yōmayru: לְעֻמָּתָם בָּרוּךְ יֹאמֵרוּ:

Those facing them say "Blessed":

ALL IN UNISON:

Boruch k'vōd Adōnoy, mim'kōmo.   בָּרוּךְ כְּבוֹד יהוה, מִמְּקוֹמוֹ.

"Blessed is the glory of HASHEM from His place."

CONGREGATION, THEN *CHAZZAN:*

Mim'kōmō hu yifen b'rachamim,   מִמְּקוֹמוֹ הוּא יִפֶן בְּרַחֲמִים,

From His place may He turn with compassion *

v'yochōn am ham'yachadim sh'mō,   וְיָחֹן עַם הַמְיַחֲדִים שְׁמוֹ,

and be gracious to the people who declare the Oneness of His Name;

erev vovōker b'chol yōm tomid,   עֶרֶב וָבֹקֶר בְּכָל יוֹם תָּמִיד,

evening and morning, every day constantly,

pa-ama-yim b'ahavo sh'ma ōm'rim: פַּעֲמַיִם בְּאַהֲבָה שְׁמַע אוֹמְרִים:

twice, with love, they proclaim the Shema. *

ALL IN UNISON:

Sh'ma yisro-ayl, Adōnoy Elōhaynu,   שְׁמַע יִשְׂרָאֵל, יהוה אֱלֹהֵינוּ,

Adōnoy e-chod.   יהוה אֶחָד.

"Hear O Israel: HASHEM is our God, HASHEM the One and Only."

CONGREGATION, THEN *CHAZZAN:*

Hu Elōhaynu, hu ovinu,   הוּא אֱלֹהֵינוּ, הוּא אָבִינוּ,

He is our God; * He is our Father;*

hu malkaynu, hu mōshi-aynu,   הוּא מַלְכֵּנוּ, הוּא מוֹשִׁיעֵנוּ,

He is our King; He is our Savior;

אַיֵּה מְקוֹם כְּבוֹדוֹ — *Where is the place of His glory?* God's glory is infinite and unbounded. Can anyone say that His glory is limited to any one place and unable to enter another?

הוּא יִפֶן בְּרַחֲמִים — *May He turn with compassion.* God's mercy causes Him to move from the throne of judgment to the throne of compassion.

עַם הַמְיַחֲדִים שְׁמוֹ... שְׁמַע אוֹמְרִים — *The people*

who declare the Oneness of His Name . . . they proclaim "Shema." With its twice-a-day declaration of the *Shema*, Israel joins in the sacred chorus of the angels — and this is sufficient merit to win God's compassion.

הוּא אֱלֹהֵינוּ — *He is our God,* i.e., He controls nature; He is our merciful Father, the Ruler of all peoples, and our only hope for salvation.

v'hu yashmi-aynu
   b'rachamov shaynis
וְהוּא יַשְׁמִיעֵנוּ
בְּרַחֲמָיו שֵׁנִית,

and He will let us hear, in His compassion, for a second time,

l'aynay kol choy,
   lihyōs lochem Laylōhim,
לְעֵינֵי כָּל חָי,
לִהְיוֹת לָכֶם לֵאלֹהִים,

in the presence of all the living, "... to be a God to you,*

ani Adōnoy Elōhaychem.
אֲנִי יהוה אֱלֹהֵיכֶם.

I am HASHEM, your God."

CHAZZAN:

Uvdivray kodsh'cho kosuv laymōr:
וּבְדִבְרֵי קָדְשְׁךָ כָּתוּב לֵאמֹר:

And in Your holy Writings the following is written:

ALL IN UNISON:

Yimlōch Adōnoy l'ōlom,
יִמְלֹךְ יהוה לְעוֹלָם,

"HASHEM shall reign forever;

Elōha-yich tziyōn l'dōr vodōr,
אֱלֹהַיִךְ צִיּוֹן לְדֹר וָדֹר,

your God, O Zion, from generation to generation.

hal'luyoh.
הַלְלוּיָהּ.

Praise God!"

CHAZZAN CONCLUDES:

לְדוֹר וָדוֹר נַגִּיד גָּדְלֶךָ וּלְנֵצַח נְצָחִים קְדֻשָּׁתְךָ נַקְדִּישׁ, וְשִׁבְחֲךָ
אֱלֹהֵינוּ מִפִּינוּ לֹא יָמוּשׁ לְעוֹלָם וָעֶד, כִּי אֵל מֶלֶךְ
גָּדוֹל וְקָדוֹשׁ אָתָּה. בָּרוּךְ אַתָּה יהוה, °הָאֵל הַקָּדוֹשׁ.
°הַמֶּלֶךְ הַקָּדוֹשׁ. — from Rosh Hashanah to Yom Kippur substitute

THE *CHAZZAN* CONTINUES tikanto shabos (P. 438) OR ato yo-tzarto (P. 441).

ATO kodōsh v'shimcho kodōsh,
אַתָּה קָדוֹשׁ וְשִׁמְךָ קָדוֹשׁ,

You are holy and Your Name is holy,

ukdōshim b'chol yōm
   y'hal'lucho, selo.
וּקְדוֹשִׁים בְּכָל יוֹם
יְהַלְלוּךָ סֶּלָה.

and holy ones praise You, every day, forever.

Boruch ato Adōnoy,
   °ho-Ayl hakodōsh.
בָּרוּךְ אַתָּה יהוה,
°הָאֵל הַקָּדוֹשׁ.

Blessed are You, HASHEM, the holy God.

FROM ROSH HASHANAH TO YOM KIPPUR SUBSTITUTE:

°hamelech hakodōsh.
°הַמֶּלֶךְ הַקָּדוֹשׁ.

the holy King.

לִהְיוֹת לָכֶם לֵאלֹהִים — *To be a God to you.* When redeeming Israel from Egypt, God said that His purpose in doing so was to be a God to the Jewish people. This too will be the purpose of of the second and final Redemption.

ON AN ORDINARY SABBATH CONTINUE HERE;
WHEN *ROSH CHODESH* FALLS ON THE SABBATH TURN TO P. 441.

■ Blessing relating to the holiness of the day: Description of the additional sacrifices for Shabbos and our yearning and desire for their reinstatement.

TIKANTO SHABOS

תִּכַּנְתָּ שַׁבָּת

You established the Sabbath;*

rotziso korb'nōseho,

רָצִיתָ קָרְבְּנוֹתֶיהָ,

found favor in its offerings;

tziviso pay-rusheho,

צִוִּיתָ פֵּרוּשֶׁיהָ

instructed regarding its commentaries*

im siduray n'socheho,

עִם סִדּוּרֵי נְסָכֶיהָ,

along with the order of its showbreads.

m'an'geho l'ōlom kovōd yincholu,

מְעַנְּגֶיהָ לְעוֹלָם כָּבוֹד יִנְחָלוּ,

Those who delight in it will inherit eternal honor,

tō-ameho cha-yim zochu,

טוֹעֲמֶיהָ חַיִּים זָכוּ,

those who savor it will merit life,

v'gam ho-ōhavim d'voreho
g'dulo bochoru,

וְגַם הָאוֹהֲבִים דְּבָרֶיהָ
גְּדֻלָּה בָּחָרוּ,

and also those who love the speech that befits it* *have chosen greatness.*

oz misinai nitztavu oleho,

אָז מִסִּינַי נִצְטַוּוּ עָלֶיהָ,

Then — from Sinai — they were instructed about it,

vat'tzavaynu Adōnoy Elōhaynu,

וַתְּצַוֵּנוּ יהוה אֱלֹהֵינוּ,

when You commanded us, HASHEM, *our God,*

l'hakriv boh korban musaf
shabos koro-uy.

לְהַקְרִיב בָּהּ קָרְבַּן מוּסַף
שַׁבָּת כָּרָאוּי.

to offer on it the Sabbath mussaf-offering properly.

Y'hi rotzōn mil'fonecho,

יְהִי רָצוֹן מִלְּפָנֶיךָ,

May it be Your will,

תִּכַּנְתָּ שַׁבָּת — *You established the Sabbath.* This paragraph introduces the concept of the special service in the Temple and concludes with the prayer that we be enabled to offer the Sabbath *mussaf* offering. The first twenty-two words begin with the letters of the Hebrew alphabet in reverse order, from the last letter to the first letter. This kabbalistic device symbolizes that after man reaches the full extent of his understanding — the last letter representing completion — he must realize that he should go back to the beginning and deepen his spiritual understanding even more.

צִוִּיתָ פֵּרוּשֶׁיהָ — [*You*] *instructed regarding its commentaries.* The numerous and complex laws of Sabbath are not clear from a superficial reading of the verses of the Torah. We know them because God instructed Moses regarding its commentaries, meaning that He taught Moses how the Scriptural verses should be understood and interpreted.

דְּבָרֶיהָ — *The speech that befits it* — because on the Sabbath one should discuss spiritual matters and not business and other mundane affairs.

Adōnoy Elōhaynu יהוה אֱלֹהֵינוּ

Vaylōhay avōsaynu, וֵאלֹהֵי אֲבוֹתֵינוּ,

HASHEM, our God and the God of our forefathers,

sheta-alaynu v'simcho l'artzaynu, שֶׁתַּעֲלֵנוּ בְשִׂמְחָה לְאַרְצֵנוּ,

that You bring us up in gladness to our Land

v'sito-aynu bigvulaynu, וְתִטָּעֵנוּ בִּגְבוּלֵנוּ,

and plant us within our boundaries.

v'shom na-ase l'fonecho וְשָׁם נַעֲשֶׂה לְפָנֶיךָ

There we will perform before You

es korb'nōs chōvōsaynu, אֶת קׇרְבְּנוֹת חוֹבוֹתֵינוּ,

our required offerings,

t'midim k'sidrom תְּמִידִים כְּסִדְרָם

the continual-offerings in their order

u-musofim k'hilchosom. וּמוּסָפִים כְּהִלְכָתָם.

and the mussaf-offerings according to their laws.

V'es musaf yōm ha-shabos ha-ze וְאֶת מוּסַף יוֹם הַשַּׁבָּת הַזֶּה

And the mussaf of this Sabbath day

na-ase v'nakriv l'fonecho נַעֲשֶׂה וְנַקְרִיב לְפָנֶיךָ
b'ahavo, בְּאַהֲבָה,

we will perform and offer to You with love

k'mitzvas r'tzōnecho, כְּמִצְוַת רְצוֹנֶךָ,

according to the commandment of Your will,

k'mō shekosavto olaynu כְּמוֹ שֶׁכָּתַבְתָּ עָלֵינוּ
b'sōrosecho, בְּתוֹרָתֶךָ,

as You have written for us in Your Torah,

al y'day mōshe avdecho, עַל יְדֵי מֹשֶׁה עַבְדֶּךָ,

through Moses, Your servant,

mipi ch'vōdecho, ko-omur: מִפִּי כְבוֹדֶךָ, כָּאָמוּר:

from Your glorious expression, as is said:

UVYŌM HA-SHABOS וּבְיוֹם הַשַּׁבָּת

"And on the Sabbath day:

sh'nay ch'vosim b'nay shono שְׁנֵי כְבָשִׂים בְּנֵי שָׁנָה,
t'mimim, תְּמִימִם,

two [male] first-year lambs, unblemished,

ushnay esrōnim sō-les וּשְׁנֵי עֶשְׂרֹנִים סֹלֶת

and two tenth-ephah of fine flour

mincho b'lulo va-shemen v'niskō.

מִנְחָה בְּלוּלָה בַשֶּׁמֶן וְנִסְכּוֹ.

for a meal-offering, mixed with olive oil, and its wine-libation.

Ōlas shabas b'shabatō,

עֹלַת שַׁבַּת בְּשַׁבַּתּוֹ,

The elevation-offering of the Sabbath must be on its particular Sabbath

al ōlas hatomid v'niskoh.

עַל עֹלַת הַתָּמִיד וְנִסְכָּהּ.

in addition to the continual elevation-offering and its wine-libation.''

■ We rejoice over the closeness of our relationship with Hashem attained through the special Shabbos offering.

YISM'CHU v'malchus'cho

יִשְׂמְחוּ בְמַלְכוּתְךָ

They shall rejoice in Your kingship* —

shōm'ray shabos v'kōr'ay ōneg,

שׁוֹמְרֵי שַׁבָּת וְקוֹרְאֵי עֹנֶג,

those who observe the Sabbath and call it a delight.

am m'kad'shay sh'vi-i,

עַם מְקַדְּשֵׁי שְׁבִיעִי,

The people that sanctifies the Seventh —

kulom yisb'u

כֻּלָּם יִשְׂבְּעוּ

v'yis-an'gu mituvecho,

וְיִתְעַנְּגוּ מִטּוּבֶךָ,

they will all be satisfied and delighted from Your goodness,

u-vash'vi-i rotziso bō v'kidashtō,

וּבַשְּׁבִיעִי רָצִיתָ בּוֹ וְקִדַּשְׁתּוֹ,

And the Seventh — You found favor in it and sanctified it.

chemdas yomim ōsō koroso,

חֶמְדַּת יָמִים אוֹתוֹ קָרָאתָ,

"Most coveted of days," You called it,

zaycher l'ma-asay v'rayshis.

זֵכֶר לְמַעֲשֵׂה בְרֵאשִׁית.

a remembrance of Creation.

■ I affirm that the sanctity of Shabbos emanates from Hashem, and I petition that the holiness of the day influence my life.

ELŌHAYNU Vaylōhay avōsaynu

אֱלֹהֵינוּ וֵאלֹהֵי אֲבוֹתֵינוּ

Our God and the God of our forefathers,

r'tzay vimnuchosaynu.

רְצֵה בִמְנוּחָתֵנוּ.

may You be pleased with our rest.

Kad'shaynu b'mitzvōsecho,

קַדְּשֵׁנוּ בְּמִצְוֹתֶיךָ,

Sanctify us with Your commandments

v'sayn chelkaynu b'sōrosecho,

וְתֵן חֶלְקֵנוּ בְּתוֹרָתֶךָ,

and grant us our share in Your Torah;

יִשְׂמְחוּ בְמַלְכוּתְךָ — They shall rejoice in Your kingship. The Sabbath reaches its pinnacle when all Jews not only perform God's will, but rejoice in it. Furthermore, they will find their joy not in the physical pleasures of the Sabbath, but in the fact that the Jewish people exist to serve and obey God.

אַתָּה יָצַרְתָּ עוֹלָמְךָ מִקֶּדֶם — You fashioned Your

sab'aynu mituvecho,　　　　　　　שַׂבְּעֵנוּ מִטּוּבֶךָ,

satisfy us from Your goodness

v'sam'chaynu bishu-osecho,　　　וְשַׂמְּחֵנוּ בִּישׁוּעָתֶךָ,

and gladden us with Your salvation,

v'tahayr libaynu l'ovd'cho be-emes.　וְטַהֵר לִבֵּנוּ לְעָבְדְּךָ בֶּאֱמֶת.

and purify our heart to serve You sincerely.

V'hanchilaynu Adōnoy Elōhaynu　וְהַנְחִילֵנוּ יהוה אֱלֹהֵינוּ

O HASHEM, our God, grant us as a heritage

b'ahavo uvrotzōn　　　　　　　בְּאַהֲבָה וּבְרָצוֹן

with love and favor,

shabas kodshecho,　　　　　　שַׁבַּת קָדְשֶׁךָ,

Your holy Sabbath

v'yonuchu vō　　　　　　　　וְיָנוּחוּ בוֹ

yisro-ayl m'kad'shay sh'mecho.　יִשְׂרָאֵל מְקַדְּשֵׁי שְׁמֶךָ.

and may Israel, the sanctifiers of Your Name, rest on it.

Boruch ato Adōnoy,　　　　　בָּרוּךְ אַתָּה יהוה,

m'kadaysh ha-shabos.　　　　מְקַדֵּשׁ הַשַּׁבָּת.

Blessed are You, HASHEM, Who sanctifies the Sabbath.

CONTINUE WITH R'tzay (P. 446.)

WHEN *ROSH CHODESH* FALL ON THE SABBATH CONTINUE HERE:

■ The blessing relating to the holiness of Shabbos when it coincides with *Rosh Chodesh:* The fusion of the sanctities of Shabbos and *Rosh Chodesh* attests to Hashem as the Creator and Director of the affairs of mankind, and the One Who grants atonement.

ATO YOTZARTO　　　　　　אַתָּה יָצַרְתָּ

ōlom'cho mikedem,　　　　　עוֹלָמְךָ מִקֶּדֶם,

You fashioned Your world from of old;*

kiliso m'lacht'cho ba-yōm hash'vi-i,　כִּלִּיתָ מְלַאכְתְּךָ בַּיּוֹם הַשְּׁבִיעִי,

You completed Your work on the seventh day.

ohavto ōsonu v'rotziso bonu,　אָהַבְתָּ אוֹתָנוּ וְרָצִיתָ בָּנוּ,

You loved us, found favor in us,

v'rōmamtonu mikol hal'shōnōs,　וְרוֹמַמְתָּנוּ מִכָּל הַלְּשׁוֹנוֹת,

and raised us above all tongues,*

---

world from of old. The *Mussaf* of Sabbath-Rosh Chodesh is the only *Shemoneh Esrei* that stresses God's role as the Creator. The monthly rebirth of the moon recalls the notion of the early idolaters that the heavenly bodies had powers of their own. On the other hand, the Sabbath is the eternal testimony that God alone

created heaven and earth from an absolute vacuum. Consequently, the Sages ordained that we declare our faith in God's Creation on the occasion of Sabbath-Rosh Chodesh.

וְרוֹמַמְתָּנוּ מִכָּל הַלְּשׁוֹנוֹת — *And raised us above all tongues.* Unlike the Sabbath service, the *Shemoneh Esrei* of the Festivals and *Rosh Chodesh*

v'kidashtonu b'mitzvōsecho,

וְקִדַּשְׁתָּנוּ בְּמִצְוֹתֶיךָ,

sanctified us through Your commandments

v'kayravtonu malkaynu
la-avōdosecho,

וְקֵרַבְתָּנוּ מַלְכֵּנוּ
לַעֲבוֹדָתֶךָ,

and drew us near to Your service, our King,

v'shimcho hagodōl v'hakodōsh
olaynu koroso.

וְשִׁמְךָ הַגָּדוֹל וְהַקָּדוֹשׁ
עָלֵינוּ קָרָאתָ.

and Your great and holy Name You proclaimed upon us.

Vatiten lonu Adōnoy Elōhaynu
b'ahavo

וַתִּתֶּן לָנוּ יהוה אֱלֹהֵינוּ
בְּאַהֲבָה,

And You gave us, HASHEM, our God, with love,

shabosōs limnucho

שַׁבָּתוֹת לִמְנוּחָה

Sabbaths for contentment

v'roshay chodoshim l'chaporo.

וְרָאשֵׁי חֳדָשִׁים לְכַפָּרָה.

and New Moons for atonement.

Ulfi shechotonu l'fonecho
anachnu va-avōsaynu,

וּלְפִי שֶׁחָטָאנוּ לְפָנֶיךָ
אֲנַחְנוּ וַאֲבוֹתֵינוּ,

But because we sinned before You — we and our forefathers —

chor'vo iraynu,

חָרְבָה עִירֵנוּ,

our City was destroyed

v'shomaym bays mikdoshaynu,

וְשָׁמֵם בֵּית מִקְדָּשֵׁנוּ,

and our Holy Temple was made desolate;

v'golo y'koraynu,

וְגָלָה יְקָרֵנוּ,

our honor was exiled

v'nutal kovōd mibays cha-yaynu,

וְנִטַּל כָּבוֹד מִבֵּית חַיֵּינוּ,

and glory was taken from the House of our life.

v'ayn anachnu y'chōlim
la-asōs chōvōsaynu

וְאֵין אֲנַחְנוּ יְכוֹלִים
לַעֲשׂוֹת חוֹבוֹתֵינוּ

So we cannot fulfill our responsibilities

b'vays b'chirosecho,

בְּבֵית בְּחִירָתֶךָ,

in Your chosen House,

baba-yis hagodōl v'hakodōsh

בַּבַּיִת הַגָּדוֹל וְהַקָּדוֹשׁ

in the great and holy House

---

includes the concept that the Jewish people were given the authority to regulate the calendar, a function that the Torah confers upon the *beis din*. In effect, by proclaiming when the months begin, the Jewish people control the very existence of the Festivals. The Sabbath, on the other hand, comes every seventh day, independent of the Jewish people and the calendar.

shenikro shimcho olov, שֶׁנִּקְרָא שִׁמְךָ עָלָיו,
upon which Your Name was called,

mip'nay ha-yod מִפְּנֵי הַיָּד
shenishtal'cho b'mikdoshecho. שֶׁנִּשְׁתַּלְּחָה בְּמִקְדָּשֶׁךָ.
because of the hand that was sent against Your Sanctuary.

Y'hi rotzōn mil'fonecho יְהִי רָצוֹן מִלְּפָנֶיךָ
May it be Your will,

Adōnoy Elōhaynu יהוה אֱלֹהֵינוּ
Vaylōhay avōsaynu, וֵאלֹהֵי אֲבוֹתֵינוּ,
HASHEM, our God and the God of our forefathers,

sheta-alaynu v'simcho l'artzaynu, שֶׁתַּעֲלֵנוּ בְשִׂמְחָה לְאַרְצֵנוּ
that You bring us up in gladness to our land

v'sito-aynu bigvulaynu, וְתִטָּעֵנוּ בִּגְבוּלֵנוּ,
and plant us within our boundaries.

v'shom na-ase l'fonecho וְשָׁם נַעֲשֶׂה לְפָנֶיךָ
There we will perform before You

es korb'nōs chōvōsaynu, אֶת קָרְבְּנוֹת חוֹבוֹתֵינוּ,
our required offerings,

t'midim k'sidrom תְּמִידִים כְּסִדְרָם,
the continual-offerings in their order

u-musofim k'hilchosom. וּמוּסָפִים כְּהִלְכָתָם.
and the mussaf-offerings according to their laws.

V'es mus'fay yōm ha-shabos ha-ze, וְאֶת מוּסְפֵי יוֹם הַשַּׁבָּת הַזֶּה
And the mussaf-offerings of this Sabbath day

v'yōm rōsh hachōdesh ha-ze, וְיוֹם רֹאשׁ הַחֹדֶשׁ הַזֶּה,
and this day of the New Moon

na-ase v'nakriv l'fonecho b'ahavo נַעֲשֶׂה וְנַקְרִיב לְפָנֶיךָ בְּאַהֲבָה,
we will perform and bring near to You with love

k'mitzvas r'tzōnecho, כְּמִצְוַת רְצוֹנֶךָ,
according to the commandment of Your will,

k'mō shekosavto olaynu כְּמוֹ שֶׁכָּתַבְתָּ עָלֵינוּ
b'sōrosecho, בְּתוֹרָתֶךָ,
as You have written for us in Your Torah,

al y'day mōshe avdecho, עַל יְדֵי מֹשֶׁה עַבְדֶּךָ,
through Moses, Your servant,

mipi ch'vōdecho, ko-omur: מִפִּי כְבוֹדֶךָ כָּאָמוּר:
from Your glorious expression, as is said:

UVYÔM HASHABOS — וּבְיוֹם הַשַּׁבָּת

"And on the Sabbath day:

sh'nay ch'vosim b'nay shono
t'mimim,

שְׁנֵי כְבָשִׂים בְּנֵי שָׁנָה, תְּמִימִם,

two [male] first-year lambs, unblemished,

ushnay esrônim sō-les

וּשְׁנֵי עֶשְׂרֹנִים סֹלֶת

and two tenth-ephah of fine flour

mincho b'lulo vashemen v'niskō.

מִנְחָה בְּלוּלָה בַשֶּׁמֶן וְנִסְכּוֹ.

for a meal-offering, mixed with olive oil, and its wine-libation.

Ōlas shabas b'shabatō,

עֹלַת שַׁבַּת בְּשַׁבַּתּוֹ,

The elevation-offering of the Sabbath must be on its particular Sabbath

al ōlas hatomid v'niskoh.

עַל עֹלַת הַתָּמִיד וְנִסְכָּהּ.

in addition to the continual elevation-offering and its wine-libation."

■ *Description of the additional sacrifices for Shabbos and* Rosh Chodesh *and our yearning and desire for their reinstatement.*

UVROSHAY chodshaychem — וּבְרָאשֵׁי חָדְשֵׁיכֶם

"On the first days of your months

takrivu ōlo Ladōnoy,

תַּקְרִיבוּ עֹלָה לַיהוה,

you are to bring an elevation-offering to HASHEM,

porim b'nay vokor sh'na-yim,
v'a-yil e-chod,

פָּרִים בְּנֵי בָקָר שְׁנַיִם, וְאַיִל אֶחָד,

two young bulls, one ram,

k'vosim b'nay shono shiv-o,
t'mimim.

כְּבָשִׂים בְּנֵי שָׁנָה שִׁבְעָה, תְּמִימִם.

seven [male] first-year lambs, unblemished."

U-minchosom v'niskayhem kimdubor,

וּמִנְחָתָם וְנִסְכֵּיהֶם כִּמְדֻבָּר,

And their meal-offerings and their wine-libations as mentioned:

sh'lōsho esrōnim lapor,

שְׁלֹשָׁה עֶשְׂרֹנִים לַפָּר,

three tenth-ephah for each bull;

ushnay esrōnim lo-o-yil,

וּשְׁנֵי עֶשְׂרֹנִים לָאַיִל,

two tenth-ephah for the ram;

v'isorōn lakeves, v'ya-yin k'niskō,

וְעִשָּׂרוֹן לַכֶּבֶשׂ, וְיַיִן כְּנִסְכּוֹ,

one tenth-ephah for each lamb; and wine for its wine-libations.

v'so-ir l'chapayr,

וְשָׂעִיר לְכַפֵּר,

A he-goat for atonement

ushnay s'midim ki'hilchosom.

וּשְׁנֵי תְמִידִים כְּהִלְכָתָם.

and two continual-offerings according to their law.

YISM'CHU v'malchus'cho   יִשְׂמְחוּ בְמַלְכוּתְךָ
They shall rejoice in Your kingship —

shôm'ray shabos v'kôr'ay ôneg,   שׁוֹמְרֵי שַׁבָּת וְקוֹרְאֵי עֹנֶג,
those who observe the Sabbath and call it a delight.

am m'kad'shay sh'vi-i,   עַם מְקַדְּשֵׁי שְׁבִיעִי,
The people that sanctifies the Seventh —

kulom yisb'u v'yis-an'gu mituvecho,   כֻּלָּם יִשְׂבְּעוּ וְיִתְעַנְּגוּ מִטּוּבֶךָ,
they will all be satisfied and delighted from Your goodness,

u-vash'vi-i rotziso bô v'kidashtô,   וּבַשְּׁבִיעִי רָצִיתָ בּוֹ וְקִדַּשְׁתּוֹ,
And the Seventh — You found favor in it and sanctified it.

chemdas yomim ôsô koroso,   חֶמְדַּת יָמִים אוֹתוֹ קָרָאתָ,
"Most coveted of days," You called it,

zaycher l'ma-asay v'rayshis.   זֵכֶר לְמַעֲשֵׂה בְרֵאשִׁית.
a remembrance of Creation.

DURING THE *CHAZZAN'S* REPETITION, THE CONGREGATION RESPONDS *OMAYN* AS INDICATED.

ELÔHAYNU Vaylôhay avôsaynu,   אֱלֹהֵינוּ וֵאלֹהֵי אֲבוֹתֵינוּ,
Our God and the God of our forefathers,

r'tzay vimnuchosaynu,   רְצֵה בִמְנוּחָתֵנוּ,
may You be pleased with our rest,

v'chadaysh olaynu   וְחַדֵּשׁ עָלֵינוּ
    b'yôm ha-shabos ha-ze   בְּיוֹם הַשַּׁבָּת הַזֶּה
    es hachôdesh ha-ze   אֶת הַחֹדֶשׁ הַזֶּה
and on this Sabbath day inaugurate this month

l'tôvo v'livrocho (Omayn),   לְטוֹבָה וְלִבְרָכָה (אָמֵן),
for good and for blessing (Amen),

l'sosôn ulsimcho (Omayn),   לְשָׂשׂוֹן וּלְשִׂמְחָה (אָמֵן),
for joy and for gladness (Amen),

lishu-o ulnechomo (Omayn),   לִישׁוּעָה וּלְנֶחָמָה (אָמֵן),
for salvation and for consolation (Amen),

l'farnoso ulchalkolo (Omayn),   לְפַרְנָסָה וּלְכַלְכָּלָה (אָמֵן),
for sustenance and for support (Amen),

l'cha-yim ulsholôm (Omayn),   לְחַיִּים וּלְשָׁלוֹם (אָמֵן),
for life and for peace (Amen).

limchilas chayt v'lislichas ovôn   לִמְחִילַת חֵטְא וְלִסְלִיחַת עָוֹן
(Omayn).   (אָמֵן).
for pardon of sin and forgiveness of iniquity (Amen).

[DURING A JEWISH LEAP YEAR ADD:]

[ulchaporas posha (Omayn).]   [וּלְכַפָּרַת פֶּשַׁע] (אָמֵן).
[and for atonement of willful sin] (Amen).

Ki v'am'cho yisro-ayl bocharto mikol ho-umōs,

כִּי בְעַמְּךָ יִשְׂרָאֵל בָּחַרְתָּ מִכָּל הָאֻמּוֹת,

For You have chosen Your people Israel from all the nations,

v'shabas kodsh'cho lohem hōdoto,

וְשַׁבַּת קָדְשְׁךָ לָהֶם הוֹדַעְתָּ,

and You made Your holy Sabbath known to them

v'chukay roshay chodoshim lohem kovoto.

וְחֻקֵּי רָאשֵׁי חֳדָשִׁים לָהֶם קָבֶעְתָּ.

and You set forth the decrees of the New Moons for them.

Boruch ato Adōnoy,

בָּרוּךְ אַתָּה יהוה,

Blessed are You, HASHEM,

m'kadaysh ha-shabos v'yisro-ayl v'roshay chodoshim.

מְקַדֵּשׁ הַשַּׁבָּת וְיִשְׂרָאֵל וְרָאשֵׁי חֳדָשִׁים.

Who sanctifies the Sabbath, Israel and the New Moons.

ON ALL SABBATHS CONTINUE HERE.

■ Fifth Blessing: Prayer for restoration of the Temple service

R'TZAY, Adōnoy Elōhaynu

רְצֵה יהוה אֱלֹהֵינוּ

Be favorable, HASHEM, our God,

b'am'cho yisro-ayl u-visfilosom,

בְּעַמְּךָ יִשְׂרָאֵל וּבִתְפִלָּתָם,

toward Your people Israel and their prayer

v'hoshayv es ho-avōdo lidvir bay-secho.

וְהָשֵׁב אֶת הָעֲבוֹדָה לִדְבִיר בֵּיתֶךָ.

and restore the service to the Holy of Holies of Your Temple.

V'i-shay yisro-ayl, usfilosom b'ahavo s'kabayl b'rotzōn,

וְאִשֵּׁי יִשְׂרָאֵל וּתְפִלָּתָם בְּאַהֲבָה תְקַבֵּל בְּרָצוֹן,

The fire-offerings of Israel and their prayer accept with love and favor,

us-hi l'rotzōn tomid avōdas yisro-ayl amecho.

וּתְהִי לְרָצוֹן תָּמִיד עֲבוֹדַת יִשְׂרָאֵל עַמֶּךָ.

and may the service of Your people Israel always be favorable to You.

V'SECHEZENO aynaynu

וְתֶחֱזֶינָה עֵינֵינוּ

May our eyes behold

b'shuv'cho l'tziyōn b'rachamim.

בְּשׁוּבְךָ לְצִיּוֹן בְּרַחֲמִים.

Your return to Zion in compassion.

Boruch ato Adōnoy, hamachazir sh'chinosō l'tziyōn.

בָּרוּךְ אַתָּה יהוה, הַמַּחֲזִיר שְׁכִינָתוֹ לְצִיּוֹן.

Blessed are You, HASHEM, Who restores His Presence unto Zion.

■ Sixth Blessing: Acknowledgment of our debt of gratitude

BOW AT Mōdim anachnu loch; STRAIGHTEN UP AT Adōnoy.
IN HIS REPETITION THE *CHAZZAN* SHOULD RECITE THE ENTIRE *MODIM* ALOUD,
WHILE THE CONGREGATION RECITES *MODIM OF THE RABBIS* (P. 448) SOFTLY.

MŌDIM anachnu loch,　　　　　מוֹדִים אֲנַחְנוּ לָךְ,
We gratefully thank You,

sho-ato hu Adōnoy Elōhaynu　　שָׁאַתָּה הוּא יהוה אֱלֹהֵינוּ
for it is You Who are HASHEM, our God,

Vaylōhay avōsaynu　　　　וֵאלֹהֵי אֲבוֹתֵינוּ
and the God of our forefathers

l'ōlom vo-ed,　　　　　　לְעוֹלָם וָעֶד,
forever and ever;

tzur cha-yaynu, mogayn yish-aynu　　צוּר חַיֵּינוּ, מָגֵן יִשְׁעֵנוּ
Rock of our lives, Shield of our salvation

ato hu l'dōr vodōr.　　　אַתָּה הוּא לְדוֹר וָדוֹר.
are You from generation to generation.

Nō-de l'cho unsapayr t'hilosecho　　נוֹדֶה לְךָ וּנְסַפֵּר תְּהִלָתֶךָ
We shall thank You and relate Your praise —

al cha-yaynu ham'surim b'yodecho,　　עַל חַיֵּינוּ הַמְּסוּרִים בְּיָדֶךָ,
for our lives, which are committed to Your power,

v'al nishmōsaynu hap'kudōs loch,　　וְעַל נִשְׁמוֹתֵינוּ הַפְּקוּדוֹת לָךְ,
and for our souls that are entrusted to You,

v'al nisecho sheb'chol yōm imonu,　　וְעַל נִסֶּיךָ שֶׁבְּכָל יוֹם עִמָּנוּ,
and for Your miracles that are with us every day,

v'al nifl'ōsecho v'tōvōsecho　　וְעַל נִפְלְאוֹתֶיךָ וְטוֹבוֹתֶיךָ
　　sheb'chol ays,　　　　שֶׁבְּכָל עֵת,
and for Your wonders and favors in every season —

erev vovōker v'tzohoro-yim.　　עֶרֶב וָבֹקֶר וְצָהֳרָיִם.
evening, morning, and afternoon.

Hatōv ki lō cholu rachamecho,　　הַטּוֹב כִּי לֹא כָלוּ רַחֲמֶיךָ,
The Beneficent One, for Your compassions were never exhausted,

v'ham'rachaym　　　　　וְהַמְרַחֵם
and the Compassionate One,

ki lō samu chasodecho,　　כִּי לֹא תַמּוּ חֲסָדֶיךָ,
for Your kindnesses never ended —

may-ōlom kivinu loch.　　מֵעוֹלָם קִוִּינוּ לָךְ.
always have we put our hope in You.

MODIM OF THE RABBIS

RECITED SOFTLY BY CONGREGATION WHILE *CHAZZAN* RECITES THE REGULAR MODIM ALOUD

MŌDIM anachnu loch,
מוֹדִים אֲנַחְנוּ לָךְ,
We gratefully thank You,

sho-ato hu Adōnoy Elōhaynu
שָׁאַתָּה הוּא יהוה אֱלֹהֵינוּ

Vaylōhay avōsaynu,
וֵאלֹהֵי אֲבוֹתֵינוּ,
for it is You Who are HASHEM, *our God and the God of our forefathers,*

Elōhay chol bosor,
אֱלֹהֵי כָל בָּשָׂר,
the God of all flesh,

yōtz'raynu, yōtzayr b'rayshis.
יוֹצְרֵנוּ, יוֹצֵר בְּרֵאשִׁית.
our Molder, the Molder of the universe.

B'rochōs v'hōdo-ōs l'shimcho
בְּרָכוֹת וְהוֹדָאוֹת לְשִׁמְךָ

hagodōl v'hakodōsh,
הַגָּדוֹל וְהַקָּדוֹשׁ,
Blessings and thanks are due Your great and holy Name

al sheheche-yisonu v'ki-yamtonu.
עַל שֶׁהֶחֱיִיתָנוּ וְקִיַּמְתָּנוּ.
for You have given us life and sustained us.

Kayn t'cha-yaynu uska-y'maynu,
כֵּן תְּחַיֵּנוּ וּתְקַיְּמֵנוּ,
So may You continue to give us life and sustain us,

v'se-esōf golu-yōsaynu
וְתֶאֱסוֹף גָּלֻיּוֹתֵינוּ

l'chatzrōs kod-shecho,
לְחַצְרוֹת קָדְשֶׁךָ,
and gather our exiles to the Courtyards of Your Sanctuary,

lishmōr chukecho v'la-asōs r'tzōnecho,
לִשְׁמוֹר חֻקֶּיךָ וְלַעֲשׂוֹת רְצוֹנֶךָ,
to observe Your decrees, to do Your will

ul-ovd'cho b'layvov sholaym,
וּלְעָבְדְּךָ בְּלֵבָב שָׁלֵם,
and to serve You wholeheartedly.

al she-anachnu mōdim loch.
עַל שֶׁאֲנַחְנוּ מוֹדִים לָךְ.
[We thank You] for inspiring us to thank You.

Boruch Ayl hahōdo-ōs.
בָּרוּךְ אֵל הַהוֹדָאוֹת.
Blessed is the God of thanksgivings.

ON CHANUKAH CONTINUE BELOW. ON ALL OTHER DAYS TURN TO P. 450.

AL hanisim, v'al hapurkon,
עַל הַנִּסִּים, וְעַל הַפֻּרְקָן,
For the miracles, and for the salvation,

v'al hag'vurōs, v'al hat'shu-ōs,
וְעַל הַגְּבוּרוֹת, וְעַל הַתְּשׁוּעוֹת,
and for the mighty deeds, and for the victories,

v'al hamilchomōs,
וְעַל הַמִּלְחָמוֹת,
and for the battles

she-osiso la-avōsaynu   שֶׁעָשִׂיתָ לַאֲבוֹתֵינוּ

which You performed for our forefathers

ba-yomim hohaym baz'man ha-ze.   בַּיָּמִים הָהֵם בַּזְּמַן הַזֶּה.

in those days, at this time.

BIMAY matisyohu ben yōchonon   בִּימֵי מַתִּתְיָהוּ בֶּן יוֹחָנָן

In the days of Mattisyahu, the son of Yochanan,

kōhayn godōl chashmōno-i u-vonov,   כֹּהֵן גָּדוֹל חַשְׁמוֹנַאי וּבָנָיו,

the High Priest, the Hasmonean, and his sons —

k'she-om'do malchus yovon   כְּשֶׁעָמְדָה מַלְכוּת יָוָן

hor'sho-o al am'cho yisro-ayl,   הָרְשָׁעָה עַל עַמְּךָ יִשְׂרָאֵל,

when the wicked Greek kingdom rose up against Your people Israel

l'hashkichom tōrosecho,   לְהַשְׁכִּיחָם תּוֹרָתֶךָ,

to make them forget Your Torah

ulha-avirom maychukay r'tzōnecho,   וּלְהַעֲבִירָם מֵחֻקֵּי רְצוֹנֶךָ.

and compel them to stray from the statutes of Your Will —

v'ato b'rachamecho horabim,   וְאַתָּה בְּרַחֲמֶיךָ הָרַבִּים,

But You, in Your abundant mercy,

omadto lohem b'ays tzorosom,   עָמַדְתָּ לָהֶם בְּעֵת צָרָתָם,

stood up for them in the time of their distress.

Ravto es rivom, danto es dinom,   רַבְתָּ אֶת רִיבָם, דַּנְתָּ אֶת דִּינָם,

You took up their grievance, You judged their claim,

nokamto es nikmosom.   נָקַמְתָּ אֶת נִקְמָתָם.

and You avenged their wrong.

mosarto gibōrim b'yad chaloshim,   מָסַרְתָּ גִבּוֹרִים בְּיַד חַלָּשִׁים,

You delivered the strong into the hand of the weak,

v'rabim b'yad m'atim,   וְרַבִּים בְּיַד מְעַטִּים,

the many into the hand of the few,

utmay-im b'yad t'hōrim,   וּטְמֵאִים בְּיַד טְהוֹרִים,

the impure into the hand of the pure,

ursho-im b'yad tzadikim   וּרְשָׁעִים בְּיַד צַדִּיקִים,

the wicked into the hand of the righteous,

v'zaydim b'yad ōs'kay sōrosecho.   וְזֵדִים בְּיַד עוֹסְקֵי תוֹרָתֶךָ.

and the wanton into the hand of the diligent students of Your Torah.

Ulcho osiso   וּלְךָ עָשִׂיתָ

shaym godōl v'kodōsh b'ōlomecho,   שֵׁם גָּדוֹל וְקָדוֹשׁ בְּעוֹלָמֶךָ,

And for Yourself You made a great and holy Name in Your world,

ul-am'cho yisro-ayl   וּלְעַמְּךָ יִשְׂרָאֵל
and for Your people Israel

osiso t'shu-o g'dōlo u-furkon   עָשִׂיתָ תְּשׁוּעָה גְדוֹלָה וּפֻרְקָן
You performed a great victory and salvation

k'ha-yōm ha-ze.   כְּהַיּוֹם הַזֶּה.
as this very day.

V'achar kayn bo-u vonecho   וְאַחַר כֵּן בָּאוּ בָנֶיךָ
   lidvir bay-secho,   לִדְבִיר בֵּיתֶךָ,
Thereafter, Your children came to the Holy of Holies of Your House,

u-finu es haycholecho,   וּפִנּוּ אֶת הֵיכָלֶךָ,
they cleansed Your Temple,

v'tiharu es mikdoshecho,   וְטִהֲרוּ אֶת מִקְדָּשֶׁךָ,
they purified the site of Your Holiness;

v'hidliku nayrōs   וְהִדְלִיקוּ נֵרוֹת
   b'chatzrōs kod-shecho,   בְּחַצְרוֹת קָדְשֶׁךָ,
and they kindled lights in the Courtyards of Your Sanctuary;

v'kov'u   וְקָבְעוּ
   sh'mōnas y'may chanuko aylu,   שְׁמוֹנַת יְמֵי חֲנֻכָּה אֵלּוּ,
and they established these eight days of Chanukah

l'hōdōs ulhalayl l'shimcho hagodōl.   לְהוֹדוֹת וּלְהַלֵּל לְשִׁמְךָ הַגָּדוֹל.
to express thanks and praise to Your great Name.

V'AL kulom yisborach v'yisrōmam   **וְעַל** כֻּלָּם יִתְבָּרַךְ וְיִתְרוֹמַם
   shimcho, malkaynu   שִׁמְךָ מַלְכֵּנוּ
For all these, may Your Name be blessed and exalted, our King,

tomid l'ōlom vo-ed.   תָּמִיד לְעוֹלָם וָעֶד.
continually forever and ever.

FROM ROSH HASHANAH TO YOM KIPPUR ADD:

Uchsōv l'cha-yim tōvim   וּכְתוֹב לְחַיִּים טוֹבִים
   kol b'nay v'risecho.   כָּל בְּנֵי בְרִיתֶךָ.
And inscribe all the children of Your covenant for a good life.

V'chōl hacha-yim yōducho selo,   וְכֹל הַחַיִּים יוֹדוּךָ סֶּלָה,
Everything alive will gratefully acknowledge You, Selah!

vihal'lu es shimcho be-emes,   וִיהַלְלוּ אֶת שִׁמְךָ בֶּאֱמֶת,
and praise Your Name sincerely,

ho-Ayl y'shu-osaynu   הָאֵל יְשׁוּעָתֵנוּ
   v'ezrosaynu selo.   וְעֶזְרָתֵנוּ סֶלָה.
O God of our salvation and help, Selah!

BEND THE KNEES AT Boruch; BOW AT ato; STRAIGHTEN UP AT Adōnoy.

Boruch ato Adōnoy,
בָּרוּךְ אַתָּה יהוה,

Blessed are You, HASHEM,

hatōv shimcho ulcho no-e l'hōdōs.
הַטּוֹב שִׁמְךָ וּלְךָ נָאֶה לְהוֹדוֹת.

Your Name is "The Beneficent One" and to You it is fitting to give thanks.

■ Seventh Blessing: Prayer for peace and harmony
amongst the Jewish people

THE *CHAZZAN* RECITES THE PRIESTLY BLESSING DURING HIS REPETITION.

אֱלֹהֵינוּ, וֵאלֹהֵי אֲבוֹתֵינוּ, בָּרְכֵנוּ בַבְּרָכָה הַמְשֻׁלֶּשֶׁת בַּתּוֹרָה הַכְּתוּבָה עַל יְדֵי מֹשֶׁה עַבְדֶּךָ, הָאֲמוּרָה מִפִּי אַהֲרֹן וּבָנָיו, כֹּהֲנִים עַם קְדוֹשֶׁךָ, כָּאָמוּר:

(kayn y'hi rotzōn – כֵּן יְהִי רָצוֹן – Cong.)
יְבָרֶכְךָ יהוה, וְיִשְׁמְרֶךָ.

(kayn y'hi rotzōn – כֵּן יְהִי רָצוֹן – Cong.)
יָאֵר יהוה פָּנָיו אֵלֶיךָ וִיחֻנֶּךָּ.

יִשָּׂא יהוה פָּנָיו אֵלֶיךָ וְיָשֵׂם לְךָ שָׁלוֹם.

(kayn y'hi rotzōn – כֵּן יְהִי רָצוֹן – Cong.)

SIM SHOLŌM tōvo uvrocho,
שִׂים שָׁלוֹם, טוֹבָה, וּבְרָכָה,

Establish peace, goodness, blessing,

chayn vochesed v'rachamim
חֵן וָחֶסֶד וְרַחֲמִים

graciousness, kindness, and compassion

olaynu v'al kol yisro-ayl amecho.
עָלֵינוּ וְעַל כָּל יִשְׂרָאֵל עַמֶּךָ.

upon us and upon all of Your people Israel.

Bor'chaynu, ovinu, kulonu k'e-chod
בָּרְכֵנוּ, אָבִינוּ, כֻּלָּנוּ כְּאֶחָד

b'ōr ponecho,
בְּאוֹר פָּנֶיךָ,

Bless us, our Father, all of us as one, with the light of Your countenance,

ki v'ōr ponecho nosato lonu,
כִּי בְאוֹר פָּנֶיךָ נָתַתָּ לָּנוּ,

Adōnoy Elōhaynu,
יהוה אֱלֹהֵינוּ,

for with the light of Your countenance You, HASHEM, our God, gave us

tōras cha-yim v'ahavas chesed,
תּוֹרַת חַיִּים וְאַהֲבַת חֶסֶד,

the Torah of life and a love of kindness,

utz-doko uvrocho v'rachamim
וּצְדָקָה וּבְרָכָה וְרַחֲמִים

v'cha-yim v'sholōm.
וְחַיִּים וְשָׁלוֹם.

righteousness, blessing, compassion, life, and peace.

V'tōv b'aynecho l'voraych
וְטוֹב בְּעֵינֶיךָ לְבָרֵךְ

es am'cho yisro-ayl,
אֶת עַמְּךָ יִשְׂרָאֵל,

And may it be good in Your eyes to bless Your people Israel

b'chol ays uvchol sho-o
bishlōmecho.

בְּכָל עֵת וּבְכָל שָׁעָה
בִּשְׁלוֹמֶךָ.

at every time and at every hour, with Your peace.

°Boruch ato Adōnoy,
ham'voraych es amō yisro-ayl
basholōm.

°בָּרוּךְ אַתָּה יהוה,
הַמְבָרֵךְ אֶת עַמּוֹ יִשְׂרָאֵל
בַּשָּׁלוֹם.

°*Blessed are You, HASHEM, Who blesses His people Israel with peace.*

° FROM ROSH HASHANAH TO YOM KIPPUR SUBSTITUTE THE FOLLOWING:

B'sayfer cha-yim b'rocho v'sholōm,
u-farnoso tōvo,

בְּסֵפֶר חַיִּים בְּרָכָה וְשָׁלוֹם,
וּפַרְנָסָה טוֹבָה,

In the book of life, blessing, and peace, and good livelihood,

nizochayr v'nikosayv l'fonecho,

נִזָּכֵר וְנִכָּתֵב לְפָנֶיךָ,

may we be remembered and inscribed before You —

anachnu v'chol am'cho
bays yisro-ayl,

אֲנַחְנוּ וְכָל עַמְּךָ
בֵּית יִשְׂרָאֵל,

we and Your entire people the Family of Israel —

l'cha-yim tōvim ulsholōm.

לְחַיִּים טוֹבִים וּלְשָׁלוֹם.

for a good life and for peace.

Boruch ato Adōnoy,
ō-se ha-sholōm.

בָּרוּךְ אַתָּה יהוה,
עוֹשֶׂה הַשָּׁלוֹם.

Blessed are You, HASHEM, Who makes the peace.

THE *CHAZZAN'S* REPETITION ENDS HERE [CONTINUE WITH *KADDISH* (P. 454)].
INDIVIDUALS CONTINUE:

Yih-yu l'rotzōn imray fi
v'hegyōn libi l'fonecho,

יִהְיוּ לְרָצוֹן אִמְרֵי פִי
וְהֶגְיוֹן לִבִּי לְפָנֶיךָ,

*May the expressions of my mouth and the thoughts of my heart
find favor before You,*

Adōnoy tzuri v'gō-ali.

יהוה צוּרִי וְגֹאֲלִי.

HASHEM, my Rock and my Redeemer.

■ I pray that, having completed my *Amidah,* I have been changed in a positive way,
especially with regard to my interpersonal relationships.

ELŌHAI, n'tzōr l'shōni mayro,

אֱלֹהַי, נְצוֹר לְשׁוֹנִי מֵרָע,

My God, guard my tongue from evil

usfosai midabayr mirmo,

וּשְׂפָתַי מִדַּבֵּר מִרְמָה,

and my lips from speaking deceitfully.

V'limkal'lai nafshi sidōm,

וְלִמְקַלְלַי נַפְשִׁי תִדּוֹם,

To those who curse me, let my soul be silent;

v'nafshi ke-ofor lakōl tih-ye.   וְנַפְשִׁי כֶּעָפָר לַכֹּל תִּהְיֶה.

and let my soul be like dust to everyone.

P'sach libi b'sōrosecho,   פְּתַח לִבִּי בְּתוֹרָתֶךָ,

Open my heart to Your Torah,

uvmitzvōsecho tirdōf nafshi.   וּבְמִצְוֹתֶיךָ תִּרְדּוֹף נַפְשִׁי.

then my soul will pursue Your commandments.

V'chol hachōsh'vim olai ro-o,   וְכָל הַחוֹשְׁבִים עָלַי רָעָה,

As for all those who design evil against me,

m'hayro hofayr atzosom   מְהֵרָה הָפֵר עֲצָתָם

speedily nullify their counsel

v'kalkayl machashavtom.   וְקַלְקֵל מַחֲשַׁבְתָּם.

and disrupt their design.

asay l'ma-an sh'mecho,   עֲשֵׂה לְמַעַן שְׁמֶךָ,

Act for Your Name's sake;

asay l'ma-an y'minecho,   עֲשֵׂה לְמַעַן יְמִינֶךָ,

act for Your right hand's sake;

asay l'ma-an k'dushosecho,   עֲשֵׂה לְמַעַן קְדֻשָּׁתֶךָ,

act for Your sanctity's sake;

asay l'ma-an tōrosecho.   עֲשֵׂה לְמַעַן תּוֹרָתֶךָ.

act for Your Torah's sake.

Lama-an yaychol'tzun y'didecho,   לְמַעַן יֵחָלְצוּן יְדִידֶיךָ,

That Your beloved ones may be given rest;

hōshi-o y'min'cho va-anayni.   הוֹשִׁיעָה יְמִינְךָ וַעֲנֵנִי.

let Your right hand save, and respond to me.

Yiy-hu l'rotzōn imray fi   יִהְיוּ לְרָצוֹן אִמְרֵי פִי

v'hegyōn libi l'fonecho,   וְהֶגְיוֹן לִבִּי לְפָנֶיךָ,

*May the expressions of my mouth and the thoughts of my heart
find favor before You,*

Adōnoy tzuri v'gō-ali.   יהוה צוּרִי וְגֹאֲלִי.

HASHEM, my Rock and my Redeemer.

BOW. TAKE THREE STEPS BACK. BOW LEFT AND SAY:

Ō-se sholōm bimrōmov,   עֹשֶׂה שָׁלוֹם בִּמְרוֹמָיו,

He Who makes peace in His heights,

BOW RIGHT AND SAY:

hu ya-a-se sholōm olaynu,   הוּא יַעֲשֶׂה שָׁלוֹם עָלֵינוּ,

may He make peace upon us,

BOW FORWARD AND SAY:

v'al kol yisro-ayl. V'imru: Omayn.   וְעַל כָּל יִשְׂרָאֵל. וְאִמְרוּ: אָמֵן.

and upon all Israel. Now respond: Amen.

Y'HI ROTZŌN mil'fonecho,
May it be Your will,

Adōnoy Elōhaynu
  Vaylōhay avōsaynu,
HASHEM, our God and the God of our forefathers,

she-yibo-ne bays hamikdosh
  bimhayro v'yomaynu,
that the Holy Temple be rebuilt, speedily in our days;

v'sayn chelkaynu b'sōrosecho,
and grant us our share in Your Torah;

v'shom na-avod-cho b'yiro,
and may we serve You there with reverence,

kimay ōlom
  uchshonim kadmōniyōs.
as in days of old and in former years.

V'or'vo Ladōnoy
  minchas y'hudo virusholo-yim
Then the offering of Judah and Jerusalem will be pleasing to HASHEM,

kimay ōlom
  uchshonim kadmōniyōs.
as in days of old and in former years.

יְהִי רָצוֹן מִלְּפָנֶיךָ

יהוה אֱלֹהֵינוּ
וֵאלֹהֵי אֲבוֹתֵינוּ,

שֶׁיִּבָּנֶה בֵּית הַמִּקְדָּשׁ
בִּמְהֵרָה בְיָמֵינוּ,

וְתֵן חֶלְקֵנוּ בְּתוֹרָתֶךָ,

וְשָׁם נַעֲבָדְךָ בְּיִרְאָה,

כִּימֵי עוֹלָם
וּכְשָׁנִים קַדְמוֹנִיּוֹת.

וְעָרְבָה לַיהוה
מִנְחַת יְהוּדָה וִירוּשָׁלָיִם,

כִּימֵי עוֹלָם
וּכְשָׁנִים קַדְמוֹנִיּוֹת.

THE INDIVIDUAL'S RECITATION OF *SHEMONEH ESREI* ENDS HERE.

REMAIN STANDING IN PLACE UNTIL THE *CHAZZAN* REACHES *KEDUSHAH* —
OR AT LEAST FOR A FEW MOMENTS — THEN TAKE THREE STEPS FORWARD.

THE *CHAZZAN* RECITES FULL *KADDISH*
(congregational responses are indicated by parentheses):

יִתְגַּדַּל וְיִתְקַדַּשׁ שְׁמֵהּ רַבָּא. (אָמֵן–Omayn). בְּעָלְמָא דִּי בְרָא
כִרְעוּתֵהּ. וְיַמְלִיךְ מַלְכוּתֵהּ, בְּחַיֵּיכוֹן וּבְיוֹמֵיכוֹן וּבְחַיֵּי דְכָל
בֵּית יִשְׂרָאֵל, בַּעֲגָלָא וּבִזְמַן קָרִיב. וְאִמְרוּ: אָמֵן.

(אָמֵן. יְהֵא שְׁמֵהּ רַבָּא מְבָרַךְ לְעָלַם וּלְעָלְמֵי עָלְמַיָּא.)
(Omayn. Y'hay sh'mayh rabo m'vorach l'olam ul-ol'may ol'ma-yo.)

יְהֵא שְׁמֵהּ רַבָּא מְבָרַךְ לְעָלַם וּלְעָלְמֵי עָלְמַיָּא. יִתְבָּרַךְ וְיִשְׁתַּבַּח
וְיִתְפָּאַר וְיִתְרוֹמַם וְיִתְנַשֵּׂא וְיִתְהַדָּר וְיִתְעַלֶּה וְיִתְהַלָּל שְׁמֵהּ
דְקֻדְשָׁא בְּרִיךְ הוּא (בְּרִיךְ הוּא – B'rich hu). °לְעֵלָּא מִן כָּל
[from Rosh Hashanah to Yom Kippur substitute – °לְעֵלָּא לְעֵלָּא מִכָּל]
בִּרְכָתָא וְשִׁירָתָא תֻּשְׁבְּחָתָא וְנֶחֱמָתָא, דַּאֲמִירָן בְּעָלְמָא. וְאִמְרוּ: אָמֵן.
(אָמֵן–Omayn).

תִּתְקַבֵּל צְלוֹתְהוֹן וּבָעוּתְהוֹן דְּכָל (בֵּית) יִשְׂרָאֵל קֳדָם אֲבוּהוֹן דִּי
בִשְׁמַיָּא. וְאִמְרוּ: אָמֵן. (Omayn – אָמֵן).

יְהֵא שְׁלָמָא רַבָּא מִן שְׁמַיָּא, וְחַיִּים עָלֵינוּ וְעַל כָּל יִשְׂרָאֵל. וְאִמְרוּ:
אָמֵן. (Omayn – אָמֵן).

Bow. Take three steps back. Bow left and say, . . . עֹשֶׂה; bow right and say, . . . הוּא יַעֲשֶׂה; bow forward and say, . . . וְעַל כָּל. Remain in place for a few moments, then take three steps forward.

עֹשֶׂה שָׁלוֹם בִּמְרוֹמָיו, הוּא יַעֲשֶׂה שָׁלוֹם עָלֵינוּ, וְעַל כָּל יִשְׂרָאֵל.
וְאִמְרוּ: אָמֵן. (Omayn – אָמֵן).

■ A hymn that acknowledges Hashem as our God, our King,
and the source of our prosperity

KAVAY el Adōnoy,   **קַוֵּה** אֶל יהוה,
> *Hope to HASHEM,*

chazak v'ya-amaytz libecho,   חֲזַק וְיַאֲמֵץ לִבֶּךָ,
v'kavay el Adōnoy.   וְקַוֵּה אֶל יהוה.
> *strengthen yourself and He will give you courage; and hope to HASHEM.*

Ayn kodōsh Kadōnoy,   אֵין קָדוֹשׁ כַּיהוה,
ki ayn biltecho,   כִּי אֵין בִּלְתֶּךָ,
> *There is none holy as HASHEM, for there is none beside You,*

v'ayn tzur Kaylōhaynu.   וְאֵין צוּר כֵּאלֹהֵינוּ.
> *and there is no Rock like our God.*

Ki mi Elō-ah mibal-aday Adōnoy,   כִּי מִי אֱלוֹהַּ מִבַּלְעֲדֵי יהוה,
> *For who is a god beside HASHEM,*

umi tzur zulosi Elōhaynu.   וּמִי צוּר זוּלָתִי אֱלֹהֵינוּ.
> *and who is a Rock except for our God.*

AYN Kaylōhaynu, ayn kadōnaynu,   **אֵין** כֵּאלֹהֵינוּ, אֵין כַּאדוֹנֵינוּ,
> *There is none like our God; there is none like our Master;*

ayn k'malkaynu, ayn k'mōshi-aynu.   אֵין כְּמַלְכֵּנוּ, אֵין כְּמוֹשִׁיעֵנוּ.
> *there is none like our King; there is none like our Savior.*

Mi Chaylōhaynu, mi chadōnaynu,   מִי כֵאלֹהֵינוּ, מִי כַאדוֹנֵינוּ,
> *Who is like our God?* Who is like our Master?*

mi ch'malkaynu, mi ch'mōshi-aynu.   מִי כְמַלְכֵּנוּ, מִי כְמוֹשִׁיעֵנוּ.
> *Who is like our King? Who is like our Savior?*

אֵין כֵּאלֹהֵינוּ . . . מִי כֵאלֹהֵינוּ — *There is none like our God. Who is like our God?* First we declare unequivocally our recognition that nothing compares to our God. Then we ask the rhetorical question: Can anyone or anything compare to Him?

Nō-de Laylōhaynu, נוֹדֶה לֵאלֹהֵינוּ,
  nō-de ladōnaynu, נוֹדֶה לַאדוֹנֵינוּ,

Let us thank our God; let us thank our Master;

nō-de l'malkaynu, נוֹדֶה לְמַלְכֵּנוּ,
  nō-de l'mōshi-aynu. נוֹדֶה לְמוֹשִׁיעֵנוּ.

let us thank our King; let us thank our Savior.

Boruch Elōhaynu, בָּרוּךְ אֱלֹהֵינוּ,
  boruch adōnaynu, בָּרוּךְ אֲדוֹנֵינוּ,

Blessed is our God; blessed is our Master;

boruch malkaynu, בָּרוּךְ מַלְכֵּנוּ,
  boruch mōshi-aynu. בָּרוּךְ מוֹשִׁיעֵנוּ.

blessed is our King; blessed is our Savior.

Ato hu Elōhaynu, אַתָּה הוּא אֱלֹהֵינוּ,
  ato hu adōnaynu, אַתָּה הוּא אֲדוֹנֵינוּ,

It is You Who is our God; it is You Who is our Master;

ato hu malkaynu, אַתָּה הוּא מַלְכֵּנוּ,
  ato hu mōshi-aynu. אַתָּה הוּא מוֹשִׁיעֵנוּ.

it is You Who is our King; it is You Who is our Savior.

ato hu she-hiktiru avōsaynu אַתָּה הוּא שֶׁהִקְטִירוּ אֲבוֹתֵינוּ
l'fonecho es k'tōres hasamim. לְפָנֶיךָ אֶת קְטֹרֶת הַסַּמִּים.

It is You before Whom our forefathers burned the spice-incense.

PITUM hak'tōres: **פִּטוּם** הַקְּטֹרֶת:

The incense mixture was formulated of [eleven spices]:*

hatzori, v'hatzipōren, הַצֳּרִי, וְהַצִּפֹּרֶן,

(1) stacte, (2) onycha,

hachelb'no, v'hal'vōno, הַחֶלְבְּנָה, וְהַלְּבוֹנָה,

(3) galbanum,* (4) frankincense —

mishkal shiv-im shiv-im mone; מִשְׁקַל שִׁבְעִים שִׁבְעִים מָנֶה;

each weighing seventy maneh;

mōr, uktzi-o, מוֹר, וּקְצִיעָה,

(5) myrrh, (6) cassia,

shibōles nayrd, v'charkōm, שִׁבֹּלֶת נֵרְדְּ, וְכַרְכֹּם,

(7) spikenard, (8) saffron —

פִּטוּם הַקְּטֹרֶת — *The incense mixture.* This passage describing the incense preparation is recited here so that a portion of Talmudic law will be studied at the conclusion of the service. It should be noted that we cannot be certain of the exact translation of the spices included in the incense.

הַחֶלְבְּנָה — *Galbanum.* The Talmud (*Kerisos* 6a) notes that galbanum has a foul odor, yet is included in the incense mixture to teach that even those who transgress are welcome to participate in the service of God.

mishkal shisho osor　　　　　מִשְׁקַל שִׁשָּׁה עָשָׂר
　　shisho osor mone;　　　　שִׁשָּׁה עָשָׂר מָנֶה;
　　　　each weighing sixteen maneh;

hakōsht sh'naym osor,　　　　הַקֹּשְׁטְ שְׁנֵים עָשָׂר,
　　　　(9) costus — twelve [maneh];

v'kilufo sh'lōsho, v'kinomōn tish-o.　וְקִלּוּפָה שְׁלֹשָׁה, וְקִנָּמוֹן תִּשְׁעָה.
　　　(10) aromatic bark — three; and (11) cinnamon — nine.

Bōris karshino tish-o kabin,　　בֹּרִית כַּרְשִׁינָה תִּשְׁעָה קַבִּין,
　　　[Additionally] Carshinah lye, nine kav;

yayn kafrisin　　　　　　　יֵין קַפְרִיסִין
　　s'in t'loso v'kabin t'loso,　סְאִין תְּלָתָא וְקַבִּין תְּלָתָא,
　　　Cyprus wine, three se'ah and three kav —

v'im ayn lō yayn kafrisin,　　וְאִם אֵין לוֹ יֵין קַפְרִיסִין,
　　　if he has no Cyprus wine,

mayvi chamar chivaryon atik,　מֵבִיא חֲמַר חִוַּרְיָן עַתִּיק,
　　　he brings old white wine;

melach s'dōmis rōva hakov;　מֶלַח סְדוֹמִית רֹבַע הַקַּב;
　　　Sodom salt, a quarter-kav;

ma-a-le oshon kol she-hu.　　מַעֲלֶה עָשָׁן כָּל שֶׁהוּא.
　　　and a minute amount of maaleh ashan. *

Rabi noson habavli ōmayr:　　רַבִּי נָתָן הַבַּבְלִי אוֹמֵר:
　　　Rabbi Nassan the Babylonian says:

af kipas ha-yardayn kol shehu.　אַף כִּפַּת הַיַּרְדֵּן כָּל שֶׁהוּא.
　　　Also a minute amount of Jordan amber.

V'im nosan boh d'vash, p'soloh.　וְאִם נָתַן בָּהּ דְּבַשׁ, פְּסָלָהּ.
　　　If he placed fruit-honey into it, he invalidated it.

V'im chisar achas mikol samoneho,　וְאִם חִסַּר אַחַת מִכָּל סַמָּנֶיהָ,
　　　But if he left out any of its spices,

cha-yov miso.　　　　　　חַיָּב מִיתָה.
　　　he is liable to the death penalty.

RABON shim-ōn ben gamli-ayl　רַבָּן שִׁמְעוֹן בֶּן גַּמְלִיאֵל
　　ōmayr:　　　　　　　　אוֹמֵר:
　　　Rabban Shimon ben Gamliel says:

Hatzori aynō elo s'rof　　　הַצֳּרִי אֵינוֹ אֶלָּא שְׂרָף
　　　The stacte is simply the sap

hanōtayf may-atzay hak'tof.　הַנּוֹטֵף מֵעֲצֵי הַקְּטָף.
　　　that drips from balsam trees.

Bōris karshino lomo hi vo-o,　　בְּרִית כַּרְשִׁינָה לָמָה הִיא בָאָה,
Why is Carshinah lye used?

k'day l'yapōs boh es hatzipōren,　　כְּדֵי לְיַפּוֹת בָּהּ אֶת הַצִפֹּרֶן,
To bleach the onycha,

k'day shet'hay no-o.　　כְּדֵי שֶׁתְּהֵא נָאָה.
to make it pleasing.

Yayn kafrisin lomo hu vo,　　יֵין קַפְרִיסִין לָמָה הוּא בָא,
Why is Cyprus wine used?

k'day lishrōs bō es hatzipōren,　　כְּדֵי לִשְׁרוֹת בּוֹ אֶת הַצִפֹּרֶן,
So that the onycha could be soaked in it,

k'day shet'hay azo.　　כְּדֵי שֶׁתְּהֵא עַזָּה.
to make it pungent.

Vahalō may ragla-yim yofin loh,　　וַהֲלֹא מֵי רַגְלַיִם יָפִין לָהּ,
Even though mei raglayim is more suitable for that,

elo she-ayn machnisin　　אֶלָּא שֶׁאֵין מַכְנִיסִין
　may ragla-yim bamikdosh　　מֵי רַגְלַיִם בַּמִּקְדָּשׁ
nevertheless they do not bring may reglayim into the Temple

mip'nay hakovōd.　　מִפְּנֵי הַכָּבוֹד.
out of respect.

HASHIR shehal'vi-yim　　**הַשִּׁיר** שֶׁהַלְוִיִּם
The [daily] song* that the Levites

ho-yu ōm'rim b'vays hamikdosh.　　הָיוּ אוֹמְרִים בְּבֵית הַמִּקְדָּשׁ.
would recite in the Temple was as follows:

Ba-yōm horishōn ho-yu ōm'rim:　　בַּיּוֹם הָרִאשׁוֹן הָיוּ אוֹמְרִים:
On the first day [of the week] they would say:

Ladōnoy ho-oretz umlō-oh,　　לַיהוה הָאָרֶץ וּמְלוֹאָהּ,
"HASHEM's is the earth and its fullness,

tayvayl v'yōsh'vay voh.　　תֵּבֵל וְיֹשְׁבֵי בָהּ.
the inhabited land and those who dwell in it."

Bashayni ho-yu ōm'rim:　　בַּשֵּׁנִי הָיוּ אוֹמְרִים:
On the second day they would say:

Godōl Adōnoy umhulol m'ōd,　　גָּדוֹל יהוה וּמְהֻלָּל מְאֹד,
"Great is HASHEM and much praised,

b'ir Elōhaynu har kodshō.　　בְּעִיר אֱלֹהֵינוּ הַר קָדְשׁוֹ.
in the city of our God, Mount of His Holiness."

הַשִּׁיר — *The [daily] song.* This mishnah
(*Tamid* 7:4) is recited here because the daily
song was chanted by the Levites at the conclusion of the incense service.

Bash'lishi ho-yu ōm'rim: בַּשְּׁלִישִׁי הָיוּ אוֹמְרִים:

On the third day they would say:

Elōhim nitzov ba-adas Ayl,   אֱלֹהִים נִצָּב בַּעֲדַת אֵל,

"God stands in the Divine assembly,

b'kerev Elōhim yishpōt.   בְּקֶרֶב אֱלֹהִים יִשְׁפֹּט.

in the midst of judges shall He judge."

Bor'vi-i ho-yu ōm'rim: בָּרְבִיעִי הָיוּ אוֹמְרִים:

On the fourth day they would say:

Ayl n'komōs Adōnoy,   אֵל נְקָמוֹת יהוה,

"O God of vengeance, HASHEM,

Ayl n'komos hōfi-a.   אֵל נְקָמוֹת הוֹפִיעַ.

O God of vengeance, appear."

Bachamishi ho-yu ōm'rim: בַּחֲמִישִׁי הָיוּ אוֹמְרִים:

On the fifth day they would say:

Harninu Laylōhim uzaynu,   הַרְנִינוּ לֵאלֹהִים עוּזֵּנוּ,

"Sing joyously to the God of our might,

hori-u Laylōhay ya-akōv.   הָרִיעוּ לֵאלֹהֵי יַעֲקֹב.

call out to the God of Jacob."

Bashishi ho-yu om'rim: בַּשִּׁשִׁי הָיוּ אוֹמְרִים:

On the sixth day they would say:

Adonoy moloch gayus lovaysh,   יהוה מָלָךְ גֵּאוּת לָבֵשׁ,

"HASHEM will have reigned, He will have donned grandeur;

lovaysh Adōnoy ōz hisazor,   לָבֵשׁ יהוה עֹז הִתְאַזָּר,

He will have donned might and girded Himself;

af tikōn tayvayl bal timōt.   אַף תִּכּוֹן תֵּבֵל בַּל תִּמּוֹט.

He even made the world firm so that it should not falter."

Ba-shabos ho-yu ōm'rim: בַּשַּׁבָּת הָיוּ אוֹמְרִים:

On the Sabbath they would say:

Mizmōr shir l'yōm ha-shabos,   מִזְמוֹר שִׁיר לְיוֹם הַשַּׁבָּת.

"A psalm, a song for the Sabbath day."

mizmōr shir le-osid lovō,   מִזְמוֹר שִׁיר לֶעָתִיד לָבֹא,

A psalm, a song for the time to come,

l'yōm shekulo shabos um'nucho   לְיוֹם שֶׁכֻּלּוֹ שַׁבָּת וּמְנוּחָה

for the day that will be entirely Sabbath and contentment

l'cha-yay ho-ōlomim.   לְחַיֵּי הָעוֹלָמִים.

for the eternal life.

TONO d'vay ayli-yohu: תָּנָא דְבֵי אֵלִיָּהוּ:

*The Academy of Elijah taught:**

Kol ha-shōne halochōs b'chol yom,   כָּל הַשּׁוֹנֶה הֲלָכוֹת בְּכָל יוֹם,

He who studies Torah laws every day

muvtoch lō shehu ben ōlom habo,   מֻבְטָח לוֹ שֶׁהוּא בֶּן עוֹלָם הַבָּא,

has the assurance that he will be in the World to Come,

shene-emar: Halichōs ōlom lō,   שֶׁנֶּאֱמַר: הֲלִיכוֹת עוֹלָם לוֹ,

as it is said, "The ways of the world are His" —

al tikray halichōs elo halochōs.   אַל תִּקְרֵי הֲלִיכוֹת, אֶלָּא הֲלָכוֹת.

do not read [halichōs] *"ways," but* [halachōs] *"laws."*

OMAR rabi el-ozor   אָמַר רַבִּי אֶלְעָזָר

omar rabi chanino: אָמַר רַבִּי חֲנִינָא:

Rabbi Elazar said on behalf of Rabbi Chanina:

Talmiday chachomim   תַּלְמִידֵי חֲכָמִים

marbim sholōm bo-ōlom,   מַרְבִּים שָׁלוֹם בָּעוֹלָם,

Torah scholars increase peace in the world,

shene-emar: שֶׁנֶּאֱמַר:

V'chol bona-yich limuday Adōnoy,   וְכָל בָּנַיִךְ לִמּוּדֵי יהוה,

as it is said: "And all your children will be students of HASHEM,

v'rav sh'lōm bono-yich,   וְרַב שְׁלוֹם בָּנָיִךְ,

and your children will have peace" —

al tikray bono-yich elo bōnoy-ich.   אַל תִּקְרֵי בָּנָיִךְ אֶלָּא בּוֹנָיִךְ.

do not read [bono-yich] *"your children," but* [bōno-yich] *"your builders."*

❖ Sholōm rov l'ōhavay sōrosecho,   שָׁלוֹם רָב לְאֹהֲבֵי תוֹרָתֶךָ,

There is abundant peace for the lovers of Your Torah,

v'ayn lomō michshōl.   וְאֵין לָמוֹ מִכְשׁוֹל.

and there is no stumbling block for them.

Y'hi sholōm b'chaylaych,   יְהִי שָׁלוֹם בְּחֵילֵךְ,

shalvo b'arm'nōsoy-ich.   שַׁלְוָה בְּאַרְמְנוֹתָיִךְ.

May there be peace within your wall, serenity within your palaces.

L'ma-an achai v'ray-oy,   לְמַעַן אַחַי וְרֵעָי,

For the sake of my brethren and comrades

adab'ro no sholōm boch.   אֲדַבְּרָה נָּא שָׁלוֹם בָּךְ.

I shall speak of peace in your midst.

תָּנָא דְבֵי אֵלִיָּהוּ — *The Academy of Elijah taught.* This homiletical teaching likens the ways of the world to the laws that govern a Jew's life on earth. Only by studying, knowing and practicing the laws of the Torah can a Jew insure himself of ultimate success.

L'ma-an bays Adōnoy Elōhaynu,   לְמַעַן בֵּית יהוה אֱלֹהֵינוּ,
For the sake of the House of HASHEM, our God,

avaksho tōv loch.   אֲבַקְשָׁה טוֹב לָךְ.
I will request your good.

Adōnoy ōz l'amō yitayn,   יהוה עֹז לְעַמּוֹ יִתֵּן,
HASHEM will give might to His people,

Adōnoy y'voraych es amō vasholōm   יהוה יְבָרֵךְ אֶת עַמּוֹ בַשָּׁלוֹם.
HASHEM will bless His people with peace.

THE RABBIS' KADDISH

IN THE PRESENCE OF A *MINYAN*, MOURNERS RECITE THE RABBIS' *KADDISH*.
MOURNER:

YISGADAL v'yiskadash   **יִתְגַּדַּל** וְיִתְקַדַּשׁ
sh'mayh rabo.   שְׁמֵהּ רַבָּא.
May His great Name grow exalted and sanctified

CONGREGATION RESPONDS: Omayn — אָמֵן

B'ol'mo di v'ro chir-usayh.   בְּעָלְמָא דִּי בְרָא כִרְעוּתֵהּ.
in the world that He created as He willed.

V'yamlich malchusayh.   וְיַמְלִיךְ מַלְכוּתֵהּ,
May He give reign to His kingship

b'cha-yaychōn uvyōmaychōn   בְּחַיֵּיכוֹן וּבְיוֹמֵיכוֹן
in your lifetimes and in your days

uvcha-yay d'chol bays yisro-ayl,   וּבְחַיֵּי דְכָל בֵּית יִשְׂרָאֵל,
and in the lifetimes of the entire Family of Israel,

ba-agolo u-vizman koriv.   בַּעֲגָלָא וּבִזְמַן קָרִיב.
swiftly and soon.

V'imru: Omayn.   וְאִמְרוּ: אָמֵן.
Now respond: Amen.

CONGREGATION RESPONDS:

Omayn. Y'hay sh'mayh rabo m'vorach   אָמֵן. יְהֵא שְׁמֵהּ רַבָּא מְבָרַךְ
l'olam ul-ol'may ol'ma-yo.   לְעָלַם וּלְעָלְמֵי עָלְמַיָּא.
Amen. May His great Name be blessed forever and ever.

MOURNER CONTINUES:

Y'hay sh'mayh rabo m'vorach   יְהֵא שְׁמֵהּ רַבָּא מְבָרַךְ
l'olam ul-ol'may ol'ma-yo,   לְעָלַם וּלְעָלְמֵי עָלְמַיָּא,
May His great Name be blessed forever and ever;

yisborach v'yishtabach v'yispo-ar   יִתְבָּרַךְ וְיִשְׁתַּבַּח וְיִתְפָּאַר
blessed, praised, glorified,

v'yisrōmam v'yisnasay   וְיִתְרוֹמַם וְיִתְנַשֵּׂא
exalted, extolled,

v'yis-hador v'yis-ale v'yis-halol   וְיִתְהַדָּר וְיִתְעַלֶּה וְיִתְהַלָּל

mighty, upraised, and lauded

sh'mayh d'kudsho b'rich hu   שְׁמֵהּ דְּקֻדְשָׁא בְּרִיךְ הוּא

be the Name of the Holy One, Blessed is He,

CONGREGATION RESPONDS:

B'rich hu.   Blessed is He.   בְּרִיךְ הוּא.

MOURNER CONTINUES:

°l'aylo min kol   °לְעֵלָּא מִן כָּל

beyond any

FROM ROSH HASHANAH TO YOM KIPPUR SUBSTITUTE:

°l'aylo l'aylo mikol   °לְעֵלָּא לְעֵלָּא מִכָּל

exceedingly beyond any

birchoso v'shiroso   בִּרְכָתָא וְשִׁירָתָא

blessing and song,

tushb'choso v'nechemoso,   תֻּשְׁבְּחָתָא וְנֶחֱמָתָא,

praise and consolation

da-amiron b'ol'mo.   דַּאֲמִירָן בְּעָלְמָא.

that are uttered in the world.

V'imru: Omayn.   וְאִמְרוּ: אָמֵן.

Now respond: Amen.

CONGREGATION RESPONDS: Omayn — אָמֵן

Al yisro-el v'al rabo-non   עַל יִשְׂרָאֵל וְעַל רַבָּנָן,

Upon Israel, and upon the teachers,

v'al talmiday-hōn,   וְעַל תַּלְמִידֵיהוֹן

v'al kol talmiday salmiday-hōn,   וְעַל כָּל תַּלְמִידֵי תַלְמִידֵיהוֹן,

their disciples and all of their disciples

v'al kol man d'os'kin b'ōrai-so,   וְעַל כָּל מָאן דְּעָסְקִין בְּאוֹרַיְתָא,

and upon all those who engage in the study of Torah,

dee v'as-ro hodayn,   דִּי בְאַתְרָא הָדֵין

v'dee b'chol asar va-asar.   וְדִי בְכָל אֲתַר וַאֲתַר.

who are here or anywhere else.

Y'hay l'hōn ulchōn sh'lomo rabo,   יְהֵא לְהוֹן וּלְכוֹן שְׁלָמָא רַבָּא,

May they and you have abundant peace,

chi-no v'chis-do v'racha-min,   חִנָּא וְחִסְדָּא וְרַחֲמִין,

grace, kindness, and mercy,

v'cha-yin arichin, um-zōnay r'vichay,   וְחַיִּין אֲרִיכִין, וּמְזוֹנֵי רְוִיחֵי,

long life, ample nourishment,

u-furkono min kodom a-vu-hōn   וּפֻרְקָנָא מִן קֳדָם אֲבוּהוֹן

and salvation from before their Father

dee vishma-yo (v'ar-o).   דִּי בִשְׁמַיָּא (וְאַרְעָא).
Who is in Heaven (and on earth).

V'imru: Omayn.   וְאִמְרוּ: אָמֵן.
Now respond: Amen.

CONGREGATION RESPONDS: Omayn — אָמֵן

Y'hay sh'lomo rabo min sh'mayo   יְהֵא שְׁלָמָא רַבָּא מִן שְׁמַיָּא,
May there be abundant peace from Heaven,

v'cha-yim olaynu v'al kol yisro-ayl.   וְחַיִּים עָלֵינוּ וְעַל כָּל יִשְׂרָאֵל.
and life, upon us and upon all Israel.

V'imru: Omayn.   וְאִמְרוּ: אָמֵן.
Now respond: Amen.

CONGREGATION RESPONDS: Omayn — אָמֵן

MOURNER BOWS, THEN TAKES THREE STEPS BACK, BOWS LEFT AND SAYS:

Ō-se sholōm bimrōmov   עֹשֶׂה שָׁלוֹם בִּמְרוֹמָיו,
He Who makes peace in His heights,

MOURNER BOWS RIGHT AND SAYS:

hu b'racha-mov ya-a-se sholōm   הוּא בְּרַחֲמָיו יַעֲשֶׂה שָׁלוֹם
   olaynu   עָלֵינוּ,
may He, in His compassion, make peace upon us,

MOURNER BOWS FORWARD AND SAYS:

v'al kol yisro-ayl. V'imru: Omayn: וְעַל כָּל יִשְׂרָאֵל. וְאִמְרוּ: אָמֵן.
and upon all Israel. Now respond: Amen.

CONGREGATION RESPONDS: Omayn — אָמֵן

MOURNER REMAINS IN PLACE FOR A FEW MOMENTS, THEN TAKES THREE STEPS FORWARD.

━━━━━━━━━━━━━━━━━━━

■ As we take leave of the synagogue and God's presence, we fortify ourselves with the resolve and commitment that the lofty ideals of prayer can be implemented and actualized in our mundane pursuits.

━━━━━━━━━━━━━━━━━━━

STAND WHILE RECITING *OLAYNU*.

OLAYNU l'shabay-ach la-adōn hakōl,   **עָלֵינוּ** לְשַׁבֵּחַ לַאֲדוֹן הַכֹּל,
It is our duty to praise the Master of all,

losays g'dulo l'yōtzayr b'rayshis,   לָתֵת גְּדֻלָּה לְיוֹצֵר בְּרֵאשִׁית,
to ascribe greatness to the Molder of primeval Creation,

shelō osonu k'gōyay ho-arotzōs,   שֶׁלֹּא עָשָׂנוּ כְּגוֹיֵי הָאֲרָצוֹת,
for He has not made us like the nations of the lands

v'lō somonu   וְלֹא שָׂמָנוּ
   k'mishp'chōs ho-adomo,   כְּמִשְׁפְּחוֹת הָאֲדָמָה.
and has not emplaced us like the families of the earth;

shelō som chelkaynu kohem,
שֶׁלֹּא שָׂם חֶלְקֵנוּ כָּהֶם,

v'gōrolaynu k'chol hamōnom
וְגוֹרָלֵנוּ כְּכָל הֲמוֹנָם.

for He has not assigned our portion like theirs nor our lot like all their multitudes.

SOME CONGREGATIONS OMIT THE PARENTHESIZED VERSE:

(Shehaym mishta-chavim
(שֶׁהֵם מִשְׁתַּחֲוִים

l'hevel vorik
לְהֶבֶל וָרִיק,

(For they bow to vanity and emptiness

u-mispal'lim el ayl lō yōshi-a.)
וּמִתְפַּלְּלִים אֶל אֵל לֹא יוֹשִׁיעַ.)

and pray to a god which helps not.)

BOW WHILE RECITING THE NEXT PHRASE.

Va-anachnu kōr'im u-mishta-chavim
וַאֲנַחְנוּ כּוֹרְעִים וּמִשְׁתַּחֲוִים

u-mōdim,
וּמוֹדִים,

But we bend our knees, bow, and acknowledge our thanks

lifnay melech malchay ham'lochim,
לִפְנֵי מֶלֶךְ מַלְכֵי הַמְּלָכִים

Hakodōsh boruch hu.
הַקָּדוֹשׁ בָּרוּךְ הוּא.

before the King Who reigns over kings, the Holy One, Blessed is He.

Shehu nōte shoma-yim
שֶׁהוּא נוֹטֶה שָׁמַיִם

v'yōsayd oretz,
וְיֹסֵד אָרֶץ,

He stretches out heaven and establishes earth's foundation,

u-mōshav y'korō
וּמוֹשַׁב יְקָרוֹ

bashoma-yim mima-al,
בַּשָּׁמַיִם מִמַּעַל,

the seat of His homage is in the heavens above

ush-chinas u-zō b'gov-hay m'rōmim.
וּשְׁכִינַת עֻזּוֹ בְּגָבְהֵי מְרוֹמִים.

and His powerful Presence is in the loftiest heights.

Hu Elōhaynu ayn ōd.
הוּא אֱלֹהֵינוּ, אֵין עוֹד.

He is our God and there is none other.

Emes malkaynu, efes zulosō,
אֱמֶת מַלְכֵּנוּ, אֶפֶס זוּלָתוֹ,

True is our King, there is nothing beside Him,

kakosuv b'sōrosō:
כַּכָּתוּב בְּתוֹרָתוֹ:

as it is written in His Torah:

V'yodato ha-yōm vaha-shayvōso
וְיָדַעְתָּ הַיּוֹם וַהֲשֵׁבֹתָ

el l'vovecho,
אֶל לְבָבֶךָ,

"You are to know this day and take to your heart

ki Adōnoy hu ho-Elōhim
כִּי יהוה הוּא הָאֱלֹהִים

that HASHEM is the only God —

ba-shoma-yim mima-al
בַּשָּׁמַיִם מִמַּעַל

v'al ho-oretz mitochas, ayn ōd.
וְעַל הָאָרֶץ מִתָּחַת, אֵין עוֹד.

in heaven above and on the earth below — there is none other."

AL KAYN n'kave l'cho
Adōnoy Elōhaynu

עַל כֵּן נְקַוֶּה לְּךָ
יהוה אֱלֹהֵינוּ

Therefore we put our hope in You, HASHEM, our God,

lirōs m'hayro b'sif-eres u-zecho,

לִרְאוֹת מְהֵרָה בְּתִפְאֶרֶת עֻזֶּךָ,

that we may soon see Your mighty splendor,

l'ha-avir gilulim min ho-oretz,

לְהַעֲבִיר גִּלּוּלִים מִן הָאָרֶץ,

to remove detestable idolatry from the earth,

v'ho-elilim korōs yikoraysun,

וְהָאֱלִילִים כָּרוֹת יִכָּרֵתוּן,

and false gods will be utterly cut off,

l'sakayn ōlom b'malchus Shadai.

לְתַקֵּן עוֹלָם בְּמַלְכוּת שַׁדַּי.

to perfect the universe through the Almighty's sovereignty.

V'chol b'nay vosor yikr'u vishmecho,

וְכָל בְּנֵי בָשָׂר יִקְרְאוּ בִשְׁמֶךָ,

Then all humanity will call upon Your Name,

l'hafnōs aylecho kol rish-ay oretz.

לְהַפְנוֹת אֵלֶיךָ כָּל רִשְׁעֵי אָרֶץ.

to turn all the earth's wicked toward You.

Yakiru v'yayd'u kol yōsh'vay sayvayl,

יַכִּירוּ וְיֵדְעוּ כָּל יוֹשְׁבֵי תֵבֵל,

All the world's inhabitants will recognize and know

ki l'cho tichra kol berech,
tishova kol loshōn.

כִּי לְךָ תִּכְרַע כָּל בֶּרֶךְ,
תִּשָּׁבַע כָּל לָשׁוֹן.

that to You every knee should bend, every tongue should swear.

L'fonecho Adōnoy Elōhaynu
yichr'u v'yipōlu,

לְפָנֶיךָ יהוה אֱלֹהֵינוּ
יִכְרְעוּ וְיִפֹּלוּ,

Before You, HASHEM, our God, they will bend every knee and cast themselves down,

v'lichvōd shimcho y'kor yitaynu,

וְלִכְבוֹד שִׁמְךָ יְקָר יִתֵּנוּ,

and to the glory of Your Name they will render homage,

vikab'lu chulom es ōl malchusecho,

וִיקַבְּלוּ כֻלָּם אֶת עוֹל מַלְכוּתֶךָ,

and they will all accept upon themselves the yoke of Your kingship

v'simlōch alayhem m'hayro
l'ōlom vo-ed.

וְתִמְלֹךְ עֲלֵיהֶם מְהֵרָה
לְעוֹלָם וָעֶד.

that You may reign over them soon and for all eternally.

Ki hamalchus shelcho hi

כִּי הַמַּלְכוּת שֶׁלְּךָ הִיא

For the kingdom is Yours

ul-ōl'may ad timlōch b'chovōd,

וּלְעוֹלְמֵי עַד תִּמְלוֹךְ בְּכָבוֹד,

and You will reign for all eternity in glory,

kakosuv b'sōrosecho:
Adōnoy yimlōch l'ōlom vo-ed.

כַּכָּתוּב בְּתוֹרָתֶךָ:
יהוה יִמְלֹךְ לְעֹלָם וָעֶד.

as it is written in Your Torah: "HASHEM shall reign for all eternity."

❖ וְנֶאֱמַר: וְהָיָה יהוה לְמֶלֶךְ

V'ne-emar: V'ho-yo Adōnoy l'melech

עַל כָּל הָאָרֶץ,

al kol ho-oretz,

And it is said: "HASHEM will be King over all the world —

בַּיוֹם הַהוּא יִהְיֶה

ba-yōm hahu yih-ye

יהוה אֶחָד וּשְׁמוֹ אֶחָד.

Adōnoy e-chod, ushmō e-chod.

on that day HASHEM will be One and His Name will be One."

SOME CONGREGATIONS RECITE THE FOLLOWING AT THIS POINT.

AL TIRO mipachad pis-ōm,

אַל תִּירָא מִפַּחַד פִּתְאֹם,

Do not fear sudden terror,

u-mishō-as r'sho-im ki sovō.

וּמִשֹּׁאַת רְשָׁעִים כִּי תָבֹא.

or the holocaust of the wicked when it comes.

Utzu aytzo v'sufor,

עֻצוּ עֵצָה וְתֻפָר,

dab'ru dovor v'lō yokum,

דַּבְּרוּ דָבָר וְלֹא יָקוּם,

Plan a conspiracy and it will be annulled; speak your piece and it shall not stand,

ki i-monu Ayl.

כִּי עִמָּנוּ אֵל.

for God is with us.

V'ad zikno ani hu,

וְעַד זִקְנָה אֲנִי הוּא,

Even till your seniority, I remain unchanged;

v'ad sayvo ani esbōl,

וְעַד שֵׂיבָה אֲנִי אֶסְבֹּל,

and even till your ripe old age, I shall endure;

ani osisi va-ani eso,

אֲנִי עָשִׂיתִי וַאֲנִי אֶשָּׂא,

va-ani esbōl va-amalayt.

וַאֲנִי אֶסְבֹּל וַאֲמַלֵּט.

I created [you] and I shall bear [you]; I shall endure and rescue.

MOURNER'S KADDISH

MOURNER:

YISGADAL v'yiskadash

יִתְגַּדַּל וְיִתְקַדַּשׁ

sh'mayh rabo.

שְׁמֵהּ רַבָּא.

May His great Name grow exalted and sanctified

CONGREGATION RESPONDS: Omayn — אָמֵן

B'ol'mo di v'ro chir-usayh.

בְּעָלְמָא דִי בְרָא כִרְעוּתֵהּ.

in the world that He created as He willed.

V'yamlich malchusayh,

וְיַמְלִיךְ מַלְכוּתֵהּ,

May He give reign to His kingship

b'cha-yaychōn uvyōmaychōn

בְּחַיֵּיכוֹן וּבְיוֹמֵיכוֹן

in your lifetimes and in your days

uvcha-yay d'chol bays yisro-ayl,

וּבְחַיֵּי דְכָל בֵּית יִשְׂרָאֵל,

and in the lifetimes of the entire Family of Israel,

ba-agolo u-vizman koriv.   בַּעֲגָלָא וּבִזְמַן קָרִיב.

swiftly and soon.

V'imru: Omayn.   וְאִמְרוּ: אָמֵן.

Now respond: Amen.

CONGREGATION RESPONDS:

Omayn. Y'hay sh'mayh rabo m'vorach   אָמֵן. יְהֵא שְׁמֵהּ רַבָּא מְבָרַךְ

l'olam ul-ol'may ol'ma-yo.   לְעָלַם וּלְעָלְמֵי עָלְמַיָּא.

Amen. May His great Name be blessed forever and ever;

MOURNER CONTINUES:

Y'hay sh'mayh rabo m'vorach   יְהֵא שְׁמֵהּ רַבָּא מְבָרַךְ

l'olam ul-ol'may ol'ma-yo,   לְעָלַם וּלְעָלְמֵי עָלְמַיָּא,

May His great Name be blessed forever and ever;

yisborach v'yishtabach v'yispo-ar   יִתְבָּרַךְ וְיִשְׁתַּבַּח וְיִתְפָּאַר

blessed, praised, glorified,

v'yisrōmam v'yisnasay   וְיִתְרוֹמַם וְיִתְנַשֵּׂא

exalted, extolled,

v'yis-hador v'yis-ale v'yis-halol   וְיִתְהַדָּר וְיִתְעַלֶּה וְיִתְהַלָּל

mighty, upraised, and lauded

sh'mayh d'kudsho b'rich hu   שְׁמֵהּ דְּקֻדְשָׁא בְּרִיךְ הוּא

be the Name of the Holy One, Blessed is He,

CONGREGATION RESPONDS:

B'rich hu.   *Blessed is He.*   בְּרִיךְ הוּא.

MOURNER CONTINUES:

°l'aylo min kol   °לְעֵלָּא מִן כָּל

beyond any

FROM ROSH HASHANAH TO YOM KIPPUR SUBSTITUTE:

°l'aylo l'aylo mikol   °לְעֵלָּא לְעֵלָּא מִכָּל

exceedingly beyond any

---

birchoso v'shiroso   בִּרְכָתָא וְשִׁירָתָא

tushb'choso v'nechemoso,   תֻּשְׁבְּחָתָא וְנֶחֱמָתָא,

blessing and song, praise and consolation

da-amiron b'ol'mo.   דַּאֲמִירָן בְּעָלְמָא.

that are uttered in the world.

V'imru: Omayn.   וְאִמְרוּ: אָמֵן.

Now respond: Amen.

CONGREGATION RESPONDS: Omayn — אָמֵן

Y'hay sh'lomo rabo min sh'mayo   יְהֵא שְׁלָמָא רַבָּא מִן שְׁמַיָּא,

May there be abundant peace from Heaven,

v'cha-yim olaynu v'al kol yisro-ayl.   וְחַיִּים עָלֵינוּ וְעַל כָּל יִשְׂרָאֵל.

and life, upon us and upon all Israel.

V'imru: Omayn:
וְאִמְרוּ: אָמֵן.

Now respond: Amen.

CONGREGATION RESPONDS: Omayn — אָמֵן

MOURNER BOWS, THEN TAKES THREE STEPS BACK, BOWS LEFT AND SAYS:

Ō-se sholōm bimrōmov
עֹשֶׂה שָׁלוֹם בִּמְרוֹמָיו,

He Who makes peace in His heights,

MOURNER BOWS RIGHT AND SAYS:

hu ya-a-se sholōm olaynu
הוּא יַעֲשֶׂה שָׁלוֹם עָלֵינוּ,

may He make peace upon us,

MOURNER BOWS FORWARD AND SAYS:

v'al kol yisro-ayl. V'imru: Omayn:
וְעַל כָּל יִשְׂרָאֵל. וְאִמְרוּ: אָמֵן.

and upon all Israel. Now respond: Amen.

CONGREGATION RESPONDS: Omayn — אָמֵן

MOURNER REMAINS IN PLACE FOR A FEW MOMENTS, THEN TAKES THREE STEPS FORWARD.

⊰ SONG OF GLORY ⊱

THE ARK IS OPENED AND THE SONG OF GLORY IS RECITED RESPONSIVELY — THE *CHAZZAN*
RECITING THE FIRST VERSE, THE CONGREGATION RECITING THE SECOND AND SO ON.

CHAZZAN:

AN-IM Z'MIRŌS
אַנְעִים זְמִירוֹת

v'shirim e-erōg,
וְשִׁירִים אֶאֱרוֹג,

I shall compose pleasant psalms and weave hymns,*

ki aylecho nafshi sa-arōg.
כִּי אֵלֶיךָ נַפְשִׁי תַעֲרוֹג.

because for You shall my soul pine.

CONGREGATION:

Nafshi chom'do b'tzayl yodecho,
נַפְשִׁי חָמְדָה בְּצֵל יָדֶךָ,

My soul desired the shelter of Your hand,

loda-as kol roz sōdecho.
לָדַעַת כָּל רָז סוֹדֶךָ.

to know every mystery of Your secret.

CHAZZAN:

Miday dab'ri bichvōdecho,
מִדֵּי דַבְּרִי בִּכְבוֹדֶךָ,

As I speak of Your glory,

hō-me libi el dōdecho.
הוֹמֶה לִבִּי אֶל דּוֹדֶיךָ.

my heart yearns for Your love.

CONGREGATION:

Al kayn adabayr b'cho nichbodōs,
עַל כֵּן אֲדַבֵּר בְּךָ נִכְבָּדוֹת,

Therefore I shall speak of Your glories,

וְשִׁירִים אֶאֱרוֹג — *And weave hymns.* Just as a
weaver unifies countless threads to make a
finished garment, so does the *paytan* [liturgical
poet] weave together words and phrases to

v'shimcho achabayd b'shiray y'didōs.　וְשִׁמְךָ אֲכַבֵּד בְּשִׁירֵי יְדִידוֹת.

and Your Name I shall honor with loving songs.

CHAZZAN:

Asap'ro ch'vōd'cho v'lō r'isicho,　אֲסַפְּרָה כְבוֹדְךָ וְלֹא רְאִיתִיךָ,

I shall relate Your glory, though I see You not;*

adam'cho achan'cho v'lō y'daticho.　אֲדַמְּךָ אֲכַנְּךָ וְלֹא יְדַעְתִּיךָ.

I shall allegorize You, I shall describe You, though I know You not.

CONGREGATION:

B'yad n'vi-echo b'sōd avodecho,　בְּיַד נְבִיאֶיךָ בְּסוֹד עֲבָדֶיךָ,

Through the hand of Your prophets,* through the counsel of Your servants;

dimiso hadar k'vōd hōdecho.　דִּמִּיתָ הֲדַר כְּבוֹד הוֹדֶךָ.

You allegorized the splendrous glory of Your power.

CHAZZAN:

G'dulos'cho ugvurosecho,　גְּדֻלָּתְךָ וּגְבוּרָתֶךָ,

kinu l'sōkef p'ulosecho.　כִּנּוּ לְתֹקֶף פְּעֻלָּתֶךָ.

Your greatness and Your strength, they described the might of Your works.

CONGREGATION:

Dimu ōs'cho v'lō ch'fi yeshcho,　דִּמּוּ אוֹתְךָ וְלֹא כְפִי יֶשְׁךָ,

They allegorized You, but not according to Your reality,

vaishavucho l'fi ma-asecho.　וַיְשַׁוּוּךָ לְפִי מַעֲשֶׂיךָ.

and they portrayed You according to Your deeds.*

CHAZZAN:

Himshilucho b'rōv chezyōnōs,　הִמְשִׁילוּךָ בְּרֹב חֶזְיוֹנוֹת,

They symbolized You in many varied visions;

hin'cho echod b'chol dimyōnōs.　הִנְּךָ אֶחָד בְּכָל דִּמְיוֹנוֹת.

yet You are a Unity* containing all the allegories.

CONGREGATION:

Va-yechezu v'cho zikno u-vacharus,　וַיֶּחֱזוּ בְךָ זִקְנָה וּבַחֲרוּת,

They envisioned in You agedness and virility,

us-ar rōsh'cho　וּשְׂעַר רֹאשְׁךָ

b'sayvo v'shacharus.　בְּשֵׂיבָה וְשַׁחֲרוּת.

and the hair of Your head as hoary and jet black.

---

compose beautiful songs of praise.

וְלֹא רְאִיתִיךָ — *Though I see You not*. We cannot see God, nor can we know His essence. The best we can do is to imagine and describe Him in human terms.

בְּיַד נְבִיאֶיךָ — *Through the hand of Your prophets*. The precedent for describing God in

human, physical terminology comes from Him — for He described Himself to the prophets in such terms.

לְפִי מַעֲשֶׂיךָ — *According to Your deeds*. It is a familiar truth that we cannot conceive of what God is; we can only know something of Him through His deeds.

CHAZZAN:

Zikno b'yōm din
   u-vacharus b'yōm k'rov

זִקְנָה בְּיוֹם דִּין
וּבַחֲרוּת בְּיוֹם קְרָב,

Aged* on judgment day and virile on the day of battle,

k'ish milchomōs yodov lō rov.

כְּאִישׁ מִלְחָמוֹת יָדָיו לוֹ רָב.

like a man of war whose powers are many.

CONGREGATION:

Chovash kōva y'shu-o b'rōshō

חָבַשׁ כְּבַע יְשׁוּעָה בְּרֹאשׁוֹ,

The hat of salvation He put on His head;

hōshi-o lō y'minō uz'rō-a kod'shō.

הוֹשִׁיעָה לוֹ יְמִינוֹ וּזְרוֹעַ קָדְשׁוֹ.

His right hand and His holy arm have helped Him.*

CHAZZAN:

Tal'lay ōrōs rōshō nimlo,

טַלְלֵי אוֹרוֹת רֹאשׁוֹ נִמְלָא,

With illuminating dewdrops His head is filled,

k'vutzōsov r'sisay loylo.

קְוֻצּוֹתָיו רְסִיסֵי לָיְלָה.

His locks are the rains of the night.

CONGREGATION:

Yispo-ayr bi ki chofaytz bi,

יִתְפָּאֵר בִּי כִּי חָפֵץ בִּי,

He shall glory in me for He desires me,

v'hu yih-ye li la-ateres tz'vi.

וְהוּא יִהְיֶה לִי לַעֲטֶרֶת צְבִי.

and He shall be for me a crown of pride.

CHAZZAN:

Kesem tohōr poz d'mus rōshō,

כֶּתֶם טָהוֹר פָּז דְּמוּת רֹאשׁוֹ,

A form of the very best gold upon his head,

v'chak al maytzach
   k'vōd shaym kodshō.

וְחַק עַל מֵצַח
כְּבוֹד שֵׁם קָדְשׁוֹ.

and carved on his forehead is His glorious, sacred Name.

CONGREGATION:

L'chayn ulchovōd tz'vi sif-oro,

לְחֵן וּלְכָבוֹד צְבִי תִפְאָרָה,

For grace and for glory* the pride of His splendor;

u-mosō lō it'ro atoro.

אֻמָּתוֹ לוֹ עִטְּרָה עֲטָרָה.

His nation crowns Him with its prayers.

הִנְּךָ אֶחָד — *Yet You are a Unity.* God is One though He appears in many guises: merciful, judgmental, old, young, warrior and so on.

זִקְנָה — *Aged.* Since the song now begins an extensive discussion of God in human terms, it changes to third person out of respect.

הוֹשִׁיעָה לוֹ יְמִינוֹ — *His right hand and His*

holy arm have helped Him. God was like a warrior winning victory through his powerful arm.

לְחֵן וּלְכָבוֹד — *For grace and for glory.* It is a mark of God's esteem for Israel that He desires its prayers and that He takes them, as it were, as a crown on His head.

CHAZZAN:

Machl'fōs rōshō k'vimay v'churōs,   מַחְלְפוֹת רֹאשׁ כְּבִימֵי בַּחֲרוּת,

The tresses of His head* are like in days of youth;

k'vutzōs'ov taltalim sh'chōrōs.   קְוֻצּוֹתָיו תַּלְתַּלִּים שְׁחוֹרוֹת.

His locks are jet-black ringlets.

CONGREGATION:

N'vay hatzedek tz'vi sif-arto,   נְוֵה הַצֶּדֶק צְבִי תִפְאַרְתּוֹ,

The Abode of righteousness is the pride of His splendor;

ya-ale no al rōsh simchosō.   יַעֲלֶה נָּא עַל רֹאשׁ שִׂמְחָתוֹ.

may He elevate it to His foremost joy.

CHAZZAN:

S'gulosō t'hi v'yodō ateres,   סְגֻלָּתוֹ תְּהִי בְיָדוֹ עֲטֶרֶת,

May His treasured nation be in His hand like a crown,

utznif m'lucho tz'vi sif-eres.   וּצְנִיף מְלוּכָה צְבִי תִפְאָרֶת.

and like a royal tiara the pride of His splendor.

CONGREGATION:

Amusim n'so-ōm ateres in'dom,   עֲמוּסִים נְשָׂאָם עֲטֶרֶת עִנְּדָם,

From infancy He bore them and affixed them as a crown,

may-asher yok'ru v'aynov kib'dom.   מֵאֲשֶׁר יָקְרוּ בְעֵינָיו כִּבְּדָם.

because they are precious in His eyes He honored them.

CHAZZAN:

P'ayrō olai uf-ayri olov,   פְּאֵרוֹ עָלַי וּפְאֵרִי עָלָיו,

His tefillin-splendor* is upon me and my tefillin-splendor is upon Him,

v'korōv aylai b'kor-i aylov.   וְקָרוֹב אֵלַי בְּקָרְאִי אֵלָיו.

and He is near to me when I call to Him.

CONGREGATION:

Tzach v'odōm lilvushō odōm,   צַח וְאָדֹם לִלְבוּשׁוֹ אָדֹם,

He is white and crimson;* His garment will be bloody red,

puro b'dorchō b'vō-ō may-edōm.   פּוּרָה בְדָרְכוֹ בְּבוֹאוֹ מֵאֱדוֹם.

when He tramples as in a press on His coming from Edom.

CHAZZAN:

Kesher t'filin her-o l'onov,   קֶשֶׁר תְּפִלִּין הֶרְאָה לֶעָנָו,

He showed the tefillin-knot* to the humble [Moses],

מַחְלְפוֹת רֹאשׁ — *The tresses of His head.* God does not change with the passage of time. His "youth" remains with Him, just as the "maturity of age" was always with Him.

פְּאֵרוֹ — *His tefillin-splendor.* Just as Israel takes pride in God, so God takes pride in Israel. The Talmud (*Berachos* 6a) expresses this idea by saying that just as Israel wears *tefillin* in which are written the praises of God, so does

God wear *tefillin*, described as His splendor, which contain Scriptural verses that praise Israel.

צַח וְאָדֹם — *He is white and crimson.* God is both compassionate, symbolized by *white*, and strict, symbolized by *crimson*. He is lenient or harsh, depending on the need.

קֶשֶׁר תְּפִלִּין — *The tefillin-knot.* When Moses asked to see [i.e., understand] God, He showed

t'munas Adōnoy l'neged aynov.   תְּמוּנַת יהוה לְנֶגֶד עֵינָיו.

the likeness of HASHEM before his eyes.

CONGREGATION:

Rōtze v'amō anovim y'fo-ayr,   רוֹצֶה בְעַמּוֹ עֲנָוִים יְפָאֵר,

He desires His people, He will glorify the humble;

yōshayv t'hilōs bom l'hispo-ayr.   יוֹשֵׁב תְּהִלּוֹת בָּם לְהִתְפָּאֵר.

enthroned upon praises, He glories with them.

CHAZZAN:

Rōsh d'vor'cho emes kōray mayrōsh,   רֹאשׁ דְּבָרְךָ אֱמֶת קוֹרֵא מֵרֹאשׁ,

The very beginning of Your word is truth — one reads it from the Torah's start;

dōr vodōr am dōreshcho d'rōsh.   דּוֹר וָדוֹר עַם דּוֹרֶשְׁךָ דְּרוֹשׁ.

the people that seeks You expounds each generation's fate.

CONGREGATION:

Shis hamōn shirai no olecho,   שִׁית הֲמוֹן שִׁירַי נָא עָלֶיךָ,

Place the multitude of my songs before You, please;

v'rinosi tikrav aylecho.   וְרִנָּתִי תִּקְרַב אֵלֶיךָ.

and my glad song bring near to You.

CHAZZAN:

T'hilosi t'hi l'rōsh'cho ateres,   תְּהִלָּתִי תְּהִי לְרֹאשְׁךָ עֲטֶרֶת,

May my praise be a crown for Your head,

usfilosi tikōn k'tōres.   וּתְפִלָּתִי תִּכּוֹן קְטֹרֶת.

and may my prayer be accepted like incense.

CONGREGATION:

Tikar shiras rosh b'aynecho,   תִּיקַר שִׁירַת רָשׁ בְּעֵינֶיךָ,

May the poor man's song be dear in Your eyes,

kashir yushar al korbonecho.   כַּשִּׁיר יוּשַׁר עַל קָרְבָּנֶיךָ.

like the song that is sung over Your offerings.

CHAZZAN:

Birchosi sa-ale l'rōsh mashbir,   בִּרְכָתִי תַעֲלֶה לְרֹאשׁ מַשְׁבִּיר,

May my blessing rise up upon the head of the Sustainer

m'chōlayl umōlid tzadik kabir.   מְחוֹלֵל וּמוֹלִיד צַדִּיק כַּבִּיר.

— Creator, Giver of life, mighty Righteous One.

CONGREGATION:

Uv'virchosi s'na-ana li rōsh,   וּבְבִרְכָתִי תְנַעֲנַע לִי רֹאשׁ,

And to my blessing, nod Your head to me,

v'ōsoh kach l'cho kivsomim rōsh.   וְאוֹתָהּ קַח לְךָ כִּבְשָׂמִים רֹאשׁ.

and take it to Yourself like the best incense.

---

him, in the simile of the Sages, the *tefillin* -knot at the back of His "head," as it were. This   indicated that not even Moses was permitted a clear vision of God's ways.

CHAZZAN:

Ye-erav no sichi olecho,
ki nafshi sa-arōg aylecho.

יֶעֱרַב נָא שִׂיחִי עָלֶיךָ,
כִּי נַפְשִׁי תַעֲרוֹג אֵלֶיךָ.

May my prayer be sweet to You, for my soul shall pine for You.

CONGREGATION:

L'CHO Adōnoy hag'dulo
v'hag'vuro v'hatif-eres
v'hanaytzach v'hahōd,

לְךָ יהוה הַגְּדֻלָּה
וְהַגְּבוּרָה וְהַתִּפְאֶרֶת
וְהַנֵּצַח וְהַהוֹד,

Yours, HASHEM, is the greatness, the strength, the splendor, the triumph, and the glory;

ki chōl ba-shoma-yim u-vo-oretz;

כִּי כֹל בַּשָּׁמַיִם וּבָאָרֶץ;

even everything in heaven and earth;

l'cho Adōnoy hamamlocho
v'hamisnasay l'chōl l'rōsh.

לְךָ יהוה הַמַּמְלָכָה
וְהַמִּתְנַשֵּׂא לְכֹל לְרֹאשׁ.

Yours, HASHEM, is the kingdom, and the sovereignty over every leader.

❖ Mi y'malayl g'vurōs Adōnoy,
yashmi-a kol t'hilosō.

❖ מִי יְמַלֵּל גְּבוּרוֹת יהוה,
יַשְׁמִיעַ כָּל תְּהִלָּתוֹ.

Who can express the mighty acts of HASHEM? Who can declare all His praise?

THE ARK IS CLOSED. IF A MOURNER IS PRESENT HE RECITES THE MOURNER'S KADDISH (P. 466).

❧ **SONG OF THE DAY** ❧

A DIFFERENT PSALM IS ASSIGNED AS THE SONG OF THE DAY FOR EACH DAY OF THE WEEK.

FOR SUNDAY

■ I remember the Shabbos daily: On the first day of Creation Hashem created the world te benefit man, and challenged him to aspire to perfection.

Ha-yōm yōm rishōn ba-shabos,

הַיּוֹם יוֹם רִאשׁוֹן בַּשַּׁבָּת,

Today is the first day* of the Sabbath,

shebō ho-yu hal'viyim
ōm'rim b'vays hamikdosh:

שֶׁבּוֹ הָיוּ הַלְוִיִּם
אוֹמְרִים בְּבֵית הַמִּקְדָּשׁ:

on which the Levites would recite in the Holy Temple.

L'DOVID mizmōr,

לְדָוִד מִזְמוֹר,

Of David a psalm.

❧ **Song of the Day**: As part of the morning Temple service, the Levites chanted a psalm that was suited to the significance of that particular day of the week. As a memorial to the Temple, these psalms have been incorporated into *Shacharis.* The introductory sentence, "Today is the first day of the Sabbath ..." enables us to fulfill the Torah's command to remember the Sabbath always. By counting the days of the week with reference to the forthcoming Sabbath we tie our existence to

the Sabbath. The Talmud (*Rosh Hashanah* 31a) explains why each of these psalms was assigned to its particular day.

הַיּוֹם יוֹם רִאשׁוֹן — *Today is the First Day.* Psalm 24 teaches that everything belongs to God. The Talmud assigns this psalm to the first day of the week because on the first day of Creation, God was the sole Being — even the angels had not yet been created. He took possession of His newly created world with the intention of ceding it to man.

Ladōnoy ho-oretz umlō-oh,
לַיהוה הָאָרֶץ וּמְלוֹאָהּ,

HASHEM's is the earth* and its fullness,

tayvayl v'yōsh'vay voh.
תֵּבֵל וְיֹשְׁבֵי בָהּ.

the inhabited land and those who dwell in it.

Ki hu al yamim y'sodoh,
כִּי הוּא עַל יַמִּים יְסָדָהּ,

v'al n'horōs y'chōn'neho.
וְעַל נְהָרוֹת יְכוֹנְנֶהָ.

For He founded it upon seas,* and established it upon rivers.

Mi ya-ale v'har Adōnoy,
מִי יַעֲלֶה בְהַר יהוה,

Who may ascend* the mountain of HASHEM,

u-mi yokum bimkōm kodshō.
וּמִי יָקוּם בִּמְקוֹם קָדְשׁוֹ.

and who may stand in the place of His sanctity?

N'ki chapa-yim u-var layvov,
נְקִי כַפַּיִם וּבַר לֵבָב,

One with clean hands* and pure heart,

asher lō noso lashov nafshi,
אֲשֶׁר לֹא נָשָׂא לַשָּׁוְא נַפְשִׁי,

v'lō nishba l'mirmo.
וְלֹא נִשְׁבַּע לְמִרְמָה.

who has not sworn in vain by My soul* and has not sworn deceitfully.

Yiso v'rocho may-ays Adōnoy,
יִשָּׂא בְרָכָה מֵאֵת יהוה,

He will receive a blessing* from HASHEM

utz'doko may-Elōhay yish-ō.
וּצְדָקָה מֵאֱלֹהֵי יִשְׁעוֹ.

and just kindness from the God of his salvation.

Ze dōr dōr'shov,
זֶה דּוֹר דֹּרְשָׁיו,

This is the generation of those who seek Him,

m'vakshay fonecho ya-akōv selo.
מְבַקְשֵׁי פָנֶיךָ יַעֲקֹב סֶלָה.

those who strive for Your Presence — Jacob, Selah.

S'u sh'orim ro-shaychem,
שְׂאוּ שְׁעָרִים רָאשֵׁיכֶם,

Raise up your heads, O gates,

v'hinos'u pischay ōlom,
וְהִנָּשְׂאוּ פִּתְחֵי עוֹלָם,

and be uplifted, you everlasting entrances,

לַה׳ הָאָרֶץ — *HASHEM's is the earth.* Since the world belongs to God, anyone who derives pleasure from His world without reciting the proper blessing expressing thanks to the Owner is regarded as a thief (*Berachos* 35a).

כִּי הוּא עַל יַמִּים יְסָדָהּ — *For He founded it upon seas.* The entire planet was covered with water until God commanded it to gather in seas and rivers and expose the dry land.

מִי יַעֲלֶה — *Who may ascend . . .?* God's most intense Presence is in the Temple, so those who wish to draw near and to perceive His splendor must be especially worthy. By exten-

sion, one who wishes to enjoy spiritual elevation must refine his behavior.

נְקִי כַפַּיִם — *One with clean hands.* This verse answers the previous question. To ascend, one must have hands clean from dishonest gain; must be honest in dealing with man; and must be reverent toward God.

נַפְשִׁי — *My soul.* God is the "speaker." He refers to one who swears falsely as having treated God's soul, as it were, with disrespect.

יִשָּׂא בְרָכָה — *He will receive a blessing.* By honoring God's Name in heart and behavior, he earns God's blessing, kindness and salvation.

v'yovō melech hakovōd.   וְיָבוֹא מֶלֶךְ הַכָּבוֹד.

so that the King of Glory may enter.

Mi ze melech hakovōd,   מִי זֶה מֶלֶךְ הַכָּבוֹד,

Who is this King of Glory? —

Adōnoy izuz v'gibōr   יהוה עִזּוּז וְגִבּוֹר,

    Adōnoy gibōr milchomo.   יהוה גִּבּוֹר מִלְחָמָה.

HASHEM, the mighty and strong, HASHEM, the strong in battle.

S'u sh'orim ro-shaychem,   ❖ שְׂאוּ שְׁעָרִים רָאשֵׁיכֶם,

    us-u pischay ōlom,   וּשְׂאוּ פִּתְחֵי עוֹלָם,

Raise up your heads, O gates, and raise up, you everlasting entrances,

v'yovō melech hakovōd.   וְיָבֹא מֶלֶךְ הַכָּבוֹד.

so that the King of Glory may enter.

Mi hu ze melech hakovōd,   מִי הוּא זֶה מֶלֶךְ הַכָּבוֹד,

Who then is the King of Glory?

Adōnoy Tz'vo-ōs,   יהוה צְבָאוֹת,

    hu melech hakovōd selo.   הוּא מֶלֶךְ הַכָּבוֹד סֶלָה.

HASHEM, Master of Legions, He is the King of Glory. Selah!

IF A MOURNER IS PRESENT, HE RECITES THE MOURNER'S *KADDISH* (PAGE 466).

FOR MONDAY

■ I remember the Shabbos daily: On the second day of Creation Hashem separated Heaven and earth. As He rules the Heavens above, so does He reign in Jerusalem.

Ha-yōm yōm shayni ba-shabos,   הַיּוֹם יוֹם שֵׁנִי בַּשַּׁבָּת,

Today is the second day* of the Sabbath,

shebō ho-yu hal'viyim   שֶׁבּוֹ הָיוּ הַלְוִיִּם

    ōm'rim b'vays hamikdosh: אוֹמְרִים בְּבֵית הַמִּקְדָּשׁ:

on which the Levites would recite in the Holy Temple:

SHIR mizmōr livnay kōrach.   שִׁיר מִזְמוֹר לִבְנֵי קֹרַח.

A song, a psalm, by the sons of Korach.

Godōl Adōnoy umhulol m'ōd,   גָּדוֹל יהוה וּמְהֻלָּל מְאֹד,

Great is HASHEM and much praised,

b'ir Elōhaynu har kodshō.   בְּעִיר אֱלֹהֵינוּ, הַר קָדְשׁוֹ.

in the city of our God, Mount of His Holiness.

Y'fay nōf m'sōs kol ho-oretz   יְפֵה נוֹף, מְשׂוֹשׂ כָּל הָאָרֶץ,

Fairest of sites, joy of all the earth

הַיּוֹם יוֹם שֵׁנִי — *Today is the second day.* Psalm 48 speaks of Jerusalem, the seat of God's holiness and kingship over the entire world. On the second day of Creation, God separated between the heavenly and earthly components of the universe and ruled over both.

har tziyōn yark'say tzofōn,
kiryas melech rov.

הַר צִיּוֹן יַרְכְּתֵי צָפוֹן,
קִרְיַת מֶלֶךְ רָב.

is Mount Zion, by the northern sides of the great king's city.

Elōhim b'arm'nōseho.
nōda l'misgov.

אֱלֹהִים בְּאַרְמְנוֹתֶיהָ
נוֹדַע לְמִשְׂגָּב.

In her palaces God is known as the Stronghold.

Ki hinay ham'lochim nō-adu
ov'ru yachdov.

כִּי הִנֵּה הַמְּלָכִים נוֹעֲדוּ,
עָבְרוּ יַחְדָּו.

For behold — the kings assembled, they came together.

Haymo ro-u kayn tomohu

הֵמָּה רָאוּ כֵּן תָּמָהוּ,

They saw and they were astounded,

nivhalu nechpozu.

נִבְהֲלוּ נֶחְפָּזוּ.

they were confounded and hastily fled.

R'odo achozosam shom,
chil kayōlaydo.

רְעָדָה אֲחָזָתַם שָׁם,
חִיל כַּיּוֹלֵדָה.

Trembling gripped them there, convulsions like a woman in birth travail.

B'ru-ach kodim
t'shabayr oniyōs tarshish.

בְּרוּחַ קָדִים
תְּשַׁבֵּר אֳנִיּוֹת תַּרְשִׁישׁ.

With an east wind You smashed the ships of Tarshish.

Ka-asher shomanu kayn ro-inu

כַּאֲשֶׁר שָׁמַעְנוּ כֵּן רָאִינוּ

As we heard,* so we saw

b'ir Adōnoy Tz'vo-ōs,
b'ir Elōhaynu,

בְּעִיר יהוה צְבָאוֹת,
בְּעִיר אֱלֹהֵינוּ,

in the city of HASHEM, Master of Legions, in the city of our God —

Elōhim y'chōn'neho ad ōlom selo.

אֱלֹהִים יְכוֹנְנֶהָ עַד עוֹלָם סֶלָה.

may God establish it to eternity, Selah!

Diminu Elōhim chasdecho,
b'kerev haycholecho.

דִּמִּינוּ אֱלֹהִים חַסְדֶּךָ,
בְּקֶרֶב הֵיכָלֶךָ.

We hoped, O God, for Your kindness, in the midst of Your Sanctuary.

K'shimcho Elōhim kayn t'hilos'cho,
al katzvay eretz,

כְּשִׁמְךָ אֱלֹהִים כֵּן תְּהִלָּתְךָ,
עַל קַצְוֵי אֶרֶץ,

Like Your Name, O God,* so is Your praise — to the ends of the earth;

tzedek mol'o y'mine-cho.

צֶדֶק מָלְאָה יְמִינֶךָ.

righteousness fills Your right hand.

כַּאֲשֶׁר שָׁמַעְנוּ — *As we heard.* From our ancestors we heard of God's miraculous salvations — but we will see similar wonders as well.

כְּשִׁמְךָ אֱלֹהִים — *Like Your Name, O God.* The prophets gave You exalted Names, and we can testify that Your praise, given You for actual

Yismach har tziyōn,

יִשְׂמַח הַר צִיּוֹן,

   togaylno b'nōs y'hudo,

תָּגֵלְנָה בְּנוֹת יְהוּדָה,

    May Mount Zion be glad, may the daughters of Judah rejoice,

l'ma-an mishpotecho.

לְמַעַן מִשְׁפָּטֶיךָ.

    because of Your judgments.

Sōbu tziyōn v'hakifuho,

סֹבּוּ צִיּוֹן וְהַקִּיפוּהָ,

   sifru migdoleho.

סִפְרוּ מִגְדָּלֶיהָ.

    Walk about Zion and encircle her, count her towers.

Shisu lib'chem l'chaylo,

❖ שִׁיתוּ לִבְּכֶם לְחֵילָה,

    Mark well in your hearts her ramparts,

pas'gu arm'nōseho,

פַּסְּגוּ אַרְמְנוֹתֶיהָ,

    raise up her palaces,

l'ma-an t'sap'ru l'dōr acharōn.

לְמַעַן תְּסַפְּרוּ לְדוֹר אַחֲרוֹן.

    that you may recount it to the succeeding generation.

Ki ze Elōhim Elōhaynu ōlom vo-ed,

כִּי זֶה אֱלֹהִים אֱלֹהֵינוּ עוֹלָם וָעֶד,

    that this is God, our God, forever and ever,

hu y'nahagaynu al mus.

הוּא יְנַהֲגֵנוּ עַל־מוּת.

    He will guide us like children.

IF A MOURNER IS PRESENT, HE RECITES THE MOURNER'S *KADDISH* (PAGE 466).

FOR TUESDAY

■ I remember the Shabbos daily: On the third day of Creation Hashem made the Earth visible. This psalm teaches that law and order are essential for its continued existence.

Ha-yōm, yōm sh'lishi ba-shabos,

הַיּוֹם יוֹם שְׁלִישִׁי בַּשַּׁבָּת,

    Today is the third day of the Sabbath,*

shebō ho-yu hal'viyim

שֶׁבּוֹ הָיוּ הַלְוִיִּם

   ōm'rim b'vays hamikdosh:

אוֹמְרִים בְּבֵית הַמִּקְדָּשׁ:

    on which the Levites would recite in the Holy Temple:

MIZMŌR l'osof,

מִזְמוֹר לְאָסָף,

    A psalm of Assaf.

Elōhim nitzov ba-adas Ayl,

אֱלֹהִים נִצָּב בַּעֲדַת אֵל,

    God stands in the Divine assembly,

---

deeds, justifies those glorious titles.

עַל־מוּת — *Like children.* This can be read as one word — עֲלָמוֹת, "youth," or as two words — עַל מוּת, "beyond death." That is, God will guide us like a father caring for his young, and will continue to guide us in the World to Come.

הַיּוֹם יוֹם שְׁלִישִׁי — *Today is the third day.* On the third day, God caused the dry land to become

visible and fit for habitation. He did so in order that man follow the Torah's laws and deal justly with other people. Therefore Psalm 82, which has as its theme the maintenance of equity and justice, a prerequisite for the continued existence of the world that was revealed on the third day, was chosen as that day's song. But this message is not limited only to courts.

b'kerev elōhim yishpōt.   בְּקֶרֶב אֱלֹהִים יִשְׁפֹּט.

in the midst of judges shall He judge.

Ad mosai tishp'tu ovel,   עַד מָתַי תִּשְׁפְּטוּ עָוֶל,

Until when* will you judge lawlessly

uf'nay r'sho-im tisu, selo.   וּפְנֵי רְשָׁעִים תִּשְׂאוּ סֶלָה.

and favor the presence of the wicked, Selah?

Shiftu dol v'yosōm,   שִׁפְטוּ דָל וְיָתוֹם,

oni vorosh hatz-diku.   עָנִי וָרָשׁ הַצְדִּיקוּ.

Judge the needy and the orphan, vindicate the poor and impoverished.

Pal'tu dal v'evyōn,   פַּלְּטוּ דַל וְאֶבְיוֹן,

miyad r'sho-im hatzilu.   מִיַּד רְשָׁעִים הַצִּילוּ.

Rescue the needy and destitute, from the hand of the wicked deliver them.

Lō yod'u v'lō yovinu,   לֹא יָדְעוּ וְלֹא יָבִינוּ,

They do not know* nor do they understand,

bachashaycho yis-halochu,   בַּחֲשֵׁכָה יִתְהַלָּכוּ,

in darkness they walk;

yimōtu kol mōs'day oretz.   יִמּוֹטוּ כָּל מוֹסְדֵי אָרֶץ.

all foundations of the earth collapse.

Ani omarti elōhim atem,   אֲנִי אָמַרְתִּי אֱלֹהִים אַתֶּם,

uvnay elyōn kulchem.   וּבְנֵי עֶלְיוֹן כֻּלְּכֶם.

I said, "You are angelic, sons of the Most High are you all."

Ochayn k'odom t'musun,   אָכֵן כְּאָדָם תְּמוּתוּן,

But like men you shall die,

uchachad hasorim tipōlu.   וּכְאַחַד הַשָּׂרִים תִּפֹּלוּ.

and like one of the princes you shall fall.

❖ Kumo Elōhim shofto ho-oretz,   ❖ קוּמָה אֱלֹהִים שָׁפְטָה הָאָרֶץ,

Arise, O God, judge the earth,

ki ato sinchal b'chol hagōyim.   כִּי אַתָּה תִנְחַל בְּכָל הַגּוֹיִם.

for You allot the heritage* among all the nations.

IF A MOURNER IS PRESENT, HE RECITES THE MOURNER'S *KADDISH* (PAGE 466).

In his own personal life, every person is a judge, for his opinions and decisions about people can affect their lives in a thousand different ways.

עַד מָתַי — *Until when ...?* The next three verses are addressed directly to judges who fail to carry out their responsibilities.

לֹא יָדְעוּ — *They do not know.* The Psalmist ex-

claims that many judges are unaware of their awesome responsibility; they walk in darkness, blinded by prejudice and selfishness.

כִּי אַתָּה תִנְחַל — *For You allot the heritage.* The Psalmist addresses God: You sought to avoid strife by allotting a fair share to all nations. Now step in to judge the earth and undo man's destructiveness.

FOR WEDNESDAY

■ I remember the Shabbos daily: On the fourth day of Creation Hashem created the sun, moon and stars. We are reminded that they, as well as the rest of Creation, are to be used in the service of Hashem.

Ha-yōm yōm r'vi-i ba-shabos,　　　　　　　הַיּוֹם יוֹם רְבִיעִי בַּשַּׁבָּת,

Today is the fourth day* of the Sabbath,

shebō ho-yu hal'viyim　　　　　　　　　שֶׁבּוֹ הָיוּ הַלְוִיִּם

ōm'rim b'vays hamikdosh:　　　　　　אוֹמְרִים בְּבֵית הַמִּקְדָּשׁ:

on which the Levites would recite in the Holy Temple:

AYL N'KOMŌS Adōnoy,　　　　　　אֵל נְקָמוֹת יהוה,

O God of vengeance, HASHEM;

Ayl n'komōs hōfi-a.　　　　　　　　אֵל נְקָמוֹת הוֹפִיעַ.

O God of vengeance, appear!

Hinosay shōfayt ho-oretz,　　　　　　הִנָּשֵׂא שֹׁפֵט הָאָרֶץ,

Arise, O Judge of the earth,

hoshayv g'mul al gay-im.　　　　　　הָשֵׁב גְּמוּל עַל גֵּאִים.

render recompense to the haughty.

Ad mosai r'sho-im, Adōnoy,　　　　　עַד מָתַי רְשָׁעִים, יהוה,

How long shall the wicked — O HASHEM —

ad mosai r'sho-im ya-alōzu.　　　　　עַד מָתַי רְשָׁעִים יַעֲלֹזוּ.

how long shall the wicked exult?

Yabi-u y'dab'ru osok,　　　　　　　יַבִּיעוּ יְדַבְּרוּ עָתָק,

They speak freely, they utter malicious falsehood,

yisam'ru kol pō-alay o-ven.　　　　יִתְאַמְּרוּ כָּל פֹּעֲלֵי אָוֶן.

they glorify themselves, all workers of iniquity.

Am'cho Adōnoy y'dak'u,　　　　　　עַמְּךָ יהוה יְדַכְּאוּ,

v'nachlos'cho y'anu.　　　　　　　וְנַחֲלָתְךָ יְעַנּוּ.

Your nation, HASHEM, they crush, and they afflict Your heritage.

Almono v'gayr yaharōgu,　　　　　אַלְמָנָה וְגֵר יַהֲרֹגוּ,

visōmim y'ratzaychu.　　　　　　וִיתוֹמִים יְרַצֵּחוּ.

The widow and the stranger they slay, and the orphans they murder.

Va-yōm'ru lō yir-e Yoh,　　　　　וַיֹּאמְרוּ לֹא יִרְאֶה יָּה,

And they say, "God will not see,

הַיּוֹם יוֹם רְבִיעִי — *Today is the fourth day.* On the fourth day, God created the sun, moon, and the stars. But instead of recognizing them as God's servants, man eventually came to regard the luminaries as independent gods that should be worshiped. Because of this idolatry, God showed Himself to be, as Psalm 94 describes Him, the God of vengeance, for despite his almost endless patience and mercy, He does not tolerate evil forever.

v'lō yovin Elōhay ya-akōv.   וְלֹא יָבִין אֱלֹהֵי יַעֲקֹב.

nor will the God of Jacob understand."

Binu bō-arim bo-om   בִּינוּ בֹּעֲרִים בָּעָם,

Understand, you boors among the people;

uchsilim mosai taskilu.   וּכְסִילִים מָתַי תַּשְׂכִּילוּ.

and you fools, when will you gain wisdom?

Hanōta ōzen ha-lō yishmo,   הֲנֹטַע אֹזֶן הֲלֹא יִשְׁמָע,

He Who implants the ear, shall He not hear?

im yōtzayr a-yin ha-lō yabit.   אִם יֹצֵר עַיִן הֲלֹא יַבִּיט.

He Who fashions the eye, shall He not see?

Hayōsayr gōyim ha-lō yōchi-ach,   הֲיֹסֵר גּוֹיִם הֲלֹא יוֹכִיחַ,

He Who chastises nations, shall He not rebuke? —

ham'lamayd odom do-as.   הַמְלַמֵּד אָדָם דָּעַת.

He Who teaches man knowledge.

Adōnoy yōday-a machsh'vōs odom,   יהוה יֹדֵעַ מַחְשְׁבוֹת אָדָם,

ki haymo hovel.   כִּי הֵמָּה הָבֶל.

HASHEM knows the thoughts of man, that they are futile.

Ashray hagever, asher t'yas'renu Yoh,   אַשְׁרֵי הַגֶּבֶר אֲשֶׁר תְּיַסְּרֶנּוּ יָּהּ,

Praiseworthy is the man* whom God disciplines,

u-mitōros'cho s'lam'denu.   וּמִתּוֹרָתְךָ תְלַמְּדֶנּוּ.

and whom You teach from Your Torah.

L'hashkit lō mimay ro,   לְהַשְׁקִיט לוֹ מִימֵי רָע,

To give him rest from the days of evil,

ad yikore lorosho shochas.   עַד יִכָּרֶה לָרָשָׁע שָׁחַת.

until a pit is dug for the wicked.

Ki lō yitōsh Adōnoy amō,   כִּי לֹא יִטֹּשׁ יהוה עַמּוֹ,

For HASHEM will not cast off His people,

v'nachalosō lō ya-azōv.   וְנַחֲלָתוֹ לֹא יַעֲזֹב.

nor will He forsake His heritage.

Ki ad tzedek yoshuv mishpot,   כִּי עַד צֶדֶק יָשׁוּב מִשְׁפָּט,

For justice shall revert to righteousness,

v'acharov kol yishray layv.   וְאַחֲרָיו כָּל יִשְׁרֵי לֵב.

and following it will be all of upright heart.

אַשְׁרֵי הַגֶּבֶר — *Praiseworthy is the man.* The wicked ask why the righteous suffer, if God truly controls everything. The Psalmist answers that God afflicts the righteous only when it is to their benefit: to chastise them, to make them realize the futility of physical pleasures, or to atone for their sins.

Mi yokum li im m'rayim,   מִי יָקוּם לִי עִם מְרֵעִים,
Who will rise up for me against evildoers?

mi yis-yatzayv li im pō-alay o-ven.   מִי יִתְיַצֵּב לִי עִם פְּעֲלֵי אָוֶן.
Who will stand up for me against the workers of iniquity?

Lulay Adōnoy ezroso li,   לוּלֵי יהוה עֶזְרָתָה לִּי,
Had HASHEM not been a help to me,

kim-at shoch'no dumo nafshi.   כִּמְעַט שָׁכְנָה דוּמָה נַפְשִׁי.
my soul would soon have dwelt in silence.

Im omarti moto ragli,   אִם אָמַרְתִּי מָטָה רַגְלִי,
If I said, "My foot falters,"

chasd'cho Adōnoy yisodayni.   חַסְדְּךָ יהוה יִסְעָדֵנִי.
Your kindness, HASHEM, supported me.

B'rōv sar-apai b'kirbi,   בְּרֹב שַׂרְעַפַּי בְּקִרְבִּי,
When my forebodings were abundant within me,

tanchumecho y'sha-ashu nafshi.   תַּנְחוּמֶיךָ יְשַׁעַשְׁעוּ נַפְשִׁי.
Your comforts cheered my soul.

hay'chovr'cho kisay havōs,   הַיְחָבְרְךָ כִּסֵּא הַוּוֹת,
Can the throne of destruction be associated with You? —

yōtzayr omol alay chōk.   יֹצֵר עָמָל עֲלֵי חֹק.
those who fashion evil into a way of life.

Yogōdu al nefesh tzadik,   יָגוֹדּוּ עַל נֶפֶשׁ צַדִּיק,
They join together against the soul of the righteous,

v'dom noki yarshi-u.   וְדָם נָקִי יַרְשִׁיעוּ.
and the blood of the innocent they condemn.

Vai-hi Adōnoy li l'misgov,   וַיְהִי יהוה לִי לְמִשְׂגָּב,
Then HASHEM became a stronghold for me,

Vaylōhai l'tzur machsi.   וֵאלֹהַי לְצוּר מַחְסִי.
and my God, the Rock of my refuge.

Va-yoshev alayhem es ōnom,   וַיָּשֶׁב עֲלֵיהֶם אֶת אוֹנָם,
He turned upon them their own violence,

uvro-osom yatzmisaym,   וּבְרָעָתָם יַצְמִיתֵם,
and with their own evil He will cut them off,

yatzmisaym Adōnoy Elōhaynu.   יַצְמִיתֵם יהוה אֱלֹהֵינוּ.
HASHEM, our God, will cut them off.

❖ L'chu n'ran'no Ladōnoy,   ❖ לְכוּ נְרַנְּנָה לַיהוה,
Come — let us sing to HASHEM,

nori-o l'tzur yishaynu.   נָרִיעָה לְצוּר יִשְׁעֵנוּ.

let us call out to the Rock of our salvation.

N'kad'mo fonov b'sōdo,   נְקַדְּמָה פָנָיו בְּתוֹדָה,

Let us greet Him with thanksgiving,

bizmirōs nori-a lō.   בִּזְמִרוֹת נָרִיעַ לוֹ.

with praiseful songs let us call out to Him.

Ki Ayl godōl Adōnoy,   כִּי אֵל גָּדוֹל יהוה,

For a great God is HASHEM,

u-melech godōl al kol elōhim: וּמֶלֶךְ גָּדוֹל עַל כָּל אֱלֹהִים.

and a great King above all heavenly powers.

IF A MOURNER IS PRESENT, HE RECITES THE MOURNER'S *KADDISH* (PAGE 466).

FOR THURSDAY

■ I remember the Shabbos daily: On the fifth day of Creation Hashem created an exciting variety of birds and fish, adding color to our world. If only man would appreciate the Divine origin of nature

Ha-yōm yōm chami-shi ba-shabos,   הַיּוֹם יוֹם חֲמִישִׁי בַּשַּׁבָּת,

Today is the fifth day of the Sabbath,

shebō ho-yu hal'viyim   שֶׁבּוֹ הָיוּ הַלְוִיִּם

ōm'rim b'vays hamikdosh: אוֹמְרִים בְּבֵית הַמִּקְדָּשׁ:

on which the Levites would recite in the Holy Temple:

LAM'NATZAYACH al hagitis l'osof.   לַמְנַצֵּחַ עַל הַגִּתִּית לְאָסָף.

For the Conductor, upon the gittis, by Assaf.

Harninu Laylōhim u-zaynu,   הַרְנִינוּ לֵאלֹהִים עוּזֵּנוּ,

Sing joyously to the God of our might,

hori-u Laylōhay ya-akōv.   הָרִיעוּ לֵאלֹהֵי יַעֲקֹב.

call out to the God of Jacob.

S'u zimro us-nu sōf,   שְׂאוּ זִמְרָה וּתְנוּ תֹף,

kinōr no-im im novel.   כִּנּוֹר נָעִים עִם נָבֶל.

Raise a song and sound the drum, the sweet harp with the lyre.

Tik-u vachōdesh shōfor,   תִּקְעוּ בַחֹדֶשׁ שׁוֹפָר,

Blow the shofar at the moon's renewal,*

הַיּוֹם יוֹם חֲמִישִׁי — *Today is the fifth day.* On the fifth day of Creation, God made the birds and the fish, which bring joy to the world. When people observe the vast variety of colorful birds and fish, they are awed by the tremendous scope of God's creative ability, and they are stirred to praise Him with songs such as Psalm 81.

תִּקְעוּ בַחֹדֶשׁ שׁוֹפָר — *Blow the shofar at the moon's renewal.* The moon's renewal is a poetic term for the first day of the lunar month, when the moon becomes visible again. This verse refers to Rosh Hashanah, which occurs on the first day of Tishrei and is the day when the *shofar* is blown.

bakese l'yōm chagaynu.　　בַּכֶּסֶה לְיוֹם חַגֵּנוּ.

at the time appointed for our festive day.

Ki chōk l'yisro-ayl hu,　　כִּי חֹק לְיִשְׂרָאֵל הוּא,

Because it is a decree for Israel,

mishpot Laylōhay ya-akōv.　　מִשְׁפָּט לֵאלֹהֵי יַעֲקֹב.

a judgment day for the God of Jacob.

Aydus bihōsayf somō,　　עֵדוּת בִּיהוֹסֵף שָׂמוֹ,

*He imposed it as a testimony for Joseph,**

b'tzaysō al eretz mitzro-yim,　　בְּצֵאתוֹ עַל אֶרֶץ מִצְרָיִם,

when he went forth over the land of Egypt —

s'fas lō yoda-ti eshmo.　　שְׂפַת לֹא יָדַעְתִּי אֶשְׁמָע.

"I understood a language I never knew!"

Hasirōsi misayvel shichmō,　　הֲסִירוֹתִי מִסֵּבֶל שִׁכְמוֹ,

I removed his shoulder from the burden,

kapov midud ta-avōr'no.　　כַּפָּיו מִדּוּד תַּעֲבֹרְנָה.

his hands let go of the kettle.

Batzoro koroso, vo-achal'tzeko,　　בַּצָּרָה קָרֵאתָ, וָאֲחַלְּצֶךָ,

In distress you called out, and I released you,

e-encho b'sayser ra-am,　　אֶעֶנְךָ בְּסֵתֶר רַעַם,

I answered you with thunder when you hid,

evchon'cho al may m'rivo selo.　　אֶבְחָנְךָ עַל מֵי מְרִיבָה, סֶלָה.

I tested you at the Waters of Strife, Selah.

Sh'ma ami v'o-ido boch,　　שְׁמַע עַמִּי וְאָעִידָה בָּךְ,

Listen, My nation, and I will attest to you;

yisro-ayl im tishma li.　　יִשְׂרָאֵל אִם תִּשְׁמַע לִי.

O Israel, if you would but listen to Me.

Lō yih-ye v'cho ayl zor,　　לֹא יִהְיֶה בְךָ אֵל זָר,

There shall be no strange god within you,

v'lō sishta-chave l'ayl naychor.　　וְלֹא תִשְׁתַּחֲוֶה לְאֵל נֵכָר.

nor shall you bow before an alien god.

Onōchi Adōnoy Elōhecho,　　אָנֹכִי יהוה אֱלֹהֶיךָ,

I am HASHEM, your God,

hama-alcho may-eretz mitzro-yim,　　הַמַּעַלְךָ מֵאֶרֶץ מִצְרָיִם,

Who elevated you from the land of Egypt,

עֵדוּת בִּיהוֹסֵף שָׂמוֹ — *He imposed it as a testimony for Joseph.* This verse is based on Joseph's life. The Talmud teaches that Joseph was released from prison and appointed viceroy of Egypt on Rosh Hashanah. In honor of that event, God ordained the *mitzvah* of *shofar* on Rosh Hashanah as a *testimony* of Joseph's freedom.

harchev picho vo-amalayhu.   הַרְחֶב פִּיךָ וַאֲמַלְאֵהוּ.

open wide your mouth* and I will fill it.

V'lō shoma ami l'kōli,   וְלֹא שָׁמַע עַמִּי לְקוֹלִי,

But My people did not heed My voice

v'yisro-ayl lō ovo li.   וְיִשְׂרָאֵל לֹא אָבָה לִי.

and Israel did not desire Me.

Vo-ashal'chayhu b'shrirus libom,   וָאֲשַׁלְּחֵהוּ בִּשְׁרִירוּת לִבָּם,

So I let them follow their heart's fantasies,

yayl'chu b'mō-atzōsayhem.   יֵלְכוּ בְּמוֹעֲצוֹתֵיהֶם.

they follow their own counsels.

Lu ami shōmay-a li,   לוּ עַמִּי שֹׁמֵעַ לִי,

If only My people would heed Me,

yisro-ayl bidrochai y'halaychu.   יִשְׂרָאֵל בִּדְרָכַי יְהַלֵּכוּ.

if Israel would walk in My ways.

Kimat ō-y'vayhem achni-a,   כִּמְעַט אוֹיְבֵיהֶם אַכְנִיעַ,

In an instant I would subdue their foes,

v'al tzorayhem oshiv yodi: וְעַל צָרֵיהֶם אָשִׁיב יָדִי.

and against their tormentors turn My hand.

M'sanay Adōnoy y'chachashu lō,   מְשַׂנְאֵי יהוה יְכַחֲשׁוּ לוֹ,

Those who hate HASHEM lie to Him —

vihi itom l'ōlom.   וִיהִי עִתָּם לְעוֹלָם.

so their destiny is eternal.

❖ Va-ya-achilayhu maychaylev chito,   ❖ וַיַּאֲכִילֵהוּ מֵחֵלֶב חִטָּה,

But He would feed him with the cream of the wheat,

u-mitzur d'vash asbi-eko.   וּמִצּוּר דְּבַשׁ אַשְׂבִּיעֶךָ.

and with honey from a rock sate you.

IF A MOURNER IS PRESENT, HE RECITES THE MOURNER'S *KADDISH* (PAGE 466).

FOR FRIDAY

■ I remember the Shabbos daily: On the sixth day, at the completion of Creation, Hashem is described as being in His full grandeur, and "dressing" Himself like a person adorned in special Sabbath clothing.

Ha-yōm yōm shishi ba-shabos,   הַיּוֹם יוֹם שִׁשִּׁי בַּשַּׁבָּת,

Today is the sixth day* of the Sabbath,

הַרְחֶב פִּיךָ — *Open wide your mouth,* with requests, and I will fulfill them. God urges Israel to ask all that its heart desires. By asking God for *everything* that he needs, a person demonstrates his faith that God's power and generosity know no bounds.

הַיּוֹם יוֹם שִׁשִּׁי — *Today is the sixth day.* Psalm 93 was designated as the song of Friday, when the footsteps of the Sabbath begin to be heard, because it describes God in His full grandeur and power as He was when He completed the six days of Creation.

shebō ho-yu hal'viyim שֶׁבּוֹ הָיוּ הַלְוִיִּם

ōm'rim b'vays hamikdosh: אוֹמְרִים בְּבֵית הַמִּקְדָּשׁ:

on which the Levites would recite in the Holy Temple:

ADŌNOY MOLOCH gay-us lovaysh יהוה מָלָךְ, גֵּאוּת לָבֵשׁ,

HASHEM will have reigned, He will have donned grandeur;*

lovaysh Adōnoy ōz hisazor, לָבֵשׁ יהוה עֹז הִתְאַזָּר,

HASHEM will have donned might and girded Himself;

af tikōn tayvayl bal timōt. אַף תִּכּוֹן תֵּבֵל בַּל תִּמּוֹט.

He even made the world firm so that it should not falter.

Nochōn kis-acho may-oz נָכוֹן כִּסְאֲךָ מֵאָז,

Your throne was established from of old,

may-ōlom oto. מֵעוֹלָם אָתָּה.

eternal are You.

Nos'u n'horōs, Adōnoy, נָשְׂאוּ נְהָרוֹת יהוה,

Like rivers they raised, O HASHEM,

nos'u n'horōs kōlom, נָשְׂאוּ נְהָרוֹת קוֹלָם,

like rivers they raised their voice;

yis-u n'horōs doch'yom. יִשְׂאוּ נְהָרוֹת דָּכְיָם.

like rivers they shall raise their destructiveness.

Mikōlōs ma-yim rabim מִקֹּלוֹת מַיִם רַבִּים,

More than the roars of many waters,

adirim mishb'ray yom, אַדִּירִים מִשְׁבְּרֵי יָם,

mightier than the waves of the sea —

adir bamorōm Adōnoy. אַדִּיר בַּמָּרוֹם יהוה.

HASHEM is mighty on high.

✥ Aydōsecho ne-emnu m'ōd ✥ עֵדֹתֶיךָ נֶאֶמְנוּ מְאֹד

Your testimonies are exceedingly trustworthy about

l'vays'cho no-avo kōdesh, לְבֵיתְךָ נָאֲוָה קֹדֶשׁ,

Your House, the Sacred Dwelling —

Adōnoy l'ōrech yomim. יהוה לְאֹרֶךְ יָמִים.

O HASHEM, may it be for lengthy days.

IF A MOURNER IS PRESENT, HE RECITES THE MOURNER'S *KADDISH* (PAGE 466).

גֵּאוּת לָבֵשׁ — *He will have donned grandeur.* God dons grandeur. This is similar to a person donning a garment; our comprehension of him is guided by the contours and quality of the garment, but the garment is hardly his essence. No matter how much of God's great- ness we think we understand, our puny intellect grasps but the minutest fraction of His infinite greatness. He does us the favor of allowing mankind this degree of perception so that we can aspire to the privilege of praising Him.

FOR THE SABBATH

■ While the Shabbos day is not mentioned in the body of this psalm, the psalm speaks of the faith in Hashem — in the face of evil — that sustained our people through the various exiles and that enables us to excitedly anticipate the "day of everlasting Sabbath."

Ha-yōm yōm shabas kōdesh,

הַיּוֹם יוֹם שַׁבַּת קֹדֶשׁ

Today is the Holy Sabbath day,

shebō ho-yu hal'viyim ōm'rim
  b'vays hamikdosh:

שֶׁבּוֹ הָיוּ הַלְוִיִּם אוֹמְרִים
בְּבֵית הַמִּקְדָּשׁ:

on which the Levites would sing in the Holy Temple:

MIZMŌR shir l'yōm ha-shabos.

מִזְמוֹר שִׁיר לְיוֹם הַשַּׁבָּת.

A psalm, a song for the Sabbath day.*

Tōv l'hōdōs Ladōnoy,
  ulzamayr l'shimcho elyōn.

טוֹב לְהֹדוֹת לַיהוה,
וּלְזַמֵּר לְשִׁמְךָ עֶלְיוֹן.

It is good to thank HASHEM and to sing praise to Your Name, O Exalted One;

L'hagid babōker chasdecho,

לְהַגִּיד בַּבֹּקֶר חַסְדֶּךָ,

to relate Your kindness in the dawn

ve-emunos'cho balaylōs.

וֶאֱמוּנָתְךָ בַּלֵּילוֹת.

and Your faith in the nights.

Alay osōr va-alay no-vel,
  alay higo-yōn b'chinōr.

עֲלֵי עָשׂוֹר וַעֲלֵי נָבֶל,
עֲלֵי הִגָּיוֹן בְּכִנּוֹר.

Upon ten-stringed instrument and lyre, with singing accompanied by a harp.

Ki simachtani Adōnoy b'fo-olecho,

כִּי שִׂמַּחְתַּנִי יהוה בְּפָעֳלֶךָ,

For You have gladdened me, HASHEM, with Your deeds;

b'ma-asay yodecho aranayn.

בְּמַעֲשֵׂי יָדֶיךָ אֲרַנֵּן.

at the works of Your Hands I sing glad song.

Ma god'lu ma-asecho Adōnoy,
  m'ōd om'ku machsh'vōsecho.

מַה גָּדְלוּ מַעֲשֶׂיךָ יהוה,
מְאֹד עָמְקוּ מַחְשְׁבֹתֶיךָ.

How great are Your deeds, HASHEM; exceedingly profound are Your thoughts.

Ish ba-ar lō yaydo,
  uchsil lō yovin es zōs.

אִישׁ בַּעַר לֹא יֵדָע,
וּכְסִיל לֹא יָבִין אֶת זֹאת.

A boor cannot know, nor can a fool understand this:

Bifrō-ach r'sho-im k'mō aysev,

בִּפְרֹחַ רְשָׁעִים כְּמוֹ עֵשֶׂב,

When the wicked bloom like grass

va-yotzitzu kol pō-alay ō-ven,

וַיָּצִיצוּ כָּל פֹּעֲלֵי אָוֶן,

and all the doers of iniquity blossom —

מִזְמוֹר שִׁיר לְיוֹם הַשַּׁבָּת — *A psalm, a song for the*   99-100 above.
Sabbath day. Psalm 92 is discussed on pages

l'hi-shom'dom aday ad.   לְהִשָּׁמְדָם עֲדֵי עַד.
it is to destroy them till eternity.

V'ato morōm l'ōlom Adōnoy.   וְאַתָּה מָרוֹם לְעֹלָם יהוה.
But You remain exalted forever, HASHEM.

Ki hinay ō-y'vecho, Adōnoy,   כִּי הִנֵּה אֹיְבֶיךָ יהוה,
For behold! — Your enemies, HASHEM,

ki hinay ō-y'vecho, yōvaydu,   כִּי הִנֵּה אֹיְבֶיךָ יֹאבֵדוּ,
for behold! — Your enemies shall perish,

yispor'du kol pō-alay ō-ven.   יִתְפָּרְדוּ כָּל פֹּעֲלֵי אָוֶן.
dispersed shall be all doers of iniquity.

Vatorem kir-aym karni,   וַתָּרֶם כִּרְאֵים קַרְנִי,
As exalted as a re'eim's shall be my pride,

balōsi b'shemen ra-anon.   בַּלֹּתִי בְּשֶׁמֶן רַעֲנָן.
I will be saturated with ever-fresh oil.

Vatabayt ayni b'shuroy,   וַתַּבֵּט עֵינִי בְּשׁוּרָי,
My eyes will see my vigilant foes;

bakomim olai m'ray-im,   בַּקָּמִים עָלַי מְרֵעִים,
when those who would harm me rise up against me,

tishma-no oznoy.   תִּשְׁמַעְנָה אָזְנָי.
my ears will hear their doom.

❖ Tzadik katomor yifroch,   צַדִּיק כַּתָּמָר יִפְרָח,
A righteous man will flourish like a date palm,

k'erez bal'vonōn yisge.   כְּאֶרֶז בַּלְּבָנוֹן יִשְׂגֶּה.
like a cedar in the Lebanon he will grow tall.

Sh'sulim b'vays Adōnoy,   שְׁתוּלִים בְּבֵית יהוה,
Planted in the House of HASHEM,

b'chatzrōs Elōhaynu yaf-richu.   בְּחַצְרוֹת אֱלֹהֵינוּ יַפְרִיחוּ.
in the Courtyards of our God they will flourish.

Ōd y'nuvun b'sayvo,   עוֹד יְנוּבוּן בְּשֵׂיבָה,
They will still be fruitful in old age,

d'shaynim v'ra-ananim yih-yu.   דְּשֵׁנִים וְרַעֲנַנִּים יִהְיוּ.
vigorous and fresh they will be —

L'hagid ki yoshor Adōnoy,   לְהַגִּיד כִּי יָשָׁר יהוה,
to declare that HASHEM is just,

tzuri v'lō avloso bō.   צוּרִי וְלֹא עַוְלָתָה בּוֹ.
my Rock in Whom there is no wrong.

IF A MOURNER IS PRESENT, HE RECITES THE MOURNER'S *KADDISH* (PAGE 466).

FROM *ROSH CHODESH* ELUL THROUGH SHEMINI ATZERES CONTINUE BELOW.
ON *ROSH CHODESH* CONTINUE ON PAGE 490.
ON CHANUKAH SOME CONGREGATIONS RECITE PSALM 30 (PAGE 282).
MANY CONGREGATIONS CONCLUDE THE SERVICE WITH *ADON OLAM* (PAGE 151).

■ *Rosh Chodesh* Elul, forty days after the incident of the Golden Calf, was the third time Moses ascended Mt. Sinai, and forty days later, on Yom Kippur, he brought with him the message of God's forgiveness. Every year we relive this momentous chapter in our history, highlighting the special opportunity for repentance and forgiveness by reciting this psalm, which contains allusions to the holidays of Rosh Hashanah, Yom Kippur, and Succos.

FROM *ROSH CHODESH* ELUL THROUGH SHEMINI ATZERES, THE FOLLOWING PSALM IS RECITED.

L'DOVID, Adōnoy ōri v'yish-i   לְדָוִד, יהוה אוֹרִי וְיִשְׁעִי,
mimi iro,   מִמִּי אִירָא,
Of David; HASHEM is my light and my salvation, whom shall I fear?

Adōnoy mo-ōz cha-yai, mimi efchod.   יהוה מָעוֹז חַיַּי, מִמִּי אֶפְחָד.
HASHEM is my life's strength, whom shall I dread?

Bikrōv olai m'ray-im   בִּקְרֹב עָלַי מְרֵעִים
When evildoers approach me

le-echōl es b'sori,   לֶאֱכֹל אֶת בְּשָׂרִי,
to devour my flesh,

tzorai v'ō-y'vai li,   צָרַי וְאֹיְבַי לִי,
my tormentors and my foes against me —

haymo kosh'lu v'nofolu.   הֵמָּה כָּשְׁלוּ וְנָפָלוּ.
it is they who stumble and fall.

Im tachane olai machane,   אִם תַּחֲנֶה עָלַי מַחֲנֶה,
lō yiro libi,   לֹא יִירָא לִבִּי,
Though an army would besiege me, my heart would not fear;

im tokum olai milchomo,   אִם תָּקוּם עָלַי מִלְחָמָה,
b'zōs ani vōtay-ach.   בְּזֹאת אֲנִי בוֹטֵחַ.
though war would arise against me, in this I trust.

Achas sho-alti may-ays Adōnoy,   אַחַת שָׁאַלְתִּי מֵאֵת יהוה,
ōsoh avakaysh,   אוֹתָהּ אֲבַקֵּשׁ,
One thing I asked of HASHEM, that shall I seek:

shivti b'vays Adōnoy kol y'may cha-yai,   שִׁבְתִּי בְּבֵית יהוה כָּל יְמֵי חַיַּי,
that I dwell in the House of HASHEM all the days of my life;

la-chazōs b'nō-am Adōnoy,   לַחֲזוֹת בְּנֹעַם יהוה,
ulvakayr b'haycholō.   וּלְבַקֵּר בְּהֵיכָלוֹ.
to behold the sweetness of HASHEM and to contemplate in His Sanctuary.

Ki yitzp'nayni b'suko b'yōm ro-o,   כִּי יִצְפְּנֵנִי בְּסֻכֹּה בְּיוֹם רָעָה,
Indeed, He will hide me in His shelter on the day of evil;

yastirayni b'sayser oholō,   יַסְתִּירֵנִי בְּסֵתֶר אָהֳלוֹ,
He will conceal me in the concealment of His Tent,

b'tzur y'rōm'mayni.   בְּצוּר יְרוֹמְמֵנִי.
He will lift me upon a rock.

V'ato yorum rōshi   וְעַתָּה יָרוּם רֹאשִׁי
al ō-y'vai s'vivōsai,   עַל אֹיְבַי סְבִיבוֹתַי,
Now my head is raised above my enemies around me,

v'ezb'cho v'oholō zivchay s'ru-o,   וְאֶזְבְּחָה בְאָהֳלוֹ זִבְחֵי תְרוּעָה,
and in His Tent I will slaughter offerings accompanied by joyous song;

oshiro va-azam'ro Ladōnoy.   אָשִׁירָה וַאֲזַמְּרָה לַיהוה.
I will sing and make music to HASHEM.

Sh'ma Adōnoy kōli ekro,   שְׁמַע יהוה קוֹלִי אֶקְרָא,
HASHEM, hear my voice when I call,

v'chonayni va-anayni.   וְחָנֵּנִי וַעֲנֵנִי.
and be gracious toward me and answer me.

L'cho omar libi bak'shu fonoy,   לְךָ אָמַר לִבִּי בַּקְּשׁוּ פָנָי,
In Your behalf, my heart has said, "Seek My Presence";

es ponecho Adōnoy avakaysh.   אֶת פָּנֶיךָ יהוה אֲבַקֵּשׁ.
Your Presence, HASHEM, do I seek.

Al tastayr ponecho mimeni,   אַל תַּסְתֵּר פָּנֶיךָ מִמֶּנִּי,
Conceal not Your Presence from me,

al tat b'af avdecho,   אַל תַּט בְּאַף עַבְדֶּךָ,
repel not Your servant in anger.

ezrosi ho-yiso,   עֶזְרָתִי הָיִיתָ,
You have been my Helper,

al tit'shayni v'al ta-azvayni,   אַל תִּטְּשֵׁנִי וְאַל תַּעַזְבֵנִי,
Elōhay yish-i.   אֱלֹהֵי יִשְׁעִי.
abandon me not, forsake me not, O God of my salvation.

Ki ovi v'imi azovuni,   כִּי אָבִי וְאִמִּי עֲזָבוּנִי,
Though my father and mother have forsaken me,

Vadōnoy ya-asfayni.   וַיהוה יַאַסְפֵנִי.
HASHEM will gather me in.

Hōrayni Adōnoy dar-kecho,   הוֹרֵנִי יהוה דַּרְכֶּךָ,
Teach me Your way, HASHEM,

un-chayni b'ōrach mi-shōr,   וּנְחֵנִי בְּאֹרַח מִישׁוֹר,
and lead me on the path of integrity,

l'ma-an shōr'roy.

because of my watchful foes.

לְמַעַן שׁוֹרְרָי.

Al tit'nayni b'nefesh tzoroy,

Deliver me not to the wishes of my tormentors,

אַל תִּתְּנֵנִי בְּנֶפֶשׁ צָרָי,

ki komu vi

ayday sheker vifay-ach chomos.

for there have arisen against me false witnesses who breathe violence.

כִּי קָמוּ בִי

עֵדֵי שֶׁקֶר, וִיפֵחַ חָמָס.

❖ Lulay he-emanti

Had I not trusted

lir-ōs b'tuv Adōnoy b'eretz cha-yim.

that I would see the goodness of HASHEM in the land of life!

❖ לוּלֵא הֶאֱמַנְתִּי

לִרְאוֹת בְּטוּב יהוה בְּאֶרֶץ חַיִּים.

Kavay el Adōnoy,

Hope to HASHEM,

קַוֵּה אֶל יהוה,

chazak v'ya-amaytz libecho,

strengthen yourself and He will give your heart courage;

חֲזַק וְיַאֲמֵץ לִבֶּךָ,

v'kavay el Adōnoy.

and hope to HASHEM.

וְקַוֵּה אֶל יהוה.

IF A MOURNER IS PRESENT, HE RECITES THE MOURNER'S *KADDISH* (PAGE 466).

■ Psalm 104: My soul bursts forth blessing Hashem; His greatness and His glory, His goodness and His wisdom are manifested in the brilliance of the world He created.

MANY CONGREGATIONS RECITE PSALM 104 ON *ROSH CHODESH*:

BOR'CHI NAFSHI es Adōnoy,

Bless HASHEM, O my soul.*

בָּרְכִי נַפְשִׁי אֶת יהוה,

Adōnoy Elōhai godalto m'ōd,

HASHEM, my God, You are very great;

יהוה אֱלֹהַי גָּדַלְתָּ מְּאֹד,

hōd v'hodor lovoshto.

You have donned majesty and splendor;

הוֹד וְהָדָר לָבָשְׁתָּ.

Ōte ōr kasalmo,

covering with light as with a garment,

עֹטֶה אוֹר כַּשַּׂלְמָה,

nōte shoma-yim kairi-o.

stretching out the heavens like a curtain.

נוֹטֶה שָׁמַיִם כַּיְרִיעָה.

בָּרְכִי נַפְשִׁי אֶת ה׳ — *Bless Hashem, O my soul.* Psalm 104 is recited on *Rosh Chodesh* because the Psalmist alludes to the new moon in the verse: "He made the moon for Festivals."

These words are not merely a casual allusion to the new month. Rather, they set the tone of this entire composition, whose main theme is God's complete mastery over every aspect of Creation. Throughout the monthly lunar cycle, the size of the moon visibly waxes and wanes,

to demonstrate dramatically that God has total mastery over His creations. No other natural phenomenon conveys this message as vividly and forcefully as the moon's cycle. Thus, the theme of the New Moon complements the theme of this entire hymn of praise to the Master of Creation.

By calling upon his soul to bless God, the Psalmist suggests that the human soul is God's great gift to man and, in effect, thanks God for

Ham'kore vama-yim aliyōsov,
הַמְקָרֶה בַמַּיִם עֲלִיּוֹתָיו,
He Who roofs His upper chambers with water;

hasom ovim r'chuvō,
הַשָּׂם עָבִים רְכוּבוֹ,
He Who makes clouds His chariot;

ham'halaych al kanfay ru-ach.
הַמְהַלֵּךְ עַל כַּנְפֵי רוּחַ.
He Who walks on winged wind.

Ōse mal-ochov ruchōs,
עֹשֶׂה מַלְאָכָיו רוּחוֹת,
He makes the winds His messengers,

m'shor'sov aysh lōhayt.
מְשָׁרְתָיו אֵשׁ לֹהֵט.
the flaming fire His attendants.

Yosad eretz al m'chōneho,
יָסַד אֶרֶץ עַל מְכוֹנֶיהָ,
He established the earth upon its foundations,

bal timōt ōlom vo-ed.
בַּל תִּמּוֹט עוֹלָם וָעֶד.
that it falter not forever and ever.

T'hōm kal'vush kisisō,
תְּהוֹם כַּלְּבוּשׁ כִּסִּיתוֹ,
The watery deep, as with a garment You covered it;

al horim ya-amdu mo-yim.
עַל הָרִים יַעַמְדוּ מָיִם.
upon the mountains, water would stand.

Min ga-aros'cho y'nusun,
מִן גַּעֲרָתְךָ יְנוּסוּן,
From Your rebuke they flee,

min kōl ra-amcho yaychofayzun.
מִן קוֹל רַעַמְךָ יֵחָפֵזוּן.
from the sound of Your thunder they rush away.

Ya-alu horim, yayr'du v'ko-ōs,
יַעֲלוּ הָרִים, יֵרְדוּ בְקָעוֹת,
They ascend mountains, they descend to valleys,

el m'kōm ze yosadto lohem.
אֶל מְקוֹם זֶה יָסַדְתָּ לָהֶם.
to the special place You founded for them.

G'vul samto bal ya-avōrun,
גְּבוּל שַׂמְתָּ בַּל יַעֲבֹרוּן,
You set a boundary they cannot overstep,

bal y'shuvun l'chasōs ho-oretz.
בַּל יְשׁוּבוּן לְכַסּוֹת הָאָרֶץ.
they cannot return to cover the earth.

Ham'shalay-ach ma-yonim
ban'cholim,
הַמְשַׁלֵּחַ מַעְיָנִים
בַּנְּחָלִים,
He sends the springs into the streams,*

bayn horim y'halaychun.
בֵּין הָרִים יְהַלֵּכוּן.
they flow between the mountains.

---

the ability to reason, articulate, and rise to
spiritual heights.

הַמְשַׁלֵּחַ מַעְיָנִים בַּנְּחָלִים — *He sends the springs
into the streams.* The Psalmist describes poeti-

Yashku kol chaisō sodoy,
They water every beast of the field,

יַשְׁקוּ כָּל חַיְתוֹ שָׂדָי,

yishb'ru f'ro-im tz'mo-om.
they quench the wild creatures' thirst.

יִשְׁבְּרוּ פְרָאִים צְמָאָם.

Alayhem ōf ha-shoma-yim yishkōn,
Near them dwell the heaven's birds,

עֲלֵיהֶם עוֹף הַשָּׁמַיִם יִשְׁכּוֹן,

mibayn ofo-yim yit'nu kōl.
from among the branches they give forth song.

מִבֵּין עֳפָאִים יִתְּנוּ קוֹל.

Mashke horim may-aliyōsov,
He waters the mountains from His upper chambers,

מַשְׁקֶה הָרִים מֵעֲלִיּוֹתָיו,

mip'ri ma-asecho tisba ho-oretz.
from the fruit of Your works the earth is sated.

מִפְּרִי מַעֲשֶׂיךָ תִּשְׂבַּע הָאָרֶץ.

Matzmi-ach chotzir lab'haymo,
He causes vegetation to sprout for the cattle,

מַצְמִיחַ חָצִיר לַבְּהֵמָה,

v'aysev la-avōdas ho-odom,
and plants through man's labor,*

וְעֵשֶׂב לַעֲבֹדַת הָאָדָם,

l'hōtzi lechem min ho-oretz.
to bring forth bread from the earth,

לְהוֹצִיא לֶחֶם מִן הָאָרֶץ.

V'ya-yin y'samach l'vav enōsh,
and wine that gladdens man's heart,*

וְיַיִן יְשַׂמַּח לְבַב אֱנוֹשׁ,

l'hatzhil ponim mishomen,
to make the face glow from oil,

לְהַצְהִיל פָּנִים מִשָּׁמֶן,

v'lechem l'vav enōsh yis-od.
and bread that sustains the heart of man.

וְלֶחֶם לְבַב אֱנוֹשׁ יִסְעָד.

Yisb'u atzay Adōnoy,
The trees of HASHEM are sated,

יִשְׂבְּעוּ עֲצֵי יהוה,

arzay l'vonōn asher noto.
the cedars of Lebanon that He has planted;

אַרְזֵי לְבָנוֹן אֲשֶׁר נָטָע.

Asher shom tziporim y'kanaynu,
there where the birds nest,

אֲשֶׁר שָׁם צִפֳּרִים יְקַנֵּנוּ,

chasido b'rōshim baysoh.
the chassidah with its home among cypresses;

חֲסִידָה בְּרוֹשִׁים בֵּיתָהּ.

---

cally how God instituted a natural system whereby the earth would be watered to provide for people and vegetation.

חָצִיר לַבְּהֵמָה וְעֵשֶׂב לַעֲבֹדַת הָאָדָם — *Vegetation ... for the cattle, and plants through man's labor.* For animals, which cannot engage in agriculture, God causes vegetation to sprout. Man, however, must labor to earn his daily bread. Before

he can partake of food, he must first sow, reap, thresh, knead, and bake his bread.

וְיַיִן יְשַׂמַּח לְבַב אֱנוֹשׁ — *And wine that gladdens man's heart.* God creates the grapes from which wine is pressed. When drunk in sensible amounts, wine gladdens the heart and drives away melancholy. It heightens the intellect and even prepares the mind for prophecy.

Horim hag'vōhim la-y'aylim,	הָרִים הַגְּבֹהִים לַיְּעֵלִים,
high mountains for the wild goats, *	
s'lo-im machse lash'fanim.	סְלָעִים מַחְסֶה לַשְׁפַנִּים.
rocks as refuge for the gophers.	
Oso yoray-ach l'mō-adim,	עָשָׂה יָרֵחַ לְמוֹעֲדִים,
He made the moon for Festivals, *	
shemesh yoda m'vō-ō.	שֶׁמֶשׁ יָדַע מְבוֹאוֹ.
the sun knows its destination.	
Toshes chōshech vihi loylo,	תָּשֶׁת חֹשֶׁךְ וִיהִי לָיְלָה,
You make darkness and it is night,	
bō sirmōs kol chaisō yo-ar.	בּוֹ תִרְמֹשׂ כָּל חַיְתוֹ יָעַר.
in which every forest beast stirs.	
Hak'firim shō-agim latoref,	הַכְּפִירִים שֹׁאֲגִים לַטָּרֶף,
The young lions roar after their prey,	
ulvakaysh may-Ayl ochlom.	וּלְבַקֵּשׁ מֵאֵל אָכְלָם.
and to seek their food from God.	
Tizrach hashemesh yay-osayfun,	תִּזְרַח הַשֶּׁמֶשׁ יֵאָסֵפוּן,
The sun rises and they are gathered in,	
v'el m'ōnōsom yirbotzun.	וְאֶל מְעוֹנֹתָם יִרְבָּצוּן.
and in their dens they crouch.	
Yaytzay odom l'fo-olō,	יֵצֵא אָדָם לְפָעֳלוֹ,
Man goes forth to his work,	
v'la-avōdosō aday orev.	וְלַעֲבֹדָתוֹ עֲדֵי עָרֶב.
and to his labor until evening.	
Mo rabu ma-asecho Adōnoy,	מָה רַבּוּ מַעֲשֶׂיךָ יהוה,
How abundant are Your works, HASHEM;	
kulom b'chochmo osiso,	כֻּלָּם בְּחָכְמָה עָשִׂיתָ,
with wisdom You made them all, *	
mol'o ho-oretz kinyonecho.	מָלְאָה הָאָרֶץ קִנְיָנֶךָ.
the earth is full of Your possessions. *	

הָרִים הַגְּבֹהִים לַיְּעֵלִים — *High mountains for the wild goats.* At first glance, the remote and barren mountains appear to serve no purpose; but in fact they were created to provide a habitat for the wild mountain goats.

Contrary to the theory that species survived only by adapting themselves to hostile environments, the Psalmist says that God created the setting to suit the needs of the species.

עָשָׂה יָרֵחַ לְמוֹעֲדִים — *He made the moon for Festivals*, i.e., the moon and its cycles were made

to facilitate the lunar calendar, upon which the Torah bases the dating of the Festivals.

כֻּלָּם בְּחָכְמָה עָשִׂיתָ — *With wisdom You made them all.* No creature evolved by chance; every one was designed by God in His *wisdom* and demonstrates His omnipotence.

מָלְאָה הָאָרֶץ קִנְיָנֶךָ — *The earth is full of Your possessions.* God did not allow a single inch to go to waste. Every spot is full of wondrous creations which testify to God's absolute mastery over the world.

Ze ha-yom godōl urchav yodo-yim,   זֶה הַיָּם, גָּדוֹל וּרְחַב יָדָיִם,
Behold this sea — great and of broad measure;

shom remes v'ayn mispor,   שָׁם רֶמֶשׂ וְאֵין מִסְפָּר,
there are creeping things without number,

cha-yōs k'tanōs im g'dōlōs.   חַיּוֹת קְטַנּוֹת עִם גְּדֹלוֹת.
small creatures and great ones.

Shom oniyōs y'halaychun,   שָׁם אֳנִיּוֹת יְהַלֵּכוּן,
There ships travel,

livyoson ze yotzarto l'sachek bō.   לִוְיָתָן זֶה יָצַרְתָּ לְשַׂחֶק בּוֹ.
this Leviathan You fashioned to sport with.

Kulom aylecho y'sabayrun,   כֻּלָּם אֵלֶיךָ יְשַׂבֵּרוּן,
All of them look to You with hope,

losays ochlom b'itō.   לָתֵת אָכְלָם בְּעִתּוֹ.
to provide their food in its [proper] time.

Titayn lohem, yilkōtun,   תִּתֵּן לָהֶם, יִלְקֹטוּן,
You give to them, they gather it in;

tiftach yod'cho, yisb'un tōv.   תִּפְתַּח יָדְךָ, יִשְׂבְּעוּן טוֹב.
You open Your hand, they are sated with good.

Tastir ponecho yibohaylun,   תַּסְתִּיר פָּנֶיךָ יִבָּהֵלוּן,
When You hide Your face, they are dismayed;

tōsayf ruchom yigvo-un   תֹּסֵף רוּחָם יִגְוָעוּן,
when You retrieve their spirit, they perish

v'el aforom y'shuvun.   וְאֶל עֲפָרָם יְשׁוּבוּן.
and to their dust they return.

T'shalach ruchacho yiboray-un   תְּשַׁלַּח רוּחֲךָ יִבָּרֵאוּן,
When You send forth Your breath, they are created,

uschadaysh p'nay adomo.   וּתְחַדֵּשׁ פְּנֵי אֲדָמָה.
and You renew the surface of the earth.

Y'hi ch'vōd Adōnoy l'ōlom,   יְהִי כְבוֹד יהוה לְעוֹלָם,
May the glory of HASHEM endure forever,

yismach Adōnoy b'ma-asov.   יִשְׂמַח יהוה בְּמַעֲשָׂיו.
let HASHEM rejoice in His works.

Hamabit lo-oretz vatir-od,   הַמַּבִּיט לָאָרֶץ וַתִּרְעָד,
He looks toward the earth and it trembles,

yiga behorim v'ye-eshonu.   יִגַּע בֶּהָרִים וְיֶעֱשָׁנוּ.
He touches the mountains and they smoke.

Oshiro Ladōnoy b'cha-yoy,
אָשִׁירָה לַיהוה בְּחַיָּי,
I will sing to HASHEM *while I live,*

azam'ro Laylōhai b'ōdi.
אֲזַמְּרָה לֵאלֹהַי בְּעוֹדִי.
I will sing praises to my God while I endure.

Ye-erav olov sichi
יֶעֱרַב עָלָיו שִׂיחִי,
May my words be sweet to Him —

onōchi esmach Badōnoy.
אָנֹכִי אֶשְׂמַח בַּיהוה.
I will rejoice in HASHEM.

Yitamu chato-im min ho-oretz
יִתַּמּוּ חַטָּאִים מִן הָאָרֶץ,
Sinners will cease from the earth,

ursho-im ōd aynom,
וּרְשָׁעִים עוֹד אֵינָם,
and the wicked will be no more —

bor'chi nafshi es Adōnoy,
בָּרְכִי נַפְשִׁי אֶת יהוה,
Bless HASHEM, *O my soul.*

hal'luyoh.
הַלְלוּיָהּ.
Praise God!

IF A MOURNER IS PRESENT, HE RECITES THE MOURNER'S *KADDISH* (PAGE 466).

◆§ DAYTIME KIDDUSH – SABBATH AND FESTIVALS ◈◆

ON THE SABBATH, INCLUDING FESTIVALS THAT FALL ON THE SABBATH, *KIDDUSH* BEGINS HERE:

V'SHOM'RU v'nay yisro-ayl
וְשָׁמְרוּ בְנֵי יִשְׂרָאֵל

es ha-shabos,
אֶת הַשַּׁבָּת,
And the Children of Israel observed the Sabbath,

la-asōs es ha-shabos l'dōrōsom
לַעֲשׂוֹת אֶת הַשַּׁבָּת לְדֹרֹתָם
to make the Sabbath for their generations

b'ris ōlom.
בְּרִית עוֹלָם.
an eternal covenant.

Bayni u-vayn b'nay yisro-ayl
בֵּינִי וּבֵין בְּנֵי יִשְׂרָאֵל
Between Me and the Children of Israel

ōs hi l'ōlom,
אוֹת הִיא לְעֹלָם,
it is a sign forever,

ki shayshes yomim oso Adōnoy
כִּי שֵׁשֶׁת יָמִים עָשָׂה יהוה
that in six days did HASHEM *make*

◆§ **The Daytime Kiddush**

The morning *Kiddush* was introduced by the Sages, and its status is subordinate to that of the Sabbath Eve *Kiddush* which is Scriptural in origin. Therefore, the morning *Kiddush* is euphemistically called "the great *Kiddush*."

Originally, it consisted only of the blessing over wine. Scriptural verses were added over the centuries. However, not all the verses are said in all congregations. In some, only the last fragment of the last verse (*Al Kayn*) is recited.

es ha-shoma-yim v'es ho-oretz,
אֶת הַשָּׁמַיִם וְאֶת הָאָרֶץ,
the heaven and the earth,

u-va-yōm hash'vi-i shovas va-yinofash.
וּבַיּוֹם הַשְּׁבִיעִי שָׁבַת וַיִּנָּפַשׁ.
and on the seventh day He rested and was refreshed.

ZOCHÔR es yōm ha-shabos
l'kad'shō.
זָכוֹר אֶת יוֹם הַשַּׁבָּת
לְקַדְּשׁוֹ.
Always remember* the Sabbath day to hallow it.

Shayshes yomim ta-avōd
שֵׁשֶׁת יָמִים תַּעֲבֹד
For six days you may labor

v'osiso kol m'lachtecho.
וְעָשִׂיתָ כָּל מְלַאכְתֶּךָ.
and do all your work.

v'yōm hash'vi-i
וְיוֹם הַשְּׁבִיעִי
But the seventh day

shabos Ladōnoy Elōhecho,
שַׁבָּת לַיהוה אֱלֹהֶיךָ,
is the Sabbath for HASHEM, Your God;

lō sa-ase chol m'locho,
לֹא תַעֲשֶׂה כָל מְלָאכָה,
you may do no work —

ato u-vincho u-vitecho
אַתָּה וּבִנְךָ וּבִתֶּךָ
you, your son and your daughter,

avd'cho va-amos'cho uvhemtecho,
עַבְדְּךָ וַאֲמָתְךָ וּבְהֶמְתֶּךָ,
your slave and your maidservant, your animal,

v'gayr'cho asher bish-orecho.
וְגֵרְךָ אֲשֶׁר בִּשְׁעָרֶיךָ.
and the stranger who is in your gates.

Ki shayshes yomim oso Adōnoy
כִּי שֵׁשֶׁת יָמִים עָשָׂה יהוה
For in six days did HASHEM make

es ha-shoma-yim v'es ho-oretz
אֶת הַשָּׁמַיִם וְאֶת הָאָרֶץ
the heaven and the earth,

es ha-yom v'es kol asher bom,
אֶת הַיָּם וְאֶת כָּל אֲשֶׁר בָּם,
the sea and all that is in them

va-yonach ba-yōm hash'vi-i,
וַיָּנַח בַּיּוֹם הַשְּׁבִיעִי,
and He rested on the seventh day;

al kayn bayrach Adōnoy
עַל כֵּן בֵּרַךְ יהוה
therefore HASHEM blessed

es yōm hashabos vai-kad'shayhu.
אֶת יוֹם הַשַּׁבָּת וַיְקַדְּשֵׁהוּ.
the Sabbath day and sanctified it.

זָכוֹר — *Always remember*. This passage the fourth commandment of the Ten Commandments, implies the positive commandments of the day.

ON FESTIVALS:

Ayle mō-aday Adōnoy   אֵלֶּה מוֹעֲדֵי יהוה

These are the appointed Festivals of HASHEM,

mikro-ay kōdesh   מִקְרָאֵי קֹדֶשׁ

holy convocations,

asher tik'ru ōsom b'mō-adom.   אֲשֶׁר תִּקְרְאוּ אֹתָם בְּמוֹעֲדָם.

which you are to proclaim in their appointed times.

Vaidabayr mōshe   וַיְדַבֵּר מֹשֶׁה

And Moses declared

es mō-aday Adōnoy   אֶת מֹעֲדֵי יהוה,

HASHEM's appointed Festivals

el b'nay yisro-ayl.   אֶל בְּנֵי יִשְׂרָאֵל.

to the Children of Israel.

Savri moronon   סַבְרִי מָרָנָן

v'rabonon v'rabōsai: וְרַבָּנָן וְרַבּוֹתַי:

By your leave, my masters, rabbis and teachers:

BORUCH ato Adōnoy   בָּרוּךְ אַתָּה יהוה

Blessed are You, HASHEM,

Elōhaynu melech ho-ōlom,   אֱלֹהֵינוּ מֶלֶךְ הָעוֹלָם,

our God, King of the universe,

bōray p'ri hagofen.   בּוֹרֵא פְּרִי הַגָּפֶן.

Who creates the fruit of the vine.

THOSE WHO HEAR THE BLESSING CONGREGATION RESPOND: Omayn — אָמֵן

ON SUCCOS, IN THE SUCCAH, ADD:

BORUCH ato Adōnoy   בָּרוּךְ אַתָּה יהוה

Blessed are You, HASHEM,

Elōhaynu melech ho-ōlom,   אֱלֹהֵינוּ מֶלֶךְ הָעוֹלָם,

our God, King of the universe,

asher kid'shonu b'mitzvōsov   אֲשֶׁר קִדְּשָׁנוּ בְּמִצְוֹתָיו

Who has sanctified us with His commandments

v'tzivonu layshayv basuko.   וְצִוָּנוּ לֵישֵׁב בַּסֻּכָּה.

and had commanded us to dwell in the succah.

THOSE WHO HEAR THE BLESSING RESPOND: Omayn — אָמֵן

THE BLESSINGS RECITED BEFORE AND AFTER THE MEAL
ARE FOUND ON PAGES 173–192 ABOVE.

The Shabbos Afternoon Service

৵৽ Shabbos Minchah

৵৽ Mutual Love

The *Minchah* of Shabbos represents the apex and ideal relationship that man, individually and collectively, can have with his Maker. It extols the close bonds of love and friendship between God and His people. The beautiful theme of "I am for my Beloved and my Beloved is for me" (*Song of Songs* 6:3) is understood by the Sages to be the expression of mutual praise and affection between God and Israel. It is the theme that is highlighted at the beginning of the central blessing of *Minchah Shemoneh Esrei*: "You are One and Your Name is One and who is like Your people Israel, one nation on earth."

Kedushas Levi notes that this beautiful theme is found often. The Torah calls the *Yom Tov* of liberation from Egypt "The Festival of Matzos" (*Deuteronomy* 16:16), and we call it Pesach / Passover. God assigns a name that extols our observance of the holiday, namely the baking of matzos and the special care to avoid any *chametz*; the Jewish people give it a name that extols God's kindness when He "passed over" the Jewish homes in Egypt and spared Israel's firstborn. In addition, the Talmud informs us that God dons *tefillin,* as it were. Israel's *tefillin* contains the *Shema*, declaring God's Oneness and uniqueness — what is contained in Hashem's *tefillin*? The Talmud responds, "Who is like Your people Israel, one nation on earth" (*II Samuel* 7:23). As we praise Him, so He praises us (*Berachos* 6a).

৵৽ Shabbos Brings Inner Peace

At first glance, the popular greeting of "Shabbat Shalom" is difficult to understand. Where is the conflict that calls for the blessing of *shalom*, peace? The Sages suggest that all week long there is a conflict between the body and the soul. The former wants to express itself not only in areas that are entirely its domain, but to go further and dominate the soul. Similarly the soul yearns for spirituality all week long, even in mundane activities and temporal activity. On Shabbos, through Torah, *zemiros* and tasty foods, ideally one is able to harmonize the balance and struggle that is raging within us.

Shabbos afternoon is most special as we have had the affect and influence of Shabbos for almost twenty-four hours. Having lived the synthesis of bodily rest and spiritual nourishment, we can appreciate the teaching that Shabbos is ¹/₆₀th of the world to come (*Berachos* 57b). Just at this time, we can appreciate the prophecy of *Zechariah* 14:9, that when the final redemption comes, all the world will recognize the Oneness of God, meaning that there are no contradictions in His behavior. The Shabbos *Minchah* alludes to the long-awaited day when

history will attain God's goal of perfection. Thus this *Shemoneh Esrei* directs our focus not only to the holiness of the Shabbos day, but to the spiritual bliss of the future.

✦§ Rest That Pleases God

In each of the four *Shemoneh Esreis* of Shabbos we beseech God רְצֵה בִמְנוּחָתֵנוּ, *be pleased with our rest*. At first glance this seems difficult. One could well understand asking God to find favor with something we do. Every *mitzvah* has its own variables that could disqualify the outcome or the action. *Tefillin* may be *passul*, or unfit, because some of the letters in the parchment might be rubbed out. A *succah* may be unfit because it does not provide enough shade or because it is situated under a tree. What, however, can go wrong with our rest, that we ask Hashem to be "pleased with our rest"?

The answer might be found in a phrase we recite in the Shabbos *Minchah Shemoneh Esrei*: "Through their [i.e., Israel's] rest they sanctify Your Name." This passage sheds light on what Shabbos rest should be; it must be the sort that would sanctify His Name. Sleeping through the Shabbos and lounging around the house or yard could hardly qualify. Clearly then, for our rest to be considered a sanctification of His Name we have to integrate all that we do with a spirituality that reflects His Name.

The enjoyment of tasty Shabbos food can be enhanced by reminding oneself that one is eating the meal in honor of Shabbos, not only to satisfy our hunger or because it is tempting. The singing of Shabbos *zemiros* serves to help us focus on both the uniqueness of the day, its laws, and the relationship between God and His people. The Torah learning that one is privileged to partake of on Shabbos can connect us to its Source, can help us transcend time, and unite us with our rich heritage, thereby making it possible not only to taste spirituality and sanctity, but to sanctify His Name and to yearn for and anticipate the Shabbos of the future, when all of mankind will appreciate the Shabbos.

⊰{ MINCHAH FOR SABBATH AND FESTIVALS }⊱

■ The alphabetic acrostic of *Ashray* motivates the supplicant to praise God, His Kingship, and His providing the needs of every living creature. The Sages highlight the importance of *Ashray* by declaring that whoever recites this psalm three times daily is directing himself towards meriting a place in the World to Come (*Berachos* 4b).

ASHRAY yōsh'vay vay-secho,

אַשְׁרֵי יוֹשְׁבֵי בֵיתֶךָ,

Praiseworthy* are those who dwell in Your house;

ōd y'hal'lucho selo.

עוֹד יְהַלְלוּךָ סֶּלָה.

may they always praise You, Selah!

Ashray ho-om shekocho lō,

אַשְׁרֵי הָעָם שֶׁכָּכָה לּוֹ,

Praiseworthy is the people for whom this is so,

ashray ho-om she-Adōnoy Elōhov.

אַשְׁרֵי הָעָם שֶׁיהוה אֱלֹהָיו.

praiseworthy is the people whose God is HASHEM.

T'hilo l'dovid,

תְּהִלָּה לְדָוִד,

A psalm of praise by David.

arōmimcho Elōhai hamelech,

אֲרוֹמִמְךָ אֱלוֹהַי הַמֶּלֶךְ,

I will exalt You, my God the King,

va-avor'cho shimcho l'ōlom vo-ed.

וַאֲבָרְכָה שִׁמְךָ לְעוֹלָם וָעֶד.

and I will bless Your Name forever and ever.

B'chol yōm avor'cheko,

בְּכָל יוֹם אֲבָרְכֶךָ,

Every day I will bless You,

va-ahal'lo shimcho l'ōlom vo-ed.

וַאֲהַלְלָה שִׁמְךָ לְעוֹלָם וָעֶד.

and I will laud Your Name forever and ever.

Godōl Adōnoy umhulol m'ōd,

גָּדוֹל יהוה וּמְהֻלָּל מְאֹד,

HASHEM is great and exceedingly lauded,

v'ligdulosō ayn chayker.

וְלִגְדֻלָּתוֹ אֵין חֵקֶר.

and His greatness is beyond investigation.

Dōr l'dōr y'shabach ma-asecho,

דּוֹר לְדוֹר יְשַׁבַּח מַעֲשֶׂיךָ,

Each generation will praise Your deeds to the next,

ugvurōsecho yagidu.

וּגְבוּרֹתֶיךָ יַגִּידוּ.

and of Your mighty deeds they will tell.

⊷§ **Minchah for Sabbath and Festivals**

The climax of the Sabbath is described in Kabbalistic literature as a time when God receives our prayers with favor, and Himself yearns for the Redemption, an aspect of the day that is reflected by the *Minchah* service. After *Ashrei*, which is recited at every *Minchah*, we recite *U'va LeTzion Goeil*, "A re-

deemer shall come to Zion," which confidently anticipates the coming of the Messiah. The Sabbath *Minchah Shemoneh Esrei* speaks of the spiritual bliss that will prevail in that time of perfection and universal recognition of God's sovereignty.

The Torah reading during the Sabbath *Minchah* includes the calling to the Torah of *Ko-*

Hadar k'vōd hōdecho,

הֲדַר כְּבוֹד הוֹדֶךָ,

The splendrous glory of Your power

v'divray nifl'ōsecho osicho.

וְדִבְרֵי נִפְלְאֹתֶיךָ אָשִׂיחָה.

and Your wondrous deeds I shall discuss.

Ve-ezuz nōr'ōsecho yōmayru,

וֶעֱזוּז נוֹרְאֹתֶיךָ יֹאמֵרוּ,

And of Your awesome power they will speak,

ugdulos'cho asap'reno.

וּגְדוּלָּתְךָ אֲסַפְּרֶנָּה.

and Your greatness I shall relate.

Zecher rav tuv'cho yabi-u,

זֵכֶר רַב טוּבְךָ יַבִּיעוּ,

A recollection of Your abundant goodness they will utter

v'tzidkos'cho y'ranaynu.

וְצִדְקָתְךָ יְרַנֵּנוּ.

and of Your righteousness they will sing exultantly.

Chanun v'rachum Adōnoy,

חַנּוּן וְרַחוּם יהוה,

Gracious and merciful is HASHEM,

erech apa-yim ugdol chosed.

אֶרֶךְ אַפַּיִם וּגְדָל חָסֶד.

slow to anger, and great in [bestowing] kindness.

Tōv Adōnoy lakōl,

טוֹב יהוה לַכֹּל,

HASHEM *is good to all,*

v'rachamov al kol ma-asov.

וְרַחֲמָיו עַל כָּל מַעֲשָׂיו.

and His mercies are on all His works.

Yōducho Adōnoy kol ma-asecho,

יוֹדוּךָ יהוה כָּל מַעֲשֶׂיךָ,

All Your works shall thank You, HASHEM,

vachasidecho y'vor'chucho.

וַחֲסִידֶיךָ יְבָרְכוּכָה.

and Your devout ones will bless You.

K'vōd malchus'cho yōmayru,

כְּבוֹד מַלְכוּתְךָ יֹאמֵרוּ,

Of the glory of Your kingdom they will speak,

ugvuros'cho y'dabayru.

וּגְבוּרָתְךָ יְדַבֵּרוּ.

and of Your power they will tell,

L'hōdi-a livnay ho-odom
g'vurōsov,

לְהוֹדִיעַ לִבְנֵי הָאָדָם
גְּבוּרֹתָיו,

to inform human beings of His mighty deeds,

uchvōd hadar malchusō.

וּכְבוֹד הֲדַר מַלְכוּתוֹ.

and the glorious splendor of His kingdom.

---

hen, Levite, and Israelite. The reading is identical to the reading on the following Monday and Thursday. The Torah reading just before the end of the Sabbath symbolizes that we will

take the Torah-imbued spirit of the Sabbath with us into the next week..

אַשְׁרֵי —*Praiseworthy.* This psalm is discussed on pages 30-33 above.

Malchus'cho malchus kol ōlomim,   מַלְכוּתְךָ מַלְכוּת כָּל עֹלָמִים,
Your kingdom is a kingdom spanning all eternities,

u-memshalt'cho b'chol dōr vodōr.   וּמֶמְשַׁלְתְּךָ בְּכָל דּוֹר וָדֹר.
and Your dominion is throughout every generation.

Sōmaych Adōnoy l'chol hanōf'lim,   סוֹמֵךְ יהוה לְכָל הַנֹּפְלִים,
HASHEM supports all the fallen ones

v'zōkayf l'chol hak'fufim.   וְזוֹקֵף לְכָל הַכְּפוּפִים.
and straightens all the bent.

Aynay chōl aylecho y'sabayru,   עֵינֵי כֹל אֵלֶיךָ יְשַׂבֵּרוּ,
The eyes of all look to You with hope

v'ato nōsayn lohem   וְאַתָּה נוֹתֵן לָהֶם
  es ochlom b'itō.   אֶת אָכְלָם בְּעִתּוֹ.
and You give them their food in its proper time.

CONCENTRATE INTENTLY WHILE RECITING THE NEXT VERSE.

Pōsay-ach es yodecho,   פּוֹתֵחַ אֶת יָדֶךָ,
  u-masbi-a l'chol chai rotzōn.   וּמַשְׂבִּיעַ לְכָל חַי רָצוֹן.
You open Your hand, and satisfy the desire of every living thing.

Tzadik Adōnoy b'chol d'rochov,   צַדִּיק יהוה בְּכָל דְּרָכָיו,
Righteous is HASHEM in all His ways

v'chosid b'chol ma-asov.   וְחָסִיד בְּכָל מַעֲשָׂיו.
and magnanimous in all His deeds.

Korōv Adōnoy l'chol kōr'ov,   קָרוֹב יהוה לְכָל קֹרְאָיו,
HASHEM is close to all who call upon Him —

l'chōl asher yikro-uhu ve-emes.   לְכֹל אֲשֶׁר יִקְרָאֻהוּ בֶאֱמֶת.
to all who call upon Him sincerely.

R'tzōn y'ray-ov ya-ase,   רְצוֹן יְרֵאָיו יַעֲשֶׂה,
The will of those who fear Him He will do,

v'es shav-osom yishma v'yōshi-aym.   וְאֶת שַׁוְעָתָם יִשְׁמַע וְיוֹשִׁיעֵם.
and their cry He will hear, and save them.

Shōmayr Adōnoy es kol ōhavov,   שׁוֹמֵר יהוה אֶת כָּל אֹהֲבָיו,
HASHEM protects all who love Him,

v'ays kol hor'sho-im yashmid.   וְאֵת כָּל הָרְשָׁעִים יַשְׁמִיד.
but all the wicked He will destroy.

❖ T'hilas Adōnoy y'daber pi,   ❖ תְּהִלַּת יהוה יְדַבֶּר פִּי,
May my mouth declare the praise of HASHEM

vi-voraych kol bosor shaym kodshō   וִיבָרֵךְ כָּל בָּשָׂר שֵׁם קָדְשׁוֹ
and may all flesh bless His Holy Name

l'ōlom vo-ed.

לְעוֹלָם וָעֶד.

forever and ever.

Va-anachnu n'voraych Yoh,

וַאֲנַחְנוּ נְבָרֵךְ יָהּ,

We will bless God

may-ato v'ad ōlom, hal'luyoh

מֵעַתָּה וְעַד עוֹלָם, הַלְלוּיָהּ.

from this time and forever. Praise God!

■ The recitation of "The Order of *Kedushah*," a central theme of U'vo L'Tziyon, is one of the merits upon which the world continues to endure (*Sotah* 49a).

UVO L'TZIYŌN gō-ayl,

וּבָא לְצִיּוֹן גּוֹאֵל,

"A redeemer shall come to Zion*

ulshovay fesha b'ya-akōv,

וּלְשָׁבֵי פֶשַׁע בְּיַעֲקֹב,

and to those of Jacob who repent from willful sin,"

n'um Adōnoy.

נְאֻם יהוה.

the words of HASHEM.

Va-ani, zōs b'risi ōsom,

וַאֲנִי, זֹאת בְּרִיתִי אוֹתָם,

omar Adōnoy,

אָמַר יהוה,

"And as for Me, this is My covenant* *with them," said* HASHEM,

ruchi asher olecho,

רוּחִי אֲשֶׁר עָלֶיךָ,

"My spirit that is upon you

udvorai asher samti b'ficho,

וּדְבָרַי אֲשֶׁר שַׂמְתִּי בְּפִיךָ,

and My words that I have placed in your mouth

lō yomushu mipicho

לֹא יָמוּשׁוּ מִפִּיךָ

u-mipi zar-acho

וּמִפִּי זַרְעֲךָ

shall not be withdrawn from your mouth, nor from the mouth of your offspring,

u-mipi zera zar-acho,

וּמִפִּי זֶרַע זַרְעֲךָ,

nor from the mouth of your offspring's offspring,"*

omar Adōnoy,

אָמַר יהוה,

said HASHEM,

may-ato v'ad ōlom.

מֵעַתָּה וְעַד עוֹלָם.

"from this moment and forever."

וּבָא לְצִיּוֹן גּוֹאֵל — *A redeemer shall come to Zion.* God pledges that Messiah will come to redeem the city Zion and the people of Israel. Not only those who remained righteous throughout the ordeal of exile will be saved, but even those who have strayed will rejoin the righteous in the glorious future, provided they return to the ways of God.

זֹאת בְּרִיתִי — *This is My covenant.* God affirms that His covenant with Israel will always re-

main in force: that His spirit [of prophecy] and His words [as written in His Torah] will remain with Israel forever.

מִפִּיךָ וּמִפִּי זַרְעֲךָ וּמִפִּי זֶרַע זַרְעֲךָ — *From your mouth, nor from the mouth of your offspring, nor from the mouth of your offspring's offspring.* Three generations are mentioned here. This is a Divine assurance that if a family produces three consecutive generations of profound Torah scholars, the blessing of Torah

❖ וְאַתָּה קָדוֹשׁ,
V'ato kodōsh,

יוֹשֵׁב תְּהִלּוֹת יִשְׂרָאֵל.
yōshayv t'hilōs yisro-ayl.

You are the Holy One, enthroned upon the praises of Israel.*

V'koro ze el ze v'omar:
וְקָרָא זֶה אֶל זֶה וְאָמַר:

And one [angel] will call another and say:

THE ENTIRE CONGREGATION SHOULD RECITE THE FOLLOWING VERSE ALOUD AND IN UNISON.

Kodōsh, kodōsh, kodōsh,
קָדוֹשׁ, קָדוֹשׁ, קָדוֹשׁ,

Adōnoy tz'vo-ōs,
יהוה צְבָאוֹת,

"Holy, holy, holy* is Hashem, Master of Legions,

m'lō chol ho-oretz k'vōdō.
מְלֹא כָל הָאָרֶץ כְּבוֹדוֹ.

the whole world is filled with His glory."

Umkab'lin dayn min dayn v'om'rin:
וּמְקַבְּלִין דֵּין מִן דֵּין וְאָמְרִין:

And they receive permission from one another and say:

Kadish bishmay m'rōmo ilo-o
קַדִּישׁ בִּשְׁמֵי מְרוֹמָא עִלָּאָה

bays sh'chin'tayh;
בֵּית שְׁכִינְתֵּהּ,

"Holy in the most exalted heaven, the abode of His Presence;

kadish al ar-o ōvad g'vurtayh;
קַדִּישׁ עַל אַרְעָא עוֹבַד גְּבוּרְתֵּהּ,

holy on earth, product of His strength;

kadish l'olam ul-ol'may ol'ma-yo,
קַדִּישׁ לְעָלַם וּלְעָלְמֵי עָלְמַיָּא,

Adonoy Tz'vo-ōs,
יהוה צְבָאוֹת,

holy forever and ever is Hashem, Master of Legions —

malyo chol ar-o ziv y'korayh.
מַלְיָא כָל אַרְעָא זִיו יְקָרֵהּ.

the entire world is filled with the radiance of His glory."

Vatiso-ayni ru-ach,
וַתִּשָּׂאֵנִי רוּחַ,

And a wind lifted me;*

vo-eshma acharai kōl ra-ash godōl:
וָאֶשְׁמַע אַחֲרַי קוֹל רַעַשׁ גָּדוֹל:

and I heard behind me the sound of a great noise:

THE ENTIRE CONGREGATION SHOULD RECITE THE FOLLOWING VERSE ALOUD AND IN UNISON.

Boruch k'vōd Adōnoy mim'kōmō.
בָּרוּךְ כְּבוֹד יהוה מִמְּקוֹמוֹ.

"Blessed is the glory of Hashem from His place."

---

knowledge will not be withdrawn from its posterity (*Bava Metzia* 85a). In a broader sense, we see the fulfillment of this blessing in the miracle that Torah greatness has remained with Israel throughout centuries of exile and flight from country to country and from continent to continent.

יוֹשֵׁב תְּהִלּוֹת יִשְׂרָאֵל — *Enthroned upon the praises of Israel.* Although God is praised by myriad angels, He values the praises of Israel above all; as the Talmud teaches (*Chullin* 90b),

the angels are not permitted to sing their praises on High until the Jews sing theirs below.

קָדוֹשׁ — *Holy.* The song of the angels is discussed on page 37 above.

וַתִּשָּׂאֵנִי רוּחַ — *And a wind lifted me.* These words were uttered by the prophet Ezekiel, after he had been commanded to undertake a difficult mission on behalf of the exiled Jew. God sent a wind to lift him and transport him to Babylon, and as he was lifted, Ezekiel heard

Untolasni rucho,　　　　　　　　　　　　　　וּנְטָלַתְנִי רוּחָא,

And a wind lifted me;

v'shim-ays basrai kol zi-a sagi　　　　וְשִׁמְעֵת בַּתְרַי קָל זִיעַ סַגִּיא

and I heard behind me the sound of the powerful movement

dimshab'chin v'om'rin:　　　　　　　　　דִּמְשַׁבְּחִין וְאָמְרִין:

of those who praised saying:

B'rich y'koro Dadōnoy　　　　　　　　　בְּרִיךְ יְקָרָא דַיהוה

"Blessed is the honor of HASHEM

may-asar bays sh'chintayh.　　　　　מֵאֲתַר בֵּית שְׁכִינְתֵּהּ.

from the place of the abode of His Presence."

THE ENTIRE CONGREGATION SHOULD RECITE THE FOLLOWING VERSE ALOUD AND IN UNISON.

Adōnoy yimlōch l'ōlom vo-ed.　　　　**יהוה יִמְלֹךְ לְעֹלָם וָעֶד.**

HASHEM shall reign for all eternity.

Adōnoy malchusayh ko-aym　　　　　יהוה מַלְכוּתֵהּ קָאֵם

HASHEM — His kingdom is established

l'olam ul-ol'may ol'ma-yo.　　　　　לְעָלַם וּלְעָלְמֵי עָלְמַיָּא.

forever and ever.

Adōnoy Elōhay avrohom　　　　　　　יהוה אֱלֹהֵי אַבְרָהָם

yitzchok v'yisro-ayl avōsaynu,　　　יִצְחָק וְיִשְׂרָאֵל אֲבֹתֵינוּ,

HASHEM, God of Abraham, Isaac, and Israel, our forefathers,

shomro zōs l'ōlom,　　　　　　　　　שָׁמְרָה זֹאת לְעוֹלָם,

may You preserve this forever

l'yaytzer machsh'vōs l'vav amecho,　　לְיֵצֶר מַחְשְׁבוֹת לְבַב עַמֶּךָ,

as the realization of the thoughts in Your people's heart,

v'hochayn l'vovom aylecho.　　　　　וְהָכֵן לְבָבָם אֵלֶיךָ.

and may You direct their heart to You.

V'hu rachum, y'chapayr ovōn　　　　וְהוּא רַחוּם, יְכַפֵּר עָוֹן

He, the Merciful One, is forgiving of iniquity

v'lō yashchis,　　　　　　　　　　　וְלֹא יַשְׁחִית,

and does not destroy;

v'hirbo l'hoshiv apō,　　　　　　　　וְהִרְבָּה לְהָשִׁיב אַפּוֹ,

frequently He withdraws His anger,

v'lō yo-ir kol chamosō.　　　　　　　וְלֹא יָעִיר כָּל חֲמָתוֹ.

not arousing His entire rage.

the song of the angels. This suggests that the person who ignores his own convenience in order to serve God can expect to climb spiritual heights beyond his normal capacity.

Ki ato Adōnoy tōv v'saloch,

כִּי אַתָּה אֲדֹנָי טוֹב וְסַלָּח,

For You, my Lord, are good and forgiving,

v'rav chesed l'chol kōr'echo.

וְרַב חֶסֶד לְכָל קֹרְאֶיךָ.

and abundantly kind to all who call upon You.

Tzidkos'cho tzedek l'ōlom,

צִדְקָתְךָ צֶדֶק לְעוֹלָם,

v'sōros'cho emes.

וְתוֹרָתְךָ אֱמֶת.

Your righteousness is righteous forever,* and Your Torah is truth.

Titayn emes l'ya-akōv,

תִּתֵּן אֱמֶת לְיַעֲקֹב,

chesed l'avrohom,

חֶסֶד לְאַבְרָהָם,

Grant truth to Jacob, kindness to Abraham,

asher nishbato la-avōsaynu

אֲשֶׁר נִשְׁבַּעְתָּ לַאֲבֹתֵינוּ

mimay kedem.

מִימֵי קֶדֶם.

as You swore to our forefathers from ancient times.

Boruch Adōnoy

בָּרוּךְ אֲדֹנָי

yōm yōm ya-amos lonu,

יוֹם יוֹם יַעֲמָס לָנוּ,

Blessed is my Lord, for every single day He burdens us [with blessings],*

ho-Ayl y'shu-osaynu selo.

הָאֵל יְשׁוּעָתֵנוּ סֶלָה.

the God of our salvation, Selah.

Adōnoy Tz'vo-ōs imonu,

יהוה צְבָאוֹת עִמָּנוּ,

HASHEM, Master of Legions, is with us,

misgov lonu Elōhay ya-akōv selo.

מִשְׂגָּב לָנוּ אֱלֹהֵי יַעֲקֹב סֶלָה.

a stronghold for us is the God of Jacob, Selah.

Adōnoy Tz'vo-ōs,

יהוה צְבָאוֹת,

HASHEM, Master of Legions,

ashray odom bōtay-ach boch.

אַשְׁרֵי אָדָם בֹּטֵחַ בָּךְ.

praiseworthy is the man who trusts in You.

Adōnoy hōshi-o,

יהוה הוֹשִׁיעָה,

HASHEM, save!

hamelech ya-ananyu v'yōm kor-aynu.

הַמֶּלֶךְ יַעֲנֵנוּ בְיוֹם קָרְאֵנוּ.

May the King answer us on the day we call.

Boruch hu Elōhaynu

בָּרוּךְ הוּא אֱלֹהֵינוּ

Blessed is He, our God,

צִדְקָתְךָ צֶדֶק לְעוֹלָם — *Your righteousness is righteous forever.* People question the ways of God because they do not see the righteous rewarded nor the wicked punished. But this question is a product of shortsightedness. God's justice is not measured in months or years. His reward lasts forever, so it does not matter if it is de-layed during the temporary stay of our souls in our earth bodies.

יַעֲמָס לָנוּ — *He burdens us [with blessings].* God gives us the daily responsibility to perform countless commandments because He desires to load us with blessings.

sheb'ro-onu lichvōdō,
שֶׁבְּרָאָנוּ לִכְבוֹדוֹ,
Who created us for His glory,

v'hivdilonu min hatō-im,
וְהִבְדִּילָנוּ מִן הַתּוֹעִים,
separated us from those who stray,

v'nosan lonu tōras emes,
וְנָתַן לָנוּ תּוֹרַת אֱמֶת,
gave us the Torah of truth

v'cha-yay ōlom nota b'sōchaynu.
וְחַיֵּי עוֹלָם נָטַע בְּתוֹכֵנוּ.
and implanted eternal life within us.

Hu yiftach libaynu b'sōroso
הוּא יִפְתַּח לִבֵּנוּ בְּתוֹרָתוֹ,
May He open our heart* through His Torah

v'yosaym b'libaynu ahavosō v'yir-oso,
וְיָשֵׂם בְּלִבֵּנוּ אַהֲבָתוֹ וְיִרְאָתוֹ
and imbue our heart with love and awe of Him

v'la-asōs r'tzōnō
וְלַעֲשׂוֹת רְצוֹנוֹ
and that we may do His will

ul-ovdō b'layvov sholaym,
וּלְעָבְדוֹ בְּלֵבָב שָׁלֵם,
and serve Him wholeheartedly,

l'ma-an lō niga lorik,
לְמַעַן לֹא נִיגַע לָרִיק,
so that we do not struggle in vain

v'lō naylayd labeholo.
וְלֹא נֵלֵד לַבֶּהָלָה.
nor produce for futility.

Y'hi rotzōn mil'fonecho
יְהִי רָצוֹן מִלְּפָנֶיךָ
May it be Your will,

Adōnoy Elōhaynu
יהוה אֱלֹהֵינוּ
Vaylōhay avōsaynu,
וֵאלֹהֵי אֲבוֹתֵינוּ,
HASHEM, our God and the God of our forefathers,

shenishmōr chukecho bo-ōlom ha-ze,
שֶׁנִּשְׁמֹר חֻקֶּיךָ בָּעוֹלָם הַזֶּה,
that we observe Your decrees in this world,

v'nizke v'nichye v'nir-e
וְנִזְכֶּה וְנִחְיֶה וְנִרְאֶה
and merit that we live and see

v'nirash tōvo uvrocho
וְנִירַשׁ טוֹבָה וּבְרָכָה
and inherit goodness and blessing

lishnay y'mōs hamoshi-ach,
לִשְׁנֵי יְמוֹת הַמָּשִׁיחַ,
in the years of Messianic times

הוּא יִפְתַּח לִבֵּנוּ — *May He open our heart.* This verse contains a major principle of the nature of Torah study. Though it is a rigorous and demanding intellectual pursuit, it cannot be mastered without pure motives, faith and love of God, and Divine help. If someone studies Torah only for the sake of the prestige it will give him to outwit less accomplished scholars, he will not succeed: His struggle for knowledge will be in vain. Or if someone has attained Torah knowledge in a commendable way, but later discards his faith, he will have lost the merit of his study — and his efforts will have proved to be futile.

ulcha-yay ho-ōlom habo.

וּלְחַיֵּי הָעוֹלָם הַבָּא.

and for the life of the World to Come.

L'ma-an y'zamercho chovōd v'lō yidōm,

לְמַעַן יְזַמֶּרְךָ כָבוֹד וְלֹא יִדֹּם,

So that my soul might sing to You and not be stilled,

Adōnoy Elōhai l'ōlom ōdeko.

יהוה אֱלֹהַי לְעוֹלָם אוֹדֶךָּ.

HASHEM, my God, forever will I thank You.

Boruch hagever
asher yivtach Badōnoy,

בָּרוּךְ הַגֶּבֶר
אֲשֶׁר יִבְטַח בַּיהוה,

Blessed is the man who trusts in HASHEM,

v'ho-yo Adōnoy mivtachō.

וְהָיָה יהוה מִבְטַחוֹ.

then HASHEM will be his security.

Bitchu Vadōnoy aday ad,

בִּטְחוּ בַיהוה עֲדֵי עַד,

Trust in HASHEM forever,

ki b'Yoh Adōnoy tzur ōlomim.

כִּי בְּיָהּ יהוה צוּר עוֹלָמִים.

for in God, HASHEM, is the strength of the worlds.

❖ v'yivt'chu v'cho yōd'ay sh'mecho,

❖ וְיִבְטְחוּ בְךָ יוֹדְעֵי שְׁמֶךָ,

Those knowing Your Name will trust in You,

ki lō ozavto dōr'shecho Adōnoy.

כִּי לֹא עָזַבְתָּ דֹרְשֶׁיךָ, יהוה.

and You forsake not those Who seek You, HASHEM.

Adōnoy chofaytz l'ma-an tzidkō,

יהוה חָפֵץ לְמַעַן צִדְקוֹ,

HASHEM desired, for the sake of its [Israel's] righteousness,

yagdil tōro v'yadir.

יַגְדִּיל תּוֹרָה וְיַאְדִּיר.

that the Torah be made great and glorious.

THE *CHAZZAN* RECITES *HALF-KADDISH.*
(Congregational responses are indicated by parentheses.)

יִתְגַּדַּל וְיִתְקַדַּשׁ שְׁמֵהּ רַבָּא. (אָמֵן—Omayn). בְּעָלְמָא דִּי בְרָא
כִרְעוּתֵהּ. וְיַמְלִיךְ מַלְכוּתֵהּ, בְּחַיֵּיכוֹן וּבְיוֹמֵיכוֹן וּבְחַיֵּי דְכָל
בֵּית יִשְׂרָאֵל, בַּעֲגָלָא וּבִזְמַן קָרִיב. וְאִמְרוּ: אָמֵן.
(אָמֵן. יְהֵא שְׁמֵהּ רַבָּא מְבָרַךְ לְעָלַם וּלְעָלְמֵי עָלְמַיָּא.)
(Omayn. Y'hay sh'mayh rabo m'vorach l'olam ul-ol'may ol'ma-yo.)
יְהֵא שְׁמֵהּ רַבָּא מְבָרַךְ לְעָלַם וּלְעָלְמֵי עָלְמַיָּא. יִתְבָּרַךְ וְיִשְׁתַּבַּח
וְיִתְפָּאַר וְיִתְרוֹמַם וְיִתְנַשֵּׂא וְיִתְהַדָּר וְיִתְעַלֶּה וְיִתְהַלָּל שְׁמֵהּ
דְּקֻדְשָׁא בְּרִיךְ הוּא (B'rich hu—בְּרִיךְ הוּא). °לְעֵלָּא מִן כָּל
[substitute לְעֵלָּא לְעֵלָּא מִכָּל°—from Rosh Hashanah to Yom Kippur
בִּרְכָתָא וְשִׁירָתָא תֻּשְׁבְּחָתָא וְנֶחֱמָתָא, דַּאֲמִירָן בְּעָלְמָא. וְאִמְרוּ: אָמֵן.
(אָמֵן—Omayn).

ON EVERY SABBATH CONTINUE BELOW; ON A FESTIVAL THAT FALLS ON A WEEKDAY, *SHEMONEH ESREI* (P. 675) IS RECITED AT THIS POINT.

CONGREGATION, THEN *CHAZZAN* :

VA-ANI s'filosi l'cho Adōnoy,　　　　וַאֲנִי תְפִלָּתִי לְךָ יהוה

　ays ratzon,　　　　　　　　　　　　עֵת רָצוֹן,

　　　As for me, may my prayer to You, HASHEM, be at an opportune time;

Elōhim b'rov chasdecho,　　　　　　אֱלֹהִים בְּרׇב חַסְדֶּךָ,

　　　　O God, in Your abundant kindness,

anayni be-emes yish-echo.　　　　עֲנֵנִי בֶּאֱמֶת יִשְׁעֶךָ.

　　　answer me with the truth of Your salvation.

⊰ REMOVAL OF THE TORAH FROM THE ARK ⊱

ALL RISE AND REMAIN STANDING UNTIL THE TORAH IS PLACED ON THE *BIMAH*.

■ After completing the morning prayer service in which man communicates with Hashem, by extolling His greatness, I prepare myself for the Torah reading — where Hashem communicates with us.

THE ARK IS OPENED. BEFORE THE TORAH IS REMOVED THE CONGREGATION RECITES:

VAIHI BINSŌ-A ho-oron　　　　וַיְהִי בִּנְסֹעַ הָאָרֹן

　va-yōmer mōshe,　　　　　　　　וַיֹּאמֶר מֹשֶׁה,

　　　When the Ark would travel, Moses would say,

kumo Adōnoy v'yofutzu ōy'vecho　　קוּמָה יהוה וְיָפֻצוּ אֹיְבֶיךָ

　　　"Arise, HASHEM, and let Your foes be scattered,

v'yonusu m'san-echo miponecho.　　וְיָנֻסוּ מְשַׂנְאֶיךָ מִפָּנֶיךָ.

　　　let those who hate You flee from You."

Ki mitziyōn taytzay sōro,　　　　כִּי מִצִּיּוֹן תֵּצֵא תוֹרָה,

　　　For from Zion the Torah will come forth

udvar Adōnoy mirusholo-yim.　　וּדְבַר יהוה מִירוּשָׁלָיִם.

　　　and the word of HASHEM from Jerusalem.

Boruch shenosan tōro　　　　　בָּרוּךְ שֶׁנָּתַן תּוֹרָה

　l'amō yisro-ayl bikdushosō.　　לְעַמּוֹ יִשְׂרָאֵל בִּקְדֻשָּׁתוֹ.

　Blessed is He Who gave the Torah to His people Israel in His holiness.

■ I pray that Hashem crown His Third Temple with mercy and love, and I declare my absolute faith in Him and His Torah.

B'RICH SH'MAYH d'moray ol'mo,　בְּרִיךְ שְׁמֵהּ דְּמָרֵא עָלְמָא,

　Blessed is the Name of the Master of the universe,

b'rich kisroch v'asroch.　　　　בְּרִיךְ כִּתְרָךְ וְאַתְרָךְ.

　　　blessed is Your crown and Your place.

Y'hay r'usoch im amoch yisro-ayl
l'olam,
יְהֵא רְעוּתָךְ עִם עַמָּךְ יִשְׂרָאֵל לְעָלַם,

May Your favor remain with Your people Israel forever;

u-furkan y'minoch achazay l'amoch
וּפֻרְקַן יְמִינָךְ אַחֲזֵי לְעַמָּךְ

may You display the salvation of Your right hand to Your people

b'vays makd'shoch
בְּבֵית מַקְדְּשָׁךְ,

in Your Holy Temple,

ul-amtuyay lono mituv n'hōroch,
וּלְאַמְטוּיֵי לָנָא מִטּוּב נְהוֹרָךְ,

and to benefit us with the goodness of Your luminescence

ulkabayl tz'lōsono b'rachamin.
וּלְקַבֵּל צְלוֹתָנָא בְּרַחֲמִין.

and to accept our prayers with mercy.

Y'hay ra-avo kodomoch
יְהֵא רַעֲוָא קֳדָמָךְ,

May it be Your will

d'sōrich lon cha-yin b'tivuso,
דְּתוֹרִיךְ לָן חַיִּין בְּטִיבוּתָא,

that You extend our lives with goodness

v'lehevay ano f'kido
b'gō tzadika-yo,
וְלֶהֱוֵי אֲנָא פְּקִידָא בְּגוֹ צַדִּיקַיָּא,

and that I be numbered among the righteous;

l'mircham olai
לְמִרְחַם עֲלַי

that You have mercy on me

ulmintar yosi v'yas kol di li,
וּלְמִנְטַר יָתִי וְיָת כָּל דִּי לִי,

and protect me, all that is mine

v'di l'amoch yisro-ayl.
וְדִי לְעַמָּךְ יִשְׂרָאֵל.

and that is Your people Israel's.

Ant hu zon l'chōlo,
umfarnays l'chōlo,
אַנְתְּ הוּא זָן לְכֹלָּא, וּמְפַרְנֵס לְכֹלָּא,

It is You Who nourishes all and sustains all;

ant hu shalit al kōlo,
אַנְתְּ הוּא שַׁלִּיט עַל כֹּלָּא,

it is You Who controls everything;

ant hu d'shalit al malcha-yo,
u-malchuso diloch hi.
אַנְתְּ הוּא דְּשַׁלִּיט עַל מַלְכַיָּא, וּמַלְכוּתָא דִּילָךְ הִיא.

it is You Who controls kings, and kingship is Yours.

Ano avdo d'kudsho b'rich hu,
אֲנָא עַבְדָּא דְּקֻדְשָׁא בְּרִיךְ הוּא,

I am a servant of the Holy One, Blessed is He,

d'sogidno kamayh
דְּסָגִידְנָא קַמֵּהּ

u-mikamo dikar ōraisayh
וּמִקַּמָּא דִּיקַר אוֹרַיְתֵהּ

and I prostrate myself before Him and before the glory of His Torah

b'chol idon v'idon. בְּכָל עִדָּן וְעִדָּן.

at all times.

Lo al enosh rochitzno, לָא עַל אֱנָשׁ רָחִיצְנָא,

Not in any man do I put trust,

v'lo al bar elohin somichno, וְלָא עַל בַּר אֱלָהִין סָמִיכְנָא,

nor on any angel do I rely —

elo be-Eloho dishma-yo, אֶלָּא בֶּאֱלָהָא דִשְׁמַיָּא,

only on the God of heaven —

d'hu Eloho k'shōt, דְּהוּא אֱלָהָא קְשׁוֹט,

Who is the God of truth,

v'ōraisayh k'shōt, unvi-ōhi k'shōt, וְאוֹרָיְתֵהּ קְשׁוֹט, וּנְבִיאוֹהִי קְשׁוֹט,

Whose Torah is truth, and whose prophets are true,

u-masgay l'mebad tav-von ukshōt. וּמַסְגֵּא לְמֶעְבַּד טַבְוָן וּקְשׁוֹט.

and Who acts liberally with kindness and truth.

Bayh ano rochitz, בֵּהּ אֲנָא רָחִיץ,

In Him do I trust,

v'lishmayh kadisho yakiro וְלִשְׁמֵהּ קַדִּישָׁא יַקִּירָא

ano aymar tushb'chon. אֲנָא אֵמַר תֻּשְׁבְּחָן.

and to His glorious and holy Name do I declare praises.

Y'hay ra-avo kodomoch, יְהֵא רַעֲוָא קֳדָמָךְ,

May it be Your will

d'siftach libo-i b'ōraiso, דְּתִפְתַּח לִבָּאִי בְּאוֹרָיְתָא,

that You open my heart to the Torah,

v'sashlim mish-alin d'libo-i, וְתַשְׁלִים מִשְׁאֲלִין דְּלִבָּאִי,

and that You fulfill the wishes of my heart

v'libo d'chol amoch yisro-ayl, וְלִבָּא דְּכָל עַמָּךְ יִשְׂרָאֵל,

and the heart of Your entire people Israel,

l'tav ulcha-yin v'lishlom. Omayn. לְטַב וּלְחַיִּין וְלִשְׁלָם. אָמֵן.

for good, for life, and for peace. Amen.

THE TORAH SCROLL IS REMOVED FROM THE ARK AND PRESENTED TO THE *CHAZZAN*, WHO
ACCEPTS IT IN HIS RIGHT ARM. THE *CHAZZAN* TURNS TO THE ARK, BOWS WHILE RAISING THE
TORAH, AND RECITES:

Gad'lu Ladōnoy iti גַּדְּלוּ לַיהוה אִתִּי

unrōm'mo sh'mō yachdov. וּנְרוֹמְמָה שְׁמוֹ יַחְדָּו.

Declare the greatness of HASHEM with me, and let us exalt His Name together.

THE *CHAZZAN* TURNS TO HIS RIGHT AND CARRIES THE TORAH TO THE *BIMAH*. THE TORAH IS
KISSED AS IT IS CARRIED TO THE *BIMAH* AND BACK TO THE ARK. THE CONGREGATION RESPONDS:

L'CHO Adōnoy hag'dulo לְךָ יהוה הַגְּדֻלָּה

Yours, HASHEM, is the greatness,

v'hag'vuro v'hatif-eres
v'hanaytzach v'hahōd,

וְהַגְּבוּרָה וְהַתִּפְאֶרֶת
וְהַנֵּצַח וְהַהוֹד,

the strength, the splendor, the triumph, and the glory;

ki chōl ba-shoma-yim u-vo-oretz,

כִּי כֹל בַּשָּׁמַיִם וּבָאָרֶץ,

even everything in heaven and earth;

l'cho Adōnoy hamamlocho

לְךָ יהוה הַמַּמְלָכָה

Yours, HASHEM, is the kingdom,

v'hamisnasay l'chōl l'rōsh.

וְהַמִּתְנַשֵּׂא לְכֹל לְרֹאשׁ.

and the sovereignty over every leader.

Rōm'mu Adōnoy Elōhaynu,

רוֹמְמוּ יהוה אֱלֹהֵינוּ,

Exalt HASHEM, our God,

v'hishta-chavu lahadōm raglov,
kodōsh hu.

וְהִשְׁתַּחֲווּ לַהֲדֹם רַגְלָיו,
קָדוֹשׁ הוּא.

and bow at His footstool; He is Holy!

Rōm'mu Adōnoy Elōhaynu,

רוֹמְמוּ יהוה אֱלֹהֵינוּ,

Exalt HASHEM, our God,

v'hishta-chavu l'har kodshō,

וְהִשְׁתַּחֲווּ לְהַר קָדְשׁוֹ,

and bow to His holy mountain;

ki kodōsh Adōnoy Elōhaynu.

כִּי קָדוֹשׁ יהוה אֱלֹהֵינוּ.

for holy is HASHEM, our God.

AV horachamim,
hu y'rachaym am amusim,

אַב הָרַחֲמִים,
הוּא יְרַחֵם עַם עֲמוּסִים,

May the Father of compassion have mercy on the people that is borne by Him,

v'yizkōr b'ris aysonim,

וְיִזְכֹּר בְּרִית אֵיתָנִים,

and may He remember the covenant of the spiritually mighty.

v'yatzil nafshōsaynu
min hasho-ōs horo-ōs,

וְיַצִּיל נַפְשׁוֹתֵינוּ
מִן הַשָּׁעוֹת הָרָעוֹת,

May He rescue our souls from the bad times,

v'yig-ar b'yaytzer hora
min han'su-im,

וְיִגְעַר בְּיֵצֶר הָרָע
מִן הַנְּשׂוּאִים,

and upbraid the Evil Inclination to leave those borne by Him,

v'yochōn ōsonu liflaytas ōlomim,

וְיָחָן אוֹתָנוּ לִפְלֵיטַת עוֹלָמִים,

graciously make us an eternal remnant,

vimalay mish-alōsaynu

וִימַלֵּא מִשְׁאֲלוֹתֵינוּ

and fulfill our requests

b'mido tōvo y'shu-o v'rachamim.

בְּמִדָּה טוֹבָה יְשׁוּעָה וְרַחֲמִים.

in good measure, for salvation and mercy.

THE TORAH IS PLACED ON THE *BIMAH* AND PREPARED FOR READING.
THE *GABBAI* USES THE FOLLOWING FORMULA TO CALL A *KOHEN* TO THE TORAH:

וְתִגָּלֶה וְתֵרָאֶה מַלְכוּתוֹ עָלֵינוּ בִּזְמַן קָרוֹב, וְיָחֹן פְּלֵיטָתֵנוּ וּפְלֵיטַת
עַמּוֹ בֵּית יִשְׂרָאֵל לְחֵן וּלְחֶסֶד וּלְרַחֲמִים וּלְרָצוֹן. וְנֹאמַר
אָמֵן. הַכֹּל הָבוּ גֹדֶל לֵאלֹהֵינוּ וּתְנוּ כָבוֹד לַתּוֹרָה.
כֹּהֵן° קְרָב, יַעֲמֹד (NAME) בֶּן (FATHER'S NAME) הַכֹּהֵן.

°IF NO *KOHEN* IS PRESENT, THE *GABBAI* SAYS:

אֵין כָּאן כֹּהֵן, יַעֲמֹד (insert name) בֶּן (father's name) יִשְׂרָאֵל (לֵוִי) בִּמְקוֹם כֹּהֵן.

בָּרוּךְ שֶׁנָּתַן תּוֹרָה לְעַמּוֹ יִשְׂרָאֵל בִּקְדֻשָּׁתוֹ.

CONGREGATION, THEN *GABBAI*:

V'atem had'vaykim   וְאַתֶּם הַדְּבֵקִים
  Badōnoy Elōhaychem,   בַּיהוה אֱלֹהֵיכֶם,
You who cling to HASHEM, your God,
cha-yim kul'chem ha-yōm.   חַיִּים כֻּלְּכֶם הַיּוֹם.
you are all alive today.

⊰[**READING OF THE TORAH**]⊱

THE READER SHOWS THE *OLEH* (PERSON CALLED TO THE TORAH) THE PLACE IN THE TORAH. THE
OLEH TOUCHES THE TORAH WITH A CORNER OF HIS *TALLIS*, OR THE BELT OR MANTLE OF THE
TORAH, AND KISSES IT.
HE THEN BEGINS THE BLESSING, BOWING AT Bor'chu AND STRAIGHTENING UP AT Adōnoy.

BOR'CHU es Adōnoy ham'vōroch.   בָּרְכוּ אֶת יהוה הַמְבֹרָךְ.
Bless HASHEM, the blessed One.

CONGREGATION, FOLLOWED BY *OLEH*, RESPONDS,
BOWING AT Boruch AND STRAIGHTENING UP AT Adōnoy.

Boruch Adōnoy ham'vōroch   בָּרוּךְ יהוה הַמְבֹרָךְ
  l'ōlom vo-ed.   לְעוֹלָם וָעֶד.
Blessed is HASHEM, the blessed One, for all eternity.

OLEH CONTINUES:

BORUCH ato Adōnoy   בָּרוּךְ אַתָּה יהוה
  Elōhaynu melech ho-ōlom,   אֱלֹהֵינוּ מֶלֶךְ הָעוֹלָם,
Blessed are You, HASHEM, our God, King of the universe,
asher bochar bonu mikol ho-amim   אֲשֶׁר בָּחַר בָּנוּ מִכָּל הָעַמִּים,
Who selected us from all the peoples
v'nosan lonu es tōrosō.   וְנָתַן לָנוּ אֶת תּוֹרָתוֹ.
and gave us His Torah.

Boruch ato Adōnoy, nōsayn hatōro.   בָּרוּךְ אַתָּה יהוה, נוֹתֵן הַתּוֹרָה.
Blessed are You, HASHEM, Giver of the Torah.

CONGREGATION RESPONDS: Omayn — אָמֵן.

AFTER HIS TORAH PORTION HAS BEEN READ, THE *OLEH* RECITES:

BORUCH ato Adōnoy   בָּרוּךְ אַתָּה יהוה

Blessed are You, HASHEM,

Elōhaynu melech ho-ōlom,   אֱלֹהֵינוּ מֶלֶךְ הָעוֹלָם,

our God, King of the universe,

asher nosan lonu tōras emes,   אֲשֶׁר נָתַן לָנוּ תּוֹרַת אֱמֶת,

Who gave us the Torah of truth

v'cha-yay ōlom nota b'sōchaynu.   וְחַיֵּי עוֹלָם נָטַע בְּתוֹכֵנוּ.

and implanted eternal life within us.

Boruch ato Adōnoy, nōsayn hatōro.   בָּרוּךְ אַתָּה יהוה, נוֹתֵן הַתּוֹרָה.

Blessed are You, HASHEM, Giver of the Torah.

CONGREGATION RESPONDS: Omayn — אָמֵן.

HAGBAHAH AND GELILAH / RAISING THE TORAH

THE TORAH IS RAISED FOR ALL TO SEE. EACH PERSON LOOKS AT THE TORAH AND RECITES ALOUD:

V'ZŌS hatōro asher som mōshe   וְזֹאת הַתּוֹרָה אֲשֶׁר שָׂם מֹשֶׁה

This is the Torah that Moses placed

lifnay b'nay yisro-ayl   לִפְנֵי בְּנֵי יִשְׂרָאֵל,

before the Children of Israel,

al pi Adōnoy b'yad mōshe.   עַל פִּי יהוה בְּיַד מֹשֶׁה.

upon the command of HASHEM, through Moses' hand.

IN MANY CONGREGATIONS THE *GABBAI* RECITES THE *KEIL MALEI RACHAMIM* PRAYER (P. 422) IN MEMORY OF THE DECEASED EITHER ON OR PRIOR TO THE *YAHRZEIT.*

RETURNING THE TORAH

THE *CHAZZAN* TAKES THE TORAH IN HIS RIGHT ARM AND RECITES:

y'hal'lu es shaym Adōnoy,   יְהַלְלוּ אֶת שֵׁם יהוה,

Let them praise the Name of HASHEM,

ki nisgov sh'mō l'vadō —   כִּי נִשְׂגָּב שְׁמוֹ לְבַדּוֹ —

for His Name alone will have been exalted —

CONGREGATION RESPONDS:

— hōdō al eretz v'shomōyim   הוֹדוֹ עַל אֶרֶץ וְשָׁמָיִם.

— His glory is above earth and heaven.

Va-yorem keren l'amō,   וַיָּרֶם קֶרֶן לְעַמּוֹ,

And He will have exalted the pride of His people,

t'hilo l'chol chasidov,   תְּהִלָּה לְכָל חֲסִידָיו,

causing praise for all His devout ones,

livnay yisro-ayl am k'rōvō, hal'luyoh.   לִבְנֵי יִשְׂרָאֵל עַם קְרֹבוֹ, הַלְלוּיָה.

for the Children of Israel, His intimate people. Praise God!

AS THE TORAH IS CARRIED TO THE ARK THE FOLLOWING PSALM IS RECITED.

L'DOVID MIZMŌR,   לְדָוִד מִזְמוֹר,
Of David a psalm:

Ladōnoy ho-oretz umlō-oh,   לַיהוה הָאָרֶץ וּמְלוֹאָהּ,
HASHEM's is the earth and its fullness,

tayvayl v'yōsh'vay voh.   תֵּבֵל וְיֹשְׁבֵי בָהּ.
the inhabited land and those who dwell in it.

Ki hu al yamim y'sodoh,   כִּי הוּא עַל יַמִּים יְסָדָהּ,
For He founded it upon seas,

v'al n'horōs y'chōn'neho.   וְעַל נְהָרוֹת יְכוֹנְנֶהָ.
and established it upon rivers.

Mi ya-ale v'har Adōnoy,   מִי יַעֲלֶה בְהַר יהוה,
Who may ascend the mountain of HASHEM,

u-mi yokum bimkōm kodshō.   וּמִי יָקוּם בִּמְקוֹם קָדְשׁוֹ.
and who may stand in the place of His sanctity?

N'ki chapa-yim u-var layvov,   נְקִי כַפַּיִם וּבַר לֵבָב,
One with clean hands and pure heart,

asher lō noso lashov nafshi   אֲשֶׁר לֹא נָשָׂא לַשָּׁוְא נַפְשִׁי
who has not sworn in vain by My soul

v'lō nishba l'mirmo.   וְלֹא נִשְׁבַּע לְמִרְמָה.
and has not sworn deceitfully.

Yiso v'rocho may-ays Adōnoy,   יִשָּׂא בְרָכָה מֵאֵת יהוה,
He will receive a blessing from HASHEM

utzdoko may-Elōhay yish-ō.   וּצְדָקָה מֵאֱלֹהֵי יִשְׁעוֹ.
and just kindness from the God of his salvation.

Ze dōr dōr'shov,   זֶה דּוֹר דֹּרְשָׁיו,
This is the generation of those who seek Him,

m'vakshay fonecho, ya-akōv, selo.   מְבַקְשֵׁי פָנֶיךָ, יַעֲקֹב, סֶלָה.
those who strive for Your Presence — Jacob, Selah.

S'u sh'orim ro-shaychem,   שְׂאוּ שְׁעָרִים רָאשֵׁיכֶם,
Raise up your heads, O gates,

v'hinos'u pischay ōlom,   וְהִנָּשְׂאוּ פִּתְחֵי עוֹלָם,
and be uplifted, you everlasting entrances,

v'yovō melech hakovōd.   וְיָבוֹא מֶלֶךְ הַכָּבוֹד.
so that the King of Glory may enter.

Mi ze melech hakovōd,   מִי זֶה מֶלֶךְ הַכָּבוֹד,
Who is this King of Glory? —

Adōnoy izuz v'gibōr,

יהוה עִזּוּז וְגִבּוֹר,

  Adōnoy gibōr milchomo.

יהוה גִּבּוֹר מִלְחָמָה.

    HASHEM, the mighty and strong, HASHEM, the strong in battle.

S'u sh'orim ro-shaychem,

שְׂאוּ שְׁעָרִים רָאשֵׁיכֶם,

    Raise up your heads, O gates,

us-u pischay ōlom,

וּשְׂאוּ פִּתְחֵי עוֹלָם,

    and raise up, you everlasting entrances,

v'yovō melech hakovōd.

וְיָבֹא מֶלֶךְ הַכָּבוֹד.

    so that the King of Glory may enter.

Mi hu ze melech hakovōd,

מִי הוּא זֶה מֶלֶךְ הַכָּבוֹד,

    Who then is the King of Glory?

Adōnoy tz'vo-ōs

יהוה צְבָאוֹת

  hu melech hakovōd, selo.

הוּא מֶלֶךְ הַכָּבוֹד, סֶלָה.

    HASHEM, Master of Legions, He is the King of Glory. Selah!

AS THE TORAH IS PLACED INTO THE ARK, THE FOLLOWING VERSES ARE RECITED:

UVNUCHŌ yōmar,

וּבְנֻחֹה יֹאמַר,

    And when it rested he would say,

shuvo Adōnoy

שׁוּבָה יהוה

  riv'vōs alfay yisro-ayl.

רִבְבוֹת אַלְפֵי יִשְׂרָאֵל.

    "Reside tranquilly, O HASHEM, among the myriad thousands of Israel."

Kumo Adōnoy limnuchosecho,

קוּמָה יהוה לִמְנוּחָתֶךָ,

    Arise, HASHEM, to Your resting place,

ato va-arōn u-zecho.

אַתָּה וַאֲרוֹן עֻזֶּךָ.

    You and the Ark of Your strength.

Kōhanecho yilb'shu tzedek,

כֹּהֲנֶיךָ יִלְבְּשׁוּ צֶדֶק,

    Let Your priests be clothed in righteousness,

vachasidecho y'ranaynu.

וַחֲסִידֶיךָ יְרַנֵּנוּ.

    and Your devout ones will sing joyously.

Ba-avur dovid avdecho,

בַּעֲבוּר דָּוִד עַבְדֶּךָ,

    For the sake of David, Your servant,

al toshayv p'nay m'shichecho.

אַל תָּשֵׁב פְּנֵי מְשִׁיחֶךָ.

    turn not away the face of Your anointed.

Ki lekach tōv nosati lochem,

כִּי לֶקַח טוֹב נָתַתִּי לָכֶם,

    For I have given you a good teaching,

tōrosi al ta-azōvu.

תּוֹרָתִי אַל תַּעֲזֹבוּ.

    do not forsake My Torah.

Aytz cha-yim hi lamachazikim boh,

❖ עֵץ חַיִּים הִיא לַמַּחֲזִיקִים בָּהּ,

    It is a tree of life for those who grasp it,

v'sōm'cheho m'u-shor.　　　　　　　　וְתֹמְכֶיהָ מְאֻשָּׁר.

and its supporters are praiseworthy.

D'rocheho darchay nō-am,　　　　　　דְּרָכֶיהָ דַרְכֵי נֹעַם,

v'chol n'sivōseho sholōm.　　　　　　וְכָל נְתִיבֹתֶיהָ שָׁלוֹם.

Its ways are ways of pleasantness and all its paths are peace.

Hashivaynu Adōnoy aylecho v'noshuvo,　הֲשִׁיבֵנוּ יהוה אֵלֶיךָ וְנָשׁוּבָה,

Bring us back to You, HASHEM, and we shall return,

chadaysh yomaynu k'kedem.　　　　　חַדֵּשׁ יָמֵינוּ כְּקֶדֶם.

renew our days as of old.

THE *CHAZZAN* RECITES *HALF-KADDISH*.

(Congregational responses are indicated by parentheses.)

יִתְגַּדַּל וְיִתְקַדַּשׁ שְׁמֵהּ רַבָּא. (אָמֵן –Omayn). בְּעָלְמָא דִּי בְרָא
כִרְעוּתֵהּ. וְיַמְלִיךְ מַלְכוּתֵהּ, בְּחַיֵּיכוֹן וּבְיוֹמֵיכוֹן וּבְחַיֵּי דְכָל
בֵּית יִשְׂרָאֵל, בַּעֲגָלָא וּבִזְמַן קָרִיב. וְאִמְרוּ: אָמֵן.
(אָמֵן. יְהֵא שְׁמֵהּ רַבָּא מְבָרַךְ לְעָלַם וּלְעָלְמֵי עָלְמַיָּא.)

(Omayn. Y'hay sh'mayh rabo m'vorach l'olam ul-ol'may ol'ma-yo.)

יְהֵא שְׁמֵהּ רַבָּא מְבָרַךְ לְעָלַם וּלְעָלְמֵי עָלְמַיָּא. יִתְבָּרַךְ וְיִשְׁתַּבַּח
וְיִתְפָּאַר וְיִתְרוֹמַם וְיִתְנַשֵּׂא וְיִתְהַדָּר וְיִתְעַלֶּה וְיִתְהַלָּל שְׁמֵהּ
דְקֻדְשָׁא בְּרִיךְ הוּא (בְּרִיךְ הוּא – B'rich hu). °לְעֵלָּא מִן כָּל
[מִכָּל לְעֵלָּא לְעֵלָּא° – from Rosh Hashanah to Yom Kippur substitute]
בִּרְכָתָא וְשִׁירָתָא תֻּשְׁבְּחָתָא וְנֶחֱמָתָא, דַּאֲמִירָן בְּעָלְמָא. וְאִמְרוּ: אָמֵן.
(אָמֵן –Omayn).

ON AN ORDINARY SABBATH AND ON THE SABBATH OF *CHOL HAMOED* CONTINUE WITH THE
SABBATH *SHEMONEH ESREI* BELOW. ON FESTIVALS, EVEN THOSE THAT FALL ON THE SABBATH, THE
FESTIVAL *SHEMONEH ESREI* (P. 675) IS RECITED.

∢ MINCHAH SHEMONEH ESREI FOR THE SABBATH ⊱

IN THE SYNAGOGUE THE *SHEMONEH ESREI* IS RECITED WHILE FACING THE ARK; ELSEWHERE IT IS
RECITED WHILE FACING THE DIRECTION OF THE LAND OF ISRAEL. TAKE THREE STEPS BACKWARD,
LEFT, RIGHT, LEFT, THEN THREE STEPS FORWARD, RIGHT, LEFT, RIGHT. REMAIN STANDING WITH
FEET TOGETHER DURING *SHEMONEH ESREI*. RECITE IT WITH QUIET DEVOTION AND WITHOUT ANY
INTERRUPTION. ALTHOUGH IT SHOULD NOT BE AUDIBLE TO OTHERS, ONE MUST PRAY LOUDLY
ENOUGH TO HEAR ONESELF.

Ki shaym Adōnoy ekro,　　　　　　כִּי שֵׁם יהוה אֶקְרָא,

hovu gōdel Laylōhaynu.　　　　　　הָבוּ גֹדֶל לֵאלֹהֵינוּ.

When I call out the Name of HASHEM, ascribe greatness to our God.

Adōnoy s'fosai tiftoch,　　　　　　אֲדֹנָי שְׂפָתַי תִּפְתָּח,

u-fi yagid t'hilosecho.　　　　　　וּפִי יַגִּיד תְּהִלָּתֶךָ.

My Lord, open my lips, that my mouth may declare Your praise.

■ **First Blessing:** In the merit of our Patriarchs whose actions reflected Godliness, Hashem pledged to always be with Israel and protect them.

BEND THE KNEES AT Boruch; BOW AT ato; STRAIGHTEN UP AT Adōnoy.

BORUCH ato Adōnoy   בָּרוּךְ אַתָּה יהוה

Blessed are You, HASHEM,

Elōhaynu Vaylōhay avōsaynu,   אֱלֹהֵינוּ וֵאלֹהֵי אֲבוֹתֵינוּ,

our God and the God of our forefathers,

Elōhay avrohom, Elōhay yitzchok,   אֱלֹהֵי אַבְרָהָם, אֱלֹהֵי יִצְחָק,

Vaylōhay ya-akōv,   וֵאלֹהֵי יַעֲקֹב,

God of Abraham, God of Isaac, and God of Jacob;

ho-Ayl hagodōl hagibōr v'hanōro,   הָאֵל הַגָּדוֹל הַגִּבּוֹר וְהַנּוֹרָא,

Ayl elyōn,   אֵל עֶלְיוֹן,

the great, mighty, and awesome God, the supreme God,

gōmayl chasodim tōvim   גּוֹמֵל חֲסָדִים טוֹבִים

v'kōnay hakōl,   וְקוֹנֵה הַכֹּל,

Who bestows beneficial kindnesses and creates everything,

v'zōchayr chasday ovōs,   וְזוֹכֵר חַסְדֵי אָבוֹת,

Who recalls the kindnesses of the Patriarchs

umayvi gō-ayl livnay v'nayhem,   וּמֵבִיא גוֹאֵל לִבְנֵי בְנֵיהֶם,

and brings a Redeemer to their children's children,

l'ma-an sh'mō b'ahavo.   לְמַעַן שְׁמוֹ בְּאַהֲבָה.

for His Name's sake, with love.

FROM ROSH HASHANAH TO YOM KIPPUR ADD:

Zochraynu l'cha-yim,   זָכְרֵנוּ לְחַיִּים,

melech chofaytz bacha-yim,   מֶלֶךְ חָפֵץ בַּחַיִּים,

Remember us for life, O King Who desires life,

v'chosvaynu b'sayfer hacha-yim,   וְכָתְבֵנוּ בְּסֵפֶר הַחַיִּים,

l'ma-ancho Elōhim cha-yim.   לְמַעַנְךָ אֱלֹהִים חַיִּים.

and inscribe us in the Book of Life — for Your sake, O Living God.

Melech ōzayr u-mōshi-a u-mogayn.   מֶלֶךְ עוֹזֵר וּמוֹשִׁיעַ וּמָגֵן.

O King, Helper, Savior, and Shield.

BEND THE KNEES AT Boruch; BOW AT ato; STRAIGHTEN UP AT Adōnoy.

Boruch ato Adōnoy,   בָּרוּךְ אַתָּה יהוה,

mogayn avrohom.   מָגֵן אַבְרָהָם.

Blessed are You, HASHEM, Shield of Abraham.

■ Second Blessing: God's might as it is manifest in nature and man

ATO gibōr l'ōlom Adōnoy,

אַתָּה גִּבּוֹר לְעוֹלָם אֲדֹנָי,

You are eternally mighty, my Lord,

m'cha-yay maysim ato,

מְחַיֵּה מֵתִים אַתָּה,

the Resuscitator of the dead are You;

rav l'hōshi-a.

רַב לְהוֹשִׁיעַ.

abundantly able to save,

BETWEEN SHEMINI ATZERES AND PESACH, ADD:

Mashiv horu-ach u-mōrid hageshem.

מַשִּׁיב הָרוּחַ וּמוֹרִיד הַגָּשֶׁם.

Who makes the wind blow and makes the rain descend;

M'chalkayl cha-yim b'chesed,

מְכַלְכֵּל חַיִּים בְּחֶסֶד,

Who sustains the living with kindness,

m'cha-yay maysim b'rachamim rabim,

מְחַיֵּה מֵתִים בְּרַחֲמִים רַבִּים,

resuscitates the dead with abundant mercy,

sōmaych nōf'lim, v'rōfay chōlim,

סוֹמֵךְ נוֹפְלִים, וְרוֹפֵא חוֹלִים,

u-matir asurim,

וּמַתִּיר אֲסוּרִים,

supports the fallen, heals the sick, releases the confined,

umka-yaym emunosō li-shaynay ofor.

וּמְקַיֵּם אֱמוּנָתוֹ לִישֵׁנֵי עָפָר.

and maintains His faith to those asleep in the dust.

Mi cho-mōcho ba-al g'vurōs,

מִי כָמוֹךָ בַּעַל גְּבוּרוֹת,

u-mi dōme loch,

וּמִי דּוֹמֶה לָךְ,

Who is like You, O Master of mighty deeds, and who is comparable to You,

melech maymis umcha-ye

מֶלֶךְ מֵמִית וּמְחַיֶּה

u-matzmi-ach y'shu-o.

וּמַצְמִיחַ יְשׁוּעָה.

O King Who causes death and restores life and makes salvation sprout!

FROM ROSH HASHANAH TO YOM KIPPUR ADD:

Mi cho-mōcho av horachamim,

מִי כָמוֹךָ אַב הָרַחֲמִים,

Who is like You, O Merciful Father,

zōchayr y'tzurov l'cha-yim
b'rachamim.

זוֹכֵר יְצוּרָיו לְחַיִּים
בְּרַחֲמִים.

Who recalls His creatures mercifully for life!

V'ne-emon ato l'hacha-yōs maysim.

וְנֶאֱמָן אַתָּה לְהַחֲיוֹת מֵתִים.

And You are faithful to resuscitate the dead.

Boruch ato Adōnoy,

בָּרוּךְ אַתָּה יהוה,

m'cha-yay hamaysim.

מְחַיֵּה הַמֵּתִים.

Blessed are You, HASHEM, Who resuscitates the dead.

■ Third Blessing: Regarding the holiness of God's Name

DURING THE *CHAZZAN'S* REPETITION, *KEDUSHAH* IS RECITED; INDIVIDUALS CONTINUE ON P. 523.

STAND WITH FEET TOGETHER AND AVOID ANY INTERRUPTIONS. RISE ON TOES WHEN SAYING
Kodōsh, kodōsh, kodōsh; Boruch; AND Yimlōch. CONGREGATION, THEN *CHAZZAN*:

N'KADAYSH es shimcho bo-ōlom,　　נְקַדֵּשׁ אֶת שִׁמְךָ בָּעוֹלָם,
We shall sanctify Your Name in this world,

k'shaym shemakdishim ōsō　　כְּשֵׁם שֶׁמַּקְדִּישִׁים אוֹתוֹ
bishmay morōm,　　בִּשְׁמֵי מָרוֹם,
just as they sanctify it in heaven above,

kakosuv al yad n'vi-echo,　　כַּכָּתוּב עַל יַד נְבִיאֶךָ,
as it is written by Your prophet,

v'koro ze el ze v'omar:　　וְקָרָא זֶה אֶל זֶה וְאָמַר:
"And one [angel] will call another and say:

ALL IN UNISON:

Kodōsh kodōsh kodōsh　　קָדוֹשׁ קָדוֹשׁ קָדוֹשׁ
Adōnoy tz'vo-ōs,　　יהוה צְבָאוֹת,
'Holy, holy, holy is HASHEM, *Master of Legions,*

m'lō chol ho-oretz k'vōdō.　　מְלֹא כָל הָאָרֶץ כְּבוֹדוֹ.
the whole world is filled with His glory.'"

CHAZZAN:

L'u-mosom boruch yōmayru:　　לְעֻמָּתָם בָּרוּךְ יֹאמֵרוּ:
Those facing them say, "Blessed":

ALL IN UNISON:

Boruch k'vōd Adōnoy, mim'kōmō.　　בָּרוּךְ כְּבוֹד יהוה, מִמְּקוֹמוֹ.
"Blessed is the glory of HASHEM *from His place."*

CHAZZAN:

Uvdivray kodsh'cho kosuv laymōr:　　וּבְדִבְרֵי קָדְשְׁךָ כָּתוּב לֵאמֹר:
And in Your holy Writings the following is written:

ALL IN UNISON:

Yimlōch Adōnoy l'ōlom,　　יִמְלֹךְ יהוה לְעוֹלָם,
*"*HASHEM *shall reign forever —*

Elōha-yich tziyōn l'dōr vodōr,　　אֱלֹהַיִךְ צִיּוֹן לְדֹר וָדֹר,
hal'luyoh.　　הַלְלוּיָהּ.
your God, O Zion — from generation to generation: Praise God!"

CHAZZAN CONCLUDES:

לְדוֹר וָדוֹר נַגִּיד גָּדְלֶךָ וּלְנֵצַח נְצָחִים קְדֻשָּׁתְךָ נַקְדִּישׁ, וְשִׁבְחֲךָ
אֱלֹהֵינוּ מִפִּינוּ לֹא יָמוּשׁ לְעוֹלָם וָעֶד, כִּי אֵל מֶלֶךְ
גָּדוֹל וְקָדוֹשׁ אָתָּה. בָּרוּךְ אַתָּה יהוה, °הָאֵל הַקָּדוֹשׁ.

°הַמֶּלֶךְ הַקָּדוֹשׁ. — from Rosh Hashanah to Yom Kippur substitute

THE *CHAZZAN* CONTINUES Ato echod (P. 523).

ATO kodōsh v'shimcho kodōsh,

אַתָּה קָדוֹשׁ וְשִׁמְךָ קָדוֹשׁ,

You are holy and Your Name is holy,

ukdōshim b'chol yōm
y'hal'lucho, selo.

וּקְדוֹשִׁים בְּכָל יוֹם
יְהַלְלוּךָ סֶּלָה.

and holy ones praise You, every day, forever.

Boruch ato Adōnoy,
°ho-Ayl hakodōsh.

בָּרוּךְ אַתָּה יהוה,
°הָאֵל הַקָּדוֹשׁ.

Blessed are You, HASHEM, the holy God.

FROM ROSH HASHANAH TO YOM KIPPUR SUBSTITUTE:

°hamelech hakodōsh.　　°הַמֶּלֶךְ הַקָּדוֹשׁ.

the holy King.

■ Fourth blessing: relating to the Holiness of the day. Shabbos is a taste of the World to Come, when the Oneness and Essence of Hashem will be fully understood and appreciated.

ATO E-CHOD v'shimcho e-chod,

אַתָּה אֶחָד וְשִׁמְךָ אֶחָד,

You are One and Your Name is One;*

u-mi k'am'cho yisro-ayl
gōy e-chod bo-oretz,

וּמִי כְּעַמְּךָ יִשְׂרָאֵל
גּוֹי אֶחָד בָּאָרֶץ,

and who is like Your people Israel, one nation on earth.*

tif-eres g'dulo, va-ateres y'shu-o,

תִּפְאֶרֶת גְּדֻלָּה, וַעֲטֶרֶת יְשׁוּעָה,

The splendor of greatness and the crown of salvation,

yōm m'nucho ukdusho
l'am'cho nosoto.

יוֹם מְנוּחָה וּקְדֻשָּׁה
לְעַמְּךָ נָתָתָּ.

the day of contentment and holiness have You given to Your people.

Avrohom yogayl, yitzchok y'ranayn,

אַבְרָהָם יָגֵל, יִצְחָק יְרַנֵּן,

Abraham would rejoice, Isaac would exalt,

ya-akōv u-vonov yonuchu vō,

יַעֲקֹב וּבָנָיו יָנוּחוּ בוֹ,

Jacob and his children would rest on it,

אַתָּה אֶחָד — *You are One.* The opening verse is a clear reference to the verse (*Zechariah* 14:9) stating that when the Final Redemption comes, all the world will recognize the Oneness of God, meaning that there are no contradictions in His behavior. As noted above, the Sabbath *Minchah* alludes to the long-awaited day when history will attain God's goal of perfection. Thus the *Minchah Shemoneh Esrei* directs our focus not only to the holiness of the Sabbath day, but to the spiritual bliss of the future.

וּמִי כְּעַמְּךָ יִשְׂרָאֵל — *And who is like Your people Israel.* Israel is unique because it alone accepted

the Torah and dedicated itself to God's service. Consequently, God awarded Israel the spiritual gifts cited in the next verse.

יַעֲקֹב וּבָנָיו יָנוּחוּ בוֹ — *Jacob and his children would rest on it.* The Sages derive from Scriptural verses that all three Patriarchs observed the Sabbath, even before the Torah was given. Only of Jacob, however, could it be said that all his children joined him in observing the day, because Abraham's Ishmael and Isaac's Esau did not join their fathers. Indeed, the descendants of Ishmael chose Friday as their day of rest, and the descendants of Esau chose Sunday.

m'nuchas ahavo un'dovo,   מְנוּחַת אַהֲבָה וּנְדָבָה,

    m'nuchas emes ve-emuno,   מְנוּחַת אֱמֶת וֶאֱמוּנָה,

a rest of love and magnanimity; a rest of truth and faith;

m'nuchas sholōm v'shalvo,   מְנוּחַת שָׁלוֹם וְשַׁלְוָה,

    v'hashkayt vo-vetach,   וְהַשְׁקֵט וָבֶטַח,

a rest of peace and serenity, and tranquility and security;

m'nuchoh sh'laymo   מְנוּחָה שְׁלֵמָה

    sho-ato rōtze boh.   שָׁאַתָּה רוֹצֶה בָּהּ.

a perfect rest in which You find favor.

Yakiru vonecho v'yayd'u   יַכִּירוּ בָנֶיךָ וְיֵדְעוּ

    ki may-it'cho hi m'nuchosom,   כִּי מֵאִתְּךָ הִיא מְנוּחָתָם,

May Your children recognize and know that from You comes their rest,

v'al m'nuchosom   וְעַל מְנוּחָתָם

    yakdishu es sh'mecho.   יַקְדִּישׁוּ אֶת שְׁמֶךָ.

and through their rest, they will sanctify Your Name.

■ I affirm that the sanctity of Shabbos emanates from Hashem,
and I petition that the holiness of the day influence my life.

ELŌHAYNU Vaylōhay avōsaynu   אֱלֹהֵינוּ וֵאלֹהֵי אֲבוֹתֵינוּ

Our God and the God of our forefathers,

r'tzay vimnuchosaynu.   רְצֵה בִמְנוּחָתֵנוּ.

may You be pleased with our rest.

Kad'shaynu b'mitzvōsecho,   קַדְּשֵׁנוּ בְּמִצְוֹתֶיךָ,

Sanctify us with Your commandments

v'sayn chelkaynu b'sōrosecho,   וְתֵן חֶלְקֵנוּ בְּתוֹרָתֶךָ,

and grant us our share in Your Torah;

sab'aynu mituvecho,   שַׂבְּעֵנוּ מִטּוּבֶךָ,

satisfy us from Your goodness

v'sam'chaynu bishu-osecho,   וְשַׂמְּחֵנוּ בִּישׁוּעָתֶךָ,

and gladden us with Your salvation,

v'tahayr libaynu l'ovd'cho be-emes.   וְטַהֵר לִבֵּנוּ לְעָבְדְּךָ בֶּאֱמֶת.

and purify our heart to serve You sincerely.

V'hanchilaynu Adōnoy Elōhaynu   וְהַנְחִילֵנוּ יהוה אֱלֹהֵינוּ

O Hashem, our God, grant us as a heritage

b'ahavo uvrotzōn   בְּאַהֲבָה וּבְרָצוֹן

with love and favor,

כִּי מֵאִתְּךָ הִיא מְנוּחָתָם — *That from You comes their rest.* The quality of our Sabbath rest, as we have just described it, is God given; and this is because God Himself rested on the Sabbath.

shabas kodshecho,
שַׁבַּת קָדְשֶׁךָ,
Your holy Sabbath

v'yonuchu vom
וְיָנוּחוּ בָם
yisro-ayl m'kad'shay sh'mecho.
יִשְׂרָאֵל מְקַדְּשֵׁי שְׁמֶךָ.
and may Israel, the sanctifiers of Your Name, rest on them.

Boruch ato Adōnoy,
בָּרוּךְ אַתָּה יהוה,
m'kadaysh hashabos.
מְקַדֵּשׁ הַשַּׁבָּת.
Blessed are You, HASHEM, Who sanctifies the Sabbath.

■ Fifth Blessing: Prayer for restoration of the Temple service

R'TZAY, Adōnoy Elōhaynu
רְצֵה יהוה אֱלֹהֵינוּ
Be favorable, HASHEM, our God,
b'am'cho yisro-ayl uvisfilosom,
בְּעַמְּךָ יִשְׂרָאֵל וּבִתְפִלָּתָם,
toward Your people Israel and their prayer,

v'hoshayv es ho-avōdo
וְהָשֵׁב אֶת הָעֲבוֹדָה
lidvir bay-secho.
לִדְבִיר בֵּיתֶךָ.
and restore the service to the Holy of Holies of Your Temple.

V'ishay yisro-ayl, usfilosom
וְאִשֵּׁי יִשְׂרָאֵל וּתְפִלָּתָם
b'ahavo s'kabayl b'rotzōn,
בְּאַהֲבָה תְקַבֵּל בְּרָצוֹן,
The fire-offerings of Israel and their prayer accept with love and favor,

us'hi l'rotzōn tomid
וּתְהִי לְרָצוֹן תָּמִיד
avōdas yisro-ayl amecho.
עֲבוֹדַת יִשְׂרָאֵל עַמֶּךָ.
and may the service of Your people Israel always be favorable to You.

■ *Yaaleh Veyavo:* We petition God to have compassion on Israel and Jerusalem,
and to reinstate the Temple service, to enable us to bring
the appropriate offerings for the particular occasion.

ON *ROSH CHODESH* AND *CHOL HAMOED* RECITE THE FOLLOWING:

ELŌHAYNU Vaylōhay avōsaynu,
אֱלֹהֵינוּ וֵאלֹהֵי אֲבוֹתֵינוּ,
Our God and the God of our forefathers,

ya-a-le v'yovō v'yagi-a v'yayro-e
יַעֲלֶה, וְיָבֹא, וְיַגִּיעַ, וְיֵרָאֶה,
may there rise, come, reach, be noted,

v'yayrotze v'yishoma v'yipokayd
וְיֵרָצֶה, וְיִשָּׁמַע, וְיִפָּקֵד,
be favored, be heard, be considered,

v'yizochayr zichrōnaynu ufikdōnaynu,
וְיִזָּכֵר זִכְרוֹנֵנוּ וּפִקְדוֹנֵנוּ,
and be remembered — the remembrance and consideration of ourselves;

v'zichrōn avōsaynu,
וְזִכְרוֹן אֲבוֹתֵינוּ,
the remembrance of our forefathers;

v'zichrōn moshi-ach ben dovid avdecho,
וְזִכְרוֹן מָשִׁיחַ בֶּן דָּוִד עַבְדֶּךָ,
the remembrance of Messiah, son of David, Your servant;

v'zichrōn y'rushola-yim   וְזִכְרוֹן יְרוּשָׁלַיִם
    ir kod-shecho,   עִיר קָדְשֶׁךָ,
the remembrance of Jerusalem, Your Holy City;

v'zichrōn kol am'cho bays yisro-ayl   וְזִכְרוֹן כָּל עַמְּךָ בֵּית יִשְׂרָאֵל
    l'fonecho,   לְפָנֶיךָ,
and the remembrance of Your entire people the Family of Israel — before You

lif-layto l'tōvo   לִפְלֵיטָה לְטוֹבָה
for deliverance, for goodness,

l'chayn ulchesed ulrachamim,   לְחֵן וּלְחֶסֶד וּלְרַחֲמִים,
for grace, for kindness, and for compassion,

l'cha-yim ulsholōm   לְחַיִּים וּלְשָׁלוֹם
for life, and for peace

──────────── ON *ROSH CHODESH* ────────────

b'yōm rōsh hachōdesh ha-ze.   בְּיוֹם רֹאשׁ הַחֹדֶשׁ הַזֶּה.
on this day of Rosh Chodesh.

──────────── ON *PESACH* ────────────

b'yōm chag hamatzōs ha-ze.   בְּיוֹם חַג הַמַּצּוֹת הַזֶּה.
on this day of the Festival of Matzos.

──────────── ON *SUCCOS* ────────────

b'yōm chag hasukōs ha-ze.   בְּיוֹם חַג הַסֻּכּוֹת הַזֶּה.
on this day of the Succos Festival.

──────────────────────────────────

Zoch'raynu Adōnoy Elōhaynu   זָכְרֵנוּ יהוה אֱלֹהֵינוּ
    bō l'tōvo,   בּוֹ לְטוֹבָה,
Remember us on it, HASHEM, our God, for goodness,

u-fokdaynu vō livrocho,   וּפָקְדֵנוּ בּוֹ לִבְרָכָה,
consider us on it for blessing

v'hōshi-aynu vō l'cha-yim.   וְהוֹשִׁיעֵנוּ בּוֹ לְחַיִּים.
and help us on it for life.

U-vidvar y'shu-o v'rachamim,   וּבִדְבַר יְשׁוּעָה וְרַחֲמִים,
In the matter of salvation and compassion,

chus v'chonaynu   חוּס וְחָנֵּנוּ
    v'rachaym olaynu v'hōshi-aynu,   וְרַחֵם עָלֵינוּ וְהוֹשִׁיעֵנוּ,
pity, be gracious and compassionate with us and help us,

ki aylecho aynaynu,   כִּי אֵלֶיךָ עֵינֵינוּ,
for our eyes are turned to You,

ki Ayl melech   כִּי אֵל מֶלֶךְ
    chanun v'rachum oto.   חַנּוּן וְרַחוּם אָתָּה.
because You are God, the gracious and compassionate King.

V'SECHEZENO aynaynu   וְתֶחֱזֶינָה עֵינֵינוּ
May our eyes behold

b'shuv'cho l'tziyōn b'rachamim.   בְּשׁוּבְךָ לְצִיּוֹן בְּרַחֲמִים.
Your return to Zion in compassion.

Boruch ato Adōnoy,   בָּרוּךְ אַתָּה יהוה,
hamachazir sh'chinosō l'tziyōn.   הַמַּחֲזִיר שְׁכִינָתוֹ לְצִיּוֹן.
Blessed are You, HASHEM, Who restores His Presence unto Zion.

■ Sixth Blessing: Acknowledgment of our debt of gratitude

BOW AT Mōdim anachnu loch; STRAIGHTEN UP AT Adōnoy.
IN HIS REPETITION THE *CHAZZAN* SHOULD RECITE THE ENTIRE *MODIM* ALOUD,
WHILE THE CONGREGATION RECITES *MODIM OF THE RABBIS* (P. 528) SOFTLY.

MŌDIM anachnu loch,   מוֹדִים אֲנַחְנוּ לָךְ,
We gratefully thank You,

sho-ato hu Adōnoy Elōhaynu   שָׁאַתָּה הוּא יהוה אֱלֹהֵינוּ
for it is You Who are HASHEM, our God,

Vaylōhay avōsaynu   וֵאלֹהֵי אֲבוֹתֵינוּ
and the God of our forefathers

l'ōlom vo-ed,   לְעוֹלָם וָעֶד,
forever and ever;

tzur cha-yaynu, mogayn yish-aynu   צוּר חַיֵּינוּ, מָגֵן יִשְׁעֵנוּ
Rock of our lives, Shield of our salvation

ato hu l'dōr vodōr.   אַתָּה הוּא לְדוֹר וָדוֹר.
are You from generation to generation.

Nō-de l'cho unsapayr t'hilosecho   נוֹדֶה לְךָ וּנְסַפֵּר תְּהִלָּתֶךָ
We shall thank You and relate Your praise —

al cha-yaynu ham'surim b'yodecho,   עַל חַיֵּינוּ הַמְּסוּרִים בְּיָדֶךָ,
for our lives, which are committed to Your power,

v'al nishmōsaynu hap'kudōs loch,   וְעַל נִשְׁמוֹתֵינוּ הַפְּקוּדוֹת לָךְ,
and for our souls that are entrusted to You,

v'al nisecho sheb'chol yōm imonu,   וְעַל נִסֶּיךָ שֶׁבְּכָל יוֹם עִמָּנוּ,
and for Your miracles that are with us every day,

v'al nifl'ōsecho v'tōvōsecho   וְעַל נִפְלְאוֹתֶיךָ וְטוֹבוֹתֶיךָ
sheb'chol ays,   שֶׁבְּכָל עֵת,
and for Your wonders and favors in every season —

erev vovōker v'tzohorō-yim.   עֶרֶב וָבֹקֶר וְצָהֳרָיִם.
evening, morning, and afternoon.

Hatōv ki lō cholu rachamecho,
הַטּוֹב כִּי לֹא כָלוּ רַחֲמֶיךָ,

The Beneficent One, for Your compassions were never exhausted,

v'ham'rachaym
וְהַמְרַחֵם

and the Compassionate One,

ki lō samu chasodecho,
כִּי לֹא תַמּוּ חֲסָדֶיךָ,

for Your kindnesses never ended —

may-ōlom kivinu loch.
מֵעוֹלָם קִוִּינוּ לָךְ.

always have we put our hope in You.

MODIM OF THE RABBIS

RECITED SOFTLY BY CONGREGATION WHILE *CHAZZAN* RECITES THE REGULAR *MODIM* ALOUD

MŌDIM anachnu loch,
מוֹדִים אֲנַחְנוּ לָךְ,

We gratefully thank You,

sho-ato hu Adōnoy Elōhaynu
שָׁאַתָּה הוּא יהוה אֱלֹהֵינוּ

Vaylōhay avōsaynu,
וֵאלֹהֵי אֲבוֹתֵינוּ,

for it is You Who are HASHEM, our God and the God of our forefathers,

Elōhay chol bosor,
אֱלֹהֵי כָל בָּשָׂר,

the God of all flesh,

yōtz'raynu, yōtzayr b'rayshis.
יוֹצְרֵנוּ, יוֹצֵר בְּרֵאשִׁית.

our Molder, the Molder of the universe.

B'rochōs v'hōdo-ōs l'shimcho
בְּרָכוֹת וְהוֹדָאוֹת לְשִׁמְךָ

hagodōl v'hakodōsh,
הַגָּדוֹל וְהַקָּדוֹשׁ,

Blessings and thanks are due Your great and holy Name

al sheheche-yisonu v'ki-yamtonu.
עַל שֶׁהֶחֱיִיתָנוּ וְקִיַּמְתָּנוּ.

for You have given us life and sustained us.

Kayn t'cha-yaynu uska-y'maynu,
כֵּן תְּחַיֵּנוּ וּתְקַיְּמֵנוּ,

So may You continue to give us life and sustain us,

v'se-esōf golu-yōsaynu
וְתֶאֱסוֹף גָּלֻיּוֹתֵינוּ

l'chatzrōs kod-shecho,
לְחַצְרוֹת קָדְשֶׁךָ,

and gather our exiles to the Courtyards of Your Sanctuary,

lishmōr chukecho v'la-asōs r'tzōnecho,
לִשְׁמוֹר חֻקֶּיךָ וְלַעֲשׂוֹת רְצוֹנֶךָ,

to observe Your decrees, to do Your will

ul-ovd'cho b'layvov sholaym,
וּלְעָבְדְּךָ בְּלֵבָב שָׁלֵם,

and to serve You wholeheartedly.

al she-anachnu mōdim loch.
עַל שֶׁאֲנַחְנוּ מוֹדִים לָךְ.

[We thank You] for inspiring us to thank You.

Boruch Ayl hahōdo-ōs.
בָּרוּךְ אֵל הַהוֹדָאוֹת.

Blessed is the God of thanksgivings.

ON CHANUKAH CONTINUE ON P. 529. ON ALL OTHER DAYS TURN TO THE BOTTOM OF P. 530.

ON CHANUKAH ADD THE FOLLOWING:

AL hanisim, v'al hapurkon,   עַל הַנִּסִּים, וְעַל הַפֻּרְקָן,

For the miracles, and for the salvation,

v'al hag'vurōs, v'al hat'shu-ōs,   וְעַל הַגְּבוּרוֹת, וְעַל הַתְּשׁוּעוֹת,

and for the mighty deeds, and for the victories,

v'al hamilchomōs,   וְעַל הַמִּלְחָמוֹת,

and for the battles

she-osiso la-avōsaynu   שֶׁעָשִׂיתָ לַאֲבוֹתֵינוּ

which You performed for our forefathers

ba-yomim hohaym baz'man ha-ze.   בַּיָּמִים הָהֵם בַּזְּמַן הַזֶּה.

in those days, at this time.

BIMAY matisyohu ben yōchonon   בִּימֵי מַתִּתְיָהוּ בֶּן יוֹחָנָן

In the days of Mattisyahu, the son of Yochanan,

kōhayn godōl chashmōno-i uvonov,   כֹּהֵן גָּדוֹל חַשְׁמוֹנַאי וּבָנָיו,

the High Priest, the Hasmonean, and his sons —

k'she-om'do malchus yovon   כְּשֶׁעָמְדָה מַלְכוּת יָוָן

hor'sho-o   הָרְשָׁעָה

when the wicked Greek kingdom rose up

al am'cho yisro-ayl,   עַל עַמְּךָ יִשְׂרָאֵל,

against Your people Israel

l'hashkichom tōrosecho,   לְהַשְׁכִּיחָם תּוֹרָתֶךָ,

to make them forget Your Torah

ulha-avirom maychukay r'tzōnecho.   וּלְהַעֲבִירָם מֵחֻקֵּי רְצוֹנֶךָ.

and compel them to stray from the statutes of Your Will.

V'ato b'rachamecho horabim,   וְאַתָּה בְּרַחֲמֶיךָ הָרַבִּים,

But you, in Your abundant mercy,

omadto lohem b'ays tzorosom,   עָמַדְתָּ לָהֶם בְּעֵת צָרָתָם,

stood up for them in the time of their distress.

Ravto es rivom, danto es dinom,   רַבְתָּ אֶת רִיבָם, דַּנְתָּ אֶת דִּינָם,

You took up their grievance, You judged their claim,

nokamto es nikmosom.   נָקַמְתָּ אֶת נִקְמָתָם.

and You avenged their wrong.

Mosarto gibōrim b'yad chaloshim,   מָסַרְתָּ גִבּוֹרִים בְּיַד חַלָּשִׁים,

You delivered the strong into the hand of the weak,

v'rabim b'yad m'atim,   וְרַבִּים בְּיַד מְעַטִּים,

the many into the hand of the few,

utmay-im b'yad t'hōrim,   וּטְמֵאִים בְּיַד טְהוֹרִים,
the impure into the hand of the pure,

ursho-im b'yad tzadikim   וּרְשָׁעִים בְּיַד צַדִּיקִים,
the wicked into the hand of the righteous,

v'zaydim b'yad ōs'kay sōrosecho.   וְזֵדִים בְּיַד עוֹסְקֵי תוֹרָתֶךָ.
and the wanton into the hand of the diligent students of Your Torah.

Ulcho osiso   וּלְךָ עָשִׂיתָ
shaym godōl v'kodōsh b'ōlomecho,   שֵׁם גָּדוֹל וְקָדוֹשׁ בְּעוֹלָמֶךָ,
And for yourself you made a great and holy Name in Your world,

ul-am'cho yisro-ayl   וּלְעַמְּךָ יִשְׂרָאֵל
and for Your people Israel

osiso t'shu-o g'dōlo u-furkon   עָשִׂיתָ תְּשׁוּעָה גְדוֹלָה וּפֻרְקָן
You performed a great victory and salvation

k'ha-yōm ha-ze.   כְּהַיּוֹם הַזֶּה.
as this very day.

V'achar kayn bo-u vonecho   וְאַחַר כֵּן בָּאוּ בָנֶיךָ
Thereafter, Your children came

lidvir bay-secho,   לִדְבִיר בֵּיתֶךָ,
to the Holy of Holies of Your House,

u-finu es haycholecho,   וּפִנּוּ אֶת הֵיכָלֶךָ,
they cleansed Your Temple,

v'tiharu es mikdoshecho,   וְטִהֲרוּ אֶת מִקְדָּשֶׁךָ,
they purified the site of Your Holiness;

v'hidliku nayrōs   וְהִדְלִיקוּ נֵרוֹת
b'chatzrōs kod-shecho,   בְּחַצְרוֹת קָדְשֶׁךָ,
and they kindled lights in the Courtyards of Your Sanctuary;

v'kov'u   וְקָבְעוּ
sh'mōnas y'may chanuko aylu,   שְׁמוֹנַת יְמֵי חֲנֻכָּה אֵלוּ,
and they established these eight days of Chanukah

l'hōdōs ulhalayl l'shimcho hagodōl.   לְהוֹדוֹת וּלְהַלֵּל לְשִׁמְךָ הַגָּדוֹל.
to express thanks and praise to Your great Name.

ON ALL DAYS CONTINUE HERE:

V'AL kulom yisborach v'yisrōmam   **וְעַל** כֻּלָּם יִתְבָּרַךְ וְיִתְרוֹמַם
shimcho, malkaynu   שִׁמְךָ מַלְכֵּנוּ
For all these, may Your Name be blessed and exalted, our King,

tomid l'ōlom vo-ed.   תָּמִיד לְעוֹלָם וָעֶד.
continually forever and ever.

FROM ROSH HASHANAH TO YOM KIPPUR ADD:

Uchsōv l'cha-yim tōvim
וּכְתוֹב לְחַיִּים טוֹבִים

kol b'nay v'risecho.
כָּל בְּנֵי בְרִיתֶךָ.

And inscribe all the children of Your covenant for a good life.

V'chōl hacha-yim yōducho selo,
וְכֹל הַחַיִּים יוֹדוּךָ סֶּלָה,

Everything alive will gratefully acknowledge You, Selah!

vihal'lu es shimcho be-emes,
וִיהַלְלוּ אֶת שִׁמְךָ בֶּאֱמֶת,

and praise Your Name sincerely,

ho-Ayl y'shu-osaynu
הָאֵל יְשׁוּעָתֵנוּ

v'ezrosaynu selo.
וְעֶזְרָתֵנוּ סֶּלָה.

O God of our salvation and help, Selah!

BEND THE KNEES AT Boruch; BOW AT ato; STRAIGHTEN UP AT Adōnoy.

Boruch ato Adōnoy,
בָּרוּךְ אַתָּה יהוה,

Blessed are You, Hashem,

hatōv shimcho ulcho no-e l'hōdōs.
הַטּוֹב שִׁמְךָ וּלְךָ נָאֶה לְהוֹדוֹת.

*Your Name is "The Beneficent One"
and to You it is fitting to give thanks.*

■ Seventh Blessing: Prayer for peace and harmony
amongst the Jewish people

SHOLŌM ROV al yisro-ayl
שָׁלוֹם רָב עַל יִשְׂרָאֵל

am'cho tosim l'ōlom,
עַמְּךָ תָּשִׂים לְעוֹלָם,

Establish abundant peace upon Your people Israel forever,

ki ato hu melech,
כִּי אַתָּה הוּא מֶלֶךְ

for You are King,

odōn l'chol ha-sholōm.
אָדוֹן לְכָל הַשָּׁלוֹם.

Master of all peace.

V'tōv b'aynecho
וְטוֹב בְּעֵינֶיךָ

And may it be good in Your eyes

l'voraych es am'cho yisro-ayl,
לְבָרֵךְ אֶת עַמְּךָ יִשְׂרָאֵל,

to bless Your people Israel

b'chol ays uvchol sho-o
בְּכָל עֵת וּבְכָל שָׁעָה

bishlōmecho.
בִּשְׁלוֹמֶךָ.

at every time and at every hour, with Your peace.

°Boruch ato Adōnoy,
ham'voraych es amō yisro-ayl
basholōm.

°בָּרוּךְ אַתָּה יהוה,
הַמְבָרֵךְ אֶת עַמּוֹ יִשְׂרָאֵל
בַּשָּׁלוֹם.

°*Blessed are You, HASHEM, Who blesses His people Israel with peace.*

° FROM ROSH HASHANAH TO YOM KIPPUR SUBSTITUTE THE FOLLOWING:

B'sayfer cha-yim b'rocho v'sholōm,
u-farnoso tōvo,

בְּסֵפֶר חַיִּים בְּרָכָה וְשָׁלוֹם,
וּפַרְנָסָה טוֹבָה,

In the book of life, blessing, and peace, and good livelihood,

nizochayr v'nikosayv l'fonecho,

נִזָּכֵר וְנִכָּתֵב לְפָנֶיךָ,

may we be remembered and inscribed before You —

anachnu v'chol am'cho
bays yisro-ayl,

אֲנַחְנוּ וְכָל עַמְּךָ
בֵּית יִשְׂרָאֵל,

we and Your entire people the Family of Israel —

l'cha-yim tōvim ulsholōm.

לְחַיִּים טוֹבִים וּלְשָׁלוֹם.

for a good life and for peace.

Boruch ato Adōnoy,
ō-se ha-sholōm.

בָּרוּךְ אַתָּה יהוה,
עוֹשֶׂה הַשָּׁלוֹם.

Blessed are You, HASHEM, Who makes the peace.

THE *CHAZZAN'S* REPETITION ENDS HERE [AND CONTINUES WITH tzidkos'cho
(BOTTOM OF P. 534)]. INDIVIDUALS CONTINUE:

Yih-yu l'rotzōn imray fi
v'hegyōn libi l'fonecho,

יִהְיוּ לְרָצוֹן אִמְרֵי פִי
וְהֶגְיוֹן לִבִּי לְפָנֶיךָ,

*May the expressions of my mouth and the thoughts of my heart
find favor before You,*

Adōnoy tzuri v'gō-ali.

יהוה צוּרִי וְגֹאֲלִי.

HASHEM, my Rock and my Redeemer.

■ I pray that having completed my *Amidah*, I have been changed in a positive way,
especially with regard to my interpersonal relationships.

ELŌHAI, n'tzōr l'shōni mayro,

אֱלֹהַי, נְצוֹר לְשׁוֹנִי מֵרָע,

My God, guard my tongue from evil

usfosai midabayr mirmo,

וּשְׂפָתַי מִדַּבֵּר מִרְמָה,

and my lips from speaking deceitfully.

V'limkal'lai nafshi sidōm,

וְלִמְקַלְלַי נַפְשִׁי תִדּוֹם,

To those who curse me, let my soul be silent;

v'nafshi ke-ofor lakōl tih-ye.

וְנַפְשִׁי כֶּעָפָר לַכֹּל תִּהְיֶה.

and let my soul be like dust to everyone.

P'sach libi b'sōrosecho,
פְּתַח לִבִּי בְּתוֹרָתֶךָ,
Open my heart to Your Torah,

uvmitzvōsecho tirdōf nafshi.
וּבְמִצְוֹתֶיךָ תִּרְדּוֹף נַפְשִׁי.
then my soul will pursue Your commandments.

V'chol hachōsh'vim olai ro-o,
וְכָל הַחוֹשְׁבִים עָלַי רָעָה,
As for all those who design evil against me,

m'hayro hofayr atzosom
מְהֵרָה הָפֵר עֲצָתָם
speedily nullify their counsel

v'kalkayl machashavtom.
וְקַלְקֵל מַחֲשַׁבְתָּם.
and disrupt their design.

Asay l'ma-an sh'mecho,
עֲשֵׂה לְמַעַן שְׁמֶךָ,
Act for Your Name's sake;

asay l'ma-an y'minecho,
עֲשֵׂה לְמַעַן יְמִינֶךָ,
act for Your right hand's sake;

asay l'ma-an k'dushosecho,
עֲשֵׂה לְמַעַן קְדֻשָּׁתֶךָ,
act for Your sanctity's sake;

asay l'ma-an tōrosecho.
עֲשֵׂה לְמַעַן תּוֹרָתֶךָ.
act for Your Torah's sake.

L'ma-an yaychol'tzun y'didecho,
לְמַעַן יֵחָלְצוּן יְדִידֶיךָ,
That Your beloved ones may be given rest;

hōshi-o y'min'cho va-anayni.
הוֹשִׁיעָה יְמִינְךָ וַעֲנֵנִי.
let Your right hand save, and respond to me.

Yih-yu l'rotzōn imray fi
יִהְיוּ לְרָצוֹן אִמְרֵי פִי
v'hegyōn libi l'fonecho,
וְהֶגְיוֹן לִבִּי לְפָנֶיךָ,
May the expressions of my mouth and the thoughts of my heart
find favor before You,

Adōnoy tzuri v'gō-ali.
יהוה צוּרִי וְגֹאֲלִי.
HASHEM, my Rock and my Redeemer.

BOW. TAKE THREE STEPS BACK. BOW LEFT AND SAY:

Ō-se sholōm bimrōmov,
עֹשֶׂה שָׁלוֹם בִּמְרוֹמָיו,
He Who makes peace in His heights,

BOW RIGHT AND SAY:

hu ya-a-se sholōm olaynu,
הוּא יַעֲשֶׂה שָׁלוֹם עָלֵינוּ,
may He make peace upon us,

BOW FORWARD AND SAY:

v'al kol yisro-ayl. V'imru: Omayn.
וְעַל כָּל יִשְׂרָאֵל. וְאִמְרוּ: אָמֵן.
and upon all Israel. Now respond: Amen.

Y'HI ROTZŌN mil'fonecho,   יְהִי רָצוֹן מִלְּפָנֶיךָ
May it be Your will,

Adōnoy Elōhaynu   יהוה אֱלֹהֵינוּ
     Vaylōhay avōsaynu,   וֵאלֹהֵי אֲבוֹתֵינוּ,
HASHEM, our God and the God of our forefathers,

she-yibo-ne bays hamikdosh   שֶׁיִּבָּנֶה בֵּית הַמִּקְדָּשׁ
     bimhayro v'yomaynu,   בִּמְהֵרָה בְיָמֵינוּ,
that the Holy Temple be rebuilt, speedily in our days;

v'sayn chelkaynu b'sōrosecho,   וְתֵן חֶלְקֵנוּ בְּתוֹרָתֶךָ,
and grant us our share in Your Torah;

v'shom na-avod-cho b'yiro,   וְשָׁם נַעֲבָדְךָ בְּיִרְאָה,
and may we serve You there with reverence,

kimay ōlom   כִּימֵי עוֹלָם
     uchshonim kadmōniyōs.   וּכְשָׁנִים קַדְמוֹנִיּוֹת.
as in days of old and in former years.

V'or'vo Ladōnoy   וְעָרְבָה לַיהוה
     minchas y'hudo virusholo-yim   מִנְחַת יְהוּדָה וִירוּשָׁלָיִם,
Then the offering of Judah and Jerusalem will be pleasing to HASHEM,

kimay ōlom   כִּימֵי עוֹלָם
     uchshonim kadmōniyōs.   וּכְשָׁנִים קַדְמוֹנִיּוֹת.
as in days of old and in former years.

THE INDIVIDUAL'S RECITATION OF *SHEMONEH ESREI* ENDS HERE.

REMAIN STANDING IN PLACE UNTIL THE *CHAZZAN* REACHES *KEDUSHAH* —
OR AT LEAST FOR A FEW MOMENTS — THEN TAKE THREE STEPS FORWARD.

━━━━━━━━━━━━━━━━

■ We affirm three basic tenents of our faith: that Hashem exists, that the Torah is
His word, and that He controls the world and repays us for our actions.

━━━━━━━━━━━━━━━━

ON MOST SABBATHS, THE FOLLOWING THREE VERSES ARE RECITED:

TZIDKOS'CHO tzedek l'ōlom,   צִדְקָתְךָ צֶדֶק לְעוֹלָם,
Your righteousness* is righteous forever.

v'sōros'cho emes.   וְתוֹרָתְךָ אֱמֶת.
and Your Torah is truth.*

צִדְקָתְךָ — *Your Righteousness.* As the Sabbath
draws to a close, the Jew becomes conscious of
the ebbing of holiness and the onset of the six
days of labor with their relative absence of
holiness and their abundance of cares. Furthermore, according to the *Zohar*, Moses,
Joseph, and David died on the Sabbath at *Minchah* time. As such thoughts and memories
dampen our spirit of Sabbath joy, we recite

three verses, each of which begins with the
words, "Your righteousness." These verses
were selected to show us how to accept the
harsher manifestations of God's justice, the
righteousness that is not only fair, but essential to man's mission on earth.

וְתוֹרָתְךָ אֱמֶת — *And Your Torah is truth.* The
righteousness and truth expressed in this verse
imply that even the harsh judgment that God

V'tzidkos'cho Elōhim, ad morōm,   וְצִדְקָתְךָ אֱלֹהִים, עַד מָרוֹם,

And Your righteousness, O God, is unto the high heavens,

asher osiso g'dōlōs,   אֲשֶׁר עָשִׂיתָ גְדֹלוֹת,

You, Who have done great things,

Elōhim mi chomōcho.   אֱלֹהִים מִי כָמוֹךָ.

O God, who is like You?

Tzidkos'cho k'har'ray ayl,   צִדְקָתְךָ כְּהַרְרֵי אֵל.

Your righteousness is like the mighty mountains —

mishpotecho t'hōm rabo,   מִשְׁפָּטֶיךָ תְּהוֹם רַבָּה,

Your judgment is like the vast deep waters.

odom uvhaymo tōshi-a, Adōnoy.   אָדָם וּבְהֵמָה תּוֹשִׁיעַ, יהוה.

Man and beast You save, HASHEM.

THE *CHAZZAN* RECITES FULL *KADDISH*

(congregational responses are indicated by parentheses):

יִתְגַּדַּל וְיִתְקַדַּשׁ שְׁמֵהּ רַבָּא. (אָמֵן –Omayn). בְּעָלְמָא דִּי בְרָא
כִרְעוּתֵהּ. וְיַמְלִיךְ מַלְכוּתֵהּ, בְּחַיֵּיכוֹן וּבְיוֹמֵיכוֹן וּבְחַיֵּי דְכָל
בֵּית יִשְׂרָאֵל, בַּעֲגָלָא וּבִזְמַן קָרִיב. וְאִמְרוּ: אָמֵן.

(אָמֵן. יְהֵא שְׁמֵהּ רַבָּא מְבָרַךְ לְעָלַם וּלְעָלְמֵי עָלְמַיָּא.)

(Omayn. Y'hay sh'mayh rabo m'vorach l'olam ul-ol'may ol'ma-yo.)

יְהֵא שְׁמֵהּ רַבָּא מְבָרַךְ לְעָלַם וּלְעָלְמֵי עָלְמַיָּא. יִתְבָּרַךְ וְיִשְׁתַּבַּח
וְיִתְפָּאַר וְיִתְרוֹמַם וְיִתְנַשֵּׂא וְיִתְהַדָּר וְיִתְעַלֶּה וְיִתְהַלָּל שְׁמֵהּ
דְּקֻדְשָׁא בְּרִיךְ הוּא (בְּרִיךְ הוּא – B'rich hu). °לְעֵלָּא מִן כָּל
[°לְעֵלָּא לְעֵלָּא מִכָּל – from Rosh Hashanah to Yom Kippur substitute]
בִּרְכָתָא וְשִׁירָתָא תֻּשְׁבְּחָתָא וְנֶחֱמָתָא, דַּאֲמִירָן בְּעָלְמָא. וְאִמְרוּ: אָמֵן.
(אָמֵן –Omayn).

sometimes imposes on man and society also emanates from His knowledge of what Creation requires. Thus, we can face the oncoming week with at least the partial comfort that events are not haphazard, rather they are totally justified.

וְצִדְקָתְךָ אֱלֹהִים עַד מָרוֹם — *And Your righteousness, O God, is unto the high heavens.* God's righteousness is seen not only in His kindness to earthbound creatures, but also in His treatment of the "high heavens." Since the moon had no light of its own, it would have seemed doomed to a dark oblivion. But God mercifully placed it in the sky so that it would reflect the sun's brilliance and thus assume a prominence of its own.

אֲשֶׁר עָשִׂיתָ גְדֹלוֹת — *You, Who have done great*

things. God's accomplishments are so great that they defy specific description.

אָדָם וּבְהֵמָה תּוֹשִׁיעַ, ה' — *Man and beast You save, HASHEM.* Every human being combines within himself both man and beast. He has an animal body and a Divine soul. Since his soul is encased in a body, God's Presence is hidden from him to a significant degree. The challenge facing man is to discern God's judgment and control even in the vast deep waters — i.e., the murkiness of this material world — and thus come to discover the Godly soul within himself.

The Talmud (*Chullin* 5b) interprets this phrase homiletically as referring to righteous people. They have the intellectual capacity of a man, but they humble themselves before God.

תִּתְקַבֵּל צְלוֹתְהוֹן וּבָעוּתְהוֹן דְּכָל (בֵּית) יִשְׂרָאֵל קֳדָם אֲבוּהוֹן דִּי
בִשְׁמַיָּא. וְאִמְרוּ: אָמֵן. (Omayn – אָמֵן).

יְהֵא שְׁלָמָא רַבָּא מִן שְׁמַיָּא, וְחַיִּים עָלֵינוּ וְעַל כָּל יִשְׂרָאֵל. וְאִמְרוּ:
אָמֵן. (Omayn – אָמֵן).

Bow. Take three steps back. Bow left and say, . . . עֹשֶׂה; bow right and say, . . . הוּא יַעֲשֶׂה; bow
forward and say, . . . וְעַל כָּל. Remain in place for a few moments, then take three steps forward.

עֹשֶׂה שָׁלוֹם בִּמְרוֹמָיו, הוּא יַעֲשֶׂה שָׁלוֹם עָלֵינוּ, וְעַל כָּל יִשְׂרָאֵל.
וְאִמְרוּ: אָמֵן. (Omayn – אָמֵן).

■ As we take leave of the synagogue and God's presence, we fortify ourselves with the
resolve and commitment that the lofty ideals of prayer can be implemented and
actualized in our mundane pursuits.

STAND WHILE RECITING *OLAYNU*.

OLAYNU l'shabay-ach la-adōn hakōl,   עָלֵינוּ לְשַׁבֵּחַ לַאֲדוֹן הַכֹּל,
It is our duty to praise the Master of all,

losays g'dulo l'yōtzayr b'rayshis,   לָתֵת גְּדֻלָּה לְיוֹצֵר בְּרֵאשִׁית,
to ascribe greatness to the Molder of primeval Creation,

shelō osonu k'gōyay ho-arotzōs,   שֶׁלֹּא עָשָׂנוּ כְּגוֹיֵי הָאֲרָצוֹת,
for He has not made us like the nations of the lands

v'lō somonu k'mishp'chōs ho-adomo,   וְלֹא שָׂמָנוּ כְּמִשְׁפְּחוֹת הָאֲדָמָה.
and has not emplaced us like the families of the earth;

shelō som chelkaynu kohem,   שֶׁלֹּא שָׂם חֶלְקֵנוּ כָּהֶם,
for He has not assigned our portion like theirs

v'gōrolaynu k'chol hamōnom   וְגֹרָלֵנוּ כְּכָל הֲמוֹנָם.
nor our lot like all their multitudes.

SOME CONGREGATIONS OMIT THE PARENTHESIZED VERSE:

(Shehaym mishta-chavim l'hevel vorik,   שֶׁהֵם מִשְׁתַּחֲוִים לְהֶבֶל וָרִיק,)
(For they bow to vanity and emptiness

u-mispal'lim el ayl lō yōshi-a.)   וּמִתְפַּלְלִים אֶל אֵל לֹא יוֹשִׁיעַ.)
and pray to a god which helps not.)

BOW WHILE RECITING THE NEXT PHRASE.

Va-anachnu kōr'im u-mishta-chavim   וַאֲנַחְנוּ כּוֹרְעִים וּמִשְׁתַּחֲוִים
u-mōdim,   וּמוֹדִים,
But we bend our knees, bow, and acknowledge our thanks

lifnay melech malchay ham'lochim,   לִפְנֵי מֶלֶךְ מַלְכֵי הַמְּלָכִים
before the King Who reigns over kings,

Hakodōsh boruch hu.   הַקָּדוֹשׁ בָּרוּךְ הוּא.
the Holy One, Blessed is He.

Shehu nōte shoma-yim v'yōsayd oretz, שֶׁהוּא נוֹטֶה שָׁמַיִם וְיוֹסֵד אָרֶץ,
He stretches out heaven and establishes earth's foundation,

u-mōshav y'korō ba-shoma-yim mima-al, וּמוֹשַׁב יְקָרוֹ בַּשָּׁמַיִם מִמַּעַל,
the seat of His homage is in the heavens above

ush-chinas u-zō b'gov-hay m'rōmim. וּשְׁכִינַת עֻזּוֹ בְּגָבְהֵי מְרוֹמִים.
and His powerful Presence is in the loftiest heights.

Hu Elōhaynu ayn ōd. הוּא אֱלֹהֵינוּ, אֵין עוֹד.
He is our God and there is none other.

Emes malkaynu, efes zulosō, אֱמֶת מַלְכֵּנוּ, אֶפֶס זוּלָתוֹ,
True is our King, there is nothing beside Him,

kakosuv b'sōrosō: כַּכָּתוּב בְּתוֹרָתוֹ:
as it is written in His Torah:

V'yodato ha-yōm vaha-shayvōso וְיָדַעְתָּ הַיּוֹם וַהֲשֵׁבֹתָ
el l'vovecho, אֶל לְבָבֶךָ,
"You are to know this day and take to your heart

ki Adōnoy hu ho-Elōhim כִּי יהוה הוּא הָאֱלֹהִים
that HASHEM is the only God —

ba-shoma-yim mima-al בַּשָּׁמַיִם מִמַּעַל
v'al ho-oretz mitochas, ayn ōd. וְעַל הָאָרֶץ מִתָּחַת, אֵין עוֹד.
in heaven above and on the earth below — there is none other."

AL KAYN n'kave l'cho עַל כֵּן נְקַוֶּה לְךָ
Adōnoy Elōhaynu יהוה אֱלֹהֵינוּ
Therefore we put our hope in You, HASHEM, our God,

lirōs m'hayro b'sif-eres u-zecho, לִרְאוֹת מְהֵרָה בְּתִפְאֶרֶת עֻזֶּךָ,
that we may soon see Your mighty splendor,

l'ha-avir gilulim min ho-oretz, לְהַעֲבִיר גִּלּוּלִים מִן הָאָרֶץ,
to remove detestable idolatry from the earth,

v'ho-elilim korōs yikoraysun, וְהָאֱלִילִים כָּרוֹת יִכָּרֵתוּן,
and false gods will be utterly cut off,

l'sakayn ōlom b'malchus Shadai. לְתַקֵּן עוֹלָם בְּמַלְכוּת שַׁדַּי.
to perfect the universe through the Almighty's sovereignty.

V'chol b'nay vosor yikr'u vishmecho, וְכָל בְּנֵי בָשָׂר יִקְרְאוּ בִשְׁמֶךָ,
Then all humanity will call upon Your Name,

l'hafnōs aylecho kol rish-ay oretz. לְהַפְנוֹת אֵלֶיךָ כָּל רִשְׁעֵי אָרֶץ.
to turn all the earth's wicked toward You.

Yakiru v'yayd'u kol yōsh'vay sayvayl, יַכִּירוּ וְיֵדְעוּ כָּל יוֹשְׁבֵי תֵבֵל,
All the world's inhabitants will recognize and know

ki l'cho tichra kol berech,
tishova kol loshōn.

כִּי לְךָ תִּכְרַע כָּל בֶּרֶךְ,
תִּשָּׁבַע כָּל לָשׁוֹן.

that to You every knee should bend, every tongue should swear.

L'fonecho Adōnoy Elōhaynu
yichr'u v'yipōlu,

לְפָנֶיךָ יהוה אֱלֹהֵינוּ
יִכְרְעוּ וְיִפֹּלוּ,

Before You, HASHEM, our God, they will bend every knee and cast themselves down,

v'lichvōd shimcho y'kor yitaynu,

וְלִכְבוֹד שִׁמְךָ יְקָר יִתֵּנוּ,

and to the glory of Your Name they will render homage,

vikab'lu chulom es ōl malchusecho,

וִיקַבְּלוּ כֻלָּם אֶת עוֹל מַלְכוּתֶךָ,

and they will all accept upon themselves the yoke of Your kingship

v'simlōch alayhem m'hayro
l'ōlom vo-ed.

וְתִמְלֹךְ עֲלֵיהֶם מְהֵרָה
לְעוֹלָם וָעֶד.

that You may reign over them soon and for all eternity.

Ki hamalchus shelcho hi

כִּי הַמַּלְכוּת שֶׁלְּךָ הִיא

For the kingdom is Yours

ul-ōl'may ad timlōch b'chovōd,

וּלְעוֹלְמֵי עַד תִּמְלוֹךְ בְּכָבוֹד,

and You will reign for all eternity in glory,

kakosuv b'sōrosecho:

כַּכָּתוּב בְּתוֹרָתֶךָ:

as it is written in Your Torah:

Adōnoy yimlōch l'ōlom vo-ed.

יהוה יִמְלֹךְ לְעֹלָם וָעֶד.

"HASHEM shall reign for all eternity."

V'ne-emar: V'ho-yo Adōnoy l'melech
al kol ho-oretz,

❖ וְנֶאֱמַר: וְהָיָה יהוה לְמֶלֶךְ
עַל כָּל הָאָרֶץ,

And it is said: "HASHEM will be King over all the world —

ba-yōm hahu yih-ye
Adōnoy e-chod, ushmō e-chod.

בַּיּוֹם הַהוּא יִהְיֶה
יהוה אֶחָד וּשְׁמוֹ אֶחָד.

on that day HASHEM will be One and His Name will be One."

SOME CONGREGATIONS RECITE THE FOLLOWING AT THIS POINT.

AL TIRO mipachad pis-ōm,

אַל תִּירָא מִפַּחַד פִּתְאֹם,

Do not fear sudden terror,

u-mishō-as r'sho-im ki sovō.

וּמִשֹּׁאַת רְשָׁעִים כִּי תָבֹא.

or the holocaust of the wicked when it comes.

U-tzu aytzo v'sufor,

עֻצוּ עֵצָה וְתֻפָר,

Plan a conspiracy and it will be annulled;

dab'ru dovor v'lō yokum,

דַּבְּרוּ דָבָר וְלֹא יָקוּם,

speak your piece and it shall not stand,

ki i-monu Ayl.   כִּי עִמָּנוּ אֵל.

for God is with us.

V'ad zikno ani hu,   וְעַד זִקְנָה אֲנִי הוּא,

Even till your seniority, I remain unchanged;

v'ad sayvo ani esbōl,   וְעַד שֵׂיבָה אֲנִי אֶסְבֹּל,

and even till your ripe old age, I shall endure;

ani osisi va-ani eso,   אֲנִי עָשִׂיתִי וַאֲנִי אֶשָּׂא,

I created [you] and I shall bear [you];

va-ani esbōl va-amalayt.   וַאֲנִי אֶסְבֹּל וַאֲמַלֵּט.

I shall endure and rescue.

MOURNER'S KADDISH

MOURNER:

YISGADAL v'yiskadash   יִתְגַּדַּל וְיִתְקַדַּשׁ

sh'mayh rabo.   שְׁמֵהּ רַבָּא.

May His great Name grow exalted and sanctified

CONGREGATION RESPONDS: Omayn — אָמֵן

B'ol'mo di v'ro chir-usayh.   בְּעָלְמָא דִּי בְרָא כִרְעוּתֵהּ.

in the world that He created as He willed.

V'yamlich malchusayh,   וְיַמְלִיךְ מַלְכוּתֵהּ,

May He give reign to His kingship

b'cha-yaychōn uvyōmaychōn   בְּחַיֵּיכוֹן וּבְיוֹמֵיכוֹן

in your lifetimes and in your days

uvcha-yay d'chol bays yisro-ayl,   וּבְחַיֵּי דְכָל בֵּית יִשְׂרָאֵל,

and in the lifetimes of the entire Family of Israel,

ba-agolo u-vizman koriv.   בַּעֲגָלָא וּבִזְמַן קָרִיב.

swiftly and soon.

V'imru: Omayn.   וְאִמְרוּ: אָמֵן.

Now respond: Amen.

CONGREGATION RESPONDS:

Omayn. Y'hay sh'mayh rabo m'vorach   אָמֵן. יְהֵא שְׁמֵהּ רַבָּא מְבָרַךְ

l'olam ul-ol'may ol'ma-yo.   לְעָלַם וּלְעָלְמֵי עָלְמַיָּא.

Amen. May His great Name be blessed forever and ever.

MOURNER CONTINUES:

Y'hay sh'mayh rabo m'vorach   יְהֵא שְׁמֵהּ רַבָּא מְבָרַךְ

l'olam ul-ol'may ol'ma-yo,   לְעָלַם וּלְעָלְמֵי עָלְמַיָּא,

May His great Name be blessed forever and ever;

yisborach v'yishtabach v'yispo-ar   יִתְבָּרַךְ וְיִשְׁתַּבַּח וְיִתְפָּאַר

blessed, praised, glorified,

v'yisrōmam v'yisnasay   וְיִתְרוֹמַם וְיִתְנַשֵּׂא

exalted, extolled,

v'yis-hador v'yis-ale v'yis-halol   וְיִתְהַדָּר וְיִתְעַלֶּה וְיִתְהַלָּל

mighty, upraised, and lauded

sh'mayh d'kudsho b'rich hu   שְׁמֵהּ דְּקֻדְשָׁא בְּרִיךְ הוּא

be the Name of the Holy One, Blessed is He,

CONGREGATION RESPONDS:

B'rich hu.   *Blessed is He.*   בְּרִיךְ הוּא.

MOURNER CONTINUES:

°l'aylo min kol   °לְעֵלָּא מִן כָּל

beyond any

FROM ROSH HASHANAH TO YOM KIPPUR SUBSTITUTE:

°l'aylo l'aylo mikol   °לְעֵלָּא לְעֵלָּא מִכָּל

exceedingly beyond any

---

birchoso v'shiroso   בִּרְכָתָא וְשִׁירָתָא

tushb'choso v'nechemoso,   תֻּשְׁבְּחָתָא וְנֶחֱמָתָא,

blessing and song, praise and consolation

da-amiron b'ol'mo.   דַּאֲמִירָן בְּעָלְמָא.

that are uttered in the world.

V'imru: Omayn.   וְאִמְרוּ: אָמֵן.

Now respond: Amen.

CONGREGATION RESPONDS: Omayn — אָמֵן

Y'hay sh'lomo rabo min sh'mayo   יְהֵא שְׁלָמָא רַבָּא מִן שְׁמַיָּא,

May there be abundant peace from Heaven,

v'cha-yim olaynu v'al kol yisro-ayl.   וְחַיִּים עָלֵינוּ וְעַל כָּל יִשְׂרָאֵל.

and life, upon us and upon all Israel.

V'imru: Omayn: וְאִמְרוּ: אָמֵן.

Now respond: Amen.

CONGREGATION RESPONDS: Omayn — אָמֵן

MOURNER BOWS, THEN TAKES THREE STEPS BACK, BOWS LEFT AND SAYS:

Ō-se sholōm bimrōmov   עֹשֶׂה שָׁלוֹם בִּמְרוֹמָיו,

He Who makes peace in His heights,

MOURNER BOWS RIGHT AND SAYS:

hu ya-a-se sholōm olaynu   הוּא יַעֲשֶׂה שָׁלוֹם עָלֵינוּ,

may He make peace upon us,

MOURNER BOWS FORWARD AND SAYS:

v'al kol yisro-ayl. V'imru: Omayn: וְעַל כָּל יִשְׂרָאֵל. וְאִמְרוּ: אָמֵן.

and upon all Israel. Now respond: Amen.

CONGREGATION RESPONDS: Omayn — אָמֵן

MOURNER REMAINS IN PLACE FOR A FEW MOMENTS, THEN TAKES THREE STEPS FORWARD.

⊰ **BORCHI NAFSHI** ⊱

THE FOLLOWING PSALMS ARE RECITED AFTER *MINCHAH* EVERY SABBATH FROM AFTER SUCCOS
UNTIL, BUT NOT INCLUDING, *SHABBOS HAGADOL* (THE SABBATH BEFORE PESACH).

■ Psalm 104: My soul bursts forth blessing Hashem; His greatness and His glory, His
goodness and His wisdom are manifested in the brilliance of the world He created.

BOR'CHI NAFSHI es Adōnoy,   בָּרְכִי נַפְשִׁי אֶת יהוה,
*Bless HASHEM, O my soul.**

Adōnoy Elōhai godalto m'ōd,   יהוה אֱלֹהַי גָּדַלְתָּ מְּאֹד,
HASHEM, my God, You are very great;

hōd v'hodor lovoshto.   הוֹד וְהָדָר לָבָשְׁתָּ.
You have donned majesty and splendor;

Ōte ōr kasalmo,   עֹטֶה אוֹר כַּשַּׂלְמָה,
covering with light as with a garment,

nōte shoma-yim kairi-o.   נוֹטֶה שָׁמַיִם כַּיְרִיעָה.
stretching out the heavens like a curtain.

Ham'kore vama-yim aliyōsov,   הַמְקָרֶה בַמַּיִם עֲלִיּוֹתָיו,
He Who roofs His upper chambers with water;

hasom ovim r'chuvō,   הַשָּׂם עָבִים רְכוּבוֹ,
He Who makes clouds His chariot;

ham'halaych al kanfay ru-ach.   הַמְהַלֵּךְ עַל כַּנְפֵי רוּחַ.
He Who walks on winged wind.

Ō-se mal-ochov ruchōs,   עֹשֶׂה מַלְאָכָיו רוּחוֹת,
He makes the winds His messengers,

m'shor'sov aysh lōhayt.   מְשָׁרְתָיו אֵשׁ לֹהֵט.
the flaming fire His attendants.

Yosad eretz al m'chōneho,   יָסַד אֶרֶץ עַל מְכוֹנֶיהָ,
He established the earth upon its foundations,

bal timōt ōlom vo-ed.   בַּל תִּמּוֹט עוֹלָם וָעֶד.
that it falter not forever and ever.

T'hōm kal'vush kisisō,   תְּהוֹם כַּלְּבוּשׁ כִּסִּיתוֹ,
The watery deep, as with a garment You covered it;

al horim ya-amdu mo-yim.   עַל הָרִים יַעַמְדוּ מָיִם.
upon the mountains, water would stand.

Min ga-aros'cho y'nusun,   מִן גַּעֲרָתְךָ יְנוּסוּן,
From Your rebuke they flee,

ה' אֶת נַפְשִׁי בָּרְכִי — *Bless Hashem, O my soul.* Psalm 104, is discussed on pages 412-415 above.

min kōl ra-amcho yaychofayzun.
מִן קוֹל רַעַמְךָ יֵחָפֵזוּן.

from the sound of Your thunder they rush away.

Ya-alu horim, yayr'du v'ko-ōs,
יַעֲלוּ הָרִים, יֵרְדוּ בְקָעוֹת,

They ascend mountains, they descend to valleys,

el m'kōm ze yosadto lohem.
אֶל מְקוֹם זֶה יָסַדְתָּ לָהֶם.

to the special place You founded for them.

G'vul samto bal ya-avōrun,
גְּבוּל שַׂמְתָּ בַּל יַעֲבֹרוּן,

You set a boundary they cannot overstep,

bal y'shuvun l'chasōs ho-oretz.
בַּל יְשׁוּבוּן לְכַסּוֹת הָאָרֶץ.

they cannot return to cover the earth.

Ham'shalay-ach ma-yonim ban'cholim,
הַמְשַׁלֵּחַ מַעְיָנִים בַּנְּחָלִים,

He sends the springs into the streams,

bayn horim y'halaychun.
בֵּין הָרִים יְהַלֵּכוּן.

they flow between the mountains.

Yashku kol chaisō sodoy,
יַשְׁקוּ כָּל חַיְתוֹ שָׂדָי,

They water every beast of the field,

yishb'ru f'ro-im tz'mo-om.
יִשְׁבְּרוּ פְרָאִים צְמָאָם.

they quench the wild creatures' thirst.

Alayhem ōf ha-shoma-yim yishkōn,
עֲלֵיהֶם עוֹף הַשָּׁמַיִם יִשְׁכּוֹן,

Near them dwell the heaven's birds,

mibayn ofo-yim yit'nu kōl.
מִבֵּין עֳפָאיִם יִתְּנוּ קוֹל.

from among the branches they give forth song.

Mashke horim may-aliyōsov,
מַשְׁקֶה הָרִים מֵעֲלִיּוֹתָיו,

He waters the mountains from His upper chambers,

mip'ri ma-asecho tisba ho-oretz.
מִפְּרִי מַעֲשֶׂיךָ תִּשְׂבַּע הָאָרֶץ.

from the fruit of Your works the earth is sated.

Matzmi-ach chotzir lab'haymo,
מַצְמִיחַ חָצִיר לַבְּהֵמָה,

He causes vegetation to sprout for the cattle,

v'aysev la-avōdas ho-odom,
וְעֵשֶׂב לַעֲבֹדַת הָאָדָם,

and plants through man's labor,

l'hōtzi lechem min ho-oretz.
לְהוֹצִיא לֶחֶם מִן הָאָרֶץ.

to bring forth bread from the earth,

V'ya-yin y'samach l'vav enōsh,
וְיַיִן יְשַׂמַּח לְבַב אֱנוֹשׁ,

and wine that gladdens man's heart,

l'hatzhil ponim mishomen,
לְהַצְהִיל פָּנִים מִשָּׁמֶן,

to make the face glow from oil,

v'lechem l'vav enōsh yis-od.
וְלֶחֶם לְבַב אֱנוֹשׁ יִסְעָד.

and bread that sustains the heart of man.

Yisb'u atzay Adōnoy,　　　יִשְׂבְּעוּ עֲצֵי יהוה,

The trees of HASHEM are sated,

arzay l'vonōn asher noto.　　　אַרְזֵי לְבָנוֹן אֲשֶׁר נָטָע.

the cedars of Lebanon that He has planted;

Asher shom tziporim y'kanaynu,　　　אֲשֶׁר שָׁם צִפֳּרִים יְקַנֵּנוּ,

there where the birds nest,

chasido b'rōshim baysoh.　　　חֲסִידָה בְּרוֹשִׁים בֵּיתָהּ.

the chassidah with its home among cypresses;

Horim hag'vōhim la-y'aylim,　　　הָרִים הַגְּבֹהִים לַיְּעֵלִים,

high mountains for the wild goats,

s'lo-im machse lash'fanim.　　　סְלָעִים מַחְסֶה לַשְׁפַנִּים.

rocks as refuge for the gophers.

Oso yoray-ach l'mō-adim,　　　עָשָׂה יָרֵחַ לְמוֹעֲדִים,

He made the moon for Festivals,

shemesh yoda m'vō-ō.　　　שֶׁמֶשׁ יָדַע מְבוֹאוֹ.

the sun knows its destination.

Toshes chōshech vihi loylo,　　　תָּשֶׁת חֹשֶׁךְ וִיהִי לָיְלָה,

You make darkness and it is night,

bō sirmōs kol chaisō yo-ar.　　　בּוֹ תִרְמֹשׂ כָּל חַיְתוֹ יָעַר.

in which every forest beast stirs.

Hak'firim shō-agim latoref,　　　הַכְּפִירִים שֹׁאֲגִים לַטָּרֶף,

The young lions roar after their prey,

ulvakaysh may-Ayl ochlom.　　　וּלְבַקֵּשׁ מֵאֵל אָכְלָם.

and to seek their food from God.

Tizrach hashemesh yay-osayfun,　　　תִּזְרַח הַשֶּׁמֶשׁ יֵאָסֵפוּן,

The sun rises and they are gathered in,

v'el m'ōnōsom yirbotzun.　　　וְאֶל מְעוֹנֹתָם יִרְבָּצוּן.

and in their dens they crouch.

Yaytzay odom l'fo-olō,　　　יֵצֵא אָדָם לְפָעֳלוֹ,

Man goes forth to his work,

v'la-avōdosō aday orev.　　　וְלַעֲבֹדָתוֹ עֲדֵי עָרֶב.

and to his labor until evening.

Mo rabu ma-asecho Adōnoy,　　　מָה רַבּוּ מַעֲשֶׂיךָ יהוה,

How abundant are Your works, HASHEM;

kulom b'chochmo osiso,　　　כֻּלָּם בְּחָכְמָה עָשִׂיתָ,

with wisdom You made them all,

mol'o ho-oretz kinyonecho.　　　מָלְאָה הָאָרֶץ קִנְיָנֶךָ.

rthe earth is full of Your possessions.

Ze ha-yom godōl urchav yodo-yim,

זֶה הַיָּם, גָּדוֹל וּרְחַב יָדָיִם,

Behold this sea — great and of broad measure;

shom remes v'ayn mispor,

שָׁם רֶמֶשׂ וְאֵין מִסְפָּר,

there are creeping things without number,

cha-yōs k'tanōs im g'dōlōs.

חַיּוֹת קְטַנּוֹת עִם גְּדֹלוֹת.

small creatures and great ones.

Shom oniyōs y'halaychun,

שָׁם אֳנִיּוֹת יְהַלֵּכוּן,

There ships travel,

livyoson ze yotzarto l'sachek bō.

לִוְיָתָן זֶה יָצַרְתָּ לְשַׂחֶק בּוֹ.

this Leviathan You fashioned to sport with.

Kulom aylecho y'sabayrun,

כֻּלָּם אֵלֶיךָ יְשַׂבֵּרוּן,

All of them look to You with hope,

losays ochlom b'itō.

לָתֵת אָכְלָם בְּעִתּוֹ.

to provide their food in its [proper] time.

Titayn lohem, yilkōtun,

תִּתֵּן לָהֶם, יִלְקֹטוּן,

You give to them, they gather it in;

tiftach yod'cho, yisb'un tōv.

תִּפְתַּח יָדְךָ, יִשְׂבְּעוּן טוֹב.

You open Your hand, they are sated with good.

Tastir ponecho yibohaylun,

תַּסְתִּיר פָּנֶיךָ יִבָּהֵלוּן,

When You hide Your face, they are dismayed;

tōsayf ruchom yigvo-un

תֹּסֵף רוּחָם יִגְוָעוּן,

when You retrieve their spirit, they perish

v'el aforom y'shuvun.

וְאֶל עֲפָרָם יְשׁוּבוּן.

and to their dust they return.

T'shalach ruchacho yiboray-un,

תְּשַׁלַּח רוּחֲךָ יִבָּרֵאוּן,

When You send forth Your breath, they are created,

uschadaysh p'nay adomo.

וּתְחַדֵּשׁ פְּנֵי אֲדָמָה.

and You renew the surface of the earth.

Y'hi ch'vōd Adōnoy l'ōlom,

יְהִי כְבוֹד יהוה לְעוֹלָם,

May the glory of HASHEM endure forever,

yismach Adōnoy b'ma-asov.

יִשְׂמַח יהוה בְּמַעֲשָׂיו.

let HASHEM rejoice in His works.

Hamabit lo-oretz vatir-od,

הַמַּבִּיט לָאָרֶץ וַתִּרְעָד,

He looks toward the earth and it trembles,

yiga behorim v'ye-eshonu.

יִגַּע בֶּהָרִים וְיֶעֱשָׁנוּ.

He touches the mountains and they smoke.

Oshiro Ladōnoy b'cha-yoy,

אָשִׁירָה לַיהוה בְּחַיָּי,

> *I will sing to HASHEM while I live,*

azam'ro Laylōhai b'ōdi.

אֲזַמְּרָה לֵאלֹהַי בְּעוֹדִי.

> *I will sing praises to my God while I endure.*

Ye-erav olov sichi

יֶעֱרַב עָלָיו שִׂיחִי,

> *May my words be sweet to Him —*

onōchi esmach Badōnoy.

אָנֹכִי אֶשְׂמַח בַּיהוה.

> *I will rejoice in HASHEM.*

Yitamu chato-im min ho-oretz

יִתַּמּוּ חַטָּאִים מִן הָאָרֶץ,

> *Sinners will cease from the earth,*

ursho-im ōd aynom,

וּרְשָׁעִים עוֹד אֵינָם,

> *and the wicked will be no more —*

bor'chi nafshi es Adōnoy,

בָּרְכִי נַפְשִׁי אֶת יהוה,

> *Bless HASHEM, O my soul.*

hal'luyoh.

הַלְלוּיָהּ.

> *Praise God!*

■ Psalm 120: We are in distress because of our exile, and we yearn to once again ascend to Jerusalem for the annual pilgrimages.

SHIR HAMA-ALOS,

שִׁיר הַמַּעֲלוֹת,

> *A song of ascents;**

el Adonoy batzoroso li,

אֶל יהוה בַּצָּרָתָה לִּי,

> *To HASHEM, in my distress,*

korosi va-ya-anayni.

קָרָאתִי וַיַּעֲנֵנִי.

> *I cried and He answered me.*

Adōnoy hatzilo nafshi

יהוה הַצִּילָה נַפְשִׁי

> *HASHEM, rescue my soul*

mis'fas sheker miloshōn r'miyo.

מִשְּׂפַת שֶׁקֶר, מִלָּשׁוֹן רְמִיָּה.

> *from lying lips, from a deceitful tongue.*

Mah yitayn l'cho uma yōsif loch,

מַה יִּתֵּן לְךָ, וּמַה יֹּסִיף לָךְ,

> *What can He give you?* and what can He add to you,*

⧉ The Song of the Ascents

The fifteen psalms (120-134), known as the Songs of Ascents, were sung in the Temple, for it was in that sacred location that the Jew was catapulted toward successively higher spiritual summits. In the Temple, Israel declared that man must not be spiritually stagnant; the world is composed of infinite degrees of goodness, and man's mission is to scale the spiritual heights which rise from earth heavenward.

These psalms do not begin, "A song of ascent" (singular), but "A song of ascents" (plural), because when the Children of Israel are worthy to ascend, they do not climb one step at a time; rather, they mount many rungs at once.

מַה יִּתֵּן לְךָ — *What can He give you?* The Psalmist addresses the tongue: What can the Almighty do, O tongue, to restrain you from doing further damage? Has He not already placed you behind two walls?

loshōn r'miyo.   לָשׁוֹן רְמִיָּה.

O deceitful tongue?

Chitzay gibōr sh'nunim   חִצֵּי גִבּוֹר שְׁנוּנִים,

[You are like] the sharp arrows of the mighty,*

im gachalay r'somim.   עִם גַּחֲלֵי רְתָמִים.

[You are to be compared] with coals of rotem-wood.*

Ō-yo li ki garti meshech,   אוֹיָה לִי כִּי גַרְתִּי מֶשֶׁךְ,

Woe unto me, for my drawn-out sojourn;

shochanti im oholay kaydor.   שָׁכַנְתִּי עִם אָהֳלֵי קֵדָר.

I dwelt with [those who inhabit] the tents of Kedar.

Rabas shoch'no loh nafshi,   רַבַּת שָׁכְנָה לָּהּ נַפְשִׁי,

Long has my soul dwelt

im sōnay sholōm.   עִם שׂוֹנֵא שָׁלוֹם.

with those who hate peace.

Ani sholōm,   אֲנִי שָׁלוֹם,

I am peace* —

v'chi adabayr, haymo lamilchomo.   וְכִי אֲדַבֵּר, הֵמָּה לַמִּלְחָמָה.

but when I speak, they are for war.*

■ Psalm 121: We recognize that Hashem is our Guardian, and we place our trust for salvation in Him alone.

SHIR LAMA-ALŌS,   שִׁיר לַמַּעֲלוֹת,

A song to the ascents:*

eso aynai el hehorim,   אֶשָּׂא עֵינַי אֶל הֶהָרִים,

I raise my eyes upon the mountains;

may-a-yin yovō ezri.   מֵאַיִן יָבֹא עֶזְרִי.

whence will come my help?

Ezri may-im Adōnoy,   עֶזְרִי מֵעִם יהוה,

My help is from HASHEM,

ōsay shoma-yim vo-oretz.   עֹשֵׂה שָׁמַיִם וָאָרֶץ.

Maker of heaven and earth.

חִצֵּי גִבּוֹר שְׁנוּנִים — *[You are like] the sharp arrows of the mighty.* Just as a bow inflicts its damage far from its source, so does the slander spread by the tongue attack its victim at a distance.

עִם גַּחֲלֵי רְתָמִים — *[You are to be compared] with coals of rotem-wood.* Charcoals of rotem-wood are especially dangerous, because long after they appear to be dead on the surface, they continue to burn within.

אֲנִי שָׁלוֹם — *I am peace.* Uppermost in my mind is a constant desire to make peace, even when circumstances force me to act belligerently.

וְכִי אֲדַבֵּר הֵמָּה לַמִּלְחָמָה — *But when I speak, they are for war.* The more I speak of peace, the more they clamor for war, because they view my attempt at rapprochement as a sign of weakness and vulnerability.

שִׁיר לַמַּעֲלוֹת — *A song to the ascents.* This song describes the means whereby Israel finds the strength to attain Godly heights and ascend to His glorious Presence.

Al yitayn lamōt raglecho,   אַל יִתֵּן לַמּוֹט רַגְלֶךָ,

He will not allow your foot to falter;

al yonum shōm'recho.   אַל יָנוּם שֹׁמְרֶךָ.

your Guardian will not slumber.

Hinay lō yonum v'lō yishon,   הִנֵּה לֹא יָנוּם וְלֹא יִישָׁן,

Behold, He neither slumbers nor sleeps —

shōmayr yisro-ayl.   שׁוֹמֵר יִשְׂרָאֵל.

the Guardian of Israel.

Adōnoy shōm'recho,   יהוה שֹׁמְרֶךָ,

HASHEM is your Guardian;

Adōnoy tzil'cho al yad y'minecho.   יהוה צִלְּךָ עַל יַד יְמִינֶךָ.

HASHEM is your Shade at your right hand.

Yōmom ha-shemesh lō yakeko,   יוֹמָם הַשֶּׁמֶשׁ לֹא יַכֶּכָּה,

By day the sun will not harm you,

v'yorayach baloylo.   וְיָרֵחַ בַּלָּיְלָה.

nor the moon by night.

Adōnoy yishmor'cho mikol ro,   יהוה יִשְׁמָרְךָ מִכָּל רָע,

HASHEM will protect you from every evil;

yishmōr es nafshecho.   יִשְׁמֹר אֶת נַפְשֶׁךָ.

He will guard your soul.

Adōnoy yishmor tzays'cho u-vō-echo,   יהוה יִשְׁמָר צֵאתְךָ וּבוֹאֶךָ,

HASHEM will guard your departure and your arrival,

may-ato v'ad ōlom.   מֵעַתָּה וְעַד עוֹלָם.

from this time and forever.

■ Psalm 122: Jerusalem is the city of a Jew's hopes and aspirations. Wherever he may be, the Jew prays for the peace of Jerusalem.

SHIR HAMA-ALŌS l'dovid   שִׁיר הַמַּעֲלוֹת, לְדָוִד,

A song of ascents, by David:*

somachti b'ōm'rim li,   שָׂמַחְתִּי בְּאֹמְרִים לִי,

I rejoiced when they said to me,

bays Adōnoy naylaych.   בֵּית יהוה נֵלֵךְ.

"Let us go to the House of HASHEM."

Ōm'dōs ho-yu rag-laynu   עֹמְדוֹת הָיוּ רַגְלֵינוּ,

Immobile stood our feet,

שִׁיר הַמַּעֲלוֹת לְדָוִד — *A song of ascents, by David.* David composed this psalm with the intention that it be recited in the Temple after it was built. The psalm describes Jerusalem as a city

where the individual experiences a personal encounter with holiness. No matter how many pilgrims come, each feels a sense of worth and elevation.

bisho-ra-yich y'rushola-yim.

בִּשְׁעָרַיִךְ יְרוּשָׁלָיִם.

within your gates, O Jerusalem.

y'rushola-yim hab'nu-yo

k'ir shechub'ro lo yachdov.

יְרוּשָׁלַיִם הַבְּנוּיָה,
כְּעִיר שֶׁחֻבְּרָה לָּהּ יַחְדָּו.

The built-up Jerusalem* is like a city that is united together.

Sheshom olu sh'votim,

שֶׁשָּׁם עָלוּ שְׁבָטִים,

For there the tribes ascended,

shivtay Yoh aydus l'yisro-ayl

שִׁבְטֵי יָהּ עֵדוּת לְיִשְׂרָאֵל,

the tribes of God, a testimony for Israel,

l'hōdōs l'shaym Adōnoy.

לְהֹדוֹת לְשֵׁם יהוה.

to give thanks to the Name of HASHEM.

Ki shomo yosh'vu chisōs l'mishpot,

כִּי שָׁמָּה יָשְׁבוּ כִסְאוֹת לְמִשְׁפָּט,

For there sat thrones of judgment,

kisōs l'vays dovid.

כִּסְאוֹת לְבֵית דָּוִד.

thrones for the House of David.

Sha-alu sh'lōm y'rushola-yim

שַׁאֲלוּ שְׁלוֹם יְרוּשָׁלָיִם,

Pray for the peace of Jerusalem;*

yishlo-yu ōhavo-yich.

יִשְׁלָיוּ אֹהֲבָיִךְ.

those who love you will be serene.

Y'hi sholōm b'chaylaych,

יְהִי שָׁלוֹם בְּחֵילֵךְ,

May there be peace within your wall,

shalvo b'arm'nōso-yich.

שַׁלְוָה בְּאַרְמְנוֹתָיִךְ.

serenity within your palaces.

L'ma-an achai v'ray-oy,

לְמַעַן אַחַי וְרֵעָי,

For the sake of my brethren and my comrades,

adab'ro no sholōm boch.

אֲדַבְּרָה נָּא שָׁלוֹם בָּךְ.

I shall speak of peace in your midst.

L'ma-an bays Adōnoy Elōhaynu,

לְמַעַן בֵּית יהוה אֱלֹהֵינוּ,

For the sake of the House of HASHEM, *our God,*

avaksho tōv loch.

אֲבַקְשָׁה טוֹב לָךְ.

I will request good for you.*

יְרוּשָׁלַיִם הַבְּנוּיָה — *The built-up Jerusalem.* David foresaw that his son Solomon would "build up" the spiritual nature of Jerusalem by constructing its most imposing edifice — the Temple.

שַׁאֲלוּ שְׁלוֹם יְרוּשָׁלַיִם — *Pray for the peace of Jerusalem.* The Jews in exile exclaim: "Pray to God for the peace of Jerusalem." Permanent peace will come to the world only with the ingathering of the exiles from the four corners of the earth. Until then Jerusalem will never experience true peace, because many nations will war over this city. The exiled Jews, those who love her, mourn over the destruction of Jerusalem and pine to see her glory reinstated.

לְמַעַן בֵּית ה' אֱלֹהֵינוּ אֲבַקְשָׁה טוֹב לָךְ — *For the sake of the House of* HASHEM, *our God, I will request good for you.* More than the Jews need

■ Psalm 123: We call out for protection from the threats — both physical and spiritual — that face us daily, and we yearn for the ultimate Redemption.

SHIR HAMA-ALŌS   שִׁיר הַמַּעֲלוֹת,

A song of ascents:

aylecho nososi es aynai,   אֵלֶיךָ נָשָׂאתִי אֶת עֵינַי,

To You* I raised my eyes,

ha-yōsh'vi bashomo-yim.   הַיֹּשְׁבִי בַּשָּׁמָיִם.

O You Who dwell in the heavens.

Hinay ch'aynay avodim   הִנֵּה כְעֵינֵי עֲבָדִים
el yad adōnayhem,   אֶל יַד אֲדוֹנֵיהֶם,

Behold! Like the eyes of servants unto their masters' hand,

k'aynay shifcho el yad g'virtoh,   כְּעֵינֵי שִׁפְחָה אֶל יַד גְּבִרְתָּהּ,

like the eyes of a maid unto her mistress' hand,

kayn aynaynu el Adōnoy Elōhaynu,   כֵּן עֵינֵינוּ אֶל יהוה אֱלֹהֵינוּ,
ad she-y'chonaynu.   עַד שֶׁיְּחָנֵּנוּ.

so are our eyes unto HASHEM, our God, until He will favor us.

Chonaynu Adōnoy chonaynu,   חָנֵּנוּ יהוה חָנֵּנוּ,

Favor us, HASHEM, favor us,

ki rav sova-nu vuz.   כִּי רַב שָׂבַעְנוּ בוּז.

for we are fully sated with contempt.*

Rabas sov'o loh nafshaynu   רַבַּת שָׂבְעָה לָּהּ נַפְשֵׁנוּ

Our soul is fully sated

hala-ag hasha-ananim,   הַלַּעַג הַשַּׁאֲנַנִּים,

with the mockery of the complacent ones,

habuz lig-ay yōnim.   הַבּוּז לִגְאֵי יוֹנִים.

with the contempt of the arrogant.*

■ Psalm 124: We acknowledge that it is Hashem Who has rescued us from the many perils that have faced us throughout our exile.

SHIR HAMA-ALŌS l'dovid,   שִׁיר הַמַּעֲלוֹת, לְדָוִד,

A song of ascents, by David:

Jerusalem, Jerusalem needs the Jews. Of what value is the Holy City and the House of HASHEM if there are no people to absorb their sacred spirit? God's Spirit dwells only where there are people who will benefit from His Presence.

אֵלֶיךָ — *To You.* The Psalmist writes from the perspective of Jews in exile, whose tragic experience has taught them that only God can help them.

כִּי רַב שָׂבַעְנוּ בוּז — *For we are fully sated with contempt.* There is no point in continuing the exile, because we have already experienced every possible form of disgrace and contempt; there is nothing more to add.

הַלַּעַג הַשַּׁאֲנַנִּים הַבּוּז לִגְאֵי יוֹנִים — *With the mockery of the complacent ones, with the contempt of the arrogant.* Israel's attempt at spiritual fulfillment and its effort to teach that life must have

Lulay Adōnoy sheho-yo lonu,

לוּלֵי יהוה שֶׁהָיָה לָנוּ,

Had not HASHEM been with us —

yōmar no yisro-ayl:

יֹאמַר נָא יִשְׂרָאֵל.

let Israel declare now!*

Lulay Adōnoy sheho-yo lonu,

לוּלֵי יהוה שֶׁהָיָה לָנוּ,

Had not HASHEM been with us

b'kum olaynu odom:

בְּקוּם עָלֵינוּ אָדָם.

when men rose up against us,

Azai cha-yim b'lo-unu

אֲזַי חַיִּים בְּלָעוּנוּ,

then they would have swallowed us alive,

bacharōs apom bonu.

בַּחֲרוֹת אַפָּם בָּנוּ.

when their anger was kindled against us.

Azai hama-yim sh'tofunu

אֲזַי הַמַּיִם שְׁטָפוּנוּ,

Then the waters would have inundated us;

nachlo ovar al nafshaynu.

נַחְלָה עָבַר עַל נַפְשֵׁנוּ.

the current would have surged across our soul.

Azai ovar al nafshaynu,

אֲזַי עָבַר עַל נַפְשֵׁנוּ,

Then they would have surged across our soul —

hama-yim hazaydōnim.

הַמַּיִם הַזֵּידוֹנִים.

the treacherous waters.

Boruch Adōnoy,

בָּרוּךְ יהוה,

Blessed is HASHEM,

shelō n'sononu teref l'shinayhem.

שֶׁלֹא נְתָנָנוּ טֶרֶף לְשִׁנֵּיהֶם.

Who did not present us as prey for their teeth.

nafshaynu k'tzipōr niml'to
mipach yōk'shim

נַפְשֵׁנוּ כְּצִפּוֹר נִמְלְטָה
מִפַּח יוֹקְשִׁים,

Our soul escaped like a bird from the hunters' snare;

hapach nishbor va-anachnu nimlot'nu.

הַפַּח נִשְׁבָּר וַאֲנַחְנוּ נִמְלָטְנוּ.

the snare broke and we escaped.

Ezraynu b'shaym Adōnoy,

עֶזְרֵנוּ בְּשֵׁם יהוה,

Our help is through the Name of HASHEM,

ōsay shoma-yim vo-oretz.

עֹשֵׂה שָׁמַיִם וָאָרֶץ.

Maker of heaven and earth.

---

a spiritual goal are greeted with derision by those who are proud of their hedonistic successes.

לוּלֵי ה' שֶׁהָיָה לָנוּ יֹאמַר נָא יִשְׂרָאֵל — *Had not HASHEM been with us — let Israel declare now!*

Let us now declare that had He not offered compassionate protection, Israel could not have survived the terrible exile. As is common in Scripture, the dire alternative is left unsaid. הַבֹּטְחִים בַּה' כְּהַר צִיּוֹן — *Those who trust in*

■ Psalm 125: God protects those who trust in Him, and saves them from the forces of evil.

SHIR HAMA-ALŌS,   **שִׁיר הַמַּעֲלוֹת,**
A song of ascents:

habōt'chim Badonōy k'har tziyōn,   הַבֹּטְחִים בַּיהוה, כְּהַר צִיּוֹן,
*Those who trust in HASHEM are like Mount Zion**

lō yimōt l'ōlom yayshayv.   לֹא יִמּוֹט לְעוֹלָם יֵשֵׁב.
that falters not, but abides forever.

Y'rushola-yim horim soviv loh,   יְרוּשָׁלַיִם הָרִים סָבִיב לָהּ,
*Jerusalem — mountains enwrap it,**

Vadōnoy soviv l'amō,   וַיהוה סָבִיב לְעַמּוֹ,
and HASHEM enwraps His people,

may-ato v'ad ōlom.   מֵעַתָּה וְעַד עוֹלָם.
from this time and forever.

Ki lō yonu-ach shayvet horesha   כִּי לֹא יָנוּחַ שֵׁבֶט הָרֶשַׁע
For the rod of wickedness shall not rest

al gōral hatzadikim   עַל גּוֹרַל הַצַּדִּיקִים,
upon the lot of the righteous,

l'ma-an lō yishl'chu hatzadikim   לְמַעַן לֹא יִשְׁלְחוּ הַצַּדִּיקִים
b'avloso y'dayhem.   בְּעַוְלָתָה יְדֵיהֶם.
so that the righteous shall not stretch their hands into iniquity.

Haytivo Adōnoy latōvim,   הֵטִיבָה יהוה לַטּוֹבִים,
Do good, HASHEM, to good people,

v'lishorim b'libōsom.   וְלִישָׁרִים בְּלִבּוֹתָם.
and to the upright in their hearts.

V'hamatim akalkalōsom,   וְהַמַּטִּים עֲקַלְקַלּוֹתָם,
But those who turn to their perverseness —

yōlichaym Adōnoy es pō-alay ho-o-ven,   יוֹלִיכֵם יהוה אֶת פֹּעֲלֵי הָאָוֶן,
HASHEM will lead them with the workers of iniquity —

sholōm al yisro-ayl.   שָׁלוֹם עַל יִשְׂרָאֵל.
*peace upon Israel.**

HASHEM *are like Mount Zion.* For God's spirit will always remain with them just as it does with Mount Zion.

יְרוּשָׁלַיִם הָרִים סָבִיב לָהּ — *Jerusalem — mountains enwrap it.* Though Jerusalem is surrounded by protective mountains that afford a tremendous strategic advantage, the Psalmist cautions the people that the city is defenseless

unless God Himself guards it.

שָׁלוֹם עַל יִשְׂרָאֵל — *Peace upon Israel.* When the corrupt element is removed from Israel, there will be no one to disturb the internal harmony of the nation. In addition to inner serenity, the nation will enjoy external peace and security.

■ Psalm 126: When the exile ends, we will return to Jerusalem triumphantly and joyously.

SHIR HAMA-ALŌS,   שִׁיר הַמַּעֲלוֹת,
A song of ascents:

b'shuv Adōnoy es shivas tziyōn,   בְּשׁוּב יהוה אֶת שִׁיבַת צִיּוֹן,
*When HASHEM will return the captivity of Zion,**

hoyinu k'chōl'mim.   הָיִינוּ כְּחֹלְמִים.
*we will be like dreamers.**

Oz yimolay s'chōk pinu,   אָז יִמָּלֵא שְׂחוֹק פִּינוּ,
ul'shōnaynu rino,   וּלְשׁוֹנֵנוּ רִנָּה,
Then our mouth will be filled with laughter and our tongue with glad song;

oz yōm'ru vagōyim   אָז יֹאמְרוּ בַגּוֹיִם,
then will they declare among the nations,

higdil Adōnoy la-asōs im ayle.   הִגְדִּיל יהוה לַעֲשׂוֹת עִם אֵלֶּה.
"HASHEM has done greatly with these."

Higdil Adōnoy la-asōs imonu,   הִגְדִּיל יהוה לַעֲשׂוֹת עִמָּנוּ,
HASHEM has done greatly with us,

ho-yinu s'maychim.   הָיִינוּ שְׂמֵחִים.
we were gladdened.

Shuvo Adōnoy es sh'visaynu,   שׁוּבָה יהוה אֶת שְׁבִיתֵנוּ,
ka-afikim banegev.   כַּאֲפִיקִים בַּנֶּגֶב.
O HASHEM — return our captivity like springs in the desert.

Hazōr'im b'dim-o, b'rino yiktzōru.   הַזֹּרְעִים בְּדִמְעָה, בְּרִנָּה יִקְצֹרוּ.
*Those who tearfully sow** will reap in glad song.*

holōch yaylaych uvocho   הָלוֹךְ יֵלֵךְ וּבָכֹה
*He walks along weeping,**

nōsay meshech hazora   נֹשֵׂא מֶשֶׁךְ הַזָּרַע,
he who bears the measure of seeds,

bō yovō v'rino, nōsay alumōsov.   בֹּא יָבֹא בְרִנָּה, נֹשֵׂא אֲלֻמֹּתָיו.
but will return in exultation, a bearer of his sheaves.

בְּשׁוּב ה׳ אֶת שִׁיבַת צִיּוֹן — *When HASHEM will return the captivity of Zion.* The Psalmist wrote prophetically about the return from the exile.

הָיִינוּ כְּחֹלְמִים — *We will be like dreamers.* When the long-awaited return to Zion finally comes to pass, the recollection of the past oppression of the exile will swiftly fade away and seem like a bad dream.

הַזֹּרְעִים בְּדִמְעָה — *Those who tearfully sow.* The Psalmist compares those whose primary con-

cern is with the study of Torah and the performance of the commandments to farmers. The seeds of Israel's spiritual mission may become drenched in tears of unbearable suffering, but the crop, the eventual harvest of homage to righteousness and truth, will be reaped in joy.

הָלוֹךְ יֵלֵךְ וּבָכֹה נֹשֵׂא מֶשֶׁךְ הַזָּרַע — *He walks along weeping, he who bears the measure of seeds.* The poor farmer weeps in fear that his precious seeds may go to waste. God sees his plight and

■ Psalm 127: We recognize that the measure of our success is determined by God, not by our own efforts. We must trust in Him to do that which is necessary for us.

SHIR HAMA-ALŌS lishlōmō;

שִׁיר הַמַּעֲלוֹת, לִשְׁלֹמֹה,

A song of ascents for Solomon:

im Adōnoy lō yivne va-yis,

אִם יהוה לֹא יִבְנֶה בַיִת,

If HASHEM will not build the house,

shov om'lu vōnov bō,

שָׁוְא עָמְלוּ בוֹנָיו בּוֹ,

in vain do its builders labor on it;

im Adōnoy lō yishmor ir,

אִם יהוה לֹא יִשְׁמָר עִיר,

if HASHEM will not guard the city,

shov shokad shōmayr.

שָׁוְא שָׁקַד שׁוֹמֵר.

in vain is the watchman vigilant.

Shov lochem mashkimay kum,

שָׁוְא לָכֶם מַשְׁכִּימֵי קוּם,

It is vain for you who rise early,

m'acharay sheves,

מְאַחֲרֵי שֶׁבֶת,

who sit up late,

ōch'lay lechem ho-atzovim,

אֹכְלֵי לֶחֶם הָעֲצָבִים,

who eat the bread of sorrows —

kayn yitayn lididō shayno.

כֵּן יִתֵּן לִידִידוֹ שֵׁנָא.

for indeed, He gives His beloved ones restful sleep.

Hinay nachalas Adōnoy bonim,

הִנֵּה נַחֲלַת יהוה בָּנִים,

Behold! The heritage of HASHEM is children;

has mercy on him, enabling him to reap a bountiful crop. So, too, exiled Israel carries the burden of spiritual seeds in a hostile world, fearful lest its efforts be wasted. Yet, God will reward its sacrifice with the bounty of the World to Come.

שִׁיר הַמַּעֲלוֹת לִשְׁלֹמֹה — *A song of ascents for Solomon*. David dedicated this psalm to Solomon, who was to build the Temple.

אִם ה' לֹא יִבְנֶה בַיִת שָׁוְא עָמְלוּ בוֹנָיו בּוֹ — *If HASHEM will not build the house, in vain do its builders labor on it*. The success of man's plans is totally dependent upon the will of God. Although David amassed resources for the construction of the Temple, God gave the privilege of carrying out the sacred project to David's son.

שָׁוְא לָכֶם מַשְׁכִּימֵי קוּם מְאַחֲרֵי שֶׁבֶת — *It is vain for you who rise early, who sit up late*. Without God's help, builders will fail, even if they work early and late and deprive themselves of food, rest, and tranquility. To His beloved ones, however, who trust in Him, and whose primary goal is spiritual growth, God will give restful sleep.

הִנֵּה נַחֲלַת ה' בָּנִים — *Behold! The heritage of HASHEM is children*. Previously, the Psalmist emphasized that human effort is in vain and that all depends upon the will of God. Nowhere is this more evident than in the bearing of children. The Talmud (*Taanis* 24a) teaches that although God granted control of many natural phenomena to the angels, He reserved for Himself control over fertility. Thus, a woman does not conceive until the precise moment that God Himself has ordained, for God bequeaths the precious heritage of children to whomever He desires.

Even after a healthy baby is born, God's constant vigilance and assistance are essential, for parents cannot train a child properly and imbue him with deep faith and strong character without Divine guidance.

Some selfish people view each additional child as an unwelcome burden. Wise parents, however, realize that every newborn infant is a precious gift from God, which enables them to participate in the process of creation. Such parents consider themselves privileged to have

sochor p'ri haboten.

שָׂכָר פְּרִי הַבָּֽטֶן.

a reward is the fruit of the womb.

K'chitzim b'yad gibōr

כְּחִצִּים בְּיַד גִּבּוֹר

Like arrows in the hand of a warrior,

kayn b'nay han'urim.

כֵּן בְּנֵי הַנְּעוּרִים.

so are the children of youth.

Ashray hagever asher milay
es ashposō may-hem,

אַשְׁרֵי הַגֶּֽבֶר אֲשֶׁר מִלֵּא
אֶת אַשְׁפָּתוֹ מֵהֶם,

Praiseworthy is the man who fills his quiver with them,

lō yay-vōshu

לֹא יֵבֹֽשׁוּ,

they shall not be shamed,

ki y'dab'ru es ō-y'vim basho-ar.

כִּי יְדַבְּרוּ אֶת אוֹיְבִים בַּשָּֽׁעַר.

when they speak with enemies in the gate.*

■ Psalm 128: The faithful, God-fearing person experiences bliss not only in the World to Come, but in this world as well.

SHIR HAMA-ALŌS

שִׁיר הַמַּעֲלוֹת,

A song of ascents:

ashray kol y'ray Adōnoy,

אַשְׁרֵי כָּל יְרֵא יהוה,

Praiseworthy is each person who fears HASHEM,*

hahōlaych bidrochov.

הַהֹלֵךְ בִּדְרָכָיו.

who walks in His paths.

Y'gi-a kapecho ki sōchayl,

יְגִֽיעַ כַּפֶּֽיךָ כִּי תֹאכֵל,

When you eat the labor of your hands,*

ashrecho v'tōv loch.

אַשְׁרֶֽיךָ וְטוֹב לָךְ.

you are praiseworthy, and it is well with you.

Esht'cho k'gefen pōriyo

אֶשְׁתְּךָ כְּגֶֽפֶן פֹּרִיָּה

Your wife shall be like a fruitful vine

---

been chosen as God's agents to raise a child, and they have unreserved confidence in God's ability and desire to assist them in their roles as parents (*R' Hirsch*).

לֹא יֵבֹֽשׁוּ כִּי יְדַבְּרוּ אֶת אוֹיְבִים בַּשָּֽׁעַר — *They shall not be shamed, when they speak with enemies in the gate.* When the youthful parents have raised their children properly, they can proudly and confidently display them in public, for their children will valiantly voice their support of what is right.

אַשְׁרֵי כָּל יְרֵא ה' — *Praiseworthy is each person who fears HASHEM.* This verse presents a verbal portrait of the genuinely righteous Jew.

Since he fears only God, no mortal can intimidate him, not even the hostile conqueror who holds him captive in exile.

יְגִֽיעַ כַּפֶּֽיךָ כִּי תֹאכֵל — *When you eat the labor of your hands.* The Rabbis repeatedly praise honest labor. Let no man say, "I will eat, and drink, and enjoy life, without bothering to support myself. I have nothing to fear, for surely they will have mercy on me in heaven [and provide for all my expenses]." As a rebuttal to this distorted thinking, Scripture states: "You bless the fruit of the labor of his hands" (*Job* 1:10), indicating that a man must toil and produce results with his own two hands. Only after man exerts effort does God send His blessing.

b'yark'say vay-secho

בְּיַרְכְּתֵי בֵיתֶךָ,

in the inner chambers of your home;

bonecho kish-silay zaysim,

בָּנֶיךָ כִּשְׁתִלֵי זֵיתִים,

your children shall be like olive shoots

soviv l'shulchonecho.

סָבִיב לְשֻׁלְחָנֶךָ.

surrounding your table.

Hinay chi chayn y'vōrach gover
y'ray Adōnoy.

הִנֵּה כִי כֵן יְבֹרַךְ גָּבֶר
יְרֵא יהוה.

Behold! For so is blessed the man who fears HASHEM.

Y'vorech'cho Adōnoy mitziyōn,

יְבָרֶכְךָ יהוה מִצִּיּוֹן,

May HASHEM bless you from Zion,

ur-ay b'tuv y'rusholo-yim,

וּרְאֵה בְּטוּב יְרוּשָׁלָיִם,

and may you gaze upon the goodness of Jerusalem,

kōl y'may cha-yecho.

כֹּל יְמֵי חַיֶּיךָ.

all the days of your life.

Ur-ay vonim l'vonecho,

וּרְאֵה בָנִים לְבָנֶיךָ,

And may you see children born to your children,

sholōm al yisro-ayl.

שָׁלוֹם עַל יִשְׂרָאֵל.

peace upon Israel.

■ Psalm 129: Reflecting on the panorama of Jewish history, we see how, with Hashem's guidance and help, we rose to every challenge and overcame every threat.

SHIR HAMA-ALŌS,

שִׁיר הַמַּעֲלוֹת,

A song of ascents:

rabas tz'roruni min'uroy,

רַבַּת צְרָרֽוּנִי מִנְּעוּרַי,

Much have they distressed me since my youth,

yōmar no yisro-ayl.

יֹאמַר נָא יִשְׂרָאֵל.

let Israel declare now.*

Rabas tz'roruni min'uroy

רַבַּת צְרָרֽוּנִי מִנְּעוּרַי

Much have they distressed me since my youth,

gam lō yoch'lu li.

גַּם לֹא יָכְלוּ לִי.

but they never conquered me.

Al gabi chor'shu chōr'shim,

עַל גַּבִּי חָרְשׁוּ חֹרְשִׁים,

On my back the plowers plowed,

he-erichu l'ma-anisom.

הֶאֱרִיכוּ לְמַעֲנִיתָם.

they lengthened their furrow.

יֹאמַר נָא יִשְׂרָאֵל — *Let Israel declare now.* Now, after centuries and millennia have elapsed, Israel looks back at its history. The Jews' ability to survive all efforts to destroy them attests that the hand of God guides the course of Israel's history and shelters the Jews from all danger.

Adōnoy tzadik,
  ki-tzaytz avōs r'sho-im.

יהוה צַדִּיק,
קִצֵּץ עֲבוֹת רְשָׁעִים.

HASHEM is righteous, He cut the ropes of the wicked.

Yayvōshu v'yisōgu ochōr
  kōl sōn'ay tziyōn.

יֵבְשׁוּ וְיִסְּגוּ אָחוֹר
כֹּל שֹׂנְאֵי צִיּוֹן.

Ashamed and turned back will be all who hate Zion.

Yih-yu kachatzir gagōs,

יִהְיוּ כַּחֲצִיר גַּגּוֹת,

They shall be like the grass on rooftops,

shekadmas sholaf yovaysh.

שֶׁקַּדְמַת שָׁלַף יָבֵשׁ.

that, even before it is plucked, withers —

Shelō milay chapō kōtzayr,

שֶׁלֹּא מִלֵּא כַפּוֹ קוֹצֵר,

with which the reaper cannot fill his hand,

v'chitznō m'amayr.

וְחִצְנוֹ מְעַמֵּר.

nor the binder of sheaves his arm.

V'lō om'ru ho-ōv'rim

וְלֹא אָמְרוּ הָעֹבְרִים,

And passers-by have never said,

birkas Adōnoy alaychem

בִּרְכַּת יהוה אֲלֵיכֶם,

"HASHEM's blessing to you;

bayrachnu eschem b'shaym Adōnoy.

בֵּרַכְנוּ אֶתְכֶם בְּשֵׁם יהוה.

we bless you in the Name of HASHEM."

■ Psalm 130: Even when we are burdened by the guilt of sin, God reaches out to us with love, compassion, and redemption — if we sincerely seek to return to Him.

SHIR HAMA-ALŌS,

שִׁיר הַמַּעֲלוֹת,

A song of ascents:

mima-amakim k'rosicho Adōnoy.

מִמַּעֲמַקִּים קְרָאתִיךָ יהוה.

From the depths I called You, HASHEM.

Adōnoy shim-o v'kōli,

אֲדֹנָי שִׁמְעָה בְקוֹלִי,

My Lord, hear my voice,

tih-yeno oz'necho kashuvōs

תִּהְיֶינָה אָזְנֶיךָ קַשֻּׁבוֹת

may Your ears be attentive

l'kōl tachanunoy.

לְקוֹל תַּחֲנוּנָי.

to the sound of my pleas.

Im avo-nōs tishmor Yoh,

אִם עֲוֹנוֹת תִּשְׁמָר יָהּ,

If You preserve iniquities, O God,*

אִם עֲוֹנוֹת תִּשְׁמָר יָהּ — *If You preserve iniquities, O God.* We cannot deny that we have sinned, | but if God preserves our sins and refuses to forgive them unless we are totally deserving,

Adōnoy mi ya-amōd.

אֲדֹנָי מִי יַעֲמֹד.

my Lord, who could survive?

Ki im'cho has'licho l'ma-an tivoray.

כִּי עִמְּךָ הַסְּלִיחָה, לְמַעַן תִּוָּרֵא.

For with You is forgiveness, that You may be feared.

Kivisi Adōnoy kiv'so nafshi,

קִוִּיתִי יהוה קִוְּתָה נַפְשִׁי,

I put confidence in HASHEM, my soul put confidence,

v'lidvorō hōchol'ti.

וְלִדְבָרוֹ הוֹחָלְתִּי.

and I hoped for His word.

Nafshi Ladōnoy, mishōm'rim labōker,

נַפְשִׁי לַאדֹנָי, מִשֹּׁמְרִים לַבֹּקֶר,

I yearn for my Lord, among those longing for the dawn,*

shōm'rim labōker.

שֹׁמְרִים לַבֹּקֶר.

those longing for the dawn.

Yachayl yisro-ayl el Adōnoy,

יַחֵל יִשְׂרָאֵל אֶל יהוה,

Let Israel hope for HASHEM,

ki im Adōnoy hachesed

כִּי עִם יהוה הַחֶסֶד,

for with HASHEM is kindness,

v'harbay imō f'dus.

וְהַרְבֵּה עִמּוֹ פְדוּת.

and with Him is abundant redemption.

V'hu yifde es yisro-ayl

וְהוּא יִפְדֶּה אֶת יִשְׂרָאֵל,

mikōl avōnōsov.

מִכֹּל עֲוֹנֹתָיו.

And He shall redeem Israel from all its iniquities.

■ Psalm 131: The righteous person is neither arrogant nor jealous of others. He knows that all success is bestowed by God according to each person's needs and mission.

SHIR HAMA-ALŌS l'dovid

שִׁיר הַמַּעֲלוֹת, לְדָוִד,

A song of ascents, by David:

Adōnoy lō govah libi,

יהוה לֹא גָבַהּ לִבִּי,

HASHEM, my heart was not proud,

v'lō romu aynai

וְלֹא רָמוּ עֵינַי,

and my eyes were not haughty,*

v'lō hilachti bigdōlōs

וְלֹא הִלַּכְתִּי בִּגְדֹלוֹת

uvnif-lo-ōs mimeni.

וּבְנִפְלָאוֹת מִמֶּנִּי.

nor did I pursue matters too great and too wondrous for me.

---

we could not survive.

נַפְשִׁי לַאדֹנָי מִשֹּׁמְרִים לַבֹּקֶר — *I* [lit. *my soul*] *yearn for my Lord, among those longing for the dawn.* I am among those who constantly look out for the first signs of the dawn of redemption.

ה' לֹא גָבַהּ לִבִּי וְלֹא רָמוּ עֵינַי — HASHEM, *my heart*

Im lō shivisi v'dōmamti nafshi,
אִם לֹא שִׁוִּיתִי וְדוֹמַמְתִּי נַפְשִׁי,
I swear that I stilled and silenced my soul,

k'gomul alay imō,
כְּגָמֻל עֲלֵי אִמּוֹ,
like a suckling child at his mother's side,

kagomul olai nafshi:
כַּגָּמֻל עָלַי נַפְשִׁי.
like the suckling child is my soul.

Yachayl yisro-ayl el Adōnoy,
יַחֵל יִשְׂרָאֵל אֶל יהוה,

may-ato v'ad ōlom.
מֵעַתָּה וְעַד עוֹלָם.

Let Israel hope to HASHEM, from this time and forever.

■ Psalm 132: Although David only laid the groundwork for the Temple's construction, it was through his merit that the Temple gates miraculously opened to allow the holy Ark to enter.

SHIR HAMA-ALŌS,
שִׁיר הַמַּעֲלוֹת,
A song of ascents.

z'chōr Adōnoy l'dovid,
זְכוֹר יהוה לְדָוִד,

ays kol u-nōsō.
אֵת כָּל עֻנּוֹתוֹ.

*O HASHEM, remember unto David all his suffering.**

Asher nishba Ladōnoy,
אֲשֶׁר נִשְׁבַּע לַיהוה,
How he swore to HASHEM,

nodar la-avir ya-akōv.
נָדַר לַאֲבִיר יַעֲקֹב.
and vowed to the Strong One of Jacob.

Im ovō b'ōhel baysi
אִם אָבֹא בְּאֹהֶל בֵּיתִי,
*"If I enter the tent of my home;**

im e-ele al eres y'tzu-oy.
אִם אֶעֱלֶה עַל עֶרֶשׂ יְצוּעָי.
if I go upon the bed that is spread for me;

Im etayn sh'nos l'aynoy,
אִם אֶתֵּן שְׁנָת לְעֵינָי,

l'afapai t'numo.
לְעַפְעַפַּי תְּנוּמָה.

if I allow sleep to my eyes, slumber to my eyelids;

Ad emtzo mokōm Ladōnoy,
עַד אֶמְצָא מָקוֹם לַיהוה,
*before I find a place for HASHEM,**

mishkonōs la-avir ya-akōv.
מִשְׁכָּנוֹת לַאֲבִיר יַעֲקֹב.
resting places for the Strong One of Jacob."

זְכוֹר ה׳ לְדָוִד אֵת כָּל עֻנּוֹתוֹ — *O HASHEM, remember unto David all his suffering*. This refers to David's longing to build the Temple and, when God told him he could not do so, his sincere and unselfish efforts to prepare the way for Solomon to accomplish the task.

אִם אָבֹא בְּאֹהֶל בֵּיתִי — *If I enter the tent of my home*. David vowed that he would not enjoy the comforts of his own home until he prepared a home for God.

עַד אֶמְצָא מָקוֹם לַה׳ — *Before I find a place for HASHEM*. David's first task was to find the place

Hinay sh'ma-anuho v'efroso,
הִנֵּה שְׁמַעֲנוּהָ בְאֶפְרָתָה,
Behold! We heard of it in Ephras,

m'tzonuho bisday yo-ar.
מְצָאנוּהָ בִּשְׂדֵי יָעַר.
we found it in the forested field.

Novō-o l'mishk'nōsov,
נָבוֹאָה לְמִשְׁכְּנוֹתָיו,
We will arrive at His Tabernacles,

nishta-chave lahadōm raglov.
נִשְׁתַּחֲוֶה לַהֲדֹם רַגְלָיו.
we will prostrate ourselves at His footstool.

Kumo Adōnoy limnuchosecho,
קוּמָה יהוה לִמְנוּחָתֶךָ,
Arise, HASHEM, to Your resting place,

ato va-arōn u-zecho.
אַתָּה וַאֲרוֹן עֻזֶּךָ.
You and the Ark of Your strength.

Kōhanecho yilb'shu tzedek,
כֹּהֲנֶיךָ יִלְבְּשׁוּ צֶדֶק,
Let Your priests be clothed in righteousness,

vachasidecho y'ranaynu.
וַחֲסִידֶיךָ יְרַנֵּנוּ.
and Your devout ones will sing joyously.

Ba-avur dovid avdecho,
בַּעֲבוּר דָּוִד עַבְדֶּךָ,
For the sake of David, Your servant,

al toshayv p'nay m'shichecho.
אַל תָּשֵׁב פְּנֵי מְשִׁיחֶךָ.
turn not away the face of Your anointed.

Nishba Adōnoy l'dovid,
נִשְׁבַּע יהוה לְדָוִד,
HASHEM has sworn to David,

emes lō yoshuv mimeno,
אֱמֶת לֹא יָשׁוּב מִמֶּנָּה,
a truth from which He will never retreat:

mip'ri vitn'cho oshis l'chisay loch.
מִפְּרִי בִטְנְךָ אָשִׁית לְכִסֵּא לָךְ.
"From the fruit of your issue I will place upon your throne.

Im yishm'ru vonecho b'risi,
אִם יִשְׁמְרוּ בָנֶיךָ בְּרִיתִי,
If your sons keep My covenant,

v'aydōsi zō alam'daym,
וְעֵדֹתִי זוֹ אֲלַמְּדֵם,
and this, My testament, that I shall teach them,

gam b'nayhem aday ad,
גַּם בְּנֵיהֶם עֲדֵי עַד,
then their sons, too, forever and ever,

yaysh'vu l'chisay loch.
יֵשְׁבוּ לְכִסֵּא לָךְ.
shall sit upon your throne."*

---

where God wished the Temple to be built.
גַּם בְּנֵיהֶם עֲדֵי עַד יֵשְׁבוּ לְכִסֵּא לָךְ — *Then their sons, too, forever and ever, shall sit upon your throne.* The royal privilege belongs to David and to his

seed for all generations. Anyone who believes in the truth of the Torah given by Moses, the master of all prophets, must believe that only those who descend from David are suited for

Ki vochar Adōnoy b'tziyōn,
    ivoh l'mōshov lō.

כִּי בָחַר יהוה בְּצִיּוֹן,
אִוָּהּ לְמוֹשָׁב לוֹ.

For HASHEM has chosen Zion, He has desired it for His habitation.

Zōs m'nuchosi aday ad,

זֹאת מְנוּחָתִי עֲדֵי עַד,

This is My resting place forever and ever,

pō ayshayv ki ivisiho.

פֹּה אֵשֵׁב כִּי אִוִּתִיהָ.

here I will dwell, for I have desired it.

Tzaydoh boraych avoraych,

צֵידָהּ בָּרֵךְ אֲבָרֵךְ,

Her sustenance I will bless abundantly;

evyōneho asbi-a lochem.

אֶבְיוֹנֶיהָ אַשְׂבִּיעַ לָחֶם.

her needy I will satisfy with food.

V'chōhaneho albish yesha,

וְכֹהֲנֶיהָ אַלְבִּישׁ יֶשַׁע,

I will clothe her priests with salvation;

vachasideho ranayn y'ranaynu.

וַחֲסִידֶיהָ רַנֵּן יְרַנֵּנוּ.

her devout ones will always sing joyously.

Shom atzmi-ach keren l'dovid,

שָׁם אַצְמִיחַ קֶרֶן לְדָוִד,

There I shall cause pride to sprout for David;

orachti nayr limshichi.

עָרַכְתִּי נֵר לִמְשִׁיחִי.

I have prepared a lamp for My anointed.

Ō-y'vov albish bōshes,

אוֹיְבָיו אַלְבִּישׁ בֹּשֶׁת,

His enemies I will clothe with shame,

v'olov yotzitz nizrō.

וְעָלָיו יָצִיץ נִזְרוֹ.

but upon him, his crown will shine.

■ Psalm 133: We long for the day when we will join with all our brethren and with God Himself to rejoice in the Holy Temple.

SHIR HAMA-ALŌS l'dovid,

שִׁיר הַמַּעֲלוֹת, לְדָוִד,

A song of ascents, by David:

hinay ma tōv u-ma no-im,

הִנֵּה מַה טּוֹב וּמַה נָּעִים,

Behold, how good and how pleasant

sheves achim gam yochad.

שֶׁבֶת אַחִים גַּם יָחַד.

is the dwelling of brothers, moreover, in unity.*

Ka-shemen hatōv al horōsh,

כַּשֶּׁמֶן הַטּוֹב עַל הָרֹאשׁ,

Like the precious oil upon the head*

---

royalty. Anyone who is not of David's distinguished seed is considered a total foreigner and alien to royalty, just as anyone who is not of Aaron's seed is totally alien to the priesthood and Temple service.

שֶׁבֶת אַחִים גַּם יָחַד — *The dwelling of brothers,*

moreover, in unity. Having spoken in the previous psalm of the Temple, David goes on to laud the idyllic state that will exist when all Jews live together in brotherly love — and unity will be in their hearts as well.

כַּשֶּׁמֶן הַטּוֹב עַל הָרֹאשׁ — *Like the precious oil upon*

yōrayd al hazokon, z'kan aharōn
יֵרֵד עַל הַזָּקָן, זְקַן אַהֲרֹן,

running down upon the beard, the beard of Aaron,

she-yōrayd al pi midōsov.
שֶׁיֹּרֵד עַל פִּי מִדּוֹתָיו.

running down over the hem of his garments.

K'tal chermōn she-yōrayd
כְּטַל חֶרְמוֹן שֶׁיֹּרֵד

al har'ray tziyōn,
עַל הַרְרֵי צִיּוֹן,

Like the dew of Hermon descending upon the mountains of Zion,

ki shom tzivo
כִּי שָׁם צִוָּה

Adōnoy es hab'rocho,
יהוה אֶת הַבְּרָכָה,

for there HASHEM has commanded the blessing.

cha-yim ad ho-ōlom.
חַיִּים עַד הָעוֹלָם.

May there be life forever!

■ Psalm 134: After describing the idyllic existence of a completely united Jewish nation, we are admonished to maintain our spiritual purity even in the gloom of dispersion and exile. We must build "houses for God" — fulfilling our mission as Jews — wherever we are and however we can.

SHIR HAMA-ALŌS,   שִׁיר הַמַּעֲלוֹת,

A song of ascents:

hinay bor'chu es Adōnoy,
הִנֵּה בָּרְכוּ אֶת יהוה,

kol avday Adōnoy,
כָּל עַבְדֵי יהוה,

Behold, bless HASHEM, all you servants of HASHEM,

ho-ōm'dim b'vays Adōnoy balaylōs.   הָעֹמְדִים בְּבֵית יהוה בַּלֵּילוֹת.

*who stand in the House of HASHEM in the nights.**

S'u y'daychem kōdesh,
שְׂאוּ יְדֵכֶם קֹדֶשׁ,

uvor'chu es Adōnoy.
וּבָרְכוּ אֶת יהוה.

Lift your hands in the Sanctuary and bless HASHEM.

Y'vorech'cho Adōnoy mitziyōn,
יְבָרֶכְךָ יהוה מִצִּיּוֹן,

ōsay shoma-yim vo-oretz.
עֹשֵׂה שָׁמַיִם וָאָרֶץ:

*May HASHEM bless you from Zion, Maker of heaven and earth.**

IN THE PRESENCE OF A *MINYAN,* MOURNERS RECITE THE MOURNER'S *KADDISH* (P. 539).
THEN, THE CONGREGATION CONTINUES WITH *ALEINU* (P. 536).

---

the head. The Psalmist likens the flow of Heavenly blessing to the precious oil with which High Priests and kings were anointed. So, too, when Jews are united in brotherhood, God's blessing will flow like a stream from Mount Hermon, the lofty mountain in the north, down to every nook and cranny of the land.

הָעֹמְדִים בְּבֵית ה' בַּלֵּילוֹת — *Who stand in the House of HASHEM in the nights.* The genuine servant of HASHEM never abandons his post.

Not only does he act as a guardian of the faith by day, i.e., in times of ease and success, but even at night, i.e., in times of adversity and gloom, he remains on guard and refuses to fall asleep at his post.

יְבָרֶכְךָ ה' מִצִּיּוֹן שֵׂה שָׁמַיִם וָאָרֶץ — *May HASHEM bless you from Zion, Maker of heaven and earth.* When man is truly deserving, God will dispense blessings upon the earth directly from Zion, where God's Presence dwells on earth.

Motzo'ei
Shabbos

⊰ MAARIV — SABBATH CONCLUSION / WEEKDAY ⊱

CONGREGATION, THEN *CHAZZAN*:

V'HU rachum y'chapayr ovon
v'lō yashchis,　　　　　　　　　**וְהוּא** רַחוּם יְכַפֵּר עָוֹן
　　　　　　　　　　　　　　　וְלֹא יַשְׁחִית,

He, the Merciful One, is forgiving of iniquity and does not destroy;

v'hirbo l'hoshiv apō　　　　　　וְהִרְבָּה לְהָשִׁיב אַפּוֹ,

frequently He withdraws His anger,

v'lō yo-ir kol chamosō.　　　　וְלֹא יָעִיר כָּל חֲמָתוֹ.

not arousing His entire rage.

Adōnoy hōshi-o　　　　　　　　יהוה הוֹשִׁיעָה,

HASHEM, *save!*

hamelech ya-anaynu v'yōm kor'aynu.　הַמֶּלֶךְ יַעֲנֵנוּ בְיוֹם קָרְאֵנוּ.

May the King answer us on the day we call.

CHAZZAN SUMMONS THE CONGREGATION TO JOIN IN THE FORTHCOMING PRAYERS.

BOR'CHU es Adōnoy ham'vōroch.　**בָּרְכוּ** אֶת יהוה הַמְבֹרָךְ.

Bless HASHEM, *the blessed One.*

CONGREGATION, FOLLOWED BY *CHAZZAN*, RESPONDS,
BOWING AT Boruch AND STRAIGHTENING UP AT Adōnoy:

Boruch Adōnoy　　　　　　　　בָּרוּךְ יהוה
ham'vōroch l'ōlom vo-ed.　　　הַמְבֹרָךְ לְעוֹלָם וָעֶד.

Blessed is HASHEM *the blessed One, for all eternity.*

■ First blessing preceding the *Shema:* We recognize God's ongoing management of the world, as He allows us to benefit from the recurring cycles of night and day.

BORUCH ato Adōnoy,　　　　**בָּרוּךְ** אַתָּה יהוה

Blessed are You, HASHEM,

Elōhaynu melech ho-ōlom,　　אֱלֹהֵינוּ מֶלֶךְ הָעוֹלָם,

our God, King of the universe,

asher bidvorō ma-ariv arovim,　אֲשֶׁר בִּדְבָרוֹ מַעֲרִיב עֲרָבִים,

Who by His word brings on evenings,

b'chochmo pōsay-ach sh'orim,　בְּחָכְמָה פּוֹתֵחַ שְׁעָרִים,

with wisdom opens gates,

u-visvuno m'shane itim,　　　וּבִתְבוּנָה מְשַׁנֶּה עִתִּים,

with understanding alters periods,

u-machalif es haz'manim,　　וּמַחֲלִיף אֶת הַזְּמַנִּים,

changes the seasons,

umsadayr es hakōchovim,　　וּמְסַדֵּר אֶת הַכּוֹכָבִים

and orders the stars

b'mishm'rōsayhem boroki-a בְּמִשְׁמְרוֹתֵיהֶם בָּרָקִיעַ
  kirtzōnō. כִּרְצוֹנוֹ.
in their heavenly constellations as He wills.

Bōray yōm voloylo, בּוֹרֵא יוֹם וָלָיְלָה,
He creates day and night,

gōlayl ōr mip'nay chōshech, גּוֹלֵל אוֹר מִפְּנֵי חֹשֶׁךְ
removing light before darkness

v'chōshech mip'nay ōr, וְחֹשֶׁךְ מִפְּנֵי אוֹר,
and darkness before light;

u-ma-avir yōm u-mayvi loylo, וּמַעֲבִיר יוֹם וּמֵבִיא לָיְלָה,
He causes day to pass and brings night,

u-mavdil bayn yōm u-vayn loylo, וּמַבְדִּיל בֵּין יוֹם וּבֵין לָיְלָה,
and separates between day and night —

Adōnoy Tz'vo-ōs sh'mō. יהוה צְבָאוֹת שְׁמוֹ.
HASHEM, Master of Legions, is His Name.

✧ Ayl chai v'ka-yom, ✧ אֵל חַי וְקַיָּם,
  tomid yimlōch olaynu תָּמִיד יִמְלוֹךְ עָלֵינוּ,
May the living and enduring God continuously reign over us,

l'ōlom vo-ed. לְעוֹלָם וָעֶד.
for all eternity.

Boruch ato Adōnoy, בָּרוּךְ אַתָּה יהוה,
  hama-ariv arovim. הַמַּעֲרִיב עֲרָבִים.
Blessed are You, HASHEM, Who brings on evenings.

CONGREGATION RESPONDS AMEN: Omayn — אָמֵן

■ Second blessing preceding the *Shema:* God's love of Israel manifested itself by His giving the Jewish people the Torah and *mitzvos*. We reciprocate with our pledge to study and observe His Torah and *mitzvos*.

AHAVAS ŌLOM אַהֲבַת עוֹלָם

[With] an eternal love

bays yisro-ayl am'cho ohovto, בֵּית יִשְׂרָאֵל עַמְּךָ אָהָבְתָּ.
have You loved the House of Israel, Your people;

tōro u-mitzvōs, תּוֹרָה וּמִצְוֹת,
  chukim u-mishpotim, חֻקִּים וּמִשְׁפָּטִים,
Torah and commandments, decrees and ordinances

ōsonu limadto אוֹתָנוּ לִמַּדְתָּ.
have You taught us.

Al kayn Adōnoy Elōhaynu, עַל כֵּן יהוה אֱלֹהֵינוּ,
Therefore HASHEM, our God,

b'shoch-vaynu uvkumaynu · בְּשָׁכְבֵּנוּ וּבְקוּמֵנוּ
upon our retiring and our arising,

nosi-ach b'chukecho, · נָשִׂיחַ בְּחֻקֶּיךָ,
we will discuss Your decrees

v'nismach b'divray sōrosecho · וְנִשְׂמַח בְּדִבְרֵי תוֹרָתֶךָ,
and we will rejoice with the words of Your Torah

uvmitzvōsecho l'ōlom vo-ed, · וּבְמִצְוֹתֶיךָ לְעוֹלָם וָעֶד,
and with Your commandments for all eternity,

ki haym cha-yaynu v'ōrech yomaynu, · כִּי הֵם חַיֵּינוּ, וְאֹרֶךְ יָמֵינוּ,
for they are our life and the length of our days

u-vohem neh-ge yōmom voloylo. · וּבָהֶם נֶהְגֶּה יוֹמָם וָלָיְלָה.
and about them we will meditate day and night.

V'ahavos'cho · וְאַהֲבָתְךָ,
al tosir mimenu l'ōlomim. · אַל תָּסִיר מִמֶּנּוּ לְעוֹלָמִים.
May You not remove Your love from us forever.

Boruch ato Adōnoy, · בָּרוּךְ אַתָּה יהוה,
ōhayv amō yisro-ayl. · אוֹהֵב עַמּוֹ יִשְׂרָאֵל.
Blessed are You, HASHEM, Who loves His people Israel.

CONGREGATION RESPONDS: Omayn — אָמֵן

THE SHEMA

■ The *Shema* is our acceptance of and submission to the absolute Sovereignty of God.

IMMEDIATELY BEFORE THE RECITATION OF THE *SHEMA*, CONCENTRATE ON FULfILLING THE POSITIVE COMMANDMENT OF RECITING THE *SHEMA* DAILY, ONCE IN THE EVENING AND ONCE IN THE MORNING. IT IS IMPORTANT TO ENUNCIATE EACH WORD CLEARLY AND NOT TO RUN WORDS TOGETHER. ONE PRAYING WITHOUT A *MINYAN* BEGINS WITH THE FOLLOWING THREE-WORD FORMULA:

Ayl melech ne-emon. · אֵל מֶלֶךְ נֶאֱמָן.
God, trustworthy King.

RECITE THE FIRST VERSE ALOUD, WITH YOUR RIGHT HAND COVERING YOUR EYES, AND CONCENTRATE INTENSELY UPON ACCEPTING GOD'S ABSOLUTE SOVEREIGNTY.

SH'MA yisro-ayl, · שְׁמַע יִשְׂרָאֵל,
Adōnoy Elōhaynu, Adōnoy e-chod. · יהוה אֱלֹהֵינוּ, יהוה אֶחָד.
Hear, O Israel: HASHEM is our God, HASHEM, the One [and Only].

In an undertone:

Boruch shaym k'vōd malchusō · בָּרוּךְ שֵׁם כְּבוֹד מַלְכוּתוֹ
l'ōlom vo-ed. · לְעוֹלָם וָעֶד.
Blessed is the Name of His glorious kingdom for all eternity.

■ We return God's love by studying His Torah and committing ourselves to observe the Torah with all our resources and being.

WHILE RECITING THE FOLLOWING PARAGRAPH, CONCENTRATE ON ACCEPTING
THE COMMANDMENT TO LOVE GOD.

V'OHAVTO ays　　　　　　　　　　אֵת **וְאָהַבְתָּ**

　Adōnoy Elōhecho,　　　　　　　יהוה ׀ אֱלֹהֶיךָ,
　　　You shall love HASHEM, *your God,*

b'chol l'vov'cho,　　　　　　　　בְּכָל לְבָבְךָ,
　　　　with all your heart,

uvchol nafsh'cho, uvchol m'ōdecho.　וּבְכָל נַפְשְׁךָ, וּבְכָל מְאֹדֶךָ.
　　　with all your soul and with all your resources.

V'ho-yu had'vorim ho-ayle,　　　וְהָיוּ הַדְּבָרִים הָאֵלֶּה,
　asher onōchi m'tzav'cho ha-yōm,　אֲשֶׁר אָנֹכִי מְצַוְּךָ הַיּוֹם,
　　　Let these matters that I command you today

al l'vovecho.　　　　　　　　　עַל לְבָבֶךָ.
　　　　　be upon your heart.

V'shinantom l'vonecho,　　　　　וְשִׁנַּנְתָּם לְבָנֶיךָ,
　　　Teach them thoroughly to your children

v'dibarto bom　　　　　　　　　וְדִבַּרְתָּ בָּם,
　　　　and speak of them

b'shivt'cho b'vaysecho,　　　　בְּשִׁבְתְּךָ בְּבֵיתֶךָ,
　uvlecht'cho vaderech　　　　וּבְלֶכְתְּךָ בַדֶּרֶךְ,
　　　while you sit in your home, while you walk on the way,

uv'shochb'cho, uvkumecho.　　וּבְשָׁכְבְּךָ וּבְקוּמֶךָ.
　　　when you retire and when you arise.

Ukshartom l'ōs al yodecho,　　וּקְשַׁרְתָּם לְאוֹת עַל יָדֶךָ,
　　And you shall bind them as a sign upon your arm

v'ho-yu l'tōtofōs bayn aynecho.　וְהָיוּ לְטֹטָפֹת בֵּין עֵינֶיךָ.
　　and they shall be tefillin between your eyes.

Uchsavtom al m'zuzōs bay-secho　וּכְתַבְתָּם עַל מְזֻזוֹת בֵּיתֶךָ,
　u-visho-recho.　　　　　　　　וּבִשְׁעָרֶיךָ.
　And write them on the doorposts of your house and upon your gates.

■ We declare our collective commitment to observe God's *mitzvos,* and the recognition
that our national success or failure is dependent on this observance.

V'HO-YO im shomō-a tishm'u　　וְהָיָה, אִם־שָׁמֹעַ תִּשְׁמְעוּ
　el mitzvōsai,　　　　　　　　　אֶל מִצְוֹתַי,
And it will come to pass that if you continually hearken to My commandments

asher onōchi　　　　　　　　　אֲשֶׁר אָנֹכִי
　m'tza-ve eschem ha-yōm,　　מְצַוֶּה אֶתְכֶם הַיּוֹם,
　　　that I command you today,

l'ahavo es Adōnoy Elōhaychem, לְאַהֲבָה אֶת יהוה אֱלֹהֵיכֶם
to love HASHEM, your God,

ul-ovdō וּלְעָבְדוֹ,
and to serve Him,

b'chol l'vavchem uvchol nafsh'chem. בְּכָל לְבַבְכֶם, וּבְכָל נַפְשְׁכֶם.
with all your heart and with all your soul —

V'nosati m'tar artz'chem b'itō, וְנָתַתִּי מְטַר אַרְצְכֶם בְּעִתּוֹ,
then I will provide rain for your land in its proper time,

yōre u-malkōsh, יוֹרֶה וּמַלְקוֹשׁ,
the early rains and the late rains,

v'osafto d'gonecho v'sirōsh'cho וְאָסַפְתָּ דְגָנֶךָ וְתִירֹשְׁךָ
v'yitzhorecho. וְיִצְהָרֶךָ.
that you may gather in your grain, your wine, and your oil.

V'nosati aysev וְנָתַתִּי עֵשֶׂב
b'sod'cho livhemtecho, בְּשָׂדְךָ לִבְהֶמְתֶּךָ,
I will provide grass in your field for your cattle

v'ochalto v'sovo-to. וְאָכַלְתָּ וְשָׂבָעְתָּ.
and you will eat and you will be satisfied.

Hi-shom'ru lochem, הִשָּׁמְרוּ לָכֶם,
Beware for yourselves,

pen yifte l'vavchem, פֶּן יִפְתֶּה לְבַבְכֶם,
lest your heart be seduced

v'sartem va-avadtem וְסַרְתֶּם וַעֲבַדְתֶּם
elōhim a-chayrim אֱלֹהִים אֲחֵרִים,
and you turn astray and serve gods of others

v'hishtachavisem lohem. וְהִשְׁתַּחֲוִיתֶם לָהֶם.
and bow to them.

V'choro af Adōnoy bochem, וְחָרָה אַף יהוה בָּכֶם,
Then the wrath of HASHEM will blaze against you;

v'otzar es ha-shoma-yim וְעָצַר אֶת הַשָּׁמַיִם,
v'lō yih-ye motor, וְלֹא יִהְיֶה מָטָר,
He will restrain the heaven so there will be no rain

v'ho-adomo lō sitayn es y'vuloh וְהָאֲדָמָה לֹא תִתֵּן אֶת יְבוּלָהּ,
and the ground will not yield its produce;

va-avadtem m'hayro וַאֲבַדְתֶּם מְהֵרָה
and you will swiftly be banished

may-al ho-oretz hatōvo מֵעַל הָאָרֶץ הַטֹּבָה
from the goodly land

asher Adōnoy nōsayn lochem.　　　　אֲשֶׁר יהוה נֹתֵן לָכֶם.

V'samtem es d'vorai ayle　　　　וְשַׂמְתֶּם אֶת דְּבָרַי אֵלֶּה,
You shall place these words of Mine

al l'vavchem v'al nafsh'chem　　　　עַל לְבַבְכֶם וְעַל נַפְשְׁכֶם,
upon your heart and upon your soul;

ukshartem ōsom l'ōs al yedchem,　　וּקְשַׁרְתֶּם אֹתָם לְאוֹת עַל יֶדְכֶם,
and you shall bind them for a sign upon your arm

v'ho-yu l'tōtofōs bayn aynaychem.　　וְהָיוּ לְטוֹטָפֹת בֵּין עֵינֵיכֶם.
and they shall be tefillin between your eyes.

V'limadtem ōsom es b'naychem,　　וְלִמַּדְתֶּם אֹתָם אֶת בְּנֵיכֶם,
You shall teach them to your children,

l'dabayr bom,　　　　　　　　לְדַבֵּר בָּם,
to discuss them,

b'shivt'cho b'vay-secho,　　　　בְּשִׁבְתְּךָ בְּבֵיתֶךָ,
uvlecht'cho vaderech,　　　　　וּבְלֶכְתְּךָ בַדֶּרֶךְ,
while you sit in your home, while you walk on the way,

uv'shochb'cho uvkumecho.　　　וּבְשָׁכְבְּךָ וּבְקוּמֶךָ.
when you retire and when you arise.

Uchsavtom al m'zuzōs bay-secho　　וּכְתַבְתָּם עַל מְזוּזוֹת בֵּיתֶךָ,
uvisho-recho.　　　　　　　וּבִשְׁעָרֶיךָ.
And write them on the doorposts of your house and upon your gates.

L'ma-an yirbu y'maychem　　　לְמַעַן יִרְבּוּ יְמֵיכֶם
vimay v'naychem　　　　　וִימֵי בְנֵיכֶם,
In order to prolong your days and the days of your children

al ho-adomo asher nishba　　עַל הָאֲדָמָה אֲשֶׁר נִשְׁבַּע
Adōnoy la-avōsaychem　　　יהוה לַאֲבֹתֵיכֶם
upon the ground that HASHEM has sworn to your ancestors

losays lohem,　　　　　　לָתֵת לָהֶם,
to give them,

kimay ha-shoma-yim al ho-oretz.　כִּימֵי הַשָּׁמַיִם עַל הָאָרֶץ.
like the days of the heavens on the earth.

■ We acknowledge the Divine providence over Israel as demonstrated by the Exodus from Egypt, thus obligating us to observe His *mitzvos*.

VA-YŌMER Adōnoy　　　　וַיֹּאמֶר יהוה
el mōshe laymōr.　　　　　אֶל מֹשֶׁה לֵּאמֹר.
And HASHEM said to Moses saying:

Dabayr el b'nay yisro-ayl
דַּבֵּר אֶל בְּנֵי יִשְׂרָאֵל,

  v'omarto alayhem,
וְאָמַרְתָּ אֲלֵהֶם,

Speak to the Children of Israel and say to them

v'osu lohem tzitzis
וְעָשׂוּ לָהֶם צִיצִת

that they are to make themselves tzitzis

al kanfay vigdayhem
עַל כַּנְפֵי בִגְדֵיהֶם

on the corners of their garments,

l'dōrōsom,
לְדֹרֹתָם,

throughout their generations.

v'nos'nu al tzitzis hakonof
וְנָתְנוּ עַל צִיצִת הַכָּנָף,

  p'sil t'chayles.
פְּתִיל תְּכֵלֶת.

And they are to place upon the tzitzis of each corner a thread of turquoise wool.

V'ho-yo lochem l'tzitzis,
וְהָיָה לָכֶם לְצִיצִת,

And it shall constitute tzitzis for you,

ur-isem ōsō
וּרְאִיתֶם אֹתוֹ,

that you may see it

uz-chartem
וּזְכַרְתֶּם

  es kol mitzvōs Adōnoy,
אֶת כָּל מִצְוֹת יהוה,

and remember all the commandments of HASHEM

va-asisem ōsom,
וַעֲשִׂיתֶם אֹתָם,

and perform them;

v'lō sosuru acharay l'vavchem
וְלֹא תָתוּרוּ אַחֲרֵי לְבַבְכֶם

  v'acharay aynaychem,
וְאַחֲרֵי עֵינֵיכֶם,

and you shall not explore after your heart and after your eyes

asher atem zōnim acharayhem.
אֲשֶׁר אַתֶּם זֹנִים אַחֲרֵיהֶם.

after which you stray.

L'ma-an tizk'ru
לְמַעַן תִּזְכְּרוּ

  va-asisem es kol mitzvōsoy,
וַעֲשִׂיתֶם אֶת כָּל מִצְוֹתָי,

So that you may remember and perform all My commandments;

vih-yisem k'dōshim Laylōhaychem.
וִהְיִיתֶם קְדֹשִׁים לֵאלֹהֵיכֶם.

and be holy to your God.

CONCENTRATE ON FULFILLING THE COMMANDMENT TO REMEMBER THE EXODUS FROM EGYPT.

Ani Adōnoy Elohaychem,
אֲנִי יהוה אֱלֹהֵיכֶם,

I am HASHEM, your God,

asher hōtzaysi eschem
אֲשֶׁר הוֹצֵאתִי אֶתְכֶם

  may-eretz mitzra-yim,
מֵאֶרֶץ מִצְרָיִם,

Who has removed you from the land of Egypt

lih-yōs lochem Laylōhim,
לִהְיוֹת לָכֶם לֵאלֹהִים,

to be a God to you;

ani Adōnoy Elōhaychem. Emes . . .   . . . אֱמֶת. אֲנִי יהוה אֱלֹהֵיכֶם

I am Hashem *your God. It is true . . .*

Chazzan repeats — **יהוה אֱלֹהֵיכֶם אֱמֶת.**

■ First blessing following *Shema:* Our national deliverance in the past, exemplified by the Egyptian Exodus, serves as a source of trust in God in difficult times, strengthening our faith and commitment in the future Redemption.

VE-EMUNO kol zōs,   **וֶאֱמוּנָה** כָּל זֹאת,

   v'ka-yom olaynu,   וְקַיָּם עָלֵינוּ,

   . . . and faithful is all this, and it is firmly established for us

ki hu Adōnoy Elōhaynu   כִּי הוּא יהוה אֱלֹהֵינוּ

   that He is Hashem *our God,*

v'ayn zulosō,   וְאֵין זוּלָתוֹ,

   and there is none but Him,

va-anachnu yisro-ayl amō.   וַאֲנַחְנוּ יִשְׂרָאֵל עַמּוֹ.

   and we are Israel, His people.

Hapōdaynu miyad m'lochim,   הַפּוֹדֵנוּ מִיַּד מְלָכִים,

   He redeems us from the power of kings,

malkaynu hagō-alaynu   מַלְכֵּנוּ הַגּוֹאֲלֵנוּ

   mikaf kol he-oritzim,   מִכַּף כָּל הֶעָרִיצִים,

   our King Who delivers us from the hand of all the cruel tyrants;

ho-Ayl hanifro lonu mitzoraynu,   הָאֵל הַנִּפְרָע לָנוּ מִצָּרֵינוּ,

   the God Who exacts vengeance for us from our foes

v'ham'shalaym g'mul   וְהַמְשַׁלֵּם גְּמוּל

   l'chol ō-y'vay nafshaynu,   לְכָל אֹיְבֵי נַפְשֵׁנוּ,

   and Who brings just retribution upon all enemies of our soul;

ho-ō-se g'dōlōs ad ayn chayker,   הָעֹשֶׂה גְדֹלוֹת עַד אֵין חֵקֶר,

   He performs great deeds that are beyond comprehension,

v'niflo-ōs ad ayn mispor,   וְנִפְלָאוֹת עַד אֵין מִסְפָּר,

   and wonders beyond number;

hasom nafshaynu bacha-yim,   הַשָּׂם נַפְשֵׁנוּ בַּחַיִּים,

   He set our soul in life

v'lō nosan lamōt raglaynu,   וְלֹא נָתַן לַמּוֹט רַגְלֵנוּ,

   and did not allow our foot to falter;

hamad-richaynu al bomōs ōy'vaynu,   הַמַּדְרִיכֵנוּ עַל בָּמוֹת אוֹיְבֵינוּ,

   He led us upon the heights of our enemies

va-yorem karnaynu al kol sōn'aynu,   וַיָּרֶם קַרְנֵנוּ עַל כָּל שׂנְאֵינוּ,

   and raised our pride above all who hate us;

ho-ōse lonu nisim un'komō b'faro,   הָעֹשֶׂה לָּנוּ נִסִּים וּנְקָמָה בְּפַרְעֹה,
He wrought for us miracles and vengeance upon Pharaoh,

ōsōs u-mōf'sim   אוֹתוֹת וּמוֹפְתִים
b'admas b'nay chom,   בְּאַדְמַת בְּנֵי חָם,
signs and wonders on the land of the offspring of Ham;

hamake b'evrosō   הַמַּכֶּה בְעֶבְרָתוֹ
kol b'chōray mitzroyim,   כָּל בְּכוֹרֵי מִצְרֵיִם,
He struck with His anger all the firstborn of Egypt

va-yōtzay es amō yisro-ayl   וַיּוֹצֵא אֶת עַמּוֹ יִשְׂרָאֵל
mitōchom,   מִתּוֹכָם
and removed His people Israel from their midst

l'chayrus ōlom,   לְחֵרוּת עוֹלָם,
to eternal freedom;

hama-avir bonov   הַמַּעֲבִיר בָּנָיו
bayn gizray yam suf,   בֵּין גִּזְרֵי יַם סוּף,
He brought His children through the split parts of the Sea of Reeds

es rōd'fayhem v'es sōn'ayhem,   אֶת רוֹדְפֵיהֶם וְאֶת שׂוֹנְאֵיהֶם
bis-hōmōs tiba.   בִּתְהוֹמוֹת טָבַע.
while their pursuers and their enemies He caused to sink into the depths.

V'ro-u vonov g'vurosō,   וְרָאוּ בָנָיו גְּבוּרָתוֹ,
When His children perceived His power,

shib'chu v'hōdu lishmō,   שִׁבְּחוּ וְהוֹדוּ לִשְׁמוֹ,
they lauded and gave grateful praise to His Name;

u-malchusō b'rotzōn   ✧ וּמַלְכוּתוֹ בְּרָצוֹן
kib'lu alayhem.   קִבְּלוּ עֲלֵיהֶם.
and His Kingship they willingly accepted upon themselves.

Mōshe uvnay yisro-ayl   מֹשֶׁה וּבְנֵי יִשְׂרָאֵל
l'cho onu shiro,   לְךָ עָנוּ שִׁירָה,
Moses and the Children of Israel exclaimed to You in song,

b'simcho rabo,   בְּשִׂמְחָה רַבָּה,
with abundant gladness —

v'om'ru chulom: וְאָמְרוּ כֻלָּם:
and they said unanimously:

MI chomōcho bo-aylim Adōnoy,   **מִי** כָמֹכָה בָּאֵלִם יהוה,
Who is like You among the heavenly powers, HASHEM!

mi komōcho nedor bakōdesh,   מִי כָּמֹכָה נֶאְדָּר בַּקֹּדֶשׁ,
Who is like You, mighty in holiness,

nōro s'hilōs, ōsay fele.   נוֹרָא תְהִלֹּת עֹשֵׂה פֶלֶא.
too awesome for praise, doing wonders!

❖ Malchus'cho ro-u vonecho   ❖ מַלְכוּתְךָ רָאוּ בָנֶיךָ
Your children beheld Your majesty,

bōkay-a yom lifnay mōshe,   בּוֹקֵעַ יָם לִפְנֵי מֹשֶׁה,
as You split the Sea before Moses,

zeh Ayli onu v'om'ru: זֶה אֵלִי עָנוּ וְאָמְרוּ:
"This is my God!" they exclaimed, then they said:

ADŌNOY yimlōch l'ōlom vo-ed.   יהוה יִמְלֹךְ לְעֹלָם וָעֶד.
"HASHEM shall reign for all eternity!"

❖ V'ne-emar: ❖ וְנֶאֱמַר:
  Ki fodo Adōnoy es ya-akōv,   כִּי פָדָה יהוה אֶת יַעֲקֹב,
And it is further said: "For HASHEM has redeemed Jacob

ug-olō miyad chozok mimenu.   וּגְאָלוֹ מִיַּד חָזָק מִמֶּנּוּ.
and delivered him from a power mightier than he."

Boruch ato Adōnoy,   בָּרוּךְ אַתָּה יהוה,
  go-al yisro-ayl.   גָּאַל יִשְׂרָאֵל.
Blessed are You, HASHEM, Who redeemed Israel.

CONGREGATION RESPONDS: Omayn — אָמֵן

■ Second blessing following *Sh'ma:* We have complete trust in the protection that God grants us always. We request His assistance to utilize the tranquility of the night for personal resolutions and to plan for a better tomorrow.

HASHKIVAYNU Adōnoy Elōhaynu   הַשְׁכִּיבֵנוּ יהוה אֱלֹהֵינוּ
  l'sholōm,   לְשָׁלוֹם,
Lay us down to sleep, HASHEM, our God, in peace,

v'ha-amidaynu malkaynu l'cha-yim,   וְהַעֲמִידֵנוּ מַלְכֵּנוּ לְחַיִּים,
raise us erect, our King, to life;

ufrōs olaynu sukas sh'lōmecho,   וּפְרוֹשׂ עָלֵינוּ סֻכַּת שְׁלוֹמֶךָ,
spread over us the shelter of Your peace;

v'sak'naynu b'aytzo tōvo   וְתַקְּנֵנוּ בְּעֵצָה טוֹבָה
  mil'fonecho,   מִלְּפָנֶיךָ,
set us aright with good counsel from before Your Presence;

v'hōshi-aynu l'ma-an sh'mecho.   וְהוֹשִׁיעֵנוּ לְמַעַן שְׁמֶךָ.
and save us for Your Name's sake.

V'hogayn ba-adaynu,   וְהָגֵן בַּעֲדֵנוּ,
Shield us,

v'hosayr may-olaynu ō-yayv,
וְהָסֵר מֵעָלֵינוּ אוֹיֵב,

dever v'cherev v'ro-ov v'yogōn,
דֶּבֶר, וְחֶרֶב, וְרָעָב, וְיָגוֹן,

remove from us foe, plague, sword, famine, and woe;

v'hosayr soton mil'fonaynu
וְהָסֵר שָׂטָן מִלְּפָנֵינוּ

u-may-acharaynu,
וּמֵאַחֲרֵינוּ,

and remove spiritual impediment from before us and from behind us,

uvtzayl k'nofecho tastiraynu,
וּבְצֵל כְּנָפֶיךָ תַּסְתִּירֵנוּ,

and in the shadow of Your wings shelter us —

ki Ayl shōm'raynu u-matzilaynu oto,
כִּי אֵל שׁוֹמְרֵנוּ וּמַצִּילֵנוּ אָתָּה,

for God Who protects and rescues us are You;

ki Ayl melech chanun v'rachum oto.
כִּי אֵל מֶלֶךְ חַנּוּן וְרַחוּם אָתָּה.

for God, the Gracious and Compassionate King, are You.

❖ Ushmōr tzaysaynu u-vō-aynu,
❖ וּשְׁמוֹר צֵאתֵנוּ וּבוֹאֵנוּ,

Safeguard our going and coming,

l'cha-yim ulsholōm.
לְחַיִּים וּלְשָׁלוֹם

for life and for peace

may-ato v'ad ōlom.
מֵעַתָּה וְעַד עוֹלָם.

from now to eternity.

Boruch ato Adōnoy,
בָּרוּךְ אַתָּה יהוה,

shōmayr amō yisro-ayl lo-ad.
שׁוֹמֵר עַמּוֹ יִשְׂרָאֵל לָעַד.

Blessed are You, HASHEM, Who protects His people Israel forever.

CONGREGATION RESPONDS: Omayn — אָמֵן

■ This prayer contains the Name of God eighteen times, corresponding to the original number of blessings in the *Amidah*. At a time and place when synagogues were in remote and unsafe areas, this prayer was substituted for the *Amidah* when it was not safe to be outside the towns after dark.

BORUCH Adōnoy l'ōlom,
בָּרוּךְ יהוה לְעוֹלָם,

omayn v'omayn.
אָמֵן וְאָמֵן.

Blessed is HASHEM forever, Amen and Amen.

Boruch Adōnoy mitziyōn,
בָּרוּךְ יהוה מִצִּיּוֹן,

Blessed is HASHEM from Zion,

shōchayn y'rusholoyim hal'luyoh.
שֹׁכֵן יְרוּשָׁלָיִם, הַלְלוּיָהּ.

Who dwells in Jerusalem, Praise God!

Boruch Adōnoy Elōhim
בָּרוּךְ יהוה אֱלֹהִים

Blessed is HASHEM, God,

Elōhay yisro-ayl,
אֱלֹהֵי יִשְׂרָאֵל,

the God of Israel,

ōsay niflo-ōs l'vadō.   עֹשֵׂה נִפְלָאוֹת לְבַדּוֹ.

Who alone does wondrous things.

U-voruch shaym k'vōdō l'ōlom,   וּבָרוּךְ שֵׁם כְּבוֹדוֹ לְעוֹלָם,

Blessed is His glorious Name forever,

v'yimolay ch'vōdō   וְיִמָּלֵא כְבוֹדוֹ

es kol ho-oretz, omayn v'omayn.   אֶת כָּל הָאָרֶץ, אָמֵן וְאָמֵן.

and may all the earth be filled with His glory, Amen and Amen.

Y'hi ch'vōd Adōnoy l'ōlom,   יְהִי כְבוֹד יהוה לְעוֹלָם,

May the glory of HASHEM endure forever,

yismach Adōnoy b'ma-asov.   יִשְׂמַח יהוה בְּמַעֲשָׂיו.

let HASHEM rejoice in His works.

Y'hi shaym Adōnoy m'vōroch,   יְהִי שֵׁם יהוה מְבֹרָךְ,

Blessed be the Name of HASHEM

may-ato v'ad ōlom.   מֵעַתָּה וְעַד עוֹלָם.

from this time and forever.

Ki lō yitōsh Adōnoy es amō   כִּי לֹא יִטּשׁ יהוה אֶת עַמּוֹ

For HASHEM will not cast off His people

ba-avur sh'mō hagodōl,   בַּעֲבוּר שְׁמוֹ הַגָּדוֹל,

for the sake of His Great Name,

ki hō-il Adōnoy   כִּי הוֹאִיל יהוה

la-asōs eschem lō l'om.   לַעֲשׂוֹת אֶתְכֶם לוֹ לְעָם.

for HASHEM has vowed to make you His own people.

Va-yar kol ho-om va-yip'lu   וַיַּרְא כָּל הָעָם וַיִּפְּלוּ

al p'nayhem,   עַל פְּנֵיהֶם,

Then the entire people saw and fell on their faces

va-yōmru, Adōnoy hu ho-Elōhim,   וַיֹּאמְרוּ, יהוה הוּא הָאֱלֹהִים,

Adōnoy hu ho-Elōhim.   יהוה הוּא הָאֱלֹהִים.

and said, "HASHEM — only He is God! HASHEM — only He is God!"

V'hoyo Adōnoy l'melech   וְהָיָה יהוה לְמֶלֶךְ

al kol ho-oretz,   עַל כָּל הָאָרֶץ,

Then HASHEM will be King over all the world,

ba-yōm hahu yih-ye   בַּיּוֹם הַהוּא יִהְיֶה

Adōnoy e-chod ush'mō e-chod.   יהוה אֶחָד וּשְׁמוֹ אֶחָד.

on that day HASHEM will be One and His Name will be One.

Y'hi chasd'cho Adōnoy olaynu,   יְהִי חַסְדְּךָ יהוה עָלֵינוּ,

ka-asher yichalnu loch.   כַּאֲשֶׁר יִחַלְנוּ לָךְ.

May Your kindness, HASHEM, be upon us, just as we awaited You.

Hōshi-aynu Adōnoy Elōhaynu,   הוֹשִׁיעֵנוּ יהוה אֱלֹהֵינוּ,
Save us, HASHEM, our God,

v'kab'tzaynu min hagō-yim,   וְקַבְּצֵנוּ מִן הַגּוֹיִם,
gather us from the nations,

l'hōdōs l'shaym kod'shecho,   לְהוֹדוֹת לְשֵׁם קָדְשֶׁךָ,
to thank Your Holy Name

l'hishtabay-ach bis-hilosecho.   לְהִשְׁתַּבֵּחַ בִּתְהִלָּתֶךָ.
and to glory in Your praise!

Kol gōyim asher osiso yovō-u   כָּל גּוֹיִם אֲשֶׁר עָשִׂיתָ יָבְוֹאוּ
All the nations that You made will come

v'yishtachavu l'fonecho Adōnoy,   וְיִשְׁתַּחֲווּ לְפָנֶיךָ אֲדֹנָי,
and bow before You, My Lord,

vichab'du lishmecho.   וִיכַבְּדוּ לִשְׁמֶךָ.
and shall glorify Your Name.

Ki godōl ato v'ōse niflo-ōs,   כִּי גָדוֹל אַתָּה וְעֹשֵׂה נִפְלָאוֹת,
For You are great and work wonders;

ato Elōhim l'vadecho.   אַתָּה אֱלֹהִים לְבַדֶּךָ.
You alone, O God.

Va-anachnu am'cho v'tzōn mar-isecho,   וַאֲנַחְנוּ עַמְּךָ וְצֹאן מַרְעִיתֶךָ,
Then we, Your people and the sheep of Your pasture,

nōde l'cho l'ōlom,   נוֹדֶה לְךָ לְעוֹלָם,
shall thank You forever;

l'dōr vodōr n'sapayr t'hilosecho.   לְדוֹר וָדֹר נְסַפֵּר תְּהִלָּתֶךָ.
for generation after generation we will relate Your praise.

Boruch Adōnoy ba-yōm,   בָּרוּךְ יהוה בַּיּוֹם,
Blessed is HASHEM by day;

boruch Adōnoy baloylo,   בָּרוּךְ יהוה בַּלָּיְלָה,
blessed is HASHEM by night;

boruch Adōnoy b'shoch'vaynu,   בָּרוּךְ יהוה בְּשָׁכְבֵנוּ,
blessed is HASHEM when we retire;

boruch Adōnoy b'kumaynu.   בָּרוּךְ יהוה בְּקוּמֵנוּ.
blessed is HASHEM when we arise.

Ki v'yod'cho nafshōs   כִּי בְיָדְךָ נַפְשׁוֹת
    hacha-yim v'hamaysim.   הַחַיִּים וְהַמֵּתִים.
For in Your hand are the souls of the living and the dead.

Asher b'yodō nefesh kol choy,   אֲשֶׁר בְּיָדוֹ נֶפֶשׁ כָּל חָי,
He in Whose hand is the soul of all the living

v'ru-ach kol b'sar ish.   וְרוּחַ כָּל בְּשַׂר אִישׁ.
and the spirit of every human being.

B'yod'cho afkid ruchi,   בְּיָדְךָ אַפְקִיד רוּחִי,
In Your hand I shall entrust my spirit,

podiso ōsi, Adōnoy Ayl emes.   פָּדִיתָה אוֹתִי, יהוה אֵל אֱמֶת.
You redeemed me, HASHEM, God of truth.

Elōhaynu, sheba-shoma-yim,   אֱלֹהֵינוּ שֶׁבַּשָּׁמַיִם
Our God, Who is in heaven,

yachayd shimcho,   יַחֵד שְׁמֶךָ,
v'ka-yaym malchus'cho tomid,   וְקַיֵּם מַלְכוּתְךָ תָמִיד,
bring unity to Your Name; establish Your kingdom forever

umlōch olaynu l'ōlom vo-ed.   וּמְלוֹךְ עָלֵינוּ לְעוֹלָם וָעֶד.
and reign over us for all eternity.

YIR-U aynaynu v'yismach libaynu   **יִרְאוּ** עֵינֵינוּ וְיִשְׂמַח לִבֵּנוּ
May our eyes see, our heart rejoice

v'sogayl nafshaynu   וְתָגֵל נַפְשֵׁנוּ
bishu-os'cho be-emes,   בִּישׁוּעָתְךָ בֶּאֱמֶת,
and our soul exult in Your salvation in truth,

be-emōr l'tziyōn molach Elōhoyich.   בֶּאֱמֹר לְצִיּוֹן מָלַךְ אֱלֹהָיִךְ.
when Zion is told, "Your God has reigned!"

Adōnoy melech, Adōnoy moloch,   יהוה מֶלֶךְ, יהוה מָלָךְ,
Adōnoy yimlōch l'ōlom vo-ed.   יהוה יִמְלֹךְ לְעֹלָם וָעֶד.
HASHEM reigns, HASHEM has reigned, HASHEM will reign for all eternity.

❖ Ki hamalchus shel'cho hi,   ❖ כִּי הַמַּלְכוּת שֶׁלְּךָ הִיא,
ul-ōl'may ad timlōch b'chovōd,   וּלְעוֹלְמֵי עַד תִּמְלוֹךְ בְּכָבוֹד,
For the kingdom is Yours and for all eternity You will reign in glory,

ki ayn lonu melech elo oto.   כִּי אֵין לָנוּ מֶלֶךְ אֶלָּא אָתָּה.
for we have no King but You.

Boruch ato Adōnoy,   בָּרוּךְ אַתָּה יהוה,
Blessed are You, HASHEM,

hamelech bichvōdō tomid   הַמֶּלֶךְ בִּכְבוֹדוֹ תָּמִיד
yimlōch olaynu l'ōlom vo-ed,   יִמְלוֹךְ עָלֵינוּ לְעוֹלָם וָעֶד,
the King in His glory — He shall constantly reign over us forever and ever,

v'al kol ma-asov.   וְעַל כָּל מַעֲשָׂיו.
and over all His creatures.

CONGREGATION RESPONDS: Omayn — אָמֵן

THE *CHAZZAN* RECITES *HALF-KADDISH*.
(Congregational responses are indicated by parentheses.)

יִתְגַּדַּל וְיִתְקַדַּשׁ שְׁמֵהּ רַבָּא. (אָמֵן – Omayn) בְּעָלְמָא דִּי בְרָא
כִרְעוּתֵהּ. וְיַמְלִיךְ מַלְכוּתֵהּ, בְּחַיֵּיכוֹן וּבְיוֹמֵיכוֹן וּבְחַיֵּי דְכָל
בֵּית יִשְׂרָאֵל, בַּעֲגָלָא וּבִזְמַן קָרִיב. וְאִמְרוּ: אָמֵן.

(אָמֵן. יְהֵא שְׁמֵהּ רַבָּא מְבָרַךְ לְעָלַם וּלְעָלְמֵי עָלְמַיָּא.)

(Omayn. Y'hay sh'mayh rabo m'vorach l'olam ul-ol'may ol'ma-yo)

יְהֵא שְׁמֵהּ רַבָּא מְבָרַךְ לְעָלַם וּלְעָלְמֵי עָלְמַיָּא. יִתְבָּרַךְ וְיִשְׁתַּבַּח
וְיִתְפָּאַר וְיִתְרוֹמַם וְיִתְנַשֵּׂא וְיִתְהַדָּר וְיִתְעַלֶּה וְיִתְהַלָּל שְׁמֵהּ
דְּקֻדְשָׁא בְּרִיךְ הוּא (בְּרִיךְ הוּא – B'rich hu) °לְעֵלָּא מִן כָּל
°לְעֵלָּא לְעֵלָּא מִכָּל] – from Rosh Hashanah to Yom Kippur substitute]
בִּרְכָתָא וְשִׁירָתָא תֻּשְׁבְּחָתָא וְנֶחֱמָתָא, דַּאֲמִירָן בְּעָלְמָא, וְאִמְרוּ: אָמֵן.
(אָמֵן – Omayn).

❧ SHEMONEH ESREI — AMIDAH ❧

IN THE SYNAGOGUE THE *SHEMONEH ESREI* IS RECITED WHILE FACING THE ARK; ELSEWHERE IT IS
RECITED WHILE FACING THE DIRECTION OF THE LAND OF ISRAEL. TAKE THREE STEPS BACKWARD,
LEFT, RIGHT, LEFT, THEN THREE STEPS FORWARD, RIGHT, LEFT, RIGHT. REMAIN STANDING WITH
FEET TOGETHER DURING *SHEMONEH ESREI*. RECITE IT WITH QUIET DEVOTION AND WITHOUT ANY
INTERRUPTION. ALTHOUGH IT SHOULD NOT BE AUDIBLE TO OTHERS, ONE MUST PRAY LOUDLY
ENOUGH TO HEAR ONESELF.

Adōnoy s'fosai tiftoch,   אֲדֹנָי שְׂפָתַי תִּפְתָּח,

My Lord, open my lips,

u-fi yagid t'hilosecho.   וּפִי יַגִּיד תְּהִלָּתֶךָ.

that my mouth may declare Your praise.

■ First Blessing: In the merit of our Patriarchs whose actions reflected Godliness,
Hashem pledged to always be with Israel and protect them.

BEND THE KNEES AT Boruch; BOW AT ato; STRAIGHTEN UP AT Adōnoy.

BORUCH ato Adōnoy   **בָּרוּךְ** אַתָּה יהוה

Blessed are You, HASHEM,

Elōhaynu Vaylōhay avōsaynu, אֱלֹהֵינוּ וֵאלֹהֵי אֲבוֹתֵינוּ,

our God and the God of our forefathers,

Elōhay avrohom, Elōhay yitzchok, אֱלֹהֵי אַבְרָהָם, אֱלֹהֵי יִצְחָק,

Vaylōhay ya-akōv,   וֵאלֹהֵי יַעֲקֹב,

God of Abraham, God of Isaac, and God of Jacob;

ho-Ayl hagodōl hagibōr v'hanōro, הָאֵל הַגָּדוֹל הַגִּבּוֹר וְהַנּוֹרָא,

Ayl elyōn,   אֵל עֶלְיוֹן,

the great, mighty, and awesome God, the supreme God,

gōmayl chasodim tōvim   גּוֹמֵל חֲסָדִים טוֹבִים

   v'kōnay hakōl,   וְקוֹנֵה הַכֹּל,

Who bestows beneficial kindnesses and creates everything,

v'zōchayr chasday ovōs,   וְזוֹכֵר חַסְדֵי אָבוֹת,

Who recalls the kindnesses of the Patriarchs

u-mayvi gō-ayl livnay v'nayhem,   וּמֵבִיא גוֹאֵל לִבְנֵי בְנֵיהֶם,

and brings a Redeemer to their children's children,

l'ma-an sh'mō b'ahavo.   לְמַעַן שְׁמוֹ בְּאַהֲבָה.

for His Name's sake, with love.

FROM ROSH HASHANAH TO YOM KIPPUR ADD:

Zochraynu l'cha-yim,   זָכְרֵנוּ לְחַיִּים,

   melech chofaytz bacha-yim,   מֶלֶךְ חָפֵץ בַּחַיִּים,

Remember us for life, O King Who desires life,

   v'chosvaynu b'sayfer hacha-yim,   וְכָתְבֵנוּ בְּסֵפֶר הַחַיִּים,

   l'ma-ancho Elōhim cha-yim.   לְמַעַנְךָ אֱלֹהִים חַיִּים.

and inscribe us in the Book of Life — for Your sake, O Living God.

Melech ōzayr u-mōshi-a u-mogayn.   מֶלֶךְ עוֹזֵר וּמוֹשִׁיעַ וּמָגֵן.

O King, Helper, Savior, and Shield.

BEND THE KNEES AT Boruch; BOW AT ato; STRAIGHTEN UP AT Adōnoy.

Boruch ato Adōnoy, mogayn avrohom.   בָּרוּךְ אַתָּה יהוה, מָגֵן אַבְרָהָם.

Blessed are You, HASHEM, Shield of Abraham.

■ Second Blessing: God's might as it is manifest in nature and man

ATO gibōr l'ōlom Adōnoy,   **אַתָּה** גִּבּוֹר לְעוֹלָם אֲדֹנָי,

You are eternally mighty, my Lord,

m'cha-yay maysim ato,   מְחַיֵּה מֵתִים אַתָּה,

the Resuscitator of the dead are You;

rav l'hōshi-a.   רַב לְהוֹשִׁיעַ.

abundantly able to save,

BETWEEN SHEMINI ATZERES AND PESACH, ADD:

Mashiv horu-ach u-mōrid hageshem.   מַשִּׁיב הָרוּחַ וּמוֹרִיד הַגֶּשֶׁם.

Who makes the wind blow and makes the rain descend;

M'chalkayl cha-yim b'chesed,   מְכַלְכֵּל חַיִּים בְּחֶסֶד,

Who sustains the living with kindness,

m'cha-yay maysim b'rachamim rabim,   מְחַיֵּה מֵתִים בְּרַחֲמִים רַבִּים,

resuscitates the dead with abundant mercy,

sōmaych nōf'lim, v'rōfay chōlim,   סוֹמֵךְ נוֹפְלִים, וְרוֹפֵא חוֹלִים,
supports the fallen, heals the sick,

u-matir asurim,   וּמַתִּיר אֲסוּרִים,
releases the confined,

umka-yaym emunosō lishaynay ofor.   וּמְקַיֵּם אֱמוּנָתוֹ לִישֵׁנֵי עָפָר.
and maintains His faith to those asleep in the dust.

Mi cho-mōcho ba-al g'vurōs,   מִי כָמוֹךָ בַּעַל גְּבוּרוֹת,
Who is like You, O Master of mighty deeds,

u-mi dōme loch,   וּמִי דּוֹמֶה לָּךְ,
and who is comparable to You,

melech maymis umcha-ye   מֶלֶךְ מֵמִית וּמְחַיֶּה
u-matzmi-ach y'shu-o.   וּמַצְמִיחַ יְשׁוּעָה.
O King Who causes death and restores life and makes salvation sprout!

FROM ROSH HASHANAH TO YOM KIPPUR ADD:

Mi cho-mōcho av horachamim,   מִי כָמוֹךָ אַב הָרַחֲמִים,
Who is like You, O Merciful Father,

zōchayr y'tzurov l'cha-yim   זוֹכֵר יְצוּרָיו לְחַיִּים
b'rachamim.   בְּרַחֲמִים.
Who recalls His creatures mercifully for life!

V'ne-emon ato l'hacha-yōs maysim.   וְנֶאֱמָן אַתָּה לְהַחֲיוֹת מֵתִים.
And You are faithful to resuscitate the dead.

Boruch ato Adōnoy,   בָּרוּךְ אַתָּה יהוה,
m'cha-yay hamaysim.   מְחַיֵּה הַמֵּתִים.
Blessed are You, HASHEM, Who resuscitates the dead.

■ Third Blessing: Regarding the holiness of God's Name

ATO kodōsh v'shimcho kodōsh,   **אַתָּה** קָדוֹשׁ וְשִׁמְךָ קָדוֹשׁ,
You are holy and Your Name is holy,

ukdōshim b'chol yōm   וּקְדוֹשִׁים בְּכָל יוֹם
y'hal'lucho, selo.   יְהַלְלוּךָ סֶּלָה.
and holy ones praise You, every day, forever.

Boruch ato Adōnoy,   בָּרוּךְ אַתָּה יהוה,
°ho-Ayl hakodōsh.   °הָאֵל הַקָּדוֹשׁ.
Blessed are You, HASHEM, the holy God.

FROM ROSH HASHANAH TO YOM KIPPUR SUBSTITUTE:

°hamelech hakodōsh.   °הַמֶּלֶךְ הַקָּדוֹשׁ.
the holy King.

■ Fourth Blessing: Supplication for the gift of intellect

ATO chōnayn l'odom da-as,   אַתָּה חוֹנֵן לְאָדָם דַּעַת,

You graciously endow man with wisdom

umlamayd le-enōsh bino.   וּמְלַמֵּד לֶאֱנוֹשׁ בִּינָה.

and teach insight to a frail mortal.

AFTER THE SABBATH OR A FESTIVAL, ADD THE FOLLOWING:

ATO chōnantonu   אַתָּה חוֹנַנְתָּנוּ

l'mada tōrosecho,   לְמַדַּע תּוֹרָתֶךְ,

You have graced us * *with intelligence to study Your Torah*

vat'lam'daynu la-asōs   וַתְּלַמְּדֵנוּ לַעֲשׂוֹת

chukay r'tzōnecho.   חֻקֵּי רְצוֹנֶךָ.

and You have taught us to perform the decrees You have willed.

Vatavdayl Adōnoy Elōhaynu   וַתַּבְדֵּל יהוה אֱלֹהֵינוּ

HASHEM, our God, You have distinguished

bayn kōdesh l'chōl,   בֵּין קֹדֶשׁ לְחוֹל,

between the sacred and the secular, *

bayn ōr l'chōshech,   בֵּין אוֹר לְחֹשֶׁךְ,

between light and darkness,

bayn yisro-ayl lo-amim,   בֵּין יִשְׂרָאֵל לָעַמִּים,

between Israel and the peoples,

bayn yōm hash'vi-i   בֵּין יוֹם הַשְּׁבִיעִי

l'shayshes y'may hama-ase.   לְשֵׁשֶׁת יְמֵי הַמַּעֲשֶׂה.

between the Seventh Day and the six days of labor.

Ovinu malkaynu hochayl olaynu   אָבִינוּ מַלְכֵּנוּ הָחֵל עָלֵינוּ

Our Father, our King, begin for us

ha-yomim habo-im likrosaynu   הַיָּמִים הַבָּאִים לִקְרָאתֵנוּ

l'sholōm,   לְשָׁלוֹם,

the days approaching us for peace,

chasuchim mikol chayt   חֲשׂוּכִים מִכָּל חֵטְא

free from all sin,

umnukim mikol ovōn   וּמְנֻקִּים מִכָּל עָוֹן

cleansed from all iniquity

umdubokim b'yiro-secho. V' ...   וּמְדֻבָּקִים בְּיִרְאָתֶךָ. וְ ...

and attached to fear of You. And ...

אַתָּה חוֹנַנְתָּנוּ — *You have graced us.* The *Hav-dalah* blessing that differentiates between the Sabbath and the weekdays is quite properly inserted in the blessing of wisdom because of the well-known dictum of the Sages: "If there is no wisdom, how can there be differentiation?" (*Yerushalmi, Berachos* 5:20).

בֵּין קֹדֶשׁ לְחוֹל — *Between the sacred and the secular.* Four distinctions are enumerated here: (1) Between the holy and the secular —

chonaynu may-it'cho   חָנֵּנוּ מֵאִתְּךָ

day-o bino v'haskayl.   דֵּעָה בִּינָה וְהַשְׂכֵּל.

endow us graciously from Yourself with wisdom, insight, and discernment.

Boruch ato Adōnoy, chōnayn hado-as.   בָּרוּךְ אַתָּה יהוה, חוֹנֵן הַדָּעַת.

Blessed are You, HASHEM, gracious Giver of wisdom.

■ Fifth Blessing: Supplication for Divine assistance in repentance

HASHIVAYNU ovinu l'sōrosecho,   הֲשִׁיבֵנוּ אָבִינוּ לְתוֹרָתֶךָ,

Bring us back, our Father, to Your Torah,

v'kor'vaynu malkaynu la-avōdosecho,   וְקָרְבֵנוּ מַלְכֵּנוּ לַעֲבוֹדָתֶךָ,

and bring us near, our King, to Your service,

v'hachaziraynu bis-shuvo sh'laymo   וְהַחֲזִירֵנוּ בִּתְשׁוּבָה שְׁלֵמָה

l'fonecho.   לְפָנֶיךָ.

and return us in perfect repentance before You.

Boruch ato Adōnoy,   בָּרוּךְ אַתָּה יהוה,

horōtze bis-shuvo.   הָרוֹצֶה בִּתְשׁוּבָה.

Blessed are You, HASHEM, Who desires repentance.

■ Sixth Blessing: Supplication for forgiveness

STRIKE THE LEFT SIDE OF THE CHEST WITH THE RIGHT FIST
WHILE RECITING THE WORDS ki chotonu AND ki foshonu.

S'LACH lonu ovinu ki chotonu,   סְלַח לָנוּ אָבִינוּ כִּי חָטָאנוּ,

Forgive us, our Father, for we have erred;

m'chal lonu malkaynu ki foshonu,   מְחַל לָנוּ מַלְכֵּנוּ כִּי פָשָׁעְנוּ,

pardon us, our King, for we have willfully sinned;

ki mōchayl v'sōlayach oto.   כִּי מוֹחֵל וְסוֹלֵחַ אָתָּה.

for You pardon and forgive.

Boruch ato Adōnoy,   בָּרוּךְ אַתָּה יהוה,

chanun hamarbe lislō-ach.   חַנּוּן הַמַּרְבֶּה לִסְלֹוחַ.

Blessed are You, HASHEM, the gracious One Who pardons abundantly.

■ Seventh Blessing: Supplication for personal redemption
from the perils and problems of daily life

R'AY v'on-yaynu, v'rivo rivaynu,   רְאֵה בְעָנְיֵנוּ, וְרִיבָה רִיבֵנוּ,

Behold our affliction, take up our grievance,

---

not the profane, but the mundane factors in life that prevent us from recognizing and achieving holiness; (2) between light and darkness, which also symbolizes the distinctions between good and evil; (3) the fact that God took Israel to be His chosen people from among all the nations; and (4) between the day that testifies to God as the Creator and the days when His Presence is less apparent.

ug-olaynu m'hayro l'ma-an sh'mecho,   וּגְאָלֵנוּ מְהֵרָה לְמַעַן שְׁמֶךָ,

and redeem us speedily for Your Name's sake,

ki gō-ayl chozok oto.   כִּי גּוֹאֵל חָזָק אָתָּה.

for You are a powerful Redeemer.

Boruch ato Adōnoy, gō-ayl yisro-ayl.   בָּרוּךְ אַתָּה יהוה, גּוֹאֵל יִשְׂרָאֵל.

Blessed are You, HASHEM, Redeemer of Israel.

■ Eighth Blessing: Supplication for health and healing of body and soul

R'FO-AYNU Adōnoy, v'nayrofay,   **רְפָאֵנוּ** יהוה וְנֵרָפֵא,

Heal us, HASHEM — then we will be healed;

hōshi-aynu v'nivoshay-o,   הוֹשִׁיעֵנוּ וְנִוָּשֵׁעָה,

save us — then we will be saved,

ki s'hilosaynu oto,   כִּי תְהִלָּתֵנוּ אָתָּה,

for You are our praise;

v'ha-alay r'fu-o sh'laymo   וְהַעֲלֵה רְפוּאָה שְׁלֵמָה

l'chol makōsaynu,   לְכָל מַכּוֹתֵינוּ,

and bring complete recovery for all our ailments,

ki Ayl melech   כִּי אֵל מֶלֶךְ

rōfay ne-emon v'rachamon oto.   רוֹפֵא נֶאֱמָן וְרַחֲמָן אָתָּה.

for You are God, King, the faithful and compassionate Healer.

Boruch ato Adōnoy,   בָּרוּךְ אַתָּה יהוה,

rōfay chōlay amō yisro-ayl.   רוֹפֵא חוֹלֵי עַמּוֹ יִשְׂרָאֵל.

Blessed are You, HASHEM, Who heals the sick of His people Israel.

■ Ninth Blessing: Supplication for a year of prosperity

FOR THE FOLLOWING BLESSING, SUMMER IS DEFINED AS THE PERIOD FROM PESACH
THROUGH *MINCHAH* OF DECEMBER 4TH (OR 5TH, IN THE YEAR BEFORE A CIVIL LEAP YEAR);
WINTER IS DEFINED AS THE REST OF THE YEAR.

BORAYCH olaynu, Adōnoy Elōhaynu,   **בָּרֵךְ** עָלֵינוּ יהוה אֱלֹהֵינוּ

es hashono ha-zōs   אֶת הַשָּׁנָה הַזֹּאת

Bless on our behalf, O HASHEM, our God, this year

v'es kol minay s'vu-oso l'tōvo,   וְאֶת כָּל מִינֵי תְבוּאָתָהּ לְטוֹבָה,

and all its kinds of crops for the best,

IN SUMMER SAY:

v'sayn b'rocho   וְתֵן בְּרָכָה

and give a blessing

IN WINTER SAY:

v'sayn tal u-motor livrocho   וְתֵן טַל וּמָטָר לִבְרָכָה

and give dew and rain for a blessing

---

al p'nay ho-adomo,   עַל פְּנֵי הָאֲדָמָה,
on the face of the earth,

v'sab'aynu mituvecho,   וְשַׂבְּעֵנוּ מִטּוּבֶךְ,
and satisfy us from Your bounty,

u-voraych sh'nosaynu   וּבָרֵךְ שְׁנָתֵנוּ
  ka-shonim hatōvōs.   כַּשָּׁנִים הַטּוֹבוֹת.
and bless our year like the best years.

Boruch ato Adōnoy,   בָּרוּךְ אַתָּה יהוה,
  m'voraych ha-shonim.   מְבָרֵךְ הַשָּׁנִים.
Blessed are You, HASHEM, Who blesses the years.

■ Tenth Blessing: Supplication for the ingathering of the exiles

---

T'KA b'shōfor godōl l'chayrusaynu,   **תְּקַע** בְּשׁוֹפָר גָּדוֹל לְחֵרוּתֵנוּ,
Sound the great shofar for our freedom,

v'so nays l'kabaytz golu-yōsaynu,   וְשָׂא נֵס לְקַבֵּץ גָּלֻיוֹתֵינוּ,
raise a banner to gather our exiles

v'kab'tzaynu yachad   וְקַבְּצֵנוּ יַחַד
  may-arba kanfōs ho-oretz.   מֵאַרְבַּע כַּנְפוֹת הָאָרֶץ.
and gather us together from the four corners of the earth.

Boruch ato Adōnoy,   בָּרוּךְ אַתָּה יהוה,
  m'kabaytz nidchay amō yisro-ayl.   מְקַבֵּץ נִדְחֵי עַמּוֹ יִשְׂרָאֵל.
Blessed are You, HASHEM, Who gathers in the dispersed of His people Israel.

■ Eleventh Blessing: Supplication for the restoration of justice to the Jewish judiciary

---

HOSHIVO shōf'taynu   **הָשִׁיבָה** שׁוֹפְטֵינוּ
  k'vorishōno   כְּבָרִאשׁוֹנָה,
Restore our judges as in earliest times

v'yō-atzaynu k'vat'chilo,   וְיוֹעֲצֵינוּ כְּבַתְּחִלָּה,
and our counselors as at first;

v'hosayr mimenu yogōn va-anocho,   וְהָסֵר מִמֶּנּוּ יָגוֹן וַאֲנָחָה,
remove from us sorrow and groan;

umlōch olaynu ato, Adōnoy, l'vad'cho   וּמְלוֹךְ עָלֵינוּ אַתָּה יהוה לְבַדְּךָ
and reign over us, You, HASHEM, alone,

b'chesed uvrachamim,   בְּחֶסֶד וּבְרַחֲמִים,
with kindness and with compassion,

v'tzad'kaynu bamishpot.   וְצַדְּקֵנוּ בַּמִּשְׁפָּט.
and justify us through judgment.

Boruch ato Adōnoy, בָּרוּךְ אַתָּה יהוה,

°melech ōhayv tz'doko u-mishpot. °מֶלֶךְ אוֹהֵב צְדָקָה וּמִשְׁפָּט.

Blessed are You, HASHEM, the King Who loves righteousness and judgment.

FROM ROSH HASHANAH TO YOM KIPPUR SUBSTITUTE:

°hamelech hamishpot. °הַמֶּלֶךְ הַמִּשְׁפָּט.

the King of Judgment.

■ Twelfh Blessing: Supplication for the eradication
of heretic influences that threaten Jewish life

V'LAMALSHINIM al t'hi sikvo, וְלַמַּלְשִׁינִים אַל תְּהִי תִקְוָה,

And for the slanderers let there be no hope;

v'chol horish-o k'rega tōvayd, וְכָל הָרִשְׁעָה כְּרֶגַע תֹּאבֵד,

and may all wickedness perish in an instant;

v'chol ō-y'vecho m'hayro yikoraysu. וְכָל אֹיְבֶיךָ מְהֵרָה יִכָּרֵתוּ.

and may all Your enemies be cut down speedily.

V'hazaydim m'hayro s'akayr וְהַזֵּדִים מְהֵרָה תְעַקֵּר

The wanton sinners — may You speedily uproot

us-shabayr usmagayr v'sachni-a וּתְשַׁבֵּר וּתְמַגֵּר וְתַכְנִיעַ

smash, cast down, and humble —

bimhayro v'yomaynu. בִּמְהֵרָה בְיָמֵינוּ.

speedily in our days.

Boruch ato Adōnoy, בָּרוּךְ אַתָּה יהוה,

shōvayr ōy'vim u-machni-a zaydim. שׁוֹבֵר אֹיְבִים וּמַכְנִיעַ זֵדִים.

Blessed are You, HASHEM, Who breaks enemies and humbles wanton sinners.

■ Thirteenth Blessing: Supplication on behalf of the righteous
and recognition of their significance

AL hatzadikim v'al hachasidim, עַל הַצַּדִּיקִים וְעַל הַחֲסִידִים,

On the righteous, on the devout,

v'al ziknay am'cho bays yisro-ayl, וְעַל זִקְנֵי עַמְּךָ בֵּית יִשְׂרָאֵל,

on the elders of Your people the Family of Israel,

v'al p'laytas sōf'rayhem, וְעַל פְּלֵיטַת סוֹפְרֵיהֶם,

on the remnant of their scholars,

v'al gayray hatzedek v'olaynu, וְעַל גֵּרֵי הַצֶּדֶק וְעָלֵינוּ,

on the righteous converts and on ourselves —

yehemu rachamecho, יֶהֱמוּ רַחֲמֶיךָ

Adōnoy Elōhaynu, יהוה אֱלֹהֵינוּ,

may Your compassion be aroused, HASHEM, our God;

v'sayn sochor tōv l'chol habōt'chim ⁣ ⁣ וְתֵן שָׂכָר טוֹב לְכָל הַבּוֹטְחִים
  b'shimcho be-emes, ⁣ ⁣ בְּשִׁמְךָ בֶּאֱמֶת,
  and give goodly reward to all who sincerely believe in Your Name;

v'sim chelkaynu imohem l'ōlom, ⁣ ⁣ וְשִׂים חֶלְקֵנוּ עִמָּהֶם לְעוֹלָם,
  and place our lot with them forever,

v'lō nayvōsh ki v'cho botoch'nu. ⁣ ⁣ וְלֹא נֵבוֹשׁ כִּי בְךָ בָּטָחְנוּ.
  and we will not feel ashamed, for we trust in You.

Boruch ato Adōnoy, ⁣ ⁣ בָּרוּךְ אַתָּה יהוה,
  mish-on umivtoch latzadikim. ⁣ ⁣ מִשְׁעָן וּמִבְטָח לַצַּדִּיקִים.
  Blessed are You, HASHEM, Mainstay and Assurance of the righteous.

■ Fourteenth Blessing: Supplication for the physical and spiritual rebuilding of Jerusalem

V'LIRUSHOLA-YIM ir'cho ⁣ ⁣ **וְלִירוּשָׁלַיִם** עִירְךָ
  b'rachamim toshuv, ⁣ ⁣ בְּרַחֲמִים תָּשׁוּב,
  And to Jerusalem, Your city, may You return in compassion,

v'sishkōn b'sōchoh ka-asher dibarto, ⁣ ⁣ וְתִשְׁכּוֹן בְּתוֹכָהּ כַּאֲשֶׁר דִּבַּרְתָּ,
  and may You rest within it, as You have spoken;

uvnay ōsoh b'korōv b'yomaynu ⁣ ⁣ וּבְנֵה אוֹתָהּ בְּקָרוֹב בְּיָמֵינוּ
  binyan ōlom, ⁣ ⁣ בִּנְיַן עוֹלָם,
  may You rebuild it soon in our days as an eternal structure,

v'chisay dovid ⁣ ⁣ וְכִסֵּא דָוִד
  m'hayro l'sōchoh tochin ⁣ ⁣ מְהֵרָה לְתוֹכָהּ תָּכִין.
  and the throne of David may You speedily establish within it.

Boruch ato Adōnoy, ⁣ ⁣ בָּרוּךְ אַתָּה יהוה,
  bōnay y'rusholo-yim. ⁣ ⁣ בּוֹנֵה יְרוּשָׁלָיִם.
  Blessed are You, HASHEM, the Builder of Jerusalem.

■ Fifteenth Blessing: Supplication that the Messiah restore the Davidic reign

ES TZEMACH dovid avd'cho ⁣ ⁣ **אֶת צֶמַח** דָּוִד עַבְדְּךָ
  m'hayro satzmi-ach, ⁣ ⁣ מְהֵרָה תַצְמִיחַ,
  The offspring of Your servant David may You speedily cause to flourish,

v'karnō torum bi-shu-osecho, ⁣ ⁣ וְקַרְנוֹ תָּרוּם בִּישׁוּעָתֶךָ,
  and enhance his pride through Your salvation,

ki lishu-os'cho kivinu kol ha-yom ⁣ ⁣ כִּי לִישׁוּעָתְךָ קִוִּינוּ כָּל הַיּוֹם.
  for we hope for Your salvation all day long.

Boruch ato Adōnoy, ⁣ ⁣ בָּרוּךְ אַתָּה יהוה,
  matzmi-ach keren y'shu-o. ⁣ ⁣ מַצְמִיחַ קֶרֶן יְשׁוּעָה.
  Blessed are You, HASHEM, Who causes the pride of salvation to flourish.

■ Sixteenth Blessing: Supplication for God's acceptance of our prayer

SH'MA KOLAYNU Adōnoy Elōhaynu, שְׁמַע קוֹלֵנוּ יהוה אֱלֹהֵינוּ,
Hear our voice, HASHEM, our God,

chus v'rachaym olaynu, חוּס וְרַחֵם עָלֵינוּ,
pity and be compassionate to us,

v'kabayl b'rachamim uvrotzōn וְקַבֵּל בְּרַחֲמִים וּבְרָצוֹן
es t'filosaynu, אֶת תְּפִלָּתֵנוּ,
and accept — with compassion and favor — our prayer,

ki Ayl shōmay-a כִּי אֵל שׁוֹמֵעַ
t'filōs v'sachanunim oto, תְּפִלּוֹת וְתַחֲנוּנִים אָתָּה.
for God Who hears prayers and supplications are You;

umil'fonecho, malkaynu, וּמִלְּפָנֶיךָ מַלְכֵּנוּ
from before Yourself, our King,

raykom al t'shivaynu, רֵיקָם אַל תְּשִׁיבֵנוּ,
turn us not away empty-handed,

ki ato shōmay-a t'filas כִּי אַתָּה שׁוֹמֵעַ תְּפִלַּת
am'cho yisro-ayl b'rachamim. עַמְּךָ יִשְׂרָאֵל בְּרַחֲמִים.
for You hear the prayer of Your people Israel with compassion.

Boruch ato Adōnoy, בָּרוּךְ אַתָּה יהוה,
shōmay-a t'filo. שׁוֹמֵעַ תְּפִלָּה.
Blessed are You, HASHEM, Who hears prayer.

■ Seventeenth Blessing: Prayer for restoration of the Temple service

R'TZAY, Adōnoy Elōhaynu רְצֵה יהוה אֱלֹהֵינוּ
Be favorable, HASHEM, our God,

b'am'cho yisro-ayl u-visfilosom, בְּעַמְּךָ יִשְׂרָאֵל וּבִתְפִלָּתָם,
toward Your people Israel and their prayer

v'hoshayv es ho-avōdo וְהָשֵׁב אֶת הָעֲבוֹדָה
lidvir bay-secho. לִדְבִיר בֵּיתֶךָ.
and restore the service to the Holy of Holies of Your Temple.

V'i-shay yisro-ayl, usfilosom וְאִשֵּׁי יִשְׂרָאֵל וּתְפִלָּתָם
b'ahavo s'kabayl b'rotzōn, בְּאַהֲבָה תְקַבֵּל בְּרָצוֹן,
The fire-offerings of Israel and their prayer accept with love and favor,

us-hi l'rotzōn tomid וּתְהִי לְרָצוֹן תָּמִיד
avōdas yisro-ayl amecho. עֲבוֹדַת יִשְׂרָאֵל עַמֶּךָ.
and may the service of Your people Israel always be favorable to You.

■ *Yaaleh Veyavo:* We petition God to have compassion on Israel and Jerusalem, and to reinstate the Temple service, to enable us to bring the appropriate offerings for the particular occasion.

ON *ROSH CHODESH* AND *CHOL HAMOED* RECITE THE FOLLOWING:

ELŌHAYNU Vaylōhay avōsaynu,　　אֱלֹהֵינוּ וֵאלֹהֵי אֲבוֹתֵינוּ,
Our God and the God of our forefathers,

ya-a-le v'yovō v'yagi-a v'yayro-e　　יַעֲלֶה, וְיָבֹא, וְיַגִּיעַ, וְיֵרָאֶה,
may there rise, come, reach, be noted,

v'yayro-tze v'yi-shoma v'yipokayd　　וְיֵרָצֶה, וְיִשָּׁמַע, וְיִפָּקֵד,
be favored, be heard, be considered,

v'yizochayr zichrōnaynu u-fikdōnaynu,　　וְיִזָּכֵר זִכְרוֹנֵנוּ וּפִקְדוֹנֵנוּ,
and be remembered — the remembrance and consideration of ourselves;

v'zichrōn avōsaynu,　　וְזִכְרוֹן אֲבוֹתֵינוּ,
the remembrance of our forefathers;

v'zichrōn moshi-ach
　ben dovid avdecho,　　וְזִכְרוֹן מָשִׁיחַ
　　　בֶּן דָּוִד עַבְדֶּךָ,
the remembrance of Messiah, son of David, Your servant;

v'zichrōn y'rushola-yim
　ir kod-shecho,　　וְזִכְרוֹן יְרוּשָׁלַיִם
　　　עִיר קָדְשֶׁךָ,
the remembrance of Jerusalem, Your Holy City;

v'zichrōn kol am'cho bays yisro-ayl　　וְזִכְרוֹן כָּל עַמְּךָ בֵּית יִשְׂרָאֵל
and the remembrance of Your entire people the Family of Israel —

l'fonecho, lif-layto l'tōvo　　לְפָנֶיךָ, לִפְלֵיטָה לְטוֹבָה
before You for deliverance, for goodness,

l'chayn ulchesed ulrachamim,　　לְחֵן וּלְחֶסֶד וּלְרַחֲמִים,
for grace, for kindness, and for compassion,

l'cha-yim ulsholōm　　לְחַיִּים וּלְשָׁלוֹם
for life, and for peace

――――― ON *ROSH CHODESH* ―――――

b'yōm rōsh hachōdesh ha-ze.　　בְּיוֹם רֹאשׁ הַחֹדֶשׁ הַזֶּה.
on this day of Rosh Chodesh.

――――― ON *PESACH* ―――――

b'yōm chag hamatzōs ha-ze.　　בְּיוֹם חַג הַמַּצּוֹת הַזֶּה.
on this day of the Festival of Matzos.

――――― ON *SUCCOS* ―――――

b'yōm chag hasukōs ha-ze.　　בְּיוֹם חַג הַסֻּכּוֹת הַזֶּה.
on this day of the Succos Festival.

Zoch'raynu Adōnoy Elōhaynu
  bō l'tōvo,
זָכְרֵנוּ יהוה אֱלֹהֵינוּ
בּוֹ לְטוֹבָה,

Remember us on it, HASHEM, our God, for goodness,

u-fokdaynu vō livrocho,
וּפָקְדֵנוּ בוֹ לִבְרָכָה,

consider us on it for blessing

v'hōshi-aynu vō l'cha-yim.
וְהוֹשִׁיעֵנוּ בוֹ לְחַיִּים.

and help us on it for life.

U-vidvar y'shu-o v'rachamim,
וּבִדְבַר יְשׁוּעָה וְרַחֲמִים,

In the matter of salvation and compassion,

chus v'chonaynu
  v'rachaym olaynu v'hōshi-aynu,
חוּס וְחָנֵּנוּ
וְרַחֵם עָלֵינוּ וְהוֹשִׁיעֵנוּ,

pity, be gracious and compassionate with us and help us,

ki aylecho aynaynu,
כִּי אֵלֶיךָ עֵינֵינוּ,

for our eyes are turned to You,

ki Ayl melech
  chanun v'rachum oto.
כִּי אֵל מֶלֶךְ
חַנּוּן וְרַחוּם אָתָּה.

because You are God, the gracious and compassionate King.

V'SECHEZENO aynaynu
וְתֶחֱזֶינָה עֵינֵינוּ

May our eyes behold

b'shuv'cho l'tziyōn b'rachamim.
בְּשׁוּבְךָ לְצִיּוֹן בְּרַחֲמִים.

Your return to Zion in compassion.

Boruch ato Adōnoy,
  hamachazir sh'chinosō l'tziyōn.
בָּרוּךְ אַתָּה יהוה,
הַמַּחֲזִיר שְׁכִינָתוֹ לְצִיּוֹן.

Blessed are You, HASHEM, Who restores His Presence unto Zion.

■ Eighteenth Blessing: Acknowledgment of our debt of gratitude

---

BOW AT Mōdim anachnu loch; STRAIGHTEN UP AT Adōnoy.

MŌDIM anachnu loch,
מוֹדִים אֲנַחְנוּ לָךְ,

We gratefully thank You,

sho-ato hu Adōnoy Elōhaynu
שָׁאַתָּה הוּא יהוה אֱלֹהֵינוּ

for it is You Who are HASHEM, our God,

Vaylōhay avōsaynu
וֵאלֹהֵי אֲבוֹתֵינוּ

and the God of our forefathers

l'ōlom vo-ed,
לְעוֹלָם וָעֶד,

forever and ever;

tzur cha-yaynu, mogayn yish-aynu
צוּר חַיֵּינוּ, מָגֵן יִשְׁעֵנוּ

Rock of our lives, Shield of our salvation

ato hu l'dōr vodōr.   אַתָּה הוּא לְדוֹר וָדוֹר.

are You from generation to generation.

Nō-de l'cho unsapayr t'hilosecho   נוֹדֶה לְּךָ וּנְסַפֵּר תְּהִלָּתֶךָ

We shall thank You and relate Your praise —

al cha-yaynu ham'surim b'yodecho,   עַל חַיֵּינוּ הַמְּסוּרִים בְּיָדֶךָ,

for our lives which are committed to Your power,

v'al nishmōsaynu hap'kudōs loch,   וְעַל נִשְׁמוֹתֵינוּ הַפְּקוּדוֹת לָךְ,

and for our souls that are entrusted to You,

v'al nisecho sheb'chol yōm imonu,   וְעַל נִסֶּיךָ שֶׁבְּכָל יוֹם עִמָּנוּ,

and for Your miracles that are with us every day,

v'al nifl'ōsecho v'tōvōsecho   וְעַל נִפְלְאוֹתֶיךָ וְטוֹבוֹתֶיךָ

   sheb'chol ays,   שֶׁבְּכָל עֵת,

and for Your wonders and favors in every season —

erev vovōker v'tzohorō-yim.   עֶרֶב וָבֹקֶר וְצָהֳרָיִם.

evening, morning, and afternoon.

Hatōv ki lō cholu rachamecho,   הַטּוֹב כִּי לֹא כָלוּ רַחֲמֶיךָ,

The Beneficent One, for Your compassions were never exhausted,

v'ham'rachaym ki lō samu chasodecho,   וְהַמְרַחֵם כִּי לֹא תַמּוּ חֲסָדֶיךָ,

and the Compassionate One, for Your kindnesses never ended —

may-ōlom kivinu loch.   מֵעוֹלָם קִוִּינוּ לָךְ.

always have we put our hope in You.

ON CHANUKAH AND PURIM CONTINUE BELOW.
ON ALL OTHER DAYS CONTINUE V'al kulom (P. 593).

AL hanisim, v'al hapurkon,   **עַל** הַנִּסִּים, וְעַל הַפֻּרְקָן,

For the miracles, and for the salvation,

v'al hag'vurōs, v'al hat'shu-ōs,   וְעַל הַגְּבוּרוֹת, וְעַל הַתְּשׁוּעוֹת,

and for the mighty deeds, and for the victories,

v'al hamilchomōs,   וְעַל הַמִּלְחָמוֹת,

and for the battles

she-osiso la-avōsaynu   שֶׁעָשִׂיתָ לַאֲבוֹתֵינוּ

which You performed for our forefathers

ba-yomim hohaym baz'man ha-ze.   בַּיָּמִים הָהֵם בַּזְּמַן הַזֶּה.

in those days, at this time.

ON CHANUKAH CONTINUE HERE; ON PURIM TURN TO P. 592.

BIMAY matisyohu ben yōchonon   **בִּימֵי** מַתִּתְיָהוּ בֶּן יוֹחָנָן

In the days of Mattisyahu, the son of Yochanan,

kōhayn godōl chashmōno-i u-vonov,   כֹּהֵן גָּדוֹל חַשְׁמוֹנַאי וּבָנָיו,

the High Priest, the Hasmonean, and his sons —

ON CHANUKAH CONTINUE HERE:

k'she-om'do malchus yovon   כְּשֶׁעָמְדָה מַלְכוּת יָוָן

     hor'sho-o al am'cho yisro-ayl,   הָרְשָׁעָה עַל עַמְּךָ יִשְׂרָאֵל,

when the wicked Greek kingdom rose up against Your people Israel

l'hashkichom tōrosecho,   לְהַשְׁכִּיחָם תּוֹרָתֶךָ,

to make them forget Your Torah

ulha-avirom maychukay r'tzōnecho,   וּלְהַעֲבִירָם מֵחֻקֵּי רְצוֹנֶךָ.

and compel them to stray from the statutes of Your Will —

v'ato b'rachamecho horabim,   וְאַתָּה בְּרַחֲמֶיךָ הָרַבִּים,

But you, in Your abundant mercy,

omadto lohem b'ays tzorosom,   עָמַדְתָּ לָהֶם בְּעֵת צָרָתָם,

stood up for them in the time of their distress.

Ravto es rivom, danto es dinom,   רַבְתָּ אֶת רִיבָם, דַּנְתָּ אֶת דִּינָם,

You took up their grievance, You judged their claim,

nokamto es nikmosom.   נָקַמְתָּ אֶת נִקְמָתָם.

and You avenged their wrong.

Mosarto gibōrim b'yad chaloshim,   מָסַרְתָּ גִבּוֹרִים בְּיַד חַלָּשִׁים,

You delivered the strong into the hand of the weak,

v'rabim b'yad m'atim,   וְרַבִּים בְּיַד מְעַטִּים,

the many into the hand of the few,

utmay-im b'yad t'hōrim,   וּטְמֵאִים בְּיַד טְהוֹרִים,

the impure into the hand of the pure,

ursho-im b'yad tzadikim   וּרְשָׁעִים בְּיַד צַדִּיקִים,

the wicked into the hand of the righteous,

v'zaydim b'yad ōs'kay sōrosecho.   וְזֵדִים בְּיַד עוֹסְקֵי תוֹרָתֶךָ.

and the wanton into the hand of the diligent students of Your Torah.

Ulcho osiso   וּלְךָ עָשִׂיתָ

For Yourself You made

shaym godōl v'kodōsh b'ōlomecho,   שֵׁם גָּדוֹל וְקָדוֹשׁ בְּעוֹלָמֶךָ,

a great and holy Name in Your world,

ul-am'cho yisro-ayl   וּלְעַמְּךָ יִשְׂרָאֵל

and for Your people Israel

osiso t'shu-o g'dōlo u-furkon   עָשִׂיתָ תְּשׁוּעָה גְדוֹלָה וּפֻרְקָן

     k'ha-yōm ha-ze.   כְּהַיּוֹם הַזֶּה.

You performed a great victory and salvation as this very day.

V'achar kayn bo-u vonecho   וְאַחַר כֵּן בָּאוּ בָנֶיךָ

     lidvir bay-secho,   לִדְבִיר בֵּיתֶךָ,

Thereafter, Your children came to the Holy of Holies of Your House,

ON CHANUKAH CONTINUE HERE:

u-finu es haycholecho,   וּפִנּוּ אֶת הֵיכָלֶךָ,
they cleansed Your Temple,

v'tiharu es mikdoshecho,   וְטִהֲרוּ אֶת מִקְדָּשֶׁךָ,
they purified the site of Your Holiness;

v'hidliku nayrôs   וְהִדְלִיקוּ נֵרוֹת
   b'chatzrôs kod-shecho,   בְּחַצְרוֹת קָדְשֶׁךָ,
and they kindled lights in the Courtyards of Your Sanctuary;

v'kov'u   וְקָבְעוּ
   sh'mônas y'may chanuko aylu,   שְׁמוֹנַת יְמֵי חֲנֻכָּה אֵלּוּ,
and they established these eight days of Chanukah

l'hôdôs ulhalayl   לְהוֹדוֹת וּלְהַלֵּל
   l'shimcho hagodôl.   לְשִׁמְךָ הַגָּדוֹל.
to express thanks and praise to Your great Name.

CONTINUE V'al kulom (P. 593).

ON PURIM CONTINUE HERE:

BIMAY mord'chai v'estayr   בִּימֵי מָרְדְּכַי וְאֶסְתֵּר
In the days of Mordechai and Esther,

b'shushan habiro,   בְּשׁוּשַׁן הַבִּירָה,
in Shushan, the capital,

k'she-omad alayhem homon horosho, כְּשֶׁעָמַד עֲלֵיהֶם הָמָן הָרָשָׁע,
when Haman, the wicked, rose up against them

bikaysh l'hashmid laharôg ul-abayd   בִּקֵּשׁ לְהַשְׁמִיד לַהֲרֹג וּלְאַבֵּד
and sought to destroy, to slay, and to exterminate

es kol ha-y'hudim,   אֶת כָּל הַיְּהוּדִים,
   mina-ar v'ad zokayn, taf v'noshim מִנַּעַר וְעַד זָקֵן, טַף וְנָשִׁים
all the Jews, young and old, infants and women,

b'yôm e-chod,   בְּיוֹם אֶחָד,
on the same day,

bishlôsho osor l'chôdesh   בִּשְׁלוֹשָׁה עָשָׂר לְחֹדֶשׁ
   sh'naym osor, hu chôdesh ador, שְׁנֵים עָשָׂר, הוּא חֹדֶשׁ אֲדָר,
on the thirteenth of the twelfth month which is the month of Adar,

ushlolom lovôz.   וּשְׁלָלָם לָבוֹז.
and to plunder their possessions.

V'ato b'rachamecho horabim   וְאַתָּה בְּרַחֲמֶיךָ הָרַבִּים
But You, in Your abundant mercy,

hayfarto es atzosô,   הֵפַרְתָּ אֶת עֲצָתוֹ,
nullified his counsel

ON PURIM CONTINUE HERE:

v'kilkalto es machashavtō, וְקִלְקַלְתָּ אֶת מַחֲשַׁבְתּוֹ,

and frustrated his intention

vaha-shayvōso lō g'mulō b'rōshō, וַהֲשֵׁבְוֹתָ לּוֹ גְּמוּלוֹ בְּרֹאשׁוֹ,

and caused his design to return upon his own head,

v'solu ōsō v'es bonov al ho-aytz. וְתָלוּ אוֹתוֹ וְאֶת בָּנָיו עַל הָעֵץ.

and they hanged him and his sons on the gallows.

V'AL kulom yisborach v'yisrōmam וְעַל כֻּלָּם יִתְבָּרַךְ וְיִתְרוֹמַם

shimcho, malkaynu שִׁמְךָ מַלְכֵּנוּ

For all these, may Your Name be blessed and exalted, our King,

tomid l'ōlom vo-ed. תָּמִיד לְעוֹלָם וָעֶד.

continually, forever and ever.

FROM ROSH HASHANAH TO YOM KIPPUR ADD:

Uchsōv l'cha-yim tōvim וּכְתוֹב לְחַיִּים טוֹבִים

kol b'nay v'risecho. כָּל בְּנֵי בְרִיתֶךָ.

And inscribe all the children of Your covenant for a good life.

V'chōl hacha-yim yōducho selo, וְכֹל הַחַיִּים יוֹדוּךָ סֶּלָה,

Everything alive will gratefully acknowledge You, Selah!

vihal'lu es shimcho be-emes, וִיהַלְלוּ אֶת שִׁמְךָ בֶּאֱמֶת,

and praise Your Name sincerely,

ho-Ayl y'shu-osaynu הָאֵל יְשׁוּעָתֵנוּ

v'ezrosaynu selo. וְעֶזְרָתֵנוּ סֶלָה.

O God of our salvation and help, Selah!

BEND THE KNEES AT Boruch; BOW AT ato; STRAIGHTEN UP AT Adōnoy.

Boruch ato Adōnoy, בָּרוּךְ אַתָּה יהוה,

hatōv shimcho הַטּוֹב שִׁמְךָ

ulcho no-e l'hōdōs. וּלְךָ נָאֶה לְהוֹדוֹת.

Blessed are You, HASHEM, Your Name is "The Beneficent One"
and to You it is fitting to give thanks.

■ Nineteenth Blessing: Prayer for peace and harmony
amongst the Jewish people

SHOLŌM ROV al yisro-ayl שָׁלוֹם רָב עַל יִשְׂרָאֵל

am'cho tosim l'ōlom, עַמְּךָ תָּשִׂים לְעוֹלָם,

Establish abundant peace upon Your people Israel forever,

ki ato hu melech,
　odōn l'chol ha-sholōm.

כִּי אַתָּה הוּא מֶלֶךְ
אָדוֹן לְכָל הַשָּׁלוֹם.

for You are King, Master of all peace.

V'tōv b'aynecho l'voraych
　es am'cho yisro-ayl,

וְטוֹב בְּעֵינֶיךָ לְבָרֵךְ
אֶת עַמְּךָ יִשְׂרָאֵל,

And may it be good in Your eyes to bless Your people Israel

b'chol ays uvchol sho-o bish-lōmecho..

בְּכָל עֵת וּבְכָל שָׁעָה בִּשְׁלוֹמֶךָ..

at every time and at every hour, with Your peace.

°Boruch ato Adōnoy,
　ham'voraych es amō yisro-ayl
　ba-sholōm.

°בָּרוּךְ אַתָּה יהוה,
הַמְבָרֵךְ אֶת עַמּוֹ יִשְׂרָאֵל
בַּשָּׁלוֹם.

°Blessed are You, HASHEM, Who blesses His people Israel with peace.

° FROM ROSH HASHANAH TO YOM KIPPUR SUBSTITUTE THE FOLLOWING:

B'sayfer cha-yim b'rocho v'sholōm,
　u-farnoso tōvo,

בְּסֵפֶר חַיִּים בְּרָכָה וְשָׁלוֹם,
וּפַרְנָסָה טוֹבָה,

In the book of life, blessing, and peace, and good livelihood,

nizochayr v'nikosayv l'fonecho,

נִזָּכֵר וְנִכָּתֵב לְפָנֶיךָ,

may we be remembered and inscribed before You —

anachnu v'chol am'cho
　bays yisro-ayl,

אֲנַחְנוּ וְכָל עַמְּךָ
בֵּית יִשְׂרָאֵל,

we and Your entire people the Family of Israel —

l'cha-yim tōvim ulsholōm.

לְחַיִּים טוֹבִים וּלְשָׁלוֹם.

for a good life and for peace.

Boruch ato Adōnoy,
　ō-se ha-sholōm.

בָּרוּךְ אַתָּה יהוה,
עוֹשֶׂה הַשָּׁלוֹם.

Blessed are You, HASHEM, Who makes the peace.

Yih-yu l'rotzōn imray fi
　v'hegyōn libi l'fonecho,

יִהְיוּ לְרָצוֹן אִמְרֵי פִי
וְהֶגְיוֹן לִבִּי לְפָנֶיךָ,

*May the expressions of my mouth and the thoughts of my heart
find favor before You,*

Adōnoy tzuri v'gō-ali.

יהוה צוּרִי וְגֹאֲלִי.

HASHEM, my Rock and my Redeemer.

■ I pray that, having completed my *Amidah*, I have been changed in a positive way,
especially with regard to my interpersonal relationships.

ELŌHAI, n'tzōr l'shōni mayro,

אֱלֹהַי, נְצוֹר לְשׁוֹנִי מֵרָע,

My God, guard my tongue from evil

usfosai midabayr mirmo,
וּשְׂפָתַי מִדַּבֵּר מִרְמָה,

and my lips from speaking deceitfully.

V'limkal'lai nafshi sidōm,
וְלִמְקַלְלַי נַפְשִׁי תִדּוֹם,

To those who curse me, let my soul be silent;

v'nafshi ke-ofor lakōl tiye.
וְנַפְשִׁי כֶּעָפָר לַכֹּל תִּהְיֶה.

and let my soul be like dust to everyone.

P'sach libi b'sōrosecho,
פְּתַח לִבִּי בְּתוֹרָתֶךָ,

Open my heart to Your Torah,

uvmitzvōsecho tirdōf nafshi.
וּבְמִצְוֹתֶיךָ תִּרְדּוֹף נַפְשִׁי.

then my soul will pursue Your commandments.

V'chol hachōsh'vim olai ro-o,
וְכָל הַחוֹשְׁבִים עָלַי רָעָה,

As for all those who design evil against me,

m'hayro hofayr atzosom
מְהֵרָה הָפֵר עֲצָתָם

speedily nullify their counsel

v'kalkayl machashavtom.
וְקַלְקֵל מַחֲשַׁבְתָּם.

and disrupt their design.

asay l'ma-an sh'mecho,
עֲשֵׂה לְמַעַן שְׁמֶךָ,

Act for Your Name's sake;

asay l'ma-an y'minecho,
עֲשֵׂה לְמַעַן יְמִינֶךָ,

act for Your right hand's sake;

asay l'ma-an k'dushosecho,
עֲשֵׂה לְמַעַן קְדֻשָּׁתֶךָ,

act for Your sanctity's sake;

asay l'ma-an tōrosecho.
עֲשֵׂה לְמַעַן תּוֹרָתֶךָ.

act for Your Torah's sake.

Lama-an yaychol'tzun y'didecho,
לְמַעַן יֵחָלְצוּן יְדִידֶיךָ,

That Your beloved ones may be given rest;

hōshi-o y'min'cho va-anayni.
הוֹשִׁיעָה יְמִינְךָ וַעֲנֵנִי.

let Your right hand save, and respond to me.

Yiyu l'rotzōn imray fi
יִהְיוּ לְרָצוֹן אִמְרֵי פִי

v'hegyōn libi l'fonecho,
וְהֶגְיוֹן לִבִּי לְפָנֶיךָ,

May the expressions of my mouth and the thoughts of my heart find favor before You,

Adōnoy tzuri v'gō-ali.
יהוה צוּרִי וְגֹאֲלִי.

HASHEM, my Rock and my Redeemer.

TAKE THREE STEPS BACK. BOW LEFT AND SAY:

Ō-se sholōm bimrōmov,
עֹשֶׂה שָׁלוֹם בִּמְרוֹמָיו,

He Who makes peace in His heights,

BOW RIGHT AND SAY:

hu ya-a-se sholōm olaynu,   הוּא יַעֲשֶׂה שָׁלוֹם עָלֵינוּ,

may He make peace upon us,

BOW FORWARD AND SAY:

v'al kol yisro-ayl. V'imru: Omayn.   וְעַל כָּל יִשְׂרָאֵל. וְאִמְרוּ: אָמֵן.

and upon all Israel. Now respond: Amen.

Y'HI ROTZŌN mil'fonecho,   יְהִי רָצוֹן מִלְּפָנֶיךָ

May it be Your will,

Adōnoy Elōhaynu   יהוה אֱלֹהֵינוּ

   Vaylōhay avōsaynu,   וֵאלֹהֵי אֲבוֹתֵינוּ,

HASHEM, our God and the God of our forefathers,

she-yibo-ne bays hamikdosh   שֶׁיִּבָּנֶה בֵּית הַמִּקְדָּשׁ

   bimhayro v'yomaynu,   בִּמְהֵרָה בְיָמֵינוּ,

that the Holy Temple be rebuilt, speedily in our days;

v'sayn chelkaynu b'sōrosecho,   וְתֵן חֶלְקֵנוּ בְּתוֹרָתֶךָ,

and grant us our share in Your Torah;

v'shom na-avod-cho b'yiro,   וְשָׁם נַעֲבָדְךָ בְּיִרְאָה,

and may we serve You there with reverence,

kimay ōlom   כִּימֵי עוֹלָם

   uchshonim kadmōniyōs.   וּכְשָׁנִים קַדְמוֹנִיּוֹת.

as in days of old and in former years.

V'or'vo Ladōnoy   וְעָרְבָה לַיהוה

   minchas y'hudo virusholo-yim מִנְחַת יְהוּדָה וִירוּשָׁלָיִם,

Then the offering of Judah and Jerusalem will be pleasing to HASHEM,

kimay ōlom   כִּימֵי עוֹלָם

   uchshonim kadmōniyōs.   וּכְשָׁנִים קַדְמוֹנִיּוֹת.

as in days of old and in former years.

SHEMONEH ESREI ENDS HERE. REMAIN STANDING IN PLACE AT LEAST FOR A FEW MOMENTS THEN TAKE THREE STEPS FORWARD.

AT THE CONCLUSION OF THE SABBATH THE SERVICE CONTINUES WITH HALF-*KADDISH* (P. 597). HOWEVER, IF A FESTIVAL (OR EREV PESACH) FALLS BEFORE THE COMING SABBATH, THE *CHAZZAN* RECITES THE FULL *KADDISH* (P. 604) AND THE SERVICE CONTINUES THERE. ON WEEKNIGHTS — EVEN AT THE CONCLUSION OF A FESTIVAL — THE SERVICE CONTINUES WITH THE FULL *KADDISH* (P. 604).

ON PURIM AND TISHAH B'AV THE FULL KADDISH (P. 604) IS RECITED. ON PURIM THE *MEGILLAH* IS THEN READ; ON TISHAH B'AV *EICHAH* IS THEN READ. ON WEEKNIGHTS, BOTH ARE FOLLOWED BY *V'ATAH KADOSH* (P. 600) AND THE SERVICE CONTINUES THERE. IF PURIM OCCURS ON *MOTZA'EI SHABBOS*, CONTINUE *VIHI NOAM* (597).

THE *CHAZZAN* RECITES *HALF-KADDISH*.

(Congregational responses are indicated by parentheses.)

יִתְגַּדֵּל וְיִתְקַדַּשׁ שְׁמֵהּ רַבָּא. (אָמֵן—Omayn). בְּעָלְמָא דִּי בְרָא
כִרְעוּתֵהּ. וְיַמְלִיךְ מַלְכוּתֵהּ, בְּחַיֵּיכוֹן וּבְיוֹמֵיכוֹן וּבְחַיֵּי דְכָל
בֵּית יִשְׂרָאֵל, בַּעֲגָלָא וּבִזְמַן קָרִיב. וְאִמְרוּ: אָמֵן.

(אָמֵן. יְהֵא שְׁמֵהּ רַבָּא מְבָרַךְ לְעָלַם וּלְעָלְמֵי עָלְמַיָּא.)

(Omayn. Y'hay sh'mayh rabo m'vorach l'olam ul-ol'may ol'ma-yo.)

יְהֵא שְׁמֵהּ רַבָּא מְבָרַךְ לְעָלַם וּלְעָלְמֵי עָלְמַיָּא. יִתְבָּרַךְ וְיִשְׁתַּבַּח
וְיִתְפָּאַר וְיִתְרוֹמַם וְיִתְנַשֵּׂא וְיִתְהַדָּר וְיִתְעַלֶּה וְיִתְהַלָּל שְׁמֵהּ
דְקֻדְשָׁא בְּרִיךְ הוּא (בְּרִיךְ הוּא – B'rich hu). °לְעֵלָּא מִן כָּל
[°לְעֵלָּא לְעֵלָּא מִכָּל] – from Rosh Hashanah to Yom Kippur substitute]
בִּרְכָתָא וְשִׁירָתָא תֻּשְׁבְּחָתָא וְנֶחֱמָתָא, דַּאֲמִירָן בְּעָלְמָא. וְאִמְרוּ: אָמֵן.
(אָמֵן—Omayn).

PRAYERS FOLLOWING MAARIV

▪ As the sanctity of Shabbos departs and the workweek begins, we implore Hashem to grant us success and protection.

VIHI nō-am Adōnoy

וִיהִי נֹעַם אֲדֹנָי

Elōhaynu olaynu,

אֱלֹהֵינוּ עָלֵינוּ,

May the pleasantness of my Lord, our God, be upon us —

uma-asay yodaynu kōn'no olaynu,

וּמַעֲשֵׂה יָדֵינוּ כּוֹנְנָה עָלֵינוּ,

and our handiwork, may You establish for us;

uma-asay yodaynu kōn'nayhu.

וּמַעֲשֵׂה יָדֵינוּ כּוֹנְנֵהוּ.

and our handiwork, may You establish.

YŌSHAYV b'sayser elyōn,

יֹשֵׁב בְּסֵתֶר עֶלְיוֹן,

Whoever sits in the refuge of the Most High,

b'tzayl Shadai yislōnon.

בְּצֵל שַׁדַּי יִתְלוֹנָן.

he shall dwell in the shadow of the Almighty.

◆§ **Maariv at the Conclusion of the Sabbath**

After *Shemoneh Esrei*, two additional prayers are recited, both of which set the tone for the transition from the Sabbath to the weekdays.

The verse *Vihi nō-am* contains two aspects of our concept of blessing. On the one hand we ask that God give us the satisfaction of "pleasantness in our handiwork," meaning that we have the freedom to be productive. On the

other hand, we ask God Himself to "establish our handiwork," meaning that we give up our independence to the will and law of God. We ask that this declaration become the framework of the workweek that now begins.

We then go on to Psalm 91, which the Talmud (*Shavuos* 150) calls the "Song of Afflictions," because it expresses prayerful confidence that God will protect us from the dangers and afflictions of life.

Ōmar Ladōnoy machsi umtzudosi,
אֹמַר לַיהוה מַחְסִי וּמְצוּדָתִי,
I will say of HASHEM, "He is my refuge and my fortress,

Elōhai evtach bō.
אֱלֹהַי אֶבְטַח בּוֹ.
my God, I will trust in Him."

Ki hu yatzil'cho mipach yokush,
כִּי הוּא יַצִּילְךָ מִפַּח יָקוּשׁ,
For He will deliver you from the ensnaring trap,

mi-dever havōs.
מִדֶּבֶר הַוּוֹת.
from devastating pestilence.

B'evrosō yosech loch,
בְּאֶבְרָתוֹ יָסֶךְ לָךְ,
With His pinion He will cover you,

v'sachas k'nofov techse,
וְתַחַת כְּנָפָיו תֶּחְסֶה,
and beneath His wings you will be protected;

tzino v'sōchayro amitō.
צִנָּה וְסֹחֵרָה אֲמִתּוֹ.
shield and armor is His truth.

Lō siro mipachad loylo,
לֹא תִירָא מִפַּחַד לָיְלָה,
You shall not fear the terror of night;

maychaytz yo-uf yōmom.
מֵחֵץ יָעוּף יוֹמָם.
nor the arrow that flies by day;

Mi-dever bo-ōfel yahalōch,
מִדֶּבֶר בָּאֹפֶל יַהֲלֹךְ,
nor the pestilence that walks in gloom;

miketev yoshud tzohoro-yim.
מִקֶּטֶב יָשׁוּד צָהֳרָיִם.
nor the destroyer who lays waste at noon.

Yipōl mitzid'cho elef,
יִפֹּל מִצִּדְּךָ אֶלֶף,
Let a thousand encamp at your side

ur'vovo miminecho,
וּרְבָבָה מִימִינֶךָ,
and a myriad at your right hand,

aylecho lō yigosh.
אֵלֶיךָ לֹא יִגָּשׁ.
but to you they shall not approach.

Rak b'aynecho sabit,
רַק בְּעֵינֶיךָ תַבִּיט,
You will merely peer with your eyes

v'shilumas r'sho-im tir-e.
וְשִׁלֻּמַת רְשָׁעִים תִּרְאֶה.
and you will see the retribution of the wicked.

Ki ato Adōnoy machsi,
כִּי אַתָּה יהוה מַחְסִי,
Because [you said,] "You, HASHEM, are my refuge,"

elyōn samto m'ōnecho.
עֶלְיוֹן שַׂמְתָּ מְעוֹנֶךָ.
you have made the Most High your dwelling place.

Lō s'une aylecho ro-o,

לֹא תְאֻנֶּה אֵלֶיךָ רָעָה,

No evil will befall you,

v'nega lō yikrav b'oholecho.

וְנֶגַע לֹא יִקְרַב בְּאָהֳלֶךָ.

nor will any plague come near your tent.

Ki mal-ochov y'tza-ve loch,

כִּי מַלְאָכָיו יְצַוֶּה לָּךְ,

He will charge His angels for you,

lishmorcho b'chol d'rochecho.

לִשְׁמָרְךָ בְּכָל דְּרָכֶיךָ.

to protect you in all your ways.

Al kapa-yim yiso-uncho,

עַל כַּפַּיִם יִשָּׂאוּנְךָ,

On [their] palms they will carry you,

pen tigōf bo-even raglecho.

פֶּן תִּגֹּף בָּאֶבֶן רַגְלֶךָ.

lest you strike your foot against a stone.

Al shachal vofesen tidrōch,

עַל שַׁחַל וָפֶתֶן תִּדְרֹךְ,

Upon the lion and the viper you will tread;

tirmōs k'fir v'sanin.

תִּרְמֹס כְּפִיר וְתַנִּין.

you will trample the young lion and the serpent.

Ki vi choshak va-afal'tayhu,

כִּי בִי חָשַׁק וַאֲפַלְּטֵהוּ,

For he has yearned for Me and I will deliver him;

asag'vayhu ki yoda sh'mi.

אֲשַׂגְּבֵהוּ כִּי יָדַע שְׁמִי.

I will elevate him because he knows My Name.

Yikro-ayni v'e-enayhu,

יִקְרָאֵנִי וְאֶעֱנֵהוּ,

He will call upon Me and I will answer him,

imō onōchi v'tzoro,

עִמּוֹ אָנֹכִי בְצָרָה,

I am with him in distress,

achal'tzayhu va-achab'dayhu.

אֲחַלְּצֵהוּ וַאֲכַבְּדֵהוּ.

I will release him and I will honor him.

Ōrech yomim asbi-ayhu,

✧ אֹרֶךְ יָמִים אַשְׂבִּיעֵהוּ,

With long life will I satisfy him,

v'ar-ayhu bishu-osi.

וְאַרְאֵהוּ בִּישׁוּעָתִי.

and I will show him My salvation.

Ōrech yomim asbi-ayhu,

אֹרֶךְ יָמִים אַשְׂבִּיעֵהוּ,

With long life will I satisfy him,

v'ar-ayhu bishu-osi.

וְאַרְאֵהוּ בִּישׁוּעָתִי.

and I will show him My salvation.

V'ATO kodōsh,
  yōshayv t'hilōs yisro-ayl.

✧ **וְאַתָּה** קָדוֹשׁ
יוֹשֵׁב תְּהִלּוֹת יִשְׂרָאֵל.

You are the Holy One, enthroned upon the praises of Israel.*

V'koro ze el ze v'omar:

וְקָרָא זֶה אֶל זֶה וְאָמַר:

And one [angel] will call another and say:

THE ENTIRE CONGREGATION SHOULD RECITE THE FOLLOWING VERSE ALOUD AND IN UNISON.

Kodōsh, kodōsh, kodōsh,
  Adōnoy tz'vo-ōs,

קָדוֹשׁ, קָדוֹשׁ, קָדוֹשׁ,
יהוה צְבָאוֹת,

"Holy, holy, holy is HASHEM, Master of Legions,

m'lō chol ho-oretz k'vōdō.

מְלֹא כָל הָאָרֶץ כְּבוֹדוֹ.

the whole world is filled with His glory."

Umkab'lin dayn min dayn v'om'rin:

וּמְקַבְּלִין דֵּין מִן דֵּין וְאָמְרִין:

And they receive permission from one another and say:

Kadish bishmay m'rōmo ilo-o
  bays sh'chin'tayh;

קַדִּישׁ בִּשְׁמֵי מְרוֹמָא עִלָּאָה
בֵּית שְׁכִינְתֵּהּ,

"Holy in the most exalted heaven, the abode of His Presence;

kadish al ar-o ōvad g'vurtayh;

קַדִּישׁ עַל אַרְעָא עוֹבַד גְּבוּרְתֵּהּ,

holy on earth, product of His strength;

kadish l'olam ul-ol'may ol'ma-yo,
  Adonoy Tz'vo-ōs,

קַדִּישׁ לְעָלַם וּלְעָלְמֵי עָלְמַיָּא,
יהוה צְבָאוֹת,

holy forever and ever is HASHEM, Master of Legions —

malyo chol ar-o ziv y'korayh.

מַלְיָא כָל אַרְעָא זִיו יְקָרֵהּ.

the entire world is filled with the radiance of His glory."

Vatiso-ayni ru-ach,

וַתִּשָּׂאֵנִי רוּחַ,

And a wind lifted me;

vo-eshma acharai
  kōl ra-ash godōl:

וָאֶשְׁמַע אַחֲרַי
קוֹל רַעַשׁ גָּדוֹל:

and I heard behind me the sound of a great noise:

THE ENTIRE CONGREGATION SHOULD RECITE THE FOLLOWING VERSE ALOUD AND IN UNISON.

Boruch k'vōd Adōnoy mim'kōmō.

בָּרוּךְ כְּבוֹד יהוה מִמְּקוֹמוֹ.

"Blessed is the glory of HASHEM from His place."

You are the Holy One

Having requested God's blessings during the forthcoming week, we now ask that the Sabbath holiness remain with us, and afford us spiritual protection throughout the week, even though the day itself is departing. Therefore we recite the verses that proclaim God's holiness on earth as well as heaven. Then we proceed to acknowledge that we were created to glorify Him and we pray that we be capable of absorbing the teachings of the Torah. For commentary see page 506.

Since these prayers refer to the six days of labor, they are not recited if a Festival (Pesach, Shavuos, Rosh Hashanah, Yom Kippur, Succos) will occur during the coming week. In that case, the holiness of the Festival suffices to infuse the week with the sanctity we long for.

Untolasni rucho,   וּנְטָלַתְנִי רוּחָא,
And a wind lifted me;

v'shim-ays basrai kol zi-a sagi   וְשָׁמְעֵת בַּתְרֵי קָל זִיעַ סַגִּיא
and I heard behind me the sound of the powerful movement

dimshab'chin v'om'rin: דִּמְשַׁבְּחִין וְאָמְרִין:
of those who praised saying:

B'rich y'koro Dadōnoy   בְּרִיךְ יְקָרָא דַיהוה
*"Blessed is the honor of H*ASHEM

may-asar bays sh'chintayh.   מֵאֲתַר בֵּית שְׁכִינְתֵּהּ.
from the place of the abode of His Presence."

THE ENTIRE CONGREGATION SHOULD RECITE THE FOLLOWING VERSE ALOUD AND IN UNISON.

Adōnoy yimlōch l'ōlom vo-ed.   יהוה יִמְלֹךְ לְעֹלָם וָעֶד.
*H*ASHEM *shall reign for all eternity.*

Adōnoy malchusayh ko-aym   יהוה מַלְכוּתֵהּ קָאֵם
*H*ASHEM *— His kingdom is established*

l'olam ul-ol'may ol'ma-yo.   לְעָלַם וּלְעָלְמֵי עָלְמַיָּא.
forever and ever.

Adōnoy Elōhay avrohom   יהוה אֱלֹהֵי אַבְרָהָם
yitzchok v'yisro-ayl avōsaynu,   יִצְחָק וְיִשְׂרָאֵל אֲבֹתֵינוּ,
*H*ASHEM, *God of Abraham, Isaac, and Israel, our forefathers,*

shomro zōs l'ōlom,   שָׁמְרָה זֹּאת לְעוֹלָם,
may You preserve this forever

l'yaytzer machsh'vōs l'vav amecho,   לְיֵצֶר מַחְשְׁבוֹת לְבַב עַמֶּךָ,
as the realization of the thoughts in Your people's heart,

v'hochayn l'vovom aylecho.   וְהָכֵן לְבָבָם אֵלֶיךָ.
and may You direct their heart to You.

V'hu rachum,   וְהוּא רַחוּם,
y'chapayr ovōn v'lō yashchis,   יְכַפֵּר עָוֹן וְלֹא יַשְׁחִית,
He, the Merciful One, is forgiving of iniquity and does not destroy;

v'hirbo l'hoshiv apō,   וְהִרְבָּה לְהָשִׁיב אַפּוֹ,
frequently He withdraws His anger,

v'lō yo-ir kol chamosō.   וְלֹא יָעִיר כָּל חֲמָתוֹ.
not arousing His entire rage.

Ki ato Adōnoy tōv v'saloch,   כִּי אַתָּה אֲדֹנָי טוֹב וְסַלָּח,
For You, my Lord, are good and forgiving,

v'rav chesed l'chol kōr'echo.   וְרַב חֶסֶד לְכָל קֹרְאֶיךָ.
and abundantly kind to all who call upon You.

Tzidkos'cho tzedek l'ōlom,

צִדְקָתְךָ צֶדֶק לְעוֹלָם,

Your righteousness is righteous forever,

v'sōros'cho emes.

וְתוֹרָתְךָ אֱמֶת.

and Your Torah is truth.

Titayn emes l'ya-akōv,

תִּתֵּן אֱמֶת לְיַעֲקֹב,

chesed l'avrohom,

חֶסֶד לְאַבְרָהָם,

Grant truth to Jacob, kindness to Abraham,

asher nishbato la-avōsaynu

אֲשֶׁר נִשְׁבַּעְתָּ לַאֲבֹתֵינוּ

mimay kedem.

מִימֵי קֶדֶם.

as You swore to our forefathers from ancient times.

Boruch Adōnoy

בָּרוּךְ אֲדֹנָי

yōm yōm ya-amos lonu,

יוֹם יוֹם יַעֲמָס לָנוּ,

Blessed is my Lord, for every single day He burdens us [with blessings],

ho-Ayl y'shu-osaynu selo.

הָאֵל יְשׁוּעָתֵנוּ סֶלָה.

the God of our salvation, Selah.

Adōnoy Tz'vo-ōs imonu,

יהוה צְבָאוֹת עִמָּנוּ,

HASHEM, Master of Legions, is with us,

misgov lonu Elōhay ya-akōv selo.

מִשְׂגָּב לָנוּ אֱלֹהֵי יַעֲקֹב סֶלָה.

a stronghold for us is the God of Jacob, Selah.

Adōnoy Tz'vo-ōs,

יהוה צְבָאוֹת,

HASHEM, Master of Legions,

ashray odom bōtay-ach boch.

אַשְׁרֵי אָדָם בֹּטֵחַ בָּךְ.

praiseworthy is the man who trusts in You.

Adōnoy hōshi-o,

יהוה הוֹשִׁיעָה,

HASHEM, save!

hamelech ya-anaynu v'yōm kor-aynu.

הַמֶּלֶךְ יַעֲנֵנוּ בְיוֹם קָרְאֵנוּ.

May the King answer us on the day we call.

Boruch hu Elōhaynu

בָּרוּךְ הוּא אֱלֹהֵינוּ

Blessed is He, our God,

sheb'ro-onu lichvōdō,

שֶׁבְּרָאָנוּ לִכְבוֹדוֹ,

Who created us for His glory,

v'hivdilonu min hatō-im,

וְהִבְדִּילָנוּ מִן הַתּוֹעִים,

separated us from those who stray,

v'nosan lonu tōras emes,

וְנָתַן לָנוּ תּוֹרַת אֱמֶת,

gave us the Torah of truth

v'cha-yay ōlom nota b'sōchaynu.

וְחַיֵּי עוֹלָם נָטַע בְּתוֹכֵנוּ.

and implanted eternal life within us.

Hu yiftach libaynu b'sōroso   הוּא יִפְתַּח לִבֵּנוּ בְּתוֹרָתוֹ,

May He open our heart through His Torah

v'yosaym b'libaynu ahavosō v'yir-osō,   וְיָשֵׂם בְּלִבֵּנוּ אַהֲבָתוֹ וְיִרְאָתוֹ

and imbue our heart with love and awe of Him

v'la-asōs r'tzōnō   וְלַעֲשׂוֹת רְצוֹנוֹ

and that we may do His will

ul-ovdō b'layvov sholaym,   וּלְעָבְדוֹ בְּלֵבָב שָׁלֵם,

and serve Him wholeheartedly,

l'ma-an lō niga lorik,   לְמַעַן לֹא נִיגַע לָרִיק,

so that we do not struggle in vain

v'lō naylayd labeholo.   וְלֹא נֵלֵד לַבֶּהָלָה.

nor produce for futility.

Y'hi rotzōn mil'fonecho   יְהִי רָצוֹן מִלְּפָנֶיךָ

May it be Your will,

Adōnoy Elōhaynu   יהוה אֱלֹהֵינוּ

Vaylōhay avōsaynu,   וֵאלֹהֵי אֲבוֹתֵינוּ,

HASHEM, our God and the God of our forefathers,

shenishmōr chukecho bo-ōlom ha-ze,   שֶׁנִּשְׁמֹר חֻקֶּיךָ בָּעוֹלָם הַזֶּה,

that we observe Your decrees in this world,

v'nizke v'nichye v'nir-e   וְנִזְכֶּה וְנִחְיֶה וְנִרְאֶה

and merit that we live and see

v'nirash tōvo uvrocho   וְנִירַשׁ טוֹבָה וּבְרָכָה

and inherit goodness and blessing

lishnay y'mōs hamoshi-ach,   לִשְׁנֵי יְמוֹת הַמָּשִׁיחַ

in the years of Messianic times

ulcha-yay ho-ōlom habo.   וּלְחַיֵּי הָעוֹלָם הַבָּא.

and for the life of the World to Come.

L'ma-an y'zamercho chovōd   לְמַעַן יְזַמֶּרְךָ כָבוֹד

v'lō yidōm,   וְלֹא יִדֹּם,

So that my soul might sing to You and not be stilled,

Adōnoy Elōhai l'ōlom ōdeko.   יהוה אֱלֹהַי לְעוֹלָם אוֹדֶךָּ.

HASHEM, my God, forever will I thank You.

Boruch hagever   בָּרוּךְ הַגֶּבֶר

asher yivtach Badōnoy,   אֲשֶׁר יִבְטַח בַּיהוה,

Blessed is the man who trusts in HASHEM,

v'ho-yo Adōnoy mivtachō.   וְהָיָה יהוה מִבְטַחוֹ.

then HASHEM will be his security.

Bitchu Vadōnoy aday ad,

בִּטְחוּ בַיהוה עֲדֵי עַד,

Trust in HASHEM forever,

ki b'Yoh Adōnoy tzur ōlomim.

כִּי בְּיָה יהוה צוּר עוֹלָמִים.

for in God, HASHEM, is the strength of the worlds.

❖ v'yivt'chu v'cho yōd'ay sh'mecho,

וְיִבְטְחוּ בְךָ יוֹדְעֵי שְׁמֶךָ,

Those knowing Your Name will trust in You,

ki lō ozavto dōr'shecho Adōnoy.

כִּי לֹא עָזַבְתָּ דֹרְשֶׁיךָ, יהוה.

and You forsake not those Who seek You, HASHEM.

Adōnoy chofaytz l'ma-an tzidkō,

יהוה חָפֵץ לְמַעַן צִדְקוֹ,

HASHEM desired, for the sake of its [Israel's] righteousness,

yagdil tōro v'yadir.

יַגְדִּיל תּוֹרָה וְיַאְדִּיר.

that the Torah be made great and glorious.

THE *CHAZZAN* RECITES FULL *KADDISH*

(congregational responses are indicated by parentheses):

יִתְגַּדַּל וְיִתְקַדַּשׁ שְׁמֵהּ רַבָּא. (Omayn – אָמֵן). בְּעָלְמָא דִּי בְרָא כִרְעוּתֵהּ. וְיַמְלִיךְ מַלְכוּתֵהּ, בְּחַיֵּיכוֹן וּבְיוֹמֵיכוֹן וּבְחַיֵּי דְכָל בֵּית יִשְׂרָאֵל, בַּעֲגָלָא וּבִזְמַן קָרִיב. וְאִמְרוּ: אָמֵן.

(אָמֵן. יְהֵא שְׁמֵהּ רַבָּא מְבָרַךְ לְעָלַם וּלְעָלְמֵי עָלְמַיָּא.)

(Omayn. Y'hay sh'mayh rabo m'vorach l'olam ulol'may ol'ma-yo.)

יְהֵא שְׁמֵהּ רַבָּא מְבָרַךְ לְעָלַם וּלְעָלְמֵי עָלְמַיָּא. יִתְבָּרַךְ וְיִשְׁתַּבַּח וְיִתְפָּאַר וְיִתְרוֹמַם וְיִתְנַשֵּׂא וְיִתְהַדָּר וְיִתְעַלֶּה וְיִתְהַלָּל שְׁמֵהּ דְּקֻדְשָׁא בְּרִיךְ הוּא (B'rich hu – בְּרִיךְ הוּא). °לְעֵלָּא מִן כָּל [substitute *from Rosh Hashanah to Yom Kippur* – °לְעֵלָּא לְעֵלָּא מִכָּל] בִּרְכָתָא וְשִׁירָתָא תֻּשְׁבְּחָתָא וְנֶחֱמָתָא, דַּאֲמִירָן בְּעָלְמָא. וְאִמְרוּ: אָמֵן. (Omayn – אָמֵן).

תִּתְקַבֵּל צְלוֹתְהוֹן וּבָעוּתְהוֹן דְּכָל (בֵּית) יִשְׂרָאֵל קֳדָם אֲבוּהוֹן דִּי בִשְׁמַיָּא. וְאִמְרוּ: אָמֵן. (Omayn – אָמֵן).

יְהֵא שְׁלָמָא רַבָּא מִן שְׁמַיָּא, וְחַיִּים עָלֵינוּ וְעַל כָּל יִשְׂרָאֵל. וְאִמְרוּ: אָמֵן. (Omayn – אָמֵן).

Bow. Take three steps back. Bow left and say, . . . עֹשֶׂה; bow right and say, . . . הוּא יַעֲשֶׂה; bow forward and say, . . . וְעַל כָּל. Remain in place for a few moments, then take three steps forward.

עֹשֶׂה שָׁלוֹם בִּמְרוֹמָיו, הוּא יַעֲשֶׂה שָׁלוֹם עָלֵינוּ, וְעַל כָּל יִשְׂרָאֵל. וְאִמְרוּ: אָמֵן. (Omayn – אָמֵן).

AT THE CONCLUSION OF THE SABBATH CONTINUE BELOW.

AT THE CONCLUSION OF A FESTIVAL CONTINUE WITH *HAVDALAH* (P. 619).

WHEN *HAVDALAH* IS NOT RECITED CONTINUE WITH *ALEINU* (P. 620).

VERSES OF BLESSING*

■ The Jew optimistically prepares himself for the forthcoming week's endeavors, reciting verses of blessing that declare Hashem as the source of all blessing.

V'YITEN L'CHO ho-Elōhim וְיִתֶּן לְךָ הָאֱלֹהִים
*And may God give you**

mital ha-shoma-yim מִטַּל הַשָּׁמַיִם
u-mishmanay ho-oretz, וּמִשְׁמַנֵּי הָאָרֶץ,
of the dew of the heavens and of the fatness of the earth,

v'rōv dogon v'sirōsh. וְרֹב דָּגָן וְתִירֹשׁ.
and abundant grain and wine.

Ya-avducho amim יַעַבְדוּךָ עַמִּים,
Peoples will serve you,

v'yishta-chavu l'cho l'umim, וְיִשְׁתַּחֲווּ לְךָ לְאֻמִּים,
and regimes will prostrate themselves to you;

hevay g'vir l'achecho, הֱוֵה גְבִיר לְאַחֶיךָ,
be a lord to your kinsmen,

v'yishta-chavu l'cho b'nay imecho, וְיִשְׁתַּחֲווּ לְךָ בְּנֵי אִמֶּךָ,
and your mother's sons will prostrate themselves to you;

ōr'recho orur אֹרְרֶיךָ אָרוּר,
they who curse you are cursed,

umvor'checho boruch. וּמְבָרְכֶיךָ בָּרוּךְ.
and they who bless you are blessed.

V'Ayl Shadai y'voraych ōs'cho וְאֵל שַׁדַּי יְבָרֵךְ אֹתְךָ
*And may the Almighty God bless you,**

v'yafr'cho v'yarbecho, וְיַפְרְךָ וְיַרְבֶּךָ,
make you fruitful and make you numerous,

v'ho-yiso lik-hal amim. וְהָיִיתָ לִקְהַל עַמִּים.
and may you be a congregation of peoples.

V'yiten l'cho es birkas avrohom, וְיִתֶּן לְךָ אֶת בִּרְכַּת אַבְרָהָם,
May He grant you the blessing of Abraham,

◆§ **Verses of Blessing**

After the main body of *Maariv*, this collection of Scriptural passages is recited. Most congregations recite them in the synagogue as part of the *Maariv* service, while others leave them for individuals to recite at home after *Havdalah*. This is primarily an anthology of blessings, beginning with those given by the Patriarch Isaac to his son Jacob. By reciting them now, on the threshold of a new week, we invoke God's blessing on the labor of the coming six days.

These verses can be divided into seven topics: (1) blessing; (2) redemption; (3) salvation; (4) knowledge of God; (5) rescue; (6) transformation of distress to relief; and (7) peace.

וְיִתֶּן לְךָ הָאֱלֹהִים — *And may God give you.* The first two verses comprise the blessings given by Isaac to Jacob at the time that Jacob posed as Esau.

וְאֵל שַׁדַּי יְבָרֵךְ אֹתְךָ — *And may the Almighty God bless you.* This verse and the next one are the blessing given by Isaac to Jacob just before

l'cho ulzar-acho itoch,
לְךָ וּלְזַרְעֲךָ אִתָּךְ,

to you and to your offspring with you,

l'risht'cho es eretz m'gurecho,
לְרִשְׁתְּךָ אֶת אֶרֶץ מְגֻרֶיךָ,

that you may possess the land of your sojourns

asher nosan Elōhim l'avrohom.
אֲשֶׁר נָתַן אֱלֹהִים לְאַבְרָהָם.

which God gave to Abraham.

May-Ayl ovicho v'ya-z'reko,
מֵאֵל אָבִיךָ וְיַעְזְרֶךָ,

It is from the God of your father and He will help you,

v'ays Shadai vi-vor'cheko,
וְאֵת שַׁדַּי וִיבָרְכֶךָ,

and with the Almighty and He will bless you —

birchōs shoma-yim may-ol,
בִּרְכֹת שָׁמַיִם מֵעָל,

blessings of heaven from above,

birchōs t'hōm rōvetzes tochas,
בִּרְכֹת תְּהוֹם רֹבֶצֶת תָּחַת,

blessings of the deep crouching below,

birchōs shoda-yim vorocham.
בִּרְכֹת שָׁדַיִם וָרָחַם.

blessings of the bosom and womb.

Birchōs ovicho gov'ru
בִּרְכֹת אָבִיךָ גָּבְרוּ

al birchōs hōrai,
עַל בִּרְכֹת הוֹרַי,

The blessings of your father* surpassed the blessings of my fathers,

ad ta-avas giv-ōs ōlom,
עַד תַּאֲוַת גִּבְעֹת עוֹלָם,

to the endless bounds of the world's hills;

tih-yeno l'rōsh yōsayf,
תִּהְיֶין לְרֹאשׁ יוֹסֵף,

let them be upon Joseph's head

ulkodkōd n'zir e-chov.
וּלְקָדְקֹד נְזִיר אֶחָיו.

and upon the head of the one separated from his brothers.

Va-ahayv'cho uvayrach'cho v'hirbecho,
וַאֲהֵבְךָ וּבֵרַכְךָ וְהִרְבֶּךָ,

And He shall love you,* and He shall bless you, and He shall make you numerous;

u-vayrach p'ri vitn'cho
וּבֵרַךְ פְּרִי בִטְנְךָ

may He bless the fruit of your womb

ufri admosecho,
וּפְרִי אַדְמָתֶךָ,

and the fruit of your land,

Jacob was sent to Paddan Aram to escape the wrath of the murderous Esau and to find himself a wife.

בִּרְכֹת אָבִיךָ — *The blessings of your father*. This verse is the climax of Jacob's blessing to Joseph, who earned the distinction of primacy among his brothers. Although all of Jacob's blessings had awesome significance, that given

to Joseph is cited here because Jacob described it as unbounded by any limits.

וַאֲהֵבְךָ — *And He shall love you*. In the last weeks of Moses' life, he exhorted and taught, warned and blessed. From here to the end of the paragraph is one of many blessings Moses pronounced as the Divine reward for Israel's loyalty to God and His commandments.

d'gon'cho v'sirōsh'cho v'yitzhorecho,　　דְּגָנֶךְ וְתִירֹשְׁךָ וְיִצְהָרֶךָ,

your grain, your wine, and your oil,

sh'gar alofecho　　שְׁגַר אֲלָפֶיךָ

v'asht'rōs tzōnecho,　　וְעַשְׁתְּרֹת צֹאנֶךָ,

the offspring of your cattle and the flocks of your sheep,

al ho-adomo　　עַל הָאֲדָמָה

on the land

asher nishba la-avōsecho lo-ses loch.　　אֲשֶׁר נִשְׁבַּע לַאֲבֹתֶיךָ לָתֶת לָךְ.

that He swore to your forefathers to give to you.

Boruch tih-ye mikol ho-amim,　　בָּרוּךְ תִּהְיֶה מִכָּל הָעַמִּים,

Blessed shall you be above all peoples;

lō yih-ye v'cho okor va-akoro,　　לֹא יִהְיֶה בְךָ עָקָר וַעֲקָרָה,

u-vivhemtecho.　　וּבִבְהֶמְתֶּךָ.

there shall not be among you a barren man or woman, nor among your cattle.

V'haysir Adōnoy mim'cho kol chōli,　　וְהֵסִיר יהוה מִמְּךָ כָּל חֳלִי,

HASHEM shall remove from you all illness;

v'chōl madvay mitzra-yim horo-im　　וְכָל מַדְוֵי מִצְרַיִם הָרָעִים

asher yoda-to　　אֲשֶׁר יָדַעְתָּ,

and all the evil sufferings of Egypt that you knew,

lō y'simom boch,　　לֹא יְשִׂימָם בָּךְ,

He shall not place upon you,

unsonom b'chol sōn'echo.　　וּנְתָנָם בְּכָל שֹׂנְאֶיךָ.

but He shall set them upon all your enemies.

HAMAL-OCH hagō-ayl ōsi　　הַמַּלְאָךְ הַגֹּאֵל אֹתִי

mikol ro,　　מִכָּל רָע,

The angel* who redeems me from all evil,

y'voraych es han'orim,　　יְבָרֵךְ אֶת הַנְּעָרִים,

may he bless the lads,

v'yikoray vohem sh'mi,　　וְיִקָּרֵא בָהֶם שְׁמִי,

and may my name be declared upon them —

v'shaym avōsai avrohom v'yitzchok,　　וְשֵׁם אֲבֹתַי אַבְרָהָם וְיִצְחָק,

and the names of my forefathers Abraham and Isaac —

הַמַּלְאָךְ — *[May] the angel*. This paragraph is devoted to blessings given by aged leaders who took pride in the growth of a young and thriving new generation. The first verse has become one of the classic blessings conferred upon children. It was given by Jacob on his deathbed to Menashe and Ephraim, the Egyptian-born children of Joseph. This is followed by Moses' proud description of the nation that he had led out of Egypt and his blessing that their future greatness should dwarf anything that had happened in the past.

v'yidgu lorōv b'kerev ho-oretz.   וְיִדְגּוּ לָרֹב בְּקֶרֶב הָאָרֶץ.
and may they proliferate abundantly like fish within the land.

Adōnoy Elōhaychem hirbo eschem,   יהוה אֱלֹהֵיכֶם הִרְבָּה אֶתְכֶם,
HASHEM, your God, has made you numerous,

v'hin'chem ha-yōm   וְהִנְּכֶם הַיּוֹם
    k'chōch'vay ha-shoma-yim lorōv.   כְּכוֹכְבֵי הַשָּׁמַיִם לָרֹב.
and behold! you are today like the stars of heaven in abundance.

Adōnoy Elōhay avōsaychem   יהוה אֱלֹהֵי אֲבוֹתֵכֶם
May HASHEM, the God of your forefathers,

yōsayf alaychem kochem   יֹסֵף עֲלֵיכֶם כָּכֶם
    elef p'omim,   אֶלֶף פְּעָמִים,
increase you a thousandfold

vi-voraych eschem   וִיבָרֵךְ אֶתְכֶם
    ka-asher diber lochem.   כַּאֲשֶׁר דִּבֶּר לָכֶם.
and bless you as He spoke to you.

BORUCH ato bo-ir,   **בָּרוּךְ** אַתָּה בָּעִיר,
Blessed are you in the city;*

u-voruch ato baso-de.   וּבָרוּךְ אַתָּה בַּשָּׂדֶה.
blessed are you in the field.

Boruch ato b'vō-echo,   בָּרוּךְ אַתָּה בְּבֹאֶךָ,
Blessed are you upon your arrival;

u-voruch ato b'tzay-secho.   וּבָרוּךְ אַתָּה בְּצֵאתֶךָ.
blessed are you upon your departure.

Boruch tan-acho umish-artecho.   בָּרוּךְ טַנְאֲךָ וּמִשְׁאַרְתֶּךָ.
Blessed is your fruit basket and your kneading trough.

Boruch p'ri vitn'cho   בָּרוּךְ פְּרִי בִטְנְךָ
Blessed is the fruit of your womb,

ufri admos'cho ufri v'hemtecho,   וּפְרִי אַדְמָתְךָ וּפְרִי בְהֶמְתֶּךָ,
the fruit of your land, and the fruit of your animal,

sh'gar alofecho v'asht'rōs tzōnecho.   שְׁגַר אֲלָפֶיךָ וְעַשְׁתְּרוֹת צֹאנֶךָ.
the offspring of your cattle and the flocks of your sheep.

Y'tzav Adōnoy it'cho   יְצַו יהוה אִתְּךָ
    es hab'rocho ba-asomecho   אֶת הַבְּרָכָה בַּאֲסָמֶיךָ
*May HASHEM command that the blessing
accompany you in your storehouse*

בָּרוּךְ אַתָּה בָּעִיר — *Blessed are you in the city.*
Moses pronounced this stirring series of blessings upon his people, telling them that if they
observed the Torah, there would be no area of
their lives that would be untouched by God's
generosity.

uvchōl mishlach yodecho,

וּבְכֹל מִשְׁלַח יָדֶךָ,

and wherever you set your hand,

u-vayrach'cho bo-oretz

וּבֵרַכְךָ בָּאָרֶץ

and may He bless you in the land

asher Adōnoy Elōhecho nōsayn loch.

אֲשֶׁר יהוה אֱלֹהֶיךָ נֹתֵן לָךְ.

that HASHEM, your God, gives you.

Yiftach Adōnoy l'cho

יִפְתַּח יהוה לְךָ

May HASHEM open for you

es ōtzorō hatōv, es ha-shoma-yim,

אֶת אוֹצָרוֹ הַטּוֹב, אֶת הַשָּׁמַיִם,

His good treasury, the heaven,

losays m'tar artz'cho b'itō

לָתֵת מְטַר אַרְצְךָ בְּעִתּוֹ,

to give you rain for your land in its time

ulvoraych ays kol ma-asay yodecho,

וּלְבָרֵךְ אֵת כָּל מַעֲשֵׂה יָדֶךָ,

and to bless your every handiwork;

v'hilviso gō-yim rabim,

וְהִלְוִיתָ גוֹיִם רַבִּים,

and may you lend many nations,

v'ato lō silve.

וְאַתָּה לֹא תִלְוֶה.

but may you not borrow.

Ki Adōnoy Elōhecho bayrach'cho

כִּי יהוה אֱלֹהֶיךָ בֵּרַכְךָ

For HASHEM, your God, will have blessed you

ka-asher diber loch,

כַּאֲשֶׁר דִּבֶּר לָךְ,

as He spoke to you;

v'ha-avat-to gō-yim rabim,

וְהַעֲבַטְתָּ גּוֹיִם רַבִּים,

and may you make many nations indebted to you,

v'ato lō sa-avōt,

וְאַתָּה לֹא תַעֲבֹט,

but may you not become indebted;

u-moshalto b'gōyim rabim,

וּמָשַׁלְתָּ בְּגוֹיִם רַבִּים,

and you will dominate many nations,

uvcho lō yimshōlu.

וּבְךָ לֹא יִמְשֹׁלוּ.

but they will not dominate you.

Ashrecho yisro-ayl, mi chomōcho,

אַשְׁרֶיךָ יִשְׂרָאֵל, מִי כָמוֹךָ,

Praiseworthy are you, O Israel,* who is like you! —

am nōsha Badōnoy,

עַם נוֹשַׁע בַּיהוה,

a people saved by God,

אַשְׁרֶיךָ יִשְׂרָאֵל — *Praiseworthy are you, O Israel*. The next two verses are Moses' last words to his people. Though they had tried him sorely during the forty years in the wilderness, and though their provocation had caused him to be denied the privilege of ever setting foot in the Land of Israel, Moses ended his life with love and praise of the nation that meant more to him than life and glory.

mogayn ezrecho,
מָגֵן עֶזְרֶךָ,

Who is the Shield of your help,

va-asher cherev ga-avosecho,
וַאֲשֶׁר חֶרֶב גַּאֲוָתֶךָ,

and Who is the Sword of your majesty.

v'yikochashu ō-y'vecho loch,
וְיִכָּחֲשׁוּ אֹיְבֶיךָ לָךְ,

Your enemies will be false with you,

v'ato al bomōsaymō sidrōch.
וְאַתָּה עַל בָּמוֹתֵימוֹ תִדְרֹךְ.

but you will tread upon their heights.

VERSES OF REDEMPTION

MOCHISI cho-ov p'sho-echo
מָחִיתִי כָעָב פְּשָׁעֶיךָ

I have blotted out* your willful sins like a thick mist

v'che-onon chatōsecho,
וְכֶעָנָן חַטֹּאתֶיךָ,

and your errors like a cloud —

shuvo aylai ki g'alticho.
שׁוּבָה אֵלַי כִּי גְאַלְתִּיךָ.

return to Me for I have redeemed you.

Ronu shoma-yim, ki oso Adōnoy,
רָנּוּ שָׁמַיִם, כִּי עָשָׂה יהוה,

Sing gladly, O heaven, for HASHEM has done so;

hori-u tachtiyōs oretz,
הָרֵיעוּ תַּחְתִּיּוֹת אָרֶץ,

exult, O depths of the earth;

pitzchu horim rino,
פִּצְחוּ הָרִים רִנָּה,

break out, O mountains, in glad song,

ya-ar v'chol aytz bō,
יַעַר וְכָל עֵץ בּוֹ,

forest and every tree within it,

ki go-al Adōnoy ya-akōv
כִּי גָאַל יהוה יַעֲקֹב

uv-yisro-ayl yispo-or.
וּבְיִשְׂרָאֵל יִתְפָּאָר.

for HASHEM has redeemed Jacob and will take pride in Israel.

Gō-alaynu Adōnoy tz'vo-ōs sh'mō,
גֹּאֲלֵנוּ יהוה צְבָאוֹת שְׁמוֹ,

Our Redeemer — HASHEM, Master of Legions, is His Name —

k'dōsh yisro-ayl.
קְדוֹשׁ יִשְׂרָאֵל.

is the Holy One of Israel.

VERSES OF SALVATION

YISRO-AYL nōsha Badōnoy
יִשְׂרָאֵל נוֹשַׁע בַּיהוה

t'shu-as ōlomim,
תְּשׁוּעַת עוֹלָמִים,

Israel is saved by* God in an everlasting salvation;

מָחִיתִי — *I have blotted out.* The section of re-demption makes clear that the basis of redemption is repentance and a return to God, which brings forgiveness of sin.

יִשְׂרָאֵל נוֹשַׁע — *Israel is saved.* The first few verses of salvation give an interesting in-sight into the nature of exile from which Israel is to be saved. Each of the first three

lō sayvōshu v'lō sikol'mu   לֹא תֵבֹשׁוּ וְלֹא תִכָּלְמוּ

they will not be shamed nor humiliated

ad ōl'may ad.   עַד עוֹלְמֵי עַד.

forever and ever.

Va-achaltem ochōl v'sovō-a,   וַאֲכַלְתֶּם אָכוֹל וְשָׂבוֹעַ,

You shall eat food and be satisfied,

v'hilaltem es shaym   וְהִלַּלְתֶּם אֶת שֵׁם

     Adōnoy Elōhaychem   יהוה אֱלֹהֵיכֶם

and you shall praise the Name of HASHEM, *your God,*

asher oso imochem l'haf-li,   אֲשֶׁר עָשָׂה עִמָּכֶם לְהַפְלִיא,

Who has done wondrously with you,

v'lō yayvōshu ami l'ōlom.   וְלֹא יֵבֹשׁוּ עַמִּי לְעוֹלָם.

and My people shall not be shamed forever.

Vidatem   וִידַעְתֶּם

     ki v'kerev yisro-ayl oni,   כִּי בְקֶרֶב יִשְׂרָאֵל אָנִי,

And you shall know that in the midst of Israel am I,

va-ani Adōnoy Elōhaychem, v'ayn ōd,   וַאֲנִי יהוה אֱלֹהֵיכֶם, וְאֵין עוֹד,

and I am HASHEM, *your God — there is none other;*

v'lō yayvōshu ami l'ōlom.   וְלֹא יֵבֹשׁוּ עַמִּי לְעוֹלָם.

and My people shall not be shamed forever.

Ki v'simcho saytzay-u   כִּי בְשִׂמְחָה תֵצֵאוּ

     uvsholōm tuvolun,   וּבְשָׁלוֹם תּוּבָלוּן,

For in gladness shall you go out and in peace shall you arrive;

hehorim v'hag'vo-ōs   הֶהָרִים וְהַגְּבָעוֹת

     yiftz'chu lifnaychem rino,   יִפְצְחוּ לִפְנֵיכֶם רִנָּה,

the mountains and the hills will break out before you in glad song

v'chol atzay haso-de yimcha-u chof.   וְכָל עֲצֵי הַשָּׂדֶה יִמְחֲאוּ כָף.

and all the trees of the field will clap hands.

Hinay Ayl y'shu-osi,   הִנֵּה אֵל יְשׁוּעָתִי,

Behold! God is my help,

evtach v'lō efchod,   אֶבְטַח וְלֹא אֶפְחָד,

I shall trust and not fear —

ki ozi v'zimros Yoh Adōnoy,   כִּי עָזִּי וְזִמְרָת יָהּ יהוה,

for God is my might and my praise — HASHEM *—*

vai-hi li li-shu-o.   וַיְהִי לִי לִישׁוּעָה.

and He was a salvation to me.

verses promises that Israel will no longer be ashamed.

Ush-avtem ma-yim b'soson,
וּשְׁאַבְתֶּם מַיִם בְּשָׂשׂוֹן,

You can draw water in joy,

mima-ai-nay hai-shu-o.
מִמַּעַיְנֵי הַיְשׁוּעָה.

from the springs of salvation.

Va-amartem ba-yōm hahu,
וַאֲמַרְתֶּם בַּיּוֹם הַהוּא,

And you shall say on that day,

hōdu Ladōnoy kir-u vishmō,
הוֹדוּ לַיהוה קִרְאוּ בִשְׁמוֹ,

"Give thanks to HASHEM, *declare His Name,*

hōdi-u vo-amim alilōsov,
הוֹדִיעוּ בָעַמִּים עֲלִילֹתָיו,

make His acts known among the peoples";

hazkiru ki nisgov sh'mō.
הַזְכִּירוּ כִּי נִשְׂגָּב שְׁמוֹ.

remind one another, for His Name is powerful.

Zam'ru Adōnoy ki gay-us oso,
זַמְּרוּ יהוה כִּי גֵאוּת עָשָׂה,

Make music to HASHEM *for He has established grandeur —*

muda-as zōs b'chol ho-oretz.
מוּדַעַת זֹאת בְּכָל הָאָרֶץ.

this is known throughout the earth.

Tzahali vorōni yōsheves tziyōn,
צַהֲלִי וָרֹנִּי יוֹשֶׁבֶת צִיּוֹן,

Exult and sing for joy, O inhabitant of Zion,

ki godōl b'kirbaych
כִּי גָדוֹל בְּקִרְבֵּךְ

k'dōsh yisro-ayl.
קְדוֹשׁ יִשְׂרָאֵל.

for the Holy One of Israel has done greatly among you.

V'omar ba-yōm hahu,
וְאָמַר בַּיּוֹם הַהוּא,

And he shall say on that day,

hinay Elōhaynu ze,
הִנֵּה אֱלֹהֵינוּ זֶה,

"Behold! this is our God,

kivinu lō v'yōshi-aynu,
קִוִּינוּ לוֹ וְיוֹשִׁיעֵנוּ,

we have hoped for Him, that He would save us —

ze Adōnoy kivinu lō,
זֶה יהוה קִוִּינוּ לוֹ,

this is HASHEM, *we have hoped for Him,*

nogilo v'nism'cho bishu-osō.
נָגִילָה וְנִשְׂמְחָה בִּישׁוּעָתוֹ.

we shall rejoice and be glad at His salvation."

VERSES OF KNOWLEDGE OF GOD

BAYS ya-akōv, l'chu v'nayl'cho
בֵּית יַעֲקֹב, לְכוּ וְנֵלְכָה

b'ōr Adōnoy.
בְּאוֹר יהוה.

O House of Jacob* — come let us go by the light of HASHEM.

בֵּית יַעֲקֹב — *O House of Jacob.* These three verses provide a definition of the salvation of which we have just spoken: Salvation is mean-ingless unless it includes knowledge of God's light, the Torah; the second of these verses teaches that one's treasure is knowledge, wis-

v'ho-yo emunas itecho

וְהָיָה אֱמוּנַת עִתֶּיךָ

The stability of your times,

chō-sen y'shu-ōs chochmas vodo-as,

חֹסֶן יְשׁוּעֹת חָכְמַת וָדָעַת,

the strength of your salvations shall be through knowledge and wisdom,

yir-as Adōnoy hi ōtzorō.

יִרְאַת יהוה הִיא אוֹצָרוֹ.

fear of God — that is one's treasure.

Vai-hi dovid l'chol d'rochov maskil

וַיְהִי דָוִד לְכָל דְּרָכָיו מַשְׂכִּיל,

And David was successful in all his ways,

Vadōnoy imō.

וַיהוה עִמּוֹ.

and HASHEM was with him.

VERSES OF RESCUE

PODO v'sholōm nafshi

פָּדָה בְשָׁלוֹם נַפְשִׁי

He redeemed* my soul in peace

mik'rov li,

מִקֳּרָב לִי,

from the battles that were upon me,

ki v'rabim ho-yu imodi.

כִּי בְרַבִּים הָיוּ עִמָּדִי.

for the sake of the multitudes who were with me.

Va-yōmer ho-om el sho-ul,

וַיֹּאמֶר הָעָם אֶל שָׁאוּל,

And the people said to Saul,

ha-yōnoson yomus

הֲיוֹנָתָן יָמוּת

"Shall Jonathan die,

asher oso

אֲשֶׁר עָשָׂה

who performed

hai-shu-o hag'dōlo ha-zōs b'yisro-ayl,

הַיְשׁוּעָה הַגְּדוֹלָה הַזֹּאת בְּיִשְׂרָאֵל,

this great salvation for Israel?

cholilo,

חָלִילָה,

A sacrilege! —

chai Adōnoy,

חַי יהוה,

as HASHEM lives,

---

dom, and fear of God; and the third verse teaches that success comes through God's help.

פָּדָה — *He redeemed.* The inclusion of the next nine verses is based on Tractate *Berachos* 55b. There the Talmud teaches that if one has had a very disturbing dream and he continues to be depressed by it, he should come before three people and tell them he has had such a dream. They are to reply with the wish that God change the implication of the dream from bad to good. Then they are to recite the following nine verses that, in effect, express the prayer that the dream's evil omen be transformed to the good, that the dreamer be rescued from distress, and he know only peace. In the context of the conclusion of the Sabbath, we change the order of the three sections. Since there is no actual distress at this moment, we begin with the verses of rescue, asking God to save us from the weekday challenges to the spiritual elevation we have absorbed during the Sabbath.

im yipōl misa-aras rōshō artzo, · · · אִם יִפֹּל מִשַּׂעֲרַת רֹאשׁוֹ אַרְצָה,
if a hair of his head falls to the ground,

ki im Elōhim oso ha-yōm ha-ze, · · · כִּי עִם אֱלֹהִים עָשָׂה הַיּוֹם הַזֶּה,
for with HASHEM has he acted this day!"

va-yifdu ho-om es yōnoson v'lō mays. · · · וַיִּפְדּוּ הָעָם אֶת יוֹנָתָן וְלֹא מֵת.
And the people redeemed Jonathan and he did not die.

Ufdu-yay Adōnoy y'shuvun, · · · וּפְדוּיֵי יהוה יְשֻׁבוּן,
Those redeemed by God will return

u-vo-u tziyōn b'rino, · · · וּבָאוּ צִיּוֹן בְּרִנָּה,
and arrive at Zion with glad song

v'simchas ōlom al rōshom, · · · וְשִׂמְחַת עוֹלָם עַל רֹאשָׁם,
and eternal gladness on their heads;

sosōn v'simcho yasigu · · · שָׂשׂוֹן וְשִׂמְחָה יַשִּׂיגוּ
joy and gladness shall they attain,

v'nosu yogōn va-anocho. · · · וְנָסוּ יָגוֹן וַאֲנָחָה.
and sorrow and groan shall flee.

VERSES OF TRANSFORMATION OF DISTRESS TO RELIEF

HOFACHTO misp'di l'mochōl li, · · · הָפַכְתָּ מִסְפְּדִי לְמָחוֹל לִי,
You have changed for me my lament into dancing;

pitachto saki vat'az'rayni simcho. · · · פִּתַּחְתָּ שַׂקִּי, וַתְּאַזְּרֵנִי שִׂמְחָה.
You undid my sackcloth and girded me with gladness.

V'lō ovo Adōnoy Elōhecho · · · וְלֹא אָבָה יהוה אֱלֹהֶיךָ
HASHEM, your God, did not wish

lishmō-a el bil-om, · · · לִשְׁמֹעַ אֶל בִּלְעָם,
to pay heed to Balaam,

va-yahafōch Adōnoy Elōhecho l'cho · · · וַיַּהֲפֹךְ יהוה אֱלֹהֶיךָ לְּךָ
and HASHEM, your God, changed for you

es hak'lolo livrocho, · · · אֶת הַקְּלָלָה לִבְרָכָה,
the curse to blessing,

ki ahayv'cho Adōnoy Elōhecho. · · · כִּי אֲהֵבְךָ יהוה אֱלֹהֶיךָ.
for HASHEM, your God, loves you.

Oz tismach b'sulo b'mochōl, · · · אָז תִּשְׂמַח בְּתוּלָה בְּמָחוֹל,
Then the maiden shall rejoice in a dance,

u-vachurim uzkaynim yachdov, · · · וּבַחֻרִים וּזְקֵנִים יַחְדָּו,
and lads and elders together;

v'hofachti evlom l'sosōn, · · · וְהָפַכְתִּי אֶבְלָם לְשָׂשׂוֹן,
and I shall change their mourning to joy,

v'nichamtim
וְנִחַמְתִּים

v'simachtim migōnom.
וְשִׂמַּחְתִּים מִיגוֹנָם.

and I shall console them and gladden them from their sorrow.

VERSES OF PEACE

BŌRAY niv s'foso-yim,
בּוֹרֵא נִיב שְׂפָתָיִם,

I create the speech of the lips:

sholōm sholōm lorochōk v'lakorōv
שָׁלוֹם שָׁלוֹם לָרָחוֹק וְלַקָּרוֹב,

"Peace, peace, for far and near,"

omar Adōnoy urfosiv.
אָמַר יהוה וּרְפָאתִיו.

says HASHEM, "and I shall heal him."

V'ru-ach lov'sho es amosai,
וְרוּחַ לָבְשָׁה אֶת עֲמָשַׂי,

A spirit clothed Amasai,

rōsh hasholishim,
רֹאשׁ הַשָּׁלִישִׁים,

head of the officers,

l'cho dovid v'im'cho ven yishai,
לְךָ דָוִיד וְעִמְּךָ בֶן יִשַׁי,

"For your sake, David, and to be with you, son of Jesse;

sholōm, sholōm l'cho,
שָׁלוֹם, שָׁלוֹם לְךָ,

peace, peace to you,

v'sholōm l'ōz'recho,
וְשָׁלוֹם לְעֹזְרֶךָ,

and peace to him who helps you,

ki azor'cho Elōhecho,
כִּי עֲזָרְךָ אֱלֹהֶיךָ,

for your God has helped you."

vaikab'laym dovid
וַיְקַבְּלֵם דָּוִיד

David accepted them

va-yit'naym b'roshay hag'dud.
וַיִּתְּנֵם בְּרָאשֵׁי הַגְּדוּד.

and appointed them heads of the band.

Va-amartem, kō le-choy,
וַאֲמַרְתֶּם, כֹּה לֶחָי,

And you shall say: "So may it be as long as you live;

v'ato sholōm u-vays'cho sholōm
וְאַתָּה שָׁלוֹם וּבֵיתְךָ שָׁלוֹם

peace for you, peace for your household,

v'chōl asher l'cho sholōm.
וְכֹל אֲשֶׁר לְךָ שָׁלוֹם.

and peace for all that is with you."

Adōnoy ōz l'amō yitayn,
יהוה עֹז לְעַמּוֹ יִתֵּן,

HASHEM will give might to His people,

Adōnoy y'voraych es amō
יהוה יְבָרֵךְ אֶת עַמּוֹ

Va-sholōm.
בַשָּׁלוֹם.

HASHEM will bless His people with peace.

OMAR rabi yōchonon: אָמַר רַבִּי יוֹחָנָן:
Rabbi Yochanan said:*

B'chol mokōm sho-ato mōtzay בְּכָל מָקוֹם שֶׁאַתָּה מוֹצֵא
Wherever you find

g'dulosō גְדֻלָתוֹ

shel hakodōsh boruch hu, שֶׁל הַקָּדוֹשׁ בָּרוּךְ הוּא,
the greatness of the Holy One, Blessed is He,

shom ato mōtzay anv'sonusō. שָׁם אַתָּה מוֹצֵא עַנְוְתָנוּתוֹ.
there you find His humility.

Dovor ze kosuv batōroh, דָּבָר זֶה כָּתוּב בַּתּוֹרָה,
This phenomenon is written in the Torah,

v'shonuy ban'vi-im, וְשָׁנוּי בַּנְּבִיאִים,
repeated in the Prophets,

umshulosh bak'suvim. וּמְשֻׁלָּשׁ בַּכְּתוּבִים.
and stated a third time in the Writings.

Kosuv batōro: כָּתוּב בַּתּוֹרָה:
It is written in the Torah:

Ki Adōnoy Elōhaychem כִּי יהוה אֱלֹהֵיכֶם
"For HASHEM, your God,

hu Elōhay ho-elōhim הוּא אֱלֹהֵי הָאֱלֹהִים
He is the God of heavenly forces

Va-adōnay ho-adōnim, וַאֲדֹנֵי הָאֲדֹנִים,
and the Master of masters,

ho-Ayl hagodōl hagibōr v'hanōro, הָאֵל הַגָּדֹל הַגִּבֹּר וְהַנּוֹרָא,
the great, mighty, and awesome God,

asher lō yiso fonim אֲשֶׁר לֹא יִשָּׂא פָנִים
v'lō yikach shōchad. וְלֹא יִקַּח שֹׁחַד.
Who shows no favoritism and accepts no bribe."

Uchsiv basrayh: וּכְתִיב בַּתְרֵהּ:
And afterwards it is written:

Ōs-e mishpat yosōm v'almono, עֹשֶׂה מִשְׁפַּט יָתוֹם וְאַלְמָנָה,
"He performs justice for orphan and widow,

אָמַר רַבִּי יוֹחָנָן — *Rabbi Yochanan said.* Although this Talmudic passage has no direct relationship to the above prayers for the coming week, it is included because it gives us confidence to pray. People have always expressed a fear, a sense of inadequacy to pray to God: What are we and who are we that we ask God to take notice of us? To this concern, Rabbi Yochanan replies with a host of Scriptural passages which show that even when God's grandeur is most apparent, He reveals His humility, meaning that He is concerned with the

Ōs-e mishpat yosōm v'almono, עֹשֶׂה מִשְׁפַּט יָתוֹם וְאַלְמָנָה,
"He performs justice for orphan and widow,

v'ōhayv gayr וְאֹהֵב גֵּר
and loves the stranger,

lo-ses lō lechem v'simlo. לָתֶת לוֹ לֶחֶם וְשִׂמְלָה.
to give him food and clothing."

shonuy ban'vi-im, dichsiv: שָׁנוּי בַּנְּבִיאִים, דִּכְתִיב:
It is repeated in the Prophets, as it is written:

Ki chō omar rom v'niso, כִּי כֹה אָמַר רָם וְנִשָּׂא,
"For so says the exalted and uplifted One,

shōchayn ad v'kodōsh sh'mō, שֹׁכֵן עַד וְקָדוֹשׁ שְׁמוֹ,
Who abides forever, and Whose Name is holy,

morōm v'kodōsh eshkōn, מָרוֹם וְקָדוֹשׁ אֶשְׁכּוֹן,
'I abide in exaltedness and holiness —

v'es dako ushfal ru-ach, וְאֶת דַּכָּא וּשְׁפַל רוּחַ,
but am with the contrite and lowly of spirit,

l'hacha-yōs ru-ach sh'folim לְהַחֲיוֹת רוּחַ שְׁפָלִים
to revive the spirit of the lowly

ulhacha-yōs layv nidko-im. וּלְהַחֲיוֹת לֵב נִדְכָּאִים.
and to revive the heart of the contrite.'"

M'shulosh bak'suvim, dichsiv: מְשֻׁלָּשׁ בַּכְּתוּבִים, דִּכְתִיב:
And it is stated a third time in the Writings, as it is written:

Shiru Laylōhim, zam'ru sh'mō, שִׁירוּ לֵאלֹהִים, זַמְּרוּ שְׁמוֹ,
"Sing to God, make music for His Name,

sōlu lorōchayv bo-arovōs, סֹלּוּ לָרֹכֵב בָּעֲרָבוֹת,
extol Him Who rides in the highest heaven,

b'Yoh sh'mō, בְּיָהּ שְׁמוֹ,
with His Name — God —

v'ilzu l'fonov. וְעִלְזוּ לְפָנָיו.
and exult before Him."

Uchsiv basrayh: וּכְתִיב בַּתְרֵהּ:
And afterwards it is written:

Avi y'sōmim v'da-yan almonōs, אֲבִי יְתוֹמִים וְדַיַּן אַלְמָנוֹת,
"Father of orphans and Judge of widows

Elōhim bim-ōn kodshō. אֱלֹהִים בִּמְעוֹן קָדְשׁוֹ.
is God in the habitation of His holiness."

---

needs and fears of even the humblest man.

Y'hi Adōnoy Elōhaynu imonu   יְהִי יהוה אֱלֹהֵינוּ עִמָּנוּ
May HASHEM, our God, be with us

ka-asher ho-yo im avōsaynu,   כַּאֲשֶׁר הָיָה עִם אֲבֹתֵינוּ,
as He was with our forefathers;

al ya-azvaynu v'al yit'shaynu.   אַל יַעַזְבֵנוּ וְאַל יִטְּשֵׁנוּ.
may He not forsake us nor cast us off.

V'atem had'vaykim   וְאַתֶּם הַדְּבֵקִים
    Badōnoy Elōhaychem,   בַּיהוה אֱלֹהֵיכֶם
You who cling to HASHEM, your God,

cha-yim kul'chem ha-yōm.   חַיִּים כֻּלְּכֶם הַיּוֹם.
are all alive today.

Ki nicham Adōnoy tziyōn,   כִּי נִחַם יהוה צִיּוֹן,
    nicham kol chorvōseho,   נִחַם כָּל חָרְבֹתֶיהָ,
For HASHEM comforts Zion, He comforts all her ruins,

va-yosem midboroh k'ayden   וַיָּשֶׂם מִדְבָּרָהּ כְּעֵדֶן
He will make her wilderness like Eden

v'arvosoh k'gan Adōnoy,   וְעַרְבָתָהּ כְּגַן יהוה,
and her wastelands like a garden of HASHEM —

sosōn v'simcho yimotzay voh,   שָׂשׂוֹן וְשִׂמְחָה יִמָּצֵא בָהּ,
joy and gladness will be found there,

tōdo v'kōl zimro.   תּוֹדָה וְקוֹל זִמְרָה.
thanksgiving and the sound of music.

Adōnoy chofaytz l'ma-an tzidkō,   יהוה חָפֵץ לְמַעַן צִדְקוֹ,
HASHEM desired, for the sake of its [Israel's] righteousness,

yagdil tōro v'yadir.   יַגְדִּיל תּוֹרָה וְיַאְדִּיר.
that the Torah be made great and glorious.

SHIR HAMA-ALŌS,   **שִׁיר הַמַּעֲלוֹת**
A song of ascents:*

ashray kol y'ray Adōnoy,   אַשְׁרֵי כָּל יְרֵא יהוה,
Praiseworthy is each person who fears HASHEM,

hahōlaych bidrochov.   הַהֹלֵךְ בִּדְרָכָיו.
who walks in His paths.

    Y'gi-a kapecho ki sōchayl,   יְגִיעַ כַּפֶּיךָ כִּי תֹאכֵל,
When you eat the labor of your hands,

ashrecho v'tōv loch.   אַשְׁרֶיךָ וְטוֹב לָךְ.
you are praiseworthy, and it is well with you.

שִׁיר הַמַּעֲלוֹת — *A song of ascents.* Psalm 128, which extols the economic and family life of one who fears God, is recited here as an exhor-tation to honesty and compassion during the ensuing week.

Esht'cho k'gefen pōri-yo
    Your wife shall be like a fruitful vine

אֶשְׁתְּךָ כְּגֶפֶן פֹּרִיָּה

b'yark'say vay-secho,
    in the inner chambers of your home;

בְּיַרְכְּתֵי בֵיתֶךָ,

bonecho kish-silay zaysim
    your children shall be like olive shoots

בָּנֶיךָ כִּשְׁתִלֵי זֵיתִים,

soviv l'shulchonecho.
    surrounding your table.

סָבִיב לְשֻׁלְחָנֶךָ.

Hinay chi chayn y'vōrach gover
   y'ray Adōnoy.
    Behold! For so is blessed the man who fears HASHEM.

הִנֵּה כִי כֵן יְבֹרַךְ גָּבֶר
יְרֵא יהוה.

Y'vorech'cho Adōnoy mitziyōn,
    May HASHEM *bless you from Zion,*

יְבָרֶכְךָ יהוה מִצִּיּוֹן,

ur-ay b'tuv y'rusholo-yim,
    and may you gaze upon the goodness of Jerusalem,

וּרְאֵה בְּטוּב יְרוּשָׁלָיִם,

kōl y'may cha-yecho.
    all the days of your life.

כֹּל יְמֵי חַיֶּיךָ.

Ur-ay vonim l'vonecho,
   sholōm al yisro-ayl.
    And may you see children born to your children, peace upon Israel.

וּרְאֵה בָנִים לְבָנֶיךָ,
שָׁלוֹם עַל יִשְׂרָאֵל.

IN SOME CONGREGATIONS MOURNERS RECITE THE MOURNER'S KADDISH (P. 623).

IN MANY CONGREGATIONS THE *CHAZZAN* RECITES *HAVDALAH*
AT THE CONCLUSION OF THE SABBATH OR OF A FESTIVAL.

סַבְרִי מָרָנָן וְרַבָּנָן וְרַבּוֹתַי:
בָּרוּךְ אַתָּה יהוה אֱלֹהֵינוּ מֶלֶךְ הָעוֹלָם, בּוֹרֵא פְּרִי הַגָּפֶן.

CONGREGATION RESPONDS: Omayn – אָמֵן.

AT THE CONCLUSION OF THE SABBATH THE FOLLOWING TWO BLESSINGS ARE RECITED.
AFTER THE FOLLOWING BLESSING SMELL THE SPICES.

בָּרוּךְ אַתָּה יהוה אֱלֹהֵינוּ מֶלֶךְ הָעוֹלָם, בּוֹרֵא מִינֵי בְשָׂמִים.

CONGREGATION RESPONDS: Omayn – אָמֵן.

AFTER THE FOLLOWING BLESSING HOLD FINGERS UP TO THE FLAME TO SEE THE REFLECTED LIGHT:*

בָּרוּךְ אַתָּה יהוה אֱלֹהֵינוּ מֶלֶךְ הָעוֹלָם, בּוֹרֵא מְאוֹרֵי הָאֵשׁ.

CONGREGATION RESPONDS: Omayn – אָמֵן.

בָּרוּךְ אַתָּה יהוה אֱלֹהֵינוּ מֶלֶךְ הָעוֹלָם, הַמַּבְדִּיל בֵּין קֹדֶשׁ לְחוֹל, בֵּין
אוֹר לְחְשֶׁךְ, בֵּין יִשְׂרָאֵל לָעַמִּים, בֵּין יוֹם הַשְּׁבִיעִי לְשֵׁשֶׁת יְמֵי
הַמַּעֲשֶׂה. בָּרוּךְ אַתָּה יהוה, הַמַּבְדִּיל בֵּין קֹדֶשׁ לְחוֹל.

CONGREGATION RESPONDS: Omayn – אָמֵן.

CHAZZAN OR SOMEONE ELSE PRESENT FOR *HAVDALAH* DRINKS MOST OF THE CUP.

BETWEEN PESACH AND SHAVUOS, THE *OMER* IS COUNTED (P. 153) AT THIS POINT.

■ As we take leave of the synagogue and God's presence, we fortify ourselves with the resolve and commitment that the lofty ideals of prayer can be implemented and actualized in our mundane pursuits.

STAND WHILE RECITING *ALEINU*.

OLAYNU l'shabay-ach la-adōn hakōl,   עָלֵינוּ לְשַׁבֵּחַ לַאֲדוֹן הַכֹּל,

It is our duty to praise the Master of all,

losays g'dulo l'yōtzayr b'rayshis,   לָתֵת גְּדֻלָּה לְיוֹצֵר בְּרֵאשִׁית,

to ascribe greatness to the Molder of primeval Creation,

shelō osonu k'gōyay ho-arotzōs,   שֶׁלֹּא עָשָׂנוּ כְּגוֹיֵי הָאֲרָצוֹת,

for He has not made us like the nations of the lands

v'lō somonu k'mishp'chōs ho-adomo,   וְלֹא שָׂמָנוּ כְּמִשְׁפְּחוֹת הָאֲדָמָה.

and has not emplaced us like the families of the earth;

shelō som chelkaynu kohem,   שֶׁלֹּא שָׂם חֶלְקֵנוּ כָּהֶם,

for He has not assigned our portion like theirs

v'gōrolaynu k'chol hamōnom   וְגוֹרָלֵנוּ כְּכָל הֲמוֹנָם.

nor our lot like all their multitudes.

SOME CONGREGATIONS OMIT THE PARENTHESIZED VERSE:

(Shehaym mishta-chavim l'hevel vorik,   (שֶׁהֵם מִשְׁתַּחֲוִים לְהֶבֶל וָרִיק,

(For they bow to vanity and emptiness

u-mispal'lim el ayl lō yōshi-a.)   וּמִתְפַּלְלִים אֶל אֵל לֹא יוֹשִׁיעַ.)

and pray to a god which helps not.)

BOW WHILE RECITING THE NEXT PHRASE.

Va-anachnu kōr'im u-mishta-chavim   וַאֲנַחְנוּ כּוֹרְעִים וּמִשְׁתַּחֲוִים
u-mōdim,   וּמוֹדִים,

But we bend our knees, bow, and acknowledge our thanks

lifnay melech malchay ham'lochim,   לִפְנֵי מֶלֶךְ מַלְכֵי הַמְּלָכִים

before the King Who reigns over kings,

hakodōsh boruch hu.   הַקָּדוֹשׁ בָּרוּךְ הוּא.

the Holy One, Blessed is He.

Shehu nōte shoma-yim v'yōsayd oretz,   שֶׁהוּא נוֹטֶה שָׁמַיִם וְיֹסֵד אָרֶץ,

He stretches out heaven and establishes earth's foundation,

u-mōshav y'korō ba-shoma-yim mima-al,   וּמוֹשַׁב יְקָרוֹ בַּשָּׁמַיִם מִמַּעַל,

the seat of His homage is in the heavens above

ush-chinas u-zō b'gov-hay m'rōmim.   וּשְׁכִינַת עֻזּוֹ בְּגָבְהֵי מְרוֹמִים.

and His powerful Presence is in the loftiest heights.

Hu Elōhaynu ayn ōd.   הוּא אֱלֹהֵינוּ, אֵין עוֹד.

He is our God and there is none other.

Emes malkaynu, efes zuloső,

אֱמֶת מַלְכֵּנוּ, אֶפֶס זוּלָתוֹ,

True is our King, there is nothing beside Him,

kakosuv b'sőroső:

כַּכָּתוּב בְּתוֹרָתוֹ:

as it is written in His Torah:

V'yodato ha-yőm vaha-shayvőso
el l'vovecho,

וְיָדַעְתָּ הַיּוֹם וַהֲשֵׁבֹתָ
אֶל לְבָבֶךָ,

"You are to know this day and take to your heart

ki Adőnoy hu ho-Előhim

כִּי יהוה הוּא הָאֱלֹהִים

that HASHEM *is the only God —*

ba-shoma-yim mima-al

בַּשָּׁמַיִם מִמַּעַל

v'al ho-oretz mitochas, ayn őd.

וְעַל הָאָרֶץ מִתָּחַת, אֵין עוֹד.

in heaven above and on the earth below — there is none other."

AL KAYN n'kave l'cho
Adőnoy Előhaynu

עַל כֵּן נְקַוֶּה לְּךָ
יהוה אֱלֹהֵינוּ

Therefore we put our hope in You, HASHEM, *our God,*

lirős m'hayro b'sif-eres u-zecho,

לִרְאוֹת מְהֵרָה בְּתִפְאֶרֶת עֻזֶּךָ,

that we may soon see Your mighty splendor,

l'ha-avir gilulim min ho-oretz,

לְהַעֲבִיר גִּלּוּלִים מִן הָאָרֶץ,

to remove detestable idolatry from the earth,

v'ho-elilim korős yikoraysun,

וְהָאֱלִילִים כָּרוֹת יִכָּרֵתוּן,

and false gods will be utterly cut off,

l'sakayn őlom b'malchus Shadai.

לְתַקֵּן עוֹלָם בְּמַלְכוּת שַׁדַּי.

to perfect the universe through the Almighty's sovereignty.

V'chol b'nay vosor yikr'u vishmecho,

וְכָל בְּנֵי בָשָׂר יִקְרְאוּ בִשְׁמֶךָ,

Then all humanity will call upon Your Name,

l'hafnős aylecho kol rish-ay oretz.

לְהַפְנוֹת אֵלֶיךָ כָּל רִשְׁעֵי אָרֶץ.

to turn all the earth's wicked toward You.

Yakiru v'yayd'u kol yősh'vay sayvayl,

יַכִּירוּ וְיֵדְעוּ כָּל יוֹשְׁבֵי תֵבֵל,

All the world's inhabitants will recognize and know

ki l'cho tichra kol berech,
tishova kol loshőn.

כִּי לְךָ תִּכְרַע כָּל בֶּרֶךְ,
תִּשָּׁבַע כָּל לָשׁוֹן.

that to You every knee should bend, every tongue should swear.

L'fonecho Adőnoy Előhaynu
yichr'u v'yipőlu,

לְפָנֶיךָ יהוה אֱלֹהֵינוּ
יִכְרְעוּ וְיִפֹּלוּ,

Before You, HASHEM, *our God, they will bend every knee and cast themselves down,*

v'lichvőd shimcho y'kor yitaynu,

וְלִכְבוֹד שִׁמְךָ יְקָר יִתֵּנוּ,

and to the glory of Your Name they will render homage,

vikab'lu chulom es ōl malchusecho, וִיקַבְּלוּ כֻלָּם אֶת עוֹל מַלְכוּתֶךָ,
and they will all accept upon themselves the yoke of Your kingship

v'simlōch alayhem m'hayro וְתִמְלֹךְ עֲלֵיהֶם מְהֵרָה
l'ōlom vo-ed. לְעוֹלָם וָעֶד.
that You may reign over them soon and for all eternity.

Ki hamalchus shel'cho hi כִּי הַמַּלְכוּת שֶׁלְּךָ הִיא
For the kingdom is Yours

ul-ōl'may ad timlōch b'chovōd, וּלְעוֹלְמֵי עַד תִּמְלוֹךְ בְּכָבוֹד,
and You will reign for all eternity in glory,

kakosuv b'sōrosecho: כַּכָּתוּב בְּתוֹרָתֶךָ:
as it is written in Your Torah:

Adōnoy yimlōch l'ōlom vo-ed. יהוה יִמְלֹךְ לְעֹלָם וָעֶד.
"HASHEM shall reign for all eternity."

V'ne-emar: V'ho-yo Adōnoy l'melech ❖ וְנֶאֱמַר: וְהָיָה יהוה לְמֶלֶךְ
al kol ho-oretz, עַל כָּל הָאָרֶץ,
And it is said: "HASHEM will be King over all the world —

ba-yōm hahu yih-ye בַּיּוֹם הַהוּא יִהְיֶה
Adōnoy e-chod, ushmō e-chod. יהוה אֶחָד וּשְׁמוֹ אֶחָד.
on that day HASHEM will be One and His Name will be One."

SOME CONGREGATIONS RECITE THE FOLLOWING AT THIS POINT.

AL TIRO mipachad pis-ōm, אַל תִּירָא מִפַּחַד פִּתְאֹם,
Do not fear sudden terror,

u-mishō-as r'sho-im ki sovō. וּמִשֹּׁאַת רְשָׁעִים כִּי תָבֹא.
or the holocaust of the wicked when it comes.

Utzu aytzo v'sufor, עֻצוּ עֵצָה וְתֻפָר,
Plan a conspiracy and it will be annulled;

dab'ru dovor v'lō yokum, דַּבְּרוּ דָבָר וְלֹא יָקוּם,
speak your piece and it shall not stand,

ki i-monu Ayl. כִּי עִמָּנוּ אֵל.
for God is with us.

V'ad zikno ani hu, וְעַד זִקְנָה אֲנִי הוּא,
Even till your seniority, I remain unchanged;

v'ad sayvo ani esbōl, וְעַד שֵׂיבָה אֲנִי אֶסְבֹּל,
and even till your ripe old age, I shall endure;

ani osisi va-ani eso, אֲנִי עָשִׂיתִי וַאֲנִי אֶשָּׂא,
I created [you] and I shall bear [you];

va-ani esbōl va-amalayt. וַאֲנִי אֶסְבֹּל וַאֲמַלֵּט.
I shall endure and rescue.

MOURNER'S KADDISH

YISGADAL v'yiskadash　　　　　יִתְגַּדַּל וְיִתְקַדַּשׁ

sh'mayh rabo.　　　　　שְׁמֵהּ רַבָּא.

May His great Name grow exalted and sanctified

CONGREGATION RESPONDS: Omayn — אָמֵן

B'ol'mo di v'ro chir-usayh.　　　　　בְּעָלְמָא דִּי בְרָא כִרְעוּתֵהּ.

in the world that He created as He willed.

V'yamlich malchusayh,　　　　　וְיַמְלִיךְ מַלְכוּתֵהּ,

May He give reign to His kingship

b'cha-yaychōn uvyōmaychōn　　　　　בְּחַיֵּיכוֹן וּבְיוֹמֵיכוֹן

in your lifetimes and in your days

uvcha-yay d'chol bays yisro-ayl,　　　　　וּבְחַיֵּי דְכָל בֵּית יִשְׂרָאֵל,

and in the lifetimes of the entire Family of Israel,

ba-agolo u-vizman koriv.　　　　　בַּעֲגָלָא וּבִזְמַן קָרִיב.

swiftly and soon.

V'imru: Omayn.　　　　　וְאִמְרוּ: אָמֵן.

Now respond: Amen.

CONGREGATION RESPONDS:

Omayn. Y'hay sh'mayh rabo m'vorach　　　אָמֵן. יְהֵא שְׁמֵהּ רַבָּא מְבָרַךְ

l'olam ul-ol'may ol'ma-yo.　　　　　לְעָלַם וּלְעָלְמֵי עָלְמַיָּא.

Amen. May His great Name be blessed forever and ever;

MOURNER CONTINUES:

Y'hay sh'mayh rabo m'vorach　　　　　יְהֵא שְׁמֵהּ רַבָּא מְבָרַךְ

l'olam ul-ol'may ol'ma-yo,　　　　　לְעָלַם וּלְעָלְמֵי עָלְמַיָּא,

May His great Name be blessed forever and ever;

yisborach v'yishtabach v'yispo-ar　　　יִתְבָּרַךְ וְיִשְׁתַּבַּח וְיִתְפָּאַר

blessed, praised, glorified,

v'yisrōmam v'yisnasay　　　　　וְיִתְרוֹמַם וְיִתְנַשֵּׂא

exalted, extolled,

v'yis-hador v'yis-ale v'yis-halol　　　וְיִתְהַדָּר וְיִתְעַלֶּה וְיִתְהַלָּל

mighty, upraised, and lauded

sh'mayh d'kudsho b'rich hu　　　　　שְׁמֵהּ דְּקֻדְשָׁא בְּרִיךְ הוּא

be the Name of the Holy One, Blessed is He,

CONGREGATION RESPONDS:

B'rich hu.　　　*Blessed is He.*　　　בְּרִיךְ הוּא.

MOURNER CONTINUES:

°l'aylo min kol   °לְעֵלָּא מִן כָּל

beyond any

FROM ROSH HASHANAH TO YOM KIPPUR SUBSTITUTE:

°l'aylo l'aylo mikol   °לְעֵלָּא לְעֵלָּא מִכָּל

exceedingly beyond any

birchoso v'shiroso   בִּרְכָתָא וְשִׁירָתָא

tushb'choso v'nechemoso,   תֻּשְׁבְּחָתָא וְנֶחֱמָתָא,

blessing and song, praise and consolation

da-amiron b'ol'mo.   דַּאֲמִירָן בְּעָלְמָא.

that are uttered in the world.

V'imru: Omayn.   וְאִמְרוּ: אָמֵן.

Now respond: Amen.

CONGREGATION RESPONDS: Omayn — אָמֵן

Y'hay sh'lomo rabo min sh'mayo   יְהֵא שְׁלָמָא רַבָּא מִן שְׁמַיָּא,

May there be abundant peace from Heaven,

v'cha-yim olaynu v'al kol yisro-ayl.   וְחַיִּים עָלֵינוּ וְעַל כָּל יִשְׂרָאֵל.

and life, upon us and upon all Israel.

V'imru: Omayn.   וְאִמְרוּ: אָמֵן.

Now respond: Amen.

CONGREGATION RESPONDS: Omayn — אָמֵן

MOURNER BOWS, THEN TAKES THREE STEPS BACK, BOWS LEFT AND SAYS:

Ō-se sholōm bimrōmov   עֹשֶׂה שָׁלוֹם בִּמְרוֹמָיו,

He Who makes peace in His heights,

MOURNER BOWS RIGHT AND SAYS:

hu ya-a-se sholōm olaynu   הוּא יַעֲשֶׂה שָׁלוֹם עָלֵינוּ,

may He make peace upon us,

MOURNER BOWS FORWARD AND SAYS:

v'al kol yisro-ayl. V'imru: Omayn.   וְעַל כָּל יִשְׂרָאֵל. וְאִמְרוּ: אָמֵן.

and upon all Israel. Now respond: Amen.

CONGREGATION RESPONDS: Omayn — אָמֵן

MOURNER REMAINS IN PLACE FOR A FEW MOMENTS, THEN TAKES THREE STEPS FORWARD.

FROM ROSH CHODESH ELUL THROUGH SHEMINI ATZERES, THE FOLLOWING PSALM IS RECITED.

L'DOVID, Adōnoy ōri v'yish-i   לְדָוִד, יהוה אוֹרִי וְיִשְׁעִי,

mimi iro,   מִמִּי אִירָא,

Of David; HASHEM is my light and my salvation, whom shall I fear?

Adōnoy mo-ōz cha-yai, mimi efchod.   יהוה מָעוֹז חַיַּי, מִמִּי אֶפְחָד.

HASHEM is my life's strength, whom shall I dread?

Bikrōv olai m'ray-im
   le-echōl es b'sori,
בִּקְרֹב עָלַי מְרֵעִים
לֶאֱכֹל אֶת בְּשָׂרִי,

When evildoers approach me to devour my flesh,

tzorai v'ō-y'vai li,
צָרַי וְאֹיְבַי לִי,

my tormentors and my foes against me —

haymo kosh'lu v'nofolu.
הֵמָּה כָשְׁלוּ וְנָפָלוּ.

it is they who stumble and fall.

Im tachane olai machane,
   lō yiro libi,
אִם תַּחֲנֶה עָלַי מַחֲנֶה,
לֹא יִירָא לִבִּי,

Though an army would besiege me, my heart would not fear;

im tokum olai milchomo,
   b'zōs ani vōtay-ach.
אִם תָּקוּם עָלַי מִלְחָמָה,
בְּזֹאת אֲנִי בוֹטֵחַ.

though war would arise against me, in this I trust.

Achas sho-alti may-ays Adōnoy,
   ōsoh avakaysh,
אַחַת שָׁאַלְתִּי מֵאֵת יהוה,
אוֹתָהּ אֲבַקֵּשׁ,

One thing I asked of HASHEM, that shall I seek:

shivti b'vays Adōnoy kol y'may cha-yai,
שִׁבְתִּי בְּבֵית יהוה כָּל יְמֵי חַיַּי,

that I dwell in the House of HASHEM all the days of my life;

la-chazōs b'nō-am Adōnoy,
   ulvakayr b'haycholō.
לַחֲזוֹת בְּנֹעַם יהוה,
וּלְבַקֵּר בְּהֵיכָלוֹ.

to behold the sweetness of HASHEM and to contemplate in His Sanctuary.

Ki yitzp'nayni b'sukō b'yōm ro-o,
כִּי יִצְפְּנֵנִי בְּסֻכֹּה בְּיוֹם רָעָה,

Indeed, He will hide me in His shelter on the day of evil;

yastirayni b'sayser oholō,
יַסְתִּירֵנִי בְּסֵתֶר אָהֳלוֹ,

He will conceal me in the concealment of His Tent,

b'tzur y'rōm'mayni.
בְּצוּר יְרוֹמְמֵנִי.

He will lift me upon a rock.

V'ato yorum rōshi
   al ō-y'vai s'vivōsai,
וְעַתָּה יָרוּם רֹאשִׁי
עַל אֹיְבַי סְבִיבוֹתַי,

Now my head is raised above my enemies around me,

v'ezb'cho v'oholō zivchay s'ru-o,
וְאֶזְבְּחָה בְאָהֳלוֹ זִבְחֵי תְרוּעָה,

and in His Tent I will slaughter offerings accompanied by joyous song;

oshiro va-azam'ro Ladōnoy.
אָשִׁירָה וַאֲזַמְּרָה לַיהוה.

I will sing and make music to HASHEM.

Sh'ma Adōnoy kōli ekro,
שְׁמַע יהוה קוֹלִי אֶקְרָא,

HASHEM, hear my voice when I call,

v'chonayni va-anayni.

וְחָנֵּנִי וַעֲנֵנִי.

and be gracious toward me and answer me.

L'cho omar libi bak'shu fonoy,

לְךָ אָמַר לִבִּי בַּקְשׁוּ פָנָי,

In Your behalf, my heart has said, "Seek My Presence";

es ponecho Adōnoy avakaysh.

אֶת פָּנֶיךָ יהוה אֲבַקֵּשׁ.

Your Presence, HASHEM, do I seek.

Al tastayr ponecho mimeni,

אַל תַּסְתֵּר פָּנֶיךָ מִמֶּנִּי,

al tat b'af avdecho,

אַל תַּט בְּאַף עַבְדֶּךָ,

Conceal not Your Presence from me, repel not Your servant in anger.

ezrosi ho-yiso,

עֶזְרָתִי הָיִיתָ,

You have been my Helper,

al tit'shayni v'al ta-azvayni,

אַל תִּטְּשֵׁנִי וְאַל תַּעַזְבֵנִי,

Elōhay yish-i.

אֱלֹהֵי יִשְׁעִי.

abandon me not, forsake me not, O God of my salvation.

Ki ovi v'imi azovuni,

כִּי אָבִי וְאִמִּי עֲזָבוּנִי,

Vadōnoy ya-asfayni.

וַיהוה יַאַסְפֵנִי.

Though my father and mother have forsaken me, HASHEM will gather me in.

Hōrayni Adōnoy dar-kecho,

הוֹרֵנִי יהוה דַּרְכֶּךָ,

Teach me Your way, HASHEM,

un-chayni b'ōrach mi-shōr,

וּנְחֵנִי בְּאֹרַח מִישׁוֹר,

l'ma-an shōr'roy.

לְמַעַן שׁוֹרְרָי.

and lead me on the path of integrity, because of my watchful foes.

Al tit'nayni b'nefesh tzoroy,

אַל תִּתְּנֵנִי בְּנֶפֶשׁ צָרָי,

Deliver me not to the wishes of my tormentors,

ki komu vi

כִּי קָמוּ בִי

ayday sheker vifay-ach chomos.

עֵדֵי שֶׁקֶר, וִיפֵחַ חָמָס.

for there have arisen against me false witnesses who breathe violence.

Lulay he-emanti

❖ לוּלֵא הֶאֱמַנְתִּי

Had I not trusted

lir-ōs b'tuv Adōnoy b'eretz cha-yim.

לִרְאוֹת בְּטוּב יהוה בְּאֶרֶץ חַיִּים.

that I would see the goodness of HASHEM in the land of life!

Kavay el Adōnoy,

קַוֵּה אֶל יהוה,

Hope to HASHEM,

chazak v'ya-amaytz libecho,

חֲזַק וְיַאֲמֵץ לִבֶּךָ,

strengthen yourself and He will give your heart courage;

v'kavay el Adōnoy.

וְקַוֵּה אֶל יהוה.

and hope to HASHEM.

IF A MOURNER IS PRESENT, HE RECITES THE MOURNER'S *KADDISH* (PAGE 623).

■ *Psalm* 49 teaches that man should use his sojourn on earth to enhance his spiritual development so that he will be better prepared for the World to Come. This concept is a source of comfort for those who have lost a close relative; therefore it is customary to recite this psalm after *Shacharis* and *Maariv* in the home of someone observing *shivah*, the seven-day period of mourning.

IN A HOUSE OF MOURNING, PSALM 49 IS RECITED:

LAM'NATZAY-ACH livnay kōrach mizmōr.

לַמְנַצֵּחַ לִבְנֵי קֹרַח מִזְמוֹר.

For the Conductor, by the sons of Korach, a psalm.

Shim-u zōs kol ho-amim,

שִׁמְעוּ זֹאת כָּל הָעַמִּים,

Hear this all you peoples,

ha-azinu kol yōsh'vay choled.

הַאֲזִינוּ כָּל יֹשְׁבֵי חָלֶד.

give ear all you dwellers of decaying earth.

Gam b'nay odom, gam b'nay ish,

גַּם בְּנֵי אָדָם, גַּם בְּנֵי אִישׁ,

Sons of Adam and sons of man alike;

yachad oshir v'evyōn.

יַחַד עָשִׁיר וְאֶבְיוֹן.

together — rich man, poor man.

Pi y'dabayr chochmōs,

פִּי יְדַבֵּר חָכְמוֹת,

My mouth shall speak wisdom,

v'hogus libi s'vunōs.

וְהָגוּת לִבִּי תְבוּנוֹת.

and the meditations of my heart are insightful.

Ate l'moshol ozni,

אַטֶּה לְמָשָׁל אָזְנִי,

I will incline my ear to the parable;

eftach b'chinōr chidosi.

אֶפְתַּח בְּכִנּוֹר חִידָתִי.

with a harp I will solve my riddle.

Lomo iro bimay ro,

לָמָּה אִירָא בִּימֵי רָע,

Why should I have to fear in days of evil,

avon akayvai y'subayni.

עֲוֹן עֲקֵבַי יְסֻבֵּנִי.

when the injunctions that I trod upon will surround me?

Habōt'chim al chaylom,

הַבֹּטְחִים עַל חֵילָם,

Those who rely on their possessions,

uvrōv osh'rom yis-halolu.

וּבְרֹב עָשְׁרָם יִתְהַלָּלוּ.

and of their great wealth they are boastful —

Och lō fodō yifde ish,

אָח לֹא פָדֹה יִפְדֶּה אִישׁ,

yet a man cannot redeem a brother,

lō yitayn Laylōhim kofrō.

לֹא יִתֵּן לֵאלֹהִים כָּפְרוֹ.

nor give to God his ransom.

V'yaykar pidyōn nafshom,

וְיֵקַר פִּדְיוֹן נַפְשָׁם,

Too costly is their soul's redemption

v'chodal l'ōlom.

וְחָדַל לְעוֹלָם.

and unattainable forever.

Vichi ōd lonetzach,

וִיחִי עוֹד לָנֶצַח,

Can one live eternally,

lō yir-e ha-shochas.

לֹא יִרְאֶה הַשָּׁחַת.

never to see the pit?

Ki yir-e chachomim yomusu,

כִּי יִרְאֶה חֲכָמִים יָמוּתוּ,

Though he sees that wise men die,*

yachad k'sil vova-ar yōvaydu,

יַחַד כְּסִיל וָבַעַר יֹאבֵדוּ,

that the foolish and boorish perish together

v'oz'vu la-achayrim chaylom.

וְעָזְבוּ לַאֲחֵרִים חֵילָם.

and leave their possessions to others — [nevertheless,]

Kirbom botaymō l'ōlom,

קִרְבָּם בָּתֵּימוֹ לְעוֹלָם,

in their imagination their houses are forever,

mish-k'nōsom l'dōr vodōr,

מִשְׁכְּנֹתָם לְדוֹר וָדֹר,

their dwellings for generation after generation;

kor'u vishmōsom
alay adomōs.

קָרְאוּ בִשְׁמוֹתָם
עֲלֵי אֲדָמוֹת.

they have proclaimed their names throughout the lands.

V'odom bikor bal yolin,

וְאָדָם בִּיקָר בַּל יָלִין,

But as for man — in glory he shall not repose,

nimshal kab'haymōs nidmu.

נִמְשַׁל כַּבְּהֵמוֹת נִדְמוּ.

he is likened to the silenced animals.

Ze darkom, kesel lomō,

זֶה דַרְכָּם, כֵּסֶל לָמוֹ,

This is their way — folly is theirs,

v'a-charayhem b'fihem yirtzu,
selo.

וְאַחֲרֵיהֶם בְּפִיהֶם יִרְצוּ,
סֶלָה.

yet of their destiny their mouths speak soothingly, Selah!

Katzōn lish-ōl shatu,

כַּצֹּאן לִשְׁאוֹל שַׁתּוּ,

Like sheep, they are destined for the Lower World,

כִּי יִרְאֶה חֲכָמִים יָמוּתוּ — *Though he sees that wise men die.* Sinners are deluded because they see that even good people die. If death grasps everyone equally, then why should the wealthy not indulge his pleasures?

mo-ves yir-aym,

מָוֶת יִרְעֵם,

death shall consume them;

va-yirdu vom y'shorim labōker,

וַיִּרְדּוּ בָם יְשָׁרִים לַבֹּקֶר,

and the upright shall dominate them at daybreak,

v'tzurom l'valōs sh'ōl

וְצוּרָם לְבַלּוֹת שְׁאוֹל

their essence is doomed to rot in the grave,

miz'vul lō.

מִזְּבֻל לוֹ.

each from his dwelling.

Ach Elōhim yifde nafshi

אַךְ אֱלֹהִים יִפְדֶּה נַפְשִׁי

miyad sh'ōl,

מִיַּד שְׁאוֹל,

But God will redeem my soul * from the grip of the Lower World,*

ki yikochayni selo.

כִּי יִקָּחֵנִי סֶלָה.

for He will take me, Selah!

Al tiro ki ya-ashir ish,

אַל תִּירָא כִּי יַעֲשִׁר אִישׁ,

Fear not when a man grows rich,

ki yirbe k'vōd bay-sō.

כִּי יִרְבֶּה כְּבוֹד בֵּיתוֹ.

when he increases the splendor of his house.

Ki lō v'mōsō yikach hakōl,

כִּי לֹא בְמוֹתוֹ יִקַּח הַכֹּל,

For upon his death he will not take anything,

lō yayrayd acharov k'vōdō.

לֹא יֵרֵד אַחֲרָיו כְּבוֹדוֹ.

his splendor will not descend after him.

Ki nafshō b'chayov y'voraych,

כִּי נַפְשׁוֹ בְּחַיָּיו יְבָרֵךְ,

Though he may bless himself in his lifetime,

v'yōducho ki saytiv loch.

וְיוֹדֻךָ כִּי תֵיטִיב לָךְ.

others will praise you if you improve yourself.

Tovō ad dōr avōsov,

תָּבוֹא עַד דּוֹר אֲבוֹתָיו,

It shall come to the generation of its fathers —

ad naytzach lō yir-u ōr.

עַד נֵצַח לֹא יִרְאוּ אוֹר.

unto eternity they shall see no light.

❖ Odom bikor v'lō yovin,

❖ אָדָם בִּיקָר וְלֹא יָבִין,

Man is glorious but understands not,

nimshal kab'haymōs nidmu.

נִמְשַׁל כַּבְּהֵמוֹת נִדְמוּ.

he is likened to the silenced animals.

IF A MOURNER IS PRESENT, HE RECITES THE MOURNER'S *KADDISH* (PAGE 623).

אַךְ אֱלֹהִים יִפְדֶּה נַפְשִׁי — *But God will redeem my soul.* Having completed his observations regarding the doom facing the wicked, the Psalmist now expresses his confidence that *he* can look forward to the splendor of the World to Come.

﴾ SANCTIFICATION OF THE MOON / KIDDUSH LEVANAH ﴿

■ I joyously greet the "Divine Presence" by acknowledging the renewal of Creation as evidenced by the renewal of the moon. My joy is compounded when I realize the potential for renewal and striving for perfection that both I and the Jewish People — who are compared to the moon — are afforded monthly.

HAL'LU-YOH, הַלְלוּיָהּ,

Praise God!

hal'lu es Adōnoy min ha-shoma-yim, הַלְלוּ אֶת יהוה מִן הַשָּׁמַיִם,

Praise HASHEM from the heavens;

hal'luhu bam'rōmim. הַלְלוּהוּ בַּמְּרוֹמִים.

praise Him in the heights.

Hal'luhu chol mal-ochov, הַלְלוּהוּ כָל מַלְאָכָיו,

hal'luhu kol tz'vo-ov. הַלְלוּהוּ כָּל צְבָאָיו.

Praise Him, all His angels; praise Him, all His legions.

Hal'luhu shemesh v'yoray-ach, הַלְלוּהוּ שֶׁמֶשׁ וְיָרֵחַ,

hal'luhu kol kōch'vay ōr. הַלְלוּהוּ כָּל כּוֹכְבֵי אוֹר.

Praise Him, sun and moon; praise Him, all bright stars.

Hal'luhu sh'may ha-shomo-yim, הַלְלוּהוּ שְׁמֵי הַשָּׁמָיִם,

Praise Him, the most exalted of the heavens

v'hama-yim asher may-al וְהַמַּיִם אֲשֶׁר מֵעַל

ha-shomo-yim. הַשָּׁמָיִם.

and the waters that are above the heavens.

Y'hal'lu es shaym Adōnoy, יְהַלְלוּ אֶת שֵׁם יהוה,

Let them praise the Name of HASHEM,

ki hu tzivo v'nivro-u. כִּי הוּא צִוָּה וְנִבְרָאוּ.

for He commanded and they were created.

Va-ya-amidaym lo-ad l'ōlom, וַיַּעֲמִידֵם לָעַד לְעוֹלָם,

And He established them forever and ever,

chok nosan v'lō ya-avōr. חָק נָתַן וְלֹא יַעֲבוֹר.

He issued a decree that will not change.

◦§ Sanctification of the Moon

The Sanctification of the Moon [*Kiddush Levanah*] has no calendrical significance. Rather, there are two bases for this ritual: The Talmud (*Sanhedrin* 42a) states that one who blesses the new moon in its proper time is regarded like one who greets God's Presence. This is because one of the ways we can recognize the existence of God is through the orderly functioning of the enormously com-plex heavenly bodies. We may note that as science unfolds more and more of the vastness of the universe, the presence of a Creator becomes more and more obvious to one who wishes to see; indeed, to deny Him is ludicrous. This phenomenon is most apparent in the cycles of the moon, because its changes are more visible than those of any other body. Thus, when we greet the moon, we greet its Creator and Guide.

SOME ADD THIS KABBALISTIC DECLARATION OF INTENT BEFORE THE BLESSING:

Harayni muchon umzumon   הֲרֵינִי מוּכָן וּמְזֻמָּן

Behold I am prepared and ready

l'ka-yaym hamitzvo   לְקַיֵּם הַמִּצְוָה

l'kadaysh hal'vono.   לְקַדֵּשׁ הַלְּבָנָה.

to perform the commandment to sanctify the moon.

L'shaym yichud kudsho   לְשֵׁם יִחוּד קֻדְשָׁא

b'rich hu ushchintayh,   בְּרִיךְ הוּא וּשְׁכִינְתֵּיהּ

For the sake of the unification of the Holy One, Blessed is He, and His Presence,

al y'day hahu tomir v'nelom,   עַל יְדֵי הַהוּא טָמִיר וְנֶעְלָם,

through Him Who is hidden and inscrutable —

b'shaym kol yisro-ayl.   בְּשֵׁם כָּל יִשְׂרָאֵל.

[I pray] in the name of all Israel.

ONE SHOULD LOOK AT THE MOON BEFORE RECITING THIS BLESSING:

BORUCH ato Adōnoy,   **בָּרוּךְ** אַתָּה יהוה,

Blessed are You, HASHEM,

Elōhaynu melech ho-ōlom,   אֱלֹהֵינוּ מֶלֶךְ הָעוֹלָם,

our God, King of the Universe,

asher b'ma-amorō boro sh'chokim,   אֲשֶׁר בְּמַאֲמָרוֹ בָּרָא שְׁחָקִים,

Who with His utterance created* the heavens,

uvru-ach piv kol tz'vo-om.   וּבְרוּחַ פִּיו כָּל צְבָאָם.

and with the breath of His mouth all their legion.

Chōk uzman nosan lohem   חֹק וּזְמַן נָתַן לָהֶם

A decree and a schedule did He give them*

shelō y'shanu es tafkidom.   שֶׁלֹּא יְשַׁנּוּ אֶת תַּפְקִידָם.

that they not alter their assigned task.

Sosim usmaychim   שָׂשִׂים וּשְׂמֵחִים

la-asōs r'tzōn kōnom,   לַעֲשׂוֹת רְצוֹן קוֹנָם,

They are joyous and glad* to perform the will of their Maker —

The second aspect of the prayer is its significance for the history of Israel. Just as the moon is reborn after a period of decline and total disappearance so, too, Israel's decline will end and its light will once again blaze to fullness.

בָּרוּךְ...אֲשֶׁר בְּמַאֲמָרוֹ בָּרָא — *Blessed ... Who with His utterance created.* God created heaven and its infinite bodies with nothing more than His word. The very existence of so many galaxies and solar systems testifies undeniably to Creation because so huge and complex a universe could not have come about by chance.

חֹק וּזְמַן נָתַן לָהֶם — *A decree and a schedule did He give them.* After creating the heavenly bodies, God set them in their specified orbits, giving each an unchangeable role in the cosmos.

שָׂשִׂים וּשְׂמֵחִים — *They are joyous and glad.* Despite the apparent tedium of their permanently assigned tasks, the heavenly bodies joyously serve their Maker because they know that by doing His will they have a role in Creation. This is a lesson to man to revel in his opportunity to serve God.

פּוֹעֵל אֱמֶת שֶׁפְּעֻלָּתוֹ אֱמֶת.
pō-ayl emes shep'ulosō emes.
the Worker of truth Whose work is truth.

וְלַלְּבָנָה אָמַר
V'lal'vono omar
שֶׁתִּתְחַדֵּשׁ עֲטֶרֶת תִּפְאֶרֶת
shetischadaysh ateres tiferes
To the moon He said that it should renew itself as a crown of splendor

לַעֲמוּסֵי בָטֶן,
la-amusay voten,
for those borne [by Him] from the womb,

שֶׁהֵם עֲתִידִים
shehaym asidim
לְהִתְחַדֵּשׁ כְּמוֹתָהּ,
l'hischadaysh k'mōsoh,
those who are destined to renew themselves like it,

וּלְפָאֵר לְיוֹצְרָם
ulfo-ayr l'yōtz'rom
עַל שֵׁם כְּבוֹד מַלְכוּתוֹ.
al shaym k'vōd malchusō.
and to glorify their Molder for the name of His glorious kingdom.

בָּרוּךְ אַתָּה יהוה,
Boruch ato Adōnoy,
מְחַדֵּשׁ חֳדָשִׁים.
m'chadaysh chodoshim.
Blessed are You, HASHEM, Who renews the months.

RECITE THREE TIMES:

BORUCH yōtz'raych, boruch ōsaych, בָּרוּךְ יוֹצְרֵךְ, בָּרוּךְ עוֹשֵׂךְ,
Blessed is your Molder; blessed is your Maker;

boruch kōnaych, boruch bōr'aych. בָּרוּךְ קוֹנֵךְ, בָּרוּךְ בּוֹרְאֵךְ.
blessed is your Owner; blessed is your Creator.

RECITE THREE TIMES:

K'shaym she-ani rōkayd k'negdaych כְּשֵׁם שֶׁאֲנִי רוֹקֵד כְּנֶגְדֵּךְ
Just as I dance* toward you

v'ayni yochōl lin-gō-a boch, וְאֵינִי יָכוֹל לִנְגּוֹעַ בָּךְ,
but cannot touch you,

kach lō yuchlu kol ō-y'vai כָּךְ לֹא יוּכְלוּ כָּל אוֹיְבַי
lin-gō-a bi l'ro-o. לִנְגּוֹעַ בִּי לְרָעָה.
so may none of my enemies be able to touch me for evil.

RECITE THREE TIMES:

Tipōl alayhem aymoso vofachad, תִּפֹּל עֲלֵיהֶם אֵימָתָה וָפַחַד,
Let fall upon them fear and terror;

bigdōl z'rō-acho yid'mu ko-oven. בִּגְדֹל זְרוֹעֲךָ יִדְּמוּ כָּאָבֶן.
at the greatness of Your arm, let them be still as stone.

כְּשֵׁם שֶׁאֲנִי רוֹקֵד — *Just as I dance.* Often in Scripture, a prophecy is accompanied by a physical act. This has the effect of making the prophecy irreversible. Here, too, we, in a sym- bolic way, exert ourselves to touch the moon while remaining on earth, and we pray that, in like fashion, the exertions of our enemies against us will be of no avail. Thus, we rein-

RECITE THREE TIMES:

Ko-oven yid'mu z'rō-acho bigdōl   כְּאֶבֶן יִדְּמוּ זְרוֹעֲךָ בִּגְדֹל

As stone let them be still,* at Your arm's greatness;

vofachad aymoso alayhem tipōl.   וָפַחַד אֵימָתָה עֲלֵיהֶם תִּפֹּל.

terror and fear, upon them let fall.

RECITE THREE TIMES:

Dovid melech yisro-ayl chai v'ka-yom.   דָּוִד מֶלֶךְ יִשְׂרָאֵל חַי וְקַיָּם.

David, King of Israel, is alive and enduring.

EXTEND GREETINGS THREE TIMES:

Sholōm alay-chem.   שָׁלוֹם עֲלֵיכֶם.

Peace upon you.*

THE PERSON WHO WAS GREETED RESPONDS:

Alay-chem sholōm.   עֲלֵיכֶם שָׁלוֹם.

Upon you, peace.

RECITE THREE TIMES:

Simon tōv u-mazol tōv y'hay lonu   סִמָּן טוֹב וּמַזָּל טוֹב יְהֵא לָנוּ

May there be a good sign and a good fortune for us

ulchol yisro-ayl, omayn.   וּלְכָל יִשְׂרָאֵל. אָמֵן.

and for all Israel. Amen.

KŌL dōdi hinay ze bo,   **קוֹל** דּוֹדִי הִנֵּה זֶה בָּא

The voice of my beloved — Behold! It came suddenly,

m'dalayg al hehorim,   מְדַלֵּג עַל הֶהָרִים

m'kapaytz al hag'vo-ōs.   מְקַפֵּץ עַל הַגְּבָעוֹת.

leaping over mountains, skipping over hills.

Dō-me dōdi litzvi   דּוֹמֶה דוֹדִי לִצְבִי

ō l'ōfer ho-ayolim,   אוֹ לְעֹפֶר הָאַיָּלִים,

My beloved is like a gazelle or a young hart.

hinay ze ōmayd achar kos'laynu,   הִנֵּה זֶה עוֹמֵד אַחַר כָּתְלֵנוּ,

Behold! He was standing behind our wall,

mashgi-ach min hachalōnōs   מַשְׁגִּיחַ מִן הַחַלֹּנוֹת,

observing through the windows,

maytzitz min hacharakim.   מֵצִיץ מִן הַחֲרַכִּים.

peering through the lattices.

---

force the point by a physical act.

כְּאֶבֶן יִדְּמוּ — *As stone let them be still.* We now repeat the previous verse, but we reverse the order of the words. This reversal implies that the natural order of nature, too, may sometimes be reversed. In other words, God will

sometimes protect us through the natural order of events; at other times He will perform open miracles to thwart those who seek our harm.

שָׁלוֹם עֲלֵיכֶם — *Peace upon you.* Various reasons are given for the inclusion of this greeting.

■ As the monthly development of the moon testifies to Hashem's direction and orchestration of nature, so do I derive optimism and faith recognizing that my deliverance comes directly from Hashem.

SHIR LAMA-ALŌS,
A song to the ascents.

שִׁיר לַמַּעֲלוֹת,

eso aynai el hehorim,
may-a-yin yovō ezri.

אֶשָּׂא עֵינַי אֶל הֶהָרִים,
מֵאַיִן יָבֹא עֶזְרִי.

I raise my eyes to the mountains; whence will come my help?

Ezri may-im Adōnoy,
ōsay shoma-yim vo-oretz.

עֶזְרִי מֵעִם יהוה,
עֹשֵׂה שָׁמַיִם וָאָרֶץ.

My help is from HASHEM, Maker of heaven and earth.

Al yitayn lamōt raglecho,
al yonum shōm'recho.

אַל יִתֵּן לַמּוֹט רַגְלֶךָ,
אַל יָנוּם שֹׁמְרֶךָ.

He will not allow your foot to falter; your Guardian will not slumber.

Hinay lō yonum v'lō yishon
shōmayr yisro-ayl.

הִנֵּה לֹא יָנוּם וְלֹא יִישָׁן,
שׁוֹמֵר יִשְׂרָאֵל.

Behold, He neither slumbers nor sleeps — the Guardian of Israel.

Adōnoy shōm'recho,

יהוה שֹׁמְרֶךָ,

HASHEM is your Guardian;

Adōnoy tzil'cho al yad y'minecho.

יהוה צִלְּךָ עַל יַד יְמִינֶךָ.

HASHEM is your Shade at your right hand.

Yōmom ha-shemesh lō yakeko,
v'yorayach baloy'lo.

יוֹמָם הַשֶּׁמֶשׁ לֹא יַכֶּכָּה,
וְיָרֵחַ בַּלָּיְלָה.

By day the sun will not harm you, nor the moon by night.

Adōnoy yishmor'cho mikol ro
yishmōr es nafshecho.

יהוה יִשְׁמָרְךָ מִכָּל רָע,
יִשְׁמֹר אֶת נַפְשֶׁךָ.

HASHEM will protect you from every evil; He will guard your soul.

Adōnoy yishmor tzays'cho u-vō-echo

יהוה יִשְׁמָר צֵאתְךָ וּבוֹאֶךָ,

HASHEM will guard your departure and your arrival,

may-ato v'ad ōlom.

מֵעַתָּה וְעַד עוֹלָם.

from this time and forever.

Having greeted the *Shechinah*, we joyously wish the blessing of peace upon one another; after cursing our enemies, then we make clear that we wish no ill to our brethren. At the beginning of Creation, as recorded in the Talmud (*Chullin* 60b), the sun and moon were of equal size. When the moon complained that two kings cannot wear the same crown — i.e., it wished to be larger than the sun — the moon was made smaller. Nevertheless, the sun continues to shine its brilliant light upon the moon, thus providing a lesson to man not to harbor a grudge against others who have wronged him. We express this resolve by wishing peace upon our fellow Jews.

HAL'LUYOH, הַלְלוּיָהּ,

hal'lu Ayl b'kod'shō, הַלְלוּ אֵל בְּקָדְשׁוֹ,

Praise God! Praise God in His Sanctuary;

hal'luhu birki-a u-zō. הַלְלוּהוּ בִּרְקִיעַ עֻזּוֹ.

praise Him in the firmament of His power.

Hal'luhu bigvurōsov, הַלְלוּהוּ בִגְבוּרֹתָיו,

Praise Him for His mighty acts;

hal'luhu k'rōv gudlō. הַלְלוּהוּ כְּרֹב גֻּדְלוֹ.

praise Him as befits His abundant greatness.

Hal'luhu b'sayka shōfor, הַלְלוּהוּ בְּתֵקַע שׁוֹפָר,

Praise Him with the blast of the shofar;

hal'luhu b'nayvel v'chinōr. הַלְלוּהוּ בְּנֵבֶל וְכִנּוֹר.

praise Him with lyre and harp.

Hal'luhu b'sōf u-mochōl, הַלְלוּהוּ בְּתֹף וּמָחוֹל,

Praise Him with drum and dance;

hal'luhu b'minim v'ugov. הַלְלוּהוּ בְּמִנִּים וְעֻגָב.

praise Him with organ and flute.

Hal'luhu b'tziltz'lay shoma, הַלְלוּהוּ בְּצִלְצְלֵי שָׁמַע,

Praise Him with clanging cymbals;

hal'luhu b'tziltz'lay s'ru-o. הַלְלוּהוּ בְּצִלְצְלֵי תְרוּעָה.

praise him with resonant trumpets.

Kōl han'shomo t'halyl Yoh, כֹּל הַנְּשָׁמָה תְּהַלֵּל יָהּ,

Let all souls praise God,

hal'luyoh. הַלְלוּיָהּ.

Praise God!

TONO d'vay rabi yishmo-ayl. **תָּנָא** דְּבֵי רַבִּי יִשְׁמָעֵאל.

The Academy of Rabbi Yishmael taught:

Ilmolay lō zochu yisro-ayl אִלְמָלֵי לֹא זָכוּ יִשְׂרָאֵל

Had Israel not been privileged

elo l'hakbil p'nay avihem אֶלָּא לְהַקְבִּיל פְּנֵי אֲבִיהֶם

sheba-shoma-yim שֶׁבַּשָּׁמַיִם

to greet the countenance of their Father in Heaven

pa-am achas bachōdesh, da-yom. פַּעַם אַחַת בַּחֹדֶשׁ, דַּיָּם.

except for once a month — it would have sufficed them.

Omar aba-yay, אָמַר אַבַּיֵּי.

Abaye said:

hilkoch tzorich l'maym'ro m'umod.

הִלְכָךְ צָרִיךְ לְמֵימְרָא מֵעֲמָד.

Therefore one must recite it while standing.

Mi zōs ōlo min hamidbor

מִי זֹאת עֹלָה מִן הַמִּדְבָּר

Who is this who rises from the desert

misrapekes al dōdoh.

מִתְרַפֶּקֶת עַל דּוֹדָהּ.

clinging to her Beloved!

VIHI ROTZŌN mil'fonecho

וִיהִי רָצוֹן מִלְּפָנֶיךָ

May it be Your will,

Adōnoy Elōhai Yaylōhay avōsai,

יהוה אֱלֹהַי וֵאלֹהֵי אֲבוֹתַי,

HASHEM, my God and the God of my forefathers,

l'malōs p'gimas hal'vono

לְמַלֹּאת פְּגִימַת הַלְּבָנָה,

to fill the flaw of the moon*

v'lō yih-ye voh shum mi-ut,

וְלֹא יִהְיֶה בָהּ שׁוּם מִעוּט,

that there be no diminution in it.

vihi ōr hal'vono k'ōr hachamo,

וִיהִי אוֹר הַלְּבָנָה כְּאוֹר הַחַמָּה,

May the light of the moon be like the light of the sun

uch-ōr shiv-as y'may v'rayshis,

וּכְאוֹר שִׁבְעַת יְמֵי בְרֵאשִׁית

and like the light of the seven days of Creation,

k'mō sheho-y'so kōdem mi-utoh,

כְּמוֹ שֶׁהָיְתָה קוֹדֶם מִעוּטָהּ,

as it was before it was diminished,

shene-emar:

שֶׁנֶּאֱמַר:

as it is said:

Es sh'nay ham'ōrōs hag'dōlim.

אֶת שְׁנֵי הַמְּאֹרֹת הַגְּדֹלִים.

"The two great luminaries."

V'yiska-yaym bonu mikro shekosuv:

וְיִתְקַיֶּם בָּנוּ מִקְרָא שֶׁכָּתוּב:

And may there be fulfilled upon us the verse that is written:

U-vikshu es Adōnoy Elōhayhem

וּבִקְשׁוּ אֶת יהוה אֱלֹהֵיהֶם,

They shall seek HASHEM, their God,

v'ays dovid malkom. Omayn.

וְאֵת דָּוִיד מַלְכָּם. אָמֵן.

and David, their king. Amen.

לְמַלֹּאת פְּגִימַת הַלְּבָנָה — *To fill the flaw of the moon.* The references to diminution of the moon and its restoration to its primeval status refer to spiritual concepts. The Sages teach that the spiritual illumination of those earliest days was concealed because God knew that man would prove unworthy of it. That was only a temporary phenomenon, however.

When the Final Redemption comes, that splendor will be returned to the earth, thus removing the stigma from the moon. Since the moon symbolizes Israel and the House of David, it is natural that man's lack of spiritual fulfillment — the concealment of the light — should be expressed in the smallness of the moon.

LAM'NATZAY-ACH bin-ginōs   לַמְנַצֵּחַ בִּנְגִינֹת
mizmōr shir.   מִזְמוֹר שִׁיר.
> *For the Conductor, upon Neginos, a psalm, a song.*

Elōhim y'chonaynu vi-vor'chaynu,   אֱלֹהִים יְחָנֵּנוּ וִיבָרְכֵנוּ,
> *May God favor us and bless us,*

yo-ayr ponov itonu selo.   יָאֵר פָּנָיו אִתָּנוּ סֶלָה.
> *may He illuminate His countenance with us, Selah.*

Loda-as bo-oretz dar-kecho,   לָדַעַת בָּאָרֶץ דַּרְכֶּךָ,
> *To make known Your way on earth,*

b'chol gō-yim y'shu-osecho.   בְּכָל גּוֹיִם יְשׁוּעָתֶךָ.
> *among all the nations Your salvation.*

Yōducho amim Elōhim,   יוֹדוּךָ עַמִּים אֱלֹהִים,
> *The peoples will acknowledge You, O God,*

yōducho amim kulom.   יוֹדוּךָ עַמִּים כֻּלָּם.
> *all of the peoples will acknowledge You.*

Yism'chu viran'nu l'umim,   יִשְׂמְחוּ וִירַנְּנוּ לְאֻמִּים,
> *Nations will be glad and sing for joy,*

ki sishpōt amim mishōr,   כִּי תִשְׁפֹּט עַמִּים מִישׁר,
> *because You will judge the peoples fairly*

ul-umim bo-oretz tanchaym selo.   וּלְאֻמִּים בָּאָרֶץ תַּנְחֵם סֶלָה.
> *and guide the nations on earth, Selah.*

Yōducho amim Elōhim,   יוֹדוּךָ עַמִּים אֱלֹהִים,
> *Then peoples will acknowledge You, O God,*

yōducho amim kulom.   יוֹדוּךָ עַמִּים כֻּלָּם.
> *the peoples will acknowledge You, all of them.*

Eretz nos'no y'vuloh,   אֶרֶץ נָתְנָה יְבוּלָהּ,
> *The earth has yielded its produce,*

y'vor'chaynu Elōhim Elōhaynu.   יְבָרְכֵנוּ אֱלֹהִים אֱלֹהֵינוּ.
> *may God, our own God, bless us.*

Y'vor'chaynu Elōhim,   יְבָרְכֵנוּ אֱלֹהִים,
> *May God bless us*

v'yir'u ōsō kol afsay oretz.   וְיִירְאוּ אוֹתוֹ כָּל אַפְסֵי אָרֶץ.
> *and may all the ends of the earth fear Him.*

IN MOST CONGREGATIONS, *ALEINU*, * (PAGE 620), FOLLOWED BY THE MOURNER'S *KADDISH*,
IS REPEATED AT THIS POINT.

עָלֵינוּ – *Aleinu*. Lest our ecstatic greeting of the moon be interpreted as worship of a heavenly body, God forbid, we recite *Aleinu*, which is our declaration that we serve only God and none other.

⟨ HAVDALAH AT SABBATH/FESTIVAL CONCLUSION ⟩⟩

■ A collection of Scriptural verses expressing the optimism of the Jew for success in his endeavors during the forthcoming week.

AT THE CONCLUSION OF THE SABBATH BEGIN HERE:
IN THE SYNAGOGUE, MOST CONGREGATIONS OMIT THE FIRST PARAGRAPH.

HINAY Ayl y'shu-osi,
הִנֵּה אֵל יְשׁוּעָתִי

Behold! God is my salvation,

evtach v'lō efchod,
אֶבְטַח וְלֹא אֶפְחָד,

I shall trust and not fear —

ki ozi v'zimros Yoh Adōnoy,
כִּי עָזִּי וְזִמְרָת יָהּ יהוה,

for God, Hashem, is my might and my praise

vai-hi li lishu-o.
וַיְהִי לִי לִישׁוּעָה.

— and He was a salvation for me.

Ush-avtem ma-yim b'sosōn,
וּשְׁאַבְתֶּם מַיִם בְּשָׂשׂוֹן,

mima-ainay hai-shu-o.
מִמַּעַיְנֵי הַיְשׁוּעָה.

You can draw water with joy, from the springs of salvation.

LaAdōnoy hai-shu-o,
לַיהוה הַיְשׁוּעָה,

Salvation is Hashem's,

al am'cho virchosecho selo.
עַל עַמְּךָ בִרְכָתֶךָ סֶּלָה.

upon Your people is Your blessing, Selah.

Adōnoy Tz'vo-ōs imonu,
יהוה צְבָאוֹת עִמָּנוּ,

Hashem, Master of legions, is with us,

misgov lonu Elōhay ya-akōv selo.
מִשְׂגָּב לָנוּ אֱלֹהֵי יַעֲקֹב סֶלָה.

a stronghold for us is the God of Jacob, Selah.

Adōnoy Tz'vo-ōs,
יהוה צְבָאוֹת,

Hashem, Master of legions,

ashray odom bōtay-ach boch.
אַשְׁרֵי אָדָם בֹּטֵחַ בָּךְ.

praised is the man who trusts in You.

Adōnoy hōshi-o,
יהוה הוֹשִׁיעָה,

Hashem save!

hamelech ya-anaynu
הַמֶּלֶךְ יַעֲנֵנוּ

v'yōm kor-aynu.
בְיוֹם קָרְאֵנוּ.

May the King answer us on the day we call.

◈ **Havdalah.** The concluding moments of the Sabbath are a time of foreboding, as holiness wanes and travail looms. Consequently, the *Havdalah* after the Sabbath includes symbols of blessing. Among them are the optimistic verses of blessing that introduce the post-Sabbath *Havdalah* and the custom to fill the cup until it overflows.

With the departure of the holy Sabbath and the onset of the workweek, it is essential that each Jew be conscious of the sharp difference between the holiness he has just been experiencing and the sharply lower level of spirituality to which he is about to descend.

La-y'hudim hoy'so ōro   לַיְּהוּדִים הָיְתָה אוֹרָה
  v'simcho, v'sosōn vikor.   וְשִׂמְחָה, וְשָׂשֹׂן וִיקָר,

For the Jews there was light, gladness, joy, and honor —

kayn tih-ye lonu.   כֵּן תִּהְיֶה לָּנוּ.

so may it be for us.

Kōs y'shu-ōs eso,   כּוֹס יְשׁוּעוֹת אֶשָּׂא,
  uvshaym Adōnoy ekro.   וּבְשֵׁם יהוה אֶקְרָא.

I will raise the cup of salvations, and I shall invoke the Name of HASHEM.*

THE FOLLOWING IS RECITED AT THE CONCLUSION OF THE SABBATH AND OF FESTIVALS:

Savri moronon v'rabonon v'rabōsai: סַבְרִי מָרָנָן וְרַבָּנָן וְרַבּוֹתַי:

By your leave, my masters, rabbis and teachers:

BORUCH ato Adōnoy,   **בָּרוּךְ** אַתָּה יהוה
  Elōhaynu melech ho-ōlom,   אֱלֹהֵינוּ מֶלֶךְ הָעוֹלָם,

Blessed are You, HASHEM, our God, King of the universe,

bōray p'ri hagofen.   בּוֹרֵא פְּרִי הַגָּפֶן.

Who creates the fruit of the vine.

ALL PRESENT RESPOND: Omayn — אָמֵן

AT THE CONCLUSION OF THE SABBATH THE FOLLOWING TWO BLESSINGS ARE RECITED.
AFTER THE FOLLOWING BLESSING SMELL THE SPICES.

BORUCH ato Adōnoy,   **בָּרוּךְ** אַתָּה יהוה
  Elōhaynu melech ho-ōlom,   אֱלֹהֵינוּ מֶלֶךְ הָעוֹלָם,

Blessed are You, HASHEM, our God, King of the universe,

bōray minay v'somim.   בּוֹרֵא מִינֵי בְשָׂמִים.

*Who creates species of fragrance.**

ALL PRESENT RESPOND: Omayn — אָמֵן

AFTER THE FOLLOWING BLESSING HOLD FINGERS UP TO THE FLAME TO SEE THE REFLECTED LIGHT:

BORUCH ato Adōnoy,   **בָּרוּךְ** אַתָּה יהוה
  Elōhaynu melech ho-ōlom,   אֱלֹהֵינוּ מֶלֶךְ הָעוֹלָם,

Blessed are You, HASHEM, our God, King of the universe,

bōray m'ōray ho-aysh.   בּוֹרֵא מְאוֹרֵי הָאֵשׁ.

*Who creates the illuminations of the fire.**

ALL PRESENT RESPOND: Omayn — אָמֵן

כּוֹס יְשׁוּעוֹת — *The cup of salvations.* When one expresses his gratitude to God, he lifts a cup of wine, symbolizing his joy at the salvations that God has granted. The upraised cup is called "the cup of salvations."

בּוֹרֵא מִינֵי בְשָׂמִים — *Who creates species of fragrance.* The reason for smelling the pleasant aroma of spices at the end of the Sabbath is to assuage oneself for the loss of the departing "additional soul" that joined him at the onset of the Sabbath.

בּוֹרֵא מְאוֹרֵי הָאֵשׁ — *Who creates the illuminations of the fire.* The Talmud (*Pesachim* 54a) gives the reason for the blessing. Fire was cre-

■ May the distinction between the holiness of Shabbos and the secular nature of the weekdays guide me to appreciate the other differences that exist in His universe.

THE FOLLOWING BLESSING IS RECITED AT THE CONCLUSION
OF THE SABBATH AND OF FESTIVALS:

BORUCH ato Adōnoy,

בָּרוּךְ אַתָּה יהוה

Blessed are You, HASHEM,

Elōhaynu melech ho-ōlom,

אֱלֹהֵינוּ מֶלֶךְ הָעוֹלָם,

our God, King of the unverse,

hamavdil bayn kōdesh l'chōl,

הַמַּבְדִּיל בֵּין קֹדֶשׁ לְחוֹל,

Who separates between holy and secular,

bayn ōr l'chōshech,

בֵּין אוֹר לְחֹשֶׁךְ,

between light and darkness,*

bayn yisro-ayl lo-amim,

בֵּין יִשְׂרָאֵל לָעַמִּים,

between Israel and the nations,

bayn yōm hash'vi-i

בֵּין יוֹם הַשְּׁבִיעִי

between the seventh day

l'shayshes y'may hama-ase.

לְשֵׁשֶׁת יְמֵי הַמַּעֲשֶׂה.

and the six days of labor.

Boruch ato Adōnoy,

בָּרוּךְ אַתָּה יהוה,

Blessed are You, HASHEM,

hamavdil bayn kōdesh l'chōl.

הַמַּבְדִּיל בֵּין קֹדֶשׁ לְחוֹל.

Who separates between holy and secular.

ALL PRESENT RESPOND: Omayn — אָמֵן

THE ONE WHO RECITED *HAVDALAH*, OR SOMEONE ELSE PRESENT FOR *HAVDALAH*, SHOULD DRINK MOST OF THE WINE FROM THE CUP, THEN EXTINGUISH THE FLAME BY POURING LEFTOVER WINE OVER IT INTO A DISH. IT IS CUSTOMARY TO DIP THE FINGERS INTO THE WINE-DISH AND TOUCH THE EYELIDS AND INNER POCKETS WITH THEM. THIS SYMBOLIZES THAT THE "LIGHT OF THE *MITZVAH*" WILL GUIDE US AND INVOKE BLESSING FOR THE COMING WEEK.

ated at the end of Adam's first Sabbath on earth. Then, God gave Adam the instinctive understanding to rub stones together in order to bring forth a fire for light and heat.

As in the case of all such blessings, one must enjoy the thing for which he thanks God, in this case, the illumination. Therefore, we hold our fingers up to the flame and gaze at its light upon our nails.

בֵּין קֹדֶשׁ לְחוֹל בֵּין אוֹר לְחֹשֶׁךְ... — *Between holy and secular, between light and darkness...*

The *holy* represents sanctity, while the *secular* is the "shell," i.e., the outer barrier that prevents people from perceiving holiness. By recognizing the difference b*etween light and darkness* one is able to discern God's wisdom, and thereby make one's own distinction between good, represented by light, and evil, represented by darkness. The awareness that God took Israel to Himself as His Chosen People should cause inexpressible joy.

Hallel

◈§ Hallel

◈§ Days of Praise

That *Hallel* is recited on the festivals may be understood by the fact that the Torah commands וְשָׂמַחְתָּ בְּחַגֶּךָ, *You shall rejoice on your festivals* (*Deuteronomy* 16:11). In the physical sense, this happiness manifests itself in the form of special food and drink, clothing, and treats for the children (see *Orach Chaim* 529). It is interesting to note, Rabbi Soloveitchik taught, that the Torah often connects happiness with being before and in the presence of Hashem as found, for example, in *Leviticus* (23:40). On Pesach, Shavuos, and Succos, the festivals when the Torah ordains a pilgrimage to Jerusalem and visiting the Temple (*Deuteronomy* 16:16), the privilege of participating in this spiritually uplifting experience elicits songs of praise and thanksgiving. While we do not yet have the Third Temple, the festivals remain the Biblically designated holy days when the Jew is privileged to have a rendezvous with Hashem, and this warrants the recitation of *Hallel*.

◈§ Whole and Half Hallel

The Talmud (*Arachin* 10b) differentiates between Pesach and Succos. Whereas on Succos the Full *Hallel* is recited each day, on Pesach it is recited only on the first two days (in Israel only on the first day). On the rest of Pesach, we recite the so-called Half-*Hallel*, or more exactly the abridged *Hallel*, which omits the first eleven verses of Psalm 115, and the first eleven verses of Psalm 116. The Talmud explains that on Succos the composition of the *mussaf* offering changed each day, thus each day has its own unique character and warrants its own recitation of *Hallel*. On Pesach, however, the sacrifices for all the days are identical. Since there is no new character, there is no independent obligation for *Hallel* after the first day(s). However, it is customary to recite *Hallel* on the rest of Pesach, since the Intermediate Days possess a flavor of the holiday — which is why many do not don *tefillin* — and the last days are *Yom Tov*. To mark the difference between an obligatory and customary *Hallel*, the latter is abridged. A second reason for abridging the *Hallel* during the remainder of Pesach will be explained below.

Rambam (*Hil. Chanukah* 3:6) explains that *Hallel* is not recited on Rosh Hashanah and Yom Kippur, because "they are days of repentance, awe, and dread, not days of excessive joy." Rabbi Chaim Soloveitchik of Brisk wonders: Why not recite *Hallel* on these days as an expression of our optimism? After all, we bathe and take haircuts in honor of Rosh Hashanah and we do not fast on that day, as we are optimistic that the Jewish nation will emerge victorious and meritorious in their judgment (*Orach Chaim* 581:4). Reb Chaim answers, based on *Psalms* 13:6: "As for me, I trust in Your kindness, my heart will rejoice in

Your salvation yet I will sing to Hashem, for He dealt kindly with me." King David declares that much though he trusts and rejoices, he will actually *sing* out in joy only after God has *dealt kindly with* him. From this we derive that one does not recite *Hallel* in *anticipation*; one recites *Hallel* only after the actual salvation has occurred.

⌐§ Reasons for Recitation

There is a difference of opinion regarding the commandment of reciting *Hallel* on the holidays. The *Be'hag — Baal Halachos Gedolos* — maintains that it is a Biblical commandment. Ramban maintains that it is part of the Biblical command to rejoice on the holidays, not necessarily a separate independent command. Rambam maintains that *Hallel* is always a Rabbinic commandment.

The second obligation for the recitation of *Hallel* is deliverance from an impending danger to the Jewish nation. *Midrash Tanchuma (Parashas Beshalach)* teaches that the Torah says: "Then Moses and the children of Israel chose to sing this song to Hashem, and they said the following." Why must the Torah include the word לֵאמֹר, *the following*? Let it simply proceed with the text of the song and we would know what they sang. Therefore the Midrash teaches that the word לֵאמֹר, literally *to say*, is meant to imply that whenever God delivers Jews from a potential disaster, they should respond with songs of praise, i.e., Hallel. This requirement to recite Hallel applies not only when the actual deliverance occurs, but annually on the anniversary of the event. We literally relive Jewish history. We not only eat matzah, receive the Torah, and reside in *succos* as the Jews of Moses' time did, but fast when they did and feast when they did.

For the same reason, *Hallel* is recited all eight days of Chanukah. While it is not a Biblically ordained festival, having occurred much after the giving of the Torah, we recite *Hallel* because of the miracle of the oil and the military victory over the Syrian-Greek oppressors.

⌐§ Purim

The Talmud (*Megillah* 14a) asks why do we not recite *Hallel* on Purim. If upon emerging from slavery to freedom we recite *Hallel* on Pesach, then surely on Purim, when we were threatened with annihilation, we should sing *Hallel*. The Talmud gives three answers. The last one is that in a sense we *do* recite *Hallel*, for the reading of *Megillas Esther* on Purim is a fulfillment of *Hallel*. While the Name of Hashem does not appear explicitly in the *Megillah,* our Rabbis teach that often the word מֶלֶךְ, *king*, refers not only to Ahasuerus, but to Hashem. For example, the beginning of Chapter 6, "That night the king could not sleep," refers to the King of kings, as well as Ahasuerus. Thus, the reading of the *Megillah* is not just the retelling of an exciting slice of history and an example of God's guiding hand, but the fulfillment of our obligation to recite *Hallel*. So much so, that *Meiri* holds that if one cannot hear the *Megillah* on Purim, one should recite *Hallel*. Although the Halachah does not follow *Meiri*'s view, his teaching helps us focus on the role of the *Megillah*. The other two reasons given

by the Talmud are that from the time the Jewish people entered their land, *Hallel* is recited only for miracles that occurred in *Eretz Yisrael*. Lastly, even after the miracle of Purim, the Jews were still subjects of King Ahasuerus, and *Hallel* is recited only if the national freedom is more complete.

◄§ My Creatures are Drowning

Yalkut Shimoni §654 gives a reason why the Full *Hallel* is not recited on the last day of Pesach, in celebration of the miraculous salvation at the Sea of Reeds, which took place on that day. When the sea was split and the Egyptian army was drowned, the angels wished to sing praise to Hashem for saving the Jewish nation, whereupon Hashem stopped them, saying, "My creatures are drowning in the sea and you wish to sing?" Thus, because of the loss of human life, albeit our enemy, we do not recite Full *Hallel* on the seventh day of Pesach. This accords with the verse, "When your enemy falls, be not glad, and when he stumbles, let your heart not be joyous" (*Proverbs* 24:17). What a powerful lesson regarding the worth, value, and potential of life!

◄§ Rosh Chodesh and Hallel

Although *Rosh Chodesh* is included in the Torah's chapter of Festivals, it is not considered a full-fledged festival because it is permissible to work on *Rosh Chodesh*. Nevertheless, it has been customary since Talmudic times to recite Half-*Hallel*. *Meiri* (*Taanis* 28b) comments that the basis of the custom was to provide a remembrance of the ceremony of sanctifying the month that was done in *Eretz Yisrael*, or simply to serve as a reminder that the day was *Rosh Chodesh*.

The halachic codifiers differ regarding whether or not a blessing should be recited prior to the *Hallel* of *Rosh Chodesh*, since it began as a custom, rather than a requirement (see *Orach Chaim* 422). Ashkenazic Jewry follows the opinion of the *Rama*, that a blessing should be recited.

◄§ On the Seder Night

Finally, it is interesting to note that the Mishnah (*Megillah* 20b) identifies *Hallel* as one of the *mitzvos* that is done only during the day and not at night. The exception to the rule is that of *Hallel* on the night of the Pesach *Seder*. Rav Hai Gaon (cited by *Ran*, on the *Rif*, *Pesachim* 26b) explains that *Hallel* on the night of the Pesach *Seder* is not in response to the occasion of the *Yom Tov* — that *Hallel* is said only during the day. Rather as the Mishnah teaches (*Pesachim* 116b), "Every year the Jew is to look upon himself as if he personally left Egypt." Therefore the motivation for the recitation of *Hallel* on the night of the Pesach *Seder* is in response to the miracle that is happening to us "now" on that night. Therefore we recite *Hallel* at night in praise for the miracle that is presently occurring.

⊰ **THE FOUR SPECIES** ⊱

■ May I be privileged to perform this commandment properly; through my waving of the Four Species in all directions, I symbolically proclaim His dominion over all.

MANY RECITE THE FOLLOWING BEFORE TAKING THE FOUR SPECIES:

Y'HI ROTZŌN mil'fonecho   יְהִי רָצוֹן מִלְּפָנֶיךָ,

Adōnoy Elōhai Vaylōhay avōsai,   יהוה אֱלֹהַי וֵאלֹהֵי אֲבוֹתַי,

May it be Your will, HASHEM, my God and the God of my forefathers,

bifri aytz hodor v'chapōs t'morim   בִּפְרִי עֵץ הָדָר, וְכַפּוֹת תְּמָרִים,

that through the fruit of the esrog tree, date-palm branches,

va-anaf aytz ovōs v'arvay nochal   וַעֲנַף עֵץ עָבוֹת, וְעַרְבֵי נָחַל,

twigs of the myrtle tree, and brook willows,

ōsiōs shimcho ham'yuchod   אוֹתִיּוֹת שִׁמְךָ הַמְיֻחָד

t'korayv e-chod el e-chod   תְּקָרֵב אֶחָד אֶל אֶחָד,

the letters of Your unified Name may become close to one another,

v'ho-yu la-achodim b'yodi   וְהָיוּ לַאֲחָדִים בְּיָדִי,

that they may become united in my hand;

v'layda aych shimcho nikro olai   וְלֵידַע אֵיךְ שִׁמְךָ נִקְרָא עָלַי,

and to make known that Your Name is called upon me,

v'yir'u migeshes aylai.   וְיִירְאוּ מִגֶּשֶׁת אֵלָי.

that [evil forces] may be fearful of approaching me.

Uv'na-anu-i ōsom   וּבְנַעֲנוּעִי אוֹתָם

tashpi-a shefa b'rochōs   תַּשְׁפִּיעַ שֶׁפַע בְּרָכוֹת

And when I wave them, may an abundant outpouring of blessing flow

mida-as elyōn linvay apiryōn   מִדַּעַת עֶלְיוֹן לִנְוֵה אַפִּרְיוֹן,

from the wisdom of the Most High to the abode of the Tabernacle,

limchōn bays elōhaynu,   לִמְכוֹן בֵּית אֱלֹהֵינוּ.

to the prepared place of the House of our God.

Us'-hay chashuvo l'fonecho   וּתְהֵא חֲשׁוּבָה לְפָנֶיךָ

mitzvas arbo-o minim aylu,   מִצְוַת אַרְבָּעָה מִינִים אֵלּוּ,

And may the mitzvah of these Four Species be reckoned before You

⊷⊱ **The Four Species**

The Torah commands the taking of the Four Species and concludes: *You shall be joyous before HASHEM . . .* (*Leviticus* 23:40). The Sages explain the connection between this *mitzvah* and joyousness:

In earlier times if a litigant's claim before the royal court was decided in his favor, he would receive a spear from the king. When he left the palace holding the king's spear aloft all knew that he had been victorious in his suit. So, too, during the Days of Awe, the Jewish people were on trial before the Heavenly Court. On Succos, "the season of joy," we celebrate our happiness that God has accepted our repentance — a confidence symbolized by the *lulav* held aloft.

k'ilu ki-yamtiho
כְּאִלּוּ קִיַּמְתֶּיהָ

b'chol p'rotōseho v'shorosheho
בְּכָל פְּרָטוֹתֶיהָ וְשָׁרָשֶׁיהָ

as if I had fulfilled it with all its particulars, roots,

v'saryag mitzvos hat'luyim boh,
וְתַרְיַ״ג מִצְוֹת הַתְּלוּיִם בָּהּ,

and the six hundred thirteen mitzvos dependent on it.

ki chavonosi l'yachado sh'mo
כִּי כַוָּנָתִי לְיַחֲדָא שְׁמָא

For my intention is to unify the Name

d'kud'sho b'rich hu ush'chin'tayh
דְּקֻדְשָׁא בְּרִיךְ הוּא וּשְׁכִינְתֵּהּ,

of the Holy One, Blessed is He, and His Presence,

bidchilu ur-chimu
בִּדְחִילוּ וּרְחִימוּ,

in awe and in love,

l'yachayd shaym yud kay bevav kay
לְיַחֵד שֵׁם י״ה בְּו״ה

b'yichudo sh'lim
בְּיִחוּדָא שְׁלִים,

to unify the Name Yud-Kei with Vav-Kei in perfect unity,

b'shaym kol yisro-ayl. Omayn.
בְּשֵׁם כָּל יִשְׂרָאֵל. אָמֵן.

in the name of all Israel; Amen.

Boruch Adōnoy l'ōlom
בָּרוּךְ יהוה לְעוֹלָם,

omayn v'omayn.
אָמֵן, וְאָמֵן.

Blessed is HASHEM forever, Amen and Amen.

THE FOUR SPECIES — LULAV, HADDASIM, ARAVOS, ESROG — ARE TAKEN IN HAND EVERY DAY OF SUCCOS, THROUGH HOSHANA RABBAH, EXCEPT ON THE SABBATH. THE LULAV-BUNDLE IS PICKED UP WITH THE RIGHT HAND, THEN THE ESROG (PITAM FACING DOWN) WITH THE LEFT. AFTER THE BLESSINGS ARE RECITED, THE ESROG IS TURNED (SO THE PITAM IS FACING UP) AND THE FOUR SPECIES ARE WAVED IN THE SIX DIRECTIONS (STRAIGHT AHEAD, RIGHT, BACK, LEFT, UP AND DOWN).

BORUCH ato Adōnoy
בָּרוּךְ אַתָּה יהוה

Elōhaynu melech ho-ōlom,
אֱלֹהֵינוּ מֶלֶךְ הָעוֹלָם,

Blessed are You, HASHEM, our God, King of the universe,

asher kid'shonu b'mitzvōsov,
אֲשֶׁר קִדְּשָׁנוּ בְּמִצְוֹתָיו,

Who has sanctified us with His commandments

v'tzivonu al n'tilas lulov.
וְצִוָּנוּ עַל נְטִילַת לוּלָב.

and has commanded us concerning the taking of a palm branch.

THE FOLLOWING BLESSING IS ADDED ONLY ON THE FIRST DAY THAT THE FOUR SPECIES ARE TAKEN.

BORUCH ato Adōnoy
בָּרוּךְ אַתָּה יהוה

Elōhaynu melech ho-ōlom,
אֱלֹהֵינוּ מֶלֶךְ הָעוֹלָם,

Blessed are You, HASHEM, our God, King of the universe,

she-heche-yonu v'ki-y'monu v'higi-onu
שֶׁהֶחֱיָנוּ וְקִיְּמָנוּ וְהִגִּיעָנוּ

laz'man ha-ze.
לַזְּמָן הַזֶּה.

Who has kept us alive, sustained us, and brought us to this season.

⊰❘ HALLEL ❘⊱

HALLEL IS RECITED AFTER THE *SHEMONEH ESREI* OF *SHACHARIS* ON FESTIVALS, CHANUKAH AND *ROSH CHODESH*. (SOME CONGREGATIONS ALSO RECITE IT FOLLOWING THE *MAARIV SHEMONEH ESREI* ON *SEDER* NIGHTS.) ON *ROSH CHODESH* (EXCEPT ON *ROSH CHODESH* TEVES) AND THE LAST SIX DAYS OF PESACH, TWO PARAGRAPHS (AS INDICATED IN THE TEXT) ARE OMITTED. [THOSE WHO WEAR *TEFILLIN*, SEE PAGE 837.]

THE *CHAZZAN* RECITES THE BLESSING. THE CONGREGATION, AFTER RESPONDING AMEN, REPEATS IT, AND CONTINUES WITH THE FIRST PSALM.

BORUCH ato Adonoy   בָּרוּךְ אַתָּה יהוה
> *Blessed are You, HASHEM,*

Elōhaynu melech ho-ōlom,   אֱלֹהֵינוּ מֶלֶךְ הָעוֹלָם,
> *our God, King of the universe,*

asher kid'shonu b'mitzvōsov   אֲשֶׁר קִדְּשָׁנוּ בְּמִצְוֹתָיו,
> *Who has sanctified us with His commandments*

v'tzivonu likrō es ha-halayl.   וְצִוָּנוּ לִקְרֹא אֶת הַהַלֵּל.
> *and has commanded us to read the Hallel.*

■ I proudly join the People of Israel in extolling Hashem as the Creator and Master of the world — particularly His ability to transform man's condition.

HAL'LUYOH,   הַלְלוּיָהּ
> *Praise God!*

hal'lu avday Adōnoy,   הַלְלוּ עַבְדֵי יהוה,
> *Give praise, you servants of HASHEM;**

hal'lu es shaym Adōnoy.   הַלְלוּ אֶת שֵׁם יהוה.
> *praise the Name of HASHEM!*

Y'hi shaym Adōnoy m'vōroch,   יְהִי שֵׁם יהוה מְבֹרָךְ,
> *Blessed be the Name of HASHEM,*

may-ato v'ad ōlom.   מֵעַתָּה וְעַד עוֹלָם.
> *from this time and forever.*

Mimizrach shemesh ad m'vō-ō,   מִמִּזְרַח שֶׁמֶשׁ עַד מְבוֹאוֹ,
> *From the rising of the sun to its setting,*

⊰৪ **Hallel**

The prophets ordained that the six psalms (113-118) of *Hallel* [literally, *praise*] be recited on each Festival, and to commemorate times of national deliverance from peril. Moreover, the Talmud (*Pesachim* 117a) states that before David redacted and incorporated these psalms into the Book of *Psalms*, *Hallel* was already known to the nation: Moses and Israel had recited it after being saved from the Egyptians at the Sea; Joshua, after defeating the kings of Canaan; Deborah and Barak, after defeating Sisera; Hezekiah, after defeating Sennacherib;

Chananyah, Mishael and Azariah, after being saved from the wicked Nebuchadnezzar; and Mordechai and Esther, after the defeat of the wicked Haman.

These psalms were singled out as the unit of praise because they contain five fundamental themes of Jewish faith: the Exodus, the Splitting of the Sea, the Giving of the Torah at Sinai, the future Resurrection of the Dead, and the coming of the Messiah.

הַלְלוּיָהּ הַלְלוּ עַבְדֵי ה׳ — *Praise God! Give praise, you servants of HASHEM.* Only after their liberation from Pharaoh's bondage could the Jews

m'hulol shaym Adōnoy.　　מְהֻלָּל שֵׁם יהוה.

HASHEM's Name is praised.

Rom al kol gōyim Adōnoy,　　רָם עַל כָּל גּוֹיִם יהוה,

High above all nations is HASHEM,

al ha-shoma-yim k'vōdō.　　עַל הַשָּׁמַיִם כְּבוֹדוֹ.

above the heavens is His glory.

Mi Kadōnoy Elōhaynu,　　מִי כַּיהוה אֱלֹהֵינוּ,

hamagbihi lo-shoves.　　הַמַּגְבִּיהִי לָשָׁבֶת.

Who is like HASHEM, our God, Who is enthroned on high —

Hamashpili lir-ōs,　　הַמַּשְׁפִּילִי לִרְאוֹת,

ba-shoma-yim u-vo-oretz.　　בַּשָּׁמַיִם וּבָאָרֶץ.

yet deigns to look upon the heaven and the earth?*

M'kimi may-ofor dol,　　מְקִימִי מֵעָפָר דָּל,

He raises the needy from the dust,

may-ashpōs yorim evyōn.　　מֵאַשְׁפֹּת יָרִים אֶבְיוֹן.

from the trash heaps He lifts the destitute.

L'hōshivi im n'divim,　　לְהוֹשִׁיבִי עִם נְדִיבִים,

im n'divay amō.　　עִם נְדִיבֵי עַמּוֹ.

To seat them with nobles, with the nobles of His people.

Mōshivi akeres haba-yis,　　מוֹשִׁיבִי עֲקֶרֶת הַבַּיִת,

He transforms the barren wife

aym habonim s'maycho,　　אֵם הַבָּנִים שְׂמֵחָה,

into a glad mother of children.

hal'luyoh.　　הַלְלוּיָהּ.

Praise God!

■ I sing in grateful appreciation and reverence, recalling the miraculous transformation of the natural order that accompanied the Exodus from Egypt and the Revelation at Sinai.

B'TZAYS yisro-ayl mimitzro-yim,　　בְּצֵאת יִשְׂרָאֵל מִמִּצְרַיִם,

When Israel went out of Egypt,*

---

be considered the *servants of HASHEM*, because they no longer vowed allegiance to any other ruler.

הַמַּשְׁפִּילִי לִרְאוֹת בַּשָּׁמַיִם וּבָאָרֶץ — *Yet deigns to look* [lit. *bends down low to see*] *upon the heaven and the earth.* This is the challenging and exciting aspect of God's relationship to man: As we act towards God, so does He react to us. If we ignore His presence, He withdraws high above the heavens; but if we welcome His

proximity, He lovingly involves Himself in every phase of our lives.

בְּצֵאת יִשְׂרָאֵל מִמִּצְרַיִם — *When Israel went out of Egypt.* The second chapter of *Hallel* continues the theme of the first chapter, which praises God for raising up the needy and destitute. Israel was thus elevated when they left Egypt and risked their lives by entering the Sea at God's command.

bays ya-akōv may-am lō-ayz.
בֵּית יַעֲקֹב מֵעַם לֹעֵז.

*Jacob's household from a people of alien tongue** —

Hoy'so y'hudo l'kod-shō,
הָיְתָה יְהוּדָה לְקָדְשׁוֹ,

*Judah became His sanctuary,**

yisro-ayl mamsh'lōsov.
יִשְׂרָאֵל מַמְשְׁלוֹתָיו.

Israel His dominions.

Ha-yom ro-o va-yonōs,
הַיָּם רָאָה וַיָּנֹס,

The sea saw and fled:

ha-yardayn yisōv l'ochōr.
הַיַּרְדֵּן יִסֹּב לְאָחוֹר.

the Jordan turned backward.

Hehorim rok'du ch'aylim,
הֶהָרִים רָקְדוּ כְאֵילִים,

*The mountains skipped like rams,**

g'vo-ōs kivnay tzōn.
גְּבָעוֹת כִּבְנֵי צֹאן.

the hills like young lambs.

Ma l'cho ha-yom ki sonus,
מַה לְּךָ הַיָּם כִּי תָנוּס,

What ails you, O sea, that you flee?

ha-yardayn tisōv l'ochōr.
הַיַּרְדֵּן תִּסֹּב לְאָחוֹר.

O Jordan, that you turn backward?

Hehorim tirk'du ch'aylim,
הֶהָרִים תִּרְקְדוּ כְאֵילִים,

O mountains, that you skip like rams?

g'vo-ōs kivnay tzōn.
גְּבָעוֹת כִּבְנֵי צֹאן.

O hills, like young lambs?

Milifnay odōn chuli oretz,
מִלִּפְנֵי אָדוֹן חוּלִי אָרֶץ,

Before the Lord's Presence — did I, the earth, tremble —

milifnay Elō-a ya-akōv.
מִלִּפְנֵי אֱלוֹהַּ יַעֲקֹב.

before the presence of the God of Jacob,

hahōf'chi hatzur agam mo-yim,
הַהֹפְכִי הַצּוּר אֲגַם מָיִם,

*Who turns the rock into a pond of water,**

chalomish l'ma-y'nō mo-yim.
חַלָּמִישׁ לְמַעְיְנוֹ מָיִם.

the flint into a flowing fountain.

בֵּית יַעֲקֹב מֵעַם לֹעֵז — *Jacob's household from a people of alien tongue.* Even the Jews who were forced to communicate with the Egyptians in the language of the land did so only under duress. Among themselves, however, they spoke only the Holy Tongue and regarded Egyptian as a foreign language.

הָיְתָה יְהוּדָה לְקָדְשׁוֹ — *Judah became His sanctuary.* God singled out the tribe of Judah to be the family of royalty, because they sanctified God's Name at the Sea of Reeds. Led by their prince,

Nachshon ben Aminadav, this tribe was the first to jump into the threatening waters (*Rosh*).

הֶהָרִים רָקְדוּ כְאֵילִים — *The mountains skipped like rams.* When Israel received the Torah, Sinai and the neighboring mountains and hills shook and trembled at the manifestation of God's Presence and the thunder and lightning that accompanied it.

הַהֹפְכִי הַצּוּר אֲגַם מָיִם — *Who turns the rock into a pond of water.* When the Jews thirsted for water in the wilderness, God instructed Moses

■ I beseech Hashem to reveal Himself, again enabling all of mankind to recognize and appreciate His true essence.

ON *ROSH CHODESH* (EXCEPT TEVES) AND THE LAST SIX DAYS OF PESACH
THE FOLLOWING PARAGRAPH IS OMITTED.

LŌ LONU, Adōnoy, lō lonu,
לֹא לָנוּ, יהוה, לֹא לָנוּ,
Not for our sake,* HASHEM, not for our sake,

ki l'shimcho tayn kovōd,
כִּי לְשִׁמְךָ תֵּן כָּבוֹד,
but for Your Name's sake give glory,*

al chasd'cho al amitecho.
עַל חַסְדְּךָ עַל אֲמִתֶּךָ.
for Your kindness and for Your truth!

Lomo yōm'ru hagōyim,
לָמָּה יֹאמְרוּ הַגּוֹיִם,
a-yay no Elōhayhem.
אַיֵּה נָא אֱלֹהֵיהֶם.
Why should the nations say, "Where is their God now?"

Vaylōhaynu va-shomo-yim,
וֵאלֹהֵינוּ בַשָּׁמָיִם,
Our God is in the heavens;

kōl asher chofaytz oso.
כֹּל אֲשֶׁר חָפֵץ עָשָׂה.
whatever He pleases, He does!

Atzabayhem kesef v'zohov,
עֲצַבֵּיהֶם כֶּסֶף וְזָהָב,
ma-asay y'day odom.
מַעֲשֵׂה יְדֵי אָדָם.
Their idols are silver and gold, the handiwork of man.

Pe lohem v'lō y'dabayru,
פֶּה לָהֶם וְלֹא יְדַבֵּרוּ,
They have a mouth, but cannot speak;

ayna-yim lohem v'lō yir-u.
עֵינַיִם לָהֶם וְלֹא יִרְאוּ.
they have eyes, but cannot see.

Ozna-yim lohem v'lō yishmo-u,
אָזְנַיִם לָהֶם וְלֹא יִשְׁמָעוּ,
They have ears, but cannot hear;

af lohem v'lō y'ri-chun.
אַף לָהֶם וְלֹא יְרִיחוּן.
they have a nose, but cannot smell.

Y'dayhem v'lō y'mi-shun,
יְדֵיהֶם וְלֹא יְמִישׁוּן,
Their hands — they cannot feel;

(*Exodus* 17:6), "You shall smite the rock and water shall come out of it, so that the people may drink."

לֹא לָנוּ — *Not for our sake.* The preceding psalm depicts the awe inspired by God's miracles. Here the Psalmist describes the aftermath of that inspiration. Although Israel remained imbued with faith, our oppressors soon began to scoff, "Where is your God?" We pray that God will intervene again in the affairs of man, not for our sake, but for His.

לֹא לָנוּ ה׳ ... כִּי לְשִׁמְךָ תֵּן כָּבוֹד — *Not for our sake, HASHEM ... but for Your Name's sake give glory.* We beg You to redeem us, not because we are personally worthy, nor because of the merit of our forefathers. Rather we urgently strive to protect Your glorious Name, so that no one can deny Your mastery and dominion.

raglayhem v'lō y'halaychu,	רַגְלֵיהֶם וְלֹא יְהַלֵּכוּ,
their feet — they cannot walk;	
lō yehgu bigrōnom.	לֹא יֶהְגּוּ בִּגְרוֹנָם.
they cannot utter a sound from their throat.	
K'mōhem yih-yu ōsayhem,	כְּמוֹהֶם יִהְיוּ עֹשֵׂיהֶם,
Those who make them should become like them,	
kōl asher bōtay-ach bohem.	כֹּל אֲשֶׁר בֹּטֵחַ בָּהֶם.
whoever trusts in them!	
❖ Yisro-ayl b'tach Badōnoy,	❖ יִשְׂרָאֵל בְּטַח בַּיהוה,
O Israel, trust in HASHEM;	
ezrom u-moginom hu.	עֶזְרָם וּמָגִנָּם הוּא.
their help and their shield is He!	
Bays aharōn bitchu Vadōnoy,	בֵּית אַהֲרֹן בִּטְחוּ בַיהוה,
House of Aaron, trust in HASHEM;	
ezrom u-moginom hu.	עֶזְרָם וּמָגִנָּם הוּא.
their help and their shield is He!	
Yir-ay Adōnoy bitchu VaAdōnoy,	יִרְאֵי יהוה בִּטְחוּ בַיהוה,
You who fear HASHEM, *trust in* HASHEM;	
ezrom u-moginom hu.	עֶזְרָם וּמָגִנָּם הוּא.
their help and their shield is He!	

■ Reciprocal appreciation: Hashem blesses Israel, and I pledge that as long as I have the gift of life, I will enthusiastically praise Hashem.

ADŌNOY z'choronu y'voraych,	יהוה זְכָרָנוּ יְבָרֵךְ,
HASHEM *Who has remembered us will bless** —	
y'voraych es bays yisro-ayl,	יְבָרֵךְ אֶת בֵּית יִשְׂרָאֵל,
He will bless the House of Israel;	
y'voraych es bays aharōn.	יְבָרֵךְ אֶת בֵּית אַהֲרֹן.
He will bless the House of Aaron;	
Y'voraych yir-ay Adōnoy,	יְבָרֵךְ יִרְאֵי יהוה,
hak'tanim im hag'dōlim.	הַקְּטַנִּים עִם הַגְּדֹלִים.
He will bless those who fear HASHEM, *the small as well as the great.*	
Yōsayf Adōnoy alaychem,	יֹסֵף יהוה עֲלֵיכֶם,
alaychem v'al b'naychem.	עֲלֵיכֶם וְעַל בְּנֵיכֶם.
May HASHEM *increase upon you, upon you and upon your children!**	

הי זְכָרָנוּ יְבָרֵךְ — HASHEM *Who has remembered us will bless.* The Psalmist expresses confidence that just as God has blessed His people in the past, so He will bless them in the future.

יֹסֵף ה׳ עֲלֵיכֶם, עֲלֵיכֶם וְעַל בְּנֵיכֶם — *May* HASHEM *increase upon you, upon you and upon your children!* The true nature of בְּרָכָה, ''blessing,'' means increase and abundance. The Psalmist

B'ruchim atem Ladōnoy,　　　　　　　　בְּרוּכִים אַתֶּם לַיהוה,

　ōsay shoma-yim vo-oretz.　　　　　עֹשֵׂה שָׁמַיִם וָאָרֶץ.

You are blessed of HASHEM, maker of heaven and earth.

Ha-shoma-yim shoma-yim Ladōnoy,　　❖ הַשָּׁמַיִם שָׁמַיִם לַיהוה,

As for the heavens — the heavens are HASHEM's,

v'ho-oretz nosan livnay odom.　　　וְהָאָרֶץ נָתַן לִבְנֵי אָדָם.

but the earth He has given to mankind.*

Lō ha-maysim y'hal'lu Yoh,　　　　לֹא הַמֵּתִים יְהַלְלוּ יָהּ,

Neither the dead can praise God,*

v'lō kol yōr'day dumo.　　　　　　וְלֹא כָּל יֹרְדֵי דוּמָה.

nor any who descend into silence;

Va-anachnu n'voraych Yoh,　　　　　וַאֲנַחְנוּ נְבָרֵךְ יָהּ,

but we will bless God

may-ato v'ad ōlom,　　　　　　　　מֵעַתָּה וְעַד עוֹלָם,

from this time and forever.

hal'luyoh.　　　　　　　　　　　　הַלְלוּיָהּ.

Bless God!

■ I invoke the name of Hashem in times of trouble and sorrow.

ON *ROSH CHODESH* (EXCEPT TEVES) AND THE LAST SIX DAYS OF PESACH
THE FOLLOWING PARAGRAPH IS OMITTED.

OHAVTI ki yishma Adōnoy　　　**אָהַבְתִּי** כִּי יִשְׁמַע יהוה

　es kōli tachanunoy.　　　　　אֶת קוֹלִי תַּחֲנוּנָי.

I love [Him],* for HASHEM hears my voice, my supplications.

Ki hito oznō li, uvyomai ekro.　כִּי הִטָּה אָזְנוֹ לִי, וּבְיָמַי אֶקְרָא.

As He has inclined His ear to me, so in my days shall I call.

---

foresaw that Israel would suffer from attrition in exile and they would fear eventual extinction. Therefore, he offers the assurance that, at the advent of Messiah, their number will increase dramatically.

הַשָּׁמַיִם שָׁמַיִם לַהּ׳ וְהָאָרֶץ נָתַן לִבְנֵי אָדָם — *As for the heavens — the heavens are HASHEM's, but the earth He has given to mankind.* Since the heavens remain under God's firm control, all celestial bodies are forced to act in accordance with His will without freedom of choice. On earth, however, man was granted the freedom to determine his own actions and beliefs.

This verse can be explained homiletically. Man need not perfect heaven because it is already dedicated to the holiness of God. But the earth is man's province. Man is bidden to perfect it and transform its material nature into something spiritual. Indeed, man was created to make the earth heavenly.

לֹא הַמֵּתִים יְהַלְלוּ יָהּ — *Neither the dead can praise God.* The people who fail to recognize God's omnipresence and influence over the world resemble the dead, who are insensitive to all external stimuli and who are oblivious to reality. However, the souls of the righteous continue to praise God even after they depart from their bodies.

אָהַבְתִּי — *I love [Him].* The Psalmist foresaw that Israel would feel completely alone in exile. The nations would taunt them, "Your prayers and pleas are worthless, because God has turned a deaf ear to you." Therefore, he composed this psalm to encourage the downcast exiles with the assurance that indeed: "HASHEM hears my voice, my supplications."

Afofuni chevlay mo-ves,
אֲפָפוּנִי חֶבְלֵי מָוֶת,
The pains of death* encircled me;

umtzoray sh'ōl m'tzo-uni,
וּמְצָרֵי שְׁאוֹל מְצָאוּנִי,
the confines of the grave have found me;

tzoro v'yogōn emtzo.
צָרָה וְיָגוֹן אֶמְצָא.
trouble and sorrow I would find.

Uvshaym Adōnoy ekro,
וּבְשֵׁם יהוה אֶקְרָא,
ono Adōnoy mal'to nafshi.
אָנָּה יהוה מַלְּטָה נַפְשִׁי.
Then I would invoke the Name of HASHEM: "Please, HASHEM, save my soul."

Chanun Adōnoy v'tzadik,
חַנּוּן יהוה וְצַדִּיק,
Vaylōhaynu m'rachaym.
וֵאלֹהֵינוּ מְרַחֵם.
Gracious is HASHEM and righteous, our God is merciful.

Shōmayr p'so-yim Adōnoy,
שֹׁמֵר פְּתָאיִם יהוה,
HASHEM protects the simple;

dalōsi v'li y'hōshi-a.
דַּלּוֹתִי וְלִי יְהוֹשִׁיעַ.
I was brought low, but He saved me.

Shuvi nafshi limnuchoychi,
שׁוּבִי נַפְשִׁי לִמְנוּחָיְכִי,
Return, my soul, to your rest;*

ki Adōnoy gomal oloychi.
כִּי יהוה גָּמַל עָלָיְכִי.
for HASHEM has been kind to you.

Ki chilatzto nafshi mimo-ves,
כִּי חִלַּצְתָּ נַפְשִׁי מִמָּוֶת,
For You have delivered my soul from death,

es ayni min dim-o,
אֶת עֵינִי מִן דִּמְעָה,
es ragli midechi.
אֶת רַגְלִי מִדֶּחִי.
my eyes from tears, my feet from stumbling.

❖ Es-halaych lifnay Adōnoy,
אֶתְהַלֵּךְ לִפְנֵי יהוה,
b'artzōs hacha-yim.
בְּאַרְצוֹת הַחַיִּים.
I shall walk before HASHEM in the lands of the living.

He-emanti ki adabayr,
הֶאֱמַנְתִּי כִּי אֲדַבֵּר,
ani onisi m'ōd.
אֲנִי עָנִיתִי מְאֹד.
I have kept faith although I say: "I suffer exceedingly."

Ani omarti v'chofzi,
אֲנִי אָמַרְתִּי בְחָפְזִי,
kol ho-odom kōzayv.
כָּל הָאָדָם כֹּזֵב.
I said in my haste: "All mankind is deceitful."

חֶבְלֵי מָוֶת — *The pains of death.* This is an apt description of the exile, when Israel is encircled by violent enemies who seek to kill them.

שׁוּבִי נַפְשִׁי לִמְנוּחָיְכִי — *Return, my soul, to your rest.* When misery and persecution upset me, I told my soul that it would find peace and

■ I invoke the name of Hashem in times of rejoicing and success.

MO OSHIV Ladōnoy,
kol tagmulōhi oloy.

מָה אָשִׁיב לַיהוה,
כָּל תַּגְמוּלוֹהִי עָלָי.

How can I repay HASHEM* for all His kindness to me?

Kōs y'shu-ōs eso,

כּוֹס יְשׁוּעוֹת אֶשָּׂא,

I will raise the cup of salvations

uvshaym Adōnoy ekro.

וּבְשֵׁם יהוה אֶקְרָא.

and the Name of HASHEM I will invoke.

N'dorai Ladōnoy ashalaym,

נְדָרַי לַיהוה אֲשַׁלֵּם,

My vows to HASHEM I will pay,

negdo no l'chol amō.

נֶגְדָה נָּא לְכָל עַמּוֹ.

in the presence, now, of His entire people.

Yokor b'aynay Adōnoy
hamovso lachasidov.

יָקָר בְּעֵינֵי יהוה
הַמָּוְתָה לַחֲסִידָיו.

Difficult in the eyes of HASHEM is the death of His devout ones.

Ono Adōnoy ki ani avdecho,

אָנָּה יהוה כִּי אֲנִי עַבְדֶּךָ,

Please, HASHEM — for I am Your servant,

ani avd'cho, ben amosecho,
pitachto l'mōsayroy.

אֲנִי עַבְדְּךָ, בֶּן אֲמָתֶךָ,
פִּתַּחְתָּ לְמוֹסֵרָי.

I am Your servant, son of Your handmaid — You have released my bonds.

❖ L'cho ezbach zevach tōdo,

❖ לְךָ אֶזְבַּח זֶבַח תּוֹדָה,

To You I will sacrifice thanksgiving offerings,

uvshaym Adōnoy ekro.

וּבְשֵׁם יהוה אֶקְרָא.

and the Name of HASHEM I will invoke.

N'dorai Ladōnoy ashalaym,

נְדָרַי לַיהוה אֲשַׁלֵּם,

My vows to HASHEM I will pay,

negdo no l'chol amō.

נֶגְדָה נָּא לְכָל עַמּוֹ.

in the presence, now, of His entire people.

B'chatzrōs bays Adōnoy,

בְּחַצְרוֹת בֵּית יהוה,

In the Courtyards of the House of HASHEM,

b'sōchaychi y'rusholo-yim,

בְּתוֹכֵכִי יְרוּשָׁלָיִם

in your midst, O Jerusalem,

hal'luyoh.

הַלְלוּיָהּ.

Praise God!

---

comfort only if it would *return* to God.
מָה אָשִׁיב לַה׳ — *How can I repay HASHEM?* What gift can I give to the King who owns everything? How can I possibly repay His acts of

kindness, for they are too numerous to recount? How can I even approach Him? He is eternal and I am finite; He is the highest, and I am the lowest!

■ The shortest chapter in Scripture depicts the universal recognition and praise of Hashem's Divine protection of the Jewish people which will prevail in Messianic times.

HAL'LU es Adōnoy, kol gōyim,
הַלְלוּ אֶת יהוה, כָּל גּוֹיִם,
Praise HASHEM,* all nations;

shab'chuhu kol ho-umim.
שַׁבְּחִוּהוּ כָּל הָאֻמִּים.
praise Him, all the states!

ki govar olaynu chasdō,
כִּי גָבַר עָלֵינוּ חַסְדּוֹ,
For His kindness has overwhelmed us,

ve-emes Adōnoy l'ōlom
וֶאֱמֶת יהוה לְעוֹלָם,
and the truth of HASHEM is eternal,

hal'luyoh.
הַלְלוּיָהּ.
Praise God!

■ I affirm that Hashem's kindness endures forever,
even at times when it is not apparent.

EACH OF THE FOLLOWING FOUR VERSES IS RECITED ALOUD BY THE *CHAZZAN.* AFTER EACH VERSE, THE CONGREGATION RESPONDS WITH THE VERSE: Hōdu Ladōnoy ki tōv, ki l'ōlom chasdō, AND THEN RECITES THE SUCCEEDING VERSE.
ON SUCCOS THE FOUR SPECIES ARE WAVED EACH TIME THE VERSE Hōdu Ladōnoy IS RECITED, AS FOLLOWS: THREE TIMES STRAIGHT AHEAD AT Hōdu; THREE TIMES TO THE RIGHT AT ki; THREE TIMES TO THE BACK AT tōv; THREE TIMES TO THE LEFT AT ki; THREE TIMES UP AT l'ōlom; AND THREE TIMES DOWN AT chasdō.

HŌDU Ladōnoy ki tōv,
הוֹדוּ לַיהוה כִּי טוֹב,
Give thanks to HASHEM for He is good;*

ki l'ōlom chasdō.
כִּי לְעוֹלָם חַסְדּוֹ.
His kindness endures forever!

Yōmar no yisro-ayl,
יֹאמַר נָא יִשְׂרָאֵל,
Let Israel say now:

ki l'ōlom chasdō.
כִּי לְעוֹלָם חַסְדּוֹ.
His kindness endures forever!

Yōm'ru no vays aharōn,
יֹאמְרוּ נָא בֵית אַהֲרֹן,
Let the House of Aaron say now:

ki l'ōlom chasdō.
כִּי לְעוֹלָם חַסְדּוֹ.
His kindness endures forever!

Yōm'ru no yir-ay Adōnoy,
יֹאמְרוּ נָא יִרְאֵי יהוה,
Let those who fear HASHEM say now:

ki l'ōlom chasdō.
כִּי לְעוֹלָם חַסְדּוֹ.
His kindness endures forever!

הַלְלוּ אֶת ה׳ — *Praise HASHEM.* The brevity of this psalm symbolizes the simplicity of the world order which will prevail after the advent of the Messiah.

הוֹדוּ לַה׳ כִּי טוֹב — *Give thanks to HASHEM for He is good.* This is a general expression of thanks to God. No matter what occurs, God is always good and everything He does is for the best,

■ I express my confidence that despite the difficult circumstances of my people, our destiny is to be triumphant, and when we experience redemption, I will recognize that all that Hashem has done has been for the good.

MIN HAMAYTZAR korosi Yoh,   מִן הַמֵּצַר קָרָאתִי יָּה,

From the straits* did I call upon God;

ononi vamerchov Yoh.   עָנָנִי בַמֶּרְחָב יָה.

God answered me with expansiveness.

Adōnoy li lō iro,   יהוה לִי לֹא אִירָא,

HASHEM is with me, I have no fear;

ma ya-ase li odom.   מַה יַּעֲשֶׂה לִי אָדָם.

how can man affect me?

Adōnoy li b'ōz'roy,   יהוה לִי בְּעֹזְרָי,

HASHEM is with me through my helpers;*

va-ani er-e v'sōn'oy.   וַאֲנִי אֶרְאֶה בְשֹׂנְאָי.

therefore I can face my foes.

Tōv la-chasōs Badōnoy,   טוֹב לַחֲסוֹת בַּיהוה,

    mib'tō-ach bo-odom.   מִבְּטֹחַ בָּאָדָם.

It is better to take refuge in HASHEM than to rely on man.*

Tōv la-chasōs Badōnoy,   טוֹב לַחֲסוֹת בַּיהוה,

    mib'tō-ach bindivim.   מִבְּטֹחַ בִּנְדִיבִים.

It is better to take refuge in HASHEM than to rely on nobles.

Kol gōyim s'vovuni,   כָּל גּוֹיִם סְבָבְוּנִי,

All the nations surround me;

b'shaym Adōnoy ki amilam.   בְּשֵׁם יהוה כִּי אֲמִילַם.

in the Name of HASHEM I cut them down!

Sabuni gam s'vovuni,   סַבְּוּנִי גַם סְבָבְוּנִי,

They encircle me, they also surround me;

b'shaym Adōnoy ki amilam.   בְּשֵׁם יהוה כִּי אֲמִילַם.

in the Name of HASHEM, I cut them down!

Sabuni chidvōrim   סַבְּוּנִי כִדְבֹרִים

They encircle me like bees,

---

even though this may not be immediately apparent to man.

מִן הַמֵּצַר — *From the straits.* This psalm expresses gratitude and confidence. Just as David himself was catapulted from his personal straits to a reign marked by accomplishment and glory, so too Israel can look forward to Divine redemption from the straits of exile

and oppression.

ה׳ לִי בְּעֹזְרָי — *HASHEM is with me through my helpers.* I have many helpers, but I place confidence in them only because HASHEM is with them. If my helpers were not granted strength by God, their assistance would be futile.

טוֹב לַחֲסוֹת בַּה׳ מִבְּטֹחַ בָּאָדָם — *It is better to take refuge in HASHEM than to rely on man.* It is far

dō-achu k'aysh kōtzim,
דֹּעֲכוּ כְּאֵשׁ קוֹצִים,

but they are extinguished as a fire does thorns;

b'shaym Adōnoy ki amilam.
בְּשֵׁם יהוה כִּי אֲמִילַם.

in the Name of HASHEM I cut them down!

Dochō d'chisani linpōl,
דָּחֹה דְחִיתַנִי לִנְפֹּל,

Vadōnoy azoroni.
וַיהוה עֲזָרָנִי.

You pushed me hard that I might fall, but HASHEM assisted me.

Ozi v'zimros Yoh, vai-hi li lishu-o.
עָזִּי וְזִמְרָת יָהּ, וַיְהִי לִי לִישׁוּעָה.

God is my might and my praise, and He was a salvation for me.

Kōl rino vishu-o,
קוֹל רִנָּה וִישׁוּעָה,

b'oholay tzadikim,
בְּאָהֳלֵי צַדִּיקִים,

The sound of rejoicing and salvation is in the tents of the righteous:

Y'min Adōnoy ōso cho-yil.
יְמִין יהוה עֹשָׂה חָיִל.

"HASHEM's right hand does valiantly.

Y'min Adōnoy rōmaymo,
יְמִין יהוה רוֹמֵמָה,

HASHEM's right hand is raised triumphantly;

y'min Adōnoy ōso cho-yil.
יְמִין יהוה עֹשָׂה חָיִל.

HASHEM's right hand does valiantly!"

Lō omus ki echye,
לֹא אָמוּת כִּי אֶחְיֶה,

va-asapayr ma-asay Yoh.
וַאֲסַפֵּר מַעֲשֵׂי יָהּ.

I shall not die! But I shall live and relate the deeds of God.

Yasōr yis'rani Yoh,
יַסֹּר יִסְּרַנִי יָּהּ,

v'lamo-ves lō n'sononi.
וְלַמָּוֶת לֹא נְתָנָנִי.

*God has chastened me exceedingly, but He did not let me die.**

Pischu li sha-aray tzedek,
פִּתְחוּ לִי שַׁעֲרֵי צֶדֶק,

Open for me the gates of righteousness,

ovō vom ō-de Yoh.
אָבֹא בָם אוֹדֶה יָהּ.

I will enter them and thank God.

Ze ha-sha-ar Ladōnoy,
זֶה הַשַּׁעַר לַיהוה,

This is the gate of HASHEM;

tzadikim yovō-u vō.
צַדִּיקִים יָבֹאוּ בוֹ.

*the righteous shall enter through it.**

---

better to put one's trust in God's protection, even without a pledge from Him, than to rely on the most profuse assurances of human beings.

יַסֹּר יִסְּרַנִי יָּהּ וְלַמָּוֶת לֹא נְתָנָנִי — *God has chastened me exceedingly, but He did not let me die.* Throughout the duration of the exile, I survived because whatever suffering God decreed was only to atone for my sins.

זֶה הַשַּׁעַר לַה׳ צַדִּיקִים יָבֹאוּ בּוֹ — *This is the gate of HASHEM; the righteous shall enter through it.* This refers to the gate of the Temple. When the exile is over, the righteous will enter through this gate, and they will thank God for answering their plea for redemption.

Ōd'cho ki anisoni,
אוֹדְךָ כִּי עֲנִיתָנִי,

vat'hi li li-shu-o.
וַתְּהִי לִי לִישׁוּעָה.

I thank You for You have answered me and become my salvation.

Ōd'cho ki anisoni,
אוֹדְךָ כִּי עֲנִיתָנִי,

vat'hi li li-shu-o.
וַתְּהִי לִי לִישׁוּעָה.

I thank You for You have answered me and become my salvation.

Even mo-asu habōnim,
אֶבֶן מָאֲסוּ הַבּוֹנִים,

ho-y'so l'rōsh pino.
הָיְתָה לְרֹאשׁ פִּנָּה.

The stone the builders despised has become the cornerstone.*

Even mo-asu habōnim,
אֶבֶן מָאֲסוּ הַבּוֹנִים,

ho-y'so l'rōsh pino.
הָיְתָה לְרֹאשׁ פִּנָּה.

The stone the builders despised has become the cornerstone.

May-ays Adōnoy ho-y'so zōs,
מֵאֵת יהוה הָיְתָה זֹּאת,

hi niflos b'aynaynu.
הִיא נִפְלָאת בְּעֵינֵינוּ.

This emanated from HASHEM; it is wondrous in our eyes.

May-ays Adōnoy ho-y'so zōs,
מֵאֵת יהוה הָיְתָה זֹּאת,

hi niflos b'aynaynu.
הִיא נִפְלָאת בְּעֵינֵינוּ.

This emanated from HASHEM; it is wondrous in our eyes.

Ze ha-yōm oso Adōnoy,
זֶה הַיּוֹם עָשָׂה יהוה,

nogilo v'nism'cho vō.
נָגִילָה וְנִשְׂמְחָה בוֹ.

This is the day HASHEM has made; let us rejoice and be glad on it.

Ze ha-yōm oso Adōnoy
זֶה הַיּוֹם עָשָׂה יהוה,

nogilo v'nism'cho vō.
נָגִילָה וְנִשְׂמְחָה בוֹ.

This is the day HASHEM has made; let us rejoice and be glad on it.

THE NEXT FOUR LINES ARE RECITED RESPONSIVELY, *CHAZZAN* THEN CONGREGATION.

ON SUCCOS THE FOUR SPECIES ARE WAVED: THREE TIMES STRAIGHT AHEAD AND THREE TIMES
TO THE RIGHT AT ono; THREE TIMES TO THE BACK AND THREE TIMES TO THE LEFT AT hōshi-o;
THREE TIMES UP AND THREE TIMES DOWN AT no.

ONO Adōnoy hōshi-o no.
אָנָּא יהוה הוֹשִׁיעָה נָּא.

Please, HASHEM, save now!

Ono Adōnoy hōshi-o no.
אָנָּא יהוה הוֹשִׁיעָה נָּא.

Please, HASHEM, save now!

Ono Adōnoy hatzlicho no.
אָנָּא יהוה הַצְלִיחָה נָּא.

Please, HASHEM, bring success now!

Ono Adōnoy hatzlicho no.
אָנָּא יהוה הַצְלִיחָה נָּא.

Please, HASHEM, bring success now.

אֶבֶן מָאֲסוּ הַבּוֹנִים הָיְתָה לְרֹאשׁ פִּנָּה — *The stone the builders despised has become the cornerstone.* This verse refers to David, who was rejected by his own father and brothers. When the prophet

BORUCH HABO b'shaym Adōnoy, בָּרוּךְ הַבָּא בְּשֵׁם יהוה,
Blessed is he who comes in the Name of HASHEM;

bayrachnuchem mibays Adōnoy. בֵּרַכְנוּכֶם מִבֵּית יהוה.
we bless you from the House of HASHEM.

Boruch habo b'shaym Adōnoy, בָּרוּךְ הַבָּא בְּשֵׁם יהוה,
Blessed is he who comes in the Name of HASHEM;

bayrachnuchem mibays Adōnoy. בֵּרַכְנוּכֶם מִבֵּית יהוה.
we bless you from the House of HASHEM.

Ayl Adōnoy va-yo-er lonu, אֵל יהוה וַיָּאֶר לָנוּ,
HASHEM is God, He illuminated for us;

isru chag ba-avōsim, אִסְרוּ חַג בַּעֲבֹתִים,
bind the festival-offering with cords

ad karnōs hamizbay-ach. עַד קַרְנוֹת הַמִּזְבֵּחַ.
until the corners of the Altar.

Ayl Adōnoy va-yo-er lonu, אֵל יהוה וַיָּאֶר לָנוּ,
HASHEM is God, He illuminated for us;

isru chag ba-avōsim, אִסְרוּ חַג בַּעֲבֹתִים,
bind the festival-offering with cords

ad karnōs hamizbay-ach. עַד קַרְנוֹת הַמִּזְבֵּחַ.
until the corners of the Altar.

Ayli ato v'ōdeko, אֵלִי אַתָּה וְאוֹדֶךָּ,
  Elōhai arōm'meko. אֱלֹהַי אֲרוֹמְמֶךָּ.
You are my God, and I will thank You; my God, I will exalt You.

Ayli ato v'ōdeko, אֵלִי אַתָּה וְאוֹדֶךָּ,
  Elōhai arōm'meko. אֱלֹהַי אֲרוֹמְמֶךָּ.
You are my God, and I will thank You; my God, I will exalt You.

ON SUCCOS THE FOUR SPECIES ARE WAVED EACH TIME THE VERSE hōdu Ladonōy IS RECITED, AS FOLLOWS: THREE TIMES STRAIGHT AHEAD AT hōdu; THREE TIMES TO THE RIGHT AT ki; THREE TIMES TO THE BACK AT tōv; THREE TIMES TO THE LEFT AT ki; THREE TIMES UP AT l'ōlom; AND THREE TIMES DOWN AT chasdō.

Hōdu Ladōnoy ki tōv, הוֹדוּ לַיהוה כִּי טוֹב,
Give thanks to HASHEM, for He is good;

ki l'ōlom chasdō. כִּי לְעוֹלָם חַסְדּוֹ.
His kindness endures forever.

Hōdu Ladōnoy ki tōv, הוֹדוּ לַיהוה כִּי טוֹב,
Give thanks to HASHEM, for He is good;

ki l'ōlom chasdō. כִּי לְעוֹלָם חַסְדּוֹ.
His kindness endures forever.

Samuel announced that one of Jesse's sons was to be anointed king, no one even thought of summoning David, who was out tending the sheep (see *I Samuel* 16:4-13).

■ The concluding blessing of *Hallel* reaffirms my belief and confidence that all mankind will join in the praise of Hashem.

Y'HAL'LUCHO Adōnoy Elōhaynu   יְהַלְלוּךָ יהוה אֱלֹהֵינוּ

kol ma-asecho,   כָּל מַעֲשֶׂיךָ,

All Your works shall praise You,* HASHEM, our God;

vachasidecho tzadikim   וַחֲסִידֶיךָ צַדִּיקִים

ōsay r'tzōnecho,   עוֹשֵׂי רְצוֹנֶךָ,

and Your devout ones, the righteous who do Your will,

v'chol am'cho bays yisro-ayl   וְכָל עַמְּךָ בֵּית יִשְׂרָאֵל

and Your entire people, the House of Israel,

b'rino yōdu vi-vor'chu   בְּרִנָּה יוֹדוּ וִיבָרְכוּ

with glad song will thank, bless,

vi-shab'chu vifo-aru virōm'mu   וִישַׁבְּחוּ וִיפָאֲרוּ וִירוֹמְמוּ

praise, glorify, exalt,

v'ya-aritzu v'yakdishu v'yamlichu   וְיַעֲרִיצוּ וְיַקְדִּישׁוּ וְיַמְלִיכוּ

extol, sanctify, and proclaim the sovereignty

es shimcho malkaynu   אֶת שִׁמְךָ מַלְכֵּנוּ.

of Your Name, our King.

Ki l'cho tōv l'hōdōs   כִּי לְךָ טוֹב לְהוֹדוֹת

For to You it is fitting to give thanks,

ulshimcho no-e l'zamayr,   וּלְשִׁמְךָ נָאֶה לְזַמֵּר,

and unto Your Name it is proper to sing praises,

ki may-ōlom v'ad ōlom ato Ayl.   כִּי מֵעוֹלָם וְעַד עוֹלָם אַתָּה אֵל.

for from this world to the World to Come You are God.

Boruch ato Adōnoy,   בָּרוּךְ אַתָּה יהוה,

melech m'hulol ba-tishbochōs.   מֶלֶךְ מְהֻלָּל בַּתִּשְׁבָּחוֹת.

Blessed are You, HASHEM, the King Who is lauded with praises.

CONGREGATION RESPONDS: Omayn — אָמֵן

ON *ROSH CHODESH* MANY RECITE THE FOLLOWING VERSE AFTER *HALLEL*:

V'avrohom zokayn bo ba-yomim   וְאַבְרָהָם זָקֵן בָּא בַּיָּמִים

Now Abraham was old, well on in years,

Vadonoy bay-rach es avrohom bakol.   וַיהוה בֵּרַךְ אֶת אַבְרָהָם בַּכֹּל.

and HASHEM had blessed Abraham with everything.

יְהַלְלוּךָ ... כָּל מַעֲשֶׂיךָ — *All Your works shall praise You.* This paragraph is a concluding blessing that sums up the broad theme of *Hallel*, that Israel and the entire universe will join in praising God. In the perfect world of the future, the entire universe, including the vast variety of human beings, will function harmoniously according to God's will. This is the highest form of praise, for without it all the beautiful spoken and sung words and songs of praise are insincere and meaningless.

The
Three Festivals

✍ The Shalosh Regalim / Three Festivals

✍ Source of Sanctity

There is a marked difference between Shabbos and the Festivals in their source of sanctity. Shabbos was sanctified by God Himself, from the seventh day of Creation. Its holiness derived from Him alone; it preceded the existence of the Jewish nation and is in no way dependent on human intervention. Accordingly, the blessing that completes the *Kiddush* and the middle blessing of the Shabbos *Amidah* is "Blessed are You, Hashem, **Who sanctifies** the Shabbos"; the day's holiness stems exclusively from Him. In sharp contrast, *Yom Tov* relates only to the Jewish nation, based upon its unique history. Furthermore, since the Festivals fall on dates in the calendar, and the Jewish calendar is fixed by the Sanhedrin, it is the Jewish people who sanctify the Festivals. Thus the blessing for the *Yom Tov Kiddush* and all the *Yom Tov Amidah* prayers is "Blessed are You, Hashem, Who sanctifies Israel and the festive seasons," i.e., Israel's holiness precedes that of the Festivals and is instrumental in making them holy.

The Festivals are entirely and exclusively for the Jewish nation, and each focuses on the special love and attention Hashem bestowed upon our people at the particular time that it commemorates. The middle blessing of every Festival *Amidah* begins with אַתָּה בְחַרְתָּנוּ, *You [God] have chosen us from all the peoples*. The Gaon of Vilna sees in this prayer a reference to Hashem's kindness to our forefathers at each respective holiday. Thus, *You have chosen us from all the peoples* refers to Pesach and God's miraculous deliverance of the Jewish people from Egypt. The Ten Plagues that subjugated the Egyptians did not effect the Jewish nation, and the splitting of the Sea of Reeds further attested to their chosenness. The next phrase, אָהַבְתָּ אוֹתָנוּ, *You loved us*, refers to Shavuos, when the Torah was given. The observance and study of Torah is the greatest sign of God's love. Finally, וְרָצִיתָ בָּנוּ, *You found favor in us*, refers to Hashem's forgiveness of Israel after the sin of the Golden Calf. Less than six week after Israel received the Ten Commandments, the people sinned grievously, but God signified His forgiveness by providing protective clouds for the repenting nation — the figurative סֻכּוֹת, or *tents*, that the Festival commemorates — the Divine sign that He *found favor* and forgave the Jewish people.

✍ Israel's Chosenness

The Sages (*Pirkei Avos* 3:18) shed light on the chosenness of Israel. "[Rabbi Akiva] used to say: Beloved is man for he was created in God's image; . . . beloved are the people Israel, for they are described as children of the Omnipresent . . . beloved are the people Israel, for a cherished utensil [i.e., the Torah] was given

to them." Rabbi Akiva differentiates between the role of man who perfected the gift of being creative in God's image, and Israel who are designated as His children.

Maimonides defines man's "image of God" as the gift of intelligence. God commanded Adam to use that intelligence to subdue, dominate, and control the earth (*Genesis* 1:28); to farm the land, mine the ore, and split the atom. Possessing intellect, Adam was able to receive communication from Hashem, Who gave him six commandments: the prohibition of murder, idolatry, sexual immorality, cursing Hashem, stealing, and the obligation to establish a judicial system. Adam failed to transmit successfully the obedience and observance of these laws. His son Cain murdered Abel (*Genesis* 4:8), and his grandson Enosh introduced idolatry (ibid. v.26). Man's slide into evil brought about the Flood, which decimated the world's people. Noah and his family were saved and it was left to him to transmit these commandments to mankind. Hashem gave Noah a seventh commandment, that of refraining from eating the organ taken from a living animal.

These commandments are known as the seven Noahide Laws, laws that apply to all of mankind, giving them meaning, purpose and dignity. But Noah, too, was unable to create an environment that respected the majesty of God and the dignity of man.

◆§ Abraham's Covenant

Abraham was different. Hashem loved him because he would transmit the way of Hashem, with justice and righteousness, to his offspring (*Genesis* 18:19). Long before the creation of the world, the Torah existed; it was the blueprint of Creation and the model for man's ideal lifestyle (*Pesachim* 54a). Hashem therefore entered into a covenant with Abraham, that began with the observance of circumcision, forging a sense of holiness onto his physical being and designating his family as God's Chosen People.

At Sinai, Hashem declared "You shall be to Me the most beloved treasure of all peoples . . . You shall be to Me a kingdom of ministers and a holy people" (*Exodus* 19:5-6). Israel was chosen to live and forge its destiny with the Torah, to imbue the world with spirituality and holiness. Most often this is accomplished by their loyal devotion to Torah and *mitzvos,* under any and all circumstances and difficulties. Furthermore, the Torah teaches that if Jews conform to the commands of the Torah, "Then all the peoples of the earth will see that the Name of HASHEM is proclaimed over you, and they will revere you" (*Deuteronomy* 8:10). The Vilna Gaon interprets the phrase "and they will revere you" to mean that your example will teach others to revere God.

◆§ Singularity of Sinai

The experience at Sinai was singular in the annals of world history. Never before nor since has an entire people experienced prophecy. Our belief in the Torah is not based on the testimony of Moses or a few other individuals who claim to have received the word of Hashem. We are loyal to the Torah because we personally received the Torah. We view our chosenness to lead a life broadened by 248 positive commandments and restricted by 365 negative commandments as a

privilege, not a burden.

Our being the chosen people is not to invoke superiority over other nations. Quite the contrary, it imposes greater responsibility upon ourselves. Throughout the Torah, the mistakes, backsliding, and weaknesses of our people are highlighted. The generation that stood at Sinai ultimately lost its chance to enter the Promised Land, due to its sins. When we fail to execute the teachings of the Torah, we are no longer deserving of a special status, as we recite in the Festival *Mussaf,* "because of our sins we were exiled from our land."

Moreover, the concept of chosenness can hardly be called "racist," if it is open to all. The Torah constantly emphasizes that the law is the same for a born Jew as for a convert. The prototype Jewish leader, King David, was a descendant of a convert, Ruth the Moabite, and the future King Messiah will be, as well. In addition the Torah shows high regard for another convert, Jethro, the father-in-law of Moses, whose wise advice is recorded in the same portion that describes the Revelation at Sinai and the Ten Commandments. Furthermore, our yearnings for the days of the *Mashiach,* writes Maimonides, is not to tyrannize over the gentiles, nor to be exalted over the nations, but to be free for the pursuit of Torah and wisdom.

The chosenness of Israel was not a temporary, conditional happening. In the covenant of circumcision, Hashem pledged that the relationship between Him and Abraham's offspring is eternal (*Genesis* 17:7). The Land of Israel, too, was given to the Jewish nation eternally. When Moses prayed for God's mercy upon Israel following the tragedy of the Golden Calf, he appealed to the potential desecration of Hashem's Name were He to terminate the Jewish people (*Exodus* 32:12), thus indicating permanence of the relationship between God and His people.

The same idea is expressed by the prophet Ezekiel who in thirty-six chapters, admonishes the Jewish people for their betrayal of the Covenant of Sinai. Their punishment was exile, which brought about a two-fold desecration of Hashem's holy Name. Firstly, the nations chided Israel that their God could not protect them. Secondly, instead of utilizing the experience of exile as a time for introspection and change, Jews "adjusted" to the exile and stopped seeing it as a punishment. Thus a further desecration of Hashem's Name emerges as the Jew in exile continues his former sinful lifestyle.

Hashem responds and declares, "Not for your sake will I redeem you, rather for the sake of My Name that Israel has desecrated." Israel will be redeemed. Israel will be brought back to its land so that Hashem's plan for the ultimate education and salvation of mankind will be realized. Finally, the Jerusalem Talmud teaches (*Sanhedrin* 10:1), and Rambam codifies (*Hil. Melachim* 8:11), that righteous gentiles have a share in the World to Come. This is why Israel's "chosenness" has not driven us to missionize and convert the rest of humanity.

⊷§ Israel and the Torah

The theme of chosenness is most often associated directly with the unique relationship of the Jewish people with the Torah. Indeed it is specifically mentioned in the daily blessing for Torah study, and the blessing that is recited when a man is called up to read from the Torah: "Blessed are You, Hashem ... Who selected us from all the peoples and gave us His Torah." Similarly, the morning

blessing before the *Shema* speaks of God's "abundant love" for Israel, and immediately thereafter beseeches "Our Father, the merciful Father, Who acts mercifully, have mercy upon us, instill in our hearts to understand and elucidate, to listen, learn, teach, safeguard, perform, and fulfill all the words of your Torah's teaching with love."

Our relationship with the Torah is far beyond an academic one that is fulfilled through the commandment to study and teach it. Rather the Torah itself is a sign of the closeness of Hashem and Israel (*Semag*, *Introduction to the Negative Commandments*). Semag refers specifically to the Oral Torah, the Mishnah and Talmud, which is the exclusive possession of the Jewish people. Other nations and religions may include the Written Torah in their Bible, but the Oral Law that was given to Moses at Sinai, together with rules of logic and textural analysis known as Hermeneutic Principles, are not studied by any other people. This is the Torah study that has primarily occupied the time and effort of Torah scholars for thousands of years.

This special bond is unique to Israel; no other people had such a relationship with their studies. The Torah is not just study; if studied properly it impacts most positively and significantly on the personality of its students. This is demonstrated by the *Taz* (*Orach Chaim* 224), who comments on the different blessings recited when one sees an individual who has excelled in secular knowledge, and one who has excelled in Torah. Upon seeing an outstanding secular scholar, one recites "Blessed are You . . . Who has *given* [שֶׁנָּתַן] of His knowledge to human beings." Upon seeing an outstanding Torah scholar, one blesses Hashem "Who has *apportioned* [שֶׁחָלַק] of His knowledge to those who fear Him." The difference between "Who has given" and "Who has apportioned," according to the *Taz*, is that when one is *given* something, the recipient does not retain anything of the donor. But when something is *apportioned*, the recipient received a part of the donor, namely some Godliness is actually absorbed by the Torah scholar, thereby impacting on his personality. One can be a great physicist, historian, or mathematician but not necessarily a good moral, ethical or honest human being. But one cannot be a Torah scholar without the Torah having forged a "Torah personality" of ideal interpersonal relations and conduct (see *Yoma* 85a).

◄§ Chosen for a Mission

In addition, the אַתָּה בְחַרְתָּנוּ, *You have chosen us,* prayer reminds us that at Sinai we were chosen for a mission, of being "a kingdom of ministers and a holy nation" (*Exodus* 19:6). This charge was given to us at Sinai. However, the *Kohanim* and Levites constitute the minority of the Jewish people; they are one tribe out of twelve, and the smallest one at that. The overwhelming majority of Jews are Israelites. Therefore, explains Rabbi Yehudah HaLevi (in *The Kuzari*), just as the role of the priests within the Jewish nation was that of teachers, similarly are we to be a nation of teachers to the rest of the world. Isaiah charged us to be "a light unto the nations." Our loyal observance of Torah and *mitzvos* has over the centuries impacted significantly on the communities about us.

This mission of being chosen to teach, to uplift all of mankind, can be substantiated by the following: The Torah teaches that many miracles occurred on the

first day that Joshua led the Jewish people across the Jordan River into the land of Canaan. One of them was that the entire Torah was to be inscribed on stones (see *Deuteronomy* 27:8), in seventy languages (*Sotah* 33b). The key point is not exactly how much was written, but rather, as symbolized by the number seventy, the responsibility to make the Torah accessible to all people.

Rashi comments on the first verse of the *Shema*, that Hashem Who now is only *our* God, meaning that only Israel worships him, will someday be acknowledged as the God of all mankind. This universalist credo, which is so important but often overlooked by centuries of anti-Semitism, is an important underlying theme of *Ata V'chartanu*, You have chosen us.

◌ Agricultural Symbolism

It is interesting to note that the Torah ties the Three Festivals to the agricultural cycle. Pesach occurs in *chodesh ha'aviv*, the month of springtime (*Deuteronomy* 16:1). Spring is the time when the earth comes to life after the winter and produce begins to grow; similarly the Exodus from Egypt represents the "spring" — the early stage — of our relationship with God. We were just beginning to grow.

Shavuos is *Chag HaBikkurim*, the holiday of the first fruits. When Hashem sends Moses to Pharaoh to redeem the Jewish people, He instructs Moses to inform the king, "Israel is Hashem's firstborn" (*Exodus* 4:22). Just as the first fruits are separated from the rest, Israel, God's "firstborn" was chosen from among the nations of the world to accept Hashem's Torah.

Finally, the third and last of the festivals is Succos. The Torah calls it *Chag HaAsif* (*Exodus* 23:16), the holiday of ingathering. Just as the farmer harvests all his crops, not just the first ones to ripen, similarly the holiday of Succos with its seventy offerings symbolizing the seventy nations teaches the all-important lesson that ultimately all of mankind will join together in recognition of Hashem. Thus the holidays themselves, according to Rabbi Benjamin Blech in his *Understanding Judaism*, reflect the development of our peoplehood and also our relationship to the rest of society.

This duality is reflected in *Aleinu*, the concluding prayer of each of the day's three prayers. *Aleinu* contains two paragraphs. The first focuses clearly on the special relationship that only Israel has at present with Hashem. "It is our duty to praise the Master of All .. for He has not made us like the nations of the lands ... He is our God and there is none other." The first paragraph clearly reflects the chosenness expressed in *Ata V'chartanu*, the singularity of Israel.

The second paragraph, however, points to the future: "Therefore we put our hope in You that we may soon see Your mighty splendor, to remove detestable idolatry from the earth, and false gods will be utterly cut off... And it is said: Hashem will be King over all the world. On that day Hashem will be One and His Name will be One."

Without fail, the Jew concludes every prayer with the ultimate hope that *Ata V'chartanu* will lead us to fulfill our mission as *Mamleches Kohanim*, a kingdom of ministers, inspiring the rest of society. *Ata V'chartanu* is thus a great challenge for the Jewish people, and we pray that we will be worthy of fulfilling it.

◈{ THE SEARCH FOR AND REMOVAL OF CHAMETZ/LEAVEN }◈

■ The Torah prohibits the Jew from owning *chametz*/leaven on Pesach. We therefore both rid and annul all *chametz* from our midst. In addition to the ridding and nullification of physical *chametz*, we are to remove arrogance and haughtiness — spiritual *chametz* — from our character.

ON THE NIGHT PRECEDING 14 NISSAN, THE NIGHT BEFORE THE PESACH *SEDER,* THE SEARCH FOR *CHAMETZ* (LEAVEN) IS MADE. IT SHOULD BE DONE WITH A CANDLE, AS SOON AS POSSIBLE AFTER NIGHTFALL. [WHEN THE FIRST *SEDER* IS ON SATURDAY NIGHT, THE SEARCH IS CONDUCTED ON THURSDAY NIGHT (13 NISSAN).] BEFORE THE SEARCH IS BEGUN, THE FOLLOWING BLESSING IS RECITED. IF SEVERAL PEOPLE ASSIST IN THE SEARCH, ONLY ONE RECITES THE BLESSING FOR ALL.

BORUCH ato Adōnoy   בָּרוּךְ אַתָּה יהוה

Elōhaynu melech ho-ōlom,   אֱלֹהֵינוּ מֶלֶךְ הָעוֹלָם,

Blessed are You, HASHEM, our God, King of the universe,

asher kid'shonu b'mitzvōsov,   אֲשֶׁר קִדְּשָׁנוּ בְּמִצְוֹתָיו,

Who has sanctified us with His commandments

v'tzivonu al bi-ur chomaytz.   וְצִוָּנוּ עַל בִּעוּר חָמֵץ.

and has commanded us concerning the removal of chametz.

ALL PRESENT RESPOND: Omayn — אָמֵן

AFTER THE SEARCH, THE *CHAMETZ* IS WRAPPED AND PUT ASIDE IN A SAFE PLACE TO BE BURNED IN THE MORNING. THEN THE FOLLOWING DECLARATION IS MADE.

KOL CHAMIRO vachami-o   כָּל חֲמִירָא וַחֲמִיעָא

d'iko virshusi   דְּאִכָּא בִרְשׁוּתִי,

Any chametz* or leaven that is in my possession,

d'lo chazitayh (d'lo chamitayh)   דְּלָא חֲזִתֵּהּ (דְּלָא חֲמִתֵּהּ)

which I have not recognized (which I have not seen),

udlo vi-artayh udlo y'dano layh,   וּדְלָא בְעַרְתֵּהּ וּדְלָא יְדַעְנָא לֵהּ,

have not removed and do not know about,

libotayl v'lehevay hefkayr   לִבָּטֵל וְלֶהֱוֵי הֶפְקֵר

k'afro d'ar-o.   כְּעַפְרָא דְאַרְעָא.

should be annulled and become ownerless, like dust of the earth.

◈§ The Search for and Removal of Chametz

Since the Torah forbids a Jew to eat *chametz* in his possession during Pesach, the Rabbis ordained a search of all homes, shops, and any other places where *chametz* may have been brought during the year. The search should be made by candlelight and therefore it should be done at night when a candle's flame is noticeable (*Pesachim* 2a). The primary *mitzvah* is the destruction of the *chametz* that will take place on the next morning, but the blessing is made at this point because the search is not merely preparation for the *mitzvah* of destroying the *chametz*, but an integral part of it.

כָּל חֲמִירָא — *Any chametz.* It is essential that all *chametz* be declared ownerless so that one not be in possession of *chametz* without knowing it. The evening declaration carefully omits any *chametz* that one wishes to retain for the next day's breakfast, the *chametz* that will be burned the next morning, and the *chametz* that will be sold to a non-Jew in the morning.

This is a legal declaration, not a prayer; therefore it must be understood. If one does not understand the Aramaic, he should recite it in a language he understands. Preferably, it should be recited by all members of the family.

IN THE MORNING, AFTER THE *CHAMETZ* HAS BEEN BURNED, THE FOLLOWING DECLARATION IS MADE.

KOL CHAMIRO vachami-o   כָּל חֲמִירָא וַחֲמִיעָא
d'iko virshusi,   דְּאִכָּא בִרְשׁוּתִי,

Any chametz or leaven that is in my possession,

da-chazitayh udlo chazitayh,   דַּחֲזִתֵהּ וּדְלָא חֲזִתֵהּ

whether I have recognized it or not,

(da-chamitayh udlo chamitayh),   (דַּחֲמִתֵהּ וּדְלָא חֲמִתֵהּ),

(whether I have seen it or not,)

d'vi-artayh udlo vi-artayh,   דְּבִעַרְתֵהּ וּדְלָא בִעַרְתֵהּ,

whether I have removed it or not,

libotayl v'lehevay hefkayr   לִבָּטֵל וְלֶהֱוֵי הֶפְקֵר
k'afro d'ar-o.   כְּעַפְרָא דְאַרְעָא.

should be annulled and become ownerless, like dust of the earth.

⊰ ERUV TAVSHILIN ⊱

WHEN FRIDAY IS A FESTIVAL DAY, AN *ERUV TAVSHILIN* IS MADE ON *EREV YOM TOV* [SEE COMMENTARY]. THE *ERUV-* FOODS ARE HELD WHILE THE FOLLOWING BLESSING AND DECLARATION ARE RECITED.

BORUCH ato Adōnoy   בָּרוּךְ אַתָּה יהוה
Elōhaynu melech ho-ōlom,   אֱלֹהֵינוּ מֶלֶךְ הָעוֹלָם,

Blessed are You, HASHEM, our God, King of the universe,

asher kid'shonu b'mitzvōsov,   אֲשֶׁר קִדְּשָׁנוּ בְּמִצְוֹתָיו,

Who has sanctified us with His commandments

v'tzivonu al mitzvas ayruv.   וְצִוָּנוּ עַל מִצְוַת עֵרוּב.

and has commanded us concerning the mitzvah of eruv.

ALL PRESENT RESPOND: Omayn — אָמֵן

BAHADAYN ayruvo   בַּהֲדֵין עֵרוּבָא
y'hay shoray lono   יְהֵא שָׁרֵא לָנָא

Through this eruv may we be permitted

⋅⋅⋅ Eruvin

The person setting up any of the three types of *eruv* must understand its purpose. Therefore, the declaration which follows the blessing — "Through this *eruv*. . ." — must be understood by the person saying it. Since the *eruv* becomes invalid if the *eruv*-food is lost, eaten up or spoiled, it is important that it be placed in a protected place until it is no longer needed.

⋅⋅⋅ Eruv Tavshilin

The Biblical prohibition against the performance of labor on Festivals (*Exodus* 12:16) does not apply to preparation of food, but the Rabbis

forbade such preparation for another day as demeaning to the Festival. If a Festival falls on a Friday, however, the Sages instituted the following device to permit preparation of fresh food for the Sabbath. The Sabbath food preparation must begin before the Festival starts, and this preparation may be continued on Friday. Thus, on the day before the Festival, one takes a *challah* or matzah along with a cooked food (such as fish, meat, or an egg), holds them while reciting the blessing and declaration, then sets them aside to be eaten on the Sabbath. This is known as *Eruv Tavshilin*, literally, *mingling of cooked foods*, since these foods

la-afuyay ulva-shulay ul-atmunay	לַאֲפוּיֵי וּלְבַשּׁוּלֵי וּלְאַטְמוּנֵי

to bake, cook, insulate,

ul-adlukay sh'rogo ul-sakono	וּלְאַדְלוּקֵי שְׁרָגָא וּלְתַקָּנָא

kindle flame, prepare,

ulmebad kol tzorkono,	וּלְמֶעְבַּד כָּל צָרְכָּנָא,

and do anything necessary

mi-yōmo tovo l'shab'so	מִיּוֹמָא טָבָא לְשַׁבְּתָא

on the Festival for the sake of the Sabbath

[lono ul-chol yisro-ayl	[לָנָא וּלְכָל יִשְׂרָאֵל
hadorim bo-ir ha-zōs].	הַדָּרִים בָּעִיר הַזֹּאת].

[for ourselves and for all Jews who live in this city].

⊰❖ ERUVEI CHATZEIROS ❖⊱

THIS *ERUV* IS REQUIRED FOR THE SABBATH, BUT NOT FOR A WEEKDAY FESTIVAL [SEE COMMENTARY].
THE *ERUV*-FOODS ARE HELD WHILE THE FOLLOWING BLESSING AND DECLARATION ARE RECITED.
[IF THE *ERUV* IS MADE FOR THE ENTIRE YEAR, THE BRACKETED PASSAGE IS ADDED.]

BORUCH ato Adōnoy	**בָּרוּךְ** אַתָּה יהוה
Elōhaynu melech ho-ōlom,	אֱלֹהֵינוּ מֶלֶךְ הָעוֹלָם,

Blessed are You, HASHEM, our God, King of the universe,

asher kid'shonu b'mitzvōsov,	אֲשֶׁר קִדְּשָׁנוּ בְּמִצְוֹתָיו,

Who has sanctified us with His commandments

v'tzivonu al mitzvas ayruv.	וְצִוָּנוּ עַל מִצְוַת עֵרוּב.

and has commanded us concerning the mitzvah of eruv.

ALL PRESENT RESPOND: Omayn — אָמֵן

BAHADAYN ayruvo	**בַּהֲדֵין** עֵרוּבָא
y'hay shoray lono	יְהֵא שָׁרֵא לָנָא

Through this eruv may we be permitted

l'apukay ul-ayulay	לְאַפּוּקֵי וּלְעַיּוּלֵי

to carry out or to carry in

min habotim le-chotzayr,	מִן הַבָּתִּים לֶחָצֵר,
u-min he-chotzayr l'votim,	וּמִן הֶחָצֵר לְבָתִּים,

from the houses to the courtyard, and from the courtyard to the houses,

---

become part of the Sabbath provisions (*Orach Chaim* 527:1-2 according to *Mishnah Berurah;* cf. *Aruch HaShulchan*).

Eruvei Chatzeiros

The Sages forbade carrying from the private domain of one person to that of another on the Sabbath. Such shared areas as courtyards, halls or staircases are regarded as separate domains, and it is forbidden to carry from private dwellings into the shared areas. The *eru-*

vei chatzeiros procedure merges all the houses opening into a shared area into one ownership. This is done by collecting a loaf of bread or a matzah from each of the families and placing all the loaves in one of the dwelling units, to symbolize that all the contributors are residents of that unit. Then all the residents may carry in all its parts on the Sabbath, as long as the breads are intact and edible at the onset of Sabbath. [This procedure does not apply to a

u-miba-yis l'va-yis,   וּמִבַּיִת לְבַיִת,

from house to house,

u-maychotzayr l'chotzayr, u-migag l'gag,   וּמֵחָצֵר לְחָצֵר, וּמִגַּג לְגַג,

from courtyard to courtyard, and from roof to roof,

kol mai ditzrich lon,   כָּל מַאי דִּצְרִיךְ לָן,

all that we require, for ourselves

ulchol yisro-ayl hadorim   וּלְכָל יִשְׂרָאֵל הַדָּרִים

   bash'chuno zu   בַּשְּׁכוּנָה זוּ

and for all Jews who live in this area

[ulchol mi she-yitōsef boh,   [וּלְכָל מִי שֶׁיִּתּוֹסֵף בָּהּ,

and to all who will move into this area,

l'chol shab'sōs hashono,   לְכָל שַׁבְּתוֹת הַשָּׁנָה,

   ul-chol yomim tōvim].   וּלְכָל יָמִים טוֹבִים]

for all the Sabbaths and Festivals of the year.

⚬⊰ ERUVEI TECHUMIN ⊱⚬

THE *ERUV*-FOOD IS PUT IN A SAFE PLACE [SEE COMMENTARY] AND THE FOLLOWING BLESSING AND DECLARATION ARE RECITED. THE APPROPRIATE BRACKETED PHRASES SHOULD BE ADDED.

BORUCH ato Adōnoy   **בָּרוּךְ** אַתָּה יהוה

   Elōhaynu melech ho-ōlom,   אֱלֹהֵינוּ מֶלֶךְ הָעוֹלָם,

Blessed are You, HASHEM, our God, King of the universe,

asher kid'shonu b'mitzvōsov,   אֲשֶׁר קִדְּשָׁנוּ בְּמִצְוֹתָיו,

Who has sanctified us with His commandments

v'tzivonu al mitzvas ayruv.   וְצִוָּנוּ עַל מִצְוַת עֵרוּב.

and has commanded us concerning the mitzvah of eruv.

ALL PRESENT RESPOND: Omayn — אָמֵן

B'ZE ho-ayruv   **בְּזֶה** הָעֵרוּב

   y'hay mutor li/lonu   יְהֵא מֻתָּר [לִי/לָנוּ]

Through this eruv may [I/we] be permitted

laylaych mimokōm ze   לֵילֵךְ מִמָּקוֹם זֶה

   alpa-yim amo l'chol ru-ach   אַלְפַּיִם אַמָּה לְכָל רוּחַ

to walk two thousand cubits in every direction from this place

b'[shabos uv]yōm tōv ze.   בְּ[שַׁבָּת וּבְ]יוֹם טוֹב זֶה.

during this [Sabbath and] Festival.

---

public thoroughfare.]

⚬⊰ **Eruvei Techumin**

On the Sabbath and Festivals, a person is forbidden to go more than 2,000 cubits from his halachically defined dwelling. By placing a sufficient amount of food for two Sabbath meals as much as 2,000 cubits from his residence, one establishes *that* place as his dwelling, and his 2,000-cubits *radius* is reckoned from there. [For a full discussion of *Eruvei Chatzeiros* and *Techumin,* see the Introduction to ArtScroll *Mishnah Eruvin.*]

❧{ FESTIVAL EVE KIDDUSH }❧

ON FRIDAY NIGHT BEGIN HERE; ON OTHER NIGHTS BEGIN BELOW.

■ I offer testimony that the purpose of Hashem's creating
the world in six days was for men to rest on the Shabbos.

THESE FOUR WORDS ARE RECITED IN AN UNDERTONE:

(Vaihi erev vaihi vōker)　　　(וַיְהִי עֶרֶב וַיְהִי בֹקֶר)

(And there was evening and there was morning)

YŌM HA-SHISHI.　　　　.יוֹם הַשִּׁשִּׁי

The sixth day.

Vaichulu ha-shoma-yim v'ho-oretz　　　וַיְכֻלּוּ הַשָּׁמַיִם וְהָאָרֶץ

v'chol tz'vo-om.　　　　.וְכָל צְבָאָם

Thus were finished the heavens and the earth, and all their array.

Vaichal Elōhim ba-yōm hash'vi-i　　　וַיְכַל אֱלֹהִים בַּיּוֹם הַשְּׁבִיעִי

On the seventh day God completed

m'lachtō asher oso,　　　　,מְלַאכְתּוֹ אֲשֶׁר עָשָׂה

His work which He had done,

va-yishbōs ba-yōm hash'vi-i　　　וַיִּשְׁבֹּת בַּיּוֹם הַשְּׁבִיעִי

and He abstained on the seventh day

mikol m'lachtō asher oso.　　　.מִכָּל מְלַאכְתּוֹ אֲשֶׁר עָשָׂה

from all His work which He had done.

Vaivorech Elōhim es　　　　וַיְבָרֶךְ אֱלֹהִים אֶת

yōm hash'vi-i vaikadaysh ōsō,　　יוֹם הַשְּׁבִיעִי וַיְקַדֵּשׁ אֹתוֹ,

God blessed the seventh day and sanctified it,

ki vō shovas miko'l m'lachtō　　　כִּי בוֹ שָׁבַת מִכָּל מְלַאכְתּוֹ

because on it He had abstained from all His work

asher boro Elōhim la-asōs.　　　.אֲשֶׁר בָּרָא אֱלֹהִים לַעֲשׂוֹת

which God created to make.

ON ALL NIGHTS CONTINUE HERE:

Savri moronon v'rabonon v'rabōsai:　　סַבְרִי מָרָנָן וְרַבָּנָן וְרַבּוֹתַי:

By your leave, my masters, rabbis and teachers:

BORUCH ato Adōnoy　　　בָּרוּךְ אַתָּה יהוה

Elōhaynu melech ho-ōlom,　　　אֱלֹהֵינוּ מֶלֶךְ הָעוֹלָם,

Blessed are You, HASHEM, our God, King of the universe,

bōray p'ri hagofen.　　　　.בּוֹרֵא פְּרִי הַגָּפֶן

Who creates the fruit of the vine.

ALL PRESENT RESPOND: Omayn — אָמֵן

KIDDUSH CONTINUES ON FOLLOWING PAGES.

BORUCH ato Adōnoy
    Elōhaynu melech ho-ōlom,
Blessed are You, HASHEM, our God, King of the universe,

בָּרוּךְ אַתָּה יהוה
אֱלֹהֵינוּ מֶלֶךְ הָעוֹלָם,

asher bochar bonu mikol om
    v'rōm'monu mikol loshōn,
Who has chosen us from every people, exalted us above every tongue,

אֲשֶׁר בָּחַר בָּנוּ מִכָּל עָם,
וְרוֹמְמָנוּ מִכָּל לָשׁוֹן,

v'kid'shonu b'mitzvōsov.
and sanctified us with His commandments.

וְקִדְּשָׁנוּ בְּמִצְוֹתָיו.

Vatiten lonu
    Adōnoy Elōhaynu b'ahavo
And You gave us, HASHEM, our God, with love

וַתִּתֶּן לָנוּ
יהוה אֱלֹהֵינוּ בְּאַהֲבָה

ON THE SABBATH ADD:

shabosōs limnucho u . . .
Sabbaths for rest, and

שַׁבָּתוֹת לִמְנוּחָה וּ . . .

mō-adim l'simcho,
    chagim uz'manim l'sosōn,
appointed Festivals for gladness, Festivals and times for joy,

מוֹעֲדִים לְשִׂמְחָה
חַגִּים וּזְמַנִּים לְשָׂשׂוֹן,

ON THE SABBATH ADD:

es yōm ha-shabos ha-ze v' . . .
this day of Sabbath and

אֶת יוֹם הַשַּׁבָּת הַזֶּה וְ . . .

——————— ON PESACH: ———————

es yōm chag hamatzōs ha-ze,
    z'man chayrusaynu,
this day of the Festival of Matzos, the time of our freedom,

אֶת יוֹם חַג הַמַּצּוֹת הַזֶּה,
זְמַן חֵרוּתֵנוּ,

——————— ON SHAVUOS: ———————

es yōm chag hashovu-ōs ha-ze,
    z'man matan tōrosaynu,
this day of the Festival of Shavuos, the time of the giving of our Torah,

אֶת יוֹם חַג הַשָּׁבֻעוֹת הַזֶּה,
זְמַן מַתַּן תּוֹרָתֵנוּ,

——————— ON SUCCOS: ———————

es yōm chag hasukōs ha-ze,
    z'man simchosaynu,
this day of the Festival of Succos, the time of our gladness.

אֶת יוֹם חַג הַסֻּכּוֹת הַזֶּה,
זְמַן שִׂמְחָתֵנוּ,

——— ON SHEMINI ATZERES AND SIMCHAS TORAH: ———

es yōm hash'mini chag ho-atzeres
ha-ze, z'man simchosaynu,
the eighth day, this Festival of the Assembly, the time of our gladness,

אֶת יוֹם הַשְּׁמִינִי חַג הָעֲצֶרֶת
הַזֶּה, זְמַן שִׂמְחָתֵנוּ,

ON THE SABBATH ADD:

b'ahavo
with love,

בְּאַהֲבָה

mikro kōdesh,

מִקְרָא קֹדֶשׁ,

    zaycher litzi-as mitzro-yim.

זֵכֶר לִיצִיאַת מִצְרָיִם.

a holy convocation, a memorial of the Exodus from Egypt.

Ki vonu vocharto,

כִּי בָנוּ בָחַרְתָּ

    v'ōsonu kidashto mikol ho-amim,

וְאוֹתָנוּ קִדַּשְׁתָּ מִכָּל הָעַמִּים,

For You have chosen us and You have sanctified us above all the peoples,

---

ON THE SABBATH ADD:

v'shabos

וְשַׁבָּת

and the Sabbath

---

u-mō-aday kod'shecho

וּמוֹעֲדֵי קָדְשֶׁךָ

and Your holy Festivals

ON THE SABBATH ADD:

b'ahavo uvrotzōn

בְּאַהֲבָה וּבְרָצוֹן

in love and in favor

---

b'simcho uvsosōn hinchaltonu:

בְּשִׂמְחָה וּבְשָׂשׂוֹן הִנְחַלְתָּנוּ.

in gladness and in joy have You granted us as a heritage.

Boruch ato Adōnoy, m'kadaysh

בָּרוּךְ אַתָּה יהוה, מְקַדֵּשׁ

Blessed are You, HASHEM, Who sanctifies

ON THE SABBATH ADD:

hashabos v' . . .

הַשַּׁבָּת וְ . . .

the Sabbath and

---

yisro-ayl v'haz'manim.

יִשְׂרָאֵל וְהַזְּמַנִּים.

Israel and the (festive) seasons.

ALL PRESENT RESPOND: Omayn — אָמֵן

ON SATURDAY NIGHT, TWO CANDLES WITH FLAMES TOUCHING ARE HELD AND THE FOLLOWING BLESSINGS ARE RECITED. AFTER THE FIRST BLESSING, HOLD THE FINGERS UP TO THE FLAMES TO SEE THE REFLECTED LIGHT.

BORUCH ato Adōnoy

בָּרוּךְ אַתָּה יהוה

    Elōhaynu melech ho-ōlom,

אֱלֹהֵינוּ מֶלֶךְ הָעוֹלָם,

Blessed are You, HASHEM, our God, King of the universe,

bōray m'ōray ho-aysh.

בּוֹרֵא מְאוֹרֵי הָאֵשׁ.

Who creates the illumination of the fire.

ALL PRESENT RESPOND: Omayn — אָמֵן

BORUCH ato Adōnoy,

בָּרוּךְ אַתָּה יהוה

    Elōhaynu melech ho-ōlom,

אֱלֹהֵינוּ מֶלֶךְ הָעוֹלָם,

Blessed are You, HASHEM, our God, King of the universe,

hamavdil bayn kōdesh l'chōl,

הַמַּבְדִּיל בֵּין קֹדֶשׁ לְחוֹל,

Who distinguishes between the sacred and secular,

bayn ōr l'chōshech,
בֵּין אוֹר לְחֹשֶׁךְ,

  bayn yisro-ayl lo-amim,
בֵּין יִשְׂרָאֵל לָעַמִּים,

between light and darkness, between Israel and the peoples,

bayn yōm hash'vi-i,
בֵּין יוֹם הַשְּׁבִיעִי

  l'shayshes y'may hama-ase,
לְשֵׁשֶׁת יְמֵי הַמַּעֲשֶׂה.

between the Seventh Day and the six days of labor.

bayn k'dushas shabos
בֵּין קְדֻשַּׁת שַׁבָּת

  likdushas yōm tōv hivdalto,
לִקְדֻשַּׁת יוֹם טוֹב הִבְדַּלְתָּ,

Between the sanctity of the Sabbath and the sanctity of the holidays
You have distinguished,

v'es yōm hash'vi-i mi-shayshes
וְאֶת יוֹם הַשְּׁבִיעִי מִשֵּׁשֶׁת

  y'may hama-ase kidashto,
יְמֵי הַמַּעֲשֶׂה קִדַּשְׁתָּ,

and the Seventh Day, from among the six days of labor You have sanctified.

hivdalto v'kidashto es
הִבְדַּלְתָּ וְקִדַּשְׁתָּ אֶת

  am'cho yisro-ayl bikdushosecho.
עַמְּךָ יִשְׂרָאֵל בִּקְדֻשָּׁתֶךָ.

You have distinguished and You have sanctified Your people Israel
with Your holiness.

Boruch ato Adōnoy
בָּרוּךְ אַתָּה יהוה,

  hamavdil bayn kōdesh l'kōdesh.
הַמַּבְדִּיל בֵּין קֹדֶשׁ לְקֹדֶשׁ.

Blessed are You, HASHEM, Who distinguishes between holiness and holiness.

ALL PRESENT RESPOND: Omayn — אָמֵן

ON SUCCOS THE FOLLOWING BLESSING IS RECITED IN THE *SUCCAH.*

BORUCH ato Adōnoy
בָּרוּךְ אַתָּה יהוה

  Elōhaynu melech ho-ōlom,
אֱלֹהֵינוּ מֶלֶךְ הָעוֹלָם,

Blessed are You, HASHEM, our God, King of the universe,

asher kid'shonu b'mitzvōsov
אֲשֶׁר קִדְּשָׁנוּ בְּמִצְוֹתָיו

Who has sanctified us with His commandments

v'tzivonu layshayv basuko.
וְצִוָּנוּ לֵישֵׁב בַּסֻּכָּה.

and has commanded us to dwell in the succah.

ALL PRESENT RESPOND: Omayn — אָמֵן

THE FOLLOWING BLESSING IS OMITTED ON THE LAST TWO NIGHTS OF PESACH.

BORUCH ato Adōnoy
בָּרוּךְ אַתָּה יהוה

  Elōhaynu melech ho-ōlom,
אֱלֹהֵינוּ מֶלֶךְ הָעוֹלָם,

Blessed are You, HASHEM, our God, King of the universe,

shehecheyonu v'ki-y'monu
שֶׁהֶחֱיָנוּ וְקִיְּמָנוּ

  v'higi-onu laz'man ha-ze.
וְהִגִּיעָנוּ לַזְּמַן הַזֶּה.

Who has kept us alive, sustained us, and brought us to this season.

ALL PRESENT RESPOND: Omayn — אָמֵן

⊰ SHEMONEH ESREI FOR THE FESTIVALS ⊱

THIS *SHEMONEH ESREI* IS RECITED AT *MAARIV, SHACHARIS* AND *MINCHAH* ON THE FESTIVAL DAYS OF
PESACH, SHAVUOS AND SUCCOS. ON *CHOL HAMOED* THE WEEKDAY (OR SABBATH) *SHEMONEH ESREI* IS
RECITED. THE *SHEMONEH ESREI* FOR *MUSSAF* MAY BE FOUND ON P. 708.

IN THE SYNAGOGUE THE *SHEMONEH ESREI* IS RECITED WHILE FACING THE ARK; ELSEWHERE IT IS RECITED
WHILE FACING THE DIRECTION OF THE LAND OF ISRAEL. TAKE THREE STEPS BACKWARD, LEFT, RIGHT, LEFT,
THEN THREE STEPS FORWARD, RIGHT, LEFT, RIGHT. REMAIN STANDING WITH FEET TOGETHER DURING
SHEMONEH ESREI. RECITE IT WITH QUIET DEVOTION AND WITHOUT ANY INTERRUPTION. ALTHOUGH IT
SHOULD NOT BE AUDIBLE TO OTHERS, ONE MUST PRAY LOUDLY ENOUGH TO HEAR ONESELF.

──────────── AT *MINCHAH*, THE FOLLOWING VERSE IS ADDED: ────────────

Ki shaym Adōnoy ekro,   כִּי שֵׁם יהוה אֶקְרָא,

   hovu gōdel Laylōhaynu.   הָבוּ גֹדֶל לֵאלֹהֵינוּ.

When I call out the Name of HASHEM, *ascribe greatness to our God.*

Adōnoy s'fosai tiftoch,   אֲדֹנָי שְׂפָתַי תִּפְתָּח,

   u-fi yagid t'hilosecho.   וּפִי יַגִּיד תְּהִלָּתֶךָ.

My Lord, open my lips, that my mouth may declare Your praise.

■ First Blessing: In the merit of our Patriarchs whose actions reflected Godliness,
   Hashem pledged to always be with Israel and protect them.

BEND THE KNEES AT Boruch; BOW AT ato; STRAIGHTEN UP AT Adōnoy.

BORUCH ato Adōnoy   בָּרוּךְ אַתָּה יהוה

Blessed are You, HASHEM,

Elōhaynu Vaylōhay avōsaynu,   אֱלֹהֵינוּ וֵאלֹהֵי אֲבוֹתֵינוּ,

our God and the God of our forefathers,

Elōhay avrohom, Elōhay yitzchok,   אֱלֹהֵי אַבְרָהָם, אֱלֹהֵי יִצְחָק,

   Vaylōhay ya-akōv,   וֵאלֹהֵי יַעֲקֹב,

God of Abraham, God of Isaac, and God of Jacob;

ho-Ayl hagodōl hagibōr v'hanōro,   הָאֵל הַגָּדוֹל הַגִּבּוֹר וְהַנּוֹרָא,

   Ayl elyōn,   אֵל עֶלְיוֹן,

the great, mighty, and awesome God, the supreme God,

gōmayl chasodim tōvim   גּוֹמֵל חֲסָדִים טוֹבִים

   v'kōnay hakōl,   וְקוֹנֵה הַכֹּל,

Who bestows beneficial kindnesses and creates everything,

v'zōchayr chasday ovōs,   וְזוֹכֵר חַסְדֵי אָבוֹת,

Who recalls the kindnesses of the Patriarchs

u-mayvi gō-ayl livnay v'nayhem,   וּמֵבִיא גוֹאֵל לִבְנֵי בְנֵיהֶם,

and brings a Redeemer to their children's children,

l'ma-an sh'mō b'ahavo.   לְמַעַן שְׁמוֹ בְּאַהֲבָה.

for His Name's sake, with love.

Melech ōzayr u-mōshi-a u-mogayn.　מֶלֶךְ עוֹזֵר וּמוֹשִׁיעַ וּמָגֵן.

O King, Helper, Savior, and Shield.

BEND THE KNEES AT *Boruch*; BOW AT *ato*; STRAIGHTEN UP AT Adōnoy.

Boruch ato Adōnoy,　בָּרוּךְ אַתָּה יהוה,

　　mogayn avrohom.　מָגֵן אַבְרָהָם.

Blessed are You, HASHEM, Shield of Abraham.

■ Second Blessing: God's might as it is manifest in nature and man

ATO gibōr l'ōlom Adōnoy,　**אַתָּה** גִבּוֹר לְעוֹלָם אֲדֹנָי,

You are eternally mighty, my Lord,

m'cha-yay maysim ato,　מְחַיֶּה מֵתִים אַתָּה,

the Resuscitator of the dead are You;

rav l'hōshi-a.　רַב לְהוֹשִׁיעַ.

abundantly able to save,

AT *MINCHAH* OF SHEMINI ATZERES; ALL PRAYERS OF SIMCHAS TORAH; AND *MAARIV* AND *SHACHARIS* OF THE FIRST DAY OF PESACH, ADD THE FOLLOWING PHRASE:

Mashiv horu-ach u-mōrid hageshem.　מַשִּׁיב הָרוּחַ וּמוֹרִיד הַגֶּשֶׁם.

Who makes the wind blow and makes the rain descend;

M'chalkayl cha-yim b'chesed,　מְכַלְכֵּל חַיִּים בְּחֶסֶד,

Who sustains the living with kindness,

m'cha-yay maysim b'rachamim rabim,　מְחַיֶּה מֵתִים בְּרַחֲמִים רַבִּים,

resuscitates the dead with abundant mercy,

sōmaych nōf'lim, v'rōfay chōlim,　סוֹמֵךְ נוֹפְלִים, וְרוֹפֵא חוֹלִים,

　　u-matir asurim,　וּמַתִּיר אֲסוּרִים,

supports the fallen, heals the sick, releases the confined,

umka-yaym emunosō li-shaynay ofor.　וּמְקַיֵּם אֱמוּנָתוֹ לִישֵׁנֵי עָפָר.

and maintains His faith to those asleep in the dust.

Mi cho-mōcho ba-al g'vurōs,　מִי כָמוֹךָ בַּעַל גְּבוּרוֹת,

　　u-mi dōme loch,　וּמִי דוֹמֶה לָּךְ,

Who is like You, O Master of mighty deeds, and who is comparable to You,

melech maymis umcha-ye　מֶלֶךְ מֵמִית וּמְחַיֶּה

　　u-matzmi-ach y'shu-o.　וּמַצְמִיחַ יְשׁוּעָה.

O King Who causes death and restores life and makes salvation sprout!

V'ne-emon ato l'hacha-yōs maysim.　וְנֶאֱמָן אַתָּה לְהַחֲיוֹת מֵתִים.

And You are faithful to resuscitate the dead.

Boruch ato Adōnoy,　בָּרוּךְ אַתָּה יהוה,

Blessed are You, HASHEM,

m'cha-yay hamaysim.   מְחַיֵּה הַמֵּתִים.

Who resuscitates the dead.

DURING THE *CHAZZAN'S* REPETITION, *KEDUSHAH* (BELOW) IS RECITED AT THIS POINT.
INDIVIDUALS CONTINUE ato kodōsh (AT THE BOTTOM OF PAGE 679).

■ Third Blessing: Regarding the holiness of God's Name

THE FOLLOWING *KEDUSHAH* IS RECITED AT *MINCHAH*; AT *SHACHARIS*, TURN TO PAGE 678.

STAND WITH FEET TOGETHER AND AVOID ANY INTERRUPTIONS. RISE ON TOES
WHEN SAYING Kodōsh, kodōsh, kodōsh; Boruch; AND Yimlōch.

CONGREGATION, THEN *CHAZZAN*:

N'KADAYSH es shimcho bo-ōlom,   נְקַדֵּשׁ אֶת שִׁמְךָ בָּעוֹלָם,

We shall sanctify Your Name in this world,

k'shaym shemakdishim ōsō   כְּשֵׁם שֶׁמַּקְדִּישִׁים אוֹתוֹ

bishmay morōm,   בִּשְׁמֵי מָרוֹם,

just as they sanctify it in heaven above,

kakosuv al yad n'vi-echo,   כַּכָּתוּב עַל יַד נְבִיאֶךָ,

as it is written by Your prophet,

v'koro ze el ze v'omar: וְקָרָא זֶה אֶל זֶה וְאָמַר:

"And one [angel] will call another and say:

ALL IN UNISON:

Kodōsh, kodōsh, kodōsh   קָדוֹשׁ קָדוֹשׁ קָדוֹשׁ

Adōnoy Tz'vo-ōs,   יהוה צְבָאוֹת,

'*Holy, holy, holy is* HASHEM, *Master of Legions,*

m'lō chol ho-oretz k'vōdō.   מְלֹא כָל הָאָרֶץ כְּבוֹדוֹ.

the whole world is filled with His glory.'"

CHAZZAN:

L'u-mosom boruch yōmayru: לְעֻמָּתָם בָּרוּךְ יֹאמֵרוּ:

Those facing them say, "Blessed":

ALL IN UNISON:

Boruch k'vōd Adōnoy, mim'kōmo.   בָּרוּךְ כְּבוֹד יהוה, מִמְּקוֹמוֹ.

"Blessed is the glory of HASHEM *from His place."*

CHAZZAN:

Uvdivray kodsh'cho kosuv laymōr: וּבְדִבְרֵי קָדְשְׁךָ כָּתוּב לֵאמֹר:

And in Your holy Writings the following is written:

ALL IN UNISON:

Yimlōch Adōnoy l'ōlom,   יִמְלֹךְ יהוה לְעוֹלָם,

*"*HASHEM *shall reign forever —*

Elōha-yich tziyōn l'dōr vodōr,   אֱלֹהַיִךְ צִיּוֹן לְדֹר וָדֹר,

hal'luyoh.   הַלְלוּיָהּ.

your God, O Zion — from generation to generation: Praise God!"

THE *CHAZZAN* CONTINUES לְדוֹר וָדוֹר (PAGE 679).

THE FOLLOWING *KEDUSHAH* IS RECITED AT *SHACHARIS*.

STAND WITH FEET TOGETHER AND AVOID ANY INTERRUPTIONS. RISE ON TOES
WHEN SAYING Kodōsh, kodōsh, kodōsh; Boruch; AND Yimlōch.

CONGREGATION, THEN *CHAZZAN*:

N'KADAYSH es shimcho bo-ōlom,　　נְקַדֵּשׁ אֶת שִׁמְךָ בָּעוֹלָם,

We shall sanctify Your Name in this world,

k'shaym shemakdishim ōsō　　כְּשֵׁם שֶׁמַּקְדִּישִׁים אוֹתוֹ

bishmay morōm,　　בִּשְׁמֵי מָרוֹם,

just as they sanctify it in heaven above,

kakosuv al yad n'vi-echo,　　כַּכָּתוּב עַל יַד נְבִיאֶךָ,

as it is written by the hand of Your prophet,

v'koro ze el ze v'omar:　　וְקָרָא זֶה אֶל זֶה וְאָמַר:

"And one [angel] will call another and say:

ALL IN UNISON:

Kodōsh, kodōsh, kodōsh　　קָדוֹשׁ קָדוֹשׁ קָדוֹשׁ

Adōnoy Tz'vo-ōs,　　יהוה צְבָאוֹת,

'Holy, holy, holy is HASHEM, *Master of Legions,*

m'lō chol ho-oretz k'vōdō.　　מְלֹא כָל הָאָרֶץ כְּבוֹדוֹ.

the whole world is filled with His glory.'"

CONGREGATION, THEN *CHAZZAN*:

Oz b'kōl ra-ash godōl　　אָז בְּקוֹל רַעַשׁ גָּדוֹל

adir v'chozok mashmi-im kōl,　　אַדִּיר וְחָזָק מַשְׁמִיעִים קוֹל,

Then, with a sound of great noise, mighty and powerful,
they make heard a voice,

misnas'im l'umas s'rofim,　　מִתְנַשְּׂאִים לְעֻמַּת שְׂרָפִים,

raising themselves toward the Seraphim;

l'u-mosom boruch yōmayru:　　לְעֻמָּתָם בָּרוּךְ יֹאמֵרוּ:

those facing them say, "Blessed . . .":

ALL IN UNISON:

Boruch k'vōd Adōnoy, mim'kōmō.　　בָּרוּךְ כְּבוֹד יהוה, מִמְּקוֹמוֹ.

"Blessed is the glory of HASHEM *from His place."*

CONGREGATION, THEN *CHAZZAN*:

Mim'kōm'cho malkaynu sōfi-a,　　מִמְּקוֹמְךָ מַלְכֵּנוּ תוֹפִיעַ,

From Your place, our King, You will appear

v'simlōch olaynu,　　וְתִמְלֹךְ עָלֵינוּ,

and reign over us,

ki m'chakim anachnu loch.　　כִּי מְחַכִּים אֲנַחְנוּ לָךְ.

for we await You.

Mosai timlōch b'tziyōn,　　מָתַי תִּמְלֹךְ בְּצִיּוֹן,

When will You reign in Zion?

b'koróv b'yomaynu,

Soon, in our days —

בְּקָרוֹב בְּיָמֵינוּ,

l'ólom vo-ed tishkón.

forever and ever — may You dwell there.

לְעוֹלָם וָעֶד תִּשְׁכּוֹן.

Tisgadal v'siskadash

May You be exalted and sanctified

תִּתְגַּדַּל וְתִתְקַדַּשׁ

b'sóch y'rushola-yim ir'cho,

within Jerusalem, Your city,

בְּתוֹךְ יְרוּשָׁלַיִם עִירָךְ,

l'dór vodór ulnaytzach n'tzochim.

from generation to generation and for all eternity.

לְדוֹר וָדוֹר וּלְנֵצַח נְצָחִים.

V'aynaynu sir-eno malchusecho,

May our eyes see Your kingdom,

וְעֵינֵינוּ תִרְאֶינָה מַלְכוּתֶךָ,

kadovor ho-omur b'shiray u-zecho,

as it is expressed in the songs of Your might,

כַּדָּבָר הָאָמוּר בְּשִׁירֵי עֻזֶּךָ,

al y'day dovid m'shi-ach tzidkecho:

written by David, Your righteous anointed:

עַל יְדֵי דָוִד מְשִׁיחַ צִדְקֶךָ:

ALL IN UNISON:

Yimlóch Adónoy l'ólom,

"HASHEM shall reign forever;

יִמְלֹךְ יהוה לְעוֹלָם,

Elóha-yich tziyón l'dór vodór,

your God, O Zion, from generation to generation.

אֱלֹהַיִךְ צִיּוֹן לְדֹר וָדֹר,

hal'luyoh.

Praise God!"

הַלְלוּיָהּ.

CHAZZAN CONCLUDES:

לְדוֹר וָדוֹר נַגִּיד גָּדְלֶךָ וּלְנֵצַח נְצָחִים קְדֻשָּׁתְךָ נַקְדִּישׁ, וְשִׁבְחֲךָ אֱלֹהֵינוּ מִפִּינוּ לֹא יָמוּשׁ לְעוֹלָם וָעֶד, כִּי אֵל מֶלֶךְ גָּדוֹל וְקָדוֹשׁ אָתָּה. בָּרוּךְ אַתָּה יהוה, הָאֵל הַקָּדוֹשׁ.

THE *CHAZZAN* CONTINUES Ato v'chartonu (P. 680).

INDIVIDUALS CONTINUE HERE:

ATO kodósh v'shimcho kodósh,

You are holy and Your Name is holy,

אַתָּה קָדוֹשׁ וְשִׁמְךָ קָדוֹשׁ,

ukdóshim b'chol yóm

y'hal'lucho, selo.

and holy ones praise You, every day, forever.

וּקְדוֹשִׁים בְּכָל יוֹם

יְהַלְלוּךָ סֶּלָה.

Boruch ato Adónoy,

ho-Ayl hakodósh.

Blessed are You, HASHEM, the holy God.

בָּרוּךְ אַתָּה יהוה,

הָאֵל הַקָּדוֹשׁ.

■ I reflect with gratitude upon the chosenness that Hashem has granted the Jewish people — endowing us with privileges as well as Divine purpose.

ATO V'CHARTONU
אַתָּה בְחַרְתָּנוּ
You have chosen us

mikol ho-amim,
מִכָּל הָעַמִּים,
from all the peoples;

ohavto ōsonu, v'rotziso bonu,
אֲהַבְתָּ אוֹתָנוּ, וְרָצִיתָ בָּנוּ,
You loved us and found favor in us;

v'rōmamtonu mikol hal'shōnōs,
וְרוֹמַמְתָּנוּ מִכָּל הַלְּשׁוֹנוֹת,
*You exalted us above all the tongues**

v'kidashtonu b'mitzvōsecho,
וְקִדַּשְׁתָּנוּ בְּמִצְוֹתֶיךָ,
*and You sanctified us with Your commandments.**

v'kayravtonu malkaynu
la-avōdosecho,
וְקֵרַבְתָּנוּ מַלְכֵּנוּ
לַעֲבוֹדָתֶךָ,
You drew us close, our King, to Your service

v'shimcho hagodōl v'hakodōsh
olaynu koroso.
וְשִׁמְךָ הַגָּדוֹל וְהַקָּדוֹשׁ
עָלֵינוּ קָרָאתָ.
*and proclaimed Your great and Holy Name upon us.**

◄§ **The Festival Prayers**

Unlike the *Shemoneh Esrei* prayers of the Sabbath that concentrate primarily on the sanctity of the day, the Festival prayers stress Israel's status as God's Chosen People. The Sabbath derives its holiness from God Who rested on the seventh day of Creation; its holiness predated Israel and is in no way dependent on the Jewish people. The Festivals, on the other hand, commemorate the history of Israel. Although the Sabbath, as the testimony to God the Creator, could exist without the Jewish people, there could not be any Festivals unless there had been a nation that was freed from Egypt, given the Torah and sheltered in the wilderness. This emphasis is apparent from the very start of the middle section of the Festival *Shemoneh Esrei,* which declares that God has chosen Israel from among the nations, a concept that is absent from the Sabbath *Shemoneh Esrei.*

Furthermore, since the Festivals are dependent on the sanctification of the months — which the Torah assigns to the Jewish courts — the Festivals are creatures of the Jewish people, as it were. Another feature unique to the Festivals is that joy is an integral part of their observance. Both of these features are reflected in the *Shemoneh Esrei.*

מִכָּל הַלְּשׁוֹנוֹת — *Above all the tongues.* Human language is capable of capturing sublime thoughts and complex ideas, but Israel was granted the language of the Torah, which encompasses God's own wisdom and which is uniquely suited to expressing concepts of holiness.

וְקִדַּשְׁתָּנוּ בְּמִצְוֹתֶיךָ — *And You sanctified us with Your commandments.* Unlike the laws of human legislatures and monarchs, the laws of the Torah infuse holiness into those who observe them.

וְשִׁמְךָ . . . עָלֵינוּ קָרָאתָ — *And proclaimed Your . . . Name upon us.* We are proud and grateful that God wished to be known as the God of Israel.

The three expressions at the beginning of this paragraph — *chosen, loved,* and *found favor* — allude to the respective historical characteristics of the three pilgrimage festivals, which will be named in וַתִּתֶּן לָנוּ, *And You gave us.* On Pesach, God chose us from among the Egyptians; on Shavuos, He showed His love for us by giving us His Torah; and on Succos, He showed us favor for forgiving the sin of the Golden Calf and bringing us into the Divine shelter.

■ This passage expresses our understanding of the difference between the greater sanctity of Shabbos as compared to the sanctity of *Yom Tov*. A primary manifestation of this distinction is the permissibility of cooking or preparing food on *Yom Tov*.

ON SATURDAY NIGHT THE FOLLOWING IS RECITED.

VATÔDI-AYNU Adōnoy Elōhaynu · וַתּוֹדִיעֵנוּ יהוה אֱלֹהֵינוּ
es mishp'tay tzidkecho, · אֶת מִשְׁפְּטֵי צִדְקֶךָ,
You have made known to us,* HASHEM, our God, Your righteous ordinances,

vat'lam'daynu la-asōs (bohem) · וַתְּלַמְּדֵנוּ לַעֲשׂוֹת (בָּהֶם)
chukay r'tzōnecho. · חֻקֵּי רְצוֹנֶךָ.
and You taught us to do the decrees of Your will.

Vatiten lonu Adōnoy Elōhaynu · וַתִּתֶּן לָנוּ יהוה אֱלֹהֵינוּ
You gave us,* HASHEM, our God,

mishpotim y'shorim v'sōrōs emes, · מִשְׁפָּטִים יְשָׁרִים וְתוֹרוֹת אֱמֶת,
chukim u-mitzvōs tōvim. · חֻקִּים וּמִצְוֹת טוֹבִים.
fair laws and true teachings, good decrees and commandments.

Vatanchilaynu z'manay sosōn · וַתַּנְחִילֵנוּ זְמַנֵּי שָׂשׂוֹן
As a heritage You gave us seasons of joy,

u-mō-aday kōdesh v'chagay n'dovo. · וּמוֹעֲדֵי קֹדֶשׁ וְחַגֵּי נְדָבָה.
appointed Festivals of holiness, and free-willed festive-offerings.*

Vatōrishaynu k'dushas shabos · וַתּוֹרִישֵׁנוּ קְדֻשַּׁת שַׁבָּת
You made us heir to the Sabbath holiness,

uchvōd mō-ayd vachagigas horegel. · וּכְבוֹד מוֹעֵד וַחֲגִיגַת הָרֶגֶל.
the appointed Festival glory, and festive-offering of the pilgrimage.

Vatavdayl Adōnoy Elōhaynu · וַתַּבְדֵּל יהוה אֱלֹהֵינוּ
You distinguished, O HASHEM, our God,

bayn kōdesh l'chōl, · בֵּין קֹדֶשׁ לְחוֹל,
between the sacred and secular,

bayn ōr l'chōshech, · בֵּין אוֹר לְחֹשֶׁךְ,
between light and darkness,

וַתּוֹדִיעֵנוּ — *You have made known to us.* Despite the great sanctity of the Festivals, they are less holy than the Sabbath, hence the requirement that *Havdalah* be recited here in *Shemoneh Esrei* and again as part of the *Kiddush*.

וַתִּתֶּן לָנוּ — *You gave us.* God gave us many commandments of various kinds: some that are comprehensible to the human mind, and others that are beyond our comprehension; some that teach us to perceive our proper role in Creation, and others that regulate all facets of our behavior in a manner that will bring us

closer to His service. The Sabbaths and Festivals are uniquely suited to inspire us with renewed sanctity to strive toward the fulfillment of the tasks God has set for us.

זְמַנֵּי שָׂשׂוֹן וּמוֹעֲדֵי קֹדֶשׁ וְחַגֵּי נְדָבָה — *Seasons of joy, appointed Festivals of holiness, and free-willed festive-offerings.* These three terms refer to three aspects of the Festivals. Firstly, they are seasons of joy as regards the agricultural cycle: Pesach comes in springtime; Shavuos ushers in the time of the first fruits; and Succos is the festive season of harvest. Secondly, they are

bayn yisro-ayl lo-amim,   בֵּין יִשְׂרָאֵל לָעַמִּים,
between Israel and the peoples,

bayn yōm hash'vi-i   בֵּין יוֹם הַשְּׁבִיעִי
l'shayshes y'may hama-ase.   לְשֵׁשֶׁת יְמֵי הַמַּעֲשֶׂה.
between the Seventh Day and six days of labor.

Bayn k'dushas shabos   בֵּין קְדֻשַּׁת שַׁבָּת
likdushas yōm tōv hivdalto,   לִקְדֻשַּׁת יוֹם טוֹב הִבְדַּלְתָּ,
Between the sanctity of the Sabbath and the sanctity of the holiday
You have distinguished;

v'es yōm hash'vi-i   וְאֶת יוֹם הַשְּׁבִיעִי
and the Seventh Day,

mi-shayshes y'may hama-ase   מִשֵּׁשֶׁת יְמֵי הַמַּעֲשֶׂה
kidashto,   קִדַּשְׁתָּ,
from among the six days of labor You have sanctified.

hivdalto v'kidashto   הִבְדַּלְתָּ וְקִדַּשְׁתָּ
es am'cho yisro-ayl   אֶת עַמְּךָ יִשְׂרָאֵל
You have distinguished and You have sanctified Your people Israel

bikdusho-secho.   בִּקְדֻשָּׁתֶךָ.
with Your holiness.

■ I express my profound appreciation for the privilege of celebrating each of the Biblical holidays with both prayer and Torah study, as well as with family and friends, thereby experiencing the joy of the day.

VATITEN LONU Adōnoy Elōhaynu   **וַתִּתֶּן לָנוּ** יהוה אֱלֹהֵינוּ
b'ahavo   בְּאַהֲבָה
And You gave us, HASHEM, our God, with love

ON THE SABBATH ADD:
shabosōs limnucho u . . .   שַׁבָּתוֹת לִמְנוּחָה וּ . . .
[Sabbaths for rest], and

mō-adim l'simcho,   מוֹעֲדִים לְשִׂמְחָה
appointed Festivals for gladness,

chagim uz'manim l'sosōn,   חַגִּים וּזְמַנִּים לְשָׂשׂוֹן,
Festivals and times for joy,

ON THE SABBATH ADD:
es yōm hashabos ha-ze v' . . .   אֶת יוֹם הַשַּׁבָּת הַזֶּה וְ . . .
this day of Sabbath and

appointed as Festivals because of their historical significance: Pesach commemorates the Exodus; Shavuos recalls the Revelation at Sinai; and Succos reminds us that God sheltered us in the wilderness. Finally these three terms recall the three kinds of offerings, expressing both

es yōm chag hamatzōs ha-ze,
z'man chayrusaynu,

אֶת יוֹם חַג הַמַּצּוֹת הַזֶּה,
זְמַן חֵרוּתֵנוּ,

this day of the Festival of Matzos, the time of our freedom,

es yōm chag hashovu-ōs ha-ze,
z'man matan tōrosaynu,

אֶת יוֹם חַג הַשָּׁבֻעוֹת הַזֶּה,
זְמַן מַתַּן תּוֹרָתֵנוּ,

this day of the Festival of Shavuos, the time of the giving of our Torah,

es yōm chag hasukōs ha-ze,
z'man simchosaynu,

אֶת יוֹם חַג הַסֻּכּוֹת הַזֶּה,
זְמַן שִׂמְחָתֵנוּ,

this day of the Festival of Succos, the time of our gladness,

es yōm hash'mini chag ho-atzeres
ha-ze, z'man simchosaynu,

אֶת יוֹם הַשְּׁמִינִי חַג הָעֲצֶרֶת
הַזֶּה, זְמַן שִׂמְחָתֵנוּ,

the eighth day, this Festival of the Assembly, the time of our gladness,

	ON THE SABBATH ADD:	
b'ahavo		בְּאַהֲבָה
	*with love,**	

mikro kōdesh,

מִקְרָא קֹדֶשׁ,

*a holy convocation,**

zaycher litzi-as mitzro-yim.

זֵכֶר לִיצִיאַת מִצְרָיִם.

a memorial of the Exodus from Egypt.

ELŌHAYNU Vaylōhay avōsaynu,

אֱלֹהֵינוּ וֵאלֹהֵי אֲבוֹתֵינוּ,

Our God and God of our forefathers,

ya-a-le v'yovō v'yagi-a v'yayro-e

יַעֲלֶה, וְיָבֹא, וְיַגִּיעַ, וְיֵרָאֶה,

may there rise, come, reach, be noted,

v'yayro-tze v'yi-shoma v'yipokayd

וְיֵרָצֶה, וְיִשָּׁמַע, וְיִפָּקֵד,

be favored, be heard, be considered,

v'yizochayr zichrōnaynu u-fikdōnaynu,

וְיִזָּכֵר זִכְרוֹנֵנוּ וּפִקְדוֹנֵנוּ,

and be remembered — the remembrance and consideration of ourselves;

v'zichrōn avōsaynu,

וְזִכְרוֹן אֲבוֹתֵינוּ,

the remembrance of our forefathers;

---

devotion and joy, that were offered by the multitudes of Jews who came to Jerusalem for each of the three annual pilgrimage Festivals.

בְּאַהֲבָה — *With love.* The extra expression of love referring only to the Sabbath denotes the particular affection with which Israel accepted

the commandments of the Sabbath. Whereas the Festival observance represents our acknowledgment of God's kindness to our ancestors, the Sabbath shows our desire to honor Him as the Creator.

מִקְרָא קֹדֶשׁ — *A holy convocation.* On these days,

v'zichrōn moshi-ach ben dovid avdecho,

וְזִכְרוֹן מָשִׁיחַ בֶּן דָּוִד עַבְדֶּךָ,

the remembrance of Messiah, son of David, Your servant;

v'zichrōn y'rushola-yim ir kod-shecho,

וְזִכְרוֹן יְרוּשָׁלַיִם עִיר קָדְשֶׁךָ,

the remembrance of Jerusalem, the City of Your Holiness;

v'zichrōn kol am'cho bays yisro-ayl l'fonecho,

וְזִכְרוֹן כָּל עַמְּךָ בֵּית יִשְׂרָאֵל לְפָנֶיךָ,

and the remembrance of Your entire people the Family of Israel — before You

lif-layto l'tōvo

לִפְלֵיטָה לְטוֹבָה

for deliverance, for goodness,

l'chayn ulchesed ulrachamim,

לְחֵן וּלְחֶסֶד וּלְרַחֲמִים,

for grace, for kindness, and for compassion,

l'cha-yim ulsholōm

לְחַיִּים וּלְשָׁלוֹם

for life, and for peace

———————— ON PESACH ————————

b'yōm chag hamatzōs ha-ze.

בְּיוֹם חַג הַמַּצּוֹת הַזֶּה.

on this day of the Festival of Matzos.

———————— ON SHAVUOS ————————

b'yōm chag hashovuos ha-ze.

בְּיוֹם חַג הַשָּׁבֻעוֹת הַזֶּה.

on this day of the Festival of Shavuos.

———————— ON SUCCOS ————————

b'yōm chag hasukōs ha-ze.

בְּיוֹם חַג הַסֻּכּוֹת הַזֶּה.

on this day of the Succos Festival.

———— ON SHEMINI ATZERES AND SIMCHAS TORAH ————

b'yōm hash'mini chag ho-atzeress ha-ze.

בְּיוֹם הַשְּׁמִינִי חַג הָעֲצֶרֶת הַזֶּה.

on the eighth day, this Festival of the Assembly.

zoch-raynu Adōnoy Elōhaynu bō l'tōvo,

זָכְרֵנוּ יהוה אֱלֹהֵינוּ בּוֹ לְטוֹבָה,

Remember us on it, HASHEM, our God, for goodness,

u-fokdaynu vō livrocho,

וּפָקְדֵנוּ בּוֹ לִבְרָכָה,

consider us on it for blessing

v'hōshi-aynu vō l'cha-yim.

וְהוֹשִׁיעֵנוּ בּוֹ לְחַיִּים.

and help us on it for life.

U-vidvar y'shu-o v'rachamim,

וּבִדְבַר יְשׁוּעָה וְרַחֲמִים,

In the matter of salvation and compassion

——————————————————————

the nation is called upon to gather for the pursuit of holiness, and to sanctify the Festival through prayer and praise to God.

chus v'chonaynu   חוּס וְחָנֵּנוּ

v'rachaym olaynu v'hōshi-aynu,   וְרַחֵם עָלֵינוּ וְהוֹשִׁיעֵנוּ,

pity, be gracious and compassionate with us and help us,

ki aylecho aynaynu,   כִּי אֵלֶיךָ עֵינֵינוּ,

for our eyes are turned to You,

ki Ayl melech chanun v'rachum oto.   כִּי אֵל מֶלֶךְ חַנּוּן וְרַחוּם אָתָּה.

because You are God, the gracious and compassionate King.

■ May the blessings, happiness and tranquility of the holidays permanently impact upon and enhance my commitment to Hashem.

V'HASI-AYNU Adōnoy Elōhaynu   וְהַשִּׂיאֵנוּ יהוה אֱלֹהֵינוּ

Bestow upon us, O Hashem, our God,

es birkas mō-adecho   אֶת בִּרְכַּת מוֹעֲדֶיךָ

the blessing of Your appointed Festivals

l'cha-yim ulsholōm,   לְחַיִּים וּלְשָׁלוֹם,

l'simcho ulsosōn,   לְשִׂמְחָה וּלְשָׂשׂוֹן,

for life and for peace, for gladness and for joy,

ka-asher rotziso   כַּאֲשֶׁר רָצִיתָ

v'omarto l'vor'chaynu,   וְאָמַרְתָּ לְבָרְכֵנוּ.

as You desired and promised to bless us.

ON THE SABBATH ADD:

Elōhaynu Vaylōhay avōsaynu   אֱלֹהֵינוּ וֵאלֹהֵי אֲבוֹתֵינוּ

Our God and the God of our forefathers,

r'tzay vimnucho-saynu.   רְצֵה בִמְנוּחָתֵנוּ

may You be pleased with our rest.

Kad'shaynu b'mitzvōsecho   קַדְּשֵׁנוּ בְּמִצְוֹתֶיךָ

v'sayn chelkaynu b'sōrosecho,   וְתֵן חֶלְקֵנוּ בְּתוֹרָתֶךָ,

Sanctify us with Your commandments and grant us our share in Your Torah;

sab'aynu mituvecho,   שַׂבְּעֵנוּ מִטּוּבֶךְ

v'sam'chaynu bi-shu-osecho,   וְשַׂמְּחֵנוּ בִּישׁוּעָתֶךָ,

satisfy us from Your goodness and gladden us with Your salvation,

v'tahayr libaynu l'ovd'cho be-emes.   וְטַהֵר לִבֵּנוּ לְעָבְדְּךָ בֶּאֱמֶת.

and purify our heart to serve You sincerely.

V'hanchilaynu Adōnoy Elōhaynu   וְהַנְחִילֵנוּ יהוה אֱלֹהֵינוּ

And grant us a heritage, O Hashem, our God —

ON THE SABBATH ADD:

b'ahavo uvrotzōn   בְּאַהֲבָה וּבְרָצוֹן

with love and with favor

b'simcho uvsosōn

בְּשִׂמְחָה וּבְשָׂשׂוֹן

with gladness and with joy —

ON THE SABBATH ADD:

shabos u . . .

שַׁבָּת וּ . . .

the Sabbath and

mō-aday kod'shecho,

מוֹעֲדֵי קָדְשֶׁךָ,

the appointed Festivals of Your holiness,

v'yism'chu v'cho yisro-ayl
m'kad'shay sh'mecho.

וְיִשְׂמְחוּ בְךָ יִשְׂרָאֵל
מְקַדְּשֵׁי שְׁמֶךָ.

and may Israel, the sanctifiers of Your Name, rejoice in You.

Boruch ato Adōnoy, m'kadaysh

בָּרוּךְ אַתָּה יהוה, מְקַדֵּשׁ

Blessed are You, HASHEM, Who sanctifies

ON THE SABBATH ADD:

hashabos v' . . .

הַשַּׁבָּת וְ . . .

the Sabbath,

yisro-ayl v'haz'manim.

יִשְׂרָאֵל וְהַזְּמַנִּים.

Israel and the (festive) seasons. *

■ Fifth Blessing: Prayer for restoration of the Temple service

R'TZAY, Adōnoy Elōhaynu

רְצֵה יהוה אֱלֹהֵינוּ

Be favorable, HASHEM, our God,

b'am'cho yisro-ayl u-visfilosom,

בְּעַמְּךָ יִשְׂרָאֵל וּבִתְפִלָּתָם,

toward Your people Israel and their prayer

v'hoshayv es ho-avōdo
lidvir bay-secho.

וְהָשֵׁב אֶת הָעֲבוֹדָה
לִדְבִיר בֵּיתֶךָ.

and restore the service to the Holy of Holies of Your Temple.

V'i-shay yisro-ayl, usfilosom
b'ahavo s'kabayl b'rotzōn,

וְאִשֵּׁי יִשְׂרָאֵל וּתְפִלָּתָם
בְּאַהֲבָה תְקַבֵּל בְּרָצוֹן,

The fire-offerings of Israel and their prayer accept with love and favor,

us-hi l'rotzōn tomid
avōdas yisro-ayl amecho.

וּתְהִי לְרָצוֹן תָּמִיד
עֲבוֹדַת יִשְׂרָאֵל עַמֶּךָ.

and may the service of Your people Israel always be favorable to You.

V'SECHEZENO aynaynu

וְתֶחֱזֶינָה עֵינֵינוּ

May our eyes behold

מְקַדֵּשׁ יִשְׂרָאֵל וְהַזְּמַנִּים — *Who sanctifies Israel and the (festive) seasons.* The use of the term "festive seasons," rather than the Scriptural term "appointed Festivals," alludes to a special feature of the Jewish calendar. The Torah ordains that Pesach must fall in the springtime; thus the Rabbinical court must take the seasons into account in formulating the calendar.

b'shuv'cho l'tziyōn b'rachamim.　　　בְּשׁוּבְךָ לְצִיּוֹן בְּרַחֲמִים.

Your return to Zion in compassion.

Boruch ato Adōnoy,　　　בָּרוּךְ אַתָּה יהוה,

hamachazir sh'chinosō l'tziyōn.　　　הַמַּחֲזִיר שְׁכִינָתוֹ לְצִיּוֹן.

Blessed are You, HASHEM, Who restores His Presence unto Zion.

■ Sixth Blessing: Acknowledgment of our debt of gratitude

BOW AT Mōdim anachnu loch; STRAIGHTEN UP AT Adōnoy.
IN HIS REPETITION THE *CHAZZAN* SHOULD RECITE THE ENTIRE *MODIM* ALOUD,
WHILE THE CONGREGATION RECITES *MODIM OF THE RABBIS* (P. 594) SOFTLY.

MŌDIM anachnu loch,　　　**מוֹדִים** אֲנַחְנוּ לָךְ,

We gratefully thank You,

sho-ato hu Adōnoy Elōhaynu　　　שָׁאַתָּה הוּא יהוה אֱלֹהֵינוּ

Vaylōhay avōsaynu l'ōlom vo-ed,　　　וֵאלֹהֵי אֲבוֹתֵינוּ לְעוֹלָם וָעֶד,

for it is You Who are HASHEM, our God, and the God of our forefathers forever and ever;

tzur cha-yaynu, mogayn yish-aynu　　　צוּר חַיֵּינוּ, מָגֵן יִשְׁעֵנוּ

Rock of our lives, Shield of our salvation

ato hu l'dōr vodōr.　　　אַתָּה הוּא לְדוֹר וָדוֹר.

are You from generation to generation.

Nō-de l'cho unsapayr t'hilosecho　　　נוֹדֶה לְּךָ וּנְסַפֵּר תְּהִלָּתֶךָ

We shall thank You and relate Your praise —

al cha-yaynu ham'surim b'yodecho,　　　עַל חַיֵּינוּ הַמְּסוּרִים בְּיָדֶךָ,

for our lives, which are committed to Your power,

v'al nishmōsaynu hap'kudōs loch,　　　וְעַל נִשְׁמוֹתֵינוּ הַפְּקוּדוֹת לָךְ,

and for our souls that are entrusted to You,

v'al nisecho sheb'chol yōm imonu,　　　וְעַל נִסֶּיךָ שֶׁבְּכָל יוֹם עִמָּנוּ,

and for Your miracles that are with us every day,

v'al nifl'ōsecho v'tōvōsecho　　　וְעַל נִפְלְאוֹתֶיךָ וְטוֹבוֹתֶיךָ

sheb'chol ays,　　　שֶׁבְּכָל עֵת,

and for Your wonders and favors in every season —

erev vovōker v'tzohoro-yim.　　　עֶרֶב וָבֹקֶר וְצָהֳרָיִם.

evening, morning, and afternoon.

Hatōv ki lō cholu rachamecho,　　　הַטּוֹב כִּי לֹא כָלוּ רַחֲמֶיךָ,

The Beneficent One, for Your compassions were never exhausted,

v'ham'rachaym ki lō samu chasodecho,　　　וְהַמְרַחֵם כִּי לֹא תַמּוּ חֲסָדֶיךָ,

and the Compassionate One, for Your kindnesses never ended —

may-ōlom kivinu loch.　　　מֵעוֹלָם קִוִּינוּ לָךְ.

always have we put our hope in You.

MODIM OF THE RABBIS

RECITED SOFTLY BY CONGREGATION WHILE *CHAZZAN* RECITES THE REGULAR MODIM ALOUD

MÔDIM anachnu loch,

מוֹדִים אֲנַחְנוּ לָךְ,

We gratefully thank You,

sho-ato hu Adônoy Elôhaynu

Vaylôhay avôsaynu,

שָׁאַתָּה הוּא יהוה אֱלֹהֵינוּ
וֵאלֹהֵי אֲבוֹתֵינוּ,

for it is You Who are HASHEM, our God and the God of our forefathers,

Elôhay chol bosor,

אֱלֹהֵי כָל בָּשָׂר,

the God of all flesh,

yôtz'raynu, yôtzayr b'rayshis.

יוֹצְרֵנוּ, יוֹצֵר בְּרֵאשִׁית.

our Molder, the Molder of the universe.

B'rochôs v'hôdo-ôs l'shimcho

hagodôl v'hakodôsh,

בְּרָכוֹת וְהוֹדָאוֹת לְשִׁמְךָ
הַגָּדוֹל וְהַקָּדוֹשׁ,

Blessings and thanks are due Your great and holy Name

al sheheche-yisonu v'ki-yamtonu.

עַל שֶׁהֶחֱיִיתָנוּ וְקִיַּמְתָּנוּ.

for You have given us life and sustained us,

Kayn t'cha-yaynu uska-y'maynu,

כֵּן תְּחַיֵּנוּ וּתְקַיְּמֵנוּ,

So may You continue to give us life and sustain us

v'se-esôf golu-yôsaynu

l'chatzrôs kod-shecho,

וְתֶאֱסוֹף גָּלֻיּוֹתֵינוּ
לְחַצְרוֹת קָדְשֶׁךָ,

and gather our exiles to the Courtyards of Your Sanctuary,

lishmôr chukecho

v'la-asôs r'tzônecho,

לִשְׁמוֹר חֻקֶּיךָ
וְלַעֲשׂוֹת רְצוֹנֶךָ,

to observe Your decrees, to do Your will

ul-ovd'cho b'layvov sholaym,

וּלְעָבְדְּךָ בְּלֵבָב שָׁלֵם,

and to serve You wholeheartedly.

al she-anachnu môdim loch.

עַל שֶׁאֲנַחְנוּ מוֹדִים לָךְ.

[We thank You] for inspiring us to thank You.

Boruch Ayl hahôdo-ôs.

בָּרוּךְ אֵל הַהוֹדָאוֹת.

Blessed is the God of thanksgivings.

V'AL kulom yisborach v'yisrômam

shimcho, malkaynu

וְעַל כֻּלָּם יִתְבָּרַךְ וְיִתְרוֹמַם
שִׁמְךָ מַלְכֵּנוּ

For all these, may Your Name be blessed and exalted, our King,

tomid l'ôlom vo-ed.

תָּמִיד לְעוֹלָם וָעֶד.

continually forever and ever.

V'chôl hacha-yim yôducho selo,

וְכֹל הַחַיִּים יוֹדוּךָ סֶּלָה,

Everything alive will gratefully acknowledge You, Selah!

vihal'lu es shimcho be-emes,

וִיהַלְלוּ אֶת שִׁמְךָ בֶּאֱמֶת,

and praise Your Name sincerely,

ho-Ayl y'shu-osaynu

v'ezrosaynu selo.

הָאֵל יְשׁוּעָתֵנוּ

וְעֶזְרָתֵנוּ סֶלָה.

O God of our salvation and help, Selah!

BEND THE KNEES AT Boruch; BOW AT ato; STRAIGHTEN UP AT Adōnoy.

Boruch ato Adōnoy,

בָּרוּךְ אַתָּה יהוה,

Blessed are You, HASHEM,

hatōv shimcho ulcho no-e l'hōdōs.

הַטּוֹב שִׁמְךָ וּלְךָ נָאֶה לְהוֹדוֹת.

Your Name is "The Beneficent One" and to You it is fitting to give thanks.

■ Seventh Blessing: Prayer for peace and harmony
amongst the Jewish people

ON SIMCHAS TORAH, MANY CONGREGATIONS RECITE THE FULL
BIRCAS KOHANIM/PRIESTLY BLESSING (P. 737) AT SHACHARIS.

AT SHACHARIS THE CHAZZAN RECITES THE PRIESTLY BLESSING DURING HIS REPETITION.

אֱלֹהֵינוּ, וֵאלֹהֵי אֲבוֹתֵינוּ, בָּרְכֵנוּ בַבְּרָכָה הַמְשֻׁלֶּשֶׁת בַּתּוֹרָה

הַכְּתוּבָה עַל יְדֵי מֹשֶׁה עַבְדֶּךָ, הָאֲמוּרָה מִפִּי אַהֲרֹן וּבָנָיו,

כֹּהֲנִים עַם קְדוֹשֶׁךָ, כָּאָמוּר:

(kayn y'hi rotzōn – בֵּן יְהִי רָצוֹן – Cong.)   יְבָרֶכְךָ יהוה, וְיִשְׁמְרֶךָ.

(kayn y'hi rotzōn – בֵּן יְהִי רָצוֹן – Cong.)   יָאֵר יהוה פָּנָיו אֵלֶיךָ וִיחֻנֶּךָּ.

יִשָּׂא יהוה פָּנָיו אֵלֶיךָ וְיָשֵׂם לְךָ שָׁלוֹם.

(kayn y'hi rotzōn – בֵּן יְהִי רָצוֹן – Cong.)

DURING SHACHARIS CONTINUE HERE;
DURING MINCHAH AND MAARIV CONTINUE Sholōm rov (MIDDLE OF P. 690):

SIM SHOLŌM tōvo uvrocho,

שִׂים שָׁלוֹם, טוֹבָה, וּבְרָכָה,

Establish peace, goodness, blessing,

chayn vochesed v'rachamim

חֵן וָחֶסֶד וְרַחֲמִים

graciousness, kindness, and compassion

olaynu v'al kol yisro-ayl amecho.

עָלֵינוּ וְעַל כָּל יִשְׂרָאֵל עַמֶּךָ.

upon us and upon all of Your people Israel.

Bor'chaynu, ovinu, kulonu k'e-chod

b'ōr ponecho,

בָּרְכֵנוּ, אָבִינוּ, כֻּלָּנוּ כְּאֶחָד

בְּאוֹר פָּנֶיךָ,

Bless us, our Father, all of us as one, with the light of Your countenance,

ki v'ōr ponecho nosato lonu,

Adōnoy Elōhaynu,

כִּי בְאוֹר פָּנֶיךָ נָתַתָּ לָּנוּ,

יהוה אֱלֹהֵינוּ,

for with the light of Your countenance, You, HASHEM, our God, gave us

tōras cha-yim v'ahavas chesed,
תּוֹרַת חַיִּים וְאַהֲבַת חֶסֶד,
the Torah of life and a love of kindness,

utz-doko uvrocho v'rachamim
v'cha-yim v'sholōm.
וּצְדָקָה וּבְרָכָה וְרַחֲמִים
וְחַיִּים וְשָׁלוֹם.
righteousness, blessing, compassion, life, and peace.

V'tōv b'aynecho l'voraych
es am'cho yisro-ayl,
וְטוֹב בְּעֵינֶיךָ לְבָרֵךְ
אֶת עַמְּךָ יִשְׂרָאֵל,
And may it be good in Your eyes to bless Your people Israel

b'chol ays uvchol sho-o
bishlōmecho.
בְּכָל עֵת וּבְכָל שָׁעָה
בִּשְׁלוֹמֶךָ.
at every time and at every hour, with Your peace.

Boruch ato Adōnoy,
בָּרוּךְ אַתָּה יהוה,
Blessed are You, HASHEM,

ham'voraych es amō yisro-ayl
ba-sholōm.
הַמְבָרֵךְ אֶת עַמּוֹ יִשְׂרָאֵל
בַּשָּׁלוֹם.
Who blesses His people Israel with peace.

CONTINUE ON PAGE 691.

———— DURING *MINCHAH* AND *MAARIV* THE FOLLOWING IS RECITED. ————

SHOLŌM ROV al yisro-ayl
am'cho tosim l'ōlom,
שָׁלוֹם רָב עַל יִשְׂרָאֵל
עַמְּךָ תָּשִׂים לְעוֹלָם,
Establish abundant peace upon Your people Israel forever,

ki ato hu melech,
odōn l'chol ha-sholōm.
כִּי אַתָּה הוּא מֶלֶךְ
אָדוֹן לְכָל הַשָּׁלוֹם.
for You are King, Master of all peace.

V'tōv b'aynecho l'voraych
es am'cho yisro-ayl,
וְטוֹב בְּעֵינֶיךָ לְבָרֵךְ
אֶת עַמְּךָ יִשְׂרָאֵל,
And may it be good in Your eyes to bless Your people Israel

b'chol ays uvchol sho-o
bish-lōmecho.
בְּכָל עֵת וּבְכָל שָׁעָה
בִּשְׁלוֹמֶךָ.
at every time and at every hour, with Your peace.

Boruch ato Adōnoy,
בָּרוּךְ אַתָּה יהוה,
Blessed are You, HASHEM,

ham'voraych es amō yisro-ayl
ba-sholōm.
הַמְבָרֵךְ אֶת עַמּוֹ יִשְׂרָאֵל
בַּשָּׁלוֹם.
Who blesses His people Israel with peace.

THE *CHAZZAN'S* REPETITION ENDS HERE. INDIVIDUALS CONTINUE THRU P. 692:

Yih-yu l'rotzōn imray fi
v'hegyōn libi l'fonecho,

יִהְיוּ לְרָצוֹן אִמְרֵי פִי
וְהֶגְיוֹן לִבִּי לְפָנֶיךָ,

*May the expressions of my mouth and the thoughts of my heart
find favor before You,*

Adōnoy tzuri v'gō-ali.

יהוה צוּרִי וְגֹאֲלִי.

HASHEM, my Rock and my Redeemer.

ELŌHAI, n'tzōr l'shōni mayro,

אֱלֹהַי, נְצוֹר לְשׁוֹנִי מֵרָע,

My God, guard my tongue from evil

usfosai midabayr mirmo,

וּשְׂפָתַי מִדַּבֵּר מִרְמָה,

and my lips from speaking deceitfully.

V'limkal'lai nafshi sidōm,

וְלִמְקַלְלַי נַפְשִׁי תִדּוֹם,

To those who curse me, let my soul be silent;

v'nafshi ke-ofor lakōl tih-ye.

וְנַפְשִׁי כֶּעָפָר לַכֹּל תִּהְיֶה.

and let my soul be like dust to everyone.

P'sach libi b'sōrosecho,

פְּתַח לִבִּי בְּתוֹרָתֶךָ,

Open my heart to Your Torah,

uvmitzvōsecho tirdōf nafshi.

וּבְמִצְוֹתֶיךָ תִּרְדּוֹף נַפְשִׁי.

then my soul will pursue Your commandments.

V'chol hachōsh'vim olai ro-o,

וְכָל הַחוֹשְׁבִים עָלַי רָעָה,

As for all those who design evil against me,

m'hayro hofayr atzosom
v'kalkayl machashavtom.

מְהֵרָה הָפֵר עֲצָתָם
וְקַלְקֵל מַחֲשַׁבְתָּם.

speedily nullify their counsel and disrupt their design.

Asay l'ma-an sh'mecho,
asay l'ma-an y'minecho,

עֲשֵׂה לְמַעַן שְׁמֶךָ,
עֲשֵׂה לְמַעַן יְמִינֶךָ,

Act for Your Name's sake; act for Your right hand's sake;

asay l'ma-an k'dushosecho,
asay l'ma-an tōrosecho.

עֲשֵׂה לְמַעַן קְדֻשָּׁתֶךָ,
עֲשֵׂה לְמַעַן תּוֹרָתֶךָ.

act for Your sanctity's sake; act for Your Torah's sake.

L'ma-an yaychol'tzun y'didecho,

לְמַעַן יֵחָלְצוּן יְדִידֶיךָ,

That Your beloved ones may be given rest;

hōshi-o y'min'cho va-anayni.

הוֹשִׁיעָה יְמִינְךָ וַעֲנֵנִי.

let Your right hand save, and respond to me.

Yih-yu l'rotzōn imray fi
v'hegyōn libi l'fonecho,

יִהְיוּ לְרָצוֹן אִמְרֵי פִי
וְהֶגְיוֹן לִבִּי לְפָנֶיךָ,

*May the expressions of my mouth and the thoughts of my heart
find favor before You,*

Adōnoy tzuri v'gō-ali.   יהוה צוּרִי וְגֹאֲלִי.

HASHEM, my Rock and my Redeemer.

BOW. TAKE THREE STEPS BACK. BOW LEFT AND SAY:

Ō-se sholōm bimrōmov,   עֹשֶׂה שָׁלוֹם בִּמְרוֹמָיו,

He Who makes peace in His heights,

BOW RIGHT AND SAY:

hu ya-a-se sholōm olaynu,   הוּא יַעֲשֶׂה שָׁלוֹם עָלֵינוּ,

may He make peace upon us,

BOW FORWARD AND SAY:

v'al kol yisro-ayl. V'imru: Omayn.   וְעַל כָּל יִשְׂרָאֵל. וְאִמְרוּ: אָמֵן.

and upon all Israel. Now respond: Amen.

Y'HI ROTZŌN mil'fonecho,   **יְהִי רָצוֹן** מִלְּפָנֶיךָ

May it be Your will,

Adōnoy Elōhaynu   יהוה אֱלֹהֵינוּ

   Vaylōhay avōsaynu,   וֵאלֹהֵי אֲבוֹתֵינוּ,

HASHEM, our God and the God of our forefathers,

she-yibo-ne bays hamikdosh   שֶׁיִּבָּנֶה בֵּית הַמִּקְדָּשׁ

   bimhayro v'yomaynu,   בִּמְהֵרָה בְיָמֵינוּ,

that the Holy Temple be rebuilt, speedily in our days;

v'sayn chelkaynu b'sōrosecho,   וְתֵן חֶלְקֵנוּ בְּתוֹרָתֶךָ,

and grant us our share in Your Torah;

v'shom na-avod-cho b'yiro,   וְשָׁם נַעֲבָדְךָ בְּיִרְאָה,

and may we serve You there with reverence,

kimay ōlom   כִּימֵי עוֹלָם

   uchshonim kadmōniyōs.   וּכְשָׁנִים קַדְמוֹנִיּוֹת.

as in days of old and in former years.

V'or'vo Ladōnoy   וְעָרְבָה לַיהוה

   minchas y'hudo virusholo-yim,   מִנְחַת יְהוּדָה וִירוּשָׁלָיִם,

Then the offering of Judah and Jerusalem will be pleasing to HASHEM,

kimay ōlom   כִּימֵי עוֹלָם

   uchshonim kadmōniyōs.   וּכְשָׁנִים קַדְמוֹנִיּוֹת.

as in days of old and in former years.

THE INDIVIDUAL'S RECITATION OF *SHEMONEH ESREI* ENDS HERE.

REMAIN STANDING IN PLACE UNTIL THE *CHAZZAN* REACHES *KEDUSHAH* —
OR AT LEAST FOR A FEW MOMENTS — THEN TAKE THREE STEPS FORWARD.

AT *SHACHARIS,* THE SERVICE CONTINUES WITH *HALLEL* (P. 647);
AT *MINCHAH,* WITH THE FULL *KADDISH* (P. 535);
AT *MAARIV,* ON THE SABBATH WITH *VAYECHULU* (P. 140),
ON A WEEKDAY WITH THE FULL *KADDISH* (143).

◄{ PRE-MUSSAF PIYUT }►

IN MOST CONGREGATIONS THE *CHAZZAN* CHANTS THE FOLLOWING PRAYER AFTER THE *HAFTARAH* BLESS-
INGS HAVE BEEN COMPLETED. HOWEVER, ON DAYS WHEN *YIZKOR* IS RECITED, IT IS USUALLY OMITTED.

YOH AYLI, v'gō-ali,   יָהּ אֵלִי, וְגוֹאֲלִי,
> O God, my God* and Redeemer,

esyatz'vo likrosecho,   אֶתְיַצְּבָה לִקְרָאתֶךָ,
> I shall stand to greet You —

ho-yo v'yih-ye, ho-yo v'hō-ve,   הָיָה וְיִהְיֶה, הָיָה וְהֹוֶה,
> Who was and Who will be, Who was and Who is —

kol gōy admosecho.   כָּל גּוֹי אַדְמָתֶךָ.
> with the entire nation on Your soil;

V'sōdo, v'lo-ōlo, v'lamincho,   וְתוֹדָה, וְלָעוֹלָה, וְלַמִּנְחָה,
    v'lachatos, v'lo-oshom,   וְלַחַטָּאת, וְלָאָשָׁם,
    v'lash'lomim,   וְלַשְּׁלָמִים,
    v'lamilu-im, kol korbonecho.   וְלַמִּלּוּאִים, כָּל קָרְבָּנֶךָ.
> and the thanksgiving-, elevation-, meal-, sin-, guilt-, peace-,
> and inauguration-offerings — Your every offering.

Z'chōr nil-o, asher nos'o,   זְכוֹר נִלְאָה אֲשֶׁר נָשָׂאָה
> Remember the exhausted [nation]* that won [Your favor],

v'hoshivoh l'admosecho.   וַהֲשִׁיבָהּ לְאַדְמָתֶךָ.
> and return her to Your soil.

Selo ahal'leko,   סֶלָה אֲהַלְלֶךָ,
> Eternally will I laud You,

b'ashray yōsh'vay vay-secho.   בְּאַשְׁרֵי יוֹשְׁבֵי בֵיתֶךָ.
> saying, "Praiseworthy are those who dwell in Your House."

DAK al dak, ad ayn nivdak,   דַּק עַל דַּק, עַד אֵין נִבְדָּק,
> Painstakingly exact,* beyond calculation —

v'lisvunosō ayn chayker.   וְלִתְבוּנָתוֹ אֵין חֵקֶר.
> to His intelligence there is no limit.

Ho-Ayl nōro, b'achas s'kiro,   הָאֵל נוֹרָא, בְּאַחַת סְקִירָה,
> The awesome God — with a single glance,*

יָהּ אֵלִי — *O God, my God.* Since *Ashrei* is one of
the most prominent of all the psalms, its recitation before the Festival *Mussaf* is introduced
with a joyous prayer that longs for the opportunity to sing it before God in the rebuilt Temple,
along with the order of sacrificial offerings.

זְכוֹר נִלְאָה — *Remember the exhausted [nation].*
Israel has been exhausted by long exile and
much travail, but she won God's favor long ago
and therefore longs for her return from exile.

דַּק עַל דַּק — *Painstakingly exact.* This refers to

the inscrutable greatness of God's awesome
judgment.

בְּאַחַת סְקִירָה — *With a single glance.* On the Day
of Judgment, "All who walk the earth pass before Him "like young sheep" (*Rosh Hashanah*
16a, 18a). When sheep were tithed, they were
released one by one through a small opening in
a corral. Similarly, although all mankind
stands before Him, God judges each person
individually, by examining that person's lifetime in a single glance.

bayn tōv lora y'vakayr.   בֵּין טוֹב לָרַע יְבַקֵּר.

He differentiates the good from bad.

V'sōdo, v'lo-ōlo, v'lamincho,   וְתוֹדָה, וְלָעוֹלָה, וְלַמִּנְחָה,
   v'lachatos, v'lo-oshom,   וְלַחַטָּאת, וְלָאָשָׁם,
   v'lash'lomim,   וְלַשְּׁלָמִים,
   v'lamilu-im, kol korbonecho.   וְלַמִּלוּאִים, כָּל קָרְבָּנֶךָ.

And the thanksgiving-, elevation-, meal-, sin-, guilt-, peace-,
and inauguration-offerings — Your every offering.

Z'chōr nil-o, asher nos'o,   זְכוֹר נִלְאָה, אֲשֶׁר נָשָׂאָה,

Remember the exhausted [nation] that won [Your favor],

v'hoshivoh l'admosecho.   וְהָשִׁיבָה לְאַדְמָתֶךָ.

and return her to Your soil.

Selo ahal'leko,   סֶלָה אֲהַלְלֶךָ,

Eternally will I laud You,

b'ashray yōsh'vay vay-secho.   בְּאַשְׁרֵי יוֹשְׁבֵי בֵיתֶךָ.

saying, "Praiseworthy are those who dwell in Your House."

ADŌN tz'vo-ōs, b'rōv p'lo-ōs,   **אֲדוֹן** צְבָאוֹת, בְּרוֹב פְּלָאוֹת,

The Lord of Legions, with abundant miracles

chibayr kol oholō.   חִבֵּר כָּל אָהֳלוֹ.

He connected His entire Tabernacle,

Binsivōs layv livlayv,   בִּנְתִיבוֹת לֵב לִבְלֵב,

and made it blossom through the thirty-two paths [of wisdom] —

hatzur tomim po-olō.   הַצּוּר תָּמִים פָּעֳלוֹ.

the Rock, His work is perfect!

V'sōdo, v'lo-ōlo, v'lamincho,   וְתוֹדָה, וְלָעוֹלָה, וְלַמִּנְחָה,
   v'lachatos, v'lo-oshom,   וְלַחַטָּאת, וְלָאָשָׁם,
   v'lash'lomim,   וְלַשְּׁלָמִים,
   v'lamilu-im, kol korbonecho.   וְלַמִּלוּאִים כָּל קָרְבָּנֶךָ.

And the thanksgiving-, elevation-, meal-, sin-, guilt-, peace-,
and inauguration-offerings — Your every offering.

Z'chōr nil-o, asher nos'o,   זְכוֹר נִלְאָה אֲשֶׁר נָשָׂאָה

Remember the exhausted [nation] that won [Your favor],

v'hoshivoh l'admosecho.   וְהָשִׁיבָה לְאַדְמָתֶךָ.

and return her to Your soil.

Selo ahal'leko,   סֶלָה אֲהַלְלֶךָ,

Eternally will I laud You,

b'ashray yōsh'vay vay-secho.   בְּאַשְׁרֵי יוֹשְׁבֵי בֵיתֶךָ.

saying, "Praiseworthy are those who dwell in Your House."

⟪ YIZKOR ⟫

■ Our prayers, charity, and acts of kindness serve as a source of merit for our departed forbears and loved ones, even as their memory continues to inspire us.

THOSE CONGREGANTS WHOSE PARENTS ARE BOTH LIVING DO NOT PARTICIPATE IN THE *YIZKOR* SERVICE, BUT LEAVE THE SYNAGOGUE AND RETURN WHEN THE CONGREGATION BEGINS *AV HARACHAMIM,* AT THE END OF *YIZKOR.*

ALTHOUGH THE FOLLOWING VERSES ARE NOT PART OF THE TRADITIONAL *YIZKOR* SERVICE, SOME CONGREGATIONS HAVE ADOPTED THE CUSTOM OF RECITING THEM RESPONSIVELY BEFORE *YIZKOR.*

ADŌNOY, mo odom vataydo-ayhu,

יְהֹוָה, מָה אָדָם וַתֵּדָעֵהוּ,

HASHEM, what is man that You recognize him?

ben enosh vat'chash'vayhu.

בֶּן אֱנוֹשׁ וַתְּחַשְּׁבֵהוּ.

The son of a frail human that You reckon with him?

Odom la-hevel domo,

אָדָם לַהֶבֶל דָּמָה,

    yomov k'tzayl ōvayr.

יָמָיו כְּצֵל עוֹבֵר.

Man is like a breath, his days are like a passing shadow.

Babōker yotzitz v'cholof,

בַּבֹּקֶר יָצִיץ וְחָלָף,

In the morning it blossoms and is rejuvenated,

lo-erev y'molayl v'yovaysh.

לָעֶרֶב יְמוֹלֵל וְיָבֵשׁ.

by evening it is cut down and brittle.

Limnōs yomaynu kayn hōda

לִמְנוֹת יָמֵינוּ כֵּן הוֹדַע,

According to the count of our days, so may You teach us;

v'novi l'vav choch-mo.

וְנָבִיא לְבַב חָכְמָה.

then we shall acquire a heart of wisdom.

Sh'mor tom ur'ay yoshor.

שְׁמָר תָּם וּרְאֵה יָשָׁר,

Safeguard the perfect and watch the upright,

ki acharis l'ish sholōm.

כִּי אַחֲרִית לְאִישׁ שָׁלוֹם.

for the destiny of that man is peace.

Ach Elōhim

אַךְ אֱלֹהִים

    yif-de nafshi mi-yad sh'ōl,

יִפְדֶּה נַפְשִׁי מִיַּד שְׁאוֹל,

But God will redeem my soul from the grip of the Lower World,

ki yikochayni selo.

כִּי יִקָּחֵנִי סֶלָה.

for He will take me, Selah!

⧉ Yizkor

The ancient custom of remembering the souls of the departed and contributing to charity in their memory is rooted in the fundamental Jewish belief in the eternity of the soul. When physical life ends, only the body dies, but the soul ascends to the realm of the spirit where it regularly attains higher levels of purity and holiness.

When this life is over, the soul can no longer perform good deeds; that method of attaining merit is the sole province of mortal man, who must struggle with the baseness and selfishness of his animal nature. But there is a way

Kolo sh'ayri ulvovi

כָּלָה שְׁאֵרִי וּלְבָבִי,

My flesh and my heart yearn —

tzur l'vovi v'chelki Elōhim l'olam.

צוּר לְבָבִי וְחֶלְקִי אֱלֹהִים לְעוֹלָם.

Rock of my heart, and my portion is God, forever.

V'yoshōv he-ofor
   al ho-oretz k'she-ho-yo,

וְיָשֹׁב הֶעָפָר
עַל הָאָרֶץ כְּשֶׁהָיָה,

Thus the dust returns to the ground as it was,

v'horu-ach toshuv
   el Ho-elōhim asher n'sonoh.

וְהָרוּחַ תָּשׁוּב
אֶל הָאֱלֹהִים אֲשֶׁר נְתָנָהּ.

and the spirit returns to God Who gave it.

YŌSHAYV b'sayser elyōn,

ישֵׁב בְּסֵתֶר עֶלְיוֹן,

Whoever sits in the refuge of the Most High,

b'tzayl Shadai yislōnon.

בְּצֵל שַׁדַּי יִתְלוֹנָן.

he shall dwell in the shadow of the Almighty.

Ōmar Ladōnoy machsi umtzudosi,
   Elōhai evtach bō.

אֹמַר לַיהוה מַחְסִי וּמְצוּדָתִי,
אֱלֹהַי אֶבְטַח בּוֹ.

I will say of HASHEM, "He is my refuge and my fortress, my God, I will trust in Him."

Ki hu yatzil'cho mipach yokush,
   mi-dever havōs.

כִּי הוּא יַצִּילְךָ מִפַּח יָקוּשׁ,
מִדֶּבֶר הַוּוֹת.

For He will deliver you from the ensnaring trap, from devastating pestilence.

B'evrosō yosech loch,
   v'sachas k'nofov techse,

בְּאֶבְרָתוֹ יָסֶךְ לָךְ,
וְתַחַת כְּנָפָיו תֶּחְסֶה,

With His pinion He will cover you, and beneath His wings you will be protected;

tzino v'sōchayro amitō.

צִנָּה וְסֹחֵרָה אֲמִתּוֹ.

shield and armor is His truth.

Lō siro mipachad loylo,
   maychaytz yo-uf yōmom.

לֹא תִירָא מִפַּחַד לָיְלָה,
מֵחֵץ יָעוּף יוֹמָם.

You shall not fear the terror of night; nor the arrow that flies by day;

Mi-dever bo-ōfel yahalōch,

מִדֶּבֶר בָּאֹפֶל יַהֲלֹךְ,

nor the pestilence that walks in gloom;

miketev yoshud tzohoro-yim.

מִקֶּטֶב יָשׁוּד צָהֳרָיִם.

nor the destroyer who lays waste at noon.

---

that the disembodied soul can derive new sources of merit. History is a continuum. If we, the living, give charity or do good deeds due to the lasting influence or in memory of a departed parent or other loved one, the merit is truly that of the soul in its spiritual realm. Moreover, God in His mercy credits our deed to the departed one because he or she too would have done the same

— were it possible. But mere intentions do not suffice; only accomplishment can achieve this purpose. The intention to give and the fulfillment of that intention are both necessary.

The original custom was to recall the names of the departed and to pledge charity on their behalf on Yom Kippur. Ashkenazic Jewry's custom of reciting *Yizkor* on the three pilgrimage

Yipōl mitzid'cho elef,

    ur'vovo miminecho,

יִפֹּל מִצִּדְּךָ אֶלֶף,

וּרְבָבָה מִימִינֶךָ,

Let a thousand encamp at your side and a myriad at your right hand,

aylecho lō yigosh.

אֵלֶיךָ לֹא יִגָּשׁ.

but to you they shall not approach.

Rak b'aynecho sabit,

    v'shilumas r'sho-im tir-e.

רַק בְּעֵינֶיךָ תַבִּיט,

וְשִׁלֻּמַת רְשָׁעִים תִּרְאֶה.

You will merely peer with your eyes and you will see the retribution of the wicked.

Ki ato Adōnoy machsi,

כִּי אַתָּה יהוה מַחְסִי,

Because [you said,] "You, HASHEM, are my refuge,"

elyōn samto m'ōnecho.

עֶלְיוֹן שַׂמְתָּ מְעוֹנֶךָ.

you have made the Most High your dwelling place.

Lō s'une aylecho ro-o,

    v'nega lō yikrav b'oholecho.

לֹא תְאֻנֶּה אֵלֶיךָ רָעָה,

וְנֶגַע לֹא יִקְרַב בְּאָהֳלֶךָ.

No evil will befall you, nor will any plague come near your tent.

Ki mal-ochov y'tza-ve loch,

    lishmorcho b'chol d'rochecho.

כִּי מַלְאָכָיו יְצַוֶּה לָּךְ,

לִשְׁמָרְךָ בְּכָל דְּרָכֶיךָ.

He will charge His angels for you, to protect you in all your ways.

Al kapa-yim yiso-uncho,

    pen tigōf bo-even raglecho.

עַל כַּפַּיִם יִשָּׂאוּנְךָ,

פֶּן תִּגֹּף בָּאֶבֶן רַגְלֶךָ.

On [their] palms they will carry you, lest you strike your foot against a stone.

Al shachal vofesen tidrōch,

עַל שַׁחַל וָפֶתֶן תִּדְרֹךְ,

Upon the lion and the viper you will tread;

tirmōs k'fir v'sanin.

תִּרְמֹס כְּפִיר וְתַנִּין.

you will trample the young lion and the serpent.

Ki vi choshak va-afal'tayhu,

כִּי בִי חָשַׁק וַאֲפַלְּטֵהוּ,

For he has yearned for Me and I will deliver him;

asag'vayhu ki yoda sh'mi.

אֲשַׂגְּבֵהוּ כִּי יָדַע שְׁמִי.

I will elevate him because he knows My Name.

Yikro-ayni v'e-enayhu,

יִקְרָאֵנִי וְאֶעֱנֵהוּ,

He will call upon Me and I will answer him,

imō onōchi v'tzoro,

    achal'tzayhu va-achab'dayhu.

עִמּוֹ אָנֹכִי בְצָרָה,

אֲחַלְּצֵהוּ וַאֲכַבְּדֵהוּ.

I am with him in distress, I will release him and I will honor him.

Festivals is of a later origin, possibly dating from the time of the Crusades when bloody massacres wiped out many Jewish communities and inflicted suffering on many others. The three Festivals, which the Torah ordains as times of charity, were chosen as times to remember the dead and pray that the generosity of the living should be a source of merit for their souls.

Ōrech yomim asbi-ayhu,
v'ar-ayhu bishu-osi.

אֹרֶךְ יָמִים אַשְׂבִּיעֵהוּ,
וְאַרְאֵהוּ בִּישׁוּעָתִי.

With long life will I satisfy him, and I will show him My salvation.

Ōrech yomim asbi-ayhu,
v'ar-ayhu bishu-osi.

אֹרֶךְ יָמִים אַשְׂבִּיעֵהוּ,
וְאַרְאֵהוּ בִּישׁוּעָתִי.

With long life will I satisfy him, and I will show him My salvation.

WHENEVER THE NAME OF THE DECEASED IS MENTIONED IT IS GIVEN IN THE FOLLOWING FORM:
THE DECEASED'S HEBREW NAME FOLLOWED BY *BEN*, SON OF — OR, *BAS*, DAUGHTER OF — THEN
THE DECEASED'S FATHER'S HEBREW NAME.

——————————— FOR ONE'S FATHER ———————————

YIZKŌR Elōhim
*May God remember**

יִזְכֹּר אֱלֹהִים

nishmas ovi mōri

נִשְׁמַת אָבִי מוֹרִי

the soul of my father, my teacher, (NAME OF THE DECEASED)

she-holach l'ōlomō,

שֶׁהָלַךְ לְעוֹלָמוֹ,

who has gone on to his world,

ba-avur sheb'li neder
etayn tz'doko ba-adō.

בַּעֲבוּר שֶׁבְּלִי נֶדֶר
אֶתֵּן צְדָקָה בַּעֲדוֹ.

because, without making a vow, I shall give to charity on his behalf.

Bis-char ze

בִּשְׂכַר זֶה

As reward for this,

t'hay nafshō tz'ruro
bitz-rōr hacha-yim

תְּהֵא נַפְשׁוֹ צְרוּרָה
בִּצְרוֹר הַחַיִּים

*may his soul be bound in the Bond of Life,**

im nish-mōs
avrohom yitzchok v'ya-akōv,

עִם נִשְׁמוֹת
אַבְרָהָם יִצְחָק וְיַעֲקֹב,

together with the souls of Abraham, Isaac, and Jacob;

soro rivko rochayl v'lay-o,

שָׂרָה רִבְקָה רָחֵל וְלֵאָה,

Sarah, Rebecca, Rachel, and Leah;

v'im sh'or tzadikim v'tzidkoniyōs
sheb'gan ayden.

וְעִם שְׁאָר צַדִּיקִים וְצִדְקָנִיּוֹת
שֶׁבְּגַן עֵדֶן.

*and together with the other righteous men and women in the Garden of Eden.**

V'nōmar: Omayn.

וְנֹאמַר: אָמֵן.

Now let us respond: Amen.

───────────────────────────────────────

יִזְכֹּר אֱלֹהִים — *May God remember.* In calling
upon God to "remember," we do not suggest
that the possibility of forgetting exists before
the All-Knowing One. Rather, we pray that in
return for our devotion and generosity, God
should take cognizance of the new source of

merit for the soul whose memory is now influ-
encing our conduct.

בִּצְרוֹר הַחַיִּים — *In the Bond of Life.* The ultimate
life is that of the spirit, which is eternal and
which is unlimited by the constraints of time
and space and the weakness of flesh. The

— FOR ONE'S MOTHER —

YIZKŌR Elōhim

יִזְכּוֹר אֱלֹהִים

May God remember

nishmas imi mōrosi

נִשְׁמַת אִמִּי מוֹרָתִי

the soul of my mother, my teacher, (NAME OF THE DECEASED)

shehol'cho l'ōlomoh,

שֶׁהָלְכָה לְעוֹלָמָהּ,

who has gone on to her world,

ba-avur sheb'li neder

בַּעֲבוּר שֶׁבְּלִי נֶדֶר

  etayn tz'doko ba-adoh.

אֶתֵּן צְדָקָה בַּעֲדָהּ.

because, without making a vow, I shall give to charity on her behalf.

Bis-char ze

בִּשְׂכַר זֶה

As reward for this,

t'hay nafshoh tz'ruro

תְּהֵא נַפְשָׁהּ צְרוּרָה

  bitz-rōr hacha-yim

בִּצְרוֹר הַחַיִּים

may her soul be bound in the Bond of Life,

im nishmōs

עִם נִשְׁמוֹת

  avrohom yitzchok v'ya-akōv,

אַבְרָהָם יִצְחָק וְיַעֲקֹב,

together with the souls of Abraham, Isaac, and Jacob;

soro rivko rochayl v'lay-o,

שָׂרָה רִבְקָה רָחֵל וְלֵאָה,

Sarah, Rebecca, Rachel, and Leah;

v'im sh'or tzadikim v'tzidkoniyōs

וְעִם שְׁאָר צַדִּיקִים וְצִדְקָנִיּוֹת

  sheb'gan ayden.

שֶׁבְּגַן עֵדֶן.

and together with the other righteous men and women in the Garden of Eden.

V'nōmar: Omayn.

וְנֹאמַר: אָמֵן.

Now let us respond: Amen.

— FOR ONE'S MALE RELATIVE —

YIZKŌR Elōhim nishmas

יִזְכּוֹר אֱלֹהִים נִשְׁמַת

May God remember the soul of

MY GRANDFATHER:	z'keini	(NAME OF THE DECEASED)	זְקֵנִי
MY UNCLE:	dōdi	(NAME OF THE DECEASED)	דּוֹדִי
MY BROTHER:	ochi	(NAME OF THE DECEASED)	אָחִי
MY SON:	b'ni	(NAME OF THE DECEASED)	בְּנִי
MY HUSBAND:	ba-ali	(NAME OF THE DECEASED)	בַּעֲלִי

greater the merit achieved by a soul during its time on earth — or as a result of our deeds in its memory — the more it is bound together with the souls of the Patriarchs and Matriarchs.

בְּגַן עֵדֶן — *In the Garden of Eden.* Although

literally this is the place where Adam and Eve lived until their sin caused them to be driven out, it is also used to refer to the spiritual paradise because it implies spiritual perfection and bliss.

she-holach l'ōlomō,
שֶׁהָלַךְ לְעוֹלָמוֹ,

who has gone on to his world,

ba-avur sheb'li neder
בַּעֲבוּר שֶׁבְּלִי נֶדֶר

etayn tz'doko ba-adō.
אֶתֵּן צְדָקָה בַּעֲדוֹ.

because, without making a vow, I shall give to charity on his behalf.

Bis-char ze
בִּשְׂכַר זֶה

As reward for this,

t'hay nafshō tz'ruro
תְּהֵא נַפְשׁוֹ צְרוּרָה

bitz-rōr hacha-yim
בִּצְרוֹר הַחַיִּים

may his soul be bound in the Bond of Life,

im nishmōs
עִם נִשְׁמוֹת

avrohom yitzchok v'ya-akōv,
אַבְרָהָם יִצְחָק וְיַעֲקֹב,

together with the souls of Abraham, Isaac, and Jacob;

soro rivko rochayl v'lay-o,
שָׂרָה רִבְקָה רָחֵל וְלֵאָה,

Sarah, Rebecca, Rachel, and Leah;

v'im sh'or tzadikim v'tzidkoniyōs
וְעִם שְׁאָר צַדִּיקִים וְצִדְקָנִיּוֹת

sheb'gan ayden.
שֶׁבְּגַן עֵדֶן.

and together with the other righteous men and women in the Garden of Eden.

V'nōmar: Omayn.
וְנֹאמַר: אָמֵן.

Now let us respond: Amen.

───────── FOR ONE'S FEMALE RELATIVE ─────────

YIZKŌR Elōhim nishmas
יִזְכֹּר אֱלֹהִים נִשְׁמַת

May God remember the soul of

MY GRANDMOTHER: z'kenti	(NAME OF THE DECEASED)	זְקֶנְתִּי
MY AUNT: dōdosi	(NAME OF THE DECEASED)	דוֹדָתִי
MY SISTER: achōsi	(NAME OF THE DECEASED)	אֲחוֹתִי
MY DAUGHTER: biti	(NAME OF THE DECEASED)	בִּתִּי
MY WIFE: ishti	(NAME OF THE DECEASED)	אִשְׁתִּי

she-hol'cho l'ōlomoh,
שֶׁהָלְכָה לְעוֹלָמָהּ,

who has gone on to her world,

ba-avur sheb'li neder
בַּעֲבוּר שֶׁבְּלִי נֶדֶר

etayn tz'doko ba-adoh.
אֶתֵּן צְדָקָה בַּעֲדָהּ.

because, without making a vow, I shall give to charity on her behalf.

Bis-char ze
בִּשְׂכַר זֶה

As reward for this,

t'hay nafshoh tz'ruro
   bitz-rōr hacha-yim

תְּהֵא נַפְשָׁהּ צְרוּרָה
בִּצְרוֹר הַחַיִּים

may her soul be bound in the Bond of Life,

im nishmōs

עִם נִשְׁמוֹת

   avrohom yitzchok v'ya-akōv,

אַבְרָהָם יִצְחָק וְיַעֲקֹב,

together with the souls of Abraham, Isaac, and Jacob;

soro rivko rochayl v'lay-o,

שָׂרָה רִבְקָה רָחֵל וְלֵאָה,

Sarah, Rebecca, Rachel, and Leah;

v'im sh'or tzadikim v'tzidkoniyōs

וְעִם שְׁאָר צַדִּיקִים וְצִדְקָנִיּוֹת

   sheb'gan ayden.

שֶׁבְּגַן עֵדֶן.

and together with the other righteous men and women in the Garden of Eden.

V'nōmar: Omayn.

וְנֹאמַר: אָמֵן.

Now let us respond: Amen.

--- FOR MARTYRS ---

YIZKŌR Elōhim

יִזְכֹּר אֱלֹהִים

May God remember

nishmōs hak'dōshim v'hat'hōrim

נִשְׁמוֹת הַקְּדוֹשִׁים וְהַטְּהוֹרִים

the souls of the holy and pure ones

she-hum'su v'shenehergu

שֶׁהוּמְתוּ וְשֶׁנֶּהֶרְגוּ

   v'shenishchatu v'shenis-r'fu

וְשֶׁנִּשְׁחֲטוּ וְשֶׁנִּשְׂרְפוּ

   v'shenit-b'u v'shenech-n'ku

וְשֶׁנִּטְבְּעוּ וְשֶׁנֶּחְנְקוּ

who were killed, murdered, slaughtered, burned, drowned, and strangled

al kidush ha-shaym

עַל קִדּוּשׁ הַשֵּׁם,

for the sanctification of the Name,

(al y'day hatzōr'rim hagermonim,

(עַל יְדֵי הַצּוֹרְרִים הַגֶּרְמָנִים

(through the hands of the German oppressors,

yimach sh'mom v'zichrom),

יִמַּח שְׁמָם וְזִכְרָם),

may their name and memory be obliterated),

ba-avur sheb'li neder

בַּעֲבוּר שֶׁבְּלִי נֶדֶר

   etayn tz'doko ba-adom.

אֶתֵּן צְדָקָה בַּעֲדָם.

because, without making a vow, I shall give to charity on their behalf.

Bis-char ze

בִּשְׂכַר זֶה

As reward for this,

ti-h'yeno nafshōsayhem

תִּהְיֶינָה נַפְשׁוֹתֵיהֶם

   tz'rurōs bitz-ror hacha-yim

צְרוּרוֹת בִּצְרוֹר הַחַיִּים

may their souls be bound in the Bond of Life,

im nishmōs

עם נִשְׁמוֹת

avrohom yitzchok v'ya-akōv,

אַבְרָהָם יִצְחָק וְיַעֲקֹב,

together with the souls of Abraham, Isaac, and Jacob;

soro rivko rochayl v'lay-o,

שָׂרָה רִבְקָה רָחֵל וְלֵאָה,

Sarah, Rebecca, Rachel, and Leah;

v'im sh'or tzadikim v'tzidkoniyōs

וְעִם שְׁאָר צַדִּיקִים וְצִדְקָנִיּוֹת

sheb'gan ayden.

שֶׁבְּגַן עֵדֶן.

and together with the other righteous men and women in the Garden of Eden.

V'nōmar: Omayn.

וְנֹאמַר: אָמֵן.

Now let us respond: Amen.

FOR MEMBERS OF ISRAEL DEFENSE FORCE

[THE FOLLOWING TEXT IS TAKEN FROM THE *MINCHAS YERUSHALAYIM SIDDUR.*]

YIZKŌR Elōhim es nishmōs

יִזְכֹּר אֱלֹהִים אֶת נִשְׁמוֹת

May God remember the souls

cha-yolay tz'vo hahagono l'yisro-ayl

חַיָּלֵי צְבָא הַהֲגָנָה לְיִשְׂרָאֵל

of the fighters of the Israel Defense Force

shemosru nafshom

שֶׁמָּסְרוּ נַפְשָׁם

who gave their lives

al k'dushas Ha-shaym,

עַל קְדֻשַׁת הַשֵּׁם,

ha-om, v'ho-oretz,

הָעָם וְהָאָרֶץ,

for the sanctification of the Name, the People, and the Land;

v'nof-lu mōs gibōrim

וְנָפְלוּ מוֹת גִּבּוֹרִים

who died a heroic death

b'milchemes ha-shichrur

בְּמִלְחֶמֶת הַשִּׁחְרוּר,

uv'ma-archōs sinai

וּבְמַעַרְכוֹת סִינַי,

in the War of Independence and the battlefields of Sinai

uv'tafkiday hagono u-vitochōn.

וּבְתַפְקִידֵי הֲגָנָה וּבִטָּחוֹן.

in missions of defense and safety.

Min'shorim kalu u-may-aroyōs govayru,

מִנְּשָׁרִים קַלּוּ, וּמֵאֲרָיוֹת גָּבֵרוּ,

They were quicker than eagles and stronger than lions

b'haycholtzom l'ezras ho-om,

בְּהֵחָלְצָם לְעֶזְרַת הָעָם,

as they volunteered to assist the people

v'hirvu b'domom hatohōr

וְהִרְווּ בְּדָמָם הַטָּהוֹר

and with their pure blood soaked

es rigvay admas kodshaynu.

אֶת רִגְבֵי אַדְמַת קָדְשֵׁנוּ.

the clods of our holy earth.

Zaycher akaydosom

זֵכֶר עֲקֵדָתָם

The memory of their self-sacrifice

uma-asay g'vurosom

וּמַעֲשֵׂי גְבוּרָתָם

and heroic deeds

lo yosufu may-itonu l'ōlomim.

לֹא יָסְוּפוּ מֵאִתְּנוּ לְעוֹלָמִים.

will never perish from us.

Tih-yeno nishmōsayhem tzrurōs
bitz-rōr hacha-yim

תִּהְיֶינָה נִשְׁמוֹתֵיהֶם צְרוּרוֹת
בִּצְרוֹר הַחַיִּים

May their souls be bound in the Bond of Life

im nishmōs

עִם נִשְׁמוֹת

avrohom yitzchok v'ya-akōv,

אַבְרָהָם יִצְחָק וְיַעֲקֹב,

together with the souls of Abraham, Isaac, and Jacob,

v'im nishmōs

וְעִם נִשְׁמוֹת

and with the souls of

sh'or gibōrei yisro-ayl uk-dōshov
sheb'gan ayden. Omayn.

שְׁאָר גִּבּוֹרֵי יִשְׂרָאֵל וּקְדוֹשָׁיו
שֶׁבְּגַּן עֵדֶן. אָמֵן.

the other Jewish heroes and martyrs who are in the Garden of Eden. Amen.

AFTER *YIZKOR* IT IS CUSTOMARY TO RECITE THE FOLLOWING PRAYERS. IT IS PERMITTED TO MENTION MANY NAMES IN THIS PRAYER, BUT IT IS PREFERABLE TO RECITE SEPARATE PRAYERS FOR MEN AND WOMEN.

———————————— FOR A MAN ————————————

AYL molay rachamim,

אֵל מָלֵא רַחֲמִים,

shōchayn bam'rōmim,

שׁוֹכֵן בַּמְּרוֹמִים,

O God, full of mercy, Who dwells on high,

ham-tzay m'nucha n'chōna

הַמְצֵא מְנוּחָה נְכוֹנָה

al kanfay Hash'china,

עַל כַּנְפֵי הַשְּׁכִינָה,

grant proper rest* on the wings of the Divine Presence* —

b'ma-alōs k'dōshim ut-hōrim

בְּמַעֲלוֹת קְדוֹשִׁים וּטְהוֹרִים

in the lofty levels of the holy and the pure ones,*

k'zō-har horoki-a mazhirim,

כְּזֹהַר הָרָקִיעַ מַזְהִירִים,

who shine like the glow of the firmament —

es nishmas

אֶת נִשְׁמַת

for the soul of (NAME OF THE DECEASED)

she-holach l-ōlomō,

שֶׁהָלַךְ לְעוֹלָמוֹ,

who has gone on to his world,

אֵל ... הַמְצֵא מְנוּחָה נְכוֹנָה — *O God, ... grant proper rest.* The fact that a soul is in Paradise does not guarantee it complete contentment. Its level there depends on its prior achievements here on earth; consequently there are as many degrees there as there are degrees of righteousness on earth. Through our prayers and deeds, we hope to earn God's compassion upon the departed soul.

עַל כַּנְפֵי הַשְּׁכִינָה — *On the wings of the Divine*

Presence. Elsewhere, where this term is used to mean Heavenly protection from danger, we say "under the wings," using the analogy of a bird spreading its protective wings over its young. In this prayer, where we speak of spiritual elevation, we reverse the analogy, comparing God's Presence to a soaring eagle that puts its young on top of its wings and carries them aloft.

קְדוֹשִׁים וּטְהוֹרִים — *The holy and the pure ones.* This is a reference to the angels.

ba-avur sheb'li neder

בַּעֲבוּר שֶׁבְּלִי נֶדֶר

because, without making a vow,

etayn tz'doko

אֶתֵּן צְדָקָה

b'ad hazkoras nishmosō.

בְּעַד הַזְכָּרַת נִשְׁמָתוֹ,

I will contribute to charity in remembrance of his soul.

B'gan ayden t'hay m'nuchosō,

בְּגַן עֵדֶן תְּהֵא מְנוּחָתוֹ,

May his resting place be in the Garden of Eden —

lo-chayn ba-al horachamim

לָכֵן בַּעַל הָרַחֲמִים

therefore may the Master of mercy

yas-tiray-hu b'sayser k'nofov

יַסְתִּירֵהוּ בְּסֵתֶר כְּנָפָיו

l'ōlomim,

לְעוֹלָמִים,

shelter him in the shelter of His wings for eternity;

v'yitz-rōr bitz-rōr hacha-yim

וְיִצְרוֹר בִּצְרוֹר הַחַיִּים

es nishmosō,

אֶת נִשְׁמָתוֹ,

and may He bind his soul in the Bond of Life.

Adonoy hu na-chalosō,

יהוה הוּא נַחֲלָתוֹ,

HASHEM *is his heritage,*

v'yonu-ach b'sholōm al mishkovō.

וְיָנוּחַ בְּשָׁלוֹם עַל מִשְׁכָּבוֹ.

and may he repose in peace on his resting place.

V'nōmar: Omayn

וְנֹאמַר: אָמֵן.

Now let us respond: Amen.

─────── FOR A WOMAN ───────

AYL molay rachamim,

אֵל מָלֵא רַחֲמִים,

shōchayn bam'rōmim,

שׁוֹכֵן בַּמְּרוֹמִים,

O God, full of mercy, Who dwells on high,

ham-tzay m'nucha n'chōna

הַמְצֵא מְנוּחָה נְכוֹנָה

al kanfay Hash'china,

עַל כַּנְפֵי הַשְּׁכִינָה,

grant proper rest on the wings of the Divine Presence —

b'ma-alōs k'dōshim ut-hōrim

בְּמַעֲלוֹת קְדוֹשִׁים וּטְהוֹרִים

in the lofty levels of the holy and the pure ones,

k'zō-har horoki-a mazhirim,

כְּזֹהַר הָרָקִיעַ מַזְהִירִים,

who shine like the glow of the firmament —

es nishmas

אֶת נִשְׁמַת

for the soul of (NAME OF THE DECEASED)

she-holcho l-ōlomoh,

שֶׁהָלְכָה לְעוֹלָמָה,

who has gone on to her world,

ba-avur sheb'li neder

בַּעֲבוּר שֶׁבְּלִי נֶדֶר

because, without making a vow,

etayn tz'doko

    b'ad hazkoras nishmosoh.

אֶתֵּן צְדָקָה

בְּעַד הַזְכָּרַת נִשְׁמָתָהּ,

I will contribute to charity in remembrance of her soul.

B'gan ayden t'hay m'nuchosoh,

בְּגַן עֵדֶן תְּהֵא מְנוּחָתָהּ,

May her resting place be in the Garden of Eden —

lo-chayn ba-al horachamim

לָכֵן בַּעַל הָרַחֲמִים

therefore may the Master of mercy

yas-tire-ho b'sayser k'nofov

    l'ōlomim,

יַסְתִּירֶהָ בְּסֵתֶר כְּנָפָיו

לְעוֹלָמִים,

shelter her in the shelter of His wings for eternity;

v'yitz-rōr bitz-rōr hacha-yim

    es nishmosoh,

וְיִצְרוֹר בִּצְרוֹר הַחַיִּים

אֶת נִשְׁמָתָהּ,

and may He bind her soul in the Bond of Life.

Adonoy hu na-chalosoh,

יהוה הוּא נַחֲלָתָהּ,

HASHEM is her heritage,

v'sonu-ach b'sholōm al mishkovoh.

וְתָנוּחַ בְּשָׁלוֹם עַל מִשְׁכָּבָהּ.

and may she repose in peace on her resting place.

V'nōmar: Omayn

וְנֹאמַר: אָמֵן.

Now let us respond: Amen.

— FOR MARTYRS —

AYL molay rachamim,

    shōchayn bam'rōmim,

אֵל מָלֵא רַחֲמִים,

שׁוֹכֵן בַּמְּרוֹמִים,

O God, full of mercy, Who dwells on high,

ham-tzay m'nucha n'chōna

    al kanfay Hash'china,

הַמְצֵא מְנוּחָה נְכוֹנָה

עַל כַּנְפֵי הַשְּׁכִינָה,

grant proper rest on the wings of the Divine Presence —

b'ma-alōs k'dōshim ut-hōrim

בְּמַעֲלוֹת קְדוֹשִׁים וּטְהוֹרִים

in the lofty levels of the holy and the pure ones,

k'zō-har horoki-a mazhirim,

כְּזֹהַר הָרָקִיעַ מַזְהִירִים,

who shine like the glow of the firmament —

es nishmōs

    hak'dōshim v'hat'horim

אֶת נִשְׁמוֹת

הַקְּדוֹשִׁים וְהַטְּהוֹרִים

for the souls of the holy and pure ones

she-hum'su v'shenehergu

    v'shenishchatu v'shenis-r'fu

    v'shenit-b'u v'shenech-n'ku

שֶׁהוּמְתוּ וְשֶׁנֶּהֶרְגוּ

וְשֶׁנִּשְׁחֲטוּ וְשֶׁנִּשְׂרְפוּ

וְשֶׁנִּטְבְּעוּ וְשֶׁנֶּחְנְקוּ

who were killed, murdered, slaughtered, burned, drowned, and strangled

al kidush ha-shaym
עַל קִדּוּשׁ הַשֵּׁם,
for the sanctification of the Name,

(al y'day hatzōr'rim hagermonim,
(עַל יְדֵי הַצוֹרְרִים הַגֶּרְמָנִים
(through the hands of the German oppressors,

yimach sh'mom v'zichrom),
יְמַח שְׁמָם וְזִכְרָם),
may their name and memory be obliterated),

ba-avur sheb'li neder
בַּעֲבוּר שֶׁבְּלִי נֶדֶר
because, without making a vow,

etayn tz'doko
אֶתֵּן צְדָקָה
b'ad hazkoras nishmōsayhem.
בְּעַד הַזְכָּרַת נִשְׁמוֹתֵיהֶם,
I shall give to charity in remembrance of their souls.

B'gan ayden t'hay m'nuchosom,
בְּגַן עֵדֶן תְּהֵא מְנוּחָתָם,
May their resting place be in the Garden of Eden —

lo-chayn ba-al horachamim
לָכֵן בַּעַל הָרַחֲמִים
therefore may the Master of mercy

yas-tiraym b'sayser k'nofov
יַסְתִּירֵם בְּסֵתֶר כְּנָפָיו
l'ōlomim,
לְעוֹלָמִים,
shelter them in the shelter of His wings for eternity;

v'yitz-rōr bitz-rōr hacha-yim
וְיִצְרוֹר בִּצְרוֹר הַחַיִּים
es nishmōsay-hem,
אֶת נִשְׁמוֹתֵיהֶם,
and may He bind their souls in the Bond of Life.

Adonoy hu na-chalosom,
יהוה הוּא נַחֲלָתָם,
HASHEM is their heritage,

v'yonuchu b'sholōm
וְיָנוּחוּ בְּשָׁלוֹם
al mishk'vōsay-hem.
עַל מִשְׁכְּבוֹתֵיהֶם,
and may they repose in peace on their resting places.

V'nōmar: Omayn
וְנֹאמַר: אָמֵן.
Now let us respond: Amen.

———————————— FOR MEMBERS OF THE ISRAEL DEFENSE FORCE ————————————

AYL molay rachamim,
אֵל מָלֵא רַחֲמִים,
shōchayn bam'rōmim,
שׁוֹכֵן בַּמְּרוֹמִים,
O God, full of mercy, Who dwells on high,

ham-tzay m'nucha n'chōna
הַמְצֵא מְנוּחָה נְכוֹנָה
al kanfay Hash'china,
עַל כַּנְפֵי הַשְּׁכִינָה,
grant proper rest on the wings of the Divine Presence —

b'ma-alōs k'dōshim ut-hōrim
בְּמַעֲלוֹת קְדוֹשִׁים וּטְהוֹרִים
in the lofty levels of the holy and the pure ones,

k'zō-har horoki-a mazhirim,   כְּזֹהַר הָרָקִיעַ מַזְהִירִים,

who shine like the glow of the firmament —

l'nishmōs cha-yolay   לְנִשְׁמוֹת חַיָלֵי

tz'vo hagono l'yisro-ayl,   צְבָא הֲגָנָה לְיִשְׂרָאֵל,

for the souls of the members of the Israel Defense Force,

asher mosru nafshom   אֲשֶׁר מָסְרוּ נַפְשָׁם

who gave up their lives

al k'dushas ha-shaym,   עַל קְדֻשַּׁת הַשֵּׁם,

v'al kibush ho-oretz.   וְעַל כִּבּוּשׁ הָאָרֶץ.

for the sanctification of the Name and the conquest of the Land.

Lo-chayn ba-al horachamim   לָכֵן בַּעַל הָרַחֲמִים

Therefore may the Master of mercy

yas-tiraym b'sayser k'nofov   יַסְתִּירֵם בְּסֵתֶר כְּנָפָיו

l'ōlomim,   לְעוֹלָמִים,

shelter them in the shelter of His wings for eternity;

v'yitz-rōr bitz-rōr hacha-yim   וְיִצְרוֹר בִּצְרוֹר הַחַיִּים

es nishmōsay-hem,   אֶת נִשְׁמוֹתֵיהֶם,

and may He bind their souls in the Bond of Life.

Adonoy hu na-chalosom,   יהוה הוּא נַחֲלָתָם,

HASHEM is their heritage,

B'gan ayden t'hay m'nuchosom,   בְּגַן עֵדֶן תְּהֵא מְנוּחָתָם,

May their resting place be in the Garden of Eden —

v'yonuchu b'sholōm   וְיָנוּחוּ בְּשָׁלוֹם

al mishk'vōsay-hem.   עַל מִשְׁכְּבוֹתֵיהֶם,

and may they repose in peace on their resting places.

V'nōmar: Omayn.   וְנֹאמַר: אָמֵן.

Now let us respond: Amen.

AT THE CONCLUSION OF THE *YIZKOR* SERVICE, IT IS CUSTOMARY FOR THE *GABBAI*
TO RECITE A PRAYER ON BEHALF OF THE RABBI OF THE CONGREGATION.

מִי שֶׁבֵּרַךְ אֲבוֹתֵינוּ אַבְרָהָם יִצְחָק וְיַעֲקֹב, מֹשֶׁה אַהֲרֹן, דָּוִד וּשְׁלֹמֹה,

הוּא יְבָרֵךְ אֶת רַבִּי (NAME) בֶּן (FATHER'S NAME) בַּעֲבוּר שֶׁיִּתֵּן

צְדָקָה בְּעַד הַנְּשָׁמוֹת שֶׁהִזְכִּיר הַיּוֹם, לִכְבוֹד הַמָּקוֹם, לִכְבוֹד הַתּוֹרָה,

ON THE SABBATH — לִכְבוֹד הַשַּׁבָּת,] לִכְבוֹד הָרֶגֶל. בִּשְׂכַר זֶה, הַקָּדוֹשׁ בָּרוּךְ

הוּא יִשְׁמְרֵהוּ וְיַצִּילֵהוּ מִכָּל צָרָה וְצוּקָה, וּמִכָּל נֶגַע וּמַחֲלָה, וְיִשְׁלַח

בְּרָכָה וְהַצְלָחָה בְּכָל מַעֲשֵׂה יָדָיו, וְיִזְכֶּה לַעֲלוֹת לָרֶגֶל, עִם כָּל יִשְׂרָאֵל

אֶחָיו. וְנֹאמַר: אָמֵן.   (CONGREGATION RESPONDS: Omayn — אָמֵן)

THE SERVICE CONTINUES WITH *AV HARACHAMIM* (P. 422).

◈{ MUSSAF FOR THE FESTIVALS }◈

THE FOLLOWING *SHEMONEH ESREI* IS RECITED ON ALL FESTIVAL DAYS, INCLUDING *CHOL HAMOED* AND
THE SABBATH. ON THE FIRST DAY OF PESACH, THE *CHAZZAN'S* REPETITION BEGINS WITH THE PRAYER
FOR DEW (P. 751); ON SHEMINI ATZERES IT BEGINS WITH THE PRAYER FOR RAIN (P. 755).

IN THE SYNAGOGUE THE *SHEMONEH ESREI* IS RECITED WHILE FACING THE ARK; ELSEWHERE IT IS RECITED
WHILE FACING THE DIRECTION OF THE LAND OF ISRAEL. TAKE THREE STEPS BACKWARD, LEFT, RIGHT, LEFT,
THEN THREE STEPS FORWARD, RIGHT, LEFT, RIGHT. REMAIN STANDING WITH FEET TOGETHER DURING
SHEMONEH ESREI. RECITE IT WITH QUIET DEVOTION AND WITHOUT ANY INTERRUPTION. ALTHOUGH IT
SHOULD NOT BE AUDIBLE TO OTHERS, ONE MUST PRAY LOUDLY ENOUGH TO HEAR ONESELF.

Ki shaym Adōnoy ekro,	כִּי שֵׁם יהוה אֶקְרָא,
hovu gōdel Laylōhaynu.	הָבוּ גֹדֶל לֵאלֹהֵינוּ.

When I call out the Name of HASHEM, ascribe greatness to our God.

Adōnoy s'fosai tiftoch,	אֲדֹנָי שְׂפָתַי תִּפְתָּח,
ufi yagid t'hilosecho.	וּפִי יַגִּיד תְּהִלָּתֶךָ.

My Lord, open my lips, that my mouth may declare Your praise.

■ **First Blessing:** In the merit of our Patriarchs whose actions reflected Godliness,
Hashem pledged to always be with Israel and protect them.

BEND THE KNEES AT Boruch; BOW AT ato; STRAIGHTEN UP AT Adōnoy.

BORUCH ato Adōnoy	**בָּרוּךְ** אַתָּה יהוה

Blessed are You, HASHEM,

Elōhaynu Vaylōhay avōsaynu,	אֱלֹהֵינוּ וֵאלֹהֵי אֲבוֹתֵינוּ,

our God and the God of our forefathers,

Elōhay avrohom, Elōhay yitzchok,	אֱלֹהֵי אַבְרָהָם, אֱלֹהֵי יִצְחָק,
Vaylōhay ya-akōv,	וֵאלֹהֵי יַעֲקֹב,

God of Abraham, God of Isaac, and God of Jacob;

ho-Ayl hagodōl hagibōr v'hanōro,	הָאֵל הַגָּדוֹל הַגִּבּוֹר וְהַנּוֹרָא,
Ayl elyōn,	אֵל עֶלְיוֹן,

the great, mighty, and awesome God, the supreme God,

gōmayl chasodim tōvim	גּוֹמֵל חֲסָדִים טוֹבִים
v'kōnay hakōl,	וְקוֹנֵה הַכֹּל,

Who bestows beneficial kindnesses and creates everything,

v'zōchayr chasday ovōs,	וְזוֹכֵר חַסְדֵי אָבוֹת,

Who recalls the kindnesses of the Patriarchs

u-mayvi gō-ayl livnay v'nayhem,	וּמֵבִיא גּוֹאֵל לִבְנֵי בְנֵיהֶם,

and brings a Redeemer to their children's children,

l'ma-an sh'mō b'ahavo.	לְמַעַן שְׁמוֹ בְּאַהֲבָה.

for His Name's sake, with love.

◈§ **Mussaf.** Just as *Shacharis* and *Minchah* respectively correspond to the morning and afternoon continual-offerings in the Temple, so does *Mussaf* correspond to the *mussaf*, or additional, offerings of the Festivals, *Rosh Chodesh* and the Sabbath.

Melech ōzayr u-mōshi-a u-mogayn.   מֶלֶךְ עוֹזֵר וּמוֹשִׁיעַ וּמָגֵן.
O King, Helper, Savior, and Shield.

BEND THE KNEES AT Boruch; BOW AT ato; STRAIGHTEN UP AT Adōnoy.

Boruch ato Adōnoy,   בָּרוּךְ אַתָּה יהוה,
mogayn avrohom.   מָגֵן אַבְרָהָם.
Blessed are You, HASHEM, Shield of Abraham.

■ Second Blessing: God's might as it is manifest in nature and man

ATO gibōr l'ōlom Adōnoy,   אַתָּה גִּבּוֹר לְעוֹלָם אֲדֹנָי,
m'cha-yay maysim ato,   מְחַיֵּה מֵתִים אַתָּה,
You are eternally mighty, my Lord, the Resuscitator of the dead are You;

rav l'hōshi-a.   רַב לְהוֹשִׁיעַ.
abundantly able to save,

ON SHEMINI ATZERES, SIMCHAS TORAH, AND THE SILENT
SHEMONEH ESREI OF THE FIRST DAY OF PESACH:

Mashiv horu-ach u-mōrid hageshem.   מַשִּׁיב הָרוּחַ וּמוֹרִיד הַגֶּשֶׁם.
Who makes the wind blow and makes the rain descend;

M'chalkayl cha-yim b'chesed,   מְכַלְכֵּל חַיִּים בְּחֶסֶד,
Who sustains the living with kindness,

m'cha-yay maysim b'rachamim rabim,   מְחַיֵּה מֵתִים בְּרַחֲמִים רַבִּים,
resuscitates the dead with abundant mercy,

sōmaych nōf'lim, v'rōfay chōlim,   סוֹמֵךְ נוֹפְלִים, וְרוֹפֵא חוֹלִים,
u-matir asurim,   וּמַתִּיר אֲסוּרִים,
supports the fallen, heals the sick, releases the confined,

umka-yaym emunosō li-shaynay ofor.   וּמְקַיֵּם אֱמוּנָתוֹ לִישֵׁנֵי עָפָר.
and maintains His faith to those asleep in the dust.

Mi cho-mōcho ba-al g'vurōs,   מִי כָמוֹךָ בַּעַל גְּבוּרוֹת,
u-mi dōme loch,   וּמִי דוֹמֶה לָּךְ,
Who is like You, O Master of mighty deeds, and who is comparable to You,

melech maymis umcha-ye   מֶלֶךְ מֵמִית וּמְחַיֶּה
u-matzmi-ach y'shu-o.   וּמַצְמִיחַ יְשׁוּעָה.
O King Who causes death and restores life and makes salvation sprout!

V'ne-emon ato l'hacha-yōs maysim.   וְנֶאֱמָן אַתָּה לְהַחֲיוֹת מֵתִים.
And You are faithful to resuscitate the dead.

Boruch ato Adōnoy,   בָּרוּךְ אַתָּה יהוה,
m'cha-yay hamaysim.   מְחַיֵּה הַמֵּתִים.
Blessed are You, HASHEM, Who resuscitates the dead.

DURING THE *CHAZZAN'S* REPETITION, *KEDUSHAH* (BELOW) IS RECITED AT THIS POINT.
INDIVIDUALS CONTINUE **ato kodŏsh** (PAGE 713).

■ Third Blessing: Regarding the holiness of God's Name

THE FOLLOWING *KEDUSHAH* IS RECITED ON FESTIVAL DAYS, SHABBOS *CHOL HAMOED*, AND
HOSHANA RABBAH; ON *CHOL HAMOED* THAT FALLS ON A WEEKDAY, TURN TO PAGE 712.

STAND WITH FEET TOGETHER AND AVOID ANY INTERRUPTIONS. RISE ON TOES
WHEN SAYING **Kodŏsh, kodŏsh, kodŏsh**; **Boruch**; AND **Yimlŏch**.

CONGREGATION, THEN *CHAZZAN*:

NA-ARITZ'CHO v'nakdish'cho　　　　　　נַעֲרִיצְךָ וְנַקְדִּישְׁךָ
We shall revere You and sanctify You

k'sŏd si-ach sarfay kŏdesh,　　　　　　כְּסוֹד שִׂיחַ שַׂרְפֵי קֹדֶשׁ,
according to the counsel of the holy Seraphim,

hamakdishim shimcho bakŏdesh,　　　　　הַמַּקְדִּישִׁים שִׁמְךָ בַּקֹּדֶשׁ,
who sanctify Your Name in the Sanctuary,

kakosuv al yad n'vi-echo,　　　　　　כַּכָּתוּב עַל יַד נְבִיאֶךָ,
as it is written by Your prophet,

v'koro ze el ze v'omar:　　　　　　וְקָרָא זֶה אֶל זֶה וְאָמַר:
"And one [angel] will call another and say:

ALL IN UNISON:

Kodŏsh kodŏsh kodŏsh　　　　　　קָדוֹשׁ קָדוֹשׁ קָדוֹשׁ
　Adŏnoy Tz'vo-ŏs,　　　　　　　יהוה צְבָאוֹת,
'Holy, holy, holy is HASHEM, Master of Legions,

m'lŏ chol ho-oretz k'vŏdŏ.　　　　　מְלֹא כָל הָאָרֶץ כְּבוֹדוֹ.
the whole world is filled with His glory.' "

CONGREGATION, THEN *CHAZZAN*:

❖ K'vŏdŏ molay ŏlom,　　　　　　כְּבוֹדוֹ מָלֵא עוֹלָם,
His glory fills the world.

m'shor'sov shŏ-alim ze lo-ze,　　　מְשָׁרְתָיו שׁוֹאֲלִים זֶה לָזֶה,
His ministering angels ask one another,

a-yay m'kŏm k'vŏdŏ,　　　　　　אַיֵּה מְקוֹם כְּבוֹדוֹ,
"Where is the place of His glory?"

l'u-mosom boruch yŏmayru:　　　　לְעֻמָּתָם בָּרוּךְ יֹאמֵרוּ:
Those facing them say "Blessed":

ALL IN UNISON:

Boruch k'vŏd Adŏnoy, mim'kŏmŏ.　　בָּרוּךְ כְּבוֹד יהוה, מִמְּקוֹמוֹ.
"Blessed is the glory of HASHEM from His place."

CONGREGATION, THEN *CHAZZAN*:

❖ Mim'kŏmŏ hu yifen b'rachamim,　　מִמְּקוֹמוֹ הוּא יִפֶן בְּרַחֲמִים,
From His place may He turn with compassion

v'yochŏn am ham'yachadim sh'mŏ,　וְיָחֹן עַם הַמְיַחֲדִים שְׁמוֹ,
and be gracious to the people who declare the Oneness of His Name;

erev vovōker b'chol yōm tomid,　　　　עֶרֶב וָבֹקֶר בְּכָל יוֹם תָּמִיד,
evening and morning, every day constantly,

pa-ama-yim b'ahavo sh'ma ōm'rim:　פַּעֲמַיִם בְּאַהֲבָה שְׁמַע אוֹמְרִים:
twice, with love, they proclaim the Shema.

ALL IN UNISON:

Sh'ma yisro-ayl, Adōnoy Elōhaynu,　שְׁמַע יִשְׂרָאֵל, יהוה אֱלֹהֵינוּ,
Adōnoy e-chod.　　　　　　　　　　יהוה אֶחָד.
"Hear O Israel: HASHEM is our God, HASHEM the One and Only."

CONGREGATION, THEN *CHAZZAN*:

Hu Elōhaynu, hu ovinu,　　　　　הוּא אֱלֹהֵינוּ, הוּא אָבִינוּ,
He is our God; He is our Father;

hu malkaynu, hu mōshi-aynu,　　הוּא מַלְכֵּנוּ, הוּא מוֹשִׁיעֵנוּ,
He is our King; He is our Savior;

v'hu yash-mi-aynu　　　　　　　וְהוּא יַשְׁמִיעֵנוּ
　　b'rachamov shaynis　　　　　בְּרַחֲמָיו שֵׁנִית,
and He will let us hear, in His compassion, for a second time,

l'aynay kol choy,　　　　　　　לְעֵינֵי כָּל חָי,
in the presence of all the living,

lihyōs lochem Laylōhim,　　　　לִהְיוֹת לָכֶם לֵאלֹהִים,
　　ani Adōnoy Elōhaychem.　　אֲנִי יהוה אֱלֹהֵיכֶם.
"... to be a God to you, I am HASHEM, your God."

SOME CONGREGATIONS OMIT THE FOLLOWING ON SHABBOS *CHOL HAMOED*:
ALL IN UNISON:

Adir adiraynu, Adōnoy adōnaynu,　אַדִּיר אַדִּירֵנוּ, יהוה אֲדֹנֵינוּ,
Mighty is our Mighty One, * HASHEM, our Master —*

mo adir shimchō b'chol ho-oretz.　מָה אַדִּיר שִׁמְךָ בְּכָל הָאָרֶץ.
how mighty is Your Name throughout the earth!

V'ho-yo Adōnoy l'melech　　　　וְהָיָה יהוה לְמֶלֶךְ
　　al kōl ho-oretz　　　　　　עַל כָּל הָאָרֶץ,
HASHEM will be King over all the world —

bayōm hahu yih-ye　　　　　　בַּיּוֹם הַהוּא יִהְיֶה
　　Adōnoy e-chod ush'mō e-chod.　יהוה אֶחָד וּשְׁמוֹ אֶחָד.
on that day HASHEM will be one and His Name will be One.

CHAZZAN:

Uvdivray kodsh'cho kosuv laymōr:　וּבְדִבְרֵי קָדְשְׁךָ כָּתוּב לֵאמֹר:
And in Your holy Writings the following is written:

אַדִּיר אַדִּירֵנוּ — *Mighty is our Mighty One*. This brief selection is added to *Kedushah* only on Festivals, because, as discussed elsewhere, they are times of special closeness between God and Israel. In this brief prayer, we exclaim our confidence that God's absolute power will ultimately be recognized by the entire human race.

ALL IN UNISON:

Yimlŏch Adŏnoy l'ŏlom,

יִמְלֹךְ יהוה לְעוֹלָם,

"HASHEM shall reign forever;

Elŏha-yich tziyŏn l'dŏr vodŏr,
hal'luyoh.

אֱלֹהַיִךְ צִיּוֹן לְדֹר וָדֹר,
הַלְלוּיָהּ.

your God, O Zion, from generation to generation. Praise God!"

CHAZZAN CONCLUDES ON TOP OF PAGE 713.

THE FOLLOWING *KEDUSHAH* IS RECITED ON *CHOL HAMOED* THAT FALLS ON A WEEKDAY.
STAND WITH FEET TOGETHER AND AVOID ANY INTERRUPTIONS. RISE ON TOES
WHEN SAYING Kodŏsh, kodŏsh, kodŏsh; Boruch; AND Yimlŏch.

CONGREGATION, THEN *CHAZZAN:*

N'KADAYSH es shimcho bo-ŏlom,

נְקַדֵּשׁ אֶת שִׁמְךָ בָּעוֹלָם,

We shall sanctify Your Name in this world,

k'shaym shemakdishim ŏsŏ
bish-may morŏm,

כְּשֵׁם שֶׁמַּקְדִּישִׁים אוֹתוֹ
בִּשְׁמֵי מָרוֹם,

just as they sanctify it in heaven above,

Kakosuv al yad n'vi-echo,

כַּכָּתוּב עַל יַד נְבִיאֶךָ,

as it is written by Your prophet,

v'koro ze el ze v'omar:

וְקָרָא זֶה אֶל זֶה וְאָמַר:

"And one [angel] will call another and say:

ALL IN UNISON:

Kodŏsh, kodŏsh, kodŏsh
Adŏnoy Tz'vo-ŏs,

קָדוֹשׁ קָדוֹשׁ קָדוֹשׁ
יהוה צְבָאוֹת,

'Holy, holy, holy is HASHEM, Master of Legions,

m'lŏ chol ho-oretz k'vŏdŏ.

מְלֹא כָל הָאָרֶץ כְּבוֹדוֹ.

the whole world is filled with His glory.'"

CHAZZAN:

L'u-mosom boruch yŏmayru:

לְעֻמָּתָם בָּרוּךְ יֹאמֵרוּ:

Those facing them say, "Blessed":

ALL IN UNISON:

Boruch k'vŏd Adŏnoy, mim'kŏmŏ.

בָּרוּךְ כְּבוֹד יהוה, מִמְּקוֹמוֹ.

"Blessed is the glory of HASHEM from His place."

CHAZZAN:

Uvdivray kodsh'cho kosuv laymŏr:

וּבְדִבְרֵי קָדְשְׁךָ כָּתוּב לֵאמֹר:

And in Your holy Writings the following is written:

ALL IN UNISON:

Yimlŏch Adŏnoy l'ŏlom,

יִמְלֹךְ יהוה לְעוֹלָם,

"HASHEM shall reign forever —

Elŏha-yich tziyŏn l'dŏr vodŏr,
hal'luyoh.

אֱלֹהַיִךְ צִיּוֹן לְדֹר וָדֹר,
הַלְלוּיָהּ.

your God, O Zion — from generation to generation: Praise God!"

לְדוֹר וָדוֹר נַגִּיד גָּדְלֶךָ וּלְנֵצַח נְצָחִים קְדֻשָּׁתְךָ נַקְדִּישׁ, וְשִׁבְחֲךָ
אֱלֹהֵינוּ מִפִּינוּ לֹא יָמוּשׁ לְעוֹלָם וָעֶד, כִּי אֵל מֶלֶךְ
גָּדוֹל וְקָדוֹשׁ אָתָּה. בָּרוּךְ אַתָּה יהוה, הָאֵל הַקָּדוֹשׁ.

THE *CHAZZAN* CONTINUES *ato v'chartonu* BELOW.

ATO kodōsh v'shimcho kodōsh,　　　　**אַתָּה** קָדוֹשׁ וְשִׁמְךָ קָדוֹשׁ,

You are holy and Your Name is holy,

ukdōshim b'chol yōm　　　　　　　　וּקְדוֹשִׁים בְּכָל יוֹם
　y'hal'lucho, selo.　　　　　　　　יְהַלְלוּךָ סֶּלָה.

and holy ones praise You, every day, forever.

Boruch ato Adōnoy,　　　　　　　　בָּרוּךְ אַתָּה יהוה,
　ho-Ayl hakodōsh.　　　　　　　　הָאֵל הַקָּדוֹשׁ.

Blessed are You, HASHEM, the holy God.

▪ I reflect with gratitude upon the chosenness that Hashem has granted the Jewish
people — endowing us with privileges as well as Divine purpose.

ATO V'CHARTONU　　　　　　　　**אַתָּה בְחַרְתָּנוּ**
　mikol ho-amim,　　　　　　　　　מִכָּל הָעַמִּים,

You have chosen us from all the peoples;

ohavto ōsonu, v'rotziso bonu,　　　　אָהַבְתָּ אוֹתָנוּ, וְרָצִיתָ בָּנוּ,

You loved us and found favor in us;

v'rōmamtonu mikol hal'shōnōs,　　　וְרוֹמַמְתָּנוּ מִכָּל הַלְּשׁוֹנוֹת,

You exalted us above all the tongues*

v'kidashtonu b'mitzvōsecho,　　　　וְקִדַּשְׁתָּנוּ בְּמִצְוֹתֶיךָ,

and You sanctified us with Your commandments.

v'kayravtonu malkaynu la-avōdosecho,　וְקֵרַבְתָּנוּ מַלְכֵּנוּ לַעֲבוֹדָתֶךָ,

You drew us close, our King, to Your service

v'shimcho hagodōl v'hakodōsh　　　וְשִׁמְךָ הַגָּדוֹל וְהַקָּדוֹשׁ
　olaynu koroso.　　　　　　　　עָלֵינוּ קָרָאתָ.

and proclaimed Your great and Holy Name upon us.

VATITEN LONU Adōnoy Elōhaynu　**וַתִּתֶּן לָנוּ** יהוה אֱלֹהֵינוּ
　b'ahavo　　　　　　　　　　בְּאַהֲבָה

And You gave us, HASHEM, our God, with love

ON THE SABBATH ADD:

shabosōs limnucho u . . .　　　　. . . שַׁבָּתוֹת לִמְנוּחָה וּ
[Sabbaths for rest], and

mō-adim l'simcho,   מוֹעֲדִים לְשִׂמְחָה

appointed Festivals for gladness,

chagim uz'manim l'sosōn,   חַגִּים וּזְמַנִּים לְשָׂשׂוֹן,

Festivals and times for joy,

ON THE SABBATH ADD:

es yōm ha-shabos ha-ze v' . . .   . . . אֶת יוֹם הַשַּׁבָּת הַזֶּה וְ

this day of Sabbath and

—— ON PESACH: ——

es yōm chag hamatzōs ha-ze,   אֶת יוֹם חַג הַמַּצּוֹת הַזֶּה,

z'man chayrusaynu,   זְמַן חֵרוּתֵנוּ,

this day of the Festival of Matzos, the time of our freedom,

—— ON SHAVUOS: ——

es yōm chag hashovu-ōs ha-ze,   אֶת יוֹם חַג הַשָּׁבֻעוֹת הַזֶּה,

z'man matan tōrosaynu,   זְמַן מַתַּן תּוֹרָתֵנוּ,

this day of the Festival of Shavuos, the time of the giving of our Torah,

---

—— ON SUCCOS: ——

es yōm chag hasukōs ha-ze,   אֶת יוֹם חַג הַסֻּכּוֹת הַזֶּה,

z'man simchosaynu,   זְמַן שִׂמְחָתֵנוּ,

this day of the Festival of Succos, the time of our gladness,

---

—— ON SHEMINI ATZERES AND SIMCHAS TORAH: ——

es yōm hash'mini chag ho-atzeres   אֶת יוֹם הַשְּׁמִינִי חַג הָעֲצֶרֶת

ha-ze, z'man simchosaynu   הַזֶּה, זְמַן שִׂמְחָתֵנוּ,

the eighth day, this Festival of the Assembly, the time of our gladness,

---

ON THE SABBATH ADD:

b'ahavo   בְּאַהֲבָה

with love,

---

mikro kōdesh,   מִקְרָא קֹדֶשׁ,

a holy convocation,

zaycher li-tzi-as mitzro-yim.   זֵכֶר לִיצִיאַת מִצְרָיִם.

a memorial of the Exodus from Egypt.

■ The realization that the optimum observance of Torah and *mitzvos* may only be performed in the Land of Israel together with the Holy Temple

---

U-MIP'NAY CHATO-AYNU   וּמִפְּנֵי חֲטָאֵינוּ

But because of our sins*

וּמִפְּנֵי חֲטָאֵינוּ — *But because of our sins.* This is a cardinal principle of Jewish faith. History is not haphazard; Israel's exile and centuries-

long distress is a result of its sins. It is axiomatic, therefore, that only repentance can reverse this process.

golinu may-artzaynu,

גָּלִינוּ מֵאַרְצֵנוּ,

we have been exiled from our Land

v'nisrachaknu may-al admosaynu.

וְנִתְרַחַקְנוּ מֵעַל אַדְמָתֵנוּ.

and sent far from our soil.

V'ayn anachnu y'chōlim la-alōs

וְאֵין אֲנַחְנוּ יְכוֹלִים לַעֲלוֹת

We cannot ascend

v'layro-ōs ulhishta-chavos l'fonecho,

וְלֵרָאוֹת וּלְהִשְׁתַּחֲוֹת לְפָנֶיךָ,

to appear and to prostrate ourselves before You,

v'la-asōs chōvōsaynu
  b'vays b'chirosecho,

וְלַעֲשׂוֹת חוֹבוֹתֵינוּ
בְּבֵית בְּחִירָתֶךָ,

and to perform our obligations in the House of Your choice,

baba-yis hagodōl v'hakodōsh

בַּבַּיִת הַגָּדוֹל וְהַקָּדוֹשׁ

in the great and holy House

shenikro shimcho olov,

שֶׁנִּקְרָא שִׁמְךָ עָלָיו,

upon which Your Name was proclaimed,

mip'nay ha-yod
  shenishtal'cho b'mikdo-shecho.

מִפְּנֵי הַיָּד
שֶׁנִּשְׁתַּלְּחָה בְּמִקְדָּשֶׁךָ.

because of the hand that was dispatched against Your Sanctuary.

Y'hi rotzōn mil'fonecho

יְהִי רָצוֹן מִלְּפָנֶיךָ

May it be Your will,

Adōnoy Elōhaynu
  Vaylōhay avōsaynu,

יהוה אֱלֹהֵינוּ
וֵאלֹהֵי אֲבוֹתֵינוּ,

HASHEM, our God and the God of our forefathers,

melech rachamon,
  shetoshuv usrachaym olaynu

מֶלֶךְ רַחֲמָן,
שֶׁתָּשׁוּב וּתְרַחֵם עָלֵינוּ

O merciful King, that You once more be compassionate upon us

v'al mikdosh'cho
  b'rachamecho horabim,

וְעַל מִקְדָּשְׁךָ
בְּרַחֲמֶיךָ הָרַבִּים,

and upon Your Sanctuary in Your abundant mercy,

v'sivnayhu m'hayro usgadayl k'vōdō.

וְתִבְנֵהוּ מְהֵרָה וּתְגַדֵּל כְּבוֹדוֹ.

and rebuild it soon and magnify its glory. *

וְתִבְנֵהוּ מְהֵרָה וּתְגַדֵּל כְּבוֹדוֹ — *And rebuild it soon and magnify its glory.* The Land of Israel and the Temple are more than geographical or architectural concepts. There is a spiritual Presence that complements the material locations on earth. When Israel sinned, the spiritual Presence withdrew because it could not tolerate the nearness of sinners. Consequently, the Jewish people were exiled from the Land that they had spiritually contaminated. Conversely, Jewish return to the Land is incomplete unless we can also bring about the return of the Divine holiness to the country and the Temple Mount. Thus we now pray that God rebuild the Temple in the sense that He return His Presence to the Land, a condition that can occur only when God's sovereignty is accepted by all, and the Jewish people

ovinu malkaynu,
אָבִינוּ מַלְכֵּנוּ,
Our Father, our King,

galay k'vōd malchus'cho olaynu m'hayro,
גַּלֵּה כְּבוֹד מַלְכוּתְךָ עָלֵינוּ מְהֵרָה,
reveal the glory of Your Kingship upon us, speedily;

v'hōfa v'hinosay olaynu
וְהוֹפַע וְהִנָּשֵׂא עָלֵינוּ
appear and be uplifted over us

l'aynay kol choy.
לְעֵינֵי כָּל חָי.
before the eyes of all the living.

V'korayv p'zuraynu mibayn hagōyim,
וְקָרֵב פְּזוּרֵינוּ מִבֵּין הַגּוֹיִם,
Draw our scattered ones near from among the nations,

unfutzōsaynu kanays mi-yark'say oretz.
וּנְפוּצוֹתֵינוּ כַּנֵּס מִיַּרְכְּתֵי אָרֶץ.
and bring in our dispersions from the ends of the earth.

Vahavi-aynu l'tziyōn ir'cho b'rino,
וַהֲבִיאֵנוּ לְצִיּוֹן עִירְךָ בְּרִנָּה,
Bring us to Zion, Your City, in glad song,

v'lirushola-yim bays mikdosh'cho b'simchas ōlom.
וְלִירוּשָׁלַיִם בֵּית מִקְדָּשְׁךָ בְּשִׂמְחַת עוֹלָם.
and to Jerusalem, home of Your Sanctuary, in eternal joy.

V'shom na-ase l'fonecho
וְשָׁם נַעֲשֶׂה לְפָנֶיךָ
There we will perform before You

es korb'nōs chōvōsaynu,
אֶת קָרְבְּנוֹת חוֹבוֹתֵינוּ,
our obligatory offerings,

t'midim k'sidrom,
תְּמִידִים כְּסִדְרָם,
the continual-offerings according to their order

u-musofim k'hilchosom.
וּמוּסָפִים כְּהִלְכָתָם.
and the additional-offerings according to their law.

—————————— ON WEEKDAYS: ——————————

V'es musaf
וְאֶת מוּסַף
and the additional-offering of

—————————— ON THE SABBATH: ——————————

v'es mus'fay yōm ha-shabos ha-ze v' . . .
וְאֶת מוּסְפֵי יוֹם הַשַּׁבָּת הַזֶּה וְ . . .
And the additional-offerings of this day of Sabbath and

are returned to their Land. Then will come the climax of our longing — that we will deserve to serve God in His Temple as He ordained in the Torah.

—————————— ON PESACH ——————————

yōm chag hamatzōs ha-ze

יוֹם חַג הַמַּצּוֹת הַזֶּה

this day of the Festival of Matzos

—————————— ON SHAVUOS ——————————

yōm chag hashovu-ōs ha-ze

יוֹם חַג הַשָּׁבֻעוֹת הַזֶּה

this day of the Festival of Shavuos

—————————— ON SUCCOS ——————————

yōm chag hasukōs ha-ze

יוֹם חַג הַסֻּכּוֹת הַזֶּה

this day of the Succos Festival

———————— ON SHEMINI ATZERES AND SIMCHAS TORAH ————————

yōm hash'mini chag ho-atzeres ha-ze

יוֹם הַשְּׁמִינִי חַג הָעֲצֶרֶת הַזֶּה

the eighth day, this Festival of the Assembly

na-ase v'nakriv l'fonecho b'ahavo

נַעֲשֶׂה וְנַקְרִיב לְפָנֶיךָ בְּאַהֲבָה

we will perform and bring near to You with love,

k'mitzvas r'tzōnecho,

כְּמִצְוַת רְצוֹנֶךָ,

according to the commandment of Your will,

k'mō shekosavto olaynu b'sōrosecho

כְּמוֹ שֶׁכָּתַבְתָּ עָלֵינוּ בְּתוֹרָתֶךָ,

as You have written for us in Your Torah,

al y'day mōshe avdecho,

עַל יְדֵי מֹשֶׁה עַבְדֶּךָ,

through Moses, Your servant,

mipi ch'vōdecho, ko-omur:

מִפִּי כְבוֹדֶךָ, כָּאָמוּר:

from Your glorious expression, as it is said:

———————— ON THE SABBATH ADD: ————————

UVYŌM HA-SHABOS

וּבְיוֹם הַשַּׁבָּת

On the Sabbath day:

sh'nay ch'vosim b'nay shono t'mimim,

שְׁנֵי כְבָשִׂים בְּנֵי שָׁנָה תְמִימִם,

two [male] first-year lambs, unblemished;

ush-nay esrōnim sō-les mincho b'lulo va-shemen, v'niskō.

וּשְׁנֵי עֶשְׂרֹנִים סֹלֶת מִנְחָה בְּלוּלָה בַשֶּׁמֶן, וְנִסְכּוֹ.

and two tenth-ephah of fine flour for a meal-offering,
mixed with olive oil, and its wine-libation.

Ōlas shabas b'shabatō,

עֹלַת שַׁבַּת בְּשַׁבַּתּוֹ,

The elevation-offering of the Sabbath must be on its particular Sabbath,

al ōlas hatomid v'nisko.

עַל עֹלַת הַתָּמִיד וְנִסְכָּהּ.

in addition to the continual elevation-offering and its wine-libation.

Ze korban shabos.

זֶה קָרְבַּן שַׁבָּת.

V'korban ha-yōm ko-omur:

וְקָרְבַּן הַיּוֹם כָּאָמוּר:

This is the offering of the Sabbath. And the offering of the day is as it is said:

■ The sanctity of the day warranted these additional offerings. May my recitation of
these verses be considered by Hashem as if they were offered.

ON THE FIRST TWO DAYS OF PESACH:

U-VACHŌDESH HORI-SHŌN,   וּבַחֹדֶשׁ הָרִאשׁוֹן
b'arbo-o osor yōm lachōdesh,   בְּאַרְבָּעָה עָשָׂר יוֹם לַחֹדֶשׁ,
And in the first month on the fourteenth day of the month —
pesach Ladōnoy.   פֶּסַח לַיהוה.
the pesach-offering to HASHEM.

U-vachami-sho osor yōm   וּבַחֲמִשָּׁה עָשָׂר יוֹם
lachōdesh ha-ze, chog,   לַחֹדֶשׁ הַזֶּה, חָג,
And on the fifteenth day of this month — a Festival;
shiv-as yomim matzōs yay-ochayl.   שִׁבְעַת יָמִים מַצּוֹת יֵאָכֵל.
for seven days, matzos are to be eaten.

Ba-yōm hori-shōn mikro kōdesh,   בַּיּוֹם הָרִאשׁוֹן מִקְרָא קֹדֶשׁ,
On the first day is a holy convocation,
kol m'leches avōdo lō sa-asu.   כָּל מְלֶאכֶת עֲבֹדָה לֹא תַעֲשׂוּ.
you may not do any laborious work.

V'hikravtem i-she ōlo Ladōnoy,   וְהִקְרַבְתֶּם אִשֶּׁה עֹלָה לַיהוה,
You are to bring a fire-offering, an elevation-offering to HASHEM,
porim b'nay vokor sh'na-yim,   פָּרִים בְּנֵי בָקָר שְׁנַיִם,
v'a-yil e-chod,   וְאַיִל אֶחָד,
two young bulls, one ram
v'shiv-o ch'vosim b'nay shono,   וְשִׁבְעָה כְבָשִׂים בְּנֵי שָׁנָה,
and seven [male] first-year lambs,
t'mimim yih-yu lochem.   תְּמִימִם יִהְיוּ לָכֶם.
they shall be unblemished for you.

U-minchosom v'nis-kayhem kimdubor,   וּמִנְחָתָם וְנִסְכֵּיהֶם כִּמְדֻבָּר,
And their meal-offerings and their wine-libations as mentioned:
sh'lōsho esrōnim lapor,   שְׁלֹשָׁה עֶשְׂרֹנִים לַפָּר,
ush-nay esrōnim lo-o-yil,   וּשְׁנֵי עֶשְׂרֹנִים לָאָיִל,
three tenth-ephah for each bull; two tenth-ephah for each ram;
v'isorōn lakeves, v'ya-yin k'niskō.   וְעִשָּׂרוֹן לַכֶּבֶשׂ, וְיַיִן כְּנִסְכּוֹ.
one tenth-ephah for each lamb; and wine for its libation.

V'so-ir l'chapayr,   וְשָׂעִיר לְכַפֵּר,
ush-nay s'midim k'hilchosom.   וּשְׁנֵי תְמִידִים כְּהִלְכָתָם.
A he-goat for atonement, and two continual-offerings according to their law.

CONTINUE ON PAGE 728.

ON *CHOL HAMOED* PESACH AND THE LAST TWO DAYS OF PESACH:

V'HIKRAVTEM i-she   וְהִקְרַבְתֶּם אִשֶּׁה
    ōlo Ladōnoy,   עֹלָה לַיהוה,

You are to bring a fire-offering, an elevation-offering to HASHEM,

porim b'nay vokor sh'na-yim,   פָּרִים בְּנֵי בָקָר שְׁנַיִם,
    v'a-yil e-chod,   וְאַיִל אֶחָד,

two young bulls, one ram

v'shiv-o ch'vosim b'nay shono,   וְשִׁבְעָה כְבָשִׂים בְּנֵי שָׁנָה,

and seven [male] first-year lambs,

t'mimim yih-yu lochem.   תְּמִימִם יִהְיוּ לָכֶם.

they shall be unblemished for you.

U-minchosom v'nis-kayhem kimdubor,   וּמִנְחָתָם וְנִסְכֵּיהֶם כִּמְדֻבָּר,

And their meal-offerings and their wine-libations as mentioned:

sh'lōsho esrōnim lapor,   שְׁלֹשָׁה עֶשְׂרֹנִים לַפָּר,

three tenth-ephah for each bull;

ush-nay esrōnim lo-o-yil,   וּשְׁנֵי עֶשְׂרֹנִים לָאָיִל,

two tenth-ephah for each ram;

v'isorōn lakeves, v'ya-yin k'niskō.   וְעִשָּׂרוֹן לַכֶּבֶשׂ, וְיַיִן כְּנִסְכּוֹ.

one tenth-ephah for each lamb; and wine for its libation.

V'so-ir l'chapayr,   וְשָׂעִיר לְכַפֵּר,

A he-goat for atonement,

ush-nay s'midim k'hilchosom.   וּשְׁנֵי תְמִידִים כְּהִלְכָתָם.

and two continual-offerings according to their law.

CONTINUE ON PAGE 728.

ON SHAVUOS:

UVYŌM HABIKURIM,   וּבְיוֹם הַבִּכּוּרִים,

And on the day of the first fruits,

b'hak-riv'chem mincho chadosho   בְּהַקְרִיבְכֶם מִנְחָה חֲדָשָׁה
    Ladōnoy,   לַיהוה,

when you bring a new meal-offering to HASHEM,

b'shovu-ōsaychem,   בְּשָׁבֻעֹתֵיכֶם,

on your Festival of Weeks;

mikro kōdesh yih-ye lochem,   מִקְרָא קֹדֶשׁ יִהְיֶה לָכֶם,

there shall be a holy convocation for you,

kol m'leches avōdo lō sa-asu.   כָּל מְלֶאכֶת עֲבֹדָה לֹא תַעֲשׂוּ.

you may not do any laborious work.

ON SHAVUOS CONTINUE HERE:

V'hikravtem ōlo
  l'ray-ach nichō-ach Ladōnoy,

וְהִקְרַבְתֶּם עוֹלָה
לְרֵיחַ נִיחֹחַ לַיהוה,

You are to bring an elevation-offering for a satisfying aroma to HASHEM;

porim b'nay vokor sh'na-yim,
  a-yil e-chod,

פָּרִים בְּנֵי בָקָר שְׁנַיִם,
אַיִל אֶחָד,

two young bulls, one ram,

shiv-o ch'vosim b'nay shono.

שִׁבְעָה כְבָשִׂים בְּנֵי שָׁנָה.

seven [male] first-year lambs.

U-minchosom v'nis-kayhem kimdubor,

וּמִנְחָתָם וְנִסְכֵּיהֶם כִּמְדֻבָּר,

And their meal-offerings and their wine-libations as mentioned:

sh'lōsho esrōnim lapor,

שְׁלֹשָׁה עֶשְׂרֹנִים לַפָּר,

three tenth-ephah for each bull;

ush-nay esrōnim lo-o-yil,

וּשְׁנֵי עֶשְׂרֹנִים לָאָיִל,

two tenth-ephah for each ram;

v'isorōn lakeves, v'ya-yin k'niskō.

וְעִשָּׂרוֹן לַכֶּבֶשׂ, וְיַיִן כְּנִסְכּוֹ.

one tenth-ephah for each lamb; and wine for its libation.

V'so-ir l'chapayr,

וְשָׂעִיר לְכַפֵּר,

A he-goat for atonement,

ush-nay s'midim k'hilchosom.

וּשְׁנֵי תְמִידִים כְּהִלְכָתָם.

and two continual-offerings according to their law.

CONTINUE ON PAGE 728.

ON THE FIRST TWO DAYS OF SUCCOS:

U-VACHAMI-SHO OSOR yōm
  lachōdesh hash'vi-i,

וּבַחֲמִשָּׁה עָשָׂר יוֹם
לַחֹדֶשׁ הַשְּׁבִיעִי,

And on the fifteenth day of the seventh month,

mikro kōdesh yih-ye lochem,

מִקְרָא קֹדֶשׁ יִהְיֶה לָכֶם,

there shall be a holy convocation for you;

kol m'leches avōdo lō sa-asu,

כָּל מְלֶאכֶת עֲבֹדָה לֹא תַעֲשׂוּ,

you may not do any laborious work;

v'chagōsem chag Ladōnoy
  shiv-as yomim.

וְחַגֹּתֶם חַג לַיהוה
שִׁבְעַת יָמִים.

and you shall celebrate a Festival to HASHEM for seven days.

V'hikravtem ōlo i-shay

וְהִקְרַבְתֶּם עֹלָה אִשֵּׁה

You are to bring an elevation-offering, a fire-offering,

ON THE FIRST TWO DAYS OF SUCCOS CONTINUE HERE:

רֵיחַ נִיחֹחַ לַיהוה,

ray-ach nichō-ach Ladōnoy,

a satisfying aroma to HASHEM;

פָּרִים בְּנֵי בָקָר שְׁלֹשָׁה עָשָׂר,

porim b'nay vokor sh'lōsho osor,

thirteen young bulls,

אֵילִם שְׁנָיִם,

aylim sh'no-yim,

two rams,

כְּבָשִׂים בְּנֵי שָׁנָה אַרְבָּעָה עָשָׂר,

k'vosim b'nay shono arbo-o osor,

fourteen [male] first-year lambs,

תְּמִימִם יִהְיוּ.

t'mimim yih-yu.

they are to be unblemished.

וּמִנְחָתָם וְנִסְכֵּיהֶם כִּמְדֻבָּר,

U-minchosom v'nis-kayhem kimdubor,

And their meal-offerings and their wine-libations as mentioned:

שְׁלֹשָׁה עֶשְׂרֹנִים לַפָּר,

sh'lōsho esrōnim lapor,

three tenth-ephah for each bull;

וּשְׁנֵי עֶשְׂרֹנִים לָאָיִל,

ush-nay esrōnim lo-o-yil,

two tenth-ephah for each ram;

וְעִשָּׂרוֹן לַכֶּבֶשׂ, וְיַיִן כְּנִסְכּוֹ.

v'isorōn lakeves, v'ya-yin k'niskō.

one tenth-ephah for each lamb; and wine for its libation.

וְשָׂעִיר לְכַפֵּר,

V'so-ir l'chapayr,

A he-goat for atonement,

וּשְׁנֵי תְמִידִים כְּהִלְכָתָם.

ush-nay s'midim k'hilchosom.

and two continual-offerings according to their law.

CONTINUE ON PAGE 728.

ON THE FIRST DAY OF *CHOL HAMOED* SUCCOS:

וּבַיּוֹם הַשֵּׁנִי,

U-VA-YŌM ha-shayni,

And on the second day:

פָּרִים בְּנֵי בָקָר שְׁנֵים עָשָׂר,

porim b'nay vokor sh'naym osor,

אֵילִם שְׁנָיִם,

aylim sh'noyim,

twelve young bulls, two rams,

כְּבָשִׂים בְּנֵי שָׁנָה אַרְבָּעָה עָשָׂר,

k'vosim b'nay shono arbo-o osor,

תְּמִימִם.

t'mimim.

fourteen [male] first-year lambs, unblemished.

וּמִנְחָתָם וְנִסְכֵּיהֶם כִּמְדֻבָּר,

U-minchosom v'nis-kayhem kimdubor,

And their meal-offerings and their wine-libations as mentioned:

שְׁלֹשָׁה עֶשְׂרֹנִים לַפָּר,

sh'lōsho esrōnim lapor,

three tenth-ephah for each bull;

ON THE FIRST DAY OF *CHOL HAMOED* SUCCOS CONTINUE HERE:

ush-nay esrōnim lo-o-yil,	וּשְׁנֵי עֶשְׂרֹנִים לָאָיִל,
two tenth-ephah for each ram;	
v'isorōn lakeves, v'ya-yin k'niskō.	וְעִשָּׂרוֹן לַכֶּבֶשׂ, וְיַיִן כְּנִסְכּוֹ.
one tenth-ephah for each lamb; and wine for its libation.	
V'so-ir l'chapayr,	וְשָׂעִיר לְכַפֵּר,
A he-goat for atonement,	
ush-nay s'midim k'hilchosom.	וּשְׁנֵי תְמִידִים כְּהִלְכָתָם.
and two continual-offerings according to their law.	
U-va-yōm hash'lishi,	וּבַיּוֹם הַשְּׁלִישִׁי,
And on the third day:	
porim ashtay osor, aylim sh'noyim,	פָּרִים עַשְׁתֵּי עָשָׂר, אֵילִם שְׁנָיִם,
eleven bulls, two rams,	
k'vosim b'nay shono arbo-o osor,	כְּבָשִׂים בְּנֵי שָׁנָה אַרְבָּעָה עָשָׂר,
t'mimim.	תְּמִימִם.
fourteen [male] first-year lambs, unblemished.	
U-minchosom v'nis-kayhem kimdubor,	וּמִנְחָתָם וְנִסְכֵּיהֶם כִּמְדֻבָּר,
And their meal-offerings and their wine-libations as mentioned:	
sh'lōsho esrōnim lapor,	שְׁלֹשָׁה עֶשְׂרֹנִים לַפָּר,
three tenth-ephah for each bull;	
ush-nay esrōnim lo-o-yil,	וּשְׁנֵי עֶשְׂרֹנִים לָאָיִל,
two tenth-ephah for each ram;	
v'isorōn lakeves, v'ya-yin k'niskō.	וְעִשָּׂרוֹן לַכֶּבֶשׂ, וְיַיִן כְּנִסְכּוֹ.
one tenth-ephah for each lamb; and wine for its libation.	
V'so-ir l'chapayr,	וְשָׂעִיר לְכַפֵּר,
A he-goat for atonement,	
ush-nay s'midim k'hilchosom.	וּשְׁנֵי תְמִידִים כְּהִלְכָתָם.
and two continual-offerings according to their law.	

CONTINUE ON PAGE 728.

ON THE SECOND DAY OF *CHOL HAMOED* SUCCOS:

U-VA-YŌM ha-sh'lishi,	**וּבַיּוֹם** הַשְּׁלִישִׁי,
And on the third day:	
porim ashtay osor, aylim sh'noyim,	פָּרִים עַשְׁתֵּי עָשָׂר, אֵילִם שְׁנָיִם,
eleven bulls, two rams,	
k'vosim b'nay shono arbo-o osor,	כְּבָשִׂים בְּנֵי שָׁנָה אַרְבָּעָה עָשָׂר,
t'mimim.	תְּמִימִם.
fourteen [male] first-year lambs, unblemished.	

ON THE SECOND DAY OF *CHOL HAMOED* SUCCOS CONTINUE HERE:

U-minchosom v'nis-kayhem kimdubor,   וּמִנְחָתָם וְנִסְכֵּיהֶם כִּמְדֻבָּר,

And their meal-offerings and their wine-libations as mentioned:

sh'lōsho esrōnim lapor,   שְׁלֹשָׁה עֶשְׂרֹנִים לַפָּר,

three tenth-ephah for each bull;

ush-nay esrōnim lo-o-yil,   וּשְׁנֵי עֶשְׂרֹנִים לָאָיִל,

two tenth-ephah for each ram;

v'isorōn lakeves, v'ya-yin k'niskō.   וְעִשָּׂרוֹן לַכֶּבֶשׂ, וְיַיִן כְּנִסְכּוֹ.

one tenth-ephah for each lamb; and wine for its libation.

V'so-ir l'chapayr,   וְשָׂעִיר לְכַפֵּר,

A he-goat for atonement,

ush-nay s'midim k'hilchosom.   וּשְׁנֵי תְמִידִים כְּהִלְכָתָם.

and two continual-offerings according to their law.

U-va-yōm hor'vi-i,   וּבַיּוֹם הָרְבִיעִי,

And on the fourth day:

porim asoro, aylim sh'noyim,   פָּרִים עֲשָׂרָה, אֵילִם שְׁנָיִם,

ten bulls, two rams,

k'vosim b'nay shono   כְּבָשִׂים בְּנֵי שָׁנָה

  arbo-o osor, t'mimim.   אַרְבָּעָה עָשָׂר, תְּמִימִם.

fourteen [male] first-year lambs, unblemished.

U-minchosom v'nis-kayhem kimdubor,   וּמִנְחָתָם וְנִסְכֵּיהֶם כִּמְדֻבָּר,

And their meal-offerings and their wine-libations as mentioned:

sh'lōsho esrōnim lapor,   שְׁלֹשָׁה עֶשְׂרֹנִים לַפָּר,

three tenth-ephah for each bull;

ush-nay esrōnim lo-o-yil,   וּשְׁנֵי עֶשְׂרֹנִים לָאָיִל,

two tenth ephah for each ram;

v'isorōn lakeves, v'ya-yin k'niskō.   וְעִשָּׂרוֹן לַכֶּבֶשׂ, וְיַיִן כְּנִסְכּוֹ.

one tenth-ephah for each lamb; and wine for its libation.

V'so-ir l'chapayr,   וְשָׂעִיר לְכַפֵּר,

A he-goat for atonement,

ush-nay s'midim k'hilchosom.   וּשְׁנֵי תְמִידִים כְּהִלְכָתָם.

and two continual-offerings according to their law.

CONTINUE ON PAGE 728.

ON THE THIRD DAY OF *CHOL HAMOED* SUCCOS:

U-VA-YŌM hor'vi-i,   **וּבַיּוֹם** הָרְבִיעִי,

And on the fourth day:

porim asoro, aylim sh'noyim,   פָּרִים עֲשָׂרָה, אֵילִם שְׁנָיִם,

ten bulls, two rams,

ON THE THIRD DAY OF *CHOL HAMOED* SUCCOS CONTINUE HERE:

k'vosim b'nay shono arbo-o osor,   כְּבָשִׂים בְּנֵי שָׁנָה אַרְבָּעָה עָשָׂר,

t'mimim.   תְּמִימִם.

fourteen [male] first-year lambs, unblemished.

U-minchosom v'nis-kayhem kimdubor,   וּמִנְחָתָם וְנִסְכֵּיהֶם כִּמְדֻבָּר,

And their meal-offerings and their wine-libations as mentioned:

sh'lōsho esrōnim lapor,   שְׁלֹשָׁה עֶשְׂרֹנִים לַפָּר,

three tenth-ephah for each bull;

ush-nay esrōnim lo-o-yil,   וּשְׁנֵי עֶשְׂרֹנִים לָאַיִל,

two tenth-ephah for each ram;

v'isorōn lakeves, v'ya-yin k'niskō.   וְעִשָּׂרוֹן לַכֶּבֶשׂ, וְיַיִן כְּנִסְכּוֹ.

one tenth-ephah for each lamb; and wine for its libation.

V'so-ir l'chapayr,   וְשָׂעִיר לְכַפֵּר,

A he-goat for atonement,

ush-nay s'midim k'hilchosom.   וּשְׁנֵי תְמִידִים כְּהִלְכָתָם.

and two continual-offerings according to their law.

U-va-yōm ha-chami-shi,   וּבַיּוֹם הַחֲמִישִׁי,

And on the fifth day:

porim tish-o, aylim sh'noyim,   פָּרִים תִּשְׁעָה, אֵילִם שְׁנָיִם,

nine bulls, two rams,

k'vosim b'nay shono arbo-o osor,   כְּבָשִׂים בְּנֵי שָׁנָה אַרְבָּעָה עָשָׂר,

t'mimim.   תְּמִימִם.

fourteen [male] first-year lambs, unblemished.

U-minchosom v'nis-kayhem kimdubor,   וּמִנְחָתָם וְנִסְכֵּיהֶם כִּמְדֻבָּר,

And their meal-offerings and their wine-libations as mentioned:

sh'lōsho esrōnim lapor,   שְׁלֹשָׁה עֶשְׂרֹנִים לַפָּר,

three tenth-ephah for each bull;

ush-nay esrōnim lo-o-yil,   וּשְׁנֵי עֶשְׂרֹנִים לָאַיִל,

two tenth ephah for each ram;

v'isorōn lakeves, v'ya-yin k'niskō.   וְעִשָּׂרוֹן לַכֶּבֶשׂ, וְיַיִן כְּנִסְכּוֹ.

one tenth-ephah for each lamb; and wine for its libation.

V'so-ir l'chapayr,   וְשָׂעִיר לְכַפֵּר,

A he-goat for atonement,

ush-nay s'midim k'hilchosom.   וּשְׁנֵי תְמִידִים כְּהִלְכָתָם.

and two continual-offerings according to their law.

CONTINUE ON PAGE 728.

ON THE FOURTH DAY OF *CHOL HAMOED* SUCCOS:

U-VA-YŌM ha-chami-shi,   וּבַיּוֹם הַחֲמִישִׁי

And on the fifth day:

porim tish-o, aylim sh'noyim,   פָּרִים תִּשְׁעָה, אֵילִם שְׁנָיִם,

nine bulls, two rams,

k'vosim b'nay shono arbo-o osor,   כְּבָשִׂים בְּנֵי שָׁנָה אַרְבָּעָה עָשָׂר,
    t'mimim.   תְּמִימִם.

fourteen [male] first-year lambs, unblemished.

U-minchosom v'nis-kayhem kimdubor,   וּמִנְחָתָם וְנִסְכֵּיהֶם כִּמְדֻבָּר,

And their meal-offerings and their wine-libations as mentioned:

sh'lōsho esrōnim lapor,   שְׁלֹשָׁה עֶשְׂרֹנִים לַפָּר,

three tenth-ephah for each bull;

ush-nay esrōnim lo-o-yil,   וּשְׁנֵי עֶשְׂרֹנִים לָאָיִל,

two tenth-ephah for each ram;

v'isorōn lakeves, v'ya-yin k'niskō.   וְעִשָּׂרוֹן לַכֶּבֶשׂ, וְיַיִן כְּנִסְכּוֹ.

one tenth-ephah for each lamb; and wine for its libation.

V'so-ir l'chapayr,   וְשָׂעִיר לְכַפֵּר,

A he-goat for atonement,

ush-nay s'midim k'hilchosom.   וּשְׁנֵי תְמִידִים כְּהִלְכָתָם.

and two continual-offerings according to their law.

U-va-yōm ha-shishi,   וּבַיּוֹם הַשִּׁשִּׁי,

And on the sixth day:

porim sh'mono, aylim sh'noyim,   פָּרִים שְׁמֹנָה, אֵילִם שְׁנָיִם,

eight bulls, two rams,

k'vosim b'nay shono arbo-o osor,   כְּבָשִׂים בְּנֵי שָׁנָה אַרְבָּעָה עָשָׂר,
    t'mimim.   תְּמִימִם.

fourteen [male] first-year lambs, unblemished.

U-minchosom v'nis-kayhem kimdubor,   וּמִנְחָתָם וְנִסְכֵּיהֶם כִּמְדֻבָּר,

And their meal-offerings and their wine-libations as mentioned:

sh'lōsho esrōnim lapor,   שְׁלֹשָׁה עֶשְׂרֹנִים לַפָּר,

three tenth-ephah for each bull;

ush-nay esrōnim lo-o-yil,   וּשְׁנֵי עֶשְׂרֹנִים לָאָיִל,

two tenth-ephah for each ram;

v'isorōn lakeves, v'ya-yin k'niskō.   וְעִשָּׂרוֹן לַכֶּבֶשׂ, וְיַיִן כְּנִסְכּוֹ.

one tenth-ephah for each lamb; and wine for its libation.

V'so-ir l'chapayr,   וְשָׂעִיר לְכַפֵּר,

A he-goat for atonement,

ON THE FOURTH DAY OF *CHOL HAMOED* SUCCOS CONTINUE HERE:

ush-nay s'midim k'hilchosom.   וּשְׁנֵי תְמִידִים כְּהִלְכָתָם.

and two continual-offerings according to their law.

CONTINUE ON PAGE 728.

ON HOSHANA RABBAH:

U-VA-YŌM ha-shishi,   **וּבַיּוֹם** הַשִּׁשִּׁי,

And on the sixth day:

porim sh'mōno, aylim sh'noyim,   פָּרִים שְׁמֹנָה, אֵילִם שְׁנָיִם,

eight bulls, two rams,

k'vosim b'nay shono arbo-o osor,   כְּבָשִׂים בְּנֵי שָׁנָה אַרְבָּעָה עָשָׂר,

t'mimim.   תְּמִימִם.

fourteen [male] first-year lambs, unblemished.

U-minchosom v'nis-kayhem kimdubor,   וּמִנְחָתָם וְנִסְכֵּיהֶם כִּמְדֻבָּר,

And their meal-offerings and their wine-libations as mentioned:

sh'lōsho esrōnim lapor,   שְׁלֹשָׁה עֶשְׂרֹנִים לַפָּר,

three tenth-ephah for each bull;

ush-nay esrōnim lo-o-yil,   וּשְׁנֵי עֶשְׂרֹנִים לָאָיִל,

two tenth-ephah for each ram;

v'isorōn lakeves, v'ya-yin k'niskō.   וְעִשָּׂרוֹן לַכֶּבֶשׂ, וְיַיִן כְּנִסְכּוֹ.

one tenth-ephah for each lamb; and wine for its libation.

V'so-ir l'chapayr,   וְשָׂעִיר לְכַפֵּר,

A he-goat for atonement,

ush-nay s'midim k'hilchosom.   וּשְׁנֵי תְמִידִים כְּהִלְכָתָם.

and two continual-offerings according to their law.

U-va-yōm hash'vi-i,   וּבַיּוֹם הַשְּׁבִיעִי,

And on the seventh day:

porim shiv-o, aylim sh'noyim,   פָּרִים שִׁבְעָה, אֵילִם שְׁנָיִם,

seven bulls, two rams,

k'vosim b'nay shono arbo-o osor,   כְּבָשִׂים בְּנֵי שָׁנָה אַרְבָּעָה עָשָׂר,

t'mimim.   תְּמִימִם.

fourteen [male] first-year lambs, unblemished.

U-minchosom v'nis-kayhem kimdubor,   וּמִנְחָתָם וְנִסְכֵּיהֶם כִּמְדֻבָּר,

And their meal-offerings and their wine-libations as mentioned:

sh'lōsho esrōnim lapor,   שְׁלֹשָׁה עֶשְׂרֹנִים לַפָּר,

three tenth-ephah for each bull;

ON HOSHANA RABBAH CONTINUE HERE:

ush-nay esrōnim lo-o-yil,　　　　　　　　וּשְׁנֵי עֶשְׂרֹנִים לָאָיִל,

two tenth-ephah for each ram;

v'isorōn lakeves, v'ya-yin k'niskō.　　　וְעִשָּׂרוֹן לַכֶּבֶשׂ, וְיַיִן כְּנִסְכּוֹ.

one tenth-ephah for each lamb; and wine for its libation.

V'so-ir l'chapayr,　　　　　　　　　　וְשָׂעִיר לְכַפֵּר,

A he-goat for atonement,

ush-nay s'midim k'hilchosom.　　　　וּשְׁנֵי תְמִידִים כְּהִלְכָתָם.

and two continual-offerings according to their law.

CONTINUE ON PAGE 728.

ON SHEMINI ATZERES AND SIMCHAS TORAH:

BA-YŌM HA-SH'MINI,　　　　　　**בַּיּוֹם הַשְּׁמִינִי,**

atzeres tih-ye lochem,　　　　　　　עֲצֶרֶת תִּהְיֶה לָכֶם,

On the eighth day, there shall be an Assembly for you,

kol m'leches avōdo lō sa-asu.　　　כָּל מְלֶאכֶת עֲבֹדָה לֹא תַעֲשׂוּ.

you may not do any laborious work.

v'hikravtem ōlo i-shay　　　　　　וְהִקְרַבְתֶּם עֹלָה אִשֵּׁה

　　rayach nichō-ach Ladōnoy,　　　רֵיחַ נִיחֹחַ לַיהוה,

You are to bring an elevation-offering, a fire-offering,

a satisfying aroma to Hashem,

par e-chod, a-yil e-chod,　　　　פַּר אֶחָד, אַיִל אֶחָד,

one bull, one ram,

k'vosim b'nay shono shiv-o,　　　כְּבָשִׂים בְּנֵי שָׁנָה שִׁבְעָה,

　　t'mimim.　　　　　　　　　　תְּמִימִם.

seven [male] first-year lambs, unblemished.

U-minchosom v'nis-kayhem kimdubor,　וּמִנְחָתָם וְנִסְכֵּיהֶם כִּמְדֻבָּר,

And their meal-offerings and their wine-libations as mentioned:

sh'lōsho esrōnim lapor,　　　　שְׁלֹשָׁה עֶשְׂרֹנִים לַפָּר,

　　ush'nay esrōnim lo-o-yil,　　וּשְׁנֵי עֶשְׂרֹנִים לָאָיִל,

three tenth-ephah for each bull; two tenth-ephah for each ram;

v'isorōn lakeves, v'ya-yin k'niskō.　וְעִשָּׂרוֹן לַכֶּבֶשׂ, וְיַיִן כְּנִסְכּוֹ.

one tenth-ephah for each lamb; and wine for its libation.

V'so-ir l'chapayr,　　　　　　　וְשָׂעִיר לְכַפֵּר,

A he-goat for atonement,

ush-nay s'midim k'hilchosom.　　וּשְׁנֵי תְמִידִים כְּהִלְכָתָם.

and two continual-offerings according to their law.

CONTINUE ON PAGE 728.

ON ALL DAYS CONTINUE HERE:

ON THE SABBATH, THE FOLLOWING PARAGRAPH IS ADDED:

YISM'CHU v'malchus'cho   **יִשְׂמְחוּ** בְמַלְכוּתְךָ
They shall rejoice in Your kingship —

shōm'ray shabos v'kōr'ay ōneg,   שׁוֹמְרֵי שַׁבָּת וְקוֹרְאֵי עֹנֶג,
those who observe the Sabbath and call it a delight.

am m'kad'shay sh'vi-i,   עַם מְקַדְּשֵׁי שְׁבִיעִי,
The people that sanctifies the Seventh —

kulom yisb'u v'yis-an'gu   כֻּלָּם יִשְׂבְּעוּ וְיִתְעַנְּגוּ
    mituvecho,   מִטּוּבֶךָ,
they will all be satisfied and delighted from Your goodness.

u-vash'vi-i rotziso bō v'kidashtō,   וּבַשְּׁבִיעִי רָצִיתָ בּוֹ וְקִדַּשְׁתּוֹ,
And the Seventh — You found favor in it and sanctified it.

chemdas yomim ōsō koroso,   חֶמְדַּת יָמִים אוֹתוֹ קָרֵאתָ,
"Most coveted of days," You called it,

zaycher l'ma-asay v'rayshis.   זֵכֶר לְמַעֲשֵׂה בְרֵאשִׁית.
a remembrance of Creation.

ELŌHAYNU Vaylōhay avōsaynu,   **אֱלֹהֵינוּ** וֵאלֹהֵי אֲבוֹתֵינוּ,
Our God and the God of our forefathers,

ON THE SABBATH SOME ADD:

r'tzay vimnuchosaynu   רְצֵה בִמְנוּחָתֵנוּ
may You be pleased with our rest

melech rachamon rachaym olaynu,   מֶלֶךְ רַחֲמָן רַחֵם עָלֵינוּ,
O merciful King, have mercy on us;

tōv u-maytiv hidoresh lonu,   טוֹב וּמֵטִיב הִדָּרֶשׁ לָנוּ,
O good and beneficent One,* let Yourself be sought out by us;

shuvo aylaynu   שׁוּבָה אֵלֵינוּ
    bahamōn rachamecho,   בַּהֲמוֹן רַחֲמֶיךָ,
return to us in Your yearning mercy

big-lal ovōs she-osu r'tzōnecho.   בִּגְלַל אָבוֹת שֶׁעָשׂוּ רְצוֹנֶךָ.
for the sake of the forefathers who did Your will.

B'nay vayscho k'vat'chilo,   בְּנֵה בֵיתְךָ כְּבַתְּחִלָּה,
Rebuild Your House as it was at first,

טוֹב וּמֵטִיב — *O good and beneficent One*. In the case of human beings, someone may be good, but not have the resources to benefit others. On the other hand, someone may benefit oth-ers by helping them do good deeds, but for himself he may prefer to indulge his sinful nature. God, however, is always perfect — He is both good and beneficent.

v'chōnayn mikdosh'cho al m'chōnō,   וְכוֹנֵן מִקְדָּשְׁךָ עַל מְכוֹנוֹ,
and establish Your Sanctuary on its prepared site;

v'har-aynu b'vinyonō   וְהַרְאֵנוּ בְּבִנְיָנוֹ,
    v'sam'chaynu b'sikunō.   וְשַׂמְּחֵנוּ בְּתִקּוּנוֹ.
show us its rebuilding and gladden us in its perfection.

V'hoshayv kōhanim la-avōdosom,   וְהָשֵׁב כֹּהֲנִים לַעֲבוֹדָתָם,
Restore the Kohanim to their service

ulvi-yim l'shirom ulzimrom,   וּלְוִיִּם לְשִׁירָם וּלְזִמְרָם,
and the Levites to their song and music;

v'hoshayv yisro-ayl linvayhem.   וְהָשֵׁב יִשְׂרָאֵל לִנְוֵיהֶם.
and restore Israel to their dwellings.

V'shom na-ale v'nayro-e   וְשָׁם נַעֲלֶה וְנֵרָאֶה
    v'nishta-chave l'fonecho,   וְנִשְׁתַּחֲוֶה לְפָנֶיךָ,
And there we will ascend and appear and prostrate ourselves before You,

b'sholōsh pa-amay r'golaynu,   בְּשָׁלֹשׁ פַּעֲמֵי רְגָלֵינוּ,
during our three pilgrimage seasons,

kakosuv b'sōrosecho.   כַּכָּתוּב בְּתוֹרָתֶךָ:
as it is written in Your Torah:

Sholōsh p'omim ba-shono   שָׁלוֹשׁ פְּעָמִים בַּשָּׁנָה,
    yayro-e chol z'chur'cho   יֵרָאֶה כָּל זְכוּרְךָ
"Three times a year all your males are to appear

es p'nay Adōnoy Elōhecho,   אֶת פְּנֵי יהוה אֱלֹהֶיךָ,
    bamokōm asher yivchor,   בַּמָּקוֹם אֲשֶׁר יִבְחָר,
before HASHEM, your God, in the place He shall choose,

b'chag hamatzōs,   בְּחַג הַמַּצּוֹת,
    uvchag hashovu-ōs,   וּבְחַג הַשָּׁבֻעוֹת,
    uvchag hasukōs,   וּבְחַג הַסֻּכּוֹת,
on the Festival of Matzos, on the Festival of Shavuos,
and on the Festival of Succos,

v'lō yayro-e   וְלֹא יֵרָאֶה
    es p'nay Adōnoy raykom.   אֶת פְּנֵי יהוה רֵיקָם.
and they shall not appear before HASHEM empty-handed.

Ish k'mat'nas yodō,   אִישׁ כְּמַתְּנַת יָדוֹ,
Every man according to the gift of his hand,

k'virkas Adōnoy Elōhecho   כְּבִרְכַּת יהוה אֱלֹהֶיךָ,
    asher nosan loch.   אֲשֶׁר נָתַן לָךְ.
according to the blessing of HASHEM, your God, that He gave you."

V'HASI-AYNU Adōnoy Elōhaynu   וְהַשִׂיאֵנוּ יהוה אֱלֹהֵינוּ

Bestow upon us, O HASHEM, our God,

es birkas mō-adecho   אֶת בִּרְכַּת מוֹעֲדֶיךָ

the blessing of Your appointed Festivals

l'cha-yim ulsholōm,   לְחַיִּים וּלְשָׁלוֹם,

   l'simcho ulsosōn,   לְשִׂמְחָה וּלְשָׂשׂוֹן,

for life and for peace, for gladness and for joy,

ka-asher rotziso   כַּאֲשֶׁר רָצִיתָ

   v'omarto l'vor'chaynu,   וְאָמַרְתָּ לְבָרְכֵנוּ.

as You desired and promised to bless us.

<table>
<tr><td colspan="2" align="center">ON THE SABBATH ADD:</td></tr>
<tr><td>Elōhaynu Vaylōhay avōsaynu</td><td>אֱלֹהֵינוּ וֵאלֹהֵי אֲבוֹתֵינוּ</td></tr>
<tr><td colspan="2" align="center">Our God and the God of our forefathers,</td></tr>
<tr><td>r'tzay vimnuchosaynu.</td><td>רְצֵה בִמְנוּחָתֵנוּ.</td></tr>
<tr><td colspan="2" align="center">may You be pleased with our rest.</td></tr>
</table>

Kad'shaynu b'mitzvōsecho   קַדְּשֵׁנוּ בְּמִצְוֹתֶיךָ

Sanctify us with Your commandments

v'sayn chelkaynu b'sōrosecho,   וְתֵן חֶלְקֵנוּ בְּתוֹרָתֶךָ,

and grant us our share in Your Torah;

sab'aynu mituvecho,   שַׂבְּעֵנוּ מִטּוּבֶךָ

satisfy us from Your goodness

v'sam'chaynu bi-shu-osecho,   וְשַׂמְּחֵנוּ בִּישׁוּעָתֶךָ,

and gladden us with Your salvation,

v'tahayr libaynu l'ovd'cho be-emes.   וְטַהֵר לִבֵּנוּ לְעָבְדְּךָ בֶּאֱמֶת.

and purify our heart to serve You sincerely.

V'hanchilaynu Adōnoy Elōhaynu   וְהַנְחִילֵנוּ יהוה אֱלֹהֵינוּ

And grant us a heritage, O HASHEM, our God —

<table>
<tr><td colspan="2" align="center">ON THE SABBATH ADD:</td></tr>
<tr><td>b'ahavo uvrotzōn</td><td>בְּאַהֲבָה וּבְרָצוֹן</td></tr>
<tr><td colspan="2" align="center">with love and with favor</td></tr>
</table>

b'simcho uvsosōn   בְּשִׂמְחָה וּבְשָׂשׂוֹן

with gladness and with joy —

<table>
<tr><td colspan="2" align="center">ON THE SABBATH ADD:</td></tr>
<tr><td>shabos u . . .</td><td>שַׁבָּת וּ . . .</td></tr>
<tr><td colspan="2" align="center">the Sabbath and</td></tr>
</table>

mō-aday kod'shecho,   מוֹעֲדֵי קָדְשֶׁךָ,

the appointed Festivals of Your holiness,

v'yism'chu v'cho yisro-ay
m'kad'shay sh'mecho.

וְיִשְׂמְחוּ בְךָ יִשְׂרָאֵל
מְקַדְּשֵׁי שְׁמֶךָ.

and may Israel, the sanctifiers of Your Name, rejoice in You.

Boruch ato Adōnoy, m'kadaysh

בָּרוּךְ אַתָּה יהוה, מְקַדֵּשׁ

Blessed are You, Hashem, Who sanctifies

ON THE SABBATH ADD:

hashabos v' . . .

הַשַּׁבָּת וְ . . .

the Sabbath,

yisro-ayl v'haz'manim.

יִשְׂרָאֵל וְהַזְּמַנִּים.

Israel and the (festive) seasons.

■ Fifth Blessing: Prayer for restoration of the Temple service

R'TZAY, Adōnoy Elōhaynu

רְצֵה יהוה אֱלֹהֵינוּ

Be favorable, Hashem, our God,

b'am'cho yisro-ayl u-visfilosom,

בְּעַמְּךָ יִשְׂרָאֵל וּבִתְפִלָּתָם,

toward Your people Israel and their prayer

v'hoshayv es ho-avōdo
lidvir bay-secho.

וְהָשֵׁב אֶת הָעֲבוֹדָה
לִדְבִיר בֵּיתֶךָ.

and restore the service to the Holy of Holies of Your Temple.

V'i-shay yisro-ayl, usfilosom

וְאִשֵּׁי יִשְׂרָאֵל וּתְפִלָּתָם

The fire-offerings of Israel and their prayer

b'ahavo s'kabayl b'rotzōn,

בְּאַהֲבָה תְקַבֵּל בְּרָצוֹן,

accept with love and favor,

us-hi l'rotzōn tomid
avōdas yisro-ayl amecho.

וּתְהִי לְרָצוֹן תָּמִיד
עֲבוֹדַת יִשְׂרָאֵל עַמֶּךָ.

and may the service of Your people Israel always be favorable to You.

ON FESTIVALS WHEN THE *KOHANIM* ASCEND TO PRONOUNCE *BIRCAS KOHANIM*, THE *CHAZZAN'S* REPETITION CONTINUES ON P. 737. DURING *CHOL HAMOED*, OR IF NO *KOHEN* IS PRESENT ON A FESTIVAL, THE *CHAZZAN'S* REPETITION CONTINUES HERE:

V'SECHEZENO aynaynu

וְתֶחֱזֶינָה עֵינֵינוּ

May our eyes behold

b'shuv'cho l'tziyōn b'rachamim.

בְּשׁוּבְךָ לְצִיּוֹן בְּרַחֲמִים.

Your return to Zion in compassion.

Boruch ato Adōnoy,
hamachazir sh'chinosō l'tziyōn.

בָּרוּךְ אַתָּה יהוה,
הַמַּחֲזִיר שְׁכִינָתוֹ לְצִיּוֹן.

Blessed are You, Hashem, Who restores His Presence unto Zion.

■ Sixth Blessing: Acknowledgment of our debt of gratitude

BOW AT Mōdim anachnu loch; STRAIGHTEN UP AT Adōnoy.
IN HIS REPETITION THE *CHAZZAN* SHOULD RECITE THE ENTIRE *MODIM* ALOUD,
WHILE THE CONGREGATION RECITES *MODIM OF THE RABBIS* (P. 733) SOFTLY.

MŌDIM anachnu loch,   **מוֹדִים** אֲנַחְנוּ לָךְ,
        We gratefully thank You,

sho-ato hu Adōnoy Elōhaynu   שָׁאַתָּה הוּא יהוה אֱלֹהֵינוּ
    Vaylōhay avōsaynu   וֵאלֹהֵי אֲבוֹתֵינוּ
   for it is You Who are HASHEM, our God, and the God of our forefathers

l'ōlom vo-ed,   לְעוֹלָם וָעֶד,
        forever and ever;

tzur cha-yaynu, mogayn yish-aynu   צוּר חַיֵּינוּ, מָגֵן יִשְׁעֵנוּ
    Rock of our lives, Shield of our salvation

ato hu l'dōr vodōr.   אַתָּה הוּא לְדוֹר וָדוֹר.
    are You from generation to generation.

Nōde l'cho unsapayr t'hilosecho   נוֹדֶה לְּךָ וּנְסַפֵּר תְּהִלָּתֶךָ
    We shall thank You and relate Your praise —

al cha-yaynu ham'surim b'yodecho,   עַל חַיֵּינוּ הַמְּסוּרִים בְּיָדֶךָ,
   for our lives, which are committed to Your power,

v'al nishmōsaynu hap'kudōs loch,   וְעַל נִשְׁמוֹתֵינוּ הַפְּקוּדוֹת לָךְ,
   and for our souls that are entrusted to You,

v'al nisecho sheb'chol yōm imonu,   וְעַל נִסֶּיךָ שֶׁבְּכָל יוֹם עִמָּנוּ,
   and for Your miracles that are with us every day,

v'al nifl'ōsecho v'tōvōsecho   וְעַל נִפְלְאוֹתֶיךָ וְטוֹבוֹתֶיךָ
    and for Your wonders and favors

sheb'chol ays,   שֶׁבְּכָל עֵת,
    in every season —

erev vovōker v'tzohoro-yim.   עֶרֶב וָבְקֶר וְצָהֳרָיִם.
    evening, morning, and afternoon.

Hatōv ki lō cholu rachamecho,   הַטּוֹב כִּי לֹא כָלוּ רַחֲמֶיךָ,
   The Beneficent One, for Your compassions were never exhausted,

v'ham'rachaym   וְהַמְרַחֵם
   ki lō samu chasodecho,   כִּי לֹא תַמּוּ חֲסָדֶיךָ,
   and the Compassionate One, for Your kindnesses never ended —

may-ōlom kivinu loch.   מֵעוֹלָם קִוִּינוּ לָךְ.
    always have we put our hope in You.

MODIM OF THE RABBIS

RECITED SOFTLY BY CONGREGATION WHILE *CHAZZAN* RECITES THE REGULAR MODIM ALOUD

MŌDIM anachnu loch,   מוֹדִים אֲנַחְנוּ לָךְ,
We gratefully thank You,

sho-ato hu Adōnoy Elōhaynu   שָׁאַתָּה הוּא יהוה אֱלֹהֵינוּ
Vaylōhay avōsaynu,   וֵאלֹהֵי אֲבוֹתֵינוּ,
for it is You Who are HASHEM, *our God and the God of our forefathers,*

Elōhay chol bosor,   אֱלֹהֵי כָל בָּשָׂר,
the God of all flesh,

yōtz'raynu, yōtzayr b'rayshis.   יוֹצְרֵנוּ, יוֹצֵר בְּרֵאשִׁית.
our Molder, the Molder of the universe.

B'rochōs v'hōdo-ōs l'shimcho   בְּרָכוֹת וְהוֹדָאוֹת לְשִׁמְךָ
hagodōl v'hakodōsh,   הַגָּדוֹל וְהַקָּדוֹשׁ,
Blessings and thanks are due Your great and holy Name

al sheheche-yisonu v'ki-yamtonu.   עַל שֶׁהֶחֱיִיתָנוּ וְקִיַּמְתָּנוּ.
for You have given us life and sustained us.

Kayn t'cha-yaynu uska-y'maynu,   כֵּן תְּחַיֵּינוּ וּתְקַיְּמֵנוּ,
So may You continue to give us life and sustain us,

v'se-esōf golu-yōsaynu   וְתֶאֱסוֹף גָּלֻיוֹתֵינוּ
l'chatzrōs kod-shecho,   לְחַצְרוֹת קָדְשֶׁךָ,
and gather our exiles to the Courtyards of Your Sanctuary,

lishmōr chukecho   לִשְׁמוֹר חֻקֶּיךָ
v'la-asōs r'tzōnecho,   וְלַעֲשׂוֹת רְצוֹנֶךָ,
to observe Your decrees, to do Your will

ul-ovd'cho b'layvov sholaym,   וּלְעָבְדְּךָ בְּלֵבָב שָׁלֵם,
and to serve You wholeheartedly.

al she-anachnu mōdim loch.   עַל שֶׁאֲנַחְנוּ מוֹדִים לָךְ.
[We thank You] for inspiring us to thank You.

Boruch Ayl hahōdo-ōs.   בָּרוּךְ אֵל הַהוֹדָאוֹת.
Blessed is the God of thanksgivings.

V'AL kulom yisborach v'yisrōmam   וְעַל כֻּלָּם יִתְבָּרַךְ וְיִתְרוֹמַם
shimcho, malkaynu   שִׁמְךָ מַלְכֵּנוּ
For all these, may Your Name be blessed and exalted, our King,

tomid l'ōlom vo-ed.   תָּמִיד לְעוֹלָם וָעֶד.
continually forever and ever.

V'chōl hacha-yim yōducho selo,   וְכֹל הַחַיִּים יוֹדוּךָ סֶּלָה,
Everything alive will gratefully acknowledge You, Selah!

vihal'lu es shimcho be-emes,
     וִיהַלְלוּ אֶת שִׁמְךָ בֶּאֱמֶת,

and praise Your Name sincerely,

ho-Ayl y'shu-osaynu
     הָאֵל יְשׁוּעָתֵנוּ

v'ezrosaynu selo.
     וְעֶזְרָתֵנוּ סֶלָה.

O God of our salvation and help, Selah!

BEND THE KNEES AT *Boruch*; BOW AT *ato*; STRAIGHTEN UP AT *Adōnoy.*

Boruch ato Adōnoy,
     בָּרוּךְ אַתָּה יהוה,

Blessed are You, HASHEM,

hatōv shimcho ulcho no-e l'hōdōs.
     הַטּוֹב שִׁמְךָ וּלְךָ נָאֶה לְהוֹדוֹת.

Your Name is "The Beneficent One" and to You it is fitting to give thanks.

■ Seventh Blessing: Prayer for peace and harmony
amongst the Jewish people

IF *KOHANIM* DO NOT ASCEND TO OFFER THE BLESSING,
THE *CHAZZAN* RECITES THE PRIESTLY BLESSING DURING HIS REPETITION.

אֱלֹהֵינוּ, וֵאלֹהֵי אֲבוֹתֵינוּ, בָּרְכֵנוּ בַבְּרָכָה הַמְשֻׁלֶּשֶׁת בַּתּוֹרָה
הַכְּתוּבָה עַל יְדֵי מֹשֶׁה עַבְדֶּךָ, הָאֲמוּרָה מִפִּי אַהֲרֹן וּבָנָיו,
כֹּהֲנִים עַם קְדוֹשֶׁךָ, כָּאָמוּר:

(kayn y'hi rotzōn – כֵּן יְהִי רָצוֹן – Cong.)   יְבָרֶכְךָ יהוה, וְיִשְׁמְרֶךָ.

(kayn y'hi rotzōn – כֵּן יְהִי רָצוֹן – Cong.)   יָאֵר יהוה פָּנָיו אֵלֶיךָ וִיחֻנֶּךָּ.

יִשָּׂא יהוה פָּנָיו אֵלֶיךָ וְיָשֵׂם לְךָ שָׁלוֹם.

(kayn y'hi rotzōn – כֵּן יְהִי רָצוֹן – Cong.)

SIM SHOLŌM tōvo uvrocho,
     שִׂים שָׁלוֹם, טוֹבָה, וּבְרָכָה,

Establish peace, goodness, blessing,

chayn vochesed v'rachamim
     חֵן וָחֶסֶד וְרַחֲמִים

graciousness, kindness, and compassion

olaynu v'al kol yisro-ayl amecho.
     עָלֵינוּ וְעַל כָּל יִשְׂרָאֵל עַמֶּךָ.

upon us and upon all of Your people Israel.

Bor'chaynu, ovinu, kulonu k'e-chod
     בָּרְכֵנוּ, אָבִינוּ, כֻּלָּנוּ כְּאֶחָד

b'ōr ponecho,
     בְּאוֹר פָּנֶיךָ,

Bless us, our Father, all of us as one, with the light of Your countenance,

ki v'ōr ponecho nosato lonu,
     כִּי בְאוֹר פָּנֶיךָ נָתַתָּ לָּנוּ,

Adōnoy Elōhaynu,
     יהוה אֱלֹהֵינוּ,

for with the light of Your countenance You, HASHEM, our God, gave us

tōras cha-yim v'ahavas chesed,
     תּוֹרַת חַיִּים וְאַהֲבַת חֶסֶד,

the Torah of life and a love of kindness,

utz-doko uvrocho v'rachamim
v'cha-yim v'sholōm.

וּצְדָקָה וּבְרָכָה וְרַחֲמִים
וְחַיִּים וְשָׁלוֹם.

righteousness, blessing, compassion, life, and peace.

V'tōv b'aynecho l'voraych
es am'cho yisro-ayl,

וְטוֹב בְּעֵינֶיךָ לְבָרֵךְ
אֶת עַמְּךָ יִשְׂרָאֵל,

And may it be good in Your eyes to bless Your people Israel

b'chol ays uvchol sho-o
bish-lōmecho.

בְּכָל עֵת וּבְכָל שָׁעָה
בִּשְׁלוֹמֶךָ.

at every time and at every hour, with Your peace.

Boruch ato Adōnoy,

בָּרוּךְ אַתָּה יהוה,

Blessed are You, HASHEM,

ham'voraych es amō yisro-ayl
ba-sholōm.

הַמְבָרֵךְ אֶת עַמּוֹ יִשְׂרָאֵל
בַּשָּׁלוֹם.

Who blesses His people Israel with peace.

THE *CHAZZAN'S* REPETITION ENDS HERE. INDIVIDUALS CONTINUE:

Yih-yu l'rotzōn imray fi
v'hegyōn libi l'fonecho,

יִהְיוּ לְרָצוֹן אִמְרֵי פִי
וְהֶגְיוֹן לִבִּי לְפָנֶיךָ,

*May the expressions of my mouth and the thoughts of my heart
find favor before You,*

Adōnoy tzuri v'gō-ali.

יהוה צוּרִי וְגֹאֲלִי.

HASHEM, my Rock and my Redeemer.

ELŌHAI, n'tzōr l'shōni mayro,

אֱלֹהַי, נְצוֹר לְשׁוֹנִי מֵרָע,

My God, guard my tongue from evil

usfosai midabayr mirmo,

וּשְׂפָתַי מִדַּבֵּר מִרְמָה,

and my lips from speaking deceitfully.

V'limkal'lai nafshi sidōm,

וְלִמְקַלְלַי נַפְשִׁי תִדּוֹם,

To those who curse me, let my soul be silent;

v'nafshi ke-ofor lakōl tih-ye.

וְנַפְשִׁי כֶּעָפָר לַכֹּל תִּהְיֶה.

and let my soul be like dust to everyone.

P'sach libi b'sōrosecho,

פְּתַח לִבִּי בְּתוֹרָתֶךָ,

Open my heart to Your Torah,

uvmitzvōsecho tirdōf nafshi.

וּבְמִצְוֹתֶיךָ תִּרְדּוֹף נַפְשִׁי.

then my soul will pursue Your commandments.

V'chol hachōsh'vim olai ro-o,

וְכָל הַחוֹשְׁבִים עָלַי רָעָה,

As for all those who design evil against me,

m'hayro hofayr atzosom

מְהֵרָה הָפֵר עֲצָתָם

speedily nullify their counsel

v'kalkayl machashavtom.

וְקַלְקֵל מַחֲשַׁבְתָּם.

and disrupt their design.

asay l'ma-an sh'mecho,

   asay l'ma-an y'minecho,

עֲשֵׂה לְמַעַן שְׁמֶךָ,
עֲשֵׂה לְמַעַן יְמִינֶךָ,

Act for Your Name's sake; act for Your right hand's sake;

asay l'ma-an k'dushosecho,

   asay l'ma-an tōrosecho.

עֲשֵׂה לְמַעַן קְדֻשָּׁתֶךָ,
עֲשֵׂה לְמַעַן תּוֹרָתֶךָ.

act for Your sanctity's sake; act for Your Torah's sake.

L'ma-an yaychol'tzun y'didecho,

לְמַעַן יֵחָלְצוּן יְדִידֶיךָ,

That Your beloved ones may be given rest;

hōshi-o y'min'cho va-anayni.

הוֹשִׁיעָה יְמִינְךָ וַעֲנֵנִי.

let Your right hand save, and respond to me.

Yih-yu l'rotzōn imray fi

   v'hegyōn libi l'fonecho,

יִהְיוּ לְרָצוֹן אִמְרֵי פִי
וְהֶגְיוֹן לִבִּי לְפָנֶיךָ,

May the expressions of my mouth and the thoughts of my heart
find favor before You,

Adōnoy tzuri v'gō-ali.

יהוה צוּרִי וְגֹאֲלִי.

HASHEM, my Rock and my Redeemer.

BOW. TAKE THREE STEPS BACK. BOW LEFT AND SAY:

Ō-se sholōm bimrōmov,

עֹשֶׂה שָׁלוֹם בִּמְרוֹמָיו,

He Who makes peace in His heights,

BOW RIGHT AND SAY:

hu ya-a-se sholōm olaynu,

הוּא יַעֲשֶׂה שָׁלוֹם עָלֵינוּ,

may He make peace upon us,

BOW FORWARD AND SAY:

v'al kol yisro-ayl. V'imru: Omayn.

וְעַל כָּל יִשְׂרָאֵל. וְאִמְרוּ: אָמֵן.

and upon all Israel. Now respond: Amen.

Y'HI ROTZŌN mil'fonecho,

יְהִי רָצוֹן מִלְּפָנֶיךָ

May it be Your will,

Adōnoy Elōhaynu

   Vaylōhay avōsaynu,

יהוה אֱלֹהֵינוּ
וֵאלֹהֵי אֲבוֹתֵינוּ,

HASHEM, our God and the God of our forefathers,

she-yibo-ne bays hamikdosh

   bimhayro v'yomaynu,

שֶׁיִּבָּנֶה בֵּית הַמִּקְדָּשׁ
בִּמְהֵרָה בְיָמֵינוּ,

that the Holy Temple be rebuilt, speedily in our days;

v'sayn chelkaynu b'sōrosecho,

וְתֵן חֶלְקֵנוּ בְּתוֹרָתֶךָ,

and grant us our share in Your Torah;

v'shom na-avod-cho b'yiro,

וְשָׁם נַעֲבָדְךָ בְּיִרְאָה,

and may we serve You there with reverence,

kimay ōlom

uchshonim kadmōniyōs.

כִּימֵי עוֹלָם

וּכְשָׁנִים קַדְמוֹנִיּוֹת.

as in days of old and in former years.

V'or'vo Ladōnoy

minchas y'hudo virusholo-yim

וְעָרְבָה לַיהוה

מִנְחַת יְהוּדָה וִירוּשָׁלָיִם,

Then the offering of Judah and Jerusalem will be pleasing to HASHEM,

kimay ōlom

uchshonim kadmōniyōs.

כִּימֵי עוֹלָם

וּכְשָׁנִים קַדְמוֹנִיּוֹת.

as in days of old and in former years.

THE INDIVIDUAL'S RECITATION OF *SHEMONEH ESREI* ENDS HERE.
REMAIN STANDING IN PLACE UNTIL THE *CHAZZAN* REACHES *KEDUSHAH* —
OR AT LEAST FOR A FEW MOMENTS — THEN TAKE THREE STEPS FORWARD.

DURING *SUCCOS*, THE *HOSHANA* PRAYERS (P. 772) ARE RECITED. AT ALL OTHER TIMES,
THE *CHAZZAN* RECITES THE FULL *KADDISH* (P. 454).
ON FESTIVAL DAYS, THE SABBATH OF *CHOL HAMOED*, AND HOSHANA RABBAH,
THE SERVICE CONTINUES THERE; ON OTHER DAYS, CONTINUE WITH *ALEINU* (P. 463).

ᵐᵉ **BIRCAS KOHANIM — THE PRIESTLY BLESSING** ᵐᵉ

WHEN THE *KOHANIM* ASCEND TO PRONOUNCE THE PRIESTLY BLESSING,
THE CONGREGATION, FOLLOWED BY THE *CHAZZAN*, RECITES:

V'SAY-ORAYV l'fonecho asirosaynu

k'ōlo uchkorbon.

וְתֶעֱרַב לְפָנֶיךָ עֲתִירָתֵנוּ

כְּעוֹלָה וּכְקָרְבָּן.

May our entreaty be pleasing before You as an elevation-offering and as a sacrifice.

Ono, rachum, b'rachamecho horabim

אָנָּא, רַחוּם, בְּרַחֲמֶיךָ הָרַבִּים

Please, O Merciful One, in Your abounding mercy

hoshayv sh'chinos'cho l'tziyōn irecho,

הָשֵׁב שְׁכִינָתְךָ לְצִיּוֹן עִירֶךָ,

return Your Shechinah to Zion, Your city,

v'sayder ho-avōdo lirusholo-yim.

וְסֵדֶר הָעֲבוֹדָה לִירוּשָׁלָיִם.

and the order of the Temple service to Jerusalem.

V'sechezeno aynaynu

b'shuv'cho l'tziyōn b'rachamim,

וְתֶחֱזֶינָה עֵינֵינוּ

בְּשׁוּבְךָ לְצִיּוֹן בְּרַחֲמִים,

And may our eyes behold when You return to Zion in mercy,

v'shom na-avodcho b'yir-o

וְשָׁם נַעֲבָדְךָ בְּיִרְאָה

that we may serve You there with awe

kimay ōlom

uchshonim kadmōniyōs.

כִּימֵי עוֹלָם

וּכְשָׁנִים קַדְמוֹנִיּוֹת.

as in days of old and as in earlier years.

ᵐᵉ**The Priestly Blessing.** The Midrash teaches that until the time of the Patriarchs, God retained for Himself the power to bless people. With the advent of the Patriarchs, He gave this awesome power to them. After they died, God declared that henceforth the *Kohanim* would bless the Jewish people. Thus, the upraised hands of the *Kohanim* are the vehicle through which God's blessing flows upon His chosen people.

CHAZZAN CONCLUDES:

Boruch ato Adōnoy,　　　　　　　　בָּרוּךְ אַתָּה יהוה,

Blessed are You, HASHEM,

she-ōs'cho l'vad'cho b'yir-o na-avōd.　שָׁאוֹתְךָ לְבַדְּךָ בְּיִרְאָה נַעֲבוֹד.

for You alone do we serve, with awe.

CONGREGATION RESPONDS: Omayn — אָמֵן

BOW AT Mōdim anachnu loch; STRAIGHTEN UP AT Adōnoy.
IN HIS REPETITION THE *CHAZZAN* SHOULD RECITE THE ENTIRE *MODIM* ALOUD,
WHILE THE CONGREGATION RECITES *MODIM OF THE RABBIS* (P. 739) SOFTLY.

MŌDIM anachnu loch,　　　　　מוֹדִים אֲנַחְנוּ לָךְ,

We gratefully thank You,

sho-ato hu Adōnoy Elōhaynu　　　שָׁאַתָּה הוּא יהוה אֱלֹהֵינוּ

　Vaylōhay avōsaynu l'ōlom vo-ed,　וֵאלֹהֵי אֲבוֹתֵינוּ לְעוֹלָם וָעֶד,

for it is You Who are HASHEM, our God, and the God of our forefathers
forever and ever;

tzur cha-yaynu, mogayn yish-aynu　צוּר חַיֵּינוּ, מָגֵן יִשְׁעֵנוּ

Rock of our lives, Shield of our salvation

ato hu l'dōr vodōr.　　　　　　אַתָּה הוּא לְדוֹר וָדוֹר.

are You from generation to generation.

Nō-de l'cho unsapayr t'hilosecho　נוֹדֶה לְּךָ וּנְסַפֵּר תְּהִלָּתֶךָ

We shall thank You and relate Your praise —

al cha-yaynu ham'surim b'yodecho,　עַל חַיֵּינוּ הַמְּסוּרִים בְּיָדֶךָ,

for our lives, which are committed to Your power,

v'al nishmōsaynu hap'kudōs loch,　וְעַל נִשְׁמוֹתֵינוּ הַפְּקוּדוֹת לָךְ,

and for our souls that are entrusted to You,

v'al nisecho sheb'chol yōm imonu,　וְעַל נִסֶּיךָ שֶׁבְּכָל יוֹם עִמָּנוּ,

and for Your miracles that are with us every day,

v'al nifl'ōsecho v'tōvōsecho　　וְעַל נִפְלְאוֹתֶיךָ וְטוֹבוֹתֶיךָ

　sheb'chol ays,　　　　　　　שֶׁבְּכָל עֵת,

and for Your wonders and favors in every season —

erev vovōker v'tzohoro-yim.　　עֶרֶב וָבֹקֶר וְצָהֳרָיִם.

evening, morning, and afternoon.

Hatōv ki lō cholu rachamecho,　הַטּוֹב כִּי לֹא כָלוּ רַחֲמֶיךָ,

The Beneficent One, for Your compassions were never exhausted,

v'ham'rachaym　　　　　　　וְהַמְרַחֵם

　ki lō samu chasodecho,　　כִּי לֹא תַמּוּ חֲסָדֶיךָ,

and the Compassionate One, for Your kindnesses never ended —

may-ōlom kivinu loch.　　　מֵעוֹלָם קִוִּינוּ לָךְ.

always have we put our hope in You.

MODIM OF THE RABBIS

RECITED SOFTLY BY CONGREGATION WHILE *CHAZZAN* RECITES THE REGULAR MODIM ALOUD

MŌDIM anachnu loch,   מוֹדִים אֲנַחְנוּ לָךְ,

We gratefully thank You,

sho-ato hu Adōnoy Elōhaynu   שָׁאַתָּה הוּא יהוה אֱלֹהֵינוּ

Vaylōhay avōsaynu,   וֵאלֹהֵי אֲבוֹתֵינוּ,

for it is You Who are HASHEM, *our God and the God of our forefathers,*

Elōhay chol bosor,   אֱלֹהֵי כָל בָּשָׂר,

the God of all flesh,

yōtz'raynu, yōtzayr b'rayshis.   יוֹצְרֵנוּ, יוֹצֵר בְּרֵאשִׁית.

our Molder, the Molder of the universe.

B'rochōs v'hōdo-ōs l'shimcho   בְּרָכוֹת וְהוֹדָאוֹת לְשִׁמְךָ

hagodōl v'hakodōsh,   הַגָּדוֹל וְהַקָּדוֹשׁ,

Blessings and thanks are due Your great and holy Name

al sheheche-yisonu v'ki-yamtonu.   עַל שֶׁהֶחֱיִיתָנוּ וְקִיַּמְתָּנוּ.

for You have given us life and sustained us.

Kayn t'cha-yaynu uska-y'maynu,   כֵּן תְּחַיֵּנוּ וּתְקַיְּמֵנוּ,

So may You continue to give us life and sustain us,

v'se-esōf golu-yōsaynu   וְתֶאֱסוֹף גָּלֻיּוֹתֵינוּ

l'chatzrōs kod-shecho,   לְחַצְרוֹת קָדְשֶׁךָ,

and gather our exiles to the Courtyards of Your Sanctuary,

lishmōr chukecho   לִשְׁמֹר חֻקֶּיךָ

v'la-asōs r'tzōnecho,   וְלַעֲשׂוֹת רְצוֹנֶךָ,

to observe Your decrees, to do Your will

ul-ovd'cho b'layvov sholaym,   וּלְעָבְדְּךָ בְּלֵבָב שָׁלֵם,

and to serve You wholeheartedly.

al she-anachnu mōdim loch.   עַל שֶׁאֲנַחְנוּ מוֹדִים לָךְ.

[We thank You] for inspiring us to thank You.

Boruch Ayl hahōdo-ōs.   בָּרוּךְ אֵל הַהוֹדָאוֹת.

Blessed is the God of thanksgivings.

V'AL kulom yisborach v'yisrōmam   וְעַל כֻּלָּם יִתְבָּרַךְ וְיִתְרוֹמַם

shimcho, malkaynu   שִׁמְךָ מַלְכֵּנוּ

For all these, may Your Name be blessed and exalted, our King,

tomid l'ōlom vo-ed.   תָּמִיד לְעוֹלָם וָעֶד.

continually forever and ever.

V'chōl hacha-yim yōducho selo,
וְכָל הַחַיִּים יוֹדֽוּךָ סֶּֽלָה,

Everything alive will gratefully acknowledge You, Selah!

vihal'lu es shimcho be-emes,
וִיהַלְלוּ אֶת שִׁמְךָ בֶּאֱמֶת,

and praise Your Name sincerely,

ho-Ayl y'shu-osaynu v'ezrosaynu selo.
הָאֵל יְשׁוּעָתֵֽנוּ וְעֶזְרָתֵֽנוּ סֶּֽלָה.

O God of our salvation and help, Selah!

BEND THE KNEES AT Boruch; BOW AT ato; STRAIGHTEN UP AT Adōnoy.

Boruch ato Adōnoy,
בָּרוּךְ אַתָּה יהוה,

Blessed are You, HASHEM,

hatōv shimcho ulcho no-e l'hōdōs.
הַטּוֹב שִׁמְךָ וּלְךָ נָאֶה לְהוֹדוֹת.

Your Name is "The Beneficent One" and to You it is fitting to give thanks.

WHILE THE *CHAZZAN* RECITES V'chōl hacha-yim, (ABOVE) THE *KOHANIM* RECITE SILENTLY:

Y'hi rotzōn mil'fonecho
יְהִי רָצוֹן מִלְּפָנֶֽיךָ,

May it be Your will,

Adōnoy Elōhaynu
יהוה אֱלֹהֵֽינוּ

Vaylōhay avōsaynu,
וֵאלֹהֵי אֲבוֹתֵֽינוּ,

HASHEM, our God and the God of our fathers,

shet'hay hab'rocho ha-zōs
שֶׁתְּהֵא הַבְּרָכָה הַזֹּאת

that this blessing

shetzivisonu l'voraych
שֶׁצִּוִּיתָֽנוּ לְבָרֵךְ

es amcho yisro-ayl
אֶת עַמְּךָ יִשְׂרָאֵל

which You have commanded us to bestow upon Your people Israel

b'rocho sh'laymo,
בְּרָכָה שְׁלֵמָה,

be a full blessing,

v'lo yih-ye vo
וְלֹא יִהְיֶה בָה

shum michshol v'ovōn
שׁוּם מִכְשׁוֹל וְעָוֹן

that there be in it neither stumbling block nor sin

may-ato v'ad ōlom.
מֵעַתָּה וְעַד עוֹלָם.

from now and forever.

CONGREGATION RESPONDS: Omayn — אָמֵן

CHAZZAN RECITES THE FOLLOWING IN AN UNDERTONE:

ELŌHAYNU Vaylōhay avōsaynu,
אֱלֹהֵֽינוּ וֵאלֹהֵי אֲבוֹתֵֽינוּ,

Our God and the God of our forefathers,

bor'chaynu vab'rocho
בָּרְכֵֽנוּ בַבְּרָכָה

ham'shuleshes batōro
הַמְשֻׁלֶּֽשֶׁת בַּתּוֹרָה

bless us with the three-verse blessing* in the Torah

אֱלֹהֵֽינוּ . . . בָּרְכֵֽנוּ בַּבְּרָכָה — *Our God . . . bless us with the . . . blessing.* We ask God, not the Kohanim, to bless us, because, as the Talmud (*Chullin* 49a) teaches, although the *Kohanim*

hak'suvo al y'day mōshe avdecho,

הַכְּתוּבָה עַל יְדֵי מֹשֶׁה עַבְדֶּךָ,

that was written by Moses, Your servant,

ho-amuro mipi aharōn u-vonov,

הָאֲמוּרָה מִפִּי אַהֲרֹן וּבָנָיו,

that was said by Aaron and his sons,

CHAZZAN RECITES THE FOLLOWING ALOUD:

KŌHANIM

כֹּהֲנִים

the Kohanim,

CONGREGATION:

am k'dōshecho — ko-omur:

עַם קְדוֹשֶׁךָ — כָּאָמוּר:

Your holy people — as it is said:

FACING THE ARK, THE KOHANIM RAISE THEIR HANDS AND BEGIN TO RECITE THE FOLLOWING BLESSING ALOUD AND IN UNISON. UPON REACHING v'tzivonu, THEY TURN TO FACE THE CONGREGATION AND COMPLETE THE BLESSING.

BORUCH ato Adōnoy

בָּרוּךְ אַתָּה יהוה

Elōhaynu melech ho-ōlom,

אֱלֹהֵינוּ מֶלֶךְ הָעוֹלָם,

Blessed are You, HASHEM, our God, King of the universe,

asher kid'shonu

אֲשֶׁר קִדְּשָׁנוּ

bikdushosō shel aharōn,

בִּקְדֻשָּׁתוֹ שֶׁל אַהֲרֹן,

Who has sanctified us with the holiness of Aaron,*

v'tzivonu l'voraych es amō

וְצִוָּנוּ לְבָרֵךְ אֶת עַמּוֹ

yisro-ayl b'ahavo.

יִשְׂרָאֵל בְּאַהֲבָה.

and has commanded us to bless His people Israel with love.*

THE CONGREGATION, BUT NOT THE CHAZZAN, RESPONDS: Omayn — אָמֵן

EACH WORD IS RECITED ALOUD BY THE CHAZZAN AND REPEATED BY THE KOHANIM:

Y'VORECH'CHO

יְבָרֶכְךָ

May [He] bless you

ADŌNOY

יהוה

— HASHEM* —

---

pronounce the words, they are merely conduits through which the blessing descends from God to the nation below. This is made clear in the Scriptural commandment, which ends with God's pledge ''and I will bless them.''

בָּרוּךְ ... בִּקְדֻשָּׁתוֹ שֶׁל אַהֲרֹן — *Blessed . . . with the holiness of Aaron.* Just as the selection of Israel as the Holy Nation is not dependent solely upon the deeds of each individual member, but on the holiness of their forebears — indeed, it is the very sanctity of the Patriarchs which imbued their descendants with a capacity for holiness — so is the sanctity of the *Kehunah* [priesthood] unique among the descendants of Aaron.

בְּאַהֲבָה — *With love.* The Kohanim are to feel

love for the congregation when they pronounce the blessings. The addition of the phrase *with love* is based upon the dictum of the *Zohar*: ''Any *Kohen* who does not have love for the congregation or for whom the congregation has no love, may not raise his hands to bless the congregation . . .''

Raising the hands is a symbol of a heart pouring forth blessing and joy from a treasure trove of happiness. Raising the hands is not a sterile act — it must be a wholehearted expression of the hope and blessing which are hidden in the soul. An ocean of inexpressible joy issues from a pure soul; and the purer the soul, the purer the blessing.

יְבָרֶכְךָ ה' — *May HASHEM bless you*, with increasing wealth and long life.

EXCEPT ON SHABBOS, THE *KOHANIM* SING AN EXTENDED CHANT BEFORE SAYING v'yishm'recho.

V'YISHM'RECHO.

וְיִשְׁמְרֶךָ.

and safeguard you. *

WHILE THE *KOHANIM* SING AN EXTENDED CHANT BEFORE SAYING v'yishm'recho,
THE CONGREGATION RECITES THE FOLLOWING SUPPLICATION IN AN UNDERTONE.

RIBÔNÔ Shel Ôlom,
Master of the world, *

רִבּוֹנוֹ שֶׁל עוֹלָם,

ani sheloch vachalômôsai sheloch.
I am Yours and my dreams are Yours.

אֲנִי שֶׁלָּךְ וַחֲלוֹמוֹתַי שֶׁלָּךְ.

Chalôm cholamti
v'ayni yôday-a ma hu.
I have dreamed a dream but I do not know what it indicates. *

חֲלוֹם חָלַמְתִּי
וְאֵינִי יוֹדֵעַ מַה הוּא.

Y'hi rotzôn mil'fonecho,
May it be Your will,

יְהִי רָצוֹן מִלְּפָנֶיךָ,

Adônoy Elôhai Vaylôhay avôsai,
HASHEM, my God and the God of my forefathers,

יהוה אֱלֹהַי וֵאלֹהֵי אֲבוֹתַי,

she-yih-yu kol chalômôsai olai
v'al kol yisro-ayl l'tôvo —
that all my dreams regarding myself and regarding all of Israel be good ones —

שֶׁיִּהְיוּ כָּל חֲלוֹמוֹתַי עָלַי
וְעַל כָּל יִשְׂרָאֵל לְטוֹבָה —

bayn shecholamti al atzmi,
those I have dreamed about myself,

בֵּין שֶׁחָלַמְתִּי עַל עַצְמִי,

u-vayn shecholamti al achayrim,
those I have dreamed about others,

וּבֵין שֶׁחָלַמְתִּי עַל אֲחֵרִים,

u-vayn shechol'mu achayrim oloy.
and those that others have dreamed about me.

וּבֵין שֶׁחָלְמוּ אֲחֵרִים עָלַי.

Im tôvim haym,
chaz'kaym v'am'tzaym,
If they are good, strengthen them, fortify them,

אִם טוֹבִים הֵם,
חַזְּקֵם וְאַמְּצֵם,

v'yiska-y'mu vi u-vohem
make them endure in me and in them

וְיִתְקַיְּמוּ בִי וּבָהֶם

וְיִשְׁמְרֶךָ — *And safeguard you.* May the above blessings be preserved against loss or attack. Only God can guarantee that no one or nothing can tamper with the gifts He confers upon His loved ones.

רִבּוֹנוֹ שֶׁל עוֹלָם — *Master of the world.* Between the verses of *Bircas Kohanim* it is customary to recite a supplication regarding dreams. The prevalent version of this supplication is virtually unchanged from the text appearing in the Talmud (*Berachos* 55b). There it appears with the following introduction:

If one had a dream but is uncertain whether the dream forebode good or evil, let him stand before the *Kohanim* at the time they spread their hands in blessing, and let him say, *Master of the world! I am Yours and my dreams are Yours . . .*

חֲלוֹם חָלַמְתִּי וְאֵינִי יוֹדֵעַ מַה הוּא — *I have dreamed a dream but I do not know what it indicates.* During sleep the soul divests itself of the corporeal garb which inhibits its free movement during the day. Thus, in his dreams, one is able to soar above his body and attain the higher spiritual forces of eternal life, yet upon awakening he will be unaware of the implications of what he has attained.

kachalōmōsov shel yōsayf hatzadik. כַּחֲלוֹמוֹתָיו שֶׁל יוֹסֵף הַצַּדִּיק.
like the dreams of the righteous Joseph.

V'im tz'richim r'fu-o, r'fo-aym וְאִם צְרִיכִים רְפוּאָה, רְפָאֵם
But if they require healing, heal them

k'chizkiyohu melech y'hudo כְּחִזְקִיָּהוּ מֶלֶךְ יְהוּדָה
maychol-yō, מֵחָלְיוֹ,
like Hezekiah king of Judah from his sickness;

uchmiryom han'vi-o mitzoratoh, וּכְמִרְיָם הַנְּבִיאָה מִצָּרַעְתָּהּ,
like Miriam the prophetess from her tzaraas;

uchna-amon mitzoratō, וּכְנַעֲמָן מִצָּרַעְתּוֹ,
like Naaman from his tzaraas;

uchmay moro al y'day וּכְמֵי מָרָה עַל יְדֵי
mōshe rabaynu, מֹשֶׁה רַבֵּנוּ,
like the waters of Marah through the hand of Moses our teacher;

uchmay y'richō al y'day elisho. וּכְמֵי יְרִיחוֹ עַל יְדֵי אֱלִישָׁע.
and like the waters of Jericho through the hand of Elisha.

Uchshaym she-hofachto וּכְשֵׁם שֶׁהָפַכְתָּ
es kil'las bil-om horosho אֶת קִלְלַת בִּלְעָם הָרָשָׁע
And just as You transformed the curse of the wicked Balaam

mik'lolo livrocho, מִקְּלָלָה לִבְרָכָה,
from a curse to a blessing,

kayn tahafōch kol chalōmōsai olai כֵּן תַּהֲפוֹךְ כָּל חֲלוֹמוֹתַי עָלַי
v'al kol yisro-ayl l'tōvo, וְעַל כָּל יִשְׂרָאֵל לְטוֹבָה,
*so may You transform all of my dreams regarding myself
and regarding all of Israel for goodness.*

v'sishm'rayni uschonayni v'sirtzayni. וְתִשְׁמְרֵנִי וּתְחָנֵּנִי וְתִרְצֵנִי.
May You protect me, may You be gracious to me, may You accept me.

CONGREGATION AND *CHAZZAN* RESPOND: Omayn — אָמֵן

EACH WORD IS RECITED ALOUD BY THE *CHAZZAN* AND REPEATED BY THE *KOHANIM:*

YO-AYR יָאֵר
May [He] illuminate

ADŌNOY יהוה
HASHEM

PONOV פָּנָיו
His countenance

AYLECHO אֵלֶיךָ
*for you**

יָאֵר ה' פָּנָיו אֵלֶיךָ — *May HASHEM illuminate His countenance for you.* This is the blessing of spiri- tual growth, the light of Torah, which is symbolized by God's "countenance."

EXCEPT ON THE SABBATH, THE *KOHANIM* SING AN EXTENDED CHANT BEFORE SAYING vi-chuneko.

VI-CHUNEKO.   וִיחֻנֶּֽךָּ

and be gracious to you. *

WHILE THE *KOHANIM* SING AN EXTENDED CHANT BEFORE SAYING vichuneko,
THE CONGREGATION RECITES THE FOLLOWING SUPPLICATION IN AN UNDERTONE.

RIBŌNŌ shel ōlom,   רִבּוֹנוֹ שֶׁל עוֹלָם,

Master of the world,

ani sheloch vachalōmōsai sheloch.   אֲנִי שֶׁלָּךְ וַחֲלוֹמוֹתַי שֶׁלָּךְ.

I am Yours and my dreams are Yours.

Chalōm cholamti   חֲלוֹם חָלַמְתִּי

v'ayni yōday-a ma hu.   וְאֵינִי יוֹדֵעַ מַה הוּא.

I have dreamed a dream but I do not know what it indicates.

Y'hi rotzōn mil'fonecho,   יְהִי רָצוֹן מִלְּפָנֶֽיךָ,

May it be Your will,

Adōnoy Elōhai Vaylōhay avōsai, יהוה אֱלֹהַי וֵאלֹהֵי אֲבוֹתַי,

HASHEM, my God and the God of my forefathers,

she-yih-yu kol chalōmōsai olai   שֶׁיִּהְיוּ כָּל חֲלוֹמוֹתַי עָלַי

v'al kol yisro-ayl l'tōvo —   וְעַל כָּל יִשְׂרָאֵל לְטוֹבָה —

that all my dreams regarding myself and regarding all of Israel be good ones —

bayn shecholamti al atzmi,   בֵּין שֶׁחָלַמְתִּי עַל עַצְמִי,

those I have dreamed about myself,

u-vayn shecholamti al achayrim, וּבֵין שֶׁחָלַמְתִּי עַל אֲחֵרִים,

those I have dreamed about others,

u-vayn shechol'mu achayrim oloy. וּבֵין שֶׁחָלְמוּ אֲחֵרִים עָלָי.

and those that others have dreamed about me.

Im tōvim haym,   אִם טוֹבִים הֵם,

chaz'kaym v'am'tzaym,   חַזְּקֵם וְאַמְּצֵם,

If they are good, strengthen them, fortify them,

v'yiska-y'mu vi u-vohem   וְיִתְקַיְּמוּ בִי וּבָהֶם

make them endure in me and in them

kachalōmōsov shel yōsayf hatzadik. כַּחֲלוֹמוֹתָיו שֶׁל יוֹסֵף הַצַּדִּיק.

like the dreams of the righteous Joseph.

V'im tz'richim r'fu-o, r'fo-aym   וְאִם צְרִיכִים רְפוּאָה, רְפָאֵם

But if they require healing, heal them

k'chizkiyohu melech y'hudo   כְּחִזְקִיָּֽהוּ מֶֽלֶךְ יְהוּדָה

maychol-yō,   מֵחָלְיוֹ,

like Hezekiah king of Judah from his sickness;

וִיחֻנֶּֽךָּ — *And be gracious to you.* May you find favor in God's eyes; alternatively, may you find favor in man's eyes, for all of a person's qualities will avail him little if others dislike him.

uchmiryom han'vi-o mitzoratoh,   וּכְמִרְיָם הַנְּבִיאָה מִצָּרַעְתָּהּ,
like Miriam the prophetess from her tzaraas;

uchna-amon mitzoratō,   וּכְנַעֲמָן מִצָּרַעְתּוֹ,
like Naaman from his tzaraas;

uchmay moro al y'day   וּכְמֵי מָרָה עַל יְדֵי
   mōshe rabaynu,   מֹשֶׁה רַבֵּנוּ,
like the waters of Marah through the hand of Moses our teacher;

uchmay y'richō al y'day elisho.   וּכְמֵי יְרִיחוֹ עַל יְדֵי אֱלִישָׁע.
and like the waters of Jericho through the hand of Elisha.

Uchshaym she-hofachto   וּכְשֵׁם שֶׁהָפַכְתָּ
And just as You transformed

es kil'las bil-om horosho   אֶת קִלְלַת בִּלְעָם הָרָשָׁע
the curse of the wicked Balaam

mik'lolo livrocho,   מִקְּלָלָה לִבְרָכָה,
from a curse to a blessing,

kayn tahafōch kol chalōmōsai olai   כֵּן תַּהֲפוֹךְ כָּל חֲלוֹמוֹתַי עָלַי
v'al kol yisro-ayl l'tōvo,   וְעַל כָּל יִשְׂרָאֵל לְטוֹבָה,
*so may You transform all of my dreams regarding myself
and regarding all of Israel for goodness.*

v'sishm'rayni uschonayni v'sirtzayni.   וְתִשְׁמְרֵנִי וּתְחָנֵּנִי וְתִרְצֵנִי.
May You protect me, may You be gracious to me, may You accept me.

CONGREGATION AND *CHAZZAN* RESPOND: Omayn — אָמֵן

EACH WORD IS RECITED ALOUD BY THE *CHAZZAN* AND REPEATED BY THE *KOHANIM*:

YISO   יִשָּׂא
May [He] turn

ADŌNOY   יהוה
— *HASHEM* —

PONOV   פָּנָיו
His countenance

AYLECHO   אֵלֶיךָ
to you*

V'YOSAYM   וְיָשֵׂם
and establish

L'CHO   לְךָ
for you

•ఄ יִשָּׂא ה׳ פָּנָיו אֵלֶיךָ ఄ• — *May [He]* HASHEM *turn His countenance to you.* May He suppress His anger against you, even if you are sinful and deserve to be punished. One's face is indicative of his attitude toward someone else. If he is angry, he will turn away from the one he dislikes. God "turns His face" toward Israel to show that He loves them.

EXCEPT ON THE SABBATH, THE *KOHANIM* SING AN EXTENDED CHANT BEFORE SAYING sholōm.

SHOLŌM

שָׁלוֹם.

peace.*

WHILE THE *KOHANIM* SING AN EXTENDED CHANT BEFORE SAYING sholōm,
THE CONGREGATION RECITES THE FOLLOWING SUPPLICATION IN AN UNDERTONE.

Y'HI ROTZŌN mil'fonecho,

יְהִי רָצוֹן מִלְּפָנֶיךָ,

May it be Your will,

Adōnoy Elōhai Vaylōhay avōsai,

יהוה אֱלֹהַי וֵאלֹהֵי אֲבוֹתַי,

HASHEM, my God and the God of my forefathers,

sheta-ase l'ma-an
k'dushas chasodecho

שֶׁתַּעֲשֶׂה לְמַעַן
קְדֻשַּׁת חֲסָדֶיךָ

that You act for the sake of the holiness of Your kindness

v'gōdel rachamecho hap'shutim,

וְגֹדֶל רַחֲמֶיךָ הַפְּשׁוּטִים,

and the greatness of Your mercies which reach out,

ulma-an tohoras shimcho hagodōl
hagibōr v'hanōro,

וּלְמַעַן טָהֳרַת שִׁמְךָ הַגָּדוֹל
הַגִּבּוֹר וְהַנּוֹרָא,

*and for the sake of the sanctity of Your Name —
the great, the mighty, and the awesome —*

ben esrim ushta-yim ōsiyōs

בֶּן עֶשְׂרִים וּשְׁתַּיִם אוֹתִיּוֹת

composed of twenty-two letters

ha-yōtz'im min hap'sukim
shel birkas kōhanim

הַיּוֹצְאִים מִן הַפְּסוּקִים
שֶׁל בִּרְכַּת כֹּהֲנִים

which derive from the verses of Bircas Kohanim

[THE DIVINE NAME THAT APPEARS HERE IN BRACKETS
SHOULD BE SCANNED WITH THE EYES BUT NOT SPOKEN.]

[אנקת״ם פסת״ם פספסי״ם דיונסי״ם]

ho-amuro mipi aharōn u-vonov
am k'dōshecho,

הָאֲמוּרָה מִפִּי אַהֲרֹן וּבָנָיו
עַם קְדוֹשֶׁךָ,

spoken by Aaron and his sons, Your holy people —

shetih-ye korōv li b'kor-i loch,

שֶׁתִּהְיֶה קָרוֹב לִי בְּקָרְאִי לָךְ,

that You be near to me when I call to You;

v'sishma t'filosi
na-akosi v'enkosi tomid,

וְתִשְׁמַע תְּפִלָּתִי
נַאֲקָתִי וְאַנְקָתִי תָּמִיד,

that You listen to my prayer, my plea, and my cry at all times,

k'shaym sheshomato

כְּשֵׁם שֶׁשָּׁמַעְתָּ

just as You listened

וְיָשֵׂם לְךָ שָׁלוֹם — *And establish for you peace.*
Peace is the seal of all blessings, because with-

out peace — prosperity, health, food, and drink
are worthless.

enkas ya-akôv t'mimecho   אֶנְקַת יַעֲקֹב תְּמִימֶךָ

to the cry of Jacob, Your perfect one,

hanikro ish tom.   הַנִּקְרָא אִישׁ תָּם.

who is called "a wholesome man."

V'siten li ulchol nafshôs baysi   וְתִתֶּן לִי וּלְכָל נַפְשׁוֹת בֵּיתִי

And may You bestow upon me and upon all the souls of my household,

m'zônôsaynu u-farnosôsaynu —   מְזוֹנוֹתֵינוּ וּפַרְנָסָתֵנוּ —

b'revach v'lô v'tzimtzum,   בְּרֶוַח וְלֹא בְצִמְצוּם,

our food and our sustenance — generously and not sparsely,

b'hatayr v'lô v'isur,   בְּהֶתֵּר וְלֹא בְאִסּוּר,

b'nachas v'lô v'tza-ar —   בְּנַחַת וְלֹא בְצַעַר —

honestly and not in forbidden fashion, pleasurably and not in pain —

mitachas yod'cho hor'chovo,   מִתַּחַת יָדְךָ הָרְחָבָה,

from beneath Your generous hand,

k'shaym shenosato   כְּשֵׁם שֶׁנָּתַתָּ

pisas lechem le-echôl   פִּסַּת לֶחֶם לֶאֱכוֹל

u-veged lilbôsh   וּבֶגֶד לִלְבּוֹשׁ

just as You gave a portion of bread to eat and clothing to wear

l'ya-akôv ovinu   לְיַעֲקֹב אָבִינוּ

hanikro ish tom.   הַנִּקְרָא אִישׁ תָּם.

to our father Jacob who is called "a wholesome man."

V'sit'naynu l'ahavo,   וְתִתְּנֵנוּ לְאַהֲבָה,

l'chayn ulchesed ulrachamim   לְחֵן וּלְחֶסֶד וּלְרַחֲמִים

And may You grant that we find love, favor, kindness, and mercy

b'aynecho uv-aynay chol rô-aynu,   בְּעֵינֶיךָ וּבְעֵינֵי כָל רוֹאֵינוּ,

in Your eyes and in the eyes of all who behold us;

v'yih-yu d'vorai   וְיִהְיוּ דְבָרַי

nishmo-im la-avôdosecho,   נִשְׁמָעִים לַעֲבוֹדָתֶךָ,

and that my words in Your service be heard;

k'shaym shenosato   כְּשֵׁם שֶׁנָּתַתָּ

es yôsayf tzadikecho —   אֶת יוֹסֵף צַדִּיקֶךָ —

just as You granted Joseph, Your righteous one —

b'sho-o shehilbi-shô oviv   בְּשָׁעָה שֶׁהִלְבִּישׁוֹ אָבִיו

at the time that his father garbed him

k'sônes pasim —   כְּתֹנֶת פַּסִּים —

in a fine woolen tunic —

l'chayn ulchesed ulrachamim   לְחֵן וּלְחֶסֶד וּלְרַחֲמִים
that he find favor, kindness, and mercy

b'aynecho uv-aynay chol rō-ov.   בְּעֵינֶיךָ וּבְעֵינֵי כָל רוֹאָיו.
in Your eyes and in the eyes of all who beheld him.

V'sa-ase imi niflo-ōs v'nisim,   וְתַעֲשֶׂה עִמִּי נִפְלָאוֹת וְנִסִּים,
ultōvo ōs,   וּלְטוֹבָה אוֹת,
May You perform wonders and miracles with me, and a goodly sign;

v'satz-lichayni bidrochai,   וְתַצְלִיחֵנִי בִּדְרָכַי,
grant me success in my ways;

v'sayn b'libi bino l'hovin ulhaskil   וְתֵן בְּלִבִּי בִּינָה לְהָבִין וּלְהַשְׂכִּיל
place in my heart the power of understanding, to understand, to be wise,

ulka-yaym es kol divray   וּלְקַיֵּם אֶת כָּל דִּבְרֵי
salmud tōrosecho v'sōdōseho,   תַלְמוּד תּוֹרָתֶךָ וְסוֹדוֹתֶיהָ,
to fulfill all the words of Your Torah's teaching and its mysteries;

v'satzilayni mish'gi-ōs,   וְתַצִּילֵנִי מִשְּׁגִיאוֹת,
save me from errors;

ustahayr ra-yōnai v'libi   וּתְטַהֵר רַעְיוֹנַי וְלִבִּי
la-avōdosecho ulyir-osecho.   לַעֲבוֹדָתֶךָ וּלְיִרְאָתֶךָ.
and purify my thinking and my heart for Your service and Your awe.

V'sa-arich yomai   וְתַאֲרִיךְ יָמַי
May You prolong my days

———— INSERT THE APPROPRIATE WORDS: ————

vimay ovi v'imi   וִימֵי אָבִי וְאִמִּי
and the days of my father, my mother,

v'ish-ti u-vonai uvnōsai   וְאִשְׁתִּי וּבָנַי וּבְנוֹתַי
my wife, my son(s), my daughter(s),

———————————————————————————

b'tōv u-vin-imōs,   בְּטוֹב וּבִנְעִימוֹת,
with goodness, with sweetness,

b'rōv ōz v'sholōm,   בְּרֹב עֹז וְשָׁלוֹם,
with an abundance of strength and peace.

omayn selo.   אָמֵן סֶלָה.
Amen: Selah.

CONGREGATION AND *CHAZZAN* RESPOND: Omayn — אָמֵן

THE *CHAZZAN* IMMEDIATELY BEGINS Sim sholōm (P. 750); THE *KOHANIM* TURN BACK TO THE
ARK, LOWER THEIR HANDS AND RECITE THEIR CONCLUDING PRAYER Ribōnō shel ōlom (P. 749);
AND THE CONGREGATION RECITES Adir bamorōm (P. 749). THEY CONCLUDE THEIR RESPECTIVE
PRAYERS SIMULTANEOUSLY WITH THE *CHAZZAN'S* CONCLUSION AND RESPOND Omayn.

— KOHANIM: —

RIBŌNŌ shel ōlom,   רִבּוֹנוֹ שֶׁל עוֹלָם,

Master of the world,

osinu ma shegozarto olaynu,   עָשִׂינוּ מַה שֶּׁגָּזַרְתָּ עָלֵינוּ,

we have done what You have decreed upon us,

af ato asay imonu   אַף אַתָּה עֲשֵׂה עִמָּנוּ

now may You also do

k'mo shehivtachtonu: כְּמָה שֶׁהִבְטַחְתָּנוּ:

as You have promised us:

Hashkifo mim'ōn kodsh'cho,   הַשְׁקִיפָה מִמְּעוֹן קׇדְשְׁךָ,

Look down from You sacred dwelling,

min ha-shoma-yim,   מִן הַשָּׁמַיִם,

from the heavens,

u-voraych es am'cho es yisro-ayl,   וּבָרֵךְ אֶת עַמְּךָ אֶת יִשְׂרָאֵל,

and bless Your people, Israel,

v'ays ho-adomo   וְאֵת הָאֲדָמָה

   asher nosato lonu —   אֲשֶׁר נָתַתָּה לָּנוּ —

and the earth which You have given us —

ka-asher nishbato la-avōsaynu —   כַּאֲשֶׁר נִשְׁבַּעְתָּ לַאֲבוֹתֵינוּ —

just as You have sworn to our fathers —

eretz zovas cholov udvosh.   אֶרֶץ זָבַת חָלָב וּדְבָשׁ.

a Land that flows with milk and honey.

— CONGREGATION: —

ADIR bamorōm,   אַדִּיר בַּמָּרוֹם,

Mighty One on high,

shōchayn bigvuro,   שׁוֹכֵן בִּגְבוּרָה,

He Who dwells in power!

ato sholōm v'shimcho sholōm.   אַתָּה שָׁלוֹם וְשִׁמְךָ שָׁלוֹם.

You are Peace and Your Name is Peace!

Y'hi rotzōn shetosim olaynu   יְהִי רָצוֹן שֶׁתָּשִׂים עָלֵינוּ

May it be acceptable that You grant us

v'al kol am'cho bays yisro-ayl   וְעַל כָּל עַמְּךָ בֵּית יִשְׂרָאֵל

and all of Your people, the House of Israel,

cha-yim uvrocho   חַיִּים וּבְרָכָה

life and blessing

l'mishmeres sholōm.   לְמִשְׁמֶרֶת שָׁלוֹם.

for a safeguard of peace.

CHAZZAN:

SIM SHOLÔM tōvo uvrocho,   שִׂים שָׁלוֹם, טוֹבָה, וּבְרָכָה,
Establish peace, goodness, blessing,

chayn vochesed v'rachamim   חֵן וָחֶסֶד וְרַחֲמִים
graciousness, kindness, and compassion

olaynu v'al kol yisro-ayl amecho.   עָלֵינוּ וְעַל כָּל יִשְׂרָאֵל עַמֶּךָ.
upon us and upon all of Your people Israel.

Bor'chaynu, ovinu, kulonu k'e-chod   בָּרְכֵנוּ, אָבִינוּ, כֻּלָּנוּ כְּאֶחָד
     b'ōr ponecho,   בְּאוֹר פָּנֶיךָ,
Bless us, our Father, all of us as one, with the light of Your countenance,

ki v'ōr ponecho nosato lonu,   כִּי בְאוֹר פָּנֶיךָ נָתַתָּ לָנוּ,
     Adōnoy Elōhaynu,   יהוה אֱלֹהֵינוּ,
for with the light of Your countenance You, HASHEM, our God, gave us

tōras cha-yim v'ahavas chesed,   תּוֹרַת חַיִּים וְאַהֲבַת חֶסֶד,
the Torah of life and a love of kindness,

utz-doko uvrocho v'rachamim   וּצְדָקָה וּבְרָכָה וְרַחֲמִים
     v'cha-yim v'sholōm.   וְחַיִּים וְשָׁלוֹם.
righteousness, blessing, compassion, life, and peace.

V'tōv b'aynecho l'voraych   וְטוֹב בְּעֵינֶיךָ לְבָרֵךְ
     es am'cho yisro-ayl,   אֶת עַמְּךָ יִשְׂרָאֵל,
And may it be good in Your eyes to bless Your people Israel

b'chol ays uvchol sho-o   בְּכָל עֵת וּבְכָל שָׁעָה
     bishlōmecho.   בִּשְׁלוֹמֶךָ.
at every time and at every hour, with Your peace.

Boruch ato Adōnoy,   בָּרוּךְ אַתָּה יהוה,
Blessed are You, HASHEM,

ham'voraych es amō yisro-ayl   הַמְבָרֵךְ אֶת עַמּוֹ יִשְׂרָאֵל
     ba-sholōm.   בַּשָּׁלוֹם.
Who blesses His people Israel with peace.

THE *CHAZZAN'S* RECITES IN AN UNDERTONE:

Yih-yu l'rotzōn imray fi   יִהְיוּ לְרָצוֹן אִמְרֵי פִי
     v'hegyōn libi l'fonecho,   וְהֶגְיוֹן לִבִּי לְפָנֶיךָ,
     Adōnoy tzuri v'gō-ali.   יהוה צוּרִי וְגֹאֲלִי.
May the expressions of my mouth and the thoughts of my heart
find favor before You, HASHEM, my Rock and my Redeemer.

DURING SUCCOS, THE *HOSHANA* PRAYERS (P. 772) ARE RECITED. AT ALL OTHER TIMES, THE *CHAZZAN* RECITES THE FULL *KADDISH* (P. 454). ON FESTIVAL DAYS, THE SABBATH OF *CHOL HAMOED*, AND HOSHANA RABBAH, THE SERVICE CONTINUES THERE; ON OTHER DAYS, CONTINUE WITH *ALEINU* (P. 463).

⪦ **PRAYER FOR DEW** ⪧

THE PRAYER FOR DEW IS RECITED BY THE *CHAZZAN* ON THE FIRST DAY OF PESACH DURING HIS REPETITION OF *MUSSAF*. THE ARK IS OPENED AND THE CONGREGATION STANDS UNTIL THE CONCLUSION OF THE PRAYER.

■ **Dew:** A blessing Hashem bestows regularly upon mankind, though we do not always merit it. It is recited on Pesach, when we were delivered, though not completely deserving of it.

Ki shaym Adōnoy ekro,   כִּי שֵׁם יהוה אֶקְרָא,

    hovu gōdel Laylōhaynu.   הָבוּ גֹדֶל לֵאלֹהֵינוּ.

When I call out the Name of HASHEM, ascribe greatness to our God.

Adōnoy s'fosai tiftoch,   אֲדֹנָי שְׂפָתַי תִּפְתָּח,

    uf-i yagid t'hilosecho.   וּפִי יַגִּיד תְּהִלָּתֶךָ.

My Lord, open my lips, that my mouth may declare Your praise.

CHAZZAN BENDS HIS KNEES AT Boruch; BOWS AT ato; STRAIGHTENS UP AT Adōnoy.

BORUCH ato Adōnoy   בָּרוּךְ אַתָּה יהוה

Blessed are You, HASHEM,

Elōhaynu Vaylōhay avōsaynu,   אֱלֹהֵינוּ וֵאלֹהֵי אֲבוֹתֵינוּ,

our God and the God of our forefathers,

Elōhay avrohom, Elōhay yitzchok,   אֱלֹהֵי אַבְרָהָם, אֱלֹהֵי יִצְחָק,

    Vaylōhay ya-akōv,   וֵאלֹהֵי יַעֲקֹב,

God of Abraham, God of Isaac, and God of Jacob;

ho-Ayl hagodōl hagibōr v'hanōro,   הָאֵל הַגָּדוֹל הַגִּבּוֹר וְהַנּוֹרָא,

    Ayl elyōn,   אֵל עֶלְיוֹן,

the great, mighty, and awesome God, the supreme God,

gōmayl chasodim tōvim   גּוֹמֵל חֲסָדִים טוֹבִים

    v'kōnay hakōl,   וְקוֹנֵה הַכֹּל,

Who bestows beneficial kindnesses and creates everything,

v'zōchayr chasday ovōs,   וְזוֹכֵר חַסְדֵי אָבוֹת,

Who recalls the kindnesses of the Patriarchs

u-mayvi gō-ayl livnay v'nayhem,   וּמֵבִיא גוֹאֵל לִבְנֵי בְנֵיהֶם,

and brings a Redeemer to their children's children,

l'ma-an sh'mō b'ahavo.   לְמַעַן שְׁמוֹ בְּאַהֲבָה.

for His Name's sake, with love.

Melech ōzayr u-mōshi-a u-mogayn.   מֶלֶךְ עוֹזֵר וּמוֹשִׁיעַ וּמָגֵן.

O King, Helper, Savior, and Shield.

⪦§ **The Prayer for Dew**

   When Isaac bestowed the Patriarchal blessing upon his son Jacob (*Genesis* Ch. 27), he intimated that Pesach, the time of redemption and of praise for God, is the time when the Heavenly chambers of dew and blessing are open. Thus, the first day of Pesach is an auspicious time to pray for dew. Moreover, the

B'DATŌ abi-o chidōs,

בְּדַעְתּוֹ אַבִּיעָה חִידוֹת,

With His consent I shall speak of mysteries.

b'am zu b'zu b'tal l'hachadōs.

בְּעַם זוּ בְּזוּ בְּטַל לְהַחֲדוֹת.

Among this people, through this [prayer], may they be made exultant by the dew.

Tal gay udsho-eho lachadōs,

טַל גֵּיא וּדְשָׁאֶיהָ לַחֲדוֹת,

Dew — bringing joy to valley and its herbage;

dotzim b'tzilō l'haychodōs.

דָּצִים בְּצִלּוֹ לְהֵחָדוֹת.

taking pleasure in His shelter to be made exultant.

Ōs yaldus tal l'hogayn l'sōlodōs.

אוֹת יַלְדוּת טַל לְהָגֵן לְתוֹלָדוֹת.

Dew is a symbol of youth[ful promise], may it protect the generations.

CHAZZAN BENDS HIS KNEES AT Boruch; BOWS AT ato; STRAIGHTENS UP AT Adōnoy.

Boruch ato Adōnoy,

בָּרוּךְ אַתָּה יהוה,

mogayn avrohom.

מָגֵן אַבְרָהָם.

Blessed are You, HASHEM, Shield of Abraham.

ATO gibōr l'ōlom Adōnoy,

אַתָּה גִּבּוֹר לְעוֹלָם אֲדֹנָי,

You are eternally mighty, my Lord,

m'cha-yay maysim ato,

מְחַיֵּה מֵתִים אַתָּה,

rav l'hōshi-a.

רַב לְהוֹשִׁיעַ.

the Resuscitator of the dead are You; abundantly able to save.

T'HŌMŌS hadōm

תְּהוֹמוֹת הֲדוֹם

lir-sisō k'sufim,

לִרְסִיסוֹ כְּסוּפִים,

The depths of the footstool yearn for His droplet,

v'chol n'ōs deshe lō nichsofim.

וְכָל נְאוֹת דֶּשֶׁא לוֹ נִכְסָפִים.

and every lush meadow yearns for it.

Tal zichrō g'vurōs mōsifim,

טַל זִכְרוֹ גְּבוּרוֹת מוֹסִיפִים,

Dew — its mention enhances [His] powers,

chokuk b'gishas musofim,

חָקוּק בְּגִישַׁת מוּסָפִים,

it is inscribed in the Mussaf prayer.

tal l'hacha-yōs bō n'kukay s'ifim.

טַל לְהַחֲיוֹת בּוֹ נְקוּקֵי סְעִיפִים.

Dew — to resuscitate with it those buried in the cleft of rocks.

Elōhaynu Vaylōhay avōsaynu,

אֱלֹהֵינוּ וֵאלֹהֵי אֲבוֹתֵינוּ,

Our God and the God of our forefathers:

TAL tayn lirtzōs artzoch,

טַל תֵּן לִרְצוֹת אַרְצָךְ,

Dew — give it to favor Your Land;

---

prayer and the season suggest the principle that Creation was designed to accommodate the dictates of the Torah: Spring, the season of gentle dew and the rejuvenation of nature, is also the time when the Jewish people was redeemed and began to blossom as a nation.

shisaynu v'rocho b'ditzoch,   שִׂיתֵנוּ בְרָכָה בְדִיצָךְ,

establish us for blessing in Your pleasure;

rōv dogon v'sirōsh b'hafritzoch,   רֹב דָּגָן וְתִירוֹשׁ בְּהַפְרִיצָךְ,

with abundant grain and wine may You strengthen [us];

kōmaym ir boh cheftzoch —   קוֹמֵם עִיר בָּהּ חֶפְצָךְ —

establish the city containing Your delight —

b'tol.   בְּטָל.

with dew.

TAL tzavay shono tōvo um-uteres,   **טַל** צַוֵּה שָׁנָה טוֹבָה וּמְעֻטֶּרֶת,

Dew — decree it for a year that is good and crowned;

p'ri ho-oretz l'go-ōn ulsif-eres,   פְּרִי הָאָרֶץ לְגָאוֹן וּלְתִפְאָרֶת,

may the fruit of the earth become the pride and splendor;

ir kasuko nōseres,   עִיר כַּסֻּכָּה נוֹתֶרֶת,

the city deserted like a booth —

simo b'yod'cho ateres —   שִׂימָהּ בְּיָדְךָ עֲטֶרֶת —

let Your hand make it a crown —

b'tol.   בְּטָל.

with dew.

TAL nōfayf alay eretz b'rucho,   **טַל** נוֹפֵף עֲלֵי אֶרֶץ בְּרוּכָה,

Dew — let it drop sweetly on the blessed Land,

mimeged shoma-yim sab'aynu v'rocho,   מִמֶּגֶד שָׁמַיִם שַׂבְּעֵנוּ בְרָכָה,

with the delicacies of heaven sate us with blessing,

l'ho-ir mitōch cha-shaycho,   לְהָאִיר מִתּוֹךְ חֲשֵׁכָה,

to enlighten from amid the darkness

kano acharecho m'shucho —   כַּנָּה אַחֲרֶיךָ מְשׁוּכָה —

the fundamental nation that is drawn after You —

b'tol.   בְּטָל.

with dew.

TAL ya-asis tzuf horim,   **טַל** יַעֲסִיס צוּף הָרִים,

Dew — let it sweeten the honey of the mountains,

t'aym bim-ōdecho muvchorim,   טְעַם בִּמְאוֹדֶךָ מֻבְחָרִים,

let the chosen [people] savor Your plenty.

chanunecho chalaytz mimasgayrim,   חֲנוּנֶיךָ חַלֵּץ מִמַּסְגֵּרִים,

Free Your favored ones from bondage;

zimro nan-im v'kōl norim —   זִמְרָה נַנְעִים וְקוֹל נָרִים —

sweetly we will sing and raise our voice —

b'tol.   בְּטָל.

with dew.

TAL vosova malay asomaynu,   **טַל** וָשׂוֹבַע מַלֵּא אֲסָמֵינוּ,

Dew — and plenty, may they fill our granaries,

hacho-ays t'chadaysh yomaynu,   הֲכָעֵת תְּחַדֵּשׁ יָמֵינוּ,

if only You would now rejuvenate our days!

dōd, k'erk'cho ha-amayd sh'maynu,   דּוֹד כְּעֶרְכְּךָ הַעֲמֵד שְׁמֵנוּ,

Beloved One, make our names enduring like Your own,

gan rove simaynu —   גַּן רָוֶה שִׂימֵנוּ —

make us like a well-watered garden —

b'tol.   בְּטָל.

with dew.

TAL bō s'voraych mozōn,   **טַל** בּוֹ תְבָרֵךְ מָזוֹן,

Dew — may You bless [our] sustenance with it,

b'mishmanaynu al y'hi rozōn,   בְּמִשְׁמַנֵּינוּ אַל יְהִי רָזוֹן,

in our abundance may there be no scarcity.

a-yumo asher hisato katzōn,   אֲיֻמָּה אֲשֶׁר הִסַּעְתָּ כַצֹּאן,

This nation that You led like sheep —

Ono tofayk loh rotzōn —   אָנָּא תָּפֵק לָהּ רָצוֹן —

please, fulfill her desire —

b'tol.   בְּטָל.

with dew.

Sho-ato hu Adōnoy Elōhaynu,   שָׁאַתָּה הוּא יהוה אֱלֹהֵינוּ,

For You are HASHEM, our God,

mashiv horu-ach u-mōrid hatol.   מַשִּׁיב הָרוּחַ וּמוֹרִיד הַטָּל.

Who makes the wind blow and makes the dew descend.

CONGREGATION THEN *CHAZZAN*:

Livrocho v'lō liklolo.   לִבְרָכָה וְלֹא לִקְלָלָה.

For blessing and not for curse.

CONGREGATION RESPONDS: Omayn — אָמֵן

CONGREGATION THEN *CHAZZAN*:

L'cha-yim v'lō l'moves.   לְחַיִּים וְלֹא לְמָוֶת.

For life and not for death.

CONGREGATION RESPONDS: Omayn — אָמֵן

CONGREGATION THEN *CHAZZAN:*

L'sōva v'lō l'rozōn.   לְשֹׂבַע וְלֹא לְרָזוֹן.

For plenty and not for scarcity.

CONGREGATION RESPONDS: Omayn — אָמֵן

THE PRAYER FOR DEW IS COMPLETED AND THE ARK IS CLOSED.
THE REPETITION CONTINUES WITH M'chalkayl cha-yim (P. 709).

ᴴ **PRAYER FOR RAIN** ᴴ

THIS PRAYER IS RECITED BY THE *CHAZZAN* ON SHEMINI ATZERES DURING HIS REPETITION OF *MUSSAF*.
THE ARK IS OPENED AND THE CONGREGATION STANDS UNTIL THE CONCLUSION OF THE PRAYER.

■ Rain: A blessing Hashem bestows upon mankind commensurate with their meritorious actions, as stated in the second paragraph of the *Shema*. Fully cognizant of our shortcomings, we beseech Hashem to remember the exemplary actions of our prestigious ancestors.

Ki shaym Adōnoy ekro,	כִּי שֵׁם יהוה אֶקְרָא,
hovu gōdel Laylōhaynu.	הָבוּ גֹדֶל לֵאלֹהֵינוּ.

When I call out the Name of HASHEM, *ascribe greatness to our God.*

Adōnoy s'fosai tiftoch,	אֲדֹנָי שְׂפָתַי תִּפְתָּח,
u-fi yagid t'hilosecho.	וּפִי יַגִּיד תְּהִלָּתֶךָ.

My Lord, open my lips, that my mouth may declare Your praise.

CHAZZAN BENDS HIS KNEES AT Boruch; BOWS AT ato; STRAIGHTENS UP AT Adōnoy.

BORUCH ato Adōnoy	**בָּרוּךְ** אַתָּה יהוה

Blessed are You, HASHEM,

Elōhaynu Vaylōhay avōsaynu,	אֱלֹהֵינוּ וֵאלֹהֵי אֲבוֹתֵינוּ,

our God and the God of our forefathers,

Elōhay avrohom, Elōhay yitzchok,	אֱלֹהֵי אַבְרָהָם, אֱלֹהֵי יִצְחָק,
Vaylōhay ya-akōv,	וֵאלֹהֵי יַעֲקֹב,

God of Abraham, God of Isaac, and God of Jacob;

ho-Ayl hagodōl hagibōr v'hanōro,	הָאֵל הַגָּדוֹל הַגִּבּוֹר וְהַנּוֹרָא,
Ayl elyōn,	אֵל עֶלְיוֹן,

the great, mighty, and awesome God, the supreme God,

gōmayl chasodim tōvim	גּוֹמֵל חֲסָדִים טוֹבִים
v'kōnayh hakōl,	וְקוֹנֵה הַכֹּל,

Who bestows beneficial kindnesses and creates everything,

v'zōchayr chasday ovōs,	וְזוֹכֵר חַסְדֵי אָבוֹת,

Who recalls the kindnesses of the Patriarchs

u-mayvi gō-ayl livnay v'nayhem,	וּמֵבִיא גוֹאֵל לִבְנֵי בְנֵיהֶם,

and brings a Redeemer to their children's children,

l'ma-an sh'mō b'ahavo.	לְמַעַן שְׁמוֹ בְּאַהֲבָה.

for His Name's sake, with love.

Melech ōzayr u-mōshi-a u-mogayn.	מֶלֶךְ עוֹזֵר וּמוֹשִׁיעַ וּמָגֵן.

O King, Helper, Savior, and Shield.

᳀ **The Prayer for Rain**

Since the fall and winter are the rainy season in the Land of Israel, and it is a country that is more dependent on rainfall than most, the Sages ordained that the prayer for rain be recited on Succos, the pilgrimage Festival which falls closest to the rainy season. Because the Festival itself is spent primarily in the *succah,* and it is re-

AF B'RI utas shaym sar motor,   אַף־בְּרִי אֻתַּת שֵׁם שַׂר מָטָר,

Af-Bri* is designated as the name of the angel of rain;

l'ha-aviv ulha-anin   לְהַעֲבִיב וּלְהַעֲנִין

    l'horik ulhamtar.   לְהָרִיק וּלְהַמְטַר.

to thicken and to form clouds, to empty them and to cause rain.

Ma-yim ibim bom gay la-atar,   מַיִם אֲבִים בָּם גֵּיא לַעֲטַר,

Water with which to crown the valley's vegetation —

l'val yu-atzoru b'nishyōn sh'tor.   לְבַל יֵעָצְרוּ בְּנִשְׁיוֹן שְׁטָר.

may it not be withheld because of our unredeemed debt.

Emunim g'nōn bom shō-alay motor.   אֱמוּנִים גְּנוֹן בָּם שׁוֹאֲלֵי מָטָר.

In the merit of the faithful Patriarchs protect the ones who pray for rain.

CHAZZAN BENDS HIS KNEES AT Boruch; BOWS AT ato; STRAIGHTENS UP AT Adōnoy.

Boruch ato Adōnoy,   בָּרוּךְ אַתָּה יהוה,

    mogayn avrohom.   מָגֵן אַבְרָהָם.

Blessed are You, HASHEM, Shield of Abraham.

CONGREGATION RESPONDS: Omayn — אָמֵן

ATO gibōr l'ōlom Adōnoy,   אַתָּה גִּבּוֹר לְעוֹלָם אֲדֹנָי,

You are eternally mighty, my Lord,

m'cha-yay maysim ato,   מְחַיֵּה מֵתִים אַתָּה,

    rav l'hōshi-a.   רַב לְהוֹשִׁיעַ.

the Resuscitator of the dead are You; abundantly able to save.

YATRI-ACH l'falayg mipeleg geshem,   יַטְרִיחַ לְפַלֵּג מִפֶּלֶג גֶּשֶׁם,

May He obligate [the Angel Af-Bri] to give us portions of the segregated rain,

l'mōgayg p'nay neshi   לְמוֹגֵג פְּנֵי נֶשִׁי

    b'tzachōs leshem.   בְּצַחוֹת לֶשֶׁם.

to soften the wasteland's face when it is dry as rock.

Ma-yim l'ad'roch kiniso b'reshem,   מַיִם לְאַדְּרָךְ כִּנִּיתָ בְּרֶשֶׁם,

With water You symbolized Your might in Scripture,

l'hargi-a b'ra-afom linfuchay neshem,   לְהַרְגִּיעַ בְּרַעֲפָם לִנְפוּחֵי נֶשֶׁם,

to soothe with its drops those in whom was blown a soul,

l'hacha-yōs mazkirim   לְהַחֲיוֹת מַזְכִּירִים

    g'vurōs hagoshem.   גְּבוּרוֹת הַגָּשֶׁם.

to keep alive the ones who recall the strengths of the rain.

---

garded as a symbol of Divine displeasure for rain to prevent people from eating and living there, it would be incongruous to pray for rain at a time when we do not want it to fall. Therefore, the prayer is recited on Shemini Atzeres, when the Scriptural commandment of *succah*-

dwelling is no longer applicable.

◆§ אַף־בְּרִי — *Af-Bri,* the name of the angel appointed over the rainclouds, is formed from the two words *Af,* "anger," and *Bri,* "health." This name alludes to the two ways in which rain

Elōhaynu vaylōhay avōsaynu,　　　　אֱלֹהֵינוּ וֵאלֹהֵי אֲבוֹתֵינוּ,
Our God and the God of our forefathers:

Z'CHŌR ov　　　　　　　　　　　　זְכוֹר אָב

nimshach acharecho kama-yim.　　נִמְשַׁךְ אַחֲרֶיךָ כַּמַּיִם.
Remember the Patriarch [Abraham], who was drawn behind You like water.

Bayrachtō k'aytz shosul　　　　　　בֵּרַכְתּוֹ כְּעֵץ שָׁתוּל

al palgay ma-yim,　　　　　　　　עַל פַּלְגֵי מָיִם,
You blessed him like a tree replanted alongside streams of water;

g'nantō, hitzaltō may-aysh u-mima-yim,　　גְּנַנְתּוֹ, הִצַּלְתּוֹ מֵאֵשׁ וּמִמָּיִם,
You shielded him, You rescued him from fire and from water;

d'rashtō b'zor-ō al kol mo-yim.　　דְּרַשְׁתּוֹ בְּזַרְעוֹ עַל כָּל מָיִם.
You tested him when he sowed upon all waters.

CONGREGATION, THEN *CHAZZAN*:

Ba-avurō al timna mo-yim.　　　　בַּעֲבוּרוֹ אַל תִּמְנַע מָיִם.
For his sake, do not hold water back!

CHAZZAN CONTINUES:

Z'CHŌR hanōlod bivsōras　　　　זְכוֹר הַנּוֹלָד בִּבְשׂוֹרַת
Remember the one [Isaac] born with the tidings of,

yukach no m'at ma-yim.　　　　　יֻקַּח נָא מְעַט מָיִם.
"Let some water be brought."

V'sachto l'hōrō l'shochatō,　　　　וְשַׂחְתָּ לְהוֹרוֹ לְשָׁחֲטוֹ,

lishpōch domō kama-yim.　　　　לִשְׁפּוֹךְ דָּמוֹ כַּמַּיִם.
You told his father to slaughter him — to spill his blood like water.

Zihayr gam hu　　　　　　　　　זָהַר גַּם הוּא

lishpōch layv kama-yim.　　　　לִשְׁפּוֹךְ לֵב כַּמַּיִם.
He too was scrupulous to pour his heart like water.

Chofar u-motzo b'ayrōs mo-yim.　　חָפַר וּמָצָא בְּאֵרוֹת מָיִם.
He dug and discovered wells of water.

CONGREGATION, THEN *CHAZZAN*:

B'tzidkō chōn chashras mo-yim.　　בְּצִדְקוֹ חֹן חַשְׁרַת מָיִם.
For the sake of his righteousness, grant abundant water!

CHAZZAN CONTINUES:

Z'CHŌR TO-an maklō　　　　　זְכוֹר טָעַן מַקְלוֹ

v'ovar yardayn ma-yim.　　　　וְעָבַר יַרְדֵּן מָיִם.
Remember the one [Jacob] who carried his staff and crossed the Jordan's water.

---

may fall. Sometimes it descends in harsh torrents and is a sign of Divine anger; at other times it falls in a beneficial manner and brings health and prosperity in its wake. The responsibilities of this angel are described in the first two stanzas of this prayer.

Yichad layv v'gol even
   mipi b'ayr ma-yim,

יִחַד לֵב וְגָל אֶבֶן
מִפִּי בְּאֵר מַיִם,

He dedicated his heart and rolled a stone off the mouth of a well of water,

k'ne-evak lō sar bolul
   may-aysh u-mima-yim.

כְּנֶאֱבַק לוֹ שַׂר בָּלוּל
מֵאֵשׁ וּמִמַּיִם.

as when he was wrestled by an angel composed of fire and water.

Lochayn hivtachtō
   he-yōs imō bo-aysh u-vamo-yim.

לָכֵן הִבְטַחְתּוֹ
הֱיוֹת עִמּוֹ בָּאֵשׁ וּבַמָּיִם.

Therefore You pledged to remain with him through fire and water.

CONGREGATION, THEN *CHAZZAN*:

Ba-avurō al timna moyim.

בַּעֲבוּרוֹ אַל תִּמְנַע מָיִם.

For his sake, do not hold water back!

CHAZZAN CONTINUES:

Z'CHŌR moshuy b'sayvas
   gōme min hama-yim.

זְכוֹר מָשׁוּי בְּתֵבַת
גֹּמֶא מִן הַמַּיִם.

Remember the one [Moses] drawn forth in a bulrush basket from the water.

Nomu dolō dolo
   v'hishko tzōn mo-yim.

נָמוּ דָּלֹה דָלָה
וְהִשְׁקָה צֹאן מָיִם.

They said, "He drew water and provided the sheep with water."

S'gulecho ays tzom'u lama-yim,

סְגוּלֶיךָ עֵת צָמְאוּ לַמַּיִם,

At the time Your treasured people thirsted for water,

al hasela hoch va-yaytz'u moyim.

עַל הַסֶּלַע הָךְ וַיֵּצְאוּ מָיִם.

he struck the rock and out came water.

CONGREGATION, THEN *CHAZZAN*:

B'tzidkō chōn chashras mo-yim.

בְּצִדְקוֹ חֹן חַשְׁרַת מָיִם.

For the sake of his righteousness, grant abundant water!

CHAZZAN CONTINUES:

Z'CHŌR p'kid shosōs

זְכוֹר פְּקִיד שָׁתוֹת

Remember the appointee [Aaron] over the Temple,

tōvayl chomaysh t'vilōs bama-yim.

טוֹבֵל חָמֵשׁ טְבִילוֹת בַּמָּיִם.

who made five immersions in the water.

Tzō-e umarchitz kapov
   b'kidush ma-yim.

צוֹעֶה וּמַרְחִיץ כַּפָּיו
בְּקִדּוּשׁ מַיִם.

He went to cleanse his hands through sanctification with water.

Kōray u-ma-ze tohoras ma-yim.

קוֹרֵא וּמַזֶּה טָהֲרַת מַיִם.

He called out and sprinkled [blood bringing] purity as with water.

Ruchak may-am pachaz kamo-yim.

רָחַק מֵעַם פַּחַז כַּמָּיִם.

He remained apart from a people of waterlike impetuosity.

CONGREGATION, THEN *CHAZZAN*:

Ba-avurō al timna mo-yim.

בַּעֲבוּרוֹ אַל תִּמְנַע מָיִם.

For his sake, do not hold water back!

CHAZZAN CONTINUES:

Z'CHŌR sh'naym osor sh'votim

זְכוֹר שְׁנֵים עָשָׂר שְׁבָטִים

Remember the twelve tribes

shehe-evarto b'gizras ma-yim,

שֶׁהֶעֱבַרְתָּ בְּגִזְרַת מַיִם,

You caused to cross through the split waters,

shehimtakto lomō m'rirus ma-yim.

שֶׁהִמְתַּקְתָּ לָמוֹ מְרִירוּת מַיִם.

for whom You sweetened the water's bitter taste.

Tōl'dōsom nishpach domom
olecho kama-yim.

תּוֹלְדוֹתָם נִשְׁפַּךְ דָּמָם
עָלֶיךָ כַּמָּיִם.

Their offspring — their blood was spilt for You like water.

Tayfen ki nafshaynu of'fu mo-yim.

תֵּפֶן כִּי נַפְשֵׁנוּ אָפְפוּ מָיִם.

Turn to us — for woes engulf our souls like water.

CONGREGATION, THEN *CHAZZAN*:

B'tzidkom chōn chashras mo-yim.

בְּצִדְקָם חֹן חַשְׁרַת מָיִם.

For the sake of their righteousness, grant abundant water!

CHAZZAN CONTINUES:

Sho-ato hu Adōnoy Elōhaynu,

שָׁאַתָּה הוּא יהוה אֱלֹהֵינוּ,

For You Are HASHEM, Our God,

mashiv horu-ach u-mōrid hagoshem.

מַשִּׁיב הָרוּחַ וּמוֹרִיד הַגָּשֶׁם.

Who makes the wind blow and makes the rain descend.

CONGREGATION THEN *CHAZZAN*:

Livrocho v'lō liklolo.

לִבְרָכָה וְלֹא לִקְלָלָה.

For blessing and not for curse.

CONGREGATION RESPONDS: Omayn — אָמֵן

CONGREGATION THEN *CHAZZAN*:

L'cha-yim v'lō l'moves.

לְחַיִּים וְלֹא לְמָוֶת.

For life and not for death.

CONGREGATION RESPONDS: Omayn — אָמֵן

CONGREGATION THEN *CHAZZAN*:

L'sōva v'lō l'rozōn.

לְשׂוֹבַע וְלֹא לְרָזוֹן.

For plenty and not for scarcity.

CONGREGATION RESPONDS: Omayn — אָמֵן

THE PRAYER FOR RAIN IS COMPLETED AND THE ARK IS CLOSED.
THE REPETITION CONTINUES WITH M'chalkayl cha-yim (P. 709).

⟜ AKDAMUS ⟞

ON THE FIRST DAY OF SHAVUOS, AFTER THE *KOHEN* HAS BEEN CALLED UP FOR THE TORAH
READING BUT BEFORE HE HAS RECITED HIS BLESSING, *AKDAMUS* IS READ RESPONSIVELY.

■ An intricate Aramaic peom extolling the virues of both Hashem and His Torah, and
our inadequecy to fully express their greatness.

CHAZZAN:

AKDOMUS milin,

v'shoro-yus shuso,

אַקְדָּמוּת מִלִּין,

וְשָׁרָיוּת שׁוּתָא,

In introduction to the words, and commencement of my speech,

avlo shokilno, harmon urshuso.

אַוְלָא שָׁקֵילְנָא, הַרְמָן וּרְשׁוּתָא.

I begin by taking authorization and permission.

CONGREGATION:

B'vovay t'ray uslos,

d'eftach b'nakshuso,

בְּבָבֵי תְּרֵי וּתְלָת,

דְּאֶפְתַּח בְּנַקְשׁוּתָא,

In two and three sections, I shall commence with trembling,

b'voray d'voray v'toray

aday l'kashi-shuso.

בִּבְרֵי דְבָרֵי וְטָרֵי

עֲדֵי לְקַשִׁישׁוּתָא.

With permission from Him Who created everything and shields it till its hoary age.

CHAZZAN:

G'vuron ol'min layh,

v'lo sipayk p'rishuso,

גְּבוּרָן עָלְמִין לֵיהּ,

וְלָא סְפֵק פְּרִישׁוּתָא,

His is eternal strength that could not be described —

g'vil ilu r'ki-ay,

k'nay kol churshoso.

גְּוִיל אִלּוּ רְקִיעֵי,

קְנֵי כָּל חוּרְשָׁתָא.

even if the heavens were parchment, and the forests quills,

CONGREGATION:

D'yō ilu yamay,

v'chol may ch'nishuso,

דְּיוֹ אִלּוּ יַמֵּי,

וְכָל מֵי כְנִישׁוּתָא,

if all oceans were ink, as well as every gathered water;

doyray ar-o sofray,

v'roshmay rashvoso.

דָּיְרֵי אַרְעָא סָפְרֵי,

וְרָשְׁמֵי רַשְׁוָתָא.

if the earth's inhabitants were scribes and recorders of initials —

CHAZZAN:

Hadar moray sh'ma-yo,

v'shalit b'yabeshto,

הֲדַר מָרֵי שְׁמַיָּא,

וְשַׁלִּיט בְּיַבֶּשְׁתָּא,

the glory of the Master of heaven and the Ruler of earth.

hokaym ol'mo y'chido-ay,
 v'chab'shayh b'chab'shuso.

הָקֵם עָלְמָא יְחִידָאֵי,
וְכַבְּשֵׁיה בְּכַבְּשׁוּתָא.

In isolation He established the earth and controlled [its expansion] with constraint.

———————— CONGREGATION: ————————

Uvlo lay-u shachl'layh,
 uvlo t'shoshuso,

וּבְלָא לֵאוּ שַׁכְלְלֵיה,
וּבְלָא תְּשָׁשׁוּתָא,

He perfected it without fatigue and without weariness,

uv-oso kalilo,
 d'lays bah m'shoshuso.

וּבְאָתָא קַלִילָא,
דְּלֵית בַּה מְשָׁשׁוּתָא.

and with a letter, slight and lacking substance.

———————— CHAZZAN: ————————

Zamayn kol avid-tayh,
 b'hach yōmay shito,

זַמֵּן כָּל עֲבִידְתֵּיה,
בְּהַךְ יוֹמֵי שִׁתָּא,

He readied all His work in those six days,

zay-hōr y'korayh ali,
 alay chors'yayh d'eshoso.

זְהוֹר יְקָרֵיה עֲלִי,
עֲלֵי כָרְסְיֵה דְּאֶשָּׁתָא.

then the splendor of His majesty ascended upon His fiery throne.

———————— CONGREGATION: ————————

Cha-yol elef alfin
 v'ribō l'shamshuso,

חַיָּל אֶלֶף אַלְפִין
וְרִבּוֹ לְשַׁמְשׁוּתָא,

A host of a thousand thousands and tens of thousands serve Him,

chad-tin n'vōt l'tzafrin,
 sagi-o t'ro-shuso.

חַדְתִּין נְבוֹט לְצַפְרִין,
סַגִּיאָה טְרָשׁוּתָא.

new ones flow forth every morning — How great is Your faithfulness!

———————— CHAZZAN: ————————

T'fay y'kidin s'rofin,
 k'lōl gapay shito,

טְפֵי יְקִידִין שְׂרָפִין,
כְּלוֹל גַּפֵּי שִׁתָּא.

Even greater are the flaming Seraphim, each one six winged,

t'aym ad yisy'hayv l'hōn,
 sh'sikin b'adishto.

טְעַם עַד יִתְיְהֵב לְהוֹן,
שְׁתִיקִין בְּאַדִשְׁתָּא.

until permission is granted them, they must be still, in total silence.

———————— CONGREGATION: ————————

Y'kab'lun dayn min dayn,
 shovay d'lo v'shash-to,

יְקַבְּלוּן דֵּין מִן דֵּין,
שָׁוֵי דְּלָא בְשַׁשְׁתָּא,

Upon receiving [permission] from one another, in unison with no delay [they chant]:

y'kar m'lay chol ar-o,
יְקַר מְלֵי כָל אַרְעָא,

lislōsay k'dushto.
לִתְלוֹתֵי קְדוּשְׁתָּא.

"All the world is filled with His glory" — after three times chanting "Holy."

— CHAZZAN: —

K'kol min kodom Shadai,
בְּקָל מִן קֳדָם שַׁדַּי,

k'kol may n'fi-shuso,
כְּקָל מֵי נְפִישׁוּתָא,

Like the sound emanating from the Almighty, like the sound of torrential waters,

k'ruvin kovayl galgalin,
כְּרוּבִין קֳבֵל גַּלְגַּלִּין,

m'rōm'min b'avshoso.
מְרוֹמְמִין בְּאַוְשָׁתָא.

Cherubim responding to galgalim, exalting in a crescendo.

— CONGREGATION: —

L'mechezay v'anpo ayn,
לְמֶחֱזֵי בְאַנְפָּא עֵין,

k'vos giray kashto,
כְּוָת גִּירֵי קַשְׁתָּא,

Seeming to the human eye like arrows flashing from a bow,

l'chol asar d'mishtal'chin,
לְכָל אֲתַר דְּמִשְׁתַּלְּחִין,

z'rizin b'ashvoso.
זְרִיזִין בְּאַשְׁוָתָא.

to every place that they are sent, they hasten anxiously.

— CHAZZAN: —

M'vor'chin b'rich y'korayh,
מְבָרְכִין בְּרִיךְ יְקָרֵיהּ,

b'chol l'shon l'chi-shuso,
בְּכָל לְשָׁן לְחִישׁוּתָא,

They chant the blessing: "Blessed is His glory" — in every spoken tongue —

may-asar bays sh'chintayh,
מֵאֲתַר בֵּית שְׁכִינְתֵּיהּ,

d'lo tz'rich b'chi-shuso.
דְּלָא צְרִיךְ בְּחִישׁוּתָא.

"From the place where His Presence dwells" — which requires no searching.

— CONGREGATION: —

N'him kol chayl m'rōmo,
נְהִים כָּל חֵיל מְרוֹמָא,

m'kal'sin bachashashto,
מְקַלְּסִין בַּחֲשַׁשְׁתָּא,

Roaring, the entire heavenly legion, praises in trepidation:

n'hiro malchusayh,
נְהִירָא מַלְכוּתֵיהּ,

l'dor v'dor l'afrashto.
לְדָר וְדָר לְאַפְרַשְׁתָּא.

"May His kingdom glow eternally from generation to generation."

— CHAZZAN: —

S'diro v'hōn k'dushto,
סְדִירָא בְהוֹן קְדוּשְׁתָּא,

v'chad cholfo shato,
וְכַד חָלְפָא שַׁעְתָּא,

*Scheduled among them is the Kedushah service,
and when the time is over,*

siyumo dil'olam,
    v'ōf lo lishvu-aso.

סִיּוּמָא דְלְעָלַם,
וְאוֹף לָא לִשְׁבוּעֲתָא.

it is forever at an end, not repeated, even after seven years.

———————— CONGREGATION: ————————

Adav y'kar achasantayh,
    chavivin, d'vikva-to,

עֲדַב יְקַר אַחֲסַנְתֵּיהּ,
חֲבִיבִין דְּבִקְבַעְתָּא,

But the portion of His precious inheritance is better, for with regularity

avidin layh chativo,
    bidnach ushkato.

עֲבִידִין לֵיהּ חֲטִיבָה,
בִּדְנַח וּשְׁקַעְתָּא.

they make Him their sole desire, at sunrise and sunset.

———————— CHAZZAN: ————————

P'rishon l'monosayh,
    l'me-bad layh r'uso,

פְּרִישָׁן לְמָנָתֵיהּ,
לְמֶעְבַּד לֵיהּ רְעוּתָא,

Designated as His portion to carry out His will,

p'rishusayh sh'vochayh,
    y'chavun b'sho-uso.

פְּרִישׁוּתֵיהּ שְׁבָחֵיהּ,
יְחַוּוּן בְּשָׁעוּתָא.

His wonders and His praises they recount at every hour.

———————— CONGREGATION: ————————

Tz'vi v'chomid v'rogig,
    d'yil-un b'lo-uso,

צְבִי וְחָמִיד וְרָגִיג,
דְּיִלְאוּן בְּלָעוּתָא,

He desired, longed, and coveted that they toil in Torah study —

tz'lōs'hōn b'chayn m'kabayl,
    v'hanyo vo-uso.

צְלוֹתְהוֹן בְּכֵן מְקַבֵּל,
וְהַנְיָא בָעוּתָא.

— therefore He accepts their prayers; their prayer is efficacious.

———————— CHAZZAN: ————————

K'tiro l'chay olmo.
    b'sogo bish-vu-aso,

קְטִירָא לְחֵי עָלְמָא,
בְּתָגָא בִּשְׁבוּעֲתָא,

They are wreathed with an oath into a crown for the Eternally Living;

kovayl y'kar tōtefto,
    y'sivo vikvi-uso.

קָבֵל יְקַר טוֹטֶפְתָּא,
יְתִיבָא בִקְבִיעוּתָא.

beside His precious tefillin, it rests with regularity.

———————— CONGREGATION: ————————

R'shimo hi gufo,
    b'chochm'so uvda-to,

רְשִׁימָא הִיא גוּפָא,
בְּחָכְמְתָא וּבְדַעְתָּא,

This is inscribed therein, with wisdom and with knowledge:

r'vu-s'hōn d'yisro-ayl,
    k'ro-ay vishmato.

רְבוּתְהוֹן דְּיִשְׂרָאֵל,
קְרָאֵי בִשְׁמַעְתָּא.

the magnitude of Israel, reciters of the Shema.

—————————— CHAZZAN: ——————————

Sh'vach ribōn ol'mo,   שְׁבַח רִבּוֹן עָלְמָא,

   amiro dachvoso,   אֲמִירָא דַכְוָתָא,

This praise of the Master of the Universe is a pure statement

sh'far alai l'chavō-yayh,   שְׁפַר עֲלַי לְחַוּוֹיֵהּ,

   b'apay mal-k'voso.   בְּאַפֵּי מַלְכְּוָתָא.

that it behooves me to declare in the presence of the kings.

—————————— CONGREGATION: ——————————

To-in u-miskan'shin   תָּאִין וּמִתְכַּנְּשִׁין,

   k'chayzu idvoso.   כְּחֵזוּ אִדְוָתָא,

The wicked come and gather, appearing like sea waves,

t'mayhin v'shoylin lah,   תְּמֵהִין וְשָׁיְלִין לַהּ,

   b'aysek osvoso.   בְּעֵסֶק אָתְוָתָא.

with wonderment they inquire of Israel regarding proofs:

—————————— CHAZZAN: ——————————

M'non u-mon hu r'chimoch,   מִנָּן וּמָאן הוּא רְחִימָךְ,

   shapiro b'rayvoso,   שַׁפִּירָא בְּרֵיוָתָא,

"Whence and Who is your Beloved, O nation of beautiful appearance,

arum b'ginayh sofis,   אֲרוּם בְּגִינֵיהּ סָפִית,

   m'dōr ary'voso.   מְדוֹר אַרְיָוָתָא.

that for His sake you perish in a lions' den?

—————————— CONGREGATION: ——————————

Y'koro v'yo-o at,   יְקָרָא וְיָאָה אַתְּ,

   in ta-arvi l'marvoso,   אִין תַּעַרְבִי לְמַרְוָתָא,

Honored and comely would you be,
if you would blend into our dominion;

r'usaych na-avid lich,   רְעוּתֵךְ נַעֲבִיד לִיךְ,

   b'chol asr'voso.   בְּכָל אַתְרָוָתָא.

we would grant your wish in every place."

—————————— CHAZZAN: ——————————

B'chochm'so m'sivoso l'hōn,   בְּחָכְמְתָא מְתִיבָתָא לְהוֹן,

   k'tzos l'hōdo-uso,   קְצָת לְהוֹדָעוּתָא,

With wisdom she responds to them in part — to let them know:

y'datun chak'min layh,   יְדַעְתּוּן חַכְּמִין לֵיהּ,

   b'isht'mōdo-uso.   בְּאִשְׁתְּמוֹדָעוּתָא.

If your wise men could but know Him with full awareness!

R'vus'chōn mo chashivo,

רְבוּתְכוֹן מָה חֲשִׁיבָא,

kovayl hahi sh'vachto,

קֳבֵל הַהִיא שְׁבַחְתָּא,

What value has your greatness compared to His praise? –

r'vuso d'yabayd li,

רְבוּתָא דְּיַעֲבֵּד לִי,

kad matyo y'shu-aso.

כַּד מַטְיָא יְשׁוּעֲתָא.

of the great things He will do for me when redemption shall arrive.

B'maysay li n'hōro,

בְּמֵיתֵי לִי נְהוֹרָא,

v'sa-chafay l'chōn bahaso,

וְתַחֲפֵי לְכוֹן בַּהֲתָא,

when He will bring me light, and you will be covered with shame;

y'korayh kad yisg'lay

יְקָרֵיהּ כַּד יִתְגְּלֵי,

b'sukfo uvgayvoso,

בְּתַקְפָּא וּבְגֵיוָתָא,

when His glory will be revealed with power and with grandeur,

Y'shalaym g'mula-yo,

יְשַׁלֵּם גְּמֻלַיָּא,

l'san-ay v'nagvoso,

לְסַנְאֵי וְנַגְוָתָא.

He will repay in kind to the haters and the isles;

tzidkoso l'am chaviv,

צִדְקָתָא לְעַם חָבִיב,

v'sagi zachvoso.

וְסַגִּיא זַכְוָתָא.

but righteousness to the people who are beloved
and abundantly meritorious,

Chadu sh'laymo b'maysayh,

חֲדוּ שְׁלֵמָא בְּמֵיתֵיהּ,

u-monay dachyoso,

וּמָנֵי דַכְיָתָא,

when He brings total joy, and pure vessels

kiry'so dirushlaym,

קִרְיְתָא דִירוּשְׁלֵם,

kad y'chanaysh galvoso.

כַּד יְכַנֵּשׁ גַּלְוָתָא.

to the city of Jerusalem as He gathers in the Exile.

Y'korayh matil alay,

יְקָרֵיהּ מַטִּיל עֲלַהּ,

b'yōmay v'layl'voso,

בְּיוֹמֵי וְלֵילָוָתָא,

His Shechinah will shelter her during days and nights,

g'nunayh l'mebad bah,

גְּנוּנֵיהּ לְמֶעְבַּד בַּהּ,

b'sushb'chon k'liloso.

בְּתוּשְׁבְּחָן כְּלִילָתָא.

His bridal canopy to be built in her crowned with praises –

─────────────── CHAZZAN: ───────────────

D'zayhōr anona-yo,

   l'mishpar kiloso,

דְּזֵיהוֹר עֲנָנַיָּא,

לְמִשְׁפַּר כִּילָתָא,

with brilliant clouds to beautify the canopy;

l'fumayh da-avidto,

   avidon m'talalto.

לְפוּמֵיהּ דַּעֲבִידְתָּא,

עֲבִידָן מְטַלַּלְתָּא.

for each according to his sacred toil, they will make a shelter.

─────────────── CONGREGATION: ───────────────

B'sachtakay d'hav pizo,

   ushva ma-aloso,

בְּתַכְתַּקֵּי דְהַב פִּיזָא,

וּשְׁבַע מַעֲלָתָא,

Upon armchairs of purest gold and seven elevations

t'chimin tzadikay,

   kodom rav po-oloso.

תְּחִימִין צַדִּיקֵי,

קֳדָם רַב פָּעֲלָתָא.

will the righteous be emplaced before Him
of many achievements.

─────────────── CHAZZAN: ───────────────

V'rayvayhōn domay

   l'sov-o chedvoso,

וְרֵיוֵיהוֹן דָּמֵי,

לְשָׂבְעָא חֶדְוָתָא,

And their appearance will resemble one as sated with joy —

r'ki-o b'zayhōrayh,

   v'chōch'vay zivoso.

רְקִיעָא בְּזֵיהוֹרֵיהּ,

וְכוֹכְבֵי זִיוָתָא.

as the heavenly expanse in its splendor and the sparkling stars.

─────────────── CONGREGATION: ───────────────

Hadoro d'lo efshar

   l'mifrat b'sif-voso,

הֲדָרָא דְלָא אֶפְשַׁר

לְמִפְרַט בְּשִׂפְוָתָא,

Beauty that cannot be detailed with lips,

v'lo isht'ma v'chomay,

   n'vi-on chezvoso.

וְלָא אִשְׁתְּמַע וְחָמֵי,

נְבִיאָן חֶזְוָתָא.

that was neither heard nor seen in prophetic visions,

─────────────── CHAZZAN: ───────────────

B'lo sholto bayh ayn,

   b'gō ayden ginso,

בְּלָא שָׁלְטָא בֵּיהּ עֵין,

בְּגוֹ עֵדֶן גִּנְתָּא,

over which no eye has reigned: the inside of the Garden of Eden.

m'ta-y'lay vay chingo,

   l'vahaday dishchinto.

מְטַיְּלֵי בֵי חִנְגָּא,

לְבַהֲדֵי דִשְׁכִינְתָּא.

In it they will find joy in a circle-dance before the Shechinah.

───────── CONGREGATION: ─────────

Alayh romzay dayn hu,
 b'ram b'emtonuso,
  To Him, they will point: "That is He!" — but with trepidation —

עֲלֵיהּ רָמְזֵי דֵּין הוּא,
 בְּרַם בְּאֵמְתָנוּתָא,

sabarno layh b'shivyon,
 t'kōf haymonuso.
  "We hoped for Him in our captivity, with a powerful faith."

שַׁבַּרְנָא לֵיהּ בְּשִׁבְיָן,
 תְּקוֹף הֵמָנוּתָא.

───────── CHAZZAN: ─────────

Yadbar lon ol'min,
 alaymin m'damuso,
  He will lead us forever — we will be youthfully vigorous —

יַדְבַּר לָן עָלְמִין,
 עָלְמִין מְדַמּוּתָא,

m'nos dilon d'mil'kadmin,
 poraysh ba-aromuso.
  our predetermined portions having been set aside with elevation.

מְנָת דִּילָן דְּמִלְּקַדְמִין,
 פָּרֵשׁ בַּאֲרָמוּתָא.

───────── CONGREGATION: ─────────

T'lulo d'livyoson,
 v'sōr tur romuso,
  The sport with the Leviathan and the ox of lofty mountains —

טְלוּלָא דְלִוְיָתָן,
 וְתוֹר טוּר רָמוּתָא.

v'chad b'chad ki sovich,
  when they will interlock with one another

וְחַד בְּחַד כִּי סָבִיךְ,

v'ovayd k'rovuso.
  and engage in combat,

וְעָבֵד קְרָבוּתָא.

───────── CHAZZAN: ─────────

B'karnōhi m'nagach b'haymōs,
 birvuso,
  with his horns the Behemoth will gore with strength;

בְּקַרְנוֹהִי מְנַגַּח בְּהֵמוֹת,
 בִּרְבוּתָא,

y'karta nun l'kivlayh,
 b'tzitzōy bigvurto.
  the fish will leap to meet him with his fins, with power.

יְקַרְטַע נוּן לְקִבְלֵיהּ,
 בְּצִיצוֹי בִּגְבוּרְתָּא.

───────── CONGREGATION: ─────────

M'korayv layh boryayh,
 b'charbayh ravr'vuso,
  Their Creator will approach them with His mighty sword.

מְקָרֵב לֵיהּ בָּרְיֵהּ,
 בְּחַרְבֵּיהּ רַבְרְבוּתָא,

aristōn l'tzadikay y'sakayn,
 v'shayruso.
  A banquet for the righteous will He prepare, and a feast.

אֲרִסְטוֹן לְצַדִּיקֵי יְתַקֵּן,
 וְשֵׁרוּתָא.

CHAZZAN:

מְסַחֲרִין עֲלֵי תַכֵּי,

M'sacharin alay sakay,

דְּכַדְכֹד וְגוּמַרְתָּא,

  d'chadkōd v'gumarto,

They will sit around tables of precious stones and gems,

נְגִידִין קַמֵּיהוֹן,

n'gidin kamayhōn,

אֲפַרְסְמוֹן נַהֲרָתָא.

  afars'mōn naharoso.

before them will be flowing rivers of balsam.

CONGREGATION:

וּמִתְפַּנְּקִין וְרָווֹ,

U-mispan'kin v'rovō,

בְּכַסֵּי רְוָיָתָא,

  b'chasay r'vo-yoso,

They will delight and drink their fill from overflowing goblets

חֲמַר מְרַת דְּמִבְּרֵאשִׁית

chamar m'ras d'mib'rayshis

נְטִיר בֵּי נַעֲוָתָא.

  n'tir bay na-avoso.

of sweet wine that since Creation was preserved in pressing tanks.

CHAZZAN:

זַכָּאִין כַּד שְׁמַעְתּוּן

Zako-in kad sh'matun

שְׁבַח דָּא שִׁירָתָא,

  sh'vach do shiroso,

O righteous ones, just as you heard the praise within this song,

קְבִיעִין כֵּן תֶּהֱווּן,

k'vi-in kayn tehevun,

בְּהַנְהוּ חֲבוּרָתָא.

  b'hanhu chavuroso.

so may you be appointed among that company,

CONGREGATION:

וְתִזְכּוּן דִּי תֵיתְבוּן,

V'sizkun di says'vun,

בְּעֵלָּא דָרָתָא,

  b'aylo doroso,

being privileged to be seated in the foremost row —

אֲרֵי תְצִיתוּן לְמִלּוֹי,

aray s'tzisun l'milōy,

דְּנָפְקִין בְּהַדְרָתָא.

  d'nofkin b'hadroso.

if you listen to His words that emanate in majesty.

CHAZZAN:

מְרוֹמָם הוּא אֱלָהִין,

M'rōmom hu Elohin,

בְּקַדְמָא וּבַתְרַיְתָא.

  b'kadmo u-vasraiso.

He is exalted — God — in the beginning and when all is done,

ALL ALOUD AND IN UNISON:

צְבִי וְאִתְרְעִי בָן,

Tz'vi v'isr'i von,

וּמְסַר לָן אוֹרַיְתָא.

  umsar lon ōraiso.

He desired and selected us, and He gave us the Torah!

⊰‖ USHPIZIN ‖⊱

UPON ENTERING THE *SUCCAH*, WE INVITE THE *USHPIZIN*-GUESTS
[THE SEVEN "FAITHFUL SHEPHERDS OF ISRAEL"] TO JOIN US.

■ Following the exalted state of spiritual purification of Yom Kippur, the Jew, according to tradition, merits the company of the seven "Faithful Shepherds." Each with his own exemplary characteristic inspires us to enhance our service of Hashem and man.

RIBŌN kol ho-ōlomim,
רִבּוֹן כָּל הָעוֹלָמִים,

y'hi rotzōn mil'fonecho
יְהִי רָצוֹן מִלְּפָנֶיךָ

Master of all the worlds, may it be Your will

shet'hay chashuvo l'fonecho
שֶׁתְּהֵא חֲשׁוּבָה לְפָנֶיךָ

mitzvas y'shivas suko zu,
מִצְוַת יְשִׁיבַת סֻכָּה זוֹ,

that this mitzvah of dwelling in the succah be reckoned before You

k'ilu ki-yamti-ho
כְּאִלּוּ קִיַּמְתִּיהָ

b'chol p'rote-ho v'dikduke-ho
בְּכָל פְּרָטֶיהָ וְדִקְדּוּקֶיהָ

as if I had fulfilled it in all its details and implications,

v'saryag mitzvos hat'luyim boh,
וְתַרְיַ"ג מִצְוֹת הַתְּלוּיִם בָּהּ,

as well as the six hundred thirteen mitzvos that are dependent upon it;

uch-ilu kivanti b'chol hakavonōs
וּכְאִלּוּ כִּוַּנְתִּי בְּכָל הַכַּוָּנוֹת

and as if I had concentrated upon all the intentions

shekiv'nu voh
שֶׁכִּוְּנוּ בָהּ

anshay ch'neses hag'dōlo.
אַנְשֵׁי כְנֶסֶת הַגְּדוֹלָה.

which the Men of the Great Assembly concentrated upon regarding it.

EACH DAY:

azamayn lis-udosi ushpizin ilo-in:
אֲזַמֵּן לִסְעֻדָתִי אֻשְׁפִּיזִין עִלָּאִין:

I invite to my meal the exalted guests:

avrohom yitzchok ya-akōv
אַבְרָהָם יִצְחָק יַעֲקֹב

yōsayf mōshe aharōn v'dovid.
יוֹסֵף מֹשֶׁה אַהֲרֹן וְדָוִד.

Abraham, Isaac, Jacob, Joseph, Moses, Aaron and David.

⊰§ **Ushpizin**

The *Zohar* teaches that for dwelling faithfully in their *succos*, the people of Israel merit the privilege of inviting and welcoming the *Shechinah* [God's Presence] and the seven "faithful shepherds" who descend from their heavenly abode in Gan Eden and enter these *succos* as exalted *ushpizin*, or guests. There they observe how their descendants fulfill the *mitzvah* of *succah* dwelling under God's protection.

These seven faithful shepherds of Israel are: Abraham, Isaac, Jacob, Joseph, Moses, Aaron and King David. All seven are guests in every *succah* throughout the seven days of the Festival,

but on each day one of them leads the others as the guest of honor.

For example, on the first day Abraham leads the other six, and that day is referred to as the "*Ushpizin* of Abraham." On the second day Isaac leads the others, the day being referred to as the "*Ushpizin* of Isaac." And so on until Hoshana Rabbah when King David is the guest of honor.

Customs regarding the invitation and associated prayers differ. Some recite the full text as presented here, while others include or omit various paragraphs. Additionally, some repeat the invitations and prayers before each meal, while others recite them only once each day.

ON THE FIRST DAY:

B'motu minoch avrohom
ushpizi ilo-i,

בְּמָטוּ מִנָּךְ אַבְרָהָם
אֻשְׁפִּיזִי עִלָּאִי,

May it please you, Abraham, my exalted guest,

d'yays-vu imi v'imoch
kol ushpizay ilo-ay,

דְּיֵתְבוּ עִמִּי וְעִמָּךְ
כָּל אֻשְׁפִּיזַי עִלָּאֵי,

that all the other exalted guests dwell here with me and with you —

yitzchok ya-akōv yōsayf
mōshe aharōn v'dovid.

יִצְחָק יַעֲקֹב יוֹסֵף
מֹשֶׁה אַהֲרֹן וְדָוִד.

Isaac, Jacob, Joseph, Moses, Aaron and David.

ON THE SECOND DAY:

B'motu minoch yitzchok ushpizi ilo-i, בְּמָטוּ מִנָּךְ יִצְחָק אֻשְׁפִּיזִי עִלָּאִי,

May it please you, Isaac, my exalted guest,

d'yays-vu imi v'imoch
kol ushpizay ilo-ay,

דְּיֵתְבוּ עִמִּי וְעִמָּךְ
כָּל אֻשְׁפִּיזַי עִלָּאֵי,

that all the other exalted guests dwell here with me and with you —

avrohom ya-akōv yōsayf
mōshe aharōn v'dovid.

אַבְרָהָם יַעֲקֹב יוֹסֵף
מֹשֶׁה אַהֲרֹן וְדָוִד.

Abraham, Jacob, Joseph, Moses, Aaron and David.

ON THE THIRD DAY:

B'motu minoch ya-akōv ushpizi ilo-i, בְּמָטוּ מִנָּךְ יַעֲקֹב אֻשְׁפִּיזִי עִלָּאִי,

May it please you, Jacob, my exalted guest,

d'yays-vu imi v'imoch
kol ushpizay ilo-ay,

דְּיֵתְבוּ עִמִּי וְעִמָּךְ
כָּל אֻשְׁפִּיזַי עִלָּאֵי,

that all the other exalted guests dwell here with me and with you —

avrohom yitzchok yōsayf
mōshe aharōn v'dovid.

אַבְרָהָם יִצְחָק יוֹסֵף
מֹשֶׁה אַהֲרֹן וְדָוִד.

Abraham, Isaac, Joseph, Moses, Aaron and David.

ON THE FOURTH DAY:

B'motu minoch yōsayf ushpizi ilo-i, בְּמָטוּ מִנָּךְ יוֹסֵף אֻשְׁפִּיזִי עִלָּאִי,

May it please you, Joseph, my exalted guest,

d'yays-vu imi v'imoch
kol ushpizay ilo-ay,

דְּיֵתְבוּ עִמִּי וְעִמָּךְ
כָּל אֻשְׁפִּיזַי עִלָּאֵי,

that all the other exalted guests dwell here with me and with you —

avrohom yitzchok ya-akov
mōshe aharōn v'dovid.

אַבְרָהָם יִצְחָק יַעֲקֹב
מֹשֶׁה אַהֲרֹן וְדָוִד.

Abraham, Isaac, Jacob, Moses, Aaron and David.

ON THE FIFTH DAY:

B'motu minoch mōshe ushpizi ilo-i,

בְּמָטוּ מִנָּךְ מֹשֶׁה אֻשְׁפִּיזִי עִלָּאֵי,

May it please you, Moses, my exalted guest,

d'yays-vu imi v'imoch
kol ushpizay ilo-ay,

דְּיֵיתְבוּ עִמִּי וְעִמָּךְ
כָּל אֻשְׁפִּיזֵי עִלָּאֵי,

that all the other exalted guests dwell here with me and with you —

avrohom yitzchok ya-akōv
yōsayf aharōn v'dovid.

אַבְרָהָם יִצְחָק יַעֲקֹב
יוֹסֵף אַהֲרֹן וְדָוִד.

Abraham, Isaac, Jacob, Joseph, Aaron and David.

ON THE SIXTH DAY:

B'motu minoch aharōn
ushpizi ilo-i,

בְּמָטוּ מִנָּךְ אַהֲרֹן
אֻשְׁפִּיזִי עִלָּאֵי,

May it please you, Aaron, my exalted guest,

d'yays-vu imi v'imoch
kol ushpizay ilo-ay,

דְּיֵיתְבוּ עִמִּי וְעִמָּךְ
כָּל אֻשְׁפִּיזֵי עִלָּאֵי,

that all the other exalted guests dwell here with me and with you —

avrohom yitzchok ya-akōv
yōsayf mōshe v'dovid.

אַבְרָהָם יִצְחָק יַעֲקֹב
יוֹסֵף מֹשֶׁה וְדָוִד.

Abraham, Isaac, Jacob, Joseph, Moses and David.

ON HOSHANA RABBAH:

B'motu minoch dovid ushpizi ilo-i,

בְּמָטוּ מִנָּךְ דָּוִד אֻשְׁפִּיזִי עִלָּאֵי,

May it please you, David, my exalted guest,

d'yays-vu imi v'imoch
kol ushpizay ilo-ay,

דְּיֵיתְבוּ עִמִּי וְעִמָּךְ
כָּל אֻשְׁפִּיזֵי עִלָּאֵי,

that all the other exalted guests dwell here with me and with you —

avrohom yitzchok ya-akōv
yōsayf mōshe v'aharōn.

אַבְרָהָם יִצְחָק יַעֲקֹב
יוֹסֵף מֹשֶׁה וְאַהֲרֹן.

Abraham, Isaac, Jacob, Joseph, Moses and Aaron.

THE NIGHTTIME FESTIVAL *KIDDUSH* APPEARS ON PAGE 671.
THE NIGHTTIME *KIDDUSH* FOR THE SABBATH OF *CHOL HAMOED* APPEARS ON PAGE 170.
THE DAYTIME KIDDUSH APPEARS ON PAGE 495.

⊰ FAREWELL TO THE SUCCAH ⊱

BEFORE LEAVING THE *SUCCAH* FOR THE LAST TIME ONE SAYS:

יְהִי רָצוֹן מִלְּפָנֶיךָ

Y'hi rotzōn mil'fonecho,

May it be Your will,*

יהוה אֱלֹהֵינוּ
וֵאלֹהֵי אֲבוֹתֵינוּ,

Adōnoy Elōhaynu
Vaylōhay avōsaynu,

HASHEM, *our God and the God of our forefathers,*

כְּשֵׁם שֶׁקִּיַּמְתִּי

k'shaym sheki-yamti

that just as I have fulfilled [the mitzvah]

וְיָשַׁבְתִּי בְּסֻכָּה זוֹ,

v'yoshavti b'suko zu,

and dwelled in this succah,

כֵּן אֶזְכֶּה לְשָׁנָה הַבָּאָה

kayn ezke l'shono habo-o

so may I merit in the coming year

לֵישֵׁב בְּסֻכַּת
עוֹרוֹ שֶׁל לִוְיָתָן.

layshayv b'sukas
ōrō shel livyoson.

to dwell in the succah of the skin of Leviathan.*

לְשָׁנָה הַבָּאָה בִּירוּשָׁלָיִם.

L'shono habo-o birusholo-yim.

Next year in Jerusalem.

⊰ HOSHANOS / הושענות ⊱

On each day of Succos: Immediately after the *chazzan's* repetition of the *Shemoneh Esrei* of *Mussaf,* special prayers called *Hoshanos* are recited. The Ark is opened and a Torah scroll is removed and carried to the *bimah* where one member of the congregation holds it. The Ark remains open and the Torah is held at the *bimah* until the conclusion of the *Hoshana* service. The *lulav* and *esrog* are held during the entire service.

Four introductory stiches are recited responsively — *chazzan* then congregation — each day. Upon completing the introductory verses the *chazzan* leads all males who are carrying a *lulav* and *esrog* around the *bimah* as he reads the day's *Hoshana* [see below] responsively with the congregation. He should time his steps to complete the circuit as he recites the last verse of the *Hoshana.*

Two factors determine which *Hoshana* is recited: (a) the day of the week; and (b) the day of the month. The accompanying diagrams record the four calendrical possibilities for the Festival of Succos, and the *Hoshana* recited in each case.

On the Sabbath: Three changes are made in the *Hoshana* service on the Sabbath: (a) Although the Ark is opened, a Torah is not removed; (b) the *bimah* is not circled; and (c) the *lulav* and *esrog* are omitted.

Farewell to the Succah

יְהִי רָצוֹן מִלְּפָנֶיךָ — *May it be Your will.* We take leave of the *succah* with a prayer that next year we can experience the joy of deliverance, so that all the symbolic holiness of the *succah* can be realized in our national and personal lives. In this brief prayer we specify only the *"succah* of the skin of the Leviathan" and the hope that we soon be in Jerusalem upon the coming of Messiah.

בְּסֻכַּת עוֹרוֹ שֶׁל לִוְיָתָן — *In the succah of the skin of Leviathan.* The Leviathan was a monstrous fish created on the fifth day of Creation. Its story is related at length in the Talmud (*Bava Basra* 74b), where it is told that the Leviathan will be slain and its flesh served as a feast to the righteous in Time to Come, and its skin used to cover the tent where the banquet will take place.

On Hoshana Rabbah: On *Hoshana Rabbah,* the seventh day of Succos, all the Torah scrolls in the Ark are brought to the *bimah,* held by members of the congregation. On this day the *bimah* is circled seven times, as seven *Hoshana* prayers are recited. After each *Hoshana,* a Scriptural verse related to the *Sefirah*-emanation of that *hakafah*-circuit is recited. When the seven circuits have been completed, additional prayers, beginning on page 797, are recited.

S	M	T	W	T	F	S
IF THE FIRST DAY OF SUCCOS FALLS ON MONDAY							
14	15 למען אמתך P. 774	16 אבן שתיה P. 775	17 אערוך שועי P. 785	18 אום אני חומה P. 777	19 אל למושעות P. 786	20 אום נצורה P. 791
21 HOSHANA RABBAH	22	23	24	25	26	27

S	M	T	W	T	F	S
IF THE FIRST DAY OF SUCCOS FALLS ON TUESDAY							
13	14	15 למען אמתך P. 774	16 אבן שתיה P. 775	17 אערוך שועי P. 785	18 * אל למושעות P. 786	19 אום נצורה P. 791
20 אדון המושיע P. 778	21 HOSHANA RABBAH	22	23	24	25	26

*Some congregations substitute אוֹם אֲנִי חוֹמָה (p. 777).

S	M	T	W	T	F	S
IF THE FIRST DAY OF SUCCOS FALLS ON THURSDAY							
11	12	13	14	15 למען אמתך P. 774	16 אבן שתיה P. 775	17 אום נצורה P. 791
18 אערוך שועי P. 785	19 אל למושעות P. 786	20 אדון המושיע P. 778	21 HOSHANA RABBAH	22	23	24

S	M	T	W	T	F	S
IF THE FIRST DAY OF SUCCOS FALLS ON THE SABBATH							
9	10	11	12	13	14	15 אום נצורה P. 791
16 למען אמתך P. 774	17 אערוך שועי P. 785	18 אבן שתיה P. 775	19 אל למושעות P. 786	20 אדון המושיע P. 778	21 HOSHANA RABBAH	22

⧏ HOSHANOS ⧐

■ As the Jewish nation was victorious over the walled city of Jericho by encircling it once daily and seven times on the seventh day of its conquest, we likewise encircle the *Bimah* and the Torah once each day and seven times on the seventh day, representing the anticipation of the victory over our oppressors and our return to Jerusalem.

EACH DAY'S *HOSHANA* SERVICE BEGINS WITH THE FOLLOWING INTRODUCTORY STANZA CHANTED RESPONSIVELY — *CHAZZAN*, THEN CONGREGATION.

HŌSHA-NO, l'ma-ancho   הוֹשַׁעְנָא, לְמַעַנְךְ

     Elōhaynu — hōsha-no.   אֱלֹהֵינוּ — הוֹשַׁעְנָא.

Please save — for Your sake, our God! Please save!

     Hōsha-no, l'ma-ancho   הוֹשַׁעְנָא, לְמַעַנְךְ

     bōr'aynu — hōsha-no.   בּוֹרְאֵנוּ — הוֹשַׁעְנָא.

Please save — for Your sake, our Creator! Please save!

     Hōsha-no, l'ma-ancho   הוֹשַׁעְנָא, לְמַעַנְךְ

     gō-alaynu — hōsha-no.   גּוֹאֲלֵנוּ — הוֹשַׁעְנָא.

Please save — for Your sake, our Redeemer! Please save!

     Hōsha-no, l'ma-ancho   הוֹשַׁעְנָא, לְמַעַנְךְ

     dōr'shaynu — hōsha-no.   דּוֹרְשֵׁנוּ — הוֹשַׁעְנָא.

Please save — for Your sake, our Attender! Please save!

L'MA-AN AMITOCH.   לְמַעַן אֲמִתָּךְ.

     For the sake of Your Truth;*

L'ma-an b'risoch   לְמַעַן בְּרִיתָךְ.

     for the sake of Your Covenant;

L'ma-an godloch v'sif-artoch.   לְמַעַן גָּדְלָךְ וְתִפְאַרְתָּךְ.

     for the sake of Your Greatness and Your Splendor;

L'ma-an dosoch.   לְמַעַן דָּתָךְ.

     for the sake of Your Mandate;

L'ma-an hōdoch.   לְמַעַן הוֹדָךְ.

     for the sake of Your Glory;

L'ma-an vi-udoch.   לְמַעַן וְעוּדָךְ.

     for the sake of Your Meeting House;

L'ma-an zichroch.   לְמַעַן זִכְרָךְ.

     For the sake of Your Mention;

L'ma-an chasdoch.   לְמַעַן חַסְדָּךְ.

     for the sake of Your Kindness;

◆§ **For the Sake of Your Truth**

Each of the *Hoshanos* comprises twenty-two verses or stanzas which follow an alphabetical pattern. In this first *Hoshana*, each verse begins with the word לְמַעַן, *For the sake of,* followed by one of many attributes of God; accordingly, it may be considered an extension of the introductory stanza which directly precedes it.

L'ma-an tuvoch.
לְמַעַן טוּבָךְ.
> *for the sake of Your Goodness;*

L'ma-an yichudoch.
לְמַעַן יִחוּדָךְ.
> *for the sake of Your Oneness;*

L'ma-an k'vōdoch.
לְמַעַן כְּבוֹדָךְ.
> *for the sake of Your Honor;*

L'ma-an limudoch.
לְמַעַן לִמּוּדָךְ.
> *for the sake of Your Teaching;*

L'ma-an malchusoch.
לְמַעַן מַלְכוּתָךְ.
> *for the sake of Your Kingship;*

L'ma-an nitzchoch.
לְמַעַן נִצְחָךְ.
> *for the sake of Your Triumph;*

L'ma-an sōdoch.
לְמַעַן סוֹדָךְ.
> *for the sake of Your Counsel;*

L'ma-an uzoch.
לְמַעַן עֻזָּךְ.
> *for the sake of Your Power;*

L'ma-an p'ayroch.
לְמַעַן פְּאֵרָךְ.
> *for the sake of Your Beauty;*

L'ma-an tzidkosoch.
לְמַעַן צִדְקָתָךְ.
> *for the sake of Your Righteousness;*

L'ma-an k'dushosoch.
לְמַעַן קְדֻשָּׁתָךְ.
> *for the sake of Your Sanctity;*

L'ma-an rachamecho horabim.
לְמַעַן רַחֲמֶיךָ הָרַבִּים.
> *for the sake of Your numerous Mercies;*

L'ma-an sh'chinosoch.
לְמַעַן שְׁכִינָתָךְ.
> *for the sake of Your Shechinah;*

L'ma-an t'hilosoch.
לְמַעַן תְּהִלָּתָךְ.
> *for the sake of Your Praise.*

DURING THE FIRST SIX DAYS OF SUCCOS CONTINUE *ani vohō* (P. 788).
ON HOSHANA RABBAH CONTINUE:

Ki omarti ōlom chesed yibo-ne.
כִּי אָמַרְתִּי עוֹלָם חֶסֶד יִבָּנֶה.
For I have said: "The world shall be built with kindness."

EVEN SH'SI-YO.
אֶבֶן שְׁתִיָּה.
> *Foundation stone;**

Bays hab'chiro.
בֵּית הַבְּחִירָה.
> *chosen Temple;*

⊷§ Foundation Stone

All twenty-two verses of this prayer are allusions to either the Holy Temple or the city of Jerusalem in which it was located. Most of the descriptive expressions are of Scriptural derivation; the remainder are of Talmudic origin.

The intent of all these verses is the same, namely: Please save (i.e., redeem) the Holy Temple from its present desolation and desecration, and from the wild foxes that prowl over it (see *Lamentations* 5:18), that it may be rebuilt, speedily in our days.

Gōren ornon.

גֹּרֶן אָרְנָן.

Arnan's granary;

D'vir hamutzno.

דְּבִיר הַמֻּצְנָע.

hidden rendezvous;

Har hamōriyo.

הַר הַמּוֹרִיָּה.

Mount Moriah;

V'har yayro-e.

וְהַר יֵרָאֶה.

Mount He-is-seen;

Z'vul tif-artecho.

זְבוּל תִּפְאַרְתֶּךָ.

residence of Your Splendor;

Chono dovid.

חָנָה דָוִד.

where David resided;

Tōv hal'vonōn.

טוֹב הַלְּבָנוֹן.

goodness of Lebanon;

Y'fay nōf m'sōs kol ho-oretz.

יְפֵה נוֹף מְשׂוֹשׂ כָּל הָאָרֶץ.

fairest of brides, joy of all the earth;

K'lilas yōfi.

כְּלִילַת יֹפִי.

perfectly beautiful;

Linas hatzedek.

לִינַת הַצֶּדֶק.

lodge of righteousness;

Mochōn l'shivtecho.

מָכוֹן לְשִׁבְתֶּךָ.

prepared for Your dwelling;

Nove sha-anon.

נָוֶה שַׁאֲנָן.

tranquil abode;

Sukas sholaym.

סֻכַּת שָׁלֵם.

Tabernacle of Salem;

Aliyas sh'votim.

עֲלִיַּת שְׁבָטִים.

pilgrimage of the tribes;

Pinas yikras.

פִּנַּת יִקְרַת.

valuable cornerstone;

Tziyōn ham'tzuyenes.

צִיּוֹן הַמְצֻיֶּנֶת.

the distinguished Zion;

Kōdesh hakodoshim.

קֹדֶשׁ הַקֳּדָשִׁים.

Holy of Holies;

Rotzuf ahavo.

רָצוּף אַהֲבָה.

decked with love;

Sh'chinas k'vōdecho.

שְׁכִינַת כְּבוֹדֶךָ.

resting place of Your Honor;

Tayl talpiyōs.

תֵּל תַּלְפִּיּוֹת.

hill of Talpios.

DURING THE FIRST SIX DAYS OF SUCCOS CONTINUE ani vohō (P. 788).

ON HOSHANA RABBAH CONTINUE:

L'cho z'rō-a im g'vuro,   לְךָ זְרוֹעַ עִם גְּבוּרָה,

Yours is the arm with strength,

to-ōz yod'cho torum y'minecho. תָּעֹז יָדְךָ תָּרוּם יְמִינֶךָ.

show us the power of Your hand, raise high Your right hand.

ŌM ANI CHŌMO.   **אוֹם אֲנִי חוֹמָה.**

Nation [that declares], "I am a wall!"*

Boro kachamo.   בָּרָה כַּחַמָּה.

Brilliant as the sun —

Gōlo v'suro.   גּוֹלָה וְסוּרָה.

yet exiled and displaced;

Dom'so l'somor.   דָּמְתָה לְתָמָר.

likened to a palm tree —

Haharugo olecho.   הַהֲרוּגָה עָלֶיךָ.

yet murdered for Your sake

V'nechesheves k'tzōn tivcho. וְנֶחְשֶׁבֶת כְּצֹאן טִבְחָה.

and regarded like a sheep for slaughter;

Z'ruyo bayn mach-ise-ho. זְרוּיָה בֵּין מַכְעִיסֶיהָ.

although scattered among her provocateurs,

Chavuko udvuko boch.   חֲבוּקָה וּדְבוּקָה בָּךְ.

she hugs and cleaves to You,

Tō-enes uloch.   טוֹעֶנֶת עֻלָּךְ.

bearing Your yoke —

Y'chido l'yachadoch.   יְחִידָה לְיַחֲדָךְ.

unique in declaring Your Oneness.

K'vusho vagōlo.   כְּבוּשָׁה בַּגוֹלָה.

While vanquished in exile,

Lōmedes yir-osoch.   לוֹמֶדֶת יִרְאָתָךְ.

she learns Your awesomeness.

M'rutas lechi.   מְרוּטַת לֶחִי.

Plucked of cheek,

N'suno l'makim.   נְתוּנָה לְמַכִּים.

given over to the whippers,

Sōveles sivloch.   סוֹבֶלֶת סִבְלָךְ.

she shoulders Your burden.

Aniyo sō-aro.   עֲנִיָּה סֹעֲרָה.

A storm-tossed pauper,

◆§ Nation [that Declares], "I am a wall!"

Many metaphors are used in Scripture and Rabbinic writing to describe the nation of Israel. Most of the epithets in this *Hoshana* are particularly applicable to Israel during its decline and exile. Material poverty is juxtaposed with spiritual wealth as the *paytan* paints a word picture depicting the firm faith of God's chosen people.

P'du-yas tōvi-yo.   פְּדוּיַת טוֹבִיָּה.
she who was redeemed by Moses.

Tzōn kodoshim.   צֹאן קָדָשִׁים.
Sacred sheep,

K'hilōs ya-akōv.   קְהִלּוֹת יַעֲקֹב.
congregations of Jacob,

R'shumim bishmecho.   רְשׁוּמִים בִּשְׁמֶךָ.
inscribed with Your Name,

Shō-agim hōsha-no.   שׁוֹאֲגִים הוֹשַׁעְנָא.
they cry, "Please save us!" —

T'muchim olecho.   תְּמוּכִים עָלֶיךָ.
they rely upon You!

DURING THE FIRST SIX DAYS OF SUCCOS CONTINUE *ani vohō* (P. 788).

ON HOSHANA RABBAH CONTINUE:

Titayn emes l'ya-akōv,   תִּתֵּן אֱמֶת לְיַעֲקֹב,
    chesed l'avrohom.   חֶסֶד לְאַבְרָהָם.
Grant truth to Jacob, kindness to Abraham.

ODŌN HAMŌSHI-A.   אָדוֹן הַמּוֹשִׁיעַ.
Lord Who saves,*

Bilt'cho ayn l'hōshi-a.   בִּלְתְּךָ אֵין לְהוֹשִׁיעַ.
other than You there is no savior.

Gibōr v'rav l'hōshi-a.   גִּבּוֹר וְרַב לְהוֹשִׁיעַ.
You are powerful and abundantly able to save.

Dalōsi v'li y'hōshi-a.   דַּלּוֹתִי וְלִי יְהוֹשִׁיעַ.
I am impoverished, yet You shall save me.

Ho-ayl hamōshi-a.   הָאֵל הַמּוֹשִׁיעַ.
God is the Savior,

U-matzil u-mōshi-a.   וּמַצִּיל וּמוֹשִׁיעַ.
He delivers and saves.

Zō-akecho tōshi-a   זוֹעֲקֶיךָ תּוֹשִׁיעַ.
Those who cry to You — save;

Chōchecho hōshi-a.   חוֹכֶיךָ הוֹשִׁיעַ.
those who yearn for You — save.

T'lo-echo tasbi-a.   טְלָאֶיךָ תַּשְׂבִּיעַ.
Satiate Your lambs,

◦§ Lord Who Saves

Every part of Creation may be assigned to one of four kingdoms or categories of existence. In ascending spiritual order they are: דּוֹמֵם, "mineral" (lit., silent]; צוֹמֵחַ, "vegetable" (lit.. sprouting); חַי, "animal" (lit., living); and מְדַבֵּר, "human" (lit., speaking).

In the Divine plan for the world, each member of one realm is capable of becoming elevated to a higher one. Indeed, this is the purpose of its existence. The minerals in the soil, water, and air are absorbed by plants, which, in turn, serve as food for the animals. Finally, these become the fare of Man. Scripture alludes

Y'vul l'hashpi-a.   יְבוּל לְהַשְׁפִּיעַ.
cause an abundance of crops,

Kol si-ach tadshay v'sōshi-a.   כָּל שִׂיחַ תַּדְשֵׁא וְתוֹשִׁיעַ.
of trees, of vegetation — save.

L'gay bal tarshi-a.   לְגַיְא בַּל תַּרְשִׁיעַ.
Do not condemn the ground,

M'godim tamtik v'sōshi-a.   מְגָדִים תַּמְתִּיק וְתוֹשִׁיעַ.
but sweeten the luscious fruits — save.

N'si-im l'hasi-a.   נְשִׂיאִים לְהַסִּיעַ.
Let the wind bring the soaring clouds,

S'i-rim l'honi-a.   שְׂעִירִים לְהָנִיעַ.
let the stormy rains be emplaced,

Anonim mil'hamni-a.   עֲנָנִים מִלְּהַמְנִיעַ.
let the clouds not be withheld,

Pōsay-ach yod umasbi-a.   פּוֹתֵחַ יָד וּמַשְׂבִּיעַ.
He Who opens a hand and satisfies,

Tz'may-echo tasbi-a.   צְמֵאֶיךָ תַּשְׂבִּיעַ.
Your thirsty ones — satisfy;

Kōr'echo tōshi-a.   קוֹרְאֶיךָ תּוֹשִׁיעַ.
Your callers — save;

R'chumecho tōshi-a.   רְחוּמֶיךָ תּוֹשִׁיעַ.
Your beloved ones — save;

Shōcharecho hōshi-a.   שׁוֹחֲרֶיךָ הוֹשִׁיעַ.
Your seekers — save;

T'mimecho tōshi-a.   תְּמִימֶיךָ תּוֹשִׁיעַ.
Your wholesome ones — save.

DURING THE FIRST SIX DAYS OF SUCCOS CONTINUE ani vohō (P. 788).

ON HOSHANA RABBAH CONTINUE:

N'imōs bi-min'cho netzach.   נְעִימוֹת בִּימִינְךָ נֶצַח.
There is delight at Your right hand for triumph.

ODOM UVHAYMO.   אָדָם וּבְהֵמָה.
Man and beast:

Bosor v'ru-ach unshomo.   בָּשָׂר וְרוּחַ וּנְשָׁמָה.
Flesh, spirit and soul;

---

to this system of elevation: *And I shall give grass [vegetable] in your field [mineral] for your cattle [animal] and you [Man] shall eat and be sated* (Deuteronomy 11:15).

But does this process of uplifting end with man? Is man the perfect being? Certainly not. Man must raise himself from the evil which fills his heart. The last words of the above verse, *and you shall eat and be sated,* tell how. This same phrase also appears as the opening of another verse which continues: *and you shall*

bless HASHEM, *your God*. Recitation of a blessing is the fulfillment of a *mitzvah*, and, as Kabbalah teaches, while study of Torah provides the soul's sustenance, the performance of *mitzvos* supplies its raiment. Man must use the baser elements of creation in the fulfillment of *mitzvos*, but he needs guidance to use them wisely.

In the next three *Hoshanos* we invoke Divine protection for all of these realms, and we pray for our own welfare — *Lord Who saves . . . save*

גִּיד וְעֶצֶם וְקַרְמָה.
Gid v'etzem v'kormo.
sinew, bone and skin;

דְּמוּת וְצֶלֶם וְרִקְמָה.
D'mus v'tzelem v'rikmo.
likeness and image — a tapestry;

הוֹד לַהֶבֶל דָּמָה.
Hōd lahevel domo.
splendor resembling futility,

וְנִמְשַׁל כַּבְּהֵמוֹת נִדְמָה.
V'nimshal kab'haymōs nidmo.
compared to the likeness of beasts —

זִיו וְתֹאַר וְקוֹמָה.
Ziv v'sō-ar v'kōmo.
luster, figure and stature.

חִדּוּשׁ פְּנֵי אֲדָמָה.
Chidush p'nay adomo.
Renew the face of the earth —

טִיעַת עֲצֵי נְשַׁמָּה.
Ti-as atzay n'shamo.
planting trees in desolate lands,

יְקָבִים וְקָמָה.
Y'kovim v'komo.
winepresses and stands of grain,

כְּרָמִים וְשִׁקְמָה.
K'romim v'shikmo.
vineyards and sycamores.

לְתֵבֵל הַמְסִיָּמָה.
L'sayvayl ham'su-yomo.
To the demarcated land —

מִטְרוֹת עֹז לְסַמְּמָה.
Mitrōs ōz l'sa-m'mo.
to heal with powerful rains,

נְשִׁיָּה לְקַיְּמָה.
N'shi-yo l'ka-y'mo.
to give life to forsaken wastes,

שִׂיחִים לְקוֹמְמָה.
Sichim l'kōm'mo.
to sustain with vegetation,

עֲדָנִים לְעָצְמָה.
Adonim l'otzmo.
to enhance with sweet fruits,

פְּרָחִים לְהַעֲצִימָה.
P'rochim l'ha-atzimo.
to invigorate with flowers.

צְמָחִים לְגָשְׁמָה.
Tz'mochim l'goshmo.
To rain on the sproutings —

קָרִים לְזָרְמָה.
Korim l'zormo.
to pour a stream of cool waters,

רְבִיבִים לְשַׁלְמָה.
R'vivim l'salmo.
to cloak with droplets,

שְׁתִיָּה לְרוֹמֲמָה.
Sh'siyo l'rōmaymo.
to elevate the thirsty earth

תְּלוּיָה עַל בְּלִימָה.
T'luyo al b'limo.
which is suspended upon silence.

---

now . . . man and beast . . . the ground [and its produce] from accursedness.

ON HOSHANA RABBAH CONTINUE:

Adōnoy adōnaynu   יְהֹוָה אֲדֹנֵינוּ
Hashem, our Lord,

mo adir shimcho b'chol ho-oretz,   מָה אַדִּיר שִׁמְךָ בְּכָל הָאָרֶץ,
how mighty is Your Name throughout the earth;

asher t'no hōd'cho al ha-shomo-yim.   אֲשֶׁר תְּנָה הוֹדְךָ עַל הַשָּׁמָיִם.
for it were fit that You place Your splendor above the heavens.

ADOMO MAY-ERER.   אֲדָמָה מֵאֵרֶר.
        Ground from accursedness;*

B'haymo mim'shakeles.   בְּהֵמָה מִמְּשַׁכֵּלֶת.
        beast from aborting;

Gōren mi-gozom.   גֹּרֶן מִגָּזָם.
        granary from gazam;

Dogon mi-dalekes.   דָּגָן מִדַּלֶּקֶת.
        grain from scorch;

Hōn mim'ayro.   הוֹן מִמְּאֵרָה.
        wealth from affliction;

V'ōchel mim'humo.   וְאֹכֶל מִמְּהוּמָה.
        food from confusion;

Za-yis mi-neshel.   זַיִת מִנֶּשֶׁל.
        olives from dropping;

Chito maychogov.   חִטָּה מֵחָגָב.
        wheat from chagav;

Teref migōvai.   טֶרֶף מִגּוֹבַי.
        nourishment from govai;

Yekev mi-yelek.   יֶקֶב מִיֶּלֶק.
        winepress from yelek;

Kerem mitōla-as.   כֶּרֶם מִתּוֹלַעַת.
        vineyard from worms;

Lekesh may-arbe.   לֶקֶשׁ מֵאַרְבֶּה.
        late crop from arbeh;

Meged mitz'lotzal.   מֶגֶד מִצְּלָצַל.
        fruit from tz'latzal;

Nefesh mibe-holo.   נֶפֶשׁ מִבֶּהָלָה.
        soul from panic;

Sōva misol-om.   שֹׂבַע מִסָּלְעָם.
        satiety from salam;

Adorim midalus.   עֲדָרִים מִדַּלּוּת.
        flocks from leanness;

◆§ **Ground from Accursedness**

   This *Hoshana* enumerates a whole litany of destructive forces that could destroy the world's food supply. Appearing on the list are eight species of locust — *gazam, chagav, govai, yelek, arbeh, tz'latzal, salam* and *chasil*.

Payrōs mi-shidofōn.

fruits from the east wind;

פֵּרוֹת מִשִּׁדָּפוֹן.

Tzōn mitz'misus.

sheep from extermination;

צֹאן מִצְּמִיתוּת.

Kotzir mik'lolo.

harvest from curse;

קָצִיר מִקְּלָלָה.

Rōv mayrozōn.

abundance from emaciation;

רֹב מֵרָזוֹן.

Shibōles mitzinomōn.

grain spikes from withering;

שִׁבֹּלֶת מִצִּנָּמוֹן.

T'vu-o maychosil.

crops from chasil.

תְּבוּאָה מֵחָסִיל.

Tzadik Adōnoy b'chol d'rochov,

צַדִּיק יהוה בְּכָל דְּרָכָיו,

Hashem *is righteous in all His ways;*

v'chosid b'chol ma-asov.

וְחָסִיד בְּכָל מַעֲשָׂיו.

magnanimous in all His deeds.

L'MA-AN AYSON

לְמַעַן אֵיתָן

hanizrak b'lahav aysh.

הַנִּזְרַק בְּלַהַב אֵשׁ.

In the merit of the courageous one* [Abraham] who was hurled into flaming fire.

L'ma-an bayn

לְמַעַן בֵּן

hane-ekad al aytzim vo-aysh.

הַנֶּעֱקַד עַל עֵצִים וָאֵשׁ.

In the merit of the son [Isaac] who was bound upon the wood near the fire.

L'ma-an gibōr

לְמַעַן גִּבּוֹר

hane-evak im sar aysh.

הַנֶּאֱבַק עִם שַׂר אֵשׁ.

In the merit of the strong one [Jacob] who wrestled with a prince of fire.

L'ma-an d'golim nochiso

לְמַעַן דְּגָלִים נָחִיתָ

b'ōr va-anan aysh.

בְּאוֹר וַעֲנַן אֵשׁ.

In the merit of the tribal banners which You guided
with a light — and a cloud — of fire.

L'ma-an hō-alo lamorōm

לְמַעַן הֶעֱלָה לַמָּרוֹם

v'nis-alo k'mal-achay aysh.

וְנִתְעַלָּה כְּמַלְאֲכֵי אֵשׁ.

In the merit of him [Moses] who was raised to the heavens
and became as exalted as angels of fire.

⊷§ **In the Merit of the Courageous One**

Who planted the seeds of superhuman fortitude and dignity with which millennia of Jews have endured hardship and privation? From whom did Israel inherit the ability to remain holy even amid holocaust? "All that happened to the Patriarchs is of prophetic significance to their descendants." For this reason, too, the Torah often relates seemingly unimportant events in the lives of our forebears.

Not only did the deeds of the Patriarchs insure the posterity of Israel, but they also

L'ma-an v'hu loch
    k'segen b'er-elay aysh.
לְמַעַן וְהוּא לָךְ
כְּסֶגֶן בְּאֶרְאֵלֵי אֵשׁ.

In the merit of him [Aaron] who was to You like a deputy at the Altars of fire.

L'ma-an zeved dib'rōs
    han'sunōs may-aysh.
לְמַעַן זֶבֶד דִּבְּרוֹת
הַנְּתוּנוֹת מֵאֵשׁ.

In the merit of the gift of Commandments presented from a fire.

L'ma-an chipuy y'ri-ōs anan aysh.
לְמַעַן חִפּוּי יְרִיעוֹת עֲנַן אֵשׁ.

In the merit of the canopy of curtains — a cloud of fire.

L'ma-an teches har
    yorad-to olov bo-aysh.
לְמַעַן טֶכֶס הַר
יָרַדְתָּ עָלָיו בָּאֵשׁ.

In the merit of the array at the mountain upon which You descended in fire.

L'ma-an y'didus ba-yis
    asher ohavto mish'may aysh.
לְמַעַן יְדִידוּת בַּיִת
אֲשֶׁר אָהַבְתָּ מִשְּׁמֵי אֵשׁ.

*In the merit of the love of the Temple
which You adored beyond heavens made of fire.*

L'ma-an komah ad shok'o ho-aysh.
לְמַעַן כָּמַהּ עַד שְׁקִעָה הָאֵשׁ.

In the merit of him [Moses] who yearned until the sinking of the fire.

L'ma-an lokach machtas aysh
    v'haysir charōn aysh.
לְמַעַן לָקַח מַחְתַּת אֵשׁ
וְהֵסִיר חֲרוֹן אֵשׁ.

*In the merit of him [Aaron] who took a fire pan
and removed an anger burning like fire.*

L'ma-an m'kanay kin-o
    g'dōlo bo-aysh.
לְמַעַן מְקַנֵּא קִנְאָה
גְדוֹלָה בָאֵשׁ.

In the merit of him [Elijah] who zealously took great vengeance with fire.

L'ma-an nof yodō
    v'yor'du avnay aysh.
לְמַעַן נָף יָדוֹ
וַיֵּרְדוּ אַבְנֵי אֵשׁ.

*In the merit of him [Joshua] who raised his hand in prayer —
and down came stones of fire.*

L'ma-an som t'lay cholov k'lil aysh.
לְמַעַן שָׂם טְלֵה חָלָב כְּלִיל אֵשׁ.

*In the merit of him [Samuel] who offered a nursing ewe
to be completely consumed by fire.*

---

inculcated into the nation's fiber the traits which engendered those deeds. A Talmudic dictum teaches that "the merits of the Patriarchs have expired." Nevertheless, the qualities of character with which their merits have imbued their offspring have not expired. Because we still exhibit Abraham's kindness, Isaac's courage, and Jacob's adherence to truth, because we follow the trails blazed by Moses and Aaron, Joshua and Samuel, David

and Solomon, because we maintain and display the unwavering faith of Daniel and his companions, we are able to pray for salvation.

This Hoshana traces the achievements of our spiritual models as they were tested with fire, and appeals for salvation in the merit of their indelible imprint upon Israel's national character.

L'ma-an omad bagŏren
  v'nisratzo vo-aysh.

לְמַעַן עָמַד בַּגֹּרֶן
וְנִתְרַצָּה בָאֵשׁ.

*In the merit of him [David] who stood in the granary
and was shown favor with fire.*

L'ma-an pilayl bo-azoro
  v'yor'do ho-aysh.

לְמַעַן פִּלֵּל בַּעֲזָרָה
וַיֵּרְדָה הָאֵשׁ.

*In the merit of him [Solomon] who prayed in the Courtyard
and down came fire.*

L'ma-an tzir olo vi'nis-alo
  b'rechev v'susay aysh.

לְמַעַן צִיר עָלָה וְנִתְעַלָּה
בְּרֶכֶב וְסוּסֵי אֵשׁ.

*In the merit of the agent [Elijah] who ascended to heaven and was exalted,
through a chariot and horses of fire.*

L'ma-an k'dŏshim
  mushlochim bo-aysh.

לְמַעַן קְדוֹשִׁים
מֻשְׁלָכִים בָּאֵשׁ.

*In the merit of holy ones [Chananiah, Mishael, and Azariah]
who were cast into the fire.*

L'ma-an ribŏ riv'von choz
  v'naharay aysh.

לְמַעַן רִבּוֹ רִבְבָן חָז
וְנַהֲרֵי אֵשׁ.

In the merit of him [Daniel] who saw myriad myriads and streams of fire.

L'ma-an shim'mŏs ir'cho
  has'rufo vo-aysh.

לְמַעַן שִׁמְמוֹת עִירָךְ
הַשְּׂרוּפָה בָאֵשׁ.

In the merit of the ruins of Your city which was devoured in fire.

L'ma-an tŏl'dŏs alufay y'hudo
  tosim k'chiyŏr aysh.

לְמַעַן תּוֹלְדוֹת אַלּוּפֵי יְהוּדָה
תָּשִׂים כְּכִיּוֹר אֵשׁ.

*In the merit of the descendants of Judah's princes
whom You will set as a flaming fire.*

L'CHO Adŏnoy hag'dulo

לְךָ יהוה הַגְּדֻלָּה

Yours, HASHEM, is the greatness,

v'hag'vuro v'hatif-eres
  v'hanaytzach v'hahŏd

וְהַגְּבוּרָה וְהַתִּפְאֶרֶת
וְהַנֵּצַח וְהַהוֹד

the strength, the splendor, the triumph, and the glory,

ki chŏl ba-shoma-yim u-vo-oretz,

כִּי כֹל בַּשָּׁמַיִם וּבָאָרֶץ,

even everything in heaven and earth;

l'cho Adŏnoy hamamlocho
  v'hamisnasay l'chŏl l'rŏsh.

לְךָ יהוה הַמַּמְלָכָה
וְהַמִּתְנַשֵּׂא לְכֹל לְרֹאשׁ.

*Yours, HASHEM, is the kingdom,
and the sovereignty over every leader.*

V'ho-yo Adōnoy l'melech   וְהָיָה יהוה לְמֶלֶךְ
   al kol ho-oretz,   עַל כָּל הָאָרֶץ,

HASHEM will be King over all the earth,

ba-yōm hahu   בַּיּוֹם הַהוּא

on that day

yih-ye Adōnoy e-chod ushmō e-chod.   יִהְיֶה יהוה אֶחָד וּשְׁמוֹ אֶחָד.

HASHEM will be One and His Name will be One.

Uvsōros'cho kosuv laymōr: וּבְתוֹרָתְךָ כָּתוּב לֵאמֹר:

And in Your Torah is written as follows:

Sh'ma yisro-ayl,   שְׁמַע יִשְׂרָאֵל,
   Adōnoy Elōhaynu Adōnoy e-chod.   יהוה אֱלֹהֵינוּ יהוה אֶחָד.

Hear, O Israel, HASHEM is our God, HASHEM is the One and Only.

Boruch shaym k'vōd malchusō   בָּרוּךְ שֵׁם כְּבוֹד מַלְכוּתוֹ
   l'ōlom vo-ed.   לְעוֹלָם וָעֶד.

Blessed is the Name of His glorious kingdom for all eternity.

ON HOSHANA RABBAH CONTINUE ani vohō (P. 788).

E-ERŌCH SHU-I.   אֶעֱרוֹךְ שׁוּעִי.

I shall arrange my prayer*

B'vays shav-i.   בְּבֵית שַׁוְעִי.

in the house of prayer:

Gilisi vatzōm pish-i.   גִּלִּיתִי בַצוֹם פִּשְׁעִי.

I have bared, on the fast day, my transgression;

D'rashticho bō l'hōshi-i.   דְּרַשְׁתִּיךָ בּוֹ לְהוֹשִׁיעִי.

I have sought You on that day for salvation.

Hakshivo l'kōl shav-i.   הַקְשִׁיבָה לְקוֹל שַׁוְעִי.

Harken to the sound of my outcry;

V'kumo v'hōshi-i.   וְקוּמָה וְהוֹשִׁיעִי.

arise and save me;

Z'chōr v'rachaym mōshi-i.   זְכוֹר וְרַחֵם מוֹשִׁיעִי.

remember and be merciful, my Savior.

Chai kayn t'sha-sh'i.   חַי כֵּן תְּשַׁעְשְׁעִי.

Living God — in Your faithfulness let me rejoice.

◆§ **I Shall Arrange my Prayer**

One must always anticipate troublesome situations and pray for salvation before oppressive times arrive (*Sanhedrin* 44b). When is the opportune time for such prayer?

"Seek HASHEM when He may be found; call to Him when He is near" (*Isaiah* 55:6). The Tal-

mud (*Rosh Hashanah* 18a) asks, "When may He be found? When is He near?" and answers, "During the Ten Days [of Awe] beginning with Rosh Hashanah and culminating with Yom Kippur."

Now Israel prays that God recall its repentance during the period when God called for it.

Tōv b'enek sh'i.   טוֹב בְּאֶנֶק שְׁעִי.
Goodly One — turn to my groan,

Yochish mōshi-i.   יָחִישׁ מוֹשִׁיעִי.
may my Savior hasten.

Kalay marshi-i.   כַּלֵּה מַרְשִׁיעִי.
Destroy the one who tempts me to sin,

L'val ōd tarshi-i.   לְבַל עוֹד תַּרְשִׁיעִי.
that he may no longer incriminate me.

Mahayr Elōhay yish-i.   מַהֵר אֱלֹהֵי יִשְׁעִי.
Hasten, God of my salvation,

Netzach l'hōshi-i.   נֶצַח לְהוֹשִׁיעִי.
eternally to save me.

So no avōn rish-i.   שָׂא נָא עֲוֹן רִשְׁעִי.
Please, pardon the iniquity of my wickedness,

Avōr al pish-i.   עֲבוֹר עַל פִּשְׁעִי.
overlook my transgression,

P'nay no l'hōshi-i.   פְּנֵה נָא לְהוֹשִׁיעִי.
turn, now, and save me.

Tzur tzadik mōshi-i.   צוּר צַדִּיק מוֹשִׁיעִי.
Rock, Righteous One, Who is my Savior —

Kabayl no shav-i.   קַבֵּל נָא שַׁוְעִי.
accept now my prayer,

Rōmaym keren yish-i.   רוֹמֵם קֶרֶן יִשְׁעִי.
elevate the pride of my salvation.

Shadai mōshi-i.   שַׁדַּי מוֹשִׁיעִי.
Almighty — my Savior,

Tōfi-a v'sōshi-i.   תּוֹפִיעַ וְתוֹשִׁיעִי.
shine Your countenance upon me and save me.

CONTINUE ani vohō (PAGE 788).

AYL L'MŌSHO-ŌS.   אֵל לְמוֹשָׁעוֹת.
O God! Bring about salvations*

B'arba sh'vu-ōs.   בְּאַרְבַּע שְׁבֻעוֹת.
because of the four oaths

Goshim b'shav-ōs.   גָּשִׁים בְּשַׁוְעוֹת.
of those who approach with pleas.

◆§ **God! Bring About Salvations**
A description of the Jews' clinging to God,   and their observance of His *mitzvos*, despite their exile.

Dōf'kay erech shu-ōs.   דּוֹפְקֵי עֶרֶךְ שׁוּעוֹת.
They knock on the doors where prayers are arranged;

Hōgay sha-a-shu-ōs.   הוֹגֵי שַׁעֲשׁוּעוֹת
they meditate upon the beloved Torah

V'chidōsom mishta-sh'ōs.   וְחִידֹתָם מִשְׁתַּעְשְׁעוֹת.
and their riddles are beloved;

Zō-akim l'hash-ōs.   זֹעֲקִים לְהַשְׁעוֹת.
they cry for attention;

Chōchay y'shu-ōs.   חוֹכֵי יְשׁוּעוֹת.
they yearn for salvation;

T'fulim boch sh'ōs.   טְפוּלִים בָּךְ שָׁעוּת.
they cling to You, to You they turn.

Yōd'ay vin sho-ōs.   יוֹדְעֵי בִין שָׁעוֹת.
They know the understanding of the hours,

Kōr'echo b'shav-ōs.   כּוֹרְעֶיךָ בְּשַׁוְעוֹת.
yet they kneel before You pleading

L'hovin sh'mu-ōs.   לְהָבִין שְׁמוּעוֹת.
that they may understand the lessons

Mipicho nishmo-ōs.   מִפִּיךָ נִשְׁמָעוֹת.
which were heard from Your mouth.

Nōsayn t'shu-ōs.   נוֹתֵן תְּשׁוּעוֹת.
O Grantor of salvations,

S'furōs mashmo-ōs.   סְפוּרוֹת מַשְׁמָעוֹת.
gather the counters

Aydus mashmi-ōs.   עֵדוּת מַשְׁמִיעוֹת.
that teach the Testimony.

Pō-ayl y'shu-ōs.   פּוֹעֵל יְשׁוּעוֹת.
O Worker of salvations,

Tzadik nōsho-ōs.   צַדִּיק נוֹשָׁעוֹת.
send [the Messiah] the righteous one who will find salvation.

Kiryas t'shu-ōs.   קִרְיַת תְּשׁוּעוֹת.
For the city of salvations,

Regesh t'shu-ōs.   רֶגֶשׁ תְּשָׁאוֹת.
swarming with masses,

Sholōsh sho-ōs.   שָׁלֹשׁ שָׁעוֹת.
during the three hours,

Tochish lis-shu-ōs.   תָּחִישׁ לִתְשׁוּעוֹת.
hasten the time of salvations.

CONTINUE ani vohō (P. 788).

AFTER EACH DAY'S *HAKAFAH*-CIRCUIT (EXCEPT ON THE SABBATH), CONTINUE:

ANI VOHŌ HŌSHI-O NO.   אֲנִי וָהוֹ הוֹשִׁיעָה נָּא.

ANI VAHŌ, bring salvation now.*

K'HŌ-SHATO AYLIM   כְּהוֹשַׁעְתָּ אֵלִים

b'lud imoch,   בְּלוּד עִמָּךְ,

As You saved the terebinths* in Lud [Egypt] along with Yourself

b'tzays'cho l'yaysha amoch,   בְּצֵאתְךָ לְיֵשַׁע עַמָּךְ,

when You went forth to save the nation —

kayn hōshano.   כֵּן הוֹשַׁעְנָא.

so save now.

K'hōshato gōy vaylōhim,   כְּהוֹשַׁעְתָּ גּוֹי וֵאלֹהִים,

d'rushim l'yaysha Elōhim,   דְּרוּשִׁים לְיֵשַׁע אֱלֹהִים,

As You saved the nation and its leaders who sought the salvations of God —

kayn hōshano.   כֵּן הוֹשַׁעְנָא.

so save now.

K'hōshato hamōn tz'vo-ōs,   כְּהוֹשַׁעְתָּ הֲמוֹן צְבָאוֹת,

v'imom mal-achay tz'vo-ōs,   וְעִמָּם מַלְאֲכֵי צְבָאוֹת,

As You saved the multitudes of hosts and with them the hosts of angels —

kayn hōshano.   כֵּן הוֹשַׁעְנָא.

so save now.

K'hōshato zakim mibays avodim,   כְּהוֹשַׁעְתָּ זַכִּים מִבֵּית עֲבָדִים,

chanun b'yodom ma-avidim,   חַנּוּן בְּיָדָם מַעֲבִידִים,

As You saved pure ones from the house of slavery,
Gracious One, from those who forced manual labor upon them —

kayn hōshano.   כֵּן הוֹשַׁעְנָא.

so save now.

K'hōshato t'vu-im b'tzul g'zorim,   כְּהוֹשַׁעְתָּ טְבוּעִים בְּצוּל גְּזָרִים,

y'kor'cho imom ma-avirim,   יְקָרְךָ עִמָּם מַעֲבִירִים,

As You saved those sinking in the depths of the rifts,
Your honor was with them when they crossed —

kayn hōshano.   כֵּן הוֹשַׁעְנָא.

so save now.

אֲנִי וָהוֹ הוֹשִׁיעָה נָּא — *ANI VAHO, bring salvation now.* The obscure terms אֲנִי וָהוֹ, "ANI VAHO," are identified as two in a series of seventy-two Divine Names, each containing three letters. The complete series is composed of the letters which make up three consecutive verses of *Exodus* (14:19-21), each of which contains exactly seventy-two letters. In the mystical formula by which these Names are formed, verses 19 and 21 are read in their proper order, while verse 20

is read backwards. The first of these seventy-two Names is וָהוֹ, and the thirty-seventh Name is אני.

◆§ As You Saved the Terebinths

This *Hoshana*, which is recited after each day's circuit [except on the Sabbath], contains various poetical allusions to the Exodus from Egypt and other incidents of God's salvation of Israel, and pleads that we be granted similar salvation.

K'hōshato kano   כְּהוֹשַׁעְתָּ כַּנָּה

m'shōreres va-yō-sha,   מְשׁוֹרֶרֶת וַיִּוָּשַׁע,

As You saved the garden which sang "He delivered,"

l'gōcho m'tzuyenes va-yivo-sha,   לְגוֹחָהּ מְצֻיֶּנֶת וַיְוָשַׁע,

regarding Him Who draws forth it is pronounced "He was delivered" –

kayn hōshano.   כֵּן הוֹשַׁעְנָא.

so save now.

K'hōshato ma-amar   כְּהוֹשַׁעְתָּ מַאֲמַר

v'hōtzaysi eschem,   וְהוֹצֵאתִי אֶתְכֶם,

As You saved with the declaration, "I shall bring you forth,"

nokuv v'hutzaysi it'chem,   נָקוּב וְהוּצֵאתִי אִתְּכֶם,

which may be interpreted, "I shall be brought forth with you" –

kayn hōshano.   כֵּן הוֹשַׁעְנָא.

so save now.

K'hōshato sōv'vay mizbay-ach,   כְּהוֹשַׁעְתָּ סוֹבְבֵי מִזְבֵּחַ,

ōm'say arovo l'hakif mizbay-ach,   עוֹמְסֵי עֲרָבָה לְהַקִּיף מִזְבֵּחַ,

As You saved those who went roundabout the Altar,

those who carry the willow to encircle the Altar –

kayn hōshano.   כֵּן הוֹשַׁעְנָא.

so save now.

K'hōshato pil-ay orōn k'huf-sha,   כְּהוֹשַׁעְתָּ פִּלְאֵי אָרוֹן כְּהֻפְשַׁע,

tzi-ayr p'leshes   צַעַר פְּלֶשֶׁת

bacharōn af v'nōsha,   בַּחֲרוֹן אַף וְנוֹשַׁע,

when you punished Philistia with flaming anger, and it was saved –

kayn hōshano.   כֵּן הוֹשַׁעְנָא.

so save now.

K'hōshato k'hilōs bovelo shilachto,   כְּהוֹשַׁעְתָּ קְהִלּוֹת בָּבֶלָה שִׁלַּחְתָּ,

rachum l'ma-anom shulachto,   רַחוּם לְמַעֲנָם שֻׁלַּחְתָּ,

As You saved the congregations which You had sent to Babylon,

Merciful One, for their sake were You also sent –

kayn hōshano.   כֵּן הוֹשַׁעְנָא.

so save now.

K'hōshato sh'vus shivtay ya-akōv,   כְּהוֹשַׁעְתָּ שְׁבוּת שִׁבְטֵי יַעֲקֹב,

As You saved the captivity of the tribes of Jacob,

toshuv v'soshiv sh'vus   תָּשׁוּב וְתָשִׁיב שְׁבוּת

oholay ya-akōv,   אָהֳלֵי יַעֲקֹב,

return and restore the captivity of the tents of Jacob,

v'hōshi-o no.

וְהוֹשִׁיעָה נָּא.

and bring salvation now.

K'hōshato shōm'ray mitzvōs,

כְּהוֹשַׁעְתָּ שׁוֹמְרֵי מִצְוֹת,

v'chōchay y'shu-ōs,

וְחוֹכֵי יְשׁוּעוֹת,

As You saved those observant of mitzvos, and hopeful for salvations —

Ayl l'mōsho-ōs, v'hōshi-o no.

אֵל לְמוֹשָׁעוֹת, וְהוֹשִׁיעָה נָּא.

O God Who brings about salvations, bring salvation now.

ANI VOHŌ HŌSHI-O NO.

אֲנִי וָהוֹ הוֹשִׁיעָה נָּא.

ANI VAHŌ, bring salvation now.

ON HOSHANA RABBAH CONTINUE tit'naynu (P. 797).

DURING THE FIRST SIX DAYS OF SUCCOS CONTINUE:

HŌSHI-O es amecho,

הוֹשִׁיעָה אֶת עַמֶּךָ,

u-voraych es nachalosecho,

וּבָרֵךְ אֶת נַחֲלָתֶךָ,

Save Your people and bless Your heritage,

ur-aym v'nas'aym ad ho-ōlom.

וּרְעֵם וְנַשְּׂאֵם עַד הָעוֹלָם.

tend them and elevate them forever.

V'yih-yu d'vorai ayle

וְיִהְיוּ דְבָרַי אֵלֶּה

asher hischananti lifnay Adōnoy,

אֲשֶׁר הִתְחַנַּנְתִּי לִפְנֵי יהוה,

May these words of mine, which I have supplicated before HASHEM,

k'rōvim el Adōnoy Elōhaynu

קְרֹבִים אֶל יהוה אֱלֹהֵינוּ

yōmom voloylo,

יוֹמָם וָלָיְלָה,

be near to HASHEM, our God, by day and by night,

la-asōs mishpat avdō

לַעֲשׂוֹת מִשְׁפַּט עַבְדּוֹ

u-mishpat amō yisro-ayl,

וּמִשְׁפַּט עַמּוֹ יִשְׂרָאֵל,

that He bring about justice for His servant and justice for His people, Israel,

d'var yōm b'yōmō.

דְּבַר יוֹם בְּיוֹמוֹ.

each day's need in its day;

L'ma-an da-as kol amay ho-oretz,

לְמַעַן דַּעַת כָּל עַמֵּי הָאָרֶץ,

that all the peoples of the earth shall know

ki Adōnoy hu ho-Elōhim,

כִּי יהוה הוּא הָאֱלֹהִים,

ayn ōd.

אֵין עוֹד.

that HASHEM is God — there is no other.

THE TORAH SCROLL IS RETURNED TO THE ARK.

ON THE FIRST TWO DAYS OF SUCCOS THE *CHAZZAN* RECITES THE FULL *KADDISH* (P. 454) AND THE SERVICE CONTINUES FROM THERE (PP. 455-490).

DURING *CHOL HAMOED* THE *CHAZZAN* RECITES THE FULL *KADDISH* (P. 454) AND THE SERVICE CONTINUES WITH *ALEINU* (P. 463).

ON THE SABBATH (WHETHER IT COINCIDES WITH YOM TOV OR WITH *CHOL HAMOED*)
THE FOLLOWING *HOSHANOS* ARE RECITED:

ŌM N'TZURO k'vovas.

אוֹם נְצוּרָה כְּבָבַת.

Nation protected* like the pupil of the eye —

Bōnenes b'dos nefesh m'shivas.

בּוֹנֶנֶת בְּדָת נֶפֶשׁ מְשִׁיבַת.

she seeks understanding of the law which restores the soul.

Gōmeres hilchōs shabos.

גּוֹמֶרֶת הִלְכוֹת שַׁבָּת.

She studies the laws of the Sabbath,

Dōreshes mas-as shabos.

דּוֹרֶשֶׁת מַשְׂאַת שַׁבָּת.

explicates the burdens of the Sabbath,

Hakōva-as alpa-yim t'chum shabos.

הַקּוֹבַעַת אַלְפַּיִם תְּחוּם שַׁבָּת.

establishes two thousand as the boundary of the Sabbath,

Umshivas regel mi-shabos.

וּמְשִׁיבַת רֶגֶל מִשַּׁבָּת.

and restrains her foot because of the Sabbath.

Zochōr v'shomōr

m'ka-yemes ba-shabos.

זָכוֹר וְשָׁמוֹר
מְקַיֶּמֶת בַּשַּׁבָּת.

"Remember" and "Safeguard" she fulfills on the Sabbath

Chosho l'mahayr bi-as shabos.

חָשָׁה לְמַהֵר בִּיאַת שַׁבָּת.

by rushing to hasten the onset of the Sabbath;

Tōrachas kōl mishisho la-shabos.

טוֹרַחַת כֹּל מִשִּׁשָׁה לַשַּׁבָּת.

by toiling throughout the six for the Sabbath;

Yōsheves u-mamtenes

ad k'lōs shabos.

יוֹשֶׁבֶת וּמַמְתֶּנֶת
עַד כְּלוֹת שַׁבָּת.

by sitting, patiently waiting until the end of the Sabbath.

Kovōd vo-ōneg kōr'o la-shabos.

כָּבוֹד וָעֹנֶג קוֹרְאָה לַשַּׁבָּת.

"Honor" and "Delight" she proclaims the Sabbath;

L'vush uchsus m'chalefes ba-shabos.

לְבוּשׁ וּכְסוּת מְחַלֶּפֶת בַּשַּׁבָּת.

clothing and raiment she changes for the Sabbath,

Ma-achol u-mishte m'chino la-shabos.

מַאֲכָל וּמִשְׁתֶּה מְכִינָה לַשַּׁבָּת.

food and drink she prepares for the Sabbath,

Nō-am m'godim man-emes la-shabos.

נֹעַם מְגָדִים מַנְעֶמֶת לַשַּׁבָּת.

of the sweetness of delicate fruits she partakes on the Sabbath,

S'udōs sholōsh m'ka-yemes ba-shabos.

סְעוּדוֹת שָׁלֹשׁ מְקַיֶּמֶת בַּשַּׁבָּת.

three meals she fulfills on the Sabbath,

⊸§ **Nation Protected**
This *Hoshana*, recited on the Sabbath, con-

tains allusions to the observance of various
mitzvos related to the Sabbath.

Al sh'tay chikorōs
בּוֹצַעַת בַּשַּׁבָּת.
בּוֹצַעַת בַּשַּׁבָּת.

עַל שְׁתֵּי כִכָּרוֹת
over two loaves she breaks bread on the Sabbath.

Pōretes arba r'shuyōs ba-shabos.
פּוֹרֶטֶת אַרְבַּע רְשֻׁיּוֹת בַּשַּׁבָּת.
She distinguishes four domains on the Sabbath.

Tzivuy hadlokas nayr
madlekes ba-shabos.
צִוּוּי הַדְלָקַת נֵר
מַדְלֶקֶת בַּשַּׁבָּת.
The command of kindling the light she fulfills for the Sabbath.

Kidush ha-yōm
m'kadeshes ba-shabos.
קִדּוּשׁ הַיּוֹם
מְקַדֶּשֶׁת בַּשַּׁבָּת.
The Sanctification of the day she recites on the Sabbath.

Renen sheva m'faleles ba-shabos.
רֶנֶן שֶׁבַע מְפַלֶּלֶת בַּשַּׁבָּת.
A seven-part prayer she prays on the Sabbath.

Shiv-o vados kōr'o va-shabos.
שִׁבְעָה בַדַּת קוֹרְאָה בַּשַּׁבָּת.
Seven portions of the Torah she reads on the Sabbath.

Tanchileno l'yōm shekulō shabos.
תַּנְחִילֶנָּה לְיוֹם שֶׁכֻּלּוֹ שַׁבָּת.
Cause her to inherit the day which will be completely a Sabbath.

ANI VOHŌ HŌSHI-O NO.   אֲנִי וָהוֹ הוֹשִׁיעָה נָּא.
Ani Vaho, *bring salvation now.*

K'HŌSHATO ODOM   כְּהוֹשַׁעְתָּ אָדָם
y'tzir kapecho l'gōn'no,
יְצִיר כַּפֶּיךָ לְגוֹנְנָה,
As You saved Adam, Your handiwork, to be his shield;

b'shabas kōdesh
himtzaysō kōfer vachanino,
בְּשַׁבַּת קֹדֶשׁ
הִמְצֵאתוֹ כְּפֶר וַחֲנִינָה,
on the holy Sabbath You brought forth for him forgiveness and grace —

kayn hōshano.
כֵּן הוֹשַׁעְנָא.
so save now.

K'hōshato gōy m'tzuyon
m'kavim chōfesh,
כְּהוֹשַׁעְתָּ גּוֹי מְצֻיָּן
מְקַוִּים חֹפֶשׁ,
As You saved the distinctive nation which sought freedom;

day-o kiv'nu lovur sh'vi-i l'nōfesh,
דֵעָה כִּוְּנוּ לָבוּר שְׁבִיעִי לְנְפֶשׁ,
with wisdom they anticipated the choice of the seventh for rest —

kayn hōshano.
כֵּן הוֹשַׁעְנָא.
so save now.

k'hōshato ho-om
nihagto katzōn l'hanchōs,
כְּהוֹשַׁעְתָּ הָעָם
נִהַגְתָּ כַּצֹּאן לְהַנְחוֹת,
As You saved the people whom You guided like a flock to contentment;

v'chōk samto b'moro
   al may m'nuchōs,
      and You issued a statute at Marah beside tranquil waters —

וְחֹק שַׂמְתָּ בְּמָרָה
עַל מֵי מְנֻחוֹת,

kayn hōshano.   כֵּן הוֹשַׁעְנָא.
         so save now.

K'hōshato z'vudecho
   b'midbar sin bamachane,
    As You saved Your portion in the encampment at the Wilderness of Sin;

כְּהוֹשַׁעְתָּ זְבוּדֶיךָ
בְּמִדְבַּר סִין בַּמַּחֲנֶה,

choch'mu
   v'lok'tu ba-shishi lechem mish-ne,
    they acted wisely and gathered double bread on the sixth —

חָכְמוּ
וְלָקְטוּ בַשִּׁשִּׁי לֶחֶם מִשְׁנֶה,

kayn hōshano.   כֵּן הוֹשַׁעְנָא.
         so save now.

K'hōshato t'fulecho
   hōru hachono b'mado-om,
     As You saved those who clung to You,
    who derived the rules of preparation through their wisdom;

כְּהוֹשַׁעְתָּ טְפוּלֶיךָ
הוֹרוּ הֲכָנָה בְּמַדָּעָם,

yishar kōchom v'hōdo lomō rō-om,   יִשַּׁר כֹּחָם וְהוֹדָה לָמוֹ רוֹעָם,
    their shepherd blessed their talent and deferred to them —

kayn hōshano.   כֵּן הוֹשַׁעְנָא.
         so save now.

K'hōshato kulk'lu b'ōneg
   mon ham'shumor,
 As You saved those You sustained on the day of delight with the guarded manna,

כְּהוֹשַׁעְתָּ כֻּלְכְּלוּ בְּעֹנֶג
מָן הַמְשֻׁמָּר,

lō hofach aynō v'raychō lō nomor,   לֹא הָפַךְ עֵינוֹ וְרֵיחוֹ לֹא נָמָר,
   whose appearance did not change and whose aroma did not sour —

kayn hōshano.   כֵּן הוֹשַׁעְנָא.
         so save now.

K'hōshato mishp'tay
   mas-ōs shabos gomoru,
   As You saved those who study the laws regarding the burdens of the Sabbath;

כְּהוֹשַׁעְתָּ מִשְׁפְּטֵי
מַשְׂאוֹת שַׁבָּת גָּמְרוּ,

nochu v'shov'su
   r'shuyōs us-chumim shomoru,
    they are content and they rest, guarding domains and boundaries —

נָחוּ וְשָׁבְתוּ
רְשֻׁיּוֹת וּתְחוּמִים שָׁמְרוּ,

kayn hōshano.   כֵּן הוֹשַׁעְנָא.
         so save now.

K'hōshato sinai hushm'u
   b'dibur r'vi-i,
   As You saved those permitted to hear the fourth pronouncement at Sinai;

כְּהוֹשַׁעְתָּ סִינַי הֻשְׁמְעוּ
בְּדִבּוּר רְבִיעִי,

inyan zochōr v'shomōr
l'kadaysh sh'vi-i,
עִנְיַן זָכוֹר וְשָׁמוֹר
לְקַדֵּשׁ שְׁבִיעִי,

the theme of "Remember" and "Safeguard" to sanctify the seventh —

kayn hōshano.
כֵּן הוֹשַׁעְנָא.

so save now.

K'hōshato puk'du y'richō
sheva l'hakayf,
כְּהוֹשַׁעְתָּ פְּקֻדוּ יְרִיחוֹ
שֶׁבַע לְהַקֵּף,

As You saved those bidden at Jericho to encircle seven times;

tzoru ad rid-toh ba-shabos l'sakayf,
צָרוּ עַד רִדְתָּהּ בַּשַּׁבָּת לְתַקֵּף,

they besieged it until its downfall on the Sabbath, to strengthen them,

kayn hōshano.
כֵּן הוֹשַׁעְנָא.

so save now.

K'hōshato kōheles v'amō
b'vays ōlomim,
כְּהוֹשַׁעְתָּ קֹהֶלֶת וְעַמּוֹ
בְּבֵית עוֹלָמִים,

As You saved Koheles [Solomon] and his people in the eternal Temple,

ritzucho b'chog'gom shiv-o
v'shiv-o yomim,
רִצּוּךְ בְּחָגְגָם שִׁבְעָה
וְשִׁבְעָה יָמִים,

they pleased You when they celebrated seven and another seven days —

kayn hōshano.
כֵּן הוֹשַׁעְנָא.

so save now.

K'hōshato shovim
ōlay gōlo l'fidyōm,
כְּהוֹשַׁעְתָּ שָׁבִים
עוֹלֵי גוֹלָה לְפִדְיוֹם,

As You saved those who returned, ascending from exile to redemption;

tōros'cho b'kor-om bechog yōm yōm,
תּוֹרָתְךָ בְּקָרְאָם בְּחַג יוֹם יוֹם,

as they read Your Torah every day of the Festival —

kayn hōshano.
כֵּן הוֹשַׁעְנָא.

so save now.

K'hōshato m'sam'checho
b'vinyan shayni ham'chudosh,
כְּהוֹשַׁעְתָּ מְשַׂמְּחֶיךָ
בְּבִנְיַן שֵׁנִי הַמְחֻדָּשׁ,

As You saved those who brought You joy with the renewed Second Temple;

nōt'lin lulov
kol shiv-o bamikdosh,
נוֹטְלִין לוּלָב
כָּל שִׁבְעָה בַּמִּקְדָּשׁ,

who took up the lulav all seven days in the Sanctuary —

kayn hōshano.
כֵּן הוֹשַׁעְנָא.

so save now.

K'hōshato chibut arovo
shabos madchim,
כְּהוֹשַׁעְתָּ חִבּוּט עֲרָבָה
שַׁבָּת מַדְחִים,

As You saved those for whom the beating of the willow overrode the Sabbath;

murbiyōs mōtzo   מַרְבִּיּוֹת מוֹצָא
  lisōd mizbay-ach manichim,   לִיסוֹד מִזְבֵּחַ מַנִּיחִים,
  those who placed Motza's branches at the base of the Altar –
kayn hōshano.   כֵּן הוֹשַׁעְנָא.
  so save now.

K'hōshato b'rakōs   כְּהוֹשַׁעְתָּ בְּרַכּוֹת
  va-arukōs ugvōhōs m'al'sim,   וַאֲרֻכּוֹת וּגְבוֹהוֹת מְעַלְּסִים,
  As You saved those who praised with supple, long and tall willows;
biftiroson   בִּפְטִירָתָן
  yōfi l'cho mizbay-ach m'kal'sim, יְפִי לְךָ מִזְבֵּחַ מְקַלְּסִים,
  who departed while extolling, "Beauty becomes you, O Altar" –
kayn hōshano.   כֵּן הוֹשַׁעְנָא.
  so save now.

K'hōshato mōdim umya-chalim   כְּהוֹשַׁעְתָּ מוֹדִים וּמְיַחֲלִים
  v'lō m'shanim,   וְלֹא מְשַׁנִּים,
  As You saved those who thanked and hoped, but never exchanged;
kulonu onu l'Yoh   כֻּלָּנוּ אָנוּ לְיָהּ
  v'aynaynu l'Yoh shōnim,   וְעֵינֵינוּ לְיָהּ שׁוֹנִים,
  like them we all cry out, "We are God's and our eyes are to God" –
kayn hōshano.   כֵּן הוֹשַׁעְנָא.
  so save now.

K'hōshato yekev machatzovecho   כְּהוֹשַׁעְתָּ יֶקֶב מַחֲצָבֶיךָ
  sōv'vim b'ra-anono,   סוֹבְבִים בְּרַעֲנָנָה,
  As You saved those who encircled Your hewn wine cellar with greenery;
rōn'nim ani vohō hōshi-o no,   רוֹנְנִים אֲנִי וָהוֹ הוֹשִׁיעָה נָּא,
  singing, "ANI VAHO, bring salvation now" –
kayn hōshano.   כֵּן הוֹשַׁעְנָא.
  so save now.

K'hōshato chayl z'rizim   כְּהוֹשַׁעְתָּ חֵיל זְרִיזִים
  m'shor'sim bimnucho,   מְשָׁרְתִים בִּמְנוּחָה,
  As You saved the army of speedy ones who serve on the day of contentment,
korban shabos koful ōlo u-mincho, קָרְבַּן שַׁבָּת כָּפוּל עוֹלָה וּמִנְחָה,
  with the doubled Sabbath offering, of burnt- and meal-offering –
kayn hōshano.   כֵּן הוֹשַׁעְנָא.
  so save now.

K'hōshato l'vi-yecho   כְּהוֹשַׁעְתָּ לְוִיֶּיךָ
  al duchonom l'harbos,   עַל דּוּכָנָם לְהַרְבַּת,
  As You saved Your Levites who sang upon their platform,

ōm'rim

אוֹמְרִים

mizmōr shir l'yōm ha-shabos,

מִזְמוֹר שִׁיר לְיוֹם הַשַּׁבָּת,

saying, "A psalm, a song, for the Sabbath day" —

kayn hōshano.

כֵּן הוֹשַׁעְנָא.

so save now.

K'hōshato nichumecho

כְּהוֹשַׁעְתָּ נְחוּמֶיךָ

b'mitzvōsecho tomid yishtash'un,

בְּמִצְוֹתֶיךָ תָּמִיד יִשְׁתַּעְשְׁעוּן,

As You saved those whom You comforted,
those who constantly find joy in Your mitzvos;

urtzaym v'hachalitzaym

וּרְצֵם וְהַחֲלִיצֵם

b'shuvo vonachas yivoshay-un,

בְּשׁוּבָה וָנַחַת יִוָּשֵׁעוּן,

so may You favor them and give them rest,
and with tranquility and contentment may they attain salvation —

kayn hōshano.

כֵּן הוֹשַׁעְנָא.

so save now.

K'hōshato sh'vus shivtay ya-akōv,

כְּהוֹשַׁעְתָּ שְׁבוּת שִׁבְטֵי יַעֲקֹב,

As You saved the captivity of the Tribes of Jacob,

toshuv v'soshiv sh'vus

תָּשׁוּב וְתָשִׁיב שְׁבוּת

oholay ya-akōv,

אָהֳלֵי יַעֲקֹב,

return and restore the captivity of Jacob's tents

v'hōshi-o no.

וְהוֹשִׁיעָה נָּא.

and bring salvation now.

K'hōshato shōm'ray mitzvōs,

כְּהוֹשַׁעְתָּ שׁוֹמְרֵי מִצְוֹת,

v'chōchay y'shu-ōs,

וְחוֹכֵי יְשׁוּעוֹת,

As You saved those observant of mitzvos, and hopeful for salvations —

Ayl l'mōsho-ōs, v'hōshi-o no.

אֵל לְמוֹשָׁעוֹת, וְהוֹשִׁיעָה נָּא.

O God Who brings about salvations, bring salvation now.

ANI VOHŌ HŌSHI-O NO.

אֲנִי וָהוֹ הוֹשִׁיעָה נָּא.

Ani Vahō, bring salvation now.

HŌSHI-O es amecho,

הוֹשִׁיעָה אֶת עַמֶּךָ,

u-voraych es nachalosecho,

וּבָרֵךְ אֶת נַחֲלָתֶךָ,

Save Your people and bless Your heritage,

ur-aym v'nas'aym ad ho-ōlom.

וּרְעֵם וְנַשְּׂאֵם עַד הָעוֹלָם.

tend them and elevate them forever.

V'yih-yu d'vorai ayle

וְיִהְיוּ דְבָרַי אֵלֶּה

asher hischananti lifnay Adōnoy,

אֲשֶׁר הִתְחַנַּנְתִּי לִפְנֵי יהוה,

May these words of mine, which I have supplicated before HASHEM,

k'rōvim el Adōnoy Elōhaynu
yōmom voloylo,

קְרֹבִים אֶל יהוה אֱלֹהֵינוּ
יוֹמָם וָלָיְלָה,

be near to HASHEM, our God, by day and by night;

la-asōs mishpat avdō
u-mishpat amō yisro-ayl,

לַעֲשׂוֹת מִשְׁפַּט עַבְדּוֹ
וּמִשְׁפַּט עַמּוֹ יִשְׂרָאֵל,

that He bring about justice for His servant and justice for His people, Israel,

d'var yōm b'yōmō.

דְּבַר יוֹם בְּיוֹמוֹ.

each day's need in its day;

L'ma-an da-as kol amay ho-oretz,

לְמַעַן דַּעַת כָּל עַמֵּי הָאָרֶץ,

that all the peoples of the earth shall know

ki Adōnoy hu ho-Elōhim,
ayn ōd.

כִּי יהוה הוּא הָאֱלֹהִים,
אֵין עוֹד.

that HASHEM is God — there is no other.

THE TORAH SCROLL IS RETURNED TO THE ARK. THE *CHAZZAN* RECITES THE FULL *KADDISH* (P. 454)
AND THE SERVICE CONTINUES FROM THERE (PP. 455-490).

ADDITIONAL PRAYERS FOR HOSHANA RABBAH

ALL CONTINUE HERE:

TIT'NAYNU l'shaym v'lis-hilo.

תִּתְּנֵנוּ לְשֵׁם וְלִתְהִלָּה.

Establish us* for fame and renown;

T'shisaynu el ha-chevel
v'el hanachalo.

תְּשִׁיתֵנוּ אֶל הַחֶבֶל
וְאֶל הַנַּחֲלָה.

place us upon our measured heritage;

T'rōm'maynu l'malo l'molo.

תְּרוֹמְמֵנוּ לְמַעְלָה לְמָעְלָה.

raise us ever higher;

T'kab'tzaynu l'vays hat'filo.

תְּקַבְּצֵנוּ לְבֵית הַתְּפִלָּה.

gather us to the House of Prayer;

Tatzivaynu
k'aytz al palgay ma-yim sh'sulo.

תַּצִּיבֵנוּ
כְּעֵץ עַל פַּלְגֵי מַיִם שְׁתוּלָה.

stand us erect, like a tree embedded by streams of water;

Tifdaynu mikol nega u-machalo.

תִּפְדֵּנוּ מִכָּל נֶגַע וּמַחֲלָה.

redeem us from every plague and sickness;

T'at'raynu b'ahavo ch'lulo.

תְּעַטְּרֵנוּ בְּאַהֲבָה כְלוּלָה.

envelop us with perfect love;

T'sam'chaynu b'vays hat'filo.

תְּשַׂמְּחֵנוּ בְּבֵית הַתְּפִלָּה.

gladden us in the House of Prayer;

◄§ **Establish Us.**
This is the first in a series of additional

Hoshanos chanted on Hoshana Rabbah after
the completion of the seven *hakafah* -circuits.

T'nahalaynu al may m'nuchōs selo.   תְּנַהֲלֵנוּ עַל מֵי מְנוּחוֹת סֶלָה.
lead us beside tranquil waters, forever;

T'mal'aynu chochmo v'sichlo.   תְּמַלְּאֵנוּ חָכְמָה וְשִׂכְלָה.
fill us with wisdom and sense;

Talbi-shaynu ōz ugdulo.   תַּלְבִּישֵׁנוּ עֹז וּגְדֻלָה.
clothe us with strength and greatness;

Tachtiraynu b'cheser k'lulo.   תַּכְתִּירֵנוּ בְּכֶתֶר כְּלוּלָה.
crown us with the perfect crown;

T'yash'raynu b'ōrach s'lulo.   תְּיַשְּׁרֵנוּ בְּאֹרַח סְלוּלָה.
set us right on the level road;

Tito-aynu b'yōsher m'silo.   תִּטָּעֵנוּ בְּיֹשֶׁר מְסִלָּה.
plant us on the straight path;

T'chonaynu b'rachamim uvchemlo.   תְּחָנֵּנוּ בְּרַחֲמִים וּבְחֶמְלָה.
grace us with mercy and pity;

Tazkiraynu b'mi zōs ōlo.   תַּזְכִּירֵנוּ בְּמִי זֹאת עוֹלָה.
remember us with "How worthy is she!";

Tōshi-aynu l'kaytz hag'ulo.   תּוֹשִׁיעֵנוּ לְקֵץ הַגְּאֻלָּה.
save us for the final End of Redemption;

T'had'raynu b'ziv hamulo.   תְּהַדְּרֵנוּ בְּזִיו הַמּוּלָה.
beautify us with the radiance of angels;

Tadbikaynu k'ayzōr chasulo.   תַּדְבִּיקֵנוּ כְּאֵזוֹר חֲתוּלָה.
cause us to cleave to You like a tightly wrapped sash;

T'gad'laynu b'yod hag'dōlo.   תְּגַדְּלֵנוּ בְּיָד הַגְּדוֹלָה.
make us great with Your great hand;

T'vi-aynu l'vays'cho b'rino v'tzoholo.   תְּבִיאֵנוּ לְבֵיתְךָ בְּרִנָּה וְצָהֳלָה.
bring us to Your Temple with joyous song and cheer;

T'am'tzaynu b'revach v'hatzolo.   תְּאַמְּצֵנוּ בְּרֶוַח וְהַצָּלָה.
strengthen us with relief and rescue;

T'ad'raynu b'even t'lulo.   תְּאַדְּרֵנוּ בְּאֶבֶן תְּלוּלָה.
adorn us with the elevated stone;

T'lab'vaynu b'vinyan ir'cho
k'vat'chilo.   תְּלַבְּבֵנוּ בְּבִנְיַן עִירְךָ כְּבַתְּחִלָּה.
hearten us with the rebuilding of Your city as of old;

T'ōr'raynu l'tziyōn b'shichlulo.   תְּעוֹרְרֵנוּ לְצִיּוֹן בְּשִׁכְלוּלָה.
awaken us to Zion in its completeness;

T'zakaynu b'nivn'so ho-ir al tiloh.   תְּזַכֵּנוּ בְּנִבְנְתָה הָעִיר עַל תִּלָּהּ.
let us merit the rebuilding of the City on its hill;

Tarbitzaynu b'sosōn v'gilo.   תַּרְבִּיצֵנוּ בְּשָׂשׂוֹן וְגִילָה.

let us recline with joy and gladness;

T'chaz'kaynu Elōhay ya-akōv selo.   תְּחַזְּקֵנוּ אֱלֹהֵי יַעֲקֹב סֶלָה.

strengthen us, O God of Jacob, Selah.

CHAZZAN, THEN CONGREGATION:

ONO HŌSHI-O NO.   **אָנָּא הוֹשִׁיעָה נָּא.**

Please bring salvation now.

ALL CONTINUE:

ONO EZŌN chin t'ayvay yish-och,   **אָנָּא אֱזוֹן** חִין תְּאֵבֵי יִשְׁעֶךָ,

Please hearken* to the plea of those who long for Your salvation;

b'arvay nachal l'shash'och,   בְּעַרְבֵי נַחַל לְשַׁעְשְׁעֶךָ,

with brook willows they bring You joy

v'hōshi-o no.   וְהוֹשִׁיעָה נָּא.

and bring salvation now.

Ono g'al kanas nit-och,   אָנָּא גְּאַל כַּנַּת נִטְעֶךָ,

Please redeem the garden of Your planting,

dumo b'tat'och,   דּוּמָה בְּטַאטְאֶךָ,

as You sweep away Dumah

v'hōshi-o no.   וְהוֹשִׁיעָה נָּא.

and bring salvation now.

Ono habayt lab'ris tiv-och,   אָנָּא הַבֵּט לַבְּרִית טִבְעֶךָ,

Please gaze upon the covenant of Your signet ring,

u-machashakay eretz b'hatbi-och,   וּמַחֲשַׁכֵּי אֶרֶץ בְּהַטְבִּיעֶךָ,

even as You sink the ones who darken the earth

v'hōshi-o no.   וְהוֹשִׁיעָה נָּא.

and bring salvation now.

Ono z'chor lonu ov yid'och,   אָנָּא זְכָר לָנוּ אָב יְדָעֶךָ,

Please recall on our behalf the Patriarch [Abraham] who perceived You;

chasd'cho lomō b'hōdi-och,   חַסְדְּךָ לָמוֹ בְּהוֹדִיעֶךָ,

may Your lovingkindness be upon them, for he made You known

v'hōshi-o no.   וְהוֹשִׁיעָה נָּא.

and bring salvation now.

◄§ **Please Hearken**

The rainy season in the Land of Israel begins almost immediately after Succos. For this reason special prayers for rain (p. 755) are recited on Shemini Atzeres. Additionally, the *Hoshanos* service of Hoshana Rabbah centers on the *aravos*, or brook-willows, a species which both depends upon and is identified with water.

The Talmud teaches that during Succos the

Heavenly Tribunal judges the world with regard to its water supply for the following year. God ordained the water-libations of Succos as a source of merit; as if He said, "Pour water before Me on this Festival, that you be blessed with the year's rains" (*Rosh Hashanah* 16a). These prayers for rain are not recited until the last day of the Festival because "rain is but a symptom of curse during Succos," for it makes it impossible to sit in the *succah* (*Taanis* 2a).

אָנָּא טְהוֹרֵי לֵב בְּהַפְלִיאָךְ,

Ono t'hōray layv b'hafli-och,

Please when you set aside the pure of heart,

יִוָּדַע כִּי הוּא פִלְאָךְ,

yivoda ki hu fil-och,

let it be known that this is Your wonder

וְהוֹשִׁיעָה נָא.

v'hōshi-o no.

and bring salvation now.

אָנָּא כַּבִּיר כֹּחַ תֶּן לָנוּ יִשְׁעָךְ,

Ono kabir kō-ach ten lonu yish-och,

Please Almighty One, grant us Your salvation,

לַאֲבוֹתֵינוּ כְּהִשָּׁבְעָךְ,

la-avōsaynu k'hi-shov'och,

as You swore to our fathers

וְהוֹשִׁיעָה נָא.

v'hōshi-o no.

and bring salvation now.

אָנָּא מַלֵּא מִשְׁאֲלוֹת
עַם מְשַׁוְּעָךְ,

Ono malay mish-alōs
am m'shav'och,

Please fulfill the requests of Your entreating people,

נֶעֱקַד בְּהַר מוֹר כְּמוֹ שִׁוְּעָךְ,

ne-ekad b'har mōr k'mō shiv'och,

as [Isaac] the one bound on the Myrrh mountain entreated You

וְהוֹשִׁיעָה נָא.

v'hōshi-o no.

and bring salvation now.

אָנָּא סַגֵּב אֶשְׁלֵי נִטְעָךְ,

Ono sagayv eshlay nit-och,

Please strengthen [Israel] the tamarisks of Your planting,

עָרִיצִים בְּהַנִיעָךְ,

oritzim b'hani-och,

as You cause the idolaters to wander

וְהוֹשִׁיעָה נָא.

v'hōshi-o no.

and bring salvation now.

אָנָּא פְּתַח לָנוּ אוֹצְרוֹת רְבָעָךְ,

Ono p'sach lonu ōtz'rōs riv-och,

Please open the treasure troves of Your rains for us,

צִיָּה מֵהֶם בְּהַרְבִּיעָךְ,

tzi-yo mayhem b'harbi-och,

as You water the parched earth from them

וְהוֹשִׁיעָה נָא.

v'hōshi-o no.

and bring salvation now.

אָנָּא קוֹרְאֶיךָ אֶרֶץ בְּרוֹעֲעָךְ,

Ono kōr'echo eretz b'rō-a-och,

Please — those who call to You, when You bring the earth destruction,

רְעֵם בְּטוּב מִרְעָךְ,

r'aym b'tuv mir-och,

shepherd them in Your goodly pastures

וְהוֹשִׁיעָה נָא.

v'hōshi-o no.

and bring salvation now.

אָנָּא שְׁעָרֶיךָ תַּעַל מִמְּשׁוֹאָךְ,

Ono sh'orecho ta-al mim'shō-och,

Please raise Your gates in the wake of Your desolation,

tayl talpiyōs b'hasi-och,   תֵּל תַּלְפִּיּוֹת בְּהַשִּׂיאָךְ,
when You exalt the Hill of Talpios

v'hōshi-o no.   וְהוֹשִׁיעָה נָּא.
and bring salvation now.

CHAZZAN, THEN CONGREGATION:

ONO AYL, NO,   אָנָּא אֵל נָא,
HŌSHANO V'HŌSHI-O NO.   הוֹשַׁעְנָא וְהוֹשִׁיעָה נָּא.

Please God, please! Save now and bring salvation now.

ALL CONTINUE:

AYL, NO, to-inu k'se ōvayd,   אֵל נָא תָּעִינוּ כְּשֶׂה אֹבֵד,
Please God! We have strayed like lost sheep;

sh'maynu mi-sifr'cho al t'abayd,   שְׁמֵנוּ מִסִּפְרְךָ אַל תְּאַבֵּד,
do not cause our name to be lost from Your Book —

hōshano v'hōshi-o no.   הוֹשַׁעְנָא וְהוֹשִׁיעָה נָּא.
save now and bring salvation now.

Ayl, no, r'ay es tzōn haharaygo,   אֵל נָא רְעֵה אֶת צֹאן הַהֲרֵגָה,
Please God! Tend the sheep of the slaughter,

k'tzufo v'olecho harugo,   קְצוּפָה וְעָלֶיךָ הֲרוּגָה,
who are the victims of wrath and are killed for Your sake —

hōshano v'hōshi-o no.   הוֹשַׁעְנָא וְהוֹשִׁיעָה נָּא.
save now and bring salvation now.

Ayl, no, tzōn'cho v'tzōn mar-isecho,   אֵל נָא צֹאנְךָ וְצֹאן מַרְעִיתֶךָ,
Please God! Your sheep and the sheep of Your pasture,

p'ulos'cho v'ra-yosecho,   פְּעֻלָּתְךָ וְרַעְיָתֶךָ,
Your accomplishment and Your beloved —

hōshano v'hōshi-o no.   הוֹשַׁעְנָא וְהוֹשִׁיעָה נָּא.
save now and bring salvation now.

Ayl, no, aniyay hatzōn,   אֵל נָא עֲנִיֵּי הַצֹּאן,
Please God! The poorest of the sheep,

sichom anay b'ays rotzōn,   שִׂיחָם עֲנֵה בְּעֵת רָצוֹן,
answer their prayers at an opportune time —

hōshano v'hōshi-o no.   הוֹשַׁעְנָא וְהוֹשִׁיעָה נָּא.
save now and bring salvation now.

Ayl, no, nōs'ay l'cho a-yin,   אֵל נָא נוֹשְׂאֵי לְךָ עַיִן,
Please God! Those who raise their eyes to You,

miskōm'mayhem yih-yu ch'a-yin,   מִתְקוֹמְמֵיהֶם יִהְיוּ כְאַיִן,
may those who rise against them be as naught —

hōshano v'hōshi-o no.

הוֹשַׁעְנָא וְהוֹשִׁיעָה נָּא.

save now and bring salvation now.

Ayl, no, limnas'chay l'cho ma-yim,

אֵל נָא לִמְנַסְּכֵי לְךָ מַיִם,

Please God! Those who pour water before You,

k'mima-ainay haishu-o
yish-avun ma-yim,

כְּמִמַּעְיְנֵי הַיְשׁוּעָה
יִשְׁאֲבוּן מָיִם,

from the springs of salvation may they draw water —

hōshano v'hōshi-o no.

הוֹשַׁעְנָא וְהוֹשִׁיעָה נָּא.

save now and bring salvation now.

Ayl, no, ya-alu l'tziyōn mōshi-im,

אֵל נָא יַעֲלוּ לְצִיּוֹן מוֹשִׁיעִים,

Please God! May saviors arise from Zion;

t'fulim b'cho uvshimcho nōsho-im,

טְפוּלִים בְּךָ וּבְשִׁמְךָ נוֹשָׁעִים,

those who cling to You and are saved in Your Name —

hōshano v'hōshi-o no.

הוֹשַׁעְנָא וְהוֹשִׁיעָה נָּא.

save now and bring salvation now.

Ayl, no, chamutz b'godim,

אֵל נָא חֲמוּץ בְּגָדִים,

Please God! With bloodied clothes,

z'ōm l'na-ayr kol bōg'dim,

זְעוֹם לְנַעֵר כָּל בּוֹגְדִים,

be enraged to shake out all the rebels —

hōshano v'hōshi-o no.

הוֹשַׁעְנָא וְהוֹשִׁיעָה נָּא.

save now and bring salvation now.

Ayl, no, v'zochōr tizkōr,

אֵל נָא וְזָכוֹר תִּזְכּוֹר,

Please God! Remember, may You remember,

han'churay b'lesech vochōr,

הַנְּכוּרֵי בְּלֶתֶךְ וָכוֹר,

those purchased for a lesech and a kor —

hōshano v'hōshi-o no.

הוֹשַׁעְנָא וְהוֹשִׁיעָה נָּא.

save now and bring salvation now.

Ayl, no, dōr'shecho b'anfay arovōs,

אֵל נָא דוֹרְשֶׁיךָ בְּעַנְפֵי עֲרָבוֹת,

Please God! Those who seek You with willow branches,

ga-yom sh'ay may-arovōs,

גַּעְיָם שְׁעֵה מֵעֲרָבוֹת,

to their cries turn, from Aravos —

hōshano v'hōshi-o no.

הוֹשַׁעְנָא וְהוֹשִׁיעָה נָּא.

save now and bring salvation now.

Ayl, no, boraych b'itur shono,

אֵל נָא בָּרֵךְ בְּעִטּוּר שָׁנָה,

Please God! With a crown bless this year;

amorai r'tzay

אֲמָרַי רְצֵה

may you find my words favorable

b'filuli b'yōm hōshano, בְּפִלּוּלִי בְּיוֹם הוֹשַׁעְנָא,

as I pray on this day of Hoshana —

hōshano v'hōshi-o no. הוֹשַׁעְנָא וְהוֹשִׁיעָה נָּא.

save now and bring salvation now.

CHAZZAN, THEN CONGREGATION:

ONO AYL, NO, אָנָּא אֵל נָא,

HŌSHANO V'HŌSHI-O NO, הוֹשַׁעְנָא וְהוֹשִׁיעָה נָּא,

OVINU OTO. אָבִינוּ אָתָּה.

Please God, please! Save now and bring salvation now, for You are our Father.

ALL CONTINUE:

L'MA-AN TOMIM b'dōrōsov, לְמַעַן תָּמִים בְּדוֹרוֹתָיו,

In the merit of [Noah] the one who was perfect in his generations,

hanimlot b'rōv tzidkōsov, הַנִּמְלָט בְּרוֹב צִדְקוֹתָיו,

he escaped by his abundant righteousness,

mutzol mi-shetef b'vō mabul ma-yim. מֻצָּל מִשֶּׁטֶף בְּבֹא מַבּוּל מָיִם.

and was rescued from inundation upon the arrival of the Flood of water.

L'ōm ani chōmo, לְאוֹם אֲנִי חוֹמָה,

For [the nation that declares,] "I am a wall,"

hōshano v'hōshi-o no, ovinu oto. הוֹשַׁעְנָא וְהוֹשִׁיעָה נָּא, אָבִינוּ אָתָּה.

may You save now and bring salvation now, for You are our Father.

L'ma-an sholaym v'chol ma-asim, לְמַעַן שָׁלֵם בְּכָל מַעֲשִׂים,

In the merit of [Abraham] the one who was perfect in all deeds,

ham'nuse ba-asoro nisim, הַמְנֻסֶּה בַּעֲשָׂרָה נִסִּים,

who was proven through ten trials;

k'shor mal-ochim nom כְּשֹׁר מַלְאָכִים נָם

yukach no m'at ma-yim. יֻקַּח נָא מְעַט מָיִם.

upon seeing the angels he said, "Let there be brought some water."

L'voro kachamo, לְבָרָה כַּחַמָּה,

For [the people] brilliant as the sun,

hōshano v'hōshi-o no, ovinu oto. הוֹשַׁעְנָא וְהוֹשִׁיעָה נָּא, אָבִינוּ אָתָּה.

may You save now and bring salvation now, for You are our Father.

L'ma-an rach v'yochid לְמַעַן רַךְ וְיָחִיד

nechenat p'ri l'may-o, נֶחֱנַט פְּרִי לְמֵאָה,

In the merit of [Isaac] the tender and only fruit which blossomed at one hundred,

---

◆§ **In the Merit of the One Who Was Perfect.**

This *Hoshana* recounts the love for God which was the hallmark of the righteous people of old. Since that *Hoshana* was a prayer for an end to Israel's suffering in exile, it men-

zo-ak a-yay ha-se l'ōlo,

זָעַק אַיֵּה הַשֶּׂה לְעוֹלָה,

who cried, "Where is the lamb for the offering?"

bis'ruhu avodov motzonu ma-yim.

בְּשָׂרְוּהוּ עֲבָדָיו מָצָאנוּ מָיִם.

His servants informed him, "We have found water."

L'gōlo v'suro,

לְגוֹלָה וְסוּרָה,

hōshano v'hōshi-o no, ovinu oto.

הוֹשַׁעְנָא וְהוֹשִׁיעָה נָּא, אָבִינוּ אָתָּה.

For the exiled and displaced, may You save now and bring salvation now,
for You are our Father.

L'ma-an kidam s'ays b'rocho,

לְמַעַן קִדַּם שְׂאֵת בְּרָכָה,

In the merit of [Jacob] the first with a gift for the blessing,

hanistam ulshimcho chiko,

הַנִּשְׂטַם וּלְשִׁמְךָ חִכָּה,

who was hated but who yearned for Your Name,

m'yachaym b'maklōs
b'shikasōs hama-yim.

מְיַחֵם בְּמַקְלוֹת
בְּשִׁקֲתוֹת הַמָּיִם.

he stimulated with rods at the troughs of water.

L'dom'so l'somor,

לְדָמְתָה לְתָמָר,

For those likened to a palm tree,

hōshano v'hōshi-o no, ovinu oto.

הוֹשַׁעְנָא וְהוֹשִׁיעָה נָּא, אָבִינוּ אָתָּה.

may You save now and bring salvation now, for You are our Father.

L'ma-an tzodak he-yōs l'cho l'chōhayn,

לְמַעַן צָדַק הֱיוֹת לְךָ לְכֹהֵן,

In the merit of [Levi] the one worthy of being Your Kohen,

kechoson p'ayr y'chahayn,

כֶּחָתָן פְּאֵר יְכַהֵן,

adorned like a bridegroom he would serve,

m'nuse b'maso
b'may m'rivas ma-yim.

מְנֻסֶּה בְּמַסָּה
בְּמֵי מְרִיבַת מָיִם.

he was proven at Massah, at Merivah's water.

L'hohor hatōv,

לְהָהָר הַטּוֹב,

For the good mountain,

hōshano v'hōshi-o no, ovinu oto.

הוֹשַׁעְנָא וְהוֹשִׁיעָה נָּא, אָבִינוּ אָתָּה.

may You save now and bring salvation now, for You are our Father.

L'ma-an pō-ar he-yōs g'vir l'echov,

לְמַעַן פֹּאַר הֱיוֹת גְּבִיר לְאֶחָיו,

In the merit of the splendrous one who would be master over his brothers,

y'hudo asher govar b'echov,

יְהוּדָה אֲשֶׁר גָּבַר בְּאֶחָיו,

Judah who ruled over his brothers,

mispar rōva midol'yov yizal ma-yim.

מִסְפַּר רְבַע מִדָּלְיָו יִזַּל מָיִם.

though he was fourth, from his buckets shall pour water.

---

tioned an incident involving fire in the life of each Patriarch. This *Hoshana* is a prayer for rain, so the biographical events are related to water.

Lō lonu ki im l'ma-ancho,
לֹא לָנוּ כִּי אִם לְמַעֲנָךְ,
Not for our sake but for Yours,

hōshano v'hōshi-o no, ovinu oto.
הוֹשַׁעְנָא וְהוֹשִׁיעָה נָא, אָבִינוּ אָתָּה.
may You save now and bring salvation now, for You are our Father.

L'ma-an onov mikōl v'ne-emon,
לְמַעַן עָנָיו מִכֹּל וְנֶאֱמָן,
In the merit of [Moses] the humblest of all and the most trusted,

asher b'tzidkō kilkayl hamon,
אֲשֶׁר בְּצִדְקוֹ כִּלְכֵּל הַמָּן,
for whose righteousness He supplied manna,

moshuch l'gō-ayl u-moshuy mima-yim.
מָשׁוּךְ לְגוֹאֵל וּמָשׁוּי מִמַּיִם.
he was drawn to be a redeemer and pulled from the water.

L'zōs hanishkofo,
לְזֹאת הַנִּשְׁקָפָה,
For the one who gazes down,

hōshano v'hōshi-o no, ovinu oto.
הוֹשַׁעְנָא וְהוֹשִׁיעָה נָא, אָבִינוּ אָתָּה.
may You save now and bring salvation now, for You are our Father.

L'ma-an samtō
לְמַעַן שַׂמְתּוֹ
k'mal-achay m'rōmim,
כְּמַלְאֲכֵי מְרוֹמִים,
In the merit of [Aaron] the one You emplaced like exalted angels,

halōvaysh u-rim v'sumim,
הַלּוֹבֵשׁ אוּרִים וְתֻמִּים,
m'tzuve lovō bamikdosh
מְצֻוֶּה לָבֹא בַּמִּקְדָּשׁ
he who, wearing the Urim and Tumim, is commanded to come to the Temple

b'kidush yoda-yim v'ragla-yim
בְּקִדּוּשׁ יָדַיִם וְרַגְלַיִם
urchitzas ma-yim.
וּרְחִיצַת מַיִם.
with sanctified hands and feet, and an immersion in water.

L'chōlas ahavo,
לְחוֹלַת אַהֲבָה,
For the one sick with love,

hōshano v'hōshi-o no, ovinu oto.
הוֹשַׁעְנָא וְהוֹשִׁיעָה נָא, אָבִינוּ אָתָּה.
may You save now and bring salvation now, for You are our Father.

L'ma-an n'vi-o
לְמַעַן נְבִיאָה
m'chōlas machana-yim,
מְחוֹלַת מַחֲנַיִם,
In the merit of [Miriam] the prophetess of the dance of the camps,

lichmayhay layv
לִכְמֵהֵי לֵב
hus'mo ayna-yim,
הוּשְׂמָה עֵינַיִם,
to those of thirsting heart she was an inspiration,

l'ragloh rotzo
לְרַגְלָהּ רָצָה
alōs voredes b'ayr ma-yim.
עֲלוֹת וְרֶדֶת בְּאֵר מַיִם.
at her feet ran, rising and descending, the well of water.

L'tōvu ōholov,

לְטוֹבוּ אֹהֳלָיו,

For the one of goodly tents,

hōshano v'hōshi-o no, ovinu oto.

הוֹשַׁעְנָא וְהוֹשִׁיעָה נָא, אָבִינוּ אָתָּה.

may You save now and bring salvation now, for You are our Father.

L'ma-an m'shorays lō mosh may-ōhel,

לְמַעַן מְשָׁרֵת לֹא מָשׁ מֵאֹהֶל,

In the merit of [Joshua] the servant who moved not from the tent,

v'ru-ach hakōdesh olov ihayl,

וְרוּחַ הַקֹּדֶשׁ עָלָיו אֹהֵל,

upon him the Holy Spirit rested,

b'ovrō va-yardayn nichr'su hama-yim.

בְּעָבְרוֹ בַיַּרְדֵּן נִכְרְתוּ הַמָּיִם.

when he crossed the Jordan, cut was the water.

L'yofo u-voro,

לְיָפֶה וּבָרָה,

For the beautiful and brilliant,

hōshano v'hōshi-o no, ovinu oto.

הוֹשַׁעְנָא וְהוֹשִׁיעָה נָא, אָבִינוּ אָתָּה.

may You save now and bring salvation now, for You are our Father.

L'ma-an limad r'ōs l'tōvo ōs,

לְמַעַן לִמַּד רְאוֹת לְטוֹבָה אוֹת,

In the merit of [Gideon] the one who showed how to perceive a good omen,

zo-ak a-yay niflo-ōs,

זָעַק אַיֵּה נִפְלָאוֹת,

he cried, "Where are Your wonders,"

mitzo tal migizo
m'lō hasayfel ma-yim.

מִצָּה טַל מִגִּזָּה
מְלֹא הַסֵּפֶל מָיִם.

from a fleece he pressed dew, a bowl full of water.

L'chalas l'vonōn,

לְכַלַּת לְבָנוֹן,

For the bride of Lebanon,

hōshano v'hōshi-o no, ovinu oto.

הוֹשַׁעְנָא וְהוֹשִׁיעָה נָא, אָבִינוּ אָתָּה.

may You save now and bring salvation now, for You are our Father.

L'ma-an k'lulay
asōs milchamtecho,

לְמַעַן כְּלוּלֵי
עֲשׂוֹת מִלְחַמְתֶּךָ,

In the merit of [Gideon's army] the dedicated fighters in Your war,

asher b'yodom tato y'shu-osecho,

אֲשֶׁר בְּיָדָם תַּתָּה יְשׁוּעָתֶךָ,

into whose hands You placed Your salvation,

tz'rufay migōy
b'lok'kom b'yodom ma-yim.

צְרוּפֵי מִגּוֹי
בְּלָקְקָם בְּיָדָם מָיִם.

proven purest of the nation by having lapped from their hand water.

L'lō vog'du voch,

לְלֹא בָגְדוּ בָךְ,

For those that did not rebel against You,

hōshano v'hōshi-o no, ovinu oto.

הוֹשַׁעְנָא וְהוֹשִׁיעָה נָא, אָבִינוּ אָתָּה.

may You save now and bring salvation now, for You are our Father.

L'ma-an yochid tzōr'rim dosh,   לְמַעַן יָחִיד צוֹרְרִים דָּשׁ,

In the merit of [Samson] the only child, who thrashed the oppressors,

asher mayrechem l'nozir hukdosh,   אֲשֶׁר מֵרֶחֶם לְנָזִיר הֻקְדַּשׁ,

sanctified from the womb as a Nazir;

mimachtaysh lechi   מִמַּכְתֵּשׁ לֶחִי

hivkato lō ma-yim.   הִבְקַעְתָּ לוֹ מָיִם.

from the hollow of a jawbone You brought him water.

L'ma-an shaym kodshecho,   לְמַעַן שֵׁם קָדְשֶׁךָ,

In the merit of Your Holy Name,

hōshano v'hōshi-o no, ovinu oto.   הוֹשַׁעְנָא וְהוֹשִׁיעָה נָּא, אָבִינוּ אָתָּה.

may You save now and bring salvation now, for You are our Father.

L'ma-an tōv hōlaych v'godayl,   לְמַעַן **טוֹב** הוֹלֵךְ וְגָדֵל,

In the merit of [Samuel] the good and increasingly exalted one

asher may-ōshek aydo chidayl,   אֲשֶׁר מֵעֹשֶׁק עֵדָה חָדֵל,

who restrained himself from robbing the flock,

b'shuv om maychayt   בְּשׁוּב עַם מֵחֲטֹא

tzov sh'ov ma-yim.   צָו שְׁאָב מָיִם.

when the people repented he bade them draw water.

L'novo kirusholo-yim,   לְ**נָ**אוָה כִּירוּשָׁלָיִם,

For the one as beautiful as Jerusalem,

hōshano v'hōshi-o no, ovinu oto.   הוֹשַׁעְנָא וְהוֹשִׁיעָה נָּא, אָבִינוּ אָתָּה.

may You save now and bring salvation now, for You are our Father.

L'ma-an cha-yoch m'charkayr b'shir,   לְמַעַן **חַיָּךְ** מְכַרְכֵּר בְּשִׁיר,

In the merit of [David] the smiling one, dancing with song,

ham'lamayd tōro b'chol k'lay shir,   הַמְלַמֵּד תּוֹרָה בְּכָל כְּלֵי שִׁיר,

who teaches Torah accompanied by every sort of instrument,

m'nasaych l'fonov   מְנַסֵּךְ לְפָנָיו

k'so-av sh'sōs ma-yim.   כִּתְאָב שְׁתוֹת מָיִם.

he poured libations before Him though he thirsted to drink water.

L'somu v'cho sivrom,   לְ**שָׂ**מוּ בְךָ סִבְרָם,

For those who place their hope in You,

hōshano v'hōshi-o no, ovinu oto.   הוֹשַׁעְנָא וְהוֹשִׁיעָה נָּא, אָבִינוּ אָתָּה.

may You save now and bring salvation now, for You are our Father.

L'ma-an zoch olo va-s'oro,   לְמַעַן **זָ**ךְ עָלָה בַסְעָרָה,

In the merit of [Elijah] the pure one who ascended in a storm wind,

ham'kanay u-mayshiv evro,   הַמְקַנֵּא וּמֵשִׁיב עֶבְרָה,

who avenged and turned back fury,

l'filulō yor'do aysh
  v'li-chacho ofor u-ma-yim.

לִפְלוּלוֹ יָרְדָה אֵשׁ
וְלִחֲכָה עָפָר וּמָיִם.

at his prayer fire descended which consumed dust and water.

L'ayneho b'raychōs,

לְעֵינֶיהָ בְּרֵכוֹת,

For the one whose eyes are [like] pools,

hōshano v'hōshi-o no, ovinu oto.

הוֹשַׁעְנָא וְהוֹשִׁיעָה נָא, אָבִינוּ אָתָּה.

may You save now and bring salvation now, for You are our Father.

L'ma-an v'shayrays be-emes l'rabō

לְמַעַן וְשֵׁרֵת בֶּאֱמֶת לְרַבּוֹ,

In the merit of [Elisha] the one who served his master earnestly,

pi sh'na-yim b'ruchō ne-etzal bō,

פִּי שְׁנַיִם בְּרוּחוֹ נֶאֱצַל בּוֹ,

a double measure of his spirit was vested in him,

b'kachtō m'nagayn
  nismal'u gayvim ma-yim.

בְּקַחְתּוֹ מְנַגֵּן
נִתְמַלְּאוּ גֵבִים מַיִם.

when he summoned a musician the cisterns were filled with water.

L'fotzu mi chomōcho,

לְפֹצוּ מִי כָמֹכָה,

For those who exclaimed, "Who is like You?"

hōshano v'hōshi-o no, ovinu oto.

הוֹשַׁעְנָא וְהוֹשִׁיעָה נָא, אָבִינוּ אָתָּה.

may You save now and bring salvation now, for You are our Father.

L'ma-an hirhayr asōs r'tzōnecho,

לְמַעַן הִרְהֵר עֲשׂוֹת רְצוֹנֶךָ,

In the merit of [Hezekiah] the one who meant to do Your will,

hamachriz t'shuvo l'tzōnecho,

הַמַּכְרִיז תְּשׁוּבָה לְצֹאנֶךָ,

he cried out, "Repentance," to Your sheep,

oz b'vō m'chorayf
  sosam aynōs ma-yim.

אָז בְּבֹא מְחָרֵף
סָתַם עֵינוֹת מָיִם.

then when the blasphemer came he sealed the springs of water.

L'tziyōn michlal yōfi,

לְצִיּוֹן מִכְלַל יֹפִי,

For Zion, perfect in beauty,

hōshano v'hōshi-o no, ovinu oto.

הוֹשַׁעְנָא וְהוֹשִׁיעָה נָא, אָבִינוּ אָתָּה.

may You save now and bring salvation now, for You are our Father.

L'ma-an d'roshucho b'sōch hagōlo,

לְמַעַן דְּרָשׁוּךָ בְּתוֹךְ הַגּוֹלָה,

In the merit of [Daniel, Chananiah, Mishael, and Azariah]
those who sought You in midst of the exile,

v'sōd'cho lomō niglo,

וְסוֹדְךָ לָמוֹ נִגְלָה,

Your secret was uncovered to them.

b'li l'hisgo-ayl
  dor'shu zayr'ōnim u-ma-yim.

בְּלִי לְהִתְגָּאֵל
דָּרְשׁוּ זֵרְעוֹנִים וּמָיִם.

Not to defile themselves they requested pulse and water.

L'kōr'echo vatzor,　　　　　　　　　　לִקוֹרְאֶיךָ בַצָּר,

For those who call in distress,

hōshano v'hōshi-o no, ovinu oto.　　　הוֹשַׁעְנָא וְהוֹשִׁיעָה נָּא, אָבִינוּ אָתָּה.

may You save now and bring salvation now, for You are our Father.

L'ma-an gomar chochmo u-vino,　　　　לְמַעַן גָּמַר חָכְמָה וּבִינָה,

In the merit of [Ezra] the one who studied wisdom and understanding,

sōfayr mohir m'falays amono,　　　　　סוֹפֵר מָהִיר מְפַלֵּשׁ אֱמָנָה,

a skillful scribe, expounder of faith,

m'chak'maynu amorim　　　　　　　　מְחַכְּמֵנוּ אֲמָרִים

ham'shulim b'rachavay ma-yim.　　　　הַמְּשׁוּלִים בְּרַחֲבֵי מָיִם.

he made us wise with sayings that are likened to expanses of water.

L'rabosi om,　　　　　　　　　　　　לְרַבָּתִי עָם,

For [the city] great with people,

hōshano v'hōshi-o no, ovinu oto.　　　הוֹשַׁעְנָא וְהוֹשִׁיעָה נָּא, אָבִינוּ אָתָּה.

may You save now and bring salvation now, for You are our Father.

L'ma-an bo-ay l'cho ha-yōm b'chol layv,　לְמַעַן בָּאֵי לְךָ הַיּוֹם בְּכָל לֵב,

*For the sake of [the present congregation] those who come to You today
with all their heart,*

shōf'chim l'cho si-ach b'lō layv volayv,　שׁוֹפְכִים לְךָ שִׂיחַ בְּלֹא לֵב וָלֵב,

pouring prayer before You with undivided heart,

shō-alim mim'cho ōz mitrōs ma-yim.　　שׁוֹאֲלִים מִמְּךָ עוֹז מִטְרוֹת מָיִם.

asking You for powerful rains of water.

L'shōr'rucho va-yom,　　　　　　　　לְשׁוֹרְרוּךָ בַיָּם,

For those who sang to You at the Sea,

hōshano v'hōshi-o no, ovinu oto.　　　הוֹשַׁעְנָא וְהוֹשִׁיעָה נָּא, אָבִינוּ אָתָּה.

may You save now and bring salvation now, for You are our Father.

L'ma-an ōm'ray yigdal sh'mecho,　　　לְמַעַן אוֹמְרֵי יִגְדַּל שְׁמֶךָ,

For the sake of those [Israel] who say, "May Your Name be exalted!"

v'haym nachalos'cho v'amecho,　　　　וְהֵם נַחֲלָתְךָ וְעַמֶּךָ,

they are Your heritage and Your people;

tz'ma-yim l'yesh-acho,　　　　　　　צְמֵאִים לִישׁוּעֶךָ,

k'eretz a-yayfo lama-yim.　　　　　　כְּאֶרֶץ עֲיֵפָה לַמָּיִם.

they thirst for Your salvation as does a land that thirsts for water.

L'sarto lomō m'nucho,　　　　　　　לְתַרְתָּ לָמוֹ מְנוּחָה,

For those for whom You scouted a resting place,

hōshano v'hōshi-o no, ovinu oto.　　　הוֹשַׁעְנָא וְהוֹשִׁיעָה נָּא, אָבִינוּ אָתָּה.

may You save now and bring salvation now, for You are our Father.

SOME PUT ASIDE THE *LULAV* AND *ESROG* AND TAKE UP THE *HOSHANA*- BUNDLE OF FIVE WILLOW
TWIGS. THIS IS HELD UNTIL IT IS BEATEN AT THE END OF THE SERVICE. OTHERS RETAIN THE *LULAV*
AND *ESROG* AND DO NOT TAKE UP THE *HOSHANA*- BUNDLE UNTIL IT IS TO BE BEATEN.

CHAZZAN, THEN CONGREGATION:

HŌSHANO, AYL NO,   הוֹשַׁעְנָא, אֵל נָא,

ONO HŌSHI-O NO.   אָנָּא הוֹשִׁיעָה נָא.

Save now, please God, please bring salvation now;

HŌSHANO, S'LACH NO,   הוֹשַׁעְנָא, סְלַח נָא

V'HATZLICHO NO,   וְהַצְלִיחָה נָא,

save now, forgive now, bring success now,

V'HŌSHI-AYNU AYL MO-U-ZAYNU.   וְהוֹשִׁיעֵנוּ אֵל מָעֻזֵּנוּ.

and save us, God, our Fortress.

ALL CONTINUE:

TA-ANE EMUNIM,   תַּעֲנֶה אֱמוּנִים,

shōf'chim l'cho layv kama-yim,   שׁוֹפְכִים לְךָ לֵב כַּמַּיִם,

Answer the faithful* who pour out their heart to You like water –

v'hōshi-o no,   וְהוֹשִׁיעָה נָא,

and bring salvation now,

l'ma-an bo vo-aysh u-vama-yim,   לְמַעַן בָּא בָאֵשׁ וּבַמַּיִם,

in the merit of [Abraham] the one who entered fire and water –

gozar v'nom yukach no m'at ma-yim,   גָּזַר וְנָם יֻקַּח נָא מְעַט מַיִם,

who decreed saying, "Let there now be taken some water";

v'hatzlicho no,   וְהַצְלִיחָה נָא,

v'hōshi-aynu Ayl mo-u-zaynu.   וְהוֹשִׁיעֵנוּ אֵל מָעֻזֵּנוּ.

and bring success now and save us, God, our Fortress.

Ta-ane d'golim, gozu gizray ma-yim,   תַּעֲנֶה דְגָלִים, גָּזוּ גִּזְרֵי מַיִם,

Answer the [Twelve] bannered [Tribes] who passed through divisions of water –

v'hōshi-o no,   וְהוֹשִׁיעָה נָא,

and bring salvation now,

l'ma-an hane-ekad   לְמַעַן הַנֶּעֱקַד

b'sha-ar ha-shoma-yim,   בְּשַׁעַר הַשָּׁמַיִם,

in the merit of [Isaac] the one bound at the gateway of Heaven,

v'shov v'chofar b'ayrōs ma-yim,   וְשָׁב וְחָפַר בְּאֵרוֹת מַיִם,

who returned and dug wells of water;

v'hatzlicho no,   וְהַצְלִיחָה נָא,

v'hōshi-aynu Ayl mo-u-zaynu.   וְהוֹשִׁיעֵנוּ אֵל מָעֻזֵּנוּ.

and bring success now and save us, God, our Fortress.

⋙ **Answer the Faithful**
Following the theme of the preceding

Hoshana, we again ask for rain in the merit of
our righteous forebears.

Ta-ane zakim, chōnim alay ma-yim,   תַּעֲנֶה זַכִּים, חוֹנִים עֲלֵי מָיִם,

Answer [the Israelites] the pure ones who encamped near the water —

v'hōshi-o no,   וְהוֹשִׁיעָה נָּא,

and bring salvation now,

l'ma-an cholok m'fatzayl maklōs   לְמַעַן חָלָק מְפַצֵּל מַקְלוֹת

   b'shikasōs hama-yim,   בְּשִׁקֲתוֹת הַמָּיִם,

in the merit of [Jacob] the smooth-skinned one who peeled rods
at the trough of water,

to-an v'gol even mib'ayr ma-yim,   טָעַן וְגָל אֶבֶן מִבְּאֵר מָיִם,

who lifted and rolled away a boulder from a well of water;

v'hatzlicho no,   וְהַצְלִיחָה נָא,

   v'hōshi-aynu Ayl mo-u-zaynu.   וְהוֹשִׁיעֵנוּ אֵל מָעוּזֵּנוּ.

and bring success now and save us, God, our Fortress.

Ta-ane y'didim, nōchalay dos   תַּעֲנֶה יְדִידִים, נוֹחֲלֵי דָת

   m'shulas ma-yim,   מְשׁוּלַת מָיִם,

Answer the beloved heirs of the mandate likened to water —

v'hōshi-o no,   וְהוֹשִׁיעָה נָּא,

and bring salvation now,

l'ma-an koru b'mish-anōsom ma-yim,   לְמַעַן כָּרוּ בְּמִשְׁעֲנוֹתָם מָיִם,

in the merit of those who dug with their staffs for water,

l'hochin lomō   לְהָכִין לָמוֹ

   ultze-etzo-aymō ma-yim,   וּלְצֶאֱצָאֵימוֹ מָיִם,

to prepare, for themselves and for their offspring, water;

v'hatzlicho no,   וְהַצְלִיחָה נָא,

   v'hōshi-aynu Ayl mo-u-zaynu.   וְהוֹשִׁיעֵנוּ אֵל מָעוּזֵּנוּ.

and bring success now and save us, God, our Fortress.

Ta-ane mischan'nim,   תַּעֲנֶה מִתְחַנְּנִים,

   k'vishimōn alay ma-yim,   כְּבִישִׁימוֹן עֲלֵי מָיִם,

Answer those who beseech as in the Wilderness for water —

v'hōshi-o no,   וְהוֹשִׁיעָה נָּא,

and bring salvation now,

l'ma-an ne-eman ba-yis   לְמַעַן נֶאֱמַן בַּיִת

in the merit of [Moses] the most trusted of the household,

maspik lo-om ma-yim.   מַסְפִּיק לָעָם מָיִם,

who supplied the people with water,

sela hoch va-yozuvu ma-yim,   סֶלַע הָךְ וַיָּזוּבוּ מָיִם,

who struck the rock and there flowed water;

v'hatzlicho no,
וְהַצְלִיחָה נָא,

v'hōshi-aynu Ayl mo-u-zaynu.
וְהוֹשִׁיעֵנוּ אֵל מָעוּזֵּנוּ.

and bring success now and save us, God, our Fortress.

Ta-ane ōnim ali v'ayr ma-yim,
תַּעֲנֶה עוֹנִים עֲלִי בְאֵר מַיִם,

Answer those who responded, "Ascend, O well of water" —

v'hōshi-o no,
וְהוֹשִׁיעָה נָא,

and bring salvation now,

l'ma-an pukad
לְמַעַן פֻּקַד

b'may m'rivas ma-yim,
בְּמֵי מְרִיבַת מַיִם,

in the merit of [Aaron] the one assigned at Merivah's waters,

tz'may-im l'hashkōsom ma-yim,
צְמֵאִים לְהַשְׁקוֹתָם מַיִם,

to give drink to those thirsting for water;

v'hatzlicho no,
וְהַצְלִיחָה נָא,

v'hōshi-aynu Ayl mo-u-zaynu.
וְהוֹשִׁיעֵנוּ אֵל מָעוּזֵּנוּ.

and bring success now and save us, God, our Fortress.

Ta-ane k'dōshim
תַּעֲנֶה קְדוֹשִׁים

m'nas'chim l'cho ma-yim,
מְנַסְּכִים לְךָ מַיִם,

Answer the holy ones who pour before You libations of water —

v'hōshi-o no,
וְהוֹשִׁיעָה נָא,

and bring salvation now,

l'ma-an rōsh m'shōr'rim
לְמַעַן רֹאשׁ מְשׁוֹרְרִים

k'so-av sh'sōs ma-yim,
כְּתָאַב שְׁתוֹת מַיִם,

in the merit of [David] the foremost singer who,
though thirsting to drink water,

shov v'nosach l'cho ma-yim,
שָׁב וְנִסַּךְ לְךָ מַיִם,

poured before You a libation of water;

v'hatzlicho no,
וְהַצְלִיחָה נָא,

v'hōshi-aynu Ayl mo-uzaynu.
וְהוֹשִׁיעֵנוּ אֵל מָעוּזֵּנוּ.

and bring success now and save us, God, our Fortress.

Ta-ane shō-alim
תַּעֲנֶה שׁוֹאֲלִים

b'ribu-a eshlay ma-yim,
בְּרִבּוּעַ אֶשְׁלֵי מַיִם,

Answer those who ask with a quartet of species planted near water —

v'hōshi-o no,
וְהוֹשִׁיעָה נָא,

and bring salvation now,

l'ma-an tayl talpiyōs mōtzo ma-yim,
לְמַעַן תֵּל תַּלְפִּיּוֹת מוֹצָא מַיִם,

in the merit of the Hill of Talpios [the Temple], source of water,

tiftach eretz v'sar-if shoma-yim,
תִּפְתַּח אֶרֶץ וְתַרְעִיף שָׁמַיִם,

may the earth open wide and the heavens give rain;

v'hátzlicho no,

וְהַצְלִיחָה נָא,

v'hōshi-aynu Ayl mo-u-zaynu.

וְהוֹשִׁיעֵנוּ אֵל מָעֻזֵּנוּ.

and bring success now and save us, God, our Fortress.

CHAZZAN, THEN CONGREGATION:

RACHEM NO

רַחֵם נָא

K'HAL ADAS Y'SHURUN,

קְהַל עֲדַת יְשֻׁרוּן,

Be merciful, please, with the congregation of Jeshurun's flock;

S'LACH UMCHAL AVŌNOM,

סְלַח וּמְחַל עֲוֹנָם,

forgive and pardon their iniquities;

V'HŌSHI-AYNU

וְהוֹשִׁיעֵנוּ

ELŌHAY YISH-AYNU.

אֱלֹהֵי יִשְׁעֵנוּ.

and save us, God of our salvation.

ALL CONTINUE:

OZ K'AYNAY AVODIM

אָז כְּעֵינֵי עֲבָדִים

el yad adōnim,

אֶל יַד אֲדוֹנִים,

Then, like the eyes of slaves* looking to their master's hand,

bonu l'fonecho n'dōnim,

בָּאנוּ לְפָנֶיךָ נְדוֹנִים,

so did we come before You for judgment —

v'hōshi-aynu Elōhay yish-aynu.

וְהוֹשִׁיעֵנוּ אֱלֹהֵי יִשְׁעֵנוּ.

so save us, God of our salvation.

Gay-e Adōnay ho-adōnim,

גֵּאֶה אֲדוֹנֵי הָאֲדוֹנִים,

nisgoru vonu m'donim,

נִתְגָּרוּ בָנוּ מְדָנִים,

Proud One, Lord of lords, they have stirred up strife within us;

doshunu uv-olunu zulos'cho adōnim,

דָּשׁוּנוּ וּבְעָלוּנוּ זוּלָתְךָ אֲדוֹנִים,

lords have trodden upon us and become our masters, excluding You —

v'hōshi-aynu Elōhay yish-aynu.

וְהוֹשִׁיעֵנוּ אֱלֹהֵי יִשְׁעֵנוּ.

so save us, God of our salvation.

Hayn gashnu ha-yōm b'sachanun,

הֵן גַּשְׁנוּ הַיּוֹם בְּתַחֲנוּן,

Indeed we have approached with supplication today,

odecho rachum v'chanun,

עָדֶיךָ רַחוּם וְחַנּוּן,

before You, O merciful and gracious One.

v'siparnu nifl'ōsecho b'shinun,

וְסִפַּרְנוּ נִפְלְאוֹתֶיךָ בְּשִׁנּוּן,

And we have recounted, and repeated Your wonders —

◦§ **Then, Like the Eyes of Slaves.**
Slaves have no avenues of support other than the largesse of their master. Like- wise, Israel has no source of sustenance other than its faith in God to Whom it turns its eyes.

וְהוֹשִׁיעֵנוּ אֱלֹהֵי יִשְׁעֵנוּ.
v'hōshi-aynu Elōhay yish-aynu.
so save us, God of our salvation.

זָבַת חָלָב וּדְבָשׁ, נָא אַל תִּיבָשׁ,
Zovas cholov udvosh, no al tivosh,
Where milk and honey flow please make not arid.

חַשְׁרַת מַיִם בְּאִבֶיהָ תֶּחְבָּשׁ,
chashras ma-yim b'ibeho techbosh,
With watering clouds clothe her produce —

וְהוֹשִׁיעֵנוּ אֱלֹהֵי יִשְׁעֵנוּ.
v'hōshi-aynu Elōhay yish-aynu.
and save us, God of our salvation.

טָעֵנוּ בִשְׁמֵנָה,
T'aynu vishmayno,
בְּיַד שִׁבְעָה וּשְׁמוֹנָה,
b'yad shiv-o ush-mōno,
Plant us in the fertile land, by the hand of seven and eight;

יָשָׁר צַדִּיק אֵל אֱמוּנָה,
yoshor tzadik Ayl emuno,
O just and righteous One, O trustworthy God —

וְהוֹשִׁיעֵנוּ אֱלֹהֵי יִשְׁעֵנוּ.
v'hōshi-aynu Elōhay yish-aynu.
and save us, God of our salvation.

כָּרַתָּ בְרִית לָאָרֶץ,
Korato v'ris lo-oretz,
עֹד כָּל יְמֵי הָאָרֶץ,
ōd kol y'may ho-oretz,
You have made a covenant with the earth, continuously, all the days of the earth,

לְבִלְתִּי פְרָץ בָּהּ פָּרֶץ,
l'vilti f'rotz boh poretz,
not to cause a breach in it —

וְהוֹשִׁיעֵנוּ אֱלֹהֵי יִשְׁעֵנוּ.
v'hōshi-aynu Elōhay yish-aynu.
so save us, God of our salvation.

מִתְחַנְּנִים עֲלֵי מַיִם,
Mischan'nim alay ma-yim,
כַּעֲרָבִים עַל יִבְלֵי מַיִם,
ka-arovim al yivlay ma-yim,
Those who supplicate for water like willows alongside streams of water;

נָא זְכָר לָמוֹ נִסּוּךְ הַמַּיִם,
no z'chor lomō nisuch hama-yim,
please, remember for their sake the libations of water —

וְהוֹשִׁיעֵנוּ אֱלֹהֵי יִשְׁעֵנוּ.
v'hōshi-aynu Elōhay yish-aynu.
and save us, God of our salvation.

שִׂיחִים בְּדֶרֶךְ מַטָּעָתָם,
Sichim b'derech mato-osom,
עוֹמְסִים בְּשַׁוְעָתָם,
ōm'sim b'shav-osom,
Trees, in the direction of their growth, they carry as they supplicate —

עֲנֵם בְּקוֹל פְּגִיעָתָם,
anaym b'kōl p'gi-osom,
respond to the sound of their entreaties —

וְהוֹשִׁיעֵנוּ אֱלֹהֵי יִשְׁעֵנוּ.
v'hōshi-aynu Elōhay yish-aynu.
and save us, God of our salvation.

Pō-ayl y'shu-ōs,   פּוֹעֵל יְשׁוּעוֹת,

   p'nay l'filulom sh'ōs,   פְּנֵה לִפְלוּלָם שְׁעוֹת,

Worker of salvations, heed their prayers and turn to them,

tzad'kaym Ayl l'mōsho-ōs,   צַדְּקֵם אֵל לְמוֹשָׁעוֹת,

adjudge them righteous, O God of salvations —

v'hōshi-aynu Elōhay yish-aynu.   וְהוֹשִׁיעֵנוּ אֱלֹהֵי יִשְׁעֵנוּ.

and save us, God of our salvation.

Kōl rigshom tisha,   קוֹל רִגְשָׁם תֵּשַׁע,

To the voices of their multitudes turn,

tiftach eretz v'yifru yesha,   תִּפְתַּח אֶרֶץ וְיִפְרוּ יֶשַׁע,

open the earth and let salvation sprout,

rav l'hōshi-a v'lō chofaytz resha,   רַב לְהוֹשִׁיעַ וְלֹא חָפֵץ רֶשַׁע,

O He Who is bounteous in salvation, and desires not wickedness —

v'hōshi-aynu Elōhay yish-aynu.   וְהוֹשִׁיעֵנוּ אֱלֹהֵי יִשְׁעֵנוּ.

and save us, God of our salvation.

CHAZZAN, THEN CONGREGATION:

SHA-ARAY SHOMA-YIM P'SACH,   שַׁעֲרֵי שָׁמַיִם פְּתַח,

Open the gates of heaven,

V'ŌTZOR'CHO HATŌV   וְאוֹצָרְךָ הַטּוֹב

LONU SIFTACH,   לָנוּ תִפְתַּח,

and Your goodly treasure trove may You open for us.

TŌSHI-AYNU   תּוֹשִׁיעֵנוּ

V'RIV AL TIMTACH,   וְרִיב אַל תִּמְתַּח,

Save us, do not let accusations be drawn out,

V'HŌSHI-AYNU   וְהוֹשִׁיעֵנוּ

ELŌHAY YISH-AYNU.   אֱלֹהֵי יִשְׁעֵנוּ.

and save us, God of our salvation.

CHAZZAN, THEN CONGREGATION:

KŌL M'VASAYR   קוֹל מְבַשֵּׂר

M'VASAYR V'ŌMAYR: מְבַשֵּׂר וְאוֹמֵר:

The voice of the herald* heralds and proclaims:

◄§ **The Voice of the Herald**

Upon concluding the prayers for rain we proclaim our faith in the resuscitation of the dead which will follow the coming of the Messiah.

This juxtaposition is based upon the Talmud and the Midrash: Greater is the day of the rains than the resuscitation of the dead. The resuscitation will benefit only the righteous, while the rains benefit both the righteous and the wicked; the resuscitation will benefit only man, while the rains benefit both man and beast.

ALL:

ŌMETZ YESH-ACHO bo, אֹמֶץ יֶשְׁעֲךָ בָּא,
The strength of Your salvations comes,

kōl dōdi hinay ze bo, קוֹל דּוֹדִי הִנֵּה זֶה בָּא,
a voice — my Beloved, behold He comes —

m'vasayr v'ōmayr. מְבַשֵּׂר וְאוֹמֵר.
heralds and proclaims.

Kōl bo b'riv'vōs kitim, קוֹל בָּא בְּרִבְבוֹת כִּתִּים,
A voice — He comes among myriad bands,

la-amōd al har hazaysim, לַעֲמוֹד עַל הַר הַזֵּיתִים,
to stand upon the Mount of Olives —

m'vasayr v'ōmayr. מְבַשֵּׂר וְאוֹמֵר.
heralds and proclaims.

Kōl gishtō ba-shōfor liska, קוֹל גִּשְׁתּוֹ בַּשׁוֹפָר לִתְקַע,
A voice — to the blast of the shofar, He draws near,

tachtov har yiboka, תַּחְתָּיו הַר יִבָּקַע,
beneath Him the mountain shall be split —

m'vasayr v'ōmayr. מְבַשֵּׂר וְאוֹמֵר.
heralds and proclaims.

Kōl dofak v'haytzitz v'zorach, קוֹל דָּפַק וְהֵצִיץ וְזָרַח,
A voice — He knocks, He peers and He shines,

u-mosh chatzi hohor mimizroch, וּמָשׁ חֲצִי הָהָר מִמִּזְרָח,
and half the mountain moves from the east —

m'vasayr v'ōmayr. מְבַשֵּׂר וְאוֹמֵר.
heralds and proclaims.

Kōl haykim milul no-omō, קוֹל הֵקִים מִלּוּל נָאֲמוֹ,
A voice — He has verified the words of His utterance,

u-vo hu v'chol k'dōshov imō, וּבָא הוּא וְכָל קְדוֹשָׁיו עִמּוֹ,
He has come, and all His holy ones with Him —

m'vasayr v'ōmayr. מְבַשֵּׂר וְאוֹמֵר.
heralds and proclaims.

Kōl ul-chol bo-ay ho-ōlom, קוֹל וּלְכָל בָּאֵי הָעוֹלָם,
A voice — to all who walk the earth,

bas kōl yi-shoma bo-ōlom, בַּת קוֹל יִשָּׁמַע בָּעוֹלָם,
a Heavenly voice is heard on the earth —

m'vasayr v'ōmayr. מְבַשֵּׂר וְאוֹמֵר.
heralds and proclaims.

Kōl zera amusay r'chomō,
קוֹל זֶרַע עֲמוּסֵי רָחֲמוֹ,
A voice — the seed borne [by Him] from the womb,

nōl'du k'yeled mim'ay imō,
נוֹלְדוּ כִּיֶלֶד מִמְּעֵי אִמּוֹ,
born like a child from its mother's innards —

m'vasayr v'ōmayr.
מְבַשֵּׂר וְאוֹמֵר.
heralds and proclaims.

Kōl cholo v'yol'do mi zōs,
קוֹל חָלָה וְיָלְדָה מִי זֹאת,
A voice — she delivered and gave birth: "Who is this?

mi shoma kozōs,
מִי שָׁמַע כָּזֹאת,
Who has heard the likes of this?" —

m'vasayr v'ōmayr.
מְבַשֵּׂר וְאוֹמֵר.
heralds and proclaims.

Kōl tohōr po-al kol ayle,
קוֹל טָהוֹר פָּעַל כָּל אֵלֶּה,
A voice — the pure One has done all these;

u-mi ro-o ko-ayle,
וּמִי רָאָה כָּאֵלֶּה,
and who has seen the likes of these? —

m'vasayr v'ōmayr.
מְבַשֵּׂר וְאוֹמֵר.
heralds and proclaims.

Kōl yesha uzman huchad,
קוֹל יֵשַׁע וּזְמַן הוּחַד,
A voice — salvation and its moment were ordained.

ha-yuchal eretz b'yōm e-chod,
הֲיוּחַל אֶרֶץ בְּיוֹם אֶחָד,
Can the earth deliver issue in a single day? —

m'vasayr v'ōmayr.
מְבַשֵּׂר וְאוֹמֵר.
heralds and proclaims.

Kōl kabir rōm vosachas,
קוֹל כַּבִּיר רוֹם וָתָחַת,
A voice — He Who is mighty above and below,

im yivoled gōy pa-am echos,
אִם יִוָּלֵד גּוֹי פַּעַם אֶחָת,
can a nation be born in a trice? —

m'vasayr v'ōmayr.
מְבַשֵּׂר וְאוֹמֵר.
heralds and proclaims.

Kōl l'ays yig-al amō no-ōr,
קוֹל לְעֵת יִגְאַל עַמּוֹ נָאוֹר,
A voice — when the resplendent One redeems His people,

v'ho-yo l'ays erev yih-ye ōr,
וְהָיָה לְעֵת עֶרֶב יִהְיֶה אוֹר,
at evening time there will be light —

m'vasayr v'ōmayr.
מְבַשֵּׂר וְאוֹמֵר.
heralds and proclaims.

Kōl mōshi-im ya-alu l'har tziyōn,
קוֹל מוֹשִׁיעִים יַעֲלוּ לְהַר צִיּוֹן,
A voice — saviors shall ascend upon Mount Zion,

ki cholo gam yol'do tziyōn,

כִּי חָלָה גַּם יָלְדָה צִיּוֹן,

for Zion has delivered and given birth

m'vasayr v'ōmayr.

מְבַשֵּׂר וְאוֹמֵר.

— heralds and proclaims.

Kōl nishma b'chol g'vulaych,

קוֹל נִשְׁמַע בְּכָל גְּבוּלֵךְ,

A voice — it is heard within all your boundaries,

harchivi m'kōm oholaych,

הַרְחִיבִי מְקוֹם אָהֳלֵךְ,

"Expand the area of your tents!" —

m'vasayr v'ōmayr.

מְבַשֵּׂר וְאוֹמֵר.

heralds and proclaims.

Kōl simi ad damesek mishk'nōsa-yich,

קוֹל שִׂימִי עַד דַּמֶּשֶׂק מִשְׁכְּנוֹתַיִךְ,

A voice — set up your dwellings until Damasek,

kab'li vona-yich uvnōsa-yich,

קַבְּלִי בָנַיִךְ וּבְנוֹתַיִךְ,

receive your sons and your daughters —

m'vasayr v'ōmayr.

מְבַשֵּׂר וְאוֹמֵר.

heralds and proclaims.

Kōl ilzi chavatzeles ha-shorōn,

קוֹל עִלְזִי חֲבַצֶּלֶת הַשָּׁרוֹן,

A voice — be joyous, O rose of Sharon,

ki komu y'shaynay chevrōn,

כִּי קָמוּ יְשֵׁנֵי חֶבְרוֹן,

for those sleeping in Hebron have arisen —

m'vasayr v'ōmayr.

מְבַשֵּׂר וְאוֹמֵר.

heralds and proclaims.

Kōl p'nu aylai v'hivosh'u,

קוֹל פְּנוּ אֵלַי וְהִוָּשֵׁעוּ,

A voice — turn to Me and you shall be saved —

ha-yōm im b'kōli sishmo-u,

הַיּוֹם אִם בְּקוֹלִי תִשְׁמָעוּ,

this very day, if you will but heed My voice —

m'vasayr v'ōmayr.

מְבַשֵּׂר וְאוֹמֵר.

heralds and proclaims.

kōl tzomach ish tzemach sh'mō,

קוֹל צָמַח אִישׁ צֶמַח שְׁמוֹ,

A voice — a man has sprouted, Tzemach is his name,

hu dovid b'atzmō,

הוּא דָוִד בְּעַצְמוֹ,

he is David himself —

m'vasayr v'ōmayr.

מְבַשֵּׂר וְאוֹמֵר.

heralds and proclaims.

Kōl kumu k'fushay ofor,

קוֹל קוּמוּ כְּפוּשֵׁי עָפָר,

A voice — arise, you who are covered with dust;

hokitzu v'ran'nu shōch'nay ofor,   הָקִיצוּ וְרַנְּנוּ שׁוֹכְנֵי עָפָר,
awake and sing, you who lie in the dust —

m'vasayr v'ōmayr.   מְבַשֵּׂר וְאוֹמֵר.
heralds and proclaims.

Kōl rabosi om b'hamlichō,   קוֹל רַבָּתִי עָם בְּהַמְלִיכוֹ,
A voice — when He rules the city great with people,

migdōl y'shu-ōs malkō,   מִגְדּוֹל יְשׁוּעוֹת מַלְכּוֹ,
His king shall be a tower of salvations —

m'vasayr v'ōmayr.   מְבַשֵּׂר וְאוֹמֵר.
heralds and proclaims.

Kōl shaym r'sho-im l'ha-avid,   קוֹל שֵׁם רְשָׁעִים לְהַאֲבִיד,
A voice — the name of the wicked He will cause to be lost,

ōse chesed limshichō l'dovid,   עֹשֶׂה חֶסֶד לִמְשִׁיחוֹ לְדָוִד,
but He will show kindness to His anointed, to David —

m'vasayr v'ōmayr.   מְבַשֵּׂר וְאוֹמֵר.
heralds and proclaims.

Kōl t'no y'shu-ōs l'am ōlom,   קוֹל תְּנָה יְשׁוּעוֹת לְעַם עוֹלָם,
A voice — grant salvations to the eternal people,

l'dovid ulzar-ō ad ōlom,   לְדָוִד וּלְזַרְעוֹ עַד עוֹלָם,
to David and to his descendants, forever —

m'vasayr v'ōmayr.   מְבַשֵּׂר וְאוֹמֵר.
heralds and proclaims.

CHAZZAN, THEN CONGREGATION, LOUDLY:

KŌL M'VASAYR   קוֹל מְבַשֵּׂר
M'VASAYR V'ŌMAYR.   מְבַשֵּׂר וְאוֹמֵר.
The voice of the herald heralds and proclaims.

KŌL M'VASAYR   קוֹל מְבַשֵּׂר
M'VASAYR V'ŌMAYR.   מְבַשֵּׂר וְאוֹמֵר.
The voice of the herald heralds and proclaims.

KŌL M'VASAYR   קוֹל מְבַשֵּׂר
M'VASAYR V'ŌMAYR.   מְבַשֵּׂר וְאוֹמֵר.
The voice of the herald heralds and proclaims.

ALL CONTINUE:

HŌSHI-O es amecho   **הוֹשִׁיעָה** אֶת עַמֶּךְ
u-voraych es nachalosecho,   וּבָרֵךְ אֶת נַחֲלָתֶךָ,
Save Your people and bless Your heritage,

ur-aym v'nas'aym ad ho-ōlom. וּרְעֵם וְנַשְּׂאֵם עַד הָעוֹלָם.

tend them and elevate them forever.

V'yih-yu d'vorai ayle וְיִהְיוּ דְבָרַי אֵלֶּה

asher his-chananti lifnay Adōnoy, אֲשֶׁר הִתְחַנַּנְתִּי לִפְנֵי יהוה,

May these words of mine, which I have supplicated before Hashem,

k'rōvim el Adōnoy Elōhaynu קְרוֹבִים אֶל יהוה אֱלֹהֵינוּ

yōmom voloylo, יוֹמָם וָלָיְלָה,

be near to Hashem, our God, by day and by night;

la-asōs mishpat avdō לַעֲשׂוֹת מִשְׁפַּט עַבְדּוֹ

u-mishpat amō yisro-ayl, וּמִשְׁפַּט עַמּוֹ יִשְׂרָאֵל,

that He bring about justice for His servant and justice for His people, Israel,

d'var yōm b'yōmō. דְּבַר יוֹם בְּיוֹמוֹ.

each day's need in its day;

L'ma-an da-as kol amay ho-oretz, לְמַעַן דַּעַת כָּל עַמֵּי הָאָרֶץ,

that all the peoples of the earth shall know

ki Adōnoy hu ho-Elōhim, ayn ōd. כִּי יהוה הוּא הָאֱלֹהִים, אֵין עוֹד.

that Hashem is God, there is no other.

BEATING THE HOSHANA-BUNDLE

THE TORAH SCROLLS ARE RETURNED TO THE ARK AND IT IS CLOSED. THE *HOSHANA*-BUNDLE IS BEATEN ON THE GROUND (FIVE TIMES ACCORDING TO SOME), AFTER WHICH THE *YEHI RATZON* IS RECITED, FOLLOWED BY THE FULL *KADDISH* (P. 454); AND THE SERVICE CONTINUES THERE. IN SOME CONGREGATIONS THE ORDER IS REVERSED, WITH *KADDISH* BEING RECITED BEFORE THE *HOSHANA*-BUNDLE IS BEATEN.

Y'HI ROTZŌN mil'fonecho יְהִי רָצוֹן מִלְּפָנֶיךָ

May it be favorable before You,

Adōnoy Elōhaynu יהוה אֱלֹהֵינוּ

Vaylōhay avōsaynu, וֵאלֹהֵי אֲבוֹתֵינוּ,

Hashem, our God and the God of our forefathers,

habōchayr binvi-im tōvim הַבּוֹחֵר בִּנְבִיאִים טוֹבִים

uvminhagayhem hatōvim, וּבְמִנְהֲגֵיהֶם הַטּוֹבִים,

He Who opts for good prophets and their good customs,

shet'kabayl b'rachamim uvrotzōn שֶׁתְּקַבֵּל בְּרַחֲמִים וּבְרָצוֹן

that You accept with mercy and favor

es t'filosaynu v'hakofōsaynu, אֶת תְּפִלָּתֵנוּ וְהַקָּפוֹתֵינוּ,

our prayer and our hakafah-circuits.

uzchor lonu וּזְכָר לָנוּ

z'chus shiv-as t'mimecho, זְכוּת שִׁבְעַת תְּמִימֶיךָ,

Remember for our sake the merit of Your seven perfect ones.

v'sosir m'chitzas habarzel   וְתָסִיר מְחִיצַת הַבַּרְזֶל

   hamafsekes baynaynu u-vaynecho,   הַמַּפְסֶקֶת בֵּינֵינוּ וּבֵינֶיךָ,

Remove the iron partition* separating us from You.

v'sa-azin shav-osaynu,   וְתַאֲזִין שַׁוְעָתֵנוּ,

Hearken to our plea

v'saytiv lonu hachasimo,   וְתֵיטִיב לָנוּ הַחֲתִימָה,

and grant us the good seal,*

tōle eretz al b'limo.   תֹּלֶה אֶרֶץ עַל בְּלִימָה.

He Who suspends the earth upon silence.

V'chosmaynu b'sayfer cha-yim tōvim.   וְחָתְמֵנוּ בְּסֵפֶר חַיִּים טוֹבִים.

Seal us in the Book of Good Life.

V'ha-yōm ha-ze titayn   וְהַיּוֹם הַזֶּה תִּתֵּן

   bish-chinas u-zecho   בִּשְׁכִינַת עֻזֶּךָ

Today may You place, with the manifestation of Your strength,

chami-sho g'vurōs m'mutokōs   חֲמִשָּׁה גְבוּרוֹת מְמֻתָּקוֹת

five strict powers which have been sweetened

al y'day chavitas arovo   עַל יְדֵי חֲבִיטַת עֲרָבָה

through the beating of willows,

minhag n'vi-echo hak'dōshim,   מִנְהַג נְבִיאֶיךָ הַקְּדוֹשִׁים,

the custom ordained by Your holy prophets.

v'sis-ōrayr ho-ahavo baynayhem,   וְתִתְעוֹרֵר הָאַהֲבָה בֵּינֵיהֶם,

May You awaken love among them

u-snash'kaynu min'shikōs picho,   וּתְנַשְּׁקֵנוּ מִנְּשִׁיקוֹת פִּיךָ,

and kiss us with the kisses of Your mouth,*

mamtekes kol hag'vurōs   מַמְתֶּקֶת כָּל הַגְּבוּרוֹת

   v'chol hadinin.   וְכָל הַדִּינִין.

which sweeten all the strict powers and all the harsh judgments.

V'so-ir lishchinas u-zecho   וְתָאִיר לִשְׁכִינַת עֻזֶּךָ

May You illuminate the manifestation of Your strength

b'shaym yud kay vov   בְּשֵׁם יוּ׳׳ד הֵ׳׳א וָא׳׳ו

with the Name Yud-Kei-Vav

מְחִיצַת הַבַּרְזֶל — *The iron partition.* Sinful acts build a partition between the sinner and the spark of holiness, which is the source of spiritual life. As one plunges deeper into sin, the partition strengthens until it is strong as iron, while the spark of holiness becomes virtually inaccessible. Only repentance can breach the partition and extricate that spark of holiness.

הַחֲתִימָה — *The seal.* On Hoshana Rabbah the final seal is placed on the verdict issued on Rosh Hashanah and tentatively sealed on Yom Kippur.

נְשִׁיקוֹת פִּיךָ — *The kisses of your mouth.* God's love for Israel is expressed (in *Song of Songs*) in terms of embrace and kisses. Embrace refers to the coupling of acts of man with acts of God through the performance of

shehu tal ōrōs talecho,

שֶׁהוּא טַל אוֹרת טַלֶּךְ,

which corresponds to the dew — Your dew is the dew of lights.

u-mishom tashpi-a shefa l'avd'cho

וּמִשָּׁם תַּשְׁפִּיעַ שֶׁפַע לְעַבְדְּךְ

From there endow Your servant,

l'avd'cho hamisnapayl l'fonecho,

הַמִּתְנַפֵּל לְפָנֶיךָ,

who prostrates himself before You,

m'chilo, sheta-arich yomai,

מְחִילָה, שֶׁתַּאֲרִיךְ יָמַי,

with forgiveness, that my days may be lengthened.

v'simchol li chato-ai

וְתִמְחָל לִי חֲטָאַי

va-avonōsai ufsho-ai,

וַעֲוֹנוֹתַי וּפְשָׁעַי,

Forgive me my sins, my iniquities, and my transgressions.

v'sifshōt y'min'cho v'yod'cho

וְתִפְשׁוֹט יְמִינְךָ וְיָדְךָ

l'kab'layni

לְקַבְּלֵנִי

Spread wide Your right arm and Your hand to accept me,

bis-shuvo sh'laymo l'fonecho.

בִּתְשׁוּבָה שְׁלֵמָה לְפָנֶיךָ.

with my whole-hearted repentance before You.

V'ōtzor'cho hatōv tiftach

וְאוֹצָרְךָ הַטּוֹב תִּפְתַּח

Open Your goodly treasure trove

l'hasbi-a ma-yim nefesh shōkayko,

לְהַשְׂבִּיעַ מַיִם נֶפֶשׁ שׁוֹקֵקָה,

to satisfy with water a thirsty soul —

k'mō shekosuv:

כְּמוֹ שֶׁכָּתוּב:

as it is written:

Yiftach Adōnoy l'cho

יִפְתַּח יהוה לְךָ

May HASHEM *open for you*

es ōtzorō hatōv es ha-shoma-yim,

אֶת אוֹצָרוֹ הַטּוֹב אֶת הַשָּׁמַיִם,

His goodly treasure trove, the heavens,

losays m'tar artz'cho b'itō

לָתֵת מְטַר אַרְצְךָ בְּעִתּוֹ

to give your land rain in its season

ulvoraych ays kol

וּלְבָרֵךְ אֶת כָּל

ma-asay yodecho.

מַעֲשֵׂה יָדֶךָ.

and to bless all of your handiwork.

Omayn.

אָמֵן.

Amen.

CHAZZAN RECITES THE FULL KADDISH (P. 454) AND THE SERVICE RESUMES THERE.

---

mitzvos and deeds of kindness. Kissing refers to the word of man uniting with the word of God through the study of the holy Torah.

⟨ THE HAKAFAH CIRCUITS OF SIMCHAS TORAH ⟩

■ A collection of verses that illustrate the greatness of Hashem. Following the seven days of rejoicing of Succos when we encircle the Torah with the Four Species, on Simchas Torah we demonstrate the apex of our joy, by encircling the *bimah* — symbolically encircling Hashem himself.

BEFORE THE ARK IS OPENED FOR THE *HAKAFOS*, THE FOLLOWING SELECTION OF VERSES
IS RECITED RESPONSIVELY:

ATO HOR'AYSO loda-as,   אַתָּה הָרְאֵתָ לָדַעַת,

You have been shown to know,

ki Adōnoy hu ho-Elōhim,   כִּי יהוה הוּא הָאֱלֹהִים,

ayn ōd mil'vadō.   אֵין עוֹד מִלְּבַדּוֹ.

that HASHEM, *He is the God, there is none beside Him.*

L'ōsay niflo-ōs g'dōlōs l'vadō,   לְעֹשֵׂה נִפְלָאוֹת גְּדֹלוֹת לְבַדּוֹ,

ki l'ōlom chasdō.   כִּי לְעוֹלָם חַסְדּוֹ.

To Him Who alone performs great wonders, for His kindness endures forever.

Ayn komōcho vo-elōhim, Adōnoy,   אֵין כָּמוֹךָ בָאֱלֹהִים, אֲדֹנָי,

There is none like You among the heavenly powers, my Lord,

v'ayn k'ma-asecho.   וְאֵין כְּמַעֲשֶׂיךָ.

and there is nothing like Your works.

Y'hi ch'vōd Adōnoy l'ōlom,   יְהִי כְבוֹד יהוה לְעוֹלָם,

yismach Adōnoy b'ma-asov.   יִשְׂמַח יהוה בְּמַעֲשָׂיו.

May the glory of HASHEM *endure forever, let* HASHEM *rejoice in His works.*

Y'hi shaym Adōnoy m'vōroch,   יְהִי שֵׁם יהוה מְבֹרָךְ,

may-ato v'ad ōlom.   מֵעַתָּה וְעַד עוֹלָם.

Blessed be the Name of HASHEM, *from this time and forever.*

Y'hi Adōnoy Elōhaynu imonu,   יְהִי יהוה אֱלֹהֵינוּ עִמָּנוּ,

May HASHEM, *our God, be with us,*

ka-asher hoyo im avōsaynu,   כַּאֲשֶׁר הָיָה עִם אֲבֹתֵינוּ,

as He was with our forefathers,

al ya-azvaynu v'al yit'shaynu.   אַל יַעַזְבֵנוּ וְאַל יִטְּשֵׁנוּ.

may He not forsake us nor cast us off.

Simchas Torah

Simchas Torah is unique among the Festivals. Technically, in the Diaspora, it is the second-day extension of Shemini Atzeres and should no more have a separate identity than the eighth day of Pesach or the second day of Shavuos. Nevertheless, the special nature of Simchas Torah — literally, celebration of the Torah — has caused it to be given a name that emphasizes the joyous nature of the day.

When God promised unsurpassed wisdom to the newly crowned Solomon, the young king celebrated with a feast for all his dear ones (*II Kings* 3:15). From this the Sages derive that one should make a feast upon completing a section of the Torah, as we do on Simchas Torah when we complete the annual public reading of the Five Books of the Torah.

Symbolic of this joy, we celebrate Simchas Torah by removing all the Torah scrolls from

V'imru, hōshi-aynu,   וְאִמְרוּ, הוֹשִׁיעֵנוּ,

    Elōhay yish-aynu,   אֱלֹהֵי יִשְׁעֵנוּ,

Say: "Save us, O God of our salvation,

v'kab'tzaynu v'hatzilaynu   וְקַבְּצֵנוּ וְהַצִּילֵנוּ

    min hagōyim,   מִן הַגּוֹיִם,

gather us and rescue us from the nations,

l'hōdōs l'shaym kod'shecho,   לְהֹדוֹת לְשֵׁם קָדְשֶׁךָ,

    l'hishtabay-ach bis-hilosecho.   לְהִשְׁתַּבֵּחַ בִּתְהִלָּתֶךָ.

to thank Your Holy Name and to glory in Your praise."

Adōnoy melech, Adōnoy moloch,   יהוה מֶלֶךְ, יהוה מָלָךְ,

    Adōnoy yimlōch l'ōlom vo-ed.   יהוה יִמְלֹךְ לְעוֹלָם וָעֶד.

HASHEM reigns, HASHEM has reigned, HASHEM shall reign for all eternity.

Adōnoy ōz l'amō yitayn,   יהוה עֹז לְעַמּוֹ יִתֵּן,

HASHEM will give might to His people,

Adōnoy y'voraych es amō va-sholōm.   יהוה יְבָרֵךְ אֶת עַמּוֹ בַשָּׁלוֹם.

HASHEM will bless His people with peace.

v'yih-yu no amoraynu l'rotzōn,   וְיִהְיוּ נָא אֲמָרֵינוּ לְרָצוֹן,

    lifnay adōn kōl.   לִפְנֵי אֲדוֹן כֹּל.

May our words find favor, we pray, before the Lord of everything.

THE ARK IS OPENED AND THE RESPONSIVE RECITATION CONTINUES:

VAY-HI BINSŌ-A ho-orōn,   **וַיְהִי בִּנְסֹעַ הָאָרֹן,**

    va-yōmer mōshe,   וַיֹּאמֶר מֹשֶׁה,

When the Ark would travel, Moses would say,

kumo Adōnoy, v'yofutzu ōy'vecho,   קוּמָה יהוה, וְיָפֻצוּ אֹיְבֶיךָ,

"Arise, HASHEM, and let Your foes be scattered;

v'yonusu m'sanecho miponecho.   וְיָנֻסוּ מְשַׂנְאֶיךָ מִפָּנֶיךָ.

let those who hate You flee from You."

kumo Adōnoy limnuchosecho,   קוּמָה יהוה לִמְנוּחָתֶךָ,

    ato va-arōn u-zecho.   אַתָּה וַאֲרוֹן עֻזֶּךָ.

Arise, HASHEM, to Your resting place, You and the Ark of Your strength.

kōhanecho yilb'shu tzedek,   כֹּהֲנֶיךָ יִלְבְּשׁוּ צֶדֶק,

    vachasidecho y'ranaynu.   וַחֲסִידֶיךָ יְרַנֵּנוּ.

*Let Your priests be clothed in righteousness,
and Your devout ones will sing joyously.*

---

the Ark and making seven *Hakafos* around the *bimah*, the table from which the Torah is read. This is done in the evening after *Maariv* and in the morning before the Torah reading.

The number seven represents spiritual completion, similar to the seventh day of the week as the Sabbath and the seven circuits around the *bimah* on Hoshana Rabbah. Thus, our seven

Ba-avur dovid avdecho,　　בַּעֲבוּר דָּוִד עַבְדֶּךָ,

For the sake of David, Your servant,

al toshayv p'nay m'shichecho.　　אַל תָּשֵׁב פְּנֵי מְשִׁיחֶךָ.

turn not away the face of Your anointed.

V'omar ba-yōm hahu,　　וְאָמַר בַּיּוֹם הַהוּא,

hinay Elōhaynu ze,　　הִנֵּה אֱלֹהֵינוּ זֶה,

He shall say on that day, "Behold! — this is our God,

kivinu lō v'yōshi-aynu,　　קִוִּינוּ לוֹ וְיוֹשִׁיעֵנוּ,

we hoped to Him and He saved us;

ze Adōnoy kivinu lō　　זֶה יהוה קִוִּינוּ לוֹ,

nogilo v'nism'cho bi-shu-osō.　　נָגִילָה וְנִשְׂמְחָה בִּישׁוּעָתוֹ.

this is HASHEM to whom we hoped, let us exult and be glad in His salvation."

Malchus'cho malchus kol ōlomim,　　מַלְכוּתְךָ מַלְכוּת כָּל עֹלָמִים,

Your kingdom is a kingdom spanning all eternities,

u-memshalt'cho b'chol dōr vodōr.　　וּמֶמְשַׁלְתְּךָ בְּכָל דּוֹר וָדֹר.

and Your dominion is throughout every generation.

Ki mitziyōn taytzay sōro,　　כִּי מִצִּיּוֹן תֵּצֵא תוֹרָה,

For from Zion the Torah will come forth,

udvar Adōnoy mirusholo-yim.　　וּדְבַר יהוה מִירוּשָׁלָיִם.

and the word of HASHEM from Jerusalem.

ALL, IN UNISON:

AV HORACHAMIM,　　אַב הָרַחֲמִים,

haytivo virtzōn'cho es tziyōn,　　הֵיטִיבָה בִרְצוֹנְךָ אֶת צִיּוֹן,

Father of compassion, do good to Zion according to Your will;

tivne chōmōs y'rusholo-yim.　　תִּבְנֶה חוֹמוֹת יְרוּשָׁלָיִם.

rebuild the walls of Jerusalem.

ki v'cho l'vad botoch'nu,　　כִּי בְךָ לְבַד בָּטָחְנוּ,

For we trust in You alone,

melech Ayl rom v'niso,　　מֶלֶךְ אֵל רָם וְנִשָּׂא,

O King, God, exalted and uplifted,

Adōn ōlomim.　　אֲדוֹן עוֹלָמִים.

Master of worlds.

ALL THE TORAH SCROLLS ARE REMOVED FROM THE ARK AND MEMBERS OF THE CONGREGATION ARE GIVEN THE HONOR OF CARRYING THEM DURING THE PROCESSION. IN SOME CONGREGATIONS, A LIT CANDLE, SYMBOLIZING THE LIGHT OF TORAH, IS PLACED IN THE ARK WHILE IT IS EMPTY.

Hakafos on Simchas Torah symbolize the completeness of our joy in the Torah.

Before the Torah scrolls are removed, the con-

gregation responsively recites the regular service for removal of the Torah scrolls, with the augmentation of additional verses.

FIRST *HAKAFAH*-CIRCUIT

AS THE TORAH SCROLLS ARE CARRIED AROUND THE *BIMAH*, EACH OF THE FOLLOWING VERSES IS RECITED BY THE *CHAZZAN* OR *HAKAFAH* LEADER AND IS THEN REPEATED BY THE CONGREGATION. IN SOME CONGREGATIONS THE THREE INTRODUCTORY VERSES (ono Adōnoy) ARE RECITED ONLY AT THE FIRST *HAKAFAH* CIRCUIT, WHILE IN OTHERS THEY ARE RECITED AT ALL *HAKAFAH*-CIRCUITS.

ONO Adōnoy, hōshi-o no.   **אָנָּא** יהוה, הוֹשִׁיעָה נָּא.
Please, HASHEM, save now!

Ono Adōnoy, hatzlicho no.   אָנָּא יהוה, הַצְלִיחָה נָא.
Please, HASHEM, bring success now!

Ono Adōnoy,   אָנָּא יהוה,
anaynu v'yōm kor'aynu.   עֲנֵנוּ בְיוֹם קָרְאֵנוּ.
Please, HASHEM, answer us on the day we call.

Elōhay horuchōs, hōshi-o no.   אֱלֹהֵי הָרוּחוֹת, הוֹשִׁיעָה נָא.
God of the spirits, save now!

Bōchayn l'vovōs, hatzlicho no.   בּוֹחֵן לְבָבוֹת, הַצְלִיחָה נָא.
Tester of hearts, bring success now!

Gō-ayl chozok,   גּוֹאֵל חָזָק,
anaynu v'yōm kor'aynu.   עֲנֵנוּ בְיוֹם קָרְאֵנוּ.
O Powerful Redeemer, answer us on the day we call!

SECOND *HAKAFAH*-CIRCUIT

Dōvayr tz'dokōs, hōshi-o no.   דּוֹבֵר צְדָקוֹת, הוֹשִׁיעָה נָא.
Speaker of righteousness, save now!

Hodur bilvushō, hatzlicho no.   הָדוּר בִּלְבוּשׁוֹ, הַצְלִיחָה נָא.
Majestic One in His garb, bring success now!

Vosik v'chosid,   וָתִיק וְחָסִיד,
anaynu v'yōm kor'aynu.   עֲנֵנוּ בְיוֹם קָרְאֵנוּ.
Faithful and Devout One, answer us on the day we call!

THIRD *HAKAFAH*-CIRCUIT

Zach v'yoshor, hōshi-o no.   זַךְ וְיָשָׁר, הוֹשִׁיעָה נָא.
Pure and Just One, save now!

Chōmayl dalim, hatzlicho no.   חוֹמֵל דַּלִּים, הַצְלִיחָה נָא.
He Who pities the poor, bring success now!

tōv u-maytiv,   טוֹב וּמֵטִיב,
anaynu v'yōm kor'aynu.   עֲנֵנוּ בְיוֹם קָרְאֵנוּ.
Good and Beneficent One, answer us on the day we call!

FOURTH *HAKAFAH*-CIRCUIT

Yōday-a machashovōs, hōshi-o no.   יוֹדֵעַ מַחֲשָׁבוֹת, הוֹשִׁיעָה נָא.
Knower of thoughts, save now!

Kabir v'no-ōr, hatzlicho no.　　　　　כַּבִּיר וְנָאוֹר, הַצְלִיחָה נָא.

Powerful and Illustrious One, bring success now!

Lōvaysh tz'dokōs,　　　　　　　　　לוֹבֵשׁ צְדָקוֹת,

anaynu v'yōm korraynu.　　　　　　עֲנֵנוּ בְיוֹם קָרְאֵנוּ.

He who garbs Himself in righteousness, answer us on the day we call!

———————— FIFTH *HAKAFAH*-CIRCUIT ————————

Melech ōlomim, hōshi-o no.　　　　מֶלֶךְ עוֹלָמִים, הוֹשִׁיעָה נָא.

Eternal King, save now!

No-ōr v'adir, hatzlicho no.　　　　　נָאוֹר וְאַדִּיר, הַצְלִיחָה נָא.

Illustrious and Mighty One, bring success now!

Sōmaych nōf'lim,　　　　　　　　　סוֹמֵךְ נוֹפְלִים,

anaynu v'yōm korraynu.　　　　　　עֲנֵנוּ בְיוֹם קָרְאֵנוּ.

Supporter of the fallen, answer us on the day we call!

———————— SIXTH *HAKAFAH*-CIRCUIT ————————

Ōzayr dalim, hōshi-o no.　　　　　עוֹזֵר דַּלִּים, הוֹשִׁיעָה נָא.

Helper of the destitute, save now!

Pōde u-matzil, hatzlicho no.　　　　פּוֹדֶה וּמַצִּיל, הַצְלִיחָה נָא.

Redeemer and Rescuer, bring success now!

Tzur ōlomim,　　　　　　　　　　צוּר עוֹלָמִים,

anaynu v'yōm kor-aynu.　　　　　　עֲנֵנוּ בְיוֹם קָרְאֵנוּ.

Eternal Rock, answer us on the day we call!

———————— SEVENTH *HAKAFAH*-CIRCUIT ————————

Kodōsh v'nōro, hōshi-o no.　　　　קָדוֹשׁ וְנוֹרָא, הוֹשִׁיעָה נָא.

Holy and awesome One, save now!

Rachum v'chanun, hatzlicho no.　　רַחוּם וְחַנּוּן, הַצְלִיחָה נָא.

Merciful and gracious One, bring success now!

Shōmayr hab'ris,　　　　　　　　שׁוֹמֵר הַבְּרִית,

anaynu v'yōm korraynu.　　　　　　עֲנֵנוּ בְיוֹם קָרְאֵנוּ.

Keeper of the covenant, answer us on the day we call!

Tōmaych t'mimim, hōshi-o no.　　תּוֹמֵךְ תְּמִימִים, הוֹשִׁיעָה נָא.

Supporter of the wholesome, save now!

Takif lo-ad, hatzlicho no.　　　　　תַּקִּיף לָעַד, הַצְלִיחָה נָא.

Eternally strong One, bring success now!

Tomim b'ma-asov,　　　　　　　　תָּמִים בְּמַעֲשָׂיו,

anaynu v'yōm korraynu.　　　　　　עֲנֵנוּ בְיוֹם קָרְאֵנוּ.

Perfect in His deeds, answer us on the day we call!

⟨⟨ KINDLING THE CHANUKAH MENORAH ⟩⟩

■ The *menorah* is lit in public to proclaim the miracle of Chanukah, which demonstrated the omnipotence of Hashem.

ALL THREE BLESSINGS ARE PRONOUNCED BEFORE KINDLING THE CHANUKAH *MENORAH* FOR THE FIRST TIME. ON ALL SUBSEQUENT NIGHTS, THE THIRD BLESSING, *SHEHECHEYANU*, IS OMITTED.

BORUCH ato Adōnoy
בָּרוּךְ אַתָּה יהוה

Elōhaynu melech ho-ōlom,
אֱלֹהֵינוּ מֶלֶךְ הָעוֹלָם,

Blessed are You, HASHEM, our God, King of the universe,

asher kid'shonu b'mitzvōsov,
אֲשֶׁר קִדְּשָׁנוּ בְּמִצְוֹתָיו,

Who has sanctified us with His commandments,

v'tzivonu l'hadlik nayr shel chanuko.
וְצִוָּנוּ לְהַדְלִיק נֵר שֶׁל חֲנֻכָּה.

and has commanded us to kindle the Chanukah light.

ALL PRESENT RESPOND: Omayn — אָמֵן

BORUCH ato Adōnoy
בָּרוּךְ אַתָּה יהוה

Elōhaynu melech ho-ōlom,
אֱלֹהֵינוּ מֶלֶךְ הָעוֹלָם,

Blessed are You, HASHEM our God, King of the universe,

she-oso nisim la-avōsaynu,
שֶׁעָשָׂה נִסִּים לַאֲבוֹתֵינוּ,

ba-yomim hohaym baz'man ha-ze.
בַּיָּמִים הָהֵם בַּזְּמַן הַזֶּה.

Who has wrought miracles for our forefathers, in those days at this season.

ALL PRESENT RESPOND: Omayn — אָמֵן

BORUCH ato Adōnoy
בָּרוּךְ אַתָּה יהוה

Elōhaynu melech ho-ōlom,
אֱלֹהֵינוּ מֶלֶךְ הָעוֹלָם,

Blessed are You, HASHEM, our God, King of the universe,

sheheche-yonu v'kiy'monu v'higi-onu
שֶׁהֶחֱיָנוּ וְקִיְּמָנוּ וְהִגִּיעָנוּ

laz'man ha-ze.
לַזְּמַן הַזֶּה.

Who has kept us alive, sustained us, and brought us to this season.

ALL PRESENT RESPOND: Omayn — אָמֵן

ON THE FIRST NIGHT, THE LIGHT TO THE EXTREME RIGHT IS KINDLED. ON EACH SUBSEQUENT NIGHT, A NEW LIGHT IS ADDED TO THE LEFT OF THE PREVIOUS NIGHT'S LIGHTS. THE NEW LIGHT IS ALWAYS KINDLED FIRST, THE ONE TO ITS RIGHT SECOND, AND SO ON. AFTER ONE LIGHT HAS BEEN KINDLED, *HANAIROS HALALU* IS RECITED. THE ADDITIONAL LIGHTS ARE KINDLED DURING ITS RECITATION.

HANAYRŌS halolu
הַנֵּרוֹת הַלָּלוּ

anachnu madlikin
אֲנַחְנוּ מַדְלִיקִין

These lights we kindle

al hanisim v'al haniflo-ōs,
עַל הַנִּסִּים וְעַל הַנִּפְלָאוֹת,

upon the miracles, the wonders,

v'al hat'shu-ōs v'al hamilchomōs,
וְעַל הַתְּשׁוּעוֹת וְעַל הַמִּלְחָמוֹת,

the salvations, and the battles

she-osiso la-avōsaynu	שֶׁעָשִׂיתָ לַאֲבוֹתֵינוּ
which You performed for our forefathers	
ba-yomim hohaym baz'man ha-ze,	בַּיָּמִים הָהֵם בַּזְּמַן הַזֶּה,
in those days at this season,	
al y'day kōhanecho hak'dōshim.	עַל יְדֵי כֹּהֲנֶיךָ הַקְּדוֹשִׁים.
through Your holy priests.	
V'chol sh'mōnas y'may chanuko,	וְכָל שְׁמוֹנַת יְמֵי חֲנֻכָּה,
During all eight days of Chanukah	
hanayrōs halolu kōdesh haym.	הַנֵּרוֹת הַלָּלוּ קֹדֶשׁ הֵם.
these lights are sacred,	
V'ayn lonu r'shus	וְאֵין לָנוּ רְשׁוּת
l'hishtamaysh bohem,	לְהִשְׁתַּמֵּשׁ בָּהֶם,
and we are not permitted to make ordinary use of them,*	
elo lir-ōsom bilvod,	אֶלָּא לִרְאוֹתָם בִּלְבָד,
but to look at them,*	
k'day l'hōdōs ulhalayl	כְּדֵי לְהוֹדוֹת וּלְהַלֵּל
l'shimcho hagodōl	לְשִׁמְךָ הַגָּדוֹל
in order to express thanks and praise to Your great Name*	
al nisecho v'al nifl'ōsecho	עַל נִסֶּיךָ וְעַל נִפְלְאוֹתֶיךָ
v'al y'shu-osecho.	וְעַל יְשׁוּעָתֶךָ.
for Your miracles, Your wonders and Your salvation.	

AFTER THE LIGHTS HAVE BEEN KINDLED, *MAOZ TZUR* IS CHANTED:

MO-ŌZ TZUR y'shu-osi,	**מָעוֹז צוּר** יְשׁוּעָתִי
l'cho no-e l'shabay-ach,	לְךָ נָאֶה לְשַׁבֵּחַ,
O mighty Rock of my salvation, to praise You is a delight.	
tikōn bays t'filosi,	תִּכּוֹן בֵּית תְּפִלָּתִי
v'shom tōdo n'zabay-ach,	וְשָׁם תּוֹדָה נְזַבֵּחַ,
Restore my House of Prayer and there we will bring a thanksgiving offering.	

וְאֵין לָנוּ רְשׁוּת לְהִשְׁתַּמֵּשׁ בָּהֶם — *And we are not permitted to make ordinary use of them.* The prohibition against enjoying the lights for any personal purpose — such as reading or doing work by their illumination — makes it manifestly clear to all that they were kindled for the sole purpose of commemorating the miracle.

In compliance with the prohibition against enjoying the lights, we light a *shamash,* (a servant) flame, which is not holy, so that any incidental pleasure that comes from the lights can be considered as coming from the *shamash.*

כְּדֵי לְהוֹדוֹת וּלְהַלֵּל לְשִׁמְךָ הַגָּדוֹל — *In order to express thanks and praise to Your great Name.* By utilizing the Chanukah lights only for the *mitzvah* and contemplating them while they burn, we make it apparent to all that our intent is to publicize the miracle and to praise God's great Name in acknowledgment of His great miracles.

◆§ **Maoz Tzur**

This *piyut* (liturgical poem) opens with a plea for the reestablishment of the Temple; the rededication of the Altar; and the renewal of the services there. It then recalls various exiles that the Jewish people endured, praises God for redeeming us from each of them, and prays for the restoration of the Temple and for the dawn of the Messianic Redemption.

l'ays tochin matbay-ach,

mitzor ham'nabay-ach,

לְעֵת תָּכִין מַטְבֵּחַ,

מִצָּר הַמְנַבֵּחַ,

When You will have prepared the slaughter for the blaspheming foe,

oz egmōr, b'shir mizmōr,

chanukas hamizbay-ach.

אָז אֶגְמוֹר, בְּשִׁיר מִזְמוֹר,

חֲנֻכַּת הַמִּזְבֵּחַ.

then I shall complete with a song of hymn the dedication of the Altar.

RO-ŌS sov'o nafshi,

b'yogōn kōchi chilo,

רָעוֹת שָׂבְעָה נַפְשִׁי,

בְּיָגוֹן כֹּחִי כִלָה,

Troubles sated my soul, when with grief my strength was consumed.

cha-yai mayr'ru b'kōshi,

b'shibud malchus eglo,

חַיַּי מֵרְרוּ בְּקֹשִׁי,

בְּשִׁעְבּוּד מַלְכוּת עֶגְלָה,

They had embittered my life with hardship, with the calf-like kingdom's bondage.

uvyodō hag'dōlo,

hōtzi es has'gulo,

וּבְיָדוֹ הַגְּדוֹלָה,

הוֹצִיא אֶת הַסְּגֻלָה,

But with His great power He brought forth the treasured ones.

chayl par-ō, v'chol zar-ō,

yor'du k'even bimtzulo.

חֵיל פַּרְעֹה, וְכָל זַרְעוֹ,

יָרְדוּ כְּאֶבֶן בִּמְצוּלָה.

Pharaoh's army and all his offspring went down like a stone into the deep.

D'VIR kodshō hevi-ani,

v'gam shom lō shokat-ti,

דְּבִיר קָדְשׁוֹ הֱבִיאַנִי,

וְגַם שָׁם לֹא שָׁקַטְתִּי,

To the abode of His holiness He brought me, but there, too, I had no rest;

u-vo nōgays v'higlani,

ki zorim ovadti,

וּבָא נוֹגֵשׂ וְהִגְלַנִי,

כִּי זָרִים עָבַדְתִּי,

and an oppressor came and exiled me. For I had served aliens,

v'yayn ra-al mosachti

kim-at she-ovarti,

וְיֵין רַעַל מָסַכְתִּי,

כִּמְעַט שֶׁעָבַרְתִּי,

and had drunk benumbing wine. Scarcely had I departed [my land]

kaytz bovel, z'rubovel,

l'kaytz shiv-im nōshoti.

קֵץ בָּבֶל, זְרֻבָּבֶל,

לְקֵץ שִׁבְעִים נוֹשַׁעְתִּי.

when at Babylonia's demise Zerubabel came.

At the end of seventy years I was saved.

K'RŌS kōmas b'rōsh,

bikaysh agogi ben ham'doso,

כְּרוֹת קוֹמַת בְּרוֹשׁ,

בִּקֵּשׁ אֲגָגִי בֶּן הַמְּדָתָא,

To sever the towering cypress sought the Aggagite, son of Hammedatha,*

כְּרוֹת קוֹמַת בְּרוֹשׁ — *To sever the towering cypress.* The Talmud (*Megillah* 10b) expounds on an ob-

scure prophecy of *Isaiah* (55:13): "In place of the thorn shall come up the cypress," the prickly

v'nih-y'so lō l'fach ulmōkaysh,
v'ga-avosō nishboso,

וְנִהְיְתָה לוֹ לְפַח וּלְמוֹקֵשׁ,
וְגַאֲוָתוֹ נִשְׁבָּתָה,

but it became a snare and a stumbling block to him and his arrogance was stilled.

rōsh y'mini nisay-so,
v'ōyayv sh'mō mochiso,

רֹאשׁ יְמִינִי נִשֵּׂאתָ,
וְאוֹיֵב שְׁמוֹ מָחִיתָ,

The head of the Benjaminite You lifted and the enemy, his name You blotted out.

rōv bonov, v'kinyonov,
al ho-aytz toliso.

רֹב בָּנָיו, וְקִנְיָנָיו,
עַל הָעֵץ תָּלִיתָ.

His numerous progeny — his possessions — on the gallows You hanged.

Y'VONIM nikb'tzu olai,
azai bimay chashmanim,

יְוָנִים נִקְבְּצוּ עָלַי,
אֲזַי בִּימֵי חַשְׁמַנִּים,

Greeks* gathered against me then in Hasmonean days.

u-for'tzu chōmōs migdolai,
v'tim'u kol hash'monim,

וּפָרְצוּ חוֹמוֹת מִגְדָּלַי,
וְטִמְּאוּ כָּל הַשְּׁמָנִים,

They breached the walls of my towers and they defiled all the oils;

u-minōsar kankanim,
na-aso nays la-shōshanim,

וּמִנּוֹתַר קַנְקַנִּים,
נַעֲשָׂה נֵס לַשּׁוֹשַׁנִּים,

and from the one remnant of the flasks a miracle was wrought for the roses.

b'nay vino, y'may sh'mōno,
kov'u shir urnonim.

בְּנֵי בִינָה, יְמֵי שְׁמוֹנָה,
קָבְעוּ שִׁיר וּרְנָנִים.

Men of insight — eight days established for song and jubilation.

CHASŌF z'rō-a kodshecho.
v'korayv kaytz hai-shu-o,

חֲשׂוֹף זְרוֹעַ קָדְשֶׁךָ,
וְקָרֵב קֵץ הַיְשׁוּעָה,

Bare Your holy arm and hasten the End for salvation.

n'kōm nikmas dam avodecho,
may-umo hor'sho-o,

נְקוֹם נִקְמַת דַּם עֲבָדֶיךָ,
מֵאֻמָּה הָרְשָׁעָה,

Avenge the vengeance of Your servant's blood from the wicked nation.

ki or'cho lonu hai-shu-o,
v'ayn kaytz limay horo-o,

כִּי אָרְכָה לָנוּ הַיְשׁוּעָה,
וְאֵין קֵץ לִימֵי הָרָעָה,

For the triumph is too long delayed for us, and there is no end to days of evil.

d'chay admōn, b'tzayl tzalmōn,
hokaym lonu rō-im shiv-o.

דְּחֵה אַדְמוֹן, בְּצֵל צַלְמוֹן,
הָקֵם לָנוּ רוֹעִים שִׁבְעָה.

Repel the Red One in the nethermost shadow and establish for us the seven shepherds.

"thorn" Haman who attempted to destroy Mordechai, the stately "cypress." But Haman's own sinister plans ensnared him and he was hung on the gallows he had prepared for Mordechai.

יְוָנִים – *Greeks*. This refers to the Syrian-Greeks, especially Antiochus IV Epiphanes, the monarch who attempted through force to impose Greek culture on the Land of Israel.

⟨ READING OF THE MEGILLAH ⟩

■ The *Megillah* reflects our realization that Hashem protects His nation Israel even in the Diaspora.

BEFORE READING *MEGILLAS ESTHER* ON PURIM [BOTH AT NIGHT AND AGAIN IN THE MORNING], THE READER RECITES THE FOLLOWING THREE BLESSINGS. THE CONGREGATION SHOULD ANSWER AMEN AFTER EACH BLESSING, AND HAVE IN MIND THAT THEY THEREBY FULFILL THE OBLIGATION OF RECITING THE BLESSINGS THEMSELVES. DURING THE MORNING READING, THEY SHOULD ALSO HAVE IN MIND THAT THE THIRD BLESSING APPLIES TO THE OTHER *MITZVOS* OF PURIM — *SHALACH MANOS,* GIFTS TO THE POOR, AND THE FESTIVE PURIM MEAL — AS WELL AS TO THE *MEGILLAH* READING.

BORUCH ato Adōnoy   בָּרוּךְ אַתָּה יהוה
Blessed are You, HASHEM,

Elōhaynu melech ho-ōlom,   אֱלֹהֵינוּ מֶלֶךְ הָעוֹלָם,
our God, King of the universe,

asher kid'shonu b'mitzvōsov,   אֲשֶׁר קִדְּשָׁנוּ בְּמִצְוֹתָיו,
Who has sanctified us with His commandments

v'tzivonu al mikro m'gilo.   וְצִוָּנוּ עַל מִקְרָא מְגִלָּה.
and has commanded us regarding the reading of the Megillah.

CONGREGATION RESPONDS: Omayn — אָמֵן

BORUCH ato Adōnoy   בָּרוּךְ אַתָּה יהוה
Blessed are You, HASHEM,

Elōhaynu melech ho-ōlom,   אֱלֹהֵינוּ מֶלֶךְ הָעוֹלָם,
our God, King of the universe,

she-oso nisim la-avōsaynu,   שֶׁעָשָׂה נִסִּים לַאֲבוֹתֵינוּ,
Who has wrought miracles for our forefathers,

ba-yomim hohaym baz'man ha-ze.   בַּיָּמִים הָהֵם בַּזְּמַן הַזֶּה.
in those days at this season.

CONGREGATION RESPONDS: Omayn — אָמֵן

BORUCH ato Adōnoy   בָּרוּךְ אַתָּה יהוה
Blessed are You, HASHEM,

Elōhaynu melech ho-ōlom,   אֱלֹהֵינוּ מֶלֶךְ הָעוֹלָם,
our God, King of the universe,

sheheche-yonu v'ki-y'monu   שֶׁהֶחֱיָנוּ וְקִיְּמָנוּ
Who has kept us alive, sustained us

v'higi-onu laz'man ha-ze.   וְהִגִּיעָנוּ לַזְּמַן הַזֶּה.
and brought us to this season.

CONGREGATION RESPONDS: Omayn — אָמֵן

THE *MEGILLAH* IS READ.

AFTER THE *MEGILLAH* READING, EACH MEMBER OF THE CONGREGATION RECITES THE FOLLOWING
BLESSING. [THIS BLESSING IS NOT RECITED UNLESS A *MINYAN* IS PRESENT FOR THE READING.]

BORUCH ato Adōnoy
בָּרוּךְ אַתָּה יהוה
Blessed are You, HASHEM,

Elōhaynu melech ho-ōlom,
אֱלֹהֵינוּ מֶלֶךְ הָעוֹלָם,
our God, King of the universe,

horov es rivaynu,
הָרָב אֶת רִיבֵנוּ,
Who takes up our grievance,

v'hadon es dinaynu,
וְהַדָּן אֶת דִּינֵנוּ,

v'hanōkaym es nikmosaynu,
וְהַנּוֹקֵם אֶת נִקְמָתֵנוּ,
judges our claim, avenges our wrong;

v'ham'shalaym g'mul
וְהַמְשַׁלֵּם גְּמוּל

l'chol ō-y'vay nafshaynu,
לְכָל אֹיְבֵי נַפְשֵׁנוּ,
Who brings just retribution upon all enemies of our soul

v'hanifro lonu mitzoraynu.
וְהַנִּפְרָע לָנוּ מִצָּרֵינוּ.
and exacts vengeance for us from our foes.

Boruch ato Adōnoy,
בָּרוּךְ אַתָּה יהוה,
Blessed are You, HASHEM,

hanifro l'amō yisro-ayl
הַנִּפְרָע לְעַמּוֹ יִשְׂרָאֵל

mikol tzorayhem,
מִכָּל צָרֵיהֶם,
Who exacts vengeance for His people Israel from all their foes,

ho-Ayl hamōshi-a.
הָאֵל הַמּוֹשִׁיעַ.
the God Who brings salvation.

CONGREGATION RESPONDS: Omayn — אָמֵן

AFTER THE NIGHTTIME *MEGILLAH* READING, THE FOLLOWING TWO PARAGRAPHS ARE RECITED.
AFTER THE DAYTIME READING, CONTINUE WITH SHOSHANAS YAAKOV, P. 836.

ASHER HAYNI atzas gōyim,
אֲשֶׁר הֵנִיא עֲצַת גּוֹיִם,
Who balked the counsel of the nations

va-yofer machsh'vōs arumim.
וַיָּפֶר מַחְשְׁבוֹת עֲרוּמִים.
and annulled the designs of the cunning,

B'kum olaynu odom rosho,
בְּקוּם עָלֵינוּ אָדָם רָשָׁע,
when a wicked man stood up against us,

naytzer zodōn mizera amolayk.
נֵצֶר זָדוֹן מִזֶּרַע עֲמָלֵק.
a wantonly evil branch of Amalek's offspring.

Go-o v'oshrō v'choro lō bōr,
גָּאָה בְעָשְׁרוֹ וְכָרָה לוֹ בוֹר,
Haughty with his wealth he dug himself a grave,

ugdulosō yok'sho lō loched.
וּגְדֻלָּתוֹ יָקְשָׁה לוֹ לָכֶד.
and his very greatness snared him in a trap.

Dimo v'nafshō lilkōd v'nilkad,   דִּמָּה בְנַפְשׁוֹ לִלְכֹּד וְנִלְכַּד,
Fancying to trap, he became entrapped;

bikaysh l'hashmid   בִּקֵּשׁ לְהַשְׁמִיד
   v'nishmad m'hayro.   וְנִשְׁמַד מְהֵרָה.
attempting to destroy, he was swiftly destroyed.

Homon hōdi-a ayvas avōsov,   הָמָן הוֹדִיעַ אֵיבַת אֲבוֹתָיו,
Haman showed his forebears' enmity,

v'ōrayr sin-as achim labonim.   וְעוֹרֵר שִׂנְאַת אַחִים לַבָּנִים.
and aroused the brotherly hate of Esau on the children.

V'lō zochar rachamay sho-ul,   וְלֹא זָכַר רַחֲמֵי שָׁאוּל,
He would not remember Saul's compassion,

ki v'chemlosō al agog nōlad ōyayv.   כִּי בְחֶמְלָתוֹ עַל אֲגָג נוֹלַד אוֹיֵב.
that through his pity on Agag the foe was born.

Zomam rosho l'hachris tzadik,   זָמַם רָשָׁע לְהַכְרִית צַדִּיק,
The wicked one conspired to cut away the righteous,

v'nilkad tomay biday tohōr.   וְנִלְכַּד טָמֵא בִּידֵי טָהוֹר.
but the impure was trapped in the pure one's hands.

Chesed govar al shig'gas ov,   חֶסֶד גָּבַר עַל שִׁגְגַת אָב,
Kindness overcame the father's error,

v'rosho hōsif chayt al chato-ov.   וְרָשָׁע הוֹסִיף חֵטְא עַל חֲטָאָיו.
and the wicked one piled sin on sins.

Toman b'libō machsh'vōs arumov,   טָמַן בְּלִבּוֹ מַחְשְׁבוֹת עֲרוּמָיו,
In his heart he hid his cunning thoughts,

va-yismakayr la-asōs ro-o.   וַיִּתְמַכֵּר לַעֲשׂוֹת רָעָה.
and devoted himself to evildoing.

Yodō sholach bikdōshay Ayl,   יָדוֹ שָׁלַח בִּקְדוֹשֵׁי אֵל,
He stretched his hand against God's holy ones,

kaspō nosan l'hachris zichrom.   כַּסְפּוֹ נָתַן לְהַכְרִית זִכְרָם.
he spent his silver to destroy their memory.

Kir-ōs mord'chai ki yotzo ketzef,   כִּרְאוֹת מָרְדְּכַי כִּי יָצָא קֶצֶף,
When Mordechai saw the wrath commence,

v'dosay homon nit'nu v'shushon.   וְדָתֵי הָמָן נִתְּנוּ בְשׁוּשָׁן.
and Haman's decrees issued in Shushan,

Lovash sak v'koshar mispayd,   לָבַשׁ שַׂק וְקָשַׁר מִסְפֵּד,
he put on sackcloth and bound himself in mourning,

v'gozar tzōm va-yayshev al ho-ayfer. וַיִּגְזַר צוֹם וַיֵּשֶׁב עַל הָאֵפֶר.

decreed a fast and sat on ashes:

Mi ze ya-amōd l'chapayr sh'gogo, מִי זֶה יַעֲמֹד לְכַפֵּר שְׁגָגָה,

"Who would arise to atone for error,

v'limchōl chatas avōn avōsaynu. וְלִמְחֹל חַטַּאת עֲוֹן אֲבוֹתֵינוּ.

to gain forgiveness for our ancestors' sins?"

Naytz porach milulov, נֵץ פָּרַח מִלּוּלָב,

A blossom bloomed from a lulav branch —

hayn hadaso om'do l'ōrayr y'shaynim. הֵן הֲדַסָּה עָמְדָה לְעוֹרֵר יְשֵׁנִים.

behold! Hadassah stood up to arouse the sleeping.

Soriseho hivhilu l'homon, סָרִיסֶיהָ הִבְהִילוּ לְהָמָן,

His servants hastened Haman,

l'hashkōsō yayn chamas taninim. לְהַשְׁקוֹתוֹ יֵין חֲמַת תַּנִּינִים.

to serve him wine of serpent's poison.

Omad b'oshrō v'nofal b'rish-ō, עָמַד בְּעָשְׁרוֹ וְנָפַל בְּרִשְׁעוֹ,

He stood tall through his wealth and toppled through his evil —

oso lō aytz v'nislo olov. עָשָׂה לוֹ עֵץ וְנִתְלָה עָלָיו.

he built the gallows on which he was hung.

Pihem pos'chu kol yōsh'vay sayvayl, פִּיהֶם פָּתְחוּ כָּל יוֹשְׁבֵי תֵבֵל,

The earth's inhabitants opened their mouths,

ki fur homon nehpach l'furaynu. כִּי פוּר הָמָן נֶהְפַּךְ לְפוּרֵנוּ.

for Haman's lot became our Purim.

Tzadik nechelatz miyad rosho, צַדִּיק נֶחֱלַץ מִיַּד רָשָׁע,

The righteous man was saved from the wicked's hand;

ō-yayv nitan tachas nafshō. אוֹיֵב נִתַּן תַּחַת נַפְשׁוֹ.

the foe was substituted for him.

Ki-y'mu alayhem la-asōs purim, קִיְּמוּ עֲלֵיהֶם לַעֲשׂוֹת פוּרִים,

They undertook to establish Purim,

v'lismō-ach b'chol shono v'shono. וְלִשְׂמֹחַ בְּכָל שָׁנָה וְשָׁנָה.

to rejoice in every single year.

Ro-iso es t'filas רָאִיתָ אֶת תְּפִלַּת

  mord'chai v'estayr, מָרְדְּכַי וְאֶסְתֵּר,

You noted the prayer of Mordechai and Esther;

homon u-vonov al ho-aytz toliso. הָמָן וּבָנָיו עַל הָעֵץ תָּלִיתָ.

Haman and his sons You hung on the gallows.

THE FOLLOWING IS RECITED AFTER BOTH *MEGILLAH* READINGS.

SHŌSHANAS ya-akōv　　　　　　　**שׁוֹשַׁנַּת** יַעֲקֹב

The rose of Jacob

tzohalo v'somaycho,　　　　　　　צָהֲלָה וְשָׂמֵחָה,

was cheerful and glad,

bir-ōsom yachad　　　　　　　בִּרְאוֹתָם יַחַד

when they jointly saw

t'chayles mord'choy.　　　　　　　תְּכֵלֶת מָרְדְּכָי.

Mordechai robed in royal blue.

T'shu-osom ho-yiso lo-netzach,　　　תְּשׁוּעָתָם הָיִיתָ לָנֶצַח,

You have been their eternal salvation,

v'sikvosom b'chol dōr vodōr.　　　וְתִקְוָתָם בְּכָל דּוֹר וָדוֹר.

and their hope throughout generations.

L'hōdi-a shekol　　　　　　　לְהוֹדִיעַ שֶׁכָּל

kōvecho lō yayvōshu,　　　　　קֹוֶיךָ לֹא יֵבֹשׁוּ,

To make known that all who hope in You will not be shamed;

v'lō yikol'mu lo-netzach　　　　וְלֹא יִכָּלְמוּ לָנֶצַח

nor ever be humiliated,

kol hachōsim boch.　　　　　　כָּל הַחוֹסִים בָּךְ.

those taking refuge in You.

Orur homon asher bikaysh l'ab'di,　　אָרוּר הָמָן אֲשֶׁר בִּקֵּשׁ לְאַבְּדִי,

Accursed be Haman who sought to destroy me,

boruch mord'chai ha-y'hudi.　　　בָּרוּךְ מָרְדְּכַי הַיְּהוּדִי.

blessed be Mordechai the Yehudi.

Aruro zeresh ayshes mafchidi,　　　אֲרוּרָה זֶרֶשׁ אֵשֶׁת מַפְחִידִי,

Accursed be Zeresh the wife of my terrorizer,

b'rucho estayr ba-adi,　　　　　בְּרוּכָה אֶסְתֵּר בַּעֲדִי,

blessed be Esther [who sacrificed] for me —

v'gam charvōno zochur latōv.　　　וְגַם חַרְבוֹנָה זָכוּר לַטּוֹב.

and Charvonah, too, be remembered for good.

◄§ *Tefillin* on *Chol HaMoed*

There are three different customs (all halachically valid) regarding the wearing of *tefillin* on *Chol HaMoed:*

a) *Tefillin* are worn but the blessings usually recited upon donning them are omitted (*Taz* to *O.C.* 31:2).

b) *Tefillin* are worn and the blessings recited, but silently *(Rama).*

c) *Tefillin* should not be worn *(Orach Chaim* 31:2 and *Vilna Gaon).*

Mishnah Berurah advises that before putting on the *tefillin* one should stipulate mentally the following: "If I am obligated to wear *tefillin* today, then I am donning them in fulfillment of my obligation; but if I am not obligated to wear *tefillin* today, then I do not intend to fulfill any *mitzvah* by donning them"; and that the blessing not be recited.

It is not proper for a congregation to follow contradictory customs. Thus, if one whose custom is not to wear *tefillin* during *Chol HaMoed* prays with a *tefillin*-wearing *minyan,* he should don *tefillin* without a blessing. Conversely, if one whose custom is to wear *tefillin* prays with a non-*tefillin*-wearing *minyan,* he should not wear his *tefillin* while praying but may don them at home before going to the synagogue *(M.B.).*

Those who wear *tefillin* customarily remove them before *Hallel.* (However, since the Torah reading of the first day of *Chol HaMoed* Pesach mentions the *mitzvah* of *tefillin,* on that day many people do not remove their *tefillin* until after the Torah reading.)

◄§ ORDER OF PUTTING ON TEFILLIN ►

MANY RECITE THE FOLLOWING DECLARATION OF INTENT BEFORE PUTTING ON *TEFILLIN:*

L'SHAYM YICHUD　　　　　　　　　**לְשֵׁם יְחוּד**

For the sake of the unification

Kudsho b'rich hu ush-chintayh　　　קֻדְשָׁא בְּרִיךְ הוּא וּשְׁכִינְתֵּהּ,

of the Holy One, Blessed is He, and His Presence,

bidchilu urchimu　　　　　　　　　בִּדְחִילוּ וּרְחִימוּ

in fear and love,

l'yachayd shaym Yud-Kay b'Vov Kay　　לְיַחֵד שֵׁם י״ה בְּו״ה

b'yi-chudcho sh'lim　　　　　　　　בְּיִחוּדָא שְׁלִים,

to unify the Name —Yud-Kei with Vav-Kei — in perfect unity

b'shaym kol yisro-ayl　　　　　　　בְּשֵׁם כָּל יִשְׂרָאֵל.

in the name of all Israel.

HIN'NI m'chavayn bahanochas t'filin　**הִנְנִי** מְכַוֵּן בַּהֲנָחַת תְּפִלִּין

Behold, in putting on tefillin

l'ka-yaym mitzvas bōr'i,　　　　　לְקַיֵּם מִצְוַת בּוֹרְאִי,

I intend to fulfill the commandment of my Creator,

shetzivonu l'honi-ach t'filin,　　　שֶׁצִּוָּנוּ לְהָנִיחַ תְּפִלִּין,

Who has commanded us to put on tefillin,

kakosuv b'sōrosō:　　　　　　　כַּכָּתוּב בְּתוֹרָתוֹ:

as is written in His Torah:

Ukshartom l'ōs al yodecho,　　　וּקְשַׁרְתָּם לְאוֹת עַל יָדֶךָ,

"Bind them as a sign upon your arm

v'ho-yu l'tōtofōs bayn aynecho.

וְהָיוּ לְטֹטָפֹת בֵּין עֵינֶיךָ.

and let them be tefillin between your eyes.''

v'haym arba parshiyōs aylu —

וְהֵם אַרְבַּע פַּרְשִׁיּוֹת אֵלּוּ —

These four portions [contained in the tefillin] —

sh'ma, v'ho-yo im shomō-a,

שְׁמַע, וְהָיָה אִם שָׁמֹעַ,

[1] "Shema"; [2] "And it will come to pass, if you will hearken";

kadesh, v'ho-yo ki y'vi-acho —

קַדֶּשׁ, וְהָיָה כִּי יְבִאֲךָ —

[3] "Sanctify"; and [4] "And it will come to pass when He shall bring you" —

she-yaysh bo-hem yi-chudō v'achdusō

שֶׁיֵּשׁ בָּהֶם יִחוּדוֹ וְאַחְדּוּתוֹ

yisborach sh'mō bo-ōlom;

יִתְבָּרַךְ שְׁמוֹ בָּעוֹלָם;

contain His Oneness and Unity, may His Name be blessed, in the universe;

v'shenizkōr nisim v'niflo-ōs

וְשֶׁנִּזְכּוֹר נִסִּים וְנִפְלָאוֹת

so that we will recall the miracles and wonders

she-oso imonu

שֶׁעָשָׂה עִמָּנוּ

b'hōtzi-onu mimitzro-yim;

בְּהוֹצִיאָנוּ מִמִּצְרָיִם;

that He did with us when He removed us from Egypt;

va-asher lō hakō-ach v'hamemsholo

וַאֲשֶׁר לוֹ הַכֹּחַ וְהַמֶּמְשָׁלָה

bo-elyōnim u-vatachtōnim

בָּעֶלְיוֹנִים וּבַתַּחְתּוֹנִים

and that He has the strength and dominion over those above and those below

la-asōs bo-hem kirtzōnō.

לַעֲשׂוֹת בָּהֶם כִּרְצוֹנוֹ.

to do with them as He wishes.

V'tzivonu l'honi-ach al ha-yod,

וְצִוָּנוּ לְהָנִיחַ עַל הַיָּד,

He has commanded us to put [tefillin] upon the arm

l'zichrōn z'rō-a han'tu-yo,

לְזִכְרוֹן זְרוֹעַ הַנְּטוּיָה,

to recall the "outstretched arm" [of the Exodus];

v'shehi neged halayv,

וְשֶׁהִיא נֶגֶד הַלֵּב,

and that it be opposite the heart

l'shabayd bo-ze

לְשַׁעְבֵּד בָּזֶה

ta-avas u-machsh'vōs libaynu

תַּאֲוַת וּמַחְשְׁבוֹת לִבֵּנוּ

thereby to subjugate the desires and thoughts of our heart

la-avōdosō, yisborach sh'mō.

לַעֲבוֹדָתוֹ, יִתְבָּרַךְ שְׁמוֹ.

to His service, may His Name be blessed;

V'al horōsh neged hamō-ach,

וְעַל הָרֹאשׁ נֶגֶד הַמּוֹחַ,

and upon the head opposite the brain,

shehan'shomo sheb'mōchi,

שֶׁהַנְּשָׁמָה שֶׁבְּמוֹחִי,

so that the soul that is in my brain,

im sh'or chushai v'chōchōsai,   עִם שְׁאָר חוּשַׁי וְכֹחוֹתַי,
together with my other senses and potentials,

kulom yih-yu m'shu-bodim   כֻּלָּם יִהְיוּ מְשֻׁעְבָּדִים
la-avōdosō, yisborach sh'mō.   לַעֲבוֹדָתוֹ, יִתְבָּרַךְ שְׁמוֹ.
may all be subjugated to His service, may His Name be blessed.

U-mi-shefa mitzvas t'filin   וּמִשֶּׁפַע מִצְוַת תְּפִלִּין
May some of the spiritual influence of the commandment of tefillin

yis-mashaych olai lih-yōs li   יִתְמַשֵּׁךְ עָלַי לִהְיוֹת לִי
be extended upon me so that I have

cha-yim arukim, v'shefa kōdesh,   חַיִּים אֲרֻכִּים, וְשֶׁפַע קֹדֶשׁ,
a long life, a flow of holiness,

u-machashovōs k'dōshōs,   וּמַחֲשָׁבוֹת קְדוֹשׁוֹת
b'li harhōr chayt v'ovōn k'lol,   בְּלִי הַרְהוֹר חֵטְא וְעָוֹן כְּלָל;
and holy thoughts, without even an inkling of sin or iniquity;

v'shelō y'fataynu   וְשֶׁלֹּא יְפַתֵּנוּ
v'lō yisgore vonu yaytzer horo,   וְלֹא יִתְגָּרֶה בָנוּ יֵצֶר הָרָע,
and that the Evil Inclination will not seduce us nor incite against us,

v'yanichaynu la-avōd es Adōnoy   וְיַנִּיחֵנוּ לַעֲבֹד אֶת יהוה
ka-asher im l'vovaynu.   כַּאֲשֶׁר עִם לְבָבֵנוּ.
and that it permit us to serve HASHEM as is our hearts' desire.

vihi rotzōn mil'fonecho,   וִיהִי רָצוֹן מִלְפָנֶיךָ,
May it be Your will,

Adōnoy Elōhaynu   יהוה אֱלֹהֵינוּ
Vaylōhay avōsaynu,   וֵאלֹהֵי אֲבוֹתֵינוּ,
HASHEM, our God and the God of our forefathers,

shet'hay chashuvo mitzvas   שֶׁתְּהֵא חֲשׁוּבָה מִצְוַת
hanochas t'filin   הֲנָחַת תְּפִלִּין
that the commandment of putting on tefillin be considered as worthy

lifnay Hakodōsh boruch hu,   לִפְנֵי הַקָּדוֹשׁ בָּרוּךְ הוּא
before the Holy One, Blessed is He,

k'ilu kiyamti-ho b'chol p'rote-ho   כְּאִלּוּ קִיַּמְתִּיהָ בְּכָל פְּרָטֶיהָ
v'dikduke-ho v'chav'nōse-ho,   וְדִקְדּוּקֶיהָ וְכַוָּנוֹתֶיהָ,
as if I had fulfilled it in all its details, implications, and intentions,

v'saryag mitzvōs hat'lu-yim boh.   וְתַרְיַ"ג מִצְוֹת הַתְּלוּיִים בָּהּ.
as well as the 613 commandments that are dependent upon it.

Omayn selo.   אָמֵן סֶלָה.
Amen, Selah.

STAND WHILE PUTTING ON *TEFILLIN*. PLACE THE ARM-*TEFILLIN* UPON THE LEFT BICEPS (OR THE RIGHT BICEPS OF ONE WHO WRITES LEFT-HANDED), HOLD IT IN PLACE READY FOR TIGHTENING, THEN RECITE THE FOLLOWING BLESSING:

BORUCH ato Adōnoy   בָּרוּךְ אַתָּה יהוה
  Elōhaynu melech ho-ōlom,   אֱלֹהֵינוּ מֶלֶךְ הָעוֹלָם,
Blessed are You, HASHEM, our God, King of the universe,

asher kid'shonu b'mitzvōsov   אֲשֶׁר קִדְּשָׁנוּ בְּמִצְוֹתָיו,
Who has sanctified us with His commandments

v'tzivonu l'honi-ach t'filin.   וְצִוָּנוּ לְהָנִיחַ תְּפִלִּין.
and has commanded us to put on tefillin.

TIGHTEN THE ARM-*TEFILLIN* IMMEDIATELY AND WRAP THE STRAP SEVEN TIMES AROUND THE ARM. WITHOUT ANY INTERRUPTION, PUT THE HEAD-*TEFILLIN* IN PLACE, ABOVE THE HAIRLINE AND OPPOSITE THE SPACE BETWEEN THE EYES. BEFORE TIGHTENING THE HEAD-*TEFILLIN*, RECITE THE FOLLOWING BLESSING:

BORUCH ato Adōnoy   בָּרוּךְ אַתָּה יהוה
  Elōhaynu melech ho-ōlom,   אֱלֹהֵינוּ מֶלֶךְ הָעוֹלָם,
Blessed are You, HASHEM, our God, King of the universe,

asher kid'shonu b'mitzvōsov,   אֲשֶׁר קִדְּשָׁנוּ בְּמִצְוֹתָיו,
Who has sanctified us with His commandments

v'tzivonu al mitzvas t'filin.   וְצִוָּנוּ עַל מִצְוַת תְּפִלִּין.
and has commanded us regarding the commandment of tefillin.

TIGHTEN THE HEAD-*TEFILLIN* IMMEDIATELY AND RECITE:

Boruch shaym k'vōd malchuso   בָּרוּךְ שֵׁם כְּבוֹד מַלְכוּתוֹ
  l'ōlom vo-ed.   לְעוֹלָם וָעֶד.
Blessed is the Name of His glorious kingdom for all eternity.

AFTER THE HEAD-*TEFILLIN* IS SECURELY IN PLACE, RECITE:

U-MAYCHOCHMOS'CHO Ayl elyōn,   וּמֵחָכְמָתְךָ אֵל עֶלְיוֹן,
  ta-atzil olai,   תַּאֲצִיל עָלַי;
From Your wisdom, O supreme God, may You imbue me;

u-mibinos'cho t'vinayni,   וּמִבִּינָתְךָ תְּבִינֵנִי;
from Your understanding give me understanding;

uvchasd'cho tagdil olai,   וּבְחַסְדְּךָ תַּגְדִּיל עָלַי;
with Your kindness do greatly with me;

u-vigvuros'cho tatzmis ō-y'vai v'komai.   וּבִגְבוּרָתְךָ תַּצְמִית אֹיְבַי וְקָמָי.
with Your power cut down my foes and rebels.

v'shemen hatōv torik   וְשֶׁמֶן הַטּוֹב תָּרִיק
  al shivo k'nay ham'nōro,   עַל שִׁבְעָה קְנֵי הַמְּנוֹרָה,
[May] You pour goodly oil upon the seven arms of the Menorah,

l'hashpi-a tuv'cho livri-yōsecho. לְהַשְׁפִּיעַ טוּבְךָ לִבְרִיּוֹתֶיךָ.

to cause Your good to flow to Your creatures.

Pōsay-ach es yodecho, פּוֹתֵחַ אֶת יָדֶךָ,

u-masbi-a l'chol chai rotzōn. וּמַשְׂבִּיעַ לְכָל חַי רָצוֹן.

[May] You open Your hand and satisfy the desire of every living thing.

THE WRAP THE STRAP THREE TIMES AROUND THE MIDDLE FINGER WHILE RECITING:

V'AYRAS-TICH li l'ōlom. וְאֵרַשְׂתִּיךְ לִי לְעוֹלָם,

I will betroth you to Me forever,

V'ayras-tich li b'tzedek uvmishpot וְאֵרַשְׂתִּיךְ לִי בְּצֶדֶק וּבְמִשְׁפָּט

uvchesed uvrachamim. וּבְחֶסֶד וּבְרַחֲמִים.

and I will betroth you to Me with righteousness, justice, kindness, and mercy.

v'ayras-tich li be-emuno, וְאֵרַשְׂתִּיךְ לִי בֶּאֱמוּנָה,

v'yoda-at es Adōnoy. וְיָדַעַתְּ אֶת יהוה.

I will betroth you to Me with fidelity, and you shall know HASHEM.

THEN WRAP THE STRAP AROUND THE HAND.

IT IS PROPER TO RECITE THE FOUR SCRIPTURAL PASSAGES THAT ARE CONTAINED IN THE *TEFILLIN* WHILE WEARING THEM. TWO OF THE PASSAGES WILL BE RECITED AS PART OF *SHEMA* (P. 362-367). THE OTHER TWO, CITED BELOW, ARE RECITED EITHER AFTER PUTTING ON THE *TEFILLIN*, OR BEFORE REMOVING THEM.

VAI-DABAYR Adōnoy וַיְדַבֵּר יהוה

el mōshe laymōr: אֶל מֹשֶׁה לֵּאמֹר:

HASHEM *spoke to Moses, saying:*

kadesh li kol b'chōr, קַדֶּשׁ לִי כָל בְּכוֹר,

Sanctify to Me every firstborn;

peter kol rechem bivnay yisro-ayl פֶּטֶר כָּל רֶחֶם בִּבְנֵי יִשְׂרָאֵל

the first issue of every womb among the Children of Israel,

bo-odom u-vab'haymo, li hu. בָּאָדָם וּבַבְּהֵמָה, לִי הוּא.

both of man and of beast, is Mine.

Va-yōmer mōshe el ho-om: וַיֹּאמֶר מֹשֶׁה אֶל הָעָם:

Moses said to the people:

zochōr es ha-yōm ha-ze זָכוֹר אֶת הַיּוֹם הַזֶּה

asher y'tzosem mimitzra-yim, אֲשֶׁר יְצָאתֶם מִמִּצְרַיִם,

Remember this day on which you departed from Egypt,

mibays avodim, מִבֵּית עֲבָדִים,

from the house of bondage,

ki b'chōzek yod כִּי בְּחֹזֶק יָד

hōtzi Adōnoy eschem mi-ze, הוֹצִיא יהוה אֶתְכֶם מִזֶּה,

for with a strong hand HASHEM *removed you from here,*

וְלֹא יֵאָכֵל חָמֵץ.

v'lō yay-ochayl chomaytz.

and therefore no chametz may be eaten.

הַיּוֹם אַתֶּם יֹצְאִים,
בְּחֹדֶשׁ הָאָבִיב.

Ha-yōm atem yōtz'im,
b'chōdesh ho-oviv.

Today you are leaving in the month of springtime.

וְהָיָה כִי יְבִיאֲךָ יהוה

V'ho-yo ki y'vi-acho Adōnoy

And it will come to pass, when HASHEM shall bring you

אֶל אֶרֶץ הַכְּנַעֲנִי וְהַחִתִּי
וְהָאֱמֹרִי וְהַחִוִּי וְהַיְבוּסִי

el eretz hak'na-ani v'ha-chiti
v'ho-emōri v'ha-chivi v'hai-vusi

to the land of the Canaanites, Hittites, Emorites, Hivvites, and Jebusites,

אֲשֶׁר נִשְׁבַּע לַאֲבֹתֶיךָ לָתֶת לָךְ,

asher nishba la-avōsecho lo-ses loch,

which He swore to your forefathers to give you —

אֶרֶץ זָבַת חָלָב וּדְבָשׁ,

eretz zovas cholov udvosh,

a land flowing with milk and honey —

וְעָבַדְתָּ אֶת הָעֲבֹדָה הַזֹּאת
בַּחֹדֶשׁ הַזֶּה.

v'ovad-to es ho-avōdo ha-zōs
ba-chōdesh ha-ze.

you shall perform this service in this month.

שִׁבְעַת יָמִים תֹּאכַל מַצֹּת,

Shivas yomim tōchal matzōs,

Seven days you shall eat matzos,

וּבַיּוֹם הַשְּׁבִיעִי חַג לַיהוה.

uva-yōm hash'vi-i chag Ladōnoy.

and on the seventh day there shall be a festival to HASHEM.

מַצּוֹת יֵאָכֵל
אֵת שִׁבְעַת הַיָּמִים,

Matzōs yay-ochayl
ays shivas ha-yomim,

Matzos shall be eaten throughout the seven days;

וְלֹא יֵרָאֶה לְךָ חָמֵץ,

v'lō yayro-e l'cho chomaytz,

no chametz may be seen in your possession

וְלֹא יֵרָאֶה לְךָ שְׂאֹר

v'lō yayro-e l'cho s'ōr

nor may leaven be seen in your possession

בְּכָל גְּבֻלֶךָ.

b'chol g'vulecho.

in all your borders.

וְהִגַּדְתָּ לְבִנְךָ
בַּיּוֹם הַהוּא לֵאמֹר:

v'higad-to l'vincho
ba-yōm hahu laymōr:

And you shall tell your son on that day, saying:

בַּעֲבוּר זֶה עָשָׂה יהוה לִי
בְּצֵאתִי מִמִּצְרָיִם.

ba-avur ze oso Adōnoy li
b'tzaysi mimitzro-yim.

"It is because of this that HASHEM acted on my behalf when I left Egypt."

V'ho-yo l'cho l'ōs al yod'cho,

וְהָיָה לְךָ לְאוֹת עַל יָדְךָ,

And it shall serve you as a sign on your arm

ulzikorōn bayn aynecho,

וּלְזִכָּרוֹן בֵּין עֵינֶיךָ,

and as a reminder between your eyes —

l'ma-an tih-ye
tōras Adōnoy b'ficho,

לְמַעַן תִּהְיֶה
תּוֹרַת יהוה בְּפִיךָ,

so that HASHEM's Torah may be in your mouth;

ki v'yod chazoko hōtzi-acho Adōnoy
mimitzro-yim.

כִּי בְּיָד חֲזָקָה הוֹצִאֲךָ יהוה
מִמִּצְרָיִם.

for with a strong hand HASHEM removed you from Egypt.

V'shomarto es hachuko ha-zōs

וְשָׁמַרְתָּ אֶת הַחֻקָּה הַזֹּאת

And you shall observe this ordinance

l'mō-adoh, mi-yomim yomimo.

לְמוֹעֲדָהּ, מִיָּמִים יָמִימָה.

at its designated time from year to year.

V'HO-YO ki y'vi-acho Adōnoy
el eretz hak'na-ani

וְהָיָה כִּי יְבִאֲךָ יהוה
אֶל אֶרֶץ הַכְּנַעֲנִי

And it shall come to pass, when HASHEM will bring you to the land of the Canaanites

ka-asher nishba l'cho v'la-avōsecho,
un'sonoh loch.

כַּאֲשֶׁר נִשְׁבַּע לְךָ וְלַאֲבֹתֶיךָ,
וּנְתָנָהּ לָךְ.

as He swore to you and to your forefathers, and will have given it to you.

V'ha-avarto kol peter rechem
Ladōnoy,

וְהַעֲבַרְתָּ כָל פֶּטֶר רֶחֶם
לַיהוה,

Then you shall set apart every first issue of the womb to HASHEM,

v'chol peter sheger b'haymo
asher yih-ye l'cho,

וְכָל פֶּטֶר שֶׁגֶר בְּהֵמָה
אֲשֶׁר יִהְיֶה לְךָ,

and every first issue that is dropped by cattle that belong to you,

haz'chorim Ladōnoy.

הַזְּכָרִים לַיהוה.

the males shall belong to HASHEM.

V'chol peter chamōr tifde v'se,

וְכָל פֶּטֶר חֲמֹר תִּפְדֶּה בְשֶׂה,

Every first issue donkey you shall redeem with a lamb or kid,

v'im lō sifde va-araftō,

וְאִם לֹא תִפְדֶּה וַעֲרַפְתּוֹ,

if you do not redeem it, then you must axe the back of its neck.

v'chōl b'chōr odom b'vonecho tifde.

וְכֹל בְּכוֹר אָדָם בְּבָנֶיךָ תִּפְדֶּה.

And you must redeem every human firstborn among your sons.

V'ho-yo ki yishol'cho vincho mochor

וְהָיָה כִּי יִשְׁאָלְךָ בִנְךָ מָחָר

And it shall be when your son asks you at some future time,

לֵאמֹר, מַה זֹּאת,

laymōr, ma zōs,

saying, "What is this?",

וְאָמַרְתָּ אֵלָיו,

v'omarto aylov,

you shall answer him,

בְּחֹזֶק יָד

b'chōzek yod

"With a strong hand

הוֹצִיאָנוּ יהוה מִמִּצְרַיִם מִבֵּית עֲבָדִים.

hōtzi-onu Adōnoy mimitzra-yim mibays avodim.

HASHEM removed us from Egypt, from the house of bondage.

וַיְהִי כִּי הִקְשָׁה פַרְעֹה לְשַׁלְּחֵנוּ,

Vaihi ki hiksho farō l'shal'chaynu,

And it happened, when Pharaoh stubbornly refused to let us go,

וַיַּהֲרֹג יהוה

va-ya-harōg Adōnoy

that HASHEM killed

כָּל בְּכוֹר בְּאֶרֶץ מִצְרַיִם,

kol b'chōr b'eretz mitz-ra-yim,

all the firstborn in the land of Egypt,

מִבְּכֹר אָדָם

mib'chōr odom

from the firstborn of man

וְעַד בְּכוֹר בְּהֵמָה.

v'ad b'chōr b'haymo.

to the firstborn of beast.

עַל כֵּן אֲנִי זֹבֵחַ לַיהוה

Al kayn ani zōvayach Ladōnoy

Therefore, I sacrifice to HASHEM

כָּל פֶּטֶר רֶחֶם הַזְּכָרִים,

kol peter rechem haz'chorim,

all first male issue of the womb,

וְכָל בְּכוֹר בָּנַי אֶפְדֶּה.

v'chol b'chōr bonai efde.

and redeem all the firstborn of my sons."

וְהָיָה לְאוֹת עַל יָדְכָה

V'ho-yo l'ōs al yod'cho

And it shall be a sign upon your arm

וּלְטוֹטָפֹת בֵּין עֵינֶיךָ,

ultōtofōs bayn aynecho,

and totafos between your eyes,

כִּי בְּחֹזֶק יָד

ki b'chōzek yod

for with a strong hand

הוֹצִיאָנוּ יהוה

hōtzi-onu Adōnoy

HASHEM removed us

מִמִּצְרָיִם.

mimitzro-yim.

from Egypt.